# THE SIXTIES

# THE SIXTIES

Cultural Revolution in Britain, France,
Italy, and the United States,
c.1958–c.1974

## ARTHUR MARWICK

BLOOMSBURY READER

LONDON · NEW DELHI · NEW YORK · SYDNEY

For copyright reasons, any images not belonging to the original author
have been removed from this book. The text has not been changed,
and may still contain references to missing images

This edition published in 2012 by Bloomsbury Reader

Bloomsbury Reader is a division of Bloomsbury Publishing Plc,

50 Bedford Square, London WC1B 3DP

ISBN: 978 1 4482 0573 8
eISBN: 978 1 4482 0542 4

Visit www.bloomsburyreader.com to find out more about our authors and their books
You will find extracts, author interviews, author events and you can sign up for
newsletters to be the first to hear about our latest releases and special offers
Printed and bound by CPI Group (UK) Ltd, Croydon, CR0 4YY

MIX
Paper from
responsible sources
FSC® C013604

# Contents

# Preface

Without the sources contained in archives and libraries the historian is nothing. Without archivists and librarians to guide him/her the historian is a blunderer, high on purpose, low on achievement. The archives I have used are listed at the end of this book. But I begin here with an expression of my immense debt of gratitude, for the warmth of their welcome as well as their unstinted assistance, to the archivists and librarians at: the Mississippi Valley Collection, Memphis State University; the Memphis and Shelby County Library Special Collections; the University of Mississippi Library Special Collections; the University of California at Los Angeles Library Special Collections; the Stanford University Library Special Collections; the Library of the Hoover Institution on War, Revolution, and Peace, Stanford University; the Bancroft Library of the University of California at Berkeley; the San Francisco Public Library Reference Section and Department of Documents; the Columbia University Rare Book and Manuscript Library; the Cornell University Library Division of Manuscript Collections, Ithaca, New York; the Schlesinger Library at Radcliffe College, Cambridge, Massachusetts; the Grayson History Research Center, University of Minnesota Libraries, St Paul (a visit which goes back to the seventies); the Institut Français d'Histoire Sociale at the Archives Nationales, Paris; the Centre de Recherches, Histoire des Mouvements Sociaux et du Syndicalisme, Paris; the Musée Nationale des Arts et Traditions Populaires, Paris; the Maison de la Villette, Paris; the Archivio Diaristico, Pieve Santo Stefano, Tuscany; the Fondazione Giangiacomo Feltrinelli, Milan; the Istituto Ferruccio Parri, Bologna; the Library of the Università dei Stranieri, Perugia; the Biblioteca dei Deputati, Rome; the Modern Records Centre, University of Warwick Library; the National Library of Scotland; and the old British Library Reading Room. It is always a pleasure to work at the Bibliothèque Nationale in Paris and at the Biblioteca Nazionale Centrale in Rome, the latter, because of its friendly bar, being the only library I know where it is easier to order a drink than a book. The New York Public Library, to use the local idiom, is something else. Nearer to base, Tony Coulson at the Open University Library has always come up with the answers I needed.

Along with archivists and librarians, historians need patient, self-crucifying colleagues.

Professor Pierre Sorlin of Paris and Bologna and Professor Dan Leab of New York went far beyond the call of comradeship in battling through a massive earlier draft of this book, annotating practically every page, every paragraph, every phrase. The book has benefited immeasurably from their ministrations, though I fear I sometimes continued to go my own way. For some very shrewd and helpful comments I am grateful to Henry Cowper, Simon Sadler, Robert Rowland, and my colleagues on the Open University Sixties Research Group. I should also make special mention of Dr Robert Lumley of University College, London, who not only gave a sparkling and informative talk to the Open University seminar, but provided me with important bibliographical information for Italy. For photocopies of important periodical material, I am indebted to my colleague Dr James Moore.

Trying out ideas in seminars and lectures is a vital element in the process by which history books come to be produced. I have had my thoughts corrected, clarified, extended, not just at the Open University seminars but in discussions at Memphis State University, the University of Perugia, the University of Reykjavik, and at Bristol, Cambridge, and Edinburgh universities. In communicating one's ideas and in receiving corrections one employs that wonderful human *tool*, language: we *use* language, language does not, as some theorists insist, use *us*.

All sources, including statistical ones, are suspect; but practically every source has some unique strength as well as many weaknesses. Much of my search has been for the responses of individuals and families in all classes to the 'cultural revolution' of which they were themselves the vital component, in letters to each other, to the press, to their MPs and Congressmen, in diaries, in memoirs. Where what they say is congruent with the frameworks established by the more quantitative sources, I have quoted them. I have made much use of magazines—for teenagers, for the aspiring lower middle class, for women, for prosperous African-Americans: undoubtedly the owners and editors had their own agendas; but so did readers. Because of problems of access and the difficulty of achieving consistent coverage over the four countries, I have made much less use of television broadcasts than I would have liked (here, as elsewhere, there is still plenty of work for others to do). Oral history, recorded scientifically by other scholars, has been very useful; I have not tried to set myself up as an oral historian, just as I have striven *not* to rely on my own recollections. Photographs, cartoons, etc. are primary sources too. Like all sources they have to be critically analysed and collated with relevant contextual information. I have tried to do this in my captions.

For a piece of comparative history, Britain, France, Italy, and the USA make a good choice, but, quite frankly, I could not seriously consider including Germany because my knowledge of German extends little beyond reading menus and ordering food and drink. The importance of comparative history was driven home for me by an American who remarked: 'Say, I never knew you guys had a sixties over there.'

The immense tasks of preparing the constantly revised latest drafts, devising systems to cope with these and with the protracted process of tracking down missing references, and preparing the finalized text for handover to the publishers were carried through with great patience and skill by Margaret Marchant, to whom I also owe a great debt. For indispensable work on early drafts I would like to thank Mandy Topham, Wendy Clarke, and Janet Andrews.

As the Open University Research Committee denied me funds for my researches, I largely financed them by taking visiting professorships at Rhodes College, Memphis, Tennessee, and at the University of Perugia. I have the warmest memories of my sojourns at both places, and I received enormous help from both my American and Italian colleagues: my thanks also to them, and in particular to Professor Piero Melograni. I am very grateful to the Arts Faculty Research Committee, which not only financed my original travel arrangements but made possible several subsequent visits to the French and Italian archives and libraries, and to Warwick and Edinburgh.

Huge amounts have been written on the sixties and, of course, I stand (I hope!) on the shoulders of previous writers. I do believe that the approaches I have taken are fresh ones, and that I have many new things to say. But that is for my readers to judge. I have always said that history must be a dialogue between the historian and readers. I express my own assumptions and conclusions clearly and trenchantly in the spirit that readers have every right to disagree with them. I have followed the usual academic conventions in making plain the evidence on which my contentions are based. In the Secondary Sources section of my Note on Sources I have confined myself to books published within the last ten years or so. These get the full citations of publisher and place of publication. Printed primary sources (emanating from within the period studied itself), and the earlier secondary sources which I have made use of, are to be found in my chapter notes, where publishers are not listed. Place of publication is London, unless otherwise stated. Books of my own are referred to in the chapter notes where they might be helpful in following up particular points. They are not listed again among the secondary sources at the end of the book. That example, perhaps, offers some insight into the way in which I have tried to make the Bibliography both manageable and useful.

Research, reflection, and writing are paramount, but a book also has to be published to the highest professional standards. I'd like to thank my publisher, George Miller, and his assistant, Shelley Cox, my editor, Sarah Barrett, and also Wendy Simpson and Peter Gibbs for reading the proofs. Finally a word of thanks to Michael Sissons, who, in bad times and good, has been my agent since 1964.

# Part I

# Introduction

# 1

# Was There a Cultural Revolution c.1958–c.1974?

*Nostalgia, Prejudice, and Debate*

Mention of 'the sixties' rouses strong emotions even in those who were already old when the sixties began and those who were not even born when the sixties ended. For some it is a golden age, for others a time when the old secure framework of morality, authority, and discipline disintegrated. In the eyes of the far left, it is the era when revolution was at hand, only to be betrayed by the feebleness of the faithful and the trickery of the enemy; to the radical right, an era of subversion and moral turpitude. What happened between the late fifties and the early seventies has been subject to political polemic, nostalgic mythologizing, and downright misrepresentation. If asked to explain the fuss, both survivors of the decade and observers of the repeated attempts subsequently to conjure it up again could probably manage to put together a list of its most striking features, which might look something like this: black civil rights; youth culture and trend-setting by young people; idealism, protest, and rebellion; the triumph of popular music based on Afro-American models and the emergence of this music as a universal language, with the Beatles as the heroes of the age; the search for inspiration in the religions of the Orient; massive changes in personal relationships and sexual behaviour; a general audacity and frankness in books and in the media, and in ordinary behaviour; relaxation in censorship; the new feminism; gay liberation; the emergence of 'the underground' and 'the counterculture'; optimism and genuine faith in the dawning of a better world.[1] They might, in addition, be able to contrast this with a list of key features of the fifties, including: rigid social hierarchy; subordination of women to men and children to parents; repressed attitudes to sex; racism; unquestioning respect for authority in the

3

family, education, government, the law, and religion, and for the nation-state, the national flag, the national anthem; Cold War hysteria; a strict formalism in language, etiquette, and dress codes; a dull and cliche-ridden popular culture, most obviously in popular music, with its boring big bands and banal ballads.

A conservative, of course, would see the fifties as a last age of morality, patriotism, law and order, respect for the family, tuneful music, and a popular culture which was pleasing, not shocking. A conservative would point out that the gross abuse of drugs began in the sixties (fashions in hard drugs have changed, but it was in the sixties that society's defences were decisively breached), aided by self-serving claptrap about the mind-expanding and enlightening qualities of psychedelic experiences; that hippie communes were often as notable for violent squabbles and lamentable hygiene as for peace and spirituality, reminding us also that after the long student occupation of the Sorbonne, that august centre of learning was found to be in a disgusting condition; that dubious theories about language and knowledge as instruments of bourgeois and patriarchal oppression were propagated, leading to the paralysing miasma of political correctness which has affected the academic world ever since. Conservatives would also argue that because of the propagation of 'progressive' ideas, crime statistics swung upwards while educational standards dived downwards. Let us listen to a couple of conservatives. Who better to lead off than Margaret Thatcher, radical right prime minister of Britain from 1979 to 1991? 'We are reaping', she declared in March 1982, 'what was sown in the sixties… fashionable theories and permissive claptrap set the scene for a society in which old values of discipline and restraint were denigrated.'[2] Defining the sixties as 'the period of dogmatic answers and trivial tracts', the American Professor Allan Bloom declared in 1986 that, intellectually, sixties theorists were as destructive as the Nazis:

> The American University in the sixties was experiencing the same dismantling of the structure of rational inquiry as had the German university in the thirties. As Hegel was said to have died in Germany in 1933, Enlightenment in America came close to breathing its last during the sixties. The fact that the universities are no longer in convulsions does not mean they have regained their health…

Most recently, a strongly hostile view of the radicals of the sixties was put forward by Professor Paul Bearman. And while, in his own introduction to *Reassessing the Sixties*, Stephen Macedo presents a very balanced account, several of his contributors take up very hostile views of radicalism, feminism, and black liberation.[3]

So, left-centre and right do seem to agree that, for good or ill, *something* significant happened in the sixties. But the disillusioned revolutionaries, the extreme left, declare that nothing very much happened. It was all just froth and empty spectacle, in which so-called counter-cultural practices were manipulated by the usual commercial interests; the distribution of economic and political power was exactly the same in the seventies as it had been in the fifties. There is a kind of 'soft left' variation of this negative view, propagated by many of those who were active in the cultural innovations of the time: 'The sixties were great—i.e. *we* were great—but of absolutely no enduring significance. Tough *you* weren't there.' That is the approach of Jim Haynes, of Traverse Theatre and Arts Lab fame, and of musician George Melly:

> Pop culture and the sixties are long gone, and all I can hope is that my resurrected book may offer those too young to remember those heady days and nights some idea of what they were about. Silly and transient they may have been, but at least they were alive, kicking and, above all, hopeful.[4]

Is it legitimate to make contrasts and comparisons between the 'fifties', the 'sixties', the 'seventies'? We readily think in decades, but that is only because we count the years as we would our fingers or our toes. In historical study we do need a concept of periods, or eras, or ages, though such periods do not automatically coincide with decades or with centuries, nor do they have any immanent or natural existence, independent of the analytical needs of historians. Periodization, the chopping up of the past into chunks or periods, is essential because the past in its entirety is so extensive and complex; but different historians will identify different chunks, depending upon their interests and the countries they are dealing with—a periodization which suits the study of Western Europe will not suit the study of Africa or Japan. The implication of periodization is that particular chunks of time contain a certain unity, in that events, attitudes, values, social hierarchies within the chosen 'period' seem to be closely integrated with each other, to share common features, and in that there are identifiable points of change when a 'period' defined in this way gives way to a 'new period'. Books covering relatively long stretches of time will usually be divided up into a number of shorter periods, indicating points of change. In his book covering the years 1914–91 Professor Eric Hobsbawm has chosen one title for the entire period of his book, *The Age of Extremes: The Short Twentieth Century 1914–1991,* and three further titles for the shorter periods he identifies within that long period: 'The Age of Catastrophe' (1914–45), 'The Golden Age' (1945–73), and 'The Landslide' (1973–91). Hobsbawm does not see the sixties as a separate period, merging the sixties with the fifties into his 'Golden Age' starting in 1945; and he is far from alone among historians in doing this.

However, my starting-point for this book is that the prima facie evidence is strong enough to warrant exploring the proposition that there was a self-contained period (though no period is hermetically sealed), commonly known as 'the sixties', of outstanding historical significance in that what happened during this period transformed social and cultural developments for the rest of the century. Two schoolteachers, writing in the first person singular in an essay looking back on their days as teenagers in sixties Liverpool, stressed the lasting effects of the upheavals, even while confessing to the naivety of some of their beliefs:

> And did all that upheaval in living standards, in attitudes and fashion have a lasting effect on the lives of the adults who were teenagers in Liverpool in the sixties? I believe it did. It gave us tolerance for new ideas, and brought us a step nearer to equality of rights, removing many prejudices of sexual, racial and moral origin. It gave us the freedom to accept or reject things on their own merits and according to our own individual preferences. I believe that

5

the sixties were a mini-renaissance in which the right of individual expression was encouraged, applauded and nurtured by a generation whose naive belief was that all we needed was love.[5]

The image of 'a mini-renaissance' is a striking one. Few historians today would contest the proposition that, viewing the past with certain social and cultural preoccupations in mind, we can identify a period in European history which we can legitimately label 'the Renaissance' (*c.*1300–*c.*1600), in which artistic standards and values, and ideas about society and the individual's relations with it, were transformed, and which thus had profound effects on succeeding centuries. The prima facie evidence is overwhelming: the city of Urbino, St Peter's in Rome, the paintings of Piero della Francesca, Giovanni Bellini, Raphael, and a hundred others, *The Prince* by Machiavelli, the plays of Shakespeare (being English, he only squeezes in after extra time). In my researches for this book I have visited archives in France, Italy, and the United States, as well as the United Kingdom. Aside from masses of archival evidence, which I shall be citing copiously in this book, I have everywhere encountered fascinating traces of the sixties, some trivial, some portentous. The Beatles and their origins are commemorated in the Café Liverpool on the boulevard Clichy in Paris, the fashion street of sixties London in the Café Carnaby on via Cusani, Milan. On my first morning in Memphis (adopted home of Elvis Presley, scene of the assassination of Martin Luther King, and location of fabulous archives of sixties sources, the Mississippi Valley collection and the Memphis and Shelby County Library Special Collections), I watched a team of black garbage collectors, with their enormous automated lorry, order an elegant white lady, trying to park her Mercedes sports coupé, to get herself and her car the hell out of their way. A later chapter will describe the appalling conditions endured by black sanitation workers in Memphis at the time of their strike in 1968. Here, in 1991, I was witnessing one enduring gain from the sixties civil rights movement. Walking across Overton Park I was immensely cheered to see goalposts for my own kind of football: previously a minority sport, 'soccer', on a nationwide basis, had come to America in the later sixties.

And Urbino... St Peter's? No. Too much of sixties architecture is awful, the low-cost public housing (much of it now demolished) disgraceful. But at least the sixties was a time of changing perceptions and objectives, a time of the first really major initiatives in regard to both the natural and the urban environment, a time of pedestrianization and the conservation of historical city centres (a time also, it must be added, of some appalling environmental disasters, which, indeed, served to strengthen the nascent environmental movements).

Naturally, developments in the sixties were affected by what had gone before in the forties and fifties: but I shall be arguing that minor and rather insignificant movements in the fifties became major and highly significant ones in the sixties; that intangible ideas in the fifties became powerful practicalities in the sixties; that the sixties were characterized by the vast number of innovative activities taking place *simultaneously*, by unprecedented *interaction* and *acceleration*. In my view the critical point of change came, as precisely as one could ever express it, in 1958–9. So, just as Hobsbawm has 'a short twentieth century', I am postulating a 'long sixties', beginning in 1958 and ending, broadly speaking—many of the new trends of the sixties continued throughout

6

the seventies, and right on to today—in 1973–4. This terminal date pretty well coincides with the one chosen by Hobsbawm for the ending of his 'Golden Age': he takes 1973 because it was the year of the international oil crisis, when the doubling of oil prices led to widespread recession and a general crisis of confidence; it was also in 1973, following the conclusion of a formal peace treaty in January, that all American troops were withdrawn from Vietnam, though Nixon continued to provide massive aid to the Saigon government. I prefer to go up to 1974 because it was only in that year that the mass of ordinary people *began* to feel the effects of the oil crisis, because some of the crucial developments initiated in the sixties only culminated then, or even later (18-year-olds in France and Italy got the vote in 1974, the year also of the referendum in Italy safeguarding the right to divorce and of the passing of abortion law reform in the French parliament), and because only in August, with Congress drastically cutting aid to Saigon and Nixon resigning, did the anti-war movement feel it was achieving victory. Justifying the choice of 1958–9 as a critical point of change will be a major aim of Part II of this book.

It is very important not to get into the position of idealizing, reifying, or anthropomorphizing periods or decades, attributing personalities to them, singling out 'good' decades from 'bad' decades. History was a more naive subject when, in the middle of the nineteenth century, Jacob Burckhardt wrote his famous *The Civilization of the Renaissance in Italy.* Seeking to express the immense significance that he attached to his period, he said that it 'must be called the leader of modern ages', explaining that he was 'treating of a civilization which is the mother of our own, and whose influence is still at work among us'.[6] Well, I shall certainly not say that 'the sixties was the mother of the nineties'—the contemporary mind rightly boggles at such crass metaphors—but I would be very tempted to say that this book is about 'the civilization of the cultural revolution in the West', were it not that I have confined myself to only four countries, Britain, France, Italy, and the USA.

I have stated the proposition which I intend to explore. There are many 'counter-propositions' among the debates which pervade all discussion of the sixties. In analysing these I shall at the same time be adding further details to my own basic proposition. We have already encountered the first of the 'counter-propositions'. Hobsbawm's 'Golden Age' begins in 1945, not 1958. Hobsbawm is in the excellent company of most economic historians, who envisage one long period of economic recovery and economic expansion beginning at the end of the war. French historians tend to speak of *les trente glorieuses,* 'the thirty glorious years', which followed the ending of the war, embracing the fifties, sixties, and seventies.[7] Historians of France and Italy (and West Germany) rightly stress that the 'economic miracles' in these countries belong to the fifties, not the sixties. My response is that if we are purely concerned with economic history, this periodization is a sensible one, but that if we are primarily interested in social and cultural developments, the growing power of young people, the particular behaviour and activities associated with them, the changes in family relationships, the new standards of sexual behaviour, then the idea of a point of change around 1958–9 begins to make great good sense after all. Economic expansion began in the fifties, but the *social* benefits came in the sixties. That does not end the matter. Italian studies concentrating on social and cultural matters have presented the years 1968–9, the years of student protests and workers' strikes, as the *beginning* of a new era of rapid change. Martin

Clark, the authoritative British historian of modern Italy, has a chapter called 'The Great Cultural Revolution' which in fact refers to the 1970s, not the 1960s.[8] My detailed counter-arguments can only emerge in the course of this book. But my quick answer here will be that such historians overemphasize the significance of the events of 1968–9, forgetting that these events were only possible because of deeper changes taking place in Italian society throughout the sixties. Finally there are those, mostly British, perhaps unduly influenced by the poet Philip Larkin's declaration that 'sexual intercourse began in 1963', who maintain that the sixties only 'began' in that year; some, in the manner of George Melly, claim also that the sixties 'ended' in 1968–9. I believe we can resolve these puzzles by thinking not just of a 'long sixties' but of that period being divided into three distinctive sub-periods, 1958–63, 1964–8/9, and 1969–74. It is on that premiss that I have structured this book, striving at the same time to bring out the links between apparently disparate activities—rock'n'roll dancing by teenagers and environmental protest by the middle-aged, for example.

The second counter-proposition, in its scholarly form, belongs almost entirely to American historians of the United States. It is the position that the things that happened in the sixties—there is full recognition that distinctive things did happen—on the whole had harmful effects on the societies in which they happened. The polemical form we have already met in the words I quoted from Margaret Thatcher. The more scholarly version, in its application to the United States, is well expressed in the title Allen J. Matusow chose for his general history of America in the period, *The Unraveling of American Society*, a theme not dissimilar to that expressed in the title of an earlier book by W. L. O'Neill, *Coming Apart*; recent versions of the 'unraveling' thesis are John M. Blum's *Years of Discord* and David Burner's *Making Peace With the 60s*. In *Destructive Generation*, former radicals Peter Collier and David Horowitz maintained that sixties developments turned American society 'into a collection of splinter groups'.[9] All of these historians were deeply sympathetic to the liberal reform policies of President J. F. Kennedy and his advisers, as they were to the entire civil rights movement. They were profoundly shocked by the assassination of Kennedy in 1963, and then by the assassinations in 1968 of Martin Luther King and of Robert Kennedy. They deplored the way in which social welfare programmes were curtailed as a result of the colossal expenditure on the Vietnam war; even more they regretted the bitter divisions in American society provoked by that war, the often violent demonstrations, and the still more violent repressions by the police. They were shocked, again, by the split in the civil rights movement after 1964, with blacks moving towards violence and separatism; shocked too by the destructive and murderous rioting in the black ghettos in the major cities. They had put faith in the liberal instincts of the Democratic party, then found that party in utter turmoil by 1968, before its defeat by Richard Nixon and the Republicans. Havoc, largely involving white students and white police, was wreaked in 1968 and 1969; attacks by the secret terrorist organization, the Weathermen, continued into 1970, which was also the year in which white student protesters were shot dead at Kent State University. Horrific events, indeed. But they were not, in my view, indications of new fractures in American society; they were indications rather that fractures which had long existed and had been too long ignored were now being brought out into the open. The Vietnam war was a tragedy and a crime; but by 1973–4 the anti-war cause had achieved a wonderful victory. Despite the advent to power of Nixon and the Republicans, welfare programmes did continue, and in some cases were actually improved. American society did not 'unravel': forms of discrimination continued, but blacks did win basic civil rights, and some prospered as never before.

It will be a major theme of this book that it is a mistake to concentrate on politics and changes of government: the social and cultural movements I am concerned with continued largely irrespective of the political complexions of governments. If we look outside America, it is true that racial discrimination got worse in both Britain and France from about 1968 onwards. It is also indisputably true that in 1969–70 a new era of terrorism and violence, 'the years of the bullet', began in Italy. We are not studying a 'golden age'—there are no golden ages—and many appalling events took place in the sixties. We may well throw up our hands in horror, but we must also make long-term assessments. Italy survived its crisis, as America did not 'come apart': on the other hand, it will be argued in this book, the true gains of the sixties proved enduring.

We now come to the most fraught field of contention when it comes to the scholarly analysis of the sixties, as well as the popular mythology. This counter-proposition is inextricably bound up with the arguments and debates which actually took place in the sixties, since most of the activists and protesters at the time themselves believed in it. At its heart lies what I shall call the Great Marxisant Fallacy: the belief that the society we inhabit is the bad bourgeois society, but that, fortunately, this society is in a state of crisis, so that the good society which lies just around the corner can be easily attained if only we work systematically to destroy the language, the values, the culture, the ideology of bourgeois society.[10] (I say 'Marxisant' because I am speaking of a broad metaphysical view about history and about how society works, derived from Marxism, but forming the basis for the structuralism, post-structuralism, and theories of ideology and language developed in the sixties.) In reality the society we live in has evolved through complex historical processes, very different from the Marxist nonsense about 'the bourgeoisie' overthrowing the feudal aristocracy. It contains genuinely democratic elements as well as gross inequalities and abuses of power; the only thing we can do is to work as systematically and rationally as possible to reform that society. In the eyes of the upholders of the Great Marxisant Fallacy, of course, that opinion condemns me as a dupe of bourgeois ideology. Practically all the activists, student protesters, hippies, yippies, Situationists, advocates of psychedelic liberation, participants in be-ins and rock festivals, proponents of free love, members of the underground, and advocates of Black Power, women's liberation, and gay liberation believed that by engaging in struggles, giving witness, or simply doing their own thing they were contributing to the final collapse of bad bourgeois society. To say that is not to withhold admiration from the activism and the idealism, nor to deny the many positive achievements of the protesters; but it is to recognize that their ultimate objectives were based on a fundamental fallacy. There was never any possibility of a revolution; there was never any possibility of a 'counter-culture' replacing 'bourgeois' culture. Modern society is highly complex with respect to the distribution of power, authority, and influence. Just as it was *not* formed by the simple overthrow of the aristocracy by the bourgeoisie, so, in its contemporary form, it does not consist simply of a bourgeois ruling class and a proletariat. Contemporary societies, as I shall stress throughout this book, are certainly class societies—using

9

'class' as the ordinary people we shall be studying (as distinct from the ideologists and activists) used the term when, say, they talked of 'upper-class education', 'upper-middle-class professions', 'lower-middle-class leisure activities', or 'working-class housing', and not in the loaded Marxist way with its assumptions of class conflict and class ideologies.

Mention of the term 'counter-culture' brings me to one of the most important aspects of the whole muddied field of controversy we are now tramping our way through. One of the most basic problems in the production and consumption of history is that many of the most important words we have to use are actually used in different ways, that is to say, have different meanings. 'Culture' is one of the classic instances. Often the word is used as a collective noun embracing opera, painting, poetry, and so on, broadly what is dealt with in the arts, entertainments, and books pages of our posher newspapers. Sometimes 'popular culture' is also spoken of, referring to films, popular music, romantic, crime, and other less ambitious fiction, and, perhaps, spectating at football matches. Sometimes in this book I use 'culture' in that way—there is no space for elaborate reformulations. But when we come to terms like 'counter-culture', 'culture' is being used in a wider sense to mean 'the network or totality of attitudes, values and practices of a particular group of human beings'. This definition is far from solving all of our problems, because much uncertainty remains as to the size of the 'group of human beings' which would be appropriate. One might speak of American culture, or of aristocratic culture, or of youth culture, or, perhaps, of Western culture, signifying 'the Western way of life'—all the attitudes and values and practices springing from the traditions of ancient Athens, modified by Christian religion, by the eighteenth-century Enlightenment, by the French Revolution, by Romanticism, by overseas conquests and colonialism, by the upheavals of the twentieth century. A single 'culture', obviously, may be very big, or it may be quite small, depending upon the context in which the concept is being used. For myself, I intend throughout this book (though such is the slippery nature of language that it is always difficult to achieve total obedience even to self-imposed rules) to use the word 'subculture' where I want to drive home the point that the 'network' I am speaking of is, in the last analysis, a part of a larger network, or culture. Thus I speak of 'youth subculture', because I do not believe that there was a 'youth culture' which ever became completely independent of, or alternative to, the larger culture involving parents, educational institutions, commercial companies, technology, and the mass media. Indeed, it is one of the absolutely fundamental contentions of this book that the essence of what happened in the sixties is that large numbers of new subcultures were created, which then expanded and interacted with each other, thus creating the pullulating flux which characterizes the era. I shall return to that, but meantime let us stick with the concept of 'counter-culture'.

The term does originate within the period (1958-74) itself: those indulging in the various practices and activities I have already listed began to feel themselves to constitute a counter-culture. It was introduced to a limited audience by a young American academic, Theodore Roszak, in an article, 'Youth and the Great Refusal', published in *The Nation* on 25 March 1968:

> The counter culture is the embryonic cultural base of New Left politics, the effort to discover new types of community, new family patterns, new sexual mores, new kinds of

livelihood, new aesthetic forms, new personal identities on the far side of power politics, the bourgeois home, and the Protestant work ethic.

The term went into wide usage when Roszak put together a number of previously published essays as a book and called the book *The Making of a Counter Culture*. Readers of the over-written and elaborately rhetorical introduction which Roszak wrote specially for this potential (and actual) bestseller perhaps did not notice how muted his claims actually were on behalf of his counter-culture: he surmised that it might *over the next four generations* 'transform this disoriented civilization of ours into something a human being can identify as home'. His counter-culture consisted of 'a strict minority of the young and a handful of their adult mentors': it was opposed to 'technocratic society', and drew its ideas from 'the psychology of alienation, oriental mysticism, psychedelic drugs, and communitarian experiments'.[11] In the same year another young professional, Charles Reich, in an even more speculative and less precise work, *The Greening of America*, suggested that adoption of the new lifestyles and new ways of thinking would completely transform the world.[12] These books give us insights into concerns of the time about the spoliation caused by the unrestrained application of technology and into some of the euphoric responses; they cannot be taken as embodying authoritative historical assessments. For myself, I accept that the term 'counter-culture' was and is widely used, and that most people have a firm sense of what it signifies: my position is that it is a convenient term, valuable if it is deployed in the manner of everyday usage but dangerous if it is taken to imply any Marxisant assumptions about the dialectic, the overthrow of bourgeois society, the triumph of the alternative society. (The theory of the dialectic, I should explain, poses a sharp conflict between existing (bourgeois) culture and an oppositional culture, this conflict resulting in a new stage in human development, a new culture or society—there is no more evidence for the existence of 'the dialectic' than there is for the existence of 'the Holy Ghost')

It is, then, perfectly legitimate to use the term 'counter-culture' to refer to the many and varied activities and values which contrasted with, or were critical of, the conventional values and modes of established society: the contrast, in slightly hackneyed common usage, is between 'counter-culture' and 'mainstream culture'. These are terms I shall occasionally use in this book, though my preference is for using the adjective, 'counter-cultural', rather than the substantive, 'counter-culture'. The crucial point is that there was no unified, integrated counter-culture, totally and consistently in opposition to mainstream culture. When I demonstrate the many commercial transactions between those who probably saw themselves as mainly belonging to counter-culture, and those who indisputably belonged to money-making mainstream culture, I am not condemning or mocking the former. We can none of us escape from the larger culture to which we belong—and, in any case, there is nothing inherently objectionable about commercial transactions. Pointing out that hippies and drop-outs, while in some ways making the most complete break from mainstream society, did absolutely nothing to further the reform, let alone the supercession, of that society is not to condemn or mock them either, but merely to point out that what is called *the* counter-culture was in reality made up of a large number of very varied subcultures. Sometimes commentators, particularly those writing on American society, make a distinction between the counterculture and 'the Movement' or 'the New Left':[13] there is no rigid distinction, but in speaking of counter-culture the emphasis is on dress, general values, lifestyles, leisure activities, while in speaking of the Movement or the New Left the preoccupation is entirely with those who were genuinely politically active and took part in protests and demonstrations. The British 'New Left', a more restricted grouping of non-dogmatic Marxists, appeared in the fifties; in France and Italy the term 'New Left' is applied to the non-Communist (but Marxisant) radical groups consolidating in the later sixties, above all the 'student movement'. These are convenient labels and it is sensible to make use of them, provided always that they are not made to carry a greater load of assumptions and implications than they can bear, and that their deployment is not made a substitute for fully substantiated explanations.

What I shall hope to demonstrate is that the various counter-cultural movements and subcultures, being ineluctably implicated in and interrelated with mainstream society while all the time expanding and interacting with each other, did not *confront* that society but *permeated* and *transformed* it. I shall also hope to convey the message that this transformation was not due solely to counter-cultural protest and activism, but also to a conjunction of developments, including economic, demographic, and technological ones, and, critically, to the existence in positions of authority of men and women of traditional enlightened and rational outlook who responded flexibly and tolerantly to counter-cultural demands: I refer to this vital component of sixties transformations as 'measured judgement', to signify (by means of the distant echo from Shakespeare) that it emanated from people in authority, people very much part of mainstream society.

The other fundamental point which I shall hope to establish, and one which perhaps most distinguishes this book from other studies of the sixties, is that most of the movements, subcultures, and new institutions which are at the heart of sixties change were thoroughly imbued with the entrepreneurial, profit-making ethic.[14] I am thinking here of boutiques, experimental theatres, art galleries, discothèques, nightclubs, 'light shows', 'head shops', photographic and model agencies, underground films, pornographic magazines. With the assistance of the great expansion in mass communications, particularly in television, the sixties was very much an age of 'spectacle': leading figures in the counter-culture became very much part of this spectacle, thereby earning both status and prestige and ordinary money. Underground film-maker Andy Warhol mixed enthusiastically with New York high society; the Arts Lab in London was visited by ambassadors and executives from multinational corporations; the book *One-Dimensional Man* (1964) by Herbert Marcuse (singled out by Roszak as one of the high priests of counter-culture) was actually funded by an American government body and the Ford Foundation. Entrepreneuralism, an entirely admirable quality when it does not depend on the direct exploitation of other human beings, was an indispensable ingredient in sixties change.

Mention of Marcuse brings me to some of the more crudely political theories about the sixties. While some believed that simply by living the counter-culture they would bring about the collapse of bourgeois society, many others stuck to the traditional Marxist view that for the revolution to occur, there had to be a revolutionary class, in the form of the working class or proletariat. Unfortunately, if there was one thing the working class manifestly did not want to do, it was to carry out a revolution. Many theories were advanced to explain its failure to fulfil its historic destiny as laid down by Marxism, and, indeed, the postmodernist emphasis on language was part of the effort to keep Marxism going. Personally, I have always thought that once Marxist theory has been shown to be simply incorrect, the sensible thing to do would be to junk the theory, rather than try to find ever more elaborate ways of shoring it up. However, many of those who would agree with me about the entrepreneuralism of the sixties would say that in fact the new popular culture, far from being critical of established values, simply formed a part of that commercialism and consumerism which seduced the workers into believing that they were perfectly contented living in existing society. Marcuse was responsible for the notion of 'repressive tolerance'—in effect, the idea that the 'measured judgement' of which I have just spoken was no more than a cunning way of keeping revolutionary sentiment and radical protest under control, while appearing to be tolerant.[15] Marcuse also argued that, failing revolutionary action on the part of the proletariat as a whole, radical students would have to act as the true agents of revolution. Candidates for playing the role of the revolutionary class being so thin on the ground, other Marxist, or neo-Marxist, or Marxisant thinkers came up with various kinds of 'new working class' they hoped would fit the bill. The 'new working class' of the French sociologist Serge Mallet was made up of the new 'white-coated', highly qualified, technological workers;[16] to the Italian Marxist in the revolutionary group Potere Operaio (Workers' Power) this elusive class was to be found among the marginal riff-raff drifting from one job to another, and particularly among the underemployed agricultural labourers of the Italian south, who often pursued whatever jobs were going in the north.[17] In this book there is no 'new working class'; nor do I dispense the magical potion of ideology (in the Marxist sense), the miracle ingredient which stops workers from acting in what are alleged to be their own class interests, and leads them instead to accept the values of bourgeois society.

My complaint about the Marxists will be that they are so busy looking for a revolution which could not happen that they miss the fact that another kind of revolution did happen (or so I shall be arguing), a 'revolution', or 'transformation' in material conditions, lifestyles, family relationships, and personal freedoms for the vast majority of ordinary people; certainly there was no political or economic revolution, no fundamental redistribution of political and economic power. Slightly hesitantly, I am calling this 'revolution' or 'transformation' a 'cultural revolution'. When I say 'cultural revolution' I very definitely do not mean 'counter-cultural revolution', although that, I recognize, is what other writers (including non-Marxist ones) have usually meant when *they have* used the term 'cultural revolution'.[18] My usage is much broader. The activities of the minorities in the 'counterculture', the New Left, the student movement, played some part in changing the lives of the majority, though there were many other factors. To me the full significance of the sixties lies not in the activities of minorities but in what happened to the majority, and *how* it happened. For me, 'cultural revolution' is a convenient shorthand term to describe that entire process. What is important is giving an accurate account of what happened, not the label one puts on that account; all labels are imperfect. A particular drawback to mine is that China during the sixties actually underwent the 'Great Proletarian Cultural Revolution' of Mao Tse-tung. This was the most complete attempt so far to put into practice the new theory that if a proletarian revolution was to be complete and irreversible, all bourgeois customs, behaviour, ideology, and language must be obliterated: with intolerable cruelty and inhumanity, all considered to be bourgeois were harried and humiliated, and put to work in crucifying labouring jobs. The cultural revolution of which I (tentatively) speak has nothing to do with the theories and practice of Chairman Mao.

There would be those, including, of course, many of the student activists of the time, who would say that changes in living standards and lifestyles for the peoples of North America and Western Europe are of little import compared with Third World movements for liberation from colonialism and dictatorships.[19] At the beginning of our period, Fidel Castro overthrew the evil, American-backed Battista dictatorship in Cuba. A young member of Castro's government, Che Guevara, gave up his comfortable post to become a leader of the oppressed against their dictatorial rulers in South America, where he eventually met his death. Portraits of Che were reproduced everywhere as he became the single greatest hero of the European and North American protest movements. The Vietnam war—the attempt of the Americans to bolster the corrupt regime in South Vietnam against Communist North Vietnam and the Communist Vietcong in South Vietnam—waging a brutal campaign against ordinary villagers, killing hostages, using napalm, defoliants and other poisons, and then carrying the bombing raids to North Vietnam was the biggest single cause of protests and demonstrations. That unspeakable oppressions and the struggles against them in the Third World received unprecedented attention from young people in the West is very much to the credit of these young people, but does not mean that these events in themselves are the most significant features of the sixties. Indeed, it is very doubtful if the periodization privileging the sixties which, I am arguing, makes sense for the Western countries has as much meaning for the Third World, where colonial struggles extended over a much longer period. Anyway, my history is as unrepentantly a history of the West as Burckhardt's was of Italy. While, incidentally, one must be unsparing in one's condemnation of the misguided and unforgivable American actions in Vietnam, one cannot fail to note that in venerating Ho Chi Minh, the North Vietnamese leader (a 'hero' to put next to Che Guevara), students were once again victims of the Great Marxisant Fallacy: in aiming at (and succeeding in) taking over the whole of Vietnam, Ho Chi Minh was no noble leader of national liberation; he was an unscrupulous Marxist totalitarian, as the sad condition of Vietnam today demonstrates.

Two other relatively minor controversies should be considered: the first concerning the significance of the events of 1968, when the barricades went up in Paris, and students and strikers succeeded in creating a condition of total paralysis in France; the second relating to the apparent hegemony in popular culture of 'Swinging Britain', and to the question of how far, in reality, popular culture continued to be controlled by America. I have already said something about the slightly different events of 1968–9 in Italy: my general answer would be that what happened in 1968 cannot be taken out of the context of other developments throughout the sixties. What was going on in Paris *looked* like an attempt at the kind of revolution predicted by Marxists: it wasn't. Nor was British dominance of popular culture as total as patriots would like to maintain: American finance was critical to many British achievements after 1964. Yet the achievements really were astonishing, and deserve careful examination.

In discussing certain widespread perceptions of the sixties which will be challenged in this book, I have steadily uncovered my own basic assumptions, and my own basic conclusions, throughout stressing that I believe the period 1958–74 to have been both unique and of special significance with regard to what came after. It is now time to set out systematically my conception of what are the fundamental and historically significant characteristics of that era.

## Characteristics of a Unique Era

System and numbers should not be sneezed at. The historian's activities are (or should be) closer to those of the scientist than to those of the novelist or poet. However, neat equations, still less general laws, do not figure in the historian's work. The interactions, convergences, 'feedback loops' uncovered by historians testify rather to the significance in their subject, as in the natural sciences, of 'chaos'.

What I set out here is a numbered list of developments, characterizing and expressing the significance of my 'cultural revolution', or 'long sixties'; some emerged out of one or more of the other developments, and most interacted with each other. There is no hierarchy of either chronological or explanatory primacy, but the ordering is not purely arbitrary: given all the complexities inherent in the way in which things do actually happen, it is intended to convey my sense of how things happened in the sixties. I mix developments in which there was a high element of willed human agency and developments in which economic, technological, or demographic imperatives were of greatest importance.

1. The formation of new subcultures and movements, generally critical of, or in opposition to, one or more aspects of established society. These ranged from experimental theatres and architectural think-tanks to New Left, civil rights, anti-war, feminist and gay rights movements, Child Poverty, Help the Homeless, and environmental protection groups.

2. Closely associated with these was an outburst of entrepreneurialism, individualism, doing your own thing. Sometimes these initiatives were supported by government or local subsidy, but in essence they were uninhibited examples of private enterprise, and in no way socialistic. I am thinking here of the founding of theatres, clubs, boutiques, modelling and photographic agencies, book shops, cafés, restaurants, art galleries, 'arts labs', pornographic and listings magazines, and design studios.

3. The rise to positions of unprecedented influence of young people, with youth subculture having a steadily increasing impact on the rest of society, dictating taste in fashion, music, and popular culture generally. Youth subculture was not monolithic: in respect to some developments one is talking of teenagers, with respect to others it may be a question of everyone under 30 or so. Such was the prestige of youth and the appeal of the youthful lifestyle that it became possible to be 'youthful' at much more advanced ages than would ever have been thought proper previously. Youth, particularly at the teenage end, created a vast market of its own in the artefacts of popular culture. But with respect to spending patterns and changing lifestyles attention

must be given to young married couples, and particularly young wives, who, of course, not many years before, had themselves belonged to youth, narrowly defined.

4. Important advances in technology: television (including Telstar, the first transatlantic transmission being made in 1962), extended and long-play records, transistor radios, electronic synthesizers, modernized telephone systems (vital to teenagers); a remarkable expansion in jet travel, as well as the complete substitution of quickly accelerating electric and diesel locomotives for steam ones; advanced consumer products such as refrigerators and washing-machines; the contraceptive pill, first available in the United States in 1961 and in Britain in 1962.

5. The advent, as a consequence in particular of the almost universal presence of television, of 'spectacle' as an integral part of the interface between life and leisure. The most rebellious action, the most obscure theories, the wildest cultural extremism, the very 'underground' itself: all operated as publicly as possible, and all, thanks to the complex interaction with commercial interests and the media, attracted the maximum publicity. Thus one extreme gesture accelerated into the next. Each spectacle had to be more extreme than the previous one.

6. Unprecedented international cultural exchange, in which, along with (for example) espresso machines from Italy, discos from France, and theatrical innovation from America, Britain, particularly with respect to pop music and fashion, film, and television, played an unprecedented role.

7. Massive improvements in material life, so that large sections of society joined the consumer society and acquired 'mod cons'; in many backward areas this involved the arrival of electricity, together with inside lavatories and properly equipped bathrooms. Those who railed, and rail, against the consumer society of the sixties forget how welcome it was to those who were only in the process of joining it. I quote from a survey which is used extensively later in the book: revisiting a peasant family belonging to a community 65 miles south of Rome in 1969 when an inside toilet had been installed—previously family members and guests had had to take to the fields—a Roman sociologist was told by the proud owner: 'I feel like a human being, like other people, not like an animal as I felt before.'[20]

8. Upheavals in race, class, and family relationships. Given the importance of the civil rights movement in America, it may seem inappropriate to run these three categories together. Indeed, in writing this book I found that I had to abandon my original plan for Part II of putting race and class together in one chapter: the race question in America was so distinctive and important that I have had to treat it on its own. None the less, I believe it is right to see the challenge to established authorities and hierarchies in human relations as one single, though multi-faceted, process, subverting the authority of the white, the upper and middle class, the husband, the father, and the male generally.

9. 'Permissiveness'—that is to say, a general sexual liberation, entailing striking changes in public and private morals and (what I am particularly keen to stress) a new frankness, openness, and indeed honesty in personal relations and modes of expression.

10. New modes of self-presentation, involving emancipation from the old canons of fashion, and

a rejoicing in the natural attributes of the human body. If some of the more fantastic forms of apparel did tend to become a kind of uniform for, say, hippies, nevertheless it remained true as never before that individuals could dress to please themselves, rather than to meet some convention as to what was suitable to a particular age, class, or profession. There was for the first time the beginnings of a recognition of the realities of human beauty (specifically, that only a small minority of both sexes are truly beautiful and that therefore this minority have a very high commercial value) as against the traditional polite fictions and evasions.

11. A participatory and uninhibited popular culture, whose central component was rock music, which in effect became a kind of universal language.

12. Original and striking (and sometimes absurd) developments in élite thought—associated with the structuralists and post-structuralists, e.g. Barthes, Foucault, Althusser, and also with Marcuse, Marshall McLuhan, etc.—and culture, as seen in pop art, conceptual art, concrete poetry, and the privileging of 'chance' in literature, art, and music. Much of the new thinking simply contributed to what I have described as the Great Marxisant Fallacy, but it was also liberating in many areas, contributing to the protest movements and to the new feminism and gay liberation. Most obviously the attacks were on consumer and technocratic society. There was an obsession with language, conceived, along with knowledge, as an instrument of bourgeois oppression. There was a revival of the anti-art notions of Dada. Many of these trends came together in the tiny but fertile revolutionary movement, Situationism.

13. The continued existence, and indeed expansion, of a liberal, progressive presence within the institutions of authority, the characteristic which I have defined as 'measured judgement'. The concept should in my view completely replace the erroneous one of 'repressive tolerance', spawned by Marcuse. Many of the exciting developments in the sixties, and much of its unique character, are due to the existence of a genuine liberal tolerance and willingness to accommodate to the new subcultures, permitting them to permeate and transform society. The social welfare advances of the sixties were largely due to the protagonists of measured judgement responding to, or often anticipating, the claims of specialist protest groups.

14. Against that, we must place the continued existence of elements of extreme reaction, concentrated in particular in the various police forces but also in certain religious bodies. While it is clear that some of the protesting movements, particularly in the later stages, deliberately set out to provoke violence, there can be no question that throughout the decade almost all instances of violence and rioting came into being because of the insensitive (or worse) behaviour of the police.

15. New concerns for civil and personal rights, and a new willingness to become involved in often risky action on behalf of these. In presenting this heading, I may seem either to be duplicating part of what is contained under heading 8, or to be crudely running together great human ventures which deserve individual treatment. But it is my belief that the major fact of the changing role and status of the black American relates both to the kind of changing circumstances which were producing modifications in class and family relationships and to the conscious protest

17

movements not just against segregation and discrimination but against the destruction of the environment, consumer society, and militaristic imperialism. Also involved are the American urban riots of 1965 and the events of 1968–9, the new feminism, and the beginnings of gay liberation.

16. The first intimations of the electrifying challenges implicit in the concept of the entire West as a collection of multicultural societies. Just when formal segregation between black and white was being dismantled in America, Britain and France acquired substantial racial minorities; a process which began in Italy in the early seventies. It is my belief that the only societies for the future are multicultural ones, societies which will exhibit to the full the vibrancy and creative potential which first bloomed in the sixties. Of all my assertions this must be the most controversial, given that everywhere today there are frequent and ugly reminders of the persistence of racism. Yet the glimpses in the sixties of what multiculturalism might entail may well prove to be the most important legacy of the cultural revolution, or mini-renaissance, of 1958-74.[21]

## Sources and Methods

A very Stonehenge of assertion there; validation will be the task of the rest of this book. My methods are those of the professional historian, a scientist, I have said, rather than a poet or novelist (though history is not a mathematical subject in the way that most of the sciences are). Society owes much to its historians: and what a lot we know about the remotest civilizations, about the strange republics which—after 1989—kept turning up in the former Soviet Union, about the origins of the Second World War, about the treatment of women in ancient Athens. The past has such a profound impact on the present, and on what will happen in the future, that an understanding of the past, a knowledge of history, is essential. We need a history supported by evidence and based on dispassionate analysis. We need a history which tells it, as nearly as humans can, as it was. We do not need a history which goes on and on about the wickedness of the bourgeoisie, or which is merely designed to support predetermined theories about language, ideology, narratives, and discourse, as agents of bourgeois hegemony.

It is an inescapable fact of the intellectual world in which we live today that there is, on the one side, the non-metaphysical, source-based, scientific history of the historians and, on the other, the metaphysical history of those committed to left-wing political causes (or, alternatively, to the nihilistic philosophy that humanity is helpless in face of the impersonal structures of bourgeois thought and language): the postmodernists, the cultural theorists.[22] (I am equally critical of right-wing metaphysical histories such as Francis Fukuyama's *The End of History and the Last Man* (1992).) Unfortunately, there are historians who feel it politic to keep one foot in each camp, and who spatter their work with the artificial vocabulary of cultural theory, 'narrative', 'discourse', and that glib verb, 'to construct'. If I do not use such words in this book, it is not because I am not aware of them, it is because I am only too aware. They all carry a whole freight of Marxist and postmodernist assumptions about the way societies work. It is terrifically important that it be understood that what I am about to say about the sixties is based on the evidence provided by a wide range of primary sources, analysed with the professional techniques of the historian, and then reflected on at length, and discussed and argued over with colleagues; and also on the evidence provided by other historians in their books (known as secondary sources) based on their work in the primary sources.

What I am definitely not prepared to do is to adopt the stance of the metaphysicians, Marxists, and cultural theorists, and tell you that the songs of the Beatles form part of a discourse which prevents blacks and workers from demanding their rights, that Antonioni's film *Blow Up* is constructed to persuade everyone that they live in the happiest of all possible worlds, and that the miniskirts of Mary Quant are 'texts' designed to make women resign themselves to bourgeois patriarchy. At times I shall have to be rather pedantic in discussing the use of such words as 'culture' and 'subculture', and 'hep', 'hip', 'hippie', 'yippie', and 'underground', but I shall not use the language of the cultural theorists. The postmodernists are right about the dangers and difficulties of language, though wrong in the conclusions they draw. Very properly, poets and novelists exploit the ambiguities and resonances of certain words and phrases; historians, however, should be explicit and precise. I shall try, though I may not fully succeed, to avoid empty metaphors and flabby clichés. Crafty rhetoric I confine (I hope!) to my chapter headings, where much has to be signified in little. Elsewhere, I shall always seek to spell things out as straightforwardly as I can. A fiendishly difficult task!

At times my quotations from the primary sources are quite long: I want to demonstrate the point that primary sources are not transparent, that, when one is looking for clear evidence, they have many weaknesses and obscurities, as well as strengths. There are many novels, many films, many artists and their works to refer to. Slick references to novels or to films which may well not be known to the reader are not helpful. Thus, in most cases I have adopted the technique of giving as much information about the novel or film as is necessary to give the reader some chance of agreeing or disagreeing with the points I am trying to make. Readers, I think, need to know the basics about the intentions of those who produced the novel or film, and need to know *what* they are saying overall, and *how* they are saying it, if my citations and (in the case of novels) quotations are to play a serious part in my developing arguments. I believe it is important to study how 'texts' are marketed and 'consumed'; I do not for one moment believe the post-structuralist claim that texts exist independently of author, artist, or director. It is a fundamental principle of mine that readers should be fully informed as to the basis upon which I am making my arguments and statements so that they are at all times free to disagree with me: I have gone on record as saying that I don't think any historian, in any one book, can ever get it more than about 80 per cent right—leaving 20 per cent which may be sheer speculation, or just downright wrong. Those who are upset over my atheism in respect to Marxism[23] tend to react as though rejecting Marxism is equivalent to snatching the crust from the starving widow's mouth, or lining trade union leaders up and shooting them. Nothing of the sort: I am just as convinced an atheist when it comes to the ideology of monetarism, market economics, and the virtues of unbridled private enterprise, and I believe in the rational study of the many evils which afflict the societies we live in, in order that effective solutions may be found as quickly as possible, and applied. I hope that outlook comes through in the pages which follow.

# 2

# If So, Why?

*Problems of Explanation*

Even supposing that my version of what happened in the sixties is broadly correct, we will still be left with the big question of *why* such movements and developments took place, and *why* they took place within this relatively short period of time. Such questions take us into the realm of causation (what 'caused' the sixties?), or, to use a term more precisely attuned to the way in which historians actually work, *explanation* (how do we 'explain' the sixties?).

Such is the nature of historical study, that it is impossible to work to a simple cause-and-effect model of this sort:

CAUSES → THE SIXTIES → CONSEQUENCES

One cannot make mechanistic distinctions between 'causes' and 'effects', because 'effects' immediately start becoming 'causes' of further effects; if we prefer the route of seeking for 'origins', we very quickly find that the 'origins' are products of some antecedent 'causes'. This book is focused on the period between 1958 and 1974. It is not intended in this short chapter to clear the ground by providing a comprehensive explanation of why it was that new developments began to take place in 1958 and the years following. Explanations will, in fact, be embedded in my discussions of these developments as we come to them. However, I do want in this chapter to say something more about the nature of historical explanation, before identifying events which took place, and ideas which were pioneered, before 1958, which undoubtedly affected developments within the sixties. Above all I will be stressing the importance of *convergence*, of the way many circumstances came together to create the unique conditions of the sixties.

First I want to set out schematically what I believe is the best way of approaching the problem of historical explanation. Essentially what I am offering here is a hierarchy of explanatory factors (these factors being capable of operating both as forces for change and as constraints upon change), organized into: (1) major forces and constraints; (2) events; (3) human agencies; and (4) convergences and contingencies.

## Major Forces And Constraints

There are three:

*(a)* Structural (geographical, demographic, economic, and technological): favourable trends in any of these will promote change; a low level of technology or a backward economy will be likely to inhibit change. We shall obviously want to look at the outcome of the wartime and postwar baby booms, leading to a great increase in the proportions of teenagers in the population, around the beginning of the sixties; at economic expansion and affluence; and at technological innovation. The growth of the multinational corporations and international trade may also be important.

*(b)* Ideological (what is believed and is possible to be believed, existing political and social philosophies): it is only when people stop believing that it is fundamentally woman's function to be a wife and mother, and to remain in the home, that changes in the role of women will be possible. Worthy of consideration are the following fifties developments: existentialism; the renewal of Marxism; the joining of Marxism to ideas of sexual liberation; the Dada-esque and revolutionary views of the Situationists; the 'Beat' philosophy; the advent of Marxist structuralism, and the founding of sociology departments in the European universities, both developments leading to an emphasis on the 'systems' or 'structures' which, allegedly, rule our lives; the emphasis, in university political science and history classes, particularly in America, on due process, public service, and democratic rights.

*(c)* Institutional (systems of government, justice, policing, voting, and education, religious organizations, working-class organizations, the family). I shall be arguing that, in combination with strong ideological prejudices against welfare legislation, the American federal system acted as a constraint upon the implementation of social welfare policies, and that the Italian system of government made the rapid and decisive implementation of any reform difficult.

### Events
It is a feature of social and cultural history as currently practised by non-metaphysical historians that proper weight is being given to the significance of events. Wars and economic crises are the most usual ones in our period. There can be no study of the sixties without consideration of the complex repercussions of the Vietnam war. The oil crisis of 1973 undoubtedly marks an ending to some of the optimistic and expansionist elements characteristic of the sixties. We should not forget the Second World War, during which great hopes were raised of a better world to follow, many of these dashed in the immediate aftermath of austerity in Europe, the Cold War, and the Nuclear Stalemate (or, looked at another way, the Threat of Mutual Annihilation).

21

## Human Agencies

Politicians, presidents, and prime ministers all aspire, by direct intervention, to alter the course of events; philanthropists and pressure groups all hope to influence them. My concern is with majorities, not minorities; but clearly we do have to take account of these individual human beings and groups of human beings, in public protests, popular culture, as well as the élite arts and high politics, who did, deliberately or otherwise, exercise some influence on the course of events.

## Convergence And Contingencies

The sharp expansion in the number of teenagers would not, of itself, have created the changes of the sixties. That needed to *coincide* with continuing affluence in America and rapid economic expansion in Europe, *and* with the new ideologies of civil rights, challenge to the family and other authorities, 'Free Speech', *and* with technological innovation, *and* with the birth of rock'n'roll. If affluence alone were responsible for the excitements and innovations of the sixties, the previous decade in the United States would be the 'swinging fifties', not the era of stuffy conformity that it actually was. An important element in sixties trends was the very reaction against that stuffiness. Continuing affluence in America was certainly necessary, but so too was the gathering experience of affluence in the European countries, making possible the new ambience of international cultural exchange. But affluence in, say, Italy did not automatically entail cultural revolution. As we shall see, Italians had to work extremely hard to profit from economic opportunity: they did this because of the new availability of consumer goods and modern conveniences. It was worth the struggle when that converted into an entirely new, and highly satisfying, lifestyle. The Vietnam war does not in itself explain the protest movements throughout America and Europe. It had to *coincide* with all the other things I've just mentioned. The advent of the Cold War had frustrated the aspirations engendered during the Second World War. As the Cold War thawed slightly, and as all those other developments took place, frustrations broke out, intensifying the movements for change. The youthfulness of John F. Kennedy originally seemed a liability to Democratic party managers. Then in the new circumstances it suddenly became an asset. Then Kennedy was shot (contingency), intensifying the potent mythology privileging youth and change.

In the third section of this chapter I shall try to weave all that together into a brief and preliminary account of why the special things (as I maintain) that happened in the sixties did happen, and why they happened in such a short space of time, 1958–74. But not everything happened in the same way in each of the four countries. This study is intended to bring out contrasts as well as comparisons.

## The Four Countries and their National Peculiarities

First, the question arises as to whether we consider the United States, spreading across the width of a whole continent, and with a population of 220 millions, to be a single society; or Italy, for that matter. For America, as it was in the fifties, there can be no missing the sharp contrasts between North and South; often, too, it is necessary to distinguish the relatively advanced milieux of California and the East coast, from the vast bulk of 'middle America'. In Italy, slightly smaller in geographical extent than Great Britain, and with a population of nearly 50 millions, economic change was accelerating at the end of the fifties, but the division between the relatively industrialized north and the backward, agriculture-based south was still very stark. France was about twice the size of Great Britain, but with the same population, of around 55 millions. Britain, like substantial parts of the United States, was very heavily industrialized; in France, in 1952, 31.8 per cent of the working population was still employed on the land (though, as in Italy, things were beginning to change rapidly), while in Italy the figure was still higher, at 42.4 per cent. When I first embarked upon my researches I thought it might be possible to draw parallels between the peasantry of southern Italy and the blacks of the American South; quickly it became apparent to me that, while race, as a problem in the European countries, was just beginning to announce itself (the outbreak in 1954 of the Algerian war for liberation from French colonial rule meant that North Africans living in France had to face an added dimension of hostility, while Britain had its first notable race riots in 1958), the race issue in America at this time had its own special character and scale which were to have a determining influence on a range of developments in the sixties.

The special character of American political structures, and the ideology they embodied, also inhibited social change initiated by human agency: in particular, America lacked a powerful, dedicated, centralized bureaucracy, the very size of the country being against this anyway. Whatever the scope of federal initiatives, these nearly always depended upon the willingness of state governments to implement them, and were usually channelled through a variety of specially created agencies. Britain, primarily because of the broad two-party acceptance of the welfare state legislation of the late forties, had the most effective system from this point of view. France had a strong central government, though with welfare policies implemented through a variety of agencies. Italy's new postwar constitution, finally ratified in 1948, expressed high aspirations, but in fact Italy lacked the strong central government needed to put such aspirations into practice. Although Rome was officially the Italian capital, it was not an unchallenged metropolitan centre in the style of Paris or London. In particular, Milan operated almost as an alternative capital. In Italy much was accomplished at local level, and community organizations, generally dominated either by the Christian Democrat party and the Catholic Church or by the Communist party, were very important. It is not my intention to place much stress on these matters, since most of the changes I am concerned with came from within society, rather than being imposed from above; but it is critical when considering the condition of the poor that, in America, political structures reinforced a prevailing ideology highly supportive of individual enterprise and therefore hostile to welfare policies,[1] while in Italy a broadly reformist ideology was frustrated by the inefficiencies of the Italian political system.

Many of the distinguishing characteristics of the different societies were legacies from the past. Britain and France had long been established as centralized nation-states. Italy, and in particular the south, had had a long history of rule by oppressive foreign dynasties, and only became a unified nation-state in the second half of the nineteenth century, under the French-speaking royal family from Piedmont; the south did not readily reconcile itself to rule from the north. Legacies from the past show themselves particularly strongly in the realm of law and order and policing. Italy and France shared in a Napoleonic tradition whereby the most prestigious branch of the police began as a part of the military; America inherited the British tradition whereby the whole idea of maintaining any kind of standing army was abhorrent, and where the police were created as a specifically civilian force.[2] America, however, retained the concept of a voluntary, non-professional militia, which became known as the National Guard—ill-trained, trigger-happy, recruiting only from those who could afford to serve, attracting the conservative and the bigoted. In France the Napoleonic tradition is represented by the Gendarmerie Nationale (numbering about 80,000 in the sixties), who are soldiers, housed in barracks with their families, and under the authority of the Ministry of Defence.[3] A smaller force than the Police Nationale (108,000 in the sixties), they tended to be less in evidence, being responsible for the policing of towns with populations of under 10,000. However, there was also a special force, the Gendarmerie Mobile, fully equipped to deal ruthlessly with civil disturbances and protests. The national police were under the control of the minister of the interior, save that the Paris police were a law unto themselves, under the control of the Paris prefect of police. In European countries, where upheavals and changes of regime have been rather more common than in Britain, there has long been a tendency to take the view that as long as the police show a general loyalty to the existing regime, they should not be supervised too closely; in other words, the police forces tend to become independent little states within the state. In France, there were effectively two little states within the state, police and gendarmes being jealous of, and very reluctant to cooperate with, each other.

Something of the arrogance of the police, and their contempt for civilian authority, can be seen in the events of March 1958 when 3,000 police marched to the French National Assembly and laid siege to it, expressing their hostility to liberal policies generally, and to any weakness in the prosecution of the war in Algeria. This action played a part in bringing down the Fourth Republic, and its replacement by the presidential regime of General de Gaulle. There was a further notorious incident in 1959, when a leading Moroccan dissident, Ben Barka, was kidnapped in front of a famous café in the university quarter of Paris, the Brasserie Lipp, and, it was presumed, murdered. Investigations revealed that the police, and in particular the Paris prefecture of police, had been involved: thus a law of July 1960 abolished the independence of the Paris police, integrating it into one single national police force.[4] The national police had its own special, and highly notorious, force, the Compagnies Républicaines de Sécurité (CRS)—founded after the Second World War, and, like the Gendarmerie Mobile, fully equipped to take repressive action against protests and disturbances; although the members of the CRS were actually civilians, their character is fully conveyed in the fact that they used army ranks, and were housed in barracks. Local control of these various types of police force was in the hands of the local prefect, who, it should be noted, was not some locally elected representative of the community but a direct appointee by the ministry of the interior.

Italy's Carabinieri were not actually part of the army, though both officers and men had to have had previous service with the regular army, while their commanding officer was always a three-star general on assignment from the regular army—that this was not an inferior, dead-end posting is shown by the fact that he could usually expect further promotion within the army.[5] The Carabinieri operated a mechanized brigade of their own, a miniature air force, and a miniature navy of coastal patrol vessels. In the main, the Carabinieri recruited from the upper echelons of Italian society: they felt a responsibility, perhaps, more to Italy's established families than to whichever politicians happened to be in power at any point. According to the constitution they were under the authority of the ministry of the interior, but in practice they paid greater heed to their commanding general and his headquarters in Rome. In the villages, the Carabinieri were the sole representatives of law and order; in the other parts of Italy they were in frequent competition and conflict with the ordinary police, formally under the control of the interior minister, but in practical terms responsible to the prefect in each of Italy's ninety-two provinces, these prefects however, ultimately being responsible to the interior minister. Operational responsibility in each province was with the *Questore*, who himself received detailed instructions from the chief of police within the interior ministry. The national police had their own, extremely brutal, analogue of the French CRS, the Célere, also founded immediately after the Second World War, when Communist subversion was particularly feared. The Carabinieri probably received more respect than the ordinary police, but the fact that they were seen as very much members of a state apart from ordinary society could be seen in the number of traditional jokes about them, similar to British jokes about the Irish, or American jokes about the Poles. Just to add to the confusion and conflict of responsibilities, there were two other police forces, the Guardia di Finanza, a body of around 40,000 charged mainly with dealing with taxation crimes and financial corruption, and the Vigili, concerned mainly with routine administrative matters.

Italy had the special problem of the powerful and highly organized criminal network (divided into different branches, with different names in different parts of southern Italy) the Mafia, which had links both to politicians and police.[6] The Fascist dictator Mussolini had waged war against the Mafia in the interwar years with some success, but members of the Mafia (because they were anti-Mussolini) attained important positions (as mayors, for instance) during the Allied invasion of Italy during the Second World War. In the postwar years, as Italian governments favoured progressive social policies, the big vested interests used the Mafia as a counterpoise to leftist politicians, while the Christian Democrat party was often prepared to ally with the Mafia against the powerful Italian Communist party; at the same time the Mafia moved into the more sophisticated areas of modern crime, such as drugs and prostitution. In the early sixties there were 'Mafia wars' between the different factions, and concerted government investigations were begun. In 1962 a standing parliamentary commission, the Anti Mafia, was appointed: its final report in 1976 revealed publicly the many contacts between the top leadership in the Mafia and the Christian Democrat party.[7]

All members of the police and paramilitary forces in both countries carried guns, making slightly ironic the title of the ordinary French constable, *gardien de la paix* (guardian of the peace). That was also the situation in the United States, where, although the British system of control of police forces by elected local authorities had been replicated, there had long been a high level of gun ownership throughout the community, and an ambience in which the almost casual use of guns by police officers was hardly questioned. The battle between the National Rifle Association, with its slogan, 'Guns don't kill people; people kill people', and Hand Gun Control Inc., with its slogan, 'Guns don't die; people do', was a very unequal one.[8] A measure of the problem can be seen in the 1968 Federal Gun Control Act, which merely prohibited the import of guns from one state to another, and their sale to minors, drug addicts, and felons. Systematic policing was made more difficult by the complexity of relationships between local, state, and federal government. The National Guards were state militias, composed exclusively of white volunteers, usually racist and right-wing in outlook, poorly trained, unprofessional in outlook, yet equipped with highly lethal weapons. They could be mobilized by the federal as well as the state authorities. At their sole disposal (though the organizations tended to be run secretively and independently) the federal authorities had the Federal Bureau of Investigation (FBI), under J. Edgar Hoover, paranoiac in his opposition to civil rights activists, particularly Martin Luther King, and the intelligence-gathering body the Central Intelligence Agency (CIA), paranoiac about un-American activities. Throughout the sixties these bodies maintained dubiously legal surveillance on protesters and activists of any sort, as, indeed, did local police forces. Well before the sixties the CIA had penetrated the main American student organizations and, indeed, ran them.[9]

The possession of guns was the defining feature of the forces of law and order in each of these three countries, a feature which determined that whenever there were major civil disturbances, loss of life was always a strong possibility. This is where police forces in Britain were fundamentally different, and why demonstrations and protests were usually of a profoundly different character. However, in Northern Ireland the Royal Irish Constabulary were armed; in the phase of extreme violence across Europe and America during and after 1968/9 Northern Ireland got its full share. Even in Britain, the attitude of leaving the police to get on with their job without asking too many questions tended to operate, though on the whole respect for the unarmed British 'bobby' was probably higher than that for the police forces in the other countries. Formally, all British police forces, save those in London, where there was direct control by the Home Secretary, were under the control of the elected local authorities. In practice the Home Secretary had always exercised *de facto* powers over the local police forces, and the Royal Commission on the Police in England and Wales, set up in January 1960, recommended that this should become *de jure*. The recommendation was implemented in the 1964 Police Act, which also made it clear that police officers had the power to act throughout the United Kingdom, not just in their own local authority areas, while reducing the total number of separate police forces.[10] It will be a theme of this book that civil disturbances in the sixties were often provoked by inappropriate, or racially prejudiced, actions on the part of the police. Events were to show that racism was often to be found in the ranks of the British police.

Proportional to their populations, Italy, followed by France, had the largest police force; then America; then Britain.[11] The police presence was always particularly evident in Italy: Italian police actions, along with those in France and America, often seemed to have a punitive quality about them, particularly in the way in which officers freely wielded their truncheons. It is important, therefore, to mention one other critical measure of civilization, in which Italy comes out with the highest honours. The Italians are justly renowned for their love of children, and it is a simple fact that, going back to the Renaissance, there was never ever any use of corporal punishment in Italian schools. Corporal punishment in schools was abolished in France in 1881; in parts of America in the sixties it was still in use in primary, though not in secondary, schools.[12] It is a severe qualification to any other claims that might be made about the rational and tolerant nature of British society that severe beating of children of all ages, in the most expensive boarding-schools as well as in the wretchedly under-equipped schools of working-class districts, continued to take place throughout the sixties and right on until the eighties.

Fear of nuclear war was a very strong emotion in the America of the fifties: in a letter drawn to my attention in the Mississippi Valley Archives, an architect cautions a Long Island client against proceeding with the building of a new house, to replace one that has been burned down: 'Do not forget the priorities affecting the securing of materials will be imposed by the government within a comparatively short time because of impending war with Russia.' Theatre programmes dating from 1956 give instructions on what to do 'in the event of an air raid alarm'.[13] American leaders, and large numbers of the American people, perceived their country as *the* major force for good in the world and as, above all, the nation with a 'manifest destiny' to oppose Communism wherever it appeared. This mission was highlighted, first by the Russian-inspired building of the Berlin Wall, in August 1961, to prevent escapes from East Berlin to West Berlin, then by the cosmic crisis of 1962, when the Russians attempted to place nuclear missiles in Cuba and were then forced to withdraw them, and continued even as relationships with Russia took on a warmer hue. Many motivations, and many mistakes, were involved in the appallingly muddled tragedy which was America's involvement in the Vietnam war, but this underlying sense of national destiny and world mission, along with the dreadful costs and the bitter controversies imbricated in the war, when television clearly showed the atrocities being committed by American forces against unarmed civilians, are factors of the utmost importance in determining certain developments in sixties America. For analogous elements of national glorification, we would have to turn to France, from 1958 ruled under a new authoritarian constitution by General de Gaulle. He, it is true, freed France in 1962 from the entanglements of the Algerian war, but the main relevancy of his presidency to our concerns is his extreme restrictiveness and conservatism in domestic policies, designed, for example, to keep working-class incomes as low as possible. Save with respect to a certain encouragement of the arts and respect for historic city centres, the regime tended to operate as something of a damper on sixties trends, though ultimately it was spectacularly challenged in the events of 1968.

Britain, prior to the sixties, though generally lauded abroad for high standards of civic loyalty and public service, for parliamentary institutions and the peaceful introduction of the welfare state, was considered philistine when it came to the arts and philosophy. Since the war, American Abstract Expressionism had dominated the art world, challenged only by *art informel* emanating from Paris and the COBRA group of artists from some of the smaller north European countries. In Europe, Marxisant conceptions of existing societies as essentially bourgeois, and of the means by which change to a better society would come about, continued to dominate; the renewal of Marxism came mainly from the publication in Italy of the ideas of Antonio Gramsci, that country's foremost twentieth-century Marxist thinker, imprisoned by Mussolini, and pioneer of the new emphasis on the alleged importance of bourgeois 'cultural hegemony', and from the transmission through Herbert Marcuse in America of the theories of the Frankfurt School of the 1920s, joining Marxist 'liberation' to the freedom from sexual repression advocated by Freud. Particularly important was the American publication of new translations of works by an early disciple of Freud, William Reich: *Sexual Revolution* and *Selected Writings* (1961); *The Importance of the Organism* (1962). The International Situationist Movement, whose leading figure was the Frenchman Guy Debord, was founded in 1957 in the little Italian town of Cosio d'Avroscia. The Situationists—the term is perhaps best understood if one thinks of the French phrase *en situation*, which has something of the force of 'in a real-life situation'—came up with the headiest mix of the main ingredients of sixties activism, protest, art, counter-culture, and fun: the 'liberation of desire'; the energetic involvement of everyone; sustained attacks on 'bourgeois society', aiming at its overthrowal. Bourgeois society was excoriated for its consumerism and the passivity of the masses; it was 'the society of spectacle', with art merely a part of consumerism. Spectacle had to be replaced by 'the construction of situations', in which 'everyone must search for what they love, for what attracts them', applying their imaginations to 'the transformation of reality', thus making everyday life 'passionate, rational, dramatic'.[14] The existentialism of Sartre was also basically Marxist in its social implications, and was particularly relevant to the new generation both in its insistence on political commitment and in its demand that people should reject 'bad faith', that is, leading lives according to the false conventions of society, and opt instead for 'authentic' existence. For young women, a special inspiration was provided by Simone de Beauvoir's *The Second Sex*, which comprehensively argued that women's roles are not determined by biology but are imposed on them by society.[15]

In America, the Beats and their philosophy became a national sensation, just a year behind rock'n'roll star Elvis Presley (who, as I shall explain further in Chapter 3, became a national figure in 1956), when Allen Ginsberg's *Howl and Other Poems,* having been confiscated by the San Francisco police in May 1957, was adjudged to 'have some redeeming social importance' and acquitted of being obscene on 3 October,[16] and Jack Kerouac's *On the Road* became a best seller.[17] The Beats all came from relatively privileged backgrounds. William Burroughs was a rich patrician from the famous office machine family, and a Harvard graduate. Ginsberg, a graduate of Columbia University, had been brought up in Patterson, New Jersey, where his father was a high school teacher and minor poet. Kerouac came from lower down in the middle class, but, on a football scholarship, got to Columbia, before dropping out. The early Beats met up in New York in the late forties. The term 'Beat', apparently, was used by a drug dealer on Times Square, New York, to describe the drifters and addicts he supplied, and the state of exalted exhaustion they achieved. To Kerouac, in 1948, the revelation came that his was 'really a Beat generation', or at least that tiny part of it which, as Ginsberg saw it, was hostile to materialism and conformist career-building. From New York, Ginsberg moved to that other vibrant centre, San Francisco, settling in North Beach.[18] There, during 1955 and 1956, poetry readings were given by figures in the 'San Francisco Poetry Renaissance', and there, in 1955, Lawrence Ferlinghetti established his City Lights Bookstore. The Beats were a serendipitous combination of New York and San

Francisco bohemia. They took on all kinds of jobs and they travelled. In 1953 Burroughs went to Tangier, where he started *The Naked Lunch* as a record of drug addiction. The couplet on the title-page of *Howl and Other Poems*, which is dedicated in part to Kerouac and Burroughs, encapsulates the Beat message for American society:

> unscrew the locks from the doors!
> unscrew the doors themselves from their jambs!

When the Beat writers became news in 1957, they were attacked by most mainstream critics; others saluted their rejection of materialistic values and seeking for a deeper meaning to life. For young people around 1960, picking out what appealed to them, Beat attitudes seemed to go well with what were understood to be existentialist ones. The term 'beatnik' is something very different. It was coined by the humorous San Francisco journalist Herb Caen, in the aftermath of the shock of the successful orbits in the autumn of 1957 of the Russian spacecraft, Sputniks I and II: beatniks were the early participants, usually bearded and wearing sandals, in the civil rights and other protests of the late fifties and early sixties.[19]

Marxism was not strong in either America or Britain, though it was in the latter that the term 'New Left' came into use to describe the response among certain intellectuals to the renewal of Marxism, represented in the founding of the *Universities and Left Review* in 1955. The name is actually rather more important than the reality, since from 1960 onwards it was appropriated by a suddenly appearing, but much more significant, movement in America. With respect to left-wing politics and ideas, America was almost totally quiescent up to the very end of the fifties. Britain did have a Labour party which had been in office from 1945 up until 1951, was to regain power again in 1964, and led the British consensus on reformist welfare policies. America had no Labour or Social Democratic party.

The question of religious practices and beliefs is relevant to both ideological and institutional constraints on social change. In France and Italy, the Catholic Church was a very strong presence. Priests in the parishes could wield enormous influence, though they were always subject to disciplining by the bishop of the diocese, whose only superior was the Pope himself. The grip of the Catholic Church on social values and private morality was particularly strong in Italy, where many who gave formal allegiance to the Communist party were deeply imbued with Catholic notions about contraception, divorce, and abortion. Anything savouring of permissiveness would meet with great resistance in Italy; and much the same was true of many areas of France. The main source of alternative social values in both countries was the Communist party, but even where it was openly anti-Catholic it tended to be puritanical and opposed to the anti-authoritarian attitudes of youth. Still, the Catholic Church was far from monolithic and unchanging. During the war the worker priest movement had started in France, and this became the core from which left-wing and Marxist ideas spread among priests in both France and Italy. Pope Pius XII, tainted with support for Fascism, was conservative to the extent of being reactionary; however, the succession in 1958 of the liberal Pope John XXIII raised hopes of a more enlightened Catholicism and the encouragement of progressive tendencies within the Church.[20]

Nonetheless, it has to be stated that throughout the sixties the Catholic Church tended to operate as a centre of opposition to all the great movements aiming towards greater freedom for ordinary human beings.

Similar comments about institutional religion can be made about certain parts of the United States—again we have to remember that different regions had different characteristics. Both traditional Catholic morality and traditional Jewish morality were very strong in certain urban areas; but the truly ponderous obstruction on the paths to new thinking and freer lifestyles was the pervasive influence across the Mid-West and the South of various brands of fundamentalist Protestantism. Christian belief was undoubtedly an important force behind the black civil rights movement, but white ministers were often obstacles; sometimes white ministers of genuinely liberal and humane outlook felt intimidated by the prejudices of their flock.[21] As late as April 1968, a Memphis cleric gave this explanation for his refusal to invite his congregation to contribute to the campaign against black poverty: 'Why do something radical and lose your job and disturb the congregation?'[22] Martin Luther King's 'letter from Birmingham Jail', discussed in Chapter 5, indicted *all* the church leaders of the town for opposing his strategy of non-violent resistance to segregation. On such important social issues as divorce and consumption of alcohol there was much hypocrisy: 'strict morality and easy divorce' and 'drinking wet and voting dry', as contemporary dissidents put it. In the South there were strict formal controls on the sale and consumption of alcohol, so that one of the quite significant, though relatively little-known, campaigns of the sixties became that of the right to 'liquor by the drink': in most places alcohol had to be purchased from a liquor store, the numbers of which were strictly regulated, there being few or none in the more salubrious suburbs, then taken in the proverbial brown bag into a bar or restaurant where a 'setup'—a mixer, or simply a glass of water, would be supplied for a ludicrous price; some of the more expensive joints could themselves supply full bottles, but never 'liquor by the drink'.

Thus Sheriff Hinds in Memphis had an undercover agent keeping an eye on liquor violations, both illegal sales and illegal pot-still production, as well as on prostitution. In the Hinds papers there exist the illiterate scrawls which the agent produced on any old scrap of paper. Under the dateline January 2 1963, we read:

> Also made a purchase at *George Harris* home at 487 jensen, he got a good layout. when you get in, he tell his customer, I got Scotch Beer Gin Bourbon Vodka are some good Posturepedic mattress 2 00 hour.
>
> There a White Lady suppose to Be Working at a *trucking Company,* that *dating Negro* for 20,000 or 30,000 a date... Oh yes that white night club down their near the state line had a private party Monday nite they say... this Negro girl Keep up with these Nite Club I will check more with her she is real nice looking And, I think Something is happening Beside Partys...[23]

You bet it was! And we get a glimpse of the reality of sex appeal across race lines, and of the lines themselves: white *lady*, Negro *girl*. Britain, with the lowest church attendance figures in Europe, was notably unaffected by Catholic puritanism, bible belt evangelicalism, or, for that matter, the bourgeois stolidity of German Christian Democracy: Britain (excluding Northern Ireland where, as in the Republic, church attendance was high) was pervaded by what can conveniently be termed 'secular Anglicanism', a tolerance originating in the Anglican Church of the eighteenth century, and spreading in more recent times to civil society. For all their conservatism and traditionalism in certain aspects, British social arrangements had long had a certain commonsense quality to them: women were subordinate to men, but then they were economically dependent; children were subordinate to their parents, but then they too were economically dependent. With the shifts in these and other circumstances and with the mounting of new challenges to tradition and authority, Britain was in many respects the country best adapted to responding tolerantly, and even to absorbing the changes and challenges. There was an obverse to all this. Not only was Britain perceived as a philistine nation in high culture, but her popular culture was derivative and second-rate, coming almost exclusively from America and, in the case of youth fashion, also from Italy. Hollywood and tin-pan alley were becoming boring and repetitive, but still exercised great power. Out of black music, combined with white country and western, white performers had spun a vigorous alternative popular music, rock'n'roll, while France was, as an expert on French popular music put it, enjoying a 'golden age', with Piaf, Tino Rossi, Chevalier, Montand, Bécaud, Brassens, les Frères Jacques, and les Compagnons de la Chanson.[24] Italy had a well-established popular music industry, independent of the American one, and bolstered by the San Remo Festival founded in 1952; the opening of the new period of international cultural exchange had indeed been signalled by the world hit, Domenico Modugno's *Volare (nel blu dipinto di blu)* (Flying—in the blue painted in blue). Britain was only in the process, in its working-class and lower-middle-class heartlands, of constructing a new popular music, derived directly from black America but with a recognizable character of its own. What happened next, in art, literature, theatre, cinema, as well as rock/pop music and popular culture, will be discussed in Chapters 3 and 10; but for the moment Britain was, relatively speaking, an empty vessel in the realm of cultural creation. That there was an empty vessel waiting to be filled—as indeed it soon was, and to overflowing—helps to explain why, in the cultural revolution about to break out, Britain assumed a surprising primacy.

## Convergence and the Forces of Change

Affluence came to America during the Second World War, and (though with many pockets of severe poverty) expanded and spread thereafter, with an acceleration towards the end of the fifties; economic recovery began in Europe from 1948 onwards. Slowly the economic basis was established for the production, consumption, and international exchange of new consumer goods. Much of the international trade in fashion and leisure items was carried on by small entrepreneurs, but there can be no doubts as to the significance of the emergence of the multinational conglomerates, of which there were very few before 1955. By 1967, 182 of the 500 largest American firms were multinational; between 1960 and 1970 their sales more than tripled.[25] The first English beer to be sold in the new British-style pubs in America came from the giant firms Watney's and Whitbread. Economic change combined with demography, specifically the 'baby boom' at the end of the Second World War, producing by the beginning of the sixties an unprecedentedly large, and unprecedentedly well-off, teenage presence, including the distinctive presence of girls, in the market-place (and young people, as capital became more readily available, could operate as producers as well as consumers). Teenagers tended to get much of the attention, but other presences were important as well: the working class, racial and ethnic minorities, the provinces (as against metropolitan dominance), and, in lesser degree to begin with, women; crucially important, though often neglected, were young and not-so-young married couples, now possessed of a comfortable margin to spend on consumer goods (one of several key novels to be examined in detail in this book is Georges Perec's *Things: A Story of the Sixties*, published in 1965 and concerned with a young couple's acquisition of, and desire for, consumer goods). The major technological developments have already been listed in the fourth of my 'characteristics of a unique era'.[26] The Watney's and Whitbread beer marketed in America was the new, easy-travelling, pasteurized, 'keg' variety, in metal barrels.

In the realm of ideology, conservative forces were strong, reinforced by the frigid influences of the Cold War, and hysteria in the United States about 'un-American' activities. Affluence and consumerism were taken as validating the perfections of existing society. However, new critiques of society were appearing in the fifties, and formed the basis for the much more rapid and extended circulation of critical ideas in the sixties: renewed Marxism, theories of Marxist protest joined to those of Freudian sexual liberation—best seen in Herbert Marcuse's *Eros and Civilization*, published in America in 1955—Marxist structuralism, Marxist sociology, Situationism, and Beat philosophy. Old racial boundaries were crossed as young whites adopted and adapted black rhythm and blues. The Second World War had been accompanied by a good deal of social upheaval. More important, as a war of heroic resistance to the evils of Nazism, and a war in which everyone participated (workers, women, blacks), it raised great hopes, and indeed promises, of substantial social change, in regard to such issues as civil rights for American blacks, or better conditions for Italian peasants.[27] In the years of struggle for economic recovery (in Europe) and of dominance by the imperatives of the Cold War, very many of these hopes had been frustrated, but they began to emerge again at the end of the fifties. Also significant, therefore, in creating certain of the movements so prominent in sixties society was the breaking out of the frustrations which had been dammed up since the early postwar years. Generally, the conservative and unchanging nature of institutions added to these frustrations. The most concentrated change took place in Britain, where the art colleges, benefiting from postwar educational growth, were particularly potent centres of innovation; but generally educational institutions (along with those of religion, policing, etc.) were very out of touch in America and the other European countries.

The unique ingredient which made it possible for all these movements to develop and expand was—in one of the most significant single examples of convergence—economic security, which underwrote innovation and daring, and minimized attendant risks. The different subcultures expanded and interacted, affecting more and more of society. In a time of affluence, and of eager commercial backers, nothing succeeded like excess. In the past, extreme movements had tended to be followed by extreme reactions. Now the old checks and balances were not operating.

Extreme positions led on to yet more extreme ones. Daring films ratified daring behaviour. Though the pill was not in fact in wide use, sexual activity became a matter for discussion, and thus a matter legitimated beyond the traditional constraints. Society seemed to offer greater possibilities than ever before for self-fulfilment, yet poverty, inequality, authoritarianism remained; hence the critiques of society got stronger and stronger. Signs of thaw in the Cold War stimulated relaxation in the more rigid nationalistic and authoritarian attitudes; the end of the Algerian war had similar effects in France.

Two contrasting features of the High Sixties are the permeation of society by new ideas, and extremely violent confrontations. The basic explanation for this lies in the emergence of a triangle of contrasting forces, ideological and institutional: (1) the new protest, innovative, and 'counter-cultural' movements; (2) the liberal and consensual elements (in some areas at least, even if they had blind spots and conservative or nationalistic attitudes in others) occupying some important positions of power (Presidents Kennedy and Johnson, and, more important, their advisers and functionaries; figures in the judiciary, broadcasting, censorship, education believing that they had to respond to a changing society; Keynesians—those of progressive economic outlook—in the civil services); (3) utterly unreformed reactionary elements, particularly in the various police forces. The Vietnam war—blind spot for many American liberals, though also opposed by many American liberals—served to focus and crystallize general anti-imperialist, anti-establishment sentiment.

Let me refer again to the Memphis Sanitation workers' strike. This was a product of longer-term grievances interacting with *both* the new black consciousness *and* determined conservative resistance. The strike shook the consciences of an important group of upper-middle-class women, already stirred by earlier events in the sixties—and, of course, there is nothing like the stink of garbage in your own backyard for promoting action. It so happened that Martin Luther King saw the strike as a cause ripe for his intervention; it happened further that King, having arrived in Memphis, was shortly afterwards assassinated. The repercussions of this microcosm of cumulation, convergence, and series of reinforcing contingencies, were immense; for one thing, the complacency of well-off Memphis whites was shattered. Many other examples, each unique but each contributing to ever-accelerating change in the sixties, will be discussed in the course of this study.

Part II

# The First Stirrings of a Cultural Revolution, 1958–1963

# 3

# New Actors, New Activities

### *The Common Currency of Change*

At the time of the 1959 general election in Britain a vulgar joke, shared by men and women, raced round the country, symbolic perhaps both of the unreconstructed sexism and political incorrectness of the time and of the more ready broaching in mixed company of risqué topics, signalled particularly forcefully in the recently released film *Room at the Top:* a woman reports that she has been raped by a candidate out canvassing for votes—it must have been the Conservative candidate, she adds—'I've never had it so good'. The phrase, actually used in circumspect fashion in a speech warning against the dangers of inflation he had given more than a year previously, had become indissolubly associated with the Conservative prime minister, Harold Macmillan, who, as 'Supermac', was perceived as presiding over a new era of consumer affluence.[1] At about the same time the *New Statesman* published a cartoon in which an old man is staring bleary-eyed at the moving images just perceptible in one of the new consumer wonders: 'No, grandpa,' his daughter is saying, 'that's the washing machine, not the television.' The almost unconsidered purchase of gadgets by ordinary families had been going on rather longer in the United States. From the first years of the Second World War, all but the substantial underclass had enjoyed an affluence which was sustained throughout the forties and fifties, whereas in European countries the fruits of recovery from the varying degrees of privation endured during the war were only just becoming available. Thus the notion of high-spending 'teenagers' as new and influential players in the market-place, creating a distinct and separate 'youth culture', appeared first in the United States, becoming a commonplace in the press and among academic sociologists from late 1957 onwards. The same notion quickly surfaced in Britain, being trumpeted in a trio of dovetailing, and much-quoted, texts of 1959–60—a market survey (*The Teenage*

*Consumer* by Mark Abrams), a novel *(Absolute Beginners* by Colin MacInnes), and a Ministry of Education White Paper, *The Youth Service in England and Wales* (usually referred to as 'The Albemarle Report').[2] Indeed, 'the teenage revolution' and 'the new youth culture' have, like 'the rise of the middle class' before them, become clattering clichés ready for collapse into the pages of an updated *1066 and All That*.

In common with all such clichés they embody much truth. Both sustained affluence and the upturn in the birth rate appeared earliest in America, but ultimately Britain, France, and Italy were also affected. Thus by the beginning of the sixties there were more teenagers, and they had more money to spend. They had their own tastes and their own leisure activities, and therefore they purchased specific products related to these activities. It was not unreasonable to perceive the totality of teenage customs and practices as constituting a separate and distinctive subculture (with, however—a point less appreciated at the time than it is today—boys and girls fulfilling distinctively different roles within that subculture). Most contemporary (and many subsequent) accounts failed to appreciate the implications of the inescapable fact that this subculture, far from constituting a self-contained package of oppositional values, was itself a product of the wider society and of the many, and sometimes contradictory, forces operating in that society. The youth subcultures of the late fifties (made up, in the different countries, of slightly different mixes of, and slightly different variations on, the same basic components) did turn out, in the light of what actually happened in the sixties, to have contained elements of true historical significance; but this was only because they interacted with, and were inflected by, other important developments, leading to a situation in which certain characteristics, once peculiar to the youth subcultures, came to pervade society as a whole. Economic and demographic changes were the structural imperatives behind the advent of the youth subcultures: but urbanization (which diminished rural isolation), mass communications (in particular, television and radio), and nationwide educational reforms, all helped to make the subcultures homogeneous within themselves.[3] The forces of parochialism and conformity were strong, and many aspects of the youth subcultures were very conservative; at the same time, even the most conservative young people could never be totally immune from all aspects (including travesties) of the new ideologies of self-expression and social criticism associated with the Beats, the existentialists, and the neo-Marxist 'New Left'. Very self-consciously in America, slightly less so in the other countries, commercial interests, backed and sometimes prodded by professional market researchers, were both seeking out and trying to create new markets: while it would be utterly absurd to see the youth subcultures as entirely, or even largely, constructed by profit-seeking entrepreneurs, it would also be absurd to ignore the extent to which they were tied in to the everyday world of consumerism and private enterprise. However, even that is not the end to a tale far more complex than the famous clichés allowed; for the successful entrepreneurs of youth subculture had themselves to be flexible and adventurous, youthful in outlook and, increasingly, in actual years.

Youth is about the least monolithic and the least stable of categories into which society can be divided. It is appropriate, for the reason just given, to start our exploration of the first stirrings of cultural revolution with the youth subcultures, which are paradigmatic cases of new actors whose new activities shortly achieved a multiplier effect, both through being treated as 'spectacle' by the media and in the eyes of non-participants, and through their convergence and interplay with the activities of other new actors; but even in their early stages of formation, the youth subcultures cannot be taken as operating in isolation from fundamental social facts, from, in particular, the facts of race and class, where much was unchanging but where there was also crucial change. Nor, though adolescence is itself naturally a time of sexual experimentation, can they be isolated from the broad changes in sexual attitudes and behaviour taking place in the wider society. Like almost all important and emotive words, 'culture', 'subculture', 'youth', and even 'teenager' are used in a variety of often imprecise ways. Already I have explained my own specialized usage in which I see 'subcultures' coming into existence, interacting, and modifying the entire 'culture', of the individual countries and, indeed, of the West as a whole, i.e. values, practices, relationships in and across the four countries; most commentators at the time spoke of 'youth *culture*', or 'teenage *culture*' (a widespread and perfectly legitimate usage which I have not totally eschewed myself), meaning the practices, values, leisure activities, and specialized purchases which they perceived as setting young people off as a separate 'class', or 'caste', or as establishing a distinctive 'teenage world'. Whether we speak of 'culture' or 'subculture' we are not, of course, envisaging one specific location in which the members of the culture or subculture can interact directly with each other. Mass communications were to be important in transmitting teenage preoccupations to the wider society; they were also essential for making possible what could genuinely be recognized as an America-wide teenage subculture, or a British, or an Italian one.

But is it *teenage* subculture, or *youth* subculture, or are the terms synonymous? If we study the many articles and books published in the various countries in the later fifties and at the beginning of the sixties, we find that attention is devoted to three slightly different categories of youth, each category being based partly on age and partly on class and educational criteria. First are the young earners, no longer at school, not yet married— these actually formed the 'teenagers' of Abrams's British survey, their actual age range being from 15 to 25 (those who were married being excluded). This was the sort of group (with the upper age limit set in the early 20s rather than 25), free of educational constraints, and, to a considerable degree, of family ones as well, which most concerned government agencies and religious bodies: this was the basic component of 'youth' as understood in Britain, France, and Italy. Second are pupils continuing in secondary education to, roughly, the end of their (strictly defined) teenage years. American surveys, less overtly cognizant of class distinctions between teenagers in full-time employment and those in high school, tended to lump both together. Third are students in various types of higher education: an age range running from the late teenage years to the early or (particularly for American postgraduate students) middle 20s. Usually studies of students are conducted separately, but sometimes commentators run all three categories together—as 'youth', or 'young people'.

However, behind all the awareness of, and concern about, youth (whatever the age range was taken to be) lay a biological phenomenon, emerging slowly across the preceding century, but accelerating with the improved nutritional standards of the postwar years: the earlier onset of puberty. More and more, becoming a teenager connoted biological change. Even with earlier marriages, the period of adolescence was lengthening. Teenagers not only had money to spend, they had, as the Albemarle Report tactfully put it, 'considerable surplus energy'.[4] By the last teenage years—the first student years—sexual energies had had time to mature into adult forms.

For the period 1958–63 the main agents in establishing new patterns of consumer sales and new standards of taste, particularly in Europe, were young, and not quite so young, married couples, with wives usually taking the initiative. All age groups shared in the sense of empowerment accorded by rising living standards and increased leisure. Provincial backwaters and unglamorous communities stirred into life. Particularly noteworthy is the opening of the revolt of certain middle-aged, middle-class Americans against the accelerating destruction of the environment brought about by a devastating combination of commercial greed and the actions of Cold War-fixated and automobile-besotted federal and local government. Improvements in living standards, and thus some potential for freedom of action, percolated through to some of the least privileged groups. Large numbers of American blacks moved from the depressed South to fairly well-paid industrial jobs in the North and West; some of those who remained began to question discrimination and degradation. Steadily, quietly, a black middle class—still openly discriminated against—grew in size and wealth, and therefore, in consumer power (this growth being clearly reflected in the black magazine *Ebony*, founded in 1945). For the moment women's spending power operated mainly within the family (though females played a special part in the teenage market with respect to fashion, cosmetics, and magazines).

In the separate sections of this chapter I take in turn: first and second, American youth subculture, then British; third, the effects on ordinary life and sexual behaviour across the varied geographical regions contained within our four countries of the spread of affluence, and of the growth of unease over the somnolent conformities of the fifties; and fourth, the particularities of the still more slowly developing youth subcultures of France and Italy, which eventually resulted in receptive ground being prepared for the British-dominated popular culture of the mid-sixties. Chapter 4 will focus on changing public attitudes towards sexual morality, and on interrelated developments in the media (mainly film) and in middlebrow (mainly novels) and élite (mainly painting) art forms; and also on class and family. Race will be the subject for Chapter 5.

### 'Your Teenager Is Big Business': 'The Disaffection of the Growing Generation'

This is a book about structural, ideological, and institutional forces and constraints, about convergence and the interaction of subcultures, and, above all, about transformations in the lives of large numbers of ordinary people. But there are always individuals who read the runes, or, more usually, half-read them, before everyone else. Just after the Second World War a young American, Eugene Gilbert, sensing the potential of the teenage market, set up Eugene Gilbert and Company to study and publicize it. The general drift of his labours is well summarized in the title of the book he published in 1957, *Advertising and Marketing to Young People*. Since much of the statistical information on the size and preferences of the teenage market was generated by Gilbert's organization, one might well reckon it to be not altogether untainted; against that, giving advice to manufacturers and advertisers was Gilbert's bread and butter, or, rather, milk and honey, so he could not afford to get it too wildly wrong. Certainly, he probably got it no more wrong than the social scientists for whom 'youth culture' was an intellectual property with enormous growth potential. Anyway, we are studying both a real phenomenon, and the perceptions of it; it is the phenomenon itself which has growing significance, but, as so often, the perceptions help to add to the significance.

The peak of the postwar baby boom came in 1947, whose progeny, of course, achieved the magic age of 13 in 1960. But the rise had started during the war, and in America in 1958 there were almost eleven million pupils in secondary schools, with nine million young persons of school age (many of them pre-teenagers) not actually at school. Gilbert almost went out of his way to stress that many of those in school (very far, of course, from being exclusively middle-class) were themselves part-time money-earners, and not simply parasites, through pocket money, upon funds earned by their fathers. Close scrutiny of the figures reveals that the greatest purchasing power did indeed lie with those who were able to earn without any of the limitations arising from being in full-time education, and that about three-quarters of those in school were almost wholly dependent on pocket money, though the proportion earning after school and during vacations had risen sharply in recent years.[5] In short, the running was being made by teenagers no longer at school, but able to command reasonable earnings; however, in spending patterns there were no significant distinctions between these front-runners and those, generally from more prosperous or more manifestly middle-class families, who did continue at school, and who were numerically in a majority. Thus, if the important new actors were not from the most highly privileged social élites, they were from the prospering middle majority of American society, certainly not from downtrodden or oppressed minorities.

*Cosmopolitan* (at that time a general-interest monthly magazine) brought out a special issue in November 1957, focused on the question, 'Are Teenagers Taking Over?'. *American Mercury*, populist and right-wing, publishing a potted version of the latest Eugene Gilbert survey, came out in September 1958 with the headline which forms the first quotation at the head of this section: '*They put "folding money" as well as small change into the till*' was the italicized opening sentence. Liberal and moderate *Harper's Magazine* followed (November 1958) with an article by Gilbert himself, declaring that his main discovery was that 'within the past decade the teenagers have become a separate and distinct group in our society'. In the same month the *New Yorker* (22 November) published the first of a two-part article by the authoritative social commentator, Dwight Macdonald, whose title, 'A Caste, a Culture, a Market', and style were in the *New Yorker* mould of gently humorous hyperbole: 'These days, merchants eye teenagers the way stockmen eye cattle'; teenagers formed 'a new American caste', evincing 'a style of life that was sui generis'. Read cautiously, these statements contained nothing that was absolutely untrue. But in fostering a sense of teenagers as unknown and unknowable aliens (only fathomable by expensive experts such as Gilbert and the social scientists), the many articles were ignoring the fact that practically all American institutions (including the public schools with their nationwide syllabus and many rituals) were working towards identifying and welcoming the differentness of teenagers (Nicholas Ray's 1955 film *Rebel Without a Cause* both presented the sensitively different teenager—played by

James Dean—and the firmly established customs and rituals of American high-school life, which, I should stress here, very strongly emphasized the separate spheres occupied by girls and boys). Few parents could have remained unaware that teenagers were special, and needs must be treated sensitively. For many years, it was true, there had been scares about teenage delinquents; but delinquents were other parents' children; and anyway the effect of all the market-speak and the sociologizing (together with the banal fact that most adult Americans actually were in quite close contact with the teenager of the species) was to shift the focus from teenagers as real or potential delinquents to teenagers as young adults in the making (if not on the make). A more solid and fact-based perspective was provided in a *Life* article of 31 August 1959, 'A New $10-Billion Power: the U.S. Teenage Consumer'. Pointing out that this purchasing power amounted to more than the total sales of General Motors, the article then located the issues which were central to teenagers as a 'separate and distinct group'—16 per cent of the expenditure went to the entertainment industry, with a substantial proportion of the rest going on fashion and grooming. Teenagers had their own distinctive entertainments (principally centred on the changing world of popular music), and they had their own modes of self-presentation, or, to put the same thing the other way round, self-identification. And that is the substance behind the colourful talk of 'a new American caste': teenagers by the late fifties had a clear self-awareness of themselves as part of an increasingly homogeneous nationwide category (the image did not, of course, coincide exactly with reality); and, along with the rest of society, they could increasingly enjoy seeing themselves as spectacle.

Gilbert's most recent survey of teenage spending was in some ways perhaps less dramatic than some of his own pronouncements, showing as it did that teenagers were both separate spenders and integrated into their families, buying for themselves, influencing purchases made on their behalf by their parents, and buying presents for their parents:

*Percentages of boys buying their own* Sports Equipment, 57; Shirts, 40; Slacks, 38; Shaving Cream, 36; Razor Blades, 27.

*Percentages of girls buying their own* Lipstick, 73; Hand Lotion, 43; Blouses, sweaters, skirts, 33; Lingerie, 31; Dresses, 27; Toilet Soap, 24.

*Percentages of teens selecting the following:* Shoes, 94; Fountain Pens, 80; Sports Equipment, 70; Radios, 55; Shampoos, 52; Watches, 47; Vacations, 38.

*Percentages of boys influencing selection of:* Shirts and slacks, 90; Shaving Cream, 49; Razor Blades, 35; Electric Razors, 26.

*Percentages of girls influencing selection of:* Blouses, skirts, 94; Dresses, 92; Lipstick, 92; Lingerie, 89; Hand Lotion, 71; Toilet Soap, 56; Permanents, 33.

That fountain pens were almost as popular as records among items purchased by teenagers (and stand high among items selected by them for purchase by their parents) indicates a certain seriousness, and, no doubt, a desire for adult status. The purchase of records, if far from universal, is of course a vital element in the subculture. Teenagers are not (in significant numbers) buying radios, but these, also vital tools in the enjoyment of particular types of music, figure prominently among items being bought for them. The strongest teenage influence is over their own self-presentation (clothing, shoes, and—for the girls—cosmetics). Alongside all this, the survey presented the information that on Mother's Day 1957 teenagers had spent $101 million, and on Father's Day $68 million, on presents for their respective parents.[6] An important component of youth subculture, and particularly female youth culture, by the beginning of the sixties not caught in this 1957 survey was the teenage magazine. The first two, *Teen* and *Dig*, appeared in 1955. By 1960 there were a dozen more, including *Teen Today, Teen World, Modern Teen, Teenville, Teentime, Sixteen, Flip, Hipcats, Teen Parade, Teen Screen, Hollywood Teenagers*, and *Confidential Teen Romances* (the special role of girls in the teen market is obvious here).

But the central component was the new popular music. Popular music for centuries was, by its very nature, specific to particular communities or nations. élite music (chamber, symphonic, operatic), however, very quickly became a universal phenomenon (in the Western world, that is), and indeed an emblem of a certain social and educational status. And while, well into the twentieth century, local communities continued to preserve their own dance forms and the music which went with them, for the aristocracy and upper bourgeoisie dance music too became international and universal. The advent of public ballrooms, together with gramophone records, radio, and, eventually, sound films, internationalized certain forms of American popular music, mainly commercialized and bastardized versions of styles generations of black Americans had evolved from white religious music.

Jazz, spontaneous and participatory, remained essentially a minority taste; the all-pervasive popular dance music (swing, ballads, crooning, etc.) was a very sophisticated commercial product, based on a fairly strict division of labour between composers and performers. Other forms of distinctive, locally based popular music continued to exist, now usually termed 'folk music'. While jazz, in its various forms, maintained a slightly separate existence, there were in America at the beginning of the fifties important developments relating to two forms of, until then, relatively uncommercialized 'folk' music: rhythm and blues (a black American form) and country and western (a white form). The new white form which emerged at this time, basically from the former, took the name of rock'n'roll. Assisted by the spread of transistor radios, as well as the development of magnetic records, rock'n'roll became the music of already affluent American teenagers, a music generally condemned by parents and leaders of opinion (families watched television, while the teenagers listened to their own radios). In deciding which records to buy, teenagers exercised choice as never before, but they were certainly not the creators of the music. The famous, and climactic, Bill Haley and the Comets not only were old, but looked it. Elvis Presley is a more portentous figure, both in that he projected a genuine youthfulness, and in that he was an amateur when he made his first recording in a do-it-yourself Memphis studio. But Elvis came to his audiences through records, films, and carefully arranged stage performances, not through performing in local clubs.

There has been much argument about 'authenticity', about the white 'purloining' of black music, and so forth. What needs to be stressed above all is that the new music was a product of exchange, of mixing of traditions, of very new influences acting upon quite old practices. In its own forms, the new music sought avidly by white teenagers (though not by them alone) was more authentic, more open, more honest, than the white popular music it began to supplant. In all cases, certain key elements lie in black America. But the popular music which had dominated the twentieth century so far had very much been a white-contrived exploitation of what were indisputably black origins. Rock'n'roll was definitely black music. Bill Haley's 'Shake, Rattle and Roll' had been written by black musician Joe Turner. 'Hound Dog', the song with which Elvis Presley made his breakthrough in 1956, had been released three years earlier by the black singer Willie Mae Thornton. But a whole vital dimension of the critical changes taking place is missed if it is not realized that, for example, Presley also brought the authentic tradition of white country music, not to mention a conviction and attack of his own, to his performances and recordings. The technological basis to the new developments has already been explained. The TV programme *American Bandstand,* broadcast nationwide by the ABC TV company on Saturday mornings from 1957 onwards and bringing the full range of musical styles to over twenty million viewers, was an important agent. But more important were the transistor radios which enabled teenagers to make their own individual listening choices. Historically, it is absolutely true that it needed white performers to secure white listeners for music which had its origins with such black performers as Chuck Berry, Fats Domino, Little Richard, and Bo Diddley. But when it came to listening in over the airwaves, it was simply impossible to maintain segregation. Most important of all, teenagers were actively involved in setting the trends of record sales.[7]

While in their listening habits young Americans were tacitly challenging racial taboos, middle America looked askance at Presley and his like, principally because of their open sexuality—thus, filmed or televised shots of Presley had to exclude his pelvic gyrations. Bill Van Dyke, resident in Los Angeles, wrote on 29 October 1957 to his parents, prosperous proprietors of a company manufacturing ironware, in Memphis, with a cutting from that day's *Los Angeles Mirror News:* the paper spoke for respectable middle-class sentiment on the West Coast, and the sentiment was obviously shared by Bill and his family:

> Sexibitionist Elvis Presley had come at last in person to a visibly palpitating, adolescent female Los Angeles to give all the little girls' libidos the jolt of their lives.
>
> Six thousand kids, predominantly feminine by a ratio of 10 to 1, jammed the Pan Pacific Auditorium to the rafters last night. They screamed their lungs out without letup as Elvis shook, bumped, and did the grinds from one side of the stage to the other until he was a quivering heap on the floor 35 minutes later.
>
> With anyone else the police would have closed the show 10 minutes after it started. But not Elvis, our new national teen-age hero.[8]

In November 1958 *American Mercury* told its readers what to think of 'Rock and Roll':

> Evidence of the systematic lowering of literary, dramatic, artistic and musical standards stare you in the face on all sides. It is obviously a major item in the brainwashing technique necessary to clinching the power of the international welfare state... That the sinister program of racial intermixture could advance so far without noticeably arousing the wrath

of American parents will forever remain a mystery.

But the testimony of these two sources is mixed. Elvis, it is recognized, however reluctantly, *is* 'our new national teen-age hero'; his commercial value is not in doubt. *American Mercury's* contorted views of rock'n'roll (the 'corrected' spelling is in itself revealing) actually makes clear just how significant the new musical practice was, as well as an awareness of the changing attitudes to race implicit in it (these being linked to the sinister advance of 'the international welfare state'!).

While overt concern over juvenile delinquency became more muted as young people were welcomed as consumers and lauded as spectacle, the notion of their being a 'caste' was often coupled in the press with some anxieties as to their attitudes towards respectable society, together with spicy references to 'Beatniks'. There was a certain uneasiness about the 'disaffection of the growing generation', as social commentator Paul Goodman put it in a book which attracted much attention when published in New York in 1960, and in London a year later, *Growing Up Absurd*. Goodman was one of the first to popularize the phrase 'Rat Race' as an image of the ruthless and dubiously moral struggle for career success. The phrase became something of a cliché in everyday newspaper and conversational discourse, connoting little more than a knowing irony, and was certainly no clarion call to activist protest—though, even so, its wide currency does indicate that an embryonic awareness of the imperfections of the American society had emerged in the fifties, an awareness which was to be kicked into life as ideas and movements interacted throughout the sixties. Goodman recognized that the overwhelming majority of young people fully accommodated to the 'Rat Race', and most other investigations found that young Americans of student age, whatever reservations they might have about the values of their parents, were in practice highly conservative and conformist (my own intention will be to highlight how, portentously, that conformity was already fraying a little at the very beginning of the sixties). Goodman saw rejection of the 'Rat Race' as the common motivation behind the (with respect to precise age) quite different minorities encompassed in what he referred to as 'Juvenile Delinquents' and 'Beats', extending the range to include also the 'English Angry Young Men'. As sources of disillusionment he cited the American TV quiz show scandal of 1959 and the parallel bribery scandal surrounding radio disc jockeys.[9] Goodman's major discovery, and a circumstance which was to be central to the expansion of student activism after 1963, was that large numbers of conformists were fascinated by the nonconformists (a limited but important aspect of the spectacle factor):

> I think that the existential reality of Beat, Angry, and Delinquent behaviour is indicated by the fact that other, earnest, young fellows who are not themselves disaffected and who are not phoney, are eager to hear about them and respect them. One cannot visit a university without being asked a hundred questions about them.[10]

Kenneth Keniston's study of young people in the slightly older age group—the student generation, basically—coincided with Goodman's in seeing them as essentially conservative, if slightly restless:

they would, he predicted, 'assure a highly stable political and social order, for few of them will be enough committed to politics to consider revolution, subversion, or even radical change'.[11] That judgement is fully borne out in the student politics and college magazines of the time. The National Interfraternity Conference at Los Angeles in December 1960 discussed 'how communism is creeping into our colleges and universities and making attempts to infiltrate the fraternity system'.[12] The Memphis State University newspaper, *Tiger Rag*, ran an editorial declaring the 'Communist threat must be fought on college campuses', with admiring references to the ultra-conservative Republican Barry Goldwater.[13] However, the same paper was extremely critical of a pamphlet entitled *Forced Racial Integration by a Memphis Attorney* as 'anti-negro, anti-semitic', 'extremist', and encouraging of 'bigotry'. A 'liberal' narrowly defeated a 'conservative' for the presidency of the students' association. However, less than one-third of students voted, evoking an editorial declaring

in the world's struggle against Communist domination it is important that we turn out for democracy, whether it be in the selection of campus leadership or in the choosing of the leadership of the Free World.

What is most striking about *Tiger Rag* is its manifest fifties-style sexism. The legend at the head of the leader column read: 'From the Campus of America's Most Beautiful Co-Eds', and every issue contained a photograph of a 'Campus Cutie'. The decisions of pairs of students to 'go steady' were thought worthy of regular report. One feature ran:

Mischievous Cupid Lets His Arrows Fly, and there's no telling who will be next.
    ... read the long list of couples below whose hearts have already been touched by his magic arrows...

Along with this sort of stuff went highly conservative moralizing. In October 1961 an editorial, 'Administration Should Act on Fraternity Party Policy', declaimed:

At Memphis State it is against the explicit policy of the university for fraternities to sponsor unscheduled and unchaperoned parties, but this policy has been violated in the past and is being violated today. These unofficial parties are an open secret on the campus. We find not so much fault in the parties as we do in the policy that ignores their existence.

In November 1963 the Women's Social Standards Committee was stressing that 'women do not drink in public places such as football games'.[14]

In discussing students generally, Keniston attributed to them seven characteristics; that some of these could apply to youth in almost any era reinforces the general impression—though with significant qualifications, as we shall see—that there was nothing very exceptional about this student generation. There was first, Keniston thought, a perceived lack of deep commitment to adult values and roles, apparent among 'even those who appear at first glance to be chiefly concerned with getting ahead and making a place for themselves'. However, that had to be balanced against 'a relative lack of rebelliousness', perhaps in part linked to a third characteristic, a 'widespread feeling of powerlessness' (distinguishing this group from the teenagers). The fourth characteristic, 'privatism' (the retreat into purely private and personal concerns, recently identified by popular sociologist David Riesman), related to the sixth, 'decline in political involvement among college youth'.[15] However, Keniston noted an exception, the exception which was to prove to rule subsequent critical developments: those students who enlisted in the direct-action desegregation campaigns. The fifth characteristic Keniston termed 'foreshortening of timespan'—a scepticism over the value of long-term career planning, which links both with the first characteristic and the last, the 'cult of experience', the seeking of (as Keniston inelegantly phrased it) 'kicks'. But having introduced this robust word, Keniston hastily added: 'Few college students go this far, even in the small group that dresses "beat", rides motorcycles, and supports the espresso bars; for most, experience is sought in ways less asocial than sex, speed, and stimulants.'[16] The foggy quality of this afterthought well captures the essence of students scarcely embarked upon the emancipation which was to be consummated well before the end of the decade. However, Goodman had written of the disaffected minority—who, he reckoned, were envied and respected by the majority—that they 'are achieving a simpler fraternity, animality, and sexuality than we have had, at least in America, in a long, long time'.[17] Again the words are slightly opaque, and lack that blunt explicitness which some years later would come readily to hand in describing student life. Presumably women must have participated in this 'animality' and 'sexuality', but in keeping with this still largely unemancipated and pre-permissive era, Goodman quite openly expressed his view that 'youth is a male problem'—'girls', he thought, simply got married.[18]

The 'exceptional elements' merited a full essay by Robert Coles, which began:

> There are today young men and women, black and white, who are going to jail for the freedom of their fellow men. They are doing radical things in novel and challenging ways; and they are doing them in every man's sight, in restaurants, in stores, in movie houses, in bus terminals, and in the obscure rural offices of voting registrars... But, they do not march with banners nor man barricades. They do not scream at other countries and their visiting leaders. They throw no bombs. They are concerned with their own country, and they want to become her true citizens. They very definitely want to change social and political customs, but they want to change them peacefully and in their time. They are not lost or confused; they know exactly what they want, and they are ready to give their lives for their goals.[19]

Mainly white 'freedom fighters' from the North joined sit-ins and demonstrations which had been sporadically developing for some years among blacks in the South. That episode will be accorded the attention it deserves in Chapter 5.

The advent to the presidency of youthful (he was 43) John F. Kennedy was undoubtedly a stimulus to outgoing activism on the part of young people, particularly through an important new initiative of 1 March 1961 echoing the British Voluntary Service Overseas (VSO), founded in 1958, and designed

> to promote world peace and friendship through a Peace Corps, which shall make available to interested countries men and women of the United States qualified for service abroad and willing to serve, under conditions of hardship if necessary, to help the peoples of such countries and areas in meeting their needs for trained manpower, and to help promote a better understanding of other peoples on the part of the American people.[20]

In talking of the Peace Corps we are again talking of a minority, this time a minority within the oldest, and last, segment of 'youth', or 'young people'—young college graduates and those (broadly) between university and marriage. A letter from a young man serving as a teacher in West Africa suggests a mix of independent-minded altruism and conventional patriotism:

> The need for education here is desperate, and the appreciation we have been getting from people on all levels is no less than astounding. Some are a little hesitant to believe that we would give up the luxuries of America, the good jobs, the money and the conveniences for that which West Africa has to offer, but they are nonetheless glad to have us... The question 'Why did you join the Peace Corps?' which has plagued us from the beginning, becomes increasingly less and less academic. One no longer has to resort to abstract philosophical arguments and platitudes (true as they might be), for I now find myself in the midst of the answer, surrounded by a situation that cries out in self-explanation. The poverty, the illiteracy, the substandard educational opportunities which are rampant in this as well as many other countries are reasons enough for anyone to want to extend his hand and heart in order that these blights might be at least partially erased.[21]

This is not a testament to unalloyed self-effacement and altruism—few documents are. In any case the idea of one generation, or certain minorities within that generation, being intrinsically nobler than their predecessors is not plausible. What can be said is that, owing to a combination of circumstances, some American young people were finding the opportunities, and were seizing these opportunities, to depart from what had been the standardized norm throughout the fifties, while those still younger, in what was generally a materialistic and self-centred way, were establishing new patterns of leisure behaviour. But there was a little more than that, which eventually became a lot more than that: with amazing suddenness, out of America's moribund Old Left there appeared a radical socialist movement of young people, Students for a Democratic Society (SDS). Marxist renewal, nuclear anxiety, a new consciousness of the evils of southern racism and admiration for demonstrators and freedom fighters, frustration with student life and consumer society all played a part. Certain Old Left figures, including Michael Harrington, shortly to become famous for his study of poverty, *The Other America* (1962), had decided to revitalize the historic socialist organization, the League for Industrial Democracy, including the setting up, in 1960, of a Student League for Industrial Democracy. But in this generation, if students were socialist at all, they were certainly not going to be led by their elders. So during 1961 students themselves, led by University of Michigan student Robert 'Al' Haber, took over, junking the archaic title for the slicker-sounding SDS. Haber brought in the editor of the Michigan student newspaper, Tom Hayden, earlier much influenced by the Beats, who did most of the writing of a sixty-four-page statement which was put before a conference of fifty-nine representatives of a dozen universities held at the United Auto Workers conference centre at Port Huron, north of Detroit.

The 'Port Huron Statement', with but one qualification, rehearsed all the major issues which were to form the essence of the New Left and the Movement throughout the High Sixties.

> We are people of this generation, bred in at least modest comfort, housed now in universities, looking uncomfortably to the world we inherit. When we were kids the United States was the wealthiest and strongest country in the world... many of us began maturing in complacency.
>
> As we grew, however, our comfort was penetrated by events too troubling to dismiss. First, the permeating and victimizing fact of human degradation, symbolized by the Southern struggle against racial bigotry, compelled most of us from silence to activism. Second, the enclosing fact of the Cold War, symbolized by the presence of the Bomb, brought awareness that we ourselves, and our friends, and millions of abstract 'others' we know more directly because of our common peril, might die at any time.[22]

Concern over the bomb, by the mid-sixties was replaced by a much more passionate concern over the Vietnam war. But all the other issues of sixties protest were there, above all the students' disaffection from their own universities, their authoritarian and cumbersome bureaucracies, their complicity in the 'corporate economy' and in weapons research, the revulsion at consumer society, and outrage at 'the actual structural separation of people from power'. A congregation of fifty-nine representatives in a trade union conference centre did not herald the conversion of still-conservative American youth, but over the years more and more young Americans were to feel compelled out of silence into activism.

### The Knitting Together of British Youth Subculture

Several different sorts of activity associated with 'youth', in the very broadest sense of the term, were taking place in the middle fifties in the different parts of Britain, among different social classes, and affecting slightly different age groups. Certain developments, such as the appearance of the Teddy boys at the beginning of the decade, attracted attention, but, in general, while Britain was admired in other countries for its high standards of public service and high levels of civic loyalty, British youth was seen as merging into the nondescript background of a culturally unimaginative, philistine, and repressed society: certainly the popular music listened to by a majority of young people, and their parents, was American, or a poor imitation; and young people with any kind of dress sense looked towards the fashions of Italy or France. This section is about how different fragments

49

of British youth subculture knitted together so that by the end of 1963 it was not just setting cultural norms for all of British society, but was about to do the same for the rest of the world.

We saw in the previous section that American commentators rated 'Angry Young Men' as components of British youth subculture. This was pushing hard against the upper limits of what could be termed 'youth', but it was true that the new opinion-formers (through their plays, books, articles, and in some cases films) and critics of society were, as a group, rather younger than had been usual in British society. The phrase 'Angry Young Man' derived from the play *Look Back in Anger*, whose author, John Osborne, was 26 when the play was first performed in 1956. Some of the other writers sometimes loosely referred to as 'Angry Young Men', though often, alternatively, as 'Kitchen Sink', working-class, or provincial (John Braine, Alan Sillitoe, David Storey, Keith Waterhouse), were still older. The young publisher Tom Maschler (the fact that one calls him 'young' indicates the sense in which these people belonged to 'youth'; he was 24 in 1957) tried, in a collection entitled *Declaration*, to bring together 'the angry young men'—'a number of young men and widely opposed writers', as he put it, 'who have burst upon the scene and are striving to change many of the values which have held good in recent years'. The authors, whose ages ranged through the 20s to the late 30s, neither mounted a coherent attack on existing British society nor particularly spoke up on behalf of young people. What the 'Angry Young Men' vogue, and, indeed, just the label itself, were taken as representing, was a fusion of the notions of 'criticism of society' and 'the young'. Characteristic of the derivative nature of much of what was newest in mid-fifties Britain, strong influences were French existentialism and the American Beat movement: *New Departures*, founded in Oxford by Mike Horovitz in 1959, featured Burroughs; other Beats figured in the mimeographed 'Tree' produced a year later by Barry Miles; Laura Mulrey later spoke of 'a mixture of the high French intellectual culture and the low American popular culture'.[23] But the peculiarly British expression of the disaffection of the (relatively) young was in terms of opposition to 'the Establishment'. Most of those who spoke critically of 'the Establishment', whether working-class in origins or not, now occupied solidly middle-class positions, and some were upper-class; ostensibly the attack was on the class basis of the British power structure, on 'the old school tie' and 'the old boy network', but it often took the form more of an attack on stuffy conventions and attitudes than on the distribution of power as such. The relevance of 'Angry Young Men' and assorted writers and intellectuals to the emergence of a coherent British youth subculture is somewhat at a remove: many in the student age group (though, as we shall see shortly, British students even in the early sixties remained a rather conservative lot), and some of those still younger, took up the cry of 'Establishment' as a kind of catch-all phrase for discontent with the way society was organized, with the subculture of the middle-aged. In this sense, it served the same function that the phrase 'Rat Race' did in the United States.

Hostility to 'the Establishment' was the most clearly articulated characteristic among the not particularly thoughtful or intellectual 'Chelsea Set', the phrase coming into usage before the middle of the fifties. Mary Quant, who was 21 in 1955 when, together with her husband-to-be, Alexander Plunkett-Green, she established Bazaar on the King's Road, Chelsea, as the first of what were to become known as 'boutiques', selling clothes which deliberately defied the conventions of established fashion, defined the Chelsea Set as including 'painters, photographers, architects, writers, socialites, actors, conmen, and superior tarts. There were racing drivers, gamblers, TV producers and advertising men.'[24] Again this scarcely suggests 'youth' as the term is most usually understood. The locations in which the Chelsea Set could be found were clubs, traditional pubs (in particular the Markham Arms on Chelsea's main thoroughfare, the King's Road), and coffee bars, specifically the new one, Fantasy, founded by an ex-solicitor, Archie McNair. Drinking alcohol was a fairly central feature and this, in theory, should have limited the set to those over the legal drinking age of 18. The fact was that young people of that age, and still younger, also congregated in the same locations, so that the Chelsea Set, though mainly focused on the young professionals of a bohemian cast, did, on its fringes at least, include teenagers. The central figures were upper-class, as indeed was Plunkett-Green. Mary Quant came from a highly intellectual and thoroughly liberal family of distant working-class origins. She had been, during her earlier years of association with the Chelsea Set, a student at Goldsmiths' Design College. Art colleges and design colleges did have students who were themselves working-class in origin, and it was possible for the odd working-class young person, of an adventurous and bohemian cast, to mingle with the Set—the more so since in public posture the Set was 'anti-Establishment'. Similar groups, strongly but not exclusively upper-class in tone, formed in other parts of the country, most notably in Oxford and Cambridge, and such university cities as Edinburgh, Exeter, and Bristol.

Art colleges and design schools were critical agencies in the evolution and expansion of youth subculture. In fact, the topic cannot be understood apart from the specificities of educational change in postwar Britain. While still really quite severely limited, opportunities had expanded for working-class children to stay on at school and then proceed to higher education, often at an art college, or, while leaving school at 15, then to pursue some form of further education, or, while going into full-time paid employment, to profit from 'day release' to undertake educational and training activities. Clubs and pubs were centres for music-making; so were art colleges. Art colleges were centres for discussions of existentialism (in however vulgarized form), Beat philosophy, and the deficiencies of 'the Establishment'. One art student of the time recalled later:

> The fact that we were technically being trained to design ceramic pots or books or theatre sets was irrelevant. You'd go to the canteen and you'd have a painter, a typographer, a film-maker, a graphic designer all at the same table.[25]

In certain parts of certain towns, folk and jazz clubs, skiffle and beat cellars, coffee bars and pubs with special music nights came into being. Depending upon exact geographical location—city centre, working-class suburb, 'bohemian' quarter, university precinct—the clientele could be drawn from one or more social classes. Reporting as early as 1 April 1957 on 'a new world of young people'—'a young people's world with its own self-made heroes'—which, 'set in the networks of skiffle parlours, jazz joints, rock and roll basements' had 'sprung up on the sleazy backstreets' of Soho, the *Daily Mail* was clear about its socially mixed composition: 'The new afterdark citizens of Soho are typists, nurses, factory workers. They are students, dreamers, bank clerks...'

This was the world investigated by middle-aged journalist Colin MacInnes, and reported on by him in certain quality magazines, and, in fictional form, in one of the (much-quoted) central texts of 1959, *Absolute Beginners*. MacInnes, in his journalism, stressed what he called the 'class-lessness' of the world of youth, a term from which, under close scrutiny, almost all meaning evaporates: what MacInnes meant was that young people from different social classes came together in the distinctive centres of youth subculture. What MacInnes, as author, insisted on in his novel was that the youth subculture he had been describing had been in existence for quite a number of years, that it was fundamentally based on the new-found affluence of youth, and that there was a sharp antagonism between the world he was proud to be bringing to the attention of middle-class readers and the world of adults, termed 'conscripts' by the characters he reported on. His first novel, *City of Spades*, published in 1958, drew attention to the existence of the West Indian community in Notting Hill. *Absolute Beginners*, set in June-July, August and September 1958, after making references to race conflict in the St Anne's district of Nottingham, culminates with the even more dramatic events in Notting Hill. In the short time-span of the book the photographer-narrator moves from taking pornographic pictures to attempting to establish himself as a trendy magazine photographer, and much of the book consists of his encounters and conversations with various colourful characters in the coffee bars and jazz clubs of Soho and Notting Hill, teenagers, blacks, personalities from newly important television. The novel opens with the narrator in conversation with the 16-year-old, all-knowing, and (significantly with regard to the authorial viewpoint) very rich The Wizard. By page 2 the narrator is reflecting:

> This teenage ball had had real splendour in the days when the kids discovered that, for the first time since centuries of kingdom come, they had money, which hitherto had always been denied to us that the best time in life to use it, namely, when you are young, and strong, and also before newspapers and telly got hold of this teenage fable and prostituted it as conscripts seem to do to everything they touch. Yes, I tell you, it had a real savage splendour in the days when we found that no-one couldn't sit on our faces anymore because we'd loot to spend at last, and our world was to be our world, the one we wanted and not standing on the doorstep of somebody else's waiting for honey, perhaps.

But what the other two famous texts of 1959–60, *The Teenage Market* by Mark Abrams and the Report of the Albemarle Committee, concentrated on unambiguously was working-class youth. On the model of Eugene Gilbert, Abrams, a middle-aged market researcher, was interested in spending power. Charged with reporting on, and making recommendations for improvements in, the youth service, the Albemarle Committee quite simply was concerned with the clients of that service, those leaving school at 15 and who remained within the purview of the youth service till the age of 20 (not in fact exclusively working-class, but the Albemarle Report does reveal that it had its main focus on those leaving secondary modern schools, which were overwhelmingly working-class). Because he was thinking entirely of those with money to spend, Abrams concentrated on those between school-leaving age of 15, i.e. the age when his 'teenagers' took up paid employment, to the time when they married, or could otherwise be presumed to have assumed adult responsibilities: he thus took the age group 15–25, subtracting from it those who were already married before the age of 25. Abrams and Albemarle were emphatically not think-ing of bohemian elements, those practising an unconventional lifestyle: they were concerned with a highly static working class following a very rigid life-cycle—money to spend while a 'teenager', a firm end to that kind of existence with marriage. There can be no doubt that the advent of a mass working-class teenage market was a crucial element in the development of youth subculture into the 1960s. Many of what were to be its most distinctive features had genuinely developed in working-class areas: skiffle and beat groups, very sharp dress on the French or Italian model (music in upper- and middle-class life and educational institutions was more usually jazz; dress, where it was not simply scruffy and unimaginative, or tweedy and utterly conventional, was more eccentric and individualized). Both Abrams and Albemarle have much to tell us about develop-ing working-class teenage subculture, and it is true that much of what they are describing was exclusively working-class. Working-class youngsters in any case had little geographical mobility (though this was true also for middle-class children at school).

But the classes certainly were not hermetically sealed: the effects of educational changes have already been mentioned; those working-class youngsters who formed skiffle or beat groups did sometimes get the chance to travel in the fulfilment of paid engagements. John Lennon, leading spirit in the skiffle group the Quarrymen, founded in 1957 when he was 16, and of course in the beat group the Beatles, established in 1960, came from a working-class background and studied at art college. His close associate Paul McCartney, lower-middle-class in origins, was drawn into the same ambience and, in a recollection of the pervasive influences of Ginsberg, Kerouac, and the American Beats, has provided an interesting insight into personal mobility between Liverpool and London:

> You'd come down to London and you'd see kids in London, students with the similar type of thing, or in Liverpool at John's art college or all this kind of stuff. Students the world over were aware of that. So when we came down here to London all we did really was plug out of the Liverpool student scene and plug into the London student scene.

'Student scene' here connotes further, or even just secondary school, education, not that of a university. One of those in this London scene was a pupil at Westminster School who, obviously, had had

> a much more privileged upbringing than ours had been, but good, it seemed to be good, they didn't seem to be a snotty crowd. So this was it: like up North, you'd be reading *On The Road* and they'd be reading *On The Road*. We'd be looking at the same kind of things.[26]

The Albemarle Committee had been appointed in October 1958, completed its report at the end of 1959, and published it in February 1960. A trifle incestuously perhaps, the Committee also kept in close touch with Abrams, but it used the figures supplied by him judiciously. Careful reading of the Report brings out that the Committee was identifying a youth subculture in the process of formation, likely to be of great significance in the early sixties, rather than one which was already fully formed. There are several references to the 'bulge' (i.e. the effects of the high postwar birth rate running year by year through the population), the major effects of which, it makes clear, are yet to come: 'For every five young people between the ages of 15 and 20 today there will be, in 1964, six young people'; in that year 'the Youth Service will be responsible for one million more young people than it had had to cater for in 1958'.[27] Abrams has to be subjected to similar careful reading. While he did argue that teenage spending power had been building up over the past thirteen years, he turns out to be as much alerting manufacturers and advertisers to a potential market in the process of formation as describing one already long in existence.

In one of several banal and derivative documents about youth appearing at this time, *The Insecure Offenders: Rebellious Youth In The Welfare State*, published in 1961, T. R. Fyvel had declared in the usual way that 'young people of today have far more money to spend than their parents ever had', and claimed that 'whole new industries... have sprung up to supply the new market, and so we have the new commercial "youth culture"'. But Abrams rather suggests that British manufacturers had as yet scarcely begun to create these 'whole new industries':

> this is a working class market, and post-war British society has little experience in providing for prosperous working-class teenagers; the latter have, therefore, in shaping their consumption standards and habits, depended very heavily on the one industrial society in the world that has such experience, i.e. the United States. For various reasons it is difficult for the middle-aged British manufacturer to adopt the styles and language and appeals of American manufacturers concerned with the teenage market....
>
> ... teenagers more than any other section of the community are looking for goods and services which are highly charged emotionally. To appreciate this is again something which is not easy for a middle-aged industrialist whose comparable enthusiasms and struggles took place in a world that died 30 or 40 years ago.[28]

MacInnes provided an impressionistic account of the range of activities and rituals, and types of person associated with the years of nascent youth subculture; Abrams and Albemarle focused on the weight of numbers which brought the evolution of British youth subculture to a state of critical mass, and on the special working-class attributes, hitherto ignored or suppressed, which by the early sixties provided the driving energy. But, this subculture was not exclusively working-class (as it was not 'classless'). Broadly, its accents were provincial and working-class, or suburban London, rather than Oxbridge or Home Counties (those in the upper-class sets already mentioned tended to adopt what came to be known as 'posh Cockney').

As with the American literature, there was heavy emphasis on the distinctiveness, and indeed separateness, of teenage subculture. In the second instalment of his survey, Abrams spoke of, 'distinctive teenage spending for distinctive teenage ends in a distinctive teenage world'.[29] Confirming the widely held assumption that young people had much more money to spend than prewar generations, the Albemarle Committee preceptively analysed the nature of this spending:

> Much of the spending is clearly—and naturally—on goods designed to impress other teenagers (e.g. dressing up) or on gregarious pursuits (e.g. coffee-bar snacks). This is spending which is, to an unusually high degree, charged with an emotional content—it helps to provide an identity or to give status or to assist in the sense of belonging to a group of contemporaries.[30]

Much advertising, the Report added, is therefore addressed 'as never before' 'specifically to teenagers and to teenagers as teenagers (as members of a named and defined group)'. While Albemarle recognized that teenagers 'acquire therefore a sense of their own economic importance and independence', and felt that they receive 'excessive public attention', it recognized more clearly than most commentators that teenagers were none the less operating within 'the wider setting of their society', characterized by general affluence and 'the pleasures' of consumer spending.

While Abrams ran quite far up the age scale in search of spenders without family commitments, Albemarle, in three paragraphs near the beginning of the Report devoted to 'Physique', gives special attention to the bottom of the age range:

> today's adolescents are taller and heavier than those of previous generations, and they mature earlier... it appears certain that puberty is occurring earlier, and that the large majority of young people now reach adolescence, as determined by physical changes, before the age of 15.

'More than one witness', this paragraph continued, 'has impressed on us his conviction that young workers have considerable surplus energy which their work, and most of the more easily available facilities for leisure, do not always satisfy.'[31] Eighteen months previously, between 15 and 19 September 1958, the *Daily Mirror* had run a series whose title, 'The Beanstalk Generation', was intended to evoke the stunning physical growth of the country's children. The first in the series, by one of the new generation of relatively young writers from working-class origins, Keith Waterhouse, was headed, 'Our Children Are Changing', and accompanied by a photograph of a teenage girl who had manifestly 'matured early'.

> She is only 13 but... already her hair has a home perm. She uses lipstick... she has been wearing a bra for a year now... she has pin-ups of Elvis Presley in her room... She is wearing nylons. She has been wearing them for two years... She is wearing high heels. She is going out on a date.

The main concern of the Albemarle Committee was that these mature youngsters would actually be the responsibility of the schools rather than the youth service. Others focused on the way in which juvenile delinquency was steadily spreading down the age scale. The Home Office Committee on Children and Young Persons did not report till October 1960, though it had actually been appointed in October 1956. By 1958 a great increase in crime in the population at large was apparent, but it was most significant in the 17-21 and 14-17 age groups, where crime rates reached the highest ever known; among the 8-14 group, too, there was a rise from 924 criminal offences per 100,000 in 1955 to 1,176 per 100,000 in 1958. The Committee set these figures within the context of, as it saw it, fifty years of war, social and cultural change, and increasingly frightening weaponry:

> During the past fifty years there has been a tremendous material, social and moral revolution in addition to the upheaval of two wars. While life has in many ways become easier and more secure, the whole future of mankind may seem frighteningly uncertain. Everyday life may be less of a struggle... but the fundamental insecurity remains with little that the individual can do about it. The material revolution... has provided more desirable objects, greater opportunity for acquiring them illegally, and considerable chances of immunity from the undesirable consequences of so doing. It is not always so clearly recognized what a complete change there has been in social and personal relationships (between classes, between sexes, and between individuals) and also in the basic assumptions which regulate behaviour. These major changes in the cultural background may well have replaced the disturbances of war as factors which contribute in themselves to instability within the family.[32]

This is all rather speculative and unspecific, but at least such considerations helped the Committee towards coming out very strongly against the restoration of judicial flogging and birching (abolished only in 1948), recommendations fully acceptable to the Macmillan government and its liberal-minded home secretary, R. A. Butler, though not to the Conservative right wing and sections of the popular press. A cartoon in the *Daily Express* of 16 November 1960 starkly presents the image of youth as juvenile delinquent. A middle-class gentleman has been assaulted by three youths, carrying cosh, chain, and open razor; they have Italian haircuts and are wearing winklepicker shoes. As the youths escape Butler, in the guise of a policeman, is addressing the victim: 'Bad luck, Sir! Never mind—if I catch the scoundrels, I'll give them a sharp tap on the head with this report!' The report is headed 'No More Birching'.

The Albemarle Committee too took up the issue of expanding teenage crime, but firmly and sensibly concluded on the note that the numbers involved were actually a tiny proportion of the total teenage population. The report did go into the question of teenage attitudes and the extent to which they represented alienation from, or active hostility to, adult society. The view left-wing publishers Macgibbon and Kee chose to project of MacInnes's novel (in the blurb for the first edition) is illuminating: they start from the fear which is so pervasive in the *Daily Express* cartoon, present MacInnes's teenagers as bright and resourceful, and end with a reference to adults as 'the enemy'. The paperback of *Absolute Beginners* was published in 1962. A review from the *Evening Standard* was quoted on the jacket:

Here, you citizens, tax payers, oldsters, you conscripts, sordid and squares, dig this—This is what you and your city and the civilisation you have made there look like to an articulate teenager. It's not very pretty if you want to know.

The Albemarle Committee on the whole played down the notion of the total alienation from adult life of teenagers, finding 'no body of evidence sufficient to suggest that teenagers as a whole have rejected family life'.

it may be that some of the recent changes in the style properties involved in young people's lives and especially in their reactions, make them readier than usual to desert, in their free time, an environment which seems 'corny' and 'square'. In spite of all this, we do not think the assumption that married life is right and desirable has yet generally been undermined.[33]

Population statistics supported this general contention, and the Committee, while recognizing the teenage period as one of 'prosperous irresponsibility', drew special attention to the popularity of early marriages. Albemarle is the voice of both 'secular Anglicanism' and 'measured judgement': its views offer clues to the ready, and relatively peaceful, acceptance of youth subculture into British society of the middle sixties.

The Committee had already recorded that it was 'left predominantly with a sense of respect and admiration for most young people's good sense, goodwill, vitality, and resilience'. It now for the first time explicitly associated British youth with characteristics it believed could be found among young people, including students, throughout other countries. The basic characteristic it identified was that of 'healthy scepticism':

to dismiss the outside world as 'square' is to some extent a natural feature of adolescence, today's rejections seem often to go beyond this, to have a peculiar edge and penetration. They suggest how strong is the *potential* idealism of young people, that idealism which is now so often baffled and turned back upon itself.[34]

The somewhat generalized rejection of the 'square' correctly identified here is in parallel with the rejection by the slightly older, and distinctly classier, age group of 'the Establishment'. The 'peculiar edge and penetration' can, very properly, be allocated mainly to the specially creative spirits, and their followers, increasingly manifesting themselves within the working class.

It was partly because of his own personal obsession that MacInnes introduced black individuals into his portrait of youth subculture. Most youth music was in some way or another black in origin; and some contemporary commentators do suggest that individual blacks were vital components in the generally bohemian and anti-establishment atmosphere. Barry Miles has confirmed that the 'hip society in Notting Hill in these days was basically very involved with West Indians'.[35] It does happen that the large seaport towns (particularly Liverpool, but also Newcastle) were markedly cosmopolitan; but there were working-class areas where no blacks were to be seen at all. And it is not possible to ignore the fact of violent conflict between white youth and racial minorities. The Albemarle Report approached the problem sensitively and exposed a certain paradox, in a subsection formally concerned with housing:

It is also important to recognise that in many industrial towns the areas with substandard housing are undergoing fundamental social changes that have sometimes led to serious disturbances among some of the young people. New and strange faces appear on the doorsteps and congregate in the streets as workers from many lands find a job and a home in Britain. The integration of these families brings problems, and has sometimes created a sense of insecurity and a fear among the established community that living standards will deteriorate further. Housing conditions do not completely explain the violence shown by some youths in these areas, and the prevalence of lawless gangs is not a new phenomenon of the slums. However, these racial outbursts present a new problem and seem paradoxical in this age when young people of all races and nationalities seem less different and share common interests such as jazz and football and often a common culture.[36]

What is certain is that it is not really possible, as Marxists have been wont to do, to present the most striking manifestations of youth subculture as representing young working-class resistance to bourgeois society (nor can signs of activity from middle-class youth be represented as entirely different 'bourgeois' phenomena).[37] Youth subculture is not exclusively working-class: across classes there is '*potential* idealism', 'healthy scepticism', condemnation both of 'squares' and 'the Establishment', as well as shared enthusiasm for certain kinds of music and certain kinds of fashion. It was easy, as the Children and Young Persons Committee had done, to imagine young people bothered by the bomb, but quite inaccurate, as a wealth of evidence demonstrated, among it this comment by a Huddersfield 15-year-old:

It's all a big skive, isn't it? All those takeover bids and that, all this yammer about old age pensions and the bomb. Nobody really cares do they? I mean, if they did, they'd do something about it.[38]

If we move to university students as a group, we find that they are particularly conservative and conformist. 'In politics there is little that is new in present-day youth,' Ferdynand Zweig concluded after conducting a survey of Oxford University students in the spring, and of Manchester University in the summer, of 1962; in danger of becoming 'cautious adults at twenty,' recorded educationalist Michael Young a year later; 'a negligible political force', characterized by a 'servility' designed to secure 'comfortable' social and economic rewards was the verdict of Professor F. Musgrove, who added, 'There is no prospect of any massive rebellion by the British young against their condition and the dominant customs, trends and institutions of our society.'[39] Zweig noted a leaning towards the politics of consensus and the moderate centre, which included the new upper-working-class or lower-middle-class student, 'rising from the ranks of the less privileged sections of society'.[40]

Noting that the new less privileged students 'resent the present rigid class structure, which bars their way to higher positions', Zweig adds that 'disapproval of class distinctions is very widespread at both universities'. But again moderation reigns:

> They do not demand the abolition of the class system, only the loosening and widening of it to allow for the full emergence of talent and merit. Greater social mobility and the abolition of educational privileges are demanded, that is all.[41]

Most notably, there appeared to be no discontent with the actual organization of the universities themselves. It was true that the British universities, recruiting a smaller proportion of the entire relevant age group than universities in America, France, or Italy (though at least as open to working-class recruits as were universities in the latter two countries), offered teaching that was both more systematic and more personalized than in the other countries.

One notable characteristic identified by Zweig, which would seem in some ways to separate students from the younger cohort of enthusiasts for the new American popular music, was hostility to America, which appears to be made up as much of snobbishness and offended patriotism, as radicalism:

> the image of the USA is not very favourable. It is the image of basically adolescent, materialistic, slightly hysterical society, run primarily by Big Business, a society exerting great pressure for conformity with little real freedom of thought, a society which can easily run amok or behave in an unpredictable way. Its excessive influence on Britain is rather resented and many are afraid that what America is today Britain may become tomorrow. President Kennedy personally is approved of and even acclaimed, mainly owing to his youthful vigour and drive... But even those students who hold a more balanced picture see shadows and clouds coming over America. This attitude to America is also a factor in the students' preference for joining Europe, as in this way, they think, Britain may be able to resist more strongly the process of Americanisation.[42]

But President Kennedy apart, British students really had little knowledge of what radicalism there was in America.

Indubitably there was a strong anti-American character about the Campaign for Nuclear Disarmament, a movement which certainly involved students (though only a minority of them)—at any one time at least half the marchers and demonstrators were young people under 25. These young people did bring to the marches some of the distinctive do-it-yourself, participatory, music-making elements of youth subculture. But the fact that most were conforming to the values of their middle-class radical families was borne out in their dress, student scruffy rather than sharply continental in the manner of working-class teenagers. Inaugurated at a well-attended meeting in the Central Hall, Westminster, on 17 February 1958, CND was the product of old-established left-wing intellectuals. That Easter there took place the first march from central

London to the nuclear missile site at Aldermaston in Berkshire. Thereafter there were annual marches from Aldermaston to London, successful up to 1963, after which enthusiasm for the campaign greatly waned. It was not a youth movement. It was not really a part of youth subculture. It does provide a link between the New Left revival of the mid-1950s, and the radical student movements of the middle and later sixties; it also provided a symbol, the upturned 'Y', and a badge, which many young protesters sported for the rest of the decade, even if not directly associated with CND. But on the whole it highlights the fact that political radicalism at this stage was a general feature neither of working-class nor of middle-class youth.[43]

Youth subculture is most obviously characterized by its dress and its music. The really significant developments in providing a distinctive, and exportable, identity for British youth took place between 1960 and the end of 1963: this was the period in which Mary Quant both went wholesale and (in late 1960) went to America, when John Stephen, the Glasgow grocer's son who, aged 19, came to London in 1956, establishing 'His Clothes' in Carnaby Street in 1958, selling sharp, but not particularly original, continental suits, became much more adventurous, and was joined by others in Carnaby Street—particularly Sally Tuffin and Marion Foale, who declared: 'We suddenly didn't want to be chic; we just wanted to be ridiculous.'[44] In 1961 Mary Quant opened a second Bazaar in Knightsbridge. None of these designers and entrepreneurs was now particularly young, but they were quite deliberately catering to the young. Skirts got shorter, and were accompanied by tights. Stockings became bold and patterned, with 1963 being declared by fashion writer Ernestine Carter 'the Year of the Leg'. That slogan was followed by 'Boots with Everything', coined by Felicity Green of the *Daily Mirror*.[45] Boots, short skirts, hipster jeans, all fashions for youthful figures, male and female, without problems to conceal. It is a matter of emphasis, of course, not complete exclusivity: the trouser suits of 1962 were not particularly aimed at youth.

In late 1960, almost three-and-a-half years before the working-class/lower-middle-class, and manifestly provincial, heralds of a surprising British hegemony in popular music, the Beatles, brought their confections to America, upper-class (by marriage) Mary Quant brought hers. Responses ranged from astonishment that the staid English could produce anything like this, to a glimmering recognition that this new English fashion was poised for universal conquest. *Life* (5 December 1960), in a feature entitled 'British Couple's Kooky Styles', remarked that 'somehow their clothes seem wackier than they are because they came from England, stronghold of the court gown, the sturdy tweed and the furled umbrella'. What *Life* singled out was the shortness of the skirts (in fact they went up to only just below the knee). *Women's Wear Daily* was altogether more percipient: 'These Britishers have a massive onslaught of talent, charm and mint-new ideas.'[46] Anticipating the way in which Mary Quant fashions would in time reach out to American young people, the American youth magazine *Seventeen* prepared a special Mary Quant spring promotion.

Mary Quant was no longer strikingly young, and she was certainly no product of the teenage cohort analysed by Abrams and Albemarle. But British youth subculture, in all its enormous influence, is only to be understood if we trace the interconnections between classes and slightly different age groups. The initial demand did come from within a youth subculture, which was predominantly working-class. That demand was met by various providers, not excluding working-class students from design and art colleges. The most successful of these was Raymond Clark, born in 1942 into a large working-class family in Oswaldtwistle, Lancashire, and educated at Salford School of Art and the Royal College of Art. He was just into his 20s when he was taken on by Alice Pollock's Quorum boutique on the King's Road as principal designer. We shall hear more of 'Ossie' Clark (from Oswaldtwistle) later. And whatever Mary Quant's origins and associations, she did very positively identify herself with youth. A statement of hers gets the balance pretty exactly (note that word 'Establishment' again):

> London led the way in the changing focus of fashion from the Establishment to the young. As a country, we were aware of the great potential of this change long before the Americans or the French. We were one step ahead from the start...[47]

Many of the same sorts of thing have to be said about the music of youth, in some ways much more commercialized, in others with even more genuine roots in working-class urban areas. Chronologically, jazz was the first black American musical form to make a significant impact on fifties Britain, most usually in the traditional, New Orleans style. The fashion was most marked among middle-class, left-wing intellectuals. But among young people, and particularly working-class young people, a kind of do-it-yourself version developed in the form of 'skiffle', employing such humble 'instruments' as broom-handles and washing-boards. Skiffle was an offshoot of traditional jazz, the first skiffle groups being sections of the jazz bands filling in the intervals by playing American folk-songs on string instruments. Dave Laing has evoked the compulsive appeal of skiffle: 'The monotonous and forceful strumming of guitars had a naive and completely unprecedented compulsion'.[48] Then came the much more trenchant influence of rock'n'roll, through imported records and through the film *Rock Around the Clock*, exhibited in Britain in 1956 and through the tour of Bill Haley and his Comets in 1957. At a time when working-class teenagers had visited on them the image of the violent Teddy boy with flick-knife and chain, British newspapers delighted in exaggerating the violence accompanying the showing of the films *Blackboard Jungle* (1955, it featuring the song 'Rock Around the Clock'), *Rock Around the Clock* (1956), and *Don't Knock the Rock* (1957). Rock'n'Roll and black blues music seem to have had a particular appeal, perhaps as 'outsider music', in working-class areas. But the working class was not an enclosed multitude, hermetically sealed from the rest of society; and, in any case, all young people are in some way outsiders. Both the sense of trend-setting in choice of records and the do-it-yourself spirit first manifested in skiffle pervaded the technical colleges, art colleges, universities, and even public schools, as well as the milieu of young workers. In Liverpool John Lennon and Paul McCartney were captivated both by rock'n'roll and by some of the black vocalists; in 1956 they became part of the local group the Quarrymen. As McCartney later recorded: 'We started off by imitating Elvis, Buddy Holly, Chuck Berry, Carl Perkins, Gene Vincent, The Coasters, The Drifters—we just copied what they did.'[49] Buddy Holly, with his group the Crickets, was an important transitional figure, writing his own songs and achieving full integration of words and music;[50] unhappily he died in an air crash in February 1959.

Of a number of groups which moved from jazz to skiffle and then to rock, the most widely known was the Shadows (with Hank Marvin), who subsequently teamed up with Cliff Richard, one of a number of young performers who adapted a kind of cheeky, music-hall presentation to skiffle and then rock. Much in the same mould were Lonnie Donegan, whose overnight success 'Rock Island Line' 'brought skiffle out of the cellars and on to the television screen', Tommy Steele, and Joe Brown and the Bruvvers. In brief, the music evolving in the British working-class clubs had more complexity than rock'n'roll and more beat than rhythm and blues. In Liverpool, apart from the Beatles, there were the Searchers and Gerry and the Pacemakers; in Manchester there were the Hollies; other groups getting attention were Freddie and the Dreamers and Herman's Hermits. In Newcastle the Alan Price Combo (later the Animals) purveyed a more purist rhythm and blues. Old-style popular music had been aimed squarely at adults, and was intended to create a mood of elegant sophistication; by the fifties, instead, the mood was becoming one of sickly sentimentality. Still, at its best, big-band swing had required 'intricate and demanding reed and brass playing'.[51] The new music was, usually, simpler to play. More important, it was played by small groups of named individuals with whom young fans could identify personally. And the subtleties and sonorous sentimentalities of the saxophone gave way to the intoxicating strumming of the electric guitar. Full transformation in Britain was not achieved till the end of 1963. The extent to which a preliminary period of change had been accomplished over 1957–9 is demonstrated by a comparison of *Melody Makers* British top ten of May 1956 and that of May 1959.[52] The latter contains six exponents (marked with asterisks), commanding the top six places, of the various types of the new small-group music, the former only one—together with teenage crooner Pat Boone and the ambiguous 'Rock and Roll Waltz'. The lists are:

*May 1956*

1. 'No Other Love'—Ronnie Hilton
2. 'Rock and Roll Waltz'—Kay Starr
3. 'Poor People of Paris'—Winifred Attwell
4. 'A Tear Fell'—Teresa Brewer
5. 'My September Love'—David Whitfield
6. 'I'll Be Home'—Pat Boone
7. 'It's Almost Tomorrow'—Dream Weavers
8. 'Only You'—Hilltoppers
9. 'Mari Title' (Man with the Golden Arm)—Billy May
10. *'Lost John'—Lonnie Donegan

*May 1959*

1. *'Living Doll'—Cliff Richard
2. *'Dream Lover'—Bobby Darin
3. *'Battle of New Orleans'—Lonnie Donegan
4. *'Lipstick on Your Collar'—Connie Francis
5. *'A Big Hunk of Love'—Elvis Presley
6. *'A Teenager in Love'—Marty Wilde

7. 'Lonely Boy'—Paul Anka
8. 'Roulette'—Russ Conway
9. 'Ragtime Country Joe'—David Seville
10. 'The Heart of a Man'—Frankie Vaughan

By the end of the fifties there were at least 300 groups in Liverpool playing regularly in pubs, clubs, and dance halls. It was still all very localized, and even those with some sort of national reputation were scarcely lavishly rewarded, as is brought out in the story told to Michael Cable by guitarist Cockney Joe Brown, who was so badly off on £15 per week that he had to go to work on the bus:

> It got really embarrassing in the end because I was supposed to be a bit of a star and people were recognising me from the telly and there I was scrambling about on the bus with me guitars over one shoulder and me stage suit over the other. I had a helluva job getting one manager to let me have a cab from the station to the theatre on expenses. Even then it was only on condition that I got a receipt every time! Can you imagine asking a London cabbie for a receipt?! What's more, I was never allowed to give more than a three penny tip.[53]

In 1960 Lennon and McCartney, together with George Harrison and Pete Best, had formed the Silver Beatles to play in such Liverpool clubs as the Cavern and the Jacaranda. Though starting in frank imitation, the group was already beginning to evolve a distinctive style, partly imposed by the line-up of three guitars and drums. That style was 'beat'. During a visit to Hamburg (venue for a number of British bands) the group were persuaded by their German impresario to introduce an element of dramatic performance into their show; they also adopted mop-top hair-cuts and collarless suits. At the beginning of the sixties the Beatles, as they were now calling themselves, were the most popular and successful group within the Liverpool beat scene, but scarcely known elsewhere in Britain (there were no local radio companies to broadcast them, no local record companies to record them). In the fifth issue of *Mersey Beat: Merseyside's Own Entertainment Paper* (31 August-14 September 1961) local journalist Bob Woller posed the question 'Why do you think the Beatles are so popular?', recalling 'that fantastic night' (27 December 1960) when the Cheshire side of the Mersey had first felt 'the impact of the act' (the word 'act' is significant).

> I think The Beatles are No 1 because they resurrected original style rock'n'roll music, the origins of which are to be found in American negro singers… here again, in The Beatles, was the stuff that screams are made of. Here was the excitement—both physical and aural—that symbolised the rebellion of youth in the Ennuied mid 50s.[54]

Charlie Gillett has described the group's vocal style as being a derivative of two American styles which had not previously been put together:

the hard rock'n'roll style like the singers Little Richard and Larry Williams, and the soft gospel call-and-response style of the Shirelles, the Drifters... Instrumentally, the Beatles were at first less inventive, producing a harsh rhythm and shrill sound comparable to some of the better American 'twist' records including Bruce Channel's 'Hey! Baby' and Buster Brown's 'Fannie Mae'.

Although the twist had been fairly successful (without the impact it had in America), the gospel-harmony groups had very little success in Britain, and the result for the British audience was a sound with a familiar rhythm and a novel vocal style. The way the Beatles echoed one another's phrases, dragged out words across several beats, shouted 'yeah', and went into falsetto cries, was received in Britain as their own invention; it seemed that Britain had finally discovered an original, indigenous rock'n'roll style.[55]

The fundamental origins of the music of the Beatles is not in doubt; in this first phase, the manner in which it was shaped and distinctively developed was due in part to the wit, inventiveness, and charm of the group, and in part to the demands of their live audiences in the clubs and dance-halls where they played. But as with Presley, so with the Beatles: in the world of rock/pop you were nothing if you were not selling on disc. Thoroughly deserved but utterly unpredictable good fortune arrived in the form of the 27-year-old gay Jewish manager of the local record shop in his father's chain, Brian Epstein. Epstein became fascinated in particular by John Lennon, and put himself forward as manager for the group. He had a clear conception of how best to project their talents; more, as a big seller of records, he was someone the record companies felt bound to listen to. Even so, five record companies turned them down before Epstein persuaded the Parlophone subsidiary of EMI, where staff man George Martin recognized the genuine musical skills of the group, to take them on. Part of the group's following was due to the sexy good looks of drummer Pete Best. But Best was replaced by the brilliant but less well-favoured Ringo Starr before 'Love Me Do' was recorded and released in October 1962.[56] It was a hit in the sense of making the lower reaches of the top twenty. 'Please, Please Me', which followed, reached second place. Epstein was then able to persuade EMI to take on several of the other south Lancashire groups he now represented: the 'Mersey sound' had arrived. By this time, all records aimed at the mass market were subject to the wonders of double and multiple-track recording. The Beatles brought with them the directness of their live performances. Their songs were not only written by themselves, but had been tested out by themselves on enthusiastic, but also exacting—and, what is more, participating—audiences. They were, in addition, among the first to signal to the mass audience the decisive switch from the individualized song of personal emotion to the truly group song, the sentimentality cut with high spirits, songs to involve an entire age group.

But actually much more than one age group. What market researchers and academic social scientists alike forget, is that the quality of 'youthfulness' is to some extent self-chosen. For generations, if not centuries, upper-class rowdies and blockheads (of the type immortalized in the Bertie Wooster of P. G. Wodehouse) practised and, in certain circumstances, perpetuated the most childish behaviour. On the whole, a university education can have the function of prolonging the patterns of youth. In part as a product of the expansion of higher education, in part through the growth of independence of choice and in rejection of the traditional adopted *gravitas* of the newly old, more and more people moving into their 20s were choosing to remain young. They too felt the intoxication of jazz, beat, or rock/pop music. On 3 January 1964 a young Cambridge don just returned from a sojourn at the University of California at Berkeley wrote to his senior colleague and sponsor at Berkeley:

> for health and sanity these last months, I've been going to twist and shake clubs which have sprung up all over London. We have a new group who may be visiting America soon, and here are worshipped as I think no other entertainer ever has been (I mean that—it's fantastic!). Called The Beatles 4 kids from Liverpool, rough, cheeky, swingy, very much war-time kids, and fully of gutsy energy. I must say I fell for their stuff when I got back. I never thought to twist and shake—but I have and I do... it is a relief to lose oneself in the unconscious hypnotic euphoria of the music.[57]

By the beginning of the sixties the way one danced rock'n'roll had become more simplified, and it was now impossible to say whether the male or the female was leading. The twist, starting in America, and arriving in Britain via Paris, became a teenage craze by early 1962—though not exclusively a teenage craze: an over-40 was quoted as saying: 'The older folks like it because you move quite separately and therefore don't have to worry about your partner's feet. And the movements are so easy...'[58] With the twist, girls (and women) had achieved complete freedom and equality on the dance floor. But the twist, unlike rock'n'roll, had to be pushed very hard in Britain by the commercial interests, led by the film companies Paramount and Columbia who mounted expensive publicity campaigns, followed by the record companies, and then the Mecca and Arthur Rank dance-hall chains.[59] In that, (a) it was an international craze, (b) it was heavily promoted by commercial interests, (c) it was essentially a youth craze, but (d) was taken up by older people, the twist is a paradigm of sixties developments in popular culture. After the twist came the 'mod' dance (more about 'mods' shortly), the shake, a dance of rapt self-absorption, with no particular partner being required. Here, looking a little ahead to May 1964, is how a student at Aberdeen University summed things up:

> It's been a good term socially, thanks to the marvellous Mersey beat, as Aberdeen like every other town in the British Isles has its local groups and we have a student group as well. The great thing now is for the societies to hire a group for an evening to have a party in the Dive in the union. This is small, dark and cellar-like and when you get it crowded with fanatically yelling and shaking people and the group pounding away, the atmosphere is terrific. The electric guitar is absolutely made for such a small stuffy hole—you can really feel the music and I find that the insistent beat results in a feeling very like being drunk. Of course it gets terribly hot—even the walls are streaming and after an hour or so of frenzied activity one feels completely limp. But this is marvellous once in a while, letting oneself go and shaking away all troubles and worries.[60]

Abrams had taken special note of the teenage magazines which were becoming a force in the market-place at the time of his researches: he mentioned *Valentine, Roxy, Marilyn,* and *Mirabelle.*[61] In the year his report was published these were joined by *Boyfriend.* These, of course, were not general teenage magazines, but magazines aimed, often in a most traditional and patronizing way, at girls, and contemporary only in their overwhelming emphasis on current pop stars and, to a lesser degree, film stars. There are pictures of male pop stars 'to cut out 'n keep'; 'free inside' there may be a 'REAL PHOTOGRAPH OF ELVIS AUTOGRAPHED FOR YOU'; there is much biographical material on pop and film stars—Tab Hunter, the Everly Brothers, Frank Sinatra, Edmund Purdom (who 'has returned from Hollywood back to British TV'); there are such features as 'ELVIS PRESLEY and the love secrets of your favourite stars', 'TOMMY STEELE and your favourite stars AT HOME', and 'DIRK BOGARDE and the film world's most thrilling love stories'; there is the usual would-be reassuring guff—in a piece on 'the girls the stars like' the information is given that 'looks don't matter'; a similar message emerges from 'CLIFF RICHARD and the other top stars talk about their dream girl'. Major advertisers are an Oxford Street firm selling engagement rings, a mail order firm offering home-based part-time employment, Cadbury's chocolate, and the Cooperative Insurance Society—offering the single woman opportunities to save for her wedding.[62]

Alongside these girls' magazines were (slightly longer-established) magazines dedicated to popular music, in particular *New Musical Express* (founded in 1952) and *Hit Parade,* founded in 1954. These, as can be seen from their letter columns, were read by males and females. Letters in *Hit Parade* tended, as was perhaps appropriate from readers who were connoisseurs rather than just fans, to celebrate American stars and condemn British imitators, but also came to recognize the emergence of distinctive British talent. In the January 1961 issue, a male reader from County Durham (clearly no master of punctuation) wrote:

It has been said over the past few months that the standard of pop music has improved. This may be so, but what has happened to such great artists as Ricky Nelson, Paul Anka and Jackie Wilson. I am very surprised that they can find no place in the British hit parade. What has happened to the record buying public of this country that they should pass over such talent for some of the poor artists of this country.

Other readers (male and female) wrote specifically of Elvis Presley: 'he is still the king of rock'n'roll'; 'he can still knock most of the young singers in this country and in the States for six'; and, more generally, 'Why are genuine rock'n'roll artists of the calibre of Chuck Berry and Jerry Lee Lewis ignored in this country? Chuck has more drive in his music than any of Britain's second-rate rock singers.' In October 1961 a reader was commenting:

Judging by the state of the charts at present it seems as if the British singers are at least holding their own against the one-time American domination. However, don't let's forget the great American vocalists without whom our own charts would be bare, and on whose voices many of our own British singers had styled themselves. For instance, Elvis Presley,

Fats Domino, Connie Francis, Buddy Holly and Eddy Cochran.

Only with British 'domination' established at the end of 1963 did British entrepreneurs (some way behind their French counterparts, as we shall see) produce genuine unisex youth magazines firmly anchored in the new musical era: *Fabulous* appeared in mid-January 1964. Actually *Fabulous* was beaten to it (by exactly a week) by a new, up-to-the-minute magazine aimed at the female teenager, *Jackie*. The older girls' magazines soon began to flag. While *Jackie* had a circulation in 1968 of 451,000, *Mirabelle* (540,000 in 1956) had fallen to 175,000. Even before the end of 1963 *Valentine* and *Roxy* had merged; and by the end of 1965 *Boyfriend* was no more.

Throughout the High Sixties, however, the new magazines were an integral part of the rock/pop-based youth subculture. Still more important were specialist radio stations, and individual television programmes. From August 1963 ITV presented the deliberately youthful rock/pop programme *Ready Steady Go*. But BBC radio at this time made no attempt to be hospitable towards youthful listeners, so that a year later the first of the 'pirate' radio stations, playing non-stop rock/pop, appeared in the shape of an old boat anchored off the Suffolk coast. A number of clubs were renowned for the live experience they offered. It was in 1963 that the Rolling Stones, whose lead singer Mick Jagger was a student at the London School of Economics, other members of the band being art students, first started their regular appearances at the Craw-Daddy Club in Richmond, south-west London. Also out in that direction was Eel Pie Island Hotel, while in Hampstead, north London, there was Klook's Kleek. Central London clubs were the Marquee and the Scene in Soho, and, in Chelsea, the Flamingo. Quickly, from France, there arrived the discothèque. Soho's famous *La Discothèque*, founded in 1954 (where early patrons were Nigel Davies, at this time working off-and-on for hairdresser Vidal Sassoon, and later known as Justin de Villeneuve, and future film star Terence Stamp, then still struggling to get into acting), was really a coffee bar.

Affluence, consumerism, changes in sexual attitudes and behaviour were affecting large sections of society, not just young people. But within the youth subculture, most certainly, 'healthy scepticism' took the form of greater openness, frankness, and contempt for adult hypocrisy; even among the more restrained and conformist, there tended to be an admiration for the more daring. These points are well brought out in a couple of interviews conducted by Charles Hamblett and Jane Deverson just at the end of the period I am currently concerned with (the interviews were actually carried out between January 1963 and June 1964). The 20-year-old daughter of a professional man, reflecting back two or three years to her school-days, commented:

> Mother says never give in to a boy because he won't respect you, you'll only go on from one lover to another and end up a tart.... You'll think you're so devastating but all the time you'll just be a cheap joke.
>
> Of course, she's right. But Sheila at school slept with her boyfriend and everyone looked up to her, there's a sort of mystique about it. You feel you're missing out on something and you're not a real woman till you've slept with a boy...

When it comes to it you're scared because they've told you, the other girls have, that it's painful… but you feel great once it's over and you want to go off and tell all your girlfriends. [63]

A general overview, and some personal reflections from a male point of view, was provided by that apparently archetypal figure, an ex-art student (19 years old at the time of the interview):

Snogging on sofas doesn't happen so much now. Teenagers are growing up, they are far more sophisticated than they used to be even a few years back. Today if they want sex they don't snog on a sofa they go to bed. It's all taken for granted.

No-one says anything about queers anymore either…

Then there is a brief interruption to this train of thought as he reflects on a former girlfriend:

She just didn't fit into my scene. I didn't even like the girl. I just wanted to fuck her all the time…

There's a boy at art school whom all the girls are mad about: a real handsome, gorgeous boy. It's funny, I'm not queer… [but]… I sometimes want to touch this beautiful boy—and I do touch him, we're like that, it's taken for granted that we will do anything we want to and no-one will think anything of it. [64]

The first really systematic survey ever of *The Sexual Behaviour of Young People*—the title of the book by Michael Schofield, Research Director of the Central Council for Health Education and organizer of the survey, published in 1965—took place just at the end of the period we are currently investigating; the age group covered was that of 15–19-year-olds. The survey showed, first—an important matter given the way in which openness and explicitness developed in the High Sixties—that most young people were very shy about discussing sexual matters. Remarks made during preliminary discussions included:

Boy: 'Nearly everything you've said we don't use the same word for.'
Boy (about masturbation): 'It's alright to ask but change the word.'
Boy (about having the interview in a church hall): 'You couldn't *say* anything there.'
Girl (about the interview): 'I would have felt funny at home.' [65]

In the group of 478 younger boys (aged 15–17) a total of 55 (11 per cent) said they had experienced sexual intercourse at least once. A total of 138 (30 per cent) of the 456 older boys (aged 17–19) reported at least one experience of sexual intercourse. The figures for the girls are much smaller. Out of 475 younger girls, 29 (6 per cent) said they had experienced sexual intercourse at least once. Of 464 older girls, the figure was 73 (16 per cent). Thus 20 per cent of all the boys in the sample had experienced sexual intercourse and 12 per cent of all the girls. Reasons for the first experience of sexual intercourse are shown in Table 3.1.

**Table 3.1**

| Reason given | Boys (%) | Girls (%) |
|---|---|---|
| Sexual appetite | 46 | 16 |
| In love | 10 | 42 |
| Curiosity | 25 | 13 |
| Drink | 3 | 9 |
| Others | 4 | 8 |
| Don't know or no answer | 12 | 12 |

The second and major conclusion, therefore, was that, while some teenagers (mostly boys) certainly were sexually active, any idea of teenagers being generally promiscuous was quite incorrect. But there was solid evidence of most types of sexual experimentation.

Government statistics did show that in 1960, 31 per cent of girls who married while in their teens were pregnant at the time of their wedding.[66] It was to this, and other similar matters of concern in polite society, that G. M. Carstairs, Professor of Psychological Medicine at the University of Edinburgh, referred in his third contribution to the prestigious Reith Lecture series for the year 1962, given on BBC radio:

I believe that we may be quite mistaken in our alarm—at times amounting almost to panic—over young people's sexual experimentation... In our religious traditions the essence of morality has sometimes appeared to consist of sexual restraint. But this was not emphasised in Christ's own teaching. For him, the cardinal virtue was *charity*, that is consideration of and concern for other people... It seems to me that our young people are rapidly turning our own society into one in which sexual experience, with precautions against conception, is becoming accepted as a sensible preliminary to marriage; a preliminary which makes it more likely that marriage, when it comes, will be a mutually considerate and mutually satisfying partnership.[67]

It wasn't really quite like that, of course. Carstairs grossly underestimated the uncomplicated hedonism of new, increasingly affluent youth, particularly male youth. But here, certainly, was the authentic voice of liberal, Christian, 'measured judgement', welcoming youth into society, not seeing it as in any way alien. With regard to actual behaviour, what we can probably say with greatest certainty is that by the early sixties a substantial teenage avant-garde of the daring—and the delinquent—had emerged, and were increasingly to set the standards for the less adventurous. The all-embracing heading to an *Evening Standard* piece (31 October 1961) read, '"TEENAGE MORALS" AND THE CORRUPTION OF THE TIMES', but really referred only to this avant-garde:

Miss Jo Drury said in her presidential address to the Association of Remand Home Superintendents and Matrons at Bournemouth today: 'Girls we are now getting have no sense of responsibility. They do not know right from wrong and there is only one subject they can talk about, and that is sex. They think that it is part of their lives'.

Mr Justice Stable, said at Lines Assizes, Lincoln, today: 'It is an accepted thing today that these young people seem to attach as much importance to the fact of sexual intercourse as they do to ordering an iced lolly.'

The association between sexual intercourse and iced lollies shows the horror certain adults felt over that central phenomenon, the earlier maturing of young people. That another adult should feel that sex should not be part of teenage girls' lives shows how far we still are from the acceptance, widespread by the beginning of the seventies, that sexual activity among young people was a fact of life.

As later sections of this book will show, changing sexual behaviour and attitudes are not simply a youth matter. But I want to end this section by, first, stressing that by the end of 1963 British youth subculture had knitted together so effectively that there were very definite, and highly liberating, patterns of behaviour and forms of self-presentation associated with it, while at the same time these were now beginning to influence the wider culture; but second, cautioning that this subculture was far from monolithic. There were different kinds of rock/pop, and rock/pop was as yet far from all-conquering. Upper-class Marianne Faithfull, who was a teenager at the beginning of the sixties frequenting coffee bars and folk clubs in Reading, has warned us that in her circles,

> Rock'n'roll in the early sixties didn't have the hip reputation it eventually acquired. Jazz was hip and blues were hip. Rock'n'roll at the time meant Billy Fury and guys with bleached blonde hair.[68]

Nothing was totally without class resonances, though style and affiliation could matter as much as class. The original 'mods' (the name coming from their enthusiasm for modern jazz) emerged from working-class east London:

> Impeccably cut Italian suits with very narrow lapels were tailor-made for them, and worn with hand-made winkle picker shoes and shirts with pointed collars. The image was completed by a short, neat Italian or French hair style, copied from foreign film stars of the day like Alain Delon—very different to the greasy Brylcreemed look of the Teddy boy.[69]

The mods switched their allegiance to certain rock/pop groups; the Who (whose lead guitarist, Pete Townshend, had studied at Ealing Art College in west London), the Small Faces (from east London), and the Animals (from Newcastle upon Tyne). They found the early Beatles too melodic and too respectable. Mod styles spread up the class structure, and working-class mods could mix in middle- and upper-class circles where obvious Teds would be excluded. In reaction against the mods there appeared the rockers, in leather jackets, not smart suits, on powerful motorbikes, not scooters, and still dancing rock'n'roll and the twist. Ritualistic rioting at English seaside resorts on bank holidays brought massive media attention—this was youth as spectacle with a vengeance. In fact these confrontations belonged only to this first phase of the formation of the British youth subculture; thereafter the terms 'mods' and 'rockers' had little salience as the youth subculture expanded, interacted with other subcultures, and permeated the wider society.

Styles of self-presentation among mods, and among those who owned to no such label, varied greatly, but what runs across the classes is the care and attention taken. An Islington apprentice printer recalled:

> Most of us had terrific hair, French style, and you spent a lot of time on it. You had to use sugar water. What you would do was wash your hair, then get a bowl of hot water, put sugar in it, then let it cool and keep stirring it up and then plaster that on your head to get it into shape...
>
> We had to go to a lot of extremes. Once I didn't go out because I put on my suit, and my shoes were a little bit dirty so I got the polish out and—disaster—I looked in the mirror and I'd splattered my shirt: So I got the hump and I didn't go out that evening; I stayed in because my shirt wasn't perfect. And I knew groups who'd get on a bus with a sheet of brown paper so they could put it on the seat so they didn't get any dirt on their suit.[70]

'Terrific hair' often implied a new kind of men's hairdresser, deliberately seeking to create new, elaborate styles for men: already at work was the man who was to become *the* name in unisex hairdressing in the High Sixties, Vidal Sassoon. No doubt there was a strong element of ritual about the way leisure time was spent, but there was certainly also a thoroughly liberated quality to it. Middle-class John Dunbar (but married to Marianne Faithfull) spoke of

> this weird Saturday night and Friday night ritual, meeting up in these pubs and exchanging lists of parties. You'd literally go to ten parties, to totally unknown houses.[71]

Our apprentice printer remembered:

> Monday was Tottenham Royal, Tuesday the Lyceum, Wednesday the Scene, or maybe stay in and wash your hair, Thursday Tottenham Royal again (because it was our own little hangout), then Friday night was 'Ready Steady Go'... Then after 'Ready Steady Go' you'd go on to the Scene later. Saturday and Sunday was either a party or the Tottenham Royal, then the next week you'd start again.[72]

To support this punishing social life, resort was had to amphetamines—Purple Hearts, French Blues, Black Bombers. The apprentice printer explained the case of Purple Hearts:

> They used to keep you going most of the night, but the only dodgy night was Sunday night because you were really tired then, so we'd take a handful and we'd be OK. There

wasn't any dope around then so we used to take speed.[73]

The metamorphosis from 'speed' to 'dope' would come soon enough. For the moment the signs were already quite clear that the spreading youth subculture was bringing together, in interaction with each other, practices associated with different social classes. Alexander Plunkett-Green had thought that Mary Quant's clothes would appeal only to the student set he was familiar with; by the early sixties he had discovered, as he put it, 'that we were interpreting the mood of the whole generation, not just smart art students'.[74] The deeper realities of class were not greatly changed. Still, an active middle-class participant in the liberated, exhausting lifestyle could genuinely record:

> It wasn't a class thing: people tended to do whatever they needed, whatever was the least hassle and the least bullshit. You had a good time, you rejected the whole philosophy you were brought up on.[75]

Writing in 1967, Vidal Sassoon said of Mary Quant that 'Mary and I had more or less grown up together' since they had met in his first Bond Street salon in 1954 when he was 26:

> She cut clothes with a brilliant flair and I tried to match her style with hair.
> All her model girls came to me. Whenever she was showing a collection, she would call me round and I would work out a hair-style to suit it. Sometimes I did not have to go around, because she would work out a design while she was under the drier in the salon, and show it to me.[76]

Sassoon had opened larger premises at 171 Bond Street in April 1959 (with a jazz group playing on the balcony at the inaugural party). Within about six months he had sensed 'the first faint whiff' of a success which stretched beyond the society and show-business clients he mainly dealt with:

> As I walked into the salon, I noticed suddenly that it was filled with people from many different worlds. There were peeresses, actresses, top models, suburban housewives having a day out in London, and quite a few kids from shops and offices.
> The rich ones had the pick of the town. The less rich—and therefore probably more discerning—had saved hard for something special. They all had come to us, presumably because they felt we would give them the best haircut.[77]

Slowly Sassoon began to take the odd male client—actors such as Terence Stamp and Peter O'Toole. But 1963, for Sassoon, was 'the Year of the Happening'. First he tried out on Mary Quant herself his idea of 'a neat, clean, swinging line', short at the back, still long at the sides; then he performed the same cut on all her models for her next show. The 'Mary Quant cut' or 'classic bob' was born, and was immediately publicized across the world.[78]

What of the sex barriers which had in fact divided the early teenage subculture? There was much male oppression still to be endured by females before the new feminism burst into flame at the very end of the decade; but, as we have seen, there was evidence that teenage girls were beginning to turn away from the stereotyped magazines of the 1950s. An inquiry conducted in the industrial city of Sheffield and reporting in 1963 found:

> There are signs that some girls are tending towards more independence in their dealings with men, and that they will not be content to sign over their lives to their husbands on marriage... they are determined to remain smart and in control of events after they have married; they are not prepared to be bowed down with lots of children, and they will expect their husbands to take a fuller share than their fathers in the running of the home.[79]

Here the teenage revolution, and the enhanced self-confidence which ensued from it, is being identified as the cause of much more profound change. The new music, and the new modes of dancing, had profound effects as well. It was not just young university lecturers who found the Beatles (and other groups) exhilarating and liberating. As the distinguished historian of pop/rock music Simon Frith has so neatly put it: 'Rock was experienced as a new sort of sexual articulation by women as well as men.'[80]

### Affluence, Sex, and the Environment

The idea that some kind of 'teenage revolution' went on entirely independent of, or in direct opposition to, adult society is inherently unlikely, particularly since the empowerment born of affluence, combined with the new opportunities for, and new forms of, self-expression, were effacing (especially for women) former boundaries between the unmarried ('youthful') and married ('adult') state. Consumer goods, in all four countries, were aimed at young and not so young married couples, and not (apart from the very specific examples already given) at teenagers; and younger married couples were themselves trend-setters. Advanced marketing and public relations techniques played their part, particularly in America, in the shaping of the teenage subculture; but, of course, they also played a far larger part in the moulding of the entire 'affluent' consumer society which America had already become. The phrase 'the affluent society' was popularized by the 1957 book of that title written by the Canadian-born economist and pillar of the American liberal-intellectual establishment, John Kenneth Galbraith, who identified the central characteristic of the affluent society as it manifested itself in the USA as the existence side by side of private affluence and public squalor. Starting from a much higher base-line, American economic growth between 1950 and 1963 was actually lower than that of any other industrialized country save Britain; none the less incomes rose steadily throughout the 1950s, and there was still plenty of mobility, and much money to be made in favoured occupations. In the same period in Britain average weekly earnings of men over 21 very nearly doubled, with increases in real earnings being somewhat less than that, since at the same time retail prices rose by about 15 per cent. France and Italy both enjoyed 'economic miracles' (i.e. sharp rises in production) between the later fifties and the early sixties. But incomes were kept under strict control: while there were modest increases in France, it is reckoned that in Italy between 1955 and 1960, despite rises in industrial production of 89 per cent and in productivity of 62 per cent, real wages actually dropped by 0.6 per cent, with unemployment remaining high at about 8 per cent.[81]

America continued to set the standards in the application of technology, engineering, 'mod cons', and consumer goods in general, to everyday life. First in overall impact, for good or ill, was the spread of car ownership, and the building of the roads and bridges for cars to drive along, as little impeded as possible. Then came television, the mighty medium of mass communication and entertainment, still a novelty in the European countries at the beginning of the 1950s. A house filled with other gadgets was much to be desired, but the actual priority for most people across all four countries was simply the occupation of a decent home. Slums in America might have more gadgets but were often as appalling as in any of the other countries. Governments did recognize that if industrial expansion was to be sustained, mass housing for the workers would have to be provided. Well ahead of mod cons, what many in all four countries required was the efficient supply of water and electricity, and the possession of proper sanitary and heating facilities.

Between 1950 and 1960 car ownership in the United States increased by over twenty-one million; over the same period 40,000 miles of interstate highways were built. Home ownership increased by over nine million. In 1946 only 7,000 families had TV sets; by 1960 the figure was over fifty million (at the same point in time 75 per cent of British families had TV sets, the figures being rather lower in both France and Italy). Affluence appeared merely to consolidate conventional, family-based America, America of the Rat Race. However, just as there was 'disaffection' among certain 'exceptional elements' in the younger generation, so we can perceive among older generations the increasing expression of uneasiness about many aspects of American society—as indeed the very coining of the phrase 'Rat Race', and the criticisms embodied in such books as *The Status Seekers* (1960) by Vance Packard, suggest. Formally family values stood unchallenged, though (as we shall see in the next chapter) more and more novels and films were presenting views of sexual morality at odds with the conventional one.

In this section I continue to recognize America's primacy in this first phase of cultural change. I start by looking at two important areas of incipient radical stirrings: resistance to the way in which both government and business were destroying the environment, natural and urban; and the questioning of fifties platitudes about the American home and women's place in it. American (rather than British) civilization was the one against which the French and the Italians measured themselves; this has to be borne in mind as I then look at developments relating to affluence and sex in France and Italy and, finally, in Britain.

Something besides rigid conformity to Cold War norms was happening among certain middle-class American women—not necessarily young ones; particularly was this so in the beautiful and lively city of San Francisco, home of other kinds of protest than that represented by the Beats, some no doubt a little cosy, some not so cosy. With the Second World War over, the city authorities had planned to tear up San Francisco's ancient cable car system (well adapted in fact to the city's many steep hills) and replace it with motor buses. Concerned citizens sprang into action, securing a referendum in 1947 in which 77 per cent of voters rejected the proposals for a total removal of the cable cars: the two main lines, north-south (with two branches at the north end) and east-west, were preserved.[82] To the east and north of San Francisco was the Bay Area, combining breathtaking natural beauty with some of the worst depredations of speculative greed and the motor car together. Here, by the end of the fifties, the three-pronged environmental threat was truly horrific: to San Francisco itself, as plans were developed to build a double-deck urban freeway within the city; to the bay, which in 1850 had measured 680 square miles, now reduced, through land reclamation and infill for various commercial purposes, to 400, and, on current projections, in danger of shrinking to 107, a mere river (a consortium of banks and land owners were planning to knock the tops off the San José mountains, with a view to rolling the spoil down into the bay, thus creating cheap land for development[83]); and to the appearance of such of the bay as might survive—already one long and undistinguished bridge, combining road and rail, ran west-east to connect with Oakland and Berkeley, now there was strong pressure for a second bridge side by side with it.[84]

During the 1950s San Francisco's city authorities accepted the conventional wisdom that urban freeways were essential to economic progress and that, in particular, there must be direct links, to inter-state highway standards, between the three main points of entry to the city—by land from the south, across the Bay Bridge from the east, and across the Golden Gate Bridge from the north. First, in a grotesque symbol of so much that was crass about fifties ideology, the railway on the lower deck of the Bay Bridge was removed so that both decks could be entirely given over to motor traffic. The city's chief administrative officer declared:

> The whole welfare of the metropolitan area is dependent on the early completion of the freeway system. The rest of the system is urgently needed now. Delay may result in stagnation within the city, and we urge every effort to expedite the construction of the freeway system, not only in San Francisco but in all metropolitan areas in the State. It is essential to their economic welfare.[85]

In that same year (1955) construction of the Embarcadero Freeway right along the shoreline of the historic port began. The double-decked structure was described by state officials as 'an ultra-modern highway facility fully separated from city traffic'; they expressed the hope that 'this type of construction will become synonymous with the city of San Francisco, restoring to its people and their visitors the opportunities of viewing the city which were lost with the departure of the ferries'[86]—the view, presumably, was that of motorists speeding along the freeway and looking in towards the city; for those actually in the city, the view out across the bay was completely obliterated by the same freeway. But the San Francisco newspapers were beginning to revolt. As early as October 1956 (when the Embarcadero Freeway was opened) the *San Francisco Chronicle* declared:

> The high-rise squalor of this abominable Autobahn will defeat all the efforts of talent and

genius to create a great civic plaza at the foot of Market Street. There is but one way to make a seemly plaza along the Embarcadero and that is to demolish the freeway and put it underground. The freeway rapes San Francisco's priceless waterfront. It is a crime which cannot be prettied up.

In 1956 Congress created the Highway Trust to accelerate the inter-state highway programme. Following this, the California Division of Highways announced plans for an extension of the Embarcadero Freeway, and for two new urban freeways, all of which would go through historic residential areas, and one of which would destroy the famous Golden Gate Park. Residents created 'a fire-storm of neighborhood protest'.[87] Meantime, the state was pressing hard for the building of the second road bridge across the bay, slightly to the north of the existing one; the San Francisco Board of Supervisors preferred a bridge to the south, to be used for some kind of local rail or 'rapid transit' system. Truly the middle-class citizens of San Francisco were stirring up a revolution: in January 1959 the Board of Supervisors withdrew their support for the urban freeways, and declared against any kind of second bay crossing, opting instead for the eventual building of a tube which would lie on the bed of the bay, and through which the projected rapid transit system would run.[88] The urban freeway building project was never revived. No second bay bridge was built. A decade later rapid transit trains were running through the tube, completely concealed under the waters of the bay. Meantime, on 29 January 1964, San Francisco's cable car system was designated as the first moving National Historic Landmark in the United States.[89]

Local groups struggling to defend their cities, as in San Francisco, had the full weight of informed opinion ('the planners'), as well as that of the most powerful commercial interests, against them. The first great national counterblast, *The Death and Life of Great American Cities*, by Jane Jacobs, a journalist married to an architect, appeared in 1961, but took some years to gain recognition as one of the great sixties classics of heresy in the face of accepted wisdom. 'The bedrock attribute of a successful city district', said Jacobs, 'is that a person must feel personally safe and secure in the street among all these strangers.'[90] The commonsense concern for the individual, vulnerable human is striking. We shall meet it again in *Silent Spring*, the second of the great pioneering environmentalist works of the early sixties, also written by a woman, and in the local environmental groups which were largely the creation of middle-class women. The opening sentence of *Death and Life of Great American Cities* was uncompromising: 'This book is an attack on current city planning and rebuilding';

> specifically on: low income projects that become worse centres of delinquency, vandalism, and general social hopelessness than the slums they were supposed to replace; civic centers that are avoided by everyone but bums... expressways that eviscerate great cities...

Jacobs saw that cities were 'different', and should not be reduced to imitating the life of small-town America. Her inspirational message was only slowly and only partially heeded:

Dull, inert cities, it is true, do contain the seeds of their own destruction and little else. But lively, diverse, intense cities contain the seeds of their own regeneration, with energy enough to carry over for problems and needs outside themselves.[91]

Between February and July 1961 two traditional conservationist and antiquarian organizations in California, the Sierra Club and the Save the Redwoods League, were merged into the newly formed, activist San Francisco Bay Association, largely through the activities of three energetic upper-middle-class women, all of them, however, as was the custom of the time, designated by reference to their prominent husbands: Mrs Clark Kerr, wife of the president of the University of California, Mrs Donald McLaughlin, wife of a member of the Board of Regents of the University of California, and Mrs Charles Gulick, wife of an economics professor.[92] Mrs Kerr (her own first name was Catherine, the other two being Sylvia and Ester) had often had the task of driving visiting dignitaries to the University of California: she had to some extent become inured to the local custom of seeing the Bay as a great economic asset ripe for continued exploitation; it was her visitors who opened her eyes to the way in which the natural beauty of the area was being spoilt. A careful appraisal of the activities of the Association was provided by the *Saturday Evening Post* (18 June 1966):

> The members of Save The Bay did their homework. They watched for every application to alter the Bay and demanded hearings for every project, then attended the hearings and testified. Both routine and under-the-counter deals began to run into trouble. Public officials dominated by real estate interests began to squirm. One applicant for a multi-million-dollar housing project that would require filling in part of the Bay accused the conservationists of being 'more interested in bird watchers than poor Negro kids.' The group investigated: The houses of the new project would not do much for poor Negroes— the price for each house ranged from 20,000 dollars to 60,000 dollars. The developer retired to the dubious argument that the ladies were leading the way for Socialism and Communism.

The concerns of the association were brought to the attention both of public and policy-makers through a publication of September 1963, which, though in the forbidding format of an academic thesis, aroused much attention: 'The Future of San Francisco Bay' by Mel Scott. The foreword explained:

> In the past the bay was so much taken for granted that there was almost no public protest when unsightly factories and dumps disfigured attractive shoreline areas or when chemical plants and careless municipalities fouled the waters of the Bay with untreated discharges. But now that population in the cities and counties bordering on the bay is increasing rapidly and the multiple pressures on urban growth threaten to destroy a magnificent national asset, a new and welcome consciousness of the unique beauty and incalculable economic worth of San Francisco Bay has begun to develop. The regional press and the radio and television networks,

77

singularly responsive to the awakened public interest in protecting the bay from further abuse, have initiated what must be a continuing effort to present the issues demanding resolution.[93]

Scott's environmentalist concern was liberally salted with sensitivity to consumerist interests. Pointing out that of the 276 miles of bay shoreline, 'scarcely four form the boundaries of water-side parks', he continued:

> In all, there are only seven city and county water-front recreation areas, two state beaches (neither of which is yet completely developed), and Angel Island, recently acquired from the Federal Government. One of the city parks, Berkeley's Aquatic Park, is cut off from the Bay by a freeway and some day may be further isolated by fills on the west side of the route. Public agencies have tended to overlook the recreational possibilities of San Francisco Bay, leaving commercial organizations to exploit or to preserve some of its natural endowments.[94]

There followed a striking anticipation of the 'heritage' developments which were to become so important in the later sixties. Referring to the potential of 'the better known commercial areas frequented by people in a holiday mood', Fisherman's Wharf in San Francisco, Jack London Square in Oakland, and restaurants and waterfront shops in Sausalito, Tiburon, and San Rafael, Scott declared that the state had basically been at fault in selling off land; the governor should set up an agency to protect the bay area and there should be a moratorium on infilling. As in so many other areas, middle-class Californians were leading the way in opening up the battle on the environment: major victories were to come in the High Sixties.

The *cause célèbre* of Overton Park in Memphis had its origins in the Cold War. A major motivation of the United States Interstate Defense Highway Act of 1956 was to ensure that the centres of major cities would be served by freeways enabling the rapid evacuation of citizens in the event of a nuclear attack. It was proposed that the new east-west leg of Interstate Highway 40 leading into the heart of Memphis would go through Overton Park, including the part occupied by the Memphis Zoo, in the pleasant, though not specially affluent residential area known as Mid-Town, an area which also housed the elegant buildings of the private Presbyterian college, South-Western. The project was immensely attractive to many different interests. None of the financial costs would fall on the city of Memphis (governed at that time by a City Commission), and only a small proportion, 10 per cent, on the state of Tennessee; 90 per cent of the costs would be met by the federal government. For the state bureaucracy both prestige and the rights of patronage were involved; for the civil engineering contractors who would benefit from that patronage the profits would be enormous; the Memphis chamber of commerce and the Downtown Association (of shop-owners and business men) argued vehemently that the prosperity of downtown business depended upon a freeway providing ready access for denizens of the suburbs which spread for mile after mile out to the east.[95] The first important document is that produced by civil engineering firm Harland Bartholomew and Associates, 'A Report Upon Inter State Highway Routes in Memphis and Shelby Co. Tennessee', dated August 1955. The firm were clearly making their plans in advance of the millions of dollars which would be released by the 1956 Highway Act. Hearings were held in Memphis on 18 April 1957 and 17 September 1957. The struggle began in July 1957 when a group of citizens formed themselves into the Committee for the Preservation of Overton Park, and it actually continued for twenty years, at times apparently fairly quiescent, then flaring up again at a number of crisis points throughout the sixties; at first the citizens had every powerful agency, and much local sentiment, against them. But, as with so many other developments of this era, what began within a microscopic subculture began to link up with other developments in other subcultures, and eventually altered government policy. By the time of the 1961 hearings, a petition of 10,000 protestors had been collected. The state roads department view at the hearings was very clearly expressed: 'We are not going to be swayed by petitions, nose counts hysteria.' The Downtown Association and the local newspaper, the *Commercial Appeal*, actually agitated for the Overton Park stretch of the freeway to be constructed before the outer eastern sections—arguing that the urgent commercial necessity was to reverse the flight to the suburbs. Meanwhile, as a consequence of earlier, less contested decisions, the construction of a north-south expressway was destroying Riverside Park by the Mississippi.

The earliest document in the campaign of resistance is a circular letter from the 'Committee for the Preservation of Overton Park' (which sometimes also referred to itself as 'Citizens to Preserve Overton Park'), addressed 'Dear Fellow-Citizen', requesting attendance at the City Commission meeting on 17 September 1957 when the freeway plan was due to be discussed: 'Not only Overton Park, but our City itself is threatened.' President of the group was the wife of a Memphis doctor, Mrs Ralph W. Handy; the secretary was Mrs Floyd F. Stoner.[96] At this stage this relatively isolated group of citizens achieved nothing: two major problems were that since the Memphis City Commission was in no way involved in the financing it was not in a strong position to take initiatives, even if its members ('commissioners') had wished to do so; secondly, both of the daily papers, the *Press Scimitar* and the *Commercial Appeal*, quite stridently supported the views of the chamber of commerce and the downtown traders. If it had merely been a matter of the destruction of a park, the protestors might well have been vanquished before they had even got properly mobilized. However, there were other considerations: beginning well to the east, the proposed new motorway spur would entail the destruction of a great deal of housing before it ever reached Overton Park; after leaving Overton Park it would then cause the razing of another swathe of housing before it reached downtown, and then almost immediately hit the massive natural obstacle of the Mississippi River. The original grand design had envisaged a new bridge at this point to enable the motorway to continue west through Arkansas, but there actually were no plans for this bridge, something the chamber of commerce and downtown shopkeepers couldn't have cared less about, since they wanted the traffic flow to stop on their doorstep, and not continue westwards towards the setting sun. Letter-writing and the circulation of protest leaflets continued: the target shifted from Memphis, to the state capital, Nashville, and to Washington itself. The first climacteric of the campaign came in March 1961, centring on an official meeting organized on the 14th of that month, at which 400 concerned citizens were kept waiting five-and-a-half hours before being allowed to voice their protests. There was a lively correspondence between the Memphis citizens, Governor Ellington of Tennessee, and the state highways commissioner, whose short, high-handed response was that any alternative to building through Overton Park would be much too expensive.

The Memphis citizens established close contact with the Washington pressure group the Citizens Committee on National Resources, whose main objective was to inject environmental concerns into housing legislation. The Memphis representative stressed the need to 'restrict the activities of the Bureau of Public Roads in their finding and taking open space areas that are used for scenic enjoyment and/or recreation'.[97] Towards the end of March another concerned Memphis citizen, Mrs Horrace Wright, sought to derive advantage from the inauguration of President Kennedy, writing to the new president with the request that he order an investigation into the project, given the waste involved and the lack of certainty over the Mississippi bridge ever being built.[98] Although the protesters were overruled in the sense that there was no formal abandonment of the project, and no abandonment of the view that the Overton Park option was the best one, they had raised enough questions to ensure that construction work in the park continued to be delayed.

Meantime a whole other dimension to the environment issue had been brought into the news by the publication of one of the great seminal classics of the sixties, *Silent Spring* by Rachel Carson (1907–64), a genetic biologist who went on to become editor-in-chief for the US Fish and Wildlife Service. Her book was about the terrible damage being done to the entire natural world by the unrestricted use of pesticides, and in fact a blistering yet moving attack on that belief in the limitless potential of technology fuelled by profit-seeking which so dominated America in the fifties (and which was also responsible for the urban spoliation I have just been discussing):

> The 'control of nature' is a phrase conceived in arrogance, born of the Neanderthal age of biology and philosophy, when it was supposed that nature exists for the convenience of man. The concepts and practices of applied entomology for the most part date from that Stone Age of Science. It is our alarming misfortune that so primitive a science has armed itself with the most modern and terrible weapons, and that in turning them against the insects it has also turned them against the earth.[99]

'What we have to face', Carson wrote, 'is not an occasional dose of poison which has accidentally got into some article of food, but a persistent and continuous poisoning of the whole human environment.' Carson was dead within two years, but she was to be spiritual grandmother to the hippies in their communes and to the whole counter-cultural rejection of technocracy, to the organic food movement, and to all the concerned scientists and other aware citizens who by the end of the decade had created a great explosion in environmental concerns. First initiatives in America, it may be noted, came from private individuals. The biggest advance in Europe so far came direct from the de Gaulle government: the Malraux Law of August 1962 turned the historic sections of French cities into conservation areas.

The first stirrings of awareness that the environment needed to be protected, in which not particularly young women were notably the leaders, was paralleled by a sense that all was not well in the American home. Betty Friedan, journalist and author of *The Feminine Mystique* (1963), the text which marked the beginning of the new feminism of the sixties, carried out her researches into what she termed 'the problem that has no name', between June 1957 and July 1962:

> Gradually, without seeing it clearly for quite a while, I came to realise that something is very wrong with the way American women are trying to live their lives today. I sensed it first as a question mark in my own life, as a wife and a mother of three small children, half-guiltily and therefore half-heartedly, almost in spite of myself, using my abilities and education in work that took me away from home... There was a strange discrepancy between the reality of our lives as women and the image to which we were trying to conform, the image I came to call the feminine mystique.[100]

The problem—though never fully articulated, never fully explored—had entered the realm of public discussion in 1960, with a CBS television programme on 'The Trapped Housewife', and a number of articles in the grander newspapers and magazines.[101] *The New York Times* (28 June 1960) put the issue neatly:

> Many young women—certainly not all—whose education plunged them into a world of ideas feel stifled in their homes. They finish their routine lives out of joint with their training. Like shut-ins, they feel left out. In the last year, the problem of the educated housewife has provided the meat of dozens of speeches made by troubled presidents of women's colleges who maintain, in face of complaints, that sixteen years of academic training is realistic training for wifehood and motherhood...
>
> Like a two-headed schizophrenic... once she wrote a paper on the Graveyard poets; now she writes notes to the milkman. Once she determined the boiling point of sulphuric acid; now she determines her boiling point with the overdue repairman... the housewife is often reduced to screams and tears... No one, it seems, is appreciative, least of all herself, of the kind of person she becomes in the process of turning from poet into shrew.

*The Feminine Mystique* was an account of the frustrations and unhappiness of educated American women unable, as 'good wives and mothers', to use their education and stretch their intelligence—'the problem that has no name'—and a criticism of the way in which American society forced women into the exclusive role of home-keepers, carers, and sexual foils to men— this role embodying what Friedan called 'the feminine mystique'. Her book was an inspiring plea for genuine equality between the sexes, in both the home and in the workplace. This was a measured feminism, warm and benevolent, offering 'A New Life Plan for Women' (the title of her final chapter):

> when women do not need to live through their husbands and children, men will not fear the love and strength of women, nor need another's weakness to prove their own

masculinity. They can finally see each other as they are. And this may be the next step in human evolution.[102]

The public reception of Friedan's book, but still more the mass of private letters received by the author (now housed in the Betty Friedan archive in Radcliffe College, Harvard University), demonstrated that the 'feminine mystique' and 'the problem that has no name' were not mere journalistic constructions. This mother of three had detected, and given expression to, yet another movement of protest breaking through fifties complacency.

An altogether jollier view of the changing aspirations of women had been provided the year before in another highly significant work of the early sixties, *Sex and the Single Girl* by Helen Gurley Brown. The author mocked the orthodox moral views purveyed by *Reader's Digest*, which wrote of the 'guilt and humiliation' of single girls 'who give in', and of how they felt constrained to move to another city 'to start again', and *Ladies' Home Journal*, which declared that if a man 'insists' the girl can either marry him or 'say no':

> I don't know about the girls in the places where these magazines are published, but I do know that where I live, there is something else a girl can say, and frequently does when a man 'insists'. And that is 'yes'. As for moving to another City to start again, if all the unmarried girls having affairs in my city alone felt called upon to do *that*, there would be the biggest population scramble since Exodus.[103]

The book was perhaps rather conventional in concentrating on tips for attracting a man, but it did boldly pose the question: 'Suppose you like girls?' The answer was wise and spirited: 'it's *your* business and I think it's a shame you have to be so surreptitious about your choice of a way of life.' Helen Gurley Brown's closing words were the authentic words of sixties freedom: 'You may marry or you may not. In today's world that is no longer the big question for women.'

It was natural that when *Paris-Match*, in the number for 8 September 1962, took cognizance of the rapid economic and social change which had taken place in France in the previous few years or so, it should use America as the benchmark. First came a reminder of what France had been like ten years previously:

> At that time the traveller who, after a long stay in the United States, found himself back in Paris would be struck with a blow to the heart. Still completely enveloped by the intense life of American cities with their unheard of prosperity, his eyes still full of pure white skyscrapers and the bright play of colours, he is back in a leaden world with, in the grey streets, only a handful of cars, all uniformly black. The women are pretty badly dressed, the men often in overalls. Passing the stunningly old-fashioned shops, our travel-ler can scarcely avoid reflecting bitterly: 'the future today belongs to the new nations. Europe can only weep amid her ruins.'

But, in fact, the article continues, France has been transformed from top to bottom. And why should that not also, it asks, be enough to change French customs from top to bottom? Towns are bigger, especially Paris, now at 8.5 millions. Average consumption is up 44 per cent. While 58 per cent still read nothing but newspapers, sales of books have gone up 28 per cent in the last six years. Shortage of housing and lack of adequate kitchen facilities are still problems, and are partly responsible for the increased consumption of convenience foods. Consumption of bread is down; people are paying more attention to their figures. Consumption of alcohol is still heavy, but much more attention is being paid to good wine.

> More of them, more young people, more attracted to the towns, better-off, more culti-
> vated, more and more fascinated by the development of modern life, such are the French
> men and French women of today... There is, according to the Institut National des
> Appellations Contrôlées [the national institution controlling wine appellations], without
> doubt a desire for social advancement, but also a phenomenon known well to manufac-
> turers of perfume: development of a sense of smell. That sense has become more delicate.
> That is why the French prefer wines with a good nose: white wines from Alsace and
> Sancerre, red wines from Burgundy and Bordeaux (above all the Médoc), and from
> Beaujolais.

Here is a very French twist to the notion of consumerism, and perhaps a rather fantastic one— colour magazines are not in themselves very authoritative sources, but fortunately, as I shall show, they can be checked against controlled survey material. The article predicted further big changes leading to 'all-out consumerism' by 1965. Overall purchasing power had increased by about 4 per cent, with lesser business executives (mainly young married women) doing best (4.7 per cent), blue-collar and white-collar workers doing pretty well (4.3 and 4.2 per cent respec-tively), and senior executives doing worst (2.8 per cent).[104]

Growing population, an enlarged proportion of young people in the population, the growth of towns: but perhaps what was really most distinctively new was the sharp decline in the rural population—the active population in agriculture and forestry had been 5.9 million in 1938, 5.58 million in 1949, and 5.03 million in 1954: by 1963 it had fallen to 3.65 million.[105] Decline in population, of course, does not necessarily mean decline in importance or decline in living stan-dards for those who remain. On the contrary, those who did remain on the land were of greater importance than ever before, enjoyed much higher living standards, and were the subject of much attention; in any case, until the 1980s half of the French population were still living in towns of fewer than 20,000 inhabitants. It was Henri Mendras's *Sociology of the French Countryside*, first published in 1959 with a third edition by 1971, which most forcefully reported on the changes in lifestyle and mental set of the French *paysan*, whom from now on I shall call simply 'farmer': 'it is not merely a change of attitude which had been demanded of him, it is a complete reorganization of his personality'.[106] Mendras then goes on to stress the key role in rural social change played by women. They were the ones who kept in touch with the changing domestic styles of the cities through the illustrated magazines. Urban life, Mendras comments, gives to women an importance which is denied to them in the traditional life of the countryside. Their

83

'effort... not to be behind the times' and 'to do as well as those in the towns' is the motor behind 'the brisk passage from one social system based on tradition' to another in which 'mass communications bring about perpetual adaptation'.[107] Farmers were assertive in a way they had never been before. 'We are dying', complained the Breton farmers in January 1960, but in February there were vigorous demonstrations throughout the country: 'The Peasant Explosion', *L'Express* called them.[108] Gaullist attempts to find answers to accommodation shortages and population pressure in the towns may not, in the longer term, have been any more successful than similar efforts in the other countries, but they were certainly vigorous and attracted much attention. In its second issue of 1960 *L'Express* had a large photograph of a block of flats at Asnieres being built during the night. This, said the accompanying article, was: 'a French triumph: forty apartments built in less than one month'.

In Italy, the material aspects of 'economic miracle' were in some ways more evident than in France, in the northern urban areas at least, where the building of flats was everywhere in evidence. During 1961 and 1962 Paolo Ammassari carried out a pioneering survey at the Fiat factories in Turin. First of all, the survey brought out the sense of enormous changes having taken place since 1955. Then it brought out the pride and satisfaction most men had in being factory workers, even though they recognized that office work carried more prestige. Almost three-quarters of the workers expressed satisfaction with their present occupations, and more than three-quarters with their present job tasks; they also expressed satisfaction with their workplace and with their contacts with other workers.[109] Can we believe this? Undoubtedly Ammassari had a strong commitment to the notion of an 'economic miracle' and its beneficial effects, and this may in some way be reflected in his results; in particular, it can be argued that he did not leave sufficient opportunity in his questionnaire for workers to express positive hostility to their working conditions. More critically, in my view, many of the workers were recent arrivals from the south, used to unemployment, insecurity, and authoritarian employers, and often anxiety-ridden over taking this plunge into the unknown north: all their instincts would lead them to express gratitude and satisfaction, and to avoid anything which might identify them as malcontents. All that said, I cannot see that Ammassari could have reason to cook his results since his own career interests (short, of course, of the thesis that we are all dupes of the bourgeoisie) were all in the direction of establishing himself as a reliable professional social scientist. Without any doubt his report is part of a widespread perception of 'miracle' and affluence. But it also supports the fact of 'never had it so good'. Italians had suffered Fascism, war, reconstruction: now quite definitely things were better than they had ever been. At the same time the dislocations in traditional patterns of behaviour caused by population movement were even greater. In 1951 the active population in agriculture, forestry, and fishing had amounted to 8.261 million, 42.2 per cent of the total active population. By 1961 numbers had dropped to 5.693 million, 29.1 per cent. For industrial employment, on the other hand, numbers had gone up from 6.290 million (32.1 per cent) to 7.963 million (40.6 per cent).

On 23 October 1960 the illustrated magazine *Epoca* began a series of articles on 'the Italian miracle'.

Ten years ago, at Turin, the worker Giovanni B arrived at the factory on a bicycle. He was dressed in a leather jacket, a pair of ancient gloves, and had a beret pulled down over his eyes. In recent months, by contrast, from the moment he leaves the house to go to work he is dressed like some office worker in a public concern or some city enterprise. He wears a fine wool suit and a tie and drives a small car which he parks in a covered car park of recent construction. Previously there were two covered parking places at the factory, one for bicycles and the second for motorbikes, but the third one, for cars, will have to be enlarged still further.

In the last few years the car has become the most obvious sign of the economic situation of the middle Italian. In the piazzas, in front of offices, at the cinema, at the theatre, hundreds, no, thousands of cars are lined up... the car, which was considered a luxury good, unnecessary, and which seemed destined only for the favourite children of respectable families, for popular singers, for owners of clinics, for big wholesalers, for stockbrokers, has sunk to the role of pure and simple means of transport. Surveyors have them, skilled workers, clerks, teachers.

There is some exaggeration here, but the general sense of expansion is not inaccurate. In all magazines tremendous emphasis is given to the building of the motorways, just getting under way in 1960. The article for 30 October discussed 'How We Live in 1960':

A hundred years after unification, the Italians are beginning to have the same tastes and to resemble each other in their houses, in how they eat and how they dress. Affluence, in its various forms, is diffusing itself throughout Italy and transforming attitudes and customs...

Perhaps the day is not far when we need no longer fear the misery and poverty, patiently endured, which made bitter and bare so many hours of our past life.

Again an exaggerated hope, but symbolic of a mood. A couple of facts clarify the picture. In 1959–60 consumption of meat was still very low: 22 kg per person per year, compared with 55 in the rest of the Common Market and 59 in the UK. Although Italy had been making washing-machines since 1953, only 3 per cent of Italian families possessed them, compared with 15 per cent in France, 21 per cent in Germany, and 60 per cent in the USA. In February 1961 *Epoca* ran its own (rather inadequate) investigation into the lives and attitudes of Italian wives. The investigators saw striking change in the fact that 'only sixty out of a hundred declared home and family most important to them'. Two out of seven were in some kind of paid employment. 'Customs, ideas, dress are all changing. Taboos are crumbling: the Italian wife has discovered sex. Sixty women out of one hundred arrive at marriage without still being virgins.' But it is then pointed out that this is not true for the south, where the old attitudes persist.[110]

The sense that traditional sexual morality was weakening comes through quite strongly in the press, though evidence is hard to find. One general sign of liberation was the launching in 1960 of the new magazine *ABC*, in this period basically a journal of politics and the arts, but notably less socially conservative than the other magazines. It put much emphasis on reports from abroad on the contraceptive pill, on liberated youth, on divorce, on daring films, plays, and novels. It also tended to publish deliberately sexy photographs of beautiful women, something which now seems disgracefully male chauvinist, but which, in the Italy of the time, was mildly provocative. *Epoca,* on 12 February 1961, had a feature on the persistence of traditional male attitudes in the south, followed on 19 February by an article on 'Unfaithful Wives', and on 26 February by extracts from letters *by* unfaithful wives. Between 1961 and 1963 Lieta Harrison, who was later to carry out a brilliant survey of the changing sexual attitudes of Italian women, carried out pioneering interviews of 169 married men, 131 married women, 167 young unmarried men, and 179 unmarried young women and girls. She published her findings in 1963 as *Le svergognate,* 'the disgraced', those, such as rape victims or child mothers who had 'lost their honour'. Much of her evidence was of continuing male oppression and prejudice, but she claimed also to have found glimmerings of change, claiming that there was a considerable contrast between the formal code, and actual behaviour. In particular, she detected signs of rebellion among younger women.[111]

In Britain, in March 1959, Dr Eustace Chesser, sponsor of the 1954 inquiry into *The Sexual, Marital and Family Relationships of the English Woman* (the title of the book published in 1956), posed the question, 'Is Chastity Outmoded?' His article appeared in the fourth edition of the British Medical Association's worthy little handbook for engaged couples, and its full title was, 'Is Chastity Outmoded? Outdated? Out?' That the question was posed indicates that we are at the point of change; that the posing of it created an avalanche of outrage and protest indicates that any change was still very limited and still very far from having gained public acceptability. *Woman's Mirror* (6 March 1959) declared itself 'stunned by the suggestions that premarital sexual intercourse might not really be a bad thing', while the unctuous pundit of the *Daily Express,* Godfrey Wynn, referred (also 6 March) to what he called Chesser's 'perilously passive doctrines': 'Almost with a sense of pride Dr Chesser quoted some dreadful figures. At least they seemed dreadful to me.' The figures were the 1954 ones that one-third of married women had indulged in premarital sexual intercourse. The *People* carried a front page headline: 'Doctors in "Free Love" Storm'. The handbook was withdrawn, though not before 200,000 copies had been sold: Chesser and his co-author, Dr Winifred de Kok, resigned from the BMA. Chesser was invited to reply to his critics on the television programme *Right to Reply*; but no right to reply was to be vouchsafed, for on reaching the studio Chesser was told the programme had been cancelled, 'for reasons of "timing"'.[112]

Much the same sort of stir was caused by the third Reith Lecture of 1962, which I have already quoted, widely simplified as presenting the view that charity was to be preferred to chastity. The fact of these traditionalist reactions is important, as is the point that all commentators were talking about premarital sex (shocking precociousness and promiscuity on the part of young people, according to the traditionalists, sensible preparation for marriage according to Chesser, Carstairs, and their ilk), not extramarital sex. Carstairs's fourth lecture was focused on 'The Changing Role of Women', but that role was seen by him as being entirely within marriage. In yet further words of balance and tolerance, welcoming change and calling for more, Carstairs prefigures some of the concerns articulated a year later by Betty Friedan—Carstairs saw

American women as generally more emancipated than British, but also more troubled:

> women are being asked to play roles which are as yet, in our society, in conflict. Society has not yet abandoned the Victorian ideal of the fully-domesticated mother and wife, destined to find her satisfactions only through service for others. Because of this lingering conception, remorselessly perpetuated by all women's magazines, women are still made to feel guilty if they seek for themselves satisfactions which come from fulfilment of their own peculiar talents and potentialities...
>
> American women, to whom equality with men in education and in work is a greater reality than it is here, are ahead of us in resolving these difficulties... But because their career expectations are greater, they suffer more from the enforced inactivity, distraction and frustrations of the child-bearing period...[113]

The period 1958–63, especially in its last years, was a time of the identifying of problems, problems that would only be fully addressed in the middle and later sixties, when Victorianism was finally laid to rest; and such notions as 'marriage', 'femininity', and 'different but equal' were probed in the most ruthless way.

## Blousons Noirs, Copains, Vitelloni: Youth in France and Italy

Laurence Wylie, an American diplomat who had spent much time in France, had identified some basic differences between the situation of American and French youth. In France there was a much more clearly articulated family framework, backed (though Wylie does not mention this) by the still very relevant traditions of the Catholic Church: French teenagers had less opportunity to develop their own specialist tastes and rituals. American children were positively encouraged to go out into society to earn extra money; in France the home circle was much more enclosed. Parents tended to take any money earned by their children: if the money was required for some particular purpose, say a motor-scooter, this had to have parental approval. At school, French boys and girls were segregated. Wylie also comments that French films about the turbulence of adolescence seemed overdone and ridiculous to Americans.[114] Yet, compared with the spate of literature in the later fifties about American teenagers, their subculture, their attitudes, their spending, in France there was only a trickle. In fact, most of the works devoted to the problems of youth appeared in the early sixties rather than the late fifties. The French focus, too, rather than being on a separate subculture, is much more upon those who are about to become, or are already becoming, adults: rather than teenagers strictly defined, French commentators were most interested in the age group 16–24 or 16–25, or, more generally, 'the under-25s'. A survey of youth conducted in the autumn of 1957 by the Institut Français d'Opinion Publique (IFOP), the results of which were written up by Françoise Giroud in *La Nouvelle Vague: portraits de la jeunesse* (1958), related to those aged between 18 and 30. Writing that 'for the first time a public opinion survey enables us to discern the psychology of the young today in France', Giroud, and the poll-takers, clearly had no sense of there being any special case for the study of teenagers. The first to recognize this case, the 39-year-old academic Alfred Sauvy, in his *La Montée des jeunes* (meaning 'The Rising Number of Young People', stressing the demographic element), was still in 1959 something of a lone voice. He warned:

> If... France does not succeed in welcoming these young people, if they find the doors closed against them, if employment is scarce in a failing economy... Such a lamentable outcome will be accompanied by political disturbances; compressed into inadequate conditions, they will explode.[115]

Commentators referred frequently to the American experience; never, at this stage, to the British.

The key texts fall into four types. Even well into the sixties there are earnest studies totally fixated on the eternal problems of adolescence and young adulthood, and quite unaware that there might be anything special about the young people of the late fifties and early sixties; this hints at the probability that there was considerable continuity in family attitudes in France. Other studies latch firmly onto the demographic factor, not so much noting the current influence of the swollen younger generation but speculating on the influence they will have in the future; some attention is given to the peculiarities of youth behaviour, and to the alleged greater sexual activity of young people, and their distancing from traditional family values. A third type of study consists of Gaullist propaganda: the baby boom had been a phenomenon of the war years, and Gaullists were proud of their role as upholders of French honour during the war; it now happened that the beginning of the great increase in numbers of young people coincided with the return to power of General de Gaulle, and if the Gaullists did not quite claim credit for this themselves, they certainly claimed a special interest in the wellbeing of young people.[116] Finally, we have the primary sources which in themselves formed a significant part of what was to prove to be a new youth movement, heralded by the radio programme *Salut les Copains* and then the revolutionary new publication of the same name, both created by Daniel Filipacchi, son of a wealthy publisher, and one of the truly important individual figures in the development of youth subculture. The more academic studies made rigorous analytical distinctions between five types of young people: young workers in agriculture; young workers in industry; young white-collar workers; secondary-school pupils; and university students.

Traditionalist gloom—darkened, it should be said, by the standard remarks about the aftermath of war and the advent of the bomb—is well represented by an article by a leading authority on economic and social matters, Pierre Lavonde, published on 12 July 1961,[117] and by two books by Antonin Bondat, *Jeunesse et famille à l'heure de l'atome* (1962) and *La Crise de la jeunesse* (1965). Despite its publication date, the last-named starts with the question of juvenile delinquency in the late fifties, going on to consider the psychological troubles of students in the same period. Young people, we are told, are either in gangs or in despair. Youth, in this sort of work, is a perennial problem to be regarded patronizingly by adults. 'Today there exists a serious youth problem' is the ponderous opening of the tract of 1962. The tone is clear: 'whatever the upheavals in social and political structures, the influence of the family remains irreplaceable'; spiritual values are all-important.[118] There is not a breath of anything that might be taken as indicating the beginnings of new youth subculture. According to Lavonde, youth 'has always been a difficult age', but is now suffering from 'a more complicated psychology than ever':

> The general climate of insecurity, born of periods of war which never end, overthrows the conditions of moral order and gives young people the sense of being isolated and of being not understood in a society which must become more community-minded.[119]

The solution, Lavonde hoped, was to be found in the government's 1961 programme of greatly expanding sporting and leisure facilities for young people. He expressed particular faith in 'holiday villages' and 'camping'.

There is something quite traditional, too, about the survey conducted by the liberal-minded weekly journal *L'Express* (31 May 1962) into the attitudes of secondary-school pupils towards the baccalauréat, though the conditions it revealed were to be germane to the unrest in the lycées endemic throughout the mid- and later sixties. What the survey brought out strongly was the immense pressure this school-leaving certificate, essential for entry into higher education, placed on both pupils and parents alike. All pupils interviewed were very tired and many were taking various medicaments. The exam could unite parents and children, but it could also divide them. Often parents gave advice and help to their children in their preparation; but in one case parents believed their child was not really working, when in fact she preferred to study cooperatively with her fellow students.

Against the perceptions of youth as problem, in various guises, there is the triumphalism of the Gaullist regime. The peerless example here is the document produced in English, mainly for consumption in the USA, *The Young Face of France* (1959). The opening is bullish:

> France is now the most dynamic country in the old continent of Europe because it possesses the largest number of young people... There are 543 children and adolescents for every 1,000 adults...

The document highlights the social policies followed by all governments since the end of the Second World War 'intended to lighten the financial burden of families'. However, taking a line with which many historians would agree, the document continues that much more important than family policies and family allowances was the 'change in the French outlook on life, which began during the darkest days of the German Occupation',[120] a change to a kind of optimism, leading to couples deliberately having larger families, in contrast with the pessimism and family limitation of the inter-war years. The text stresses the youthfulness and innovativeness of parents as well as of children. The French family 'remains the basic social unit, with an irreplaceable role in the children's education', yet 'at the same time it is changing. The home has become younger and gayer... Family *mores* are becoming more democratic.' The final section, in pointing away from teenagers towards young married couples, makes a point which recurs again and again in a wide variety of French sources. Its title is 'Young Marriages Spell Confidence in the Future', and the final section reads:

We have now come full circle from France's bumper crop of babies to parents who themselves are young. The school child, the young apprentice, and the university student are working hard to enjoy a wide variety of leisure activities. Self-reliant and outgoing, these young people are keenly interested in the problems of their time. The young face of France is turned with confidence toward the future.

Well, perhaps. We are on more solid ground with the 1961 IFOP survey of 1,623 young people between the ages of 16 and 24. The results were published in another of the key texts, Jacques Duquesne's *Les 16–24 ans*. With marvellous French directness Duquesne homes in on the matter of appearance, his opening words being 'Look at him',

> long hair which falls into an open collar, a lost expression, a somewhat rough old *blouson* (because he has just come from a Rock or Twist concert at the Palais des Sports), narrow trousers moulded to his legs and losing themselves in his cowboy boots. Such is the portrait of the youth of today that books, articles, and films have finally impressed upon our imagination.[121]

The same youths, he continues, are to be found everywhere, *blousons noirs* or *blousons dorés* in France, *vitelloni* in Italy. No mention is made of the United Kingdom; the pervading influence, the author declares, is that of the United States. From the survey proper, the conclusion emerged that young agricultural workers, 13 per cent of the age group, were the least assimilated to this model of youth; young workers, 28 per cent of the age group, were still surprisingly 'unintegrated' into the new model; while young white-collar workers, 23 per cent, were the 'most modernized', with university students and secondary school pupils rating about the same but being more ready to voice new ideas. The survey detected few signs of revolt, expressing the idea, introduced at the very beginning of this chapter, that young people are part of society, rather than in flat opposition to it: 'the ideas and institutions' which young people accept 'are precisely those created by modern life'. The materialist, consumerist vein is very apparent: money, considered from the point of view of what it can buy in the realms of security and comfort, was rated the most important element in life, after health. At the same time, the survey did detect 'individualism' as a 'very striking feature of youth'.[122]

One of the most perceptive accounts of the early stages of the formation of a youth subculture is to be found in what is said about young people in the survey of a small community in Brittany organized by the sociologist Edgar Morin.

> Simultaneously they have equipped themselves with, or are in the process of equip ping themselves with, two means of communication which give them a relative independence from the adult world and allow them to withdraw completely into their own universe: on the one hand motorized transport, in the shape of the moped, or even for some who are not necessarily upper-class, a small second hand car, given by parents as a reward for success in the *bac*, or a consolation for failure; on the other hand a form of

telecommunication, in the shape of the personalized transistor radio (which each individual keeps continuously turned on); for four or five years now, there has been an expanding production of tiny transistorized record players, more portable than musical; the tape recorder has only appeared among the upper echelons.

Thus the adolescents of Plodémet from now on have the same equipment, the same passwords... *vachement, terrible...* the same antennae, the same culture as urban youth. They feel the same winds of change, not the first wind which arrives in Saint-Germain-des-Prés, Saint-Tropez, Megère, but the powerful trade winds of the West which now blow across the entire country.[123]

That the series History Day by Day *(L'Histoire au jour le jour)* should in 1962 publish the selection *La Génération du Twist et la presse française* was in itself significant. The opening piece, by a member of the French senate, André Maroselli, starts pungently, though with an emphasis on the immediate future rather than the present, in declaring that the growing youth generation would 'inevitably' bring about 'the revolution of the sixties'. It was not until April 1964 that the popular illustrated magazine *Paris-Match* awoke, and tried to awake its readers, to the significant presence of five million young people in the age range 16–24: 'They will be our rulers tomorrow.' 'These young people,' the article continued, 'born and living in a world full of change, would soon be voters, but above all they are purchasers.' They also, *Paris-Match* claimed, had none of the traditional respect for marriage as a means towards consolidating and perpetuating the family, and they were much more sexually active than the young of any previous generation. A couple of months earlier the right-wing businessmen's think-tank the Centre d'études Politiques et Civiques (cepec) had produced some papers on the youth problem, demonstrating that the notion of a 'demographic explosion'—leading to 33 per cent of the French population in 1964 being under 20, and giving critical 'purchasing power' to 'nineteen million under-25s'—had become commonplace. The commercial implications of a burgeoning youth subculture were now fully appreciated: 'Who today is not seeking out "the youth style" in order to supply fabric for shirts, electric guitars or tons of newsprint?' Nobody, said the speaker, can be insensible to 'this new demagoguery of youth'.[124]

The CEPEC papers were published in a book edited by Michel de Saint-Pierre, *La Jeunesse d'aujourd'hui*, which also contained the responses to questionnaires Saint-Pierre had sent out to the young people via the magazine *C'est à Dire* and to schools and universities. The question 'Do you like your school or university education?' received a deluge of criticisms of the baccalauréat, one typical reply being: 'The Bachot is a stupid exam and the government itself knows this'. Another comment read:

And like the way in which secondary education is carried out. I find the system suffocating and overpowering and I would like a little more freedom for pupils with regard to their studies, their careers, and indeed for themselves personally.

There were repeated comments on the weakness in the organization of the schools themselves and on the shortages of equipment (also the shortness of vacations!). Complaints also concerned the lack of teaching of civic matters, the absence of time devoted to sports, and 'the total lack of objectivity, notably on the teaching of history and literature'. None of these remarks was specifically political. However, as a man of the right himself, Saint-Pierre obviously took pleasure in reporting comments which suggested, probably correctly, that right-wing sentiments were quite strong among privileged French youth. 'Albert Camus', wrote one respondent, 'died much too soon... and M. Jean-Paul Sartre has lived far too long.' Another wrote: 'Algeria should have remained French. Historically Algeria was French.' A more general condemnation of the education system ran as follows:

> It is very obvious there is no way I can pretend to be satisfied with the way in which our education is carried out, from infant school to university, because of its infection by the communist virus. That frequently shows itself in a direct, explicit manner; there are teachers who frankly declare themselves to be communists and who openly make propaganda; more often, alas, it is implicit and insidious. Fighting effectively against this diffusion of destructive materials is very difficult.[125]

It was true that sections of French academic life were pervaded by a general acceptance of Marxism as containing essential truths about history and the organization of society, and that some teachers tended to be militantly secularist, in a way which might be offensive to those with strong religious or right-wing affiliations.

At first sight France appeared a more politicized country than Britain, where the Suez crisis of 1956 passed with remarkably little in the way of after-effects, while France continued to be convulsed by the Algerian war and the 1958 referendum over the return to presidential power of General de Gaulle, and where there were well-organized student sections closely associated with the political parties. Overall French student involvement in left-wing politics was probably no greater than that in Britain, such as it was, manifested in the activities of CND. But French protests were generally (in the correct sense of that much-misused term) more dramatic. The Union National des Etudiants de France (UNEF), though not able to take up a position on the Algerian war itself, did fight a generally successful battle (using the courts when necessary) against government attempts to limit deferment of conscription to fight in the Algerian war.[126] There were many street demonstrations (involving both young people and adults), first against the war and then, when de Gaulle brought the war to a close, against the militarist OAS, formed in February 1961 to fight to keep Algeria French. At the major anti-OAS demonstration of 8 February 1962 a police charge at the Charonne metro station resulted in nine demonstrators, all members of the French Communist party, being crushed to death. Throughout the sixties police brutality was to be a constant element in provoking protest by young people, but it would be quite wrong to see young people in France as at this stage a major force of political dissent, let alone revolution. On the other hand, the growing dissatisfaction with the content of education, and with the environment in which, and the facilities with which, it was purveyed is a significant phenomenon of the opening years of the decade.

Saint-Pierre had also asked the question 'What opinion do you have of your parents' genera-tion?' A 'not negligible minority', he reported, respected their parents. One respondent made a fine distinction: 'I belong to the tendency who respect and love their parents, having found them to be friends and educators, but *not buddies [copains].*' Other respondents said it was too easy to criticize the older generation, but questioned whether the younger could do any better. However, the majority ('Alas,' Saint-Pierre comments) were very critical. 'Our parents? They mean well, but they are soft!' 'A lifeless generation, without ideals, happily ensconced amid their comforts.'[127] A separate survey conducted by *Nouveau Candide* sought out the attitudes of 15-year-old girls towards their parents. The sense of divide is very strong, there being no wish at all for parents to be *copains*. All rejected the idea of their parents mixing with them and their friends at their own parties and dances. Dancing for the older generation might be acceptable in nightclubs with their own friends of their own age, though parents should anyway stop dancing at the age of 35. Great horror was expressed at fathers playing young men and flirting with young girls.[128]

The famous French jazz drummer Moustache (François Galepides) identified 1958 as the year of the arrival of rock in France, or, more certainly, 'the year in which we took to playing rock as well as jazz'.[129] It was in the autumn of 1959 that the commercial radio station Europe No. 1 took the decision to create a programme specially for young people. Its title was *Salut les Copains*, whose full richness of meaning is perhaps best brought out by the fact that in December 1959 the same title was taken by a mimeographed monthly magazine, published on the outskirts of Paris, and intended to serve as a link between young French conscripts (particularly in Algeria) and civilians[130]—'Hi Buddies!' might be the best translation. Broadcast once a week at five in the afternoon (just the right time for pupils returning from school), *Salut les Copains* began with a little jingle, set to the Big Ben sequence, which was to become etched into the consciousness of a whole generation:

> Cinq heures à Londres, c'est l'heure du thé
> Cinq heures en France, c'est SLC.

Looking back, almost three years later, in the pilot edition of his magazine also called *Salut les Copains*, Daniel Filipacchi, the moving spirit behind the new radio programme, wrote:

> It was something new for France. At that time rock was not particularly popular here. To begin with *Salut les Copains* was generally ignored, but after the hazards of our début, a massive post proved that, throughout France, and in Belgium and in Switzerland, thou-sands of young boys and girls were delighted to be able to listen regularly to 'their' radio programme.[131]

Filipacchi then pins down what the new development was, before going on to make what readers by now will find a most familiar point, that youth was not on another planet in relation to young married couples:

> For the first time in a world established and led by the over-20s, the under-20s had the right to speak. And the result was not so bad, since recent statistics have demonstrated

93

that the broadcasts are just as much listened to by people over twenty and who are often, quite simply, 'parents'.

'The important thing', Filipacchi concluded,

> was to demonstrate to those who seemed not to know it, that youth is not an illness and that teenagers *[les teenagers]* are not necessarily mental defectives or hysterics.

Although the music most often featured in the early days of the radio programme was jazz— Filipacchi himself at that time being a great jazz enthusiast—gradually, a little behind the analogous movement in Britain, rock/pop began to take over. The other theme stressed in the early conversations among teenagers, which were a distinctive feature of the programme, was the wide class range of audiences and participants:

> Pupils from the Lycée Janson-de-Sailly, daughters of the medical practitioners of the sixteenth *arrondissement,* black-collar workers in Belleville [Paris's most distinctively work-ing-class area] find the same refuge in rhythm.[132]

Filipacchi then went on to claim that this new venture of a magazine was the product of the clamour of 'heaps of Copains demanding their own magazine. This number is a one-off venture, but if it goes well it will become a monthly when the new school term begins. If it does not, then an annual album will be produced with the finest photos we can put together.'

The emphasis is very much on the participation of the *Copains,* something unique to France, and on the centrality of rock/pop music:

> There it is. In any case, it is very important that, as with the broadcasts, you don't leave us in a fog, that you let us know and let those around you know. The hundreds of *Copains* who have participated in the broadcasts from Europe No. 1 proved that they are capable of designing an interesting and well-balanced programme. We need to enlarge our team, which is why it is important that you respond personally and that you get your friends to respond to our questionnaire which you will find on page 67...
>
> This number is dedicated principally to music because music, undoubtedly, is our unifying characteristic, and in that sphere we can be sure of not getting it wrong.

'But why not take up other subjects?' Filipacchi asks. Make use of the questionnaire, he insists, 'and don't hold back on the criticism. True friends speak everything that is in their minds.' The intention both to meet the special tastes of young people, and to treat them as fully integrated members of society is clear: measured judgement, or, in French, the *juste milieu,* the perfect compromise.

The content of this first issue, in effect, had three components: stories and pictures relating to pop music stars, the words of some current hits, and the advertisements, about a quarter of which are themselves for records, record-players, or musical equipment. What were presumed to be the strongest-selling features were, in fact, picked out on the cover, itself dominated by a photograph of Johnny Hallyday: 'the words of your favourites songs'; 'Ray Charles and Fats Domino'; 'Sylvie in Colour!!!'; 'Rock! Twist! Rock!'; 'For and Against Vince Taylor'; 'If You Sing Like Me... by Brenda Lee'; and 'Don't Forget Eddie Mitchell'. The 72-page package is completed with further advertisements, a pictorial item on two concerts at Olympia, the hit parade, and 'the Questionnaire'. Johnny Hallyday makes a selection of nine records, which include one by himself, one by Duke Ellington, and one by the French black jazz musician, Les McCann, and one by Cliff Richard and the Shadows: Hallyday goes out of his way to praise the Shadows 'theirs is serious work, English work', while noting that some of Cliff Richard's material falls 'into the category of syrup'. The hit parade covers the period 1 January-31 May 1962, and is divided into a section on singers and a section on songs. With regard to the former, Johnny Hallyday is No. 1, Elvis Presley No. 4.

The link with the radio programme is maintained with a two-page section featuring a discussion between several *copains*. First the participants are introduced, then they discuss what their parents would think if they saw the photo of them all together, before going on to talk about their preferences with regard to writers, actors, and so on. Francis (aged 19), formerly a counter assistant in the department store Prisunic, is now beginning to appear in films; his father is a commercial director. Philippe (aged 20) is a medical student, his parents book-sellers. Josée (aged 15) is a 'student' (presumably still at school), her mother a company director. Christian (aged 18) is a print worker, his father a computer operator and a musician. Jean-Michel (aged 18) is a guitarist, his father a foreman in a motor car factory, his mother a primary school teacher.... The inclusion of parents' professions is striking, indicating again that, along with its emphasis on the independence and responsibility of youth, *Salut les Copains* was anxious to maintain the image of close integration into the family.

The first, allegedly one-off, issue was a hit: subsequent issues maintained the basic formula, putting the heaviest emphasis on rock/pop music, but adding interviews with film and theatrical stars, and a widening range of features. The taped discussions among *copains* continued, and indeed were regularly cited in articles and books as the genuine voice of young people. In issue no. 3 of October 1962, a group of girls discussed what they looked for in boys, with the following issue having the boys talking about what they looked for in girls. In these early issues one can already trace the growing interest in British rock/pop, though the continuing background influence of American-originated music is very apparent. Issue no. 4 of November 1962 featured the visit to Paris of the Shadows, and actually went so far as to say that 'they are considered by many to be the best rock band in the world'. The December issue focused equally on 'The Legend of James Dean' and on 'Cliff Richard: The Idol of Young England'; in June 1963 there was a big piece on 'Cliff Richard in England'. In between (January 1963) there was a discussion of Helen Shapiro, 'who with Cliff Richard reigns over English teenagers'. The theme of international cultural exchange is continued with a feature in July 1963 on the visit to Paris of 'the Italian National Idol of Rock', Adriano Celentano. Through the invaluable advertisements one can also track the emergence of boutiques for young people: Chez Caddy is joined by two Prévac shops, one in rue St Lazare and one in avenue du General Leclerc.

For the pilot number of *Salut les Copains* Filipacchi had had 50,000 copies printed; within a year the magazine had a circulation of one million. Inevitably there were imitators, or, more accurately, rivals, this being France where the two great vested interests, the Catholic Church and the French Communist party, could not permit a mere private entrepreneur to seduce the youth of the country. The first into battle were the Communists, their most impressive monthly, *Nous les Garçons et les Filles*, appearing in May 1963. The pin-up on the cover was 'New Wave' film star Jean-Paul Belmondo; there was a centrefold of the rock/pop stars Françoise Hardy and Claude Nougaro. There were sections on film, song, theatre, books, 'discs', and male and female fashion. The discs were discussed in the order 'Folk', 'Classic', 'Jazz', and 'Varieties', the heading which included rock/pop. The emphasis on rock/pop was to increase, but the magazine always included a much wider range of topics than *Salut les Copains*. The ripples from that pioneering enterprise were, however, evident in the opening words of the first editorial of *Nous les Garçons et les Filles*: 'Salut les garçons et les filles'. The target audience is defined as the 'under-21s': having insisted that the magazine will cater for their special interests, the editorial, remembering its party affiliations, hastened to add that such interests, of course, could not be separated from worldwide political issues. Very much in the fashion of *Salut les Copains*, the editorial concluded by begging readers to write in with their views. 'Special interests' were covered by articles on Belmondo, on pop/rock stars Lenny Escudero, Françoise Hardy, and Claude Nougaro, and on spy novels; 'worldwide political issues' by an article calling for the abolition of military service, one on the deaths and injuries caused by boxing, and one on holidays, directed towards the social statistic that one young person in two in France never had any holiday. Unlike *Salut les Copains*, this Communist youth magazine sported an American-style comics section.

The culminating event in this early emergence of a distinctive French youth subculture was the open air concert at La Nation in Paris, organized by Filipacchi and his collaborator Frank Ténot to coincide with the beginning of the great national cycling event, the Tour de France, and with Johnny Hallyday as the leading performer. Taking place over the night of 22–3 June, the concert was expected to attract 20–30,000 participants. In fact it attracted five times that number, together with 2,000 police, and a vast amount of viciously hostile comment in the conservative press. 'There are laws,' said *Paris Presse*, 'police and courts. It's time to make use of them before the savages of the place de la Nation turn the nation's future upside down.' 'What difference', asked *Figaro*, 'is there between the twist… and Hitler's speeches in the Reichstag, apart from the leaning towards music?' But vicious or not, here was clear recognition that a new power was abroad in the land. And, in three articles in the utterly sober *Le Monde*, the distinguished sociologist Edgar Morin welcomed the exciting new manifestation of the presence of youth.[133]

In the second issue of *Nous les Garçons et les Filles* the swing towards more rock/pop was very evident: pop star Sheila is on the cover, inside there is a page devoted to Françoise Hardy songs and the disc section is now headed by 'Varieties', in fact exclusively rock/pop: Claude, François, Sheila, Charles Aznavour, Richard Anthony, Johnny Hallyday, Catherine Sauvage, Joel Holmes, Lenny Escudero, Claude Nougaro, les Fantômes, Françoise Hardy, les Champions, les Spotnicks. The main 'political' article is about young Germans and 'making friends of hereditary enemies'.

The main pinup picture inside is of les Fantômes. There are two pages of 'beauty tips for girls preparing for summer'. A feature in the September issue recalls some of the recorded discussions of *Salut les Copains:* a report on an inquiry instituted the previous month into relations between boys and girls. This report continues in the next issues, where there is also a very prescient feature on an important issue we have already noted: 'Don't shoot the prof', about the scandal of pupils returning to inadequate, overcrowded schools. The combined July/August issue had had on its cover, in a marvellous combination of symbols, a picture of Johnny Hallyday on a scooter with a gorgeous young female admirer, captioned 'Where Are You Going, Johnny?'. The cover of the December issue featured the new young tearaway American film star, Steve McQueen. But inside there was a more significant portent of things to come: listed no. 3 among the month's albums was the Beatles.

The French Catholic Church had launched its own youth magazines back in 1937: they came out weekly, one for boys, *Coeurs Vaillants* (Valiant Hearts), and one for girls, *âmes Vaillantes* (Valiant Spirits). About a third of each issue was taken up with comic strips ('adventure' rather than 'humour'), and a further substantial proportion with heavily illustrated stories. The features were far from trendy, not even elevating, but simply worthy. Matters of sex never appeared in the advice columns. The fashion page in the final issue of *Ames Vaillantes* was on 'the Scottish fashion that will be very much in vogue this winter'. The lay-out was poor, and the paper cheap. In the issues of both magazines for 3 October 1963 were announcements of the replacements which would appear the following week: *J2 Jeunesse*, for boys, and *J2 Magazine*, 'the paper for the modern girl', 'the paper for the girl who's in the swim'. High quality was promised (as well it might be), as well as colour photographs and, in *J2 Magazine*, 'feminine features: coiffure, fashion, etiquette, knitting...'

The first numbers of the new weeklies were not very different from their predecessors—the important point I shall be making is the way in which they were in fact forced to change. The first issue of *J2 Magazine* had on its cover two wholesome girls apparently drinking champagne. 'Here's to you! Here's to me! Here's to *J2 Magazine!*', they are apparently saying. Inside there are pictures of a celebratory fête at Enghien, a distinctly non-rock event, addressed by his excellency Mgr Malbois, auxiliary bishop of Versailles. The two new magazines, the auxiliary bishop declares with much truth, 'are not papers like the others'.

> In addition to comic strips, titbits of information, games, you will find new reports on current events, and articles which will help you to live as complete young Christians of 1963.

The one concession to the times was a half-page devoted to 'records of today', though in fact, this quickly manifests itself as the first blow in the war against rock music (known in France and Italy as 'yé-yé') which the producers of the magazine all obviously felt they had to fight. The feature begins: 'USA: After the twist, the madison, the hully-gully... what will they come up with next?' The first record mentioned is by 'les Sunlights' (a pop group made up of three Italian brothers and a Belgian). 'This purrs along gently but with little life and a technique which is always laborious.' The other record noticed is by 'les Landsman', two boys and a girl (there is a picture of the girl) with—this is clearly seen as a sign of grace—nonelectric guitars: 'We find les Landsman totally likeable.' Finally, there is great praise for an album of 'American folk blues' recorded from a 1962 tour of France by Memphis Slim, Willie Dixon, T-Bone Walker, and John Lee Hooker, which is described as 'standing out astonishingly… in the light of recent developments' (by which is meant, obviously, 'the twist, the madison, the hully-gully…').

Readers opening the next issue of *J2 Magazine* were immediately greeted by a three-quarter-page photograph of Gilbert Bécaud, currently having a great success at Olympia. The purpose of the accompanying article is to praise the mature Bécaud, who has abandoned his wild behaviour of the late fifties, and contrast him with 'very young stars, carried in a few days to the height of success' but, allegedly, lacking in 'stamina, professionalism perhaps also talent'. *'Even the young themselves'*, the article continues, have greeted Sylvie Vartan and Dick Rivers with whistles, flying objects, or 'glacial coldness'. Two pages of this October issue are devoted to the radio programme *Balzac 100 Deuxfois,* apparently the acceptable alternative to Filipacchi's programme, broadcast on Radio Luxembourg at 2.30 (the title was simply an elaborate version of the programme's telephone number Balzac 100 100). The programme is defined thus:

> There is first of all music of the kind young people like; reports on all subjects: recording sessions of singers: a magazine in which all young people can express views: investigations, debates, interviews on many subjects (schools, work, sport, leisure, etc.).

More and more the paper is being forced to try to have it both ways: claiming not to be against rock as such, but only against the inadequacies of most performers. Sheila is given quite favourable treatment, the nearest yet to the kind of enthusiastic puff regularly appearing in *Salut les Copains*. But out of five records, *J2*'s record feature of 14 November mentions only one rock record and then slightingly: 'les Fingers' are said to 'belong to the cohort of mercenaries of the electric guitar'. For the following issue *J2 Magazine* had managed to get hold of four ghastly photographs of fat, ugly, and maladroit members of the public doing the twist on an RTF television show. For once, the headline seemed apposite: 'When the RTF Does the Twist… The RTF Does the Twist… It's Not Pretty, Not Pretty…'. The record section had to admit, rather grudgingly, that the best-sellers of the moment were Sheila and Johnny Hallyday; also featured were Cliff Richard and the Shadows, described as 'idols from across the Channel'. The following week's column began with a leading question: 'Wouldn't you like to learn pretty songs, songs which you would be happy later to teach to your little sister or to your little brother?'—in contrast, obviously, to yé-yé songs. However, the real world of youth was catching up. As in the analogous issue of the Communist party's *Nous les Garçons et les Filles,* the last *J2 Magazine* for 1963, in its record column, gives unique prominence to 'les Beatles', including a photograph of the group from the sleeve of the record *The Beatles Hits.* This Catholic paper for girls had all but capitulated:

> It is beyond doubt that a triumphant future awaits The Beatles in France. As triumphant

as that of Cliff and his Shadows? Why not? Their new LP offers seven unedited titles and remakes of seven American hits. One either likes or dislikes this cocktail of Western, of rock, and of Irish ballads; a cocktail enlivened with plenty of punch and humour... English, that comes from within itself!

By the end of 1963 *Salut les Copains* had just barely recognized, without special comment, the arrival of the Beatles on the hit parade of most successful foreign songs (with the new year that was to change sharply). Inside the December issue of the Communist *Nous les Garçons et les Filles,* the one featuring Steve McQueen on the cover, the Beatles album was the third of those listed in the record column; it was glossed as 'No. 1 in England'. There was also a full-page commercial advertisement, made up of cuttings from various French newspapers featuring 'Beatlemania', 'the "magnificent" Beatles', and 'the purity and absence of technical trickery in the sound'.

Rumours, then, of the British invasion to come, but no word at all about Mary Quant and the new British fashions. The French might look to America for popular culture, but when it came to fashion felt no need to look elsewhere than Paris. And in fact Paris had a youthful genius of its own. Yves St Laurent was born in 1937 into an upper-class colonial family in Morocco. In 1955, aged 18, he won a French fashion competition with his design for a cocktail dress. He was snapped up by Dior, then the most prestigious name in the traditional fashion world. In 1957 Dior died: a convergence of circumstances had made it possible for 'the painfully shy 21-year-old boy wonder' (to use the press cliché of the time) to emerge as the validator of the truth that, as in Britain, and as in America, even in France this was indeed a time of opportunity for the young. However, as design director at the house of Dior, St Laurent was still aiming at the conventional market, rather than the unconventional one opened up by Mary Quant. That meant that his first trapeze collection of 1958 had an international success beyond anything yet achieved by the English designer. St Laurent himself then set off much more boldly in the direction of the startling and the youthful, but with a much less commercial success, and rather to the displeasure of his employers. They probably felt some relief when he was called up for national service; when he had a nervous breakdown and was invalided out of the army they seized the opportunity to terminate his contract. But this was not an era in which youthful genius was to be denied; as with the Beatles and Brian Epstein, there was a sharp entrepreneur waiting in the wings. Artists' agent Pierre Bergé took charge of the distressed young man isolated in the military psychiatric hospital, and encouraged him to sue Dior for wrongful dismissal. With the resultant award of £48,000 the new fashion house of Yves St Laurent was established in 1962. St Laurent could now go determinedly after the youth market. However, he was shortly to have a rival in the much older (though in social background much humbler) André Courrèges (b. 1923), son of a butler to an English family, trained engineer, and then, starting at the bottom, member of the Balenciaga fashion house. Courreges opened his own house in 1961, but it was three years before his definitively youthful styles began to emerge. Mary Quant was miles ahead of both Frenchmen.[134]

The French youth magazines provide evidence almost impossible to find elsewhere, but I must stress that radio continued to be far more influential and to reach far larger audiences, influencing young conscripts in remote parts of Algeria. Radio, as a vital component of French youth subculture, developed alongside the use of the telephone by young people, who, apart from communicating with each other, made great use in France of the new facility whereby they could phone in to certain programmes and hear their voices immediately broadcast.[135]

At first there were no youth magazines in Italy comparable with the French ones, the only serious contender being the Communist party's *Nuova Generazione,* founded in 1958; then in November 1963 a straight imitator of *Salut les Copains, Ciao Amici,* was launched. Concern about young people and their music took longer to manifest itself. In the early months of 1960 Margherita Nicotra, a married woman in her 30s living in Catania, recorded in her diary her hostility to the new music festivals and the 'hullabaloo' of the music they transmitted, and her dislike of the electric guitar.[136] On 2 July 1961 *Epoca* published a four-page photo-feature 'The Obsessives of Rock', deploying the pejorative word which was coming widely into use to denote rock performers, *urlatori* ('yellers', so that, indeed, *cantante urlatore* came to be the normal phrase for 'pop-singer'). One picture of a girl dancing was captioned: 'She submits to the *urlatori* as if in a trance'.

> In decline in the United States, rock continues to triumph in Europe: out of every ten records sold in the old continent, four are dedicated to this frenetic art, which by now has its own rigorously defined ritual. Age: 13 to 20. Dress: excessively tight trousers, jerkin or sports shirt, possibly frayed and, in any case, dirty; comb for titivating dishevelled hair. When the group plays it is obligatory to writhe, yell, and whistle. The day set aside is Saturday.

The writer, spectacularly wrong in his remark on the decline of rock, goes on to remark that the style of dancing is that characteristic of blacks, but that these rock dances 'do not possess the original gracefulness' and so only produce an 'ugly translation'. The prejudice and class basis of these judgements is fully brought out in a contrasting photograph of the 1961 debutantes ball at the Vienna Opera. The comment is: 'In stupefying contrast with these obsessive images, here is the vision of the delicate grace of a traditional waltz.' Such comments abounded in the popular illustrated magazines. Rock is said to be inevitably accompanied by scenes of wild behaviour, the tearing up of seats, and the smashing of windows (respectable Italy was five years behind the voicing of similar comments in Britain over the advent of rock'n'roll). Significantly, no photographs backed up the tales of rampaging youth. Still more significantly, what the photographs *do* bring out most graphically is the emancipatory effect on young females of the new music and the new dancing.

What there was in the way of teenage subculture in Italy at this time was fractured and derivative. The taste for rock music was still a fairly specialized one, the *urlatori* treated as a deviant minority. The undisputed giant was still Domenico Modugno. Popular music was dominated by the music festivals, particularly San Remo, and by transmissions from them on radio and television; these, together, tended to tame and homogenize indigenous Italian rock singers: wild and sexy Adriano Celentano was a fairly unique figure, most Italian pop songs, notably those of teenager Bobby Solo ('the Italian Elvis'), being heavily sentimental. A later commentator was to contrast the rapid development of British music, as it welcomed the most virile American performers, with the Italian preference for the sentimental and sugary: 'While England... was maturing the revolution of the following decade, under the direct influence of Chuck Berry, Bo Diddley and Jerry Lee Lewis, the influences on Italian music were those of Frankie Avalon, Paul Anka, Pat Boone and, above all, The Everly Brothers.'[137] Thus far, there were no magazines on the model of *Salut les Copains,* though there were, as in Britain, music magazines such as *Musica Jazz* and *Sorrisi e Canzoni.*

Some sections of Italian youth were politicized as in France, and Communist party and Catholic youth organizations were even stronger. There was no cause anything like the equivalent of the Algerian crisis, though young people were prominent in the highly effective demonstrations of June and July 1960 which prevented the extreme right-winger Tambroni from forming a government.[138] The survey carried out in January 1963 of young people aged between 15 and the early 20s (average age 17.5) in the middle schools, technical schools, and grammar schools of Pavia and Voghera in western Lombardy did not indicate any striking change as compared with a similar survey carried out in January 1953. In fact, after the title chosen for the published results, *Young People of the Sixties,* the content of the book is something of a let-down. Families are smaller and less authoritarian and young people are making more choices independently of their parents.[139] The effects of newly arrived affluence are apparent in that the interviewees seemed more secure, more able to make rational judgements, and all looked forward to owning a car; in addition the 1963 survey had a question about TV viewing, a subject not worth broaching in 1953. The interviewees seemed themselves to have no perceptions of a teenage subculture in formation, though what look like some hastily added footnotes wax indignant about the advent of 'a new decadent mass culture' (not a specifically teenage one). What the survey does bring out—and this is a good note on which to end this opening survey of the formation and consolidation of the youth subcultures which were to permeate the ideologies and practices of the High Sixties—is the universal disenchantment with school, seen merely as a necessary evil on the way towards achieving the desperately needed leaving certificate or diploma.[140]

However, throughout this chapter I have been at pains to stress two points. First, that simultaneously with 'the teenage revolution' and 'the new youth culture', there was a not dissimilar activism among the young married, and, indeed, the middle-aged, specifically with reference to sexual attitudes and behaviour, the role of women, and the environment. Second, that we must never forget the economic developments which underpinned the other changes. To have devoted this opening chapter in my study of the first stirrings of cultural revolution, 1958–63, exclusively to youth would have been to distort how things actually happened.

# 4

# Art, Morality, and Social Relations

*Reflecting Change—and Reinforcing It*

Where do morals come from? Does human sexual behaviour, in fact, change very much? Self-evidently there is a difference between, on the one side, the outward face of society, the moral code which if seen to be broken will bring more or less serious consequences for the transgressors, informally within the community or peer group, if not actually at law, and, on the other, what individuals actually get up to in private. Change has taken place when what once had to be concealed can be done quite openly, or perhaps even be boasted about. In this era of investigations and surveys it is also possible to establish convincingly that, apart from the changing public face (though, of course, the two are interlinked), behaviour among private individuals did change greatly over the sixties. As in so many other spheres, it was a question of change first of all taking place within certain groups or subcultures, then spreading to the wider society. Traditional morality was very largely maintained through community, family, and peer group pressure, and fear: fear of divine wrath, fear of public humiliation, fear of pregnancy. As pressures diminished and fears were overcome, so actual behaviour changed. The codes for the peer group are influenced, though certainly not set, by legislators, both the formal and Shelley's unacknowledged kind (poets in his day, the media in ours),[1] by the wider framework of laws, by changes in reading matter and in entertainments. Identifying particular points of change, and the agents which bring them about, is not the same as postulating apocalyptic change in spheres where, inevitably, changes accumulate over time. People do not on one evening say to each other, 'It would be great to go to bed together, but of course we can't because that would be immoral', then suddenly, the following evening, leap into bed with each other on the grounds that morals have changed. What one can do is to identify certain distinct changes in books and films, and in the laws governing both.

This book presents the sixties as a time of the emergence and interaction of many new subcultures and movements of change. The previous chapter focused on change as embodied in the behaviour of young people, and in that of some of their elders too. Inevitably it discussed the new music associated, in the first instance, with youth subculture. This chapter focuses on change as seen in, and as affected by, some of society's other cultural products, what can least confusingly be referred to as 'the arts'. The arts, as I understand them, are produced as responses to a fundamental human craving for play, colour, display, beauty, and the world of the imagination; they are produced under conditions affected by prevailing conventions and social circumstances, but they are also produced by a minority of identifiable individuals, possessed of special skills, talents, or even genius, supported, usually, by various forms of commercial organization—produced in short, by the talented minority for the less talented majority to enjoy in their leisure time. Some art, indeed, does no more than divert or entertain, some is merely exploitative, aimed squarely at cravings for violence, romance, or pornography. But most of us expect a little more of art, expect it to enlarge, or deepen our view of the world, to introduce us to new ways of looking at things, or at the very least to make us pause and think.

Across the four countries we are studying, and across all age groups, the changes which were most evident at the beginning of the sixties were in material conditions, social relations, and sexual morality. Material conditions impinge on class distinctions but do not necessarily alter them significantly. The British working class was the oldest, most firmly established (as a proportion of the population), largest, and most class-aware in the world. Britain, at the beginning of the sixties, was very evidently still divided into an upper class, various subdivisions of the middle classes, and a distinctive working class. But high levels of employment, improving material conditions, and social services and amenities had given members of the working class a confidence and sense of self-worth they had not possessed before the war. As a delegate of the Transport and General Workers' Union put it as early as 1949: 'Let there be no mistake about it, we have made substantial progress in working-class conditions during the life-time of this Government.'[2] Two years later, a plumber interviewed by sociologist Josephine Klein rejoiced:

> there is now so much work to be done and so little unemployment so if the boss rattles at you or threatens you with the sack you can just up and leave. There is no poverty any more so that makes a lot of difference.[3]

Significant affluence, in fact, came with the Conservative governments of the succeeding decade. Educational reform resulted in unprecedented numbers of working-class, lower-middle-class, and above all provincial figures from the younger generation achieving posts, principally in the arts and in the media, where they could express the indignities of class (on behalf of their parents as well as themselves), or at the very least bring the experiences of working-class and provincial life to the literary market-place.

In America the excessively wealthy upper class, with its own élite educational institutions, was quite sharply cut off from the rest of society, though this was only beginning to be fully recognized. In a lecture delivered in 1960 a psychologist, who incidentally was quite unambiguous in recognizing the existence of an American social hierarchy consisting of 'the upper class', 'the middle class', and 'lower class', expatiated on the problems of the middle class:

> Unlike individuals in the 'leisure class', or aristocracy, who inherit their positions of distinction in both the social and financial worlds, the middle-class individual usually has to achieve his position in the manufacturing or business world, and always must achieve it in the professional world. He must strive toward the attainment of long-postponed goals, and compete effectively with others who are similarly striving.[4]

A later pioneering study of social mobility by the distinguished academic Stephan Thernstrom confirmed the image of an entrenched upper class at the top of American society: 'To be born into a wealthy family was a great advantage; it markedly increased one's chances of becoming wealthy, and of entering a highly desirable occupation.'[5] But, Thernstrom continued:

> Below that level, however, the influence of family background was considerably weaker. In the competition for position and property, the sons of holders of moderate amounts of property fared only a little better than youths from propertyless homes.[6]

The notion of America having a long, mobile, middle aggregation was persuasively expressed in a famous book published just at the end of the period we are now studying. In *Beyond the Melting Pot* (1963), Nathan Glazer and Patrick Moynihan, presenting the familiar vision of American society as being divided, not basically into classes, but into a large number of 'status groups', unveiled 'middle America', essentially a unifying state of mind, characterized by opposition to civil rights, the peace movement, the student movement, 'welfare intellectuals', and so on. It was true that old ethnic communities were beginning to lose much of their special identity. Towards the end of the 1950s large numbers of foreign-language newspapers ceased publication, or were transliterated into English-language organs. An exchange of letters between the White House and a leader of the Boston Italian community, in which claims for special Italian representation in the Kennedy administration are lightly dismissed, already has an anachronistic air.[7] None the less, the moment when Glazer and Moynihan identified 'Middle America' was the moment when challenges to that state of mind were being mounted from within. Though the convention of the time was to stress identity of conditions and outlook between, in an equally conventional euphemism, 'white-collar' and 'blue-collar' workers, later social investigation was to suggest that homogeneous ethnic communities were often also homogeneously, and quite distinctively, working-class. John Bodnar, in a major study of a steel-making town in Pennsylvania, published in 1973, produced this perception of great change, and no change, in the town as it was at the end of the 1950s:

> The children of Steeltown's newcomers now dominated the town. The community was almost entirely working-class and, consequently, much of the residential separation characteristic of the past was gone. Blacks, Italians, and Slavs could be found everywhere.

104

Seven of the ten council members were Slavic, Italian, or blacks and no company officials or old-stock served on it or the school board any longer. With its older homes and smokey mills, the town became the resting place for southern Europeans and an increasing number of blacks who were unable or unwilling to leave. Steeltown now belonged to the newcomers. No one else wanted it.[8]

America was undoubtedly affluent, and it was mobile: both entailed a definite fluidity in social relations. But America was also governed by myths about class relationships; some of these myths were just now beginning to be pierced. But above all, of course, the realm in which truly significant change was beginning to take place was that of race relationships—a full analysis of that vital topic will be presented in Chapter 5.

The crucial phenomena in both Italy and France were the 'economic miracles' of the late 1950s, and the rapid movements of population away from agriculture to industry and the towns. Before the war, the working class in both countries had been relatively small and isolated and lacking in influence. As the working class expanded in both countries it gained in solidarity and self-confidence, benefiting too from social welfare reforms and the high levels of economic activity. The evidence of change was very striking: former peasants from the Italian south taking on new jobs and learning new ways in the Italian cities of the north; massive housing constructions both in these cities and in many of the cities of France. But working-class earnings in both countries were kept under very strict control, and employment was by no means steady and continuous. Various conventions of Italian and French life meant that class distinctions were not so obvious as in Britain. But in France and Italy, as much as in Britain (and indeed in America), there were very apparent distinctions between the upper class (or 'high bourgeoisie') at the top, various kinds of middle class in the middle ('middle' and 'lesser bourgeoisie'), and the working class and agricultural labourers at the bottom. Fewer farmers, however, often meant much more prosperous ones, fully integrating themselves with the middle class. Social classes, and the lines of demarcation between them, do not alter readily. This was a time of change in proportions, in attitudes and in relationships, rather than in basic frameworks. Submerged or slighted social groups were becoming more visible and more assertive. In all countries it had been a convention that class was not something to be talked about openly: the key feature of the early sixties was that class was becoming something that it was increasingly difficult to ignore.

Writers, artists, entertainers were all in some way sensitive to the changes in material conditions and social relationships, and all served to publicize, ratify, dramatize—or to provoke debate over—these changes. So too, of course, with sex. But in no society—the conventions of style, and genre, and modes of communication apart—do artists have complete freedom to express their personal or social vision. All four of our countries had quite elaborate censorship systems covering books, stage performances, film, broadcasting, artistic exhibits, and indeed ordinary utterances, all ultimately sanctioned by law but operating at various levels and under various agencies; American film censorship, for instance, was essentially in the hands of the film industry itself; originally established by the British film industry, the British film censorship operated independently of, though generally in a fairly close relationship with, the British industry; in France and Italy it was very much a matter of national law, though in both countries, and in the United States, the Church was a strong restrictive force.

Different art forms have different possibilities and different limitations in dealing with sexual matters. A novel—all words—cannot present a rounded, visual representation of a breathing, living nude, or almost-nude. On the other hand, a film (unless employing a desperately elaborate voice-over) cannot present a description exactly embracing the anatomy and sensation of, say, a French kiss or penile penetration. Film has many more devices for simulating reality than a play, together with all the possibilities of close-up, editing, and so on. To attempt to represent graphically in a film, and still more so in a play, something that might just be described in a novel would be to hazard something that even today might be regarded as very profoundly shocking. Censorship, as it affected the different forms, was inevitably inflected by such considerations. Censors, too, tended to feel that what might possibly be safe in the hands of an educated minority could quite definitely not be allowed to fall into the hands of the great uneducated majority: hardback books in limited editions might be left uninterfered with, but paperback editions, and above all films, would have to be scrutinized very closely. Traditionally the concern of censorship was with the maintenance of the established order (to which, of course, uncontrolled sexuality could always be seen as a threat). As at the middle fifties in all four countries, openly subversive (or, in the US, 'un-American') topics could not be broached in films. Blasphemy was taboo. There could be no undermining of, or presenting of alternatives to, Christian morality, the family, or monogamous heterosexual sex—which itself might be hinted at, or accepted as implicit, but not openly represented. Novels had always recognized the facts of lust, seduction, adultery, and illegitimacy; sex acts (between male and female) were usually presented briefly and schematically or, often, in highly conventionalized romantic/erotic prose. All of this had changed utterly, on both sides of the Atlantic, in all four countries, by the early seventies. The rational reform of censorship, the abolition of all absurd restrictions, was one of the great achievements of governments and peoples in the 1960s—with those of Britain very much in the lead. Thanks to the meticulous research of Tony Aldgate we now have a very full picture of how the censorship of theatre and cinema operated in Britain between 1955 and 1965, and the nature of the changes which took place.[9]

Dr Aldgate is at pains to stress how strong the censorship still was in 1965 and is sceptical about my claims that there was sweeping change. Actually, I see what happened between 1958 (a more significant date than 1955, in my view) and 1963 as merely a beginning—a contested beginning, but one which none the less led directly and at accelerating speed towards the great transformations by the end of the decade. So it is worth spending a moment reflecting upon the nature of censorship. Censorship is not generally treated warmly by the sort of people who write historical works; nor, inevitably, is its cause served well by the fundamentalist fanatics who are its frantic upholders. Censorship has always been a crucial weapon in the hands of absolutisms, empires, oligarchies. It has often been foolish, and sometimes vicious. There is no question, as I made clear a few paragraphs back, that the four societies we are dealing with were still very much class societies, in which a distinctive upper class had disproportionate influence, and in which the working class occupied a distinctly subordinate position. Special institutions such as the churches and the police exercised undue influence. Most of those in power, without doubt, had a strong disposition towards the maintenance of the status quo. Yet conventions as to what is proper behaviour arise from society as well as from the state. The censorship systems were subject to the manifold pressures generated by pluralistic societies. They operated through due processes of law, or through the decisions of autonomous censorship boards. I am not myself totally opposed to the view that societies have a right to set boundaries against what they, from time to time, deem to be offensive, dangerous, or deeply upsetting. Unfortunately, censorship systems are very imperfect mechanisms for implementing the views of society. Still, close scrutiny of the actions of censors and the reasons they gave for them during our period do indicate an intention (misconceived or not) to respond to the sensitivities of the public at large. What is certainly true is that, perceiving those sensitivities to be changing, the censorship itself also changed. There is no question (as Tony Aldgate rightly stresses) of any directly linear, increasingly triumphant, abolition of censorship during the sixties: but quite certainly, whatever the rights and wrongs of the philosophical issues I have just raised, a study of censorship, integrated closely with a study of the changing agenda of writers and artists themselves, does demonstrate change in the wider society.

It is because of the particular importance of the emergence of a cohort of working-class, lower-middle-class, and provincial writers in Britain from the late fifties onwards, together with particularly sensitive changes in theatre and, above all, film censorship, that I start off with what is sometimes referred to as 'the British New Wave'. The phrase was coined in echo of the French *nouvelle vague* of distinctive new films of around the same time, to refer to what was seen as an analogous breakthrough in the production of British films. However, while the *nouvelle vague* was essentially a revolution in style, and entirely filmic, the British New Wave was based on the arrival of a strong working-class presence in the theatre and novels, quickly transferring to film (assisted by well-disposed mediators from the established social classes) and directly expressive of new social forces; an important contributory element was the establishment of new provincial theatres, a development planned during the wartime 'cultural renaissance', though not fully realized in practical terms until well into the 1950s. I then, in the next section, look at changing literary censorship across all four countries. This leads to a study of the largely autonomous, though of course not absolutely independent, transformation in the content and style of novels in America, France, and Italy. The fifth section takes the films of these three countries, never as closely intertwined with literary sources as were the new wave films of Britain. The artistic products paraded here are of great interest for the social circumstances to which they refer, but they are also of interest in themselves as direct manifestations of taste, sensitivity, and cultural achievement. When, in the final section of this chapter, I move from novels and films to paintings and sculpture, I shall be concerned to trace the links between these artefacts and changing societies, but above all I shall be interested in them as expressions of change in themselves. The contention by the end of the book will be that all contemporary art is sixties art: that all the new art in our galleries today is organically related to the revivals, revisions, and full-blooded revolutions of the sixties. As this claim may seem preposterous, let me make clear the limitations within which it is set. Modernism in the arts, evidently, goes back to at least the beginning of the century. Dada goes back to the time of the First World War, Surrealism to the interwar years. Over the same period the ideas of Freud, and of Marx, became commonplace. Earlier twentieth-century art, as I see it, insofar as it is agressively modernist, is conceived within abstract metaphysical frameworks of little practical application. Sixties art has a new explicitness, a new democratic impulse, a new absence of metaphysical pretentiousness.

## The British 'New Wave'

Before I turn to the cohort of individuals of working-class, lower-middle-class, and provincial backgrounds upon whose writings the British New Wave was securely established, I must give attention to one crucial film of 1959, *Room at the Top* (both because of its content and style and because of the special accommodation it achieved with the British Board of Film Censors and its recently appointed secretary, John Trevelyan), and to two other significant ones, *I'm All Right Jack* and *Sapphire*, in this *annus mirabilis* of British film-making. *Room at the Top*, based on John Braine's novel of the same name, published in March 1957, was actually completed in 1958, though not released until January 1959. *Sapphire* was the creation of respected and well-established film director Basil Dearden. Dearden had made an honourable attempt to touch on the problem of racial prejudice in *Pool of London* (1950), but in the rather oblique and unsatisfactory manner of the time. *Sapphire* was a direct response to the Notting Hill race riots of August 1958, and was unique in bringing to the screen a whole varied community of blacks, inevitably in a much more graphic and telling style than even Colin MacInnes had achieved in his novels. Unlike *Room at the Top, I'm All Right Jack,* and the vast majority of British films of the time, *Sapphire,* essentially a murder mystery in which the denouement concerns the fact that the murdered woman is not in fact white, was shot in colour. In an article in *Kine Weekly* in December 1958, Dearden explained that his idea was to throw the sombre London background 'into contrast with the sudden splashes of colour introduced by the coloured people themselves'.

*I'm All Right Jack* features some of the same characters as had appeared in the rather conventional 1956 film *Private's Progress*, made by long-established film makers the Boulting Brothers, but is in all respects a different order of film. The Boulting Brothers, while having made their full quota of vacuous comedies, have also shown a rare gift for producing the occasional film which really hit, or even anticipated, a historical moment. Roy Boulting has stated that he and his brother had become very conscious of the shifts in class relationships, and wanted to record them in this new film[10] (in somewhat jaundiced fashion, as it turned out). That the intention was to create a highly deliberate and historically sensitive social satire is made clear by the very self-conscious pre-credit sequence, sketching the history of the decline of the old upper class since 1945, when it had been securely based in the world of finance, to the present, when its representatives are, somewhat shoddily, involved in industry. Ian Carmichael plays Stanley, an earnest and gormless young man, who has been 'brought up a gentleman'. At his university appointments board he is told that what is required above all is 'an air of confidence'. We see the elegant aristocratic household of Stanley's great-aunt (Margaret Rutherford), where the maid is addressed curtly as 'Spencer'. Stanley is rejected for a string of 'suitable' appointments, and finally his uncle (Dennis Price), unknown to Stanley, fiddles him into a manual job in the factory that he owns. The great-aunt's comment is: 'I expect you just supervise, dear.' But Stanley goes to work with a fork-lift truck (the uncle, for nefarious reasons to do with an arms deal with a shady Arab, intends that Stanley should create a strike). The atmosphere on the factory floor, the working-class accents and attitudes, are beautifully established, with the minimum of satirical exaggeration. Left-wing commentators at the time were outraged by the character of Kite (Peter Sellers), the Communist shop steward. Kite has high intellectual aspirations: he speaks in a stilted, polysyllabic, and in the end unsparingly ill-educated fashion: and that surely was the point—Kite with his immensely laudable aspirations has, in fact, been educationally stunted by the class society in which he grew up. Kite refers proudly to the week he spent at a summer school at Balliol (which he mispronounces exquisitely—long 'a' instead of short, Bahl-liol not Baylliol); Balliol—of the Oxford colleges one of the poshest, most academically demanding, yet most liberal in entry policy—is an important symbol in the British class structure. Kite takes Stanley home to tea, and offers him lodgings. Compared with the austere working-class house of the 1948 Ealing drama *It Always Rains on Sunday*, the Kite household betrays some signs of affluence. Stanley is a little taken aback by the tea, even more by the Australian burgundy which is brought out in special celebration, and utterly appalled by Kite's verbosity. But he is captivated by Kite's daughter Cynthia (Liz Fraser), a spindle-polisher: he takes the lodgings. The contrast between upper-class twit and working-class dumb blonde is cruelly done: 'Are them your own teeth?' she asks. 'You keep them so nice and white.'

Personnel manager at the factory is Major Hitchcock, played by Terry-Thomas with that matchless plummy accent and manner which makes one suspect that the major either hasn't quite made it into the upper class or else has come down slightly in the world. In the best of many memorable lines, Hitchcock describes Kite, to whom in public he has to show the utmost consideration, as 'the sort of chap who sleeps in his vest'. Kite calls the inevitable strike. Stanley is sent back to work on his own by his great-aunt: 'unheard of that a gentleman should go on strike. Officers don't mutiny,' she says. In the kind of class-transcending scene which was a cliche of British films (and perhaps of British life, too), the mildly obsequious but plain-speaking and self-assured Mrs Kite (Irene Handl) gets on famously with the condescending but patently human great-aunt. Stanley breaks the picket lines (both police and pickets are shown as behaving in a most restrained 'British' way) and is sent to Coventry by Kite and his fellow workers. The shady deal planned by Stanley's uncle and the ghastly Mr de Vere Cox (Richard Attenborough), whose accent, at moments of crisis, reveals his lower-class origins, progresses.

The film's climax comes in a television programme (sign of the times!) in which Stanley, the scales having dropped from his eyes, denounces both his uncle ('You're a bounder') and Kite. But virtue does not triumph. Bosses and workers are exonerated and continue their dishonest, workshy ways. Realistically, the film recognizes the barrier of class in not having Stanley marry Cynthia: he is bundled off to the terrors of a nudist camp—a neat touch, since one of the more unimaginative aspects of early permissiveness, and relaxation of film censorship, was the appearance of (very stilted) nudist camp films. *I'm All Right Jack,* with its ruthlessly, rudely and hilariously painted picture of a snobbish, arrogant and corrupt upper class and a pigheaded, workshy working class, with some rather unhappy middle-class elements in between, is at some distance from the serious working-class dramas which were to follow but it is of a piece with a growing openness in addressing some of the realities of class.

John Braine, at the time, was accounted one of the 'angry young men'. Born in 1922, he was well into his 30s when his first novel was published. Provincial (throughout his life he spoke with a strong Yorkshire accent), he had just a slightly more complex background and life story than the cohort of writers we will come to shortly. His father, as a child, had worked half-time in the Yorkshire woollen mills, but by the time the future novelist was born, the father had moved into the borders of the upper working class and the lower middle class, as a sewage works supervisor; John Braine's mother was a librarian. The fact that the family were Catholic made the young Braine something of an outsider in his native Bradford. He left his Catholic grammar school at 16, taking up various marginal white-collar jobs, before also ending up as a librarian, in Bingley. The war, and illness, substantially affected his career. He served as a telegraphist in the Royal Navy from 1942 to 1951, before being invalided out with TB. He was in any case attempting to establish himself as a freelance writer in London when a further attack of TB between 1952 and 1954 encouraged him to concentrate on literary creation.

Braine has said that the first seeds of his novel *Room at the Top* came when the sight of a rich man in an expensive car set him wondering how one achieved such a position. The significance of the film, it seems to me, can best be brought out by making some comparisons between it and the novel upon which it is based. In crudest outline, the basic plot for both texts is the same, and was, of course, laid down by the novel. Joe Lampton, son of a mill-worker, having acquired an accountancy qualification while a prisoner-of-war in Germany, comes in 1947 from working-class Dufton in Yorkshire to the city of Warley (changed in the film, since a real Warley did exist near Halifax, to Warnley, but presumably modelled on Bradford) to take up a post in the city accountant's office under the chief accountant, Hoylake. He becomes involved both with Alice Aisgill, an 'older woman' married to a prosperous businessman, and with Susan Brown, daughter of the richest and most powerful man in the area, who is himself married to a member of the aristocracy. He ditches Alice to marry Susan and thus goes straight to 'the top'. Alice kills herself in a horrific car accident. The novel is retrospective in mode, the rich man in the early 1950s looking back on his first arrival in Warley and the events which then unfold across twenty-nine short chapters sequentially up to Joe's engagement to Susan (she is pregnant by him) and his final parting from Alice (very matter-of-fact in the novel); there are occasional references back to childhood, war experiences, and postwar cronies in Dufton. Chapter 30, the final chapter, is twice as long as any previous chapter, and three, four, or five times as long as most: in it Joe hears of Alice's suicide, goes on a long drunken binge in which he has sex with a working-class girl, Mavis, manages through his military experience to inflict considerable damage on Mavis's boyfriend and his companion who try unsuccessfully to beat him up, and finally collapses, to be rescued by friends who tell him that nobody blames him for the death of Alice: ' "Oh my God," I said, "that's the trouble" '—the last words of the book. The novel, then, concerns loss of innocence, the moral compromises involved in getting to the top ('the muck one's forced to wade through to get what one wants'), the ambiguities and contradictions of different kinds of love (Joe *is* in love with Susan, towards whom he is both fastidious and protective; his love for Alice is a combination of friendship and profound sensuality), and the material circumstance of postwar Britain, including some rather muted elements of social criticism.

In sexual content the novel was not really more shocking than many which had been published earlier in the century, but it was down-to-earth and naturalistic, somewhat in the manner of other so-called 'angry young men', William Cooper and Kingsley Amis, and it did deal explicitly with the realities of class and income differences. In short, it fitted well into current literary fashion and was published by the highly respectable publishers Eyre and Spottiswoode. The critics reacted enthusiastically: 'If you want to know the way in which the young products of the Welfare State are feeling and reacting,' wrote Richard Lester in the *Evening Standard*, '*Room at the Top* will tell you.' Hard-cover sales amounted to 34,000 (greatly assisted, according to the publishers, by a mention on the BBC television programme *Panorama)*, there was serialization in the *Daily Express*, and a book club edition sold 125,000; Penguin Books offered for the paperback rights on 7 May, and the deal was concluded by 15 May 1957.[11] This was in advance of the purchase of film rights by John and James Woolf, sons of one of the great pioneers of the British commercial film, and proprietors of the small Romulus and Remus companies: these specialized in serious films which, often because of their sexual content, were usually awarded X certificates, which tended to mean fairly limited exhibition. Their legitimate aspiration was both to make money and earn prestige as the makers of serious and innovative films. In proceeding with the film, the Woolfs employed three very competent professionals—Jack Clayton to direct, Neil Patterson to write the screenplay, and Mario Nascimbene to compose the music—and one highly distinguished one—cameraman Freddie Francis. It was thought that no British actress could carry off (or, perhaps, would be acceptable in) scenes of mature and illicit sensuality, whereas the French actress Simone Signoret carried with her the aura of French X certificate films. Thus Alice Aisgill became French, while Lawrence Harvey (Lithuanian by origin), who had had several screen roles but little critical acclaim, was signed up to play the key role of Joe Lampton. Penguin held up publication of their paperback till the spring of 1959, after the film had been released, so that as 'the book of the film' it had sales of 300,000. But the truly outstanding success was that of the film itself: advertised as 'A Savage Story of Lust and Ambition—The Film of John Braine's Scorching Best-seller', it played to packed houses across the country. It generally received high critical praise, both at home and abroad. A leading trade magazine, in its 'Reviews for Showmen, provided this epigraph: 'Outstanding British Adult offering and obvious money-spinner'. The novel was essentially a middle-brow cultural artefact, receiving the status both of 'bestseller' (the term is relative, and did not denote truly massive sales in the Britain of the time) and of being a work of serious social realism. Being reckoned (accurately) 'revolutionary' in content (if not in style), the film gained considerable high art status as well as being a very successful artefact of popular mass culture.

There had been no censorship problems with the novel, but the film—any film—had to be made within the framework established by the censorship. Film-makers, if they knew they were likely to be treading upon forbidden ground, were accustomed to work in close cooperation with the censors, receiving guidance at every stage as to what was likely to be acceptable, thus avoiding the expense of shooting sequences which might have to be cut or replaced, or even whole films which would not be granted a certificate at all. The middle fifties were years of unusually high tension between the board and certain film producers: broadly, the censorship was being accused of being out of touch with changes in society (including the threat of overly conventional films from the new medium, television), of unduly favouring foreign films, particularly American ones, and of being glaringly inconsistent. By early 1958 there was almost a crisis of confidence, when a new secretary to the board was appointed, John Trevelyan, member of the same upper-class family as produced the historian G. M. Trevelyan. Tony Aldgate's researches have brought out three crucial points: first, Trevelyan, as a figure potentially able to command the support both of the board of censors and of the film producers, was in a position to establish unprecedented control of the censorship process; second, he quickly developed clear ideas about establishing a genre of adult British films of high intellectual quality (comparable to that long established in France); thirdly, the Woolf brothers themselves exploited their own respected position in the British film industry and their deep knowledge of the censorship process with great skill and daring.[12] Immediately after his appointment Trevelyan was confronted with two tricky propositions: the proposed film of John Osborne's *Look Back in Anger*, submitted, in the usual way, in the form of a pre-production script, and *Room at the Top*. But (as Aldgate's researches have established) *Room at the Top* was not in script form, but, unprecedentedly, was being submitted as an almost finalized film at 'fine cut' stage, when the picture and magnetic soundtrack are still separate, to make possible last-minute editing before combining the two into a final show print.[13]

Trevelyan genuinely admired the film; also (as the Woolfs had gambled) he shrank from imposing the punitive costs which would be involved in substantial reshooting of the film. Most important, as the correspondence between himself and the film's makers brings out, he was very ready to recognize that within a very short space of time what was acceptable to public mores had considerably changed. None the less, there were changes which he was determined to have made. Many of the desired alterations were exclusively concerned with what Trevelyan at one point referred to as 'language'. Objections were raised to: 'he can shove it up his waistcoat'; 'damn you to hell you stupid bitch'; 'have a quick bash'; 'an old whore like that'; 'educated and moral bitch'; 'don't waste your lust'; and a general reduction in the use of 'bitch', 'bloody', and 'bastard' was called for. In the end practically everything got through, with 'witch' being substituted for 'bitch', and 'time' for 'lust' in the phrases quoted. The Woolfs had shown an understanding of the censor's likely reactions, and also fidelity to the letter of the novel, in not filming Alice's death directly but simply having it reported; but in the report Trevelyan insisted on having the word 'scalped' removed, despite John Woolf's protests. All these changes required some minor re-dubbing of the soundtrack. Only one alteration to the narrative content of the film was enforced. Joe's sexual couplings with Alice and Susan were obviously integral to the plot, but that with Mavis was held to be one too many. Substituting a sequence in which the encounter was no longer explicitly sexual did involve some difficult reshooting.[14] The film was then passed for release with an X certificate.

Some reviewers seemed to be rather surprised we should have passed the film as it was without cuts, but we still think that it is perfectly acceptable for the 'X' category, and indeed the sort of film that we would like to see in this.[15]

This comment of Trevelyan's identifies him as the very embodiment of what I have referred to as 'measured judgement'. None the less, Trevelyan was very aware of how far he had gone, and he deliberately employed the little-used facility for sending censorship examiners to observe audience responses to early showings of the film. One commented: 'I am not surprised that people have talked about the frankness of the dialogue—certainly the most "adult" we have allowed in a non-continental film.'[16]

Some of the changes between novel and film were, inevitably, dictated by the medium itself: the number of characters has to be cut down, interior monologues on the whole have to be removed, resulting in one case in Charles, an old Dufton crony, becoming a new friend and fairly constant companion, acquired in Warnley. But my main purpose here is to bring out how changes, not enforced in this way, served in the film to concentrate and intensify certain particular meanings, above all for mass (largely working-class) audiences. By collapsing, altering, and frequently developing material in the novel, the film concentrates on two major and two lesser preoccupations (or 'meanings'). The major ones are: class power, class rigidities, and the possibility of social mobility; and sex, frankly presented and still more frankly discussed. The issues of moral integrity, loss of innocence, and so on are reduced to incidental elements in the early sex scenes with Alice, and emerge, in a romantically charged manner quite different from the novel, in the last sex scenes with her at the seaside cottage, and very fully in Joe's manifestations of guilt after Alice's death; in fact the ambivalence and contradictions of love as presented in the novel disappear in the film, to be replaced by a categorical assertion that Joe's true love is for Alice, his love for Susan really non-existent, the better of course to bring out first, the predatory character of Joe and second, that though social mobility is possible up one avenue, the class power retained by Aisgill can still destroy true love. The film gives very strong representations of the physical differences in social environments. While Joe Lampton in the novel was fastidious and self-questioning, Joe Lampton in the film is straightforwardly predatory, a figure much more likely to make a strong impact on mass audiences. Almost every sequence of the film makes a clear statement about class or about sex, and sometimes both; no such analysis could be applied to the chapters of the novel.

From its opening shot the film commands attention by a combination of stark visual image and powerful, almost screaming, soundtrack (train whistle, then 'mobility theme'). What we see is a pair of shoeless feet silhouetted in the window of a railway compartment. Then we take in Joe Lampton luxuriously sprawled behind his newspaper. The theme of this long opening sequence, over which the credits now begin to roll, is clearly that of social mobility, represented in a direct spatial way. A distant shot of Warnley prominently features Brown's engineering factory. Not a word is spoken as Joe takes a taxi to the city treasurer's office. As Joe, in the second sequence, enters the office the camera hints at the second major preoccupation of the film by registering the tremendous sexual excitement of the secretaries working there as they take in Lawrence Harvey's handsome presence. For seconds he is deliberately held in profile. Although the action does, somewhat shakily, take place in 1947 (the plot requires frequent references to the war), we are clearly in present time; the opening of the novel, on the other hand, had firmly established the retrospective mode. This second sequence has no analogue in the novel. Joe meets his new boss, Mr Hoylake (Raymond Huntley), who immediately drives home the major purposes of these opening sequences, telling Joe he will now 'meet a different class of people'; Joe's awareness of the contrast, the residual but ambivalent pride in his working-class origins, emerges in his response that the people of Dufton are 'not exactly savages'. Joe is introduced to Charles, with whom he will share digs in the vicinity of the better part of town, 't'top'. In a short sequence Joe sees Susan Brown with the upper-class, ex-RAF Cambridge student Jack Wales and his Lagonda (it had been an Aston Martin in the novel). Nascimbene's music expresses Joe's envious thoughts while Charles comments, 'That's not for you, lad.' Back in the digs Joe verbally establishes the working-class environment from which he is escaping: the Sunday treat was 'fish and chips wrapped in a greasy *News of the World;* then in a classic statement of the nature of working-class life-chances, he declares that living in Dufton 'seemed like a lifetime's sentence'. But then, in an utterance which really was revolutionary (there is no precise analogue in the novel, only various details meticulously presented here and there), Charles establishes the limits of middle-class life, as distinct from the upper-class amplitude of life represented by Jack and Susan and 't'top', which he indicates from the window.

In the next sequence, set with great physicality in the lower-class ambience of a dog-track, with in the distance a factory belonging to 'old millionaire Brown', the point is made that while officers like Jack Wales would be awarded a cross, similar heroism by other ranks would win only a medal. Critics rightly latched onto this as evidence of the film's message about class antagonism; in the novel the point is made much later on as an incidental aside by a minor character and without reference to Jack Wales. The dog-track sequence has great importance in the structure of the film, for it is here that the Joe Lampton scheme for grading women is given great prominence. In the novel the scheme had been something of a joke shared by Joe and Charles in their Dufton days: there the grading was entirely by sex appeal, the argument being that rich and successful men got their women from the top grade, others having to make do with lesser grades (the humorous, if no doubt male chauvinist, aspect is brought out in the rumination that since grade one women were so extremely good in bed, it was just as well their husbands had inherited money, since they would have had no energy left for earning it). In the film an important shift has been made towards aligning the grades with the *woman's* social class. While in the novel the fastidious Joe Lampton had not been sure that Susan rated above a grade two, in the film he unambiguously rates her grade one, stressing her upper-class position rather than her sex appeal—indeed, the word he uses to describe her at this juncture is 'wholesome'. ('You lust after her,' Charles insists. 'Well partly that,' Joe admits.) An attractive actress in the part of a working-class patron of the dog-track is written off as grade ten. All of this, today, sounds disgracefully sexist: but the hard truths about physical appearance and sex appeal, and the links between sex and class, had scarcely been considered appropriate subject-matter for British films, or for polite conversation; they were to become a commonplace in the exuberant but sometimes cruel sixties.

The next substantial sequence is one which again I wish to contrast with the analogue in the novel. It is quite early in the novel that Joe goes back on a routine Christmas visit to the aunt in

Dufton who had brought him up after both his parents were killed in a bombing raid. In the book, Joe's aunt is questioning him about his marriage prospects.

> 'There's a girl named Susan Brown,' I said. 'I've taken her out a few times. She's rather attractive.'
>
> 'Who is she?'
>
> 'Her father owns a factory near Leddersford. He's on the Warnley Council.'
>
> She looked at me with a curious pity. 'Money marries money, lad. Be careful she doesn't break your heart. Is she really a nice lass, though?'
>
> 'She's lovely,' I said. 'Not just lovely to look at—she's sweet and innocent and good.'
>
> 'I bet she doesn't work for a living either, or else does a job for pin money. What good's a girl like that to you? Get one of your own class, lad, go to your own people.'
>
> I poured myself another cup of tea. I didn't like its taste any longer; it was too strong, stuffy and pungent like old sacking. 'If I want her, I'll have her.'
>
> 'I wonder how fond you really are of her,' Aunt Emily said sadly.
>
> 'I love her. I'm going to marry her.' But I felt shamefaced as I spoke the words.[17]

In the film Joe's much later visit to his aunt (sequence 22) is brought about because, in a plot twist absent from the novel, he has been offered a very good job in Dufton. (He soon discovers that this has been engineered by Brown, to try to separate him from Susan.) The indoor sequence is preceded by one in which a series of external scenes bring out the working-class physicality of Dufton: a distant train whistle suggests both desolation and the possibility of mobility. To reinforce the working-class wisdom, and to stress the discrepancy in the class positions of Joe and Susan, an uncle is added to the cast (a crucial decision since, as noted, films usually *drop* characters). Joe tells them both: 'Warnley's a different kind of town, with a different sort of people.' Aunt Emily expresses wholehearted moral condemnation: 'I ask you about a lass, and all you tell me is about her father's brass.' With Auntie making the moral points, the class lines are left to Uncle: 'Money marries money'; 'Stick to your own people'. Joe, 'shamefaced' in the novel, responds vigorously with a line which is nowhere to be found in the original: 'Oh that's all old-fashioned that class stuff. Things have changed since the war. I'm as good as the next man.'

Class positions are very clearly delineated in the group sequence at the civic ball, where Joe is very thoroughly put down, with Susan in some distress but unable to do anything. It is followed by a sequence between Joe and Susan alone together, and then immediately by the third great dramatic set-piece, which is also entirely sexual. This is the sequence in which Joe seduces Susan. The film has been running for rather more than an hour; there is three-quarters of an hour still to go. In the novel the seduction does not come till chapter 27, and then it comes about rather as a by-product of a quarrel over the manner in which Joe will finally break with Alice than as the culmination of a deliberate seduction campaign, as it is presented in the film. Here, the seduction of Susan is much more central and is presented in clichés which audiences probably found it easy to engage with. Joe's demand is: 'It's what all the Joes want… The thing any girl would do for the man she loves.' Susan's reaction at the moment of surrender is: 'Joe, be gentle with me.'

Afterwards, Joe is sunk in post-coital gloom, irritated while Susan prances around chirpily asking, 'Do I look different?' In the middle of the sequence there had been yet another of the cuts which Jack Clayton deployed so well, to a brief shot of Alice and her closest friend, Elspeth, drinking gin, Elspeth trying to console Alice with the comment, 'He was a coarse brute.'

Then we come to the melodramatic sequence (sequence 37) in the Conservative Club where Brown simultaneously offers to buy Joe off and, if he refuses, threatens also to 'break' him (the sequence broadly follows the novel, but departs from it in the crude emphasis on class power). Joe does refuse, but he is actually more believable in the novel, since he has already effectively decided that his affair with Alice is over. (Wouldn't Brown's offer—in the film—have been good enough to enable him to take Alice and defy Aisgill? This is the one place where the film's reductionism with respect to the nature of love brings it near to trouble. But obviously we are meant to read the episode as honourable working-class contempt for class power.) Then comes the theatrical switch (faithful to the novel): Susan is pregnant, and Joe is to marry her as quickly as possible.

Brown has insisted that Joe must irrevocably break with Alice, 'an old whore like her' (another of the phrases the censor had been unable to obliterate). Joe sees Alice for the last time and breaks the news in what comes over as an unspeakably callous fashion ('I'm going to marry Susan,' he keeps repeating, without elaboration). In the novel Joe is less than totally distracted, indeed is still slightly detached, at the news of Alice's horrible death, which in the film hits him with devastating force. He gets drunk, self-consciously and wryly observing himself in the novel, but the censors made sure that film audiences were left with the impression that he does not have sex with the girl he picks up, Mavis. In compensation, however, Mavis's boyfriend has an additional line which ironically reflects on the way Joe has already moved up in the world: 'You stick to your own class,' he says.

What this painstaking comparison of the novel and film brings out is that the film concentrates, strengthens, and clarifies the meanings in respect of class and sex; which is what makes it such a crucial one in the fulcrum months of 1958–9; usually films dilute the meanings of the originals on which they are based—the other potentially 'tricky proposition', *Look Back in Anger*, was to prove a notorious example, emerging as a shapeless, toothless, film.

Braine was a figure of the later fifties; but the first of my cohort of new (sixties) writers shares enough of the characteristics of a John Braine to set him slightly apart also. Alan Sillitoe was born into the highly deprived family of a tannery labourer. He left school in 1942 at the age of 14 and went to work first in the Raleigh bicycle factory in Nottingham, then with a plywood manufacturer, and subsequently with an engineering firm. As had been the case with John Braine, the war had a considerable effect on the development of his career. Sillitoe became a cadet in the Air Training Corps, seizing the unique opportunity to study new skills. As soon as he was old enough, he joined the RAF and, in the immediate postwar years, was sent out as a radio operator to Malaya. There is another strange link with Braine in that while in Malaya he contracted TB. He was in hospital for a year in 1948, and tried his hand at various pieces of writing. Sillitoe was now certainly no typical representative of the working class: with his RAF pension he deliberately established himself as a writer, working briefly in Nottingham, then in south-east France, and finally in Majorca. For some years he had been fascinated by the theme of the irresponsible hedonism of Saturday night and the slow, ineluctable patterns of life, represented by Sunday morning. This became the topic of his first novel, *Saturday Night and Sunday Morning*, published in October 1958, just three months before the release of the film *Room at the Top*. Ten years later, Sillitoe wrote that 'the greatest inaccuracy was ever to call the book a "working-class novel" for it is really nothing of the sort. It is simply a novel…'[18] On the other hand, of course, working-class figures were the figures he knew; the working-class milieu was the proper setting for his story—in that sense the novel was a working-class novel. It was also far more radical than Braine's novel, and played its part, in the more restricted circle of novel-readers, in the growing acceptance of the importance of hitherto neglected geographical and social sections of British society, as also of continually expanding sexual frankness. The screen rights were bought by Woodfall Films, the new company founded by John Osborne and avant-garde theatre director Tony Richardson, ostensibly to allow the voices of anger, kitchen sink, provinces, and working-class to be heard, but backed by Canadian producer Harry Saltzman, who made no secret of his wish to turn an honest penny or two out of the new fashions. The director was Karel Reisz, who had been a leading figure in the 'new cinema' documentary movement of the fifties. Sillitoe himself was commissioned to write the screenplay. A poet and a writer, Sillitoe had no affinity with cinema, and the final script, as ever in the world of film, was a team effort, with (of course) the British Board of Film Censors playing their part.

The novel (I am using the Star paperback edition of 1975) opens with young factory worker Arthur Seaton getting outrageously drunk on a Saturday night. He then goes off to bed with Brenda, the wife of an older workmate, Jack. We come to Monday, and the factory, in Chapter 2:

> Arthur walked into a huge corridor, searching an inside pocket for his clocking-in card and noticing, as on every morning since he was fifteen—except for a two-year break in the Army—the factory smell of oil-suds, machinery, and shaved steel that surrounded you with an air in which pimples grew and prospered on your face and shoulders, that would have turned you into one big pimple if you did not spend half-an-hour over the scullery sink every night getting rid of the biggest bastards. What a life, he thought. Hard work and good wages and a smell all day that turns your guts.[19]

In the brilliant unobtrusive third-person narrative, we are quickly apprised not just of Arthur's wit and perception but also of his cheerfully callous amorality. By Chapter 4, Brenda is pregnant:

> Last night Brenda cried like a baby and he mopped the tears from her eyes with one hand and caught the runnings of his own cold with the other, so that she thought he was crying too, and went into the house somewhat contented. But as soon as he was out of earshot he started laughing, drunk to himself and all the world, until he crept upstairs in his stockinged-feet, set his Teddy suit on the number-one hanger, and slept sounder than any log.[20]

We meet Aunt Ada and a whole host of working-class characters of all ages, many on the fringes of criminality: almost every conversation is suffused with the threat or reality of violence. Chapter 6 begins with Brenda in a zinc bath about to abort with the help of a bottle of gin ('the other stuff not having worked'). It ends with Arthur about to get into bed with Brenda's younger sister, Winnie: 'Never had an evening begun so sadly and ended so well, he reflected, peeling off his socks.' It is made clear that the action of the book takes place while the Korean war is being fought; and Arthur does his two weeks' reserve training. He has a lazy contempt for the older generation of workers who had all the fight crushed out of them by the Depression; he has a more active contempt for society and all its institutions.

> They were angling for another war now, with the Russians this time. But they did go so far as to promise that it would be a short one, a few big flashes and it would be over. What a lark! We'd be fighting side-by-side with the Germans that had been bombing us in the last war. What do they take us for? Bloody fools, but one of these days they'd be wrong. They think they've settled our hashes with their insurance cards and television sets, but I'll be one of them to turn round on 'em and let them see how wrong they are... Other faces as well: the snot-gobbling gett that teks my income tax, the swivel-eyed swine that collects our rent, the big-headed bastard that gets my goat when he asks me to go to union meetings or sign a paper against what's happening in Kenya. As if I cared![21]

Chapter 10 opens with Arthur having a drink with both Brenda and Winnie. He leaves them and goes off to another pub. There (we are now two-thirds of the way through the novel) he for the first time encounters the 19-year-old Doreen (she works in a hairnet factory) and makes a date with her. 'As he walked silently up the hill', we read at the end of the same short chapter, 'towards Winnie's he hoped Doreen would not forget her date with him tomorrow night, that she would not keep him waiting too long at the cinema.' In the next chapter we learn that he 'did not see Doreen often, because his weeks and weekends were divided between Brenda and Winnie.' To Doreen's disappointment he takes her to the Goose Fair on Thursday evening, reserving the popular Saturday for his two older women. At the fair Winnie's husband, a soldier, and a fellow soldier, attempt to wreak vengeance on Arthur, but fail. It is another chapter before they catch up with him. Even then, it is made clear that thanks to his own strength and agility he could again have escaped. But he stands his ground, and is eventually savagely beaten up. He manages to make it to a pub where, by chance, he encounters Doreen, just before passing out. Here Part I, 'Saturday Night', ends. Part II, 'Sunday Morning', takes up a mere three chapters, plus the brief Chapter 16 which consists of Arthur's musings—he and Doreen are to be married in three months' time—as he sits by the canal fishing.

No film maker was going to be able to do another *Room at the Top*, and Woodfall duly submitted their initial scenario treatment to the British Board of Film Censors in November 1959. Tony Aldgate has given a precise and detailed account of the reactions of two examiners, and then of the exchanges which followed between Trevelyan and the film's producers. Sillitoe protested at the time, and has done so since, about what he regarded as harsh and unnecessary censorship restrictions. The censorship process was protracted, but in essence the objections came down to four topics: (the inevitable) 'language'; sex scenes which were 'too revealing'; the 'slap-happy and successful termination of pregnancy'; and the violence of Arthur's beating-up. Trevelyan's explanation of his continued hostility to 'language' may seem specious, or hypocritical, or patronizing, or it may contain a glint of concern for the audiences he felt he had to represent:

> I appreciate that words of this kind are normal in the speech of the type of people that the film is about but I have always found, strange though it may seem, that these are the very people who most object to this kind of thing on the screen.[22]

With regard to the abortion scene, Trevelyan explained that this

> shows a rather casual attitude to abortion and suggests to the young that if they get into difficulties all they need is to find a kind-hearted older woman who has a lot of children... I must ask you to bear in mind that this film is likely to be seen by a considerable number of young people of 16 to 20 years of age, and to recognise that social responsibility is called for.

In general, the language, in the film as finally made, was toned down—'bogger', for instance, being replaced by 'beggar'. The bed scenes and the beating-up were kept within what Trevelyan considered reasonable limits (essentially the limits set by *Room at the Top*—though sex in *Saturday Night and Sunday Morning* was more obviously joyful than in the somewhat grim *Room at the Top*). The one really big change was in the abortion episode: we are left in no doubt that the attempt with hot water and gin has failed, and that Brenda eventually decides against a £40 abortion.

Woodfall Films' first publicity handout in February 1960 (the film was released in October 1960), headed 'Big Chance for Young Artists' (neither Albert Finney nor Shirley Anne Field was widely known at that time), described Arthur Seaton as 'a convention-smashing, working-class Don Juan, who works as a machine operator, and revolts against the squalor and monotony of life in a grimy Midlands suburb by living louder and faster than everyone else'.[23] When the film appeared, *Daily Cinema* informed the trade of a

> compelling story and first-class performances in a film that should appeal to the class cinemas (for the quality of its production) and to industrial halls (for its identifiable truth about working-class life). It'll do a bomb![24]

In fact the distributors were initially hostile, and it was only 'with the unexpected failure and withdrawal of a film from the Warner Theatre, Leicester Square, that a gap suddenly appeared for *Saturday Night and Sunday Morning*, which opened there on 26 October 1960'.[25] It did indeed 'do a bomb!'

The essential, and novel, ambience of the film is established in an important pre-credit sequence where we see Arthur at his lathe. In *Room at the Top*, factories were seen only as distant smoking chimneys, or in one brief visit when Joe is looking for an executive job; here we are right in the middle of as good a visual representation of Sillitoe's pungent prose as one could get. This scene, with Arthur's interior monologue, establishes some important points: not just the grinding nature of the work ('no wonder I've allus got a bad back') but Arthur's easy mastery of it as he counts off the number of cylinders drilled and remarks that he will be able to take time off shortly for a cigarette; the contrast between Arthur's independence and energy and the older workers— 'they got ground down before the war and never recovered'; and, above all, his comments upon organized society in general: 'Don't let the bastards grind you down, that's one thing I've learned'; and, again, at the end of the scene: 'I'd like to see anyone grind me down. All I'm out for is a good time. All the rest is propaganda.'

Then, in fairly quick succession, we have Saturday evening tea at home: steak, not bacon and egg as in the novel (rationing had ended, and eating habits greatly changed between the early and late fifties); the pub scene which opened the novel—with a rock/pop group again driving home that we are in the late fifties; the bed scene with Brenda (Rachel Roberts); and Sunday morning: working-class street with one car in it. Sunday lunchtime, and Arthur is in the pub with Aunt Ada and her son Bert (film version). Bert is a miner, very much in his Sunday best, and in this scene pieces of dialogue from the novel are skilfully incorporated to create an atmosphere of a solid, almost prosperous working class. There is a sexist joke (about throwing a bitchy woman into the Trent), a class joke (about how 'our Ethel' conned a rich man into buying her drinks), and an important reference to the way life has improved since the war, combined with a piece of verbal violence (Bert relates that he had threatened a fellow miner going on about the good old days with his pick—'I'll cleave your stupid head open'). The incident in which Arthur now picks up Doreen is done with breathtaking ease and believability. Doreen is unequivocally working-class, and has a *factory* job—if this did not make her totally unique in British films so far, she certainly, in contrast to the figure of fun which is Cynthia in *I'm All Right Jack*, comes over as an individual human being.

Sunday afternoon, fishing by the canal, with Bert there as well, so that Arthur can deliver to him an adaptation of the famous lines which do not come till the beginning of Chapter 15 in the novel: 'I work for the factory, the insurance, the income tax. After they've robbed you, you get called up into the Army and shot to death.' The scene closes on the words: 'I dunno—work tomorrow', and there is an effective cut to factory and street exteriors. The relationship with Doreen, as I have noted, is given a central emphasis it does not have in the novel. In the novel, Doreen's mother is slightly odd, and has an Indian lover; in the film she is a straightforward, respectable working-class woman. Doreen is given a friend, Betty, non-existent in the novel, so that there can be a foursome at Doreen's house, with Bert linked to Betty, and Arthur's relation-ship with Doreen presented in a much more conventional boyfriend/girlfriend fashion. This is not necessarily to criticize the film: the filtering out of the eccentricities and ambiguities of Sillitoe's novel gave the film, with its unequivocally rebellious pronouncements, a much greater impact with mass audiences. The abortion attempt is done differently, but various other scenes bringing out Arthur's independence, not to say anti-social, characteristics are retained from the novel. He lies at every opportunity; he introduces a mouse into the factory; he takes the side of a

120

strange derelict character who breaks a shop window; and he shoots the gossiping neighbour, Mrs Bull, in the backside with his air-gun. But the film offers only an echo of the quite powerful feminist protest entered by Brenda in the novel: 'You're getting off light, aren't you?' she says to Arthur.

In his first attempt at a screenplay, Sillitoe had had great problems in bringing the film to a satisfactory close. The ending finally arrived at was an effective one. Arthur is sitting on the grass with Doreen, a new council housing estate in the background. Doreen expresses her determination to have a new house 'with a bathroom and everything'. Arthur stands up: 'Me and Bert used to roam all over these hills when we were kids—there won't be a blade of grass left soon.' He hurls a stone in the general direction of the housing estate. 'What did you do that for?' she asks. 'It won't be the last one I'll throw' is his stubborn rejoinder; but then, gently, 'Come on duck, let's go down.'

Sillitoe's voice, in both film and novel, was without question one of dissent, individualistic, anarchistic dissent, rather than the stereotyped dissent of organized Communism or socialism—a voice that was increasingly to be associated with the many developing subcultures of the sixties. The next Woodfall-Sillitoe film to come before the censorship was *The Loneliness of the Long Distance Runner,* based on a prize-winning short story published in 1959. The story is about a borstal boy who is also an accomplished long distance runner. A liberal-minded governor hopes to demonstrate his liberalism and bring glory upon himself and his institution by putting the boy forward for a race. The boy is well out in front when he demonstrates his contempt for all authority by simply refusing to complete the race. At least one examiner, with that eccentricity which certainly does seem to be an occupational hazard of all censors, found the story 'blatant and very trying Communist propaganda'.[26] But the fact is that no serious case was made for censoring the film on such grounds, and the prolonged censorship negotiations once again were concentrated on the matter of 'language'. The film got its X certificate in time to be released in late 1962. Undoubtedly such a certificate still implied a strong element of censorship with respect to who could actually see the film. But, though we would judge things differently today, for me, the overwhelmingly significant point is that a new type of serious British film was coming before the British public, and with the constructive support of the chief film censor.

The other writers I wish to concentrate on are: Willis Hall, author of the play *The Long and the Short and the Tall* (1958), and Keith Waterhouse, journalist and author of the novel *Billy Liar* (1959), both born in Leeds in 1929, and joint authors of the stage play of *Billy Liar* (1960); Stan Barstow, born in 1928 the son of a Yorkshire miner, educated at grammar school, and author of the novel *A Kind of Loving* (1960); David Storey, born in 1933 also the son of a Yorkshire miner, also educated at grammar school but then at the Slade School of Fine Art; Shelagh Delaney, who, born into a shop-keeping family in working-class Salford in 1939, left school at 16, author of the play *A Taste of Honey* (1958); and the much older Bill Naughton, lorry-driver and author of the radio play (1962) then stage play (1963) *Alfie,* and of the stage play *All in Good Time* (1963).

Stan Barstow's novel *A Kind of Loving* is set in the marcher lands running from the respectable working class into the lower-middle class. The narrator, Victor, is a draughtsman (who subsequently takes a job in a music shop) with high cultural ambitions. His father is a miner, earning

£20 a week. One relative is a foreman in an engineering factory, others have middle-class jobs. There is a general atmosphere of modest material comfort and of high respect for education. Victor fancies himself in love with a girl who works in his office, Ingrid, then quickly finds that he is thoroughly bored with, and indeed actively dislikes, her constant chatter about television and television game shows, but continues to be driven along partly by a sense of lust, partly by a sense of there being no escape.

> She wants me as she's got me if the only other way is not having me at all; as for me, there's times when I feel I never want to see her again and others when all I want is to take all her clothes off and roll her on a bed. Only we don't go that far. I don't know what she'd say if I offered and I'm not daft enough to take the risk if she was willing. Only I can't help thinking about it.[27]

This is two-thirds of the way through the book; both are still virgins. Eventually they do go 'all the way', though only once—any moves towards repeat performances are frustrated by Vic's embarrassment over actually going into a shop to buy condoms. Nevertheless, Vic has got Ingrid pregnant. They marry, with Ingrid's quite prosperous middle-class father behaving with great sensitivity and commonsense. Vic has been reflecting bitterly throughout on how the last thing he really wants is marriage to Ingrid. She loses the baby. But the book ends with him reconciled to his lot: 'we might find a kind of loving to carry us through.'

> What it boils down to is you've got to do your best and hope for the same. Do what you think's right and you'll be doing like millions of poor sods all over the world are doing.[28]

*A Kind of Loving* was enthusiastically received by the critics as a warm, honest, account of life in the Yorkshire coalfield. Clearly it was a prime candidate for conversion into a British film of the new type. Waterhouse and Hall were already establishing a reputation as writers who together could turn their hands to almost anything, including successful screenplays. Producer Joseph Janni commissioned them to produce a screenplay out of Barstow's novel. This ran into the usual (fairly amicable) arguments with the censor,[29] at least as much, it must be said, because of the screenwriters' determination to create a film in the mould of *Room at the Top* and *Saturday Night and Sunday Morning* as because of any general fidelity to the themes of the original novel. Barstow's book had been extremely frank in describing Vic's thought processes, but the fateful coupling is dismissed in less than three lines: 'it happens. I don't have to force her or even persuade her really; she seems as ready as I am; and it's not till after that we stop and think about it.' Apart from the prohibited 'Christ', the novel had little in the way of 'language'—Barstow was presenting an environment of civilized and justly proud people. A novel which consisted almost exclusively of Vic's meticulous account of his confused desires and aspirations obviously required much changing for the cinema. Waterhouse and Hall went still further than the screenplays of *Room at the Top* and *Saturday Night and Sunday Morning* in totally inventing a new character, Geoff, to act as Vic's confidant. Ingrid's agreeable father disappears, but her mother, not very pleasant in the novel but generally overruled by her husband and in any case only encountered towards the very end of the book, assumes a central role from early on in the film, as an uncultured middle-class snob. The damage done by the marriage to Vic's cultural aspirations is hammered home in a way that it is not in the novel. There are more, and more extended, sex scenes, and, partly perhaps in the nature of the medium, they are more palpable than anything in the novel. Trevelyan called for restraint here and for changes in 'language' and for the deletion of certain phrases which were entirely the work of Waterhouse and Hall. Even so, in the completed film, released early in 1962, there was far more overt sexual activity and far more bad language than ever there had been in the novel. However, the phrase spoken by Ingrid which satirists (not the censors) mockingly latched onto, and which caused the film to be banned in the Soviet Union, came straight from the novel: 'Something that should have happened hasn't.' And the one matter of real substance which bothered the censors did have its origins in the novel: Vic had consulted an allegedly all-knowing acquaintance, Willy, about contraception, though in fact had failed to do anything about it. It is not clear whether the objections of Trevelyan and his colleagues were that any publicizing of contraception would encourage promiscuity, or simply that any mention of the matter flouted ordinary decorum. In the end the topic was featured as a great joke. Vic and the newly-created Geoff stand outside a chemist's shop waiting for the moment when Vic can count on being served by a male shop-assistant. Finally Vic nips in, just as a dragon-like female emerges from the back shop. A few moments later Vic comes out of the shop clutching a bottle of Lucozade. Here, none the less, was a clear advance in the frank presentation of the less glamorous facts of life. This, along with Ingrid's discussion of her missed period, and the constant difficulties the couple had in finding any place to be alone together, spoke directly to Britain's increasingly sexually active youth.

Waterhouse and Hall had established themselves as playwrights before becoming successful screenwriters. British theatre, particularly provincial and avant-garde theatre, was almost as closely bound in with the new wave films as were the new working-class provincial novels. So we must now cast a glance at the condition of theatre censorship in Britain. Being the responsibility of a dignitary with the title 'lord chamberlain', theatre censorship was particularly easy to ridicule; and, since theatre performances could be altered on the spot in defiance of prior censorship in a way in which films could not, the topic of theatre censorship had a particular spice of its own. Great battles had been fought over successive John Osborne plays, first *Look Back in Anger* and then, still more intensely, *The Entertainer*. Actually over this same period the lord chamberlain did make one big concession, accepting that the topic of homosexuality could not be outlawed from theatre, though violent portrayals, male embraces, or treatments not central to the plot still would be. A first test for this recent relaxation came with the astonishingly precocious play *A Taste of Honey*, written by 18-year-old Shelagh Delaney, apparently under the stimulus of having seen a play by Terence Rattigan. The play was accepted for production by the experimental Theatre Workshop under the avant-garde director Joan Littlewood at the Theatre Royal in east London in late May 1958. It was strikingly original, a play appropriate to the opening of a period of rapid change; that it secured a stage production was also a sign of change—and not in the sour sense intended by apoplectic *Spectator* theatre critic Alan Brien (16 June 1958):

Twenty, ten, or even five years ago, before a senile society began to fawn upon the youth which is about to devour it, such a play would have remained written in green longhand in a school exercise book on the top of the bedroom wardrobe.

Certainly, though, one aspect of Delaney's potential commercial appeal can be seen in the various nicknames she was given by the press: 'teenager of the week', 'the Françoise Sagan of Salford', and (of course) 'an angry young woman'.[30]

The play focuses on a mother/daughter relationship, a single mother and a teenage daughter. The mother leads a rootless existence, but when a wealthy younger man, a constant admirer, proposes marriage she accepts. It then transpires that the daughter, Jo, has become involved with a black seaman. Nevertheless the mother (Helen) goes off with her new husband, leaving Jo to fend for herself. What had seemed like a secure relationship for Jo collapses: the seaman disappears, leaving her pregnant. Jo finds another young man, Geof, and brings him home to live with her. Geof, it becomes clear, has no sexual interest in women, and, apparently, some orientation towards men. Yet he is very anxious to settle down with Jo, and particularly keen to look after the baby when it arrives. Just as it had seemed that, in truly progressive fashion, the black seaman was being integrated into the play, so it seems that Geof has found acceptance. But again the play takes an alienating, and highly effective twist. Helen and her husband reappear, offering a home for Jo and her child since the husband is very ready to adopt Jo's child. Jo's labour pains arrive and she is taken off to hospital. Helen stays behind to inform Geof that she and her husband are going to take care of Jo and the child. This is evidently a crushing blow for Geof, who has come over as a highly sympathetic character. The burden of the censor's criticism was that, while it was recognized that Geof had to be homosexual, his homosexuality should be played down as much as possible. In the end the play was licensed on condition that Helen's reference to Geof as 'a castrated little clown' was cut, and Geof's own speech revealing his sexual orientation was considerably toned down. After its initial run, *A Taste of Honey* was revived at the Theatre Royal on 21 January 1959, transferring within less than a month to Wyndham's Theatre in the West End. Here the play ran for nearly a year, subsequently running for over a year in New York, from 4 October 1960. The British cultural invasion of America, so central to the High Sixties, came from various directions.

Clearly, *A Taste of Honey* had to be made into a film, and Tony Richardson was very keen to do so. A screenplay was presented to the Board of British Film Censors in May 1960. It may be noted in passing that none of the censors, theatre or film, had the slightest problem with the fact that the father of Jo's expected child was black. The matters the film censors concentrated on were: the usual (though this time relatively minor) one of language; Geof's homosexuality; and Jo's extreme youth (it was insisted that she should not appear to be under 16).[31] In fact Jo was played by the 19-year-old daughter of a Liverpool grocer, an astonishing newcomer with unconventional and highly expressive looks, Rita Tushingham. And in the event enough of Jo's quizzing of Geof as to his sexual orientation remained to make the point persuasively, particularly in the performance of another newcomer, Murray Melvin. But the most important single feature of this film, shot on location in Manchester, was that its two leading protagonists were women. Practically all of the other new wave films, though there were strong female characters in *Billy Liar* (played by Julie Christie) and *Saturday Night and Sunday Morning* and *This Sporting Life* (both played by Rachel Roberts), were essentially presented from the male point of view. One other exception was *The L-Shaped Room,* a 1962 Romulus film directed by Bryan Forbes of East End working-class origins, from the novel by Lynne Reid Banks, in which the self-contained character played by Leslie Caron makes her own independent decision to go ahead and have her illegitimate child.

Willis Hall's play *The Disciplines of War* (quickly renamed *The Long and the Short and the Tall)* was first presented by the Oxford Theatre Group at the 1958 Edinburgh Festival Fringe. It then moved successively to the Nottingham Playhouse (one of the new provincial theatres, originally planned during the war), to the Royal Court, London, and to the New Theatre in the West End. It concerned a clutch of working-class soldiers serving in the Malayan jungle. In respect of the fact that the characters were soldiers, the lord chamberlain was remarkably lenient in his treatment of 'language'. Hall now teamed up with Waterhouse in converting the latter's novel *Billy Liar* into a play. Billy is a shy and somewhat inadequate young man who seeks escape from an uncomprehending father and an uncongenial job in a series of wild fantasies. He is uncomfortable with women. Liz, a sympathetic but highly independent and adventurous character, penetrates his bluff when she invites him to leave with her for London, and he proves not to have the courage to face up to such an undertaking. In respect of its North Country, working-class provenance, the lord chamberlain was again relatively liberal with respect to language. The original Liz was pretty direct in manner, and in a scene where she seemed to be offering the prospect of sex to Billy, the question of contraception had come up. The lord chamberlain ruled inflexibly that all mention of contraception must be rigorously excluded from the play. Unlike all of the other literary artefacts discussed here, *Billy Liar* was intended as a conventional West End presentation, opening at the Cambridge Theatre on 13 September 1960, with Albert Finney as Billy. Still, it qualified as a slice of North Country life, and it ran for eighteen months: so it too was scheduled for conversion into a film. Meantime *A Kind of Loving,* with the same team of Waterhouse and Hall, backed by producer Joseph Janni, and director John Schlesinger, had, as we have seen, managed to get in a joke about contraception. In some ways matters proceeded smoothly on *Billy Liar* which, unlike any of the other films discussed so far, was given an A, not an X certificate. But while in the play, Liz had been able to inform Billy that she was not '*virgo intacta*', this had to be replaced in the film by the line 'You know there have been others, don't you?' And all attempts to reintroduce mention of contraception were resisted. *Billy Liar* did have the one enormous asset of Julie Christie in the role of Liz.

Bill Naughton was considerably older than the other writers discussed here, though indisputably working-class in origins. Born in Ireland in 1910, in 1914 he had come over with his family to Bolton, Lancashire, where his father took a job in the pits, while other members of the family found employment in the cotton mills. Naughton himself became a lorry-driver; amidst the changing lifestyles of the late fifties he began to occupy his overnight stops with the writing of plays. The radio play *Alfie Elkins and His Little Life* was first presented on the BBC Third Programme on the late evening of 7 January 1962. Alfie is a promiscuous Cockney lad: towards the end of the play he gets a married woman into trouble and feels bound to fix up an abortion for her in his own home. Audience research found that some listeners found the programme 'difficult to stomach' and some protested openly, one neatly declaring it 'not so much kitchen sink as kitchen garbage bin'.[32] But—demonstrating that the Third Programme's basically middle-class audience of 1962 was far from prudish—audience reaction was overwhelmingly favourable; the play was given two further airings.

Naughton's decision to expand the play for stage presentation automatically brought it within the purview of the lord chamberlain. Naughton already had a play, *All in Good Time,* about the slightly *risqué* subject of a working-class marriage in Bolton almost ruined by the bridegroom's attack of impotence, which had occasioned some brushes with the lord chamberlain, committed to the experimental repertory theatre the Mermaid, recently established in the City of London by actor Bernard Miles. *Alfie,* as the stage play was renamed, naturally also had brushes with the lord chamberlain; in the end the abortion remained, but had to be carried out off-stage. What, to me, stands out most of all, is the open recognition by the censorship that people's attitudes to sexual matters had recently been changing greatly. During negotiations the lord chamberlain's office explained 'that it was realised that the basic facts of life were nowadays discussed freely in any company'; later the office conceded 'the acceptance by most people these days of any subject for discussion—VD, homosexuality, etc...'[33] Once the play had reached the stage an official was dispatched to check on whether Miles and Naughton had in fact kept to the terms of their licence. He reported that: 'generally speaking, *and for these days,* there was nothing to which real objection would be taken...'[34]

Now back to what may be regarded as the last of the new wave films (before British cinema magnificently exploded into many different genres), *This Sporting Life* (1963), based on the novel by David Storey. Storey had actually earned a living as a rugby league footballer—most vicious and most unglamorous of the football codes, and confined to certain areas of the industrial north. He used this experience as the basis for the novel, published in 1960. The brutal existence, the crude financial interests, and above all the complex emotional relationship between the inarticulate young former miner and professional player, Arthur Machin, and his landlady, are magnificently evoked. The film is as great an aesthetic success as the novel. It is about the pain and the pride of being working-class, though of course the rugby league footballer is scarcely a typical figure. This is not really a film speaking directly about sex or about class in the manner of the others I have been discussing; it is a film with a working-class hero, and also a working-class heroine, and one which continues the process of making the working class *visible.*

If *This Sporting Life* was the culminating film of the British new wave, it may also be regarded as one of the world's best fifty films ever made—up there, in the British context, with *The Third Man* and *The Red Shoes.* David Storey evolved his own screenplay, tauter and more directly tragic than the novel. The producer was Karel Reisz, who had directed *Saturday Night and Sunday Morning.* The director was another figure from the fifties documentary film movement, the upper-class socialist Lindsay Anderson, whose first feature film this was. These two formed the basis of the production company Independent Artists, which operated within the framework of the J. Arthur Rank organization. The cameraman was Denys Coop. Anderson's often-expressed political views were, in my view, almost total clap-trap, but as a film-maker he was a genius. The first five minutes of the film, if only one knew, contain almost its entire essence (I know of nothing like it till the pre-credit sequence of *The Long Good Friday*, almost twenty years later): in the opening shots we see a brutally violent rugby league football game in which Frank Machin (there were a lot of Arthurs around at the time, so, because in particular of Arthur Seaton, Machin had to become Frank) stands tall; a brief cut to Machin down the pit drilling coal; shots of Machin in his digs with his widowed landlady, Mrs Margaret Hammond, and her two kids; short scenes incorporating all the main characters in the film; Mrs Hammond bitterly rebuffing Machin's attempts at friendship; back to the football field. Machin is smashed to the ground with a mouthful of broken teeth. It is Christmas Eve; Machin is anxious to get patched up for the party being given that evening by Weaver, owner of the local engineering factory, and of the City football club.

In the dentist's chair Machin floats away under a general anaesthetic. The rapid cutting technique (which would not have been out of place in a film of twenty years later) continues—'flashbacks', we only fully realize when, several sequences later, we find Machin still in the dentist's chair. We get the first sustained dialogue between Machin and Mrs Hammond: it is the deeply tragic, yet immensely human and spirited dialogue of a working-lass, *film noir* Beatrice and Benedick ('I don't want you poking your nose in my affairs,' she says. 'I don't poke mine in yours. I've got some pride'). The performances by Rachel Roberts and Richard Harris are unsurpassable. We are at a dance: for practically no reason at all Machin takes an over-confident over-dressed male dancer outside and smashes his face in. This is a film about deep rage against life, and also a rampant, individualistic invincibility, reminiscent at times of Arthur Seaton (Machin) and about a profoundly, disablingly bitter sense of loss (Mrs Hammond).

We continue in past time; not till three-quarters of the way through the film do we arrive back at Christmas Eve. Through sad old Johnston (William Hartnell), who acts as a scout, Machin gets a trial with City. Mrs Hammond spurns his entreaties for her to come and watch him. She takes her children to her husband's grave; we discover that she keeps his boots perennially polished. Becoming, to her immediate regret, a little more forthcoming, she tells Machin, 'When Eric died, my world went out.' In the trial Machin plays commandingly and wickedly, deliberately breaking the nose of one of his own players, for which the opposition hooker is sent off. He holds out for a thousand-pound signing-on fee. In one of those theatrical sudden-reversal scenes reminiscent of the Conservative Club scene in *Room at the Top* it seems that he won't get it, till the all-powerful Weaver (Alan Badel) emerges as his champion. Driving him home, Weaver, after telling Machin he's now 'property of the City', reveals that Mr Hammond had been killed in his factory, a horrible death which had almost certainly been suicide—so Mrs Hammond had got no compensation. Machin is desperate to show off his cheque to Mrs Hammond, desperate for her admiration. 'Guess how much I'm worth,' he says, trying to coax some response out of her. 'Thruppence,' she responds. 'Careful,' he says, with a deep, gloomy, irony. 'Can't go on cracking jokes like that—might do yourself an injury' 'More than I got when my husband died,' is her even more bitter rejoinder. 'Some people have luck made for them,' she continues. 'Some people make luck for themselves' (a sentiment he expresses strongly throughout the film). 'About time you took that ton of rock off your shoulders,' he concludes.

Machin buys a large car. He takes Mrs Hammond and the children out into the country. She begins to enjoy a game of catch. For the first time, she smiles. Later, at home she comes into his bedroom to make his bed, not realizing he is still there. It seems that the big sex scene is upon us. She shouts harshly to her little daughter to go away and play outside. But, though obviously tempted, she herself—we realize a few scenes later—breaks away from him. Mrs Weaver makes advances to Machin, but he rejects her. We arrive back at Christmas Eve. At the Christmas party we learn from the City chairman (played by Arthur Lowe) that Weaver no longer favours Machin—'He thought he owned you'—and is angered by Machin's independent-mindedness. An attractive younger woman makes advances. In the only full-blooded recognition in the film that we are on the fringes of the permissive society, she says, 'Let's go upstairs and find an empty room.' Machin spurns her and goes home profoundly depressed, all his arrogance crushed. For the first time in the film Margaret Hammond addresses him as Frank. She recalls her happy times as a munitions worker in the war (a constant point of reference for British films, however revolutionary!). 'Come to bed with me,' he says. 'But, just for Christmas mind,' she admonishes. We follow them to the bedroom door, which in good Victorian fashion is closed in our faces. There is not one sex scene in the whole film. The only minor problem the censors had was with Anderson's realistic shots of rugby league players in (and out of) the bath after a game: a few too-revealing frames had to be clipped.[35] (Still the amount of male flesh on view was something of an innovation for the time—and something probably only Lindsay Anderson of film directors of the time would have particularly wished to show.)

Frank buys Margaret a fur coat, and takes her out to an expensive restaurant, where, it happens, the Weavers are also dining. He behaves abominably, arrogantly contemptuous towards the waiters. Margaret is deeply embarrassed. Mrs Weaver expresses her pity for her; Weaver pointedly ignores him. Maurice (Colin Blakely), a fellow player and Frank's closest friend, gets married. At the wedding, Margaret goes into the blackest depression. 'I thought you were beginning to feel happy,' Frank complains. 'Everybody says I'm your slut,' she replies. He hits her. Relations between them are now worse than ever. She refers to him as 'a great ape on the football field' ('That's what we are,' Maurice advises quietly). To Frank's 'I need you', she responds with, 'I want you to go.' When he cries, 'I love you', she spits in his face. He leaves and settles into an appalling boarding-house (where Johnson, now apparently dead, had lived). There is a further series of brilliantly appropriate flashbacks. After several days Frank returns to his former lodgings. Margaret has been taken off to hospital; she has had a brain haemorrhage. In the hospital Frank sits lovingly at her bedside, but she dies without recovering consciousness. Frank goes back to the house, refusing to accept her death, believing she will still be there. (This is quite a sharp departure from the novel.) There is not a single visual mix in this technically outstanding film, but there are several astute sound mixes. We now hear the brutal shouts of the football crowd a few instants before we are back again on the football field. Emotionally devastated, Frank is incapable of playing with his accustomed ruthlessness. He takes a heavy blow from an opposition player, and he is booed and jeered by the crowd. On that note the film ends.

The period of the new wave was also the period of the emergence of Harold Pinter, born

1920, son of an East London Jewish tailor, who after grammar school became a professional actor. Pinter, a playwright influential in British cinema as well as theatre throughout the sixties, was at a different pole from the gritty northern realism of the new wave. Manifestly influenced by Beckett, he used the banal, everyday repetitions of language to explore the ways in which power relationships between human beings can shift, often quite frighteningly. Also within the new wave period there appeared a gloriously bawdy film representation of the picaresque classic Henry Fielding's *Tom Jones* (1963, directed by Tony Richardson and featuring Albert Finney).

Not all challenges to established society came from the bottom of society. Later I shall want to say much about experimental theatre, which was often confined to a very small élite minority. One élite group which emerged from Cambridge University was to prove of special significance, the group made up of Peter Cook, Jonathan Miller, Alan Bennett, and Dudley Moore which took the review *Beyond the Fringe* to the Edinburgh Festival Fringe, and then eventually to the West End. This presented in witty and potent form the anti-establishment ideas circulating velocitously in the late fifties; it was also sensitive to the issue of class—in one sketch, Peter Cook and Jonathan Miller point out that they are upper-class, while Alan Bennett and Dudley Moore are working-class, yet, they say, with heavy intentional irony, they can all 'work together'. The Establishment Club was founded in London as a home for similar anti-establishment revues: very much the product of an élite university, but bringing in the more adventurous elements from the youth subculture. Views are mixed as to how genuinely liberal the upper-class figure Sir Hugh Carlton Greene, who became director-general of the BBC in 1960, really was; one can, I think, detect some of the same qualities of 'measured judgement' as also made Trevelyan at the British Board of Film Censors sensitive to the changes taking place in society. Certainly the first ever television programme genuinely satirizing current affairs, *That Was The Week That Was*, appearing in 1962, could not have done so without his support. It came from the makers of the current affairs programme *Tonight*, but drew upon some of the young university graduates involved in *Beyond the Fringe* and the Establishment Club. The 'satire boom' lasted no longer than the 'new wave', but was, as it were, its junior partner in making public and explicit important changes in British attitudes and values.

## Literary Censorship

Three slightly different trends were very apparent in both America and Britain in the final years of the fifties and early sixties: a number of new novels were published which were perceived by contemporaries as being franker and more daring in the way they dealt with sexual matters, while at almost the same time (if anything, the former development came first) changes in literary censorship made possible not only a continuation and exaggeration of the trend but also the publication and circulation of older books which had previously been banned as subverting public morality; the third trend was that both kinds of book (which if confined to limited hardback editions might not have excited the authorities too much) were appearing in paperback for a mass market—for the sixties 'paperback revolution' had already begun. Certain branches of French literature had long been perceived in the Anglo-Saxon countries as being much more daring than anything permitted in home products; and the great controversial English-language books of the interwar years, *Lady Chatterley's Lover*, and the *Tropics* books of Henry Miller, were available in Paris (in the euphemistically titled 'Travellers' Companion Library', profitable invention of the stalwart pornographer Maurice Girodias and his Olympia Press). But arguably there was also a new sexual note in some of the more distinctive novels of the fifties, that note being very evident in *Bonjour tristesse* by Françoise Sagan (1955). Literary censorship in France, apparently quiescent, could be arbitrary, and if anything was applied with greater rigour under the Gaullist regime after 1958—this cuts two ways, however, since attempted censorship brought the issue into greater prominence. In Italy, strictest control was echoed by least change. What is very worthy of note is the attention both French and Italian journals gave to the (as they saw it) profound changes taking place in Britain, for long perceived as the model of staid decorum.

With reason, one might add: in 1955 a shopkeeper in a lower-class part of London was sentenced to two months in prison for having in stock *Lady Chatterley's Lover*.[36] This is the book which, almost simultaneously, became the subject of crucial legal actions in both Britain and America. In Britain the essential prerequisite was an actual change in the law. Credit for the new Obscene Publications Act, which allowed 'literary merit', as vouched for by acknowledged experts, as a possible defence against prosecution for obscenity goes to the then backbench Labour MP Roy Jenkins. Jenkins had shown great pertinacity and skill in making use of his luck in winning a private members' ballot, which provides the fortunate backbencher with the rare opportunity to introduce legislation. Without, however, wide recognition in governing circles that Victorian taboos could not be upheld in the late 1950s, it would not have succeeded in getting through all its parliamentary stages during the year 1958; the new law came into effect on 21 July 1959. In America an important criterion was whether a book was pure enough to be sent through the post, thus giving the American post office an important role; essentially decisions lay in the hands of the courts, depending upon how they interpreted the first amendment guaranteeing freedom of speech. A case of 1955–7 established that the notion that 'redeeming social importance' might be used as a defence, and indeed this was the defence used in the 1957 trial in San Francisco of Allen Ginsberg's *Howl*.[37] Deciding that it too would make use of this defence, Grove Press of New York brought out an unexpurgated edition of *Lady Chatterley's Lover* in the spring of 1959, when it was at once challenged by the post office: 'If this book is not filth', asked the postmaster-general, 'pray tell me what filth is.'[38] The book was duly banned, but Grove Press took immediate counter-action to restrain the postmaster-general from preventing distribution. In the US District Court, Southern District of New York, Judge Bryan ruled on 21 July 1959 that *Lady Chatterley* could be shipped through the mails, noting: 'the record... indicates general acceptance of the book', and concluding:

> These trends appear in all media of public expression, in the kind of language used and the subjects discussed in polite society, in pictures, advertisements and dress, and in other ways familiar to see. Today such things are generally tolerated whether we approve or not.[39]

This is the argument which is applied also in film censorship: people's attitudes are changing, thus the interpretation of censorship must change also. It is a self-reinforcing process, of course: people become more open, more explicit, less ashamed, less clandestine, in what they read and watch and in what they do; relaxation in censorship, greater daring in the materials available to them, legitimizes the changes in behaviour, and encourages further development towards freedom and permissiveness.

However, the fact that we are still only in the period of first stirrings of change is driven home by the way in which battle continued to rage backwards and forwards well into the early sixties. The American government immediately appealed against Bryan's ruling. However, the US Court of Appeals, declaring on 26 March 1960: 'this is a major and distinguished novel, and Lawrence one of the great writers of the age', upheld what may be termed Bryan's historic judgment.[40] Certainly those American magazines which fifteen months earlier had identified the power of the teenager were now preoccupied with the significance for public morality of the *Lady Chatterley* case. Grove Press had marketed the book at an expensive $6, but several other publishing outfits immediately jumped in with extremely cheap editions, including that of the Tabloid Publishing Company in New England which brought out an edition in newspaper format for selling on street corners at 25 cents:[41] thus did the decisions of elevated lawgivers run straight to the hearts and minds of the general public.

It was in the latter half of 1959 that Penguin Books, an infinitely more reputable and respectable organization than any of the American ones just mentioned, decided to mark the thirtieth anniversary (falling on the following year) of Lawrence's death, and the twenty-fifth of Penguin's birth, with eight Lawrence titles, including an unexpurgated *Lady Chatterley's Lover*. Of this, 200,000 copies were printed, but held back while a dozen copies were sent to the Director of Public Prosecutions. Although the DPP had recently decided, in some recognition of the changing attitudes to which I have referred several times, not to prosecute the British edition of *Lolita*, brought out by Weidenfeld and Nicolson in 1959, he did decide to prosecute the Lawrence which, in contrast to the elegant euphemisms of Nabokov, was loaded with the four-letter words which sections of the British public found deliriously exciting in print, but which by a widely accepted convention were held to be beyond the pale of civilized life. Thus it came to pass that the most celebrated and illuminating show trial of this critical time of change, was held at the Old Bailey during five days in November 1960.[42]

Some of the statements of the expert defence witnesses read comically today: they were at pains to stress that *Lady Chatterley's Lover* is 'hygienic' and 'wholesome'; it was a book 'Christians ought to read', 'a guide to young people about to get married', with, according to the bishop of Woolwich, the adultery between Lady Chatterley and her gamekeeper being 'an act of holy communion'. But such comedy was nothing to the ludicrous opening address to the jury by prosecution barrister Mervyn Griffith-Jones, which aroused great hilarity at the time and has continued to do so ever since:

> You may think that one of the ways in which you can read this book, and test it from the
> most Liberal outlook, is to ask yourselves the question, when you have read it through,

would you approve of your young sons, young daughters—because girls can read as well as boys—reading this book. Is it a book that you would have lying around in your own house? Is it a book that you would even wish your wife or your servants to read?

Unwittingly, poor, befuddled Griffith-Jones had stumbled on the fact that, while formally proceedings were about how far explicit descriptions of sexual acts could be published, and, therefore, discussed, this trial also had a class dimension. The defence stressed the extent to which Penguin Books had pioneered the supply to the working classes of classic books; their star expert witness, Richard Hoggart, spoke very much as a son of the working class. The jury (five of whom had had difficulty in just reading the oath) acquitted *Lady Chatterley* of obscenity; printing hundreds of thousands of new copies (two million were sold within the year), Penguin added a blurb referring triumphantly to the trial: 'it was not just a legal tussle, but a conflict of generation and class.' A new openness about class, together with actual changes in class relationships are critical aspects of the sixties. For the moment I want to concentrate on the way in which the content of newly published novels was changing, particularly in the United States, where a new kind of explicitness was rather more evident, and came earlier, than was the case in Britain.

Novels could be 'liberated' (and 'liberating', my argument in part is—though the censors and the censorious were still saying 'pornographic') in two ways. First, they could integrate into the narrative behaviour and acts which violated traditional morality. Beyond question, sexual relations outside marriage, illegitimate births, and so on were not new in literature, and certainly featured quite prominently in the works of novelists established well before the late fifties— Graham Greene and Somerset Maugham, for instance, not to mention, say, Colette in France or Moravia in Italy. But there could be quite a difference with regard to the amount of emphasis placed on illicit couplings, or their centrality to the plot; more, there could be the introduction of activities that had previously remained largely taboo—sex with an under-age girl (as in *Lolita);* sex between teenagers; sex between blacks and whites; sex as a completely casual and/or joyful activity (without the portentousness that traditionally had to be associated with it); homosexual (and bisexual) activities; masturbation (female as well as male); oral sex, anal sex, and sex described by a woman, from a woman's point of view, often dispassionately, or (most shocking of all) humorously; the comedy, and the magic, of tumescence and detumescence, in nipples as well as genitals, and from all angles.

Secondly (and this was really the more critical feature), there could be much more detailed, explicit (and therefore potentially arousing) descriptions of these activities, perhaps, though not necessarily, employing some of the taboo words. Nineteenth-century novelists might take you to the bedroom door, but no further: twentieth-century novelists certainly went further, but did not usually go into detail. All sorts of daring things had been done before by isolated and banned authors like D. H. Lawrence and Henry Miller; though the defence steered clear of it, and the prosecution failed to perceive it, *Lady Chatterley's Lover* did in fact contain an explicit scene of buggery; in Henry Miller sex was not only almost continuous, but presented in lavish detail; what was new in the later fifties was that this kind of material was entering into a considerable number of mainstream novels, and was being integrated into straightforward accounts of recognizable everyday life. (Miller's characters were bohemians and drop-outs; *Lady Chatterley*, as everyone knows, is simply an everyday story of aristocrats and their gamekeepers.) There was a totally new emphasis on genitalia, their mechanics, functions, and the exact sensations they produce.

In the spring of 1961 Grove Press published a hardback edition of *Tropic of Cancer*. Again there came the automatic response from the post office; but on 13 June the attempt to ban the Miller novel, at national level, from the US mails was abandoned. However, the finely balanced situation which persisted until around 1964 is demonstrated by the bans on the book enforced in Florida, Illinois, and New York State; legal proceedings were also instituted in California, Massachusetts, and Wisconsin, where in each case the book was ruled not obscene. Despite the California ruling, Los Angeles tried to maintain a local ban. On 9 October 1961 a Los Angeles bookstore owner, Bradley Reed Smith, sold a copy to a plainclothes policeman; on 23 February 1962 he was sent to prison for thirty days. The prosecution had said of defence witnesses that they 'were a fringe element believing in unbridled licentiousness and obscenity'. The star prosecution witness was Frank C. Baxter, Professor Emeritus of English at the University of Southern California and a nationally known television performer. 'This book', he announced, 'is purposely and determinedly obscene and purposefully and determinedly shocking.' *Tropic of Cancer was* 'below the twilight zone where the matter of acceptability is debated'. If the book depicted the life of an average Los Angeles citizen, he would welcome 'with great joy the hydrogen bomb'. More tellingly (and this is of serious historical interest) Baxter noted that the defence had been unable to produce a single woman to speak for the book. 'No woman in her right mind would defend it'; half the community, he told the jury, had been unrepresented by the defence.[43]

Outside the courtroom a man identified as J. D. Mercer, owner of Cosmo Book Sales of San Francisco, had been handing out cards advertising mail order copies of *Tropic of Cancer* for $2 paperback and $7.80 hardback. 'Should it be banned and your right to read it denied', he had another offer as well: 'mail 25 cents for illustrated brochure of "unusual" adult sex books and gay color physic art photos and nude statuettes. Many hard to get items.' But, having ordered the jury out, the judge addressed this fine representative of the American entrepreneurial spirit: 'you have a right to attend, this being a public trial. But you certainly don't have a right to solicit sales of this book. I order you to refrain from further activity in the court room, outside the court room or in the corridor.'[44] Actually, support for the book was far from confined to a fringe element to which neither the *Los Angeles Times* nor even the *Daily Bruin*, the student newspaper of the University of California at Los Angeles, belonged. The latter, in rather inelegant English, expressed a quite moderate view: 'It's a pretty rowdy, obscene, lively—it's a pretty wild book… the "Tropic" but it has so many redeeming features to it, that the obscenity is overruled.' The *Los Angeles Times* pressed the familiar 'the times they are achangin'' argument: 'Man's drive for self-expression, which over the centuries has built his monuments, does not stay within set bounds; the creations which yesterday were the detested and the obscene, become the classics of today.'[45] A distinguished British elder statesman of literature and philosophy, long domiciled in California, reinforced the point, while at the same time tagging on a mild joke at Miller's expense:

It is… difficult for me to take too seriously the righteous indignation of those who would

133

like to censor such books as 'Lady Chatterley's Lover' and 'Tropic of Cancer'. So far as I am concerned, the worst that can be said of Henry Miller's stylistic and powerful novel is that, in many passages, it makes sex appear so extremely unattractive that impressionable young people might be driven by the reading of it into a revulsion of puritanism.[46]

The writer was Aldous Huxley. *Paris-Match* caught up with Lady Chatterley in November 1960, remarking that publication had essentially been authorized by 'a revolution in British morals', adding the explanation that 'the war, the aeroplane and cultural exchange with the continent had liberated the British from their ancient Victorian complex'. My thesis that 1958 marks a definite point of change, and 1960 one of sustained and accelerating change, is given support by Table 4.1

**Table 4.1** *Publication dates*

|  | France | USA | UK |
|---|---|---|---|
| *Lady Chatterley* (unexpurgated) | 1929 | 1959 | 1960 |
| *Tropic of Cancer* | 1934 | 1961 | 1963 |
| *Tropic of Capricorn* | 1939 | 1962 | 1964 |
| *The Ginger Man* (unexpurgated) | 1955 | 1965 | 1963 |
| *Lolita* | 1953 | 1958 | 1959 |
| *The Naked Lunch* | 1959 | 1962 | 1964 |

### New Modes in American, French, and Italian Novels

More important, however, than the dates of publication of certain notorious books are the content, attitude, and modes of expression of certain new novels. For the United States I have selected three key examples for detailed attention: *Rabbit, Run* (1960), by John Updike; *Another Country* (1962), by James Baldwin; *The Group* (1963), by Mary McCarthy. I then, much more briefly, refer to some other books which are in themselves highly innovative and also form components of certain wider movements of cultural and social change.

In the previous section I referred to the new range of 'liberated' sexual activities and attitudes beginning to be presented fully in novels without attracting the prohibitions of the censorship. Abundantly obvious in the novels of John Updike (b. 1932), these characteristics were not in any way extraneous or designed for pornographic effect; they were simply part of the meticulous observations of the inadequate, frustrating, inglorious lives he chronicled. For the fictional Harry 'Rabbit' Angstrom, who first appeared in *Rabbit, Run*, American marriage was no more idyllic than it was for the very real Betty Friedan. John Updike was very much the white Northern Protestant, the son of a mathematics teacher, born and brought up in Pennsylvania. He studied at Harvard, where he majored in English, but also displayed great talent as a graphic artist and cartoonist; he spent a year at the Ruskin School of Drawing and Fine Art at Oxford. For nearly two years he worked on the *New Yorker*, subsequently bringing to his novel-writing the keen and cynical eye of a successful contributor to that journal. At the same time he had a deep commitment to Protestant religious morality. He published one collection of poems, prior to his first short novel, *The Poor-house Fair* (1959), which is marked by a strong element of social purpose.[47]

*Rabbit, Run* is set in 1959, when Rabbit, 26 years old, six feet three inches tall, formerly a star basketball player, has a wife who drinks, a two-year-old son, a too-small flat, and a job demonstrating a kitchen gadget called the MagiPeel Peeler in five-and-dime stores. His wife Janice

> is a small woman whose skin tends toward olive and looks tight, as if something swelling inside is straining against her littleness. Just yesterday, it seems to him, she stopped being pretty. With the addition of two short wrinkles at the corners, her mouth has become greedy; and her hair has thinned, so he keeps thinking of her skull under it.[48]

Rabbit goes off aimlessly in his car, sleeping briefly in it, then crashing out at the house of his former basketball coach. The dull particularities of driving, and of the music on the radio, are bluntly recorded:

> It takes him a half-hour to pick his way through Lancaster. On 222 he drives south through Refton, Hessdale, New Providence, and Quarryville, through Mechanics Grove and Unicorn and then a long stretch so dull and unmarked he doesn't know he's entered Maryland until he hits Oakwood. On the radio he hears 'No other arms, No other lips', 'Stagger Lee', a commercial for Rayko Clear Plastic Seat Covers, 'If I Didn't Care' by Connie Francis, a commercial for Radio-Controlled Garage Door Operators, 'I Ran All The Way Home Just To Say I'm Sorry'... news (President Eisenhower and Prime Minister Harold Macmillan began a series of talks in Gettysburg, Tibetans baffle Chinese Communists in Lhasa...[49]

And this enormous sentence continues for almost another half page in the same laconic vein. Later: 'the music on the radio slowly freezes; the rock and roll for kids cools into old standards and show tunes and comforting songs from the forties.' The coach arranges a meeting with a couple of women, Margaret ('Rabbit is amazed that Margaret is just another Janice—that same shallow density, that stubborn smallness'), and Ruth ('She is fat alongside Margaret, but not *that* fat. Chunky, more. But tall. She has flat blue eyes in square-cut sockets. Her thighs fill the front of her dress so that even standing up she has a lap. Her hair, kind of a dirty ginger colour, is bundled in a roll at the back of her head'). Rabbit goes back to Ruth's apartment with her. Several pages follow of disenchanted description of their subsequent activities, not excluding other more basic bodily functions, and including Ruth's thoroughly clinical commentaries, such as: 'Don't try to prove you're a lover on me. Just come and go.' He stays the night. She likes him: ''Cause you haven't given up. In your stupid way you're still fighting.' He goes out for food, for her to cook for lunch.

> He brings back Hot Dogs in cellophane, a package of frozen lima beans, a package of frozen french fries, a quart of milk, a jar of relish, a loaf of raisin bread, a ball of cheese wrapped in red cellophane, and, on top of the bag, a Ma Sweitzer's shoo-fly pie. It all costs $2.43. As she brings the things out of the bag in her tiny stained kitchen, Ruth says,

135

'You're kind of a bland eater.'[50]

He returns to his own home, and bumps into the Reverend Eccles, the trendy, popularizing minister of the church Janice's family belong to. Eccles has shown a keen interest in Rabbit, and his failing marriage. At Eccles's home, Rabbit meets the minister's wife, Lucy. After some desultory conversation, she recognizes him as the man who has disappeared, leaving wife and son.

'Right,' he says smartly and, in a mindless follow-through, a kind of... of coordination, she having on the drop of his answer turned with trim dismissal away from him again, slaps! her inviting ass. Not hard; a cupping hit, rebuke and fond pat both, well-placed on the pocket.

She is shocked, but at that moment her husband comes downstairs.

Her backside had felt so good, just right, dense yet springy, kind of smacked back. He supposes she'll tell, which will finish him here. Just as well. He doesn't know why he's here anyway.[51]

Immediately, Eccles and his wife get into a quarrel, so that the ass-smacking incident gets forgotten.

Rabbit is still living with Ruth. Updike lets us share her thoughts about Rabbit, and about former lovers. Rabbit

was a menace, for all his mildness. Still he did have the mildness and was the first man she ever met who did. You felt at least you were *there* for him instead of being something pasted on the inside of their dirty heads. God, she used to hate them with their wet mouths and little laughs but when she had it with Harry she kind of forgave them all, it was only half their fault, they were a kind of wall she kept battering against because she knew there was something there and all of a sudden with Harry there it was and it made everything that had gone before seem pretty unreal... They seemed sort of vague, as if she had kept her eyes shut, vague and pathetic and eager, wanting some business their wives wouldn't give, a few army words or a whimper or that business with the mouth.[52]

Rabbit clearly inspires deep affection, in Janice, in Ruth, in his former coach, in the Reverend Eccles. But the search for sex and emotional security apart, he is aimless. He was once good at basketball; now he is good at nothing.

Harry's parents are Lutherans attending the church of the stern, unbending Reverend Kruppenbach. The Reverend Eccles sees Harry's desertion of his wife as a problem between the two congregations, and first visits Harry's parents, and then Kruppenbach. Janice goes into labour, and it is the Reverend Eccles who gets word of this through to Harry. He leaves Ruth asleep and runs all the way to the hospital, where he is kept waiting:

136

He does not expect the fruit of Janice's pain to make a very human noise. His idea grows, that it will be a monster, a monster of his making. The thrust whereby it was conceived becomes confused in his mind with the perverted entry a few hours ago he made into Ruth. Momentarily drained of lust, he stares at the remembered contortions to which it has driven him. His life seems a sequence of grotesque poses assumed to no purpose—a magic dance empty of belief.[53]

Janice greets him with great affection. Rabbit goes back to the flat, and he and his son keep house till Janice can return. She does so, and the strain of living with a baby and a two-year-old son quickly becomes too much for Rabbit. He doesn't drink himself, but he forces his wife, against her will, to turn to drink again. He tries to force himself on her, then dresses and leaves her in anger and frustration. She gets to sleep, but next day takes to drinking again. While enthusiastically waiting for Harry to return, she carries on drinking. Trying to bath her new baby, she lets her drown. Harry has been trying to phone home. Finally he gets through to the Reverend Eccles. Once again Rabbit comes home. But at the funeral of the drowned baby he feels that everyone is blaming him. Once again he breaks away, and ends up ringing the bell of Ruth's apartment. Ruth is pregnant. You're bad all round, you're Mister Death, she tells him. But she'd be ready to marry him if he'd divorce Janice. Rabbit goes out, ostensibly to buy some food. But then, once again, he makes a break for it. The book ends: '... he runs. Ah: runs. Runs.'

Downbeat, and frequently almost disgusting, *Rabbit, Run* is at times highly erotic—which is the point I particularly want to stress in my continuing discussion of changing public morality. Very early in the book we read of Rabbit's early sexual encounters with Janice, before they are married (it transpires, indeed, that she was pregnant before they got married).

> She made him keep his eyes shut. Then with a shiver come as soon as he was in, her inside softly grainy, like a silk slipper. Lying side by side on this other girl's bed, feeling lost, having done the final thing; the walls silver and the fading day's gold.

On his first long aimless car drive, he muses on women:

> That wonderful way they have of coming forward around you when they want it. Otherwise just fat weight. Funny how the passionate ones are often tight and dry and the slow ones wet. They want you up and hard on their little ledge. The thing is play them until just a touch. You can tell: their skin under the fur gets all loose like a puppy's neck.[54]

Besides such accounts, the inclusion of 'fuck', 'fucking', and 'cunt', used entirely as expletives and not in the earnest manner of D. H. Lawrence, now seems tame, though it did not seem so at the time.

Much in the book forms meticulous comment on the America of 1959. As well as lists of popular songs played on the radio, there are lists of films which Rabbit and Ruth go to see. Supermarkets, we learn, are driving little grocery stores out of business, making them stay open all night. A new drive-in bank faces the antique YMCA. Overall *Rabbit, Run* is an indictment of the blank materialism of commercial life. More specifically, Kruppenbach represents strict Protestant religion; young Jack Eccles is to be seen as a compromiser, who cannot be taken seriously. The towns of Mount Judge and Brewer are imaginary. In a completely matter-of-fact way—and this is what makes it a novel of its changing times—*Rabbit, Run* is a novel of male and female lust and unbuttoned male and female reflections on sexual experience; it is, however, confined to lower-middle-class whites in southeastern Pennsylvania.

James Baldwin's *Another Country* (1962) had the same sexual explicitness, but was infinitely more audacious in that much of the sex was interracial, and that homosexuality and bisexuality are openly recognized. Baldwin, born into the black community in Harlem, New York City, in 1924, had published a successful first novel, calling upon his experiences as a boy preacher in Harlem, *Go Tell It on the Mountain* (1953). His second novel, *Giovanni's Room* (1955), confined to white characters, had broached the question of homosexual love. Baldwin's purposes were deeply serious: 'the artist', he declared, 'cannot allow any consideration to supersede his responsibility to reveal all that he can possibly discover concerning the mystery of the human being.'[55] *Another Country*, then, shares with *Rabbit, Run* a deadly seriousness of purpose, and, indeed, traces of the same theological elements. It can be linked to Updike's novel, too, and to the general points I made in the previous chapter about the stirrings of disaffection apparent in America at the beginning of the sixties, in its criticisms of the vacuous commercialism of American society: it is the upper-class Cass (formerly Clarissa) Silenski, most conventionally respectable of all the main characters in the book, who describes New York as 'getting uglier all the time', and 'a perfect example of free enterprise gone mad', and who, towards the end of the book, says of America: 'This isn't a country at all, it's a collection of football players and Eagle Scouts. Cowards. We think we are happy. We are not. We are doomed.'[56]

But Baldwin's masterpiece has a range and force which goes beyond Updike's meticulous, poetic parable. *Another Country* constitutes a fascinating interweaving of themes, only just beginning to announce themselves as Baldwin was writing, which we now recognize as being among the most distinctive of the entire period up to the beginning of the 1970s. First, of course, is race relations—continuing hurts *and* visions of change. Baldwin was to become increasingly active in the civil rights and black liberation movements. Almost immediately after *Another Country* he published the polemical, documentary work *The Fire Next Time* (1963—originally published, under a different title, in the *New Yorker)*, couched in the form of two letters. The first is addressed to a young black male (Baldwin's nephew) on the centenary of the Emancipation Proclamation, which, manifestly, has failed to set blacks free. Baldwin attacks (this is central to *Another Country*) 'the important assumption... that black men are inferior to white men'. The second letter is an autobiographical account in three parts, recollections of growing up in Harlem, an evaluation of the Black Moslems, and a statement of personal belief. The Black Moslem Elijah Muhammad is defined as a charismatic and disciplined leader who 'refuses to accept the white man's definitions'. Yet Baldwin does have a vision that 'white and black may be able to end the racial nightmare of our country and change the history of the world'. But, more immediately, his account of growing up in Harlem analyses the process of learning to be black and the need to fight in 'a white country, an Anglo-Teutonic anti-sexual country'.[57]

The notion of the need to subvert an 'anti-sexual' country lies at the heart of vast tracts of *Another Country*, and accounts for the complaint of one critic that there is 'something offensive for everyone'.[58] If the barriers and indignities of race form one encompassing theme, the other is of the paramountcy of sex, of the absolute legitimacy of sexual activity at all times, in all circumstances, and of all types and combinations. Apart from Cass and her husband Richard, all of the other characters live in a demi-world where utter promiscuity is a norm, but where also, in Baldwin's great erotic set pieces, sexual adventuring is an integral part of self-discovery and the search for authenticity—the noble cry and suspect excuse which was to be heard so often throughout the High Sixties. Baldwin anticipates the calls for gay liberation which only began to be insistently voiced at the very end of the decade. As an adolescent in Alabama, rich white kid Eric Jones is in love with a black boy, Leroy: 'I don't know why people can't do what they want to do; what *harm* are we doing to anybody?' More, Baldwin anticipates the later gender-bending orthodoxy that masculinity and femininity are not fixed states: the apparently dedicated heterosexual Vivaldo Moore ends up in bed with Eric, whose relationship with Yves is presented as the most selfless and noble in the book, and Eric, apparently totally homosexual, finds himself making love to Cass.

The complaint about the novel being 'a series of occasions for talk and fornication'[59] is not without foundation. There is so much direct speech that at times one feels one is reading a play. The characters declaim dramatically to each other, exploring their every emotion. There are sudden switches of mood: characters weep, or are struck by fear. 'Lurid' is not quite the right word: the novel is, in the purely neutral and descriptive sense of the term, 'loud'; loud, not in the style of the music often cited in the novel, traditional jazz, blues, modern jazz, and the occasional Shostakovich, but in the style of the music which was *shortly* to come to dominate all kinds of social gatherings, that loud, insistent rock/pop which was the product of the mingling of black and white talents. In a very profound way *Another Country* has the *sound* of the sixties: there is an inordinate amount of verbalizing; it screams about inhumanity, violence, disgust, self-exploration, authenticity. There is a certain conscious modernity in that much of the talk is taken up with discussing the successful (but banal, it is suggested) novel written by Richard, and the uncompleted novel being written by Vivaldo, but in general the screams are the screams of the inarticulate: the novel is prefaced by a quotation from Henry James about the abysmal mystery of what the inarticulate feel, want, and suppose themselves to be saying. Much of the popular culture, and some of the high, of the sixties was devoted to giving some kind of voice to those who had never been heard before.

Book I, entitled 'Easy Rider', is prefaced by a quotation from W. C. Handy, the black musician often credited with having invented the blues. Black former jazz musician, Rufus Scott, is down on his luck; on the opening page he is scrutinized carefully by a policeman; on the fourth page he is remembering his Harlem youth, and 'the white policeman who had taught him how to hate'. With an almost uncanny anticipation of the way in which the police were to be the principal instigators of most of the special violence of the sixties, Baldwin has policemen silently looming up throughout the book—'all policemen,' we are informed much later, 'were bright enough to know who they were working for and they were not working, anywhere in the world, for the powerless'. But quickly we go back seven months and into the first set piece, Rufus's first sexual encounter with a thirty-something blonde woman, who makes a play for him at a Harlem jazz club, and whom he recognizes as southern poor white. They go on to a party, and the action takes place there, fairly publicly.

> Yes, he was high; everything he did he watched himself doing, and he began to feel a tenderness for Leona which he had not expected to feel. He tried, with himself, to make amends for what he was doing—for what he was doing to her. Everything seemed to take a very long time. He got hung up on her breasts, standing out like mounds of yellow cream, and the tough, brown, tasty nipples, playing and nuzzling and nibbling while she moaned and whimpered and her knees sagged. He gently lowered them to the floor, pulling her on top of him. He held her tightly at the hip and the shoulder. Part of him was worried about the host and hostess and the other people in the room but another part of him could not stop the crazy thing which had begun... She began to cry. *I told you*, he moaned, *I'd give you something to cry about*, and, at once, he felt himself strangling, about to explode or die. A moan and a curse tore through him while he beat her with all the strength he had and felt the venom shoot out of him, enough for a hundred black-white babies.
>
> He lay on his back, breathing hard. He heard music coming from the room inside, and a whistle on the river. He was frightened and his throat dry. The air was chilly where he was wet.[60]

During the course of Book I, Rufus behaves brutally towards Leona; she disappears (taken away from him, we learn later, by her appalled southern white family and put in an asylum). Rufus has the friendship and support of Brooklyn-born, white working-class Vivaldo Moore, indefatigable pursuer of prostitutes of all colours, trying to set himself up as a novelist, and of the white couple made up of working-class Richard Silenski, now become successful novelist and television writer, and upper-class Cass. The careful attention to the realities of class, and to the sort of social mixing taking place among the more bohemian elements in all classes, is one of the less noticed features of the novel, but one which is again sensitive to changes actually beginning to take place in America at that time. But deeper barriers between white and black are too great. Rufus drowns himself, and his death is to brood over the rest of the novel. Book I ends with the set-piece coupling between Vivaldo and Rufus's younger sister, Ida.

Book II, 'Any Day Now', is prefaced by a quotation from Conrad. It opens with Eric and Yves together in the south of France, enjoying a lovers' idyll. There are flashbacks to Eric's adolescent relationship with LeRoy, and his first meeting with Yves. As is to be the case throughout the remainder of the book, the set pieces of homosexual lovemaking are to be much less crudely graphic, and much more colourfully flamboyant, than the heterosexual ones. They have indeed something of the reticence and obfuscation that in earlier times had characterized conventionally prudish descriptions of heterosexual encounters. Baldwin has all the deep seriousness of D. H. Lawrence; at times the unconscious humour of his passionate earnestness borders on that of *Lady Chatterley's Lover* itself.

Eric has had some success playing small parts in American films made in France, and has been offered a part in a New York play. He is returning immediately to America; Yves is to follow later. Eric had been part of the same bohemian scene as Vivaldo, Richard, and Cass; and he is affectionately welcomed back by all of them. He is horrified to hear of the death of Rufus, with whom, it would appear, he had had a homosexual encounter. The last of the major characters of the book is Ellis, a very rich impresario, who is managing Richard's transition from novel-writing to the glittering world of television. Cass (echoes of Betty Friedan) is becoming disenchanted with her life as a housewife and mother of two, and also with Richard and his apparently talentless sell-out to commercialism. She tells Vivaldo that he 'may become a real writer', while Richard 'never will be'.

> 'He's a carpenter's son,' she said, 'the fifth son of a carpenter who came from Poland. Maybe that's why it's so important. A hundred years ago he'd have been like his father and opened a carpenter's shop. But now he's got to be a writer and help Steve Ellis sell convictions and soap.' Ferociously, she ground out her cigarette.[61]

It is Cass who deliberately telephones, and visits, Eric. It is made abundantly clear that it is she, the older married woman, who is seeking out this younger, beautiful, man. He explains clearly to her that he is in love with Yves. This coupling is dealt with without the usual colour and detail. We also learn in Book II that Ida and Ellis are having an affair: but this is at second-hand, and there are no descriptions.

Book III has the consciously biblical title, 'Toward Bethlehem', and is prefaced by lines from Shakespeare's Sonnet LXV; it is a mere two chapters long, less than a quarter of the length of either of the other two books. Chapter 1 opens with the shock of Vivaldo dreaming that he is in bed with Rufus, and finding that in fact he is in bed with Eric. The scene of physical love between Vivaldo and Eric spreads over five pages, in which a complexly verbose uncertainty is created as to just exactly what they do to each other. The conclusion may sound as though it is intended as parody, but one fears it is in deadly earnest:

> They opened their eyes and looked at each other. Eric's dark blue eyes were very clear and candid, but there was a terrible fear in their depth, too, waiting. Vivaldo said, 'It was wonderful for me, Eric.' He watched Eric's face. 'Was it for you?'
>
> 'Yes,' Eric said, and he blushed. They spoke in whispers. 'I suppose that I needed it, more than I knew.'[62]

Shortly afterwards, Vivaldo is back with Ida. There has been much stress between them. There seems to be a scene of reconciliation. It is certainly the most powerful scene in the novel. No physical sex, but a violent and crudely explicit account from Ida of how she blames whites for the death of her brother Rufus, and how she has taken her revenge on whites in general, and on Ellis in particular.

I used to see the way white men watched me, like dogs. And I thought about what I could do to them. How I hated them, the way they looked, and the things they'd say, all dressed up in their damn white skin, and their clothes just so, and their little weak, white pricks jumping in their drawers. You could do any damn thing with them if you just led them along, because they wanted to do something dirty and they knew that you knew how. All black people knew that. Only, the polite ones didn't say dirty. They said real. I used to wonder what in the world they did in bed, white people I mean, between themselves, to get them so sick because they are sick...[63]

That is the tone of the novel, even if the final four-page chapter is calm and cheerful: Yves flies to New York; Eric is smilingly waiting for him at the airport. Summing up these two novels: there is little humour in *Rabbit, Run;* there is absolutely none in *Another Country.*

One of the things that made Mary McCarthy's *The Group* (1963) so shocking was that it was coolly funny in its treatment of sex. Worse, not only was the author a woman but, at the age of 51, she was a long-established member of the liberal literary establishment. *The Group* is not by some radical young newcomer, nor is it about the contemporary youth or beat scene. It is not, in its essence, time-specific at all, though formally it deals with what happens in the seven years after 1933 to a group of graduates from the upper-class women's college Vassar. There is nothing strongly feminist about the novel: the young women all tend to innocence, and look towards men to initiate them into what have remained the mysteries of sex. The hilarious, downbeat account of how Dottie Renfrew brought about her own seduction, which comes as early as Chapter 2, still has the power to shock: it ranks as the classic gateway to sixties candour, explicitness, and simple joy in sex, without the purple passages and romantic posturing:

She had never seen *that* part of a man, except in statuary and once, at the age of six, when she had interrupted Daddy in his bath, but she had a suspicion that it would be something ugly and darkly inflamed, surrounded by coarse hair. Hence, she had been very grateful for being spared the sight of it, which she did not think she could have borne, and she held her breath as a strange body climbed on hers, shrinking. 'Open your legs,' he commanded, and her legs obediently fell apart. His hands squeezed her down there, rubbing and strok-ing; her legs fell further apart, and she started to make weak, moaning noises, almost as if she wanted him to stop. He took his hand away, thank heaven, and fumbled for a second; then she felt it, the thing she feared, being guided into her as she braced herself and stiff-ened. 'Relax,' he whispered. 'You're ready.' It was surprisingly warm and smooth, but it hurt terribly, pushing and stabbing. 'Damn it,' he said. 'Relax. You're making it harder.' Just then, Dottie screamed faintly; it had gone all the way in. He put his hand over her mouth and then settled her legs around him and commenced to move it back and forth inside her. At first, it hurt so that she flinched at each stroke and tried to pull back, but this only seemed to make him more determined. Then, while she was still praying for it to be over, surprise of surprises, she started to like it a little... Then, all of a sudden, she seemed to explode in a series of long, uncontrollable contractions that embarrassed her, like the hiccups, the moment they were over, for it was as if she had forgotten Dick as a person; and he, as if he sensed this, pulled quickly away from her and thrust that part of himself onto her stomach, where it pushed and pounded at her flesh. Then he too jerked and moaned, and Dottie felt something damp and sticky running down the hill of her belly.

Minutes passed; the room was absolutely still; through the sky-light Dottie could see the moon. She lay there, with Dick's weight still on her, suspecting that something had gone wrong, probably her fault… She was ashamed of the happiness she had felt. Evidently, he had not found her satisfactory as a partner or else he would say something. Perhaps the woman was not supposed to move?[64]

The initiation continues; later Dottie's thoughts turn to whom she will confide in, and how much she will say. The next chapter includes an uninhibited, anatomically explicit, and extremely funny description of Dottie being fitted up with a contraceptive diaphragm. While the group as a whole shares the same mirth-creating naivety and inexperience, not all are as straightforward as Dottie. Hypocrisies, stratagems, and cant are all ruthlessly exposed, along with the many other trials and tribulations of a young woman's life. Priss Crockett had got married to Sloan, and had one son, Stephen.

As the wife of a paediatrician, she was bitterly ashamed that Stephen, at the age of two-and-a-half, was not able to control his bowels. He not only made evil-smelling messes in his bed, at naptime, but he sometimes soiled his pants here in the Park, which was why she sought out this isolated bench, rather than take him to the playground. Or he did it—like last week-end—in his bathing-trunks on the beach at the Oyster Bay clubhouse, in front of the whole summer colony, who were sunning and having cocktails. Sloan, even though he was a doctor, was extremely annoyed whenever Stephen did it in public, but he would never help Priss clean Stephen up or do anything to relieve her embarrassment.[65]

Mary McCarthy's novel was coolness itself, but she was soon to be throwing herself passionately into the anti-Vietnam war campaign.

*The Group* was denounced publicly by many critics for its 'shocking' sex scenes. Privately, Camilla Van Dyke, my voice of mid-South middlebrow opinion, expressed her revulsion in a letter to her parents:

I read the first 50 pages, was so nauseated by its dirt for dirt's sake that I took it right back to Doubleday [booksellers]… It's shameful that Vassar has to be the butt of such a work.[66]

A lady novelist in California took a more profit-orientated view, wondering in a letter to a friend if perhaps she should try to emulate what she called 'the bitch book': 'I don't think we need books of this sort, but if Mary McCarthy can do it, then I should at least try for these lovely $ that seem to be under that manure.'[67] But it was a book which people read (this is not always the case) as well as denounced—presumably because it was indeed a book women could identify with. It reached the American best-seller list, and in the same year had hardback publication in Britain, followed in 1964 by paperback publication.

These three books contained descriptions of a sort which could not have been published a year or two earlier; they are also, in different ways, responses to changes which were beginning to take place in American society. They are not isolated examples; many other books of striking audacity and originality were being published at the same time. Ken Kesey produced *One Flew Over the Cuckoo's Nest* (1962), which enjoyed considerable success as something of a cult novel, featuring a bitter struggle within an asylum between 'the Big Nurse' and the lusty, profane patient, R. P. McMurphy, who brings gambling, wine, and women into the ward; in suggesting that those declared mad are merely the socially troublesome, it paralleled the ideas of Michel Foucault and R. D. Laing (discussed in Chapter 7) which became very influential by the end of the decade. Kesey then turned most of his attention towards becoming a stylesetter for much of Californian psychedelia, seeking new forms of expression induced by drugs, and forming the specialists in LSD freak-outs, the Merry Pranksters.[68] *Catch-22* (1962) by Joseph Heller was more consciously modernistic than any of the other novels I have mentioned, with the time-order deliberately scrambled; it was a cynical, unheroic account, full of profanity and obscenity, of the American bomber campaign over Italy in the Second World War. It was much more enthusiastically received in Britain than in America, where it only became a best-seller in the 1970s after the book was filmed.[69] Initial success also eluded *The Sot-Weed Factor* (1960) by John Barth (b. 1930). The novel is based on an actual 1708 satirical poem of the same name, written by Ebenezer Cooke, the self-proclaimed poet laureate of the Maryland colony. As Arthur D. Casciato explains:

> Barth felt, for two reasons, that it was futile to write traditional realistic fiction: first, because all possibilities of plot had been exhausted, and, second, because realism did not exactly represent reality but 'a kind of true representation of the distortion we all make of life. In other words... a representation of a representation of life.' In *The Sot-Weed Factor*, Barth gives this screw another turn, presenting his own farcical distortion of historical documents, themselves a distortion of 'real' life in colonial Maryland. For example, Barth transforms the Pocahontas and Captain John Smith legend into a ribald tale of an impenetrable virgin and a Sacred Eggplant. His source for this version is a document, supposedly genuine, called *The Privie Journall of Sir Henry Burlingame*.[70]

A range of serious and innovative works, then. Neither of these terms could be applied to the exploitative work which for some commentators has symbolized the change in public morals of the early sixties as expressed through fiction: *The Carpetbaggers* (1961), the fifth production of popular novelist Harold Robbins (the pen name of Harold Rubins). Based loosely on the life of the millionaire recluse Howard Hughes, the novel is described on its flyleaf as follows:

> The story of a millionaire who was soft enough to buy a film company because of one woman and hard enough to make more millions after she died. The story of the whore he

made a star, of the heroes he bought and sold. The story of Hollywood at its most flamboyant and big business at its biggest.

The novel was famous for its alternating scenes of sadism and of sex. Actually, the sex scenes, when compared with some of those I have just been quoting, are old-fashioned in the extreme in their use of traditional circumlocutions. The main protagonist is Jonas Cord. At the beginning of the novel his father, a prosperous factory owner, has stolen his girlfriend, Rina, and married her. Jonas had himself got no further with Rina than being masturbated by her into his handkerchief—this is rendered in heavy code: 'Then suddenly, I felt an exquisite pain rushing from the base of my spine and I almost climbed halfway out of the seat.' The father drops dead, and Rina, briefly, comes back to Jonas in his bedroom:

> '… look at yourself, Jonas. Look at yourself lusting for your father's wife!' I didn't have to look to know she was right… together we plunged into the fiery pleasures of our own particular hell.[71]

The coupling of two relatively minor characters, David and Rosa, is a true classic of old-style prurience, and can fittingly serve here to bring out how innovative indeed were Updike, Baldwin, McCarthy and the others in their direct treatment of sex:

> David came out of the water and collapsed on the blanket. He rolled over on his side and watched her running up the beach toward him. He held his breath. She was so much a woman that he had almost forgotten she was also a doctor…
>
> She came down into his arms, her mouth tasting of ocean salt. His hand found her breast inside her bathing suit. He felt a shiver run through her as the nipple grew in his palm, then her fingers were on his thigh, capturing his manhood.[72]

The novel has a conventionally sloppy ending, with Jonas being reunited with his long-lost own true love. Hardback publication followed in Britain in 1962, with paperback publication in 1964. Exploitative and ill-written though it was, the point does remain that, a few years before, it almost certainly could not have been published in that form.

On the whole, the new American novels were more daring, more explicit, in their treatment of major issues, particularly sex, than the British novels I discussed near the beginning of the chapter, whose main originality lay in making the working class clearly visible, and whose treatment of sex, though frank, was fairly discreet. The point is confirmed as I turn to Ireland, the setting for the first two novels by Edna O'Brien, born and brought up in the west of Ireland. O'Brien herself, like her main character by the time of the third novel, moved to London, the setting for most of her later works. In comparison with the novels I have just been discussing, *The Country Girls* (1960) seems totally innocent, and *The Lonely Girl* (1962—published in America, and in the Penguin paperback of 1964 which I have used, as *The Girl with Green Eyes)* seems almost as innocent. The most striking aspect of the sexual preferences of Kait, and her friend Baba, and one which was really very sensitive to the way one aspect of sexual relationships was to develop in the permissive sixties, is that they associate entirely with older men. At one point Kait reflects 'that young men with their big knees and their awkward voices, bored me'. The whole of the latter part of the book is taken up with Kait's first complete love affair, with a documentary film-maker called Eugene. The novel is utterly frank in making it clear that she is completely overwhelmed by him, completely helpless in his presence. But she is frightened of sex, and when she does lose her virginity (a full account, incorporating what was still the novelty of a female record of female experience, by a female, with the inevitable foregrounding of male tumescence and detumescence) she doesn't like it very much: 'I felt no pleasure, just some strange satisfaction that I had done what I was born to do.' She is deeply in love, and she enjoys everything about love, except for sex. She begins to understand the learning process she is going through:

> Up to then I thought that being one with him in bed meant being one with him in life, but I knew now that I was mistaken, and that lovers are strangers, in between times.[73]

Although it makes her desperately miserable, she comes to see that parting from Eugene is inevitable. By the end of the novel she is sharing a bed-sitting-room in Bayswater, in west London, with Baba, and at night is studying English at London University (she is on the fringes of that young London which, though not classless, was characterized by a mixing of classes).

> If I saw him again I would run to kiss him, but even if I didn't see him I have a picture of him in my mind, walking through the woods, saying, in answer to my fear that he might leave me, that the experience of knowing love and of being destined, one day, to remember it, is the common lot of most people.

The last sentence of the book reads:

> What Baba doesn't know is that I am finding my feet, and when I'm able to talk I imagine that I won't be so alone, or so very far away from the world he tried to draw me into, too soon.[74]

Edna O'Brien was the harbinger of quite a tide of fairly explicit women's novels in Britain: in Ireland, her own books were banned. Under the title *The Girl With Green Eyes* this second novel of Edna O'Brien's was made into a film, with the central role being played by Rita Tushingham.

All these 'Anglo-Saxon' novels were concerned with the moral and social problems of contemporary society. They are not 'metaphysical'. Novels concerned with contemporary moral and social problems were also published in considerable numbers in France and Italy; it is with such novels that I am concerned in this chapter. However, it is important to register here the great significance in France, and to a lesser extent in Italy, of metaphysical movements in literature, and more generally of the grouping of writers into schools or movements, defined by abstract labels. In Britain in the fifties, the labels had been of rather narrow scope: 'the

Movement', 'Angry Young Men', 'Kitchen Sink'. In France, whatever the mass of ordinary readers might be reading, the dominant intellectual movement at the time of the war and immediately after was Existentialism, and novels of Sartre and Camus were seen to fit readily under that label. The new literary movement of the mid-fifties was that of the *nouveau roman* (new novel), partly linked to the philosophical movement which emerged in the early 1960s as 'Structuralism'. The *nouveau roman* sought—on the Marxist argument that the traditional novel which created character, told a story, expressed ideas about society, and so on, was bourgeois— to eschew all of these things, by stressing ambiguities of character, disrupting time sequences, and offering the reader different versions of the same events, sometimes concentrating on the minute description of inanimate physical objects. Such metaphysical preoccupations will be the concern of Chapter 7.

The French novel in this early period of rapid change on which I wish to concentrate is *Les Petits Enfants du siècle* (1961) by Christiane Rochefort.[75] In his *French Literature in the Twentieth Century* Christopher Robinson detects a trend in which youth and the values of teenage society become more and more important in French literature, referring critically to 'these facile glorifications of contemporary self-indulgence'.[76] The reference is specifically to the work of Françoise Sagan, but Robinson, quite mistakenly, puts Rochefort in the same category. Actually Rochefort was about twice Sagan's age, and from a very different social background. Forty-one in 1958 when she published her first novel, *Le Repos du guerrier*, she came from a militant working-class family (her father served for three years with the Republicans fighting against Franco) and earned her living from journalism and public relations, spending fifteen years as press attaché to the Cannes film festival.[77] *Le Repos du guerrier*, a frank but scarcely explicit account in first-person narrative of an *adult* woman's infatuation with a drunken ne'er-do-well, enjoyed a *succès de scandale* and by 1961 had sold 265,000 copies, becoming (with the useful support of Brigitte Bardot) a popular film in 1962. It presents an early version of the perception, a commonplace among feminists ten years later, that the sexual attractiveness of certain men is a dangerous drug, and a terrible trap.

*Les Petits Enfants du siècle* is also a first-person narrative, this time recounted by a working-class girl, living in an appalling multi-storey housing estate on the outskirts of Paris, who by the end of the story is 17, but who gives a child's-eye view of family life with two parents and eleven children from the time of her going to school onwards. Rochefort had discarded two alternative titles, *Malthus* and *Une vraie petite maman*. The first of these abandoned titles perhaps offers some excuse for those right-wing critics who welcomed the novel (erroneously) as a devastating attack on the way family allowances encouraged the feckless to have far too many children. The title actually chosen, together with interviews given at the time and the general orientation of Rochefort's career, points to much wider and much subtler meanings.[78] Among many other things, *Les Petits Enfants du siècle* is a protest against working-class women being treated as mere breeding-machines: mother has a new child so that father (who works in a mustard factory) can have a new car. Josyane, still pre-pubescent, has one absolutely transporting experience (cunnilingus, it is perfectly clear from the text) with Guido, Italian labourer on a local building site. Josyane's cold-eyed appraisal of the stupidities of adults and, as she grows older, of how to turn to her own advantage the sexual exigencies of the boys around her, are chillingly accurate and chillingly funny (from one boy she demands cunnilingus as a precondition for full sex). She meets a more cultured youth—but he is killed in the Algerian war. At 17 she falls in love, gets pregnant, and married. She has swallowed the drug, fallen into the trap. With regard to the value of *Les Petits Enfants du siècle* as a source, a vital consideration is that the author had the skilled journalist's eye for contemporary detail, and sensitivity to changing trends. Together with Rachel Mizraki she was responsible for producing, within a year of its English publication, a French translation of John Lennon's *In His Own Write*, prefaced by a very funny 'Intraduction [sic] des traditrices'.[79] Though *Les Petits Enfants du siècle* did not enjoy the commercial success of Rochefort's first novel, it was third on the French best-seller lists in May 1961, and won the Prix du Roman Populiste as well as being on the shortlist for the 1961 Prix Goncourt; it was not filmed, and my suggestion that it anticipated perceptions which were only widely articulated a decade later is borne out by the way in which it was finally adapted for French television only in May 1974.[80]

Sloganizing and theorizing are very strong elements in the philosophy and politics of the sixties. But more important, both in the longer term and for the wider society, was the explosive, doing-your-own-thing originality: Rochefort, who fitted into no fashion or movement, exemplifies this, like David Hockney in painting. *Les Petits Enfants du siècle* can be seen as marking a conscious break from the *nouveau roman* to whose restraint and good taste the gusto and vulgarity of Rochefort marked a direct challenge; at the same time she was absolutely on the crest of a new tide of oral writing in which the traditional constraints of correct French were totally abandoned. All-pervasive are both the sense of government eager to finance youth and rampant consumerism. As a priority family, Josyane tells us, hers have a fine flat. 'While mother is preparing the dinner, father returns and immediately switches on the telly; they eat; father and boys watch the telly, she and mother do the washing up... they have a bathroom, the washing-machine arrived when the twins were born'. The accounts both of a massive housebuilding construction site and of a young Italian working on it are in accordance with the specific facts of the economic miracle in both countries. The treatment of sex is extremely frank, though not detailed in the manner of the American novels. With respect to the eventual explosion of feminism, *Les Petits Enfants* really is quite revolutionary: apart from the cunning and intelligence of the girl narrator herself and the feebleness of most of the male characters and their refusal to play any part in domestic chores, the central position given to cunnilingus could be said to be the 'myth of the vaginal orgasm' seven years *avant la lettre* (Anna Koedt's famous tract not being written until 1968[81]).

Her next novel, *Les Stances à Sophie* (1963) (Sophie's Stanzas—the American translation of 1965 was crassly titled *Cats Don't Care for Money*) was a disillusioned story of a marriage and a divorce. The strong note of protest is apparent in the opening paragraph:

The thing about all of us poor girls is that we are never told anything. We land right in it without accurate information. When you meet Mr What's-his-name he is totally established, solid as a rock in appearance, and it seems that it has always been like that with men, that it will always continue to be so, and there is no reason why anything should change. It is in the nature of things. It's what everyone says, and, at once, one believes it: what can we do, with no other sources of information? Sometimes, one is a bit surprised: it is after all a bit much; but, to realise how stupid it is one needs to have time and a very clear head. Meantime, we have to try. In particular with regard to these fellows who form, so to speak, our natural field of manoeuvres, and towards whom, because we are ruled by our own unfortunate confusion, we show a weakness which addles our mind and throws us into contradictions, if not into total imbecility.

In Italy, at the end of the fifties, the dominant movement in all forms of literary and cinematic expression was that known as *neorealismo* ('new realism'); in the early sixties, novelists whose purposes were still essentially social and moral began to break with neo-realism, turning to allegory and other forms of non-naturalistic representation. At the same time there appeared the beginnings of a more fundamentalist, more abstract, more metaphysical movement, strongly influenced by developments in France and Germany, rather clumsily referred to as the *neoavanguardia*. Actually, the Italian language itself provided the perfect formulation for one of the first productions of this movement, the 1961 anthology of poetry entitled *I novissimi* ('the very newest'). The most distinguished figure was the philosopher Umberto Eco, the leading literary figure was Edoardo Sanguineti, while one of the youngest was Nanni Balestrini, a strong exponent of Eco's ideas about ambiguity and openness of interpretation being the defining features of modernist art. These figures of the *avanguardia* kept closely in touch with the founders of *Tel Quel*, the new French journal established in 1961 to represent the ideas of structuralism and the *nouveau roman*. In 1963 they formed themselves into Gruppo 63, very consciously echoing the left-wing and avant-garde German group formed after the war, Gruppe 47.

The major neo-realist writers still dominating the scene at the end of the fifties were Pavese, Calvino, and Moravia. A classic of neo-realism, by a writer who was to become a key figure in the changing Italian literature of the 1960s, is the collection of nine documentary essays on his home town of Racalmuto in Sicily, published in 1956, by Leonardo Sciascia, *Le parrochie di Regalpetra* (The Parishes of Regalpetra, Sciascia's fictional name for Racalmuto). In 1961 Sciascia published the first of four novels of a new type, for which he was to become famous. In Italy the genre is known as the *giallo*, literally 'yellow', the popular term for the detective story. But these are 'detective stories' with a difference. All of them concern the corruption of Sicilian life and the central role of the Mafia in business and politics; in none of them is a murderer ever brought to justice. The form was established by *Il giorno della civetta* (The Day of the Owl, 1961). I have reserved for full treatment in its proper chronological place, in Part III, the second, *A ciascuno il suo*, of 1966 (rendered in the American translation of 1968 as *A Man's Share*, though *To Each His Own Desserts* would be a more accurate translation).

At this point, I want to focus on two authors, hitherto unknown, belonging totally to this new phase in cultural history and whose unique qualities dazzled the Italian literary scene—and for whom Italian literary critics have never been able to find adequate labels. Because their work is in some way related to the Italian economic miracle, they are sometimes referred to as 'industrial' or 'commercial' novelists. But such terms are deeply inadequate, since both writers go far beyond the naturalism of the traditional novel. They are Lucio Mastronardi—his *Il calzolaio di Vigerano* and, more specifically, *Il maestro di Vigerano* were both published in book form in 1962—and Luciano Bianciardi, whose *La vita agra* was also published in 1962. Some critics referred to Mastronardi's style as 'grotesque'. I would certainly term him 'modernist', while Bianciardi is in some ways almost postmodernist. Though the term is, to the best of my knowledge, unknown to Italian criticism, I am very tempted to borrow from later English writing—exemplified by Angela Carter and Salman Rushdie—the phrase 'magic realism' implying a dynamic inventiveness in expressing moral and social truths which goes far beyond realism. At any rate they were highly original, while what they wrote was palpably related to current social change.

How individual creative works come to be produced and marketed—the personal and circumstantial factors, as well as the deeper cultural ones—is always a matter of interest. A most influential literary figure of the time, arbiter of taste, and 'mediator' (as the cultural theorists would say), was Elio Vittorini. Towards the end of January 1956 Vittorini received a letter which included the following:

> I am a young man of twenty-five and from at least the age of ten have been interested in literature... Verga, Pirandello,... Hemingway and Steinbeck, the Americans... For five years I have been writing and reading, reading and writing. Writers are born, but they also need to be developed, they say.[82]

In letters, and in the occasional meeting, Vittorini encouraged the young Mastronardi to get down to writing a novel. What was to become *Il calzolaio di Vigerano* (The Shoemaker of Vigerano) was begun in the winter of 1956/57. As it got under way, Bianciardi came out with his first book, *Il lavoro culturale* (Cultural Work), a work of criticism, not fiction, published in 1957. Vittorini, together with Italo Calvino, was planning to bring out a new literary magazine, *Il Menabò* (the Italian word for the dummy, or preliminary mock-up produced by a printer, or editor), which was launched in 1959. Vigerano is a town of 50,000 inhabitants in Lombardy, on the borders between the rich agricultural lands of the Lombardy plains and the industrial areas developing around the city of Milan. Mastronardi was born there in 1930. His father, who came from the south of Italy, had occupied the respectable lower-middle-class job of school inspector, but as an opponent of Fascism had suffered imprisonment and beatings, and had been suspended from his job. After the war he was something of a hero, and was elected to the local council on the Italian Communist party list, but he remained very much an individualist. Mastronardi's mother was a schoolmistress in Vigerano. Mastronardi himself was something of a disappointment to his father, failing to secure entry to grammar school; in an attempt to stop his son from wasting his time on politics, Mastronardi senior instructed the local Communist party not to accept his son's membership subscription. Continuing on his rather lowly trajectory, Mastronardi in 1949 became a primary schoolteacher; however, he did subsequently, as a mature student, gain entry to the University of Pavia.

The helping hands Vittorini and Calvino were offering to Mastronardi became an almighty shove when, in the very first issue of *Il Menabò* they published the complete text of *Il calzolaio*, a short novel of about 132 pages, together with a small dossier on the author. Mastronardi continued to work on *Il maestro di Vigerano* which, as already noted, was published in 1962 along with *Il calzolaio* in book format.[83] Like almost all of the Italian writers and film-makers I will be discussing, Mastronardi was Marxist in his basic assumptions about how societies operate and develop; at the same time he was fully conversant with the authoritarian character and absurdities of the Italian Communist party, and aware of how thoroughly tedious a straightforward story with a Marxist message would be.

On the opening page of *Il calzolaio* the third-person narrative introduces Mario Sala (always known as Nicca) who comes from the town's oldest family of independent shoemakers. Immediately the sense of tradition is reinforced by a loving description of the town's central square, with its frescoes by Leonardo da Vinci. Then to the contrasting phenomenon that lies at the heart of the novel: the big Edison electrical installation on the River Ticino. Mario, his wife Luisa, and practically everyone else, all engaged in shoemaking, work furiously day and night, in awful conditions. Big companies are being formed. Mario himself invests everything he has managed to save up in a project of Pelagatta, the owner of one of the new combines, to form the Pelagatta-Sala company. The period covered by the novel is that from the middle thirties to the end of the Second World War. The theme is of rapid industrialization and commercial expansion, and the desperation of almost everyone to share in this, at whatever cost to health, love, and private life. Most critics took it that, though put back fifteen or twenty years in time, the 'economic miracle' Mastronardi was attacking so angrily was really the economic miracle of the late fifties. Fine new roads are being built, there is a bypass round the town—certainly the building of the *autostrade* was much boasted of in the Italy of the early sixties. Mario is called up to serve with Mussolini's armies in Albania. Luisa, and the various caricatured characters of the novel, continue to work and to cheat. But at least Mario is doing much better in material things, described with the heavy irony and crude comedy which are among Mastronardi's characteristics: 'he had soup made of the arses of four different animals, three not being enough, so that he also included the arse of a piglet; he washed in milk, and did the washing with soap; he took colour photographs...'. The very last lines of the novel bring out in grotesquely comic way how Mario is still desperately doing everything to maximize his income:

> As the last minutes were running out before the first church bells of the morning, Mario got dressed, and bicycled down to the station, in time for the first morning train. He established himself among the salesmen at the exit, staring into the faces of the passengers, crying:
>
> 'Shoes at cut price? Leather goods, fur, all kinds of footwear?... Follow me!'

This is a very Italian novel (indeed one of the values to the historian is the contrast with the sort of different contextual matters which would preoccupy an American, a French, or a British novelist). What might be called the 'establishment myth' of the time when Mastronardi was actually writing was that Italy, at the end of the war, had made a complete break with the bad old authoritarian days of Fascism (there *was* truth in this, of course). By setting the economic miracle which actually took place in the late fifties in the Fascist period, Mastronardi is making the point that with respect to class hierarchies, and the distribution of economic power, nothing has really changed. *Il maestro* (The Schoolmaster), the more rewarding source for historians, is, however, set firmly in the contemporary period: towards the end of the book the narrator, *Il maestro*, Antonio Mombelli, is in a cafe where he selects *Volare* on the jukebox—'the voice of Modugno expanded into the air'. The complete trilogy was very unusual, but part of a movement just then developing in Italy, in that it made extensive use of local dialect words (the pocket edition containing the entire trilogy (including *Il meridionale di Vigerano)* has a glossary extending to eight closely printed double-column pages).

*Il maestro* is almost in diary format, though without any precise dates. Antonio notes that he has a wife, Ada, and a son, Rino. On the opening page he records a disagreement with his wife: she wants to go out to work, to earn money which he admits would be very useful to the household economy, but for him the idea that the wife of a *piccolo borghese* (petty bourgeois) should enter a factory was insupportable. He and Ada see a French film in which such a wife escapes from her provincial husband, and sets up in a life of luxury and immorality in Paris. Antonio is very conscious of the comparison. Constantly Mastronardi is mocking Antonio, and all his fellow-teachers, as being outdated, incompetent, overly bureaucratic. There are squabbles between the two teachers' unions, given the comic names of 'Snuse' and 'Snase'. Antonio is bored and uneasy with himself and his wife. The seventh section of the book, perhaps representing the seventh diary entry, begins: 'Sunday has also passed by. Another long useless day has died away'. The next 'entry' starts: 'The full one hundred and sixty-eight hours have gone by. Another Sunday has come to an end. What have I done with these one hundred and sixty-eight hours?' He works out that he has spent twenty-five actually teaching in school, and twenty-five in preparing his lessons. He has spent sixty-odd in sleep, half-a-dozen in eating, and so on. At the beginning of section 10 we encounter the most insistently grotesque theme in the whole book: his wife is obsessed by the toes on his feet, so that he too becomes obsessed with them (and with other people's as well). 'It came about that I would show her my bare feet with the same emotion that I would show her my member.' Ashamed of the lethargy of the school, he is bitten with enthusiasm for the economic miracle all around him. He lets his colleagues know that he intends to leave to become an industrialist. However, the only way he can get a job is by taking one in the factory owned by his wife's brother. He tries to compensate for the rueful reflection that he is now an employee of his wife and brother-in-law by turning his hand to everything and working all hours of the day—he gets up at six, the first part of his day's work finishes towards one o'clock, the second starts at two and lasts till eight, the third begins at nine. However, when he bumps into some of his old colleagues during their school holiday, he feels very proud: 'I work.' Ada, he feels, has become more masculine. He reflects that he has 'lost another skill, that of making love twice a week. We do it only on Saturday night or Sunday morning.' However, Ada is pregnant. A son is born with red hair. It can't be his, he is completely certain. The baby dies and he feels very happy about that.

His grip on life becomes less and less secure. He finds he has spent a whole night sitting on the lavatory seat. He has shot his mouth off about where money is kept at the factory, and one of his old colleagues records what he says on a pocket tape-recorder. The (rather small) sum of 800 lire goes missing from the factory. Antonio is brought before the lawyer Racalmuto (a character who had featured in the previous novel as well). Racalmuto has the tape-recorder and it is Antonio's voice which issues from it, confirming his guilt. He is excluded from the factory, but he reflects that for all the hours he put in he didn't really do anything useful. His humiliation continues as Ada puts him on a daily allowance; now he really has time to kill. He enrols in two courses. One, on Africa, is described very humorously: it will enable him to deal with the tsetse fly, with snake-bites, and so on. But the other aims at preparing him to take the advanced examination which would entitle him to become a school inspector. Entry 17, the last in Part II, is very long and is mainly taken up with a treatise on speech, said to have been written by a colleague of the author: here of course we very much have the modernist, or even postmodernist, technique of inserting 'documents' within the text. He gets fifty marks out of fifty in his exam, and is welcomed back to the school (where he takes up the special role of a teacher always at the disposition of the headmaster).

Part III opens with the reflection that this is his twentieth year at school; as in his first year, the teachers are squabbling over who should have the privilege, or perk, of teaching the son of an industrialist. He continues to worry over the paternity of the dead baby; however, he consoles himself that his son Rino is doing very well, and will become a civil servant, class A, earning the appropriate class A salary. But he has seen his wife going about with a businessman with red hair; he takes to stalking them. He looks at an array of pistols in a shop window, but finally buys a hammer. Outside a room in which Ada and the businessman are together, he hears Ada crying out in sexual pleasure. He touches his 'member', limp and dried up. ' "It's only good for pissing," I said to myself.' He attacks Ada with the hammer. While she is dying, she tells him she has always been unfaithful to him, but that the red-haired baby had been his, while Rino was not. That we are very far from being in a realistic story is made still clearer by the fact that no consequences follow for Antonio from his act of murder.

A colleague at school tells him of a fat, unattractive young woman he knows, who would be glad to marry Antonio, and would bring with her the sum of eight million lire. A number of conversations at school are recorded, all designed by Mastronardi to show how complacent and outdated school is. School—the bad old Italy—is counterpointed with the new bustling, commercial Italy, in which people keep talking about coefficients, which is even worse. As in the earlier novel, Mastronardi from time to time refers, by way of genuine contrast, to the historic beauty of the town square. Specific mention is made of the Bramante tower, which, Antonio reflects, will last for another 500 years. But in his description, early in *Il maestro*, of the corso Milano as it is today, his anger against the recent industrialization comes through very strongly:

I was taking a walk as evening sweetly descended, and the moon rose; in front of me the long corso Milano, packed with bicycles and cars and people, hurrying in lines; this hurrying, and this forming up in lines, it seemed to me expressed the full significance of their lives. And my own walk had a significance too, I thought. But I didn't know what significance to attribute to my walk. Perhaps the hurrying by these people formed the culmination of something, of some action, while I was walking without any goal... my thoughts turned to money. Banknotes which owe their value to the fact that they are backed by gold; if they were not backed by gold they would be worth nothing. So, there was something analogous about the hurrying about of the crowd around me: beneath it there was gold; while beneath my walk there was nothing nothing nothing!

Rino insists that they go to Ada's grave, which is in a cemetery for the poor. It transpires that Rino has been guilty of indecent acts with a pederast, and he is taken off to a house of correction. On a train Antonio encounters the lawyer Racalmuto: they have a conversation which consists entirely of numbers. The last sections of the book are particularly episodic, with various signs of the times: much talk of numbers and coefficients; a politician touting for votes; the Modugno song already mentioned; the Vigerano football team is compared to Real Madrid, but the coach is going to sell Vigerano's star player. The novel ends with Antonio reflecting that, given the sum of money involved, he probably will marry the fat, unattractive Rosa.

*Il calzolaio* sold 30,000 copies; *Il meridionale* sold about the same; and *Il maestro* was hovering around the same figure when, in the spring of 1963, at a meeting in Rome with producer Dino De Laurentiis it was decided to make *Il maestro* into a film, directed by Elio Petri and starring the popular idol Alberto Sordi and the distinguished English actress Claire Bloom. Something of Mastronardi's circumstances may be deduced from his letter of 26 June 1963 to Calvino saying that he was now going to buy a car and take driving lessons.[84] In fact, Mastronardi never became very wealthy, and after *Il meridionale* his talent seemed to dry up. In 1979 he committed suicide by throwing himself into the River Ticino. None of his books has been translated into English.

Bianciardi's *La vita agra* is an extremely funny novel, and much more of a popular success. An American translation by Eric Mosbacher, *It's a Hard Life*, appeared in 1964, published in London in 1965 (a literal translation would be *The Bitter Life*). The novel contains much name-dropping, and many quotations from different sources, including English ones, incorporated in the text. In the original Italian these were not specifically identified or acknowledged, but in the American and British editions quotations from J. P. Donleavy's *The Ginger Man* and from William Faulkner's *A Fable* are clearly identified and fulsomely acknowledged.[85]

The opening chapter is about the author's life as a research student in Rome, with much name-dropping and philosophizing. The chapter ends with an old lady in a bar shouting (what she shouts, we will discover later, was very relevant to questions about abortion which began to be asked insistently a few years later): 'This country of Jesuits. But did you know that last year there were 800,000 back-street abortions in Italy? Did you? Country of shit.' The second chapter continues this highly coloured account of bohemian life. Then there is a break, which signals clearly that here we have a modernist, or even postmodernist, novel:

> It wasn't like that, certainly, but that's how ten years ago I would have been able to think and write about the evening... at the artist's house. I would have thought and I would have written of it like an angry beatnik *[bitinicco]*, ten years ago, when Mr Jacques Querouaques [the famous Beat author is rendered in this curious way in the original Italian] had possibly not even learned how to put his trousers on. I would have, but I hadn't the time and I hadn't the money...[86]

The next page announces that he has attempted a 'linguistic mélange', including, it proves, not so much dialects from different parts of Italy, but dialects from different eras in Italian history. But he has also written, he says, a traditional novel with the traditional features. The novel, in fact, is very loosely constructed, consisting of episodes from his life and various external events (such as a mine explosion, an opportunity to express anger at callous capitalists). While he is working as a journalist, his editor tells him that he is determined to move on from neo-realism to realism—realism, he says, can be taken no further than Visconti's film *La terra trema*. The narrator visualizes the end of the modern civilization of consumerism, with sex replacing consumerism.

> The only great need would be that of coupling, of discovering the hundred and seventy-five possibilities of connecting up a man and a woman, and inventing a few more. To unite standing up, sitting down, flat out, face downwards, kneeling, crouching, upside-down. To penetrate by vagina, rectum, mouth, in writing, by telegraph, between the breasts, in the armpit, to practise irrumation, fellatio, podication, cunnilingus, and troilism.[87]

The next pages are hilarious, with a particularly funny description of the bureaucratic obstacles to joining the Communist party. He describes himself and his girlfriend as a couple of eccentrics, himself with a duffle-coat and long beard. He gets work doing translations from the English, and there is plenty of it because the Common Market is in sight and the economic miracle on the way—though, he adds, the workers 'still get a boot up the arse'. He mentions that a book he is working on is about the British prime minister Sir Anthony Eden and the Suez crisis. He says he himself wants to retell the story of the Italian miracle, hackneyed and much worked-over though it is.

> There has been a rise in production, gross and net, in the national product, both total and *per capita*, in employment, both absolutely and relatively, in the number of cars on the road and of electrical appliances in the home, in the rate for call girls, the hourly wage, tram fares, and the total number of passengers who buy them, the consumption of chickens, the discount rate, average life expectancy, average height, average health, average productivity and the average time of the Tour of Italy.
> All the averages are up, they say contentedly... There will be a flood of needs never heard of before. Those without cars will get them, and then there will be two per family, and then for each individual, and a television for everyone, two television sets, two refrigerators, two washing machines, three radios, an electric razor, bathroom scales, a hairdryer, a bidet and hot water.[88]

The lavatorial comes through at the beginning of the penultimate chapter, when he discusses his regular fifteen-minute daily bathroom visit at 11 a.m. He reads the paper, which is the opposite of the advice given by his father, who said that on such visits you must concentrate.

I respect this... When I went in after him there was a strong, virile smell, mixed with tobacco, the smell of daddy... I understood at once that only a full-grown man, with a wife and family, could smell like that.[89]

He is not capable of creating such an ambience, only the smell. The final chapter mainly concentrates on his agreeable domestic relations with his wife Anna, but ends with a complex and vulgar play on words. He is drowsily sitting up in bed waiting for Anna to join him, and is musing on a translation from English into Italian. It's a matter of a shell which has 'plopped into a parachute'. For 'plopped' he reckons he should use the colloquial Tuscan word *sbotto*, 'burst'. But what can he do with the phrase: 'The soft blob of light plopped and burst on the open page'? This time he'll use 'dripped' (like a tap)—*gocciò*—and the standard word for burst, *si ruppi*. Just like the light Anna is putting out before joining him in bed. Then the joke: 'And I too, quite soon, *sbotto e gocciò* (burst and drip).

The novels of Alberto Moravia had over decades been well known for bringing in illicit sex, but never described in any detail. The vulgar, hilarious, disrespectful treatment of sex by Mastronardi and Bianciardi was completely new, something which we can quite positively identify with changes in the wider society.

### 'Movies Have Suddenly Become More "Frank" "Adult" or "Dirty"'

The products of Hollywood could not be as frank as the products of the Grove Press. Still, *Life* magazine at the end of February 1960 was introducing its readers to 'the bold and risky world of "adult" movies', citing such recent films as *Suddenly Last Summer, Anatomy of a Murder, The Best of Everything, A Summer Place, Blue Denim, It Started with a Kiss,* and *North by Northwest* in support of its contention that there was 'a general awareness that American movies have suddenly become more "frank", "adult", or "dirty"'. But, it added, 'the populace... hasn't seen anything yet'.

> The production schedule for the months ahead bodes a full diet of films that would not have been permitted even a year ago. Two of John O'Hara's most libido-centred novels, *Butterfield 8* and *From the Terrace,* are now being shot. Director Billy Wilder's new film, *The Apartment,* is the story of a young man who rises swiftly in his firm by lending his apartment to his bosses for their dalliance after the working day... even *Lolita* will go into production this spring. Stanley Kubrick will direct filming of Vladimir Nabokov's wildly controversial novel about an older man and a 12-year-old girl touring the country motels together—surely the epitome of that ancient movie blurb, 'The Picture They Said Couldn't Be Made!'
>
> 'Why, the times are almost ripe,' Billy Wilder says sardonically, 'for a movie about a young man who has a passionate love affair with his mother. At the end he learns that she is not his mother and he commits suicide.'

*Life* did not mention a 1959 film which, as much as any, demonstrates that 'the times are changing, though not too much'—*Pillow Talk*, starring Doris Day and Rock Hudson. In visual presentation, starting with the stunningly stylized credit sequence, featuring a pair of beds and a pair of pillows, the film was very much in the slick, attention-grabbing mode which by the mid-sixties audiences had become very familiar with, but which was still quite novel in 1959; the accompanying music, however, is very much pre-rock, big-band stuff. Rock Hudson plays a successful composer of popular songs, and very old hat (i.e. mainstream forties and fifties) they are. When he and Doris Day go for what is represented as an avant-garde night out, the music is Latin American. The Rock Hudson character is a calculating seducer of women. Doris Day, playing an interior designer, shares a party line with him and is driven to distraction by his endless conversations with his various girlfriends. When the songwriter discovers that the unknown woman he shares his telephone with is in fact very attractive, he makes a clever play for her, pretending to be a naive and gentlemanly Texan. To himself he confides, 'I'd say five or six dates ought to do it.' The most famous sequence in the film has each in the bath and communicating by telephone. Originally, there was to have been the visual joke of Rock Hudson putting his hand through the split screen and into her bath; but the Hays Office, the film industry's own censor, would not allow this. Of course, Rock Hudson fails in his seduction plan, and the film ends with the couple about to marry in the traditional respectable way.

Even *Lolita* could not be described as an 'explicit' film, though, as with the other films mentioned by *Life*, the implications of the actualities of human behaviour were quite clearly spelled out. *Pillow Talk* was in the venerable tradition of the comedy of manners; the more striking characteristic of the Hollywood films of 1959 and after was the portrayal of shocking events in shabby environments, as in *Anatomy of a Murder*.

One cannot chart movements and styles in American films, as one can in French and Italian. American films were produced by a highly sophisticated industry. If they were now more 'frank', 'adult', or 'dirty' this was because the industry, like Judge Bryan, perceived that standards of taste were changing, that 'vapid boy-and-girl plots', as the *Life* article put it, aimed, it said, at bolstering family values in a time of postwar anxiety, no longer met the expectations of audiences. In France, this sub-period of 'first stirrings' coincided exactly with the self-conscious movement which can quite precisely be termed *la nouvelle vague*. This was a movement created by a group of dedicated and self-confident film makers, but one which enjoyed some commercial success only because of a convergence of certain circumstances and perceptions. Young people in France were bored with the tired entertainments patronized by their parents, and eager to welcome new artistic forms. It was a persuasive selling-point that the makers of the new wave films were themselves very young by conventional standards. Second, on the economic front there was both the perception by many producers that spending money on several low-budget features was a more rational policy than investing everything in a traditional lavish venture and the consideration that governments were prepared to offer financial support to the makers of high-quality films. Thirdly, there was already in France something of an intellectual upheaval, a questioning of traditional narrative structures, stemming from the coming onto the market of, and excited discussions about, the *nouveau roman*. The single most important shared characteristic of *nouvelle vague* films is that they represented the personal vision of one individual, the director (as distinct from being industry- or team-produced to tell stories and represent 'reality' in accordance with the conventions of the film industry). Thus such films implied the autonomy of film as an artistic form, and tended to be full of self-conscious references to other films (particularly to the Hollywood genre of the gangster film, or to films made by directors held to have exercised their own artistic autonomy, such as Hitchcock, Hawkes, and Ford). In a useful distinction which we owe to Pierre Sorlin, these were 'modern' films in contrast to the 'classic' films of Hollywood.[90] Much of their importance, therefore, lies in the realm of ideas, but they also offered sets of images, and set the style for the young people and young marrieds who were becoming the arbiters of taste as we move towards the High Sixties. Also, many were implicated in the new, franker representation of sexual matters— not, perhaps, quite so new in France since the Roger Vadim-Brigitte Bardot partnership had begun in 1955. Be that as it may, Louis Malle's *Les Amants* of 1958, in which Jeanne Moreau plays a society woman who, in turn, acts out the roles of a variety of uninhibited female characters, was widely discussed as opening up new areas of sexual frankness, and, indeed, enjoyed a *succès de scandale*. Increasing frankness, in fact, brought a reaction from the Gaullist regime, again demonstrating that we are not yet in a time of unrestrained march towards permissiveness: decrees 61 and 62 of 18 January 1961 added new powers and constraints to the censorship.[91]

In an article published in the summer of 1960 the Italian critic Morando Morandini wrote that Italian film producers in 1959 'began, timidly enough, to embark on a slightly bolder policy largely as a result of the French example. This year films are being made in Italy which two or three years ago could not have been attempted. Fear of censorship is an issue which no longer holds water...'[92] Actually, in the remarkable renaissance which Italian film-making enjoyed from 1959 into the middle sixties, two different movements coexisted. Neo-realism had been the mode of the Italian films which achieved international success in the years immediately after the war, and neo-realism emerged transformed in two films by Visconti: the historical *Il gattopardo*, the film of Giuseppe Tomasi di Lampedusa's famous novel set in the time of the Risorgimento; and *Rocco e i suoi fratelli*, a film located among the newly arrived southern immigrants in the suburbs of Milan (the date being given precisely as October 1955). But two other films announced the arrival on the Italian screen of the director as autonomous author: *La dolce vita* (1959) by the already well-established Federico Fellini, and *L'avventura* (1960) by the less well-known Michelangelo Antonioni. Taking these four films together, one could very reasonably conclude that 1959–60 was a watershed year in Italian film-making. In its particular form of realism, *Rocco* is operatic in quality and the story quickly veers away from the basics of working-class life to the boxing exploits of Rocco (Alain Delon)—none the less it played a substantial part in the process of making the working-class visible. The enduring images from *Il gattopardo* are of the cruelties, not the heroism, of war (in particular a military execution in the centre of a small town), and, above all, of the jars full of urine, an inescapable adjunct to an elegant aristocratic ball. Both films tell lucid and dramatic stories. The other two films are completely 'modern', episodic, lacking narrative structure, following through the internal thought processes of the director, evocative in mood, never making direct statements, full of striking images whose significance is not immediately fully graspable. *La dolce vita* begins with such an image: a statue of Christ being towed by an aeroplane. The central figure, Marcello (played by Marcello Mastroianni), is an alienated journalist, without faith in anything;

international star Anouk Aimée is Maddelena in the film, with all the ambiguity and resonance that name implies; we see Marcello in his disordered and apparently promiscuous personal life, and then in a kind of random odyssey, including night clubs, house parties, and an orgy, through the world of the Roman aristocracy.

*La dolce vita* could appropriately be called 'permissive'. There were no explicit scenes of sexual intercourse, but the orgy scene certainly looked thoroughly decadent, and a number of other scenes were highly suggestive. For the traditionalist Catholic there was much that seemed blasphemous. But what I want to stress first of all is the relationship of the film to the Italian class structure. Italy still had an upper class, mainly composed of industrial, commercial, academic, and political figures, but with at its heart, giving it tone, various titled elements from older aristocracies. It was this truth which *La dolce vita* thrust down people's throats. Fellini's casual, unstructured style was meant to give a kind of documentary sense of things actually happening. Thus most of the characters were given the first names of the actors who played them. The aristocrats were played by real aristocrats; altogether there were eight titled individuals in the film. The Principe Mascaldini was played by Principe Vadim Wolkonsky; Don Eugenio Mascaldini by Principe Don Eugenio Ruspoli di Poggio Suasa; and Don Giovanni Mascaldini by Conte Ivenda Dobrzensky. 'The lady in the white coat' was played by Donna Doris Pignatelli, Principessa di Monteroduni; 'the sleeping duchess' was played by Contessa Elisabetta Cini. This portrayal of a dissolute aristocratic core to the upper class gave great offence. Fellini recounted how, immediately after the gala showing in Milan, an irate aristocrat challenged him to a duel. The organization which zealously guarded the sanctity of titles, the Commissione Araldico-Geneologica, censured the eight aristocrats who had taken part in the film. The class issue was openly addressed in the Catholic journal *Osservatore Romano* of 14 February 1960, which declared that the film narrowed things down to one question: 'Is it true or not true... that among the Roman nobility and the rich there shine out examples of charity and generosity, as in all the other classes? Apparently it is not true.' The writer notes that Fellini does not film immorality and crime among what he calls 'the petty bourgeoisie and proletariat', only 'aristocratic and plutocratic; transgression'.

> *L'Unità* [the Communist party daily paper] wants to deny that Roman nobility and the rich do provide examples of charity and generosity apparent in hospitals, orphanages, refuges, schools, colleges, which carry the names of benefactors and noble families, who are celebrated also in the names of the streets in our city...[93]

The writer, it may be noted, quite openly recognizes the existence of a very stratified class structure, and to that extent might be said to be confirming the image presented by Fellini. The phrase 'Roman nobility' is also noteworthy; the heart of the aristocracy is seen as being centred on the Eternal City. The defence of the 'nobility' and 'rich' is highly paternalistic. Those who said that Italy of the monarchy and Mussolini, of the interwar years, still lived would seem to have had a point. The association of Fellini with the Communist paper *L'Unità* is significant. All in all this is a potent, and representative document showing how *La dolce vita* was (rightly) perceived as an attack on the decadence and, more important, continued existence of the old upper class. A powerful class, too, in its association with its industrial and commercial elements, most of whom were also very hostile to the film. A group of leading industrialists were among the first of many to call for the film to be banned and for all copies to be sequestrated.

*La dolce vita*, and the reactions it aroused, have, then, to be considered first of all with respect to the question of class. However, there is no doubt that much of the fuss concerned 'moral' issues, what were seen as sexual looseness and degeneracy, irreligious behaviour and blasphemy. The ubiquitous Vittorini declared the film to be deeply moral and 'profoundly Catholic': it was not, he said, advocating promiscuity, but condemning the failure to maintain the sanctity of sex; it was posing deep questions about Catholic behaviour and belief.[94] One influential Catholic publication—the voice of measured judgement—recognized 'the fundamental poetic sincerity of Fellini in his portrait of this vicious and empty life'.[95] But there can be no question that Catholic organizations were among the most eager in calling for the film's seizure and banning. And protests came not just from professional guardians of the faith but from ordinary lay members, one of whom protested in *Osservatore Romano* (5 March 1960) about: the long opening sequence with 'the statue which is flown over a terrace on which several women who are almost completely undressed are sunbathing', which, he said, 'is a grave offence against the symbols of the faith'; the long scene 'which pretends to present an apparition of the Madonna'; the scene with Anita Ekberg dressed up in the clothes of a priest.

Fellini made one other acute observation of contemporary Italian society. While in Britain the glory days of the illustrated magazine were now over (*Picture Post* ceased publication in 1957), Italian illustrated magazines—such as *Epoca* and *Panorama*—were becoming more and more important (and, indeed, I have made extensive use of them in writing this book), as also were the photographers who supplied them with their main raw material. The cast list for *La dolce vita* features a character Paparazzo, immediately followed by three more characters who are simply identified as 'second photographer', 'third photographer', 'fourth photographer'. In the film Paparazzo and his rivals are featured as intrusive, sensation-seeking, and generally a confounded nuisance to ordinary citizens. 'Paparazzi' quickly became an international term for intrusive newspaper and magazine photographers.

Before general release, *La dolce vita* had two gala premières, first in Rome, and then in Milan, premières attended by the very class Fellini was attacking, and for whom ticket prices were very high. The Rome première passed reasonably uneventfully. At the Milan première another aristocrat spat on him, and then screamed at him, 'Disgraceful, disgraceful!' The film had been interrupted by members of the audience shouting: 'It's contemptible, it's filth, it's lies', followed up, intriguingly, by 'Viva Italia'. One man complained later that at the orgy scene, his wife had got up and left, disgusted. As the cinema emptied people shouted at Fellini, 'Your film is disgusting!', and, again very revealingly, 'Communist!' Among the many celebrities present was the diva Maria Callas; although she made no comment, it was said that she appeared to have been scandalized by the film. But Fellini also recorded that a woman stopped him at the exit: 'On behalf of Milan, I am ashamed of the reception given to your film.' This and the many shouts of appreciation Fellini said compensated him for the generally bad reception. Of the torrent of telephone calls and telegrams which followed, there were, he claimed, more in favour of the film than against it. However, when Marcello Mastroianni popped into a bar to make a telephone call 'he was recognized by two characters standing by a luxury motor who shouted at him, "coward, vagabond, idler, communist!" '[96]

*La dolce vita* broke all box office records. Questions were raised about the film in parliament, where again there were many calls for it to be banned. Obviously many factors, and counter-factors, contributed to the enormous commercial success. Without doubt, many ordinary Italian people were shocked by the film, some enjoying the experience, others being outraged. Probably as many were confused by it; but the fact was that it was a film people felt they had to see—not just intellectuals, but everybody. The confused nature of some of the responses to *La dolce vita* is most strikingly illustrated in that of the state broadcasting corporation, RAI: it refused to broadcast *music* from the film.[97]

The main protagonist in *L'avventura* is a young woman, Claudia, who, as played by Monica Vitti, comes over as a strong and sympathetic character. Her best friend, Anna, played by Lea Massari, has a sexual relationship with Sandro, played by Gabriele Ferzetti, but refuses to marry him. Early in the film Anna and Claudia go together to Sandro's gorgeous flat on the tiny Tibertina island in the middle of the Tiber. While Claudia waits in the street outside, Anna suddenly makes a passionate assault on Sandro. 'But your friend is down there, waiting for you,' Sandro protests feebly. 'She'll wait,' says Anna coldly. As they go into a clinch, there is a cut to Claudia pacing up and down outside. Anna's father is a diplomat, and it is clear that she and Sandro, and the various friends who now go off on a yacht trip to a desolate volcanic island off the west coast, belong to the same upper class as is featured in Fellini's film. Claudia, who accompanies them, seems rather out of place, much more full of life and joy than the others, who are constantly fractious. We learn late in the film that she comes from a poor background. Again class, and the continuing power, but increasing decadence, of the upper class is an issue. On the island, Anna disappears; the rest of the film ('the adventure') concerns the fruitless search for her. Claudia takes it very seriously, and is determined to follow up every lead which the police come up with. Sandro simply tags along, supine rather than predatory. She tries to reject him several times, but he simply clings. Following a particular lead, they end up in Noto in Sicily.

Antonioni, it should be stressed, was not concerned to present a well-made story: his concern is with the reactions of the characters, which he attempts to observe dispassionately. There is an empty factory and a deserted town, then the bustling town of Noto. The contrasts between Rome, at the beginning of the film, the desolate island, Noto and Sicilian seascapes are very striking. 'In this film', as Antonioni himself put it, 'the landscape is a component of primary importance.'[98] Despite herself, Claudia feels herself physically drawn to Sandro. It transpires that he had once been a highly creative architect, but had given that up for the much more lucrative accounting job of providing estimates for architectural projects: Sandro, the main upper-class protagonist, is to be seen as decadent in this respect as in his readiness to exploit every sexual opportunity without apparently showing any real passion or commitment.

The scene which some critics were to characterize as one of the most erotic ever filmed is headed in the screenplay 'The Road to Noto and Abandoned Village'. Their car stops and

Sandro and Claudia get out. The screenplay then runs as follows:

> She turns to look at Sandro and it is she who kisses him. When they break apart, they stretch out on the grass. Sandro begins again to kiss Claudia, once, twice, three times, violently.
> Mix.
> Claudia lazily awakens from the embrace in which sleep had gathered her up... they are both a little dishevelled. They begin to move but only to take up more comfortable positions. Meanwhile, languorously, she utters little feminine moans.[99]

That's it. Once again it's a case of sex with all the clothes on (even if a little dishevelled). But certainly there can be no question as to the enormous sexual charge Monica Vitti puts into what is really quite a short scene. The last sequences of the film take place at an elegant weekend party. Claudia has become so involved with Sandro that she recognizes that, despite herself, she now hopes that Anna will never be found. Sandro, it is clear, will not go back to being an architect, but will continue to provide his remunerative estimating service for his powerful boss. Claudia goes early to bed and comes down the following morning to find that Sandro has been unable to refuse the offer of a casual sexual encounter, and is stretched out on a couch with the woman he has picked up (both again fully clothed!). The final scene takes place out of doors. Sandro is on a bench, slumped in guilty gloom. It is Claudia who makes the gesture of forgiveness, touching his hair as the film ends. She might seem to be the conventional put-upon loving woman, but in this deeply moving conclusion we see her once again as the individualist, the person capable of making decisions, the noble figure in contrast to Sandro who does little more than let things happen to him.

In their different ways all four films were quite strong meat, though *Il gattopardo* and *Rocco e i suoi fratelli* did not raise such storms as the other two, and *L'avventura* was marginally less controversial than *La dolce vita*. *Rocco e i suoi fratelli* was first shown at the Venice film festival, and then premiered at the Capitol, Milan, on 14 October 1960, when there was nothing like the protests which had accompanied the showing of *La dolce vita;* nevertheless it was actually the authorities in Milan who took it upon themselves to impose a local ban on the film. The situation at national level is fairly straightforward. In June 1960 the minister responsible for public entertainments sent a letter of bitter complaint to the president of the board of film censorship. Publication of the letter was followed by a massive press debate. In an article of typically Italian opacity entitled 'Cinema, Morals and Liberty', the intellectual journal *Il Contemporaneo* based its case for complete freedom for Antonioni, Fellini, and Visconti on what it saw as critical changes in the relationship between men and women.

> in our country this relationship is in a phase of great, and sometimes rapid, transformation. From that there follows, naturally, disequilibrium, contradiction, bitter conflict, with respect to which we demand for the artist the right to investigate and to represent, the right to contribute to a more explicit awareness of problems which for so long have

been regarded as taboo by the official morality of our country; and so we claim the right to experience, the work of these artists [Antonioni, Visconti, Fellini, etc.], and to criticize and discuss them, and also eventually perhaps to reject them. It is not with censorship or repression that one corrects the substance of things, but, on the contrary, only with free discussion. Giving space to these new themes, the arguments, these new areas of social investigation is exactly what our ruling class fears so much.[100]

The upshot was a new censorship law of 21 April 1962 directed towards banning films 'offensive to good custom, by the inclusion of elements contrary to common feelings of modesty and decency, tending towards disturbing ordinary morality and the institution of the family…'; also to be banned were films encouraging suicide, criminal activities, or disturbance of public order. A special section governed films which could not be shown to those under 18 and therefore could not be repeated on television. In many sections of Italian society notions of what was 'proper' were much stronger than in Britain or America; thus the censorship was not necessarily at variance with important parts of popular opinion. That these are, as in America, years of struggle between traditionalism and permissiveness, is brought out by the way in which a number of films (including *Rocco, L'avventura* and *La notte),* even if accepted by the national censorship, could be subject to local bans. While censorship was being relaxed in America and Britain, then, it would appear that it was being tightened up in Italy as well as in France. Undoubtedly the situation in France and Italy was different from that in America and Britain, and decisive changes in official morality had to wait a few more years. At the same time, however, it has to be noted that the would-be tightening of the censorship was brought about by the greater explicitness in certain major films, and the struggle in fact continued to be a very public one, especially in Italy, where Antonioni proceeded with further modernistic experiments in *La notte* (1960) and *L'eclisse* (1962), as did Fellini with *8½* (1963).

In all four countries the press, and sometimes television, commented on the changes taking place in novels, films, and censorship, but in a detached, and sometimes critical way, rather as with the commentaries on the new popular music. Despite the satire boom, it cannot be said that permissiveness had yet made any great inroads into the general correctness, not to say stuffiness, of press and television.

## The Explosion of Art

Artists have never set out simply to give a direct representation of the world around them. They have always been governed by certain conventions, or 'schemata' (the term was coined by the distinguished art historian E. H. Gombrich in his famous book *Art and Illusion),* these schemata changing from era to era. Throughout most of the history of Western art, paintings were consciously composed in the studio—though Constable and Turner at times, and then, most particularly, the Impressionists, with their desire to capture exactly the play of light, came closest to trying to capture a direct representation of nature. But clearly the Western tradition up to and including the Impressionists did involve the convincing representation of real scenes, real objects, real human beings. Since the late nineteenth century the arts (literature and music, of course, as well as painting and sculpture) have been dominated by a different tradition, that of Modernism, itself based on the conviction that a new era of cataclysmic change demands a new art, and that instead of merely echoing 'reality', art should create a separate 'reality' of its own. Among the characteristics this new art may display are: *(a)* a rejection of mimesis (imitation of the 'real' world), representationalism (direct representation of the 'real' world) and figurism (direct representation of figures and objects); *(b)* the explicit and self-conscious recognition that the arts are an artificial convention or game, consisting of words on a page, paint on a canvas, etc.; and *(c)* the deliberate presentation of often shocking disruptions of the order, sequences, and harmonies of traditional forms. The great era in which almost all the basic forms of Modernism in art were laid out came before the First World War. Particular periods or decades since have attracted particular attention for specific developments—the growth of Surrealism in the interwar years, for instance.

For a proper understanding of what was novel and what was derivative about sixties art, attention must be given to the movement known as Dada, a deliberately meaningless term for what was at first intended as a kind of 'anti-art', a protest against the corrupt and complacent society out of which the horrific slaughter of the First World War had emerged. Early members were Jean Arp, Francis Picabia, and Man Ray. Particularly important are Marcel Duchamp, who had anticipated Dada with his exhibition of 'ready-mades' before the First World War (and, most notoriously, his presentation in New York in 1915 of a urinal as *'Fontaine* by R. Mutt'), and Kurt Schwitters, who used ordinary scraps from urban life (bus tickets, torn newspaper, cartons, broken bits of wood or metal) found in the street outside his home in collages or relief montages. More, perhaps, than any Modernist forms so far, Dada questioned the very nature of art itself, being, in that sense 'conceptual'. Duchamp was also, with the Russian constructivist Naum Gabo, a pioneer of kinetic art (three-dimensional structures with moving elements); in interwar America, Alexander Calder was an enthusiastic protagonist of this art form.

So, how important are the 1960s? A few years ago (to help finance the research for this book) I ran a weekly seminar in a small American college on 'Society and Culture in Western Europe since 1945'. As a basic art history text book I used Edward Lucie-Smith's *Movements in Art Since 1945*.[101] This illuminating and reliable book contains 249 reproductions of works of art: I decided to offer my class a rough and simple statistical analysis concerned with the significance of the 1960s, in the eyes at least of this distinguished art historian. In order not to load things too much in favour of 'the sixties', as I have defined them, I limited my search to the fourteen years 1958–70, and excluded all works, even though produced within the period, if the artists concerned had established reputations which had clearly culminated well before 1958 (thus I excluded paintings by Magritte, the Belgian Surrealist, Rothko, the American abstract expressionist, and David Smith, who in the 1950s brought abstraction into sculpture, first producing 'drawings in metal', then assemblages of quite large chunks of metal).[102] I hesitated long over Victor Vasarely, born as long ago as 1908, but eventually included him since his optical works only began to attract attention at the beginning of the sixties. I then compared the total I arrived at for these fourteen years with the totals for the fourteen years 1945-57 and the thirteen years 1971-83.

Subsequently I divided the 'sixties' total between the six years 1958–63 (our present concern) and the seven years 1964–70 (dealt with in Chapter 7). Of course, there may have been a number of artificial constraints on Lucie-Smith's selection. As a kind of cross-check, accordingly, I did a similar simple analysis of the paintings reproduced in the catalogue for the Tate Gallery exhibition, *Forty Years of Modern Art 1945–1985*, held in 1986. The results are shown in Table 4.2.

**Table 4.2**

|  | Lucie-Smith | Tate Gallery |
|---|---|---|
| Pre-1918 | 3 | n.a. |
| 1945–57 | 61 | 25 |
| 1958–70 | 137 | 35 |
| 1958–63 | 63 | 21 |
| 1964–70 | 75* | 15* |
| 1971–83 | 32 | 20 |
| Excluded from survey | 16 | 6 |
| TOTAL | 250 | 77 |

\* Including cover picture.

The Tate Gallery catalogue does not quite give the overwhelming weighting to the 'sixties' that is apparent in Lucie-Smith; none the less the broad impression is the same. Probably because there is a slight orientation towards British painting, the Tate Gallery catalogue privileges the period I have labelled 'the first stirrings of a cultural revolution'. There is nothing magical or conclusive about these figures, but they do give grounds for maintaining that (always within the broader contexts of the long-term development of Modernism) the sixties was a period of important artistic innovation, and for referring to the years 1958–63 as ones of 'art explosion'.

Within Modernism there are many separate 'isms', individual works of art, of course, often manifesting several different 'isms'. The explosion I am speaking of came about when certain developments out of older movements, together with some of the more recent movements, came to a kind of climax, when certain movements seemed to cross-fertilize each other, and when some completely new movements and positions emerged. Throughout this book I lay stress on the unprecedented level of international cultural exchange, beginning in the late fifties and accelerating thereafter; but it is important to be aware that sometimes remarkably similar art movements could start in different countries without there ever having been any direct influence of the art of one country upon the other. Even within our quite brief period there is a great profusion of labels; some artists liked to see themselves grouped under a particular identity; others wished to assert how different they were from fellow artists. There is the matter of an artist's own personal talent; there is the matter of the other factors, institutional and accidental, which enable him or her to establish a reputation: for the younger artists in Britain, postwar educational change and the central role of the art schools were institutional factors of particular importance (and ones which lie behind many of the other cultural developments of the sixties). Often a reason for artists binding together in schools (in a different sense of the word) or groups was that this enabled them to get their work shown in a group exhibition. Otherwise, much depended upon the preferences and market calculations of privately owned galleries. However, it was critical to the kind of success which results in an artist being featured in a work like that of Lucie-Smith, or represented in a retrospective exhibition, that an artist manages to get his or her work purchased by public galleries, municipal or national. With respect to subsidized public galleries prepared to purchase contemporary works, Europe (and for once this included Britain) was in advance of America. But the United States did have some very wealthy privately funded public galleries, some of them (such as the Albright Knox Gallery in Buffalo) following very avant-garde purchasing policies; and both under the New Deal policies of the 1930s and during the Second World War, some small, non-profit-making galleries were set up: the Richmond Arts Centre across the bay from San Francisco was a famous example. With the advent of the Kennedy administration, the new Secretary of Labor Arthur J. Goldberg proposed a six-point partnership for the arts, declaring: 'we must come to accept the arts as a new community responsibility... alongside the already accepted responsibilities for health, education, and welfare.'[103]

The most important international centres for the production and sale of new art were New York, launched on the migration of artists from Hitler's Europe, and Paris, now feeling its traditional eminence to be under threat from this new transatlantic rival. The dominant 'ism' in New York at the end of the war was abstract expressionism (including what at the time was often referred to as action painting—important figures are Rothko, Gorky, and Pollock); later developments are sometimes described as post-painterly abstraction, colour-field painting, and/or hard-edge abstraction. In the mid-1950s a rather different type of art, associated particularly with Jasper Johns (b. 1930) and Robert Rauschenberg (b. 1925), began to emerge, initially referred to as neo-Dada or, in some of its aspects, as Junk Art. Johns's illusionistic painting of such familiar objects as the American flag or his bronze replicas of beer cans conjured up memories of Marcel Duchamp and his ready-mades. Rauschenberg produced what he called 'combine painting' in which a painted surface is combined with various found objects; sometimes these became three-dimensional structures. This time memories were stirred of the collages and assemblages in which in the 1920s Kurt Schwitters (usually catalogued as a Dada artist) incorporated fragments of a variety of materials found in the street. Modern movements have often involved a range of modes of expression: poetry, music, and drama, for example, as well as painting and sculpture. Rauschenberg had long been associated with the Merce Cunningham Dance Company, performing, as well as designing props and scenery. In common with other neo-Dada artists of the period he was also influenced by the American avant-garde composer John Cage, who saw art as intended to 'unfocus the spectator's mind, not something closed and apart, but to make the spectator more open, more aware of self and environment'. This was not a new notion, even in traditional art; but we will see it as an increasingly strong impulse behind many of the movements in art and multi-media activities which burgeoned in the sixties. A number of 'happenings' were organized in the 1950s, culminating in Allan Kaprow's *18 Happenings in 6 Parts*, presented in 1959 at the Reuben Art Gallery in New York. Another artist of the mid-fifties who came to be included in the broad movement soon to be known as Pop Art was Ray Johnson (b. 1927) who produced his famous portrait in collage form of *Elvis Presley* in 1955 and of *James Dean* in 1958.

166

On the whole the American abstract expressionist painting of the immediate postwar years was spurned by Paris, and had little or no influence on continental Europe; it did however—partly through the London exhibition of 1956, *Modern Art in the United States,* whose final room was devoted to abstract expressionism—affect a number of British artists, most importantly Alan Davie (b. 1920), a product of the Edinburgh College of Art. In Paris the great giants of twentieth-century art, Picasso, Braque, Matisse, and the Spaniard Miro, still held sway. Among the emerging middle generation of French artists the main 'isms' were *art informel,* a *mélange* of various Modernist styles boasting a lack of formal structure, and *tachisme,* featuring bold, thick blocks of colour in which occasionally vaguely representational elements could be discerned. The leading figure in this generation was Jean Dubuffet: he sometimes described his form of *art informel* as *art brut,* to encompass his fascination with the primitive, including children's art and graffiti; he is particularly noted for the way in which he explored the possibilities offered by different kinds of materials and surfaces. It is this characteristic which distinguishes the best Italian work of the postwar period, particularly that of Alberto Burri, whose importance, as both precursor of and participant in the movements of the sixties, it seems to me, has not always been sufficiently recognized. Burri was a doctor, taken prisoner by the Americans while serving in the Italian army: it was while in a prison camp in Texas that he first began to paint in 1944. He made use of sacking and old rags, explaining that these materials reminded him of the blood-soaked bandages he had seen in wartime—though unrelentingly abstract, his works were intended to convey a deep sense of anguish. However, they impress too by the sheer aesthetics of their appearance: one is struck, as Lucie-Smith so acutely puts it, by 'their good taste, their easy sensuousness'.[104] The other Italian who calls for mention is Lucio Fontana, celebrated across the postwar years for the series of paintings, each one nearly always called *Spatial Concept,* of all-white canvases with slashes in them.

A number of individual British artists (most notably Francis Bacon and the sculptor Henry Moore—utterly different in their artistic aims and output) achieved international renown in the postwar years, but the first completely innovative *collective* development was the emergence of Pop Art in the middle fifties. British Pop Art sprang from two very different sources, the one organized and intellectual, the other personal and inspirational. The intellectual element came from a coterie of artists and critics, including Eduardo Paolozzi (b. 1924 to an Edinburgh family of Italian ice-cream merchants), Reyner Banham (architectural historian, critic, and journalist), Lawrence Alloway (art critic), and Peter and Alison Smithson (both architects), who, calling themselves the Independent Group, were from 1952 holding meetings at the recently formed Institute of Contemporary Art (ICA)—itself an important institutional agent in transmitting avant-garde art to a broader and younger public. The preoccupation of the Independent Group was with the consumer goods, mass communications, and urban lifestyles so manifest in the America of the time, though scarcely yet present in Britain. In 1956 the group organized an exhibition at the Whitechapel Art Gallery (henceforth an important venue for introducing new ideas in art) entitled 'This Is Tomorrow', an exhibition as much about the artefacts of American urban culture (which is what the organizers meant by 'pop') as it was about representations of, or artistic references to, that culture (what came to be known as Pop Art). In the entrance, however, was what is often regarded as the prototype British Pop Art painting, reproduced also as a catalogue illustration and poster for the exhibition: *Just What Is It That Makes Today's Homes So Different, So Appealing?* by Richard Hamilton (b. 1922). Contrary to the impression which may be derived from the frequent reproduction of this seminal work, it was quite a small (26 × 25 cm) collage on paper, featuring cutouts of a male body-builder (represented as holding a giant lollipop, with POP written on it), and of a nude female pin-up; there are also representations of a television set, a tape recorder, a vacuum cleaner, a Ford motor company crest, a teen magazine, and a cinema. The new art, Hamilton declared a year later, should be characterized by 'popularity, transience, expandability, wit, sexiness, gimmickry and glamour; it must be low-cost, mass produced, young and Big Business.'[105]

The spontaneous, and much more youthful, element came from a group of students at the Royal College of Art. At the time of the 'This Is Tomorrow' exhibition, Peter Blake (b. 1932) was in the final year of his postgraduate studies when he painted *Children Reading Comics*, described in the Royal Academy Pop Art exhibition of 1991 as 'typical of his approach in its affectionate acceptance of popular art forms and its nostalgic recreation of a moment from his own youth'.[106] In general, Blake's art 'combined folk art styles such as fairground painting with imagery drawn both from Victoriana and from his idols among his contemporaries, such as pop singers, pinups, and film stars'.[107] Meantime, older fellow student Joe Tillson (b. 1928) was beginning to produce his distinctive toy-like painted constructions. A third RCA student, Richard Smith (b. 1931), shared a studio with Blake during 1957–9. Smith embodies international cultural exchange, and the elements of still-enduring American cultural hegemony. He actually went to America in 1959, thus coming directly into contact with such artists as Jasper Johns. Smith produced work which was much more abstract than that of Blake and Tillson, but often incorporating references to cigarette packaging and the colour photography of glossy magazines.

In the movements and 'isms' of modern art, critics and publicists have often played conspicuous roles (the analytical, the explicit, the reflexive are noteworthy characteristics of cultural movements in the sixties, from the French *nouvelle vague* at the beginning of the decade to 'art and language' at the end of it). On 27 October 1960 the critic Pierre Restany brought together a number of established artists in Paris to form the *Nouveau Réalistes*.[108] The founder-members of the group were Arman (it is quite common for French cultural figures to identify themselves by a single name), Raymond Hains (b. 1926), Yves Klein, Martial Raysse, Daniel Spoerri (b. 1930), Jean Tinguely (1925–91), Jacques de la Villeglé (b. 1926) and the Italian Mimmo Rotella (b. 1918); these were subsequently joined by César (b. 1921), Niki de Saint-Phalle (b. 1930), and Christo (b. 1935). Restany declared the aims of the group to be purely sociological (an interesting anticipation of one of the things Georges Perec was to say about *Les Choses*, the 1965 novel to which we shall later give detailed attention); theirs was an art concerned with the reality of the new urban environment. This concern expressed itself in two distinct ways: those who separated themselves into a subgroup of *affichistes* created their pictures out of layers of torn posters; most of those to whom the term *nouveau réaliste* is generally applied produced three-dimensional creations out of various objects found in consumer society (thus showing considerable resemblance to one branch of independently developing American Pop Art). The works produced by the *affichistes* are known as *décollages,* a form of artistic representation which actually goes back to the early

168

Cubists before, and the Dadaists during, the First World War. Among the most striking are those by Rotella. *Il Punto e Mezzo* (136 x 184 cm) of 1962 consists of a tattered poster advertising the famous Turin vermouth, *Punt e Mes,* with pieces of older posters showing through, and the actual name of the drink almost obliterated by squares of officially stamped brown paper which has been pasted on top; the picture is dominated by the dramatic commercial art image of a complete sphere and a half sphere. The title of the picture is correct Italian for 'one-and-a-half points'; the original vermouth was created in a Turin café famous as a centre for trading in stocks and shares—*punt e mes,* in Turin dialect, refers to one-and-a-half points as in the movement of stocks and shares. *Viva America* (décollage on canvas, 85 x 89 cm) of 1963 uses one complete and about a quarter of another identical poster of a bust of John F. Kennedy against an American flag, both posters being a little tattered, and Kennedy's head being partly obscured by another brown paper overlay. The largely obscured words on the original poster are in Italian, so, apart from any other meanings, the work is making a left-wing protest against American interventionism in Italian politics (on behalf of the Christian Democrats and their allies and in opposition to the Communists).

Although the group had no organic connection with American art movements, references to America are frequent. Among the three-dimensional works were what Arman called his *poubelles* (dustbins), which were Plexiglas containers filled with discarded objects: a famous one of 1961 is called *Jim Dine's Poubelle,* and contains former possessions of the American artist. Arman also produced *Accumulations,* large numbers of one particular type of object contained in various kinds of container: *Madison Avenue* (1962) is a collection of stylish high-heeled shoes. Among the *nouveau réaliste* productions which today can be found collected together in the Pompidou Centre, attention is inevitably drawn to the large constructions by Niki de Saint-Phalle. *Crucifixion* (1963) is described as consisting of 'various objects on painted polyester'. It is a vast, vulgar doll, suspended in crucifixion position, revealing a great mass of pubic hair. One is reminded of the 'blasphemy' of Fellini. The fascinating and wittily eccentric sculptures of Jean Tinguely are contrived out of all sorts of junk. *Nouveau réalisme,* like the first Pop Art, is a direct comment on the consumer society already well established in America, and now beginning to be established in Western Europe. While the first British and American work seems to range from deep affection to neutral comment, the French (and Italian) work seems to move very quickly from neutral comment to strong implied criticism—of, at the very least, overproduction, waste, and conspicuous consumption. Tinguely's malfunctioning and functionless machines (an important one of 1960 being titled *Homage to New York)* are surely a satirical commentary on faith in the new technology and the systems approach (both of which the British Independent Group genuinely admired). Rotella had been around for quite a long time, and was anyway associated with the Paris New Realists. Just beginning to emerge in Italy itself was one of the most innovative of all sixties artists, Michelangelo Pistoletto. Pistoletto put together assemblages of mirrors, and life-size photographic figures, the mirrors amplifying the composition in various ways, not least of which was the incorporation of the spectator himself or herself. Obviously such a construction will contain many meanings, but in so far as the photographic images are of contemporary people in contemporary fashion, Pistoletto joins, at least tangentially, with the other artists I have been discussing here, commentating on contemporary society in its most blatant consumerist aspects, and on the new mores and fashions.

Yves Klein died in 1962 at the age of 34. Jazz musician and judo expert as well as painter, he is most important as publicist, as creator of some highly dramatic action paintings (he used a flame-thrower, and also the action of rain on prepared canvases), and as sponsor of some highly distinctive happenings. He belongs utterly to the world of neo-Dada, of anti-art, rather than to that of *Nouveau réalisme*. His most famous creations were the *Anthropométries* (1959–61), when he had twenty musicians play his own *Monotone Symphony*, a single note held for ten minutes, alternating with ten minutes' silence, while naked girls smeared with blue paint flung themselves on a canvas spread on the floor. The ceremony was filmed (and could be viewed at the fascinating Yves Klein retrospective exhibition held at the Hayward Gallery in London in 1995). Rivalling Klein in extremism was the Italian Piero Manzoni (1929–68). I mentioned the lavatorial element in Bianciardi's *La vita agra*. Manzoni, who experimented with body art, performance art, and conceptual art, is most notorious for his series of tins of his own excrement: *Merda d'artista* (1961).[109]

The Paris New Realists were established artists before ever they came together in the new group which was to be so important in sixties art. As a force in the world art scene, London and Britain still came well behind both Paris and the United States. But now developments began to take place analogous to those in rock/pop music: American influences of various sorts were still definitely present, but more and more receding into the background, while specifically British— and, to a considerable degree, provincial British—innovation came more and more into the foreground. The dominant note was of furious experimentation, of several different 'isms' being pursued simultaneously, and of the merging of styles; colour-field abstraction, for instance, moved into what had formerly been thought of as 'sculpture'; figurative elements begin to show themselves in what appeared to be abstract painting. Special exhibitions succeeded each other with almost bewildering rapidity, accompanied by what, for Britain, was unusual media attention to avant-garde art, and by policy statements often incomprehensible and sometimes meaningless (as artists using words to be reflexive about visual works frequently are). In 1959 Richard Smith joined Robyn Denny and Ralph Rumney in organizing the 'Place' exhibition at the ICA, displaying large works which were directly derivative from American colour-field abstraction. The group were radical in that they hoped to bypass the dealer system through organizing these exhibitions on their own, and also in that they invoked the principles of the French Situationist movement (Dadaist, anti-consumer society, revolutionary). The effect of the exhibition itself was largely sensuous, described thus by Frances Spalding: 'Large, human-sized canvases of standard-ized dimensions and colours (red, green, white and black) were arranged to form corridors and vistas. The intention was to create a total environment, to give the visitor the sensation of being inside a space generated by the colours.'[110] Denny organized two further 'Situation' exhibitions in 1960 and 1961.

Much more important, and much more genuinely innovative, was the 'Young Contemporaries' exhibition of student art held early in 1961, which introduced what must really be called post-Pop Art, much more varied than the original Pop Art and much more open to

170

influences outside Pop strictly defined. The use of the term 'young', as I noted at some length in Chapter 3, depends very much upon the activity involved. These were young adults, not teenagers, but they were younger than any of the New Wave writers, apart from Shelagh Delaney, and really not much older than the Beatles and other rising rock/pop stars. After music, it was the art world which demonstrated most clearly that this was an age in which opportunity lay wide open to the young. Among the young artists were Derek Boshier and David Hockney, both born in 1937, and Patrick Caulfield, born in 1936—on average, thus, just under 25 years old at this time. In the main Caulfield and Boshier, in slightly different ways, took their images from contemporary consumer society, but in a manner which is both witty and clearly deeply critical of that society. *First Toothpaste Painting* (1962) by Boshier was the first in a series obviously referring to the gimmicky introduction of a new striped toothpaste, opening up issues about the manipulative nature of advertising. Hockney's freshly playful paintings, combining abstract and figurative elements, frankly reminiscent of Dubuffet, contain strongly personal and autobiographical elements, his own homosexuality being strongly hinted at in *Going to Be a Queen Tonight* (1960), *Bertha Alias Bernie* (1961), and *We Two Boys Together Clinging* (1961). Hockney with 'his dyed blond hair, owlish glasses, and gold lamé jacket'[111] became a symbol of the new, more approachable art, as the Beatles were the symbol of the new popular music. More purely Pop works (though generally of a complex and sophisticated type) continued, principally from the hands of Richard Hamilton and Peter Blake.

In 1963 the Whitechapel Gallery held the first public exhibition of the brightly painted welded metal constructions of Anthony Caro, followed in Battersea Park by the exhibition, 'Sculpture: Open Air Exhibition of Contemporary British and American Works'. The Battersea exhibition featured most notably the American David Smith, as well as Caro and some of those British sculptors who were soon to be known as the 'new generation' group (Barry Flanagan, Richard Long, and Tony Cragg). Caro (b. 1924) had gone through something of a personal revolution, and was also something of a revolutionary influence himself on subsequent British art: certainly, as a charismatic figure of the sixties he must rank with Hockney. Educated at upper-class Charterhouse and Christ's College, Cambridge, Caro subsequently studied at the (much lower-class) Regent Street Polytechnic and the (relatively classless) Royal Academy Schools. His apprenticeship as a sculptor was served between 1951 and 1953 as an assistant to Henry Moore. Caro visited the United States in 1959, where he was deeply influenced in particular by the colour-field abstractions of Kenneth Noland, by the abstract metal constructions of David Smith, and by the theories of the critic Clement Greenberg, the apostle of Abstract Expressionism as the 'post-painterly' culmination of Modernism. Back in Britain in 1960 Caro adopted a complete change of style, 'making totally abstract welded metal sculptures of an open, spatial kind which stood directly on the floor without any bases, and which were painted in brilliant colours'.[112] Striking early examples are *Twenty-four Hours* (1960), and *Early One Morning* (1962). Caro had a two-day-a-week teaching post at St Martin's School of Art, where he exerted a very powerful influence, though sometimes as much by reaction as by example.

In 1962 and 1963 the private Gallery One held exhibitions of the black-and-white optical work of Bridget Riley (b. 1931). Vasarely had long pioneered optical art, and this mode was also being developed in the United States. But, as can happen, Riley was actually oblivious to these

171

developments when, after experimenting with fairly conventional landscapes, which, however, had the distinctive feature of appearing to be disintegrating before the viewers' eyes, she produced her first purely optical work, *Movement in Squares* (1961, tempera on board). Modern art tends to demand some kind of participation by the viewer beyond that of traditional art; a very explicit demand for participation is a characteristic both of major social movements in the sixties and of much sixties art. That Riley's Op Art demanded participation is made clear in the catalogue to the 1963 Gallery One exhibition:

> We are faced with an inexorable yet almost imperceptible variation of linear elements and units. So smooth is the change that it does not allow the eye to organise the series of units into stable, larger entities in which it might linger and rest. There is a constant tug-of-war between shifting and crumbling patterns, but at a certain point this relentless attack on our lazy viewing habits peels our eyes into a new and crystal clear sensibility.[113]

With respect to what became known as 'happenings', precedence probably belongs to Klein in Paris, though I have already mentioned Allan Kaprow (b. 1927) and his *18 Happenings in 6 Parts* in New York in the autumn of 1959. These, of course, emblematize both the highly participatory nature of art and the breaking down of the distinctions between the visual arts and such other art forms as drama. Also in New York, and under the prestigious auspices of the Museum of Modern Art, there was held the most significant exhibition of the time, 'The Art of Assemblage', in 1961. In essence, assemblage abolishes the distinction between painting and sculpture. Pop Art in America now entered what is usually described as its classic phase, on the one side involving assemblages of many kinds, though most often created from the junk of contemporary society, or meticulous replicas thereof, and on the other two-dimensional works featuring advertising images, strip cartoons, and representations of the idols of popular culture. Leading figures of the latter tendency are Andy Warhol (1928–87), with his silk-screen productions of such icons as Marilyn Monroe, Roy Lichtenstein (b. 1923), with his painted simulations of the heroes and heroines from newspaper comic strips, James Rosenquist (b. 1933), using glossy billboard advertising images in such paintings as *I Love You With My Ford* (1961), and Tom Wesselman (b. 1931), with his still lifes featuring such products as Coca-Cola and Lucky Strike cigarettes and his 'Great American Nude' series. The leading figure in the 'assemblage' tendency is Claes Oldenburg (b. 1929), whose subjects ranged from junk food to consumer durables, often in gigantic scale and made of vinyl stuffed with kapok. Jim Dine staged *Car Crash* (1959–60) both as a happening and then as a permanent assemblage.[114] Another centre of American Pop Art was California, where Ed Kienholz (b. 1927) was an active promoter through the private gallery which he jointly ran. Kienholz produced assemblages of assemblages, which he called 'Tableaux', which enveloped the spectator, or through which he or she can walk. Kienholz's multiple assemblages are examples of what is sometimes referred to as 'funk art', art with such a bizarre, sick quality that it suggests overt criticism of contemporary society (essentially the *raison d'etre* of Dada, of course). This element is more characteristic of American three-dimensional Pop Art than of two-dimensional, which in the main seems to be a celebration, or else neutral recording, of contemporary American cultural practices and icons.

Much of the art I have been discussing was arresting, some shocking. One of the most alarming of the early pieces of funk art was the American Bruce Conner's assemblage *Couch* (1963), a decaying Victorian sofa on which there appears to be a rotting and dismembered corpse. There are strong elements of political protest, but these cannot really be said to be a general characteristic of this period of the first stirrings of a cultural revolution, though of course, such movements as the Campaign for Nuclear Disarmament produced powerful graphic art in support of the cause. But then, of all the complex and opaque sources historians have to make use of, the works of creative artists (including novelists) are the most ambiguous and difficult to interpret. The painting and sculpture of 1958–63, however, does make certain insistent suggestions. Affluence, consumerism, and aggressive advertising are now so pervasive that they have impinged heavily on the artistic consciousness. Sexuality—straight and gay—is openly, even brazenly, treated. Questioning and experimentation ranges over the symbols of established religion, the nature of art and its relations to society, and the materials and genres used. And, as in almost every other social and cultural (though not political) activity, a noteworthy proportion of leading practitioners are younger than ever before.

In Chapter 1 I set out sixteen distinctive characteristics of the cultural revolution which took place in the long sixties. We are still concerned only with the earliest phase of that revolution, but in this chapter we have discussed aspects of Theme 8 (developments in class relations) and of Themes 1, 2, 5, 6, 9, and 12 (new movements in film, literature and art; art as 'spectacle'; international cultural exchange; intimations of 'permissiveness' in novels and films).

# 5

# Race

T he experience of the Second World War had demonstrated that in America racial segregation was not exclusive to the South. Segregation arose whenever substantial numbers of
blacks came in contact with whites, as in the army. In the years after the war, industry in the
North and the far West (particularly California) prospered, while the southern staples, particularly cotton production, continued to decline: the result was further substantial movements of
blacks into areas formerly almost exclusively white. But it was, of course, in the South that segregation was rigidly underpinned by a variety of state and community laws; and it was in the South,
in the 1950s, that the drama-filled episodes, involving challenges to segregation, took place. The
three national bodies supporting the advancement of blacks (with whites prominent in their leadership) were all based in the North: the National Association for the Advancement of Colored
People (NAACP), the Congress of Racial Equality (CORE), and the Urban League (concerned
particularly with living and employment conditions among blacks in inner-city areas). The civil
rights episodes in the South were sporadic and isolated: the one would-be coordinating body was
the Southern Christian Leadership Conference (SCLC), organ of respectable churchgoing
blacks, strong on moral fervour and oratorical frenzy, both qualities very apparent in the public
persona of the Reverend Martin Luther King.

Black protest, black violence (there had always been white violence against blacks), and
changing relationships between blacks and whites are the central feature of American history in
the 1960s. These processes took place at different levels and in different forms; some became part
of the sixties spectacle, some remained out of the glare of public attention. In this chapter we shall
look at the way in which the relatively isolated (though in themselves important) episodes of the

fifties, largely confined to the South, merged into a powerful and often very destructive movement affecting the Union as a whole. The 'unravelling of America' thesis is predicated on the notion that there was an optimistic northern liberal consensus that segregation, and deeply rooted racial inequality, were southern aberrations which could steadily be eradicated from the American scene. The 'unravelling' came as the inadequacies of this consensus were exposed and unresolved racial turmoil came to dominate the North. But if there was optimism and consensus, they were based on ignorance; the problems were already there in the North and the West: stark truths were forcefully revealed in the later sixties, but northern whites could not in any case have averted their gaze for ever. In fact, many northern whites were just as racist as their southern counterparts; some simply felt a contempt for the South with respect to both its white and black populations; as many in the South mocked northerners as hypocrites, and gloated whenever they too became embroiled in problems of race. Finally, while the governing racial tension was undoubtedly that between Afro-Americans and white Americans, other tensions centred on Jews, native American Indians, Chinese and Japanese Americans, and Mexican immigrants. America did not unravel, though cherished illusions—about constitutional freedoms and the melting-pot that never was, for instance—undoubtedly did. Facing facts is not always pleasant and easy: *that* was the phenomenon of the sixties. That many of the worst facts remain fully in evidence today does not diminish the significance of the sixties as the time of crucial change.

Among the processes involved were: legislation, at federal, state, or community level—judicial rulings prescribing integration and proscribing segregation, and attempts to enforce these, not always (despite the occasional deployment of military force) successful; demonstrations, boycotts, and civil disobedience on the part of blacks; formal negotiation between whites and blacks through permanent community relations and a multiplicity of ad hoc committees; changes in everyday relationships (greater assertiveness, greater visibility on the part of blacks, greater tolerance on the part of whites, for instance); the intervention of activists from the North, usually but not necessarily white—freedom riders, participants in voter-registration programmes; the racist and obstructive reactions of many whites, often leading to further counter-actions. There is no lack of heroism and drama, and it is not surprising that most accounts highlight the odd dramatic victories and the tragically vicious cruelty and violence of white reaction. Where peaceful gains were ostensibly made, and indeed were felt by the blacks involved to be definite gains, they could often be hedged about by what now seem humiliating provisos and conditions.

Even the South was not a monolith with respect to race relations. Civic leaders in Maryland, Atlanta, Kentucky, and Tennessee considered themselves more civilized in such matters than the inhabitants of the 'deep' South; Mississippi, Alabama, and rural Louisiana being thought particularly unreconstructed. Memphis, on the left bank of the Mississippi, tucked into the south-west corner of Tennessee with Arkansas across the river and Mississippi to the south, heart of the 'mid-South', a commercial centre proud of its bosky parkways and absence of smokestack industry, makes a good vantage-point (typical, to begin with, of the more restrained white racism, though later falling behind the more flexible white populations in, for example, Atlanta, Georgia). The city fathers were openly boastful of what they saw as tranquil relations between the races. But Memphis was the first stopping-point for poor black agrarian workers driven off the failing cotton fields; worse, while able-bodied blacks continued northwards towards St Louis, they left their wives, children, and elderly dependants behind in the rapidly forming slums in the southern sections of the city. At the core of Memphis's ruling élite was a group of self-styled 'moderates' (their extreme racist opponents referred to them as 'a small group of self-serving moderates'), paternalistic in their attitudes towards blacks and, while largely oblivious to deteriorating ghetto conditions, much more sensitive than their fellow citizens to the protest movement and developments taking place elsewhere in the South. The genuinely civilized and tolerant spirit of many of the Memphis moderates owed much to the strong influence of Scottish Presbyterianism among many of the richer citizens.

Throughout the periods of black awakening and black activism the issues of segregation and integration in housing remained among the most intractable. Crude prejudice and the naked workings of the market continued to create a whirlwind. If a black family moved into a white neighbourhood, the value in the market of nearby white properties dropped. Whites would try to squeeze the new arrivals out, but if they failed some would take the opportunity to sell out before there was any catastrophic fall in prices. Whites moving out, together with falling prices, might encourage more blacks to move in. A mobile property market always means profits for estate agents. Sometimes the process was helped along. Whether it was or not, remaining whites began to feel under pressure. Without racial prejudice, of course, there would have been no problem. But, in the world as it was, for ordinary hard-working whites this new pressure often was a problem. In cities like Memphis whites expected black leaders to understand the problem, and looked to organizations such as the Urban League, and charities distributing food and clothing to blacks, to make sure that blacks did not move into white areas. However, one aspect of growing black self-confidence in the late fifties was that some of the more prosperous blacks did begin to move into the more desirable housing only to be found in white neighbourhoods. In 1958 this was happening in the Memphis residential area of Glen View. With the firm intention of ousting the blacks, white residents formed the Glen View Clan Inc. The Clan (the overtones were probably intended to be more of Scottish cosiness than of the brutality of the Ku Klux Klan) immediately enlisted the support, in maintaining the existing racial 'balance' (some balance!), of the Urban League, at the same time threatening that members would cut off contributions to the major Memphis umbrella charity organization, Shelby United Neighbors (SUN), which itself channelled funds to the League. In June 1958 Edwin Dalstrom, a retired business executive and prominent white leader of the Urban League in Memphis, received a letter from the Clan inviting his support, since the writers understood that he was 'opposed to Negroes disrupting long-established homes in Glen View and economic loss entailed thereby.' A hand-written letter from 'Glen View Residents' arrived at the beginning of July:

We of the Glen View Community and our friends in all sections of the city are watching with interest to see what you as head of the Urban League, can do through the League to secure the removal of three negro families on Glen View Avenue. As you know, they were settled there by underhanded, treacherous methods....

If you will put the matter squarely before your members, making clear the withdrawal of support for League from many former contributors, we believe the earnest, responsible members will put their heads together and devise some method to remove these unwanted intruders from our district.

If this cannot be done, then more citizens than ever will feel justified in with holding [sic] pledges to S.U.N.

May we hear from you at some early date telling us of the position the League takes on this matter?

Such a letter 'would do much also to eradicate the popular impression that the League is backing the NAACP'. Glen View Clan propaganda spoke militaristically, but undoubtedly sincerely, of 'the Planned Negro Invasion'.[1]

The city had set up a Race Relations Committee in 1956. A document compiled by its successor (the Committee on Community Relations) reveals the dreadful problems of those years, and remarks that it was 'a commentary on the earlier interracial climate' that some of the committee's 'white members were unwilling to meet with Negroes'. It became necessary to divide the Race Relations Committee into two subcommittees, which met separately and then negotiated through chosen delegates. The emissaries for the white and black subcommittees met frequently and gradually became the committee itself. There follows a firm indication of the explosive implications of the term 'moderate':

> The Race Relations committee had become sufficiently 'moderate' to arouse suspicion in the emotional atmosphere of 1958. When a prominent banker became its chairman, he was threatened with dismissal by his board of directors and, in the ensuing unpleasantness, the Committee itself dissolved.[2]

However, the determination of the 'moderates' is apparent in the fact that on 26 January 1959 a new Memphis Committee on Community Relations was established: 'to provide a meeting place for calm discussion and such responsible action as may be agreed upon to preserve order, under law, as interpreted by courts of competent jurisdiction and the peace, happiness and continued progress of the great and growing city of Memphis and all of its people'.[3] The omission of the term 'race' and the use of the comfortable 'all of its people' are typical of Memphis.

One of the most strongly 'moderate' (i.e., one of the most progressive) members of the original committee was the Jewish rabbi James Wax, whose private papers provide invaluable insights into the opinions and motives of committee members. With practically the sole exception of Wax, the 'moderate' members really were far from progressive, concerned above all to restore what they had perceived as 'tranquillity' before blacks had started demonstrating, and the Supreme Court had started ruling, against segregation. They were anxious not to be seen breaking the law, they were anxious for harmonious relations between whites and blacks, they must be distinguished from rabid anti-black racists, and they were willing to make some concessions, but they were deeply hostile to complete integration. 'Uncle Toms' would be an unfair epithet for the longer-established black members, but almost all of them, including the much-trusted Reverend

J. A. McDaniel, a black minister and leading figure in the Urban League, preferred (or had no choice but) to stay within the limits set by the white moderates.

Soon after the formation of the original committee in 1956 the black subcommittee produced a 'Statement of Principles'. These show how conservative and carefully selective these blacks were, and how unwilling to do anything upsetting to the prejudices of whites; but they also show the crucial encouragement that (white!) Supreme Court decisions had given to those blacks who were most anxious to avoid disruption and illegality. The first principle called for 'the maintenance of peace and tranquillity', and, striking that strong note of local patriotism which, throughout the troubles of the sixties, can never be totally discounted, applauded 'industrial and economic advance'. The second read as follows:

> However much any of us would like to reconstruct the world in his own image, any attempt to do so is unrealistic and fanciful. Decisions on the matters of race in our community cannot be good decisions or lasting ones unless honest and sincere attention is given to varying points of view. In short, the members of neither the white or Negro group can solve our problems by unilateral speaking or doing.[4]

After stating that for years they had obeyed laws to which they were opposed, because they believed in the principle of the rule of law, Principle IV continued: 'We believe that the law as interpreted by the Supreme Court should be obeyed and that our country should take steps towards compliance.' But then the next almost self-contradictory principle revealed the awful dilemma of intelligent, educated blacks wishing to make real if limited advances for their people, while operating within an environment utterly imbued with racism:

> We recognise that history, tradition, habit and folkways make it difficult for any of our citizens to accept Principle IV. We agree that any program of action must take cognisance of these factors—but we also agree that we cannot permit these factors to result in eternal delay, hedging, and avoidance. We want to move together but we feel we have an obligation to move.

The sixth principle expressed temporary acceptance of the split into two separate subcommittees based on race. The black moderates called for unification as soon as possible, not on the basis of equal rights, but rather appealing to white sentiment in arguing that this would be a means of restraining extremists (both black and white). The final principle, returning to the note of local patriotism, declares 'a planned, positive programme' necessary 'for a greater and finer Memphis'.[5]

It is easy to see how Memphis, from having been notable for having 'harmonious' race relations (of a sort) in the early fifties, became a storm-centre of black protest by the later sixties. This change, the change from a false calm, based on profound inequality, to open and honest—though alas, very violent—confrontation is very much an integral part of the story of the sixties. White moderates were anxious that there should be no open split in the white position. The chairman of the original committee, William W. Scott, vice-president of the National Board of

Commerce, was constantly trying to mediate between the conservatives and the moderates. Leading Memphis lawyer Lucius E. Burch brought all his professional skills to bear in making statements of fence-sitting opacity. On 28 May 1956, he wrote to Wax:

> In the meetings of our Committee of Moderates, I have formed the opinion that your interpretation of the word 'moderate' involves more than a yearning for a return to the status quo ante... It seems to me our committee is suffering greatly from the fact that the more liberal members are letting the more conservative members establish a quantitative superiority in argument.[6]

Burch supported the black statement of principles. A letter to the chairman a couple of days earlier seems to be expressing his hope that white members will show similar moderation: 'I have read the statement with great interest and approval. I only hope that our committee can measure up to the standard that they have set.'[7]

Two years later 'moderation' appeared to be wilting in the face of increased black activism. On 30 October 1958 Burch wrote to several of the moderates:

> The increased wave of bombings, violence, threats and demonstrations is bound to worry every thoughtful citizen. Perhaps, worse, suspicion and tension are increasing between the white and Negro citizens, and there is no present method for mutual and restrained discussion of the problems which have to be solved. There are those who believe that a large part of the trouble is to be found in the fact that the only articulate leadership which has emerged consists of the extremists of both races. There are very many Negroes who neither expect nor urge complete integration tomorrow or the day after, and there are very many white citizens who have become reconciled to the belief that the decrees of the Supreme Court of the United States can neither be ignored permanently or criticised out of existence.[8]

The re-formed committee contained the usual pillars of the Memphis moderate establishment, Burch (now chairman) and Scott, as well as Wax and the editors of the two Memphis daily newspapers, Frank Ahlgren and Edward Meeman, and the mayor, Edmund Orgill. Orgill was almost the prototype of the relaxed, friendly, rational southern moderate—not a supporter of full integration, but happy to attend social occasions with black leaders; his own private papers contain a clutch of hate letters (which he shrugged off) provoked by a newspaper photograph showing him sitting down to dinner with certain prominent blacks.[9] Most of the black members of the new committee were of the old type, but there was one new figure, younger, highly assertive in the manner of the coming generation of black leaders, not a preacher, but a highly successful lawyer, Russell B. Sugarmon. Formally Memphis was a highly religious city, though among themselves some of the white moderates derived considerable amusement from black religious fervour. On behalf of black preachers it could be said that they were often the most aware of, and most outspoken over, material deprivation in the black slums (an issue largely ignored by white moderates), and the most active in local community relations projects. One such project contacted the new committee soon after its formation, respectfully drawing attention to the appalling living conditions in a slum area in north Memphis. Burch's reactions are illuminating. To the black organizers of the local project he responded sympathetically, promising that the committee would take note of the problems. But to Wax he sent a private note: 'Jimmy, Do you know any of these people? The organisation seems to be pretty loaded with preachers.'[10]

Sugarmon was aware of the deficiencies in the black membership of the committee, anxious to get away from overly moderate preachers, and keen to secure representation for ordinary working blacks; he also (a reliable sign that we are now entering the sixties) wanted to secure a voice for black *women*. In January 1960 Sugarmon formally proposed the addition of four blacks. One was a fellow lawyer: but there was also a figure from the black lower middle class (a cashier at the black Tri-State Bank), one from the working class (a union representative from the agricultural machinery company, International Harvester), and a woman (the wife of a dentist). Wax was totally in favour of admitting the proposed new members, but the other whites were worried that they would form an activist fringe, and that the committee as a whole would then seem extremist in the eyes of white Memphis in general. Meeman at first supported Wax, but with much hesitation. It was conservative black member McDaniel who produced the most negative and the most sanctimonious reply: 'After prayerful consideration I abstain from casting my vote for them for the same reason that I would not vote for members of the white group that I felt held the same views.' This spurred a change of response from Meeman:

> Since learning the vote of J. A. McDaniel... I would like to change my vote to agree with him. I have great respect for Mac's sensitiveness to the needs of our situation and will defer to his judgement.
>
> I do think that we can later include people of little compromising disposition, both whites and Negroes, when we have made a public declaration which will make it clear that no member is bound by streams that may be represented on the committee.[11]

In fact black representation on the committee did steadily become more activist.

The first major task the Community Relations Committee set itself was the establishment of a series of working committees to study 'areas in which friction and violence may result', looking both at the problems in Memphis and at the way the issues were handled in other southern communities. The areas were: public transportation; public libraries colleges, universities, and schools; parks, playgrounds, zoos, museums, art galleries, and community centres; and housing. The second major action was to try to persuade the mayor and commissioners of the city of Memphis to increase the number of blacks in local government.

The housing report had nothing constructive to offer, but could not avoid a typically Memphian note of self-congratulation A general feeling of the Committee was that, on a comparative basis, Memphis has been rather fortunate in not having any appreciable violence or unruly disturbances in the clash of races.' The library study revealed that Memphis had a full-blown segregation policy, with one branch reserved for blacks only and all other branches for whites only. 'Special permission has been granted on occasion for Negroes to use the reference files at the Front Street Branch for research projects.' The recommendation, endorsed by the full committee, was that the Memphis Public Library should 'move toward granting an equal use of the Public Library facilities in Memphis to all citizens without distinction or discrimination, beginning at the adult level and gradually including all ages'. What was forcing the hands of whites on the committee was the intensified phase of black activism in all areas where segregation was most blatant. There were now black members of the committee (notably the Reverend H. C. Nabritt) who were ready to give open support to demonstrations by blacks. By mid-1960, after a series of blacks had been arrested for sitting where they pleased, buses were fully integrated. Demonstrations at Overton Park Zoo resulted in desegregation there by the autumn of the same year. Library demonstrations continued into early 1961, when the committee's recommendations were finally implemented.[12] Nabritt told a *Wall Street Journal* investigator: 'Every advancement we've had can be attributed at least in part to demonstrations of Mime some sort—sit-ins, marches, stay-at-homes.' The report continued:

> Reverend Nabritt is a member of a biracial committee set up on an informal basis some months ago to ease racial frictions quietly, sometimes secretly. He and other Negro leaders confirm that an agreement has been reached with merchants to desegregate downtown store facilities, eating places, restrooms, drinking fountains—on or before next Feb. 20. Memphis newspapers have made no comment on the plans, and white leaders are also keeping mum about them.
>
> The agreement to integrate store facilities was based on a compromise. The Negroes agreed to stop sit-ins during the Christmas rush and Jan. 7 sales events provided they were promised action by Feb. 20, says H. T. Lockard, state NAACP president…

After the beginning of the autumn term fourteen black students had been enrolled in formerly all-white schools; a mere three weeks previously three municipal golf courses had been desegregated; and within the previous week the Memphis Park Commission had produced a ten-year plan of 'gradual desegregation for parks and playgrounds, producing (not surprisingly) the reaction from black leaders that this was far too slow.[13]

A sort of an advance was already taking place at Memphis State University. Legally, as a result of events in the fifties, the university was bound to end its exclusion of blacks, and had indeed in the autumn of 1958 agreed to admit eight black students who had passed the entrance examination. However, the president of the university had attempted to go back even on this by claiming that he feared there would be violence if the blacks were actually admitted. The State Board of Education, accordingly, imposed a one-year delay. However, the United States Supreme Court subsequently ruled in another case that fear of violence did not constitute a legal reason for delaying integration, and the local federal court then ruled that the university must accept the students. To get at the sad, acid realities of the situation, I cannot do better than quote from the student newspaper, *Tiger Rag*, and from one of the two major Memphis newspapers.[14] Under the front page headline 'Eight Negroes Enrol as Students at MSU', and a subheading

181

noting that 'eight negroes', together with 4,800 others, had begun classes, *Tiger Rag* reported:

Last Friday MSU experienced first classroom integration. Throughout the day, several Memphis Police Patrol Cars and Private Detectives lingered in the hallowed halls and roamed over the campus. About four detectives were still observing the first week of school here Monday.

'We hope it continues to work without incident', President J. Millard Smith commented. 'We took all legal steps available to prevent it, but finally the courts said we had to do it and we hope it works out'.

General Student body attitude was one of avoiding the Negroes.

'I don't like it, but anything said or done wouldn't help matters any,' one student commented. Many had similar comments.

The Negroes were also instructed to avoid white student meeting places including the Student Center and the Cafeteria. They reportedly agreed and left the campus almost immediately after their classes which end at noon each day.

Additionally, there was a self-congratulatory editorial on the 'reserved manner' of the black students, who are described as a credit to Memphis and to the South'. Thereafter the issue disappears for some considerable time from the pages of this student newspaper.

Under the headline 'First Day of Integration at Memphis State', the *Commercial Appeal* offered an only slightly less heart rending account:

The negroes said several white students spoke to them briefly, always in a friendly manner. The whites were quoted as saying things like 'hello', and 'how are you doing?'.

Typical remarks from white students.

Joy Bailey, senior, of 3947 Graceland: 'I am not going to let it bother me. I plan to be a teacher and I can't see ruining a whole education system just to make trouble for a few Colored students.'

David Shearer, sophomore, of 4364 Ridgewood: 'I am definitely against it, but I am not going to start any trouble. I am willing to let things ride as they are.'

David Litscombe, senior, of 3788 Cardinal: 'It doesn't even concern me. They are here and that is all there is to it.'

Schedules of the negroes are arranged so that they will finish all classes by noon this first semester. They said they will go home after classes.

After classes today, the students returned to Dean Pratt's office for a question-answer session about their first day impressions.

Negroes said things went well for them. Then they bought some school materials thru student leaders who went to the book store for them. Books and materials cost an average $35.

Previously the negroes had agreed not to enter the school cafeteria or the student den. They said they would sit in a special section m Crump Stadium for football games. They said they will not take physical education or Air Forces ROTC courses.

Between classes they will use special lounge facilities -the girls to the office of Dean of Women... and the boys in the browsing room of the library.

This news story, of course, is addressed particularly to the concerns of the Memphis parents of white students: 'lounge facilities' is genteel middle American for lavatories.

Still, by early 1962 it did seem to northern observers that considerable change had taken place in the South, though against continuing hostility. The *Wall Street Journal* report I have already quoted, based on interviews 'with scores of businessmen, government officials., Negro and white leaders, students and men-m-the street in six Dixie states summed up the general situation knowledgeably:

> Though the sit-ins, freedom rides, boycotts and mass marches have churned up fresh bitterness in race relations in some communities, such as Jackson, Mississippi and New Orleans, the demonstrations more often have convinced Southern whites that the segregation fight is futile and a time for compromise has arrived...
>
> 'Most of us didn't want any part of the trouble that cities round us have been experiencing,' says a white member of a secret Macon businessmen's committee which spear-headed the integration drive

After its up-beat record of progress in Memphis, the report turned back to the more intransigent town of Macon, Georgia:

> Standing on a street corner in Macon, Barbara Brickill, a 19-year-old book-keeper who described herself as 'against integration', says bitterly: 'Negroes ought to keep their place. I know they have to improve themselves, but they don't have to eat with us to do that. And I'd hate to see my little brother have to go to school with them.' Then as an afterthought, she adds: 'I guess it's going to come sooner or later, though.'

In the deep South there was high drama yet to come. But first I must turn to the incident in Greensboro, North Carolina, which marks the start of the renewed activism of 1960. It appears that the four black first-year students of North Carolina Agricultural and Technical College who staged a sit-down at the Woolworth's lunch counter on 1 February were only faintly aware of the sit-ins elsewhere in the South in the later fifties. Local black leaders contacted CORE in New York, and representatives were sent immediately. Shortly afterwards Martin Luther King arrived. The Greensboro incident precipitated two developments. First, led by like-minded students at seven other black colleges, sit-ins began immediately to take place in other southern cities, becoming, by April, an unprecedentedly widespread and coordinated wave of black action. When we think of the sixties we think of student protests, and the students we usually have in mind are French students on the Paris barricades in 1968, or perhaps white American students at Berkeley in 1964. Yet, historically, the most important single set of student protests was that of the southern black colleges in 1960 comprising sit-ins, demonstrations, and a march of about 4,000 students on the Louisiana capital, Baton Rouge.[15] These students differed crucially from the docile (though undoubtedly courageous and desperately hard-working) black students who had gained entry to Memphis State University—very conscious of the sacrifices their parents had made, they felt obliged to accept the segregation that existed within the university in order to be sure of securing their degrees. The second development was the founding over the Easter weekend of the Student Non-violent Co-ordinating Committee (SNCC—pronounced 'snick'), very much, as the title suggests, a group of young people, though it began under the auspices of SCLC. SNCC, as a body of active staff workers, always remained limited to about 100, but was to offer a vital link with white students in the North who felt the call to play their part in the fight against segregation. The first freedom riders, two busloads of whom left Washington on 4 May 1961, consisted of young blacks and older whites of the traditional pacifist type: they were organized by James Farmer, formerly of the NAACP, who had become national director of CORE at the end of January. These first freedom riders met with the kind of ferocious brutality which was to be stamped indelibly on the imagery of the mid-sixties civil rights movements in the South. The objective of the riders in the two buses was to break the rigid segregation imposed in bus stations. Outside Anniston, Alabama, on 14 May one of the buses was destroyed by fire, and vicious mob attacks took place in Birmingham and Montgomery, where on 17 May this particular foray came to an end. It was SNCC which took the initiative in continuing the ride to Jackson, Mississippi. Some representatives of CORE and SCLC joined in. Federal support went as far as the provision of a National Guard escort; but local law prevailed in Jackson, where twenty-seven of the riders were arrested and sentenced to sixty days in prison.[16]

The freedom rides were essentially initiated from outside the South; however, in later 1961 there were signs that ordinary blacks of all ages in the most backward parts of the South were beginning to stir. Such a place was Albany, Georgia: the initiative came from two SNCC workers who, in alliance with the local NAACP and shortly involving Martin Luther King, formed the Albany Movement. King was briefly arrested in mid-December and again in July 1962, during an episode in which the police led the way in manifestations of extreme white violence. Ordinary blacks stood up well, but although, as a result of the freedom rides, the Inter State Commerce Commission had ordered the desegregation of bus and railway stations on 22 September 1961, desegregation was not in fact implemented. That summarizes much of the essence of the civil rights story at this time: white racism exposed more clearly than ever, black consciousness moving to new levels, but few, if any, real victories.

Greensboro and its sequels impinged on the sensibilities of white students in the North. Although this was the time of the formation of the SDS (Students for a Democratic Society), soon very active in the civil rights as well as the peace movement (leading figure Tom Hayden was arrested in the first Albany demonstration), many of those who took to marching, or indeed put their lives at risk by joining in the later freedom rides, were mainstream, middle-class young people. We have already encountered Memphis editor and 'moderate' Ed Meeman. Meeman was giving financial support to a Latvian American who had studied at the exclusive Phillips Exeter Academy and was now at posh East Coast Amherst College. This student had lived in the South, and shared the 'moderate' racist assumptions of Meeman and his like. His careful explanation to Meeman of a Good Friday 1960 demonstration in Washington organized by some Amherst students is therefore extremely interesting (his easiest, though not his most honest, course would have been simply to dismiss the demonstration as the work of an activist minority). One of the two main student leaders had explained the demonstrations as follows:

> My friends and my self felt that we, as students, should do something to demonstrate our sympathy and give our assistance to the Southern sit-ins... Simultaneously, the Student Council, Christian Association, and The Student Newspaper proposed a march on Washington on Friday 15, in order to show our fellow students in the South that we supported their fight for human dignity...
>
> The students who picketed were Christian, Jew and Atheist... All had withstood the censure of a large segment of the student body and many had disobeyed their parents' wishes in coming.

That statement was enclosed in the second of the two letters received by Meeman. The first, dated 14 April 1960, clearly records the anguished and contradictory emotions of a young man who feels strong ties to the South:

> Tomorrow morning Amherst College shall hit the headlines. I am very sorry I could not write sooner and forewarn you...
>
> I realise that all the students will get from your side is bitter feelings, for we are outsiders to the South. I brought up that objection when the plan was first discussed. Unfortunately I also had to concede that the Southerners will never act to improve the lot—I should not use that unfortunate cliché—of the Negro without pressure from outside. I regret very much that so much hard feeling has to be stirred up by controversies like this. I KNOW how many of you feel down there, both white and Colored. I feel that in many respects the students parading in Washington tomorrow will be trampling on your rights. But somehow I believe that something should be done to restore the dignity of the Southern Negro. And whatever is done will be painful to many people. All change is painful.

The second letter, dated 20 April 1960, contained the following:

> I feel that the important thing is the thoughts of the people involved. Although this sit-in strike business, and sympathy for the 'down-trodden' Negroes of the South is beginning to look too much like another fad that sweeps the campuses, I believe that the members who went from Amherst to Washington to sweat in the sun for eight hours while the tourists peered at them were somewhat sure that they knew what they were doing.

Well, I realise that it would be foolish for me to expect you to write about them. I don't... I have lived in the South and know very well that the situation is not as simple as many of the people like to picture it. I have expressed an open sympathy with the sincere men involved in it—but only to them personally. I have donated a little money to help them, that is all.[17]

The first student freedom rides began in the later summer of 1961. At UCLA oral testimony was recorded at the time from the eleven students who left Los Angeles on 9 August 1961 for the Houston freedom ride (they were joined by seven others in Houston itself). One recorded that he thought non-violent integration 'as much of an answer as had so far been evolved to fight the segregationists in the South, and, also, in the rest of the country'. Also, he continued, 'I felt that I didn't want to look back ten or twenty years from now and see certain milestones pass such as integration in inter state travel, and know that I could have been a part of them and yet have not made the effort to do so even though I had believed in them thoroughly.' He explained that he was very interested in going into politics, but equally was 'interested in learning more about myself'; he considered himself to be 'not really left wing', but perceived his central concern as being with civil liberties and civil rights; he was a dedicated follower of the recently elected Kennedy administration.[18] In Jackson, segregation with respect to inter-state travel was centred in the Greyhound Bus Company waiting-rooms; in Houston it centred on the Union Railway Station, hence the decision to travel by train. This particular piece of oral testimony provides an excellent analysis of the tensions of the trip, personality problems being as prominent as political idealism; inevitably there was a tendency to turn towards the consumption of alcohol. There is an even better description of the daunting experience of being gaoled almost immediately on arrival in Houston. The students were beaten up by the other prisoners, whose own racist attitudes always had sexual overtones: 'All they want is to sleep with white women. You know that's all they want.' The student then comments that to the other prisoners 'the whole thing' was 'intermarriage or interracial sex, and it just kept cropping up all the time'. The other main preoccupations of the ordinary prisoners were whether the freedom riders were 'Jewish or queers'. One prisoner expressed apparent regret at the Anniston bus burning: ' "That's right. That's right," he said, "I'm against violence of any kind. It's terrible, horrible. But if I catch a Nigger going to school with my daughter, I'll kill him." '

One could define the essential characteristics of this early phase up to late 1963 as being the achievement of universal visibility on the part of those determined to reveal and contest the injustices suffered by blacks, and the revelation that these injustices were so deeply imbri-cated in so many different aspects of American society that trying to overcome them was going to involve violence, destruction, and much more in the way of positive action than even the most liberal politicians had envisaged in the early years of the decade. There were symbolic acts of great drama and potency, some undoubted changes in physical reality and even shifts in attitudes, but the major configurations of the race divide essentially remained unaltered. Integration at Memphis State University (and at other institutions outside the

186

'deep South') was a low-key affair. Two of the most stirring episodes of 1962–3 concerned integration at two of the deep South's most important public universities, 'Ole Miss.', that is, Mississippi University at Oxford, Mississippi, and the University of Alabama at Tuscaloosa. These few episodes coincided with the most intense episode in the freedom rides, the voter registration campaign in south-west Mississippi, led by one of the young blacks coming to the fore in SNCC, Robert Moses (who had been profoundly affected by seeing the Greensboro episode on television). The challenge at 'Ole Miss.' was embodied in James H. Meredith, one of the legendary figures of the sixties black awakening. The vigorously resisted enrolment of Meredith took several days in September 1962, involved appalling violence, with two dead and hundreds injured, and was in the end only achieved through the intervention of federal troops. The continuing sadness of 'Ole Miss.', the tragic backwardness of its own white students, together with some perceptive hints of genuine changes to come, are contained in a sensitive article by Thomas Buckley in the *New York Times* of Sunday 21 October 1962:

> Oxford, Miss., Oct. 20 Virtually all 4,638 white students at the University of Mississippi exist in an isolation more profound than that which they impose on the one Negro student, James H. Meredith... Faculty members and other observers believe that Mr Meredith's presence on the campus is forcing the white students to think seriously for the first time about the racial issue and their attitudes toward it.
>
> If this view is correct—and many interviews and other data suggest it is—the white students before long may find their position less tolerable than Mr Meredith finds his.
>
> In that case, new violence will be directed against him, or, more likely, the barriers will be breached.
>
> Even so, given the intensity of feeling about Mr Meredith, the first student to shake his hand or join him for coffee in the cafeteria will be courageous. There are many reports that even a smile or a nod in his direction has resulted in a student's being punched or cursed.

If 'Ole Miss.' students were ultra-conservative, as was the university management and a considerable proportion of the academic staff, the university included a very progressive branch of the American Association of University Professors. On 3 October the University of Mississippi Chapter of the AAUP publicly announced this resolution: 'Riots, weapons and agitators have no place at a university'. At the end of the month the National Council of the AAUP resolved: 'The deplorable events which took place in Oxford, Mississippi, would not have occurred if the political authorities of the State had supported the University in adhering to the law of the land and its academic obligations.' The dichotomy expressed here was somewhat sharp, given that (to say the least) the attitude of 'the University' had been ambiguous. On 9 October the secretary-treasurer of the University of Mississippi Chapter had felt constrained to write to the university chancellor objecting to an article in the university magazine by the director of the university news service, entitled 'Ole Miss. Refuses to Sleep'—which, the secretary-treasurer protested, was effectively accusing members of the AAUP of saying that Ole Miss. was dead. Her letter continued:

> The most flagrant falsehood concerning the riot, however, occurs in the third paragraph. The author unconditionally states that, 'Almost all the rioters were outsiders...' To the knowledge of many members of this chapter who were eyewitnesses of the riot, this statement simply is not true.[19]

The letter goes on to point out that in the aftermath of the riots many members of staff, as well as quite a number of students, left the university community:

> Finally, there is the appallingly gratuitous and slanderous scatter-gun attack on former faculty members, with the equally irresponsible praise of those who remain. Aside from the short-comings pointed out above, we feel that the overall attitude of this article conforms to and even encourages an unfortunate outlook on the part of many people in our state, a predisposition to see our neighbors in other parts of the country as dishonest, scheming and merely self-interested when they find faults in us.

While students had avoided taking coffee with Meredith, the AAUP secretary had been one of three members of the academic staff ostentatiously to have coffee with him immediately after his successful entry into the university. Shortly, the Mississippi University Chapter of the AAUP was pointing out that, in the aftermath of desegregation and in the interests of communication between professors from former all-white universities and from former all-black universities, care would have to be taken in the selection of hotels for meetings and conventions of learned societies. For the 1964 convention of the executive committee of the south-central Modern Languages Association it would be necessary to choose 'a hotel in a city where all members of the Association will be taken as guests with no embarrassment to anyone'. The agony of sympathetic whites was recognized by the *New York Times* in a sensitive article published in mid-January 1963, which noted that not even Meredith had 'experienced the abuse to which some whites have been subjected':

> Slander, intimidation and threats have been directed at moderates and liberals on the campus. And the campaign shows no sign of abating.
>
> One white student has been driven from the university. A few others remain only because of stubborn refusal to surrender. Even the parents of the dissenters have been brought under pressure.
>
> The family of one student who had befriended Mr. Meredith reportedly was pressed to such lengths recently that it sought to ease the situation by saying the youth had suffered a 'nervous breakdown' and therefore was not responsible for his actions.
>
> Faculty members have received threatening telephone calls and scurrilous letters.

The area of the university cafeteria in which they usually sit is referred to by students as 'the Communist section'. The little daughter of a professor who had invited Mr. Meredith to dinner received a black doll last month at a school party. The accompanying card read, 'A Nigger lover'.[20]

By the spring of 1963 there had been three years of unprecedented black involvement and activism in the South, unprecedented in both intensity and geographical extent. It is possible to distinguish the various shades of black activism and opinion, as it is of white. We have already seen abundant evidence of white viciousness—towards fellow whites as well as blacks. Majority white responses ranged from the expressed intention of paying formal observance to desegregation laws only so that black/white relationships could continue as before, to deliberate ploys for avoiding desegregation (such as closing parks and libraries), to boycotting businesses which did desegregate, to open (and often murderous) violence against civil rights workers and blacks (including children) in general, and to the formation of white supremacist organizations. Blacks in the mean time supplemented marches and sit-ins with economic boycotts of their own. While black activism continued to be largely non-violent, it was inevitable that by 1962 (year of the publication of *Another Country*) trends towards violence and triumphalism were becoming apparent. The documentary evidence for black economic action ranges from the sophisticated campaign statements of the NAACP to badly typed and mimeographed single sheets, several of these collected in the files of Sheriff Hinds. Here is an example, which, under the handwritten heading 'COMRADE', runs from proposed action against white boycotts, to generous recognition of white support, to rejoicing in violence, to triumphalism and the scent of victory:

LAST MONTH THE WHITE PEOPLE OF NORTH MISSISSIPPI, EASTERN ARKANSAS, AND WEST TENNESSEE SET ABOUT TO BOYCOTT THE AUTOMOBILE SALES COMPANY OF MEMPHIS AND TRAILER SALES DIVISION OF AUTOMOBILE SALES COMPANY OF WEST MEMPHIS, ARKANSAS. WE KNOW THAT ALL YOU GOOD FELLOWMEN WILL IGNORE THIS BOYCOTT BUT WE ARE ASKING YOU TO EXTEND SPECIAL EFFORTS TO HAVE ALL YOUR FRIENDS AND NEIGHBORS IGNORE THIS STUPID, BIGOTED BOYCOTT.

We must do ALL our business with AUTOMOBILE SALES COMPANY (BOTH IN MEMPHIS AND WEST MEMPHIS) in order to prevent what happened to one of our good friends, Shainbergs Department Store in Whitehaven, Tennessee. Unfortunately, Shainbergs was forced to close their store in Whitehaven because of the conduct of the bigoted white people in your area. You must make special effort to buy all your automobiles and house trailers from our friends to show the white people that they are at the economical mercy of the Negro and the Negro sympathizer.

Automobile Sales Company has a staff of Negroes—Negro Sales Manager Charlie Washburn is always ready to serve you—he is our patriot all the way and will put the white people in their place. You will find a staff of Negro salesmen, Negro secretary and office workers always at your

189

service. Mr. Iver Schmidt, owner of both these companies, is not a Negro, but Mr. Schmidt is one of our most honored and helpful servants. He has for some time now made special effort to provide the negro with a good income—which in turn provides us with contributions to carry on our work in these times when we are forging ahead with tremendous speed.

The sit-ins are coming along nicely. The sickly whites are trying to fight back, but most of them realize that it is a futile fight as we have the Federal Government behind us and the Federal District Courts are rendering decision in our favor every day. The northern states know who they are fooling with—even the northern policemen are in actual fear of us.[21]

White supremacists were obsessed by race, 'inter-breeding', and 'Communism'. One expressive summary of the consequences of integrating schools ironically contains a recognition that children are themselves free of racial prejudice:

This the Communists would most certainly welcome. The United States would then be doomed! What nation has survived substantial inbreeding of the Negro? NONE!!...

Some 'do-gooders' will say: 'Your children don't have to marry Negroes just because they go to school with them.' But you should remember that the children are not aware of the consequences. They will accept the Negro socially if they go to school with him. It may be the immediate result will not be intermarriage, but it will come. Family and continued associations will give the communists the desired results.[22]

Here is a reader's letter in the *Albany Herald* of 20 February 1963:

the ultimate goal of the Negro is not co-education, equal opportunity of employment or elimination of discrimination, all products of their own lack of personal pride, dignity and resourcefulness. Their ultimate ambition is only the inter-breeding of the races and elimination of the Negro race from the face of the earth, and sacrificing the white in so doing. This is preached in the churches in which they pretend to worship...

The newest white supremacist organization chose a straightforward name, White Citizens' Council. It came north to attack the moderates of Memphis, Dallas, and Atlanta:

The door to race mixing has been opened in Memphis by a clique of politicians and moderates. Using a combination of stealth and force, these collaborators with the NAACP have engineered a shameful surrender on the very borders of unyielding Mississippi, upon whose pro-segregation white citizens much of the cotton center's economic life depends...

Everyone who wants to do something specific to help our beleaguered friends in Memphis, Dallas and Atlanta get rid of integration is urged to contact this publication immediately. We have a plan.[23]

Citizens' Council advertisments in June 1963 invited white readers to address this question; 'Ask Yourself This Important Question: What Have I Personally Done to *Maintain Segregation?*'

> If the answer disturbs you, probe deeper and decide what you are willing to do to preserve racial harmony in Selma and Dallas County [in Alabama]... six dollars will make both you and your wife members of an organization which has already given Selma nine years of Racial harmony since 'Black Monday'.

It was also in 1963 that some of the worst hate leaflets produced by the Council began to appear. The first White Citizens' Council meeting in Memphis, held at the King Cotton Hotel in November 1961, was regarded by the Memphis city fathers as an unwarranted intrusion from the reactionary deep South. Sheriff Hinds made sure that Operator A (whose name, reassuringly, was Muldoon) was installed thirty minutes before the meeting began. Operator A recorded an attendance of approximately 250, 'most of them ranging in age from 40 up to 75. There were not over three under 40 years of age...'[24] Police and press colluded in ridiculing the citizens as a geriatric group of anti-Memphis cranks. Operator A did, however, think that the group could be dangerous, and Sheriff Hinds undertook to maintain surveillance on them.

The Memphis establishment may have behaved here in accordance with its better traditions, but ordinary white Memphians remained unenthusiastic about civil rights. In advance of the presidential election of 1964, the monthly paper of the Memphis Typographical Union 'added up the score' with respect to the two candidates, Johnson and Goldwater, taking a strongly liberal line in coming out totally in support of Johnson. The final item in the tally, however, was something less than uncompromisingly liberal:

> *Civil Rights*—politicians of both parties have pushed hard for civil rights laws for a dozen years. Don't forget that 80% of the Republicans in congress voted for the newest such law. As one astute observer remarks, 'Who are you going to blame the most—those who carried the ball, or those who kicked it?'[25]

Some whites, then, believed themselves to be in favour of change, though in fact they had no vision of total integration and equality. Some whites resisted change with greater or less violence. For many there was a sullen recognition that change was taking place, would continue, and could not effectively be resisted: but such people, perceiving the sharing of lunch counters and library facilities as revolutionary, had no understanding of the meaning of complete integration and equality—that was simply unthinkable. A further group of whites, who to some extent overlapped with the most conservative of the 'moderates', felt that with the formal abolition of segregation 'normal' relations would be resumed, with (as they saw it) whites sticking to their customary practices and blacks to theirs. This view was implicit in many of the utterances of Memphis civic leaders; it was explicit in the leaders of the *Albany Herald,* which, after declaring support for the removal of seven Albany 'local ordinances providing for legal compulsion in the observance of racial segregation', applauded individual citizens establishing 'their own codes of social conduct':

> From the outset of the racial disturbances which Negro integrationists have inflicted upon the country since November 1961, this newspaper has maintained that the ultimate solution would lay not with bodies politic, and not even with the courts with their interpretative findings as to law, but finally with individuals, making their own judgements, choosing their own associates and thereby establishing a community code of conduct...
>
> As individuals, Albanians—of both races—may now continue to practice their segregated customs and to restore the sanity of racial harmony which was so ruthlessly and calculatingly disturbed in this peaceful community by those seeking not a workable racial order, but personal publicity—and profit.[26]

The following day, an editorial in the same paper regretted the desegregation of the city's two main libraries. 'These decisions are disappointing because we see them rendered timidly, without suitable public explanation and in direct reproach of a social principle to which a majority of Albanians had candidly pledged themselves despite hardship.' What the hardship was one can only wonder, but it was becoming customary to represent segregationists as noble spirits standing out against a fashionable tide. The city commissioners of Albany actually carried through integration in the two city libraries in a most peculiar way. Under the plan, whites and blacks who had held library cards before the closure of the libraries could together borrow books, but to prevent them from sitting down and reading them together all seats were removed. The humorist Harry Golden referred to this as 'vertical integration', and further suggested that blacks wishing to overcome the segregation which still existed in theatres should 'borrow' a white child and then gain access to white-only sections by posing as the child's servant.[27]

In Washington the Kennedy administration, perceived as symbolizing the will to change in American society, had a genuine commitment to civil rights, perhaps voiced most explicitly by the Attorney-General Robert Kennedy; at the same time the president, conscious anyway of his minuscule majority in the popular vote and of the segregationist sentiments of much of the Democratic party in the South, was very wary of arousing the hostility of powerful interest groups. But whatever the theories of states' rights, the disturbances and the violence were so great that federal initiatives were rendered unavoidable. The first major intervention was purely verbal. On 28 February 1963 Kennedy issued 'The White House Special Message on Civil Rights', promulgated under six headings: the right to vote; the right to education; the intended extension and expansion of the commission of civil rights; the right to employment; desegregation of public accommodations; and finally, other uses of federal funds (for the armed forces, in housing, and in combating police brutality). The message concluded:

> The various steps which have been undertaken or which are proposed in this Message do not constitute a final answer to the problems of race discrimination in this country. They do constitute a list of priorities—steps which can be taken by the Executive Branch and measures which can be enacted by the 88th Congress...

In addition, it is my hope that this message will lend encouragement to those state and local governments—and to private organizations, corporations and individuals—who share my concern over the gap between our precepts and our practises. This is an affair in which every individual who asks what he can do for his country should be able and willing to take part.[28]

The message was carefully crafted, not least in this final resonant echo of Kennedy's inauguration speech ('ask not what your country can do for you—ask what you can do for your country').

The climax at the University of Alabama came on n June 1963, when Governor George Wallace, who had seen that there was much political advantage to be gained from furiously waving the segregationist flag, personally barred the entrance to the university. The next day, over in Mississippi, Medgar Evers, a leading black activist in the voter registration campaign, was shot dead. In between had come, after Albany, the next major stage in the public life of Martin Luther King, the concerted effort at Birmingham, Alabama, to crack segregation there, widely regarded as being about the most stringently and viciously enforced in the entire South. King was arrested on Good Friday, and it was while he was in Birmingham Jail that a newspaper report of a denunciation by white clerics of his actions provoked him into writing one of his most resonant texts, the 'Letter from Birmingham Jail', begun on the borders of the newspaper, concluded on toilet paper, and smuggled out by his supporters.[29] The four bishops, one rabbi, and three ministers had criticized Governor Wallace's inauguration speech in January in which he had invoked 'Segregation Forever!', and had gone as far as to admit black leaders to their churches—in specially roped-off areas! Under the heading 'White Clergymen Urge Local Negroes to Withdraw from Demonstrations', the Birmingham *News* of 13 April printed their statement:

> Just as we formerly pointed out that 'hatred and violence have no sanction in our religious and political traditions', we also point out that such actions as incite hatred and violence, however technically peaceful those actions may be, have not contributed to the resolution of our local problems. We do not believe that those days of new hope are days when extreme measures are justified in Birmingham.

The 'Letter from Birmingham Jail', dated 16 April and addressed to 'My Dear Fellow Clergymen', was printed first as a pamphlet by the Quaker organization the Friends Service Committee and then, slightly revised, in King's *Why We Can't Wait* of 1964. 'Never before have I written so long a letter,' King explained towards the letter's end:

> I'm afraid it is much too long to take your precious time. I can assure you that it would have been much shorter if I had been writing from a comfortable desk, but what else can one do when he is alone in a narrow jail cell, other than write long letters, think long thoughts and pray long prayers?[30]

Long or not, this letter is a marvellously direct document which faithfully sets out the situation in Birmingham, places the civil rights movement in its international context, defines King's Christianity and its relationship to that of the white clergy, and coins the perfect description of sixties activists in all spheres in referring to himself as a 'creative extremist'. It begins:

> While confined here in the Birmingham city jail I came across your recent statement calling my present activities 'unwise and untimely'...

I think I should indicate why I am here in Birmingham, since you have been influenced by the view which argues against 'outsiders coming in'... I, along with several members of my staff, am here because I was invited here...

But more basically, I am in Birmingham because injustice is here...

... Birmingham is probably the most thoroughly segregated city in the United States... There have been more unsolved bombings of Negro homes and churches in Birmingham than in any other city in the nation. These are the hard, brutal facts of the case. On the basis of these conditions, Negro leaders sought to negotiate with the city fathers. But the latter consistently refused to engage in good-faith negotiation.

Then, last September, came the opportunity to talk with the leaders of Birmingham's economic community. In the course of the negotiations, certain promises were made by the merchants—for example, to remove the stores' humiliating racial signs. On the basis of these promises, the Reverend Fred Shuttleworth and the leaders of the Alabama Christian Movement for Human Rights agreed to a moratorium on all demonstrations. As the weeks and months went by, we realized that we were the victims of a broken promise. A few signs, briefly removed, returned; the others remained.

As in so many past experiences, our hope had been blasted, and the shadow of deep disappointment settled upon us. We had no alternative except to prepare for direct action, whereby we would present our very bodies as a means of laying our case before the conscience of the local and national community...

You may well ask: 'Why direct action? Long sit-ins, marches and so forth? Isn't negotiation a better path?' You are quite right in calling for negotiation. Indeed, this is the very purpose of direct action. Non violent direct action seeks to create such a crisis and foster such a tension that a community which has constantly refused to negotiate is forced to confront the issue...

The nations of Asia and Africa are moving at jet-like speed toward gaining political independence, but we still creep at horse-and-buggy pace toward gaining a cup of coffee at a lunch counter. Perhaps it is easy for those who have never felt the stinging darts of segregation to say, 'Wait'. But when you have seen the vicious mobs lynch your mothers and fathers at will and drown your sisters and brothers at whim; when you have seen hate-filled policemen curse, kick and even kill your black brothers and sisters; when you see the vast majority of your twenty million Negro brothers smothering in an airtight cage of poverty in the midst of an affluent society; when you suddenly find your tongue twisted and your speech stammering as you seek to explain to your six-year-old daughter why she can't go to the public amusement park that has just been advertised on television, and see tears welling up in her eyes when she is told that Funtown is closed to colored children, and see ominous clouds of inferiority beginning to form in her little mental sky, and see her beginning to distort her personality by developing an unconscious bitterness toward white people... when you are humiliated day in and day out by nagging signs reading 'White' and 'Colored'...—then you will understand why we find it difficult to wait...

In no sense do I advocate evading or defying the law, as would the radical segregationists. That would lead to anarchy. One who breaks an unjust law must do so openly, lovingly, and with a willingness to accept the penalty...

But though I was initially disappointed at being categorized as an extremist, as I continued to think about the matter I gradually gained a measure of satisfaction from the label... Jesus Christ was an extremist for love, truth and goodness... Perhaps the South, the nation and the world are in dire need of creative extremists.[31]

Over the weekend there was telephonic communication between King's wife and President Kennedy. As in Albany, King was quickly released. His fundamental strategy was that of meticulously organized, scrupulously nonviolent marches involving (in particular) black children. There can be no doubting the bravery shown by the blacks, in particular the children, in facing the Birmingham police under their notorious chief, Bull Connor, though till May, in fact, Connor showed an unexpected restraint. On 2 May, around 1,000 black children, marching in dignified style from their Baptist church into the town centre, were arrested. The following day Connor unleashed one of his most frightening weapons, his dogs. The television pictures that evening of dogs savaging peaceful demonstrators delivered another particularly potent lesson to the nation about the realities of racial discrimination. The Kennedy administration had hoped to steer well clear of any direct involvement, but on 5 May the assistant attorney-general arrived to take personal charge of negotiations with white civic and business leaders. None the less, it appeared that with Connor's police reinforced by state troopers sent in by Governor Wallace, the most violent encounter thus far would take place on 7 May. Robert Kennedy felt constrained to intervene, threatening the intervention of federal troops. The negotiations now came to a rapid conclusion, and King announced the formal concession of desegregation as a 'great victory'. But formal victory did not equal security for blacks in the streets and in their homes. If anything, the white reaction intensified: there were bombings and attempted shootings in Birmingham, and then throughout the South.

Television had played an important part in helping to spread black protest, and in informing liberal citizens in northern cities of the brutalities of southern officialdom. The president was reluctant to go on television over the race issue: that would be to project himself directly into the thick of southern conflicts. It was the University of Alabama issue which forced his hand. 11 June 1963 is indeed a climactic date, as national guardsmen secured the entry, against the personal resistance of Governor Wallace (backed of course by his state troopers), of two black students into the University of Alabama; that evening the president appeared on television to explain the federal actions. He first stated the facts:

This afternoon, following a series of threats and defiant statements, the presence of Alabama National Guardsmen was required on the University of Alabama to carry out the final and unequivocal order of the US District Court of the Northern District of Alabama. That order called for the admission of two clearly qualified young Alabama residents who happen to have been born Negro.

'America today', said the president, 'is committed to the world-wide struggle for freedom',

and when Americans are sent to Vietnam or West Berlin, we do not ask for whites only. It ought to be possible, therefore, for American students of any color to attend any public institution they select without having to be backed up by troops. It ought to be possible for consumers of any color to receive equal service in places of public accommodation, such as hotels and restaurants and theaters and retail stores, without being forced to resort to demonstrations in the street, and it ought to be possible for American citizens of any color to register and vote in a free election without interference or fear of reprisal.

The president then went on to list the still-existing statutory disadvantages suffered by 'the Negro'. He promised that he would ask Congress the very next week to take action. Progress was being made in education, 'but the pace is very slow'. 'We have a right', he continued, 'to expect that the Negro community will be responsible, will uphold the law, but they have a right to expect that the law will be fair...'

Partly in response to southern white sensibilities and partly in recognition of the objective fact that protests and demonstrations were now taking place in northern cities, Kennedy defined the problem as pertaining to the North as well as to the South. The point was seized upon by southern newspapers, the *Memphis Commercial Appeal* reporting the television address under the headline 'This Is a Problem Which Faces All—the North as Well as the South'.[32] Not only was that now abundantly true, it was perceived to be true. However, it is only proper to record here that in the national political sphere, the concerted opposition to the president's projected civil rights legislation came from a group of southern senators and congressmen.

### The North as well as the South, and the West too

Nineteen sixty-three was the year in which the experience acquired in protests and boycotts, and the tactics developed, particularly by Martin Luther King, in the South were applied in the major cities of the North. There were demonstrations relating to both jobs and schools in Los Angeles, Philadelphia, and St Louis; there were school boycotts in New York, Chicago, and Boston. Legally sanctioned segregation in public places seems now, at the end of the twentieth century, to belong to an archaic world; discrimination in employment, education, and housing, alas, still seems to be very much with us. These, of course, were the focal issues in the North.

Southerners resented northern interferences in southern race relations, and rejoiced in the growing evidence of race problems in the North; this comes through very strongly in the Van

Dyke family correspondence. Early in September 1962, Bill's parents had sent him a clipping attacking the freedom riders with the usual southern combination of patronizing superiority and sheer venom. In return Bill sent a piece from the *Los Angeles Times* of 17 September, giving free rein to all the fears embodied in the headline, 'Great Negro Tide Surges into Melting Pot of the West'. In January 1963 the city of Berkeley was voting on the question of racial discrimination in housing. In reporting on this, Bill repeated the usual comforting mantra about racial prejudice being a complex matter (the opposite, of course, is true: racial prejudice itself is a very simple matter; it is the ramifications in housing, employment, etc, which can become complex). He also gave vent to another, age-old racial prejudice, anti-semitism:

> It just proves again that there are no simple solutions to the problems of racial preju-dice—in the South or anywhere else. It was rumored last week that a Negro couple were shown an apartment in our building and you should have heard the screams from some of the enlightened New York Jews who live here![33]

According to the Los Angeles County Commission on Human Relations, 'Most of the tensions in Los Angeles County center around housing'. The commission's programme varied 'from trying to prepare communities such as Inglewood and West Los Angeles for the entry of minority groups, to trying to stabilize communities into which minority groups have already made an entry', the 'basic minority groups' being 'Negro' and 'Mexican-American'; but there were also 'Puerto Ricans, Filipinos, American Indians, Jews' (staggering, though at least thoroughly honest, that Jews should be listed in this way), 'and the largest concentration of Japanese-Americans in continental U.S.' Apart from Hawaii, Los Angeles County was the most cosmopolitan area in the entire nation, with one in every five inhabitants belonging to a minority group. However, there was no doubt in the minds of the commission as to where the most significant problem lay: the arrival every month of 2,000–2,500 blacks. Accordingly it summoned a meeting of black and white leaders for 6 June 1963 at the Statler-Hilton Hotel. The commission had no investigative or enforcement powers, so its work was 'almost entirely educational'. It was specially concerned with trying to moderate in specific situations of high tension 'such as those which arise when a minority group family moves into a new neighborhood for the first time'.[34] The Statler-Hilton meeting gave overt recognition to a problem, but it could hardly be expected to come up with solutions.

The situation in California was a curious confusion of *de facto* and *de jure* elements. The predominating fact was that black ghettos and manifest discrimination in housing already existed, despite state laws of 1957 (the Hawkins Law) and 1959 (the Unruh Law) outlawing racial discrimination in housing. There was in fact a powerful movement, led by real estate agents, to rescind these very laws. Then, in 1963, a further law (the Rumford Law) was enacted, its first chapter declaring: 'The practise of discrimination because of race, color, religion, national origins, or ancestry in housing accommodations is declared to be against public policy.' The Hawkins, Unruh, and Rumford laws together formed the 'fair housing laws' and are a tribute to the strong liberal tradition in California. Now the real estate lobby drew up 'Proposition 14', which, in accordance with California electoral law, was added to the ballot papers in the forth-coming elections. If successful it would effectively abrogate the fair housing laws. Proposition 14 read: 'Neither the State nor any subdivision or agency thereof shall deny, limit or abridge, directly or indirectly, the right of any person, who is willing or desires to sell, lease or rent any part or all of his real property, to decline to sell, lease or rent such property to such person or persons as he, in his absolute discretion, chooses.' The arguments, the subterfuges, the lies, envel-oping the question of segregation in housing are fully revealed in the 1961 hearings of the California State Committee on the matter. Charles Shattuck was a past president of the California Real Estate Association. Now chairman of the Association's Racial Relations Committee, he explained:

> We have had several members in the various groups representing the Negro population of the community in which we have been discussing this matter. Eventually maybe it will come about. But up to the present time it has not... We have both minority interests, but also, Gentlemen, we have majority interests to look out for. Both groups have got to he heard; both groups have got to be treated fairly if we are going to get along with one another as we always have...

The chair, McMillan, interrupted at this point to clarify that this traditional arrangement of 'getting along with one another' was in fact segregation. Shattuck agreed that critics did perceive it as segregation, but in his view it was simply a means of finding housing for blacks in 'suitable areas—those portions of the City that are of that character, rightfully should be theirs, and we would be glad to have them have it, and be glad to have them be realtors'. But, he continued, 'we are not going to be a party to the salt and peppering of the whole community'. The admirably liberal chair at once demanded to know the meaning of this phrase. Rather than a definition, Shattuck provided a somewhat shambling rehearsal of old tunes:

> I mean this, that it has been my observation that birds of a feather flock together pretty much as a matter of nature and I don't care how much you may try to pass laws, but the amount of human ills that kings and parliaments can cure is very small indeed. If you start to try to—it is a question of price, everybody says because the reason people don't want Negroes to move into a district, will say, is because of the change in values.[35]

'The reason', Shattuck elaborated in response to a further interruption from the chair, 'is that if they move in, the white people just move out. That's all. They move out. They just don't care to stay there...'

Assemblyman Knox joined in on behalf of the virtuous black all-American lawn-mowing householder:

> I just wondered how it would injure a neighborhood—you said you wanted to protect neighborhoods—to have a Negro family or group of good character whose children

198

were neat and attended school and mowed their lawns and minded their business—how does that hurt a neighborhood?

SHATTUCK: Well, it doesn't hurt the neighborhood if you are thinking of it in terms of dollars and cents. But it does render the neighborhood to many people one in which they will no longer care to live because many people, as I tried to say a moment ago, they are all victims of our social habits, social restrictions and conditions, I don't care who we are. The average white man, let's be frank about it, the average white family simply is not going to stay in a mixed neighborhood any longer than they have to. That's the truth of the matter. Let's face it.

KNOX: As a matter of fact, in a number of neighborhoods in California, one, two or three Negro families have moved in and they haven't become ghettos in every case, have they?

SHATTUCK: No, but they—if you give them time, they will become black.

KNOX: Don't you think it's better and more salutary, if people learn to realise that there isn't any real difference. Wouldn't that be the better way, in the long run, to solve the problem?

SHATTUCK: I'm not quite that hopeful myself. I think it takes a long time. I've never yet seen a neighborhood where the Negroes have moved into it, that given time, you gradually find you can't sell it to anybody but those Negro or minority groups. Whites just won't buy any more. They'll go elsewhere...

Shattuck's muddled phrases are a telling representation of muddled, muddy reality; Knox's is the luminous voice of measured judgement.

There were campaigns against Proposition 14 as well as for it. Film stars were prominent, and the massive city-wide rally organized by 'Westside Citizens against Proposition 14' (a very white organization) was chaired by the distinguished film actor Burt Lancaster. The debates and rallies continued till the election of 1964, when a majority of citizens did vote for Proposition 14, but then the California Supreme Court immediately declared it unconstitutional. Thus, at the end of this opening phase of heightened racial action and tension, California had laws prohibiting discrimination in housing, and a Supreme Court which upheld those laws, while at the same time ghettos were becoming more crowded and whites were fighting harder than ever to keep blacks out of all-white neighbourhoods. Similar conditions existed in northern cities where existing black populations were being steadily augmented, though there were distinctive local variations: in cities where there already were well-defined ethnic enclaves, of, say, Irish-, Polish-, or Italian-Americans, resistance to any black entry into such areas was particularly vigorous. However, the big 'spectacles' of 1963 in the northern cities focused mainly on schools and on jobs—these issues are more public, more easily identified than the more diffused and often highly secretive issue of housing segregation. School boycotts were organized in New York, Chicago, and Boston; demonstrations relating to schools and jobs took place in Los Angeles, Philadelphia, and St Louis. According to the Justice Department, there were 1,412 separate demonstrations through-out North and South during the summer of 1963.[36] Martin Luther King and the Southern

Christian Leadership Conference was at the heart of many of the 1963 demonstrations, but in Los Angeles the running was made by the Negro Leaders Committee, which organized its first demonstration on 24 June 1963 as part of its 'drive for complete integration in education, housing and employment'. The specific target was the Board of Education, singled out 'because we have had no co-operation from them in discrimination or negotiation for our minimum requirements'.[37]

Police brutality towards blacks had long been a commonplace (though formally frowned upon in cities that prided themselves on the stability of traditional race relations): as black activism against discrimination intensified, instances of police brutality both increased and were more widely reported, especially on television. It was during 1963 that the Los Angeles Human Relations Commission felt obliged to set up a special committee to fight police brutality. Earlier, the commission had frequently been called upon to mediate between police and black protesters.

> Police brutality is on the increase! Scarcely a day goes by that does not see a sadist in uniform descend with his club on the head of a Negro citizen, haul him into jail on some artificial charge, or submit him to humiliating search and detention for some minor traffic violation.
>
> Their favourite victims are teenage youths, but they are not above manhandling young and old, male and female. These facts rarely get into the daily papers, but *every adult and child in the Negro community knows that they are true.*[38]

In California during the war, the treatment of Japanese-Americans had been vicious. The situation remained fraught in the sixties, but the evidence in the vast Japanese-American research project in the UCLA Library Special Collections does suggest a gradual improvement in relationships. On the mainland there were just over a quarter of a million Japanese-Americans, more than half of them in California. The *New York Times* of 21 October 1962 referred to 'the heroic World War II combat record of Nisei [i.e. American-born Japanese-American] soldiers in American uniform', while the Japanese-American Citizens' League recorded a number of successes in a pamphlet produced in July 1966. The refusal early in 1965 in Wyoming of a licence for a marriage involving a Nisei girl led to the repeal of the Wyoming Miscegenation Statute. Amendments to immigration law in January 1966 resulted in the Japanese being eligible for entry to the United States on the same basis as everybody else. It is clear that the league, while referring to the contemporary 'frustrations and... miseries' of black Americans, sees the persecution of Japanese-Americans as now being over: they were 'the victims of racist exploitation and persecution not so long ago'.[39]

*The* other race issue was that of relationships with Mexicans (often domiciled in America, but denied American citizenship)—though the relationship here was much more fundamentally economic, it being a question of relations between white ranchers and fruit-growers, and powerless labourers driven to seek work to avoid starvation for themselves and their families. On the whole the white employers preferred employing desperate, docile Mexicans, prepared to endure the most back-breaking work and appalling employment conditions. A curious twist among our first stirrings of change is the beginnings of a movement in favour of the employment of what were called 'domestics', that is to say white farm labourers. This movement was beginning to affect some of the farmers' associations by the end of 1960. For example, bulletin 41 of the Coachella Valley Farmers Association (1 December 1960) recommended: 'cheerfully hire every willing and able domestic who applies for a job. We all agree that he deserves the job if he is qualified. Don't try to evade this responsibility in any circumstance.' Further, 'you must hire women if they can perform the work the national [i.e. Mexican] is doing'. And, 'you must furnish housing if the domestic is a single man'. In other words, finally, 'you must do as much for the domestic as you are doing for the foreign worker'.[40] On 2 March 1961 the *Los Angeles Times* took up the plight of the white farm labourer, referring to the (apparently) more satisfactory conditions obtaining for the Mexican: 'Just south of El Centro, lettuce grower Danny Danenberg maintains a model camp in which 1,200 Mexican nationals (vaceros) can live comfortably in sanitary and rather pleasant surroundings when they are not working in the fields.' The 'vacero', the article continued, 'works hard, performing mostly "strop" labor in such crops as lettuce, onions, carrots, asparagus and melons. Growers claim it would be impossible to find large numbers of domestics... to do the same back-breaking work.' Thus it was that the white labourers created a new union, the Agricultural Workers Organising Committee. These issues were to become major themes during the turbulent 'High Sixties'.

1963 is the year in which race issues come to be seen to be national, not purely southern, ones. If anything, it could be said that in the South, although there was much extreme racist violence, which was in many ways to get worse in the succeeding years, there was some sense of optimism among 'moderates', and a fair amount of reluctant acceptance that change in race relations was happening and would continue to happen; while in the North the sense was more of a problem that had suddenly reared up to confront an unwarranted complacency. *Newsweek,* on 8 July, when John F. and Robert Kennedy were striving to talk their civil rights programme—and particularly the proposal to have discrimination outlawed in all businesses servicing the public—through fervid opposition in Congress, gave a detailed account of the delicate balance pertaining that summer. From the South, it said, 'the news, more often than not, was heartening'. In the light of subsequent events, this, and the account of events in the North which followed, seems overly optimistic. Yet peaceful accommodation was not yet utterly out of the question, though, in Robert Kennedy's words to Congress, quoted in the article:

If we fail to act promptly and wisely at this crucial point... the ugly forces of disorder and violence will surely rise... and grave doubts will be thrown on the very premise of American democracy.

The article stressed the peacefulness of demonstration in the North:

In the North, across the nation, demonstrators marched against discrimination. But they marched in peace. Some 300 walked in Los Angeles, 400 in Portland, Ore., 1,000 in Philadelphia. In Boston Common, 3,000 stood for two hours under a blazing sun to chant, clap, and pray for assassinated NAACP leader Medgar Evers.

And in Detroit, with the blessing of state, and city officials, 125,000 marched the streets bloodied by race riots twenty years previously. There was no trouble. The trouble was, the article surmised, that, though marches might be peaceful, if they remained merely demonstrations and nothing actually changed, there would be trouble. On 29 July *Newsweek* summed up:

> History would mark it: the summer of 1963 was a time of revolution, the season when 19 million U.S. Negroes demanded payment of the century-old promissory note called the Emancipation Proclamation.

Blacks had become visible; blacks had become newsworthy. Mainstream magazines (*Time* and *Life* as well as *Newsweek*) began to describe the black plight in great and sympathetic detail, and to poll black views of whites, and also white reactions. The 'March on Washington for Jobs and Freedom' of 28 August was the greatest spectacle yet in the campaign for black civil rights, rounded off with one of the most frequently re-televised speeches ever, Martin Luther King's 'I Have a Dream'. But the march also brought fully into the open the split between the activities of SNCC and the older, liberal, civil rights movement. At the same time the consciences of many young white Americans—as noble and selfless as any in the world—were stirred as never before.

For its 'the Negro in America' issue of 29 July 1963 *Newsweek* employed the Harris polling organization to interview a sample of 1,157 black men and women across the nation, while their own reporters concentrated on 100 top black leaders. It presented the following conclusions:

> The wave of protest is an authentic, deep-seated broadly based revolution. It has won the allegiance of vast majorities of Negroes wherever they live and whatever their age or economic lot. Its leaders are militant partly by choice—and partly because they have no choice. The Negro wants no less than an end to discrimination in all its forms...
>
> The revolution is anti-Jim Crow—not anti-white. Negroes have their doubts about the white man; two in five think he wants to keep them down, and one Negro in five is so deeply alienated he is not sure he would fight for the U.S. in a war. But Negroes overwhelmingly reject the anti-white separatist doctrine of the Black Muslims. Most think the white man is better than he used to be and will get better still.
>
> The revolt is committed to non-violence—though one Negro in five thinks some violence is inevitable...
>
> The revolt has deep roots in the world of the American Negro. That world was born in the rural South, where Negroes still live in old, unpainted shacks...

But the Negro has been moving steadily from the country into town... The Negro has been moving North as well—an exodus that will continue. Southern Negroes are no longer so sure the North is the other side of Jordan, but two in five would go if they could.

Sometimes the Negro escapes the worst of the ghetto—if not to a $40,000 house with a pool in Atlanta's Collier Heights or a terraced luxury apartment in Harlem, at least to that citadel of the American dream that nearly every Negro now shares: a home of his own.

If he is not lucky, a Negro winds up in the slums, where the unemployment rate soars to 25 per cent, where families crack and break, where one family in eight sees its kids forced out of school by need or lured out by the streets where even the crime rate, though rampant, pays poorly ($5 for a stolen $90 suit), where numbers runners sell hope, saloons and narcotics pushers peddle oblivion, and nationalist street-corner orators fan the coals of alienation.

The fight is not so much a revolution of despair—Negroes tend to feel they are doing better all around than they were five years ago—as a revolution of soaring expectations. It is, in a sense, a television revolution. There is a TV set in nine Negro homes out of ten, putting out an antenna that senses the white world, and its ways as never before. In a world of hungering men, even a soap commercial can throw sparks of revolt if its setting is a modern suburban kitchen...

*Newsweek* here may have been importing its own consumerist philosophy and faith in economic progress as the great mover and shaker, but it did also dig up a rich trove of personal experiences of discrimination: 'As a kid I hated myself because I was black,' said Richard Macon of Detroit, 'because black to me meant the other side of the tracks, third-class citizenship, [taking] the brunt of the jokes.' One doctor recalled: 'I had to walk five miles to school. I passed three white schools on the way to this broken-down shack.' 'In military service', said Charlie Jones of Chicago, 'I had whites spit at me and scream "Nigger"; I was headed overseas, and the thought of fighting and possibly dying for nothing made me feel that I was fighting without a cause.' 'It sears you and burns you,' said Mrs Ruth M. Batson of Roxbury, Mass. 'When I was 10 years old, I went to buy lunch at a restaurant in Boston, and they served me raw hot dogs. I will never, never forget that humiliation, of paying for those raw frankfurters.' 'It feels like being punished for something you didn't do', said a railroad yardman in New Orleans.

General grievances were ranked in order. At the top stood white business, blamed for salary discrimination; only one black in three felt he would get equal pay for equal work. Next, blacks singled out real estate companies for restricting housing and for charging them higher rents; more than half (68 per cent in the North) felt they would pay higher rents than whites for the same housing. Next, blacks criticized state and local governments for denying them public jobs. Finally, one black in ten blamed unions for keeping them out of skilled jobs, especially in the building trades and in the North. Blacks recognized education as the ladder to equality: 97 per cent wanted their children to complete high school, but were frustrated by the realities of discrimination. One out of five black families had had a child drop out of high school. Almost half (47 per cent) felt that even without drop-outs their children were not getting as good an education as whites.

Just how far the problem was now a northern problem was made clear in this geography lesson:

> Forty-seventh Street, just west of Cottage Grove on Chicago's South Side, is the heart of one of the largest black ghettos in the whole U.S. Some 80,000 Negroes live there in raucous noise and rotting filth, in teeming misery and grinding poverty. At the corner of 47th and Langley, a dingy record shop blares nonstop jazz. Down the street is a shoe repair shop, but everybody knows the backroom is a bookie joint.
>
> By day, 47th Street swarms with kids in tattered cotton trousers and grimy T-shirts. They play on the side streets under the porches of the tumbledown shacks or in the gaping doorways of the ancient tenements, where the broken windows are stuffed with rags and newspapers. By night, 47th Street is a grown-up world, tired old men leaning against the parking meters talking idly of nothing, younger men and women heading for the gaudy, neon-bright bars, where a prostitute can be picked up for $4. (A few blocks farther west the neighborhood gets a bit better, and the price is $5)...

Questions about what blacks thought of whites revealed some interesting variations by class. At the lower end of the economic scale blacks tended to be very distrustful of the white man and his motives: only one in four thought the white man sincerely wanted to see his condition improve. Forty-one per cent thought the whites wanted 'to keep the Negro in his place', and 17 per cent said that whites simply didn't care. At the upper economic levels, and among the Negro leadership group, the degree of trust rose, though not overwhelmingly. Middle- and upper-income blacks of the North gave the whites a 53 per cent 'favorable vote', while the figure for their counterparts in the South was 45 per cent. The leadership group voted 'favorable' by a bare majority. There were perceptive comments about how whites had been 'pushed into patterns of discrimination by fear—fear of losing his job to a Negro, fear of intermarriage, even fear of losing a servile class to wait on him'.

> Morris Narcisse Jr. of New Orleans said: 'The poor white man especially thinks a Negro might get his job.' John Fontenot of Los Angeles observed: 'they think they going to get too many two-toned babies.' 'They're afraid they'll lose their maids,' said Richard Harris, a Louisville, Ky., trackman.

Others reckoned that whites just naturally wanted to feel superior.

> 'Without the Negro, the white man has no one to look down on,' said Mae Powell of Washington, D.C. 'He certainly can't look down on the Jew. The Jew made an ass of

him.' 'White men have gotten so they think they own the whole world', said Mable Ratcliff, a Brooklyn laundress. 'They are not going to settle for smiles and talk, no!'

For all that *Newsweek* detected optimism, and that familiar pride in a common American heritage. Fifty-two per cent thought the white man's attitude toward blacks had improved over the last five years, and 73 per cent felt his attitude would continue to improve in the next five.

The American white man has a conscience and the non-violent method appeals to that conscience. Nobody tolerates kicking a man when he's down. 'Like Medgar Evers, no one condones shooting a man in the back,' was a typical response.

The survey then concluded: 'All in all, the Negro puts more trust in the white man's government and institutions than he does in the individual.' It then added some interesting observations on Catholics, Jews, and black racism:

Of all whites, Roman Catholic priests who conduct extensive and little publicised settlement work in Negro communities, are most trusted (by 55 per cent of Negroes). Contrary to supposition, Negroes think well of Jews. But the Negro himself is not free from bias. Puerto Ricans are considered harmful (by 20 per cent, with 70 per cent saying they are not sure)...

For its 21 October issue, *Newsweek* polled white opinion in the same thorough way it had polled black opinion. Two fascinating statistical tables were published, 'Whites Say Yes' and 'Whites Say No' (see Tables 5.1 and 5.2).

**Table 5.1** *Whites say* Yes

|  | Nationwide | South | Whites who have had social contact with Negroes |
|---|---|---|---|
| Should the law guarantee Negroes equal rights to white people in: |  |  |  |
| job opportunities? | 80 | 62 | 87 |
| voting? | 95 | 92 | 96 |
| using buses and trains? | 91 | 80 | 94 |
| using restaurants and lunch counters? | 79 | 49 | 80 |
| giving their children integrated schooling? | 75 | 43 | 90 |
| Do you favor JFK's civil rights bill? | 63 | 31 | 81 |
| Do you favor the bill's provision giving Negroes the right to any public accommodation? | 66 | 29 | 83 |
| Would you favor creating a federal fair employment practices commission? | 62 | 40 | 71 |

**Table 5.2** *Whites say* No

| | Nationwide | South | Whites who have had social contact with Negroes |
|---|---|---|---|
| Would you favor a quota system guaranteeing Negroes (10% of the nation) 10% of the jobs? | 81 | 80 | 84 |
| Do you agree Negroes should get preference in job openings to make up for discrimination? | 97 | 97 | 97 |
| Would you favor a Federal law forbidding discrimination in housing against Negroes? | 56 | 80 | 35 |
| If you were in the Negro's position, do you think you would be justified to: sit-in at lunch counters? | 67 | 84 | 49 |
| boycott products whose manufacturers don't hire enough Negroes? | 55 | 66 | 43 |
| lie down in front of trucks at construction sites to protest hiring discrimination? | 91 | 94 | 87 |
| go to jail to protest discrimination? | 56 | 75 | 37 |
| Should the Federal government have more power to make sure Negroes can register and vote? | 43 | 69 | 34 |

Accompanying the tables was a rich crop of white comments:

'They're God's children as well as the white man, and should be given the same rights,' said Miss Judith Ann Jacobs, who teaches an almost all-Negro class in an elementary school in Boston, Mass. But open housing? 'Even though I'm in favor of them living in better housing districts, I personally would not want to have them live next door to me.'

'Everybody is created equal in the sight of God,' said Mrs. Mark Woodson of Bell, Calif. 'My daughter is in college with Negroes and Orientals now; we don't go by color at all.' Well, yes, she would be concerned if her daughter dated a Negro, or brought one home for supper.

'I wouldn't get too upset if Negroes moved into this neighborhood,' said Bill Harber, a retired laborer in Gary, Ind. Afterthought: 'But I'd try to move to an area without them.'

*Newsweek* was certain that white America's direction was unquestionably forward, towards equality for all races, but it could not conceal a vicious, and thoroughly threatening, note of dissent in the South (not that the deeper prejudices of northerners, just revealed, were a good omen either).

Certainly there is no national impulse to revert to past and greater prejudices. White

America endorses the Supreme Court's 1954 decision to end school segregation by almost 2 to 1. Charles E. Drewett, a 42-year-old junior executive in Crestwood, Mo., summed up the majority feeling: 'We have a Constitution. We might as well live up to it. Same thing with our religion... Otherwise, throw them both out.' Moreover, white America gives ringing endorsements to the two historic Presidential decisions to use Federal forces to carry out Federal court decisions being defied by state governors.

On all three counts, however, the South—which has been fighting history for a long time—still dissents. White Southerners reject the Supreme Court school-desegregation decision by a majority of 64 per cent; reject Eisenhower's move by 55 per cent; reject Mr. Kennedy's stand by 63 per cent. Thinking back over the Little Rock crisis, a house-wife in Cosby, Tenn., said 'He should have let the citizens drive the niggers out of Arkansas.' Of the decisions to use troops to protect James Meredith, Tom A. Hall of Beaumont, Texas, said 'I think each state should handle their own affairs. That nigger cost us a lot of money'.

The original 'March on Washington', that of 1941, never took place: pioneer black leader A. Philip Randolph successfully used the threat to secure some Fair Employment concessions from President Roosevelt. In November 1962 Randolph proposed the same strategy. In the climate of outrage over the events in Birmingham, Alabama, the proposal turned into an organized plan, and during the spring and summer of marches and demonstrations in North, South, and West it came to be seen as an appropriate culmination to a momentous year. Both the march and the civil rights bill on which President Kennedy and his brother Robert were working were issues at the White House conference on 22 June 1963 to which the President summoned all the major black leaders. Also present, in addition to King, Randolph, Roy Wilkins of the NAACP, James Farmer of CORE, Whitney Young of the National Urban League, and John Lewis of SNCC, were white trade union leader Walter Reuther, Stephen Currier, millionaire president of the philanthropic Taconic Foundation, Vice-President Lyndon Johnson, and Robert Kennedy. The president was opposed to the march, fearing it might sink his civil rights bill: 'Some of these people', he explained, 'are looking for an excuse to be against us; and I don't want to give any of them a chance to say, "Yes, I'm for the bill, but I'm damned if I will vote for it at the point of a gun." '[41] By the end of the meeting the president was persuaded that it would be impossible to call off the march, so he exerted all his influence to ensure that it would be kept under careful control by a specially established United Civil Rights Leadership Council, backed by $800,000 raised by Currier. The speech John Lewis proposed to make was censored, but even so seemed too 'revolutionary' to the liberals; other elements in SNCC were completely disenchanted by the liberal, 'establishment' nature of the march, though even they recognized that for downtrodden southern blacks the march of a quarter of a million (including, actually, at least 75,000 whites) from the Washington monument to the Lincoln memorial, on 28 August 1963, was a marvellous consciousness-raising exercise.[42] Martin Luther King was the last of the speakers to address those assembled in front of the Lincoln memorial. His appeal was to the Declaration of Independence, the Constitution, and Abraham Lincoln's Emancipation Declaration. His peroration was in his most emotional, revivalist style:

> I say to you today, my friends, so even though we face the difficulties of today and tomor-row, I still have a dream. It is a dream deeply rooted in the American dream. I have a dream that one day this nation will rise up and live out the true meaning of its creed—we hold these truths to be self-evident, that all men are created equal. I have a dream that one day on the red hills of Georgia, the sons of former slaves and the sons of former slave-owners will be able to sit down together at the table of brotherhood...
>
> When we allow freedom to ring, when we let it ring from every village and every hamlet, from every state and every city, we will be able to speed up that day when all of God's children—black men and white men, Jews and gentiles, Protestants and Catholics—will be able to join hands and sing in the words of the old Negro spiritual, 'Free at last, free at last; thank God almighty, we are free at last'.[43]

Throughout the country's major universities, civil rights activism intensified. In November 1963 staff and students of the University of California at Los Angeles formed the University Civil Rights Committee, which aimed 'to achieve with all urgency and unity the integration of Negro and all other minority citizens in the life of the Los Angeles city and county Commission... through processes of negotiation and direct, non-violent action'.[44] Across the country plans began to be made for campaigns the following summer. The basis had been laid for the summer of 1964, 'Freedom Summer'.

## Europe

Citizens of the European countries derived a distant knowledge of the American race problem from Hollywood films in which they saw blacks as servants, or, sometimes, musicians. Jazz and its black performers were special interests of many French intellectuals, and some British ones: in both coun-tries there was to be found a sense of superiority over the Americans and what were seen as their barbarous racial practices. The most dramatic of the events I have just been describing were reported above all in Italy, where, because of extensive emigration across the Atlantic, there always had been a particular interest in American affairs. Accounts, for example, of 'the War of Oxford' were generally sympathetic to James Meredith and to those struggling for civil rights.[45] On 12 January 1964, *Epoca* noted that the American magazine *Time* had named Martin Luther King 'Man of the Year':

> Thanks to men like King, 1963, from the tragedies of Birmingham and Montgomery to the grand march of 200 thousand on Washington, has been the year of an incredible black 'revolution': the 19 million black Americans have obtained, with respect to civil rights, more than in the preceding hundred years.

Italy itself, at this time, had no non-white population, though some observers did accuse the

Italians of north-central Italy of racist prejudice against (often darker-skinned) Italians from the south and Sicily. Italy also had a severe ethnic problem in the Alto Adige (or South Tyrol), where some elements in the substantial Austrian minority were at this time resorting to terrorism. The existence of this minority was due to Italy's having been on the winning side in the First World War; the absence of any non-white minority was due to the failure of the Fascist dictator, Mussolini, in his avowed aim of establishing a new Roman empire in North Africa.

The French and the British, on the other hand, had been highly successful imperial powers. At the end of the fifties France was engaged in a vicious war against Algerians fighting for their independence: none the less native Algerians, as well as French colonials *(pieds-noirs)*, could come freely to France; this was also true of the natives of the French overseas territories which were treated as if they were departments of metropolitan France—Guinea, Guadeloupe, Martinique, and Réunion. British politicians and publicists expressed great pride in the way in which the former empire was being converted into a Commonwealth: the only restrictions upon the entry into Britain of non-white and white citizens of the Commonwealth were those imposed by the home countries themselves. As a curious offshoot of the love-hate relationship which had long existed between the British and the Irish, citizens of the Republic of Ireland were free to settle in Britain with the same rights as British citizens. As Britain began to show some of the characteristic features of an affluent society, most notably labour shortages in the less salubrious and more menial jobs, immigration by non-white Commonwealth citizens, which had been steady but not very significant in the early fifties, began to accelerate. The 1961 census showed that the number of people in Britain born abroad had increased by about 40 per cent since 1951. In the three years 1960–2 total net immigration amounted to some 388,000 people, about three-quarters of them from the Commonwealth and nearly half from the West Indies.

The overall picture with regard to non-white immigration can be seen from Table 5.3.[46] At the 1961 census about 2.1 million residents in England and Wales were reported to have been born outside the United Kingdom—rather under one third of them in other Commonwealth countries, about the same number in what was now the Irish Republic, and the rest in a range of countries, principally Germany, Poland, the United States, and Russia.

**Table 5.3** *Net immigration from colonies and New Commonwealth, 1 January 1948–30 June 1962*

| Period | West Indies | India | Pakistan | Others | Total |
|--------|-------------|-------|----------|--------|-------|
| 1948–53 | 14,000 | 2,500 | 1,500 | 10,000 | 28,000 |
| 1954 | 11,000 | 800 | 500 | 6,000 | 18,300 |
| 1955 | 27,550 | 5,800 | 1,850 | 7,500 | 42,700 |
| 1956 | 29,800 | 5,600 | 2,050 | 9,400 | 46,850 |
| 1957 | 23,000 | 6,600 | 5,200 | 7,600 | 42,400 |
| 1958 | 15,000 | 6,200 | 4,700 | 3,950 | 29,850 |
| 1959 | 16,400 | 2,950 | 850 | 1,400 | 21,600 |
| 1960 | 49,650 | 5,900 | 2,500 | –350 | 57,700 |
| 1961 | 66,300 | 23,750 | 25,100 | 21,250 | 136,400 |

In Chapter 3, I said something of the influence of black West Indians on the new subcultures developing in British cities: settlement was very uneven—some cities had streets and districts which were overwhelmingly Afro-Caribbean, many others never saw a black face (see Table 5.4). No other town, in August 1958, had more than 1,500 West Indians; many had none.

**Table 5.4** *Numbers of West Indians in various English cities*

| City | 1953 | August 1958 |
|------|------|-------------|
| London | 15,000 | 40,000 |
| Birmingham | 8,000 | 30,000 |
| Manchester | 2,000 | 4,000 |
| Nottingham | 2,000 | 3,000 |
| Sheffield | < 1,500 | 3,000 |
| Leeds | < 1,500 | 3,000 |
| Liverpool | < 1,500 | 3,000 |
| Wolverhampton | < 1,500 | 3,000 |
| Bristol | < 1,500 | 2,000 |

France had long been a much more cosmopolitan country than Britain, and one facet of the economic miracle was the large number of Italians and Spaniards who had jobs in France, particularly on building sites. The complete picture is well brought out in Table 5.5.[47]

In theory, France had a systematic policy, operated through the National Office of Immigration (ONI) which had been set up in 1945. Whereas liberal and left-wing opinion in Britain was opposed to any kind of regulation of immigration, in France the Left tended to believe that control of immigration was necessary so that it could be related in an orderly way to the particular needs of the French economy. But although this theory was widely shared, immigration into France was really completely haphazard (partly because the immigrants themselves preferred to have as little to do with officialdom as possible).

**Table 5.5** *Number of immigrants in France in 1962, by country of origin*

| Country of origin | No. | % |
|-------------------|-----|---|
| EEC | 770,796 | 35.52 |
| Italy | 628,956 | 28.98 |
| Spain | 441,658 | 20.35 |
| Portugal | 50,010 | 2.30 |
| Yugoslavia | 21,314 | 0.98 |
| Poland | 177,181 | 8.16 |
| North Africa: | 410,373 | 18.91 |
|   Algeria | 350,484 | 16.15 |
|   Morocco | 33,320 | 1.53 |
|   Tunisia | 26,569 | 1.22 |
| TOTAL | 2,169,665 | |

In Britain, non-white immigrants tended to take over older housing in specific areas in specific towns; in France they tended to congregate in *bidonvilles,* shanty towns, in which living conditions were the worst in Europe.[48] It seems that many West Indians (as the figures show, Asians are not of great significance in the late fifties) came to Britain (or really to England) with high hopes, some even feeling that they were coming to 'the mother country'. That ignorance and prejudice about black people existed, and was directly encountered, particularly when the new arrivals sought accommodation, was a shock. The phrase commonly in use at the time was 'colour bar': well-intentioned, well-educated Britons liked to believe that there was no colour bar, but the new arrivals were very aware that there was. From late 1957 a group of West Indian activists began meeting to discuss the issues of unemployment, housing, and the colour bar. This resulted in March 1958 in the founding of the *West Indian Gazette,* edited by the Trinidadian Claudia Jones; the first number declared: 'West Indians in Britain form a community with its own special wants and problems which our paper alone would allow us to meet.'[49] Actually, as Dilip Hero has pointed out, the West Indian communities in Britain at this time were fragmented, with each loyal to its own island. It was in fact residence in Britain, and the common experience of racial discrimination, which began to produce a distinctive West Indian identity, with a number of specifically West Indian organizations. Certain important events, first of all the riots of August and September 1958, helped in this process, which in its own small way was as characteristic of Britain in the early sixties as was black consciousness-raising and activism of America in the early sixties.

Most of the quite small number of Afro-Caribbeans in Nottingham (they formed well under 1 per cent of the population) lived in the St Ann's district. Teddy boys, fully demonstrating the antisocial tendencies for which they had been notorious throughout the fifties, occasionally provoked minor incidents. In the few weeks before August 1958 at least a dozen black men had been beaten up and robbed by Teddy boys with the police apparently showing little inclination to try to catch the culprits. On Friday 22 August an Afro-Caribbean got into an argument with his white woman friend and hit her. A limited scuffle spread to the whole pub, in which there was an overwhelming preponderance of whites. The few blacks were badly beaten up. The following evening a group of Afro-Caribbeans armed with knives and razors turned up at the pub. They went into the attack at closing time and injured six whites. As always in such circumstances word spread quickly, no doubt being embellished along the way. A mob of 1,500 whites launched a counter-attack with razors, knives, palings, and bottles. Eight people, including policemen, were badly enough injured to need hospital treatment.[50]

Already there had been incidents in Notting Hill. In a way which was to become familiar in all countries, the news conveyed by radio and television of events in St Ann's, Nottingham, acted as an incitement in Notting Hill and the surrounding districts, collectively known as North Kensington. Certain extreme right-wing groups already had offices in the area and had been organizing meetings, as well as distributing leaflets and scrawling slogans, all to the basic refrain of 'keep Britain white'. The news from Nottingham set a gang of Teddy boys off on a violent spree of seeking out and assaulting blacks, using a variety of offensive weapons, with the result that at least five blacks were left unconscious on the pavements. The following Saturday, 30

August, was the peak day of combined violence in both Nottingham and Notting Hill. However, when a crowd of 3,000–4,000 whites gathered at the junction of St Ann's Well Road, Pease Hill Road, and Pym Street in Nottingham, there were no blacks in sight: their leaders had instructed them to stay indoors throughout the weekend. Then the white mob turned on the police, blaming them for having protected blacks the previous Saturday. Anything that happened in Nottingham was totally eclipsed by the widespread and vicious violence against black persons and property in Notting Hill. Shortly before midnight a gang of about 200 whites attacked blacks in the vicinity of Bramley Road; one property was set on fire. The following day, Sunday, a mob of 600 or so broke into black houses, assaulting the inhabitants with a fiercesome array of weapons and shouting particularly offensive slogans, most notably, 'Lynch the blacks'. The assaults and skirmishes spread far beyond Notting Hill itself and to the furthest extremities of North Kensington.[51]

It will be recalled that Teddy boys were not held in high regard by press, public, or police. So although, perhaps inevitably, blacks were not fully satisfied with police responses, fairly firm action was taken against the main perpetrators of the violence. In mid-September nine white ringleaders were given sentences of four years in prison by Judge Salmon (another representative of measured judgement). Certainly the climax of viciousness was soon over, though sporadic and less horrific activity continued for another fortnight. More significant than police action were black efforts at self-defence. Vigilante groups were formed to patrol the area in cars; more imaginatively, escorts were organized for black employees on London Transport buses and tubes who had to set out for, or return from, work very early or very late: by the end of September even the aftermath of the riot was over. But, as with so many other aspects of British life in 1958, a new era had begun. The British had become conscious that they too had a race relations problem; and West Indians had become conscious that they formed an embattled community.

The West Indian authorities (from December 1958 brought together in the new West Indies Federation) recognized the true nature of what was happening by expanding the British Caribbean Welfare Service into the Migrant Services Division and appointing two community development officers to organize and co-ordinate efforts on behalf of West Indians in Britain. At the beginning of 1959 a number of West Indian organizations in Greater London were brought together into the West Indian Standing Conference (WISC). West Indian settlement was actually more significant in Wolverhampton and the surrounding area than it was in Nottingham, and it was in this part of the Midlands that the West Indian Caribbean Association was founded, also in 1959. In 1960 a West Indian Standing Conference was set up in Birmingham. The process by which West Indians developed their own organizations and increasingly looked to them rather than to the existing British political parties was greatly accelerated by government policies on immigration, which I shall discuss in a moment. For the time being there remained quite high hopes of multiracial action against racism (and indeed, as in America, the number of whites consciously committed to opposing racism did increase throughout the sixties). By mid-1961 a number of multiracial groups had affiliated to the WISC, which now comprised a total of eighteen organizations. Of an executive committee of nine in 1962 four members were white, giving this body a character somewhat reminiscent of the American Urban League. But, as government policy hardened against black immigration, and as blacks themselves became more self-confident, the situation a year later was that the white members had withdrawn.[52]

The awareness of certain intellectuals and academics that a new problem had arrived in their midst was signalled by the founding in 1958 of the Institute of Race Relations, whose objective was stated in very neutral terms—'to encourage and facilitate the study of the relations between races everywhere'—but whose purpose was undoubtedly to find means of resolving racial tensions. It was under the auspices of this institute, and under the impact of the events in Nottingham and North Kensington, that James Wickenden brought out, as early as October 1958, a brief report on *Colour in Britain*. It 'is as well to be clear', this report stated firmly, 'that the disease is not the presence of coloured people in Britain but hostile reactions to their presence'. Wickenden spoke for an important element of genuinely liberal and non-racist white sentiment, shrewd about the nature of the problem, naive in suggesting possible solutions. He believed that some limitation upon immigration was desirable, but that it would be undesirable for Britain—as distinct from the home countries—to impose such limitations:

> Without precise information, conclusions must be tentative. But it does appear that the danger lies where a concentration of immigrants has formed too quickly for an area's capacity to absorb them. Where this occurs there has been violence and the danger of violence and hostility will always be present. As a short-term measure it is therefore surely desirable to keep the number of immigrants to a level which can be absorbed. This applies both to the country as a whole and to particular areas. But the restrictions should not come from Britain.[53]

Wickenden explained how both Pakistan and India did set up hurdles which in effect limited emigration from their countries, but that the Caribbean governments (where, of course, the overwhelming majority of immigrants at this stage came from) were unwilling to do anything of this sort. He went on to note that the British government had already said that it would enforce law and order with the strictest rigour, including the deportation of blacks convicted of certain crimes:

> Information about conditions in Britain is needed in the countries from which emigration occurs. In Britain the long-term remedy is education, by which is meant not only education in schools but the task of stimulating and informing public opinion. And legislation should, surely, be neither ahead of overwhelming public opinion nor far behind.[54]

An ambiguous final sentence, to be sure. What, anyway, was 'overwhelming public opinion'? For white Britons it depended on where you lived—in an area of immigrant settlement, or far away from it. A minority of deep-dyed racists were, as in America, obsessed by perceived sexual aspects; for the rest, the basic issues were of housing and employment. The generally liberal-minded Labour MP for the Coventry North constituency, Maurice Edelman, shared some of the sentiments of Wickenden, unwisely perhaps making these known in the very right-wing, and anti-immigrant, *Daily Mail*, where his reasonably balanced article was given the provocative title 'Should We Let Them Keep Pouring In?'[55] The article was obviously picked up by one of the American ultra-racist organizations and circulated to its members, so that among the eleven letters in support of restricting immigration (there were none expressing an opposite view) received by Edelman there was actually an illiterate and ill-spelt one from Chicago:

> you and all English citizen of the White race are going to have more trouble with them as long as they are around you can see the trouble we have with them at Little Rock and other Places it isn't Education they are fighting for in the United States or any other Place in the World but Sex they want to change the color of their skin and only way that it can be done is through Negroes and Whites marrying...

On the whole, my impression is that there is nothing quite as crude as this among expressions of opinion by British racists. However, a letter from West Kensington read as follows:

> The West Indians increase quicker than the Japanese or Indians and with the present population alone, in 10 years time this country will be half black.
> With a little out of work, it will be unsafe for women to go out at night. In our district the negroes have enormous new cars. Where do they get their money? They don't earn it.

Another correspondent from the same part of London expressed the view that the recent riots were 'inevitable' and 'probably basically sexual':

> Quite frankly white people have lots to lose from mixed marriages—the production not of white skinned 'English roses', but of coloured people with thick lips, fuzzy hair and rather bulbous eyes—they may have nice characters, but ours is the more civilised appearance.

The little concession on the question of character seems terribly English.

Where sex comes up it is not usually in connection with some general theory about miscegenation or the sexual appetites of non-whites, but with regard to observed incidents (whether or not accurately observed). The evidence suggests that many British girls and young women did find West Indian men very attractive. In her important survey of Brixton, South London, Sheila Patterson provided an appendix of stories from local newspapers describing cases in which white girls had apparently cohabited willingly with West Indian men. In Brixton and in Notting Hill in particular there were already thriving West Indian clubs. These were patronized by West Indian males, by West Indian males with their white girlfriends, and, sometimes, by unattached white women; they were scarcely patronized at all by West Indian women.[56] Wickenden was one of those who openly referred critically to 'wide boys' and 'flashy elements'.[57] Sheila Patterson was told by a female social worker in 1959:

Local people don't like the coloured men's attitude to women. You can't go along certain streets, even in broad daylight, without every second one making remarks and suggestions, whether you look the type or not. And local people say they are getting more noisy and aggressive as the numbers go up. They now feel so established in Brixton that they can do what they like.[58]

'Whether you look the type or not' is an interesting phrase, suggesting, apart from an ingrained snobbishness, that indeed there were young women who welcomed the attentions of the West Indians (and why not?).

Only one of the newspaper stories quoted by Sheila Patterson refers to an English girl actively resisting the (alleged) advances of a black man. The heading was 'Coloured Man Pestered Bus Queue Girl' (from the *South London Advertiser* of 9 March 1959):

A Brixton coloured man took hold of a girl's arm in a bus queue—and kept on annoying her although she showed resentment. He was given the maximum penalty at Lambeth on Monday for using insulting behaviour. H.A. 45 pleaded not guilty. A police officer said he saw A. in a bus queue standing behind a teenaged white girl. 'I saw him touch her back and place his hand on her shoulder. I could see from the expression on her face that she resented his action'... Giving evidence, A. said: 'I did not hound her at all. She was wearing something with many names written on, and I was reading them out. William, Joseph, John.' He said that the officer grabbed his arm and tried to twist it. The magistrate said: 'I have no doubt you were making a nuisance of yourself with the girl'. He asked his clerk what was the maximum penalty, and was told it was a £2 fine.

What actually happened we will never know. The prejudice of the magistrate is clear enough, but then the 45-year-old black man was, by his own account, behaving in a rather un-British way (are not bus queues sacred—and silent?). But compare the reactions here, and the size of the fine, to what could have happened at this time in any part of the American deep South.

That many blacks encountered a colour bar when seeking accommodation is not in question. Here I am concerned with white attitudes with respect to housing. Sheila Patterson quotes a Brixton woman in the summer of 1957 as remarking: 'Our street is getting "hot"—the blacks are beginning to move in and we'll have to sell while the going's good.' A Gallup poll in September 1958 found that of Londoners questioned as to their reactions if 'coloured people' came to live next door, 11 per cent would definitely move, 16 per cent might do so, and 73 per cent would not move. However, to the question 'Would you move if coloured people came to live in great numbers in your district?', 28 per cent said they would definitely move, another 28 per cent said they might do so, while 44 per cent said they would not move. Since a further poll in 1961 produced very similar results, it might reasonably be concluded that sheer unadulterated racial prejudice, as seen in objecting to a single black neighbour, was relatively rare, but that, as in many instances in America, purely racial elements were compounded by a fear of dropping house values, and of being swamped in an alien culture.[59]

On employment the position is mixed. Wickenden found that many employers welcomed West Indian workers, finding them efficient and hardworking. Quite certainly blacks did have experience of being told that jobs were filled, then finding the same jobs continuing to be advertised as vacant. The local labour exchange in Nottingham started treating blacks and whites separately, and whites were prone to presuming that when a black left the counter with a card this was for an actual job when it was only for an interview. Without there being much justification, many whites obviously feared that blacks were menacing their own job security, or at least undercutting wages.[60] There were incidents of racist abuse at the workplace (yet it may be noted that both the novel and the film *Saturday Night and Sunday Morning* featured one—though just one—apparently fully integrated black on the factory floor in Nottingham). Wickenden notes that some pubs and dance halls did try to impose colour bars, but that this practice was not widespread and that it was nearly always frowned upon by local magistrates (who had the power to refuse licences).

Harold Macmillan's Conservative government achieved an increased majority in the 'Never had it so good' election of 1959, and the position of those who advocated restrictions on immigration was thus greatly strengthened. Anything that stirs up righteous indignation and plays to people's fears is good for selling newspapers: the popular press (as with the *Daily Mail* article I have already referred to) strongly featured the need for, and imminence of, legislation to restrict immigration. With government intentions given such wide publicity, immigrants already in Britain naturally made hurried arrangements to bring in their families, relatives, and friends while there was yet time. In one year, 1959–60, the number of West Indian immigrants tripled, from 16,400 to 49,650. The Commonwealth Immigrants Bill was announced during 1961. Now, immigration from India and Pakistan, which till this time had been relatively insignificant, began to accelerate phenomenally: by the second half of 1962 more immigrants were coming from the Asian subcontinent than from the West Indies. It would probably be fair to say that the bill did have the overwhelming support of British public opinion: according to a Gallup poll in June 1961 67 per cent were in favour of restrictions on immigration, 6 per cent wanted a complete halt to all immigration, while 21 per cent were for the continuation of free entry. The bill was bitterly fought in Parliament by the Labour leadership, though as it passed into law on 27 February 1962 a number of Labour MPs abstained.[61] The act instituted a quota system for Commonwealth immigrants, with vouchers for those who actually had jobs or who were possessed of special skills; the fact that the Irish were exempted from its terms was widely held, rightly in the main, to highlight the racist nature of the legislation.

Apart from turning the race issue from a relatively small one into a very large one, by stimulating the enormous rush of immigrants to get into the country, the act also had the effect of producing an unprecedented unity between the different non-white groups. The Committee of Afro-Asian-Caribbean organizations (CAACO) was formed, and in Birmingham, for the first time ever, 450 West Indians, Asians, and whites marched against the new legislation under the auspices of the interracial Co-ordinating Committee Against Racial Discrimination (CCARD). During 1962 CCARD organized petitions for legislation against racial discrimination and incitement to racial hatred. There were the lineaments here of the American civil rights campaign; while the Labour party withdrew from its outright opposition to controls on immigration, it also announced plans for anti-racist legislation. And the American civil rights demonstrations, often to be seen on television, did indeed have their influence on developments in Britain. Paul Stephenson, a young man born in Bristol of West Indian parentage, had, in the spring of 1963, just returned from a three-month tour of America in which he had closely studied the civil rights campaign; now, as an official of the Bristol West Indian Development Council, he was anxious to apply what he had learned to British circumstances. He got his opportunity in April 1963 when the Bristol Omnibus Company refused employment to a West Indian applicant, on the basis of 'no coloureds'. Stephenson, in true deep South style, organized a boycott of the buses (though it should be noted that the colour bar was against employment, not against non-whites actually travelling on the buses). What counted was not actually any serious economic pressure on the bus company, but the national attention which the boycott attracted. By sheer serendipity the management gave in on 28 August, the very day of Martin Luther King's march on Washington.[62] It was a tiny episode, in a country where racial matters could scarcely really be compared to those in America, yet it did show that race, racial discrimination, and campaigns for equal rights were becoming a universal in the Western world; this was to become more and more true throughout the sixties.

As the non-white population expanded, tensions spread into other areas of social provision, notably education. There were now also explicit white condemnations of Asians, just as there had been of West Indians, particularly since the same geographical pattern was followed of Asians congregating in particular parts of particular cities. Southall in west London was one such area, so that very quickly a white Southall Residents Association came into existence. This association called for an immediate stop to immigration, declaring

> their whole way of life threatened and endangered by a flood of immigrants who were generally illiterate, dirty and completely unsuited and unused to our way of life. They overcrowd their properties to an alarming degree, create slums, endanger public health, and subject their neighbours to a life of misery, annoyance, abuse and bitterness...[63]

Segregated facilities had existed in some factories throughout the fifties, but without by any means being solely related to Asian workers, tended to increase as the number of non-whites rose.

> Segregated facilities, or requests for them from local workers, have been noted in a wide variety of industries and establishments over the last decade or so, usually in relation to toilet facilities, but sometimes to canteen arrangements. In general, these situations have arisen at the early stages of employment of immigrants and they have been resolved in a number of ways: for instance by firmness or tact on the managerial side; by special briefing during induction; by union or immigrant group protests.

A few white workers complain that Asians are dirtying the lavatories. The management is then persuaded to introduce separate toilets for Asians. In one instance when Asians had voluntarily used their own toilets for a month, white workers were forced to concede that the Asian toilets were cleaner than their own and the practice was discontinued.[64]

This account adds that such problems (even though the prejudice could be shown to be unfounded) continued well after 1963.

Wickenden's report on race in Britain in 1958, I suggested, betrayed a certain naivety—a naivety that would be impossible by the late sixties when race had become a much more central and complex issue. There is even greater naivety in a relatively early French account, *The French and Racism*, published in 1965, though referring to the late fifties and early sixties. On the basis of a small sample of Algerians, blacks, Jews, and gypsies, it rated different aspects of French racism according to seriousness. It also (this is what seems particularly naive) supported these ratings with quotations from white observers who, however, instead of being a representative sample of the population, turn out to be committed anti-racists.[65] The most widespread aspect of racism, getting a rating of 69, was what the survey called 'hostile prejudice'. A young female school teacher from Châteauroux is quoted on the effects of this hostile prejudice in education: 'All these prejudices, so much in evidence today, nourish racism, perpetuate stupidity and ignorance of the unknown. They are dangerous because they are absorbed by the children.' The educational system itself, according to this testimony, was a menace. But, according to a girl at a lycée in Rouen, lack of education was an equal menace: 'in France today racial prejudice still exists, and, above all, among the least educated layers of society.' 'Contempt' (rating 41) came next, then 'suspicion and fear' (rating 20). On this second point a solicitor from Chartres is brought in to testify:

> There is a certain orchestration by the reactionary press, with constant repetition of pejorative epithets. In this way racism takes the form of suspicion, the overwhelming sentiment in everyday life.

Hatred (18) is rated next, followed by indifference (15). A Nantes housewife is quoted on indifference:

> I don't see, in my circle, active racial discrimination, but a passive racism: we just leave the Algerians and Blacks to live in poverty, while showing a total lack of interest in them.

Last on the list are 'physical repugnance' (12) and 'paternalism' (10). In support of the former, a chemistry student in Paris is quoted as saying:

> On public transport, one can see the disgusted looks some people have when in contact with Blacks. The little people who make up the great mass of the French people, don't think of themselves as racists. But when they come in contact with a Black, an Algerian, even an Italian or a Spaniard, they always look disgusted...

218

On paternalism, an engineer from Aix-en-Provence is quoted as saying: 'Racism today in France takes a condescending, paternalist form. This kind of unconscious racism, alas, is often widespread among the left.'

This survey scarcely conveys more than that racism was widespread but took many, and sometimes quite subtle, forms. There is one rather more penetrating comment from a doctor in Paris about the way in which the Algerian revolt was in itself changing perceptions of Algerians:

> By their revolution, the Algerians have transformed the contempt that many people had for them into a feeling of hatred. And I believe that that form of racism (though no doubt more dangerous in the short term) none the less represents a certain advance. Hatred represents a sort of equality between man and man.[66]

The upshot for Algerians was devastating: they tended to be treated both as racially inferior and as enemies of the state. In the autumn of 1961 they had a curfew imposed on them, and the government closed down many of the clubs, bars, and cafés which they frequented. The explanation the minister of the interior, Roger Frey, gave to the National Assembly neatly summarizes the plight of Algerians: the policy, he said, was designed to protect 'honest' French Muslims and to distinguish them from 'criminals'.[67] On 17 October an Algerian protest march was viciously attacked by the Paris police, who used guns and clubs and then threw bodies into the Seine— possibly as many as 300. Violence in the sixties, as this chapter has made plain, was not confined to 1968–9; it was almost always provoked, and largely perpetrated, by the police. The Algerian war finally came to an end in 1962, the terms of settlement being defined in the Evian agreements. Under the agreements, in typically French fashion, an official employment agency (ONAMO) was established as the channel through which Algerians were permitted to come to France; in fact Algerians, in typically Algerian fashion, preferred to come as 'tourists', then look for work. Pressures built up, tensions increased, so that by April 1964 the government felt forced into a new policy, to be discussed later in this book.

In France's economic miracle, employment was not too much of an issue. The real scandal was living conditions. Juliette Minces, author of *Foreign Workers in France*, not actually published till 1973, but dealing with the late fifties and early sixties, prints the fascinating account of an Algerian, a middle-aged married man, who came to France in 1956:

> At first I lived with my brother in the 19th arrondissement. But I didn't stay there long. I met up with a cousin who lived in the *bidonville* [shanty town] of Nanterre. There I could have a *barraque* [shack] and with that, my wife and children were able to come and join me. I thought this was a lot better. At least I had a home and I had my children. I had bought wood and other stuff for 100,000 francs, and I built the *barraque*. That was in 1957. The land belonged to the local authority. All the Algerians helped me build it. Not only those from my village; others as well, because after all, we were all brothers. Besides, two-thirds of the *barraques* were occupied by Algerians. The others by Tunisians.
>
> We stayed there until the day the *barraque* was burned down. Before that, I had asked

Workers' Public Assistance to re-house us since we were eight in the *barraque*. They came to take a look. They came hundreds of times. But they never did anything. It was only when we were burned out that we were re-housed. It was in winter. No one knows how it happened. Perhaps it was a butane gas container which started the fire. In any case it spread everywhere. 80 to 85 *barraques* were burned down. That was a lot: in the *bidonville*, there were nearly 200 *barraques*. So, we were taken to the biggest building in Nanterre. It was the old hospital. The hospital was divided into cells. These cells were allocated to 35 families. Two or three cells per family. To begin with I was given 3 cells. For 8 persons. Later, when some people had left, I was given one more cell. So now I had four. Like that, we got along. I stayed there for six years.[68]

A family of eight living in three cells in a medieval hospital building! The account continues, and as policy changed in 1964 so the circumstances of the family also changed. But here we have been concerned only with the first beginnings of race as a problem in France and Britain. Later developments belong to later in the book.

Opinions differ as to how far the lot of southern Italians arriving in the north (particularly in Turin and Milan) can be likened to that of North Africans in France. There *were* differences and it does no good to a comparative investigation of this sort to ignore them. Italians from the south *were* Italian citizens, and it was in the interests of all Italian governments to stress the unity of the country, though, in truth, the historical experiences of north and south had been very different: as one-time Renaissance city-states, Florence, Venice, Milan, and many others were centres of European civilization; while Turin had been the elegant and sophisticated capital of Piedmont; although the cities of the south had an elegance of their own, the whole of the south had for too long been under the rule of a decadent Spanish dynasty; industrialization had come to the north, while the south remained predominantly a backward peasant economy. Some of the dialects spoken in the south were closer to Spanish or Greek than to 'educated Italian'—that is, an artificial language based on literary Tuscan (the language of Petrarch and Dante); but then there were several dialects in the north as well. Over the years, some southerners had become assimilated into northern life in a manner that was not really possible for most North Africans in France. The hostility of northerners to immigrants from the south (ranging from mild resentment to hatred) was in large measure class hostility—prosperous bourgeois and affluent worker versus uncultured, poverty-stricken peasant— but it did also contain elements that can only be described as racist.

I shall focus first on an account provided by a southerner of his 1961 journey from home to seek work in Turin, and then on the most pressing issue of all, housing for southern immigrants. The first-hand account, oddly, is rendered in the third person, as if its author were seeking to give universal validity to his personal experience.

After a long wait the train finally arrives, and the fugitive, amidst bitter commotion and good wishes to do well, leaves, in one instant everything seemingly becoming sad, around him his parents are on the verge of tears, the train gives a brutal snort like an enormous monster which has just snatched up someone to carry them off afar. Having made his final wave from the window to his family and friends, he has the greatest difficulty in finding a seat... In the depths of the carriage there is much shouting. One can see that it is a group of around ten people; when one of them sees the fugitive approaching, he guesses from the numbers of suitcases he's carrying that he's one of them and invites him to take a seat... He soon learns that the group is bound for Genoa with a collective ticket; he would like to have made the entire journey with his new friends, but he is bound for Turin, the city he had preferred because he had heard it spoken of so much by friends who had already tried this adventure, but now he almost repented of this choice, having here travelled so far from his own region... after many hours of journeying evening came, everyone thought about having a snack, after which the shouting became ever less animated and frequent till everyone dozed off and so for almost all of the rest of the night nobody any longer took any interest in the stations at which they stopped, knowing that the half-way point was still far away... The fugitives slept as best they could, practically one on top of the other on the rickety wooden benches; all they wanted to do was sleep, but without succeeding, wanting to sleep in order not to think. They were fathers of families who had had to leave their homes as soon they possibly could with only a few thousand lire apart from their train tickets, while the wives and children would only eat if they could do it on credit...

It's dawn, the train stops in a station and lots of people get on, they are workers and clerks who work in the nearby city: the fugitive is awakened by voices close by... but the dialect is new to him and he doesn't understand it, he lifts his gaze towards them and notes in the severe expressions a sense of superiority and contempt towards the others, and for you? he asks himself, not understanding the cause of this, relaxing with the thought that it is only his impression. After a short while they arrive at Genoa, exchanging many greetings with his companions of the journey, soon seeing them disappear each one with his suitcase...

Before the departure the only seats are taken, he would have liked to have exchanged a few words, but didn't dare, seeing that the incomers sat in silence, perhaps because their eyes were fixed on the luggage of the fugitives and understood who they were, where they came from and what they wanted to do where they were going, he for his part felt and behaved like a guest. The other fugitives also remained in silence, and the northerners spoke only amongst themselves in the unknown dialect.[69]

The author of that account is too literate to be typical; but then the illiterate provide no accounts at all. The directness and the sensitivity suggest that it provides real insights into the feelings of the immigrants from the south. It was published in Goffredo Foffi's classic piece of innovative research, *L'immigrazione meridionale a Torino* (Southern immigration in Turin). Foffi also provided stark data on the sort of accommodation immigrants could expect to find once they arrived in Turin. In general, conditions in Turin did not sink to the depths obtaining in Rome, Milan, and Genoa, where there were shanty towns as bad as those in France, variously termed *borgati*, or *coree*, or, in good honest French, *bidonvilles*. When the southerners began to arrive in substantial numbers in the early fifties they had found lodgings in old slum property, basements, attics, and crumbling farmhouses on the outskirts of the city. Something of a shanty town did grow up in the corso Polonia. However, this was razed to the ground in 1956 in preparation for the celebrations of the centenary of Italian unification—Turin was (nearly) united Italy's first capital at a time when Rome still belonged to the papacy. In general the authorities in Turin (like, incidentally, local and national authorities in Britain) were anxious to ensure that there would be no shanty towns (as existed in France, the USA, and other parts of Italy). In the late fifties massive building programmes produced high-rise flats for the workers: but, Foffi tells us, 'more or less racist' notice-boards indicated that these were barred to immigrants.[70] In the early sixties nearly 140,000 southerners were living in overcrowded conditions in seriously substandard accommodation: attics, basements, slum houses destined for demolition, and crumbling old farmhouses. Speculators were buying up old blocks of flats, charging high rents, and turning a blind eye to subletting. The majority of one- or two-room flats had no basic services at all; many gave on to balconies which were in imminent danger of collapsing. Often lavatories, situated in corridors, had to serve forty to fifty people. Foffi gives the notorious example of *la cartera* (the paper mill) on corso Regio Parco, a four-storey 'barracks' with narrow corridors on each floor into which each lodging opened, and four lavatories to each floor—'as bad as anything in Rome or the south'.[71]

Basic living conditions in the south could scarcely be attributed to racism (though they could be attributed to northern neglect of the south—as well as corruption in the south). Let us put it this way: running our eyes across our four countries there undoubtedly is, at a range of intensities, racism—but what is perhaps also fundamental is population movement, creating new stresses in already overcrowded cities. Even then we have to record also the positive aspects. What we have noted throughout Part II have been movements, and statements, of protest: by CORE and by SNCC, by Martin Luther King, and the French Movement Against Racism; by James Baldwin, and by Goffredo Foffi.

Part III

# The High Sixties, 1964–1969

# 6

# Acts of God and Acts of Government

## *Structural Imperatives*

This chapter relates back to what I said in Chapter 2 about causation and explanations in history, and deals with politics and state action, with economics and technology, and with democracy and social structure.

On 22 November 1963 the American president, John F. Kennedy, was assassinated in Dallas, Texas. Countless thousands mourned. If he had been too much of a politician to be an unstinting champion of good causes, he had done enough to attract the undying hatred of racists and reactionaries, and to be celebrated around the world as a youthful leader for a youthful age. His civil rights legislation was at an advanced stage. Had the assassin's bullet destroyed all that? In fact Kennedy's successor, Vice-President Lyndon B. Johnson, aided by a landslide victory in the presidential election of 1964, was able with ease to carry through not only the civil rights legislation but a whole programme of social and economic reform aimed at what Johnson called 'the great society'. Kennedy had been an upholder of American world power. Shortly after his election he had been involved in the Bay of Pigs fiasco, an abortive attempt to invade Communist Cuba. In October 1962 he had faced down the Soviet Premier Khrushchev and forced the removal of Soviet missiles from Cuba. And he had begun the involvement of American forces in trying to shore up the regime in South Vietnam, against increasingly threatening and successful Communist North Vietnam. Alas, as Johnson enacted Kennedy's civil rights and social legislation with interest, so he compounded the Vietnam policy, involving America in a war which divided the nation, and which in the rest of the world stood as an abhorrent symbol of American militarism and imperialism. In both Britain and Italy, governments acquired more of a liberal-left character, though no government dared openly oppose American foreign policy. In Italy, the system was of governments gradually shifting in composition; the first centre-left government, consisting of the Christian Democrats, the Social Democrats (a moderate, even conservative, party made up of those who had split from the original Italian Socialist party), and the Republicans, was formed in March 1962; after December 1963 the authentic Socialists were part of the government. In Britain, the Labour party gained power with a tiny majority in 1964, securing a comfortable majority in 1966. France remained under the sometimes repressive regime of de Gaulle, yet government policies were greatly influenced by the 'énarques', the all-powerful civil servants, graduates of the école Nationale d'Administration, who espoused the liberal Keynesian ideas which had come strongly into fashion by the end of the 1950s. Do assassinations, changes of government, even acts of Congress and Parliament, make any difference? That there were powers beyond the control of man was shown by the Italian floods of October 1966, which wreaked havoc upon the urban gems of Florence and Venice; however, long-term social development was scarcely affected, the main social significance of the disasters being that they drew attention to the dedication of the young people who put in long hours on restoration work. The remarkable flourish of social legislation in all four countries in the sixties certainly did have social consequences, though these were both secondary to the major economic and technological developments and inhibited by institutional circumstances and the persistence of conservative ideologies.

Technology was at its most potent in the workplace, affecting population movements and earnings, as new industries replaced old. It also provided the basis for the new consumer lifestyles. New production techniques brought down the price of consumer goods while making it possible to pay higher wages. The massive impingement of technology on society affected the urban landscape and rural environment, the working day, domestic chores and the pursuit of leisure, the role of women, and the nature of education. All societies, and governments, made much noise about the significance of science and technology; all, equally, showed little sense of what science could and could not achieve, and still less of how to ensure that the maximum benefits were obtained from the immense potential of science and technology. Technology was a vital component in the way societies developed in the 1960s, but development was haphazard and largely uncontrolled. Each January the American magazine *Time* announced its man of the previous year. In 1961 the magazine, at least recognizing that science is a collaborative, cumulative pursuit, chose a collectivity, fifteen American scientists: 'Statesmen and Savants, Builders and even Priests are their servants... Science is at the apogee of its power.'[1]

John F. Kennedy had greeted his election as president with the slogan of the 'new frontier', an image which was meant as much as anything to denote technological innovation. Some years later, seeking election in 1964, Harold Wilson spoke of 'the white heat of technology'. Kennedy promised to overhaul the lead which the Russians had established in the space race; the putting of a man on the moon in 1969 stood as a potent symbol of the utter triumph of American technology; space technology did also have some spinoffs for consumer society. Both the United States and Russia were spending 3 per cent of Gross National Product on scientific research; Britain, which continued to have a distinguished record in the winning of Nobel prizes for science, was spending 2.3 per cent; France was spending 1.5 per cent (which can be compared with the 1.8 per cent spent by West Germany). American dominance was far from absolute, but something of its extent can be seen from the fact that the United States sold five times more patents to France than France sold to the United States.[2] Perhaps the most important technology-based industry for the transformation of ordinary life was that of mass communications. It may be noted that the SECAM system for colour television was actually invented in France. Colour techniques for both film and television greatly improved, and colour television was just beginning to be widely available in Western Europe at the end of the decade. Systems for the reproduction of music in the home also advanced rapidly; synthesizing and other technical developments in the production of music brought consequences, including 'cross-over' between classical and popular music.

The growth of technology-based industries accelerated the move from country to town, especially in Italy. With technology-based industry came the so-called 'white-coat worker', who worked in clean conditions and without the hard physical effort which had been the distinguishing characteristic of traditional working-class occupations. The shift away from an emphasis on brute force facilitated the entry of women into the workplace. The building of vast petrochemical complexes, nuclear reactors, and new port facilities did nothing to improve the environment. The rapid industrial development of Mestre, the land-based extension of Venice, cast something of a shadow over that beautiful and much-suffering city. Many technological complexes were situated in what had hitherto been beautiful open countryside. Some of the big installations in southern Italy were genuinely intended to bring economic benefits to the local people; alas, as we shall increasingly see, even deliberate and well-intentioned acts of government often went sour. Much of Italy's new prosperity, in fact, depended on highly individualistic enterprises: tiny back-street businesses selling and above all repairing scooters (one of the great technological developments of the late forties, only fully exploited in the sixties), washing-machines, refrigerators. New industrial building techniques made possible the construction of the high-rise estates which housed both former slum-dwellers and immigrants pouring in to work in the newer industries. Hastily built high-rise domestic dwellings were quickly to prove one of the worst social evils of the decade.

Many new items became commonplace in domestic life, bringing undoubted benefits with them: synthetic fabrics, such as Dacron and Lycra; aerosol sprays; disinfectants and detergents; frozen foods; new plastics and polishes. The British end of the giant multinational conglomerate Unilever had set up its first research establishments in the aftermath of the Second World War. By 1963 there were three, when a fourth was established at Welwyn, to accommodate a team from Port Sunlight investigating problems of texture and flavour in oils and fats and problems relating to ice-cream. The capacity released at Port Sunlight was used for expanded research on detergents. The research was needed, for detergents were already choking up the country's sewers with foam; however, by 1965 a method was found of breaking down detergents biologically. The hazards of aerosols were not yet appreciated, though, as we have seen, pollution of the environment by the unrestrained wonders of science was already being challenged by that characteristic product of sixties activism and social concern, the new environmental movement.

If there is one set of technological developments which can challenge those in mass communications with respect to effects on ordinary life and human relationships, it is in the realm of contraception. The modern era in contraception was actually heralded by the international medical conference held in Tokyo in 1955. The intra-uterine device for contraceptive purposes had been experimented with in the 1920s and 1930s, but had produced such disastrous side-effects that it had been abandoned. At the Tokyo conference the Japanese reported the successful reintroduction of the device. At the same conference the American biologist Gregory Pincus reported his successes with hormonal oral contraceptives. The process by which ovulation is initiated, controlled, and regulated had been understood for fifty years. In the mid-1930s synthetic oestrogens were developed which could prevent the release of pituitary gonadotrophins, so that ovulation would be inhibited and conception controlled. Still lacking, however, was a cheap source of synthetic progesterone-like steroids. Then in the 1940s another American biologist, C. L. Markert, demonstrated that certain plants, particularly the Mexican yam, were rich sources of steroids from which orally effective progestogens could be synthesized cheaply. It was during the year before the Tokyo conference that Pincus and his colleagues successfully tried out the combined oestrogen-progestogen product in Puerto Rico. In 1960 the US Food and Drugs Administration approved the first birth-control pill, Enovid, as safe for use.[3] Always, though, there is a time-lag between scientific discovery and general usage. Later we shall have to examine the rather slow and halting process whereby new forms of contraception became widely disseminated; and we shall see that, although there is an obvious link between contraception and permissiveness, other, non-technological factors contributed to the liberalization of sexual attitudes.

Cultural and social change, while influenced by human agency, by contingency and convergence, takes place within the opportunities offered, and the constraints imposed, by structural, ideological, and institutional circumstances. Structural circumstances are basically those of demography, technology, and economics. Statistical tables can make the eyes glaze, and the spirit wither, but they are often the easiest way of presenting economic imperatives. And interrogating them closely can actually be quite interesting. In so far as life got better between the middle fifties and the middle seventies, the basic engine was economic growth. Even within the four countries we are concerned with, growth rates varied quite considerably (*rates* of growth don't tell everything, of course; it is easier to have a high rate of growth if you start from a low baseline). To get as full a picture with as wide a range of comparisons as possible, let us look at growth rates in the major industrialized countries (See Table 6.1).[4]

**Table 6.1** *Annual average growth rates of real gross domestic product (%)*

| Country | 1950–60 | | 1960–70 | |
| --- | --- | --- | --- | --- |
| | Total | Per capita | Total | Per capita |
| Japan | 8.0 | 6.8 | 10.6 | 9.4 |
| USA | 2.9 | 1.2 | 4.6 | 3.2 |
| UK | 2.7 | 2.3 | 2.8 | 2.1 |
| West Germany | 7.7 | 6.6 | 4.6 | 3.6 |
| France | 4.4 | 3.5 | 5.7 | 4.6 |
| Belgium | 2.7 | 2.0 | 4.5 | 3.9 |
| Netherlands | 4.6 | 3.3 | 5.3 | 4.0 |
| Sweden | 3.6 | 2.9 | 4.3 | 3.5 |
| Italy | 5.5 | 4.9 | 5.2 | 4.4 |

What we are most interested in are the figures in the third and fourth columns, and the extent to which they show increased growth rates as compared with the 1950s. We can note, first of all, that the highest rates all round are achieved by the two countries most devastated at the end of the Second World War, Japan and Germany. Starting from the highest plateau, America had not been specially impressive in the 1950s, but shows a distinct upward turn in the 1960s. Britain is the country with the poorest record, with only a slight upturn in total output and a fall in output per individual person. This is undoubtedly an indicator of growing economic problems, but we can readily see that it did not affect the sense of prosperity of the individual Briton when we learn that in Italy (which with respect to rates of growth is far superior) average earnings in manufacturing industry were 50.5p per hour, or £911 per year, whereas in Britain they were 56.6p per hour, or £1,263 per year. Growth rates in France and Italy are better than those of any other European country except the Netherlands, and better now than those of West Germany.

There is a great deal a table like this does *not* tell us, for example the different wage levels in Britain and in Italy. Government and business in both France and Italy strove to keep wages as low as possible. In 1962 sporadic strikes in north Italy culminated in June in a mass strike at Fiat. Later other metalworkers joined in and there were a number of violent clashes. Violent riots and running battles between demonstrators and police took place in the piazza Statuto in Turin from Saturday 7 July to late into the night of Monday 9 July. Urban violence was not unknown in democratic postwar Italy. In the summer of 1960 there had been clashes in which six demonstrators had been shot dead by the police, and more than twenty seriously wounded. But the 1960 demonstrations looked to the past in that they were directed against the threat of a Fascist element entering the government; the 1962 demonstrations marked the threshold of an era (roughly 'the sixties') in which workers were exerting all their power to secure a share of Italy's growing prosperity. Improving economic circumstances encouraged trade union action; trade union action helped further to improve wages. Between 1959 and 1962 the number of hours lost from industrial disputes rose from 16 million to nearly 58 million. This first wave of strikes reached its climax in 1963, which resulted in the workers gaining new collective bargaining agreements.[5] Throughout the sixties, up to the events of 1968, there was repeated industrial action in France against the deflationary, wage-controlling, and welfare-cutting policies of the de Gaulle government. And, whatever Table 6.1 may suggest, earnings in America remained considerably higher than elsewhere.

Proponents of the 'unravelling of America' thesis point to the fluctuations in the American economy in the 1960s, the slowing down of growth in the middle of the decade, the sense of many, particularly industrial workers, that they were no longer sharing in American prosperity, and the inflationary effects of the Vietnam war. It is certainly true that in contrast with the forties and fifties, a time of newfound prosperity and steady, if slow, growth in affluence, the sixties was a time of perceived economic instability; yet to see the sixties in America as anything other than a period of considerable affluence would be absurd. Like Britain before her, America was finding that it simply was not possible to prevent new countries entering the world marketplace and challenging the easy supremacy she had once enjoyed. The US share of world trade in 1948 amounted to 25 per cent; it was less than 15 per cent in 1964, and just over 10 per cent at the end of the decade. There were general problems for the long-term

229

future of the American economy. In the later sixties there was a lower sense of optimism and security in America than in the European countries. But from the point of view of ordinary life the most important facts were the enormous inequalities built into American society, and above all the division between the races. There was certainly nothing new about extreme poverty in American society, and in fact over the sixties the numbers of those in poverty (i.e. on less than half of average earnings) declined, from 22.4 per cent of the population in 1959 to 12.5 per cent in 1972. The extent to which poverty was tied up with race can be seen from the fact that in 1959 56 per cent of non-whites were in poverty; by 1972 the figure had dropped to 30.9 per cent. The equivalent figures for whites are, in 1959 18.1 per cent, and in 1972, 9.9 per cent. America was the country which most obviously had an under-class, that is to say a class of poor people whose poverty was due to a variety of circumstances rather than just to being the lowest social class (as in 'working class', or 'peasant class'). Table 6.2 gives a breakdown of who constituted the poor in America in 1972.[6]

**Table 6.2** *The American poor in 1972*

| What kind of people | % |
|---|---|
| White | 9.9 |
| Black | 30.9 |
| Mexican | 28.9 |
| Puerto Rican | 32.2 |
| Male head of family | 8 |
| Female head of family | 3.9 |
| *Education of family head* | |
| <8 years | 18 |
| High school | 6 |
| College | 2 |
| Rural farm | 20 |
| Rural non-farm | 15 |
| Central city | 1.2 |
| *Age* | |
| < 15 | 18 |
| 16–64 | 18 |
| >65 | 12 |

There is still much to say about racial prejudice and racial violence, but the overall statistics do show gains for blacks. In 1959 the median income of black male employees was 59 per cent of that of white male employees; by 1969 that figure had gone up to 67 per cent (still a very long way from equality, of course). Black gains were particularly strong in white-collar jobs (Table 6.3). It may be noted that one consequence of the rapid gains made by black women was that white women found it increasingly difficult to find maids. In 1960, 36 per cent of black women were in domestic service; by 1970 this figure had dropped to 15 per cent.[7]

**Table 6.3** *Employment in white-collar jobs (%)*

| Labour force | 1960 | 1970 |
|---|---|---|
| Black male | 11 | 17 |
| White male | 37 | 40 |
| Black female | 17 | 32 |
| White female | 59 | 61 |

In Italy the crucial structural factors, apart from the steady spread of affluence and the consequent rise in consumption (which I shall come to in a moment), were the movement from agricultural occupations (or simply unemployment in a rural setting) to industrial employment, the movement from the south to the north, and the continuing but changing inequality between north and south (Table 6.4). The most striking statistic is that of the decline in the numbers involved in agriculture, forestry, and fishing, with a steep decline from 42.2 per cent of the active population in 1951 to 29.5 per cent in 1961, with a further steady decline to 17.2 per cent in 1971. In 1951 there had actually been more people employed in the rural and fishing sector than in industry. The increase in those employed in industry is not by any means as striking: an increase of over 8 per cent between 1951 and 1961, and then an increase of slightly less than 4 per cent up to 1971. It is a feature of modern economies to have a high proportion of the active population employed in the services sector, though it does have to be added that traditionally Italy always had a rather bloated bureaucracy. Anyway, the increasing size of this sector is easy to see. If we continue the series to 1978, we would find that by that stage the services sector, at 48.0 per cent, had actually overtaken the industrial sector, at 37.5 per cent. Now all these figures are percentages of the *active* population. It is another sign of a modern economy that the proportion of those non-active is considerably greater than the proportion of those who are active. The non-active category primarily comprises children and old people. In the earlier periods there would also be a substantial proportion of non-working wives, but as we shall see later, a notable feature of the sixties is the accelerating entry of women into the active sector—a development that partially cancels out both the increasing number of young people staying longer in education and the growing number of older people (to some extent due to better nutrition and medical services).

**Table 6.4** *Italy: employment by sector*

| Sector | 1951 | | 1961 | | 1971 | |
|---|---|---|---|---|---|---|
| | 000 | % | 000 | % | 000 | % |
| Agriculture, forestry, fishing | 8,261 | 42.2 | 5,693 | 29.5 | 3,423 | 17.2 |
| Industry | 6,290 | 32.1 | 7,693 | 40.6 | 8,350 | 44.4 |
| Services | 5,026 | 25.7 | 5,936 | 30.3 | 7,238 | 38.4 |
| Total active | 19,577 | 41.2 | 19,592 | 38.7 | 18,831 | 34.8 |
| Total non-active | 27,939 | 58.8 | 31,032 | 61.3 | 35,306 | 65.2 |
| TOTAL | 47,516 | 100 | 50,624 | 100 | 54,137 | 100 |

*Source:* Antonio Gambino et al., *Dal '68 a oggi: come siamo e come eravamo* (Bari, 1979), 184.

The demographic statistics set out in Table 6.5, in addition to making the basic division between the north and the south (taken, as usual, together with the islands), divides the north into three. First, the north-west, which basically consists of what is often called the 'industrial triangle', Milan, Turin, Genoa—we will see the phenomenal growth in this area; then the northeast, which includes Venice but which is largely made up of the foothills of the Alps—we will see that this actually loses population in the fifties, recovering again in the 1960s; and the north-central—which includes Rome, and which grows only marginally in the fifties, but, as a major government and service sector centre, quite considerably in the sixties.[8]

**Table 6.5** *Italy: increases and decreases in population*

|  | Natural increase 1951–61 | Balance of migration inwards and outwards 1951–71 | Natural increase 1961–71 | Balance of migration inwards and outwards 1961–71 |
|---|---|---|---|---|
| North-west | 316,710 | 1,131,519 (+9.08%) | 688,970 | 1,075,487 (+7.65%) |
| North-east | 543,119 | −428,920 (−5.18%) | 574,117 | 140,309 (+1.45%) |
| Central | 597,543 | 86,156 (+0.95%) | 692,057 | 309,628 (+3.13%) |
| South and islands | 2,607,372 | −2,054,359 (−11.6%) | 2,476,894 | −2,090,970 (−11.5%) |
| TOTAL FOR ITALY | 4,064,744 | −1,319,604 (−2.72%) | 4,432,038 | −565,545 (−1.09%) |

Table 6.5 is a fascinating one. From the first column you can see that in the busiest industrial area (the north-west, 'industrial triangle') the birth rate (the natural rate of increase) is lowest, while it is high in the less industrialized areas, and above all in the south. We can safely say, I think, that birth control of some sort is being practised in the north-west, while the Catholic embargo on any form of fertility control is still very strong in the south. Apart from the phenomenal migration into the north-west (which reached its peak at the end of the fifties and runs at a slightly lower level throughout the sixties), we can see the heavy population losses of the south, consistently at 11.6 per cent or 11.5 per cent. In the sixties, southern immigrants are going to all parts of north and central Italy, rather than just to the north-west (stirring up, I may say, racial prejudice every-where against southerners). Italians, as we can see from the final line, are still seeking work overseas, though in the sixties (a sign of the generally booming Italian economy) the figure falls by considerably more than half.

Most of the modern industry was in the centre-north, while manufacture in the south was largely confined to traditional consumer goods: food and tobacco, clothing and footwear, hides and skins. What the south desperately needed was industrial investment. And indeed the sixties are characterized by a serious effort to address this problem. In 1961, industrial investment in the centre-north was still a good 25 per cent higher than that in the south; but by 1971 invest-ment in the south was more than double that in the north and, though total investment fell away slightly, remained nearly at that proportion in 1975.[9] Accordingly, increases in real income (from a much lower baseline) were higher in all regions of the south, save for Campania and

Puglia, than in the centre-north: across the south between 1963 and 1974 the average annual increase was 4.2 per cent, compared with 3.8 per cent in the centre-north. Taking per capita income in Italy as a whole as 100 in 1974, it was still only 68.8 in the south as against 116.8 in the centre-north.[10]

Everywhere, while the prices of food and other necessities steadily rose the prices of small cars, in relation to earning power, fell, and the many products of the new technology, such as television sets and washing-machines, were, despite inflation, actually costing less. In Italy, to take what was probably the most extreme example, between 1953 and 1965 prices of groceries and meat, in real terms, went up by more than 20 per cent; fresh vegetables went up by more than 30 per cent; fresh fish by more than 35 per cent; and fruit by more than 25 per cent. But furniture and electrical gadgets came down by 26 per cent, and cars by 33 per cent.

Chapters 8 and 9 will fill out in rich detail what all this actually meant for the lives of people in different parts of Italy; here, before we move further into our study of the High Sixties, it is important to get the basic numbers and proportions sorted out. We turn now to some of the vital statistics for France. Italy for a century had considered itself overpopulated, and even at the end of our period still had an excess of workers going abroad in search of employment. France, from at least the time of the First World War, had feared herself to be underpopulated. The situation with regard to immigrants into France was explained in the previous chapter. But the whole demographic pattern in France had been changed to a more striking degree, given past history, than in any other country. Before the Second World War France was averaging 600,000 births per year. From 1946 to 1950 the average figure was 850,000 per year; thereafter this stabilized at around 800,000. Paris before the war had been the selfish city, seen by the rest of France as putting luxury before family life, and certainly producing the fewest children of any part of France.[11] Now that was turned topsyturvy: Paris had a fecundity rate of 40 per cent, compared with 24 per cent for all of the rest of France. Overall the size of French families stabilized at two to three children; the end had come both for one-child families and for the very large ones that could still be found in rural areas in the prewar years.[12] The 'baby boom' was responsible for nearly two-thirds of the increase in population, between 1947 and 1957, from 40.3 million to 44.3 million. Between 1946 and 1957 the proportion of people under 20 in the population rose from 29.5 per cent to 31.7 per cent. Yet while overall population increased significantly, the number of those in employment remained steady at around 20 million, the same as at the beginning of the century, and actually one million fewer than in 1926–30. It is the same point as I made in connection with Italy: in a sophisticated society there are more young people (because they are staying on in education) and more old people (because they are living longer) being supported by a proportionately smaller active population.[13] Within this active population, the key fact was the decline in numbers working in agriculture. Those working in industry increased, but not in any very striking way. More striking, really, were the increases in those employed in commerce and services, and in the provision of basic consumer goods such as food, drink, and clothing. The exact proportions are made clear in Table 6.6.

**Table 6.6** *France: active population in millions, by sector*

| Sector | 1954 | 1963 | 1968 |
|---|---|---|---|
| Agriculture and forests | 5,030 | 3,650 | 2,950 |
| Industry | 5,550 | 5,920 | 5,852 |
| Food, drink, and clothing | 1,320 | 1,670 | 2,000 |
| Transport, commerce, services | 4,430 | 5,110 | 5,800 |
| Other | 2,920 | 3,380 | 3,550 |
| TOTAL ACTIVE POPULATION | 19,250 | 19,730 | 20,150 |

*Source:* Andrée Gauron, *Histoire économique et sociale de la cinquième république*, i (Paris, 1983), 20–1.

Increased purchasing power is the other major structural phenomenon. The effects of the 'economic miracle' are reflected in the way in which overall disposable income increased by 4.9 per cent in real terms between 1959 and 1963; economic fluctuations and the restrictionist policies of Gaullism are reflected in the way in which the figure for 1963–9 drops to 3.2 per cent (though it is significant enough, for all that); and the post-Gaullist phase is reflected in the again higher figure of 4.5 per cent for the period 1969–73. The differing figures for major categories are set out in Table 6.7 (it must always be remembered that those in the higher occupations already had much higher salaries).

**Table 6.7** *France: percentage growth in disposable income, 1959–1973 (i.e. net salaries)*

| | 1959–63 | 1963–9 | 1969–73 |
|---|---|---|---|
| Top executives | 2.8 | 2.9 | 3.5 |
| Middle management | 4.7 | 2.7 | 2.7 |
| White-collar workers | 4.2 | 3.0 | 4.4 |
| Workers (*ouvriers*) | 4.3 | 3.0 | 4.9 |

*Source:* Gauron, *Histoire économique et sociale*, i. 95.

The salient facts for Britain can be quickly summarized. In 1951 the average weekly earnings of men over 21 had stood at £8.30 per week. A decade later the figure had almost doubled, to £15.35; in 1966 it was £20.30, in 1968 £23.00, in 1969 £24.80, in 1970 £28.05, and in 1971 £30.93. In looking at these money wages, inflation does have to be taken into account. Between 1955 and 1960 retail prices rose by 15 per cent; and by 1969 they were 63 per cent higher than in 1955. But against that, weekly wage *rates* rose 25 per cent between 1955 and 1960, and had risen by 88 per cent in 1969. When overtime is taken into account, we find average weekly *earnings* rose 34 per cent between 1955 and 1960, and 130 per cent between 1955 and 1969. This last figure was almost exactly matched by the average earnings of middle-class salaried employees, which rose by 127 per cent between 1955 and 1969. The overall picture can be grasped from Table 6.8. The very slight drop in consumer expenditure at the end of our period may be noted. Everything taken together, while British incomes were probably still higher than those in France and Italy, the signs are that as a result of the transformations of the sixties—which were continued in France and Italy just as Britain began to suffer more and more from her chronic economic weaknesses—the British would shortly fall behind.

**Table 6.8** *Britain: disposable income and consumer expenditure, at constant 1970 prices, in pounds sterling*

|  | 1951 | 1961 | 1971 | 1972 | 1973 | 1974 |
|---|---|---|---|---|---|---|
| Personal disposable income | 390 | 532 | 638 | 680 | 719 | 724 |
| Consumer expenditure | 385 | 486 | 578 | 611 | 638 | 637 |

*Source:* Central Statistical Office, *National Income and Expenditure* (1975).

Consumerism is too often treated as a blind force, transforming the lives of everyone in identical, impersonal ways. Or, in the eyes of counter-cultural critics, it is a seductive evil in the manner in which it substitutes commercial tinsel for true values, and diverts the masses from their real interests. No question but that the manufacturing-marketing-advertising complex was carefully constructed to maximize wants and keep demand high. But consumers were not complete puppets. As we survey the statistics, we must also bring into the reckoning two important movements of the High Sixties: the consumer movement itself, challenging the big manufacturers and the shops, seeking out bargains, exposing exploitation; and the growing concern for (significantly, a new phrase of the mid-sixties) the 'quality of life'. I do not want to exaggerate what were minority movements, but I want to draw attention to the fact that consumers did have their champions, whose exploits often became part of media spectacle. In 1965 Ralph Nader launched his attack on the poor safety record of American automobiles with *Unsafe at Any Speed*, with another American champion coming forward three years later when Sidney Margoles published *The Innocent Consumer versus the Exploiters*.[14] As Nader put it, striking a note already struck by Rachel Carson, and to be repeated insistently by the end of the decade: 'A great problem of contemporary life is how to control the power of economic interests which ignore the harmful effects of their applied science and technology.'

Finally, in this statistical underpinning for things to come, let us look at the figures for the numbers of women in paid employment. One problem is that the statistics can be served up in two rather different ways, and sometimes the sources are not absolutely clear as to which is being used. One can give the percentage of the total workforce, or the percentage for any particular sector, or profession, who are women. Alternatively, one can do it the other way round and take the percentage of the total number of women who are in employment, or in some particular type of employment. The latter method is the one usually followed, but there still remain problems of whether or not part-time work is included. Surveys have actually shown that many married women preferred simply to have part-time work, so it seems reasonable to include that. Even so, the percentage of all women working actually fell slightly in France, with the growth of affluence, up till the middle sixties; it began to increase thereafter. In Italy, many women who had worked in agriculture lost their jobs with the move to the towns. The overall figures, therefore, are all the more impressive: the percentage of women in paid employment in 1951 was 27.5 per cent; by 1963 it was 30.6 per cent, and it continued thereafter. The French figures, when adjusted for part-time employment, are: 1951, 31.5 per cent; 1960, 34.1 per cent; 1966, 36.5 per cent. The French figures are actually quite high throughout: 1954, 43.9 per cent; 1962, 42.6 per cent; 1964, 40.2 per cent. In Britain, the figure in 1965 was already as high as 50 per cent; but in 1972 this had only gone up marginally to 53 per cent.[15] One other statistic is noteworthy, though it did not begin to affect relations between the sexes until well into the seventies. Throughout history, although a slightly higher number of male than female children are born, females have always been in an excess in the population because of the greater vulnerability of male children and, above all, because of the loss of males in war. Young French conscripts died in the Algerian war up until 1962, and American ones throughout most of the period in Vietnam. At the beginning of the seventies females were still in excess in all populations, but for the first time in age groups under 45, and particularly in the mating age groups, men were now beginning to be in excess.[16]

### *The Great Society, the Civilized Society, and Other Places*

On 1 February 1962 President Kennedy had delivered a message to Congress on 'public welfare', the first presidential message in American history devoted entirely to this subject. Shortly this was followed by the publication of one of the famous books signalling the first stirrings of change at the beginning of the sixties, *The Other America: Poverty in the United States*, by Michael Harrington. The ever-alert Dwight MacDonald gave the book a push and a spin by summarizing its main findings in his usual scintillating way in a *New Yorker* article entitled 'Our Invisible Poor'. But Harrington, indeed, was well able to speak for himself:

> The United States in the sixties contains an affluent society within its borders, millions and tens of millions enjoy the highest standard of life the world has ever known. This blessing is mixed. It is built upon a peculiarly distorted economy, one that often proliferates pseudo-needs rather than satisfying human needs. For some, it has resulted in a sense of spiritual emptiness, of alienation. Yet a man would be a fool to prefer hunger to satiety, and the material gains at least open up the possibility of a rich and full existence.
>
> At the same time, the United States contains an under-developed nation, a culture of poverty. Its inhabitants do not suffer the extreme privation of the peasants of Asia or the Tribesmen of Africa, yet the mechanism of the misery is similar. They are beyond history, beyond progress, sunk in a paralysing, maiming routine.
>
> The new nations, however, have one advantage: poverty is so general and so extreme that it is the passion of the entire society to obliterate it. Every resource, every policy, is measured by its effect on the lowest and most impoverished. There is a gigantic mobilization of the spirit of the society: aspiration becomes a national purpose that penetrates to every village and motivates a historic transformation.
>
> But this country seems to be caught in a paradox. Because its poverty is not so deadly, because so many are enjoying a decent standard of life, there are indifference and

blindness to the plight of the poor.

The problem, then, is to a great extent one of vision. The nation of the well-off must be able to see through the wall of affluence and recognise the alien citizens on the other side.[17]

Harrington was a socialist, and a good deal to the left of most of Kennedy's advisers and consultants. But they too believed that such an affluent society could solve the problem of poverty and, indeed, that it was an affront to 'their' America that poverty should exist at all. On 25 July Kennedy signed into law what were formally the Public Welfare Amendments to the Social Security Act of 1935, more generally known as the Social Service Amendments. Basically these amendments provided greatly increased federal support (75 per cent of the cost) to the states for the provision of job training, placement, and counselling for those on public assistance. The president declared them 'the most far-reaching revision of our public welfare programme since it was enacted in 1935'.[18] He planned to go further than these rather traditional measures: 'Now look,' he is reported as having said to Walter Heller, the chairman of his council of economic advisers in December 1962, 'I want to go beyond the things that have already been accomplished. Give me the facts and figures on the things we still have to do. For example, what about the poverty problem in the United States?' Heller had his staff prepare a memo on 'the poverty cycle' which was circulated to members of the government in the autumn.[19] Not long before his assassination Kennedy had asked for the preparation of 'a set of measures which might be woven into a basic attack on the problems of poverty and waste of human resources, as part of the 1964 legislative programme'. Johnson, on hearing of these proposals, was apparently very enthusiastic about them. In his State of the Union message of January 1964, the new president announced a thirteen-point programme which would declare 'unconditional war on poverty', a 'domestic enemy which threatens the strength of our nation and the welfare of our people'. In May, in a speech at the University of Michigan, he announced that out of such a war on poverty there would be created 'the great society'.[20]

The concept of 'the civilized society' was that of the home secretary in the British Labour government, Roy Jenkins, and appears a little later, specifically referring to the British legislation of 1967 and 1968 dealing with matters other than those of basic poverty. Britain at that time still had Europe's most fully developed welfare state, established not in the sixties but in the immediate postwar years (it is no part of the purpose of this book to argue that all developments enhancing the lives of the people happened in the sixties). The immediate postwar years, too, are the crucial ones for the development of the welfare state in France; but in Italy those same years were, in the words of Maurizio Ferrera, ones of 'lost opportunity'[21]—institutional and ideological constraints were too pervasive for the achievement of anything more than a slight amplification of existing measures. America's limited, insurance-based social security system originated in 1935 as part of Roosevelt's New Deal. Truly it was only in the sixties that welfare measures on anything like a European scale were introduced; and much of the real expansion in the American system came after 1968 when a conservative president was in office, Richard Nixon (demonstrating once more that emphasizing the political composition of governments is not always the best way of illuminating social history). In Britain during the sixties there were improvements and amplifications to the existing system. In France there were certain modifications, some of them designed to reduce government spending; the important point is that the fundamentals of the French system were maintained and, because of generally favourable economic conditions, served the French people well. In Italy the sixties was a time of elevated talk. Social Democrats and Socialists, as they came into government, as well as the more progressive Christian Democrats they joined, spoke of radical overhaul of the very patchy welfare system; but once more, institutional and ideological constraints ensured that little resulted beyond reforms on paper. The chronology of welfare in Italy is rather different from that of the other countries, with the period of the establishment of a welfare state only commencing in 1968, and most of the major reforms coming in the 1970s.

In all four countries the ideology of progressive liberalism, enhanced, especially in Britain, by a kind of socialism, was strong, though everywhere (least in Britain) competing with other ideologies (of self-help conservatism and private charitable action, for example). Britain already had the structure and infrastructure of a welfare state, so that welfare reforms generally were delivered to those they were aimed at. America and Italy were constantly having to manufacture new mechanisms; these had to compete with existing vested interests. Such social legislation as existed was in no way affected by the major intellectual developments of the time—neo-Marxist, structuralist, post-structuralist—which I shall be discussing in the next chapter. The deliberate actions of government were frequently frustrated, and often had none of the results hoped of them. But politicians' pronouncements in favour, and sometimes implementation, of welfare reforms in the 1960s were an important characteristic of the time. Some of what was done was brought about by the actions and involvement of the people themselves—most obviously in the interaction between the civil rights movement and the American government's 'war on poverty', or in Italian and French trade union activism. Government policies, or, perhaps more often, the expressed intentions of government, then further legitimized popular action.

Let us start with the British 'welfare state'. The phrase itself is used in a variety of ways, most loosely of all when it is used to define an entire society; thus, in some of the American literature 'welfare state' is used as a generic term for all the developed societies after 1945. Greater exactness can be achieved if the term is limited to one *part* of society, the complex of schemes and services through which the central government, together with the local authorities, assumes responsibility for dealing with all of the different types of social problem which beset individual citizens. Thus a country could be said (at the beginning of the sixties) to have 'a comprehensive welfare state', as in Britain, 'a patchy and inadequate one', as in Italy, or 'a very limited one', as in the United States. The British welfare state was concerned with four major problems. Most fundamental of these was that of income or *social security*: people can fail to have enough to live on through being unemployed, through being unemployable, through being too old, through having too many children, through being injured, through being pregnant, and through being ill. But if people are ill, they do not just need an income while they are out of work, they need treatment: the second problem was that of the provision of *medical services*. Sickness, in the past, had often been engendered by bad housing; good housing for everyone, in any case, was the mark of a civilized society. *Housing*, then, was the third problem to be dealt with by the welfare state. If individuals were to participate fully in a civilized society they would also require a decent *education*—the fourth problem. But what point was there in having national insurance benefits, free medical care, decent housing, and effective schooling if there were no jobs? It was a fundamental assumption of the war and postwar period that all the different pieces of welfare state legislation should be backed up by an economic policy deliberately designed to create jobs and *avoid unemployment*. *Care of children* had aspects relating to all of these problems, but could also be seen as a problem in its own right. Enthusiasts for the welfare state ideal, including both professional experts and left-wing politicians, argued that the welfare state should also be responsible for the *environment, consumer protection,* and the *arts.*

Central to the British social security system was national insurance, absolutely 'universalist' in principle, in that every employed person had to make the same flat-rate contribution, everyone in return receiving the same flat-rate benefits when their employment was interrupted. In addition to national insurance there was national assistance, basically for those unable (because, e.g. they were already quite old when the scheme came into existence) to make the required number of contributions to national insurance. By the late fifties it had become clear that while flat-rate contributions to national insurance were quite burdensome for the lowest-paid, the flat-rate benefits themselves were falling far behind the sort of income expected within an affluent society. In 1959 the Conservatives introduced a new scheme whereby better-off employees paid an additional graduated contribution which in return qualified for an additional earnings-related pension. Employers, provided they paid a higher flat-rate contribution, were permitted to contract out of the scheme if they offered their own employees an adequate pension scheme, protected on change of employment. The new principle was actually extended by the Labour government in 1966 when it introduced earnings-related contributions and benefits to cover the first six months of loss of earnings from causes other than retirement. One major contribution to income security was the Redundancy Payments Act of 1965, which laid down that lump-sum payments, financed partly by the employer and partly by compulsory contributions from all insured employees, must be paid to employees with over two years' service dismissed simply because of a change in the employer's requirements or circumstances.

The most important piece of welfare legislation of the sixties was the Ministry of Social Security Act of 1966, which (among other things) replaced national assistance, still seen by many as a degrading dole handed out by the state, by supplementary benefits, which sounded more like something to which a legitimate claim could be established. The growing view in official Labour as well as Conservative circles was that the universalist principle of 1945 was in reality wasteful of resources in that it spread inadequate benefits too thinly across the entire nation, giving a little to those who had no need, and too little to those who were in deep need. Thus, supplementary benefits both depended upon a means test and were administered in a flexible way, with much depending upon the discretion of local officials. Payable to those not in full-time employment, supplementary benefits were intended to bring income up to a scale calculated according to the number and age of the dependent children, together with a rent allowance. Humane and sensitive in many respects (great efforts were made to bring to the attention of the deprived the benefits

239

to which they were entitled), the scheme as it worked in practice had two particularly obnoxious features. First was the bureaucratic device of the 'wage-stop' designed to ensure that supplementary benefits did not act as an encouragement to the work-shy. Those who, when in employment, earned less than the income normally provided by supplementary benefits were deliberately, when out of work, paid a level of benefits slightly below their potential earnings when in work. Such people were placed in a poverty trap from which, short of a miraculous change in their employment prospects, there was no prospect of escape. Second was the 'cohabitation rule': single, separated, or divorced women claiming benefits, often for the support of their children, could have their benefits stopped if the snoopers of the Department of Health and Social Security discovered that they were in fact cohabiting with a man who could then be held to be providing them with financial support. But the main story is of the deliberate seeking-out of sources of deprivation ignored in the original welfare state of 1945–8: the Rating Act of 1966 allowed for rate rebates for those in need and the National Insurance (Old Persons and Widows Pensions and Attendance Allowance) Act of 1970 directed new benefits towards the disabled and very old.

The experience of the National Health Service suggested that some commercialism and freedom from the universalist control of the state could coexist with the maintenance of the ideal of a high-level national service. Medical insurance schemes, offering both care in private nursing homes and access to pay beds in the NHS hospitals, greatly expanded: they had about a million members at the beginning of the seventies, compared with only 50,000 at the end of the forties. Supporters of such schemes argued that they actually brought more resources within the national system; opponents argued, probably with greater salience, that they enabled the wealthy to jump the queue for treatment of non-acute conditions. A major problem for the NHS in its first dozen years was the desperate shortage of hospitals. To this, because of government miscalculation, was added by the late fifties a shortage of doctors. In the sixties genuine attempts were made to deal with both problems. A ten-year hospital-building programme was announced by the Conservatives in 1962; the shortage of General Practitioners reached a peak in the middle sixties when many doctors had more than the maximum permitted number of 3,500 patients on their lists. But after 1966, special additional allowances were earmarked for practices in certain designated areas, and by 1971 the average number of patients per doctor was down to 2,421. Attempts to expand private practice, it may be noted, were not greatly successful at this time. A new private scheme launched by the British Medical Association in 1965 came to an unlamented demise within three years. Doctors within the NHS had meantime gained a more generous system of remuneration, which in particular tended to reward the better and more progressive doctors. The British NHS was unique in that it was free at point of service (in other Western countries payment almost always had to be disbursed first, then subsequently reclaimed in whole or in part). But the demand for treatment, and above all for medicines, seemed nearly bottomless. At first the Labour government abolished the charges for medical prescriptions which had been introduced in the fifties, but in 1968 charges for medicines were reintroduced, together with dental charges amounting to half the cost of the treatment.

One sphere in which British society had always shown itself to be particularly uncaring was that of mental health. The epoch-making Mental Health Act of 1959, which brought a new flexibility and informality to the treatment of mental disorder, could not of itself carry through a revolution. In the sixties there were disclosures of ill-treatment of mental patients in some of the large, badly managed, and under-staffed institutions. These were followed by the setting up of the Hospital Advisory Service, and a general move towards attending more closely to the plight of mental patients.

Five Acts of Parliament provided the bases for Roy Jenkins's notion of Britain as the 'Civilized Society'. In October 1965 capital punishment was suspended for five years, and in 1969 abolition was made permanent (this put Britain on a par with Italy, where, it should be recognized, Catholicism placed a premium on the sanctity of human life, and ahead of America and France). Liberal MP David Steel was responsible for the Abortion Reform Bill, which, with the support of the government and several Conservatives, passed into law in 1967. The new act merely required that two doctors should certify that an abortion was necessary on medical or psychological grounds; and it authorized abortions on the National Health Service. The National Health Service (Family Planning) Act of the same year empowered local authorities to provide (without charge) contraceptives and contraceptive advice. Also in 1967, thanks to the efforts of Labour MP Leo Abse, the Sexual Offences Act decriminalized homosexual acts between consenting adults in private. Clause 1 of the Divorce Reform Act of 1969 tore apart the shrouds of centuries:

> After the commencement of this Act the sole ground on which a petition for divorce may be presented to the court by either party to a marriage shall be that the marriage has broken down irretrievably.

Henceforth, if a couple had lived apart for two years, and both consented, they had a right to divorce, If separation had lasted five years, then either partner was entitled to a divorce, even if the other did not agree. As we shall see in Chapter 13, all of this legislation relating to sexual matters aroused the admiration of reformers in the other three countries struggling to bring about similar changes there.

The British welfare state operated through the existing apparatus of British central government, expanded greatly where necessary; though far from unified in the way in which it was administered, and in the ways in which individuals secured benefits, it did have behind it the combined resources raised by British governments through general taxation; even national insurance did not really operate as a completely self-contained, self-financing insurance fund insulated from other government revenues. In France and Italy, on the contrary, although both countries were affected by the movement of opinion arising from the war experience strongly favouring unified social provision for all citizens, the principle was maintained of establishing separate funds for different types of social provision; still more was this the case in the United States. In France and Italy, too, there were established traditions of social provision having been made specifically and separately for certain occupational categories, rather than for citizens as a whole, and of creating special elected or nominated agencies, at local or regional level, to administer such schemes. In France, the basic ideal behind the postwar provisions was that of solidarity, or universality. Benefits were intended to be flat-rate, but, in contrast with the British scheme, contributions were

graduated according to income. The subsequent history of welfare provision is the rather contradictory one of attempts to move closer to the ideal of the unified scheme, the introduction of
graduated benefits, and attempts to control costs, particularly at times of financial crisis. The main
ministries responsible for social welfare were the ministry for public health and population, the
ministry of labour and social security, the ministry for ex-servicemen and war victims, and the
ministry for reconstruction and housing. But other ministries were also involved, in particular the
ministry of agriculture, which was responsible for welfare schemes for agricultural workers and
others exploiting the land. Medical aid existed for those not covered by social security: acting
retrospectively, this never covered more than 80 per cent of actual costs. Up until 1967 funds for
what in France were regarded as the main categories of *social insurance, illness, old age,* and *family*
were held by, on the one hand, the national social security fund and, on the other, a series of local
and departmental funds—the primary funds for social assurance (sickness and old age) and the
funds for family allowances. These local funds each had administrative councils consisting of from
16 to 36 members (48 in Paris), of whom three-quarters were representatives of the employees.
One expert describes the period from the 1950s to 1967 as one of 'a mosaic of systems'.[22]

There was a notable expansion of coverage in the sixties, but in no very systematic fashion;
in 1961 sickness insurance was extended to independent agricultural employers, and in 1966 to
small commercial employers. A major development was the establishment after May 1960 of an
inter-ministerial co-ordinating committee, under the chairmanship of the minister of labour. In
January 1966 the ministry for public health and population and the ministry of labour and social
security were merged into one ministry of social affairs. The system of national and local funds
was also reorganized. From 1967 onwards there was at the apex a new central agency for the
organization of social security (ACOSS). Below this there were three (instead of one, as before)
national funds; and at the bottom were two series of funds at local and departmental levels. The
administrative councils were reduced in size and the powers of employees curtailed.

The broad developments in the main aspects of French social security can be seen in
Table 6.9. Family allowances, ever since the First World War, had been a traditional concern
of French governments. The diminishing percentage taken by family benefits is an indicator
of the general spread of affluence and decline in need, and also of a targeting of benefits to
where they were really required. The other figures do represent a real rise in benefits (rather
than, e.g. in the case of the last one, a rise in actual unemployment).

**Table 6.9** *Percentages of total national income
spent on different aspects of welfare*

|              | 1960 | 1970 |
|--------------|------|------|
| Old age      | 35.1 | 41.7 |
| Health       | 34.1 | 37.0 |
| Family       | 29.4 | 18.8 |
| Unemployment | 1.3  | 2.0  |

*Source:* Jean-Pierre Dumont, *La Sécurité sociale toujours
en chantier* (Paris, 1981), 40.

242

The Italian system was still more fragmented than the French, and a good deal less developed. Maurizio Ferrera refers to 'the lost opportunity of the post-war years';[23] the new postwar Italian constitution represented a break with the past, but the actual implementation of welfare legislation depended upon which particular pressure groups were in the ascendancy, negotiations between different factions in parliament, and the overcoming of strong resistance from vested interests. Additionally, the years immediately following the war were ones of severe economic crisis. If these were years of hopes unfulfilled, the immediately succeeding ones (1949–54) can be described as those of 'institutional straightening out',[24] when some of the welfare schemes promised at the end of the war began to be put into full operation. The same source describes the period from the mid-fifties to 1967 as 'the years of development'—clearly not singling out the sixties as a specially important decade. The years 1968–75 are described as 'the years of social mobilization'. Undoubtedly piecemeal reforms run through the fifties as well as the sixties: the basic system of 'mutual assurance' (for interruption of earnings) was extended to farmers working their own land in 1956, to small artisan employers in 1957, and to small commercial employers in 1960; retirement pensions were brought to each of these groups in 1957, 1959, and 1966 respectively. A ministry of health was created in 1958. However, the sixties (up to the end of 1967) can be distinguished from the fifties both with respect to the larger proportions of gross national product allocated to welfare schemes and, more significantly, with respect to the more ambitious schemes being mooted. Being mooted, it has to be recognized, often did not mean being achieved. Characteristically, new funds would be set up, but lacking any guarantee, given the extent of local resistance and local corruption, that benefits would actually be paid to those they were intended for. In 1963 the integration fund for wage-earners was established to provide unemployment benefits for those in unstable industries: Law 77 of 1963 made benefits available to building workers, and Law 322 to country workers in the south.

If I were to draw a crude parallel between Italy and Britain, I would say that what happened in Italy with respect to social welfare was a kind of rough analogue of what happened in Britain during the Second World War: from the top, with the advent into Italian government of the Social Democrats and then the Socialists, there was much planning and publicizing of a unified welfare state; from the bottom, workers became conscious of their power, of the indignities they had suffered, and began to demand a welfare state (exactly as it happened in Britain during the war).

> The sixties represent years in which the bases seem to be laid in our country for a political programme of social services, intended as services for the entire public and no longer directed solely at the neediest section of the population, but at all citizens... With the launch of the manifesto of the Centre-Left in 1963/64, a new phase began, that of a national programme which, even if in many aspects it remained words rather than deeds, nonetheless opened up a political debate which had remained closed throughout the fifties.[25]

In Britain, then, a universalist welfare state being both modified and further developed; in France, a welfare state of a slightly different sort continuing to be developed; in Italy, the bases for a universalist welfare state only in the process of being discussed and advanced; in America? Before I attempt to assess what all the legislation, all the administrative devices, all the theories and aspirations actually meant for people living in the different societies, I want to return to the main features of the American 'great society', whose two keynote acts, both becoming law in 1964, were the Civil Rights Act (which, apart from declaring discrimination illegal in public places, in housing, and in education, also declared it illegal in employment and set up an enforcement mechanism in the form of the Equal Employment Opportunity Commission), and the Economic Opportunity Act. Inevitably, a new agency, a new factotum, and all sorts of new programmes had to be created. The new agency was the Office of Economic Opportunity (OEO), an independent federal agency, the new factotum being its director, former presidential adviser Sargent Shriver, now directly responsible to the president, while the programmes all had titles which could well have been dreamed up by advertising copywriters and were designed to fulfil the basic principle that there should be 'maximum feasible participation' on the part of the poor themselves. The essence of the act, the agency, and the programmes is contained in the very American word 'opportunity'. Johnson had announced: 'We are not content to accept the endless growth of relief roles or welfare roles. We want to offer the forgotten fifth of our people opportunity, not doles.' Shriver declared: 'I'm not at all interested in running a hand-out programme, or a "something for nothing" programme.'[26]

The central objectives of the Office of Equal Opportunity were to be achieved through a plethora of Community Action Plans, which, it was hoped, would involve the local authorities and the poor themselves. Operation Head Start was a project to take under-privileged children out of their slum environment and from under the feet of their parents for preschool training. The Upward Bound Programme was intended to enable bright slum children to go to college. There was a Job Corps for school drop-outs, and a kind of domestic Peace Corps, Volunteers in Service to America (VISTA). More immediately appropriate were the special programmes of grants and loans to low-income rural families and migrant workers. There were two fundamental ideological and institutional problems. Opinion polls consistently showed that ordinary Americans were very much against taxpayers' money being spent on any kind of welfare scheme. To that extent, Johnson's 'great society' initiative was a brave one; but the resources made available through the Office of Economic Opportunity were grossly inadequate. The liberal Republican mayor of New York, John Lindsay, claimed that to solve the problems of deprivation in New York City would require $10 billion a year for five years. The Office of Economic Opportunity was allocated around $75 million for its entire programme. It never received more than 1.5 per cent of the federal budget, or one-third of 1 per cent of gross national product. If all the funds available had got directly to the poor (which they did not) each poor person would have received $50–$70 a year.[27] The other problem was that the programmes had to be operated through the local authorities, and through those who put themselves forward as the representatives of the poor. Mayors found the programmes a fruitful source of patronage, while ambitious local civil rights leaders could also turn the programmes to their own political advantage. Much of the inadequate funding went on political objectives, rather than to the poor. Detailed examples of how all this worked out in practice, or failed to work out, will be given in Chapter 8.

Probably the most directly useful initiative from the point of view of the poor was the 1964 Food Stamp Act. The existing scheme, under the Agriculture Act of 1949, was really designed to help farmers get rid of their surplus food through dumping it on the poor. This new act separated the interests of the poor from those of the farmers. Certified low-income families could purchase stamps at substantial savings: for example, a family of four with a monthly income of $100 could buy $78 worth of stamps for $44. One problem, characteristic of the American ideology of self-help, was that some poor people simply could not afford to buy the stamps in the first place. Another was that, in accordance with the same free-enterprise ideology, the scheme was not compulsory, so that many communities did not participate, while each state was free to set its own eligibility requirements, giving rise to many unfair variations. Food stamps, however, became a widely (and unpleasantly) featured target of the reactionary right, a further confirmation that, for all their failings, they were a genuine boon to the poor.

Another genuinely constructive development, hotly contested by the official representatives of the medical profession, the American Medical Association, and the medical insurance companies, appeared in the 'Medicare' amendments to the Social Security Act, which became law on 30 July 1965. Medicare—in essence hospital and medical insurance—was aimed exclusively at old-age pensioners. The hospital insurance was compulsory, and financed by an increase in social security taxes. Enrolment in the medical plan was voluntary, and paid for by a monthly premium of $3. The costs for old people, therefore, were quite high, especially since the schemes did not in fact cover all medical and hospital expenses. Still, in the American environment of free-market medicine and rapacious doctors, the possibility of falling ill was one of the great fears in American society. The upshot of the Medicare amendments was that 'a large number of older people received medical and hospital care that previously they could not have obtained, or that otherwise would have exhausted their savings'.[28] The Medicaid amendments, passing into law on the same day, also had considerable impact: the federal government provided grants to the states so that the recipients of federally aided assistance could receive proper medical and hospital services. In addition, the service could be extended to those not actually on public assistance, but still too poor to afford their own treatment. Previously those dependent upon charity for medical care had to endure humiliating conditions. Now, in theory, Medicaid recipients could choose their doctors and hospitals. In practice

**Table 6.10** *American government expenditure on various social services as a percentage of gross domestic product*

| Social service | 1955 | 1960 | 1965 | 1970 |
|---|---|---|---|---|
| Means-tested old-age benefits | 0.4 | 0.4 | 0.3 | 0.3 |
| Non-means-tested social security | 1.2 | 2.2 | 2.6 | 3.2 |
| Unemployment insurance | 0.5 | 0.6 | 0.5 | 0.4 |
| Other income maintenance programmes | 0.4 | 0.4 | 0.7 | 1.4 |
| Health care | 0.8 | 0.9 | 1.0 | 1.7 |

*Source:* Peter Flora and Arnold J. HeidenKammer, *The Development of Welfare States in Europe and America* (New Brunswick, NJ, 1981), 109.

many doctors and hospitals refused to treat Medicaid patients, so often the care they received was much below what it should have been. The limitations in the American system are very apparent; none the less the 'great society' must be credited with advances upon anything that had gone before. Such improvements as were effected in the condition of the poor were achieved against strong resistance. Congress in 1967 attempted to freeze family payments

**Table 6.11** *Public income maintenance expenditure as percentages of gross domestic product at current prices, with the rankings of various countries*

| Country | 1962 | 1972 |
|---|---|---|
| Austria (1962–73) | 14.1 (1) | 15.3 (1) |
| France | 11.8 (3) | 12.4 (4) |
| Germany (1962–73) | 11.9 (2) | 12.4 (4) |
| Italy | 7.5 (7) | 0.4 (6) |
| Japan (1961–73) | 2.1 (17) | 2.8 (17) |
| Sweden | 6.0 (10) | 9.3 (10) |
| UK | 5.7 (11) | 7.7 (11) |
| USA | 5.5 (12) | 7.4 (12) |

*Source:* Flora and HeidenKammer, *Development of Welfare States,* 87.

**Table 6.12** *Total expenditures for health services in various countries as percentages of gross national product*

| Country | Year | % of GNP | Year | % of GNP | Year | % rate of change |
|---|---|---|---|---|---|---|
| Canada | 1961 | 6.0 | 1969 | 7.3 | 1961–9 | 13.2 |
| USA | 1961–2 | 5.8 | 1969 | 6.8 | 1962–9 | 10.1 |
| Sweden | 1962 | 5.4 | 1969 | 6.7 | 1962–9 | 14.0 |
| Netherlands | 1963 | 4.8 | 1969 | 5.9 | 1963–9 | 16.1 |
| West Germany | 1961 | 4.5 | 1969 | 5.7 | 1961–9 | 10.3 |
| France | 1963 | 4.4 | 1969 | 5.7 | 1963–9 | 14.9 |
| UK | 1961–2 | 4.2 | 1969 | 4.8 | 1962–9 | 9.5 |

*Source:* Flora and HeidenKammer, *Development of Welfare States,* 88.

made in respect of dependent children, this in fact being resisted by President Johnson. The improvements, though modest, were real. It has been reckoned that the combined effect of increased spending on social welfare, food stamps, Medicare and Medicaid was to take 38 per cent of the poor—five million households—out of poverty in 1965.[29] Overall, however, it cannot be said that the American figures are particularly impressive, as Table 6.10 shows.

To bring out the full implications of everything that I have said in this section so far, we need comparative statistics (see Table 6.11). It may be noted that two countries famed at the time for their welfare states, Sweden and Britain, come fairly low down. Although these countries had more comprehensive services than any other, the benefits actually paid tended to be on the low side (see Table 6.12).

It should be noted that the figures in this table represent total expenditures, i.e. they include private expenditure (we saw from Table 6.10 that American government expenditure on health care was only 1.7 per cent of GDP in 1970). The figures also reflect the high cost of medical services in certain countries (particularly, of course, the US). What we can see is that Britain, though providing the most comprehensive health service for the entire population, is falling behind other countries with respect to the proportion of resources devoted to health. The Italian record was so poor at this time that it is not even included in Table 6.12: in 1967, government expenditure on health services in Italy amounted to 1.1 per cent of gross domestic product.[30] However, the changing attitudes of the sixties were important. We shall find that the years from 1968 into the early seventies are universally regarded in Italy as being the years of the establishment of a true welfare state. We shall also find that, contrary to the myth of a conservative reaction at the end of the sixties, welfare provision for poor Americans did on the whole continue to improve during this period. The most intractable problem in all countries—and one which comes to prominence from time to time throughout this book—was that of providing decent housing accommodation for all citizens.

## Class and Education Systems

Class figured prominently in the avant-garde writing of the 1960s, behind most of which lay the basic assumption that the societies of the day were 'bad societies', dominated by the bourgeois class and contaminated throughout by bourgeois ideology; those societies, the theory went, must be replaced by better societies, this being brought about by the working class overthrowing the bourgeois class. This was the basic Marxist fantasy, but since it had singularly failed to come about, and since there was considerable contempt among intellectuals for Stalinist Russia and for the conformist Western Communist parties, many new variations were invented, particularly, as we shall see in the next chapter, with respect to the crucial significance of language as allegedly an irresistible vehicle of bourgeois values. Whatever the variations, much political and social commentary and debate was written as if all the Western societies were basically divided between a bourgeoisie (often rendered in English as 'middle class') and a proletariat or working class. My own contentions are that societies in the 1960s certainly were divided into a number of large aggregations which can very appropriately be termed 'classes', that we can only understand the many important things that were happening in the sixties if we have a clear conception of the nature of these classes and the relationships between them, but that neither Marxism nor Weberian sociology actually provide useful analyses of these.

My starting-point is with the overwhelming evidence that the societies we are studying divide up into broad aggregates of individuals and families, these aggregates being distinguished from each other by inequalities in wealth, income, power (or at least access to it), authority, prestige, freedom, lifestyles, and life chances, including prospects of mobility into a different aggregate of individuals and families. Each aggregate is distinguished within itself by an interlinked series of disadvantages or privileges: in one aggregate, for example, which it is not fanciful to envisage as occupying a 'low' position in society, powerlessness is linked to poverty, to low-grade living and health conditions, to poor education, to insignificant opportunities for moving 'upwards' in society; in another aggregate, 'high' in society, considerable wealth is linked to a particular type of education which is linked to the easy attainment of positions of power. In general, individuals and families within each aggregate will tend to associate more with others in that aggregate than with individuals and families outside it; those within a particular aggregate will tend to have common attitudes, common ways of doing things, though this does not mean that there may not be national attitudes and customs shared throughout all aggregates, nor that there may not be sharp differences on political and intellectual matters within aggregates. The existence of these aggregates, or at least some of them (most usually, the one immediately 'above' and the one immediately 'below') is actually perceived by those living in the societies studied, and they are usually referred to as 'classes'. To me it is obvious that it is best to use this fraught word 'class' in the way that people in the societies studied used it, rather than allying it with complete abstractions, such as 'proletariat' and 'bourgeoisie', which have little salience for people actually living in the societies concerned. In Marxism and in Weberian sociology, classes are defined by relationships to so-called 'modes of production' and by their role in alleged historical processes; but classes as they actually impinge on the lives of real people, and as perceived by them when they use such terms as 'upper class' or 'working class', are far better seen as being formed by particular combinations of historical circumstances, and being defined both by people's perceptions of them and by the range of inequalities they embody.[31]

The first fact which emerges when this approach is followed is that in each of the four countries being studied there is a distinctive upper class, which coincides neither with the landed aristocracy of former days nor with the bourgeoisie which, according to Marxist theory, was supposed to overthrow it. Depending upon the historical circumstances which had affected the different countries, the upper class was a varying amalgam of aristocratic elements (it being borne constantly in mind that there had always been a process of creating aristocrats out of those who had made their way upwards without owning land—and that in America the phrases used were more likely to be 'old money', 'old stock', or, perhaps, 'patricians') and successful elements from commerce, industry, and government. While earnest works of sociology often ignored the existence of an upper class of this sort, it cannot be concealed in novels and films which, if they are not to be rejected by readers and audiences, have to capture society as it actually is (we have already had intimations of an upper class in the films *Room at the Top, La dolce vita* and *L'avventura*, and there are several in the highly significant novels of Alison Lurie[32]). One of the most consistent features of the upper class is that it has its own educational institutions, which is why I have chosen to bring up the question of class again in this chapter.

In all four societies it is fairly easy to mark out those who are working-class, i.e. are so perceived by others and by themselves, and have very distinctive characteristics with respect to working conditions, lifestyles, and life chances. The other significant class occupying a lowly place in certain societies is that which may loosely be called 'the peasantry', but which is more precisely pinned down by the term 'agricultural workers', since a 'peasant' could be an independent landowner. From our economic statistics, we have seen that the size of this class was already in sharp decline by the 1960s, with some of its former members moving into the towns to form part of the working class. Variations and differences should not be neglected, but on the whole, within each society, both the working class and the upper class are relatively homogeneous. But what is equally true for all four societies is that, contrary to all the mythology of *the* middle class as the villains behind the evils of 'bourgeois society', the middle class is the most heterogeneous, in social origins, in levels of education, in income, in access to positions of power and influence. At the very least, one has to envisage in all four countries, apart from a middle middle class, an upper middle class which shares some of the privileges of the upper class and a lower middle class which is in many respects very close to the working class.

Race was the most obvious divide in American society, but it would be a complete mistake to think that class distinctions did not also exist. Given the strong resistance to housing integration that we have already noted, it was clear that even the most prosperous blacks were as yet scarcely incorporated within the national class structure. We have to envisage two pyramids: the main national class system with a small, very rich, and very powerful upper class at the top, an upper middle class, and then a long range of status groups within the middle class down to the poorer white-collar elements; then a generally prospering working class, linked in many aspects of ideology and, indeed, spending power to elements in the middle class, though usually separated out by workplace conditions; and then a disproportionately large under class of unfortunates compared with our other countries, save for southern Italy; the second pyramid consists of the black middle class, working class, and under class. Into that neat two-pyramid model we have to inject the complexities of America's 'ethnic' heritage. Studies from the sixties and onwards showed that America's much-vaunted 'melting-pot' had not greatly affected the formation of lower-middle-class and working-class neighbourhoods composed almost exclusively of single ethnic groups such as Italians or Poles. Lifestyles in such neighbourhoods were often very distinctively working-class, but generally prevailing ideologies were the highly conservative ones of what was about to be discovered as 'middle America'.

A study of Kansas City conducted towards the end of the decade found that 'the status distinction most commonly used to divide the vast middle ranges of the status hierarchy was based upon occupation and can be called the '*collar color line*'. In the words of one Kansas City woman, 'people who work in offices and wear white collars generally have more status than people who work in factories, work with their hands and are what you call blue-collar workers.'[33] But the authors felt that the demarcation line was probably less sharp in many other American cities. They found that many blue-collar families who were prosperous and maintained relatively high living standards were accepted as social equals by white-collar families. A study of Levitt Town found a self-confident community which mixed blue-collar and white-collar occupations, and where the main fears were of an influx of blacks; blacks of clear middle-class culture were just about acceptable, by contrast with manifestly 'lower-class' blacks.[34] The sense of there being an upper middle class on one side and the poor on the other is very apparent in the explanation given by a carpenter (almost a decade later, but valid for the sixties, I believe) for his lack of interest in a presidential election. 'Are you kidding?' he asked:

Vote for what. You got to be an idiot to believe them political commercials. It's money that runs this country. Hell, even our welfare system is meant to give jobs to all them sociologists, social workers, bureaucrats, and political hacks. Welfare is a welfare system for the educated, upper-middle class. That's what the liberal moaning for the poor is really about. It's for their own jobs. No politician is going to change that. Poverty is a growing business. I just laugh at it and don't get involved.[35]

At around the same time, the *New York Times* was quite unequivocal in defining the district of Marquette Park in Chicago as 'an all-white, ethnic, working-class neighborhood'; the problem was that it was 'on the expanding edge of a poverty-stricken black community'. The wife of an electrician explained the attitude of herself and her neighbours: 'it's not even integration they fear but their homes are all people have. This is not a community where people dabble in stocks and bonds. This is all they have, their only security.'[36] Race: in America one just can't get away from it. And clearly it does not coincide with class lines. In some fascinating material collected in the middle sixties among Detroit auto workers, John C. Leggatt found *both* racial antagonism *and* a sense of belonging to the working class, or to the poor. He asked black workers which people they felt were neglected by city officials. Among the responses he got were the following: 'poor people in general, but it's a little harder on Negroes than most'; 'Negroes don't get the breaks that they deserve'; 'Negroes, especially in the city services such as tree clipping, spraying, unpaved alleys, and things like that'; 'They try to keep us Negroes back far enough so that they will always have us working for them'; 'I realize that people have to help themselves, but look at the colored districts. Coloreds who earn the same as whites can't get properties in nice districts. The line is drawn so you can't get property'. The same question put to white workers produced these responses: 'Lower-class folks like Italians, Polish, Negroes, and Southerners'; 'Poor people'; 'White working-class people don't get things as would Negroes. For example, the police are tougher on white working people who have dogs in the neighbourhood'; 'They don't pay attention to the needs of working men. They want to keep him in the lowest place they can.'[37]

In America, then, there was *both* a sense of a quite wide-ranging 'middle America' *and* a sense of the existence of a distinctive working class. In all three European countries certain sociologists were talking of *'embourgeoisement'*, envisaging affluence as turning the working class into the middle class. Detailed empirical studies and evidence from people themselves showed this thesis to be largely nonsense. In Italy in particular, and some parts of France, far from a traditional working class merging into the middle class, working-class communities came into being for the first time, as former agricultural workers moved to the towns and cities. Certain Marxists, disillusioned with the failure of the 'old' working class to fulfil its 'historic role', identified at least two kinds of 'new working class' in which they placed their faith. In France, Serge Mallet used the term to embrace all the technical, white-coated, and minor managerial posts which had been proliferating up to the mid-1960s.[38] But the technicians and managers scarcely proved a better bet than the traditional working class, and the term 'new working class' came to be applied more often to the truly underprivileged, the labourers or permanently unemployed from southern Italy seeking work in the north, casual workers generally, migrants, blacks, and other racial minorities, and the deprived generally.[39] Empirical studies bring out that those in manual occupations felt a strong sense of working-class *awareness* (i.e., they were very aware that they were working-class in working conditions and lifestyles, and very different in these respects from the middle class), but not much working-class *consciousness* (i.e. consciousness that they ought, as Marxist theory decreed, to be in constant struggle against the middle class in order to overthrow it). Alain Touraine's classic study of *Working-class Consciousness,* carried out right in the middle of the sixties, provides strong supporting evidence. Building workers, Touraine found, 'reveal a type of consciousness strongly oriented towards their job experience. They regard themselves as producers more than wage-earners; they are more sensitive to the labour market than to the power of the boss.' Mining was the only sector in which a majority found working conditions unsatisfactory. Miners did express their work situation in terms of classes more frequently than other workers, but, Touraine continued, it would be more true to say that they were oriented towards the practical improvement of conditions than to class consciousness.[40] In a later opinion survey— still valid, I believe, for the 1960s—a middle-aged electrician expressed views about the specific working-class nature of his work, and about problems of social mobility for workers:

> I get up at 5.55. It takes me an hour to get to the factory at Vitry. A works bus picks me up 500 metres from here and brings me back at 5.30 p.m. At the factory, we never talk about personal matters. Conversation centres on football, cards and telly... Those who are interested in politics keep to themselves and form a ghetto. It's exhausting.[41]

Replying to a question about how work *ought* to be organized in the factory, he continued:

> First of all, it is scandalous to ask men to produce something without them knowing what purpose it serves. Workers should have the economic situation explained to them; then, workers' councils, made up of delegates, should decide the level and quality of production. That would end the power of the technocrats and put the whole hierarchy in question. But it is difficult to talk about this with your mates; most of the time they say: 'There you are, you are on your hobby-horse again...'

Clearly this was an exceptionally politically conscious worker, but in any case no British or American worker would have used any such word as *prolo* ('prole' in British usage being purely and simply a term of abuse and contempt), as he did in dealing with the question about the possibility of escaping from the working-class condition:

> The son of the *prolo*, in the majority of cases, turns towards a technical career. By making many sacrifices he might become a professional engineer. But since he has nothing at all to lean on, he feels bound to conform to the utmost.

A top manager (upper-middle-class in my terminology) recognized, from the other direction, the separation of classes. There were problems over the employees who are sometimes congenial, but with whom our status as executives does not permit us to sympathize, for society lives in such a way, imposes such a form of relationships, that such sympathies can only be 'platonic'; and then besides, they themselves, 'the employees' (I too am an 'employee', but no one says so, above all I am a director)... don't wish it. To them we are part of a monster called MANAGEMENT, for we are the ones who say: 'You must work longer, harder, more quickly, no, you do not deserve a rise. No, we do not have enough money to share out. We can't give it to you.'[42]

Britain was the most blatantly hierarchical society of the four, though the notion that Britain was uniquely a class society while the other three were not is sheer myth. France, America, and Italy were all pervaded to some degree by a tradition of republicanism, France very strongly by a tradition of *égalité* and citizenship, and America by one of individual enterprise and social mobility. In real terms, inequalities were actually greatest in Italy. But it was certainly in Britain that straightforward class labels were most widely used and in Britain that people most readily identified themselves, and others, with a particular class label. Regularly throughout the sixties interviews and opinion polls showed that well over 90 per cent of the population recognized the existence of social classes. When, on one typical occasion, a representative sample were asked, without prompting, to allocate themselves to a social class, 67 per cent said they were 'working-class' and 29 per cent said they were 'middle-class'. Of the remainder, 1 per cent said 'upper-working-class', 1 per cent said 'lower-middle-class', and 1 per cent said 'upper-class'; this left only 1 per cent unable to allocate themselves to any one of the traditional classes, including 'one twenty-five-stone eccentric' who said he belonged to the 'sporting class'. When pressed to allocate themselves to the 'upper' or 'lower' parts of the class, most were reluctant to do so: only 3 per cent of the middle class moved themselves up into the 'upper middle class', with 4 per cent moving themselves down into the 'lower middle class'; 10 per cent of the working class moved themselves up into the 'upper working class', with only 4 per cent allocating themselves to the 'lower working class'. This suggests a very strong awareness of the broad divisions between the traditional social classes (or 'aggregates', as I was calling them when we began this discussion), rather than a sensitivity to the subtle distinctions between different occupations, so often insisted upon by social scientists.[43]

In his study *Middle Class Families* (1968), based on Swansea, Colin Bell neatly summarized a distinction between those who had made it into the upper class and those who remained in the middle class: Swansea, he wrote, 'may appear in the first chapters of the autobiographies of the famous; but rarely appears in the last'. Awareness of the distinction between middle class and working class is brought out in two contrasting career autobiographies. A 38-year-old chemist remarked that there had been a time 'when I used to think that I was a cliché—the working class boy who made good, a member of the new middle class, the meritocratic technocrat'. The 'whole question of identity' had been 'very difficult for me and my kind'. This was no longer a problem 'because I now think I know where I am going'. If, he concluded, 'I can get another couple of notches up I will be able to send the boys to a boarding school.' The family of a 39-year-old wholesaler, on the other hand, had 'always been comfortably off'. As he was the eldest, it had always been assumed that he, at least, 'would go into Dad's business'. Describing those now working for him in his warehouses, he remarked that 'about twenty-two men' were 'what you would call working class'.[44]

Older working-class communities continued to exist in the sixties. Writing of Huddersfield, Brian Jackson stressed the continuing importance of the working men's clubs, noting that there were very few businessmen or small tradesmen in the clubs, and that those few preferred to keep a very low profile. The view in Huddersfield was:

> They've got their own clubs and political clubs. It's all working men here. And like even the pub, the club has the atmosphere of the working man's home: 'I never go into a pub at all now. Clubs are more sociable like. Look at this. I couldn't rest my legs across a chair in t'pub. Here it is like being at home. As long as I don't put me feet on t'seat I'm alright.'[45]

There was a clear boundary to the community of mill workers; floor managers, clerical workers, and minor officials were excluded. While they attracted a general dislike and mistrust, there was, Dennis Marsden found, 'a grudging respect' for the mill-owners. You could, said Jackson, 'trace a line through Huddersfield marking the point where the gap showed between middle-class and working-class life'.[46]

A celebrated survey of 'the affluent worker' in Luton, covering assembly-line workers at Vauxhall Motors, machine operators, and craftsmen servicing machines at the Skefco's Ball Bearing Company, and process workers and craftsmen engaged in process maintenance at Laporte Chemicals, did suggest some fragmentation of traditional working-class images and some blurring of class lines.[47] Fourteen per cent claimed for themselves definite 'middle-class' status, while 8 per cent took the view that they could be described equally well as 'working'-class or 'middle'-class. Yet 67 per cent had no difficulty in allocating themselves to the 'working class'. Actually these 'affluent' workers were still a million miles away from middle-class job satisfactions or from middle-class aspirations after social mobility. The Luton workers stressed the unpleasantness of their work, giving the high pay as its only advantage (70 per cent of white-collar workers, by contrast, did not mention pay and two-fifths—the highest single group—gave the nature of their work as their greatest source of satisfaction). The Luton workers expressed no very strong feelings against separate canteens: 'I don't like the idea of the boss breathing down my neck at mealtimes,' said one; 'We wouldn't want *them* listening into my conversation,' said another. All three of the Luton firms encouraged promotion from the shop floor to supervisory, technical, and managerial grades. But in fact, the mass of the labour force did not 'think of themselves as one day likely to become something more than merely wage workers'.

But is it really correct, well into the second half of the twentieth century, to talk of an upper class in each of these countries? An alternative view, very strongly canvassed in sociological circles in the 1960s, was that one should examine, not one consolidated upper class, but the different élites which ran society (business élite, political élite, even labour élite). A seminal publication was *Beyond the Ruling Class* (1963) by Suzanne Keller. However, while Keller's position was that the various élites dominating different aspects of society were not synonymous with an upper class, she did recognize that a disproportionate number of members of the élites would come from an upper class: 'For élite recruitment as a whole social class will be a variable rather than a constant element.'[48] My elaboration of this is simply that belonging to the upper class remained, in the sixties, a peculiarly important variable, though the weighting differed in each of the four countries studied, being least in America and greatest in Britain. Unless one were struck down by peculiar and unusual circumstance, to be upper-class was to have an easeful amplitude of life based on generous economic resources. Not all members of the upper class necessarily occupied positions of great power and status, but the point about being upper class was that one had ready access to such positions if one desired them: one belonged to the class from which élites most readily recruited. In no country (certainly not Britain) was the upper class a closed caste. Standards and lifestyles were set by the oldest established elements. New recruits had to adopt these standards and lifestyles, and permanent socialization into the upper class was achieved through particular educational institutions.

The self-image of the American upper class could be seen in the page upon page devoted by newspapers to society gossip, above all in the *New York Times*. Here are to be found paragraph after paragraph on balls and dinner parties, and, above all, on forthcoming marriages. A bride-groom, we read, is a Phi Beta Kappa graduate of Harvard and an alumnus of the Harvard Law School, and his father is a partner in a Philadelphia law firm; a prospective bride 'was presented to Society at St. Vincent's Debutante Ball in Rye'.[49] Early in 1960 *Life* interviewed two young men on 'the Debutante Circuit', David Treherne-Thomas, an offshoot of the British steel manu-facturing family Richard Thomas, and Peter Monroe-Smith, great-grandson of the founders of the L. G. Smith and Brothers Typewriter Company, the latter declaring: 'you must be conserva-tive and carefully groomed. This is what draws the line between real society and the new-rich and we will keep them out at all costs.'[50] Even within the upper class there were status distinctions, but new wealth could always quickly socialize itself into respectability. Both points were tacitly recog-nized in *The Amy Vanderbilt Complete Book of Etiquette*, which first remarked, 'The upper class see social pushiness as the trait of the new rich', but also recorded: 'In Los Angeles, according to one observer, the basic rule is to defer to old money, and when that fails, defer to money'.[51] What such works actually say is not necessarily always accurate: the point is the clear recognition of the existence of an upper class, even if exact definitions vary slightly.

In her social survey of the English country town Banbury, north of Oxford, conducted between 1948 and 1951, Margaret Stacey was quite clear about the existence of upper-class people in the area. A second survey, conducted between 1966 and 1968, spoke of the existence of 'three social levels' but effectively confirmed the continuing existence of an upper class. There are plenty of examples of a British upper-class self-image. Among those interviewed by Ronald Blythe for *Akenfield: A Study of Rural Life* (1969) was a leading local lady who was a magistrate and chairman of the bench: 'I suppose we would be called upper class—in fact, we could hardly be called anything else.'[52] Relaxing in his magnificent country mansion, the well-connected Labour cabinet minister R. H. S. Crossman entered into his diary on 8 January 1967 a piece of heart-searching which also encompasses the essence of being in at least the outer circles of the upper class:

> Prescote is magnificent now the grey skies have blown off. I am sitting here in comfort
> and am therefore bound to wonder whether that fierce old Tory, my brother Geoffrey, is
> reasonable when he says that I can't be a socialist and have a farm which makes good
> profits. I tell him the two are compatible provided that as a member of the government
> I'm ready to vote for a socialist policy to take those profits away and even, in a last resort,
> to confiscate the property. Nevertheless that isn't a complete answer. Having Prescote
> deeply affects my life. It's not merely that I'm more detached than my colleagues, able to
> judge things more dispassionately and look forward to retirement, its more crudely that
> I'm comfortably off now and have no worries about money. I can eat, drink and buy what
> I like as well as adding 170 acres to Prescote Manor Farm. Anne and I have a facility of
> freedom and an amplitude of life here which cuts us off from the vast mass of people.[53]

In setting the social framework for the High Sixties, the most important topic to discuss here
is that of the special upper-class educational institutions. The British 'public schools' were, and
still are, notorious, actually being extremely expensive and very exclusive private boarding
schools. But America, too, had its exclusive, upper-class private boarding-schools, some, as with
their counterparts in Britain, historic foundations converted in the nineteenth century into
centres for training those born to rule, or deliberate new creations for that same purpose.
Examples are: Philips Academy, Andover, Massachusetts (1778, converted into an exclusive
upper-class school about a hundred years later), Hill School, Pottstown, Pennsylvania (1851), and
St Paul's School, Concorde, New Hampshire (1856).[54] A special social cachet attaches to certain
eastern universities belonging to the 'Ivy League'. Actually, there were still further refinements
within the individual universities. A Harvard student already in, or well on the way into, the
upper class, would have rooms in exclusive Harvard Yard. Yale had an exclusive, aristocratic,
secret society, Skull and Bones. Important events, particularly for the purpose of socializing new
recruits into the upper class, were the lavish picnics held on a private St Lawrence River island:

> Of course, if the initiate has grown up in a Bones family and gone to picnics on the island
> all of his life, the vision—the introduction to powerful people, the fine manners, the
> strong bonds—is less awesome. But to the non-hereditary slots in a Bones class of 15, the
> outsiders—frequently the football captain, the editors of the *Yale Daily News*, a brilliant
> scholar, a charismatic student politician—the Island experience comes out as seductive
> revelation: those powerful people want me, want my talents, my services; perhaps they
> even want my genes. Play along with their rules and I can become one of them.[55]

Only a minority of all British public schools were truly upper-class. The core was formed by
what were known as the 'Clarendon Schools', the prestigious schools investigated by the
Clarendon Commission in 1861–4: Eton, Winchester, Westminster, Charterhouse, St Paul's,
Merchant Taylors, Harrow, Rugby, and Shrewsbury; by the 1960s perhaps as many again

enjoyed similar prestige. Oxford and Cambridge were the most prestigious universities, but certain colleges within these universities were particularly aristocratic, for example, Balliol, Trinity, and Magdalen, Oxford, and King's, Cambridge; by the sixties these colleges were welcoming middle- and even working-class products of postwar educational reform, but within them they still had exclusive, high-spending clubs, for those born to such privileges.

The exclusive schools in Britain, and the exclusive schools and universities in America, were private institutions (governments in Britain had assumed responsibility for universities). In France and Italy many of the most exclusive educational institutions were formally within the public domain, though there were also highly prestigious private institutions, particularly in Italy, where the Catholic Church remained an important patron of education. Although both France and Italy were republics in which an officially recognized aristocracy no longer existed, many families in both countries boasted the aristocratic *particule (de* in France, *di* in Italy), and some still boasted aristocratic titles dating from various eras in the past ('Count' being the most common title in both countries). The word *bourgeois,* as used in everyday French, is ambiguous (as is *borghese* in Italian), and can refer to someone of mediocre rather than elevated position; but the overwhelming majority of what were recognized as upper-class families belonged to what would have been called the *haute bourgeoisie;* style and tone, however, were set by an aristocratic core (in France firmly based in Paris, in Italy mainly based in Rome, but also to be found in such centres as Milan, Venice, Florence, and Naples). Secondary schools leading on to higher education are known in both countries by variations on the same word *(lycée* in France, *liceo* in Italy—here, for simplicity, I shall confine myself to using the French version). Even within the public system, as I have just hinted, certain lycées carried exceptional prestige: usually these were either residential, requiring high boarding fees, or situated in exclusive areas in major cities, thus requiring pupils to take expensive lodgings: classic examples are the lycées Louis le Grand and Henri IV in Paris. The French *grandes écoles,* which lead to top jobs in the state, the professions, industry, and commerce, were genuinely subject to competitive entry, but those who had been to the best lycées and, if necessary, could afford to stay in Paris and resit the entry examination, were at a considerable advantage. Before the war *Sciences Po* had been a private and extremely influential college of political sciences, but now it too was within the state system. In Italy, the favoured places for young members of the upper class bent on exploiting their connections to the full in public life or the commercial world (usually both) were the law faculties of Rome or Milan universities.

These basic points about the upper class and upper-class education are vital to understanding social and cultural change, and the limits upon it, throughout the sixties, though in fact the upper-class educational institutions were scarcely touched by the reforms of the decade. These reforms were essentially of two kinds: first, those aimed at expanding the provision of higher education—the intended beneficiaries being young people from the middle and lower ranges of the middle class, and the working class; second, reforms aimed at improving and expanding schooling for the working class or, in America, blacks.

The race issue apart, America in the sixties had the fairest and most comprehensive educational system. The expectation throughout the United States was that schooling would run from the ages of 5 to 17, though among deprived families it was often a much shorter period than this. For all families, apart from those who chose to send their children to private schools, schooling was free, and in most parts of middle America facilities and equipment were of a high standard; it was in poor, and of course black, areas that standards could be very low. At the end of the fifties the average number of years spent in formal education in the United States was 12.90; next came the UK, with 10.96; France was close behind, with 10.74; while Italy was a poor fourth, with 8.86. In America 40 per cent of 18–19-year-olds were in higher education, a far higher proportion than in any of the European countries.[56] Private universities and colleges could be very expensive; it was common for even middle-class students to work their way through college—which may or may not have been related to the fact that standards were generally lower than in European universities. Free places were available in many of the state universities, some of which had very high academic reputations. Generally, the story of the sixties is of an expansion in university education provided by the states.

The universal American high-school system avoided the problem of streaming (the placing of pupils of allegedly different abilities in different classes or schools) which was seriously worrying educational reformers in all three European countries by the beginning of the sixties. In all three countries various options, including fee-paying education, were on offer, but for the majority education was free, and compulsory to the age of 15. A combination of educational orthodoxy and class prejudice had resulted everywhere in a system where academically more proficient children (generally those from fairly comfortable middle-class backgrounds) went to lycées or grammar schools, while the less academically proficient (usually those from working-class families) went to some form of 'modern school', which certainly did not lead to higher education and often only led (and seemed designed to lead) to an inferior working-class occupation. A special scandal in Italy was the large number of children from deprived backgrounds who received an inadequate and repetitive schooling at elementary level and then were simply thrown out of the system at this stage for their alleged failure to make any progress.

Actually there were more real improvements in Italian elementary and secondary education throughout the sixties than in any other area of social provision, though not enough to head off protests from those rather more fortunate students who were rapidly developing sensitive social consciences. A major law of December 1962 aimed to end any kind of streaming in elementary education. The trouble remained that the labels of 'middle schools', 'higher middle schools', 'higher secondary schools' and 'secondary schools of second grade' covered very different standards of education, some leading to university, some leading only to technical colleges, some leading pretty well nowhere. Even in 1967 only 84.8 per cent of those in the 11–14 age group were in school (the comparable figure for France is 99.3 per cent). The broad statistics do demonstrate improvement, though very imperfect improvement. In 1959–60 only 51 per cent of 13-year-olds were in school: that figure had risen to 74 per cent in 1966–7. Yet in that later year still only 35.2 per cent of the relevant age group were at secondary school—though officially, according to the reform of 1962, the school leaving age should have gone up to 16. In 1959–60 30.4 per cent of these children aged between 14 and 18 were still in compulsory schooling (1.8 per cent not even having left elementary school, with 28.6 per cent in middle school); 69.6 per

**Table 6.13** *How father's occupation affected progress through the education system of every 1,000 pupils leaving elementary school, Italy, 1949–1967*

| Educational level | Entrepreneurs and higher professions | Executives or white-collar workers | Self-employed workers | Workers | Average for all occupations |
|---|---|---|---|---|---|
| Elementary | 1,000 | 1,000 | 1,000 | 1,000 | 1,000 |
| Middle school | 844 | 787 | 236 | 172 | 229 |
| Higher middle school | 765 | 701 | 166 | 108 | 170 |
| Certificate of completion of upper middle studies | 651 | 563 | 122 | 54 | 123 |
| First year university | 402 | 351 | 63 | 24 | 70 |
| University degree | 192 | 158 | 23 | 5 | 29 |
| Average no. of years of study | 13 | 12 | 6 | 6 | 6 |

*Source:* Fiorella Padoa Schioppa, *Scuola e classi sociali in Italia* (1974), 18.

cent were at higher secondary schools. In 1966–7 the percentage not yet having left elementary school had fallen to 0.7 per cent; those in middle school had dropped to 20.5 per cent, while 78.8 per cent were now in secondary school. New secondary schools, officially given the title of lycée, were being opened, but most of them were of a 'modern', 'technical' character, and were thus generally seen to be inferior to older-established lycées of a grammar-school type.[57]

The miasma which lay over Italian middle, secondary, and higher education was its continuing class basis, as seen in Table 6.13. The facts jump out from this table, although, being averaged over the years 1949–67, it does not recognize the very substantial advances which had been made by 1967. One can see how heavily the odds were stacked against the ordinary working-class child: out of every 1,000, only 172 got into middle school, only 24 got into university, and only five actually graduated. One can see also how ineffective the university system was in general, with only 192 out of the 402 most privileged entrants to university getting a degree.

The fact was that Italian university education was pretty appalling. The senior academics at the most prestigious universities were mainly upper-class figures themselves, and more concerned with their careers outside the universities than with any academic duties. Most of the basic teaching was done by assistants of much lower status. Facilities were generally overcrowded and inadequate. Many students were in any case enrolled for social and professional rather than educational reasons. Substantial university building programmes were carried out during the sixties and, together with improvements further down the system, this did mean that more students were going to university, and more were achieving degrees. Between 1962 and 1969 the total number of graduates doubled. Much of the expansion, however, was among students who were in work during the day and took evening classes. This group was to prove one of the most disgruntled as political consciousness and awareness of grievances rose among students of all types. In addition, as we shall see, certain specific legislation aroused great hostility.

Towards the end of the fifties in France it was estimated that, while over 80 per cent of children from the managerial and professional classes went on to secondary education, only 21 per cent of those from working-class backgrounds and 13 per cent from agriculture backgrounds did so.[38] Extensive educational reforms were carried through in 1959. The school leaving age was to go up to 16 with effect from 1967, and a determined effort was made to end streaming. First of all, a new kind of secondary school was established, the *collèges d'enseignement général* (CEGs); these were supposed to enjoy parity of status with the lycées, whose entrance examinations were at the same time abolished. In 1963 it was decided to introduce a new kind of comprehensive middle school, the *colleges d'enseignement secondaire* (CES). The intention proved stronger than the achievement, however: the first 1,500 CESs were not finished until 1968. But the French system, as we have seen, was considerably superior to the Italian. All those who achieved their *baccalauréat* (secondary school leaving certificate) were entitled to go to university. Numbers of university entrants rose rapidly, putting great pressure on existing facilities and creating serious tensions, despite a considerable university building programme. One problem was that such new developments as the University of Paris at Nanterre and the student residences at Antony on the southern outskirts of Paris looked, and often were, austere and second-rate.

The British authorities should perhaps be given some credit for realism in that the raising of the school leaving age to 16 was not announced until the middle sixties, and not implemented until the beginning of the seventies. Streaming in England and Wales was institutionalized in the 11-plus exam, whose results determined whether children should be sent to secondary modern schools or grammar schools (originally there had been plans to build technical schools but these never materialized). Children from secure middle-class backgrounds had the usual advantages while less-well-prepared children from working-class backgrounds were going to secondary modern schools, and into dead ends. By 1964 sociologists, psychologists, social egalitarians, and all those who stood for what I have called measured judgement were producing overwhelming arguments against selection; these were embodied in the Newsome Report on Secondary Education of 1963. The new Labour government in July 1965 issued Circular 10/65 calling upon all local authorities to submit proposals for establishing non-selective 'comprehensive schools'. Much depended on the local authorities, so that for the time being grammar schools—which, it must be recognized, had acted as important agents of change in bringing able people from working-class backgrounds into positions of influence—continued in existence.

Also in 1963 there appeared the Robbins Report on Higher Education, which roundly declared that a university place should be available for every student capable of profiting from it. Expansion of university places and university opportunities was more real in Britain than in any of the other countries, where the story of higher education was one of rising consciousness meeting intensifying frustration. In Britain there genuinely was a continuation and acceleration of the processes which had brought working-class figures so dramatically into novels, theatre, and film at the beginning of the decade. Many colleges, particularly in the spheres of art and design, were upgraded, as were teacher training colleges; quasi-university status was given to leading colleges of technology—rechristened polytechnics, their degrees were awarded by one *national* body (a sharp break with tradition), the Council for National Academic Awards (CNAA), founded in 1964; certain colleges of higher technology became full universities, and a whole clutch of totally new universities was created: Sussex, York, Kent at Canterbury, Warwick, Lancaster, East Anglia at Norwich, Essex at Colchester, and Stirling. The British education system remained grossly inequitable, but no more so than those of France and Italy; in most aspects it was less democratic than that in the United States, but students who reached university (and an increasing proportion of them *were* working-class) were better treated than anywhere else in the world. For almost all students not only was tuition free, but public grants almost met living expenses. Teacher-student ratios were remarkably low, and the systematic education provided was far ahead of the casual lectures in overcrowded halls too frequently delivered in the other three countries.

We are now fully embarked on our study of the High Sixties: change accelerates, resistance weakens, yet serious confrontations sharpen. All of this is inexplicable without an understanding of the new, but contested, developments up to the end of 1963, discussed in Part II. It also requires an understanding of the main structural, ideological, and institutional circumstances, subject-matter of this chapter. Political developments, still often placed at the centre of accounts of the sixties, are of relatively minor importance. Still, the powerful government initiatives in welfare and education were significant products of changing ideologies. We have to understand them too before we work our way through from spectacular new philosophies and artistic practices (discussed in the next chapter), and transformations in living standards and personal relations, to the apogee of rock music, pop fashion, hippiedom and the underground, to riots and violent confrontation, and to the events of 1968–9.

# 7

# 'Pushing Paradigms to Their Utmost Limits', or 'Creative Extremism'

## *Structuralism, Conceptualism, and Indeterminacy*

*North American Gurus and Left-Bank Luminaries: 'Repressive Tolerance', the 'Global Village', and 'the Death of the Author'*

'Creative extremism' was the phrase Martin Luther King used to apply to his own policy of organizing non-violent demonstrations. It could equally be applied to the ferment of radically challenging theories and philosophies produced, most notably, in the high-prestige academic institutes of the Left Bank in Paris, in North America (the USA and Canada), and, to some extent, as a consequence of the deliberately fostered interaction between avant-garde academics in America and in France. In all periods there are individual thinkers putting forward ideas which develop further, or flatly contradict, those of their predecessors. Usually checks and balances operate (the academic world is a cautious and conservative one): radical ideas are hotly contested; years pass before new paradigms become fully established. In the early sixties the ideas which had been advanced in the fifties—neo-Marxist, 'structuralist', libertarian, anti-bourgeois (in both Beat literature and *nouveau roman)*—began to be woven together, to reinforce each other, to be developed into ever more radical stances.

With the development of a large number of different but interlinked subcultures, all characterized by a trend toward freedom and permissiveness, and the growth of relatively informal modes of communication—television, magazines, experimental theatre—the circulation of ideas

261

was more rapid and the demand for the novel and the spectacular more intense than they had ever been. There was a restraining worthiness about some of the critical, anti-establishment thinking of the fifties. In the sixties worthiness faded, and flights of philosophical speculation became more and more daring. Writing at the end of the seventies about structuralism (which, he said, 'can be viewed as the extreme and radical formalization of social scientific arrogance') and post-structuralism, the French sociologist Michel Crozier referred to 'a special French logical and even absolutist trend that tends to push the basic paradigm to its utmost limit'.[1] This 'absolutist trend', partly because of general circumstances already described, partly because of the particular workings of the élite network of Left Bank intellectuals, came to its fullest intensity in the sixties.

The theories of Marcuse, Lévi-Strauss, Barthes, Lacan, Althusser, Foucault, Derrida, and perhaps, though less certainly, McLuhan and even Leary, merit close attention; first because, though often opaque and full of a specially created jargon, they were responses to the changing societies of their day; second because they did, though usually in trivialized and sloganized form, directly influence students and others involved in the various protest movements and demonstrations of the later sixties; third because in their very daring and extravagance they expressed an important aspect of sixties intellectual culture; and fourth because (possibly excluding McLuhan, and certainly Leary) they are intellectually highly exciting and challenging, and have continued—in a form which can conveniently be identified as 'postmodernism'—to exercise a strong influence on the intellectual world of today. It would be a sad day indeed if philosophers could not push their ideas to the furthest extremes, and a still sadder one if they could not criticize all aspects of society. The philosophers of the sixties opened up important new areas for study (semiotics, the study of signs, for instance), and focused attention on issues which had not always been treated seriously enough (such as language), though they were not necessarily alone in either of these things. But there was one orthodoxy they did not challenge: the broad view of history, and of social relationships, developed by Karl Marx. While both Marcuse and the French luminaries disavowed the economic determinism of what Marcuse's associates had called 'vulgar Marxism', with the post-structuralists substituting language for economics as a primary force, they retained the epochal view of history, and of how one epoch gives way to another, which Marx had inherited from Hegel, and also the Marxist notion of how the dominant class in each epoch maintains its position by imposing its ideology on all other classes. All were very critical of the Soviet Union, and the French philosophers condemned the official Marxism of the French Communist party, but all believed that the current epoch was that of bourgeois society, with a prevailing bourgeois (or capitalist) ideology which was by definition duplicitous, and that this society must be opposed in all its aspects so that a better, alternative society could take its place. That kind of schematic view of history belongs to nineteenth-century philosophy of history: its 'metaphysical' perspective is not supported by the work of serious professional historians who see the division of the past into epochs, or periods, as simply an analytical convenience, not as a representation of something which has an a priori existence. That the sixties thinkers never seriously questioned this perspective rather weakens their theories, particularly those which are directly dependent upon Marxist assumptions. Marx made many perceptive comments, but the whole field of history and social relationships is so large and complex that it simply is not possible for one individual to produce one model, or general framework, or set of laws. The sixties intellectuals I am concerned with tended to see Marx as occupying a role analogous to that of Darwin in the biological sciences; no one could actually occupy such a role.

Marx observed that liberal institutions and liberal ideas frequently masked the realities of a system which was deeply oppressive of the majority. The structuralists and post-structuralists joined with Marx in seeking for the hidden realities and deeper structures operating in society. They pushed their conclusions to ultimate extremes. Thus the sensible observation that all human activities are in some way *influenced* by the society or culture within which they live becomes the dogma that all such activities are socially or culturally *constructed*. The sensible observation that readers, or audiences, often bring their own preconceptions and imaginings to bear on the 'text' they read (novels, etc.) or watch (films, etc.) becomes the dogma that texts are autonomous, that there is no author. The sensible observation that language is very important to the way in which we frame our thoughts, and that most of what we know comes, not from direct observation, but from someone else's writing or speech, becomes the dogma that everything is *constructed* within language. The sensible observation that those with power, authority, wealth, and education have generally tried to have things their own way becomes the dogma that the central subject in the study of human societies, past and present, is power, and that what is thought of as 'knowledge' is merely a means of preserving power. The sensible observation that most people find work a necessity, that it both gives them their sense of identity and is also frequently burdensome, is turned into the dogma that work is an evil imposed by a vicious system.

Extreme or even absurd ideas can yield good literature, good art, good philosophy, but they make for lousy history; and they may not provide the best basis for practical guidance on current political problems. As things actually happened, most of them percolated to a wider activist audience in the form of slogans and catch-phrases. Young people might seem to have expanding educational opportunities and fairly liberal university authorities, but even if it appeared that their aspirations were being met, in truth this was simply 'repressive tolerance' (it is my view, as I have already indicated, that Marcuse got it exactly wrong—vicious police forces, and certain reactionary groups apart, authority in the sixties was characterized by the existence of strongly liberal elements practising that 'measured judgement' which helped to make the era such a creative one). Soviet and Western society were on a course of 'convergence': Russian totalitarianism was little worse than the 'democratic totalitarianism' (another of Marcuse's phrases) of the United States. Mass communications (television, radio, films, advertising) were now so all-pervasive and all-powerful that 'the medium is the message' and the world (both phrases came from McLuhan) was now a 'global village'. (What I shall have to say in this chapter about experimental theatre, and in the next about particular developments in rural France and Italy, will indicate the strong qualifications which have to be placed on that sweeping generalization.) Even in the most traditional medium, the written text, the message no longer came from an identifiable individual: it became fashionable to talk of 'the death of the author'. The catch-phrase for those adopting the path of expanded consciousness through drug-taking, and challenge to established society by dropping out of it, was that of the least distinguished but not least influential of the gurus, Timothy Leary: 'tune in, turn on, and drop out'. The slogans, of course, have much of the wit and sparkle which is a characteristic of sixties thought. The most sinister slogan was not that of any philosopher, but of the chairman of the Chinese Communist party and head of the Chinese government, Mao Tse-tung. Mao's 'Cultural Revolution' began in 1965: aiming to destroy all vestiges of bourgeois culture and behaviour, it was greatly admired by those who wished to eradicate bourgeois values and bourgeois language in the West.

Partly because they saw all cultural products as manifestations of bourgeois ideology, the neo-Marxists were very sensitive to the artificiality of some of the traditional boundaries between different disciplines and between different artistic practices. They were pioneers in the study of popular culture; and their writings are paralleled in the various artistic practices (taken up in other sections of this chapter) where, for instance, different art forms were sometimes blended into one performance or happening, painting merged into sculpture, and language into art, and where the lines between élite and popular culture became blurred.

Marcuse was an expatriate German from the Frankfurt School of reformed Marxism, which had sought to retain the intellectual hegemony of Marxism through jettisoning 'vulgar Marxism', and had become firmly established in American academic life in the 1930s. There is a delightful irony about the second career which the future excoriator of repressive American society led between 1941 and 1950: he was an intelligence analyst for the American government. However, Marcuse's true vocation lay in continuing to develop the neo-Marxist approaches of the Frankfurt School towards the analysis of contemporary societies, and the function of the aesthetic. He achieved international fame with *Eros and Civilization* (1955), which I have already identified as a key work in the intellectual legacy of the fifties, so important in shaping the new subcultures of the sixties, and whose very title is a reminder of the Frankfurt School's programme of amalgamating Freudian ideas of sexuality and the subconscious with Marxism. Marcuse presented advanced industrial society as a repressive society whose gods were work and power, productivity and performance, destructive of the individual whose wholeness could only be preserved through the aesthetic imagination. There was, Marcuse thought, little difference between the United States and Soviet Russia, an argument advanced in his *Soviet Marxism: A Critical Analysis* (1958). To him, both systems revealed the common features of late industrial civilization, where centralization and regimentation crushed individual enterprise. *One-Dimensional Man: Studies in the Ideology of Advanced Industrial Society* (1964) continued the attack on the dehumanizing nature of contemporary society; it was a positive incitement to the permissiveness already developing in universities and elsewhere, since it identified libertarianism as the only road to freedom. The book was very much addressed to affluent, and perhaps bored and guilty, American university students. It argued that, by manipulating the mass media in order to provoke trivial needs and desires which are easy to satisfy, capitalism had applied an opiate to the discontent of the oppressed. The necessary revolution could only be carried out by an alliance of students who refused to be brainwashed and the dispossessed poor—very much the formula tried, though not very successfully, in the student and worker demonstrations of 1967–9. With respect to my point about 'measured judgement', and the existence of genuinely tolerant (and not at all repressive) elements within the establishment, it is noteworthy that this call for revolution in the streets was funded (as the preface to *One-Dimensional Man* acknowledges) through grants from the American Council of Learned Societies, the Louis M. Rabinsky Foundation, the Rockefeller Foundation, and the Social Science Research Council, bastions of the liberal establishment.

No question, however, but that Marcuse was intensely popular with his own students, first at Brandeis from 1954 and then at San Diego from 1965; and he was himself very much a political activist, expressing himself fiercely on the Cuban missile crisis of 1962 (accusing Kennedy of warmongering), civil rights, American support for the Brazilian military coup in 1964, and, of course, Vietnam. One of his former students, Angela Davis, herself an important black and feminist activist whom we shall encounter again shortly, described his charisma as follows:

When Marcuse walked onto the platform... his presence dominated everything. There was something imposing about him that evoked total silence and attention when he appeared, without his having to pronounce a single word. The students had a rare respect for him. Their concentration was not only total during the entire hour as he paced back and forth as he lectured, but if at the sound of the bell Marcuse had not finished, the rattling of papers would not begin until he had formally closed the lecture.[2]

Marcuse spoke of 'democratic totalitarianism' in the United States, and in 1965 he published his essay on 'Repressive Tolerance' (dedicated 'to my students at Brandeis University'):[3] the tolerance of liberals is 'deceptive and promotes co-ordination [i.e. false social unity]', and serves 'to contain... change, not promote it'. The force of such concepts was to counter any hope of compromise between often liberal university authorities and protesting students, providing the latter with an intellectual justification for rejecting compromise: addressing '4,000 enthusiastic students' at Berkeley, Marcuse, accompanied by Angela Davis, attacked 'the oppressive nature of the society' and 'urged using the university as a base for organizing forces' to change society.

One of the themes which runs through this book is that of international cultural exchange. When it came to philosophical and political ideas the busiest trade route was that between America and Paris, revered among American intellectuals and quality newspapers as a centre of Western culture. In 1958 Marcuse gave lectures in French at the école des Hautes études, where one of the dominant figures, director from the following year, was the Marxist literary critic, sociologist, and 'genetic structuralist' Lucien Goldmann. Marcuse was also in Paris, as it happened, during the events of May 1968. 'Marxist theory—it exists,' he told *L'Express*. Revolutionary student Daniel Cohn-Bendit, founder of the radical March 22nd Movement, delivered a mighty put-down (exaggerated, I think):

Some people have tried to force Marcuse on us as a mentor: that is a joke. None of us has read Marcuse. Some read Marx, of course, perhaps Bakunin, and of the moderates, Althusser, Mao, Guevara, Lefebvre [Marxist historian]. Nearly all of the militants of the March 22nd Movement have read Sartre.[4]

The dominant intellectual figure in postwar Paris was undoubtedly Jean-Paul Sartre. 'Existentialism' was the vogue word in France and abroad: for those participants in the developing youth subcultures of the late 1950s who had intellectual aspirations, Existentialism was the thing. What Existentialism at this level entailed was expressing yourself through your actions, taking responsibility for these actions, and, above all, a strong sense of political commitment. The appeal of Existentialism conceived in this way was enhanced by Sartre's long-term partnership with Simone de Beauvoir, author of *The Second Sex*, which argued that what was thought of as feminine was not in fact biological, but imposed by society. Both Sartre and de Beauvoir were very strongly Marxist in general outlook, and were closely associated with such radical causes as opposition to the Algerian war. They continued to have enormous influence, not least in Britain, where acquaintanceship with the newer fashions coming to eclipse Existentialism was much patchier than it was in certain élite circles in the United States. The younger Parisian thinkers (Barthes, Derrida, etc.— also Marxist in general outlook) acknowledged Sartre's powerful sway;[5] as the new fashion took over, differences with Sartre were exaggerated, post-structuralism in particular being (misleadingly) presented in the intellectual columns of the newspapers as acknowledging no authorities and having no political commitment; 'structuralism' was the word which replaced 'Existentialism', though the latter philosophy continued to have a large following. Most of the figures I am about to discuss here were fairly happy to accept the label, and the prestige it brought with it, until the later sixties, when the term 'post-structuralism' began to be used, particularly by Barthes, Foucault, and Derrida, to stress their novelty, their continuing trendiness, and their hostility to the rigidity of early structuralism; they tended, however, to become more and more uncompromisingly Marxist, notably (though not Derrida) expressing their admiration for Mao Tse-tung's 'Cultural Revolution'. The individuals who produced structuralism and post-structuralism came from the higher bourgeoisie, and in some cases from that part of it which formed the white colonial class in Algeria, went to upper-class educational institutions, and themselves took up positions of prestige and power within France's centralized higher education system. The central institution was the école Normale Supérieure, but the network of intellectual Marxism drew in other élite institutions. French newspapers are almost as interested in philosophical fashion as they are in *haute couture*. Structuralism rose and rose through prestigious university connections, the higher journalism, literary prizes, intellectual journals, public lectures, and reviews. On 1 July 1967 *La Quinzaine Littéraire* published a cartoon by Maurice Henry modelled on the famous and once shocking painting by Manet, 'Le Déjeuner sur l'herbe structuraliste', depicting Claude Lévi-Strauss, Jacques Lacan, Roland Barthes, and Michel Foucault.

Claude Lévi-Strauss, who, while in America in the 1940s, put together the linguistic theories of the Swiss Ferdinand de Saussure (who had died in 1913), and of the Russian-born Roman Jakobson, with his own not very extensive anthropological work on primitive kinship patterns, was the first structuralist. He was born in Brussels in 1908, the son of an artist, and he studied philosophy in Paris between 1927 and 1932; his interest in philosophy remained strong during his empirical researches in social anthropology. He took up a post at São Paulo in Brazil, such fieldwork as he did being carried out entirely in the American continent. He remained in South America until 1939, then spent most of the Second World War in the United States, returning to

Paris only in 1948. The book which had such a powerful influence on Lévi-Strauss was Saussure's *Cours de linguistique générale*, published in Lausanne in 1916. Saussure had given courses of lectures on general linguistics from 1906 to 1911. Though there was clearly time for him to do so, he never wrote up his ideas in a coherent book (I feel bound to comment here that it is always easier to launch ideas in lectures than to organize them into a persuasive and thoroughly substantiated book). When, after Saussure's death, a couple of colleagues decided to publish his lectures, they could find no notes. In order, therefore, to construct *Cours de linguistique générale* they resorted to notes kept by former students of Saussure. (Again, I feel bound to comment that I would hate to be represented after my death by notes students had taken of lectures given by me.) Certainly, the book as published is disorganized and incoherent—though no doubt a prime exemplification of the thesis of 'the death of the author'. Saussure made a mountain out of the commonplace (as he himself admitted) that there is no intrinsic relationship between the *signifier* (the word) and the *signified* (what the word 'means'). Words, he argued, can only have meaning within the entire language system of which they are a part; they derive their meaning from their *difference* from other words. This language system, he asserted (there is certainly nothing in the way of proof), is external to human beings, arising instead from the power structure of society.[6] Words, it seems to me, derive their meaning from their usage, and thus Saussure's speculations seem utterly unnecessary. Be that as it may, it is certainly true that Saussurean ideas have not been accepted by the authorities of modern linguistics, Chomsky, Lyons, Lepschy, and Pinker.[7]

The revelation which came to Lévi-Strauss was that kinship patterns, and indeed all other human practices, were 'structures' in exactly the same way that languages, according to the *Cours de linguistique générale*, were 'structures' or systems. The first outline of these new 'discoveries' appeared in *Les Structures élémentaires de la parenté* (Elementary Structures of Kinship), published in 1949 while Existentialism was still all the rage, and Sartre the ruling sage. The structuralist position was fully stated in *Anthropologie structurale* of 1958, which had considerable influence within French academic circles—not least on Fernand Braudel and the *Annales* school of historians, at the école des Hautes Etudes. An important intermediary was Lucien Goldmann (b. Bucharest, July 1913), a confirmed Marxist and disciple of Lukacs (b. Budapest, April 1885), the most influential Marxist literary critic of the twentieth century (setting the fashion by which literary works are valued according to the extent to which, overtly or covertly, they advance a revolutionary agenda). Goldmann was already developing what he termed 'genetic structuralism', an attempt to integrate the historical context, or 'genesis', of literary works with the ideological structures governing their authors, exemplified in his *Le Dieu caché* (1956), a study of Pascal and Racine. Goldmann's is not one of the magic names of the sixties, but in the rise of neo-Marxist structuralism he figures as an important power-broker and publicist.

Structuralism emerged from academia and landed on the dinner tables of the French chattering classes with the publication in 1962 of Lévi-Strauss's *La Pensée sauvage* (The Primitive Mind); included in this most modish of books was an undisguised attack on Sartre, signalling Lévi-Strauss's bid to have his structuralism replace Sartre's Existentialism. Structuralism was the fashion; but it was not universally recognized as marking an advance in scholarship. Towards the end of the decade, the British anthropologist Edmund Leach wrote of Lévi-Strauss:

The outstanding characteristic of his writing, whether in French or English, is that it is difficult to understand; his sociological theories combine baffling complexity with overwhelming erudition. Some readers even suspect that they are being treated to a confidence trick. Even now, despite his immense prestige, the critics among his professional colleagues still outnumber the disciples.[8]

Such comments, it seems to me, can readily be made about all of the structuralists and post-structuralists (and indeed have been made, even by friendly critics). But, that said, it cannot be denied that one of the truly magical names is that of Roland Barthes, very much an upper-class figure, born in Cherbourg in November 1915, the son of a naval officer. He moved from one élite Parisian school, Lycée Montaigne, to one of the most exclusive of all, Lycée Louis le Grand, then studied classics at the Sorbonne between 1935 and 1939. After teaching for one year at the newly opened lycée in Biarritz he was able to get back to Paris, with appointments at the lycées Voltaire and Carnot. He suffered serious illness, but at least, with respect to the centralized intellectual and educational establishment, he was on the inside track: between 1948 and 1954 he successively held appointments as assistant librarian and then teacher at the French Institute in Bucharest, reader at the University of Alexandria, official of the Direction Générale des Relations Culturelles, and educational officer at the Centre National de la Recherche Scientifique. His first book, *Le Degré zéro de l'écriture*, appeared in 1953. Demonstrating how much he was still under the influence of Sartre, Barthes spoke of it as 'an attempt to impart a Marxist dimension to the existentialist notion of commitment'. He did have some useful, if not stunningly original, things to say, pointing out that in intellectual writing the 'adoption of a particular vocabulary signifies a prior adhesion to certain arguments while sparing one the trouble of stating them'. The fundamental proposition behind the title was that all current writing was contaminated with bourgeois values, and that, to get back to 'degree zero' (a truly objective position), all that contamination, manifested in the language used, would have to be scraped away—a nearly impossible task. The following year he published a study of the early nineteenth-century French historian Michelet, *Michelet par lui-même*: from the mid-sixties onwards Barthes, and others of like mind, were to mount increasingly strident attacks on history as written by professional historians—declaring it, in the essay 'History and Discourse', to be mere bourgeois ideology[9]—apparently unaware that the modern discipline of history is far removed from the romantic rhetoric of such writers as Michelet.

Barthes was more stimulating when he responded to consumer society and modern advertising techniques: in 1957 came *Mythologies*, mainly a collection of articles previously published in the intellectual review *Les Lettres Nouvelles*, focused on the values and attitudes implicit in the variety of messages with which our culture bombards us. Though Barthes added some concluding material, the collection scarcely stands up as a carefully developed and structured contribution to knowledge. The articles are chatty in style, often very short, and sometimes rather simplistic. In one much-cited one (Barthes is best known through selections of his most spectacular essays) he remarks that while at the barber's he had picked up a copy of *Paris-Match*, on the cover of which was a picture of a black soldier in the French army saluting the French flag: Barthes does not ask any questions about the authenticity or provenance of the photograph (is it a real soldier or a model? to what comment or article within the magazine does the picture relate? what editorial decisions were involved?) but simply offers the excruciatingly trite explanation that the hidden intention of the picture is to tell us how happy black soldiers are with French colonialism.[10]

Shortly, Barthes moved into positions of real influence. From 1960 to 1962 he was chairman of social and economic sciences at the école des Hautes études, becoming in the latter year director of studies, with a seminar in 'Sociology of Signs, Symbols and Representations', the base from which he developed the new discipline of semiology, the study of signs. He presented another much-anthologized essay, 'Eléments de Sémiologie', in 1964, and the collection *L'Empire des signes* in 1970. The desire to grapple with the barrage of signs and signals which assail us in consumer society was a laudable one: unfortunately Barthes always ended up with the answers he started out with—everything was part of 'capitalist ideology'.

Barthes was a participant in that transatlantic exchange which was so critical to the constant acceleration of ideas further and further into the extra-rational. In his *On Racine* (1963) he had argued that literary criticism must escape from its biographical focus and concentrate instead on the nature of the text in and for itself. Invited to join a symposium representative of the American and French avant garde (Marcel Duchamp, Alain RobbeGrillet, John Cage, Merce Cunningham) on the theme of closing the gap between élite and popular culture, which was to be published in the American journal *Aspen*, Barthes developed these ideas into what was to be another famous essay, 'The Death of the Author' (supposedly engaging with the symposium theme in that the traditional author could be seen as an élite figure). Not wishing to waste yet another of these short bursts of inspiration, Barthes republished the article, in French, in the journal *Mantéia* in 1968. Once again we have the familiar story of the author as simply purveyor of capitalist ideology, set within the equally hackneyed epochal view of history:

> The author is a modern figure, a product of our society in so far as, emerging from the Middle Ages with English empiricism, French rationalism, and the personal faith of the Reformation, it discovered the prestige of the individual, of, as it is more nobly put, the 'human person. It is thus logical that in literature it should be this positivism, the epitome and culmination of capitalist ideology, which has attached the greatest importance to the 'person' of the author.

The essay ends with the following dramatic statement, stressing that with regard to the meaning of a text, it is the reader who is all-important: 'a text's unity lies not in its origins but in its destination... the birth of the reader must be at the cost of the death of the Author.'[11] Barthes, as friendly critics recognized, was 'a difficult, and ambiguous writer'.[12] He threw out brilliant ideas but produced no large-scale, systematic work. Although he claimed to have moved away from the commitment of Sartre, he actually did share in what is often the finest quality of most thinkers of the sixties, a sense of passion and purpose in arousing people to what he saw as the evils of his time: he wanted to alert people to the 'mesh of words that prevents us from seeing what is really happening' and to 'the distortions created by the way verbal communication works'.[13]

Contemporaneously with structuralism, and closely related to it, there emerged the *nouveau roman*. Sartre was a novelist and playwright as well as a philosopher; the writers of the new novel, who saw themselves as in revolt against Sartrean humanism and commitment, produced theoretical treatises as well as novels. Among the leading early proponents of the new novel were Nathalie Sarraute (b. 1902), Claude Simon (b. 1913), Marguerite Duras (b. 1914), Robert Pinget (b. 1919), Alain Robbe-Grillet (b. 1922), and Michel Butor (b. 1922): almost inevitably the modishness and sectarianism which is one of the less fetching aspects of creative extremism led, just as structuralism was to be supplanted by post-structuralism, to the utterly uncompromising version of the early sixties being termed the *nouveau nouveau roman*.[14] The critical point about the new novelists (and still more the 'new new' novelists) is that, like all of the other intellectuals discussed in this chapter, their driving force was radical hostility, Marxist or neo-Marxist, to existing society: the enemy was the bourgeoisie, bourgeois 'liberal humanism', and in this particular case 'the bourgeois novel', which was seen as having achieved its apogee in the mid-nineteenth century. Neo-Marxist critics of history placed the establishment of professional history, in fact a development of the late nineteenth century and the twentieth century, in the same period. The fundamental aim of the new novel was to deny everything that went to make up the traditional novel: there would be no linear narrative, no plot, no suspense, no characters with defined identities; events would be recounted in the arbitrary mode of the human mind, stretched, abridged, repeated; meaning would come, not from individual passages of realism, but from the novel as an entity.

Openly welcoming the theories of Barthes, the new novelists strove for a 'degree zero' free of bourgeois contamination. From the structuralism of Lévi-Strauss, they took the notion of *bricolage*, literally 'cobbling together', to mean bits and pieces of myths and cultural stereotypes which could be incorporated in the structure of the novel.[15] The late fifties, as we have seen, was a particularly welcoming time for young genius, and Paris could certainly be very kind to the young, especially those with the right background and the right backing. Philippe Jayause was born at Bordeaux in November 1936, into a factory-owning family with the suitably upper-class preoccupations of hunting and shooting. In 1957, at the age of 20 and under the name of Philippe Sollers, he published the brief work (35 pages), *Le Défi*. In 1958 this was awarded the literary prize, the Prix Fénélon, just as Sollers published his first novel, *Une Curieuse Solitude*. The critical acclaim was led by two established literary figures, Emile Henriot and Louis Aragon.[16] A number of other senior figures now joined with Sollers in founding the new journal which perhaps best expressed the distinctive intellectual trends of sixties Paris, *Tel Quel*. The first number, published in the spring of 1960, uncompromisingly declared its faith in Marxism, structuralism, and an apparently puristic commitment to literature.

Robbe-Grillet was also associated with the new magazine, but since he was perhaps as much anarchist as Marxist, he soon found himself squeezed out. He remained the major theorist on behalf of the new novel, as well as its leading practitioner. Born in 1922 in Brittany, Robbe-Grillet came from a right-wing, anti-Semitic, anglophobe bourgeois family. He trained as a scientist, and originally embarked on a career in agronomy. Completed in 1949, his first novel,

*Un Régicide,* was not published until 1978, well after his name had become established. His *Les Gommes* of 1953 won the 1954 Prix Fénélon, which helped to pave the way to his becoming literary director of the important publishing house Editions de Minuit. In 1955 his *Le Voyeur* was awarded the Prix des Critiques (the prize won by Françoise Sagan in 1954). *La Jalousie* (1957) was attacked by most critics, who deemed it unreadable. But in the intellectual world he attracted much attention with his 1958 essay, 'Nature, humanisme, tragédie' in the *Nouvelle Revue Française,* for two reasons: in the manner of Barthes, he attacked the use of metaphor and warned about the hidden values encoded in language, while along the way managing to attack two of the great literary landmarks, *La Nausée* by Sartre, and *L'étranger* by Camus. The publication of *Dans le labyrinthe* in 1959 is said to mark the transition from the *nouveau roman* to the *nouveau nouveau roman.* Broadly the change meant still more of the same, with a heightened emphasis on the autonomy of the text, the absence of the author, and arbitrary shifts in the use of pronouns, 'indeterminacy' (a key notion in all the arts, here implying a fundamental role for the reader in selecting meaning), together with a more aggressive eroticism (challenging bourgeois morality of course, but in fact also part of the worldwide change in mores we noted in, for example, John Updike and Mary McCarthy).

Meantime that genteel leader of, and guide to, taste among aspiring young middle-class couples, *L'Express,* had commissioned Robbe-Grillet to write a series on the new novel. This was reprinted in book form in 1963 as *Pour un nouveau roman.* Robbe-Grillet had written:

> Story-telling, as it is understood by our academic critics—and, following them, many readers—represents an orderly world. That order, which is perceived as being natural, is tied to a whole system, rationalist and systematic, whose expansion corresponds with the taking of power by the bourgeois class. In that first half of the nineteenth century, which saw the apogee—with *La Comédie humaine*—of a narrative form which for many remains a paradise lost of the novel, several important certainties held sway: in particular a confidence that the arrangement of things was both just and universal.[17]

It was that confidence, of course, which the new novel set out to subvert. It must, he said, be primarily literary, but it may finally serve the revolution. Robbe-Grillet became a public figure in other ways as well. He wrote the script for the new wave film directed by Alain Resnais, *L'Année dernière à Marienbad* (1960), a great success in France and a cult film abroad, winner of the 1961 Golden Lion at Venice: a man and a woman are staying at the same hotel; he insists that they had met the previous year at Marienbad and made passionate love; she has no recollection of this, but as he gives his version she begins to form images of herself with him in Marienbad until, in a moment of awareness, she realizes that the place in her mind is the place where she is at present. Robbe-Grillet demonstrated his own involvement in public events by signing a manifesto against the continuation of the Algerian war, and in favour of independence for the Algerians, the *Manifeste des 121.* More films followed: *L'Immortelle* of 1963 which won the Prix Louis Delluc; *Trans-Europ-Express* in 1966; and *L'Homme qui ment* in 1968.

That Robbe-Grillet and the other new novelist had great literary gifts cannot possibly be denied: the effects they produced, exhilarating or tedious (at one extreme was choisisme, the exclusive concentration on inanimate things, in preference to human beings), were the results they very deliberately and skilfully aimed to produce. Robbe-Grillet's *La Maison de rendez-vous* (1965),[18] again a novel of the workings of the mind, is certainly not tedious, being loaded with all the ingredients of the classic exploitation novel: Lady Ava's *Villa Bleu* in Hong Kong, trafficking in drugs and girls, murder, espionage, sensual musings. *La Route de Flandres* by Claude Simon, based on his experiences as an escaped French soldier at the time of the fall of France, is an intensely rich novel, but deliberately restricted to what the central character could have been aware of (the omniscient narrator of the bourgeois novel was anathema to the new novelists). Yet so complex were the themes that in the final stages of the writing, Simon told the literary critic J. A. E. Loubère, he used coloured threads to represent each one, 'weaving them together to make the design visible to his own eyes'.[19] But Sollers is the man we have to watch. His novel *Parc* (1961), which won the Prix Medici, was reckoned to be in the *nouveau roman* mode. But in 1964 and 1965—after escaping military service in Algeria thanks to the personal intervention of de Gaulle's minister of culture, André Malraux[20]—he violently attacked first Robbe-Grillet then the *nouveau roman* itself, accusing it of 'academicism' and 'false avant-gardism'[21]. His allegiance, and that of *Tel Quel,* was with Foucault, Barthes, Lacan, Althusser, and thoroughly Marxist post-structuralism. He developed the theory of the 'revolutionary text', a mode of production which subverts bourgeois ideology by attacking the conventions of realism. Sollers experimented with drugs, then in 1968 showed his solidarity with Mao by beginning to learn Chinese.

Louis Althusser came from the French colonial class, being born in Algiers in October 1918. He was a brilliant pupil in Algiers, Marseilles, and Lyon, and so proceeded to the école Normale Supérieure, where he studied philosophy. After barely surviving the war, which he spent almost entirely in concentration camps, he returned in 1948 to the heart of the French academic élite as a teacher at the école Normale Supérieure, where he joined Lévi-Strauss; over the years that august institution steadily became the central bank of Marxist-structuralism. Just at the time when the New Left in Britain was seeking to escape from the harsh realities of Soviet Marxism by turning to the 'humanist' works of the young Marx, Althusser was uncompromising in declaring humanism to be alien to Marxism: the real subjects of history, he declared, were not human beings but the structural relationships between productive forces. Lévi-Strauss, in one of his bitter exchanges with that humanist Marxist, Sartre, had said: 'Whatever meaning and movement history displays is imparted and endowed not by historical actors, but by the totality of rule systems within which they are located and enmeshed.'[22] It may be noted that this great debate was ignored by the overwhelming majority of professional historians, just as they eschewed Lévi-Strauss's metaphysical use of the word 'history', while quietly continuing to avoid both extremes: historical explanation, their patient professional work implied, involves a balance—varying according to the specific topic—between structural, ideological, and institutional forces, willed actions, and contingency. The leading figure among the coming generation of *Annales* historians, François Furet, remarked at the time on 'the specifically French mutual contamination that has taken place between Marxism and structuralism'.[23]

Jacques Lacan was born in Paris in 1901, and trained in medicine and psychiatry; but he was always drawn to metaphysical issues, the very stuff of 'creative extremism'. From 1953 onwards he was giving weekly and sometimes twice-weekly lectures for the general public at the Sorbonne, in which he stressed the importance of the subconscious: he insisted that people are not the autonomous thinkers and actors they believe themselves to be, every action having a deeper meaning, often so threatening that people work desperately to keep it hidden; he referred repeatedly to the hidden 'desire' lying behind actions. To Freud he added Saussure (via Lévi-Strauss), coming to the view that the subconscious was structured as, allegedly, a language, signifying that subconscious desires are not those of the individual 'subject' but of the (bourgeois) power structure of the society to which the subject belongs. All of this impressed Althusser immensely, and so in 1963 Lacan was invited to move his lectures to the école Normale Supérieure. Not everyone was so impressed, however, and in the same year Lacan was expelled from the International Psychoanalytic Association on account of his unorthodox practice and teaching methods. That Lacan was no outsider was demonstrated by the way in which within a year he had founded his own école Freudiennne de Paris. No more than Barthes could Lacan produce a coherent, systematic monograph; for his first book, *écrits* (1966), he brought together a miscellaneous collection of earlier papers. As an admiring biographer admits, this disorganized, obscurely written book is 'extraordinarily difficult to read'.[24] Already, with the article 'Freud and Lacan' (1964), Althusser had begun to bring together Marxism and Lacan's version of Freud. Althusser, too, published collections of articles rather than monographs. His contribution was to insist on the inescapability of ideology: no political, economic, or social revolution would be valid without a complete destruction of bourgeois ideology. All texts had to be 'psychoanalysed' in order to reveal the bourgeois power structure underlying, and the bourgeois desires being repressed in, them. Althusser presented his ideas in articles published in *La Pensée* and *La Nouvelle Critique*.[25] *Lire le Capitale*, published in the same year, was a collaborative venture which claimed to reveal the structure which lay behind what Marx actually said. In 1968 he published *Lénin et la philosophie*. Together these form the three key texts of Althusserian Marxist structuralism.[26]

Michel Foucault was born in 1926, the son of a surgeon in Poitiers. A brilliant pupil, where should he study but at the école Normale Supérieure (under Althusser)? He took a degree in philosophy in 1948, added one in psychology in 1950, and then a diploma in psychopathology in 1952. For three years after 1952 he continued his researches, spending long periods of time observing psychiatric practice in mental hospitals. He gave classes at the école Normale Supérieure on psychopathology and published a short book, *Maladie mentale et personalité* (1954). The first part gave a solid account of psychiatric theory, defining hysteria, paranoia, neurosis, psychosis, and so on. The second part attempted to situate the theme of mental illness in a social and historical perspective, following strongly Marxisant lines, though stressing that the links are complex and not direct, and that social alienation and mental alienation should not be confused with each other: ultimately Foucault traced mental illnesses back to 'contradictions' in the patient's social environment. Foucault, distracted by a difficult love affair with the musician Jean Barraqué, had taken a post in the French department at the University of Uppsala in Sweden. Uppsala turned out to be a very puritanical place, not in any way the liberated sexual paradise Foucault had hoped for, though since his family kept him well supplied with money, he could indulge in a high lifestyle. What he did find in the university library was a marvellous collection of books on medical theory and practice, particularly with reference to mental illness, dating back to the Renaissance. Working intensively on this collection he began to produce his massive *Folie et déraison*.[27]

Bored with Uppsala, Foucault used his establishment contacts in Paris to get himself appointed director of the French Institute in Poland. The Communist regime there was at that time up to its very worst tricks, and Foucault, caught in a compromising homosexual situation, had to beat a hasty retreat. While based briefly in Hamburg, he completed *Folie et déraison*. But what should he do with it? His Paris contacts recommended that he submit it for the degree of *doctorat d'état* (which would secure him a senior post in a French university), while warning him that the work would not be acceptable as philosophy. It wasn't really history either; however, an influential academic friend, Georges Canguilhem, agreed to sponsor it as a thesis in history of science. Foucault had this work successfully presented for a *doctorat d'état*, while the leading literary and publishing figure, and amateur historian, Philippe Ariès, accepted it for publication in a collection he was editing at the publishers Plon. The published book, which presented a highly metaphysical view of 'the Classical Age' as a separate historical epoch with distinct modes of thought, brought to an end by the French Revolution, did not get more attention than one would expect for such a title, but among the most enthusiastic reviews was one by Roland Barthes, and there was also a favourable review in *Annales* by Fernand Braudel. In Britain Richard Howard, later to translate the book, gave it a good review in the *Times Literary Supplement*. Foucault himself produced a drastically reduced version, only half the length of the original, which was published in 1964. This was the version Howard translated under the title *Madness and Civilization* (1966). The series it appeared in was entitled 'Studies in Existentialism and Phenomenology', demonstrating that the British had yet to sort out their structuralism from their Existentialism—or perhaps it was Foucault who had not yet done this, or perhaps there wasn't such a difference, if Existentialism was taken to include strong Marxist commitment. The main impact of the book, on both sides of the Channel and both sides of the Atlantic, was to foster the idea that madness is only what the ideology of a particular age defines as madness, an idea which resonated in counter-cultural circles throughout the sixties.

Equipped with his *doctorat*, Foucault took up the position of head of the philosophy department at the University of Clermont-Ferrand. As was (and is) the widespread custom among French academics, he did not move to this industrial city in the provinces, but maintained his residence on the rue du Docteur-Finlay in the 15th arrondissement in Paris. Foucault was a man of wide literary and artistic interests. In 1962 he joined Barthes on the editorial board of the intellectual journal *Critique*. In 1963 he was the leading spirit in a celebrated colloquium on the novel and poetry organized by *Tel Quel*, and in the same year he published both a book on the little-known French surrealist writer Raymond Roussel, attracting the attention of RobbeGrillet, and another major work, *Naissance de la clinique: une archéologie du regard médical* (1963), focusing on the first fifty years of the new epoch, as Foucault saw it, inaugurated by the French Revolution, and the rise of the medical science created by the bourgeois ideology of that age. The main title was straightforward—*Birth of the Clinic: regard médical* literally means 'medical look', or 'the way doctors looked at their subject'. Though there is no linguistic justification for this, English-speaking fans of Foucault always subsequently translated *regard* as 'gaze', claiming, in the usual metaphysical way, that the invention of a new word has created a telling new concept. The use of the word 'archaeology' was intended to bolster Foucault's implicit claim that he was producing a deep 'structuralist' analysis of how the new medical science came into being; he liked the word and very soon was using it again, with the same intentions. He was a dramatic lecturer, and acquired a strong student following (note again how important young people are as consumers, as well as protesters, and how keen some of their elders are to be associated with them: he dressed strikingly in a black corduroy suit, white turtleneck sweaters, and a green cape).[28] At the same time his membership of the French academic establishment was confirmed in 1966 with his appointment to a major government commission on the teaching of literature and science, the commission which led to the famous Fouchet reforms of 1967. *Les Mots et les choses: archéologie des sciences humaines* (1966) (published in English in 1970 as *The Order of Things, a* title which Foucault actually preferred) was about how 'knowledge', a relativist product of bourgeois culture, comes into existence. Foucault also joined in the attack on the bourgeois notion that any significance attached to the individual human 'subject' or historical actor. Only the modern 'human sciences' put the individual 'human subject' at the centre of things; Foucault suggested that this had not always been so, and would not long continue to be so. The concluding paragraph of the book contained two particularly striking sentences: 'As the archaeology of our thought easily shows, man is an invention of recent date. And perhaps one nearing its end.'

Although Foucault was an important academic and central figure in Parisian intellectual circles, none of his books had sold in any numbers. Not surprisingly, in April 1966 the publisher Gallimard simply printed 3,500 copies of *Les Mots et les choses*. Within a week they sold out. Regular reprintings followed. 'Foucault commes des petits pains' ('Foucault is selling like hot cakes') was the heading to a *Nouvel Observateur* article devoted to the best-sellers of the summer of 1966. It was, naturally, the apocalyptic view of the individual human being about to disappear as a focal point of knowledge which seized the attention of the press; that and the general idea that structuralism was now the height of fashion, with Existentialism distinctly old-hat. Into the discourse (normal neutral usage) of trendy academics came 'discourse' (the technical, loaded usage of Foucault) and 'discursive', meaning 'pertaining to the system', usually the entire bourgeois culture, though some specialists liked to fancy that there were several, usually competing, discourses relating to different subcultures. Many academics came to feel that job prospects were best served by liberal use of the words without understanding that they implied an essentially Marxist perception of history and society.

Foucault, it should be added at once, had absolutely no liking for the French Communist party or its Stalinist leaders; in his exchanges with Sartre, he seemed to be disavowing Marxism itself. Sartre had just published *La Critique de la raison dialectique*, which, among other things, attempted to re-establish a pre-Althusserian Marxism and a belief in the importance of individual human action. In a further interview, under the fairly typical title 'Man, Is He Dead?', in *Arts et Loisirs*, Foucault declared:

> *La Critique de la raison dialectique* is the magnificent and pathetic effort of a nineteenth-century man to conceive of the twentieth century. In this sense, Sartre is the last Hegelian, and even, I would say, the last Marxist.

Actually, Foucault's writings, like those of most French intellectuals of the time, continued to be thoroughly imbued with Marxism. In pronouncements of the seventies (when, certainly, his political stance had taken a more radical and activist turn) he made it clear that he had always been a Marxist in the sense in which I have defined that term. In one interview he said that he was forever quoting Marx, though without using quotation marks, just as a physicist would do in taking for granted the discoveries of Newton or Einstein (the untenable, in my view, association of Marx with Newton and Einstein is the very essence of the great Marxisant fallacy). In another, he declared: 'One might even wonder what difference there could ultimately be between being a historian and being a Marxist.'[29] What an appalling confession it is that Foucault (and Lacan, and Robbe-Grillet, and the rest) could never see beyond the horizon determined by Marx.

A lighter touch was shown by the celebrated New Wave film-maker Jean-Luc Godard, whose film *La Chinoise* of 1967 poked fun at *Les Mots et les choses*. In an interview, Godard said that it was against people like 'Reverend Foucault' that he wanted to make films:

> If I don't particularly like Foucault it is because of his saying, 'At such and such a period they thought...' That's fine with me, but how can we be so sure? That is exactly why we try to make films; to prevent future Foucaults from presumptuously saying things like that.[30]

That Foucault, despite his attacks on Sartre and on orthodox Marxism, did have a strong sense of political commitment, even though he had never so far participated in radical activity, is apparent in an interview he gave to a Swedish magazine in March 1968:

> I think that a rigorous, theoretical analysis of the way in which economic, political, and ideological structures function is one of the necessary conditions for political action, insofar as political action is a way of manipulating and possibly changing, drastically disrupting, and transforming structures... I do not consider that structuralism is an armchair activity for intellectuals; I think it can and must be integrated with practice.[31]

Foucault was happy for the time being to be lauded as one of the leading figures in structuralism—perhaps, indeed, the leading figure, the top intellectual and true successor to Sartre; but by 1969 he was beginning to reject the structuralist label. In *L'Archéologie du savoir* (1969)—in English, *The Archaeology of Knowledge* (1972)—he was writing what was in many ways both a development, and correction, of *Les Mots et les choses*, presenting, perfectly formed, the concepts of 'discursive practices', said to govern what knowledge is actually possible in a given era—a reasonable idea when not pushed to extremes—and 'discursive formations', the actual bodies of knowledge: thus, it is maintained, historians can never get near the truth since they are constrained by the discursive practices of bourgeois society. He was tired of Clermont-Ferrand, and anxious to get a senior post in Paris. Meantime, again through high-placed connections, he took a teaching post in Tunis, where the new book was completed ahead of the events of May 1968. In Tunis he became embroiled in an awkward situation, which he faced with great courage and sensitivity. Some of his own students took part in anti-government riots which also had a marked anti-Semitic character. Foucault abhorred anti-Semitism, but he felt a prior obligation to shelter his students and testify on their behalf.[32] He was back briefly in Paris at the end of May (having missed the first exciting outbreak of the 'events'), where he joined in a meeting of Leftist politicians (including Mendès-France and Mitterrand) who were hoping for the fall of de Gaulle. His famous (if not altogether lucid) comment, on seeing a cohort of marching students was: 'They are not making a revolution; they are a revolution.'[33]

The student troubles in Paris had actually begun in the bleak surroundings of Nanterre on the western outskirts of Paris, but much of the most dramatic action had been concentrated in the Latin Quarter, where the most prestigious university institutions were situated. One of the most constructive responses of the government to criticisms of existing higher education was to establish a new university college out in the eastern suburbs of Paris, in the forest of Vincennes— the Centre Expérimental de Vincennes. The government's Orientation Commission, charged with making the initial appointments, and beginning work in October 1968, included Canguilhem, Le Roy Ladurie, Barthes, and Derrida. Canguilhem chose Foucault for the chair of philosophy; however, there was much opposition to this because Foucault was thought, particularly by members of the Communist party, to be too much of an establishment man—to be, indeed, a Gaullist.[34] But Foucault was unstoppable, and his appointment became effective from 1 December 1968.

The University of Paris at Vincennes quickly became a brilliant centre for advanced thinking in many subjects—and for teaching adult students. The influence of Foucault and his fellow-thinkers on the events of 1968 was at most indirect. The various chalked-up slogans of the Sorbonne in May 1968 were generally not complimentary towards teachers of any sort: *Les structures ne descendent pas dans les rues* (Structures do not take to the streets) was one.[35] Later, when Foucault invited Lacan to lecture at Vincennes, the latter did not find his student audiences very congenial. Walking out, he made the celebrated utterance: 'What you long for, as revolutionaries, is a master. You will get one.'[36] Structuralism did provide some slogans about 'the system', about language and ideology, and served to give a shining new image to a Marxism tarnished by the discredited French Communist party. For its part, student activism and its apparent successes induced a sort of unity among the various types of left-wing intellectuals, and for Foucault himself had a definite rationalizing effect. Early in 1969 he played a prominent part in a meeting of left-wing intellectuals and politicians at the famous hall of La Mutualité, Sartre also being present. It was only in the post-1969 years of liberation and excess that Foucault became more actively radical, identifying with gay liberation and with Maoism. Meanwhile he was also preoccupied with attaining the pinnacle of academic success, election to the Collège de France. Much of the work for which he was to be most famous—*Discipline and*

*Punish* and *The History of Sexuality*—was yet to come.

Jacques Derrida was born in Algeria in 1930. He studied at the école Normale Supérieure, then from 1960 to 1964 taught at the Sorbonne, before returning in 1965 to teach history of philosophy at the école Normale Supérieure. Derrida was an agreeably mischievous figure, responsible for the spread of 'deconstruction' as a mode of analysing literary texts, and inventor of *différance* (with an 'a' in the final syllable, not the normal 'e'). According to Saussure, words acquired their meaning through their *differences* from each other within the language system. Derrida—who published three major works in 1967, *La Voix et phénomène* (Speech and Phenomenon), *Vécriture et la différence* (Writing and Difference), and *De la grammatologie* (About Grammatology)—added that in addition meaning only came to a reader after delay, or deferral. The concept of *différance* is intended to combine these two points. Derrida is a vital figure in the international circulation of ideas I have referred to several times. The paper he delivered at Johns Hopkins University in 1966, 'Structure, Sign and Play in the Discourse of the Human Sciences', initiated the fashion for deconstruction in America. Subsequently he divided his time between Paris and the USA.[37]

While the French 'new novel' and the early ideas of Barthes were taking shape in the 1950s, the dominant literary mode in Italy was still 'new realism'. Thus in the world of ideas there was an even sharper break at the beginning of the sixties in Italy than in France, with the appearance of 'neo-avant-gardism', 'experimental modernism', 'the new poetics'. The preoccupations are very much those of the French figures I have been discussing: semiology, the 'decentring' (or death) of the individual subject, a complete break with commercialism and bourgeois traditionalism (with regard to the last point, the Italians acknowledged a debt to the German writers, who in setting up Gruppe 47 immediately after the war had sought a total rupture with the past). Among the major new figures were Umberto Eco (b. 1932), philosophy graduate, author of a dissertation on medieval society and thought (in some ways his intellectual career, including in particular his philosophical excursion into history, parallels that of Foucault), deviser of a tape in homage to James Joyce, interpreter of Modernism, student of contemporary popular culture, and Italy's first major semiologist, and Nanni Balestrini (b. 1935), contributor to the 1961 anthology of poetry, *I Novissimi*. One of the most prestigious figures of the older generation, Italo Calvino (1923–85), was already in the 1950s delving in his novels into the worlds of fantasy, myth, and allegory: but it was in the sixties that he turned to novels dealing with the creation of the cosmos— *Ti con zero* (Time and the Hunter) and *Cosmicomici*—works which seemed to echo Foucault's ideas about the insignificance of humanity in the total history of the universe. Eco began to receive something of the same attention attracted in France by his contemporaries there, with the publication of the *Opera aperta: forma e indeterminazione nelle poetiche contemporanee* (1962), whose basic thesis was that modernist works are characterized by 'openness', that is to say, their meaning is very much open to the individual interpretation of the individual reader. Eco is the most directly influential figure, perhaps second only to Barthes, in popularizing the idea of the systematic, scholarly analysis of the many different aspects of popular culture. (It may be noted, however, that his analysis of the James Bond phenomenon relates to the fifties novels by Ian Fleming, rather than to the sixties films featuring Sean Connery.) The two major works developing his structuralist and semiological interests were *La struttura assente* (1968, English translation The

Absent Structure) and *Le forme del contenuto* (1971, The Forms of the Content).

Balestrini was born into a prosperous Milan family; his mother was German, and the family avoided the worst of the war on Lake Como, where Balestrini went to a private school. He refused to follow his father into engineering, becoming instead a poet and publisher, a member of the new avant garde, dedicated to a literature which, in rupturing the accepted relationship between language and meaning, forswearing narrative content, and abandoning literary craftsmanship, would in itself embody a comment on the nakedly commercial conditions of all production in late capitalist society; the echo of the intentions of the 'new novelists' in France is strong. Along with Eco, Balestrini was active in founding Gruppe 63, which apart from the conscious echo of the German Gruppo 47, kept in close touch with the *Tel Quel* group in Paris. Between 1966 and 1968 Balestrini programmed his computer to produce poetry—the ultimate in literature as commodity. His first novel, *Tristano* (1966), consists of ten chapters of ten paragraphs each of twenty-four lines; the paragraphs are culled either from romances or from technical handbooks. There is formal perfection, but interpretation, as Eco argued should be the case, is in the hands of the reader. As we shall discover shortly, rumblings of severe discontent were apparent in the Italian secondary schools, and then the universities, from 1966 onwards. In the climactic year of 1968, when it looked as though there might be unity between students and workers, Gruppo 63 perceived how remote its new avant-garde theories were from real anticapitalist action, and disbanded. Balestrini helped found Potere Operaio (Workers' Power) and participated actively in the demonstrations of 1968 and 1969: it is with these demonstrations, centred on the Fiat plant in Turin, that his second and rather more naturalistic novel, to be discussed in a later chapter, is concerned.[38]

Attention to the significance of popular culture (and in this case that of the mass media) is the major point of contact between the various figures we have been studying, from Marcuse to Barthes to Eco, and another North American, who from 1964 onwards was undoubtedly a central figure in some of the key beliefs of the sixties, Marshall McLuhan; his famous notion that 'the medium is the message' is similar, though in a rather simplistic way, to the central notion of the structuralists, post-structuralists, and semiologists, that language determines ideas rather than the other way about. McLuhan was born in Edmonton, Alberta, in Canada, in July 1911 (dying in Toronto in December 1980). He did his postgraduate work in England, taking a Ph.D. at Cambridge in 1942 on 'The Place of Thomas Nashe in the Learning of His Time'; his interests were very much in literature, literary criticism, and the study of rhetoric. He became a convert to Catholicism, and his lifelong devotion to that faith rather singles him out from the radical commitment of the other thinkers discussed in this chapter. During a career of teaching English at the universities of Wisconsin and St Louis, he switched from the Renaissance to the modern period, concentrating on Eliot, Pound, Yeats, Wyndham Lewis, and above all Joyce. He developed the theory that 'the artist picks up the message of cultural and technical challenge decades before its transforming impact occurs; he then builds models, or "Noah's arks", for facing the change that is ahead.'

McLuhan's first book, published in 1951, was *The Mechanical Bride*. His declamatory, metaphysical, and not always very meaningful style can be seen in his comment on the crucial importance of technology: 'Technology is an abstract tyrant that carries its ravages into deeper recesses of the psyche than did the sabre-tooth tiger or the grizzly bear.' In 1962 he moved closer to national and international attention with *The Gutenberg Galaxy*, on the significance of the invention of printing in moving communication from an oral to a verbal basis. The book was again declamatory in style and composed of a series of rather loosely connected short chapters. As Claude Bissell has put it:

> The very form of the book—short sections preceded by arresting and dogmatic summaries, long quotations from a wide variety of sources, puns and verbal play—embodied the qualities of discontinuity, simultaneity, and multiple association to be found in an oral culture.[39]

The University of Toronto (he was teaching within the university at the Catholic St Michael's College) set him up in the Centre for Culture and Technology: through his seminars there he directly influenced many students, and established contacts throughout the world. The book which brought him to the centre of the international stage was *Understanding Media* (1964), which heralded what McLuhan saw as the decisive breakaway from print culture into that of the technological mass media, while establishing McLuhan himself as an authority on popular culture. Electronic communications, he said, had created a world of instant awareness in which a sense of private identity was untenable; or, as critic Harold Rosenberg put it, McLuhan was saying good-bye 'to Gutenberg and the Renaissance', to 'typographic man'; to 'the self-centred individual'.[40] Thus interpreted, McLuhan stands with the French neo-Marxists in the decentring of the subject. Once more, the book is poorly constructed—a loose series of short chapters, full of strong statements, some of which seem rather banal. The message seems to be partly pessimistic—humanity's domination by technology—and part-optimistic—recognition of the potentially liberating influence of technology. This notion of interdependence through the mass media was encapsulated in the other of McLuhan's over-quoted phrases 'global village', woven into the title of the 1968 publication *War and Peace in the Global Village*.

The other North American 'philosopher' (or 'guru', to use the idiom of the day) of the sixties everyone has heard of is Timothy Leary. Leary's intellectual legacy was minuscule, even less significant than that of McLuhan; and, of course, it bears no comparison with that of the European intellectuals I have been discussing. But Leary, the principal proselytizer on behalf of the cause that psychedelic drugs were not simply enjoyable but, through the revelations they induced, positively beneficial to the future development of humankind, was an influence on sixties attitudes we cannot ignore. Without Leary drug-taking would still have been an important component of many sixties subcultures; but Leary, a Harvard academic of considerable distinction, was the man who gave the lead, and the apparently scientific validation, to the many who thought, or affected to think, that drugs were a means to the good society, as others thought that aim was to be achieved by the destruction of bourgeois ideology. Leary was a prime exponent of one of the kinds of ultimate extremism produced, and in some degree cherished, in the sixties.

Born in Massachusetts in 1920, Leary in 1950 took a Ph.D. in clinical psychology at the University of California at Berkeley. In 1958 he joined the Harvard Center for Research in Personality. It was in August 1960 that he had 'the deepest religious experience of my life' after eating seven 'sacred mushrooms', an experience which he repeated over fifty times in the next three years. In a lecture delivered in Philadelphia on 30 August 1963, he explained:

A profound transcendent experience should leave in its wake a changed man and a changed life. Since my illumination of August, 1960, I have devoted most of my energies to try to understand the revelatory potentialities of the human nervous system and to make these insights available to others.[41]

A few months earlier, in June 1963, together with like-minded colleagues, he had founded the *Psychedelic Review*. The editorial in the first issue declared, with some echoes of Marcuse, together with that faith in technology which McLuhan partially manifested:

The synthesis of consciousness-expanding substances which we regard as one of the most outstanding achievements of technological society, has now provided us with a means of transcending and overcoming many of the distortions which operate in the very society that has brought about such substances. It is now possible to affirm the general character of our social technocracy without succumbing to its totalitarian demands. The creation and furtherance of internal freedom for large numbers of people through the intelligent use of psychedelic substances are now a practical reality.[42]

Leary repeatedly insisted that the psychedelic revelations he claimed to have had matched up with established scientific knowledge. 'We are, of course', he continued, 'at the very beginning of our research into these implications. A new experiential language and perhaps even new metaphors for the Great Plan will develop.' To this he shortly added:

remember that God (however you define the Higher Power) produced that wonderful molecule, that extraordinarily powerful organic substance we call LSD, just as surely as 'He' created the rose, or the sun, or the complex cluster of molecules you insist on calling 'your self'.[43]

At Harvard Leary had been experimenting, not with LSD, the synthetic psychedelic drug only just becoming widely known, but with psilocybin, the chemical derivative of 'sacred mushrooms', which he administered to himself and to volunteers at the university. The university authorities were unhappy about this, and when Leary refused to desist he was asked to leave. Meantime he had published a piece entitled 'The Fifth Freedom: The Right to Get High':

Make no mistake, the effect of consciousness-expanding drugs will be to transform our concepts of human nature, human potentialities, existence. The game is about to be

281

changed, ladies and gentlemen. Man is about to make use of that fabulous electrical network he carries around in his skull. Present social establishments had better be prepared for change. Our favourite concepts are standing in the way of a flood tide of 2 billion years building up. The verbal dam is collapsing. Head for the hills, or prepare your intellectual craft to flow with the current.[44]

With Richard Alpert, Leary now set up the privately funded International Foundation for Internal Freedom. Leary himself was no drop-out. He spoke up both in support of psychedelic experiences and radical political causes, and was several times arrested. He was a classic example of the middle-aged man who identified with the new youth subcultures: 'psychedelic drugs', he said, 'are the medium of the young.'[45] Sex was a central part of it all. 'One of the great purposes of an LSD session', he said in a famous interview in *Playboy* (September 1966), 'is sexual union. The more expanded your consciousness, the further out you can move beyond your mind—the deeper, the richer, the longer, and more meaningful your sexual communion.' Leary went to the extremes of permissiveness; but he was absolute in his belief in the rightness of heterosexuality. 'The fact is', he told *Playboy*, 'that LSD is a specific *cure* for homosexuality.' He told a story (risible in the extreme, though apparently utterly serious) about a lesbian:

she was very active sexually, but all of her energy was devoted to making it with girls. She was at an LSD session at one of our cottages and went down to the beach and saw this young man in a bathing suit and—flash!—for the first time in her life the cellular electricity was flowing in her body and it bridged the gap. Her subsequent sexual choices were almost exclusively members of the opposite sex.

*Playboy* taxed Leary with the claim that many taking LSD were dropping out, becoming absolutely useless to themselves and society. Leary's reply included the following:

There *is* an LSD drop-out problem, but it's nothing to worry about. It's something to cheer. The lesson I have learned from over 300 LSD sessions, and which I have been passing on to others, can be stated in six syllables: turn on, tune in, drop out. 'Turn on' means to contact the ancient energies and wisdoms that are built into your nervous system. They provide unspeakable pleasure and revelation. 'Tune in' means to harness and communicate these new perspectives in a harmonious dance with the external world. 'Drop out' means to detach yourself from the tribal game.[46]

As an apostle of sexual permissiveness Leary is often linked to W. R. Reich and Marcuse, and all three are linked with Norman O. Brown, whose ponderings, following Freud, on the evil consequences of sexual repression, and the need to avoid it at all costs, began in the mid-fifties, and surfaced in a curious ragbag of quotations under the title, *Life Against Death*.[47] 'I have not hesitated', Brown wrote, 'to pursue new ideas to their ultimate "mad" consequences, knowing that Freud too seemed mad', sounding a note we have heard already and will hear again.

Whether the ordinary kind of sexual permissiveness really owed anything to Brown's message on repression is highly doubtful, but certainly for the counter-cultural advanced guard who went in for permissiveness in a massive, systematic, and commercial fashion, Brown lined up with the other three in providing the kind of pretentious endorsement much loved by earnest hedonists.

Britain, producer of so much that was innovative in sixties popular culture, had no charismatic advocate of psychedelic revelation, no attention-grabbing theorist of mass communications, and no great philosopher busy decentring the subject and elevating the significance of language. The one individual to achieve guru status and fame on the Left Bank was the Scottish psychiatrist, R. D. Laing (b. Glasgow 1927), though, significantly for my insistence on the survival power of Sartrean ideas, he saw himself as an 'existentialist' rather than a 'structuralist'. His first book, *The Divided Self: An Existential Study in Sanity and Madness,* attracted attention for casting doubt on the way conventional psychiatrists diagnosed 'schizophrenia', and still more for criticism of that 'bourgeois institution', the family. What was perceived as 'madness' could be caused, Laing said, by the strains of family life. A reasonable wish to withdraw from family life could seem disturbing to the family, who, in turn, might find doctors, especially psychiatrists, only too ready to collude in pinning the label 'mad' on any individual behaving oddly by the family's standards. In his major work, *Sanity, Madness and the Family,* written in collaboration with A. A. Esterson and published in 1964, Laing offered case histories showing how communications within the family could become so disrupted that an individual member might seek refuge in madness.

In the preface to the second edition published in 1970, Laing and Esterson clarified that they were not accepting that the condition of 'schizophrenia' actually existed, and that what was thought to be schizophrenia could have wider social causes as well as family ones. The original edition was published by the Tavistock Clinic in its series 'Studies in Existentialism and Phenomenology'. Laing had become sufficiently well known for paperback publishers Penguin Books to commission a 'Penguin Original': *The Politics of Experience and the Bird of Paradise* (1967), among other things, suggested that the schizophrenic might simply be someone who had been unable to suppress his normal instincts and conform to an abnormal society. In his preface Laing wrote:

> There is little conjunction of truth and social 'reality'. Around us are pseudo-events, to which we adjust with a false consciousness adapted to see these events as true and real, and even as beautiful. In the society of men the truth resides now less in what things are than in what they are not. Our social realities are so ugly if seen in the light of exiled truth, and beauty is almost no longer possible if it is not a lie.
>
> What is to be done? We who are still half alive, living in the often fibrillating heart-land of a senescent capitalism—can we do more than reflect the decay around and within us? Can we do more than sing our sad and bitter songs of disillusion and defeat?

If precise meaning is not always clear, the Marxist influences are—'false consciousness', 'senescent capitalism'. As great visionaries sharing his own unhappy perceptions, Laing cited Marx, Kierkegaard, Nietzsche, Freud, Heidegger, Tillich, and Sartre, referring also to

Foucault's *Madness and Civilization*, recently published in the same Tavistock series. With Foucault, Laing was presenting madness, not as an objective condition, but simply as what society decreed to be madness, and thus raising questions about the nature of 'normality'. He was, he said, getting away from the clinical medical understanding of madness, seeing it instead in 'existential social terms'. Much of the book was taken up with little stories about Laing's patients; the second half, 'Bird of Paradise', was probably written under the influence of LSD. The book was immensely popular, many of the student generation feeling that it spoke directly to them.[48] Laing's consulting-room in exclusive Wimpole Street had chairs scattered around in disorderly fashion. He once explained that he was aiming at 'a kind of improvisational theatre where the encounter between doctor and patient can take place spontaneously'.[49] Most of his patients found such consultations deeply comforting. From 1965 to 1970 he helped run Kingsley Hall, a residential treatment hostel, providing innovative therapy. He played a major part in the 'Dialectics of Liberation congress' at London's Round House in July 1967, where leading speakers were Marcuse, Ginsberg, and Black Power spokesman Stokely Carmichael. By the later sixties he was in communication with the Left Bank luminaries, particularly Lacan. Laing, a genuinely sensitive and sympathetic person, came to be seen as leader of what was called 'the Anti-Psychiatry movement', and something of a hero of the Left, along with Marcuse at one end of the age spectrum and Che Guevara at the other. His latest, authoritative biographer, Jungian analyst John Clay, writes: 'Few psychiatrists, psychoanalysts and psychotherapists since the 1960s have not been affected by his pronouncements and modified their thinking and practice as a result.'[50] Laing's profoundest message was that of understanding those thought to be mad, truly a message from the best side of sixties thinking. He got many things wrong, particularly his attribution of the condition called schizophrenia to family and social circumstances—a mistake very much in tune with the banal side of sixties thinking.

The ideas of structuralism and post-structuralism had little effect on British intellectual life within the period up to the end of the sixties. Matters were different in the United States, where some academics were always ready to embrace new fashions. The critical event was the conference at Johns Hopkins University in October 1966 on 'The Languages of Criticism and the Sciences of Man' (already referred to), at which the speakers included Barthes and Lacan as well as Derrida. One who was greatly influenced was the apparently conservative literary critic J. Hillis Miller. In 1971 there appeared a collection edited by Miller, *Aspects of Narrative*. The preface by Miller himself is dominated by references to structuralism, to Barthes, and to *Tel Quel;* the first four papers had been read at a conference directed by Professor Paul de Man, the second paper being by Edward Said, both to be leading figures in the American postmodernism of the future. A critical moment was to come in 1972 when Miller left Johns Hopkins for Yale University, where he became chairman of the English department in 1976. A colleague from the French department was Paul de Man. The rise and rise of the 'Yale of School of Criticism' was about to begin: but that, from our point of view, is simply a relatively distant legacy of this particular sixties cultural development.

Existentialism, though popular with the young, was not being renewed at source. But other philosophical concerns continued. When in 1967 Richard Rorty published a collection entitled *The Linguistic Turn: Recent Essays in Philosophical Method,* he was not referring to the theories of language associated with the structuralists and post-structuralists, but to the empirical philosophy of the previous thirty-five years: the philosophers featured included Gilbert Ryle, Stuart Hampshire, and Peter Strawson. Meantime, in what the structuralists excoriated as the 'humanist tradition', John Rawls (b. 1921), professor of philosophy at Harvard since 1962, was publishing a number of essays, brought together in the publication of 1971, *A Theory of Justice.* This large and rich book developed the brilliantly simple idea that the fair society would be a society in which the rules were put forward by those who had no idea what their own economic position would be in that society. This is measured judgement at its highest: this is the spirit which informed the praiseworthy, if circumscribed, welfare legislation described in the previous chapter.

Traditional liberalism was indeed still a strong force throughout the 1960s. It is not easy, as I have pointed out once or twice, to draw rigid lines between, say, 'established society' and 'the alternative society', between 'majority culture' and 'underground culture', or between all the different forms of liberalism on one side and all those of radical fundamentalism on the other: many liberals supported student protest and opposed American intervention in Vietnam. Althusser was a loyal and even obsequious member of the French Communist party, seen by many radicals as a conservative force; all of the Left Bank luminaries were firmly integrated into the French academic establishment. However, if we are to penetrate to the core of structuralism and post-structuralism with respect to what was indicated in terms of political action, the fundamental point, taken up by student protesters and other activist groups, was that mere political revolution, a mere seizure of power by progressive forces, would not be enough: the very belief structures, and therefore the language systems which controlled them, must be destroyed, and totally replaced. In both commonsense ways (which may have had little to do with structuralist theorizing), and sometimes in more absurd ones, new attention was paid to the language used in relations between the races and then between the sexes. The actual practical example of the destruction of all existing structures, ideological and linguistic as well as economic and political, appeared to be the 'Cultural Revolution' begun in 1965 by Mao Tse-tung in China. Philippe Sollers, Foucault, and others were enthusiasts. 'Maoism' became quite a fashionable political stance; in Italy radical protesters were known as *cinesi* ('Chinese'). Various other protest movements, including the 'Situationists', took some of their ideas from the leading thinkers. Structuralism and post-structuralism did provide a kind of intellectual underpinning for radical fundamentalism, though the most direct influence (despite Cohn-Bendit!) was Marcuse's view that the prosperity and liberalism of Western society were in fact repressive. Much of what was said was complete nonsense (Sollers, like many others, became completely disillusioned with China in the mid-seventies); the nonsense was to have a continuing influence in patterning what were to be the hipsters, miniskirts, maxiskirts, topless bathing-suits, and hot-pants of academia, that is, deconstruction, sociology of knowledge, semiology, semiotics, cultural studies, feminist studies, new historicism, discourse theory, cultural materialism, and postmodernism in general.

## Art, Poetry, Music, and Architecture of the High Sixties

I have already spoken of an 'art explosion' in the early sixties. Some of the daring things being essayed then had already been tried in the fifties, and indeed as far back as the Dada movement of the First World War. Characteristically of this era of almost instantaneous interchange and of high expectation that change could only be followed by further change, art of the middle and later sixties was more of the same, only more so. Over the half-dozen years from 1964 to the end of the decade it is easy to pick out, without any of the ambiguity or counter-reaction of the first stirrings of change, absolutely distinctive and characteristic features which, first, continued to dominate the arts for the rest of the century, second, ran right through every artistic and creative endeavour (art and architecture, painting, sculpture, poetry, music, theatre), and, third, are also apparent in the everyday world of the media, consumerism, and dinner-table conversation. These characteristics can be defined under eight headings:

### 1. Cross-over

The term implies the intermixing of élite and popular art, already most obviously apparent in Pop Art and *nouveau réalisme*. As we have just seen, many of the great intellectuals of the time were fascinated by popular culture and the mass media. Classical musicians have long borrowed from folk music and, from at least the 1920s, from jazz: but, in fact, in the sixties the effort was much more concentrated and much more concerted; furthermore, the movement was two-way. The arts did not necessarily become more comprehensible to the majority, but the leading artists, poets, musicians wanted to show conspicuous concern for the majority and awareness of the cultural forms they favoured.

### 2. The Blurring of boundaries

Not this time the blurring between élite and popular art, but that between the different individual art forms: between art and sculpture, between art and poetry, between music and drama, and so on. Within the visual and plastic arts, paintings are two-dimensional, sculptures three-dimensional. 'Assemblages' (including 'mobiles'—assemblages which move, in the breeze or because power-driven) again dated back to Dada, and to movements of the interwar years and of the fifties: three-dimensional, more than paintings, they were not exactly sculptures. The history of the assemblage, the ultimate in the withering away of the distinction between painter and sculptor, was a venerable fifty-year one, but in the middle sixties ideas for assemblages proliferated, and among new artists the assemblage (of some sort) became the preferred means through which to make a statement. There is a blurring too (attempted, if not always realized) between art and poetry: 'concrete poetry', in its more traditional, two-dimensional form, is graphic design, shapes on the page; in a yet more extreme form it is three-dimensional shape, sculpture. Music invades drama; the odd 'happenings' of the fifties become the ubiquitous multimedia events of the mid-sixties. The sense of overlap and blurring of boundaries was enhanced by the existence of the term *musique concrète* (see below), something rather different, yet perhaps not so different in spirit. There was also 'concrete art', abstract painting involving the serial development of colour, or colours merging into each other.

### 3. Conceptualism

The heading is a vague one, yet absolutely central in that it pushes towards ultimate extremes in privileging the idea or concept over any direct representation, and in invoking the unavoidable involvement of language (the only way in which concepts can be expressed, or made explicit).

### 4.Indeterminacy or the Aleatoric

These elaborate words cover the notions of chance elements being incorporated into works of art and of there being uncertainty (in the way Eco identified) about the meaning or meanings of particular works, with the reader, viewer, listener having a part in selecting meanings.

### 5. Participation

There is a link here to the previous heading, but the participation of reader, viewer, listener, or audience could be so pronounced as to become a major element in a work, as in certain types of theatre calling for audience-participation, or in an assemblage composed of mirrors.

### 6. Technology

Mobile assemblages, assemblages with flashing lights, assemblages made out of the products of technology were all obvious examples, while *musique concrète* (taped music based on natural sounds), then electronic music (produced entirely by electronic means), were particularly stunning ones. Drug-induced perceptions (which to Leary were among technology's most splendid products) played some part across all the arts. Psychedelic 'light shows' became an almost essential adjunct to counter-cultural rock/pop music.

### 7. Radical criticism, Revolutionary stances

A large proportion of sixties creative work was deliberately intended to be 'counter-cultural', profoundly critical of 'bourgeois', or 'consumerist' society. Many artists were Marxist, several were very familiar with the newer modifications and extensions of Marxism, with the theories of Marcuse and the Left Bank luminaries. Linked to revolutionary purposes was the notion of art as research, research which would expose the failings of existing society. A 'work of art' (the phrase itself was said to be a bourgeois one) was not to be distinguished from a philosophical tract, or, for that matter, from a piece of historical writing. All could be described as 'experiments', or 'interpretations', or 'texts'.

### 8. Social and Cultural practices (particularly 'Counter-Cultural' ones) as 'Spectacle'

However revolutionary or 'counter-cultural' in intention, it was very difficult for practitioners of the arts to escape from the circumstance that everything was being produced within a society in which there was a steadily growing appetite for the new, and an entire commercial and techno-logical apparatus devoted to focusing attention on, and marketing, the daring and exciting. Individual artists were brought into the limelight much in the manner of the great intellectual figures; on the whole, the more extreme the better. Radical artists deplored this trend—to them 'spectacle-ism' was yet another regrettable feature of commercialized bourgeois society.

I noted earlier that Edward Lucie-Smith, in his *Movements in Art since 1945,* reproduces seventy-five works from the 'High Sixties'. Most of the artists, of course, had produced distinctive works prior to the sixties, and all of the movements or 'isms' defined by Lucie-Smith had had their prototypes, or had even been brought into existence, much earlier; some of the sharpest and most daring shifts came at the end of the fifties and the beginning of the sixties; nevertheless the middle and later sixties stand out as a time both of culmination and of ever-accelerating innovation—perhaps also of pushing paradigms to their utmost limits, and beyond. It seems likely that more new labels for types of art were invented in this period (prefixes and suffixes—earth art, *arte povera*—as much as 'isms'), and certain that more were in use simultaneously, than in any comparable period before, and probably since. The profusion of labels is a measure of the heavily reflexive, conceptualizing quality of much art, of the insistence that practically everything, whatever the conventional critic might think, could be classified as 'art', and of the determination to be for ever different. Some labels seemed to overlap in signification, others appeared very elastic; many artists had several labels applied to them, others moved from one label to another, perhaps denying former allegiances (as Foucault came to deny that he was a structuralist). Most artists shared in the independent spirit of the sixties, so that some preferred no label at all, or abandoned a particular label as soon as others began to use it. Still, the use of labels which do authentically belong to the period can be useful in bringing out the special features of painting and sculpture in the sixties, and the characteristics they shared with the other arts, élite and popular.

Art is always in some sense international, but it was now clearly affected by the increased velocity of international exchange. It will be necessary both to stray beyond the confines of my four chosen countries and also to stress the new influence of those whom the French and Italians referred to as 'the Anglo-Saxons' (the Americans and the British). If British popular music and British fashion held pole position in this period, it would probably be correct to say that it was 'Anglo-Saxon' art in this sense which held the equivalent position. Generally, the swing was from two-dimensional painting to assemblages, mixed-media art, including happenings, and art which simply appeared to be unworked materials of various sorts just left lying around, holes dug in the ground, or anything else the artist decided to call 'art'. A number of developments in two-dimensional painting were important: more complex and individualistic Pop Art, with the spotlight focusing especially on the absolutely individualist exploits of David Hockney; the development of what the critics came to term 'painterly abstraction' towards 'concrete art' and towards greater use of optical illusion (this could also be seen in Pop Art); and, at the very end of the decade, the appearance of new, highly charged illusionism of the traditional kind, 'super-realism'. The favoured labels were 'land art', 'earth art', *'arte povera'* and, covering both assemblages and painting, 'conceptualism' and 'minimalism'.

The artist who commanded attention, who was spectacle in the manner of Foucault, Marcuse, McLuhan, or Leary (not to mention the Beatles, the Who, and mods and rockers), was Andy Warhol. If we want to penetrate the ideological nostalgia about the sixties as a time when 'bourgeois' society and culture could have been overthrown, we can scarcely do better than look at the life and antics of Andy Warhol. Warhol, we saw, was to the fore just at the time when Pop Art decisively took over the headlines, ousting the various forms of Abstract Expressionist and 'painterly' art. He now went on to produce a very distinctive form of Pop Art, based on silk-screen reproduction and the bludgeoning use of repetition. He also moved into what he and others labelled 'underground' movies. What could be more revolutionary than 'underground', with all its connotations of clandestinity, of art so rebellious that it must conceal itself, until the time is ripe for open revolution, from 'bourgeois' eyes and spies? In fact, what Warhol wanted above all was attention: for him there was no point in being shocking if there was no one around to be shocked. Once again it is a case of not being misled by words: Warhol's 'underground' had the sense of 'bohemian', 'fringe', 'experimental', 'avant garde'. Warhol provided spectacle for some of America's richest and most aristocratic people: he himself, while also having his own particular coterie of peculiar people, mingled exultantly with leaders of fashion and wealthy trendies, with 'the beautiful people'. Those things, and those people, who were fashionable in New York, San Francisco, and Los Angeles were of course anathema to large sections of the American public, and Warhol products, towards the end of the decade, were subject to seizure and censorship. Warhol was profoundly innovative and profoundly shocking; he was at the epicentre of what was most distinctive about the arts and entertainments in the sixties—but that was not politically revolutionary, nor part of a coherent counter-culture about to overthrow traditional 'bourgeois' culture. Indeed, Warhol was one of the most notable among the capitalis-tic horde of individualistic entrepreneurs—designers, impresarios, theatre directors, shopkeepers, agents, club-owners—who made a vital contribution to the transformation of life in the sixties. Though undoubtedly concerned with worldly success, Warhol was also deeply serious; he would otherwise not have spent so much time making films which, for the unenthusiastic, were notable mostly for their interminable length and unutterable boringness. In another melancholy, though actually an entirely contingent way, Warhol seemed to symbolize an age, or perhaps just a year—1968. For 1968 was the year in which first Martin Luther King and then Robert Kennedy, candidate for the Democratic presidential nomination, were shot dead: Warhol was actually shot the day before Kennedy, and only managed to cling on to life by the very narrowest of margins. Already his films were exploiting, and contributing to, the accelerating wave of permissiveness.

Andrew Warhola was born to working-class Slovakian parents in Pittsburgh Pennsylvania, on 6 August 1928; subsequently he was to deduct anything from one to five years from his age.[51] In the fifties he became Andy Warhol, an extremely prosperous designer and illustrator for the fashion magazines, and for the advertising industry generally. He was going bald, had a pudgy nose, and weird, almost albino colouring. To ensure that he would always attract attention he took to wearing grey or white wigs. He was sexually attracted to both men and women, though more and more actively to the former. At the very end of 1963 he moved to a spacious fourth-floor loft at 231 East 47th Street, between Second and Third Avenues, not far from Grand Central Station. Redecorated mainly in silver, this became studio, and meeting, partying, and sometimes sleeping, place for all those associated with, or interested in, avant-garde Pop move-ments in the arts. If expanding and interacting youth subculture had been a key agent of change at the beginning of the decade, what can reasonably be called Pop subculture was very important in the middle of the decade. Of the various clubs, theatres, galleries, 'labs' which formed the physical locations for this subculture, Warhol's loft, quickly named 'the Factory', was among the most important. Warhol continued with his repetitious screen prints, then, with his Brillo boxes, moved into three-dimensional work, while from the summer of 1963 he was experimenting with film. Warhol, like Marcuse, McLuhan, and Leary, was always good for the remark which can be quoted again and again. Unlike the others, however, he did not always mean what he said, intending, like the Beatles in some of their remarks, to be mockingly misleading. However, the famous remark 'Machines have less problems. I'd like to be a machine, wouldn't you?' articulates directly with his manner of work in both of the media just mentioned. His art works very much were mechanically (and often, also collaboratively) produced: apart from the selection of the images and the tints to be given to them there was no artistic intervention by Warhol, and certainly no shaping or painting. The term 'the Factory' was entirely appropriate. Though some people thought that the three-dimensional Brillo boxes were actual Brillo boxes, they were in fact manufactured from scratch, but again in a very mechanical way. Films, clearly, are machine-made; but more than this, Warhol's method was simply to place the camera in position and then let it run without any further intervention from him. Thus there are very strong elements of chance and indeterminacy, as well as perhaps even a whiff of the death of the author.

Above all Warhol perceived that with conceptual art (and here the term 'art' includes his films) you could outrage people and gain enormous publicity through people simply being made aware of the concept, without ever having actually to view the painting, sculpture, or film. The Warhol exhibition which opened at the Stable Gallery, New York, on 21 April 1964 was in itself a concept. It was his first exhibition of his three-dimensional grocery carton 'sculptures'—boxes for Kellogg's Cornflakes, Heinz ketchup, etc., as well as Brillo pads. Warhol first had carpenters make wooden boxes of exactly the appropriate size; then one of his young male associates, known as Billy Name, painted the boxes in a light colour. After that, Warhol and his closest male associate, Gerard Malanga (himself definitely a creative contributor to much of Warhol's work), would silk-screen the sides of the boxes, reproducing the original graphic designs. In the exhibition itself Warhol crammed the gallery with his manufactured boxes distributed in different kinds of rows and stacks, so that the gallery had the appearance of a wholesaler's warehouse. If the gallery itself was a concept, the individual exhibits, given how little creative labour had gone into them, could well be described as 'minimalist'. The boxes did not sell particularly well, but the exhibition generated tremendous publicity.

The link between Warhol's first multi-reel film, *Sleep*, an eight-hour study from fixed camera positions of a male friend of Warhol's asleep in his bed at night, and painting, as traditionally understood, is relatively clear: there is a long tradition in Western art of paintings of sleeping subjects. *Sleep* was shown for four nights in January 1964 at the Gramercy Arts Theater, and in June at the Cinema Theater in Los Angeles, where it provoked angry scenes among the bored majority of the audience. Two more 'motionless' films followed, each about half an hour in length: *Eat*, which showed fellow artist Robert Indiana eating a mushroom, and *Blow Job*, which is fixed entirely on the face of the young man who is having this sexual act performed on him by a number of other males. From February 1965 Warhol began making sound films, improvised, and still with the same static camera. *The Life of Juanita Castro* satirized the Cuban communist leader Fidel Castro, while *Vinyl* was a spoof on British novelist Anthony Burgess's novel about excessively violent youth in a future society, *A Clockwork Orange*. Warhol's films got fairly regular exposure in movie art houses, not making money but always getting attention. He collected his own group of 'stars', and also the rock band Velvet Underground, with which he put on psyche- delic light shows, both in New York and on the West Coast. He attended many society events. In 1966 he produced a film which was considerably more sophisticated than anything that had gone before, *Chelsea Girls*. This contained seven hours of film, eight black-and-white reels, and four colour ones. As two reels were projected simultaneously, the actual viewing time was three and a half hours. It is a slow film, featuring drugged and drug-taking dropouts and snatches of desultory conversation. One small section is satirical in intent, referring to the Vietnam war, and American paranoia over North Vietnam, and featuring a North Vietnamese female agent; there is a lot of semi-nudity, but the only moment of shock was when a male character apparently being approached in a sado-masochistic way by a female character, rolled over and accidentally offered a brief flash of his flaccid penis.

*Chelsea Girls* had an opening week's run at a small art cinema in New York, Cinémathèque, in September 1966, with a further week in October and then a further sixteen days in November, prior to a transfer for two weeks to the midtown Manhattan art cinema, the Cinema Rendezvous. From there it moved successively to two mainstream cinemas. Following both good and bad reviews it was booked into Los Angeles, Dallas, Washington, San Diego, and Kansas City. Within two sentences, the *New York Times*, 2 December 1966, expressed both sides: 'At its best, "the Chelsea Girls" is a travelogue of hell—a grotesque menagerie of lost souls whimpering in a psychedelic moonscape of neon red and fluorescent blue. At its worst it is a bunch of home movies in which Mr Warhol's friends, asked to do something for the camera, can think of nothing much to do.' Now, quite definitely, 'Warhol became one of the most sought-after guests on the social circuit.'[52] On 28 November 1967 he joined such people as Robert Kennedy, Frank Sinatra, Norman Mailer, and Gloria Vanderbilt among the select 500 invited to socialite novelist Truman Capote's priapic social event, his black and white masked ball. In October 1967 the Institute of Contemporary Art in Boston mounted an exhibition of Warhol's paintings, along with showings of his early films, and a mixed-media evening with the Velvet Underground. Wherever it was shown, *Chelsea Girls* made money, but then on 30 May it was seized by Boston Vice Squad detec- tives: it was that accidental flash of penis that had done it. With respect to explicit sex and full frontal nudity Warhol's films had really been rather coy, but now he wanted to do something which would fully justify the brilliant title he had lighted on, *Fuck*. The star he hoped to secure was Jim Morrison, the sexy lead singer of the rock/pop group the Doors. Morrison failed to show up, and all others, when it came to it, refused to perform the crucial act. In January 1968 Warhol embarked on his first venture shot out of doors on location, the film which became *Lonesome Cowboys*. Apparently he had ideas of achieving a really big box office success, though as usual he left the film to develop by chance, without prior scripting. FBI agents kept a close eye on the filming, and then on the film itself at its premier at the San Francisco Film Festival on 1 November 1968. The FBI agents reported:

All of the males in the cast displayed homosexual tendencies and conducted themselves toward one another in an effeminate manner... Many of the cast portrayed their parts as if in a stupor from marijuana, drugs, or alcohol... later in the movie the cowboys went out to the ranch owned by the woman. On their arrival, they took her from her horse, removed her clothes and sexually assaulted her. During this time her private parts were exposed to the audience... The position of the male and female suggested an act of cunnilingus; however, the act was not portrayed in full view of the camera... Another scene depicted a cowboy fondling the nipples of another cowboy... There was no plot to the film and no development of the characters... Obscene words, phrases and gestures were used throughout the film.[53]

Before that, on Monday 3 June, Warhol was shot at the Factory by Valeria Solanas, an occasional visitor to the Factory and best known for her SCUM manifesto (SCUM being the 'Society for Cutting Up Men'). Very dangerously ill for a time, Warhol was able to appear in public again on 5 September. Just before *Lonesome Cowboys* was released, he at last got back to working on the film with the brilliant title, although the title was in fact changed to *Blue Movie*. With *Lonesome Cowboys* and *Blue Movie* Warhol moved entirely away from the earlier motionless pictures: the central act in *Blue Movie* was not simulated. However, Warhol was not alone in the production of blue movies, himself noting that by this post-climacteric year (1969) of the sixties, 'all sorts of dirty movies' were appearing.[54] *Blue Movie* in fact played for a week; on 31 July 1969 New York City police seized the film, which was shortly declared to be obscene.

Something of David Hockney's role as a public figure has already been hinted at. He travelled the world; he settled in California, where he shared in something of the popularity generally being accorded at that time to figures from the British arts and entertainments, British satirists and British actors; but he was never so well known on the European continent, probably because he so much went his own way, eschewing the fashion for pushing further and further into extremism. As he put it:

I have stopped bothering about modern art, in that at one time you would be frightened of doing things in painting because you would consider them most reactionary. I stopped believing that it's possible for art to progress only in a stylistic way.[55]

Hockney represented brilliant youth and the potential a brilliant youth had for making money; he represented the rise of the provincial (he was a lower-middle-class lad from Bradford in Yorkshire, the town, incidentally, which had provided the setting for *Room at the Top)*, and, above all, a nonconformist (he was a vegetarian, a conscientious objector, and gay). Hockney was very knowledgeable about contemporary painting, but he remained unconcerned about theories on the nature of art, Marxism, structuralism and post-structuralism, and language which so obsessed so many of his contemporaries. Through the influence of an older fellow student at the Royal College of Art, R. B. Kitaj, an American-born 'Anglo-Saxon' who had already experienced the real world as a sailor and soldier, Hockney developed an eclecticism and inventiveness reminiscent at times of Picasso; he drew upon Pop Art, incorporated photographic images, switched from oil paint to acrylic, rejected the fashionable contempt for the pretty, and evinced a mighty disrespect for the canons of wisdom handed down in the colleges. In a much later conversation with Peter Webb, he remarked:

> I have always been aware that there is a great pleasure in seeing. I tend to make things charming because that's my way, but often it's a bit of a disguise. I'm not afraid if they are pretty, I like pretty pictures. I tend to think that my view of the world is a bit oriental—I share their view of the tragic. Tragedy is a literary concept, not a visual one.[56]

Hockney, though continuously experimenting and diversifying, became the painter of consumer society in its most extreme form, that found in southern California. 'When I flew over San Bernardino', he recorded, 'and looked down and saw the swimming-pools of the houses, I was more thrilled than I had ever been arriving at any other city.'[57] His renderings of swimming-pools, houses (exteriors and interiors), his portraits, often double portraits set in contemporary interiors, may at first sight seem dull, but they almost always have some irony, some humour, some psychological penetration, which make them instantly and uniquely recognizable as Hockneys. R. B. Kitaj remained far less well known than Hockney; still more individualistic, and quite definitely cerebral in his wish to bring into his painting the quality of modern poetry, he is a fine example of pure sixties individualism, his reputation steadily growing in later decades.[58]

Among continental Europeans the artist as celebrity, renowned for his spectacular ideas, had been Yves Klein; following his early death, the two most dramatic figures were Michelangelo Pistoletto in Italy and Joseph Beuys in Germany. Pistoletto had quickly diversified from his mirror paintings to a range of stunning sculptures and assemblages, still sometimes employing optical effects, usually with a title indicating some deep conceptual problem: for example, *Painting for Eating* (1965), *Structure for Talking while Standing, Spear Under the Bed* (both 1965/66), *A Cubic Metre of Infinity* and *Pear Shaped Body-Mirror* (both 1966), and *Atlas Globe* (1966–8). Beuys had been a pilot in the German air force during the Second World War, and was severely injured in an air crash. In his sixties assemblages he took to making particular use of felt and fat, which for him had particular symbolic significance, as well as (frequently) bottles and instruments reminiscent of a hospital. Both Pistoletto and Beuys were included in an exhibition mounted at Genoa in 1967 by the Italian art critic Germano Celant. Celant coined the term 'art povera' (the correct Italian word is actually *arte; povera* means 'poor') to cover the work of Pistoletto, Beuys, and a considerable range of artists from New York, the Netherlands, three English cities, West Germany, and Italy. He had in fact borrowed the term from a particular type of experimental theatre, then enjoying much intellectual acclaim, *Théâtre pauvre*, pioneered by the eminent Polish director Grotowski, and notable for its lack of any of the normal props or other accessories. Whether there really was an organic connection between the kinds of art selected by Celant and this kind of theatre, or whether the wish to express unity in artistic endeavour was stronger than the reality, may remain an open question: certainly, this art was 'poor' in that it was assembled out of basic materials without, apparently, great effort being put into fashioning or designing. Celant did admit: 'There are other critical definitions, the best known being: conceptual art, earthworks, raw materialist microemotive art, antiform.'[59] Celant took a strong neo-Marxist line: 'this book does not attempt to be objective since the awareness of objectivity is false conciousness.' His conclusion stressed the magical, transcendental qualities of the works he had selected.

> The artist-alchemist organizes living and vegetable matter into magic things, working to discover the root of things, in order to re-find them and extol them... What interests him... is the discovery, the exposition, the insurrection of the magic and marvellous value of natural elements.

One of the Americans featured by Celant was Carl André, who, in keeping with the internationalism I keep harking back to, did most of his work in Europe. André became most noted for his installations consisting of basic materials placed on the floor, timbers or building bricks. Such 'art', in a rather obvious way, poses general questions about what 'art' is; it is also, in an obvious way, 'minimalist'. Behind minimalism lies the notion of somehow stripping art down to its essentials, purifying it, removing all the conventional trappings and associations. André's *Equivalent VII*, which caused a perhaps slightly synthetic outcry when exhibited at the Tate Gallery, London, in 1976, was actually produced in 1966. The point about much conceptual art (all minimalist art is conceptual, though not all conceptual art is minimalist), as Andy Warhol had realized, is that you only have to *hear* about the art object to be outraged, you do not actually have to come and see it. Among British artists, Celant included Barry Flanagan (b. Wales in 1941), and Richard Long (b. Bristol in 1945), both members of the 'New Generation' of sculptors profoundly influenced by Anthony Caro—the title came from the group exhibition held at the Whitechapel Art Gallery in east London in 1965. Looking back on the New Generation group a quarter of a century later, the conservative art critic Peter Fuller put matters sourly, if wittily:

> Caro had declared that sculpture could be anything; but his rebellious pupils took him more literally than he intended. Barry Flanagan and Nicholas Pope reduced the art to placement of barely worked materials. Others started digging holes, taking photographs, and even walks, and calling that sculpture too.[60]

That, from a hostile perspective, captures a central notion about art in the High Sixties: that art could be anything pushed to, or beyond, the utmost limits. Flanagan's work was certainly highly distinctive, and is always immediately recognizable, basically consisting of coloured hessian sacks filled with paper, foam, or sand: before Celant tried to bring everything together as art povera, this was variously described as Process Art, Anti-form, or Postminimalist. Flanagan then moved into Temporal Art, constructions which are dismantled after being viewed. Long was an Earth Art man: he presented maps and photographs of landscape as well as arrangements of stones. Leading American figures in Environmental and Earth Art were Michael Heizer and Robert Smithson: such art was particularly in vogue in fashion-conscious America in 1969, as Pop Art seemed to go into decline. The arrival of Conceptual Art among the *bien pensant* in Europe was signalled by the tour across the continent in the first half of 1969 of the exhibition 'When Attitudes Become Form': this exhibition ended up at the very avant-garde

Institute of Contemporary Arts in London during August and September 1969.

Andy Warhol took us away from mere assemblages, Earth Art, conceptualism, etc, and into film and light shows. All through the later sixties there were examples of Happenings and Performance Art. Such art moves across the boundaries towards theatre. I shall return to Performance Art, and a particular offshoot of it, Body Art, in which the artist's own body is involved, in the final part of this book. But it is now time to turn in the direction of poetry, a possible bridge being provided by the London Institute of Contemporary Arts Exhibition of 1965, 'Between Poetry and Painting', which, among other things, demonstrated how poetry could form into distinctive shapes, like some paintings. Such poetry attracted to itself one of these labels which we keep finding in different contexts in the sixties: 'Concrete Poetry'. Actually, what claimed to be 'the first international exhibition of concrete and kinetic poetry' had taken place the previous year not all that far away, in Cambridge, organized by Michael Weaver. Weaver distinguished between three kinds of concrete poetry: visual (or optic), phonetic (or sound), and kinetic (moving in a visual succession), and argued that concrete poetry was related either to the constructivist or to the expressionist tradition in art. 'The constructivist poem results from an arrangement of materials according to a scheme or system set up by the poet which must be adhered to on its own terms (permutational poems). In the expressionist poem, the poet arranges his material according to an intuitive structure.'[61]

Some authorities credit a 21-year-old Italian aristocrat, Carlo Belloli, with producing the first concrete poems, though in fact a sort of concrete poetry was being produced in the United States in the 1930s by e. e. cummings. Belloli wrote and displayed his TESTI-POEMI MURALI (mural poetic texts), and in 1959 enunciated his theory of audiovisualism (which sounds pretty like concrete poetry, though Belloli declared that his work was something different). The actual term 'concrete poetry' had been coined in the 1950s by poets working in two different locations far out on the periphery of the intellectual world I am concerned with in this book: the Brazilian brothers Agusto and Haroldo de Campos, and the Swiss Eugen Gomringer. Towards the end of the fifties, it was Germany which emerged as the most important centre of this poetry. From being an avant-garde movement for those in the know, concrete poetry, in a way we have seen so often, became in the sixties *the* most modish form of poetry. The leader of the concrete poetry movement in Italy, typically an artist as well as a poet, was Arrigo Lora Totino, who directed the poetry review *Modulo*, and helped Carol Belloli to establish the Museum of Contemporary Poetry in Turin. Only the Italian language could offer the perfect title for the way in which the poets contributing to the anthology saw themselves, *I Novissimi* (the very newest), edited by Nanni Balestrini and Alfredo Guidiani. In their Introduction the editors spoke of the 'falsity' of the official Italian language. Another poet associated with Gruppo 63, Lamberto Pignotti, put forward the concept of 'technological poetry', which would use the mass media to get poetry to the masses.[62]

The French schoolteacher (he taught German at a lycée in Amiens, where he had been born in 1928) and the leading international protagonist of concrete poetry, Pierre Garnier, preferred the term *spatialisme*. 'Spatial' and 'spatialism' are words which crop up with respect to many different art forms in the sixties—assemblages and floor displays took up space in a way that traditional paintings did not. In January 1963 Garnier issued his first 'manifesto for new poetry, visual and acoustic *(phonique)'.*[63] In this manifesto we encounter the ideas separately put forward by the Pop Artists and *nouveau réalistes* (Garnier wanted a poetry which will 'reach people'), Marshall McLuhan, Andy Warhol, and many others ('the era of the book seems past', 'now the medium creates poetry as much as the poet does'), and all those who argued for the involvement of reader and viewer in the work of art. A second manifesto in the following issue (30 May 1963) showed the same concern with slippages and changes in the meanings of words found, for example, in Barthes and Derrida:

> The art of visual poetry consists of getting the word to no longer coincide with the word. Drawn out, deformed by the other words nearby, the word sometimes gets quite notice-ably out of adjustment with itself.[64]

Both the determined effort to blur boundaries between different art forms, and the rejoicing in the possibilities of a machine can be seen in the 'action poetry' of Bernard Heidsieck, which in some respects moves towards performance art or happenings. With the familiar mixture of excit-ing clarity, mysticism, and mud, Heidsieck explained: 'places of "actions" or auditions take the place of the written page: stage, street, listening room, studio.' The action poem is made from 'anything that the poem authorizes to take… the voice, the cry, the gesture, the act, the noise, the sound, the silence, everything and anything'. The use of the tape recorder gives 'a certain angle more exact, perhaps, of reality, which the machine authorizes'.[65]

It was a fundamental feature of the arts in the sixties that no particular literary or artistic movement came anywhere near establishing a monopoly. Recurring preoccupations concern the nature of words, and, as in Pop Art and the early *nouveau roman*, the 'thingness of things'. The first tendency may be seen in the poetry of Yves Bonnefoy (b. Tours in 1923) for whom a certain restricted list of words were felt as 'essences'; the second by Francis Ponge, who 'will spend three pages getting inside the skin of an apricot, or twenty or so describing "the prawn in all its states" '.[66]

A central sixties irony, already exposed in our discussions of Andy Warhol, strongly affected many poets: they both wanted to be and boasted of being 'underground' poets, yet they also wanted to establish maximum contact with 'the masses', not easy to do if you are literally out of sight. The fifties Beat tradition of poetry readings and poetry and jazz, developing into poetry and light shows, poetry and happenings, expanded greatly in the High Sixties. Underground poetry could scarcely have found a more visible venue than the massive Albert Hall in London for the 1965 'International Poetry Incarnation', seen as the grand climax of underground poetry by its anthologist, Michael Horovitz.[67] Some poetry was openly political (American racism and American policy in Vietnam being frequent targets), some was ferociously savage (in Britain, George MacBeth represented the former and Ted Hughes the latter). Poetry became interna-tional and cosmopolitan as never before. Poets, like others, raised questions about who was really mad, about how insanity is defined in society; out of the five quotations from various authors which preface *Delusions, etc* (1972) by the alcoholic American poet John Berryman, one concludes: 'the most mentally deranged people are certainly those who see in others indications of insanity they do not notice in themselves.'

The 'rise' of the provinces, of remote regions and minor nationalities, involving the emergence of new purchasers and new, insistent voices, was an important force behind the turbulent interactions between the new intellectual and cultural movements of the sixties. It is instructive to look at what was happening to poetry in Scotland. The 'Scottish Literary Renaissance' began in the 1920s, paralleling the not utterly dissimilar black 'Harlem Renaissance'; in the postwar years a high critical reputation was enjoyed by Hugh MacDiarmid (1892–1978), Robert Garrioch (b. 1909), Norman MacCaig (b. 1910), and Edwin Morgan (b. 1920), all active figures in a clearly visible Scottish bohemia. What happened in the sixties was that the wider Scottish society (traditionally governed by strongly puritan tenets), or at least parts of it, was brought into a closer alignment with this bohemia, while the poets themselves developed a new self-awareness and confidence. Edwin Morgan, in discussing the 1960s, speaks of 'the sort of seriousness or awareness that Scottish poetry has been jolted into (as opposed to certain stereotypes of "entertainment" and "character" which have always been available)'.[68] The poet George Mackay Brown (1921–96) emerged into a more public light, being joined by Alan Jackson and, later, by Alan Bold (b. 1942) who in his early works at least was a conscious carrier of MacDiarmid's Marxist torch. Morgan records 'poems with monsters—death, alcoholism, war, heroin, the atom'.[69] Morgan and Ian Hamilton Finlay were important figures in the concrete poetry movement. Analogous developments, involving such poets as Dannie Abse, took place in Wales. Writing in the poetry magazine *Agenda*, the English poet Kathleen Raine stated: 'much fine verse is being written in Scotland and for a like density of good poets one would have to go to Wales.'[70] Poetry magazines proliferated throughout the provinces and nationalities of the British Isles. In 1967 one of these, *Phoenix*, moved to Belfast in Northern Ireland: among the local poets published by *Phoenix*, one was very quickly to rise to international fame, Seamus Heaney (b. 1939).

The term 'concrete' was also applied to a particular type of music—with, however, rather different connotations from those of both concrete poetry and concrete painting, though concrete music did share with concrete poetry the element of mechanical production. As already mentioned, concrete music depended on natural sounds, the next development being electronic music in which the sounds were entirely generated electronically. A further ingredient experimented with in the postwar years was that of indeterminacy, to use the word of the crucially important figure of the 1950s, the American musician John Cage, who was also involved in happenings and other aspects of the cultural movements I have been discussing. 'Aleatoric' is another word meaning the incorporation of chance elements. As in poetry, more traditional, or certainly less extreme, modes continued to be pursued; I shall concentrate here on a quintet of musicians whose work and attitudes help to illuminate particularly important developments and interactions in the sixties: Karlheinz Stockhausen, Luigi Nono, Pierre Boulez, Leonard Bernstein, and Steve Reich.

This is a book about Britain, France, Italy, and the United States. However, there is no way I can dodge starting this discussion with a German composer, Karlheinz Stockhausen, practitioner of serial music (music based not on the traditional tonic scales, but on ordered arrangements of pitches, rhythm, and other musical elements), electronic, and aleatoric music, admired by the

Beatles and admirer of John Lennon and the American West Coast rock/pop groups the Mothers of Invention and the Grateful Dead; in a manner not unreminiscent of David Hockney, Stockhausen showed no special respect for musical tradition and history.[71] He was born in 1928 near Cologne. In the fifties he was associated with the French concrete music group, and then with the first electronic music studio at the West German radio headquarters in Cologne. His earliest compositions at the Cologne studio, *Study I* (1953) and *Study II* (1954), were among the first examples of pure electronic music. It was in the sixties that he began to make provision for the performers themselves to influence the composition. *Hymnen* (1966–7), for orchestra and electronic sounds, was a recomposition of several national anthems into a single universal anthem. *Stimmung* (Tuning), played at the 1970 World's Fair in Japan, scored for six vocalists with microphone, contains texts consisting of names, words, days of the week, in German and English, and excerpts from German and Japanese poetry. The notion of world unity was such a consistent one with Stockhausen that when Tim Nevill published a collection of Stockhausen's writings in 1989 he titled it *Towards a Cosmic Music*. Stockhausen's world philosophy comes out clearly in his 'Manifesto for the Young', originally published in the *Journal Musical* of Paris on 16 June 1968 (when the famous Parisian 'events' of 1968 were still at high intensity):

Once again we are revolutionizing—but throughout the entire world this time. We are now setting ourselves the highest possible goal: a development of consciousness where the whole of humanity is at stake...

The higher self should provide reason with something to think about, receiving its impulse from the intuitive consciousness which is in turn fed by the higher and higher consciousness, linking every individual consciousness with supra-personal cosmic consciousness.

The rationalists will ultimately lose their unholy wars because they are ossified and lack the higher being's supra-consciousness. We are ruled by generals, business magnates, statisticians, political functionaries, religious fanatics, trade union leaders, and specialists in administration—but what else can we expect?... What has all that to do with music? Totality is at issue here. If we comprehend that, we will also produce the right music, making people aware of the whole.[72]

Stockhausen was a genius, and his place in history is not in doubt. Many others at this time in the sixties, including the Beatles and Timothy Leary, believed in one way or another in this 'supra-personal cosmic consciousness', and shared in the denunciation of rationality. The wilder beliefs of some of the major figures of the sixties did little harm; but they are the insignificant accompaniment to the real achievements of that decade. Early in 1969 Stockhausen was in Madison, Connecticut, completing a work commissioned by Leonard Bernstein, the brilliant matinee-idol conductor of the New York Philharmonic Orchestra. Stockhausen drove over to New York, where a friend's apartment was to be the location for preliminary discussions about a joint concert involving Stockhausen and the Beatles. But bad weather delayed the arrival of the other party: Stockhausen returned to Connecticut and the discussions were never taken up again.[73]

Again, as with Pistoletto and Beuys, it seems appropriate to pair an Italian with a German. Luigi Nono (1924-90), born in Venice, was the leading Italian composer of serial, electronic, and aleatoric music. His commitment to everything that was most advanced in music was sealed by his marriage to Schoenberg's daughter Nuria in 1955. Nono also exemplified the extreme left-wing commitment of so many sixties intellectuals. His chamber opera *Intolleranza 1960*, premiered in Venice in 1961, attacked facism, racial segregation, and the atom bomb, and ends with the world being flooded and destroyed. The chorus then sings:

> You who are being immersed in the floods,
> with rivers swept away
> think
> also about the terrible times that you have escaped.
> Let us go, changing countries more often than shoes,
> through class wars, dispirited
> that all there is is injustice.[74]

Marxist revolution with a vengeance! The performance was stormed by neo-Fascists, and a riot ensued between them and the Communists. The work survived, and reappeared ten years later as *Intolleranza 1970*. World political concerns are again obvious in the dramatic cantata of 1962, *Suponte di Hiroshima*. Nono's enthusiasm for the Chinese 'cultural revolution' led to him giving his daughter a Chinese name, and composing, in honour of her birth, *Per Bastiana Tai-yang Cheng (1967)*; this aleatoric work required magnetic tape and three instrumental groups playing in quarter-tones.

Against the universalist and political enthusiasms of Stockhausen and Nono stood the severity and rationalism of Pierre Boulez, son of a wealthy steel manufacturer, born at Montbrison, France, in March 1925. After studying maths, engineering, and music, Boulez in 1947, at the age of 22, became the music director of the Classical Theatre Company founded by the celebrated actor Jean-Louis Barrault. Seven years later Boulez founded his own series of avant-garde concerts, the Concerts Marigny. In his book on 'Thinking about Music Today' published in 1963 *(Penser la musique aujourd'hui)* Boulez noted that Debussy had advised, 'Go right down to the naked flesh of emotion', adding that he himself advised, 'Go right down to the naked flesh of the evidence'. The final words of the book were: 'Over and over again I have repeated: music is a science as much as an art; who can melt these two together in the same crucible, if not Imagination, that "queen of human faculties"!' Throughout the sixties Boulez had a sparkling international career, both as an 'extremist' composer of twelve-note serial music and as a charismatic conductor; in 1966 he was the specially featured composer at the Edinburgh Festival.

Leonard Bernstein, born 1918 in Lawrence, Massachusetts, believed in (as he expressed it in the title to the collection of writings published in 1966) *The Infinite Variety of Music*. He had composed the popular musical of 1957, *West Side Story*, which became a film in 1961. Very catholic, an enthusiast for cross-over between élite and popular music, he was not an enthusiast for the music of the four other composers discussed here. He was, he said in his book, sceptical about the 'much-proclaimed Death of Tonality':

> I am a fanatic music lover. I can't live one day without hearing music, playing it, studying it, or thinking about it. And all this is quite apart from my professional role as musician; I am a fan, a committed member of the musical public. I confess, freely though unhappily, that at this moment, as of this writing, God forgive me, I have far more pleasure in following the musical adventures of Simon & Garfunkel or of The Association singing 'Along Comes Mary' than I have in most of what is being written now by the whole community of 'avant garde' composers. This may not be true a year from now, or even by the time these words appear in print; but right now, on the 21 June, 1966, that is how I feel. Pop music seems to be the only area where there is to be found unabashed vitality, the fun of invention, the feeling of fresh air. Everything else seems suddenly old-fashioned: electronic music, serialism, chance music—they have already acquired the musty odor of academicism. Even jazz seems to have ground to a painful halt. And tonal music lies in abeyance, dormant.[75]

Whether or not a musician entered the realm of popular music, his earnings could be large, for even the most uncomprising avant-garde élite music had its place in the arts market of established society. In 1971 Boulez replaced Bernstein as the director of the New York Philharmonic Orchestra.

My fifth musician is Steve Reich, born in New York in October 1936, and usually labelled a 'minimalist', since his emphases were on repetition (a not too distant echo of Warhol) and extreme reduction of musical means. In his early work—produced in the early sixties, for Reich really is a sixties composer, though his international reputation was only consolidated in the seventies—he relied heavily on the written word (crossing of boundaries once more), especially the words of American poets William Carlos Williams, Charles Olsen, and Robert Creeley. But soon, moving towards chance and the unpremeditated, he began using speeches, sports commentaries, and so on as the basis for tape pieces. He used tapes in composing the soundtrack tape for Robert Wilson's experimental film of 1964 *The Plastic Haircut*. He also provided music for several San Francisco Mime Troupe productions. Experimenting in 1965 with tape loops, he noticed that two tape recorders did not run at the same speed, thus producing a time shift between the two loops.

> Two loops are lined up in unison and then gradually move completely out of phase with each other, and then back into unison. The experience of that musical process is, above all else, impersonal; *it* just goes *its* way. Another aspect is its precision; there is nothing left to chance whatsoever. Once the process has been set up it inexorably works itself out.[76]

This may sound like the opposite of the aleatoric, though whether 'chance' was really being excluded is a matter of opinion: the point is that Reich, John Cage, the concrete poets, were all trying to exclude human influences, which were being equated with 'non-objective bourgeois contamination'—daft, but if it produced exciting art, so what? Phase shifting was employed in the first half of *It's Gonna Rain,* a tape piece of 1965, mainly based on excerpts recorded by Reich from a black minister preaching about the Deluge. *Melodica* (1966) instead of words, used the children's toy instrument, the melodica. This was Reich's last tape piece before he turned to live performance music.

*Come Out* was performed in New York City Hall in 1966 as part of a benefit conference on behalf of imprisoned black activists, the 'Harlem Six'. *Piano Phase* (1967) featured two pianists moving out of phase. *Pendulum Music* (1968) was composed for microphones, amplifiers, speakers, and performers—in effect an electronic, multimedia event. Like many intellectuals, Reich turned towards the Third World. He had been studying African music since 1963, and in 1970 went to Africa to study drumming.[77]

> In 1963 I decided I had to play in all my own compositions, though I am a very techni-
> cally limited performer. These limits focused my composing on just that music that was
> natural to my abilities and inclinations as a performer. This resulted in an ensemble
> music where all the parts are identical, and relatively simple. Complexity arises out of the
> scant rhythmic relationships of one player to another.[78]

This development, whereby Reich had his own 'group' to play his own music, mirrored the similar trend in rock/pop initiated, the other way round, by the Beatles, who had moved rapidly from playing the black rhythm and blues classics to composing their own numbers.

Here I must add yet one more name, that of black American jazz saxophonist John Coltrane (1926–67), who also had his own 'group', and whose career was symbolic of several of the developments discussed in this book. Jazz, in many ways the quintessence of the aleatoric, had been the preferred musical form of many among the youthful avant garde of the early sixties. The unparalleled international reputation gained by the John Coltrane quartet among mid-sixties élite concert-goers, in the Netherlands, in Germany, in Japan—practically everywhere, in fact, save the UK, on which he turned his back after 1961[79]—is a classic instance of cross-over, as it is of the new eminence (not just visibility) attainable by a black.

Avant-garde music involved a much tinier proportion of the concert-going public than avant-garde art did with respect to gallery-goers. The rather exceptional case of Nono's *Intolleranza 1960* apart, it was much easier for controversy and publicity to be generated around art objects which could be described in a few words than around musical works which could not. The overwhelming majority of those going to classical concerts, tuning in to classical music on the radio, or listening to classical records were interested only in the traditional repertory, roughly from Mozart to Shostakovitch. Educational advance, growing affluence, social change, meant that the audience for traditional classical music was steadily growing. Although there were light shows and live rock music in Warhol's Factory, through much of the day the music being blared out from records was operatic.[80] One change in taste in the later sixties which is worthy of note was the turning towards 'early music' (basically music of the seventeenth and early eighteenth centuries), with performance and recording of this music on 'early' instruments, instruments of the period in which the music was composed. Of course, there were the same commercial pressures as were affecting all the arts we have been discussing; recording companies were engaged on a constant search for new products, and, with Bernstein's feelings about atonal music being widely shared, the search had to be directed backwards rather than forwards; still the (relative) turning away from the Romantic classics of the later nineteenth century and the search for authenticity in performance can reasonably be linked to the spirit of dissent and innovation apparent in other cultural spheres.

The experimental music Bernstein disliked did no more harm than the experiments of Carl André or the philosophy of Foucault; and people could always steer clear of them. It was rather different with the cultural extremism of architects: what architects put up, people had to put up with; what architects built, people had to live with, and often live in. An important point about Warhol's underground films was that, compared with the standard Hollywood commercial film, their costs were minute. To a degree, one can generalize that the lower the financial investment, the higher the possibilities of aesthetic innovation. For architecture, that equation simply does not hold true; architecture, the building of buildings, is always an expensive pursuit.

The sixties do not stand out as a golden age in architecture, nor as a unique one, nor as one of dazzling innovation. In general, trends which had become well established in the fifties continued into the sixties, which often meant ugly and unfriendly public buildings and shoddily built workers' flats, isolated and lacking in basic amenities. But if there were no signs at the beginning of the decade of the sorts of striking changes taking place in other spheres, by the end of the decade there had been enough in the way of protest to ensure the beginnings of a radical change in planning and architectural policies; and there had been some successes in both public and domestic building. It is, indeed, necessary to distinguish between the two kinds of building, and to look at the rather different records of the countries we are studying. Italy and France had suffered the greatest physical devastation in the war, but Britain was not very far behind. In all three countries shortage of housing was a major social problem in the postwar years, and continued to be one in the sixties. Economic recovery helped to make the problem easier to deal with, but at the same time involved massive shifts in population in Italy and France; there were great movements of population in the United States as well, particularly the migration of blacks from the South to the North and West. We have already noted the severe housing problems suffered by ethnic minorities (including Italians from the south) in all four countries. But in the forties and fifties housing was often a problem for ordinary white populations as well, not always eased by slum clearance and redevelopment schemes brought about by a mixture of concerns for family welfare, commercial profit, and general prestige. Such schemes intensified from the end of the fifties, and there is much to criticize in the house-building programmes as they continued into the sixties: but one stark fact is inescapable—people did have to be housed. A monumental problem had seemed to call for monumental solutions; and, as it happened, the single major intellectual influence upon domestic architecture was that of the Swiss architect Le Corbusier, who in the interwar years had enunciated his notions of massive 'habitational units', elevating family homes to the level of public monuments.

There can be no question about American primacy in public architecture, created by the multiplicity of affluent corporations, public bodies, and individuals eager to memorialize themselves in conspicuous and stylish buildings. America had the space—or, alternatively, in city centre areas like Manhattan it had land so precious that high-density, high-rise buildings were a necessity, and there was a premium on building ones which would cast a shadow over close neighbours, rather than themselves being cast in shadow; America had the spirit of adventure; America had the plurality of interests and traditions; and America's native corps of architects was constantly enhanced and stimulated by the arrival of brilliant architects from the rest of the world—the other twentieth-century architects to rival Le Corbusier, the Germans Mies van der Rohe and Walter Gropius, were but the most famous of many immigrants. Mies is not a figure of the sixties in the way that Foucault or, say, Eco are, but he continued to design major buildings in this decade; perhaps, as one might say of Foucault, it is the lesser followers who are the repetitive bores. There can be no denying the impact of the stark Chicago Lake Shore Apartments of 1949–51, or of the New York Seagram Building (designed by Mies with his principal American disciple, Phillip Johnson): too many repetitions ceased to be striking, and became rather oppressive. The case against Mies, put with all his usual forensic flair by the famous architecture critic Lewis Mumford, is unfair, but captures well what was going wrong with so much of the urban environment as it continued to be developed in the sixties:

> Mies van der Rohe used the facilities offered by steel and glass to create elegant monuments of nothingness. They had the dry style of machine forms without the contents. His own chaste taste gave these hollow glass shells a crystalline purity of form; but they existed alone in the Platonic world of his imagination and had no relation to site, climate, insulation, function, or internal activity; indeed, they completely turn their backs on these realities just as the rigidly arranged chairs of his living rooms openly disregarded the necessary intimacies and informalities of conversation. This was the apotheosis of the compulsive, bureaucratic spirit. Its emptiness and hollowness were more expressive than van der Rohe's admirers realised.[81]

A much-quoted aphorism from the German master was 'Less is more'. The inventive Philadelphia architect Robert Venturi (b. 1925), very much a figure of the sixties, responded with 'Less is a bore',[82] which on the whole could stand as a motto for much of the most creative and inspiring side of the art and thought of the sixties. Venturi's was the true voice of the decade of protest and respect for the rights of the ordinary citizen. His important book *Complexity and Contradiction in Architecture* (1966) called for 'accommodation' to the needs of ordinary people, for compromise, multiplicity, and irony. But the architectural establishment, and the big money, was against him: he received few commissions and was unsuccessful in competitions—his partner, John Rauch, counselled, 'Don't take it so hard. You're only a failure. I'm an assistant failure.'[83] Venturi's reaction against puritanism, and his inclusion in his buildings of the widest range of elements, can be seen in his Football Hall of Fame (1968), which incorporates a Las Vegas-style illuminated billboard, and his Lied House, Long Beach Island, New Jersey (1966–9), where the painted house number 9 is five feet high; both have very strong Pop Art elements. Nothing is perfect, and the inclusiveness of Venturi was itself eventually to lead to the empty eclectism of much postmodernist architecture.

The third of the European giants from the interwar years who continued to influence American architecture in the 1960s was the German-born Walter Gropius, who made his mark both as a teacher at Harvard and as the architect of such buildings as that awful hulk dominating Park Avenue in New York, the Pan Am Building of 1958. Among his pupils was I. M. Pei (b. 1917), responsible for a number of striking high-tech buildings, from the Mile High Center at Denver, Colorado, to the Hancock Tower, Boston (1969), using reflecting glass and a slender steel mullion system. Gropius stressed the importance of team work in architecture, and one should really speak of 'I. M. Pei and Associates', as one should speak of Eero Saarinen and Associates, Paul Rudolph and Associates, and the inseparable Kevin Roche, John Dinkeloo, and Associates—to single out four partnerships which in their own distinctive ways gave new life and character to the 'Bauhaus' inheritance from Mies and Gropius. Saarinen was responsible for Dulles International Airport, near Washington, for the TWA terminal at Kennedy International Airport, near New York, for the famous Arch at St Louis, and for the CBS building in New York with its vertical-striped, science-fiction character. Rudolph was particularly noted for his Art and Architecture building at Yale University, where 'violent contrasts of scale and colossal piers in rough corduroy concrete gave the whole building a vaguely primitive air', and his Boston Government Services Building, 'where curved stairs and cascades of platforms were linked to spiralling towers'.[84] Kevin Roche and John Dinkeloo were responsible for the Ford Foundation building in New York and the Knights of Columbus Hall, New Haven, Connecticut, the sorts of work for which American architecture critic Vincent Scully coined the term 'paramilitary dandyism', and the College Life Insurance building, Indiana, which moved William J. R. Curtis to comment on 'the eerie surealism of their sliced glass pyramids'.[85] Strong but nuanced criticisms of many of these buildings were published by Charles Jencks in his *Modern Movements in Architecture,* completed in 1971, published in 1973, and more monotone ones by Brent C. Brolin in his *The Failure of Modern Architecture* of 1976. Brolin prints a picture of the Avenue of the Americas in New York City, as it was rebuilt in the 1960s with the tall thin 'space-age' buildings designed, or inspired, by Saarinen, intending them to seem sterile and intimidating. But, as with so much of what was created in the sixties, their impact is much more complex than that.

Some splendid domestic architecture in the spirit of Le Corbusier's 'habitational units' was created, but almost exclusively for privileged families. José Luis Sert, who had been a friend and collaborator of Le Corbusier and who succeeded Gropius as head of the Harvard Architecture School, was responsible for one of the most humane, well-appointed high-rise housing schemes: the three tower blocks of his Peabody Terraces provided perfect accommodation for married students at Harvard. Equally agreeable and comfortable was Robert Venturi's old people's home, Guild House, built for the Quakers in Philadelphia between 1962–6. But the considerably less happy story of public housing for the poor is symbolized in the well-known history of Minoru Yamasaki's low-cost Pruitt-Igoe housing scheme in St Louis. Poorly constructed with shoddy materials, this unlovely and unloved complex was by the end of the decade being subject to vandalism and arson attacks; in 1972 the authorities dynamited it.[86]

Italy has never needed lessons in architecture from anyone, and remained remarkably insulated from the least desirable legacies of the international movement in architecture, in particular from developments in the United States; since Italy is not a natural steel-producing country, architects made do with what could be achieved with reinforced concrete alone. In common with most European countries, including Scotland, but not England, Italy had a long tradition of substantial buildings (up to seven floors) divided up into flats. Housing policies immediately after the war very much fitted the pattern of general social policy I outlined in Chapter 6: blocks of flats were raised very quickly, but so quickly that they very soon revealed the kinds of flaws that were only becoming apparent in America and Britain in the 1960s. A reappraisal took place in the 1950s, and henceforth much greater care was taken over public housing projects. Thus, for a number of reasons Italian public housing of the 1960s compares very favourably with that built in other countries. Italian Marxist architects were more genuinely in contact with the needs of the Italian people than were idealistic followers of Le Corbusier in the other countries.[87] The blocks of flats laid out in the Tiburtino district of Rome on an irregular plan and crowned with tiled, sloping roofs, were a great achievement.

Two of Italy's most significant skyscrapers had already been completed in Milan before the end of the fifties. The first, the Pirelli building by Gio Ponti, also involved the most important figure in Italian public architecture of the 1960s, the engineer Pier Luigi Nervi (1891–1978). The other was the twenty-six-storey Torre Velasca by Ernesto Rogers and Enrico Peressutti: the top six storeys, which, in a fine Italian affirmation of the value of urban life, were devoted to family accommodation, were supported on buttresses and overhung the rest of the building, thus echoing the contours of such medieval predecessors as Florence's Palazzo Vecchio. Nervi was responsible for a series of magnificent exhibition halls, sports stadiums, factories, and motorways. Other Italian architects of particular note were Carlo Scarpa and Giancarlo de Carlo. The latter somehow managed to echo, in a completely modern idiom, the Renaissance jewel of Urbino with his student residences for the university of that city, built between 1962 and 1969.[88]

The sixties do not particularly stand out in French architectural history. The housing estates *(grands ensembles)* built, as in Italy, as rapidly as possible in the postwar years were recognized not to have been a great success. There was then a phase, from the middle fifties onwards, of the building of more imaginative suburban developments and new towns, though often to lamentably low standards of materials and workmanship. French administrators were, on the whole, notable for their clear-headed recognition of economic needs. Between 1957 and 1963 the main Paris airport at Orly, just south of the city, was completely reconstructed. In the middle sixties attention began to be given to the inefficiencies inherent in the location of the main food markets, Les Halles, in the centre of Paris. But General de Gaulle was opposed to anything extremist in the way of modern building, and certainly to anything in the nature of a skyscraper. France's most exciting new ventures in architecture come only after the ousting of de Gaulle.

In Britain the story of public housing in the sixties was largely that of 'redevelopment', that is to say the destruction of close-knit older communities for the poor trade-off of disruptive urban motorways and badly designed and shoddily built high-rise housing, culminating in disaster when, in 1968, a gas explosion brought the collapse of Ronan Point, a systems-built tower block in east London. Some sensitively conceived, family-friendly estates were built, a good example being Ralph Erskine's carefully integrated Byker development in Newcastle; and by the end of the decade a new emphasis on conservation and a halt to the building of high-rise public housing had been introduced. The Lillington Street estate in Pimlico, London, built by Darbourne and Darke between 1967 and 1973, was widely recognized as sensitive and successful. But overall it has to be recognized that in public housing what was built in the sixties sadly aggravated the appalling legacy of the fifties. This undated letter from around November or December 1968 to the Labour MP for Coventry North perhaps says more than any architectural critic could:

> I am writing to you on behalf of my council flat exchange, as I have filled the form in for an exchange five months ago and I also had a visit from my councillor. As you see I am four stories *[sic]* high and there is no lift. I was under the doctor quite awhile before I had my first child, as you see I am only seven stone in weight and pulling a large pram up four flights of stairs it is doing a big damage to my health...[89]

But the cultural expansion of the 1960s also created demands for the building and extending of universities, and for the building of theatres. Stylistically, one could make a rough distinction between the monumental terrace style of Sir Denys Lasdun, as seen in the University of East Anglia and the National Theatre, and the gentler, more flexible style of say Sir Basil Spence with his Sussex University, strongly influenced by Le Corbusier's Jaoul houses in Paris and discreetly blending echoes of a Roman colosseum into a magnificent landscape. There had, of course, to be something going on in Liverpool, and that was the construction, between 1960 and 1967, of Frederick Gibberd's Roman Catholic cathedral: this striking building unfortunately suffered, like so many ambitious housing schemes, from financial constraints, and the impressive 'crown of thorns' which surmounts the circular building became the butt of local jokes as 'the Mersey funnel'. The first custom-built open stage theatre was that for the Chichester Festival, completed in 1961 by the firm of Powell and Moya.

Less noted at the time were a number of buildings designed by Scottish-born, Liverpool-educated James Stirling, within the partnership he had formed with James Gowan: the Engineeering building at Leicester University (completed 1964), the Cambridge University History Faculty (finished 1968), and the student residences at Oxford, the Florey Building (1966–71), which Jencks seized on as a summation of Stirling's previous work:

> It has the sharp visual contrast of Leicester, the shimmering prismatic glass versus bright red tile. It has the sloping section and circulation discipline of Cambridge, the exposed exhaust stacks and elevator towers of all his projects and that uncanny fragmented geometry—here five eighths of an octagon which is stretched round the public rooms and given a strong sense of enclosure. The forms, while not directly derivative, remind one more of those which clothed the heroic functions of post-revolutionary Russia, than they connote musings of Oxford undergraduate life.[90]

That for some, of course, was the trouble.

Cultural extremism pushed to the limits and beyond, crossing over boundaries; there were little failures and big failures; but, overall, efforts in the arts echoed and inspired the much more profound changes which were taking place throughout society.

## Experimental Theatre: Mighty Atom of Change

Warhol sometimes claimed some great political purpose for his films—opposition to the Vietnam war was a good one—though, amid the fazed-out faces and bare bottoms it was quite impossible to discern any such purpose; and Warhol, anyway, could very well have been kidding. Marxist political theatre—'agitprop'—was a recognized tool of world revolution, but everywhere unsuccessful, and dead on its feet by the mid-1960s: practically everyone found it as boring as many people found Warhol's films. Commercial films changed greatly in content over the sixties, and played an important part in ratifying changes in manners and morals; but, a few exceptions (mainly art films) apart, theirs was never a revolutionary message. Rock/pop music was probably the greatest single force in general liberation and encouragement of self-expression, but even in its underground version, even in songs advocating drug-taking, rejection of authority, opposition to the war in Vietnam, it was not a consistent radical form. A few not very enthralling paintings apart, the visual arts, however strong their attack on bourgeois artistic conventions, did not raise specific political issues. Some poetry was political, and poetry readings could generate political fervour, but mainly among a tiny minority of the already committed. To protest, music (whatever radical views a Stockhausen or a Bernstein might espouse) had to be allied to words, as, of course, it was in Nono's operas. Music, indeed, was frequently enlisted by experimental theatre (one of its characteristics) to fortify subversive messages.

Experimental theatre, almost by definition, was limited to tiny and usually élite audiences. None the less, I shall argue that experimental theatre had a special place in that effervescent mix of interlinking subcultures which by the end of the decade had transformed the societies of the Western world, and that it had identifiable effects on subsequent social and cultural developments. The theatres, clubs, restaurants, pubs, and festivals in which experimental drama took place, or from which it sallied forth into the streets, were important physical locations round which a particular subculture, itself overlapping with several other subcultures, could cohere. There was 'alternative theatre', 'underground theatre', 'street theatre'; less menacingly, there was 'fringe theatre'. There was also travelling theatre, most admirably in Free Southern Theater, an interracial company loosely associated with the voter registration campaign in the 'Freedom Summer' of 1964. I take them all together under the heading 'experimental theatre' because in the immense flux of the sixties it was quite impossible for even the most thoroughly anti-bourgeois protagonists to maintain a counter-cultural purity, and for the most unflinchingly alternative of alternative theatres to avoid state subsidy or commercial sponsorship, or to prevent the most pampered of the rich from attending their performances. From Peter Schumann, founder of Bread and Puppet Theatre, declaring in the early sixties, 'The audience which doesn't go to the theatre is always the best audience', to the young David Hare of the British Portable Theatre, insisting in the early seventies, 'Our aggressiveness is immensely conscious. I suppose it stems from a basic contempt for people who go to the theatre', radical figures excoriated their audiences, but they couldn't keep them away.[91]

Experimental theatre suggests theatre 'in the open' or 'in the round', without the traditional proscenium arch dividing actors from audience. The most extreme experimental plays would certainly require a non-conventional setting; but it was possible for experimental plays to be put on in a traditional theatre. This section will concentrate on a range of theatres outside the established metropolitan ones and the commercial circuits linked to them (though it should be noted that sometimes plays from the most experimental of backgrounds ended up in such theatres): provincial, fringe, 'off-Broadway', as well as the new theatrical spaces which proliferated throughout the sixties. An interesting case in point is the Royal Court Theatre, a traditional theatre in miniature, some way from London's West End (actually, appropriately for the sixties, at the London end of the King's Road, Chelsea), but location for many of the most avant-garde plays, including, in the fifties, both Osborne's *Look Back in Anger* and the plays of Samuel Beckett; but the Royal Court also opened during the sixties a 'Theatre Upstairs', a club theatre in the round.

Intriguingly, the experimental theatre of the sixties was in large measure an invention of the Americans, with the further twist, however, that American experimental theatre received far more acclaim in Europe (above all France) than it did in its home country. The most important pioneering groups were Living Theatre (founded 1946), Playwrights' Theatre Inc., San Francisco (founded 1958), Cafe La Mama (founded 1961), Open Theatre (founded 1963), and Bread and Puppet Theatre (founded 1963–4). Then there was Joseph Papp's New York Shakespeare Festival Public Theatre (founded 1967), Richard Schechner's Performance Group (1968), the Manhattan Project, The Theater of the Ridiculous, Caravan Theatre in Boston, and the San Francisco Mime Troupe. The single greatest intellectual influence was that of Jerzy Grotowski, with his Polish Laboratory Theatre and the notion of 'poor theatre', that is theatre stripped down and bare, without the conventional scenery and props—'minimalist' theatre, you could say. Behind Grotowski were a French director and a German playwright from the same period as Mies van der Rohe and Walter Gropius: Antonin Artaud (1896–1948), who had called for a return to the primitive and the ritualistic in drama, a conception sometimes represented by the term 'theatre of cruelty', and Bertolt Brecht (1898–1956), responsible for the 'alienation effect' by which any attempt at naturalism or illusionism was dispensed with, Brecht making no pretence that he was doing anything other than presenting a piece of theatre, and certainly not a slice of actual life.

A fourth influence from within the world of theatre was the expatriate Irish dramatist Samuel Beckett (b. 1906), who wrote mainly in French, posing a permanent doubt as to whether at any time life is worth having—a form of drama usually labelled 'theatre of the absurd'. From outside the world of theatre strictly defined came the influence of the 'happenings', pioneered in the 1950s by such American figures as Allan Kaprow and Jim Dine (from the visual arts) and John Cage (from music), together with notions of 'indeterminacy', or improvisation. Jean-Jacques Lebel, author of *Le Happening* (Paris 1966), was involved in happenings in Paris in 1963 and 1964, and Allan Kaprow mounted one at the Théâtre des Nations in July 1963. The influence of the

Beats was strong in the San Francisco Playwrights' Theatre which, according to Lawrence Ferlinghetti, sought out 'unconventional and uncompromising mss by unproduced playwrights or poets'.[92]

Up to a point, what happened in the sixties was a spilling over of frustration, a revival of aspirations first raised in wartime. It is a fact that in several countries communal theatres were planned in the war years. Thus it is not entirely fortuitous that the married couple Judith Malina and Julian Beck should have set up Living Theatre in New York in 1946. For years it played to a minority of a minority of a minority, then, within a few weeks of the opening on 15 July 1959, it achieved national notoriety and international acclaim with Jack Gelber's classic play of drug-dealing, in the presentation of which jazz was an integral feature, *The Connection*. Beck and Malina were thoroughgoing radicals, always ready to take Living Theatre on to the streets to fight political issues. In March 1962 Beck's World-Wide General Strike for Peace took the form of a sit-down in Times Square in protest against President Kennedy's resumption of nuclear testing in the atmosphere. Reacting in their usual manner, the police punctured Beck's lung; Joseph Chaikin, leading player in *The Connection*, was arrested. The next attention-focusing production was *Brig*, set in a beyond-hope military prison. Historically, the Inland Revenue Service has been a most useful arm of the American federal government (delivering nemesis to Al Capone, for example), and it was this agency which on 17 October 1963 closed down not just *Brig* but the entire company.

Between 1964 and 1968 Living Theatre was in exile, travelling around Europe. Their *Frankenstein* opened in Venice in September 1965, leading not long afterwards to the company's deportation from Italy. James Roose-Evans, in the late sixties distinguished director at the Hampstead Theatre Club, provides a description of the production:

*Frankenstein* is a collage of Grand Guignol, shadow-play, Yoga, meditation, gymnastics, howls, grunts and groans: as though set in the Chamber of Horrors at Madame Tussaud's waxworks, we see, on various platforms erected within the outline of a human head, people being crucified, lynched, guillotined, buried alive, their hearts transplanted. What takes place on the multiple stage is the reporting of yesterday and today, riotings in streets of Paris and Chicago... For four or five hours the audience is likely to be battered, bored, stimulated, provoked, assaulted...[93]

Finally back in New York in 1968, Malina and Beck used the Brooklyn Academy of Music for the audience-involving performance described as like 'a modern Dionysian rite', in which first actors then audience tore off their clothes. The cry with which Judith Malina led her naked audience out into the Brooklyn streets takes some unpacking (the notion of New York intellectuals clamouring for tractors is particularly intriguing): 'I demand everything—total love, an end to all forms of violence and cruelty such as money, prisons, people doing work they hate. We can have tractors and food and joy. I demand it now!'[94]

In 1969 Living Theatre was in London, based at the Roundhouse, once an engine shed, converted by socialist playwright Arnold Wesker into a theatre for political plays (which inevitably flopped), and subsequently used for all kinds of experimental shows, including the nude show *Oh, Calcutta!*. Richard Neville, then editor of the underground magazine Oz, provides a colourful account of the production called *Paradise Now:*

> A steamy, scriptless tableau of writhing bodies, exhorting and stamping. Limbs disen-tangle themselves and figures leap from stage to chairs and berate the audience... The swarthy tribe of many colours roam the aisles and urge us all to fight The System. Women leap into laps, their buttocks criss-crossed with Band-aids and mottled with bruises. Driven from their seats, most of the audience roamed the floor in confusion. Many either shake their fists at the cast, or rush for exits. Others join in, kiss their neighbours, even strip...
>
> The abuse kept coming. 'You're all boring bourgeois fuckwits' was the gist of it. 'While you deny your primal selves and your thirst for liberation, you are helping enslave the Whole World...' A man of awesome endowment prowled along our row screaming abuse...[95]

That, coming right at the end of the decade, was experimental theatre at its most extreme; within a year Living Theatre had disbanded.

The first ever black play (black author, black characters, black director) to be produced on Broadway was Lorrraine Hanbury's *A Raisin in the Sun* of 1959. Though the ambience was very much that of the prospering black middle class, this was an important event in black cultural history. Just as important is the fact that the person who founded and inspired Cafe La Mama, set up in a basement in New York's East Village, was a black woman, Ellen Stewart. Cafe La Mama existed to provide opportunity for new talent of all types (including director Tom O'Horgan and writers James Rado and Gerome Ragni, all later famous because of their association with *Hair);* more than any other group it went for total integration of music (and dance) with drama. Naturally it remained unsung on Manhattan and unknown elsewhere. But the La Mama tour of 1965 to Paris (where it had sufficient recognition from the US government to be granted use of the American Center for Students and Artists[96]), Denmark, and Sweden turned the company into a cult, and the East Village basement into a place of pilgrimage for avant-garde directors from Europe. La Mama played its part in the critique of Great Society values and of the expanding, and vicious, American involvement in Vietnam. One of its greatest public successes was Jean-Claude van Itallie's *America Hurrah*—a satire on American imperialism. The close interconnections (which did not exclude sharp rivalries) between the groups is demonstrated by Joseph Chaikin's move from the Living Theatre to set up Open Theatre (also in New York); Chaikin employed many women directors and writers, including Megan Terry, whose *Viet Rock* was first presented, in the spring of 1966, at Cafe La Mama. Barbara Gerrson's *MacBird* presented President Johnson as the murderer of J. F. Kennedy. As small venues multiplied, so did performances featuring violence, drug-taking, nudity, simulated sex, and, in Greenwich Village in 1968, an actual act of homosex-ual fellatio.[97]

The early training of Peter Schumann, born in German Silesia in 1934, was in the sculptural arts. He arrived in New York at the time of Kaprow's and Dine's happenings, and he did his first theatrical work at the Living Theatre. In 1963 he founded the Moosach Puppet Theatre: then he came across the material celastic, which made possible the fourteen-foot tall puppets, held aloft on a stick, which were to be the performers in what he now created as the Bread and Puppet Theatre, based at a loft in Delancey Street, Lower Manhattan. At the end of performances, bread was distributed to the audience. Schumann explained: 'We named our theatre the Bread and Puppet because we felt that the theatre should be as basic as bread.'[98] Austere and Germanic (he never changed his nationality) Schumann had in extreme degree the would-be counter-culturalist's hostility towards his audience. His biographer, Stefan Brecht, tells us that he had

> a critical attitude toward the common man; greedy celebrator of Thanksgiving, callow killer abroad, receptive listener to presidential addresses promising him the Great Society but promoting war, patriotic father of victim soldiers, crier for meat. By '67, the common man turns from selected audience to subject matter of his theatre.[99]

Audiences at Delancey Street

> consisted mainly of sympathizers, adherents or fellow travellers of the Peace and other Resistance movements, more or less genteel and often professional people, politically radical or liberal, but more the latter, college students or college educated: people whose views and feelings largely coincided and at any rate did not clash with what they discerned as the views and feeling of his theatre, who watched his shows with a good warm feeling, and they did not come to be instructed or altered or brought up short or troubled in their minds in any way, but rather to be confirmed.[100]

The first Bread and Puppet Peace demonstration took place on 3 March 1964. The beginning of US bombing of North Vietnam in February 1965 brought the Greenwich Village Puppet Parade in March. Here is a report from the FBI files:

> On March 6, 1965, Special Agents of the Federal Bureau of Investigation observed a demonstration which was co-sponsored by the Greenwich Village Peace Center and the Bread and Puppet Theatre. The demonstration consisted of twenty-three persons walking as a group through the Greenwich Village Area of New York City carrying signs protesting the war in Vietnam and America's alleged use of 'dirty bombs' therein. Ten of the demonstrators wore Halloween-type masks, eight carried poles to which were attached grotesque masks and four carried poles with skeletons atop for the purpose of dramatizing the horrors of war. The demonstration started at 1:00 pm and ended at 3:00 pm. There were no incidents or arrests.[101]

A month later Bread and Puppet Theatre were participating in a march on Washington to end the war in Vietnam, and then again in a similar march in November. Bread and Puppet appeared in many anti-Vietnam war demonstrations. In the Fifth Avenue, New York, march of November 1966 they were joined by Allen Ginsberg, and by a gaggle of hippies who had a sound truck playing music by the Supremes, the Byrds, and the Beatles. While Living Theatre was very largely taken over by the international hippie movement, Schumann hated the hippie scene, and Bread and Puppet tended to fade out of street demonstrations in 1967.

Artistic recognition in America for the Bread and Puppet Theatre came with the production of *Fire*, between January and June 1966, the first of three plays dealing directly with Vietnam. But even when the company was invited to perform at the Nancy theatrical festival in April 1968, Schumann maintained his stern, unbending attitude towards success. One of the actors commented: 'we still felt obscure, because of Peter's insistence that the world was evil and success wasn't in the vocabulary. To be a success or a modest success, shit on it, was essentially his attitude.'[102] In fact they were lionized by French intellectuals (while having little success in Britain); Marie Cardinale, in her novel *La Clé sur la porte* (1971), which is essentially reportage on youth and associated subcultures in Paris after 1968, singles out as icons of the time the Beatles, the Rolling Stones, Jimi Hendrix—and the Bread and Puppet Theatre.

Joseph Papp, passionate advocate of free public theatre, established his New York Shakespeare Festival Public Theatre in 1967, with the intention of imitating the London branch of the Royal Shakespeare Company in putting on contemporary productions. His festival opened on 29 October 1967 with Rado and Ragni's *American Tribal Love-Rock Musical* (directed by Gerald Freedman). The first production moved to a nightclub, then, completely restructured by former Cafe La Mama director Tom O'Horgan, emerged on Broadway as *Hair*. The original production, under Papp's auspices, met with cries of outrage and indignation from Papp's Public Theatre subscribers. Even greater outrage greeted the rock *Hamlet* which followed. In a press interview Papp recorded:

> There was never a performance during the run of our first three plays at which anywhere from five to fifty people didn't storm out of their seats in protest. We even developed a spot in *Hamlet* to accommodate these angry departures.[103]

Papp made it clear that he was interested not in middle-class Broadway audiences, but in the youth who were in some way concerned with contemporary issues.

The great figures who provided the intellectual and on-the-ground drive behind French experimental theatre were all active well before 1960: Jean Vilar, Roger Planchon, Maurice Sarrazin, Jean Dasté. But the man who ensured that experimental theatre would be an important force throughout France was General de Gaulle, who returned to power in 1958 with an utterly genuine commitment to the wartime ideal of reconstructing a vibrant national culture. A policy of decentralization, with subsidized *centres dramatiques* and *maisons de culture* throughout the country, was instituted immediately by André Malraux, minister of culture, and followed through by his successor. Sarrazin put on contemporary plays in Toulouse; Dasté was even more radical in Saint-Etienne; Vilar directed the Avignon Festival from its foundation in 1947 to his death at the age of 59 in 1971—it flourished in the later sixties. In 1966 Vilar expanded the festival from a fortnight to a month, bringing in such companies as Planchon's Théâtre de la Cité de Villeurbane and Maurice Béjart's Ballet du XXᵉ siècle. The festival had been confined within the Court of Honour in the Palace of the Popes, but Planchon insisted on moving outside: Jean Lacouture of *Le Monde* remarked, 'Avignon is no longer a city which has a festival, but a festival which has a city.'[104] In Avignon, as elsewhere, 1968 was a year of excitement and even riot. One protest play by the French company Le Théâtre du Chêne Noir was banned, while the hippies of Living Theatre shocked the locals. Eventually Living Theatre withdrew. Things were still more adventurous in 1969 when the workers' co-operative theatre, Théâtre du Soleil, under Ariane Mnouchkine, toured with *Les Clowns* in a mobile fairground booth.

The Marxist, dialectical view of society, that the bad, bourgeois society contains within it antithetical, alternative, or working-class (whether new or old working-class, or a working-class vanguard of students, as Marcuse posited) elements which will eventually overthrow existing society, replacing it with a good alternative society, is simply wrong; and the efforts of Foucault, Barthes, and the others to make Marxism more subtle and persuasive, by specifically making language the most important sphere (in addition to economic and political power) through which the bourgeoisie maintained its control, simply compounded the error. It became modish to believe, not so much that if you wanted to change the economic and political power structure of society you must change social and cultural practices as well, but rather that if you did change social and cultural practices that would bring about the complete transformation of society, including the distribution of economic and political power. In fact, there was indeed over the sixties, for reasons which went far beyond the actions of those who claimed to be counter-cultural, considerable change. Societies were transformed; but economic and political structures were not—experience suggests that while economic and political structures can be modified, quickly and successfully transforming them into something totally different is not a realistic possibility. Dialectical theory is misleading in suggesting that all aspects of existing society, from government and economic institutions, to bodies of knowledge, education, values, the arts and entertainments, form a monolith, bolstering bourgeois rule, while all critical or alternative manifestations must be part of the revolutionary counter-monolith, which is bound eventually to replace the bourgeois one. Movements and ideas of the sixties were phenomenally innovative, phenomenally liberating at the personal level; but that does not mean that they were ever likely to succeed in, or were necessarily always aimed at, overthrowing existing society. Experimental theatre did mount the most fundamental attacks on the received ways of doing practically everything, mocked consumer society, attacked American imperialist policies, and tried, sometimes in the most embarrassing ways, to force individual members of audiences out of their stuffy conformity, but it never formed an oppositional monolith; on the other hand, at many points it retained integral links with established society. This was true, we have seen, of Gaullist France; it was true in America, where 'off-Broadway' expanded and prospered and where, in any case, many middle-class people both opposed the Vietnam war and supported black civil rights.

Britain offered a paradigm of the way in which theatrical innovation advanced across a broad front, in the new civic theatres which were essentially a legacy of the war (in the first years the Coventry Belgrade Theatre did premières of the *Wesker Trilogy*, *Breakout* by Bill Owen, *Never Had*

*It So Good* by John Wiles, *The Lion in Love* by Shelagh Delaney—not *Paradise Now* certainly, but quite definitely experimental), in the slightly older proscenium-arch experimental theatres (Royal Court, Arts, Hampstead), in certain of the big subsidized companies (especially Peter Brook's Royal Shakespeare Company), and in the new spaces, the Traverse in Edinburgh, the Open Space (founded by the American sponsor of Theatre of Cruelty, Charles Marowitz), the Arts Lab. Theatre Workshop, very much in the older agitprop tradition, achieved a permanent home in a traditional suburban theatre in working-class east London, The Theatre Royal, Stratford East. *Oh! What a Lovely War* (1963) brought music-hall techniques to a bitterly satirical critique of the inefficiency and corruption of generals and politicians in the First World War. Labour arts minister Jenny Lee was anxious to involve Littlewood in touring theatre, but found her 'so very much in mid air that it is difficult for her best friends in the municipalities to help her'.[105]

Let us spend a little time at the Traverse Theatre, in itself one of the most important subcultural developments of the time, but also a perfect miniature of the semi-capitalistic, non-dialectical interrelationships which are central to an understanding of the sixties.[106] In Edinburgh, brilliant individual initiatives had turned the general artistic legacy of the war into something palpable and magnificent: the Edinburgh International Festival of Music and the Arts, launched in 1947. Around that festival there grew up a 'fringe', dozens of little experimental theatre groups which sought their place in the sun (or more often rain) for the three summer weeks of the festival. A coordinating body, the Fringe Society, was founded immediately after the festival of 1958, and was fully in operation for the festival of 1959. Edinburgh already had quite a developed bohemian (mainly literary) life, focused on certain pubs. Also, there was a prestigious university, with a fairly cosmopolitan student population, and an innovative art college. Something of a longing was created for the excitements of festival time to be prolonged throughout the year. William Burroughs wrote an amusing account to Allen Ginsberg about one of the important pre-Traverse events, the International Writers' Conference in the summer of 1962 in what Burroughs called 'Edinberg':

'All heroin and homosexuality' said Hugh MacDiarmid, greatest living Scotch poet he calls himself 'these people belong in jail not on the lecture platform...' By 'these people' he means Trochi and the militant homosexual Dutch delegate and myself—What an old fool he is with his kilts and his Scotch nationalism at this point...[107]

Already established in Edinburgh was the Texan (actually born in Louisiana) ex-serviceman Jim Haynes (b. 1933), who with money from his father had set up the all-the-year-round Paperback Book Shop, used additionally during the festival as a venue for fringe theatrical events. The other immediate inspiration behind the idea of some kind of permanent arts club was Richard Demarco, an art teacher and son of an Edinburgh-Italian ice cream family. It is important to stress the late fifties origins, as Demarco did when he remarked: 'You would be wrong to think the Traverse idea was born to the sound of the Beatles. We were a pre-Beatles phenomenon.'[108] Other important founding figures were Tom Mitchell, owner of the crumbling five-storey, seventeenth-century building, once a brothel, which was to house the new theatre, John Calder, the avant-garde publisher, John Martin, an established commercial artist, Andrew Elliott, a lawyer, Jim Walker, an accountant, John Malcolm, an actor who had performed in the Paperback, and the actor, stage manager, and director Terry Lane. The Traverse Theatre Club was formed in the autumn of 1962 with a constitution which evoked fifties earnestness rather than sixties exuberance: 'The object of the club shall be to present serious theatre productions of a type not usually presented for economic reasons. And renderings and encouragement of music, Scottish and other poetry and folk music, pottery, sculpture, painting, books and art.'[109] The choice of plays for the opening of the theatre (26 December 1962) was also earnest, *Orisons* by Bernando Arrabal and *Huis Clos* by Sartre, but quite inadvertently the second performance turned into a happening when the actress Colette O'Neill was accidentally stabbed with a paperknife, and seriously wounded. From the publicity point of view, there could have been no better start.

The Traverse was a bohemian middle-class enclave, surrounded by a very middle-class, puritanical, and generally hostile city. That it challenged prevailing values there can be no doubt. During the 1963 festival Haynes and Calder organized a drama conference in one of the buildings belonging to the university, at which they provided a deliberately organized happening, involving the very brief appearance of a naked young woman. The press, and some strongly puritanical members of Edinburgh's city council expressed outrage over this. There were many complaints about after-hours drinking in the Traverse bar. In the summer of 1965 the MP for West Edinburgh expressed in the House of Commons his 'grave misgivings about the way in which public money was being spent at Edinburgh's Traverse Theatre Club... and in staging plays... which are barred from performance in the ordinary theatres of the country on the grounds of obscenity or for any other reasons'.[110] Within the management committee, inevitably, there were splits. Haynes was a consistently controversial figure, and often completely at odds with other members of the committee. At the annual general meeting on 27 April 1966, held as usual on university premises, Haynes declared that 'if members did not like his choice of plays, then he suggested that they started their own theatre and he would join it'.[111] By the summer, Haynes's connection with the theatre was effectively severed, with Haynes himself settled in London. The Traverse production of *Ubu in Chains* at the 1967 festival caused outrage, mainly because the designer Gerald Scarfe had dressed up Ma and Pa Ubu to look like huge female and male genital organs respectively. In 1967 there was much protest about a series of plays by Paul Foster, particularly one called *Balls* in which the cast consisted entirely of two tennis balls swinging above an empty stage. In February 1968 the biggest scandal of all was created when a student group put on *Mass in F*, in which a young woman recounted her sexual exploits while sitting on the stage stripped to the waist, with the actors around her engaging in a variety of unprepossessing activities.

The basic aim of putting on plays which the commercial theatre would not touch was rigorously pursued, with the result that the theatre was constantly on the verge of financial crisis. The building itself (one of the attractions for many) was dingy and crumbling (declared unsafe, it had to be vacated in 1969). A July 1966 Scottish Arts Council report on the theatre began:

Obviously a theatre like the Traverse has its own special characteristics and any attempt

315

to use neon lights or 'Glitter it up' would destroy it entirely, and, of course, its air of improvisation is part of its charm, but there is… a line of demarcation between these characteristics and sordidness.[112]

An offer from a large brewing concern to take over the running of catering and the bar was firmly rejected. In fact, the theatre survived through subsidies from the Scottish Arts Council and subventions from the lawyers and accountants who served on its committee. By 1966 the Arts Council subsidy was running at a rate of £7,000 a year. Even the Edinburgh city council contributed small sums. A powerful figure in the second half of the decade was Nicholas Fairbairn, a flamboyant but extremely conservative, even reactionary, advocate (who later became a Conservative MP). The Traverse did not make money in the way in which the Beatles or even Andy Warhol made money. But there was an obvious line of business whereby successful productions were sold on to other theatres, often in London. A committee statement of January 1964 declared it not to be in the interest of members for the Traverse 'to become a cheap try-out theatre for a commercial London management'; none the less much prestige, and some income, was derived from transfers elsewhere. After the early years of mainly putting on classics of contemporary European drama, more and more new works were tried out. The Traverse was one of those sixties institutions which provided opportunities for new talent, particularly among playwrights, but also among actors, several of whom, including Tom Conti, subsequently became famous.

Haynes was an entrepreneur; the dominant figure in the years after his departure, Max Stafford-Clark, was himself a theatrical director. Stafford-Clark, who took six weeks' absence in January 1968 to work with the La Mama company in New York, led the way towards the kind of creative extremism represented in particular by Living Theatre. At the end of April 1968 he produced a paper which, while recognizing that the 'most important single aspect of the Traverse's work is the encouragement and development of new playwrights', argued: 'it's time the Traverse experimented in another direction as well.'

> For some time different groups in Europe and America have been trying to find a new theatre language—new ways of presenting plays. Simply, there is a growing dissatisfaction with actors standing on a stage speaking speeches and people sitting in an audience listening; this 'movement' is groping towards additional methods of expressing emotion and feeling: through noises, through dance movement and through greater physical involvement. Jerzy Grotowski in Poland is the Arch Druid of this whole movement and the La Mama and the Open Theatre have picked up many of their techniques and exercises from him.[113]

Stafford-Clark commented that the only director in Britain touching on these areas was Peter Brook of the Royal Shakespeare Company, as exemplified in his *Marat/Sade* and *US*. A month later Stafford-Clark produced a statement redolent of the way in which the ideas of the Left Bank luminaries were being absorbed:

The inter-relationship between the convention of language and the rule of morality is a field in which ambiguity can be used to advantage by anybody concerned with the arts. Thus a writer who wants to alter the structure of morality can do so by containing his polemic in a syntax which is, in itself, an alteration, an alteration to the structure of language that runs parallel to mood structure. His obscenities will surmount morality that much more effectively if they take place without sentence, plot or any other moral linguistic setting. Set in a story, positioned so that they can be seen to illustrate a moral point in a rational way, they will be acceptable to conventional minds. Such minds know that while syntax and convention of form remain intact their house of cards remains unthreatened. Such minds can accept the use of violence in art as illustration to a moral or rational point. In a rational setting, violence has its excuse and can be indulged thoroughly with comparative threat to established order.

When a critic says 'it was done badly' and he really means 'it was rude' it may be taken that a man situated at a significant point in the maintenance of power has felt his world shift a little under his feet. In that case, things are going well. We have not failed our public.[114]

Like Haynes, Stafford-Clark, a very gifted director, who subsequently developed his career still further at the Royal Court, had his (often bitter) differences with the Traverse committee, few of whom would have made much of that statement. Taken loosely, the statement is a call for exciting and innovative theatrical presentation; analysed rigorously, it is nonsense—established society was no house of cards and, while experimental theatre had an important role in transforming attitudes and values, it never seriously threatened the blowing down of the alleged 'house of cards'. If we are to appreciate the brilliance of sixties artistic products we have to separate them from their claims to accuracy of political and social analysis. We must not judge art as we judge history—though, ironically, avant-garde thinkers claimed that the two were the same thing. An example of the Stafford-Clark philosophy and practice (which actually preceded this statement) was the May 1968 production of Megan Terry's *Comings and Goings*, which involved elaborate activities between actors and audience, the latter being in a position to stop and start the action by the raising of a baton.

Drug-pushers and takers infiltrated the Traverse in 1964, but on the whole the club remained remarkably clear of that particular facet of sixties life. More conspicuously, the Traverse was a place where one could practically observe the sexual revolution taking place. The whole building, bar, dining-room, tiny theatre, art gallery, seemed suffused by sex, an energetic lead being given by several of the most prominent Traverse figures. Most obviously, the place seemed filled with attractive young women and predatory men. Writing of 1965–6, Joyce McMillan puts it well:

Sex was all the rage at the Traverse, and sexual frankness a strong motif of many of the early productions; but the ethos at the time was very much to do with uninhibited access to pretty young women...[115]

317

The Traverse came very close to losing its liquor licence in the spring of 1964, but thereafter it began to play a part in establishing what for Scotland was a new kind of sociable drinking, accompanied by the rock/pop hits of the day on the juke box. The Traverse also established a pattern of being open on Sundays, while closed on Mondays.

Before the final break with Edinburgh Jim Haynes, with the help of the secretary of the Arts Council, Arnold Goodman, established a second Traverse in the Jeanetta Cochrane theatre in London. He was also (May 1966) awarded the Whitbread prize for outstanding service to British theatre—richly deserved, but not exactly the appropriate accolade for an enemy of society—which, of course, Haynes, like Warhol, never was. Haynes was involved in the founding of *IT (International Times)*, which can be described as an underground newspaper—it was concerned with the preoccupations of the protest movement as well as with sex and drugs rather than political revolution. Haynes was also involved in the founding of the multimedia Arts Lab. Perhaps the most important single production there was *Vagina Rex and the Gas Oven* (1969) by the writer, director and actress Jane Arden. Employing strobe lights and other multimedia effects, this alternately surreal and mystical montage explored a woman's attempt to come to terms with her own sense of inferiority imposed on her by society. The Arts Lab could quite justly represent itself as the focal point of the underground; and it had failed to get the endorsement of that embodiment of the liberal great and good, Arnold Goodman. On the other hand, it did have the support of the arts minister in the Labour government, Jenny Lee. Among its first financial supporters were leading media people Peter Brook, Tim Baumont, Fred Zimmerman, Fenella Fielding, Tom Stoppard, John Schlesinger, Doris Lessing, Kenneth Tynan, and David Frost. Haynes, again like Warhol in New York, was mixing with the beautiful (and very rich) people, Monica Vitti, Antonioni, and Paul McCartney, famously dressed as an Arab, for example, at a celebrated party held at the Roundhouse. And the Arts Lab was on the itinerary of every ambassador and affluent visitor to swinging London.[116]

The position of Peter Brook's Royal Shakespeare Company is perhaps even more fascinating. Brook put on a 'theatre of cruelty' season in 1964, then in February 1968 he put on *US*, his company being joined by the fabulous Grotowski. Brook himself explained the background to the production:

> The birth of *US* was allied to the reaction of a group of us who quite suddenly felt that Vietnam was more powerful, more acute, more insistent a situation than any drama that already existed between covers...
>
> We were interested in a theatre of confrontation. In current events, what confronts what, who confronts who? In the case of Vietnam, it is reasonable to say that everyone is concerned, yet none is concerned; if everyone could hold in his mind through one single day both the horror of Vietnam and the normal life he is leading, the tension between the two would be intolerable... We wanted actors to explore every aspect of this contradiction, so that instead of excusing or condoling an audience, they could be what an actor is always supposed to be, the audience's representative, who is trained and prepared to go further than the spectator, down a path the spectator knows to be his own.[117]

That last sentence in itself is revealing: Brook envisaged taking his audience with him, not violently challenging its prejudices. And, of course, he was right. This director of a subsidized national theatre was certainly putting on an experimental and a political play; but its success was due to the fact that a large number of British middle-class people shared in the repugnance for the Vietnam war.

The lord chamberlain had wanted to ban *US,* but, one member of the establishment talking to another, the chairman of the RSC board of governors, George Farmer, persuaded him that *US* was in fact a responsible production. The lord chamberlain did ban *Macbird* from production in Britain, on the grounds that it was unfriendly to a friendly power.

Government initiatives were important in Italy in the fifties, where, parallelling the welfare reforms of that decade, state-subsidized permanent civic theatres *(teatri stabili)* were established in the main cities—there were six by 1960. But at the same time, the Italian police were the most brutal in suppressing plays which were politically or morally suspect; as we saw, Living Theatre were deported in 1965. Italy had some very distinguished theatrical figures: Giorgio Strehler, co-founder of the Piccolo Teatro della Città di Milano as far back as 1947; Eugenio Barba, who, in 1964, went off to Norway to found the world-renowned experimental Odin Teatret in Oslo; and, of course, the absurdest comic playwright, Dario Fo. In May 1965 the profession itself conducted an investigation into why there was no really thriving contemporary theatre in Italy as there was in other Western countries. The basic explanation that emerged was that of the Italian language problem: each part of Italy had its own version of Italian, so that it had long been customary in the theatre to use a stilted, artificial, 'universal' Italian.[118] Despite the expulsion of Living Theatre, signs that experimental theatre was gaining in importance were apparent in late 1965. *Epoca* of 26 December declared, 'In 1966 we'll all be performing', reporting that avant-garde theatre had finally arrived in Italy following upon the clamorous experiments in France, America, and Great Britain; Italian theatre directors would be forcing their audiences into participating and there would be happenings. In November 1966 a number of leading figures in theatre and film issued a manifesto on 'the New Theatre':

> Theatre must be able to achieve an absolute and total oppositional struggle... We do not
> believe in purely verbal challenges. On the contrary, we believe that we can use theatre
> to instill doubt, to destroy conventions, to tear off masks, and to get new ideas moving.
> We believe in a theatre full of interrogatives, full of manifestos, whether true or false, full
> of contemporary gestures.[119]

From this emerged what was known as 'theatre of protest' *(contestazione),* which was to merge into the activist movements of 1968–9. Little theatres were being founded everywhere, often in working-class suburbs, though many were short-lived: none the less, the expansion in theatre audiences was striking and sustained—between 1965 and 1977 there was a 400 per cent increase.[120] These theatres used the language of the locality, not the stilted, artificial, literary Italian. Looking back from 1971, Giancarlo Nanni, who founded Gruppo Space, made a point central to the significance of experimental theatre. Theatre, he said, is 'one of the few media, if not the only one, which can still function independently of the culture industry'.[121] Direct, individualistic theatre, newly minted in every performance, was the best antidote to the homogenizing influences of the commercial mass media: it was, you might say, 'theatre of the village' versus 'the global village'. The experimentalists found it essential to fight free of subsidy and supervision by national or local government, and then, also, from the embrace of the massively powerful Italian Communist party. In 1968 Dario Fo founded La Nuova Scena, which he ran as a private club to exclude the police; after each performance there would be a discussion with the audience. Two famous productions were *Grand Pantomine with Flags and Small and Medium-Sized Puppets* (1968) and *Accidental Death of an Anarchist* (1969). Fo could not help the worldwide success of this latter play from making him a lot of money. Splitting from the Communist party, he formed what was to be Italy's most important alternative theatre circuit, II Collettivo Teatrale la Commune (1970).

Because Italy was most backward, most priest-ridden, and most patriarchal, it was actually the first country to give birth, in December 1966, to a fundamentalist (though tiny) women's liberation movement, the Union for the Démystification of Male Authority (DEMAU). The feminist Theatre Maddalena was founded in Rome in 1971, two to three years behind analogous developments in America and Britain.

Experimental theatre was an essential ingredient in the bubbling mix of interlinked subcultures which made the period so uniquely distinctive. Rock music was the most important agent of mediation across traditional boundaries. But experimental theatre comes a close second: it brought members of the theatre-going upper and middle classes into contact with the tenets and practices of 'the underground' and the 'alternative culture'. It brought together into one indissoluble whole happenings, popular music, dance, and drama. Perhaps even more important, experimental theatre was a most potent riposte to electronic mass society, to the concept of the global village: it represented the doing-your-own-thing, participatory, aspect of sixties subcultures too often forgotten in general sociological accounts of the rise of consumer society; it embodied that reaction against mindless commercialism and mass marketing (though, given the interpenetrative nature of society that I have already stressed, there was no stopping some products of experimental theatre from becoming commercial hits) to be found somewhere in most sixties subcultures. And experimental theatre was intimately involved in the great protest movements of the time.

Legacies in the world of intellect and theatre-going are obvious. During the seventies and eighties there were throughout the Western world far more experimental companies than had ever existed in the sixties: experimental theatre became part of the standard theatrical diet. In 'straight' theatre, the experimentalists' incorporation of music became normal practice. Much experimental theatre was preoccupied with the theories of Marcuse and with the notions of language and identity emanating from the luminaries of the Left Bank. Beyond the confines of the theatre, therefore, experimental theatre transmitted the latest thinking to the minority interested in such matters.

What of the great liberation movements? As off-Broadway expanded, (white-run) companies put on more and more plays featuring black characters—throughout the decade there were four such plays off-Broadway to every one on Broadway. In 1966 the Negro Ensemble Company was launched, not altogether cut off from established society in so far as it received a grant of

$1,200,000 from the Ford Foundation for its first three years. At the very end of the sixties there was a great flurry of creation of (often short-lived) all-black companies. Clearly these developments were of importance to black writers, actors, and directors. But when one contemplates the majesty and the tragedy of the black civil rights movement, and what was achieved by other means, it becomes difficult to allot any real prominence to experimental theatre; most important were the travelling theatres, including the company already mentioned, and also one based on all-black Howard University in Washington, to which future black novelist Toni Morrison belonged.

With women's liberation the story is very different—for at least four reasons. First, the sorts of politically charged issues experimental theatre often dealt with were close to the kinds of arguments feminists themselves wished to advance. Second, experimental theatre offered new forms of expression just when feminists were feeling that their own theatre must be a new kind of theatre. Third, the communal spirit and collective creation of experimental theatre was highly congenial to women's liberationists. Fourth, and critically important, experimental theatre offered women roles as writers and directors to a degree never seen in conventional theatre. But, fifth, as they gathered experience and confidence, women became more sensitive to the barriers still closed against them and felt compelled to break away and form companies of their own, directly proselytizing on behalf of the feminist cause.[122] It is important not to exaggerate. The creation of feminist theatre owed more to the wider feminist movement (discussed in a later chapter) than it did to experimental theatre; none the less experimental theatre played an important ancillary role.

Gay Liberation was slower to get moving than Women's Liberation, and, as with black liberation, the links with experimental theatre are tenuous and problematic. The number of plays both on and off-Broadway, presenting gays as accepted members of society, increased throughout the sixties, with lift-off coming in the 1967–8 season; but the off-Broadway plays had long runs, the Broadway ones disastrously short ones. Mart Crowley's *The Boys in the Band* (1968), which had a long run off-Broadway, 'treated the American theatre to its most outspoken homosexual play in a year of revolutionary theatre. It presented a compelling and naturalistic portrait of the "gay" world.'[123] Colin Spencer's *Spitting Image* had its premier at the Hampstead Theatre Club in north London on 9 September 1968, directed by James Roose-Evans. From 1968 to 1969 it had a forty-nine-day run off-Broadway. The review in *Critical Digest* (24 March 1969) ran as follows:

> *Spitting Image* is a continually funny, literate (British, you know) farce-revue on an unlikely homosexual miracle. But it is most vital for its accurate satirical anti-conformist versus the establishment jabs.[124]

The basic joke was of the male homosexual couple conceiving a child. Theatre, at its more experimental end, had some influence in altering attitudes towards gays; but this is a peripheral influence compared with the organic interconnection between feminist agitation and experimental theatre.

Experimental theatre, minority activity though it always was, was involved in the general liberation of everyday life which I see as lying at the core of the social transformations of 1958–9 to 1973–4. A minute yet portentous example, confined effectively to Britain, is the way in which the experimental companies' practice of performing on Sundays (and closing on Mondays) contributed to the liberalizing of the British Sunday. More crucially, it was the repeated challenges of experimental theatre which forced the relaxation of theatrical censorship everywhere. The precipitating event for the abolition of the lord chamberlain's powers in Britain was, on 31 March 1968, the banning of, and threat of police action against, the performance at the Royal Court Upstairs of *Early Morning* by Edward Bond. Bond, overtly Marxist, was one of the great dramatic talents of sixties Britain—a name to put alongside that of Harold Pinter. *Early Morning* put historical personages—Victoria and Albert, Disraeli and Florence Nightingale (played by Marianne Faithfull)—into non-historical situations to suggest the sadism and corruption of Britain's ruling class. In scene xii Florence is dressed up as a man; in the background are six dead bodies—three hanged, three shot:

VICTORIA: If they knew you were a woman there'd be a scandal, but if they believe you're a man they'll think I'm just a normal lonely widow...
FLORENCE: I'm the first hangwoman in history—public hangwoman, that is. It's part of our war effort. And if we're being emancipated we must be consistent. So we take over any man's job that's suitable.[125]

The linkages are not necessarily direct, but the steady weakening of censorship in a variety of areas is undoubtedly articulated with that growing permissiveness which was a majority, not a minority, phenomenon.

Audiences for fringe and alternative performances were often well-heeled and highly conventional: the mighty atom of experimental theatre brought permissiveness and rebellion within their purview. Experimental theatre was the embodiment of cross-over in all senses of that term, being performed in pubs, cafés, in the streets, and in working-class suburbs. It involved music and dance and the incorporation of film projection, puppets, and masks. The cross-over with popular music was strongly represented in the rock musical *Tommy* (1969) by Pete Townshend and the Who. A central document is the musical *Hair*. Here is what American man-of-the-theatre and protagonist of Theatre of Cruelty Charles Marowitz said about *Hair* when it opened in London in November 1968, on the very day after theatrical censorship in Britain had ended:

Every so often a show comes along which consolidates some part of the *Zeitgeist* and whose significance is less in what it is than the time at which it arrives... *Hair* is such a show. It is the cohesion of a dozen contemporary trends, the most dominant of which are hip culture, drug-enthusiasm, the Cage concepts of Indeterminacy and the Marcusian theory of protest. *Hair* is about everything that is going on at the moment.[126]

Marowitz then concentrated on O'Horgan's achievements in transforming the original show,

322

referring to the director as 'the élan vital behind the La Mama Company', and concluding that, 'in *Hair*, the La Mama style has been fully realised'.

> It is a breakthrough in the musical form because it has, quite literally, shattered the musical comedy conventions. Its lyrics, as Leonard Bernstein rightly complains, are like laundry-lists, but the diction of the twentieth century is slogans and shibboleths.

After this distant evocation of Roland Barthes, Marowitz corroborates one of my main points—this product of experimental theatre represents, not a dialectical confrontation, but a significant body of American opinion:

> It would be ridiculous to see this show simply as a formalistic advance in the theatre (though no one I have read has quite recognized this aspect of it), for it is a great deal more. It is the most powerful piece of anti-war propaganda yet to come out of America and, unlike the Living Theatre's po-faced essays on similar themes, *Hair* makes its point through comedy and celebration. Without Vietnam and the American repugnance to that war, the show could never have come into being... It is a jubilant assertion of the American revolutionary genius which twenty years of repressive 'democracy' has not been able to snuff out.

Experimental theatre articulated what was already within society, not something exterior to it. It did indeed challenge, and it helped to modify, 'repressive democracy'. And experimental theatre represented a direct and personal response to the totalizing pressures of a multinational commercialism operating through the electronic media.

# 8

# Affluence, Poverty, Permissiveness

## *'Mod Cons' and Consumerism in Italy and France*

Since the Second World War the majority of Americans had been better off than ever before; there were more haves than have-nots. In Western Europe living standards were lower across all classes, and while these were generally rising, all three of our European countries contained substantial groupings of working-class, lower-middle-class, and agricultural workers whose living standards remained modest. Serious poverty was prevalent in southern Italy, very bare living conditions were to be encountered in parts of rural France. Britain, living up to its traditional image as the country of moderation, had the most even spread of prosperity (though, in accordance with another traditional image, also a very rich upper class); but Britain was not immune to the growth of that seeming concomitant of affluence, the underclass, those who had little hope of even a steady working-class job, those who were the victims of personal misfortune. As we have seen in Chapter 6, the major forces at work in all four countries were economic growth, technological innovation, liberal and socialist ideology, and government intervention— these, and particularly the last, faced a variety of institutional obstacles. This chapter looks at outcomes which can be summarized under four headings:

1. The bringing of the basic amenities and conveniences of modern urban life to remote areas (an aspect of sixties development which has received too little attention).
2. The matching of new commodities, themselves vital elements in transforming lifestyles, to increased incomes (this development, usually referred to as 'consumerism', has almost had too much attention—or, rather, the word has been thrown around as if sufficient unto itself).
3. The stirrings of conscience which provoked the poverty programmes and social reforms.

4. The accelerating liberation in personal relationships as permissive philosophies interchanged with material wellbeing.

Marcuse and many other commentators then and since represented consumerism as entailing standardization, homogenization, and the crushing of individualism and good taste; worse, it signified the swamping of all idealism and protest in a tide of gross materialism, particularly offensive when many were bypassed by affluence. Certainly there was no obvious increase in revolutionary zeal in the backward areas of southern Italy and rural France; to the inhabitants, and indeed to observers more humane and less fanatical than Marcuse, the arrival of inside lavatories and of bathrooms may have seemed a more relevant blessing.

For change in rural Italy, the best single source is the three-part social survey conducted by the American sociologist Feliks Gross (with the assistance of Professor G. N. del Monte of the department of sociology at Rome University) in the village of Bonagente, about 80 km south of Rome; the first survey took place in 1957–8, the second in 1969, and the third in 1971.[1] The survey of 1957–8 made clear both the lack of amenities in the village itself and the contrast between the existence of at least basic facilities within the village and their total absence in the habitations dotted about the surrounding countryside. Within what was called La Città (the historic walled centre of the village) there was running water, electricity, and flushing water-closets. Outside the walls there was no running water and no electricity. There were either earth-closets or no lavatory facilities at all (in which case calls of nature were calls *to* nature, in fact to the open fields). For the whole district, the fundamental problem was that of the absence of any kind of road system. The most important economic and cultural centre for the area was the small town of Celestino, but the only road led to the lesser town of Albani. Because of the lack of electricity, farmers and farm workers did not even have radio contact with the outside world (so much for McLuhan and his 'global village'). In his interview with Gross, the mayor (a member of the Italian Socialist party) put matters succinctly:

> Bonagente is about 60–80 km from Rome, but it seems that it is about 80,000 km. We are living in very primitive conditions and I don't know if we really belong to a civilized country, or whether we should be considered as a part of the African region.... We have not enough direct communication with Rome and with other great cities such as Naples.

For the majority the only point of contact with the outside world was Albani, visited on market days and saints' days. Only a very small number of artisans and better-off farmers were able to exploit one of the most distinctive early products of the economic miracle, motor-scooters; the others used donkeys, or walked. Only landowners, public officials, and a few other professionals visited Rome or Naples.

By 1969 economic expansion, and public enterprise, had effected a stunning transformation. Gross reported:

> By now, the Bonagentesi of the countryside *(contadini)* have roads, electricity and

water. There is plenty of employment and with few exceptions, the older people have their old age pensions. Thus, generally speaking, the major immediate and intermediate collective goals that the *contadini* of the fields were talking about in 1957 have been achieved.

Lack of personal transport had been a big problem at that time. On Sunday 7 September 1969, Gross counted, on one of the piazzas within the town, thirty-one parked cars, with twenty-seven on another, and six along a street. He saw no donkeys at all. He summarized the change as follows:

> Eleven years ago in Bonagente, there were two automobiles, both of an ancient vintage, kept in working condition thanks only to the Italian mechanical genius. Today, according to estimates, 20–25 per cent of all families of the entire Commune of Bonagente own cars; mostly the agile Fiat Cinquecento and Seicento, unusually well adapted to the village roads and hills, inexpensive and economic to operate, and mechanically simple. Most of the families, with few exceptions, have some kind of motorized transportation, such as a Vespa [motor-scooter], a motorcycle, or a small three-wheel Lurgoncino, used as a kind of pickup truck.

Gross identified the fundamental basis of change as the availability of work, without however highlighting the one big blot on this happy consummation: the work was only to be found eighty kilometres away, in Rome itself, or in the industrial parks spreading south from Rome along the recently built *autostrada del sole*. Gross did report that the trek towards work began as early as four o'clock in the morning, but gave that an optimistic gloss. There was an early-morning bus, then between six and seven he saw various car-pools being formed: 'I could see men and women hurrying to the meeting points, all decently dressed, all in shoes, none in the traditional sandals prevalent in 1957.' Unquestionably these gains were tangible—but won in the traditional working-class way, by long hours and back-breaking effort.

However, Sunday 7 September was the day of the Madonna del Soccorso Perpetuo (the Madonna of Constant Assistance). Since this was the day on which locals from all over Italy returned to their family homes, the number of cars was exceptional.

> After the religious celebrations and processions, some pilgrims gather at a small piazza, perhaps 500 of them, while others struggle through the traffic jam in their automobiles. A long line of vehicles stretches to the valley.
>
> In a small bar large groups of friends, families and neighbors have gathered. Their dress is modern, no different than in Rome, although a couple of old people wear with pride the traditional costumes made out of velvet and corduroy.... Otherwise, the clothing of the guests is modern, no different than that of the Romans.... The heavy and expensive coral necklaces women used to wear twelve years ago with their Sunday dresses seem to have disappeared.

In contrast to 1957, now almost everyone had radios, and most people had both radio and television. Attitudes to money, Gross reported, had changed, though people were still careful spenders. Most people

> will tell you that they do not remember such prosperity before. Now money is spent: they buy land, build homes, buy automobiles, refrigerators, radios and television sets, wire their houses. There is a general faith that prosperity and employment will continue.

Among those interviewed by Gross was Celestino Bruno, a cobbler and First World War veteran:

> BRUNO: We eat far better. Meat, which at one time was eaten rarely, is eaten today almost every day. The worker has advanced greatly, has plenty of clothing, plenty to eat.
> GROSS: When I was here twelve years ago, people always mentioned that there was no water or electricity in the countryside.
> BRUNO: We have all that. We have water. We have five litres of water per minute. This is an amount greater than we need, especially for the countryside. What I wanted to say is that we have an abundance of water. Electricity? We have it now in all farm houses. Now they build roads in the countryside, roads for cars. Generally, what is now has never been before.
> GROSS: Do you think that it is better now than it was twelve years ago when I was here?
> BRUNO: Of course we are better off now, there is no question. Today there is no misery any more; all have work. The workers save money today. There is no unemployment. It is easy to find work. They pay well. And here in the province of Frosinone, we have five hundred thousand inhabitants and about one hundred thousand registered cars. According to that figure, almost every five persons have an automobile. This is a very basic broad evolution.

Professor Del Monte provided Gross with this graphic report:

> During another trip, a friend who is also a peasant, showed me his toilet; leading the way, he said with pride: 'We have a toilet, the Roman type...' It was all plastered with tiles. I asked him: *you* remember not so long ago—we used to go in the middle of the field—not to a toilet. How do you feel today, when you go to the toilet?' Said he: 'I feel like a human being, like the others, not like an animal, as I felt before.'

The tone is so insistently upbeat that one might well entertain suspicions that Gross had elicited from his interviewees the responses he wanted. It is also true that the Italian media throughout the sixties did feature stories about the tremendous transformations taking place in Italian life: certainly phrases about Italy as a whole having had a 'great evolution' sound borrowed. If the Gross survey had been conducted entirely in 1969 and afterwards, one might well distrust the references to how primitive matters were only a dozen years previously. But the first survey was conducted independently in 1957–8, when Gross could not have known what was going to happen in the years ahead. So the strong image of very rapid and concentrated change is based on fairly independent empirical evidence. That the changes in provision of amenities, facilities, modern conveniences, and consumer goods did take place here (and all over Italy) can be substantiated from a good range of quantitative material (much of which I have already summarized in Chapter 6). One has only to reflect for a moment to realize that the change from no toilets to modern bathrooms, from no radios to television sets, from scratching an arduous existence from stony, windy land to having industrial employment and money in the pocket, would strike people with all the drama expressed in these interviews. Gross had no special vested interest in exaggerating change: American influence in Italy actually waned substantially in the sixties, and the sort of left-wing interests which the Americans had previously opposed were getting stronger. No source tells the whole truth; Gross may well have mustered his quotations to create maximum effect: but taking other sources into account, we can, I think, see in the Gross survey reliable support for one of my basic points: that change in the sixties was not simply about fringe minorities, but affected substantial numbers of previously neglected ordinary people.

Another of my basic points is also supported: the notion of extreme change contained within the best of traditional frameworks. That is one implication of the following observation from Gross, though there are perhaps other disturbing resonances, to which I shall return at the end of this section:

> In La Città the local stores are located in the ancient stone houses as they were in 1957. Inside, however, the stores are far better equipped; they are filled with food and wares unknown before. The impact of American industry in the standardization of quality, weight, and packaging and the improved display of merchandise, is also evident here. There is an abundance of boxes of cookies, chocolate, tea, coffee, canned fish—all in attractive colourful wrappings.

The emphasis among interviewees is very much on the availability of meat, rather than on prepackaged foods. But in further justification for taking Gross's account as authentic and unexaggerated, it should be noted that he does record that there were still parts of the countryside which the new amenities had not yet reached: the people in these areas felt embarrassed over their primitive conditions, presumably through an awareness of the great changes taking place elsewhere. The constraints upon these changes—absolutely crucial in transforming the lives of ordinary people, but certainly not revolutionary in abolishing what neo-Marxists saw as the curse of work—the curse satirized in Lucio Mastronardi's *Il calzolaio*—were expressed by a level-headed former inhabitant of Bonagente, by 1969 working as a bus-driver in Rome:

> Bonagente has changed. Great progress has been made. But the progress has not been made because facts have changed. The advance has been made thanks to the sacrifices. Take as an example: instead of eating meat three times a week, they will eat it once a week

and build a small house to make life better. They sacrifice themselves by rising in the morning at 4 o'clock and commuting to Rome to work. They return at night and sleep a few hours. They sacrifice plenty because they are a hard-working people. They are a tough, stubborn people; they want to work; they are used to a rigorous life; they discharge their duties and are willing to make sacrifices. That way, the country becomes more civilized.

Corroboration of Gross's main findings can be found in a variety of sources. Especially valuable for showing the physical reality of change—roads, house-building (some of it chaotic), baths and bathroom fixtures, refrigerators, television sets *and* (frequently frivolous) television programmes—is the collection of videos at the Istituto Regionale Ferruccio Parri in Bologna, made by various organizations and including one TV programme from 1988, *Il sessantotto* (Nineteen Sixty-Eight), which, far from being confined to one year, is a visual survey of the sixties. A 1989 film by the Coop Emilia-Veneto, directed by Louisa Cigognetti, with the collaboration of Pierre Sorlin, records both physical evidence and some fascinating interviews.[2] A group of elderly ladies from the rural hinterland describe life as it was before the economic miracle and the development of the sixties; their testimony, backed with still photographs, is very much of the primitiveness of living conditions, even here in the north. The proprietor of an electrical shop then gives his own account of the way in which the sale of electrical goods suddenly exploded in the sixties. Most important, and in confirmation of what is really the crucial point in the Gross survey, he lays special stress on the arrival of bathrooms and modern toilet facilities.

From 1951 to 1975 the proportion of personal disposable income spent on modern consumer goods and services, and also on transport, steadily increased, while the *proportion* spent on foodstuffs and other necessities declined. The trends are broadly the same in both the centre-north and the south, though the proportion spent on food, beverages, and tobacco is consistently higher in the south, showing that it continues to lag behind as a consumer economy. Still, at constant prices, expenditure on private consumption does steadily rise in the south, sometimes at a greater rate than in the north, though never catching up in absolute terms. The increasing importance—and availability—of transport can be seen in the fact that, by 1971, over 11 per cent of individual expenditure in the centre-north was going on this, and about 10 per cent in the south. At the same date over a fifth of expenditure in the north was going on 'other goods and services'—electrical goods, modern conveniences and the installation thereof, hair-dressing and beauty treatments, as well as banking, insurance, etc; the proportion in the south was not much less, and had surpassed that level by 1975.

Quite fortuitously we have an analogue for France of Gross's three-stage survey of a rural village between the fifties and the seventies, also conducted by an American—in this case a survey of a village in the Vaucluse, in southeastern France, presented in three successive editions, 1957, 1964 and 1974. Laurence Wylie, the academic I quoted in Chapter 3, briefly American cultural attaché in Paris, had lived in the village of Peyrane during 1950 and 1951, and he reports on changes which have taken place by the end of the fifties, and again by 1972. The account is rather impressionistic, and not based on systematic interviews, yet his comments on changes in living standards and lifestyles, and the changed attitudes of the villagers towards these by the end of the sixties, though rather general, are sharply observed:

I now realise why the noon apéritif group has disappeared: Peyrane has ceased to be a tight little community in which such a group plays an essential role. The Peyranais no longer feel themselves to be—in fact no longer are—a unit functioning as autonomously as possible in defence against the Outside World; they have become an integral part of the world they once staunchly resisted.[3]

Much more systematic evidence is available in the survey conducted in 1965 by a team of researchers under the direction of the celebrated sociologist Edgar Morin in the small Brittany community of Plodémet (population 3,700, spread out over the countryside, with a small historic centre, or *bourg*). As an agricultural region, Brittany was in decline: the growth areas were in transport, manufacture of domestic gadgets, and food production. The whole of the countryside, the report said, 'was undergoing a metamorphosis just when we were carrying out our survey'.

> The microcosm of Plodémet is in motion. The village, the countryside are putting on a new skin. Hamlets are dying. Houses for the retired and for holidaymakers are multiplying.[4]

New roads were being built, and the very landscape itself was physically altering as hills were flattened for motorways and the old *chemins creux* (farm lanes below surface level) were obliterated. A crucial section of the study reported on 'The Revolution in Domestic Conveniences and the Spirit of Consumerism'. The first wave of the acquisition of basic conveniences had occurred between 1950 and 1962. Now, interior toilets, showers, sometimes even baths were being installed; people were buying refrigerators and washing-machines. The first television set arrived in 1962; by 1965 there were 221 (in a total of 1,000 households).

> Rural houses began to imitate the layout of bourgeois houses (kitchen-living room, dining room for special occasions, bedrooms). In the *bourg* and even in the countryside, the style of furnishing changed, became more varied; side by side with the search for comfort went the search for decoration and ornamentation.[5]

People were becoming less stingy in their use of domestic resources, no longer waiting for almost complete darkness before putting on lights; no longer waiting for the depths of winter before turning on radiators.

The survey noted that the village *charcutier* was altering his wares: instead of the humbler meat products, he was making his own *pâté*, selling dairy products, factory-made *charcuterie*, and—sign of the times—chickens, roasted on an electric spit. He had plans to provide ready-cooked gastronomic dishes *(plats cuisinés)* for summer visitors. Domestic diets were becoming richer and more varied. Gruel disappeared; pancakes, traditionally the staple of the poor, came back, but with elaborate fillings, as a delicacy; potatoes were still a basic item, but people began to eat steaks, vegetables, desserts, and even cheeses (formerly, under an ancient Breton culinary taboo, considered too disgusting to eat). Italian ravioli and packaged paella began to make their appearance at the grocers. Dietary concerns (largely among women) and gastronomic expectations (largely among men) emerged. Among young people the gamut of drinks expanded (beer, fizzy drinks, Muscadet, whisky, aperitifs) just as alcoholism declined.

The strongest indications of personal emancipation springing from material change and challenges to ancient custom (such as the cheese taboo) came in matters of self-presentation:

> The traditional neglect of both personal dress during the working week is being replaced by daily preoccupation with hygiene, health, and fastidiousness in dress. While the grand old man Tota Poulhan boasted of the robustness of his teeth, completely black and never sullied by toothpaste (despite the efforts of a hospital sister when Toto found himself confined to a hospital bed), care of the teeth, the feet, the nails, and the use of shampoo became the norm among young people. Women dropped the old style of dressing in favour of a variety of outfits (frocks, suits, trousers), began using make-up and other beauty products, and visited the hair stylist. Men too, though more slowly, moved in the direction of variety and fashion.[6]

Although Morin declared that Plodémet had 'taken the route to bungaloid civilization', Plodémet remained unshakeably French and Breton, as Peyrane remained French and Vauclusean, and Bonagente southern Italian. Affluence, consumerism, and international exchange broadened choices. In 1964 Plodémet's Café des Droits de l'Homme installed its first espresso coffee-machine (bought secondhand). About a dozen well-off families set the standards in changing preferences and expanding choices. The trend-setters were not youth, but the married under-forties. Morin described the top families:

> they have maids, they make use of and decorate their reception room, they are trying to develop the correct style of dressing, of manners, of dealing with other people; some are collectors (most often of antique furniture, but also of paintings, old pistols, rare stones in the case of Dr Lévi, old mechanical gadgets in the case of the dentist).[7]

This may not, at first sight, suggest much in the way of loosening of conventions: for these partic-ular people, however, these are new lifestyles, and the correct behaviour was derived from newspapers, periodicals, and magazines, particularly the journal *L'Express,* and from television, rather than from tradition and family. At the same time, what Morin calls an 'agricultural meta-morphosis' was taking place: the old peasantry was being replaced by the farmer/technicians, whose lifestyles were also affected strongly by the new consumerism. Once again he picks out young married couples, and above all young women, as the principal agents of change—though the focus on marriage and consumer goods indicates that rural France is some distance from the America of Betty Friedan:

> The personality of the countrywoman is undergoing a mutation.... It is the young women who profit from the new freedom of choice. While the boys above all desire a nice little

woman, pleasant and serious, the girls impose certain conditions, demanding a combination of a loving disposition, a step up the social ladder, recognition of their domestic sovereignty, and a comfortable home.[8]

In this (in general) admirably objective social survey, Morin's own sentiments do at times come through as dated and sentimental in a peculiarly French way. But what he says is based on a large number of genuine interviews. Clearly a new aspiration on the part of women, supported by their menfolk, is in itself an important phenomenon. What is critical is the convergence of consumer desire, growing affluence, and the technological progress which yielded the domestic conveniences. Quite early in the book Morin quotes two conversations, the first with an oldish man: ' "By comparison with the old days? There has been change, certainly." "What change?" "From everything to everything... In everything." ' A 40-year-old photographer put it this way: 'There are heaps of things which have changed. What about young people, for example, and motorcars, enormously. Oh, I don't know what has changed, oh, everything has changed!'

It may be noted that in 1965 some people were expressing aspirations for, and probably expectation of, sharp improvement in living standards, rather than giving a factual statement that such change had already arrived. Across the country living conditions continued to get better but, almost inevitably, the pace of change slackened. As we have seen, the Gaullist regime did strive consciously to keep wages down; perhaps, too, there is a grudging quality in the French, not to be found, say, among most Italians. Anyway, in a survey at the end of the decade 44 per cent reckoned that they were better off than five years previously, while as many as 32 per cent thought they were worse off (this compares with a figure of 15 per cent in Italy saying they were worse off[9]). This same survey in *L'Express* (21–8 September 1968) produced a number of individual family biographies. M. Robert B. was an agricultural worker, aged 42, with a wife Simone, aged 38, and six children. He is paid Fr.950 a month for twelve months, with double pay in one month and certain bonuses. To supplement the family income his wife does a little outside housework. In total, including family allowances, the household has an income of about Fr.1,900 per month. Electricity, being paid for by the farmer who owns the house, is free, and there is no rent.

> In the kitchen there is a veritable arsenal of modern machines: an electric waffle iron, an electric mixer, coffee mill, and mincer, a 250-litre refrigerator, a butane gas cooker, and a washing machine. All bought on credit. In the rest of the house, emptiness, with the exception of a transistor radio. Their pride is their car, a 4L also on credit. 'It's the prosperity, and us, we want to catch a little of it. By working hard, we have now got there.'

The survey found that life was less easy for a city wage-earner, M. Pierre M., aged 45, an employee in a food-processing factory in a Paris suburb. He has three sons, and earns Fr.499.40 a fortnight. Monique, his wife, does two hours a day of house-cleaning to augment their income. Their total, per month, is Fr.1,365.49.

> They find it tough. They live in a three-room unfurnished flat, without a bathroom, in a

very old building, paying Fr.100 a month (the three boys all have to sleep in the one room). They have a refrigerator, electric cooker, and television. 'We have bought everything on credit. We have a basic principle: when the instalments on one gadget are paid off, we immediately buy another one.' She makes some clothes herself; clothes are passed from boy to boy (they are aged 15, 13, and 9). She says: 'On Sundays, from time to time, the boys go to the pictures. Us, we go for a walk, play cards with neighbours. Or else my husband stays at home doing odd jobs about the house.' Holidays are with a cousin in a little village in the Sarthe. 'It's not the seaside, but the three boys enjoy themselves.' M. M. reckons he's better off than he was ten years ago, though conscious of rising prices.

According to the survey, it was white-collar workers who were most discontented. M. Pierre G., son of an agricultural worker, had risen to the position of salaried executive in a commercial firm, earns Fr.2,800 a month, with Fr.1,000 for the thirteenth month, which, with family allowances for his two children aged 7 and 2, rises to about Fr.3,150 a month. He has a four-room fourth-floor flat without lift, in the outer suburbs of Paris. He has a week's holiday at Easter, which he spends at home, and four weeks in the summer, when he books a holiday away from home. They have a refrigerator, a cooker (with four burners, the latest model), a washing-machine, a rotisserie, a camera, a television, a three-band transistor radio, a record-player, thirty-odd records, 100-odd books. Madame G. gave up work as a secretary on the birth of her second child, but would like to take up part-time work 'in order not just to go on dreaming about the luxury world presented in the women's magazines'. They are 'profoundly dissatisfied'. M. Patrice D., aged 30, is an industrial designer; his wife, 28, is a secretary in a record company. They live at Bois-Colombes, near Paris, have one 4-year-old child. M. D. gets Fr.1,900 per month over thirteen months, and a holiday bonus of Fr.1,100. She gets Fr.1,555 over thirteen months, and a holiday bonus of Fr.900. This gives them a total of Fr.3,818 per month. They run a Simca 500—'it is beyond our means, but it is our only luxury'. Their television has been bought on credit. They have, the survey continues, 'a battery of modern conveniences, plus a record player, an ordinary camera and a film camera, a hair-dryer, and a radio in the car. But she dreams of a bigger apartment, holidays away from relatives, better clothes, fine books.' She believes that, because of rising prices, their living standard is going down. For the final interview, the survey again slipped a little down the social scale, to Claude and Geneviève S.: aged 32, he is an employee in a big Paris shop, earning Fr.1,050 per month. They have three children. She is 28 and, apart from looking after her own children, she carries out the French version of babysitting by taking in other people's children in her own flat after dinner twice a week. With family allowances, they make Fr.1,530 a month. Half of this goes on food; they have a small refrigerator, a secondhand television, and no car. Mme S. dreams of having a washing-machine.

The growth in the possession of consumer goods, and the manner in which these very quickly come to be accepted as basics, is very clear. In a general trend throughout the Western countries, French characteristics continue to stick out: generally the French were worse off for household gadgets, as well as for baths and showers, than the inhabitants of other West European countries; but the French ate much better than anyone else (with the French worker spending 43 per cent of his income on food); the French also smoked a lot, but were surpassed in this by the Italians. *L'Express* commented: 'The French destroy themselves with their forks. And also with their nerves.' Even at the end of 1967 only 53.5 per cent of French households had television.

Individual cases provide much illumination, but to be sure that we have a correct general picture, it is necessary to consider the global statistics. Economic historian Jean Fourastié gives the figures for expenditure on a considerable variety of consumer goods and services (radios, television sets, gramophones, still and film cameras; materials for sport, camping, hunting, and fishing; theatre and cinema tickets, radio and television licences; newspapers, reviews, and books; games, toys, musical instruments—see Table 8.1). Again the overall picture is abundantly clear. Whatever minor grievances people might have, the evidence is of a continuingly wider acquisition of consumer goods of all sorts, and of higher expenditures on entertainment and leisure, of, one could say, an easier and fuller life. Working-class percentages of expenditure swung away (though not overwhelmingly so!) from basic foods, and also clothing, to other items.[10]

**Table 8.1** *Expenditure on consumer goods*

| Year | Millions of francs at current values | Millions of francs at 1974 values | Index of volume of consumer goods and services |
|------|------|------|------|
| 1949 | 3,623 | 13.1 | 100 |
| 1959 | 11,524 | 31.2 | 166.6 |
| 1970 | 38,834 | 47.6 | 363.5 |
| 1974 | 66,178 | 66.2 | 504.1 |

*Source:* Jean Fourastié, *Les Trente glorieuses* (Paris, 1979), 125.

It is change both in working-class occupations and attitudes and in the remoter rural areas that I want to stress. As a survey carried out in 1965 demonstrated, levels of optimism were much higher among those in 'modern' industries than among those in traditional industries.[11] In her autobiography, published in 1974, Thérèse Jolly brings out the continuing hardships endured by sheep farmers. But although she is herself only 36 she is clear that her children get an infinitely better education than her generation did. And twice she insists on what an enormous boon to her television is.[12]

For the many, including the many in the more backward parts of France and Italy, the sun of affluence shone as never before during the High Sixties. It is proper to start with that sunshine. But we get a misleading weather map if we do not remind ourselves that even, and indeed particularly, in the richest of our four countries, it was in certain areas a case of showers as much as sunshine.

### Poverty in the United States

Without doubt, the War on Poverty was inspired by good intentions. Without doubt, a good deal of good was accomplished. Without doubt also, a good deal of money was squandered, and the allocation and distribution of funds became arenas for political ambition and corrupt practice. By the end of the decade the policies associated with the War on Poverty were being heavily criticized, and later investigations were critical of the lack of precision and pragmatism, particularly in the American programmes but also in welfare programmes elsewhere: an authoritative survey of nine Western countries published in 1974 reported: 'well-meaning hope has been more instrumental than critical analysis in the process of policy formulation; and, while policies have had positive results, there is general agreement that these results appear small in relation to policy objectives.'[13] Poverty was most obvious among blacks in the South and, increasingly, among blacks in the urban ghettos: it was an achievement both of private investigations in the sixties and of government agencies that the facts were brought to the attention of a wider public. Another notable pool of misery, given some prominence in the sixties, was that of the Mexican agricultural workers *(braceros)* in California. And over the sixties the plight of Puerto Ricans, mostly living in the big cities, became increasingly evident. But there were also poor whites, scraping a living, or not, in the remoter parts, mainly along the borders between North and South. Some commentators felt that the definition of poverty might be too low: overall, living standards did rise for most people as the economy continued to expand throughout the sixties, but it seemed to remain a basic fact of life that the poorest 20 per cent in America earned a consistent 5 per cent of the total income.[14] Referring to the objectives of the Economic Opportunities Act of 1964, another, massive survey, confined to American families over the years 1968–72, remarked that 'few people would now claim that the progress in realization of the goal has been rapid', continuing: 'Humans and their institutions and social systems are not simple and are far from being understood well enough to make the intent to eliminate poverty equivalent to the reduction of poverty.'[15] First I intend to look at black poverty, both its nature and attitudes towards it, then at conditions among the Mexican *braceros*, and finally at the poor whites. Then I shall examine some specific examples of how the poverty programmes and the policies of the Office of Economic Opportunity went wrong.

According to federal statistics, Tunica County in northern Mississippi was the most poverty-stricken county in the entire United States. It offers an interesting case study of changing attitudes over the High Sixties, though only to a lesser degree of changing material conditions. On 30 November 1964 the Memphis *Press-Scimitar* ran a folksy survey of Tunica. The article is so redolent of continuing white refusal to face the realities of black poverty, of continuing white prejudices about the happy fecklessness of blacks, of white complacency over their own generosity, and of white denial of any possible white guilt, that it deserves extensive quotation: it would be funny were it not so tragic. A separate panel in the middle of the first page establishes the down-home tone of local patriotism:

> Tunica County has some of the Mid-south's best fishing. Fishing is a casual thing for many residents of the county, and it's easy to catch a mess of fish to eat. Hunting is a major sport and game graces many tables.

The article itself largely takes the form of individual pen portraits interspersed with brief quotations:

335

Bill McClintock is a young planter who operates a big plantation successfully. He uses machinery and doesn't need many workers. He said he has 25 houses on his plantation and occupants of 23 of them live rent free. 'I'm supposed to get rent from two of the houses,' McClintock said. 'But I never collect it. So all of them live rent-free.'

There is then a cross heading reading, 'Elderly man says he lives well'.

Sidney Dye lives in one of McClintock's houses. He is an elderly Negro man who does some work, said he lives well. He lives in the same cabin with Beatrice Crawford, a friend who has been a cook for the McClintock's [sic] for many years and gets paid.

McClintock came by the house and picked up Dye in his truck to go duck hunting. Dye rowed the boat and got paid for it.

The perceived need to bring out that a black cook actually got paid for her cooking, and that her live-in lover (this bit is deliberately featured as an indirect commentary on casual black morality) got money for rowing a boat for his boss, provides rich unwitting testimony to uneasy and slightly aggressive white self-justification.

Next comes an interview with a former planter, now president of Tunica County Bank. This planter turned banker declared that it was a 'misconception' that mechanization had put 'Negroes' out of work: 'labor' left first, he maintained in a somewhat eccentric reading of recent economic history, thus forcing the farmers to mechanize. The following cross-heading makes the plaintive complaint, 'Couldn't Find Wood Splitters'. This little section featured the tribulations of the white Phillips couple, publishers of the local paper, *The Tunica Times Democrat,* in building themselves a new home:

Mrs. Phillips said they cut down a pecan tree and have been wanting the wood split up for firewood for the new home. She said they have tried for 8 weeks to get someone to split the wood at $1 an hour. No takers.

The article continued:

Many welfare checks are cashed at the stores. Negroes spend money as they get it... Perry said a couple of Negroes have savings accounts but they are the exceptions. One planter told of a Negro tenant who cleared $5,000 after selling up. He said three weeks later the tenant was back to borrow money. He had bought a car, tv set and other things and all the money was gone.

Special tv antennas to pick up Memphis stations can be seen on top of many cabins in the cotton. Also, big cars are parked in front of many of the shacks. Many Negroes have garden patches and their own livestock for meat.

The next cross heading is: '6,000 Leave in about 20 Years':

It's true that many Negroes, an estimated 6,000 in about 20 years, have left Tunica County, while the white population has increased slightly.

Towards the end the article turns towards the question of race relations: the protests and demonstrations discussed in Chapter 5 might never have happened.

> Tunica has had no racial strife and is still segregated. Some restaurants have special rooms for Negroes. There have been no churches burned in the county and there are a number of new-looking churches on plantations, usually built with white aid. White and Negro residents are proud of the two Negro schools. The Rosa Foot school has 2,805 students and is newer and larger than the white high school. The Negro school includes all 12 grades and several additions have been made... Friday was homecoming day, with Rosa Foot High playing Hernando in football. There was a fine parade in downtown Tunica, enjoyed by whites and Negroes alike. There were two bands, the Rosa Foot, and the Mount Bayou, and numerous pretty floats. White police handled traffic for the Negro parade...

Shortly there is a further cross heading, 'Little Recreation for Whites':

> Tunica County has little in the way of recreation for whites, no country club or golf course. Some of the well-to-do belong to the Memphis Country Club and other clubs. From the county seat here, it's 40 miles to Memphis on straight but narrow Highway 6.
>
> There are honky-tonks for Negroes and as long as they behave the law doesn't bother them. Beer is legal. There are the usual crap games. There is little serious crime.

That the availability to blacks of beer in their own segregated honky-tonks was considered worthy of note is in itself worthy of note; the whole question of liberation, drink, and the South will be discussed shortly.

The article ends with a reference to the unwillingness of white planters to say how much they are earning, together with a proud affirmation:

> The well-to-do planters in this country generally don't like to say how many acres they have. They are courteous but some didn't want to be quoted. But everybody I met, white and Negro alike, says that Tunica County is not the nation's poorest. In fact, they don't believe they are poor at all.

Five years later very different attitudes are apparent both in a series of articles on poverty by high-quality professional journalist Barney DuBois in the other Memphis paper, the *Commercial Appeal,* and in the extensive correspondence which ran in the letter columns throughout the series. The third article (29 July 1969) examined rural poverty, reporting a Citizen's Board of Enquiry into hunger and malnutrition in the United States as recording that at least forty-five counties in the mid-South had families living in poverty, that is to say having less than $3,500 a year for a family of four. The director of emergency food and medical services in Mississippi County, Arkansas, under the office of Equal Opportunities, was quoted as saying: 'When I taught school last year, children would come to school so hungry they vomited water.' He continued:

> Poverty workers have found one epidemic in at least three sections of the county, and if you don't do something about the cause, outdoor toilets, then medical treatment is no good.
>
> Other medical problems in rural areas result from the massive infestation of poorly kept tenement buildings by insects, rats and even weevils.

In some houses, the report continued, it is impossible to store food because of the competition for it 'between human and non human residents of the building'. There was a strong emphasis in the articles on the plight of those who had migrated from the country areas to the slums of Memphis. The fourth article (30 July 1969) was headed by a photograph of a black child lying on a bench, with a bottle of water beside his head; the caption read: 'Sometimes, A Bottle of Water is "Lunch" for the Poor.' The article itself was titled: 'Improper Diet Saps Away Poor's Health'. The article supplies graphic personal detail; there is also evidence of the poverty programme (operating, however, in an extremely haphazard way) having some effect, though scarcely enough:

> In early 1968 Nedom Harris and his family decided Coldwater Miss. was no longer to their liking. So they moved to Memphis. No easy choice for 20 people. But they managed it and found a place to live—at 275 Gayoso. Two rooms.
>
> The next step was to find work, which would provide money, with which to buy food. Twenty people eat a lot. Only one found work, however, Jimmy Harris, 19, fourth-grade dropout, got a job as a machine shop laborer at $1.60 an hour. You can't feed 20 people in Memphis on $1.60 an hour especially when the first $21.50 each month is for rent, and the next $10 to $20 is for utilities, twice that in winter. And car-fare, too. The Nedom Harris family went hungry. sometimes one meal a day, sometimes none. Never any milk. Never any juice. Mostly fatback and cereal.
>
> Besides Jimmy, the worker, the rest of the people in Nedom Harris' family are women and children. Mostly children. Some babies. Mr. Harris, almost 80, was almost a baby himself. 'I've been pretty hungry to be working,' Jimmy says. 'But I been hungrier not working. Leaving out in the morning time and wouldn't hardly make it back. It hurt best at the evening when you get back. That's when it hurt hard', says Jimmy. If you didn't have no money, you didn't eat.
>
> The family was discovered by a worker for Memphis Area Project-South, who immediately placed the family on the food supplement program of MAP-South and St. Jude Children's Research Hospital. Mrs. Harris was helped to apply for Aid for Dependent Children. She now gets $105 monthly. The program has helped, but the family occasionally goes hungry.

Malnutrition was a fundamental problem. Under the cumbersome local operation of federal legislation, resources were allocated through the MAP-South organization, the acronym standing for Memphis Area Project, with a food supplement programme being operated by the St Jude Children's Research Hospital; the other main resource was the Federal Food Stamp Program. There is a wealth of information and implication in the second quotation from the article whose very episodic character mirrors the muddled, hit-and-miss (mostly miss) nature of the poverty programmes; Dr Walters and his like are subaltern members of the great army representing liberal compassion and measured judgement.

Dr Thomas Walters of St Jude has said that of the poverty children he has studied in Memphis, more than half have had mild or moderate forms of anaemia. Nearly half have been below weight and height norms. Almost two in every 10 have had smaller than normal head circumferences, sometimes a sign of at least mild mental retardation. More than 80 percent have had tooth decay, and another 37 percent have had abscessed teeth.

It is documented that poor people live on a low protein, high carbohydrate, low iron, marginal vitamin intake. Malnutrition in Memphis is a socio-economic problem, says Dr Walters.

I don't know what the hell these statistics are for. We can't survey them any more than we've already done. If there's one malnourished baby, there's something wrong. If there's more than one, there's just that much more wrong.

He says the suburban mother would be vitally concerned if one of her children was greater than two standard deviations off the norms in height or weight. She'd be shocked, he says, if her child's head circumference were small, or if he had a mild degree of anaemia.

The 29 July article on rural poverty concentrated on Mississippi County, Arkansas, Fayette County, Tennessee, and that familiar territory, Tunica County, Mississippi. A feature of the series was the collection of well-composed and striking photographs; Tunica County was represented by a photograph of the old stove which was the only means of heating and cooking in one of the dilapidated cabins inhabited by blacks—this was to feature in the subsequent controversy in the letters columns. Much of the concern was with the population pouring from these rural areas into the south Memphis ghetto. Able-bodied workers continued on further north towards St Louis and Chicago, dumping their dependants in Memphis. A senior social worker for Memphis Area Project South, himself black, commented on the influx: 'You can see the old clunkers on the expressways on Sunday, and they're full of people, usually nine or ten. Well, them people ain't out for no Sunday drive like you are. They're moving to Memphis.' The 'tragedy', as he put it, is that:

In Mississippi, or Arkansas, they understood the rules. They knew the rules and could handle them, at least a little bit. But they come here, and it requires a degree of sophistication they just lack. When you come to an urban community, the rules change. But they

339

come in here and they can't even read the street signs, or bus signs, or fill out applications or follow written instructions. They come here and get lost.

The series aroused so much interest that it was reprinted in pamphlet form. From the selection of letters published on 17 August 1969 it is clear that consciences were aroused; however, there were also hostile reactions. One reader claimed that the 'Tunica stove' had on it a cooking pot of high quality which, the letter continued, exposed the owners of the stove as being much more affluent than they were pretending. It is not surprising that the MAP-South and St Jude's Hospital programme received no funds from the city of Memphis. However, the voice of the less bigoted younger generation of whites comes through strongly in a letter from a 24-year-old white former Mississippi farm boy, also published on 23 August:

> My color earned more and my money let me into places my black brother wasn't allowed. It doesn't take many instances of this to force a black man to make the choice between becoming a black radical or a humble good Nigger. And now some whites have the gall to criticise both the young black radical for possessing great pride and the older humble black for his lack of pride.

Out of such attitudes a new multiculturalism was to be slowly built.

Memphis had one of the biggest and most rapidly expanding medical complexes in the entire United States; but the system, dominated by three major private general-care hospitals with denominational affiliations, Baptist, Methodist, and Catholic (St Joseph), were concerned almost entirely with the privileged and did nothing for the region's slum-dwellers. Characteristic of the changing mood towards the end of the decade—and quite bravely, given that, as the newspaper itself put it, the health industry was one of Memphis's biggest—the *Commercial Appeal* on 16 November 1969 published an article entitled 'The Sick Giant'. Despite their high status, this article pointed out, less than 1 per cent of the cases handled by these hospitals concerned life-threatening conditions. Boldly, the need was identified for 'Neighborhood health centers'. The article went to the heart of the harsh economic truth for the local poor:

> When a person is run over by a truck or has a heart attack, he doesn't care where he is taken, just so he gets help. If he's fortunate, insurance will keep him from going bankrupt. Such is not the case with the poor. Surprisingly enough a large number of people of the poverty level admitted to city hospitals have some insurance, this is a small policy that pays maybe $10 of an $80 bill.

The overcrowded, understaffed, and inadequately equipped public hospitals in Memphis were run by the University of Tennessee Medical School. The scandalous contrast between affluence and poverty was addressed by the local press in late 1967:[16] 'Why in 1967—in an era which sees the majority of the population insisting on good medical care as a right and not a luxury—does such a situation exist?' Basically, the answer was: a shortage of $20 million. One hundred and five University of Tennessee physicians spent about 20 per cent of their time on public cases; for patients the waiting time was appalling:

> Mrs Patty Cooper of 788 King Alley was slumped in a chair in the admission room. Her 2-year-old was climbing around on her lap and pulling on her shoulders. Her 4-year-old was whimpering to go home and her 8-year-old was fidgeting restlessly. It was 1 p.m. She and the children had been going back and forth through the hospital red tape since 9 a.m. The children had eaten all of the sandwiches she had packed, and drunk all of the vacuum bottle milk and were getting hungry. 'I've got a half of a sandwich left, I don't know what I'm going to do with them if I have to wait much longer', she sighed.

Clearly the fault did not lie with the dean of the medical school, who sympathetically expounded the deficiencies of the system he had to run, and deplored the overcrowded wards: 'There's no room there for human dignity. It's awful.' The reporter described the maternity ward as looking 'like a dungeon': most women were kept in for only twenty-four hours after delivery, as against seventy-two hours in private hospitals.

There was no question, of course, of treatment, however inadequate, being free. Patients complained of hospitals hounding them for money, getting court orders for direct deductions from pay packets, and putting matters in the hands of collection agencies (which themselves deducted 40 per cent from whatever was collected). 'We try not to garnish [i.e. go to court for direct deductions],' the hospital superintendent told the reporter. 'But we send people bills and they go a year without acknowledging them and we have to do something. It is better for us if they will call our financial counsellors and work out some sort of instalment plan.'

Compared with the great swathes of destitution among blacks in the South, the problem of the almost limitless supply of desperate Mexican labour, leading to the shameless exploitation of both the *braceros* and white American farm workers, was a fairly specific and well-defined problem. It was featured strongly by the growing radical movements in California, some of whose members saw in such downtrodden labour a potentially revolutionary force,[17] and it offers an interesting study of the interaction between different protest movements. Not much was done for starving Mexicans, the numbers of them securing employment in fact dropping sharply, from 112,000 in 1964 to 8,700 in 1966—wise commentators pointed out that the real requirement was for economic aid direct to Mexico. The main federal initiative came in the form of enforcement of a Department of Labor ruling that before a foreign worker could be employed, an American one must be offered $1.60 an hour. Civil rights groups, church organizations, SDS, and the Los Angeles branch of SNCC came together with the National Farm Workers' Association (the Mexican workers' organization created in 1963 largely through the heroic efforts of César Chavez) to organize national boycotts of the major producers such as Delano (grapes) and Schenley (tinned fruit, wines), and to arrange a massive march on the state capital, Sacramento, in March 1966.

There was no possibility of an insurrection, though, as usual, the police did their best, attacking the marchers throughout with extremes of brutality. On 7 April Schenley and the other companies recognized the National Farm Workers' Association, with the result that the national boycott was called off. In fact, 1966 was the year of critical change in the matter of the abuse of farm workers by the big companies. Protests and violence continued, but the battle for public opinion was being won. On 15 July 1970 *El Maleriado* ('the voice of the farm worker') reported that chain-stores in the big cities were now carrying only union-approved grapes.

The *Commercial Appeal* 1969 series on poverty had featured a photograph of a white mother and son, with the caption: 'When You Find Listless Children, You Find Hunger' (31 July 1969). Towards the end of the sixties more and more attention was directed towards poor whites. Actually, when President Johnson set out on his 'poverty tour' in April and May 1964, he did visit a number of notorious poor white areas, with his first visit being to unemployed whites in South Bend, Indiana, where the Studebaker factory had closed down the previous December, and then on to Cumberland, Maryland. He also visited East Kentucky, reputed to be 'the poorest all-white area in the world, with a per capita income in 1959 of $300 per annum, and 70% of the 10,000 population unemployed'.[18] Both in the county seat, Inez (pop. 600), and in the other main community, Worfield (pop. 400), running water was only being installed in 1969. Visiting Inez in April 1964, the president had his conversation with one local fully reported:

> Tom Fletcher told the President how he had quit school in the third grade. He grew up working in a sawmill, but no longer has a regular job. He worked four days in a sawmill last month at the rate of $4 a day. When he isn't working, he said, he scratches for coal from the surface of the mountains around his home. He earned about $400 last year.
>
> 'How do you live?' the President asked. Fletcher said the family 'exists' on distribution of surplus foods. Like their father, Fletcher's two eldest children, one eight and one seven, dropped out of school long ago. Some of the other six children are in school and some are pre-school age.[19]

LBJ was reported as expressing pity, and offering this exhortation: 'Now remember, I want you to keep these kids in school.' The President then, in what was featured as 'a tour of the front lines of his war against poverty campaign', proceeded to West Virginia.

A Scripts-Howard syndicated item of 9 April 1964 described East Kentucky as 'the place where the war on poverty will be won or lost'.

> The creek is a sullen cauldron of filth. Here in Eastern Kentucky trucks haul coal, not refuse. The traditional means of disposing of mine camp waste is to throw it into the nearest waterway. But the household rubbish that chokes Marrowbone Creek is nothing to the tons of spoil from the strip mines that have profaned it. The creek is a noisome sewer—but it is wholly appropriate to the community it serves.
>
> Hellier once was a booming community. It had a bank and a city hall and a brick high school. The city hall is now a gutted ruin. Marrowbone Valley doesn't have enough people or enough money even to support a decent complement of city hall drones. The bank is a bank no longer. It is a dwelling now, occupied by a couple who share it with a

huge vault they have never been able to open.[20]

In September 1968 the Memphis *Press-Scimitar* ran a series on 'The White Face of Poverty'. The conclusion in the first article (16 September) was that most towns and cities had areas, usually near factory complexes, where low-income whites congregated. Washington Butler, the black executive director of the Memphis and Shelby County War on Poverty Committee, expressed the view that the 'indicators of poverty are general and cross racial lines', with the 'real symptoms' not being racial but 'things like low income, poor health, low level of education, low employability, female heads of households, the elderly in many cases'. However, he agreed, black poverty was much more visible than white.

The aggregate statistics I cited in Chapter 6 demonstrated that poverty did diminish in the United States in the second half of the 1960s, and the newspaper reports I have been quoting, while clearly indicating the continuance of appalling conditions, also show changes in the attitudes of some (though by no means all) middle-class whites. Still, there is no escaping the fact that the War on Poverty was nothing like the success its progenitors had hoped: too little, too fragmented, too tied in with politics, both of the conventional kind and of the new radical activist kind. A syndicated column, *Your Money's Worth*, in late 1964 provided an informed commentary on the War on Poverty—the writer (5 November 1964) told how she 'telephoned a Washington official to ask who could outline for me the full range of federal programmes now under way to combat poverty and its causes'.

More than two hours, at least a half-dozen federal agencies and 20 bureaucrats later, I gave up in disgust—not much wiser than when I had placed the first call. This incident dramatizes one vital question about our national war on poverty: who is running the show? It also raises a more serious question: How can we ultimately win the poverty war if we allow it to remain a string of disconnected skirmishes and departmental battles?[21]

The insistence that the poor themselves should be involved in administering the poverty programmes was a fine tribute to American democratic idealism, but paid little heed to the reality of alienation and hopelessness in the slums, while playing straight into the hands of politicians and vote-collectors. Another syndicated columnist reporting from Washington on 7 May 1966 declared: 'Efforts to get poor people to vote for their representatives on local poverty boards so far have been a colossal flop.' In yet another syndicated column from Washington it was reported that the head of the neighbourhood organization in the University of Chicago area had charged that Chicago mayor Richard D. Daley's anti-poverty committee 'reads like the fund-raising list of the Democratic party... six ward committee men, 31 tied to city hall. Not one person living in the poverty belt', adding, 'in Chicago, there is no war on poverty. There is only more of the ancient, galling war against the poor.' Adam Clayton Powell was a notorious black politician, Mayor Daley a notorious right-wing Democratic machine politician.

In February 1968 the Memphis *Press-Scimitar* ran an eight-part series on 'The State of Welfare'.

The article of 12 February concentrated on the second of the two biggest state programmes, Aid to Families with Dependent Children, ADC (the largest programme was Old Age Aid). ADC was funded to the extent of 75 per cent by the federal government, 20 per cent by the state, and 5 per cent by the local government. To secure benefit, mothers had to be at least 21; thus, so the article reported, a 19-year-old mother had to resort to prostitution. Birth-control equipment was made available—quite enlightened for Memphis—but only after the birth of the first child—not quite so enlightened. The second article (13 February) explained that the benefit rates ran from $90 a month for one child, to $150 a month for five children; no further supplementation was paid beyond the fifth child. Hence the sad plight of Mrs Annie Davis and her eleven children:

> They get $150 a month plus some money the mother earns at work. On Monday of last week her children—ranging in age from two to sixteen—ate rice for breakfast. They ate rice Tuesday, Wednesday and Thursday. Friday's breakfast was canned mackerel (13 cents a can)—and rice. For dinner they generally have more rice and beans, or biscuits and smoked jowl, or rice with margarine—a treat—and more mackerel. They seldom have eggs and rarely have fruit juice and milk…
>
> Mrs Davis can make up to the state's $422 a month before any money is deducted from her public assistance check. She works three days a week as a domestic, having a free child-care arrangement with another mother, who works the days Mrs Davis keeps her children.

A major problem in a city like Memphis was the tardiness in actually getting any poverty projects going. On 16 August the *Press-Scimitar* reported that the Memphis Area Project-South had begun on 1 January; three days earlier the *Commercial Appeal* had remarked that the War on Poverty seemed 'to be getting going at last', with the appointment of Washington Butler as executive director. This good news was accompanied by a photograph relating to the Summer Youth Achievement Project. The photograph itself was captioned 'Young Work Crews Spruce Up Memphis Public Housing Projects'; the less good news was that every face in the picture is white.

Even leaving out the various charitable organizations which cooperated, overlapped, and competed with the War on Poverty programme, its administration was complex enough. The Memphis programme was responsible to the main War on Poverty federal office in Atlanta, but the immediate authority lay with a committee of local citizens, mainly white, who endeavoured to exercise control over the self-consciously radical black executive director, Washington Butler: there were then specific programmes seeking greater or lesser autonomy for themselves, such as the Memphis Area Project-South and the Neighborhood Organizing Project. By August 1967 two of the black 'aides' working for the Memphis Area Project-South had acquired a reputation with the Citizens' Committee for being radical agitators, and were suspected of having been involved in that summer's bout of rioting. The entire Memphis Area Project-South was supportive of the two men, while Washington Butler was quite happy to support the demand that the men be given a hearing by the Citizens' Committee. But the committee, unsurprisingly, ordered the men removed from the Project-South payroll 'on ground of being identified with organizations whose purposes don't coincide with those of the War on Poverty'.[22] Butler was very much a distinctive late-sixties figure, with his beard, Afro hairstyle, and dashiki (West African-style shirt). Explicit federal policy was that the poor themselves should be actively involved in the poverty programmes; Butler's policies, verging on black consciousness-raising, were not exactly what federal officials had in mind. He found himself under attack both from the Memphis Committee and from the office in Atlanta. Butler probably was not a particularly efficient administrator, but, as a generally sympathetic account in the *Commercial Appeal* put it, bringing us back to the heart of the matter, the War on Poverty agency 'is a nightmarish tangle of agency lines, programs and projects. Sometimes it seems on the verge of strangling on red tape produced by itself and by the federal, city, county and state governments.'

Butler not only had to face opposition from the committee of Memphis citizens and from federal representatives, but found the city's white middle-class clerics resistant when he appealed to them to enlist help from their congregations in the battle against poverty. One Southern Baptist cleric responded that: 'Helping the poverty program is something I'm afraid wouldn't be digested by most people in our congregation. So if we do anything, it would have to be on an individual level' Several clergymen said they would be unable to ask 'such a thing' of their congregations.[23] Tangled administration, conflicting ideologies, indifference and hostility from local white middle-class Christians: perhaps the wonder is that the War on Poverty achieved so much.


## Family and Other Affairs

The reasons for there being happy families and unhappy families or some individuals being happy within the family, and some not, or some marriages lasting and some breaking up, or some individuals making their lives almost entirely outside the family framework, may depend more upon individual genetic make-up, contingency, and personal circumstance than on historical developments. Many forces combined to make the High Sixties a time of aspiration after self-fulfilment, at all levels and in all age groups. Self-fulfilment could mean liberation within the family or liberation outside the family: we have to look at what was happening in the family as well as what was happening to the family. There is a valid broad generalization to be made about a trend, dating back well before the sixties and continuing well beyond them, towards a breakdown of the traditional lifelong marriage; and it may be that in the long view the single most significant identifiable consequence of the developments of the sixties was a substantial contribution to that trend. But for the sixties the starting point is the search for self-fulfilment, with or without the polemics about the evils of repression, remembering that physical constraints (such as the ones I listed at the beginning of Chapter 4), and sometimes ideological ones, meant that self-fulfilment was by no means available to everyone; remembering also that self-fulfilment for one person can mean a destruction of economic and psychological security for another.

Though the new assertiveness and innovativeness of youth at the end of the 1950s was an important factor in change, it is wrong to perceive generational conflict as a simple, autonomous force, or to overstate the significance of youthful actors as agents for change in comparison with the major consumers, young and not-so-young married couples. It is essential also to bear in mind that within the space of a decade toddlers become teenagers, and teenagers may become married couples. Moral attitudes and social etiquette were themselves changing all the time, and changing at different speeds in the different parts of the various countries we are studying. In this section I shall start with young children and their relationships with their parents. I shall then look at teenagers, students, their attitudes and activities, which can be perceived as sometimes autonomous, sometimes within a broad family framework, present or hoped for in the future. There is a clear interaction between changing personal behaviour on the one side and, on the other, the rapidly increasing publicization of personal and sexual issues—in the press, in new kinds of journals and radio and television programmes, in the campaigns of pressure groups on behalf of contraception, divorce, and abortion. The press reported on factual changes in behaviour, and made such changes seem more publicly acceptable. Issues which, to different extents in different places, had been taboo entered the public domain. It is this framework of growing public discussion of matters relating to marriage, family, and sex which takes up the middle part of this section. Finally, I turn to the actual behaviour of adults themselves, inside and outside marriage. Within and across all four countries the patterns are complex: but overall there is one broad configuration characterizing the High Sixties everywhere.

Dr Benjamin Spock's *The Commonsense Book of Baby and Child Care*, the classic advocacy of a relaxed and permissive approach in the upbringing of children, had been published as far back as 1946. The valid simplification might be that, as in so many other areas, the revolution adumbrated during and after the Second World War became universalized in the 1960s—and was certainly a matter commanding much public attention, since Spock himself became a central figure in the American political turmoil of the times, and part of the demonology of the anti-liberal reaction. For concrete evidence of change we have to advance a little beyond babyhood, and we find that change extends from family into school. Laurence Wylie described the change, focusing upon the 5-year-old Dédou Faire he had known in Peyrane in the 1950s, and another Dédou Faire, nephew of the former, whom he encountered in his final survey.

> Twenty years ago the five-year-old Dédou Faire might occasionally have talked back to his mother; he might even have been impudent to another adult, if he were verbally clever—and stayed out of reach of a punishing hand. Fundamentally Dédou expected to obey his elders, however. In the single classroom for two dozen 4-to-6-year olds, the discipline was stern but was such effective training that in the upper classroom one scarcely heard a whisper. This year I saw Dédou's nephew, another Dédou Faire, having a tantrum in the street in front of his house; his mother seemed completely indifferent to what in the past would have been a neighborhood scandal. In school, children now speak more freely, just as at home they take part in adult conversations without being regularly silenced with the traditional 'Mange et tais-toi!'.

Wylie then went on to discuss older children and teenagers:

346

The loss of control is even more obvious with older children, especially with adolescents who in increasing numbers go to the city every day, some to work, some to continue their education. A few parents try desperately—and unhappily—to enforce traditional patterns of authority and hierarchy, but in most families there is acceptance, though tinged perhaps with nostalgia, of the young people's new independence. Village parents may be shocked by their children's involvement with city schoolmates in the Lycée revolts of recent years, but at the same time they rather wonderingly admire the daring of the young in confronting authority.

Wylie perceived that greater tolerance, greater permissiveness, did not necessarily undermine the family, could indeed strengthen it. He noted that parents and teachers were often puzzled and uncertain, but added that 'at home people have learned to tolerate—even to enjoy—a less authoritarian social atmosphere'. He then summed up:

> Despite the evolution in human relations, the families I know in both the provinces and Paris seem more unified than before. The belief in hierarchy has given way to a concern for each individual's will, a mutual respect, a tolerance of differences that I would never have thought possible.[24]

Corroboration aplenty is provided by the many sociological surveys, several of which I cited in Chapter 3. However, the magnificent resource centre the Maison de la Villette has a rich collection of testimony from the working-class families who grew up in the surrounding Porte de la Villette area on the northern fringes of Paris. Lulu, born in December 1943 into a working-class family, herself a social worker by the time of her interview in 1985, picked out the sixties as specially significant *(marquantes)*, and her acquisition at the age of 14 of a moped: 'that gave us absolutely complete freedom and I believe that it was from that moment on that our parents had a great deal more difficulty in keeping control of us.'[25]

Similar things were happening in Britain. In a survey of forty-eight working-class wives from Kentish Town in London and forty-eight middle-class wives from West Hampstead in north London, it emerged that 62 per cent of the middle-class wives felt that they gave their children much greater freedom than their mothers had given them, while 69 per cent of the working-class mothers felt they were bringing up their children differently from the way in which they had been brought up, which in 80 per cent of cases meant 'less restriction and more understanding'. Some of the working-class wives drew attention to the ways in which they were more relaxed than their parents:

> 'My parents were always on at me. In fact my father used to really knock me about. I certainly hope not to be like that,' said the wife of a sheet-metal worker. 'My Dad was a really hard man,' said a labourer's wife, 'There was no affection in him. We are not like that at all.' 'My Mum was out all the time,' said a bus driver's wife. 'I know she had to but she never seemed to be thinking of me. I really concentrate on my children.'[26]

The middle-class wives were satisfied that their housing was adequate to the needs of their children, and that there were suitable places for their children to play; the working-class wives were less happy, particularly about places to play.

Later, in Britain in particular but also in the United States, evidence of falling educational standards was to lead to attacks on the alleged introduction of 'progressive' (that is, undisciplined, 'child-centred', and ineffectual) education in the sixties. It is true, as we shall see in Chapter 10, that education's own form of creative extremism was vigorously argued for in the later sixties, less true that it was put very extensively into practice.

For older children, naturally, much attention in all countries tended to focus on sexual behaviour. However, the distinguished journalist and intellectual Evelyne Sullerot, in collaboration with two other women journalists, towards the end of the decade carried out a fascinating survey into the career aspirations of some of the 15–18-year-old readers of the monthly magazine *Christiane*.[27] Marie-Claude, aged 15 and at school in the west of France, said that she definitely intended to take a job as an adult 'because that would enable me to meet other people exercising a profession'. She would stop working once she had more than two children. Once the children were grown up, she would want herself to begin studying again. She said that she had consulted her mother (clear evidence, here, of close family ties), who had expressed her own view that a woman with children must remain at home, because the children depend on her for their education. Fernande, a chemistry student in Paris, said that she would have no wish at all to give up a job which she herself had chosen and liked, even for the sake of a husband and children. A woman, she insisted, has a right to a life outside of the home and to a certain independence: 'I do not conceive marriage as a form of slavery and I believe that every woman has the right to do what she likes doing.'

Agnès, a college student and future nursery nurse, declared roundly that 'a job is the means to personal freedom'. Once she had a job, she would earn her own living, and she would have the satisfaction of knowing that she was capable of doing something, of carrying out responsibilities in society. In her opinion a job was just as important to a girl as to a boy and she had no intention of giving up work if she got married. A rather more complicated case was that of Marie-Odile, from a rural family. She was, she said, one of many from her kind of rural background classified as being without a job. Because of family problems, she had been forced to stay at home working on her parents' farm. Her life so far had been occupied learning about farm work at home, taking a number of educational courses, and involving herself in a young people's movement. Until now, she had not been aware of the gap left by the lack of a true profession. 'It is terrible to feel oneself useless to society when one is young and full of life and idealism.'

> As soon as I can leave home, I will give up farm work for a complete change of direction. I believe it is impossible to be truly adult if one does not have a profession. It is important for every human being to have a definite vocation within society, to feel of use. A job is as important for a man as for a woman, because each is of equal value as a human being.

Lydia, aged 16, in eastern France studying for a professional diploma to become a dental assistant, expressed herself in a more religious mode: 'Working permits us to participate in the work of God in the world, and to help the world to advance.' The next interviewee, Chantelle, pupil at a lycée in the north, revealed a very strong social conscience: 'We should never forget that there are thousands of girls of our age who are obliged to work simply to earn their living. For them, very often, a job is not in any way a matter of personal liberation.' In general, the sense of independence and strong personal commitment comes through very strongly, though the persistence of class influences is clear from the way in which these qualities tended to be less strongly marked in those in working-class or rural situations.

Inevitably, independent-mindedness showed itself in other, more self-indulgent ways. One might well suspect the motives lying behind the publication of a book of interviews entitled *Ten Girls Who Rise at Midday*, the author being a male novelist.[28] However, one can well imagine the interviewees quite enjoying making the remarks attributed to them, which do chime in with developments discussed in this chapter: explicitness about sexuality, and an openness (discussed in Chapter 9) about the power of physical beauty. The author claims (probably correctly) that the girls, aged between 16 and 18, represent a new phenomenon of the age, though the way he puts it is outdated and offensive in equal measure—all, he says, are beautiful, but none is a whore or a kept woman. The question he puts to Sophie perfectly illuminates one of those differences between the French language and English which so complicates the issue of growing explicitness. 'You are beautiful and you know it. You exploit that, don't you? What I mean to say is: *êtes-vous allumeuse?*' With the aid of a very traditional French word, the question can be put with a certain delicacy: what was now becoming widespread contemporary usage in Britain would have required him to say: 'Are you a prick-teaser?' The conversation (as recorded in the book) continued as follows, starting with her response to this question: 'I love it when someone lusts after me.'

You are sitting in a cafe, you cross your legs. Someone is watching you. What do you feel?

Let's think… I am sitting… I cross my legs… It depends on the man who's watching me. If he is good looking, then I do get a little excited.

And if he is ugly? Think carefully. An ugly man who lusts after you…

That's exciting as well, because I know that he won't have me. He hasn't a hope, and I'm not taking any risk.

Arlette, aged 16, and Dominique, aged 18, both live far out in the Paris suburbs and have long metro and bus journeys. They remark of people on the metro, 'You'd think they'd never seen mini skirts.' Arlette says she has just read the latest sensational sexy novel, *Emmanuelle*—just the interesting pages, marked up by the friend who lent it to her. However, for these young women, obviously scarcely members of the *jeunesse dorée*, there were strict limits on their freedom. Dominique lamented that she had still not even visited London. 'Everybody goes there, except me, because my father won't let me.' There is a voyeurist quality to the book, a mild rather than an overt sexual explicitness; just another element in that framework of public discussion and knowledge which I will examine in more detail shortly.

Much more powerful as direct evidence is the survey carried out by Lieta Harrison between

February 1964 and August 1965, of 1,047 teenage girls in the cities and surrounding country areas of Milan, Turin, Rome, and Palermo, and 225 of the girls' mothers. Of the girls, 181 came from Milan (and its surroundings), 66 from Turin, 160 from Palermo and its surroundings, and 640 from Rome.[29] Table 8.2 gives the breakdown by age and occupation.

**Table 8.2**

| Age | Studying | Married | Working | Total |
|-----|----------|---------|---------|-------|
| 13 | 81 | 3 | | 84 |
| 14 | 184 | 8 | 12 | 204 |
| 15 | 256 | 1 | 25 | 282 |
| 16 | 129 | 5 | 52 | 186 |
| 17 | 83 | 2 | 27 | 112 |
| 18 | 64 | 7 | 31 | 102 |
| 19 | 28 | 13 | 36 | 77 |
| TOTAL | 825 | 36 | 186 | 1,047 |

Franka, 15, at school, had an immediate complaint about the ambience of ignorance in which she was brought up:

It is now three years since I began menstruating but I did not know what it was, my mother had told me nothing and continued not to want to tell me anything. Everybody thinks it is indispensable for my life that I should know exactly when the kings of Rome were born, but they won't tell me how I was born.... Every month I put the same question to my mother, and every month she gave me the same reply: 'It means that you are a woman.'

In this case a separate interview had been secured with Franka's mother, a housewife:

I did try to help Franka, from the time when she seemed not to be interested in anything else, but I hoped her friends would give her the answers. The truth is that I was embarrassed. Why should it be me that has to explain things to her?... Her science teacher could do it. How can I explain things when I don't understand them myself very well. Don't laugh, it's not enough to be married, not enough to have children. My ignorance is a great burden on me. No, I think it's right that I shouldn't say anything to Franka; I don't want to destroy her innocence.

ST, an 18-year-old student, said that when she was very young (certainly younger than 12) the parish priest asked her if she engaged in 'impure acts'. Not knowing what these were, she replied 'No', but then at the age of 12 she did begin to masturbate, but she still replied 'No' to the priest; in any case, since she was afraid of going to hell she soon gave up. Of the entire sample, 53 per cent owned to masturbating between the ages of 12 and 13; of these, 74 per cent then gave up, while 26 per cent continued; 14 per cent of the total said they had done it after heavy petting.

It was when the inquiry moved on to the questions of attitudes towards marriage, and of current sexual behaviour, that the new independent-mindedness of this generation, still brought up though it was in appalling ignorance, becomes clear. Sixty-two per cent of the total said they did not want to get married. AL, a 16-year-old grammar school girl, said: 'No, I don't want to ever surrender my decisions, or what I want to do, or to be forced to live under someone else's rules.' RM, a 17-year-old student on a commercial course, said: 'In general marriage just seems like part of the system, nothing else. It's all a matter of calculation, and when something is calcu-lated it is not a matter of true feelings. That's why I don't want to get married.' Perhaps ES, a 16-year-old apprentice shop assistant in a dress shop, and therefore probably of a lower social class than the other two, was more realistic: 'For the time being, no, but perhaps in ten years' time. For now I want to enjoy being young and I don't want to sacrifice myself to a husband.'

Lieta Harrison herself reported that all her interviewees showed an unsentimental attitude towards sex; and, she added, unlike girls of that age ten years before, they showed no sense of guilt about it. Of the entire sample, 22 per cent had had full sexual experiences, 2 per cent at the age of 13, 9 per cent at 14, 17 per cent at 15, and 72 per cent between the ages of 16 and 19. Blame was cast on the male partner by 19 per cent, accusing him of violence, blackmail, or getting them drunk. Only 14 per cent knew, in the language of Harrison, 'how to avoid preg-nancy': 39 per cent believed themselves to be safe, but that, according to Harrison, was just superstition. To the straight question: 'Is it moral to have premarital sex?', Laura, a 17-year-old grammar school student, gave a resounding 'Yes':

> it is our elders who behave scandalously. All you grown-ups make a great fuss over any sexual activities attributed to us young people. Previously women were kept under lock and key and had no hope of sexual relations until after marriage; but the boys, even the very youngest, had total freedom and so queued up at the brothels.
>
> The unfortunate girls got married to men who, at the least, were twice their age. But society didn't regard that as scandalous. It was right and proper if a child-wife was married to an old man; right and proper too if boys frequented brothels until they had achieved the economic position from which they had society's permission to get married. Now when girls no longer marry old men and boys no longer go to brothels, society says that is scandalous and accuses us of immorality. I don't consider myself immoral: I've done it, perhaps because everybody does it and perhaps because I believe it's something one ought to do. Also, nature wants you to do it, waiting is contrary to nature.

Not all answers were as forthright as that one, but none said that premarital sex was definitely immoral: one said it would be all right for a 30-year-old independent woman, but it was not right for her while she was dependent on her father. The one who came nearest to condemnation said that this was because she had seen friends 'ruin themselves for nothing'. Another confessed that she was frightened of sex. There was a reference to the persistence of traditional male attitudes towards sex: abstinence, one girl said, was not a question of morals but of convenience—Italian men still wanted their wives to be virgins. Another answer was that premarital sex was neither moral nor immoral, just stupid: the girl saying this admitted to having had sex two years previously she said when 'her head had been filled with comic books'.

The strongest voices of maturity and independence come through in reply to questions about whether those who had had sex had been forced into it by their boyfriends. AP, a 17-year-old art student, replied: 'Absolutely not; if my boyfriend had been the type who says "Do it or I'll leave you", I would have been the one to leave him.' Of those with sexual experience, 40 per cent said they were not thinking of marrying the partner concerned, while 22 per cent said that they certainly would be marrying him. The remaining 38 per cent—a statistic which perhaps contradicts some of the earlier conclusions about independent-mindedness—said that they did want to marry their partner but they did not dare bring the subject up.

The combination of greater sexual adventurousness with ignorance about contraception inevitably entailed a good number of unintended births. Previously the shame attached to these would have meant many babies being given up for adoption, even if a forced marriage had taken place. An obstetrician interviewed by Harrison declared that there were as many child wives as ever, but the difference was that now many more were keeping the child. Apparently there was less recourse among the young to abortion; this was mainly a remedy for older married women who already had too many children. Traditional taboos and prejudices still had force in Italy. In these interviews we can see quite a mix of attitudes. But taken together the interviews are strong evidence of changes in both attitudes and behaviour. The tone throughout is remarkably rational: sex is important, sex is not a matter of shame; but sex is certainly not an obsession; there is no glorifying of promiscuity.

Interesting comparisons and contrasts can be made with the more traditional and conventional parts of America. Issues of the Memphis State University student newspaper, *Tiger Rag*, show both the persistence of stuffy attitudes and the stirrings of strong student reactions. First, however, the intriguing protest of two 15-year-old girls in Detroit against a still far from fully emancipated American cinema industry and, reinforced by parental support, the success of that protest. Twice the two girls made attempts to enter the art movie cinema where *Georgy Girl*, described in the local press as the 'sexually candid British film', was being shown. To the general manager of the art house chain owning the cinema, whose policy was to admit only those over 18, the two girls wrote:

> Let me assure you that at the tender age of 15 we know, and have known for a long time, all about sex… It's an insult to our intellect that we are allowed to see the loud, fake Hollywood movies that are totally unrealistic and harmful, as they give us a distorted picture of life. Your foreign films are very realistic, truthful and on the whole of great value to us.

The cinema manager phoned the mother of one of the girls, who said that she herself had seen the film and had indeed recommended it to her daughter. The manager gave the girls free passes for the film, declaring: 'I wish I'd had your letter in my possession countless times in the past when I've had to contend with professional do-gooders worried about the corruptive possibilities of foreign films, which have long treated sex with more candor and realism than American films.'[30] Despite the earlier liberalization of American film censorship, *Georgy Girl* could only be shown to all-age audiences in a version with all the franker passages cut out; it could only be shown uncut in the art movie houses, where the over-18 rule had to be strictly maintained.

In the issue for 15 March 1964 *Tiger Rag* set up the talking-point that 'Many magazines and newspapers have commented on the decay of American morals and the weakening of social mores', inviting comment from students and teaching staff. Apparently the still very staid members of this mid-South university agreed to the proposition. Shortly, however, there followed a feature criticizing the regulations governing women's dormitories. The general rule was that everybody had to be in by 10.30, with extensions to 1.00 a.m. on Fridays and Saturdays. Freshers had to be in by 8.00 p.m., with possible extensions to 10.30 on four occasions per term if they had earned exceptionally good marks in class. In October an editorial announced: 'Sex mores, attitudes on religion and living habits are undergoing drastic revisions.' In fact, there was formally a revision in the other direction, it being ruled that all social events must be approved in advance by the office of the dean of women. The rules on chaperons (!) were tightened: 'Graduate assistants are outlawed as possible chaperons, and all parents and alumni must have been out of school three years to chaperon.' In January the women students were reported as welcoming the use of parents as chaperons rather than ones drawn from the academic staff. In the middle of the month a signed article by a woman student appeared under the title: 'College Officials Put Hex on Sex: Students Say It's Here to Stay'.

> At Vassar their lady prexy stated emphatically that 'nice girls don't' and the reply came back just as swiftly 'Yes they do'. In magazine articles and books the surveys and interviews exposed the 'new morality'. Whether students do or don't in the final analysis is a personal decision.

At the end of September a *Tiger Rag* editorial attacked the policy which prevented women from living off campus, save with parents or close relatives, declaring it 'a clear violation of the right of personal choice and is a slap at the maturity and morality of all university women'. This was followed by an editorial insisting that 'out-of-date, discriminatory rules for women must be abolished'. The theme continued in December:

> Colleges and unions across the country are having to loosen ironclad rules dictated by the morality of earlier generations. Students today make their own morality, despite university efforts, and universities are finally realising that they cannot impose stiff morality codes on students. For this reason Antioch College has adopted a complete open house policy.... Amherst allows 52 open dormitory hours a week and Rochester offers unlimited hours in fraternal housing and 20 hours a week in women's residences. At Stanford

University, students have organised the Stanford Sexual Rights Forum which advocates that women's regulations be abolished entirely and that truly co-ed housing be established, with students choosing roommates of either sex. These ideas seem very extreme, but extreme or not, they reflect a nationwide trend.

The issue continued to be aired in 1967, and in February a discussion session was organized between the newspaper and the university. An editorial representative of *Tiger Rag* 'proposed greater freedom for co-eds providing door keys to sophomore women with the grade point average of 2.5; dorm keys to fresher and senior women who are not on probation and abolition of room checks'. But Mrs Morris Graves drew applause and laughter from an audience consisting mostly of women students when she countered with: 'I don't agree at all with this new point, since the idea of greater freedom for co-eds is generally voiced by young, unmarried males.'[31]

In March 1968 *Tiger Rag* coupled an editorial on 'New Morality' with a questionnaire. Results were published the following week. The women students polled ranged in age from seventeen to thirty-eight: three-quarters of them said they were still virgins. Male students ranged in age from seventeen to twenty-nine: only 10 per cent of them, or so they said, were virgins. Among the questions, 'I live up to some religious standards about sex' produced a response of 'True' from women by a ratio of 7 to 1, and the response of 'False' from men by a ratio of 2 to 1. The statement 'I am embarrassed by discussions concerning sex' was rejected by women by a majority of 13 to 1; apparently there was marginally more embarrassment among men, who rejected the proposition 'by a slightly smaller majority'.[32] This rather silly and not particularly illuminating survey does, however, reveal some important points. It expressed the trend towards openness in sexual matters; the survey was conducted by students themselves; it did let everyone know, including the more backward and bashful, that sexual activity was definitely happening. The extent to which change had taken place over the latter part of the decade is well expressed in an editorial in February 1969, now calling for the complete abolition of dormitory hours: the remark of Mrs Morris Graves of three years previously was recalled, with the comment: 'Of course, such a remark would not terminate the dialogue today; we would simply ask, "What's so strange about that?" '[33] The virtue of focusing on Memphis State arises from the fact that this mid-South university was a hard case: if change in sexual matters was taking place here, it was certainly taking place across the nation, something, of course, recognized in the *Tiger Rag* quotation from December 1966, and something which is fully documented in the archives of other universities, and in the secondary sources.[34]

We have seen the difficulties intelligent Italian girls had in trying to acquire the basic facts of life. One should never underestimate word of mouth as a major means of communication, just as one should never take too readily what is being said in the press as transparent evidence of what people are actually doing. None the less, there can be no question as to the role of the media throughout the middle and late sixties in bringing into open debate matters which had once been for specialist journals or private whisperings. In Britain the era of the illustrated magazines had come to an end with the demise of *Picture Post* in the late fifties (only partially replaced by the emergence of the colour magazines associated with the quality Sunday newspapers), and much of the function of publicizing changing mores was in the hands of first the cinema, then television. But illustrated magazines continued to have a major function in the United States, France, and Italy. In America, *Time* and *Life* continued to lead the field (there is something apple-pie about *Playboy*, nude centrefolds and all, but undoubtedly it does respond to changing values), with *Ebony*, the magazine for blacks, becoming steadily more influential. And in 1965 Helen Gurley Brown took over the failing old-style *Cosmopolitan* and relaunched it as a magazine propagating the philosophy of *Sex and the Single Girl*. In France, *L'Express* changed its nature in a most important way in 1964—from being a narrowly political weekly newspaper, it became a general-interest magazine—as did the Italian magazine *ABC*, which had only been founded in 1960. A special importance attaches to the longer-established women's magazines (this goes for Britain as well), which also changed their character somewhat, most obviously perhaps in France. These magazines all featured the major legislative issues of contraception, divorce, and abortion, ran frequent features on 'the new morality', discussed the sexual behaviour both of young people and of adults, and frequently took a look at what was going on in other countries (Scandinavia, and then Britain, often being represented as the countries where libertarianism was now rampant).

*ABC* was launched in June 1960, as a fairly straightforward tabloid news magazine (no covers). Over a period of just over a year, from spring 1964 to the summer of 1965, it became increasingly preoccupied with issues of sexual behaviour, and also lost the last traces of censoriousness, throwing itself more and more upon the side of sexual liberation. The issue of 5 September 1965 was the crucial one in which the cause of divorce reform was taken up, with a major article entitled 'The Divorce of Common Sense', calling for government action on behalf of what it described as the four million 'outlaws of marriage', including both unhappy couples and their children. That *ABC* was genuinely involved with the great society-shaking issues of the day was made clear when two subsequent numbers included articles on what was declared to be Italy's own 'race problem', likening the status of immigrants from southern Italy to that of American blacks.

That *ABC* was *the* with-it magazine of sixties Italy is brought out in the last issue of 1965, which identified the three 'S's of soccer: 'sex, shekels, sport' *(sesso, soldi, sport)*—such a statement would never have appeared in the magazine as it was up till the middle of 1964. In the spring of 1966 the biggest meeting yet in support of the right to divorce was held in Milan, when 3,000 people filled the Teatro Lirico: *ABC* was now working closely with the Italian League for the Establishment of Divorce, whose spokesman in the Italian parliament was Loris Fortuna. The issue of 1 May 1966 was largely devoted to the matter of divorce, with a verbatim report of the proceedings at Milan. In its own arguments for divorce, the magazine played the 'times change' theme, noting that when divorce had first been mooted twelve years previously

The daily newspapers published vigorous protests from Catholic associations, indignant letters from old maids and timorous family men and other writers very diligent in the cause of defending the indissolubility of the chains of marriage.

355

But public opinion had changed rapidly over the last ten years. This was *ABC* at its best (and, as events were eventually to show, at its most influential).

The leading women's magazine in Italy was *Grazia*. However, even though fundamentalist feminism (on, it must be said, a very small scale) appeared in Italy as early as December 1966, *Grazia* remained very conventional, and only began to address the major issues to do with family and sex during the turmoil of 1968–9. Between June 1966 and May 1967 *ABC* ran a series of articles by Milana Mileni, whose astonishingly explicit novel *La ragazza di nome Giulio* (The Girl Called Jules) of 1964, had been seized by the authorities, with Milani herself being given six months' suspended prison sentence for obscenity. The articles were published in book form in October 1967 as *Italia Sexy*. One of her articles was a pioneering one on the sexual harassment working women were subject to from their bosses; others were 'We say no to marriage' and 'We are all for divorce'. The article which provided the title for the entire collection declared sex to be the key to everything, and nudity a good thing in itself. It attempted to pin down the current situation in Italy as a mixture of sexual openness and continuing faith in the Catholic Church:

> We are truly bemused, but also happy: Italian youth is better than certain guardians of morality would like it to appear. In essence, the boys and girls of today, with their clear and explicit ideas, fit perfectly into the immense carousel of life, not standing apart from it, but being involved in it. Italy has entered into the great international scene, has ceased to be provincial: the phrase 'Italia Sexy' is not important in itself, and none need be shocked by it. 'Italia Sexy' means a young Italy, an Italy in the avant garde, conscious of its vitality and its problems, an Italy without its blindfolds, without taboos, without hypocrisy. I have tried also to listen to our churchmen. It is not lying to say that with us Catholicism has its place.[35]

It was around 1965–6 that the French women's magazines, *Elle, Marie-Claire*, etc., began to adapt to the new currents. Françoise Giroud recognized this in an article entitled 'A Civilized Couple':

> In November 1946, women did not have lovers. At any rate, use of the prettiest word in the French language was banned from magazines aimed at women. In November 1966, addressing the same audience, *Elle* has no fear of instructing women on 'how to succeed in your sex life': similarly with *Marie-Claire*, and the other magazines.[36]

In August 1966 *Marie-Claire* gave its full attention to London, under the heading 'Love and the Miniskirt'. After discussing the fashion scene, the article continued, in a perhaps peculiarly French perception of the British:

> Men have discovered women (and vice versa) and in rejecting the idea that love is a sin they have discovered that it is a pleasure... They all have long hair: mummy, daddy and baby. One time in three daddies and mummies are not married.[37]

356

Another major article in the same issue was 'The Pill, Your Husband and You' by évelyne Sullerot, billed as 'the champion of the new feminism'. In previous issues readers, representatives of the Church and members of the French parliament had expressed their views on this issue. Sullerot pointed out that 90 per cent of French women practised what she referred to as 'the interrupted act' and, if that didn't work, abortion. In May 1966 *L'Express* focused attention on one of Paris's only two family planning clinics. The article explains that twelve names appear on the appointment list every day, from Monday to Saturday. They are lucky, the article continues, to live in the vicinity of one the eighty centres of the French Family Planning Movement (MFPF). The most recent one had been founded for the use of University of Paris students. So far 85,000 French women 'have been able to benefit from one of the most important revolutions of our epoch'. The three methods in use, the article explains, are the diaphragm, the coil, and the pill. But there are enormous difficulties in getting over the information; many women are so embarrassed about the matter that they come pretending to have some illness. The article then provides a number of horror stories explaining why French women, particularly working-class ones, were so intimidated over the issue of birth control. In one case a woman had gone to an old doctor in a working-class Paris suburb: 'Doctor, I have three children, hardly any income, and a minute flat. I would like to avoid a fourth birth for at least three or four years.' To this the doctor replied: 'Naturally, you are not married?' 'That's not the problem.' 'Then', the doctor responded, concluding the consultation, 'what is the problem?'[38]

The issue of 8–14 August 1966 had a photograph of the pill on its cover, announcing an article on the history of French laws on contraception, and of the development of the French birth-control movement. It was in 1958 that Dr Marie-Andrée Lagroua-Weill-Hallé had turned her own small organization, Maternité Heureuse (Happy Maternity), into the MFPF, opening the first centre in Grenoble in 1961. By August 1966 the MFPF, given some prestige by having as presidents three 1965 Nobel prize-winners, Professors François Jacob, André Lwoff, and Jacques Monod, had eighty-five centres, and employed 400 doctors. Strictly speaking the centres were illegal, but such was the discrepancy between the letter of the law and the spirit of most of those in authority that since 1958 there had been no prosecutions. In 1960 a government commission had been set up to study 'problems of the family' and had recommended new legislation concerning 'the right to happiness and emancipation of women, through freedom of choice with respect to motherhood'. However in 1962 the old guard of the French medical profession insisted on a declaration that, with respect to contraception, 'Doctors have no role to play and no function to perform'. Younger voices in the profession began to be heard, and in 1965 the faculties of medicine at Tours and Lyon set up teaching courses in contraception. Liberal forces were stirring in the French Church. When the fundamentalist Jesuit Father Naïdenoff wrote in a Catholic review: 'Even if the child dies of hunger, he will have died surrounded by tenderness, which is better than dying anonymously before birth; the traumatic effect, the moral injury of contraception is much more serious', he was reproved by his ecclesiastical superiors. *L'Express* identified several leading politicians who now supported birth control, particularly, among the Gaullists, Lucien Neuwirth, Mme Suzanne Ploux and Mme Odette Launay, as well as the socialist François Mitterrand.[39]

In July 1967 *L'Express* was celebrating Neuwirth's victory in the Assembly, where he achieved the legalization of the sale of contraceptives, though not to anyone under 21 without parental consent (Neuwirth had argued for an age limit of 18). 'After his victory', the article said, 'M. Neuwirth believed he had brought France out of the Middle Ages', but the article felt bound to conclude on a pessimistic note, quoting some very reactionary views on the subject. A Dr Jean Coumaros had apparently been loudly applauded when he asked rhetorically: 'Have husbands dreamt that henceforth it will be the wife who holds the absolute power whether or not to have a child, by taking the pill, without the husband's knowledge?' A Dr Hébert had expressed his concern at what he called, 'the flame of eroticism which menaces the country'. The pill had been on sale in Italy since October 1964, though officially for certain disorders, not for contraceptive purposes; by 1968 there were 135,000 users. In May 1967 *Epoca* reported that the government's own national health council favoured abrogating the law which prohibited propaganda on behalf of contraception, and that meantime millions of Italian women were still waiting a directive from the Catholic Church on this matter.[40]

For all the discussion in the fashionable magazines, for all the new consumerist enthusiasms of young married women, and for all the efflorescence of youth, ignorance and prudery remained strong in rural areas. The Plodémet survey discovered 'a vast cloak of modesty' covering every-thing concerning sex, including 'birth control', a term which was still unknown in 1965—indeed a young woman of the *bourg* believed that it concerned advice on breast-feeding. The survey found that women were simply not prepared to discuss such questions: a 24-year-old elementary school teacher said, 'Nobody speaks of such things, not even young women among themselves.' A young woman doctor on holiday in the summer of 1965 who tried to discuss the matter found that women simply evaded it: 'Couples continued according to the old ways, practising coitus interruptus as a means of limiting births (with some rare exceptions, such as the woman with five children who had no idea how to stop the process), but never considered family planning.'[41]

One of the major events ensuring that it was very difficult in the High Sixties to avoid discus-sions of sexual matters was the massive survey carried out in the United States by Masters and Johnson.[42] This, inevitably, filled all the various organs of communication in the United States itself, but was also featured in the various European magazines. It was a routine news item at the end of August 1966 in *L'Express* which began with a reference to Masters and Johnson, remarking that in America 'All veils are lifted'. The paragraph was headed 'The Sex Life of the French', and, after claiming, somewhat speciously, that on any medical issue Americans routinely answered questions on their sex life, added that this was simply untrue in France. It noted that in the few existing French surveys wives would say that they had had sex twice in the previous week, whereas husbands would say five times. Once again the continuing delicacy of the French language is worth noting: the phrase used is of the wife 'receiving the *hommages* of her husband'. French fascination with the uninhibited nature of the Americans showed itself again in the last *L'Express* issue of 1966, where there was an article entitled 'Foire au flirt à New York' (Fair for Pick-ups in New York), on the new singles bars opening up in New York and known there, the article claimed, as 'body exchanges'; women, the article said, were the hunters.[43]

*L'Express* had changed its format from that of a forbidding-looking newspaper to that of an illustrated magazine in September 1964. And what more suitable subject for the new magazine than London, and the new longhaired fashion being adopted by young British men? Presented with a photograph of a London street filled with long-haired young people readers were invited to pick out the one girl. The next issue reported a national survey which suggested that politics was no longer a main concern of French people, the concern now being with individual wellbeing. The second issue of 1966 featured 'Love in Freedom', an article about sexual liberation in Sweden, commenting that the French had yet to engage in a free debate about sexual attitudes. It reported the results of a survey showing that 80 per cent of the French people had had no sexual education whatsoever, and that 92 per cent were ignorant about female contraception. A second article about Sweden followed in the next issue: in general the tone was sympathetic, and we can see here *L'Express* beginning to emulate *ABC* in Italy in playing its part in publicizing the more advanced ideas of sexual liberation.

One well-established means of obtaining some information on sexual matters was the 'agony aunt' columns to be found in journals in all four countries; generally, however, these remained very traditional and 'correct' in the advice they gave, till the end of the decade at least. An interesting variation was the 'experiment in psycho-sociology' inaugurated on Radio Luxembourg in May 1967 by Ménie Grégoire, in the programme entitled *Les crises de la vie* (The Crises of Life), broadcast between 2.30 and 3.30 in the afternoon to a regular audience of two million. Grégoire received a vast number of letters from her listeners, from which two major conclusions emerge: there definitely was now a greater frankness in speaking about intimate matters; and an enormous amount of ignorance about sexual matters still persisted. Grégoire gave the following detailed findings: 90 per cent of the letters revealing problems with respect to homosexuality came from men; 50 per cent of all letters from adult men and women concerned sex; 30 per cent of these revealed fundamental ignorance of the facts of life; 20 per cent were about first love, 15 per cent about premarital sex; 5 per cent arose from parents prohibiting encounters with the opposite sex.

America, as always, offered the greatest mix of attitudes and practices. In economic terms American teenagers had the greatest freedom, though they might also be governed by taboos as severe as any to be found in Europe. Levels of sexual awareness were generally high, but religious sanctions strong with regard to such matters as abortion. It was in 1967 that abortion became a matter of public debate in the United States. It is perhaps typical of that bible-thumping country that one of the most important private organizations was the Clergy Counselling Service for Problem Pregnancies, basically a group of Protestant and Jewish clergymen first established in New York during 1967. Shortly there was a similar group in Los Angeles.

The Clergy Counselling Service pointed out: 'Social workers know a young woman often first seeks a minister, confident he who serves God will be charitable or that the followers of Jesus Christ will not throw stones.' There is quite a collection of publications and ephemera relating to abortion in the Special Collections at the University of California at Los Angeles. A typescript report headed 'Abortion Programme Given In Long Beach' refers to several such programmes being mounted, and literature distributed, by two active feminists.[44] Also in 1967 a local press in Berkeley issued *The Case For Legalised Abortion Now*, by Alan F. Guttmacher. The publishers' preface certainly contained no more than the normal exaggeration:

> An intense drama is evolving in America over the issue of abortion. While it has been used increasingly as a form of birth control, abortion has remained illegal. The reform movement therefore is rising. It now directly confronts holders of the historical view that abortion is murder. The first tangible evidence that it has gained strength came with the approval of a more liberal abortion law by the Colorado Legislature in 1967. But in other states it has been promptly suppressed. In the two most populous ones, New York and California, legislative bills advocating reform have met vigorous opposition.[45]

Magazines were more likely places for conveying advice as to what was now acceptable behaviour than formal guides to etiquette. However, there is much to be gleaned from the various editions of the popular British publication *Lady Behave*, written by Anne Edwards and Drusilla Beyfus. The original edition in 1956 had been very conscious of 'the remarkable change in manners over the last twenty years'. As spelled out, this 'remarkable change' does not come over as altogether earth-shattering:

> British royalty has entered into the middle classes. Hereditary peers have gone into trade. A Foreign Minister dropped an aitch here and there and didn't give two pins. The aim of the new schooling is to rate everyone's son by his brains rather than his background. The 'lady' who was the jewel of the old social order is today often the 'lady' who advertises for a job as a cook-housekeeper.[46]

This original edition had a section on 'The New Woman': in the 1957 reprint two brief subsections were added to this, 'Getting a Job' and 'Having a Baby'. In this form the book came out in paperback in 1964. Then in 1969 came *Lady Behave: A Guide to Modern Manners for the 1970s*. This combined a completely new introduction with selections 'From the Introduction to the First Edition' (of 1956)—wisely and significantly dropping the illustrations of 'remarkable change' I have just quoted. The new Introduction began:

> It might be supposed that the immense social changes which have occurred over the last ten years would have made a revised edition of a book on etiquette a very slim volume. The ideal of a classless society, the growing independence and equality of women, the respect for honesty in speech and social behaviour, the general climate of tolerance to what was earlier taboo, and the emphasis on self-expression in individual behaviour, must surely make nonsense of the concept of etiquette. On the contrary. We find that this volume is fatter than ever… The overlapping and the intermingling of the old and the new, the acceptance of the unconventional approach alongside the traditional, makes a sure-footed path through the current complexities of social behaviour more hazardous than ever.[47]

The original edition had had a section on 'The New Frankness in Speech', beginning with 'The Death of the Little White Lie'. In the 1969 edition this was replaced by the more direct 'Frankness in Speech':

> It seems inconceivable that when we first wrote this book, the use of the word 'bloody' on television caused a public furore. One of the significant changes in manners over the past few years has been the liberalization of attitudes towards what can be said in mixed company. Candour, frankness and honesty in conversation have become admired attributes... Television, film, certain newspapers and weekly magazines, novels and plays and autobiographies have for many people broken down the taboos on what can be discussed in public. Particularly this relates to the old inadmissibles, intimate sexual experiences, detailed descriptions of violence and every kind of physical expression and emotion.[48]

The emphasis on magazines and other publications is right. We noted the changes in novels and films in Chapter 4. Changes in what could be presented on television were much more noticeable in Britain than in the other countries. Lord Hill, chairman of the Independent Television Authority, gave a view from the top in 1966. Asked, 'Has there been a new outlook on morality?' he replied:

> There has. A sizeable number of people in our society now take a permissive view of sex. Love-making, they argue, has nothing to do with morals. Now this presents a serious problem to the ITA. Like it or dislike it, this new outlook is a significant fact in some sections of our society.[49]

Emancipated thinking, and living, are strongly evident in the collection of interviews, *Talking to Women*, published by Nell Dunn in 1965 (her BBC TV play, *Up the Junction*, about uninhibited women factory workers who treated men as sex objects, was one of the more striking examples of the 'new outlook on morality'). Then in 1968 Beyfus published a series of interviews with married women. What comes through is a certain amount of independent-mindedness and aspiration, though within a framework of fairly traditional attitudes about the roles of men and women—on the part of men as well as of women. Lily had left comprehensive school at 16, worked as a hair dresser, then married Mac, a skilled worker in shopfitting and decorating. They had been married five years and had three children. Mac had been earning an average of £1,500 a year but then, partly because of illness, had fallen on hard times and now had a wage of £13 a week. They were living in two rooms in cold-water premises in a semi-detached property near Wandsworth, in south London. It had taken four years to pay off the hire purchase on a three-piece suite, which in fact was too large to fit into either of the two rooms. The debt had also been paid off on the refrigerator, the electric cooker, and television; but as the household income fell the television had been sold, and replaced by a rented one. Remarking that some people 'are content to live on £13 a week and struggle along for years', Lily declared that she couldn't live like that: 'That's why I've got a job to help out.'

What I intend doing with my money if it's possible—I get £10 a week for a five-day week—is some towards the rent arrears, some shoes for myself and then some clothes for the children—socks, pants they need. I shall keep on with the job because I enjoy it. I'd fight if I have to give it up. I gives me a break from the children, it gives them a break from me, shouting at them all the time. I'll be a better person for it. We'll need to save a bit. Part of my money will go into the bank just the same as his does. It's combined money to us, not his or mine.[50]

Hers was an office job; the children went to a day nursery.

Most conventional, perhaps, was the wife, now in her mid-20s, who had left a secondary modern at 15, and whose 31-year-old husband, a linesman working on high pylons, was often away from their semi-detached in a housing estate outside Bedford: but if she was clearly dependent on her husband, she obviously did not accept that there was full satisfaction to be found in bringing up a family:

What is so awful about being without him is continually having children and women around. You talk differently to them as [sic] you do to a man. You get to long to rush out into the road and have a sensible conversation with an adult, if you can still think of a sensible remark that is... When he's away I don't go out on my own. I have been asked to the pictures by a man friend, but even though I knew he didn't mean anything by it, I wouldn't go. I'd feel terrible, I wouldn't know what to say, on my own.

Frances, in her late 20s, a computer programmer married for two and a half years to a business man in his early thirties, and with two children, sounds the most emancipated, or at any rate uninhibited:

When Tom is away what I do frequently want, and I admit this, is a quick screw. But everybody, of course, expects me to be feminine, and want to get involved thereafter. I don't. I'm like a man about this. I need a screw every so often and I like to have it and get it over with a cheerio. But since men don't expect a woman to feel like this, you can't. You get yourself horribly tied up. So I masturbate. This serves.

Most grandly independent was Elizabeth, in her late 30s, a consultant psychiatrist running departments in two hospitals; she had been married eighteen years to a prosperous solicitor, now in his mid-40s; of their three children two were away at boarding-school, one still a baby:

I can't go back if I give up my post. I do the sort of job that is undertaken by a man—and I have a number of highly trained men working for me. In my profession I have applied for fairly high posts for which numbers of first-class men applicants have been rejected. Once I withdraw and resign I can't go back.... If I could drop out for a year or so to see what it is like I would. But indeed now I feel I couldn't take the risk.

'No, she couldn't,' her husband agreed. But he offered an entirely different line of reasoning: 'Whilst she is at work she is the equal of any man in her profession, the equivalent of anybody. Once off her own ground she might not find it so easy to justify herself.'[51]

In the same year Hannah Gavron published her *The Captive Wife: Conflicts of Housebound Mothers*. Both working-class and middle-class wives were asked whether they felt that their marriages were more equal than those of their parents. Of the middle-class wives, 64 per cent said that they were, by which they meant that they had more independence within the marriage than their mothers had had. Among the working-class wives 56 per cent replied affirmatively, but what they meant was that they felt closer to their husbands than they felt their mothers had been to their fathers. In general, fathers in both social classes seemed to be taking on more of the family responsibilities. There was discontent and stress in all families: working-class mothers in particular often felt isolated. 'What is needed above all', Gavron concluded, 'is some deliberate attempt to re-integrate women in all their many roles with the central activities of society'.[52]

The best source for the changing sexual attitudes and behaviour of adult Italian women is another survey carried out in 1969 by Lieta Harrison: this time she interviewed 528 young married women (in the age range 23–40) in Milan, Rome, and Palermo, and their mothers. One has to be careful with some of the contrasts, of course: women in their 50s and 60s may express different attitudes about sex from what they might have done when they were in their 20s or 30s. It is also striking that the younger women seem to have become emancipated in their sexual attitudes after rather than before marriage; 66 per cent said that the question of sexual attraction was not relevant at the actual time of marriage. A 29-year-old Rome housewife said that she had not thought at all about sexual attractiveness at the time of her marriage; a 33-year-old Milan housewife said that she didn't really know how to answer—she had married her husband for other reasons; a 29-year-old Milan housewife said that she had tried not to think about such things 'because I had received an education in which all of that was a sin'. But then, of course, almost all these women would have been married well before the 1960s, so what we find in the survey is not just a change in attitudes as compared with their mothers, but a change in attitudes taking place during their married life in the sixties. Of the 528 young wives, 478 said sex was fundamental to a woman's life; of the 528 mothers only 168 said the same, and 360 denied that sex had the importance attributed to it in the Italy of the late sixties. Of the mothers, 67 per cent thought that sex was right only within marriage, while only 13.2 per cent of the daughters thought this. A 40-year-old Roman housewife, with a job as a white-collar worker, argued that if 'the union between husband and wife is not satisfying it is human to search elsewhere'. A housewife of 26 declared: 'Marriage is a bureaucratic fact, sexual attraction is an instinctive fact and thus perfectly legitimate.' Among the mothers 70.4 per cent considered premarital sexual experience to be wrong, compared with only 18.5 per cent of the daughters. A 32-year-old Milan housewife put it this way: 'If you arrive prepared there's no shock. Marriage is already very serious; having overcome the problem of sexual relations is a great help.'[53]

The comments of the older women make sad testimony to the dismal state of marital relations in traditional Italian society. A 64-year-old Milanese housewife said of sex: 'For me it was always an unpleasant duty'. Another woman, ten years her junior, said: 'Soon the man is bored with what he gets at home—after two or three years at the most.' Both sets were asked to identify what most reinforces a marriage. The daughters (22.3 per cent of them chose this) put satisfactory sexual relations at the top of the list; the older women put this at the very bottom. But perhaps an even sadder reflection on the emptiness of the traditional marriage is contained in the contrast between the daughters putting 'communication and talking' second top in the list (20.5 per cent chose this), and the mothers putting this third bottom. What the mothers thought most vital to success in a marriage (another tragic revelation) was tolerance and patience on their own part. Of the 528 daughters, 149 had had affairs outside marriage, 48 from Milan, 76 from Rome, and 26 in the Sicilian capital. An office worker of 28 declared belligerently (and very sensibly): 'By his decision we stopped sexual relations for two years: without reason he had decided to neglect me, but I am young and have the right to a normal life, so I have a lover.'[54]

French women polled in 1971 said quite clearly that they were very aware that over the previous five years their sexual lives had become much more liberated.[55] There is no such thing as uninterrupted progress, no such thing as complete happiness. But for an overall assessment of the way in which life was fuller towards the end of the sixties than it had been in 1957, one can turn to the assessments emerging from a poll of a random sample from the more than 10 million French people in the age group 15–29 published in February 1969 (see Table 8.3). On the question of sexual fidelity, a married woman of 29 said that this was above all important on the part of the wife, but then added that 'if one is in fact good-looking oneself, and one is neglected by one's husband then it's hard to achieve'. A female student of 21 was quite forthright: 'It's a question of purely intellectual fidelity, that which consists in having confidence and in giving total confidence. Physical fidelity is nothing more than a pure formality.' In the overall survey there was no great change in the general belief in the need for fidelity, the most significant shift being away from the idea that fidelity was particularly important on the part of women. The poll also showed that people now felt very much freer in a wide range of personal and social activities, that they felt happier, that they felt that the late sixties was a better time in which to live, and that they felt materially much better off.

**Table 8.3** *Is fidelity essential?*

|  | 1968–9 | 1957 |
| --- | --- | --- |
| Equally for both | 86% | 82% |
| Only for the woman | 2% | 9% |
| Not essential | 5% | 4% |

*Source: L'Express,* 17–23 Feb. 1969.

Personal diaries are rare sources, in both senses of the term. Obviously, most people do not keep diaries; no single diary can ever be assumed to be representative. Still, after the broad averages, there is always value in hearing a single voice speaking. It seems likely that Loredana Valmori, a housewife living in Sesto Fiorentino near Florence, was turned towards the idea of keeping a diary first by the death of her mother, then by the discovery in May 1964 that her husband, Eolo, didn't love her. Here are some extracts covering almost a year from Christmas 1965, which she had spent with her in-laws:

25 December 1965: Thus the day passed; Eolo returned at 8, we had dinner there, watched television and then came home. We made love, some moments which made me forget everything and restored me to tranquillity. But it was not like it once was; hurried, routine, without those kisses which steal the heart, uniting body and soul in love! I cannot be controlled, I love too much, give too much, and want too much, a man needs, or at least mine does, his liberty, his friends and his games, from which I am excluded. Always I feel this void, the void of a love which I lack, the love of a father.

14 February 1966. Arriving home we went to bed... Soon afterwards happily to sleep!

May 1966. We have a new gas cooker and a refrigerator.

1 June 1966... Today I fell asleep and if I go out now tomorrow the house will be in a mess. Eolo would be sure to be angry with me. So many useless tears or a little stupidity: so now I will get on with my work realizing that it is never possible to have a moment's peace, in this world of ours!... here in Italy we are too much slaves of tradition, while we women are the ones who bow our heads down lowest. If I had been more bird-brained than I am, we would not have this lovely house which is certainly better than many people have. But evidently such things don't matter too much to a man... With mother dead, I have nothing, only him. And he is nasty, or maybe he is mad, in America they would call this 'mental cruelty'.[56]

The entry for 30 November 1966 is entirely taken up with the flooding of the city where she had been born, Florence: 'So much fear, desperation, ruin, tears... Florence, my dear, beautiful Florence, no longer exists.' She and her husband had gone to the little street where she had grown up: 'complete silence. Everyone seems to be dead.' They returned to Sesto Fiorentino tired and depressed. Then she adds that other places apart from Florence have suffered, the entry ending 'The deluge of 1966'. At Christmas 1966 they acquire a television of their own. From December 1967 to March 1973 there are no entries: we then learn that the couple are prospering, have paid off their house, and have a fine new car.

There are no golden ages. There are certainly no prescriptions for happiness. Even where the majority enjoy good fortune, the unfortunate cannot be ignored. None the less, in this chapter we have traversed the range of transformations, material and mental, in the lives of ordinary people which form the core of the cultural revolution of the sixties.

# 9

# Beauty, Booze, and the Built Environment

### The Truth about Beauty

'Openness', 'explicitness', 'frankness' are words I have used several times to define the characteristically new attitudes of the middle and later sixties. These words apply very strongly to the way in which personal appearance was re-evaluated. Traditionally, 'beauty' had been a matter fraught with confusion and ambiguity. There was a great reluctance to make a rational distinction between beauty of physical appearance and beauty as denoting the highest moral virtue, or beauty as used with reference to a person's personality or character. Guides on personal appearance go well back into the past, and were wont to console those whose external appearance might not be all that was desired with the advice that provided they made every effort, their 'inner beauty' would shine through. Like most resonant words, 'beauty' has several usages. The problem was that people liked to slip from one usage to another: you praised someone for beauty of character, and somehow that praise was transferred to represent that that person was beautiful of appearance (even though anyone with half-decent eyesight could see that this simply wasn't true). In part, obviously, such attitudes were related to the ordinary courtesies and decencies of civilized life: it was polite to affect to find someone beautiful, even if they manifestly were not; it was obviously in very bad taste indeed to say openly that someone was plain or ugly.[1]

There was also great confusion between beauty in the sense, on the one side, of the natural physical appearance one is born with, the beauty which is a gift from one's genes, and, on the other, of fashion, make-up, and 'beauty care'. It was, of course, a basic tenet of the fashion

366

industry that if you were in fashion, then you were beautiful; if you were not in fashion, then you were ugly. Actually—though this could not be admitted—it was perfectly possible for someone to be ugly and yet in the height of fashion, and for someone else to be strikingly beautiful yet out of fashion. Fashions manifestly did change, and so a very stubborn myth developed, reinforced by Marxist and post-structuralist propaganda about everything being 'culturally constructed', that beauty was entirely relative: that what was considered beautiful in one age would not necessarily be so considered in another, that standards of beauty changed from age to age. If, instead of simply looking at what painters painted or fashions writers decreed, we look at how people actually behaved in past ages, the myth quickly disintegrates. Ordinary, lustful men and women tended to prefer persons of the opposite sex possessed of natural beauty and direct sex appeal to those who were merely in the height of fashion: for part of the nineteenth century red hair was held to be a disadvantage to a woman, yet a man could still easily spot whether a red-haired woman was pretty or not.[2] Sarah Bernhardt, in her late teens and early twenties, was lusted after by practically every wealthy man in Paris: yet she was skinny, and had a long nose, when (so we are told) the fashion type of the time called for plumpness and a round face.

There are different types of physical appearance—'Latin', 'Nordic', 'English Rose', 'Oriental', 'Afro', and so on. All of these types contain beautiful specimens, as well as personable, plain, and ugly ones. There is not, in any particular era, one type of beauty; beautiful people are the finest examples of their own particular type. Beautiful people are those whose beauty is recognized by practically everyone. Of course, we all have our own particular tastes; someone we love may appear beautiful *to us*, though not to many others. 'Beauty is in the eye of the beholder' is one of those banal pieces of folk wisdom which says nothing of significance. The beauty which counts, the beauty which has value, is the beauty which is in the eye of (almost) all beholders. And this beauty is *not* more than skin deep—it is a stunning, purely surface, purely physical quality.

For all the pretences, for all the confusions, the desirability—that is to say the value—of sheer basic, biological, physical beauty had always been recognized. Those who could afford it went for it: Catherine the Great with her handsome young guardsmen, Charles II with his well-chosen mistresses. The lure of beauty was widely recognized, though in societies where the fight to maintain and extend the family's position was tough, this lure would often be seen as a dangerous one. In certain sorts of occupations, those I have, in my *Beauty in History*, designated as the four 's's, 'showbiz', 'selling', 'service', and 'sex', a beautiful appearance was a definite asset. For several centuries, being an actress or a salesgirl was simply a deliberate prelude to a life as a courtesan. For women, exploiting their beauty inevitably entailed a sexual transaction. This was not necessarily so with men. The good-looking peasant always had the chance of becoming a footman. As the department stores developed in the nineteenth century, salesmen with a good appearance were very much in demand. Photography and then film expanded the audience for the different types of beauty. As beauty became a saleable commodity to mass audiences, the element of personal sexual transaction began to diminish. The greatest problem for polite society was that of age and ageing. Everybody had always known that as human beings grow older they get less and less physically attractive; anything in human external appearance that suggests decay or death will seem the opposite of beautiful. Much of fashion, much of the 'beauty industry' (using beauty in that rather technical way), accordingly, was directed towards enabling those growing older to put as good a face and figure on it as possible.

For the sake of clarity, I make a distinction between what I shall call the 'traditional' view of beauty, and the 'modern' one. In the traditional view—and elements of that view persist today—there was perennial confusion between beauty as surface, physical attribute and beauty as moral value; in traditional society, the major status characteristics were wealth and social position—beauty, apart from being an enticement to the sin of lust, was seen as a menace to both of these. Gabriel de Minut in his *Of Beauty* of 1587 stated that physical beauty could give rise to 'the pollution and contamination of vice and ordure'. David de Flurance Rivault in *The Art of Beautification* of 1608 spoke of 'the beauty which rules over our affections, dominates our will, and enslaves our liberty, causing unbelievable desires, excesses of passion and fires of sensuality'. In *Some Reflections on Marriage* of 1700, Mary Astell remarked: 'There's no great odds between his marrying for the Love of Money, or for the Love of beauty, the man does not Act according to Reason in either case; but is governed by irregular Appetites.' The sense of the power, and menace, of sheer physical beauty is well expressed in an old peasant saying from the Franche-Comté: 'When one has a beautiful wife, one has no fine pigs. Why? Because the pigs, instead of eating, spend all their time staring at her.'[3]

One important product of the interacting changes, and challenges to previous conventions, becoming apparent in the late fifties and accelerating from around 1964 onwards was the triumph of the 'modern' view of beauty, of physical beauty, detached altogether from moral judgements, wealth, and class—you could be poor but also beautiful; though beauty continued to be a major ingredient in sex appeal, it was now, even for women, a saleable commodity which did not also automatically entail the selling of the body. This 'modern' conception of beauty, of beauty as 'an autonomous status characteristic', did not of course fill the hearts and minds of every single individual (traditional evaluations and confusions continue to this day), but as never before it dominated society at large, in its public mores, its newspapers, its advertisements, its television programmes, its social, cultural, and political behaviour. More and more people behaved as if they recognized that 'mere' physical beauty had a particular value of its own. Male beauty was increasingly recognized as having something of the same significance that had always (despite the conventions and the confusions) attached to female beauty. In the middle and later 1960s beauty was universally praised and sought after; it had achieved a kind of parity with wealth and status, and certainly was no enemy to either.

With the acceleration of international cultural exchange it was natural that there should be international love affairs, and sometimes international weddings, all publicized by the press and thus drawing attention to beauty in all its international glamour and variety. Triangular, quadrilateral, and still more complicated entanglements were an expected feature in Hollywood, but there was a European (indeed genuinely international) dimension to the affairs and romances breaking out in the new *dolce vita* of world cinema, bringing together the names of French film director Roger Vadim, his first great protégée, Brigitte Bardot, Annette Stroyberg, Sacha Distel, Yves Montand, Marilyn Monroe, and Montand's wife, Simone Signoret. The affair between British photographer David Bailey and British model Jean

Shrimpton, both international celebrities, was followed by Bailey's marriage to Catherine Deneuve, French film star of international eminence. A soppy little story carried by *Paris-Match* in September 1965 about a couple of slightly less well-known individuals exemplifies both the interrelationship between travel, personal beauty, and the phenomenon of the international beauty competition and also the role of the illustrated press in bringing outstandingly beautiful, though relatively unknown, young people within the purview of everyone. The article is entitled: 'The One Who Has Conquered the Most Beautiful Girl in the World: A French Student':

> Three years ago Roland Cottrey, who had just passed his final school examinations, was on holiday near Séte. The Finger family happened to be passing through: Ingrid and her parents, citizens of Furth, a town near Nuremberg, were looking for a camping ground for the duration of their holiday.
>
> And, beneath the sun of Hérault, the lightning struck. Ingrid and Roland together spent four weeks of bliss: swimming, volleyball, water skiing. When the holiday ended, Roland was already calling Ingrid by her family pet name, Ingelé [in French, 'little hedgehog']. He spent the Christmas vacation at Furth. She met his parents in Paris. In the meantime Ingrid entered the Studio Suzanne, the school for models in Nuremberg. Her file contains her measurements: Height 1m 70, weight 55 kg, bust 91 cm, waist 58 cm, hips 91 cm. And these perfect proportions contributed to her successive elections in 1965 as Miss Munich, Miss Bavaria, and, on 14 May last, Miss Germany. Invited to Palm Beach, she walked off finally with the supreme accolade: the title of Miss International Beauty. Ingrid received the prize of ten thousand dollars, a gown of white silk, bracelets, a necklace and earrings. She wears that gown every evening and sleeps in her jewels. But she has deposited her ten thousand dollars in the bank: in two years' time, she will marry Roland, who is finishing his studies at L'école Nationale Supérieure de Chimie in Paris. The ten thousand dollars, they will be the dowry which Miss Beauty offers to the little Ingrid.[4]

In folk tales throughout the ages, heroines have been 'beautiful' and heroes 'handsome': photographs accompanying the article establish beyond doubt that in that respect at least, this story was no fiction: for readers of both sexes, here were very beautiful young people indeed.

In the 1950s the only challenges to the great Hollywood sex goddesses, and particularly to Marilyn Monroe, had come from European stars appearing initially in European films: first Gina Lollobrigida and then Vadim's 'discovery', Brigitte Bardot. The sexuality of these two actresses was as directly evident as that of Marilyn Monroe herself. More to our present purpose is the case of Monica Vitti, star of a series of Antonioni films from 1959 onwards. Vitti had a long Roman nose, a lean, intensely sensitive look, and struck audiences at the time as being 'different'; she was a symbol of the recognition that beauty comes in many types. Along with Vitti there appeared for international audiences a rather special type of mature Italian male beauty, in the person of Marcello Mastroianni.

As new types of beauty, both male and female, forced their way on to the screens of some commercial cinemas, Hollywood itself began to see the virtues of international film-making, where the low costs and high talents of European countries could be exploited. Paramount's 1960 film about alleged female collaborators in the Second World War, *Five Branded Women*, was a classic in the genre of exploitation movies—films which, often behind the façade of an apparently serious topic, pandered to the audience's appetite for sex or violence or both—then coming into vogue. It called for five actresses who, appearing with their hair shorn, required a very high level of natural beauty. *Life* (11 April 1960) reported:

> Paramount's latest wartime picture is a good example of the new international look in movie making. It was produced by Italy's Dino De Laurentiis, directed by America's Martin Ritt, and photographed in Italy and Austria. Its five shorn actresses were recruited from three countries—two each from the US and Italy, one from France.

On 28 January 1966 the cover story announced by *Life* over a photograph of Catherine Spaak was simply 'The New Beauties'. In the table of contents the story was given as 'Film Beauties of Europe: The Common Market Has a Full Stock of Glamor'. Most revealing of all was the title at the head of the actual story inside: 'The New Freewheeling Film Beauties of Europe'. In the comments attributed to, or made about, these actresses, uninhibited expression is given to the notion of the autonomous value of beauty; the talents of these strikingly different women, it is made clear, lie almost exclusively in their personal appearance. Italy's Marilou Tolo, 22, whose 'tawny good looks made her a fashion model at fifteen, a TV page girl at sixteen and a starlet at seventeen, has never had a camera problem'. Austria's Marisa Mell recognizes where she is, and why, at the age of 24, in protesting: 'I can be more than my eyes and legs.' Most direct is Catherine Deneuve: 'I owe my start in movies entirely to my face and body'.

British stars, each with particular qualities of beauty of their own, gained international renown as well: Julie Christie and Vanessa Redgrave; Peter O'Toole, Terence Stamp, Michael York, and Sean Connery. If ever it was true that in each era one particular style of beauty is favoured above all others (and the evidence is that, in real life, outstanding beauty in whatever style has always had devastating effects), that truth was utterly destroyed in the 1960s, with films, and of course television, presenting beauty in its many varieties (I shall come to non-Caucasian types shortly). In discussing both the stars of his film *Blow-Up* and the successful real-life London-based photographers upon whom it was in part based, Antonioni said: 'They are the heroes of the age, they have invented the new canons of beauty.'[5] Actually, they had not, in my view, invented new canons of beauty, but had revealed what many had known previously though prevented by prevailing ideologies from saying: that beauty comes in different types and is to be found in males as well as females. With regard to the new male beauties, the blurb to photographer David Bailey's *David Bailey's Box of Pin-ups* (1965) is intriguing and revealing:

> David Bailey is fascinated by tinsel—a bright, brittle quality, the more appealing because it tarnishes so soon. He has photographed the people who in England today seem

glamorous to him... Surprisingly few are female—Bailey's standards here are so rigorous that only four girls qualify, all of whom are professional models. But in the age of Mick Jagger, it is the boys who are the pin-ups: and Bailey's pictures give them all the inward, self-sufficient look of Narcissus.[6]

In many ways the world of the American female model was the most conventional and conservative: but along with Lauren Hutton and Cheryl Tiegs, with the healthy California look, there appeared on the scene Wilhelmina (daughter of a German-American Chicago butcher), a big girl with a constant weight problem, who has none the less been described as 'America's greatest model of the sixties',[7] and the tall (she was 6 ft. 1 in.) and strange Countess Vera von Lehndorff, who in the late sixties became world-famous as the model Verushka.[8]

In discussing 'Frankness in Speech' in *Lady Behave*, Anne Edwards and Drusilla Beyfus advised extreme discretion in referring to the delicate matter of the relationship between age and looks, though their own words were frank to the extent of being brutal: 'Those likely to smile a superior smile should be reminded that the two controlling factors in a woman's life, love and looks, are strictly related to age.'[9] Delicacy and discretion were not the characteristics of young people, who saw little need for the polite conventions which skirted the real facts of beauty, ageing, and ugliness, and none for fashions designed to conceal the imperfections of age. It would be absurd to argue that young people consciously adopted what I have called the 'modern' evaluation of beauty, or that in the way they dressed they were issuing a conscious manifesto on behalf of that approach. Young people were very aware of image and identity, which was often a very different thing from showing off natural beauty, or the lack of it. But what is true is that the attitudes and behaviour of youth ran counter to those conventions which had continued to bolster the 'traditional' evaluation of beauty. The new fashions looked best on the young and beautiful; they tended to expose the imperfections of all the rest. A woman was no longer pretty simply by virtue of being a woman, and a man could no longer be sure that he would be measured entirely on his achievements, not his looks.

Because of rising living standards and better medical care, young people growing up in the later fifties and early sixties were stronger and healthier than ever before. Those born with a good bone structure and balanced features were less likely now to fall victim along the way to some wasting or deforming disease, or even to bad teeth. Thus the proportion of beautiful people in the population did go up. More important, the proportion of the personable, those whose attractiveness lay in their healthy youthfulness and general vivacity, rather than any rare distinction of beauty, also went up. Of course, physical handicaps of many sorts persisted, but the toll of deficiency diseases and congenital deformities declined.

If there were more beautiful young people around, and very many more lively and personable ones, can one also argue that the youthful fashions of the sixties were simply designed to enable these young people to show off their natural attributes in the most direct way? Such an argument would not be incorrect, but, given the complex processes which always lie behind fashion changes, it would be incomplete. However, for our present purposes the crucial point is that the distinctive styles of the sixties did not conceal imperfections, nor did they establish a

371

model silhouette which could then be widely imitated (as the crinoline, for instance, did); what they did do was to expose natural endowments. Tight, unpleated, hip-slung trousers, based on the traditional American blue jeans, admirably suited shapely young men but did nothing to hide scrawny legs or protuberant stomachs. The attention to male fashion, and therefore to male personal appearance, is of great significance. However, it may be noted that, although the general shape of the male leg was now shown off, the leg itself remained concealed. For females, there was almost no concealment in the miniskirt, or hot pants.

It is probably true that all fashion in some way or another serves an erotic purpose, but miniskirts were quite explicitly and directly sexual, drawing the eye as they did high up on the thigh; on a young woman with shapely legs they were ravishing. Hot pants were equally revealing, though (despite the name) not so erotically enticing. Then, having gone through the process of exaggeration, fashion now went through that of reaction, and dress lengths were shortly back where they had been in Edwardian times. That is the internal logic of fashion; but fashion would never again conspire against natural display of the endowments of beauty.

Of course, there were many reasons for girls to wear what they did: they might desire to shock, they might desire to allure, or they might simply desire to be informal and comfortable, as when wearing a male football jersey as a miniskirt, or a pair of jeans. A prime example of fashion's inherent tendency towards exaggeration, and the stress of the times on unadorned sexuality, was the invention by Rudi Gernreich in California in 1964 of the topless bathing costume. It was a few more years before common sense and convenience, and a rejection of the pointless taboos of conventional society, led many women at bathing beaches simply to leave off the tops of their bikinis. For some women who in the later sixties and early seventies gave up wearing brassières it was a matter of political protest (brassières, somewhat illogically, being equated with male oppression of women), for others it was a matter of comfort and convenience, and for still others again part of a realization that (something feminists ignored) for males there were few more enticing sights than the moving contours of breasts, clearly apparent through a thin fabric, unconstrained by a brassière.

Fashion was not fixed forever in the sixties, but continued to evolve, change, go backwards. But no one fashion ever again set one universal convention as it had previously done; women and men could pick and choose what they thought suited them personally, and it was now open to a woman to choose the style which quite nakedly showed off her best features. Whatever the motivations and intentions, this did in fact involve a recognition of the intense power of beautiful natural endowments, as distinct from the artificialities of fashion and costume. I do not wish to overstate the case for 'naturalness' because, with all the concentration on personal appearance, there was also a vogue for one particular device which can scarcely be described as natural, the wig. But the fundamental consideration remains, and was well summed up by the *New York Times* fashion reporter Marilyn Bender in 1967:

> The purpose of fashion used to be dissimulation, the pretence that women were pretty, had perfect bodies, romantic spirits and that they were essentially helpless. Pop fashion, like pop art, lays the subject on the line. Fatty knees, wrinkled elbows, ruthless natures are exposed for all to see.

Or, as *Life* put it at the end of the decade: 'Fashions came and went—instantly—but the basics were dependably conspicuous.'[10]

In making beauty a matter of public interest and concern, an important part was played by the explosion in mass communications, particularly television and the new style of advertising associated with Madison Avenue in New York, but also developing semi-independently in Paris and in London. Advertising may well be thought the very soul of deceit, the sworn enemy of frankness and openness. But the new advertising of the sixties was also bold, uninhibited, witty, naturalistic, and rather in the manner of some of the sixties novels, explicit, and, of course, fully exploitative of the appeal of a beautiful face and figure, whether female or male. The beauty was that of anonymous models rather than of people of established status (though modelling quickly became a means of achieving status). The new advertising was involving, rather than distant and authoritarian; it advertised the artefacts of the consumer society rather than the quack medicines of the past. International beauties continued to be recruited into everyone's consciousness through film, but television, situated in the family sitting room, is far more intimate and engaging than film: in that process of comparison, contrast, and choice on which all sexual selection, in some degree, is based, the beautiful person on the small screen in the sitting-room is an even more disturbing phenomenon than the beautiful person at some distance on the large screen.

The new fashions displayed the natural endowments of youth, just as the new internationalism displayed the varieties of beauty from many different countries. How did all this affect the Afro-Americans, whose role is so important in so many other of the developments discussed in this book? My main source is *Ebony*, by the end of the 1950s a large and lavishly produced monthly colour magazine, owned by a black family and produced by a mixed staff on which blacks were in a majority, selling three-quarters of a million copies, and probably reaching a total of 5,000,000 readers.[11] The quality of the writing and of the photojournalism in *Ebony* is very high indeed; the tone is liberal, commonsense, strongly in favour of black civil rights, and deeply proud of black achievements within the framework of American society. (To see *Ebony*, or any other journal for that matter, as the voice of all blacks would, of course, be absurd.) Consistently, there is throughout a very heavy emphasis on questions of personal appearance, discussed at two quite different levels. Most of the items are relatively trivial in nature, though informed with a sharp practicality and wit, apparently being mainly aimed at black women exercised by the problems of securing a husband; but some articles firmly tie in the question of personal appearance with that of civil rights—as blacks become more assertive and more powerful, it is argued, they must present an appearance of which all blacks can be proud.

*Ebony* carried a large number of advertisements featuring black models; it also carried a very large number of advertisements for hair-straighteners, skin-whiteners, and many other beauty aids designed to help blacks look as much like whites as possible. The orthodoxy had been that black women, if not black men, should always straighten their hair. As well as regular articles on grooming and make-up and on fashion, there were frequent articles on beauty competitions, on the personal appearance of famous black women, on 'best-dressed Negro women', on such questions as 'What is the best age for beauty?' (treated with typical wit—'beauty experts say women, like wines, improve with age', but 'science, skin specialists, even Doctor Kinsey, have not succeeded in dousing the average male's enthusiasm for a young bustling companion'[12]), and each year, in June, an article on 'eligible bachelors'. These last features do not in any way, as one might at first imagine, take the line that men should be assessed on their looks—in fact most of those selected were earnest, bespectacled, and distinctly unglamorous, what they stood for being primarily economic success; the cutting edge of every article was what these men were looking for in a woman. Yet even in this exercise *Ebony* managed some of its usual double-edged wit: 'Baseball player Willy McCorey, 24,' one of the 1962 eligible bachelors, 'of the San Francisco Giants, describes his ideal woman as sports minded, honest and understanding, with charm and beauty. Being a realist he says he'll sacrifice a little beauty if the woman has all the other qualities.' The summing up for 1964 was: 'As with last year's round-up, the bachelors placed a premium on brains and personality but admitted that beauty still rates a strong consideration.' The summary for the following year gives the same emphasis to intellectual and other sterling qualities, but then adds with significant use of block capitals, 'NOT ONE OBJECTS TO BEAUTY'.[13]

At the core of all this lies the assumption (never in any way stated explicitly) that a black woman will have a struggle to attain even a plain, though economically successful and upwardly mobile, black man, and that indeed (this is very deeply buried in the text) she will be lucky to do so. Her energy should be directed to making herself as much like a white woman as possible. It is recognized that a black man may occasionally marry a white woman; this will happen when the black man is economically very successful so that the marriage will actually represent an economic and social advancement for the white woman concerned. The question is not broached of whether it is a sign of status for a black man to manage to marry a white woman; nor is there any hint of the even more distressing possibility that black men might actually find most white women more beautiful than most black women. However, in December 1965 there was a sad letter from a black girl ('I'm considered pretty') lamenting that black men were going after white women and ignoring black ones, while white men were definitely not going after black girls. When, at the end of the decade, Hollywood did get round to treating this issue, in *Guess Who's Coming to Dinner* (an honourable and witty film, though reviewed by one black critic as 'warmed over white shit'), the relationship was black man-white woman, the man mature and very successful, the woman very young.

The successful black women featured by *Ebony* all had the 'whitified' look; this is particularly evident on the cover and illustrated article of October 1961 on—and the pun may have been intended—'*Ebony* Fashion Fair Beauties'. Wherever black girls did well in beauty competitions open to both blacks and whites *Ebony* was there reporting enthusiastically; invariably what the black girls won was never more than a consolation prize, but then, as seen in *Ebony's* highly professional photography, they were never particularly beautiful (in the 'modern' sense of external physical beauty). The puzzle is explained when it is appreciated that these competitions featured 'talent'—usually singing ability—as well as mere physical beauty. In the summer of 1965 a 'Negro girl' did win a victory of sorts, but again the story, under the heading of 'Negro Girl in "Miss America" Race: Voice Student Wins "Miss Rochester" title', was more revealing than the editors seemed to realize:

Sarah says she didn't know measurements were 36, 24, 35 until judges told her, adds: 'I guess they are right.' Classmate Carol Gane was Sarah's runner-up for title. Second balloting gave title to Sarah after a tie between the two. Girls were judged on five qualities: bathing suit appearance, talent (50%), formal gown appearance, charm and poise. Said one judge: It was close between Carol and Sarah. But Sarah placed very high on talent.'

My deduction from all this would be that black women were not really expected to look beautiful, though they were expected to be able to sing. Some black women, of course, *were* very beautiful, and in the less prejudiced international scene at the Cannes Film Festival black models won titles as International Queen of the Cannes Film Festival in 1959, and again in 1960.

It is 1966 which emerges as the fulcrum year, and I can set this up nicely by referring to an article entitled 'Instant Hair' in the November 1965 issue of *Ebony*. This, significantly enough, was a witty and light-hearted article on a topic which had always been of deathly seriousness for black women. Referring to her own 'crowning glory', the author notes that, in imitation of 'the Beatle Baez look' (in her own way the American singer of protest songs Joan Baez had an impact comparable to that of the Beatles), whites were now straightening out their curly hair: 'the finest human hair is European... American hair, they say, is too brittle for wig-making. And Negro hair? We are basically consumers, remember? Not producers.' The article is essentially a celebration of the many varieties of wig now available. What is most significant is that this article provoked a pointed, and even angry, reader's letter, published in the January 1966 issue:

It seems to me there is an on-going need for practical fashion and beauty information for women of color. I am sick of seeing negro women 'lift' make-ups intended for the 'natural' look on white skin, transformed to the 'unnatural' look on us.... I have seen enough bleached blondes to make me everlastingly determined not to lead this one life in such a horrifying, stupefying and shocking manner. Nor will white lipstick ever enhance the natural beauty of my lips.... With a daughter approaching her teens, I've become very conscious of this especially when she asks, is it true, blondes have more fun? Maybe—but who the devil wants to be the object of it, especially behind one's back?

In the very next issue (no doubt planned several months in advance) *Ebony* nevertheless plunged straight on with a full-colour cover entitled 'Are Negro Girls Getting Prettier?'. The six models on the cover and most of the women photographed inside were of the usual *Ebony* type. The verbal message inside was along the lines: 'Experts say better nutrition, grooming, know-how have brought improvement.' Gone, claimed the article 'are the spindly legs, sagging bosoms, unruly rumps and ungroomed heads that marred many a potential lovely of yester year. Such common flaws have been displaced by a feminine refinement, both facial and physical, that has elevated today's young lady of hue to a place of prominence among the most pulchritudinous.'

The article provoked some stinging letters: The first quoted below is essentially traditional in attitude, but the other three are bombshells:

How dare you? We Negro women are the only women in the world who don't get any praise for our beauty. Now you decide to write an article called, 'Are Negro Girls Getting Prettier?' We have been pretty all along. Just up until a few years ago we had no access to cosmetics, wigs, etc. White women have been using these things for years, and could afford them I might add. I suggest you rephrase your article to: 'Are Negro People (male or female) Getting Smarter?' According to that article you published, no—dumber.

Your February, 1966 issue of the magazine asks the question: Are Negro Girls Getting Prettier?' Why don't you put some Negro girls so we can see (instead of half white)? Are you ashamed of the Negro girl? Or do you go along with the white man's premise that a Negro can only be good-looking when he/she is mixed with the white race?

The cover of your (Feb.) issue delivered today made me (and a lot of other people I'll wager) wince. It should be titled 'Are Negro Girls Getting Whiter?' Come to my high school and I'll show you some girls to photograph who will illustrate, I believe, that Negro girls have always been pretty.

Yes, Negro girls are getting prettier! But your cover is a refutation of the statement. The majority of us are dark brown with bold features. The girls on your cover do illustrate various types of beauty. You have, however, omitted several other beautiful types which are much more typical of our people.

In June 1966 *Ebony* made the break. The cover heading was: 'The Natural Look; New Mode for Negro Women'. The cover photograph was of a stunningly beautiful black woman, an exquisitely proportioned and intensely appealing face, surmounted by close-cropped fuzzy hair. For once this was no model or blues singer; it was Diana Smith, a 20-year-old Chicago civil rights worker. The main article inside is headed: 'The Natural Look: Many Negro Women Reject White Standards of Beauty'.

A Frenchman who had been in this country but a short time was astonished to encounter on the street one day a shapely, brown-skinned woman whose close-cropped, rough textured hair was in marked contrast to that of Brigitte Bardot—or any other woman he's ever seen. Intrigued by her extraordinarily curly locks, he rushed up to her and blurted in Gallic impulsiveness: 'But I thought only Negro *men* had kinky hair!'

His prior observation had not been entirely incorrect, for, throughout the ages, American women of color have conspired to conceal the fact that their hair is not quite like any other. This key element in the black female's mystique was, until recently, challenged only by a few bold bohemians, a handful of entertainers and dancing ethnologists like Pearl Primus, whose identification with the exotic placed them beyond the pale of convention. But for the girl in the street—the coed, the career woman, the housewife, the matron and even the maid who had been born with 'bad' or kinky hair, the straightening comb and chemical processes seemingly offered the only true paths to social salvation.

Not so today, for an increasing number of Negro women are turning their backs on traditional concepts of style and beauty by wearing their hair in its naturally kinky state. Though they remain a relatively small group, confined primarily to the trend-making cities of New York and Chicago, they are frequently outspoken, and always aware of definite reasons why they decided to 'go natural'.

'We, as black women, must realise that there is beauty in what we are, without having to make ourselves into something we aren't', contends Suzi Hill, 23-year-old staff field worker with the Southern Christian Leadership Conference.

'Economics is a part of it too,' notes Diana Smith, 20, another stalwart at King's urban headquarters where natural hair has become a badge of honor. 'It's a shame, but many poor Negro housewives take money that should be grocery money and use it to get their hair done. Now that wigs have come along, I see kids whose families are on Welfare, wearing them to high school—wigs and raggedy coats.'

Of the letters printed in reaction to this article (in the August issue), eight expressed strong hostility to the idea of the natural look, seven strong support, though one of these noted that opinion among those with whom the writer had discussed the matter was overwhelmingly against; two further letters did not express an opinion either way. The arguments against tended to ask why, since white women spent hours beautifying themselves, and usually started out with hair whose 'natural state is stringy and straggly', black women should not do the same, or suggested that the next stage would be grass huts and 'rings through our noses'. The most positive response with respect to the natural look actually being appealing, as distinct from racially correct, came from a white, male reader:

To me the women photographed to illustrate it were among the most beautiful I had ever seen. The 'white standards of beauty' they reject are the same standards that choke our cities and suburbs with garish ugliness. May we all become more natural... in every way!

The most pungent female expression of hostility was:

It may not be a secret that our hair is of the so-called 'bad' type and gives us trouble some times, but let's assure this: 'We don't have to go around PROVING it!'

Over a year later *Ebony* returned to the topic, with the cover featuring 'Natural Hair—New Symbol of Race Pride', but this time showing leading male singers and actors. For the first time reference is made to the new slogan of the black liberation movement, 'Black is Beautiful'. An appreciation was developing that to attain some kind of acceptability it was not necessary for black women to pass themselves off as imitation white women, and that some black women were extremely beautiful in their own right and in their own style. Inevitably, many blacks, men and women, like many whites, remained plain or ugly. And just as the miniskirt and hot pants of the sixties gave way to other fashions, so many black women continued to opt for Caucasian hair styles. (It should be noted that many blacks have a considerable admixture of white genes, with the result that their hair is often naturally straight anyway.) The enduring point is that new choices had been opened up, and beauty was being recognized as a natural physical quality, not something related to the slavish imitation of convention.

The actual personal appearance of men, as well as their clothing styles, was receiving more and more attention. In March 1964 a top film actor had this written about him:

> While most people who have seen him agree that his boyish face belies his 37 years, they would disagree with his self-appraisal of 'averageness'. At six-foot-two, he is four inches taller than the average American male and there is nothing average about the feline grace of contained power with which he moves his mean frame across the stage or screen. Undoubtedly one of Poitier's biggest assets in today's climate of changing racial values is the dark complexion of his handsome, clean-cut face.

Sidney Poitier had himself modestly said: 'I am blessed with a kind of physical averageness that fits Negroes between 18 and 40. I look like what producers are looking for.'[14] The real point was that Poitier's colour was no longer an obstacle to the perception on all sides that he was a very handsome man. And whatever the confusion still attending black women in America, one, a young woman from Detroit, had established herself on the European scene by mid-1966 as one of the most photographed models of the time: Donyale Luna.

This really does drive home the point that the many varieties of beauty were now being recognized. Such being the way of the fashion industry, and such the way of the mass media, it is true that one type might be very strongly featured at one point in time and another at another; but many many different types of beauty were in and out of the headlines throughout the sixties. There was less pressure than ever before to conform to dictates and conventions in this matter.

The rise of the photographic model is intimately connected with the striking developments in advertising. Of similar importance in creating job opportunities for the good-looking were the growth of television commercials, of television soap operas and situation comedies, and of public relations, the advent of boutiques, and of mass eating-places aimed at young customers, the boom in pop music. The sense of the growing marketability of beauty is revealed in the establishment in the late fifties of agencies of various sorts, and especially modelling agencies, for example that of Catherine Harle in Paris, or Lucie Clayton in London.

Jean Shrimpton was born in November 1942, her father at that time being in the RAF. He was a businessman in the building trade, but with his wife owned a seventy-five-acre farm in Buckinghamshire. Jean Shrimpton, therefore, came from the lower fringes of the upper class; she went to a convent school and was brought up with horses—in David Bailey's words, 'a county chick, all MGs, Daddie, and chinless wonders'. A social phenomenon of the postwar world had been the way in which the upper class had moved into the various branches of the media and advertising (as well as more traditional pursuits such as banking, accountancy, and the higher levels of the law). The term 'model', though it did have a 'straight' usage, was also widely used to denote an expensive prostitute (in a famous letter to *The Times* at the height of the 1963 Profumo affair, whose central protagonist was the high-class prostitute Christine Keeler, always referred to in the press as a 'model', Lucie Clayton wrote that she presumed it would be only fair if the models in her agency took to referring to Christine Keeler as 'the well-known journalist'), but modelling was already recognized as a proper career for a respectable upper-class English girl, and the rewards of photographic modelling were already much higher than those of the more traditional mannequins. However, like so many others, in 1960 the 18-year-old Jean Shrimpton enrolled for a course in shorthand and typing.[15]

There are plenty of family snaps of Jean Shrimpton from a very early age. She was very much in the upper-class English style, long-legged and slim, with a lovely innocently sexy face. She was also well brought up and shy; possibly, belonging to an affluent environment in which most of the girls were personable and well groomed, she was not fully aware of her own beauty. Others were. While sitting in the lunchtime sun in Hyde Park she was spotted and approached by film director Cy Enfield and persuaded to meet his producer; however, the latter turned her down. She was then approached by a photographer: taking the cue, and being both fed up with shorthand and typing and under no pressing necessity to earn her own living, she enrolled at a school for models.

It is customary in guides to modelling to say that models do not have to be stunning beauties—indeed, Shrimpton says this herself in her own *The Truth about Modelling*. It is also always pointed out that photographic models have to be on the slim side since it is one of the quirks of the camera that it represents a person as if with an additional fine layer of flesh, making them look heavier than they really are. But this scarcely adds up to a case that models are socially constructed, or manufactured by the media: they sell on what they look like in their photographs, that is to say, with this 'extra layer of flesh', so it is absurd to argue that a new style of scrawniness was being created. Anyway, as I have shown elsewhere, throughout history slimness has always been highly regarded, fatness never praised.[16] The notion that almost anyone, given the right circumstances, can be constructed into a model is perhaps best met by Jean Shrimpton's own fairly gentle words: 'a heavy jaw-line, or squashy or bumpy nose is not helpful', and the eyes 'mustn't squint or disappear when you laugh'.[17] Certainly there is a quality of being photogenic which, it seems, some people have and some people do not; but, principally, being photogenic means being able to be natural in front of the camera, not freezing—a matter essentially of character and training.

Shrimpton went to a good modelling school, she signed up with a top agent, Lucie Clayton, she had contacts, she was beautiful, she was photogenic. Of course, the competition was fierce, but it is not really particularly surprising that she was quickly in great demand. The way she put it herself in 1964 is very fair, provided one recognizes 'gawky' as a highly relative term: 'one of the reasons for my success was that my gawky looks just happened to fit the fashion trend three years ago. Now the casual clothes and fashion I helped to publicise are in every shop.'[18] Without her association with David Bailey, Jean Shrimpton would probably have led at least a moderately successful career as a photographic model. They moved in the same circles, of course, and Bailey was not immediately struck by her potential; she seemed too inexperienced. But when they did team up he exerted an enormous influence over her, and it seems reasonable to accept her own estimate that he played a crucial part in her rise to a position of being for several years the world's top model.[19]

Lesley Hornby was born (in 1949) into an entirely different family background, not working-class, as was often said, but essentially suburban lower-middle-class. Her father's job (he was a master craftsman from Bolton) was no doubt in essence upper-working-class, but his postwar employment at the MGM studios near London gave him a rather higher status and income. The family owned their own house in the quintessentially lower-middle-class London suburb of Neasden, and they had their own car. Lesley's mother had come from a poor background, and had worked as a shop assistant in Woolworths; she had been a most attractive woman (she got engaged four times), and, not being able to afford make-up, used to put soot from the fireplace round her eyes, and always pinched her cheeks before entering a room. Twiggy—she was not called this in her childhood but, contrary to what is often said, she had acquired this nickname before being launched as a model—was much more involved in the real youth revolution of the time than Shrimpton, making her own dresses in order to conform to the style of her own partic-ular group. She claims that she 'really hated what I looked like as a teenager... In all these pictures of me at around twelve I am wearing a brassière with Kleenex stuffed in.' None the less, such were her neat figure and stunning looks that several people already thought that she was, or ought to be, a model.[20]

In March 1965, when she was fifteen and a half, and still at school, she met Nigel John Davies, or Justin de Villeneuve, as he was already calling himself. He was 25 and came from an incontrovertibly working-class family. At the time of his meeting with Twiggy he was working on an antiques stall with Graham Morris-Jones, with whom he also had a partnership in interior decoration. Justin de Villeneuve's rise obviously owed much to personality, intelligence, and guts; but, arguably, the particular roles he fulfilled were dependent on the fact that he was extremely good-looking. In his own description of his partnership with Morris-Jones he said: 'He was an architect, he did the jobs, and I was the front man, I would talk the deal and wear the nice clothes. I always looked smart. First impressions are important.'[21] Twiggy met Justin at the hair-dresser's where his brother Tony was working. Twiggy's reaction was: 'I thought he was lovely. Everyone liked him—everyone always does.' Justin's reactions: 'There was this lovely little girl, so tiny and so beautiful. She was breathtaking.'[22] It happened that Tony had a friend who dabbled in photography, and Twiggy was taken down to Wimbledon Common to pose for a few shots. Justin claimed (admittedly later, but there seems no reason to doubt the testimony): 'When I saw her being photographed on Wimbledon Common that day, that was the moment I knew I would crack it. I knew a few models and I had seen them work before, and Twiggy just had something about her that was absolutely right. And she was a kid of fifteen.' Twiggy continued to live at home while Justin adopted a paternalistic managerial role towards her, taking her first of all to one of the great progenitors of sixties fashion, Biba.[23]

It was Tony, before there was any hint of actual public success, who invented the name 'Twiggy', though Justin generally referred to her as 'Princess'. And it was actually quite indepen-dently of Justin that, while Twiggy was buying herself an old fur, a photographer—seeing her as she looked before there was even any question of her being constructed into a public figure—took a photo of her for an article in *London Look* about young girls wearing old clothes. Twiggy had a natural affinity for clothes and a natural talent for making them; Justin wasn't the only person to think that she had a great future as a model. But modelling schools would not accept anyone less than 5 ft. 7 in. tall or with less than a 33-in. hip. Photographer Michel Molyneux, to whom Twiggy was introduced by Justin, advised them to go to *Queen*, but she was not warmly received there. Justin's male friends appreciated the trousers which Twiggy was able to run up quickly, and it was decided that together they would open a boutique. Twiggy was taken up by Susan Robbins of *Woman's Mirror*, one of the new magazines featuring youthful fashion; the fashion editor, Prudence Glynn, thought Twiggy was too small, but took her on for head shots featuring the beautiful face. At this stage, then, Twiggy's extraordinary beauty was very widely recognized, but she was running up against a prejudice or convention about the appropriate size for a model; on the other hand, youth was very much the rage, and the trend in fashion was towards the sort of things that would look perfect on her. Maybe an element of artifice and grooming did help to resolve the impasse. Twiggy had an eight-hour session at the exclusive hairdresser, Leonard, the time being largely taken up with repeated drying out, to see if the very, very short style being designed for her was exactly right.[24]

She definitely was photogenic. She was photographed in her new style by Barry Lategan, who was already booking her for modelling jobs, when Deirdre McSharry, fashion editor of the *Daily Express*, saw the Lategan pictures. Two pictures were taken at the *Express*, which then devoted a whole page to this message: 'This is the face of '66—Twiggy, the Cockney kid with the face to launch a thousand shops and she's only sixteen.' This might not have meant too much, since only a short time before McSharry had written of Donyale Luna as *the* look of 1966. But since Twiggy really was both beautiful and different, that article did launch her career: a visit to Paris, the launching of the Twiggy line, and the stupendous visit to the United States.[25]

Without their looks, Shrimpton and Twiggy would have been nowhere. This was essentially true of the many new film stars of the period, some of whom I have referred to already. With the famous male beauties of the period the process leading to success was slightly different. The photographers Terence Donovan and David Bailey undoubtedly had talent, as had such actors as Terence Stamp, David Hemmings, Michael Caine, and Sean Connery. In a wider historical perspective the most important characteristic of all of them is that they came from solidly working-class backgrounds. Two considerations emerge. First, with regard to these uniquely successful working-class products, it seems reasonable to argue that, while the basic ingredients of success were talent and opportunity offered by the current cultural context, personal beauty operated as a characteristic which could out-trump, as it were, the old imperatives of class. Secondly—the point I am most keen to establish here—because most of these highly socially mobile and successful males were in fact personally beautiful, beauty then came to be seen as a necessary or at least likely component of success.

Of the Beatles, Paul McCartney was beautiful, George Harrison was good-looking in a rather conventional way, John Lennon was personable and sensitive-looking, Ringo Starr was less well favoured. Particular 'looks' slavishly created in imitation of some famous and beautiful female had long been known; but the idea of a male, Beatle look was relatively new, and testifies to the way in which masculine appearance was now becoming almost as relevant a consideration as feminine appearance. In fact, the two great points of reference in this respect were the Beatle look and the John F. Kennedy look, to which I shall return shortly. More generally, pop groups of all types, travelling around the country, often attracting enormous audiences, offered standards of male appearance with which large numbers of young females in the audience could compare the boys known to them.

It was actually in Portugal that the footballer George Best was christened 'the footballing Beatle'. But many of the assessments of him in England essentially saw him in similar terms: as a handsome, sexy mass entertainer, with a particular appeal for youth, and above all female youth. In a reference to Pelé, the brilliant but rather plain Brazilian star who dominated the footballing scene in these years, Best remarked: 'If I'd been born ugly you would never have heard of Pelé. I don't mean that women weakened me or anything like that, I simply mean that without them I might have concentrated more on the game and therefore lasted longer in the game.'[26] Muhammad Ali was another sportsman who fused sporting prowess with male beauty. The consequence of all this was to put a premium on male good looks. Most men did not have the looks of Terence Stamp, David Bailey, George Best, or Muhammad Ali, and almost none had their talent; but as opportunities expanded in all the ramifications of advertising, public relations, popular culture, discos, British-style pubs, and so on, those who did have the appearance of a Poitier or a Connery stood in line for at least a modest advancement.

But what I am talking of is opportunities for the beautiful, not of embargoes against the plain or ugly; vibrant, febrile societies gobbled up talent in whatever physical shape it came. But, crucially, the old dishonesties, the old confusions between talent, or other qualities, and mere physical appearance, were disappearing. If someone was actually ugly, it was now more acceptable simply to say so. Already in the early 1960s Barbra Streisand was on the way to becoming 'America's biggest female box-office personality'.[27] She had had a hard time of it in acting school, where her prominent Jewish nose made her an unlikely candidate for the conventional juvenile lead; she therefore turned to exploiting her remarkable singing voice. In her first Broadway roles she was deliberately cast as the plain girl, beginning the show with lamentations as to her lot. Her first outstanding success, *Funny Girl* (which became an Academy Award-winning film), opened with the chorus singing 'If a Girl Isn't Pretty'; in one of her song hits she lamented 'Nobody Makes a Pass at Me'. In interviews Streisand repeatedly harped upon her own perception of her lack of good looks.[28] No doubt this was a publicity gimmick, but there does seem to have been some insecurity:

> She genuinely fears that her looks are too great a handicap for her talent to overcome. 'I'd like to be beautiful but sometimes I think I am strangely put together.' When someone talking to her avoids her eyes, she gets upset... 'I think he can't bear to look at me. They always write about me as the girl with the Fu Manchu fingernails and nose as long as an ant-eater's. This hurts far more than if they wrote that I was a terrible singer—which they never did.'

That was from an interview in 1966 when Streisand was already becoming well established. Four years later she made this sad comment: 'There is this joke about a girl who went to the hair-dresser and said, "Give me a Barbra Streisand look." So he took the hairbrush and broke her nose. I guess I do have a strange face.'[29] This is not to deny for one moment that Streisand's vital-ity and talent, and no doubt her acceptable figure, rendered her attractive to many men; there are many articles praising her appearance—for instance *Le Figaro* in December 1965 spoke of her 'slightly clownish, yet seductive face'[30]—and she has since had many highly publicized affairs with some of the world's most eligible men. The point is the openness and, in a sense, honesty. What most commentators were saying was that because of the talent, and the personality, the looks began to cease to matter. But all the time a distinction was being made between Streisand's immense and indisputable talent and her looks. No longer was it an essential convention that one must pretend to find the successful star also supremely beautiful.

The central idea in this section is that one of the most distinctive, though perhaps least observed, features of the High Sixties was the critical change in the way in which personal appearance was evaluated. In direct support of this contention I seek concrete evidence in three areas: the empirical studies carried out by university psychology departments during the period; the guides to grooming which flourished more than ever before; and the worlds of business and political life. Academic research into new areas may profoundly change the way research, and perhaps teaching, are conducted, and may eventually affect society, through, say, technological innovation, or new theories or new social policy. But very often academic research follows, rather than leads, the social fashion. The critical breakthrough in this area of research came in the early 1970s, with continued development into the second half of the 1970s. The changes of the 1960s had drawn attention to beauty as a characteristic of high value, and had brought it to the atten-tion of academics as a suitable subject for investigation.

Now the sorts of experiments conducted by psychologists, social psychologists and sociolo-gists, since essentially they take the form of students being asked to give their reactions to other students of various degrees of personal beauty, deal with personal inclination rather than with actual behaviour or public mores. Since it is my opinion that personal inclination has remained relatively unchanged, while public mores and, to a degree, actual behaviour have changed quite considerably, I would not expect anything surprising to emerge from these experiments: they perhaps tell us, rather, about some of the timeless features of human response and character. Their significance, however, is threefold: first, as already noted, the fact that so many experi-ments of this sort were being carried out, and the historical period in which they were being carried out; secondly, the assumptions which the researchers brought to bear in their experi-ments; thirdly, the fact that these experiments made public truths about the nature of beauty which many in the past may have surmised but which were not part of public orthodoxy, thus reinforcing the 'modern' evaluation of beauty. If one compares the very few studies up to and including (publication in) 1960 with the studies published from 1968 onwards, there is an assur-ance and even ruthlessness in the latter about what can be defined as physically attractive or not physically attractive, whereas there is a hesitancy, or perhaps rather benign naivety, about the earlier studies.

The question of the significance of personal appearance impinges on three spheres: public life, life chances, and personal life (marriage, etc.). Sociological and psychological investigators have on the whole ignored the first sphere. Before the 1960s, only fairly obvious generalizations existed in regard to the second. With regard to the third sphere, the orthodoxy was that propagated in a 1952 article by Erving Goffman. This orthodoxy, the 'matching hypothesis', very much mirrored the orthodoxy of 1950s society as a whole. In Goffman's summary:

> a proposal of marriage in our society tends to be a way in which a man sums up his social attributes and suggests to a woman that hers are not so much better as to preclude a merger or a partnership in these matters.

It also involved the premiss that a plain person will choose another plain person, a slightly more attractive person a slightly more attractive partner, and so on; in other words, the levels of attractiveness will match each other in marriage choices.[31]

The work of crucial significance in the mid-1960s was that which suggested that, on the contrary, what both men and women really wanted was a partner of high physical attractiveness, whatever their own level of attractiveness. This in turn led to a dispute over whether in fact men and women really react in the same way over this particular issue. In the sphere of life chances, the research of the early 1970s suggested that it was generally thought that people of high physical attractiveness would be more successful in life, and that indeed in an empirical situation good-looking female students would be graded more favourably than less attractive ones.[32] Let us now look at some of the detail in regard to these contentions and debates.

The experiment which seemed to refute the 'matching hypothesis' was reported on in 1966.[33] The experiment sounds fun for those who organized it; it was obviously fun for some of the subjects and presumably quite painful for others. College freshmen were invited to buy tickets for what was billed as a 'computer dance'—a dance where they would be paired with an ideal partner selected by computer. In fact the students were secretly rated in advance on personality, intelligence, and social skill and then also, as they purchased their tickets, on physical attractiveness. They were then paired on a random basis, save that great pains were taken to avoid a short man dancing with a tall woman. According to the Goffman hypothesis, students who obtained, by chance, partners whose social desirability level was the same as their own would like each other more than those who were fixed up with partners whose social desirability levels were inferior or superior to their own. Half-way through the dance the students filled in questionnaires containing questions relating to how much the subject liked his or her partner and whether he or she would like to continue the relationship. Follow-up interviews four to six months later established whether or not the relationships had indeed been continued. The conclusion was clear: the only apparent determinant of how much each student liked his or her partner, how much he or she wanted to see the partner again, and how often they did in fact see each other again was how physically attractive the partner was. The more physically attractive the partner, the more he or she was liked.

Attempts to find additional factors which might possibly predict attraction were not successful; for example, students with exceptional social skills and intelligence levels were not liked any better than those with lower levels. Nevertheless, the correlation between physical attractiveness and liking was not perfect: a perfect correlation would be represented by the figure 1; in fact it came out at 0.78 for the choices made by men, and 0.69 for those made by the women. A further group of researchers seized on this discrepancy to argue that in fact this showed that women are significantly less affected by physical attractiveness in men than men are by physical attractiveness in women. The variation is 9 per cent and I suppose whether one regards that as significant or not is to some extent a matter of opinion. The most judicious summing up would probably be that, in the particular conditions of this experiment, physical attractiveness quite clearly was the key element for both men and women, but in slightly lesser degree for women than for men. These researchers then conducted an experiment of their own using photographs divided into three levels of attractiveness, particular care being taken 'to include extremely attractive and extremely unattractive pictures in the sample'. As well as being given the photographs of potential partners, subjects (again students—being involved in experiments of this sort was clearly an occupational risk at certain American universities) were given (invented) descriptions of their attitudes, the experiment being designed to assess the weighting of physical attractiveness as against attitude similarity. To their own satisfaction at least, the experimenters came to the conclusion that 'physical attractiveness is a more important determinant of opposite-sex attraction for males than for females'. This may well be so; personally I would give greater credence to an experiment based on actual meetings than one based on photographs, and I would suspect that students in this experiment were likely to give the answers they felt they ought to give rather than responding in a deep and genuine way. Nevertheless, it is true that even the computer dance experiment did show some differential between male and female reactions.

The same researchers also made the rather obvious case that the subjects in the computer dance experiment were not constrained by the pressures and inhibitions of real life (that, however, was presumably the point of the experiment, and it is in that that its principal value lies). The same point was made, perhaps more effectively, by another group reporting in 1971.[34] The point stressed by both groups of researchers was that the computer dance situation minimized, indeed practically obliterated, the risks of rejection. As the 1971 report nicely put it, those who by chance secured partners more attractive than themselves were 'assured not only of social contact, but of the fruits of social courtesy norms for the duration of the dance'. In addition, 'those who had achieved their ideal goal of a physically attractive partner may have shown more interest in *retaining* it than they might have shown in trying to *attain* it initially'. These researchers conducted two experiments to see whether the matching principle might reassert itself if the individual were required actively to *choose* a partner, rather than simply evaluate one already provided, and to discover what the effects would be if the possibility of rejection by a desirable partner was emphasized. Their conclusion was still that physically attractive partners were markedly preferred by everyone, women as well as men, but that *within* this general trend it was apparent that men and women of lesser attractiveness did tend to choose less attractive partners than did the highly attractive students.

A number of other experiments in the early seventies examined these aspects further. Huston (1973) again found the ubiquitous effect that, overall, men generally preferred to date the most physically attractive women, but that this was most pronounced when they were assured of acceptance; subjects who were not guaranteed acceptance believed that the highly physically attractive women would be significantly less likely to want them as a date than would either the moderately attractive or the unattractive women.[35] Or, in the calculating prose of this type of discourse:

> As in any bargaining situation the participants in the dating game have to learn the range of outcomes available to them. Being turned down or never asked for a date is embarrassing and frustrating, and the less attractive individuals, in order to avoid further frustration, possibly learn to stop trying for the most desirable and unavailable dates.[36]

Here, then, we have two types of experiment. The first, the computer dance, probes people's private inclinations: what they would do if there were not constraints, including their own unattractiveness, upon them. The second type of experiment brings in the effects of that sort of personal constraint. A third sort of experiment examines people who are already committed to genuine real-life relationships, either engaged or going steady. Here it was found, not surprisingly, that people of relatively similar levels of attractiveness tend overwhelmingly to associate with each other, and that such other factors as attitude similarity and role compatibility came into play. In the cold jargon:

> The results indicate that physical attractiveness, both as subjectively experienced and objectively measured, operates in accordance with exchange-market rules. Individuals with equal market value for physical attractiveness are more likely to associate in an intimate relationship such as premarital engagement than individuals with disparate values.[37]

Let us now turn to the experiments which cast light on the relationship between a beautiful appearance and a person's life chances. Dion, Berscheid, and Walster conducted an experiment (reported in 1972) in which sixty students, thirty males and thirty females, were asked to predict the personality and life chances of persons represented to them in photographs.[38] The researchers had prepared twelve sets of three pictures, half of women, half of men, of different levels of physical attractiveness. Half of the mixed group were given female photographs to respond to, half male photographs, i.e. some of the subjects were rating people of the opposite sex, some people of their own sex. The subjects were told that the purpose of the study was to compare their ability, as untrained college students, to make accurate predictions, compared with that of trained graduates. The experiment unambiguously showed that both male and female students, regardless of whether they were responding to male or female photographs, assumed that physically attractive persons possessed more socially desirable personalities than unattractive ones, and predicted that their lives would be happier and more successful in both the social and professional sphere. Dion, Berscheid, and Walster entitled their report 'What Is Beautiful Is Good', which could, of course, be seen as taking us right back to Plato and the most thoroughgoing traditionalism. In my view, however, they should have entitled the article 'What Is Beautiful Is

Successful', the qualifications for and attributes of success discussed by them being in fact highly secular and very far removed from traditional ideas about godliness and truth.

Although most studies confirmed the very positive advantages of being good-looking, it is relevant here to bring in some of the areas where being good-looking could seem to have adverse effects. For instance, Prebs and Adinolfi showed that being too pretty could activate envy and operate as a liability for both males and females looking for a college room-mate. Accused swindlers could be seen as more dangerous and given longer sentences when they were attractive, as compared with those who were unattractive, though for most crimes where attractiveness is not an obvious asset in commissioning the crime, attractive defendants were treated more leniently.[39] Dermer and Thiel showed that when rated by unattractive raters, attractive people may be perceived as vain and egotistical, as likely to have extramarital affairs and seek divorce, and as unsympathetic to the oppressed of the world.[40] Clearly, what is being said here is not that what is beautiful is good, but simply that in evildoing, beautiful people are once again likely to be more successful than unattractive ones: they are seen as more accomplished swindlers, more successful in sexual adventures. Some studies simply concentrated on the long-held suspicion that, in an essentially male-dominated world, beautiful female students were likely to have advantages over less beautiful ones. Results of experiments suggested that on the whole real academic ability, irrespective of looks, would be recognized, but that at the bottom of the scale, where the essay is in fact quite bad, beautiful girls will get some compensation while others will not.

From the foregoing brief survey of academic research I wish to stress two facets. First, that the concerted study of the subject of personal appearance essentially begins in the 1960s and then accelerates into the 1970s, as the transformations of the sixties, and the new explicitness about beauty, began to impinge upon academia. Secondly, beauty is now, in a cool and dispassionate way, far removed from the excitement and confusions of the traditional view, and is clearly recognized as a characteristic of high value in the lives people lead in the late twentieth century.

I want now to turn to the 'beauty', or rather 'grooming', guides of the sixties, to see whether, in comparison with such guides in earlier periods, their nature and tone has changed in a way which can be taken as consonant with the other changes I have been discussing. In the late nineteenth century one clear sign that a modern evaluation of beauty was gaining at the expense of the traditional one was the replacement in grooming guides of any suggestion that attention to personal appearance was a frailty which needed to be apologized for, by the categorical insistence that making the most of her physical appearance was a woman's absolute duty. Elements of joyfulness had appeared from the twenties on, but the great change of the sixties was that all the agonizing and the moralizing disappeared. While one French *Encyclopedia of Beauty and Well-being* boasted on its first page about cutting the 'pseudo-philosophical verbiage', most guides in fact simply plunged straight in, taking it for granted that for women (to stick with them for the moment) nothing is more natural and sensible than having an interest in their personal appearance. Some go as far as to insist—rightly, in the light of the other developments we have been discussing—that a good personal appearance is essential for social and business success; others lay as much emphasis on the notion that making up or dressing up is fun, the sort of fun every woman will instinctively wish to indulge in. There is no suggestion either that this is a stern duty, or that it is an indulgence which needs to be excused. What, however, is most often also stressed is the relationship between a good appearance and sexual attractiveness. No longer is there any suggestion that to be too beautiful is to be suspect because too sexy: sex is in itself a good thing, fun, like making up; and the relationship between sex and personal appearance is openly acknowledged.[41]

It would be wrong to expect beauty guides to be totally 'realistic', after the style of the academic articles reporting on psychological research that we have just been considering; a beauty guide which says that all it is offering is a little self-amusement, which will not in reality make a woman look terribly different, will not sell many copies. That said, there is, compared with the fifties and earlier, a much greater realism: there is greater restraint and accuracy in the description of cosmetics and what they can actually do. Nowadays, said one guide, women asked only the believable from cosmetics, and for that reason advertisers tended to give scientific information in their advertisements (no doubt government regulation played its part also).[42]

It would be absurd to claim that the word 'beauty' was now being used exclusively in the 'modern' sense, as an autonomous physical characteristic with a very high value of its own. 'Beauty' was used very much to mean self-presentation, involving grooming, make-up, and fashion; it was still also often used to mean the entire personality, as in 'Beauty is an attitude of mind'. However, it is noticeable that some books do speak of, for example, 'poise', 'personality', 'charm', or 'good grooming', recognizing that these are the qualities that can be achieved by skill and effort, while natural beauty really is something rather different.[43]

Now, of course, there were the styles already mentioned, associated with, for example, Jean Shrimpton or Twiggy, and a strong emphasis on the youthful, girlish look. Women who felt the need to follow the particular fashion of the hour were helped to do this by the fashion and grooming pages of the many magazines and periodicals. But in the less ephemeral publications the overwhelming stress is on health and fitness, dieting and slimming, not in order to achieve an artificial appearance but in order to give natural qualities the best opportunity of shining through. Injunctions about the need to keep strictly in fashion are on the whole replaced by the line that each individual person has a style of their own. 'Natural' in this context is inevitably a relative term. Some may argue that slimming is not really natural. All guides recognize, with Jean Shrimpton, that the achievement of an appearance of the natural might in fact depend quite strongly on artifice. All guides took pride in the democratic fact that such artifices were now more widely available to all social classes than ever before.[44] And I would seriously distort the facts if I did not mention the great attention, especially, as it happens, in France, now being given to cosmetic medicine and cosmetic surgery. Historically, slim legs have always been thought beautiful, save that, since for most centuries legs were scarcely on view at all, not a great deal of attention was given to the issue. Sixties styles did focus attention on beautiful legs, and therefore, of course, on their opposite: hence in particular the discussions of treatment for the condition which French medical cosmeticians defined as 'cellulite', though other medical figures denied its existence.[45]

A feature of the modern evaluation of beauty is an attention to male beauty as well as female.

In the 1960s and afterwards, the tonnage of material aimed at women continued to outweigh by far that aimed at men; but none the less the sixties were marked by significant changes, most obvious in the grooming and fashion articles specifically aimed at men in a number of magazines, but also apparent in guides exclusively concerned with masculine appearance, and also in special sections in guides primarily aimed at women. How much attention most men actually paid to the advice directed at them, or, indeed, how aware of it many of them were is not an issue here; the point is that such advice existed, as never before. Two major aspects of a man's life, it was argued, now required him to pay great attention to his personal appearance: his sexual activities and his business and professional life.[46] A man's appeal, according to one French manual, no longer depended solely upon his intellectual, financial and social attributes. A man conscious that he had made the most of his appearance, it continued, who was relaxed and lively, in good health and attractive, would easily win over one who is tired, fat, or who had obvious physical flaws. The man who exploits, says another French guide, all that fashion, industry and medicine have to offer will do best in both his professional and his private life; if he is confident in his appearance he will open many doors and many hearts.[47]

One might surmise that the man who had had to go to great lengths in the attempt to alter his personal appearance might not be all that confident; the all-important unwitting testimony is that the man who is already good-looking will be at an advantage. By the sixties, service itself was no longer a major source of employment (though servants with the right style and appearance were more highly prized than ever by those who could afford them), but service trades were expanding in all directions. The most obvious new occupation was that of male model— Catherine Harlé's agency in Paris started taking on male models in 1957—but the whole pop, fashion, leisure, public relations world was pervaded by an atmosphere which put a premium on a good appearance. Formerly the chief of protocol at the White House had tended to be a venerable type, strong on stuffiness, skilled in diplomacy: the new 36-year-old incumbent of 1965, together with his good-looking wife, formed an attractive team, looking 'like the former college prom queen and football captain at a five-year class reunion.[48] Even in the orthodox business world, appearance was counting for more and more, a summary of the situation as it existed at the end of the decade being set out in an elaborate French textbook entitled *Professional Success*, which drew mainly on American experience:

> For very many years, in business, little value was accorded to self-presentation, demeanour, and appearance in general. However, modern companies have completely revised their outlook on this point and they attach growing importance to the physical appearance of their executives.[49]

No doubt being personable was more crucial than being truly beautiful; but at the same time opportunities for the beautiful were greatly expanding.

For many jobs, of course, other qualities were far more vital than good looks, and many ill-favoured men continued to hold positions of power and responsibility. Job opportunities—not all of which were specially dependent on a beautiful appearance—were continuing to expand for women (though some of the more important developments did not come till the seventies). But it was very clear that, even more exclusively than with men, service, media, and public relations posts required beauty: two areas of employment which later drew unfavourable attention for their evident assumption that only beautiful women were suitable were those of the television presenter—Barbara Walters, the USA's most famous female presenter, had briefly been a model—and the 'air hostess' (as the term was in the sixties). For a woman to achieve a senior position anywhere outside traditional female professions (such as hospital care), and a position of real power anywhere, was still most unusual. What part looks played in the careers of the few who did achieve such status is a subject suitable, if attacked with rigour and empiricism rather than fashionable theory, for further analysis. I simply note that the two leading women in the British Labour government, 1964–70, Jenny Lee and Barbara Castle, and the first woman university dean (at Brest, 1968) in France (subsequently, 1976, minister for universities), Alice Saunier-Seïté, were all considerable beauties in their day.[50]

But it is to the world of male politics I now wish to turn. Events in the United States partly reflected the trends I have been discussing, partly accelerated them, and, in addition, created a potent metaphor for the political desirability of youthful good looks in the 'Kennedy image'. When in the late summer of 1959 it appeared that John F. Kennedy might beat Hubert Humphrey for the Democratic presidential nomination, the attention of the media, in the traditional way, was focused entirely on Kennedy's beautiful wife, Jackie.[51] As it happened, Kennedy's rival, like many politicians before him, was not an impressive example of male pulchritude. As W. L. O'Neill wrote of Humphrey a decade later, when the days of discreet silence about the harsh facts of personal appearance were truly over: 'He was overweight, and with his big balding dome, square little chin, and rat-trap mouth, offered a rather comic appearance.'[52] Kennedy's youthful good looks were at the time thought by the professionals to be a disadvantage, signifying nothing other than inexperience. Only with the first televised encounter between Kennedy and Nixon did the notion of the special appeal of good looks begin to be canvassed. Yet, even at the time of the new president's first visit to Canada, most of the attention remained on the beauty of the presidential consort; however, a Canadian (female presumably, though this is not made clear) was reported as saying of Kennedy, 'He's just a living doll!'[53] Kennedy's victory, and the fact that as president he was much in the public eye, helped to ratify the association, to which the other trends we have noted were favourable, between beauty and success; and Kennedy himself, more particularly after his assassination, became a metaphor for that success.

In May 1965 *Life* put on its cover John Lindsay, the Republican aspirant to the mayorship of New York. The article inside declared:

> With youthful verve and the long-legged grace of a heron, John Vliet Lindsay, six feet three inches tall, strode into the race for Mayor of New York and Republicans all over the country broke into ear-to-ear smiles... Lindsay is 43 years old and possesses enormous personal charm... Women surround him quickly. Their eyes light up as they try to prolong his handshake, a reaction that inevitably reminds many of Jack Kennedy's campaign days.[54]

Within less than a year, the spotlight was on a candidate, also Republican, for the governorship of California:

> The speaker stands tall on the rostrum, gazing across a thicket of scarlet carnations in the ballroom of San Diego's El Cortez Hotel. Every seat at every table is taken; every eye is eagerly fixed on him. Across the twenty feet that separate the dais from the first row of tables he looks almost twenty years younger than the fifty-four he is. The sober brown suit, the tapered white collar, the discreet tie are impeccable. His face is tanned, his smile dazzling. Not a hair is out of place (and not a gray strand is visible). He looks strong and youthful and vigorous. He has that new, clear, young look in American politics—the charisma of a John F. Kennedy, a John Lindsay, a Mark Hatfield.[55]

The candidate was the former actor and television presenter Ronald Reagan.

Reagan was shortly to win the governorship against the Democratic incumbent Edmund G. Brown, leaving Brown to complain bitterly about 'two-dimensional politics', 'package politics', and the evil influence of television: in doing so he pinned down Reagan's possession of a very valuable asset in his appearance (though also, to be fully accurate, in his voice):

> For two-dimensional politics, Reagan is also blessed with surface features that are immediately appealing: a resonant voice with a tone of natural sincerity and just the right touch of boyishness, a hairline as unmoving as the Maginot Line, and a ruggedly handsome face that is neither unusual enough to jar the viewer nor so deeply wrinkled that it can't be smoothed out with make-up. He will be sixty—the same age as Humphrey—but most Californians would probably guess, on the basis of *appearance*, that he is 10–15 years younger than the former Vice-President.[56]

Two-dimensional or not, the trend was set.

The association of Reagan with Kennedy may seem odd, perhaps even offensive. But the matter is a non-ideological one. Kennedy is simply a metaphor for beauty as an autonomous characteristic which, independent of political programmes or ideas, has political value (which is not to say that it is an *essential* ingredient of success—a quick role-call of presidents and prime ministers since Kennedy will immediately establish that; the argument is not that Kennedy made beauty indispensable, but that he ratified the association between beauty and success). It may be undesirable that looks should have this value; or it may in fact be an advantage that looks should be openly considered, as a prelude to separating them out from more worthwhile characteristics such as integrity or wisdom. Commercialism, misrepresentation, two-dimensional politics and the meretricious packaging of just about everything were inescapable facets of sixties society. Yet there was an admirable honesty, too, in facing up more squarely than ever before to the facts of human physical endowment. To medieval man, deformity or disability was a sign of evil; in more recent centuries they were matters to be politely ignored. It was, as we shall see, at the very end of the sixties that governments instituted the policies that have resulted in special, and quite explicitly advertised, facilities for the disabled.

All through the High Sixties the Memphis State University paper, *Tiger Rag*, remained a bastion of down-home American attitudes towards women and beauty. At the head of its leader column, it declared its editorial content to be coming 'From the Campus of America's Most Beautiful Co-eds'. In every issue there was a 'Campus Cutie'. Not until 10 May 1968 was there a letter asking why no blacks ever appeared among the Campus Cuties; the reply revealed that female students desiring to compete for this signal honour had to put themselves forward, filling out applications available in the *Tiger Rag* office; black women, unsurprisingly, never put themselves forward. In July a white woman student took over as editor, and in September the Campus Cuties item disappeared. In November an article on black unity criticized the apathy of black women 'hung up on this good-hair-is-straight-hair bit'.[57] On 14 January 1969 there appeared the first solo photograph of an individually identifiable black woman—the heading was 'MSU Journalist Gets Red Carpet Treatment', and the story line was about a journalism student 'feted in Abilene, Kansas, while doing research on juvenile rehabilitation'.

### Pick-Me-Ups and Pick-Ups

So relaxed and so liberated in so many ways, the British continued to bemuse visitors, and irritate many of their own people, with a licensing system governing the consumption of alcoholic drinks which went back deep into the past, but which had taken its final shape during the First World War when measures were enacted to ensure that overindulgence did not interfere with the war effort. In France and Italy intoxicating liquors were on sale in every most minuscule café, and throughout whatever hours the place chose to stay open. In Britain, the pubs did not open till 11 in the morning (12 noon in Scotland), then closed at 2.30 or 3 in the afternoon, opening again at 5 or 6, then closing at some time between 10 p.m. (in Scotland) and 11 p.m. (in London)—a few areas exercised the 'local option' to remain alcohol-free. Only a small proportion of restaurants (generally the more expensive ones) had special licences permitting them to serve alcohol with food; the overwhelming majority of cafés and eating-places were prohibited from serving alcohol. A modest reform in 1964 permitted ten minutes' 'drinking-up time', after 3 p.m. or 10 p.m., or whatever the closing hour was, in which drinks already purchased could be (and had to be) consumed. Previously all glasses had had to be empty at the actual legal closing time. Consuming drink after the ten minutes was, for both customer and landlord, a serious offence. In England more limited licensing hours operated on Sundays; in Scotland and Wales the pubs were closed, but an archaic system existed whereby bars attached to hotels were permitted to serve 'bona fide' travellers, who were supposed to sign a register indicating that they had travelled more than three miles—by the second half of the sixties the letter of the law was being extensively flouted, with certain bars being openly known as places where one could drink on Sunday, traveller or no. In England there were various kinds of drinking clubs, with more or less lax membership rules, which permitted those in the know to continue drinking when the pubs were shut. Another wrinkle in the licensing legislation made it possible for certain premises offering some kind of snack to serve alcohol for one hour beyond whatever the legal time was in the particular locality.

For visitors, and others wishing to enjoy themselves in a relaxed way, the curfews in the afternoon, in the evening, and on Sundays seemed very much at odds with the new swinging British image, but in fact revealed much about the continuing strength of older attitudes and prejudices.

In half of the United States the laws governing drinking were almost as relaxed as those in France and Italy, though, compared even with Britain, there were stronger efforts to prevent drinking among young people. In Britain the lowest legal age for consuming alcohol was 18 (the absolute ban on young children entering pubs was a serious problem for people, particularly tourists, with families; this apparent hostility to children marked a sharp distinction between social life in the Latin countries and in the Anglo-Saxon ones): in the United States the legal age for drinking ranged from 18 to 21 and, in some states, even higher. However, it was throughout the South that the liquor-licensing systems made Britain seem a model of rationality and good sense, and starkly revealed the deep sense within the American psyche that taking a drink was clear evidence of godlessness.

Among all the liberation struggles of the sixties, that to civilize the American South with respect to moderate social drinking has been the most neglected, though in fact it was of considerable importance, and had a number of ramifications beyond what might be assumed. A work of history describes and analyses; it does not pass moral judgements. None the less, in dealing with a topic of this sort it would be cavalier to ignore the unchallengeable evidence of the grave damage done by alcohol abuse; and it should not be denied that, on a range of grounds, alcohol consumption among young people should be discouraged. Having said all that, one can make a relatively neutral point about the separation of young people from adult society. While I have recognized the vital importance of the new initiatives being taken by young people from the end of the fifties onwards, I have also tried to resist both a too ready acceptance of notions of generational conflict and approaches which fail to recognize the importance of young adults and married couples in bringing about social change. American liquor laws, together with the unavailability of alcohol to students on certain college campuses, meant that in some parts of America there was a divide much less evident elsewhere. Many southern states had 'bone-dry' laws under which individual counties and cities could exercise the option of imposing total prohibition.

Depending on the locality, the fight to liberalize the drink laws had different focal points. In Memphis the two main ones were the exclusion of liquor stores from most of the more prosperous, suburban parts of the city, and the absence of facilities for the purchase of 'liquor by the drink' and 'mixed drinks', either in existing hotel and club bars or in 'open bars'. Already by 1960 the city's dedicated moderates were moving in favour of liquor reform: basically the arguments were economic—Memphis needed to attract conventions, tourists, and investment in new hotels. Others craved a touch of civilization and sophistication (New Orleans was always an object of some envy on this score). Mayor Edmund Orgill noted:

> Sale of mixed drinks would make possible places which would provide entertainment and fine food. We certainly don't want anything which would lower the city's moral

standards... We are so conservative that we lack the color, the excitement, the entertainment, the variety of eating places, which could make us attractive for many as a convention site.[58]

In October 1960 the question of open bars was discussed by the five-man City Licensing Commission. On the whole, the commission was in favour of 'limited and controlled open bars', but they feared to come out openly and say so. As one pro-reform journalist put it:

> they turned pale at the thought of the political consequences of taking such a stand. It's politically akin to denouncing your mother in public or spitting on the American Flag.[59]

One official actually advanced the democratic argument: 'In my own opinion, it is discrimination when citizens who cannot afford to belong to private clubs... and want to have a mixed drink in the bar are denied the privilege.'[60]

From 1964 onwards the political fears abated, and the matter was more and more openly debated, with both Memphis newspapers actively in favour of reform. At the same time, undercover policemen still sought to entrap those selling liquor illegally, and prosecutions continued. It was easy, however, for the press, in any case constantly putting the arguments for the economic benefits and for a more exciting and civilized society, to make these prosecutions look ridiculous, especially since proprietors usually tried to shift the blame onto the black bar staff. Even some of the judges seemed to be shifting to the side of reform. In December 1964 a *Press-Scimitar* editorial lamented that because of the Memphis liquor laws the owners of the Hilton hotel chain had decided not to build a Hilton in Memphis. Already, it had reported the complaints of visitors about not being able to buy mixed drinks at Memphis airport. However, when this matter was being discussed by the county's legislative delegation, the largest crowd in years turned out at the county courts to oppose any legalizing of the sale of mixed drinks in Memphis.[61]

The *Commercial Appeal* led the campaign for the wider diffusion of liquor stores throughout Memphis, and the matter was discussed by the city commissioners in April 1965. A strong plea was raised that the 'antiquated boundaries be done away with or extended'. But there was strong opposition from those who wished to keep the residential areas uncontaminated, and from the fundamentalist Christians. Dissent was expressed by the pastor of the Eudora Baptist church 'whose comments were seconded in a chorus of "Amens" from several other Baptist preachers in the audience'. The motion for change was defeated by four to one.[62] Next month Vice Squad Inspector Eugene Barkstale was reported in the *Commercial Appeal* as having bought drinks at the Rivermont club:

> Henry Neal, 45, of 3582 Pankey Lane, the bartender, and Fred Smith, 37 of 368-A South Fourth, a waiter, was cited for violating City and State Liquor laws. Mr Neal was released after posting $301 in bonds. Mr Smith remained in jail last night. Both are Negroes...
> Harry Snow, Rivermont Club manager, said employees are instructed not to accept

cash for drinks but that Mr Smith disobeyed orders. He will be discharged, Mr Snow said. Mr Neal and Mr Smith are scheduled to receive a hearing in City Court at 9 a.m. today.[63]

The American people had always been geographically very mobile, as families went in search of better opportunities and new livelihoods. In the sixties, people often travelled in search of more interesting or more luxurious holidays. Tourism was a great force making for a loosening of the licensing laws. Already, Florida was recognized as being 'among the wettest of the Southern states', and it was noticeable that most usually relaxation appeared first in the various resort towns. In general the Carolinas, both North and South, were bastions of the brown bag and the set-up; but the elegant old port city of Charleston was a rather more agreeable place in which to drink. As liberalization began to take place the contradictions and inconsistencies of the various laws began to seem more absurd; and it became easier to mock openly southern traditions of 'legally dry but bootleg wet', or 'voting dry but drinking wet'. Mississippi offered many benchmarks of obscurantism and, one could almost say, barbarism. It was therefore something of an event in 1966 when state-wide prohibition was ended there, leaving decisions to the individual counties and creating the kind of muddled situation endemic elsewhere in the South: both package sales and mixed drinks were now allowed in restaurants and private clubs; liquor by the drink could be obtained in cocktail lounges in what were called 'resort areas' (i.e. tourist spots); thirty-eight counties opted to go wet (two of them subsequently changing their minds and reverting to prohibition), forty-two remained dry; four others, because of technicalities, were half-and-half. Liquor by the drink was legalized in the Tennessee state capital, and rival city to Memphis, Nashville, in 1967, in the urban areas and resort communities of Virginia in 1968, and (because of a change in the Arkansas state law) across the Mississippi in West Memphis in 1969.[64] The owner of the Wonder City Restaurant there was very keen to exploit the change, but the proprietor of Watkins Café had serious doubts. 'I've been polling my customers,' the former said, 'and most of them seem to favor it.' He continued:

I personally would rather see folk buying a drink instead of a bottle. If we do qualify [i.e. by local vote] here at Wonder City, naturally I'll be going after some of that Memphis business, since they don't serve mixed drinks over there.

The latter feared good old mid-South bible-thumping hypocrisy:

My trade is almost exclusively local business and I just don't believe West Memphians are ready to sit down in a restaurant in their own home town and order a drink. I may be 100 per cent wrong, but I just don't want to face the financial risk and criticism from some of my church member customers.

The Watkins Café proprietor went on to admit that in the past his café had permitted 'brown bagging', but added that that 'was not the same thing as serving drinks over the bar'.[65]

A *Press-Scimitar* staff writer enjoyed himself in reporting a debate in March 1967, which brings out the weird thinking evoked by the issue of strong drink, but also shows how much had changed since 1960 when believers in liberalization felt it wise to keep quiet.

'Liquor by the drink' gagged some and went down smoothly for others as the hotly disputed issue flared back and forth last night at the Memphis Open Forum meeting held at First Congregational Church.
The issue aroused strong emotions and stimulated argument about other topical issues, such as the 10 Commandments, evolution and over eating.

Following total condemnation of the liquor trade by a Baptist pastor—'booze is the mother of crime'—there came a most eccentric advocacy of alcohol. France and England, the speaker said, are

two nations which have high alcohol consumption per capita rates, but which have made valuable contributions to civilisation.
On the other hand, he said, India and China—both having low consumption per capita rates because of religious taboos—have made very few contributions. He added:
'Germany had its lower rate of consumption when Hitler was dictator, and as you know Hitler was a tee-totaller and Herman Goering didn't drink—he was a dope addict.'

The comedy continued, with the report concluding with another strange appeal to history:

A woman in the audience assailed [the claim that] 'Overeating is as immoral as overdrinking,' saying: 'Overeating doesn't hurt you in the head.'
When Dr Pollard pointed out that there is more per capita drinking today and a higher crime rate as a result, he was questioned by a young man in the audience who gave statistics contending the reverse was true. The young man added: 'I have a resolution in my hands from the Methodist Convention from 1850, which censured Methodist ministers for no longer selling moonshine whiskey to the congregation after services.'[66]

Following a petition drawn up by those favouring liquor by the drink, a referendum was held in Memphis in August 1967. However, tradition was still strong, or perhaps, more accurately, the traditionalists were still more committed than the reformers: against the petition there were 61,827, for it, 52,240—a majority against change of 9,587; 41 per cent of those eligible voted. A further petition in 1969 produced a further referendum. This time 47 per cent voted, giving a majority for reform of 74,758 to 64,887 against. Serving liquor by the drink in Memphis began on 15 December 1969; the important social implications of this will be discussed in the final part of this book. Meantime, in June 1968 the boundaries limiting liquor stores to the central areas of Memphis had been removed. As there was to be no increase in the actual number of liquor stores, the outcome was simply redistribution. No liquor store could be less than 500 ft. from a church, a school, a park, a library, or another liquor store.[67]

In moving geographically, many Memphis liquor stores changed in character: 'Trying to build a "Neighborhood" clientele of housewives and their commuting husbands, liquor dealers moving their stores out of the crowded downtown section of Memphis are going in for a classy atmosphere, self-service and enough variety to tempt customers with wide tastes and the money to indulge them.'

> Owners are moving from cramped in-town locations with scuffed linoleum floors and counters which kept unruly customers a safe distance from the shelves into wide-open, well-lighted, carpeted school-boy-clean establishments in suburban shopping centers.
>
> Proprietors familiar with a furtive 'Gimme a half-pint of Thunderbird' are learning to respond with grace to a soft plea for help in choosing a wine to go with the fish. Or finding a scotch which will taste expensive when the boss comes to dinner but doesn't cost more than a salesman can afford.
>
> Wines are getting special treatment. Many dealers who kept mostly half-pints of cheap port are stocking up on expensive imports and high quality domestics.
>
> Joseph A. Lucchesi Sr. describes himself as a pioneer in importing fine wines to Memphis and says he now does a substantial business in imports at his store at 74 Union. He will build a special wine room in the rear of a new store at 3988 North Thomas.
>
> Mr Lucchesi, who can deliver a one-hour lecture on wines in three minutes said he'll stock books and other literature about wines, and will 'show customers the difference between wines of high quality and inferior wines'.[68]

Again we see how sixties changes often became part of a chain reaction. Liberalizing the rules governing the zoning of liquor stores contributed to new, more civilized patterns of liquor consumption. The advent of liquor by the glass was, in Memphis and other similar places, to facilitate the arrival of the singles bars already being established in New York and California.

No changes were required in the New York liquor licensing laws to facilitate the arrival of what quickly became known as 'singles bars' (sometimes also, more vulgarly, as 'body shops' or 'body exchanges'). Essentially these were upmarket versions of traditional New York Irish bars, combining bar service with relatively informal restaurant facilities, and aiming specially at attracting unattached women. As we shall see in the next chapter, there was at this time something of a fashion for English-style pubs, and to some extent the two trends merged with and cross-fertilized each other. However, I think the singles bar can safely be accounted a product of a specific American talent for identifying a new market and designing the perfect facility to meet it. The favoured location was the Upper East Side, and the two bars (both founded in 1965) which quickly became legendary were T.G.I. Friday's and Maxwell's Plum. The former name was a take-off from the traditional Irish pub featuring the owner's initials and surname (e.g. P. J. Clarke's, nearer midtown, which, while retaining the traditional model of bar at the front, closed-off restaurant at the back, and legendary middle-aged barmen, did also appeal to the newly fashionable young clientele). In Friday's and Maxwell's Plum, bar and restaurant occupied essentially the same space and were staffed by handsome young college students. Let us consult some contemporary sources. *Broadman's Social Guide to New York Bars* explained its purpose thus: 'For singles, separated, divorced, and one nighters: where to go what to wear how to connect.' Part I is entitled 'Approaching the Watering Hole', and is divided into short chapters on, for example, 'Sex for the Liberated Separated', 'How to Say Hello', and 'For Women Only'. In this chapter we read:

> The majority of watering holes on the Upper East Side, from 60 to 86th streets, on First, Second, and Third avenues, have evening specials for women on weekdays and brunches for everybody on Sundays. The evening specials starting at the cocktail hour (5:00) usually consist of drinks at half-price or free. And the reason is obvious. Gals attract the men. And the men are the spenders....
>
> Most of the women over 30 that we've talked to either firmly state, 'I don't sit at bars (alone),' or 'I just haven't got the courage to be put on display'. It makes a lot of sense. Having the odd-balls making pitches, snide remarks, and taking your being there as an invitation to bed, is pretty hard to stomach. *But times are changing and so is the thinking.* Bars, saloons, and bar-restaurants in the better neighborhoods are perfectly acceptable meeting places. Instead of staying home nights, steeping in self-pity and bemoaning the scarcity of eligible men, more women... are going out to local watering holes.

P. J. Clarke's makes an early appearance in Part II, 'The Watering Holes':

> As 'in' Irish, He-man bars go, P. J. Clarke's has to be near the top of the list. It's one of those three-deep bar places that attracts out-of-work actors, working actors, the model that did that ad in *Cosmopolitan*, the advertising creative guys that laid out the ad, the account executives and—the majority—those who come to stand at the bar next to them.
>
> Especially you gals who have been looking for a place where the men are part of the Beautiful People or arty set.

Shortly we come to Friday's, 'one of the oldest singles pubs on the strip':

> Wednesday, Friday, and Saturday are *the* nights. But get there about 8:00 or you'll have a tough time getting into the place. And when you do get in, you'll find Friday's no different in atmosphere—chequered tablecloths; juke-box music; hanging Tiffany lamps; young, moustached (or 'stached', as they say) waiters; and long beat-up wooden bar—from any other pub on the strip. Don't be disappointed, though, because the girl-meets-boy syndrome is in full gear at the bar.

Maxwell's Plum is featured as '*the* East Side showplace establishment. If you're a guy from 24 to 40-plus or a gal over 21 but not quite 40, Maxwell's is a must.'[69]

Myra Waldo's *Restaurant Guide to New York City and Vicinity* also features most of the same places, but in addition includes the more hippie Max's Kansas City Steak House (between

398

Midtown and Greenwich Village), stressing the strong element of 'spectacle' involved in the appeal of these places.[70] Max's Kansas City 'is a hang out for long-haired hippies. Max's food is fairly good, but the atmosphere and people are more interesting...' The entry ends reassuringly: 'Incidentally, despite the bizarre dress of the clientele, the hippies are generally well behaved as a rule and all is quite respectable.' Max's Kansas City was in fact a favoured hang-out of the Warhol crowd.[71]

British-style pubs (the Edinburgh Castle and the Rose and Crown were famous in San Francisco) and singles bars spread to other urban centres in the United States. In the French and Italian press, singles bars were commented upon as Anglo-Saxon curiosities; nothing exactly analogous appeared in France or Italy before the end of the sixties—perhaps they were not so much needed. Nor were many specifically new locales created in Britain (as distinct from fully-fledged restaurants): certain traditional pubs in certain privileged areas (near universities or in traditional bohemian quarters) suddenly became very lively, packed with young people and often, for the first time, introducing jukeboxes; particularly well known in the metropolis were the Flask in Hampstead (which resolutely resisted the jukebox) and the Chelsea Potter on the King's Road in Chelsea. In many ways this was a last golden age for the British pub.

All decent-sized towns in both France and Italy had been reasonably well supplied with agreeable places in which to eat or drink. Still, there had been plenty of room for improvement in the backward and poverty-stricken areas. Let us have a last piece of testimony from Bonagente:

> In 1957, we did not have all the bars and inns we have today. When you return to Bonagente, you will find the Trattoria of Camillo. Every evening you will find twenty or thirty people over there. They play cards, drink a bottle of wine, speak about their work, exchange ideas, and also speak about politics. That is a 'good time'—leisure. The same happens in the inn of Cherubini, which has been opened for only two years. We have still other taverns at Lago Profondo and at Birio where people meet in the evenings...[72]

Fairly humble and still rustic stuff, no doubt. But for all the variations of location, clientele, and tempo, one can see that a common atmosphere of affluence and of joy in living was spreading to all parts of the four countries we are studying. As more and more non-British restaurants opened in Britain, a greater interest was also being taken in more imaginative cuisine within the home. A pioneering figure was Elizabeth David, who had produced books on Mediterranean, Italian, and French provincial cooking during the 1950s. In 1965 she opened the first of the shops which sold high-quality (mainly French) kitchen equipment. While Britain strove to catch up with the traditions of France and Italy, the French took a leap in a new direction: I'll discuss *la nouvelle cuisine* in the next chapter.

All the developments of the High Sixties had their negative sides, and often an exaggerated, even hysterical emptiness. Some commentators of both right and left have been harsh. Speaking of Italy, Ernesto Galli della Loggia has written:

In a few years a gangsterish speculation threw itself upon the peninsula and swamped it in its misdeeds.

The Italian scene, the countryside within which for centuries the Italians had lived, was destroyed and disfigured for ever: hundreds and hundreds of kilometres of coasts, ancient towns and communes, prestigious historical centres, entire islands, woods, moors, and alpine valleys, disappeared or became unrecognizable.

The workers gained, della Loggia admits, but, he says, 'at the expense of their historic identity'. He goes on to identify 'a series of typical images' of this new, unfortunate age: the television quiz show pitched at the collective psychosis, the annual summer exodus to the holiday cabin at one of the popular resorts; three-quarters of the year spent on organizing Christmas, symbol of an ephemeral miracle. The new heroes are the 'spectral personages of show business'. These are international phenomena, but at their most virulent and destructive in Italy, because Italy was governed by a Catholic ruling class 'not only incapable to the ultimate degree of dominating and organizing these phenomena, but destined to be swept away by them'.[73] This strikes me as a harsh judgement. In so far as conditions were the tougher in Italy, the achievements were the greater. There were obstacles to desirable change, and incentives to callousness and exploitation, in all countries. This chapter seeks to show the ways in which opportunities did expand, both on the material level, and with respect to self-expression and freedom from the constraints of custom. But we are not far enough into this book for an overall assessment. The most truly stirring events of the sixties have yet to be discussed.

### Pedestrian Precincts and Swinging City Centres

Commercial interests led both Memphis newspapers to take a liberal stand on liquor, resulting eventually in an improvement in the quality of life for ordinary citizens. The same instincts led them to aggressive support for the destruction of Overton Park, a much more vital component of high-quality life for the local people. However, the environmental movement, though terribly fragmented, was now under way. The High Sixties is a time of private and commercial responses to environmental problems often being in conflict with each other, of increasingly positive initiatives by ordinary citizens, and of more frequent, if sometimes contradictory, interventions by governments. Historically, the United States had pioneered certain aspects of protection of the countryside, the first National Parks having been set aside in the nineteenth century. With respect to the new kind of urban planning, not predicated upon the primary necessity of free movement for the motor car, most of the initiatives were European. The first pedestrian-only street in the motor car age had been established in Essen in Germany in the 1930s; the first extensive experiment in the new age took place in Copenhagen, where the five continuous streets collectively known as Strøget were first closed to traffic in 1962, this innovation being made permanent from 1964. Here I resume the stories of San Francisco and San Francisco Bay and of Overton Park, Memphis. Then I turn to France, where the dysfunctional central situation of the traditional market, Les Halles, together with concern over a particularly crumbling and decrepit section of the Beaubourg *quartier* to the east, merged with Gaullist commercial ambitions, and then in turn provoked resistance from people, publicists, and opposition politicians, and where pedestrianization schemes began to be developed in provincial towns; to the United Kingdom, where much 'urban renewal' of the most disastrous sort continued, but where pedestrianization was pioneered ahead of France and Italy; and to Italy where a unique urban heritage was menaced by a fanatical commitment to the internal combustion engine, and where environmental initiatives were late and reluctant. Finally back to the United States, where the sad and shabby saga of Beale Street, Memphis only just eclipses those of the rest of down-town 'redevelopment', and of the predatorily expanding medical centre, but where, also, Atlanta was creating a unique combination of historic preservation and a total post-modern city centre.

California's middle-class protesters carried California's middle-class legislators with them, and in 1965 a California State Act established the Bay Conservation and Development Commission, described in a US Department of Transportation report as 'the first major step anywhere in the United States toward an enforceable regional plan embracing several counties and dozens of cities', which 'promises to become a catalyst, stimulating efforts here and elsewhere to transform the chaos of metropolitan sprawl into rational, comprehensive planning of an orderly, efficient, beautiful and humane environment'. No doubt the universal promise was never fulfilled, but between 1965 and 1969 local legislators were deluged with letters supporting the environmental protection initiatives and calling for stronger ones. A second State Act in 1969 made the commission permanent and gave it stronger powers.[74]

In Memphis the next flurry of activity came in 1964, by which time the protesters had estab-lished themselves as a pressure group to be feared, rather than a minor nuisance to be dismissed. They were increasingly subjected to mocking fire from the two newspapers: 'Let's stick to the facts about the expressway' said a *Press-Scimitar* editorial of 19 June 1964—the facts, it seemed, were all on the side of the wisdom of building the expressway and ignoring sentimental pleas on behalf of the park. Within a week of this editorial Mrs Handy received an unpleasant hand-printed anony-mous letter, in an envelope postmarked 25 June 1964:

DEAR MARIE, I HATE TO SEE YOU MAKE SUCH A FOOL OF YOURSELF OVER THE EXPRESS-WAY. WHY DO YOU THINK THE CITY PLANNERS HAVE ANYTHING BUT THE BEST INTEREST FOR THE CITY? EXPERTS PLAN THE ROUTE AND YOU GARBLE THE FACTS SO THAT ALL PEOPLE FEEL IS PITY FOR YOU. IF YOU PERSIST IN SUCH AN ABSURDITY NOONE WILL HAVE CONFIDENCE IN ANYTHING YOU DO OR SAY INCLUDING YOUR FAMILY. WISEUP AND FIND A MORE SUITABLE HOBBY.

AN INTERESTED FRIEND.[75]

Needless to say, the redoubtable Mrs Handy took such contemptible communications in her stride. A vigorous correspondence with city and state officials ensued.[76] Officialdom was unmoved:

It is easy to assert that the trees of Overton park are invaluable and should be spared at any cost, but those who control the expenditure of the tax dollars, both state and federal, which finance the interstate highway system, cannot responsibly accept this point of view.[77]

However, if there was no change on the local political scene, big changes were taking place in Washington. The Department of Transport Act of 1966 transferred the Federal Bureau of Roads (fanatics for building interstate highways whatever the environmental consequences) from the Department of Commerce into the new Department of Transport. The Transport Act declared it to be 'the National Policy that special efforts should be made to preserve the natural beauty of the countryside and public parks and recreation lands':

> After the effective date of this Act, the Secretary shall not approve any programme or project which requires the use of any land from a public park, recreation area, etc. unless there is no feasible and prudent alternative to the use of such land.

Given the complex division of powers within the United States, not to mention the ambiguities within the phrase 'no feasible and prudent alternative', and given the entrenched attitudes and interests of powerful forces in both Nashville and Memphis, this did not by any means entail victory for the Committee of Citizens to preserve Overton Park, but it did mean that if they chose to go to law they had a solid basis on which to fight in the Federal Courts. The case of the protesters was further helped when the National Environmental Protection Act was signed into federal law in January 1970.

Much of the Memphis establishment remained committed to the building of the expressway, but on their side the protesters had the services of the brilliant Memphis lawyer, Charles Newman. In these real life legal proceedings there was no dramatic *dénouement* in the style of such TV programmes as LA *Law* or *Ironside*. The suit was appealed through the various levels of the Federal Judicial system till it reached the Supreme Court in 1971, where there was no conclusive ruling. Meanwhile Nixon's secretary of transportation, John Volpe, who had previously approved the freeway plan, though with significant qualification as to its design,[78] totally rejected it. The magnificence of the victory won so far—houses had been destroyed, but Overton Park had still not been touched, and the State Highway Authorities were prohibited by Court Order from encroaching nearer than one mile from the edge of the park—is brought out by the violent sentiments still being expressed within Memphis itself. The president of the Union Planters Bank and also of the Memphis Chamber of Commerce declared it an 'outrage that the road isn't permitted to be completed. It is a major inhibiting factor in downtown growth'. The *Press-Scimitar* produced the heading 'Environmentalists Spilling Blood': 'The spilled innocent blood is that of those unfortunate individuals killed on overcrowded Memphis streets—who would still be alive if the expressway had been built through Overton Park, as it was originally scheduled to be constructed years ago'.[79] The expressway was never built: Overton Park was saved. Meantime the House of Representatives was beginning hearings on 'The Quality of Urban Life', while, in 1968, the American Institute of Architects established an Urban Design and Development Group. On 8

April 1969 the institute adopted a statement calling for 'renewal and development of our existing cities', and 'particularly a commitment to the creation of a humane environment for all our people'.[80]

Drastic urban reconstruction at the behest of the state was very much in the French tradition; somehow there had always been an acceptable balance between ruthlessness and good taste—at least as far as prosperous inhabitants and tourists were concerned, if not for the poor whose quarters were torn down in the name of progress. Massive building projects were in the hands of the Sociétés d'économie Mixte, companies financed by a mixture of public and private money: the consequence was a steady population movement from city centres to arid suburbs. Then in 1962 there came a striking example of the positive, 'one-nation' side of Gaullism (comparable with the initiative on provincial theatres): the Malraux Act introduced conservation areas *(secteurs sauvegardés),* historic areas which were not only to be preserved but enhanced. An Act of 1967 compelled all towns of over 10,000 inhabitants to produce plans demonstrating how they were dealing with issues of conservation. Unfortunately, commercialization continued to compete with environmentalism and respect for the rights of traditional communities, and many areas, particularly working-class ones, were exempted from planning controls.[81]

By the beginning of the sixties the circular motorway round the city of Paris, the *périphérique,* was already under construction, and parts of the banks of the Seine were being converted for the rapid movement of private cars. A major perceived obstacle to ongoing modernization was the old, congested market in the centre of Paris, Les Halles, whose elegant pavilions, ironically enough, dated from exactly the same period, that of Napoleon III, as the major boulevard system of Baron Haussmann who had destroyed so much of old Paris. Les Halles was situated in an area of small restaurants and bars, a place of romantic attraction to both Parisians and tourists alike. However, it undoubtedly imposed heavy traffic burdens upon a wide surrounding area, was itself inefficient, and (it was claimed) lacked proper standards of hygiene. The basic idea was to move the market to the outer suburbs, and to redevelop the area vacated. All of this was placed in the hands of a government commission attached to the prime minister but involving representatives of the city of Paris as well as of the state. A decree of 1 December 1961 provided for the acquisition of the land on which Les Halles itself was built, at the very ungenerous price of twenty francs a square metre. A decree of 13 July 1962 made Rungis, well up the River Seine, the designated home of the new market. A further decree of 2 December 1963 made provision for the compulsory purchase of land surrounding the old market. It was expected that developments both in Paris and out at Rungis would be completed by the end of 1967, with the entire transfer of the market facilities taking place at the beginning of 1968. It was intended that the initial government commission would shortly hand over to a Société d'économie Mixte, composed of equal numbers of representatives from the state, the professional experts, and the various Parisian organizations—an ideal Gaullist combination of state and commercial interests; the cost of the entire plan was estimated at 370 million new francs. Rejoicing in the favourable vote for the whole programme obtained at the Paris municipal council on 13 November 1963, Amédé Brousset, National Assembly deputy for Paris, commented sarcastically on the environmentalist sentiments of certain Paris councillors, referring to a historic session in which, one after the other, St Louis, Philippe le Bel, Louis XIV and Napoleon were invoked and, in which tender-hearted councillors expressed concern on behalf of the *clochards* [the famous Parisian street-sleeping down-and-outs], particularly *habitués* of the les Halles area, without extending their solicitude to the ladies selling their charms in the rue Saint-Denis.

To preserve Les Halles, Brousset said, was to preserve 'the surrounding slums'. Rungis, on the other hand, offered the ideal location, seven kilometres from the Porte d'Italie, the southern entrance to the city of Paris, and near the recently constructed motorway, the Autoroute du Sud.[82]

Brousset put this case in a lecture to foreign diplomats on 21 May 1964. The pressing question, he said, was: if the market did have to be removed, what was going to be put in its place? In his address, subsequently published as a publicity booklet, Brousset presented the official vision, weighed down with his own ponderous sarcasm:

> Personally and for many years I have never separated the need to move les Halles outside of Paris from the need to renovate the space thus liberated and to have thought about that very carefully well in advance of the final closure of the market. So I find it utterly natural everyone is worried, and is asking questions, about what will take the place of the twelve pavilions which are going to disappear and of the five hectares thus freed, especially if there are no restrictions....
>
> Some people will want a vast five-hectare meadow reserved for the little birds; some want to construct a stadium; there are ministers who dream of installing their ministries; the University wants to establish itself on both sides of the river. Fortunately there are others sensitive to history. Saint-Eustache will rise grander than ever. The Bourse du Commerce and its Italianate tower are safeguarded. There will be a swimming-pool, leisure grounds, shops, workshops for artisans; there will be food and other wholesale businesses, a flower market; underground parking with 20,000 places and, in prospect, hotels for ordinary tourists. While beyond the Boulevard Sevastopol, against the horizon there will stand out the city of artisans and artists.[83]

Brousset expressed the very essence of Gaullism, invoking the glories of France, quoting from *The Death and Life of the Great American Cities* to point up the awful warning of America where urban centres had simply been left to decay, and blowing the trumpet for the renovating powers of private enterprise.

To the east of the Les Halles area, between it and the Marais, the seventeenth-century quarter which, thanks in part to private initiative, was then undergoing restoration, was a small derelict patch known as the Plateau Beaubourg. Here ancient cottages had crumbled, or had been burned to the ground, leaving an eyesore on which people parked their cars. Although there were fine six-storey buildings in the rest of the Beaubourg quarter, the streets on both sides of the Boulevard Sévastopol were both brash and squalid. There was a story that de Gaulle himself had been offended by the prostitutes openly plying their trade in the rue Saint Denis (referred to sarcastically by Brousset) and had insisted that they should all be swept away.[84]

It was perfectly reasonable for the authorities to argue that, since the removal of the markets inevitably required action over what was to replace them, action should at the same time be taken with regard to the Beaubourg area. But despite the visionary scene conjured up by Brousset, it was clear that the government commission and its successor, the Société d'économie Mixte, intended extensive demolition, and the introduction of large-scale commercial development. There was enormous hostility from ordinary citizens and growing uneasiness among planners and politicians, as a more humane concept of urban planning began to find acceptance. The protesters also had the support of a press characterized more by measured judgement than enthusiasm for Gaullist commercialism.[85] The definitive decisions which led to the relatively humane Les Halles-Beaubourg development as we know it today were not taken till the mid-seventies, but in retrospect the municipal council meeting of 6 July 1967 can be seen as a critical moment. Convening at 4.15 p.m., the meeting lasted until 5.45 a.m. In the end the council rejected the notion of a commercial centre, banned any high-rise buildings, and expressed determination to preserve 'the cultural and educational vocation of the quarter'.[86] Models representing the existing plans of the Société d'Économie Mixte d'Aménagement des Halles were put on view in the Hotel de Ville: 6,000 Parisians came to look and, almost to a man or woman, indicated their hostility. Meeting on 13 March 1968, the council decided to abandon all existing plans and set up a new commission of elected members. On 24 October the council adopted the project drawn up by this commission. This envisaged a vast subterranean forum, installed around the proposed new interchange station Châtelet-Les Halles, linking the old metro with the new suburban express railway (RER), while the area of Les Halles itself was to be transformed into a vast pedestrian space, encircled by renovated housing, an international business centre, a large library, and some hotels—effectively, the library (which went to the Beaubourg) apart, what we have today.

Outside Paris, the first French city to take up the new concern for the urban environment was Rouen. The initiative was from above rather than below, and the target was as much the elimination of traffic jams as the protection of the city centre. Deputy Mayor Bernard Canu called for action in 1966; in 1967 a protected-sector plan, with facilities for pedestrians, was drawn up, under the provisions of the 1962 Malraux Law. In April 1968 the newly elected mayor, M. Lecanuet, together with architects and town planners, visited Sweden. The chief architect of Norwich, demonstrating clearly the rapid circulation of cultural ideas, gave a lecture on what was being achieved in his city. Public involvement now began to grow: strongly supported by the main local newspaper *Paris-Normandie*, Canu, towards the end of 1969, won agreement for the establishment of a pedestrian area centred on the rue du Gros Horloge, which starts from the magnificent medieval clock. The first phase of the project was implemented in May 1970, when a municipal order prohibited general traffic movements and regulated the entry of delivery vans. The streets were repaved in a manner we are now all familiar with: pavements eliminated, since pedestrians could now roam at will.[87] We tend to think of France as having always had a form of outdoor café society not indigenous to the Anglo-Saxon countries. The words of the OECD report on Rouen give us pause, and again remind us of how much of what we take for granted today actually originated in the sixties:

> The first measures, in May 1970, coincided with a dry spell of weather and met with popular approval from the start. The three cafés near the Gros Horloge were allowed to bring out chairs and tables into the street and several retailers set up display and sale counters.

The second phase began on 15 September, and embodied a more elaborate approach, with the relaying of paving stones in peacock-tail patterns and the installation of new street lighting.[88]

If anything, the Italians are more addicted to their modes of personal transport even than the French, and more insistent on getting right to their destinations without any need at all to walk. However, after a law of April 1963 had given cities (optional) environmental powers, a much stronger one of 6 August 1967 made provision for the safeguarding of urban areas 'of historical or artistic character, or of particular environmental value'. A further law of 19 November 1968 laid down rules for zones of special value with respect to history, the environment, or natural beauty.[89] Bologna, where the Communist local authority was a splendid example of what Italian Communism, at the local and practical level, could achieve, was the leader in imaginative and sensitive environmental policies, and the first city to take action under the 1963 Act. In 1966 conservation orders were placed on the historic city centre, which in 1968 became Italy's first pedestrian precinct *(isola pedonale)*. Restoring the historic buildings of the city centre—suffering both from age and the bombing raids of the Second World War—was a massive operation. The inhabitants were moved to 'parking houses' erected on cleared sites on the edge of the central area, being given the option of moving back into the restored central area once the work was completed—without regard to the great enhancement in property values which had meantime taken place. One of the team of foreign architects who came to study this experiment was deeply impressed (whether he fully understood what was going on may be a different matter):

> In visiting one area we were particularly struck by the fact that the architect who showed us around was known to all the inhabitants who greeted him and frequently asked his advice on various matters. This was obviously a secure community, intimately related to their environment and this relationship was emphasised by the provision of small gardens in the middle of city blocks previously choked with 'temporary' structures or by the display in various buildings of archeological items found on their sites during the course of the work.[90]

In Perugia the central street, the corso Vanucci, which runs the length of the plateau on which the old city is built, from the cathedral to the ramparts, was closed to traffic during daylight hours; even in Rome, where futurist intoxication with the motor car had created total contempt for the interests of pedestrians, the third city plan of November 1968 designated certain parts of historic Rome as pedestrian-only areas. These were only beginnings, the major developments coming in the early seventies.

The brutalist attacks on the British urban environment had begun in the 1950s; many of them continued, and were intensified, throughout the 1960s—the destruction of Victorian Birmingham is a case in point. However, it was also in the High Sixties that protest movements against 'urban renewal' and in favour of conservation began to mobilize and that, indeed, official conservation agencies began to be set up. The city of Norwich, with its beautiful cathedral close, its castle, and, perhaps most important, its lively and innovative college of art, was the pioneer. In 1967 the city adopted the first British plan for the pedestrianization of central city streets, testimony in this case not so much to creative British thought as to openness to continental experimentation—the city planner had previously toured four European cities. First London Street was closed to motor traffic, followed a year later by Lower Goat Lane, Dove Street, and White Lion Street. These, as their names suggest, could all lay some claim to historic origins; the claim to fame of Carnaby Street in London lay entirely in the present, but as other cities began to follow the Norwich example, this centre of sixties fashion was closed to traffic during the daytime hours. History, however, is no simple tale of the good and the bad; some critics have blamed the subsequent decline of Carnaby Street into an emporium of tourist tat on this exclusion of normal traffic. At government level the Civic Amenities Act of 1967 was followed by the revised Town and Country Planning Act of 1968, the basis for expanding environmental initiatives at the end of the decade.[91]

From plans that (as these things go) succeeded, let us turn to one of the most striking examples of failure in urban planning. Beale Street for today's visitor to Memphis is a shocking disappointment, especially if that visitor is already familiar with Bourbon Street and the French quarter in New Orleans. By the middle of the sixties there was, at federal level, a strong wish to give overt recognition to black American cultural achievements. Within Memphis, too, there was a perception that at least some token recognition of Beale Street as birthplace of the blues not only could be claimed as a generous civil rights initiative but might also be good for the tourist trade. The problem was that among influential Memphians, including the few blacks as well as the much larger and more powerful number of whites, there was no sense of how a shabby and run-down street, to the south of the city centre and therefore on the fringes of the main black ghetto, could be revived and restored. For whites and blacks, 'urban renewal' meant tearing down old buildings and replacing them with money-making modern ones. Among Memphis civil leaders there was a total aversion to the spending of citizens' money on any such programme. What they did like to do was to get a hold of any federal money available: the easiest and most profitable way of deploying that money was in knocking buildings down—there was, anyway, a feeling that rebuilding ought to be left to private enterprise.

In the summer and autumn of 1965 the local congressman was working hard to have Beale Street declared a National Landmark. As he wrote to the leading black citizen G. W. Lee, 'I feel that if this is done it certainly will be a tribute to the contribution of the American Negro to the nation.'[92] The street was so designated in May 1966, and the dedication ceremony took place on 28 October that year. But this was all good intention and window-dressing, with no backup of the kind that really counted. Some of the people who acted so vigorously to preserve Overton Park also had a genuine sense of the significance of Beale Street, but there was no concerted popular movement as there was in resistance to the freeway project. Some of the interest was rather academic, and some eccentric in true 'doing your own thing', half-hippie, half-commercial, sixties style. There was strong interest from the Memphis State University history department, where an oral history project was established in April 1966.

From July 1965 Memphis had a claim on federal money for what was presented as a Beale Street urban renewal programme, receiving an advance of $462,425 in the middle of that month. What was really intended came through clearly in a statement of March 1966 by the executive director of the Downtown Association: 'I think the real purpose of urban renewal is to make funds available to private enterprise to help it acquire land for needed improvements.'[93] G. W. Lee was at the head of a group of black investors who produced their own 'Negro Plan'. This envisaged one massive new building whose ground floor would house the Tri-State Bank:

> above the ground floor will rise three storeys of parking space and two storeys of office area, with the top nine floors as motel units. The proposed building is expected to produce nearly six times as much annual tax revenue as the properties currently on the site.[94]

It was left for the white Jewish proprietor of the cheap menswear shop, Lansky Bros, to draw attention to the last point powerful interests were concerned with:

> You're forgetting one thing. If you tear down all these buildings you will no longer have Beale Street, and you will defeat your purpose.[95]

There were efforts at resistance from Lansky and many of the other local traders, but they faced the same autocratic and money-grabbing attitude from officialdom as had faced the Overton Park protesters, and black businessmen certainly were not in agreement with the white protesters. The Memphis chapter of the (black) National Business League adopted a resolution critical of those opposed to the planned redevelopment, once again demonstrating unexpected cross-currents to the race issue:

> 'As a racial group we have been moved and removed in urban renewal programmes,' the resolution says. 'Now, for the first time when a Negro group seeks to build and participate in the removal and renewal of an area which will displace a group of white merchants, a loud cry is made against the whole concept of urban renewal. If this concept is fair and legal when Negroes are removed, congruously it is fair when whites are removed. For the sad truth is that if the urban renewal plans were dropped tomorrow, no one would be sadder or more sick than the "Beale Street merchants" who say they oppose. For they are a part of a dying street that vitally needs help from some outside source.'[96]

At the beginning of February, the executive director of the Memphis housing authority declared that 'private business is eager to step in with new development if urban renewal clears the way'.[97] The owner of the York Army Sporting Goods Co. was reported as saying: 'We protest this. We have been in that location sixty years. It is profitable.' The indefatigable and far-sighted Lansky suggested that the housing authority investigate the possibility of urban renewal in the Central Station-Union Station area further to the south, rather than the Beale Street area.[98] At the beginning of March about twenty of the aggrieved local traders met with the housing authority director, who told them that the plans were still in 'the "jelling" state':

> Generally, the Beale Street Urban Renewal Project calls for a sweeping revamping and revitalization of Beale, with new buildings for commercial use, a pedestrian mall, a night club district, enlargement of Handy Park and other changes.[99]

The 'grand opening' of the 'New Beale Street East night spot' was no great harbinger of change, as this new venue was entirely inside the existing Sheraton Motor Inn, out on the fringes of the area. Ewald and Associates, the planners, publicly offered the estimate that every dollar spent by government on this sort of project would engender sixteen dollars for private enterprise.[100] According to the executive director of the Memphis housing authority, the area was 'earmarked to become the entertainment center of Memphis'. It was to become 'another gaslight square as exists in St Louis, or another French Quarter [New Orleans] type tourist attraction'. A 'New Beale Street' was to be created, 'with much of the flavor of the Beale of W. C. Handy's day remaining and the probability that it will become a real tourist attraction.' It was to be the first project in Memphis 'to combine conservation with demolition'. The jumble of heritage wannabe and straight profit-seeking went on, and on. Buildings would be preserved, including those 'which have some historical significance, such as the site of Pee Wee's Saloon, where Handy wrote the "Memphis Blues"'. But the 'anchor of the project' was to be the new Memphis Light Gas and Water Division administrative building.

> Other plans have been discussed to refurbish Beale Street as a sort of gas light area, with places attractive to tourists. It is expected that pawn shops and other colorful places on Beale will be kept. Many of the present business places would be improved.[101]

In March 1967 the *Press-Scimitar* featured an article on the 'Dramatic Contrast Between Old and New Memphis', in which

> our new Civic Center's modernistic stone and glass towers rise from wide, landscaped promenades, cheek-by-jowl with the shabby little row of ancient stores on North Main, soon to be razed in the name of progress.
>
> At the other end of Main, there is controversy about the direction of change. Sam Hunsaker, advertising consultant of 214 S. Cleveland, has a somewhat different perspective:
> 'I knew Beale Street in the early twenties. How distinctly I remember the foyers of

furniture stores and others—each with a victrola back near the door playing Negro songs which I was never able to find in the music shops. Terrific! I used to cruise Beale almost every night with tremendous fascination. I have been away more than 30 years. Returning to Beale for a bout of nostalgia—it wasn't there!... That era should be preserved as a Memphis landmark! We should reconstruct it just as Williamsburg has been reconstructed. Let MLGW put up their fancy building—but couldn't we set aside a block or two for the real old Beale Street? Not the New Orleans French Quarter touch—it couldn't be that—but the tawdry, loud, native, Negro flavor of this historic landmark.'[102]

However, the paper dismissed this 'different perspective' as 'romantic'.

Well before 1968 Beale Street was *en route* from being merely a run-down, tawdry street to being the even more dismal demolition zone it was by the end of the decade. The gloom was intensified by certain events of 1968 (discussed in Chapter 11). The big march organized by Martin Luther King in connection with the sanitation workers' strike passed that way, and the rioting was particularly severe on Beale Street, with the white-owned businesses being attacked. Then the assassination of King took place not far away in the Lorraine Motel in the all-black ghetto to the south. This atrocity cast a shadow over whatever enthusiasm there had been for genuine renovation. By 1970 1,500 people had been driven from the area, and most of the white businesses had gone.[103] In the new decade Memphis caught a whiff of the new fashion for pedestrianization; and the struggle between sentiment and cupidity continued.

Civic inertia in Memphis may be contrasted with the release of energy which the advance of civil rights seemed to provoke in Atlanta. Atlanta had no Beale Street and it had no Mississippi waterfront (shamefully neglected in Memphis), but it did have its romantically named central thoroughfare, Peachtree Street, and as the railway age gave way totally to that of the automobile, the Memphis authorities discovered another asset, known by the end of the decade as Underground Atlanta. Atlanta had grown up as a railway city, the railway running into a natural gulch. Steadily this gulch was bridged over, and then built over. Still, in the early sixties the 'Underground Atlanta' thus formed was not thought to be of interest or value. Celestine Sibleif's *Peachtree Street, USA: An Affectionate Portrait of Atlanta*, published in 1963, has a style matched to its title, but is in an illuminating source all the same:

This is upper-deck Peachtree Street. There is another. Beneath the pavement of street and sidewalk and the hauled-up earth of the little park lie the rail-road tracks, which shaped and ordered so much of Atlanta's history and geography, including the start of its most famous street. No visitors and only a limited number of citizens know this down-under world of granite-block streets, iron rails and black faced dusty buildings. By day it is the freight entrance to downtown stores and office buildings and is alive with the movement of trucks and trains, of whistling workmen swinging boxes and crates about. Shafts of sunlight shimmering with dust motes sift down around viaducts and alleyways to illuminate it by day. At night it is deserted. Commerce relinquishes its hold on this world and it is taken over by derelicts, by drunks and doorway sleepers. 'Bus Stop Bill', a bleary-eyed citizen whose profession is mooching car fare, comes home from a hard day at the bus stops with a bottle of muscatel for his stomach's sake and an exciting evening of eluding the police patrol on its regular pick-up journeys through the area.

Despite its sinister appearance there's little crime down here. The old winos and rummies who regard it as home are not quarrelsome. They ask only to be let alone, a snug cranny against the winter rain or cold, the comfort of the misty, tomblike chill when summer heat bears down on the pavements above.[104]

Within ten years Underground Atlanta had become the first place hosts thought of taking their visitors to see. As a guidebook published in 1978 put it: 'This charming "City Beneath the City" is an authentic restoration of the shops, saloons, cafés, cobble stones, banks, and ware-houses of our fast-and-loose young rail-road days and a wonderful welter of restaurants, night clubs, shops, exhibits, museum, and special attractions have been added'—including wax works.[105] But at the same time Atlanta went inspirationally modern. To quote the same guide-book, on 'the complex that changed Atlanta's skyline (and the world's mind about Atlanta)':

Peachtree Center, our vibrant new-as-tomorrow city within a city, is one of the premier stars in our downtown crown. Architect John Portman created this soaring world with its coordinated structures, parks, plazas, outdoor cafés, restaurants, and lounges, theatres and night clubs, offices and shops. And the whole world is copying.[106]

In the High Sixties the environment was nothing like as high up political agendas as it is today. Atrocious development plans continued to be commissioned and implemented. But there were a number of very solid achievements, in large measure due to an unprecedented activism on the part of ordinary citizens, though usually transmitted through a refreshing willingness to think again on the part of many politicians and planners. Practical achievement was essentially at local level, yet environmentalism, as much as rock music or anti-Vietnam war protest, was international. Key events were the Venice conference of May 1964, which produced the International Charter on Conservation and Restoration, and the Council of Europe Convention at Bath in October 1966. The 1964 charter opened up a new vision of the historical monument as an integrated entity, relating to peoples rather than rulers.[107]

Of course such a concept, as we have seen throughout this section, could inspire the profit-conscious heritage business, rather than genuine environmentalism. None the less, the decade which had opened with Rachel Carson setting down her anxieties about what was happening to the natural world was to end with thoroughly thought-out international initiatives relating to all aspects of environmental concern.

411

# 10

# National and Other Identities

## Les Années Anglaises?

The notion of the irresistible force of Americanization, and specifically the Americanization of Western Europe, has been with us for a long time. J. B. Priestley, novelist and pundit, detected strong American influences in the Britain of the 1930s; Americanization has been represented as being particularly potent in France and Italy during and after the Second World War. Marxists, disappointed—as ever—in the failure of the West European working classes to do their duty by history, were wont to invoke Americanization as the seductive force sapping the revolutionary energies of the workers. More recently, commentators of all faiths have come to recognize a general modernization, as distinct from a specific Americanization, as a process affecting the behaviour and political attitudes of people in all advanced countries.[1] At the same time, it would be absurd not to recognize the primacy of black American music, of white American commercialized popular music, and of Hollywood films. The rise of particular forms of British pop culture has to be set within that framework. Did these forms actually break out of the framework in the High Sixties? Certainly British popular culture enjoyed unprecedented prestige and influence during this period; so the first topic to be explored in this chapter is that of popular culture across the four countries with specific reference to British initiatives and British influence. The second section examines the world of the hippies, the drop-outs, and the 'underground'; is this a world in which American hegemony cannot be challenged? Then to two areas where sixties innovations, or rather alleged sixties innovations, have subsequently come in for much criticism as having gravely weakened the fabric of society: education and responses to crime. The criticisms are raised only in Britain and America: only the two 'Anglo-Saxon' countries, apparently, had 'progressives' and 'do-gooders'. All four nations, in fact, retained national traditions, national peculiarities, special fields of achievement and excellence, and it is my purpose to bring these out, particularly in the final section of this chapter, even as I stress also that all peoples in the West went through the same unique transforming experiences.

My title for this section is taken from some articles published in *Le Monde* in the summer of 1986 by the journalist Michel Winock, reprinted as *Chronique des années soixante* (Chronicle of the Sixties). In explication of this phrase 'the English years', Winock wrote:

> If one flag deserves to fly over the hot-pot of the sixties, no doubt that it should be the Union Jack. That England which the continentals imagine to be always corseted and controlled by Victorian principles was putting the *the* into the youth of the world.[2]

The Union Jack, of course, is the British, not the English, flag; what Winock meant to speak of was 'the British years'. This is a considered verdict ten years after the event; but there is a mass of testimony from the decade itself to the same effect. In May 1966 *L'Express* declared that Great Britain is the country 'where the wind of today blows most strongly'. Just over a year later the same paper remarked: 'Thanks to The Beatles, to the Rolling Stones, England rules over international Pop Music; their young actors are the best in the world.' The American magazine *Time* brought out a special issue in April 1966 devoted to 'Swinging London', that city being described by *Epoca* in Italy as 'the happiest and the most electric city in Europe, and the most nonconformist'.[3] That the driving influence was the youth subculture whose 'knitting together' I described in Chapter 3 was widely recognized, as it was by Winock in his phrase about 'putting the *the* into the youth of the world'. Eight months later, in July 1966, *Epoca*, half in horror, half in grudging admiration, published an article on 'This Madness of English Youth':

> five million young people under twenty-one have subverted all the customs and conventions of British society; they have broken the barriers of language and of class; they dress up, they make a noise, and they are rebelling against the rules governing reticence and modesty about sex. What do they want? Nothing, save to live in this way.

The article went on to mention that the discothèque had practically taken the place of the nightclub. There was a mention of Mary Quant, and a picture of Carnaby Street and John Stephen's boutique.[4]

If there was one single critical event in the establishment of the hegemony of youth-inspired British popular culture, it was the two-week tour of the United States by the Beatles in February 1964, consolidated by the second longer tour commencing on 19 August of that year. The first releases in the US, which Capitol had passed on to minor companies, had not sold particularly well, and an engagement at the Paris Olympia from 16 January to 4 February had been less than enthusiastically received. It took lobbying and planning, and commercial pressure from EMI, to ensure the conditions for success in America; but in fact the true basis had already been securely laid. A year of hit records and television appearances in Britain, together with a performance at *Sunday Night at the London Palladium* on 13 October 1963, led to the emergence between October

413

and December of the phenomenon of 'Beatlemania' among the group's adoring pre-teen and teenage fans. The Beatles' conquest of Great Britain was ratified by their appearance at a Royal Command Performance at the Prince of Wales Theatre, London. The sight of screaming fans, and of the Beatles themselves, telegenic and always ready with laconic and wittily debunking remarks, delivered in broad Liverpudlian accents, became one of the earliest sixties 'spectacles'. In the States the first records could be purchased, even if only by the most advanced and enthusiastic fans; more important, the Beatles themselves with all their charm, and the astounding reactions they provoked, could be seen on American television. The importance of Brian Epstein has already been mentioned; Epstein lobbied, EMI applied commercial pressure—and Capitol could discern the makings of international stars.[5]

When *I Want to Hold Your Hand* was released in the States on 26 December, Capitol put a full-strength publicity campaign behind it. The LP *Meet the Beatles!* was issued on 20 January 1964, and a re-release of *Please Please Me* ten days later. On 1 February *I Want to Hold Your Hand* was top of the hit parade in America, a week *before* the Beatles themselves arrived. That Capitol had pulled out all the stops in what no one has ever claimed was a totally innocent business had undoubtedly helped; the free media publicity secured by the group helped further; but there is no doubt that the novelty and freshness of the group's approach which still captivated the British, young and not so young, also captivated American record-buyers. The arrival of the Beatles in America revealed that Beatlemania had also arrived; adoring mobs of youngsters gave them a reception at Kennedy Airport which was quickly flashed around the world. On 9 February the group appeared live on *The Ed Sullivan Show*, watched by a record seventy-three million audience—clearly the Beatles already had an appeal, or at least an interest, for far more than teens and pre-teens. Sandwiched between that performance and a second appearance on the same prestigious television show, the Beatles performed at the cathedral of upper- and middle-class classical concert-going, Carnegie Hall. In March, *Twist and Shout* and *Can't Buy Me Love* were issued in the United States in advance of British release. In April, with *Can't Buy Me Love*, the Beatles held the other four top positions in the American hit parade, something unprecedented and of course highly newsworthy, and also a further eleven places in the top 100. On the second visit to America, 19 August to 20 September, billed as their 'first American tour', they gave twenty-one live shows and one TV performance, starting at the Hollywood Bowl and concluding with a refusal to perform at Gator Bowl, Jacksonville, Florida, without a guarantee that the audience would be unsegregated.[6] The Beatles owed almost everything to black music; many took them, legitimately enough, as symbolizing youthful radicalism, though they were never more than what one might call 'honorary' members of the movement; like many others they dipped in and out of 'counter-cultural' events, being obviously also part—why not?—of the highly commercialized rock/pop scene.

However, although the Beatles made the first and critical breakthrough for British performers in America, they might not necessarily have lasted beyond the glorious year of 1964. There were many challenges to their preeminence, particularly from the Rolling Stones, and the real essence of their achievement is that in a period when British groups really did dominate (though, as new American groups came to the fore, far from monopolize) the Beatles, continually

414

innovating, remained the most widely recognized and celebrated group till they themselves chose to disband in 1970. Their impact in America reached to strange places: as early as 1964 a librarian at Yale University wrote to Allen Ginsberg, with reference to the next presidential election: 'I have enregistered to vote and am starting a write-in campaign for The Beatles.'[7] The joke was intended to be taken at least half-seriously. The tour promoter, Arthur Howes, had no doubts as to the unique achievement of the Beatles, but, it must be noted, he expressed his admiration in the crudest business terms:

> The biggest thing The Beatles did was to open up the American market to all British artists. Nobody had ever been able to get in before The Beatles. They alone did it. I had brought over lots of American stars, but nobody had gone over there. They just weren't interested. By opening up the States, The Beatles made an enormous amount of money for this country.[8]

That was undoubtedly one big consideration in, and often a major public justification for, the award of MBEs in June 1965; within the mind of Labour Prime Minister Harold Wilson, who did participate in the cultural vibrations of the sixties to the extent of inviting figures from both élite and popular culture to his Downing Street parties, it was probably impossible to separate out genuine admiration from a politician's desire to be seen in close proximity to the country's most popular personalities.

In 1964 the Beatles were involved in the making of their first film; in 1965 they gave up touring and live performances. From 1966, in an indispensable alliance with George Martin, they made increasingly complex recordings dependent upon the most sophisticated studio resources. A Beatles song was always instantly recognizable, yet the variety of styles they essayed seemed almost endless. Of three 1965 hits, *Help!* was fairly reminiscent of the earlier Beatles, *Ticket to Ride* was psychologically deeper than anything they had yet recorded and, with respect to 'sheer sound... extraordinary for its time—massive with chiming electric guitars, weighty rhythm, and rumbling floor tom-toms',[9] while *Yesterday* has been described by Charlie Gillett as 'a tritely sentimental ballad'—a judgement which must be balanced against the fact that classical composer Peter Maxwell Davies thought highly enough of it to arrange it as a guitar solo.[10] It is in part because of their very variousness that the Beatles have so often been spoken of as the voice of the age—while the Americans Bob Dylan and Joan Baez were much more closely identified with the civil rights and student protest movements. With Beatles songs direct links between lyrics and current events are not easy to find. In general, it was a case of music and lyrics together constructing—constantly changing—moods which never failed, it seemed, to evoke responses in large numbers of listeners of the day. Their music was eclectic, yet insistently experimental, and indeed extremist—very much in keeping with the other expressive modes I have been discussing throughout this book. In their Britishness they were, as we saw, part of a greater transition whereby hitherto invisible swathes of British society became visible and assertive. This transition, subject of course to particular national circumstances, had its universal aspects, and the Beatles, in their demeanour as well as in their songs, appealed to all who were touched by that transition.[11] The song which most directly expressed the new class-defying tide of individualistic enterprise in Britain is *Paperback Writer* (released in America on 13 May 1966 and in the UK on 10 June), whose lyric alludes to the current trend-setting writers, film stars, and fashion designers. The Beatles had a marijuana period, and an LSD and psychedelic period (drugs not always being essential for psychedelic effects). The effects of pot-smoking were apparent in *Paperback Writer*, in *If I Needed Someone*, which was also strongly influenced by George Harrison's interest in Indian music, and, most notably, in *The Word*. The LSD period coincided with the period of increasingly complex singles—notably *Strawberry Fields Forever* and *Penny Lane*, released, in one of the great bargains of all time, on opposite sides of the same record, in February 1967—and the great LPs, above all *Sergeant Pepper's Lonely Hearts Club Band* (1967).[12] A 'dramatic cycle' rather than 'simply a chain of songs', it uses a full symphony orchestra, draws upon Indian influences, and in its totality is an expression of drug-expanded consciousness.[13] Further LPs followed, and also one of the most memorable of all singles, *Hey Jude* (1968).

George Harrison went to India in September 1966 to study music with Ravi Shankar. Oriental mysticism, transcendental meditation, Indian music and apparel were all coming into fashion among youth, counter-cultural, and protest groups. From August 1967 the Beatles had as their spiritual adviser the Maharaja Mahesh Yogi. Of explicit political commitment there is not a great deal in Beatles songs: the single most obviously associated with one particular contemporary outlook on the world's problems, *All You Need Is Love*, was one of the more banal; *Revolution 1*, first released on the obverse of *Hey Jude*, and *Revolution 9*, part of the LP *The Beatles* (November 1968), were both, in their verbal messages, confused and contradictory, and were bitterly attacked by the Left. John Lennon had wanted to register the Paris events of May 1968;[14] given how these and other events actually turned out, the partially drug-induced chaos of the record was perhaps after all quite close to reality.

The Beatles made the breakthrough into America. Other British bands quickly followed. Would they have done so anyway? Given that these other groups were products and voices of that great transition of which I have already spoken, one has to say that it is possible. One can go no further than that, since the Beatles were very nearly an irresistible phenomenon. What does have to be stressed is that the rock/pop aspect of 'the British years' comprised many, many more performers than just the Beatles, though their only real rivals were the Rolling Stones. When the Rolling Stones were founded, Mick Jagger, lead singer, was a student at the London School of Economics, and two other members were at the Sidcup Art School. In order to distinguish them from the endearing Beatles, their manager Andrew Oldham encouraged them to project a wild and anti-social image. Oldham took them to America to record, and both their first British number one, *It's All Over Now*, and their first American top ten hit, *Time Is on My Side*, were recorded in Chicago.[15] Their most powerful records, from 1965 onwards, were made in the RCA studio in Hollywood: *Satisfaction*, *Paint It Black*, *Honky Tonk Woman*. As Charlie Gillett puts it:

by the end of the sixties, the Rolling Stones had virtually created a new category for themselves; having moved on from the Chuck Berry/Bo Diddley/Muddy Waters boogie blues, through the soul influence of Solomon Burke and Don Cobay, which represented the entire panorama of the past fifteen years of black dance music, they welded it all to lyrics which enabled a young white audience to identify themselves with the messages. And all this, while continuing to ignore 'the rules' by which popular entertainers traditionally found acceptance in the media. So far as anyone could tell from the outside, the Rolling Stones did not care what anyone thought about them, and this insolence gave them great strength.[16]

Importantly, the Rolling Stones, like the Beatles, had stamina; the latter lasted till 1970, the former apparently forever. At one time the Animals, with lead singer Eric Burdon, looked like challengers, but the group began to fall apart in 1966. The Who aimed at a wild image similar to that of the Rolling Stones. With their guitarist and songwriter Pete Townshend, they, along with the Kinks, with singer and songwriter Ray Davies, specialized in explicit comment on the contemporary scene. The Yardbirds were only totally successful while they retained their brilliant guitarist Eric Clapton.[17]

Rather as the sexual liberation of the time was somewhat too much of a male monopoly (or so feminists were to complain), rock/pop was very much a male monopoly. Most innovative of the female performers was Dusty Springfield, her *You Don't Have to Say You Love Me* being a huge international hit in 1966; working-class Sandie Shaw was a very appealing singer of uncontroversial material. The Rolling Stones made their records in the States, and the Beatles often released theirs there first. However, an interesting insight into the strength of the British position in pop music is given by the way in which two Americans, P. J. Proby and Jimi Hendrix, came to be presented as essentially British stars. Hendrix, a black born in Seattle in 1942, was talent-spotted in Greenwich Village by Chas Chandler, bass player with the Animals, who recruited him to London and managed him in a partnership with the Animals' manager, Mike Jeffreys. Hendrix was a brilliant guitarist, singing songs which seemed closely related to the protests of the time. Having made his name in Britain, he did in fact return to America. He died of a drugs overdose in 1970. Proby was the embodiment of the aggressive rock soloist, crowning his act by bursting out of his tight-fitting trousers.

At the age of 13, blind black prodigy Stevie Wonder (b. Detroit 1950) had topped the American charts, playing harmonica and singing the jazz soul song *Fingertips Part 2*. His *Uptight* (1965) and version of Bob Dylan's antiwar song *Blowing in the Wind* (1966) were hits in the UK as well as the USA. He emerges as a classic exponent of the multiculturalism inherent in rock/pop, his *A Place in the Sun* (1966) being influenced by the Beatles as well as Dylan.[18]

What about the reception of British rock/pop in France and Italy? There were empty seats at the Olympia appearances of the Beatles in January and February 1964, and the main French newspapers were unenthusiastic. However, that well-known verdict does not take into account the enormous enthusiasm in the specialist youth magazines (including the Catholic ones introduced in Chapter 3). One teenager, an aspiring rock singer at the time, in an oral interview twenty-one years later, admitted his lack of interest at the time, and then his subsequent embarrassment over the poor public reception given to the Beatles:

417

The Beatles at Olympia, I have to say frankly, I couldn't believe that they were The Beatles. If you press me, they didn't interest me at all. I went to hear Sylvie Vartan and Trini Lopez who sang *If I Had a Hammer,* that was how France was at the time, it's queer speaking of it like this, but that is how one has to speak.[19]

The Catholic magazines had been forced to accept the Beatles, and by February 1965 they had to accept the Rolling Stones as well. *J2 Jeunes* reviewed the LP *Around and Around:*

> twelve titles, each one more stunning than the other, but in a good sense. If ever there was a secret of the Rolling Stones, it is that of rhythm and all of the publicity about their long hair does not in any way reflect on their sincerity.[20]

Special significance attaches to the January 1965 issue of *Salut les Copains,* which actually announced itself as 'a very American number' while in fact, presumably in spite of the intentions of the editors, it conclusively demonstrated the complete reversal of the old American hegemony over Britain. This comes out clearly in the records reviewed, in the substantial article 'The Beatles in America', and in the usual recorded discussion among a selection of readers, this time on the question 'French Rock or Anglo-Saxon Rock?'. Throughout this discussion the participants overwhelmingly spoke of British performers to the exclusion of American ones. Thus Régis, 15 years old, declared that, apart from Eddy Mitchell and, occasionally, Johnny Hallyday and Sylvie Vartan,

> no one can equal the Rolling Stones, the Beatles, the Animals, the Kinks and all the English groups. I find them better than the Americans, for since Elvis Presley has taken to singing with violins and the greats (Buddy Holly and Eddy Cochran) have gone, it is across the Channel that one finds truth.

Some of the young people defended French singers, but none defended the Americans, apart from a few who recalled Presley, Ray Charles, and Chuck Berry. The first choice of Chantal, 17 years old, fell on 'Johnny' (i.e. Hallyday). Her response was:

> You forget something, you anglophiles, which is that I would never have become interested in rock if it had been sung solely in English. And all my friends are like me. Those who are not as badly bitten as I am, when I get them to listen to *Salut les Copains* [the radio programme], shout out in horror every time an English disc is played, *unless perhaps it is the Beatles.* [My italics.]

Among the older generation, there were some who had recognized the special talent of the Beatles: in 1965 less than a year after the publication in Britain of John Lennon's *In His Own Write,* the novelist Christiane Rochefort, together with Michel Misraki, had published *John Lennon en flagrant délire: tentative désespérée de traduction par Christiane Rochefort et Michel Misraki* (John Lennon in Fragrant Delirium: A Desperate Attempt at Translation by Christiane Rochefort and Michel Misraki). The admiration was genuine, the desperation induced by the impossibility of translating Lennon's puns. One can distinguish among the older generation in France two types of reaction to the Beatles: either the group are represented as the least gifted of a new and regrettable type of music with its associated mania, or they are seen as embodying an entirely British reaction against the general tedium of British life. When the Beatles, on their second visit to France, had a season at the Palais des Sports in Paris in June 1965, *L'Express* announced, or perhaps boasted, 'France is one of the only countries in the western hemisphere to have refused to have recognized their genius'. In fact, the words used *(boudé leur génie)* carry the implication that the French were 'sulking', so perhaps *L'Express* intended them critically.[21] The visit actually was a great success, which the French press had to recognize, whether in serious or ironic tones. Henceforth, a French historian of the Beatles recorded, whether one was enthusiastic or not, it was impossible to ignore the group as 'an important sociocultural phenomenon'.[22] Indeed, the article in *L'Express* had concluded: 'The Beatles phenomenon is positive... they are evangelists.' A study conducted at this time of one section of provincial youth found that the popular performers were the Modern Jazz Quartet, les Compagnons de la Chanson, the French pop stars Salvatore Adamo, Hallyday, Vartan, etc., and, on the same level of popularity, the Beatles and the Rolling Stones.[23]

In Italy, to begin with, there was a very wide chasm between conventional opinion, as expressed in the main magazines I have been using, *Epoca, Oggi, Panorama, L'Espresso* and the main newspapers, and that of the youth subculture and more radical elements, as expressed in *Ciao Amici, BIG,* and *ABC*. It was *BIG* which presented the Beatles as the symbol of the struggle of young people against the older generation. Under the title 'Youth Be on Guard', the editor-in-chief wrote on 3 December 1965:

> The world of school is in eruption. Not a day passes without the newspapers reporting matters relating to the problems of public education, finally brought into the light of day and literally brought out into the streets, after years of dangerous silence and pernicious indifference... Pupils have, finally, grasped this state of affairs and have started agitating, demanding their sacred rights...; responding to a questionnaire the majority of young people have indicated their preferred personalities to be our dear, *simpaticissimi* friends the Beatles. This demonstrates that sometimes long hair and a particular type of music can also represent the symbol of an aspiration towards liberty and democracy.

Both *BIG* and *Ciao Amici* used the term 'first victory' to celebrate, in March 1966, the first Beatles programme on Italian television. While in June 1966 the Rome newspaper *Il Messaggero*, reporting on the second visit of the Beatles to Paris, had spoken of 'moderate success' and 'many empty seats', and while *Epoca* and the other magazines had continued to censure what it called the 'narcissistic' mode of the Beatles, the Rolling Stones, the Who and the Yardbirds, following the Italian tour of June 1965 there was almost universal recognition that the Beatles were 'a living legend'—which did not exclude continuing critical comments and references to the fact that sales in France and Italy continued to be, in relative terms, much lower than in the United States.

There is no point in pretending that the Beatles captivated everyone; but their significance was acknowledged by pretty well everybody who paid attention to the news, and within their own constituency they topped the polls, perhaps in part because they still had the power to annoy the staid and middle-aged. In certain parts of the American Middle West their success was relatively limited.[24] Once again a letter from Bill Van Dyke indicates the reservations of people like himself and his family, while clearly demonstrating that theirs is not a majority view. In September 1964 he wrote specifically to his family about the film *A Hard Day's Night*: 'I cut out the reviews of The Beatles' movie last month because I was so amazed at the all-out praise.'[25] In an admiring interview of Lennon by a high-profile journalist of the time, Maureen Cleave of the *London Evening Standard,* the following appeared:

> Experience has sown few seeds of doubt in him: not that his mind is closed, but it's closed round whatever he believes at the time. 'Christianity will go', he said 'it will vanish and shrink. I needn't argue about that, I'm right and I will be proved right. We are more popular than Jesus now; I don't know which will go first—rock'n'roll or Christianity—Jesus was all right but his disciples were thick and ordinary. It's them twisting it that ruins it for me.' He is reading extensively about religion.[26]

Virtually four months behind the times, but just a couple of weeks before the Beatles' third tour of the USA, the American magazine *Datebook* (29 July 1966) published the juicy first phrase of the fourth sentence, familiar to everyone, causing an outcry among Christian fundamentalists. When this third, unhappy (and last) American tour began on 12 August Lennon had to apologize publicly for his remark about Jesus.[27] As might be expected, *Tiger Rag*, the student newspaper at Memphis State University, continued to be agnostic and even mocking in its comments on British popular music in general, and the Beatles in particular. However, in early 1968 a national poll among college students in the magazine *Look* demonstrated that the Beatles 'continue to capture the imagination of college students': 'The Beatles grew up right along with us… They are like the great scribes of our era.' *Tiger Rag* signalled its concurrence with this view.[28] It was indeed a widely held view towards the end of 'the British years'. In 1969, Carl Pelz judged:

> The phenomenal impact of rock during the late 1960s is directly related to the impact of one group, The Beatles. This group by itself has generated more public enthusiasm and more activity in the music industry than any individual or group in rock history, even more than Elvis Presley generated when he appeared in 1956.[29]

The Beatles, and British rock/pop music generally, had a significance which went beyond the confines of popular music itself. Within a purely British context, the direct impact of the Beatles on popular music was impressive. Britain had become a major player; British groups commanded attention in America. But Britain did not, of course, achieve anything like the total dominance over the Americans that the Americans had exerted over Britain in the fifties. The most remarkable sign of direct British influence was the deliberate creation in the United States of the group the Monkees, designed to project the fetching, playful qualities associated with the Beatles—not that this prevented them from producing one of the most memorable hits of the later sixties, *I'm a Believer*.[30] But if we can talk of an American dominance in the fifties, and a British pre-eminence through most of the High Sixties, we have to recognize also a whole new wave of innovative American groups from California, and particularly the Bay area, in the later sixties, groups to which the Beatles, in their eclectic way, were instantly responsive, and groups which had a strong influence on the Rolling Stones. I shall discuss these in the next section when I turn to the hippies, 'flower power', and the 'Summer of Love', all born in the USA.

The other major element giving rise to the notion of 'the British years' was pop fashion. Making headway against the highly organized American popular music industry was a considerable achievement. With clothes, things were very different. In one sense, America was a pushover; in another, there might have been no scope at all for British success. The Americans, even at their most informal, are inveterate uniform-wearers. There was also a small battalion committed to the outrageous, catered for in 1964 by Rudi Gernreich, the Californian designer who in 1964 produced the topless bathing-suit. It was all or nothing. The British had either to break the uniform codes or retreat. In fact the British designers did have a considerable success. There was much stronger resistance in France and Italy, which had their entrenched traditions of innovative fashion. In the end, as with rock/pop, British influence showed itself, to a greater or lesser degree, in two distinct ways: that of the spectacle and the symbol, concentrating on the major celebrities among designers and models, and that of liberating ordinary lives by removing the tyranny of uniforms and traditional fashion, and bringing in colour and sexiness.

The names to put alongside the internationally renowned rock/pop groups I have just been discussing are Mary Quant, John Stephen, and Barbara Hulanicki, who had opened the first Biba boutique in Abingdon Road in Kensington, just west of central London, in 1963, subsequently moving to more sophisticated Kensington Church Street. The credit for getting things going definitely belongs to Quant, but Biba, priding itself on very competitive pricing, was still more of a democratic influence. Ossie Clark, definitely one of the beautiful people of Swinging London, producer of exclusive, expensive models, in many ways the essence of sixties cultural extremism (black ciré trouser suit with see-through shirt, 1964; swimsuit with hold-ups, 1965; Pierrot coat, 1967), was much less of an international influence. In fact, the other international figures were the models Jean Shrimpton and Twiggy. The style of Mary Quant came to the attention of those in France of a cosmopolitan and adventurously youthful cast at almost exactly the same time as the youth magazines were writing of the coming success of the Beatles; *Paris-Match* distanced itself a little, stressing the eccentric, Anglo-Saxon characteristics of the style: 'a little "beatnik", a little "kooky", a little "dandy"'.[31] The popularity, though certainly a limited one, of the abandoned, youthful British fashions can be traced in the youth magazines, while the major press organs were primarily concerned with continuing to boost the French fashion industry. In a fashion preview for the year 1965, *L'Express* ignored British fashion; there was, it was true, a rather novel discussion of male fashion, but here the designer given most attention was

Pierre Cardin. Where specifically youthful fashion was being discussed, the French papers saw no need to go beyond the names of Yves Saint-Laurent and André Courrèges. However, at the end of 1966, *L'Express* unwittingly gave away the fact that, whatever the attitudes of the press, whatever the official decrees of fashion, the British styles had had a considerable impact. *L'Express* spoke of fashion now being 'liberated from the London delirium, which no longer inspires anything but boredom', perhaps failing to see that in declaring French fashion 'liberated' it was admitting that previously it had been 'conquered'. By December 1966 *L'Express* was recognizing the supremacy of first Shrimpton and then Twiggy: 'Twiggy is the teenage idol of 66 as the "Shrimp" was the teenage idol of 65.' In March 1966 *Salut les Copains* presented a large-scale analysis of the clothes of Carnaby Street.[32]

It is an article of faith to this day amongst French commentators that the miniskirt was invented, not by Quant, but by Courréges. It is true that in the international fashion exchange the French were at a disadvantage compared with the British, in that, where pop and youth fashion was concerned, as distinct from old-style *haute couture*, the British, partly for language reasons, partly because American commercial interests had already singled out British pop products as highly desirable investment prospects, had a much more direct and much more highly publicized road to America. The miniskirt was almost a logical response to sexual liberation and the new emphasis on the attractions of the natural physical attributes of youth, including neat bottoms and slim legs: Courréges undoubtedly conceived of the same idea at around the same time as Quant, but without question it was Quant who, quite independently, was responsible for it as a fashion, launched in September 1965, which swept the world. French fashion historian Yvonne Deslandres attributed the first models to Quant, but claimed that Courréges followed up with much more stylish versions—which probably puts matters fairly.[33] It was in the same year that Vidal Sassoon, Quant's accomplice in the 'youthquake' in style, opened his first hairdressing shop on Madison Avenue in New York. Already Ailsa Garland of *Vogue* had said to him: 'You've done it, Vidal! You've changed the shape of heads all over the world. At last hair is going to look like hair again!' The pioneers were entrepreneurs and money-makers, certainly not direct purveyors to factory workers, shopgirls, secretaries, students and hippies (though the fashions did indeed very quickly reach all of these).[34]

Although feminists were shortly to speak darkly of it as merely pandering to evil male appetites, the miniskirt, soon almost always worn with tights, was a very popular, and even tenacious, fashion, being worn and argued over after the advent of hot pants (very short shorts) and then, in the classic fashion pattern of extreme innovation followed by extreme reaction, the maxiskirt, which reached to the ankles. As with the Beatles, there was a certain resistance in mid-America, the Memphis *Press-Scimitar* declaring on 6 March 1967: 'Memphis women say down with the miniskirt.' However, market pressures were clearly going the other way, with respectable department stores like Famous and Peck & Peck selling out of the new fashion. The 30-something daughter of the Van Dykes wrote to her parents, on returning to Arkansas after a visit to Los Angeles:

We saw the teeny-boppers in their mini-skirts and fishnet stockings in Los Angeles, but I didn't believe the more conservative Middle West would be caught dead in such gear. I must be wrong. Yesterday I went to Famous... I looked at everything between $15 and $100, and there wasn't a single dress I even wanted to try on. Everything is made for the junior figure... cut too short... Even my favourite Peck & Peck has deserted me for the mini-mod.[35]

In Tennessee, mothers of girls suspended from school for wearing skirts adjudged by the school principal as being too short 'claimed it was impossible to find school clothing in style and still meet the... hemline rule'—this as late as September 1969. The miniskirt controversies in America, indeed, pick out sharply some of the main themes of this book: reactionary, sex-obsessed attitudes from school and police authorities; sensible attitudes from judges; relaxed and joky attitudes from the 'moderate' press, with an almost inevitable invocation of the primacy of London. Many school boards ruled that girls could not wear skirts more than five inches above the knee. The principal of the Tennessee school insisted

> that observation was the whole point of the board's ruling, because the school has open stairways. The fact that girls are sometimes at the top and boys at the bottom creates what [the principal] described as 'a distraction from the educational process'.[36]

A survey of the police across the country in April 1970 revealed that 91 per cent thought that miniskirts increased the likelihood of rape. The police claimed:

> Since the introduction of the miniskirt in 1964, rape was up 68 per cent in the United States, 90 per cent in England... Miniskirts obviously were not the only factor involved. The same period witnessed a general relaxation of public moral standards, a greater permissiveness in movies and television, loosening of controls over pornography, and a trend toward nudity in the theater and nightclubs. It was also a time of social tension and widespread alienation, of increased use of drugs and alcohol. Any or all of these things may have been as important as short skirts in providing the last straw of stimulation that pushes men across the line between legal lust and criminal rape.

Many sex crimes, the police conceded, were 'by nuts', but

> 98 per cent of the police officers agreed that perfectly normal but emotionally immature boys are sometimes goaded into criminal attacks by the sensory arousal resulting from feminine attire that offers a tantalising striptease view of intimate areas.

Apparently the newspaper reporting them had some sympathy for these arguments, since the report concluded with what the paper called 'a thoughtful footnote' from the vice squad commander of a large western city: 'Fathers and husbands, he said, are derelict in their duty when they fail to warn daughters and wives against clothing styles that some males may find provocative.'[37] In January 1971 a sheriff in Minnesota sacked a female clerk in his office for wearing a miniskirt which broke his severe dress code, limited to one inch above the centre of the kneecap. For schoolgirls the news was good. The county superior court judge in Tennessee ruled in favour of the mothers of the three suspended girls, rejecting the school board's five-inch rule in favour of a seven-inch one, while noting that 'girls come in several shapes and sizes—and that skirt measuring is "not an exact science" '.[38]

Once again the Italians, after a brief period of indifference, became enthusiastic about the British fashion. In April 1967 several boutiques described as being in 'the Carnaby style' were opened inside the large Standa department store in the centre of Milan—they were given rather eccentric and (it must be said) notably undemocratic titles: 'Lord Kingsay', 'Lady Ellen', 'Portofino Beach' (resort of Italy's 'beautiful people'). *Ciao Amici* reported:

CARNABY A MILANO... You enter and have the real impression of finding yourself in London, Carnaby Street: there has been so much talk of this extraordinarily famous *[famosissima]* street that by now we know every nook and cranny, the ambience, the colours, all that marvellous caravanserai of fashion, of modern taste, of with-it ideas *[idee IN]*... The ground floor of the shop has been transformed into an exact copy of Carnaby Street... Here you can dress yourself exactly like our friends from across the Channel... The sales girls are pretty and, needless to say, dressed in miniskirts.[39]

The same number contained an interview with Mary Quant—'the creator of the most with-it fashion in the world... She invented the miniskirt.' A month earlier *Epoca* had announced 'the arrival of the queen of the miniskirt' and, a few weeks later, the arrival of 'Twiggy, the doll with the freckles', 'the inspiration of the new fashion'. A British consortium, composed principally of John Stephen, Mary Quant, and the Beatles, opened six boutiques in the via Margutta, one of Rome's most elegant streets, inhabited by aristocrats and successful artists, who put up a tremendous fight against this intrusion of 'in' fashion.[40] The new British empire had made a priceless conquest; but local tastes and traditions can be tenacious against even the most powerful commercial forces: within three years all the boutiques had closed, being replaced by top-class art and antique dealers.

The image of imperial conquest was actually used by the American magazine *Life*, in commenting, at around the same time as the arrival of the British boutiques in Italy, on the continuing hegemony of British fashion over American:

Any hopes chauvinistic Americans have nourished that swinging London was slowing down a bit as a trend-setter have been soundly squashed by Britain's latest export—Twiggy—all 91 pounds of her... she has in two short weeks almost converted this colony for the British Empire.[41]

Once again, the *Press-Scimitar* leader-writer sought to conceal his puzzlement in the familiar dated clichés and folk-tales:

She speaks inelegant English. She is something less than sexy, which her admirers not only admit but brag about. And she regularly wears mini-skirted garments that offer no warmth to her knobbly knees. Skinny, sexless Twiggy, however, generates great excitement among clothes designers, fashion photographers and sundry promoters whose thought processes the average American doesn't even pretend to understand. These inscrutable types undoubtedly will make her U.S. visit a howling financial success. But we less sophisticated types hardly can resist her either. She excites among hospitable Americans the reaction that follows the discovery on their doorstep of any skinny, scantily clad youngster: 'Laud sakes, we've got to get that child fattened up and put her in some decent clothes before she leaves here!'[42]

In 1964 British designers Mary Quant and Jean Muir had claimed that Paris fashion was now out of date: John Bates was developing pantsuits and catsuits, sold in his boutique Varon, while a few brave spirits in London were trying out topless dresses. But French fashion designers did not suddenly go bankrupt; nor did Italian; nor did American; any assertion of British primacy has to be placed within a context in which a governing feature was an international exchange of ideas and styles. In 1964 Pierre Cardin in Paris produced his 'space-age' collection. In 1965 youth styles were produced in France by Courreges and Saint-Laurent, and in America by Betsey Johnson, Geoffrey Beene, and Anne Fogarty. Op Art was adopted by Mary Quant in 1964 but taken up by Courreges in 1966, the year when Saint-Laurent opened his own off-the-peg chain, Rive Gauche. In 1967 Italian designers Pucci and Fiorucci were to the fore in the development of 'ethnic, hippie fashions'. Still, the British primacy was real enough, though it did not outlast 'the British years'; the French, Italian, and American press reported and commented on British fashion, and the spectacle associated with it, to an extent and in a manner that simply was not the case for the fashion produced in their own countries. Important boutiques for men were Lord John and I Was Lord Kitchener's Valet. British fashion certainly did not obliterate that of the other countries, but it was the most 'in'.

So apparently was British cinema: this is 'the British hour', said *Epoca:*

> Everyone gets their turn. In cinema things go in cycles by which, as in poker, the hand
> passes from one country's film industry to another. We have already had the Italian hour,
> then the American, then the Russian, then the German, then once more the American,
> then the French, then once more the Italian. Today it's the British hour… for two years,
> in the international market, they have had success after success.[43]

But if, once more, we are talking about *market* success, should we not be looking at where the investment came from? As long ago as 1974 the distinguished Irish film critic Alexander Walker, in his *Hollywood England*, mocked British pretensions on the ground that the famous British films of the High Sixties were almost entirely financed from the United States.[44] Film enthusiasts understandably don't like to miss any opportunity of attacking the negative attitudes towards film which prevail in Great Britain: investors reluctant to invest, governments grudging and minimalist. But it is scarcely fair to visit the sins of moneybags and ministries on the cameramen, editors, producers, screenwriters, directors, and actors who actually made the films. Indeed, it would be much more logical to argue that British achievements would have been still greater had there been internal financing on a rational and organized basis. Further, the point has to be made that the films discussed in Chapter 4, the films that were themselves an integral part of the first stirrings of the cultural revolution, and which thrust themselves into a commanding seller's position in the world market, *were* largely British-financed. Thereafter Americans were eager enough to invest in films which—this was their prime selling-point—were distinctively and unambiguously British.

It is true that British film production suffered badly in the seventies when American investment was drastically reduced, but that does not alter the fact that throughout the High Sixties a remarkably diverse array of outstandingly successful, and utterly British, films was turned out, all in some way closely in touch with the great transitions in British society of the time. Films made in a British environment always carry with them distinctive traces of the British social and cultural context, as novels written in a particular country carry rare clues as to social arrangements and deeper values in that country—a point I return to in the final section of this chapter. Film, in certain respects, is inherently an international medium, and it was as susceptible as popular music to the effects of international interaction. There had, for instance, been an established tradition of Franco-Italian coproductions; the first of the Italian-produced and directed 'Spaghetti westerns' was made in 1964; and endgame was perhaps reached in January 1967 with *Blow-Up*, financed by Metro Goldwyn Mayer, directed by the Italian director Antonioni, and made in England with an entirely British cast. To complicate things further, two of the most innovative directors domiciled in Britain at the time, Joseph Losey and Richard Lester, were American-born.

But let us look at the 'success after success' identified by *Epoca*, which show the range of genres now replacing the social comment films of the New Wave. Apart from *A Taste of Honey, Billy Liar,* and *The Servant* (1963, directed by Joseph Losey), it mentions *Darling* (1965, John Schlesinger), *Tom Jones* (1963, Tony Richardson), and *The Ipcress File* (1965, Sidney J. Furie). *Tom Jones* was set in the eighteenth century, being based on Henry Fielding's picaresque novel, but it was redolent of the rumbustious, hedonistic, sexually liberated spirit then breaking out in British society. Heading the all-British cast was the new working-class star, Albert Finney. This film was totally financed by the American company United Artists, but it should also be pointed out that United Artists did not belong to the Hollywood studio system, but had always been a company specializing in independent and innovative productions. United Artists, it may be noted, also put up the money for the first Beatles film, *A Hard Day's Night*. In so far as the film musical was an American genre, *A Hard Day's Night* can rightly be described as 'derivative'; but it was, up to a point, congruent with the slice-of-life character of the British New Wave films, highly original in replacing the cliché of a rags-to-riches biopic with a jokey, slightly surrealistic presentation of the Beatles as themselves—wealthy and adored—in the Britain of the day. The film had originally been planned as a publicity exercise, but that plan was overtaken by the fame the group had achieved before the film went into production. *A Hard Day's Night* nicely captured the allure and

426

humour of this provincial, working-class/lower-middle-class group with its own directly composed music: that's what made it—together with the sexual charge delivered to young females.[45] *Darling* I shall return to in a moment. *The Ipcress File* is a slice-of-life spy story, the spy being perky, working-class Harry Palmer, played authentically by working-class Michael Caine, struggling to make a not very glamorous living and done down by his upper-class bosses.

An altogether more glamorous fictional figure was the upper-class Commander James Bond, the invention of novelist Ian Fleming. Fleming's novels about Secret Agent 007 ('licensed to kill'), extremely popular towards the end of the fifties (and for the next thirty-odd years), fitted the traditional stereotype of snobbish, upper-class England, and were much commented on in France and analysed by Umberto Eco in Italy.[46] They are full of sex (or implied sex), violence, and a snobbish knowingness about the luxuries of life. In 1961 Harry Saltzman had joined with the American producer Albert 'Cubby' Broccoli in buying the options on all the Bond novels except *Casino Royale,* which Fleming had already sold, and set up a six-picture contract with United Artists. Three suave screen heroes were considered for the part of James Bond: Patrick McGoohan, Richard Johnson, and Roger Moore. But Broccoli had taken a liking to Sean Connery in, of all things, the 1959 Disney film *Darby O'Gill and the Little People.* Fleming's *de haut en bas* reaction to Connery was that he 'was looking for Commander James Bond, not an overgrown stuntman'. Connery, a former milk delivery man in Edinburgh, spoke with the accent of his native city—one which, however, is slow and easy to follow, and suggests a certain mid-Atlantic quality. Film director Terrence Young undertook to induct Connery into the patrician sensibilities of Commander Bond; it was Connery himself who decided to play the role tongue-in-cheek and who wrote in some of the ironic one-liners which became the distinguishing feature of the role.[47]

The British film industry had not, on the whole, been notable for producing renowned international pin-ups. On the other hand, it was at this time a world leader in special effects. Sean Connery did become an international star; so also did Peter Sellers, essentially a character actor, who had made an enormous impression on American audiences with the United Artists-financed *The Mouse That Roared* of 1959. The Hollywood director Stanley Kubrick came to London to make two films with Sellers, *Lolita* (1962) and the incisive satire on those American leaders who cheerfully contemplated nuclear engagement, *Dr Strangelove or, How I Learned to Stop Worrying and Love the Bomb* (1964). The third new-style British international star born at this time was Julie Christie, who seemed the embodiment of the independent, swinging, short-skirted, knee-booted young English female. After *Billy Liar,* she was the unscrupulous, success-seeking young woman in *Darling,* and then the spirited Bathsheba in *Far From the Madding Crowd* (1967) from the Thomas Hardy novel—all three of these films were directed by John Schlesinger. This last film also featured one of the sexy new working-class male leads, Terence Stamp. Former French *nouvelle vague* film-maker François Truffaut came to England to make his *Fahrenheit 451* (1966), about a book-destroying future society, with Julie Christie. The film was based on a novel by Ray Bradbury—science fiction joined with *verismo* espionage stories as one of the most vibrant literary genres in the Britain of the day.

As we have seen, *Georgy Girl* (1966), while considered risqué in the United States, appealed to

427

certain teenage girls there as speaking more directly to them than the American films of the time. It relates to the new honesty about beauty and physical attractiveness which I discussed in the previous chapter. A successful pop song from the film's sound track explained Georgy's plight. Played by Lynn Redgrave, she was a plump, pudding-faced girl, in contrast to her devastatingly sexy and utterly ruthless flatmate, played by Charlotte Rampling. When the latter gets pregnant she has no compunction over abandoning her baby, while sturdy Georgy Girl is happy to adopt it. Yet another slice of life from mid-sixties Britain. What mid-sixties Britain—as lived through the Traverse Theatre, discothèques, the Arts Lab, parties which everyone gatecrashed, and the pubs in which they learned about the parties—was particularly notable for was unrestricted male licentiousness. The film about this, whose early origins I have already discussed, was *Alfie* (1966) directed by Lewis Gilbert, and starring Michael Caine—now to begin his irresistible rise. It has become something of a platitude that after 1970, with the rise of the new feminism, such a film, which, Alexander Walker said, 'would have been dubbed a crude propaganda tract for chauvinist male pigs', could never again have been made. Whether that means that *Alfie* is a shallow, time-bound film—or even whether the statement is actually true—is less certain. Alfie is presented as neither good nor bad, simply as a type representative of the new permissive society, a working-class libertine who is more systematic, and more successful, than Arthur Seaton in *Saturday Night and Sunday Morning* and, unlike Seaton, not prepared to make any final concession to marriage and domesticity; there is a sad abortion scene, and the final note is of loneliness, not fulfilment. With the publicity slogan, 'Is every man an Alfie? Ask any woman', the film was immensely popular in America as well as Britain, apparently with women as much as men. There was an appealing spin-off song, sung as a separate hit single in Britain by Cilla Black from Liverpool, and dubbed onto the soundtrack of the American version of the film by Cher.[48]

A trio of best films about uninhibited, permissive Britain (there were many others) is completed by *Smashing Time* (1967, directed by Desmond Davis and starring Rita Tushingham), about two provincial girls who come to swinging London, getting caught up in the fashion and the parties. Earlier in 1967 *Accident* had been released, directed by Joseph Losey with a screenplay by Harold Pinter (from the novel by Nicholas Moseley). Brilliantly structured (beginning and ending with the car crash indicated in the title), beautifully scripted, this film, with its young aristocrat (Michael York) and Oxford dons (Dirk Bogarde and Stanley Baker), is a long way from the New Wave films of the beginning of the decade; far more critically, it was a far cry, in its utterly persuasive explorations of the realities and ambiguities of human behaviour, from previous eras of British film-making. Britain, it could be said, was ready for *the* film of the London-centred international cultural revolution of the sixties, *Blow-Up*, by the Italian director Antonioni. According to MGM's press release: 'The story is set against the world of fashion, dolly girls, pop groups, beat clubs, models, parties, and above all, the "in" photographers who more than anyone have promoted the city's new image.' The prospering celebrity photographer Thomas, played by working-class David Hemmings, is an Alfie with talent. Antonioni had his own preoccupations with questions about the nature of reality, yet the film gives clear representations of the beautiful people's London of the time. The strong narrative component of the film is in the form of a kind of thriller: the blow-up of a photograph Thomas has taken in a deserted park seems to reveal a murder; an elegant young lady (Vanessa Redgrave) attempts to retrieve the photograph. One scene which attracted much attention involved Hemmings tumbling around the floor with some scantily clad teeny-boppers. In the final sequence Thomas watches a mimed tennis match, his eyes mechanically following the invisible ball backwards and forwards; the noise of the ball being struck comes onto the sound-track, but still no ball can be seen. Within a visually rich series of images operating on many levels, the dialogue itself is very effective, and very British: it was largely written by another playwright making his name on the London stage, Edward Bond.

Lindsay Anderson's *If* (1968—the title carries a deliberate allusion to Kipling's poem of that name, not intended to be flattering) starts naturalistically in a public school (i.e. an expensive private boarding-school), with three rebellious boys being subjected to brutal punishment (at this time secondary school pupils were rebelling all over France and Italy, but with regard to the punishment of children these countries had, since the 1880s and the Renaissance, respectively, reached levels of civilization still to be attained in Britain); the film then moves into a surreal climax of considerable symbolic force, when the founder's day celebration is bombed and machine-gunned by the rebel boys. In a grittily British cultural and commercial environment still hostile to film, *If* nearly perished. The producers, Memorial Enterprises, founded by sixties prodigy Albert Finney and headed by the older actor Michael Medwin, could not find investors. Ultimately the American company Paramount did put up the money, but even then exhibition was confined to the Paramount cinema in London. There—a poke in the nose for British philistines—it enjoyed sufficient commercial success for the ABC circuit to agree to national release in 1969.[49] Lindsay Anderson's penchant for the exposure of male genitalia was once again frustrated by the censor—rather strangely, since no cuts had been made to the quite lavish exposure in the fight between two nude males in the film of D. H. Lawrence's *Women in Love,* also of 1968.

The youth magazines in France expressed great enthusiasm for British films; the adult magazines were rather more restrained. Already in April 1963, *Paris-Match* acknowledged the 'powerful sexual attraction' of Sean Connery, but *L'Express* found the Bond film *Goldfinger* 'infantile and a shattering assault on the senses', and, while giving a great deal of attention to Ian Fleming as novelist, completely ignored Connery. *The Ipcress File* passed almost unnoticed, *L'Express* explaining: 'There is an incompatibility of spirit between the Cannes Festival and the English actor Michael Caine.'[50] The mainstream magazines talked a great deal about Losey, Lester, Schlesinger, Richardson, and Anderson, whom they represented as being *almost* the equals of Godard, Truffaut, Malle, and the other fashionable French directors of the day. Even more attention was given to Julie Christie. She was on the cover of *Marie-Claire* on 1 May 1966 with the legend 'Julie Christie: her prodigious success', the article inside placing her alongside Garbo, Dietrich, Harlow, Monroe, and Bardot. *Salut les Copains,* however, kept young readers fully informed about new British films. It devoted a whole review to *What's New, Pussycat?,* Clive Donner's wonderfully funny 1965 film about a sexually liberated Europe and about the realities of age and personal appearance, with Peter Sellers in one of his most extravagant roles ('Is she prettier than me?' his despairing wife in the film asks. 'Jesus, I am prettier than you,' the Sellers character replies).

After the masterpieces of Lester, here is a crazily funny film by Clive Donner, full of the most unbridled and the cleverest humour. Quite simply you will be doubled up.[51]

*What's New, Pussycat?* was filmed by a French cameraman in Paris, on American money, the production company being the (relatively) independent-minded United Artists. The initial idea came from old-style Hollywood producer Charles K. Feldman, who personally sank quite a lot of his own money into the project. He was determined to involve British comic actor Peter Sellers, formerly of the fifties cult radio programme *The Goon Show*, but now just emerging as an international film star. Feldman also hoped to secure American pin-up Warren Beatty, whose habitual telephone greeting to young women provided the film's title. Beatty, however, was not available, and his part went to British pin-up Peter O'Toole. The cast was completed by three international beauties, Romy Schneider, Capucine, and Ursula Andress, and one American one, Paula Prentiss. To direct the film, Feldman engaged British television director Clive Donner (a very significant development at a time when the golden age of British television had already arrived). For the screenplay, he signed up Woody Allen, then a stand-up comic in New York. However, Peter O'Toole has provided a version of the scripting which stresses the British contribution:

> We began with a brilliant, sketchy, Perelmanesque script by Woody Allen, who is a genius. Then things got a little neurotic, with lots of politics and infighting and general treachery and finally—with the ghost of W. C. Fields hovering over our heads—we improvised the whole thing from start to finish. There were areas in the script that were undeveloped, which is the norm with most films: you cast first and write afterwards. I actually wrote with my own fair hand about three-fifths of the script. When I say 'wrote' I mean that we'd meet at ten in the morning—Sellers and I and Clive Donner, the direc-tor—and sit around talking and hoping. Sellers had the ideas, I did the words and Clive was the arbitrator. We jotted things down on the back of contraceptives and off we went...[52]

Allen, who had a role in the film as the perennially unsuccessful male chasing attractive young females, did not appreciate the butchery of his script, but was consoled by the fame and fortune which the film brought him.

The film was released on 23 June 1965. The music was written by American popular song writer Burt Bacharach; the theme song was sung by budding Welsh sex symbol Tom Jones. *What's New, Pussycat?* was the biggest international comedy success of 1965. Film historian Alexander Walker has written that the film

> mustered the largest group of Kooks hitherto seen on the screen and rushed them through a series of barely linked situations that resembled *La Ronde* with the brakes off. It was good-omened entertainment for what was then being perceived—though not yet offi-cially dubbed—as the 'swinging sixties', with their erratic, way-out, do-your-own-thing

sense of accelerating anarchy.... The film's huge box-office success—which overcame notices of extreme hostility from the New York critics, who called it 'salacious', 'leering', 'over-sexed', and, at its most modest, 'distasteful'—was largely credited to Sellers' artfulness.[53]

The sixties, of course, was the first great age of international coproductions. But it is very much a part of these *années anglaises* that this Franco-American film should come over so strongly as a British film.

But for the French both *Alfie*, the film and the character, and Michael Caine were just too British. The film won 'a special prize' at the Cannes Festival, but that, *L'Express* explained, 'was enough for a vulgar film'.

Besides, who in France, knows Michael Caine? In London, where he is taken for an actor of genius, his large dark glasses, his tight stomach and his air of always being in the clouds produces ravaging effects. In spite of this appearance and of his thirty-three years, he is starting on a career as a juvenile lead.

He had been made, the magazine said, by his part as Harry Palmer in *The Ipcress File*, particularly by his laid-back manner: 'To play the role of an anti hero, one had to find the anti-actor.' The public, 'tired of the inhumanity of James Bond and company', *L'Express* continued, quite errone-ously—the public was far from tired of James Bond and obviously appreciated the tongue-in-cheek humour of Connery, which *L'Express* evidently missed—'cannot resist the human failings of Harry Palmer'—a shrewd enough comment. The writer was fascinated, and clearly thought that readers would be too, by the fact that acting was Caine's thirty-sixth occupation, the others having been essentially proletarian in character. Also with Caine's lifestyle, obviously perceived as continuing to be proletarian, living in a working-class district (Elephant and Castle, south of the Thames in London) near his elderly mother, continuing to go to football matches with Terence Stamp, and continuing to cook meals in his flat for young women he hoped to have his wicked way with. 'For, with the anti-actor, as with the anti-hero, cooking is the means of seduc-tion.' There was then a reference to the film *The Wrong Box* (Bryan Forbes, 1966)—one of those comedies which were perhaps among Britain's greatest contribution to human happiness during the sixties—followed by references to the big-budget films Caine was now making in Hollywood. After stressing his sense of humour, the article ended: 'Michael Caine has won everything. Save for the best actor prize at the Cannes Festival.'[54]

Youth and mainstream magazines were in much closer agreement in Italy. *Ciao Amici* gave Britain first place for cinema as well as for music. The Communist youth magazine *Nuova Generazione* consistently and totally ignored British popular culture, but singled out for praise Peter Brook's film of his theatrical production *Marat-Sade*, and *Accident* by Joseph Losey, 'the great English director', to whose *The Servant* it also gave special praise. *Ciao Amici* declared James Bond 'the most popular personality of 1965'.[55] The reference to Peter Brook recalls that a number of British films drew their inspiration from theatre. At this time, when, as I have already explained, the lines between 'experimental' theatre and 'middle-class' theatre were blurring, British theatre, too was enjoying a very high reputation, particularly with the Americans. This is made abundantly clear in a range of sources, including letters home from American academics holidaying or researching in London preserved in the Bancroft Library at Berkeley.[56] (American academics tended also to lyricize about British pubs, for imitations of which, as we saw in the previous chapter, there was quite a fashion in parts of America during the later sixties, and reported by *Time*, 3 June 1966, in an article entitled 'British Style Pubs'.) Under the headline 'English Theater tries everything—and becomes the finest in the world', a correspondent for *Life* (20 May 1966), singling out *Saved* by Edward Bond, *The Homecoming* by Harold Pinter, *Marat/Sade*, and *The Killing of Sister George*, the play by Frank Marcus, which came out about lesbianism, declared that 'London's excitement draws famous, adventurous directors'. It added that the 'National Theater, founded only three years ago, is already the finest and most versatile acting company in the world'.

*Life* spoke also of the high quality of the plays televised by the BBC and ITV. The main showcase, and also an opening onto the consummating cultural revolution of the High Sixties, was the BBC's Wednesday Night Play. Nell Dunn was one of those upper-class young ladies who got swept up in Swinging London, who contributed to the new openness about female sexuality, and who took an utterly genuine interest in working-class behaviour, working-class values, and working-class speech patterns, bringing up her own child in the working-class area of Battersea, across the river from Chelsea. The title, *Up the Junction*, of her first book, a collection of sketches (1963), refers to Clapham Junction in Battersea. Adapted as a Wednesday Play in 1965, it caused an outcry for its abortion scene; in fact, its true significance lies in the way that women are protrayed as the predators, the men the sex objects. Another important Wednesday Play author was working-class but Oxford-educated, Dennis Potter, whose *Vote, Vote, Vote for Nigel Barton* took a working-class lad through Oxford into Labour politics. However, the sensation was *Cathy Come Home* (November 1966), written by Jeremy Sandford and directed by Ken Loach, the story of a young mother moving from one squalid lodging to another, then into a hostel for the homeless before finally being evicted and having her children taken away from her. Through a combination of sheer serendipity and the articulation of a profound social conscience among many, particularly young, British people, the broadcasting of this play coincided with the founding of the voluntary organization on behalf of the homeless, Shelter.

The liberalizing influence of the BBC Director-General, Sir Hugh Greene, has already been noted. Under his aegis a number of comedy series with an unconventional, disturbing edge to their social comment had been broadcast. The ultimate came in 1966 in the form of *Till Death Us Do Part*, written by working-class Johnny Speight and featuring the ultra-conservative working man, Alf Garnett (played by Warren Mitchell), constantly in furious contention with his layabout, Labour-voting son-in-law and his stolid wife, Else.[57] *Till Death Us Do Part* infuriated all opponents of the permissive society, though, with the delicious irony that lay at the core of the show, Alf Garnett himself was the most vociferous opponent of permissiveness. *Till Death Us Do Part* dared to portray Alf Garnett openly, and shockingly, as the racist too many British people actually were. It had a regular audience of over seventeen million, and was enthusiastically commented on by the critics. On the whole, cultural traffic in television was still largely one-way—from America, with such lurid soap operas as *Peyton Place* holding strong positions in European viewing patterns. What brought the almost mythic status of British television internationally was the BBC's last black-and-white drama series, *The Forsyte Saga* (1967), fashioned from the distinctly lower-middle brow novels of John Galsworthy, set between the late Victorian period and the 1920s, but with a brilliant cast of actors. In 1971 London Weekend Television broadcast the first episode of *Upstairs Downstairs,* a series based on the careful delineation of the hierarchy within an aristocratic Edwardian household and, in international fame, the successor to *The Forsyte Saga.* However, the truly revolutionary transfer was that of (an American version of) *Till Death Us Do Part* to American television screens.

At the end of the 1966–7 football season a number of less famous British clubs (such as Scotland's Ayr United) came over to America to play exhibition games as part of a plan to institute professional football (always known in the States as 'soccer', though in Britain this is a basically upper-class term used to distinguish association football from 'rugger' or rugby football) as a mass spectator sport in America. With the relaxation in the sixties of the all-American ethic, closely identified with the all-American games of (gridiron) football and baseball, football had developed among ethnic groups from Europe and Latin America, but to Americans 'soccer' was essentially a British game. In British professional football a real beginning-of-the-sixties style of campaign, fought by the Professional Footballers' Association under the leadership of Jimmy Hill, had in 1961 secured the abolition of the maximum wage, which had preserved football in aspic as an essentially working-class occupation. In 1963 the Victorian master-servant transfer system was also brought to an end. The best players could now join other high-paid entertainers in the world of spectacle. In 1966 England hosted and, with a genuinely entertaining team, won the football World Cup. Football crossed over, to occupy the leisure time of people of all social classes as well as ordinary workers. In sports facilities of all types, the continental European countries were well in advance of Britain, making possible their people's direct participation in sporting activities, with Britain remaining too much a country of spectators and pub pundits. While, in Italy, women played football to international level, females in Britain were officially prohibited from playing football after the age of puberty. Across our four countries, the sixties marked only a first stage in a great liberalization of sport, in the direct entry of individuals into sporting activities, whether aerobics or tennis, hill-walking or lunchtime football. Individuals had more leisure; stereotypes about the age at which one stopped sporting activity were weakening; more people aspired after a youthful and fit appearance; sport was a means of self-expression; taboos about activities appropriate to females were being overthrown. The big expansion comes in the seventies. But meantime things were changing in America. 'Soccer' was taken up in colleges and in schools. A kind of British rivalry between 'soccer' and 'rugger', advertised in British-style pubs as 'a game for roughs played by gentlemen', was introduced. The attempt to bring in professional soccer as a spectator sport went ahead, but failed within a few years. None the less the effects within American society were considerable. Soccer was a game that boys and girls could play without requiring the superhuman qualities required in American football and baseball, and without risking the brutal injuries which were a feature of the former. The holding

433

of the football World Cup in the United States in 1994 was just one more legacy of 'the British years'.

Apart perhaps from hippies setting up communes in America, or setting out for India and Afghanistan, for young people London was the city to visit, to enjoy the swinging scene, to luxuriate in the sense of freedom, sometimes to have abortions. I must avoid jingoistic excess. Several times I have argued that there was no impermeable barrier between 'counter-culture' and 'mainstream' culture. The values, activities, and associations of some figures within both cultures were far from admirable: a particularly reprehensible *nostalgie de la boue* which beset the upper class led to a fraternization between society figures of various sorts and the Kray brothers, evilly vicious criminals from the East End of London, who were finally arrested in 1968 for murders, large-scale fraud, extortion and intimidation.[58] There was a louche side to sixties libertarianism, with fools claiming to find such people as the Krays entertaining and authentic, but it does not need to be overstated. It happens that the Krays were around, but their significance in regard to the major issues of historical change was—like that of John Profumo and Christine Keeler before them—negligible. Some scandals—as we shall see in the next chapter—do illuminate important matters. Most do not. With regard to the lively cultural activities I have already described, both private individuals and government were, with the sad exception of films, eager to invest, though not everyone found Britain swinging, or London full of beautiful people. Terence Stamp, devastatingly handsome star of *Far From the Madding Crowd*, tells the story which can neatly end this section:

> I had booked a table at Wheeler's in Old Compton Street for supper that evening. It was the original eating house of the chain and the table on the first floor beside the open fire was my favourite corner. Jean [Shrimpton] ordered a sole Véronique, I, a Colbert. We shared a beetroot and watercress salad. Next to us was a middle-aged American couple, their voices marking them as tourists.
>
> The man said rather loudly, 'We haven't seen any of these beautiful people we read about in *Time Magazine*, Shirley.'[59]

## Hippies, Yippies, and other Beings

The sixties was a time of liberation for majorities in all Western countries, when teenage girls, supported by their mothers, could wear skirts as short as they pleased and get to see films which spoke directly to them, such as *Georgy Girl*, when young professional men (and old ones for that matter) could wear clothes as colourful as they chose and hair as long as they liked, when formerly underemployed labourers from the Italian south could enjoy the excitements of metropolitan life in Milan, when young women on the dance floor no longer had to 'follow', no longer felt a relentless pressure to acquire a husband, and could reasonably expect that when they did, that husband would help with the household chores, when more people than ever before had decent accommodation, enough to eat, direct contact with what was going on in the world, and perhaps even the beginnings of an environment where human needs were not totally sacrificed to the car. There were other things people could do. Professor Lewis Yablonsky, a distinguished sociologist in his late thirties when in 1967 he conducted a systematic personal investigation of hippie communities all across America, reckoned that at that time there were 200,000 'visible and identifiable hippie dropouts' in the United States ('hippie' was the widely used label; hippies themselves, as I've mentioned, called themselves 'heads' or 'freaks'). To this he added a further 200,000 whom he described as 'visible teeny-boppers, part-time summer and weekend hippies'. Then there were several hundred thousand students, young executives, and professional people 'who use psychedelic drugs, interact, and closely associate with totally dropped-out hippies, yet maintain 9–5 jobs or student status'. If we adopt these very wide parameters, we are still talking about considerably less than 0.1 per cent of the total American population. If we focus only on those living in hippie communes, we have a figure which is a fifth of that. Minorities, of course, can be very important; but we are here talking of a very tiny minority. However, Yablonsky also brought out another statistic which illuminates a feature which is central to understanding what was happening in the sixties. Those who had some sympathies with the hippies and what they stood for—'fellow-travellers', Yablonsky calls them (not altogether happily, perhaps since one of the things hippies tended to do was, literally, to travel, at least till they found a satisfactory commune, while these sympathizers who did not, as Yablonsky put it, 'use psychedelic drugs in any regular way or make the scene personally', remained immobile in their conventional occupations)—numbered another few millions.[60] Millions of students also sympathized with many of the aims of the student radicals—yet would never themselves become involved in combat with a policeman, just as many millions of ordinary people came to feel that blacks could simply not be treated any longer in the way they had been treated under formal segregation—though never themselves taking part in a demonstration or a sit-in.

It is with the 200,000 of those I am inclined to call 'full-time' hippies that I am concerned here, and, less intensely, with the perhaps further 200,000 in Europe. International cultural exchange is a process I have constantly emphasized. In some ways the hippies were the most international of all the phenomena associated with the sixties, and it is in dealing with them that my decision to concentrate on four specific countries begins to seem particularly vulnerable—some of the putative 200,000, as we shall see, did not belong to any of my four countries. Was the hippie essentially an American invention? What was a hippie? How did the term originate? The notion of the 'bohemian' is a useful one (as, in a different context, is that of the 'fringe'). The bohemian is 'different', defies convention, but is not necessarily thereby engaged in trying to subvert 'bourgeois' society. The Beats of the fifties were particularly potent rebels in that the ideas and attitudes they generated continued to exert influence throughout the sixties, but they were bohemian in that their central commitment was to art, basically novels and poetry, not to social, still less political, causes. The Beats produced a language, a distinctive badge of their kind of bohemia: 'swinging' as a term of praise implying 'liberated in all the best sorts of ways', 'tea' for 'marijuana', 'dig' for 'enjoy' or 'like', 'hep' for 'most up to the moment, most in tune with the latest Beat ideas'. Those who became hippies were deeply influenced, consciously or unconsciously, by the Beats but also, as a different generation, were eager to have them written off as dated and superseded. By the mid-sixties, if you were up-to-the-minute, you said 'hip', not 'hep'.[61]

The linguistic origins are indisputably American. However, while recognizing America as its birthplace, a French commentator highly critical of the whole hippie movement insisted that the European wave was originated in Britain by the Albert Hall underground poetry festival.[62] And in the American sources, in keeping with what I was saying in the previous section, we find the view being quite strongly expressed that the hip place to be is London, with descriptions being given of hip households, which seem very like embryonic hippie communities.[63] Yet, at the same time, on the continent of Europe, groups of a nonconformist, broadly counter-cultural type were appearing, noticeably in countries which, thoroughly decent and respectable, had long harboured a Dadaist alter ego (Denmark, Sweden, the Netherlands, West Germany, Switzerland): most important were the Provos (originating in the Netherlands) and the Situationists (mainly in France and Italy). The first Provo manifesto was promulgated in Amsterdam in July 1965, advancing the teasing concept of the 'provotariat', ambiguously activist/non-activist:

The proletariat is the slave of the politicians... it has joined its old enemy the bourgeoisie, and now constitutes with the bourgeoisie a huge grey mass... We live in a monolithic, sick society in which the creative individual is the exception. Big boss, capitalism, communists impose on us, tell us what we should do, what we should consume... But the provotariat wants to be itself.[64]

One magnificent early Provo gesture was the provision of 50,000 white bicycles for free use in Amsterdam.[65] Both groups were activist, had a clear philosophy condemnatory of capitalist and consumerist society, and often had a wonderful Dadaist wit. In general, it would be true to say that the counter-cultural/anti-capitalist/anti-imperialist milieu in Europe offered a less pronounced divide than the American one between hippies and activist protesters. London was the great entrepot, with continentals pouring in from one direction, Americans, partly to savour hip and swinging London, partly as a staging-post for Europe and the Orient, from the other.[66]

So, to answer the question I left dangling, yes, full-time hippies are essentially an American phenomenon. Corroborating details of importance are that American hippiedom, unlike the European movements, had two spectacular, news-commanding leading spirits, Timothy Leary and Ken Kesey; and these two figures had begun their proselytizing well before 1965. Indeed, some commentators date the beginning of the hippie movement to Kesey's abandonment of novel-writing in favour of setting up his Merry Pranksters and instituting his 'acid tests'. The adjective 'hip' did not develop into the substantive 'hippie' till the spring of 1967, the key moment being the publication in the intellectual, left-leaning, even crusading magazine *Ramparts* of an article entitled 'The Social History of the Hippies'. Dozens of press reports followed, remarking on the weird-looking people who were congregating, not in the West Village (of Greenwich Village, New York), traditional home of bohemians and Beats, but the East Village; not in the North Beach area of San Francisco, but in the more central Haight-Ashbury; not in cities at all, but on the slopes of the Big Sur, the mountain to the north-west of Los Angeles, and in the rural parts of north California. Activists and protesters continued to think of themselves as hip and to use phrases such as 'hip people', 'hip neighbours', and 'hip community', but distanced themselves from the inactive drop-outs by refusing the label 'hippie'.

What, then, distinguished a hippie? The essential ingredients were LSD, and everything associated with it, and 'nature'. LSD was used, as Yablonsky explained, as the 'personal key to cosmic consciousness and universal unity'. 'Grass' or 'pot' was a more basic staple of everyday life, smoked communally, to cement the 'circle of friendly love'.[67] The faith in LSD, of course, was totally misguided. So also was the notion that cities were artificial and that there must, in the words of hippie philosopher Stan Russell, be a return to the 'natural condition that underlies man-made cultures and societies'.[68] Rock/pop music was there too, but then that was a universal language extending far beyond the domain of the hippies. The Haight-Ashbury district, inevitably known as Hashbury, generated its own particular style. Already one of the main bastions of American resistance to conquest by the Beatles, prior to the fabrication of the Monkees, had been the Beach Boys (founded in 1961), who extolled the semi-drop-out lifestyle (in vacations at least) of the south California beaches. Now bands deliberately at odds with the slick presentation of conventional rock/pop radio, openly smoking grass while producing the music, proudly related to the local Hashbury scene. Groups emerged whose style, attuned to the psychedelic, hip subculture, strongly influenced both the Beatles and the Rolling Stones: the Grateful Dead (lead singer Jerry Garcia), Jefferson Airplane, Mother Earth, and Big Brother and the Holding Company, featuring Janis Joplin. These bands lived the communal Hashbury life and joined in the quintessential hippie denunciations of 'the plastic world'. They played in the big traditional dance-halls of San Francisco, now fitted with strobe lights to give the obligatory psychedelic effects, the Fillmore, the Avalon, Winterland, and Carousel. Their genuine aversion for mainstream commercialism was not in doubt; but there is no counter-culture uncontaminated with mainstream culture: soon, for the groups that became world-renowned, there were record contracts, soon there was loads of money.[69]

Flowers expressed the beautiful essence of nature and the exact opposite of the plastic. 'Flower power' was the elemental power of nature, against that represented by police truncheons and mace, and by napalm and all the horrid weaponry of the Vietnam war. No sooner had the word 'hippie' come into fashion than it was joined by the label 'flower children'. In the middle of the Hashbury there was a strip of grass, the Panhandle. The elegant Golden Gate Park was not far away. Hippies and flower children, under the inspiration in particular of Kesey, organized happenings, be-ins, love-ins, and smoke-ins. They provided press and television with magnificent spectacle. Journalist Tom Wolfe, having already introduced the middle-class reading public to the fashionable figures of the earlier sixties, including the Beatles and Andy Warhol, in his collection of essays, *The Kandy-Kolored Tangerine-Flake Streamline Baby* (1965), now, in his *Electronic Kool-Aid Acid Test* (1968), brought the excesses of the hippie scene, and particularly the role of Ken Kesey, to that same audience. 'At any one time' the Haight-Ashbury, Yablonsky wrote,

> is almost a fantasy land of sights and sounds. Flute players in robes. Micro-minied girls in boots, without bras, obviously aware of a kind of sexual attractiveness, swing down the street. There are consciously dirty teenagers and under fed youths who come from upper-middle-class families. Some seem to be beating their parents up obliquely by literally

starving and begging. On the same scene are wiser, older 'heads'—… philosophers of the movement. These bearded figures (some in their late thirties and forties) smile straight ahead as they walk down the street, many in flowing robes with 'hip' crosses round their necks.[70]

San Francisco resident Lois Rather wrote of the antique military jackets, the African or Indian robes and ground-sweeping pioneer calico skirts, the boots or bare feet. The summer of 1967 was the 'Summer of Love'. Apart from Golden Gate Park, there were hippie gatherings in the Grand Canyon and in Central Park, New York.[71] Scott Mackenzie produced the hit single *San Francisco:* 'If you're going to San Francisco, be sure to wear some flowers in your hair.' There was a genuine community of a kind, and a voluntary organization called the Diggers supplied food, clothing, and even hospital care for starving or sick hippies. But on 16 May 1968 *Time* ran a story, 'Wilting Flowers':

> love has fled the Hashbury. Although anti-draft hipsters recently held an amorous assembly knee-deep in a pool by City Hall, love has been replaced by cynical commercialism, loneliness and fear, sporadic brutality and growing militance.

The love had never been all-encompassing; what was happening now was a general move by the true, full-time hippies away from the cities and into rural communes. *Newsweek* fifteen months later (18 August 1969) announced 'The Year of the Commune'.

Although the hippie subculture had its own (increasingly commercialized) music, both the Beatles and the Rolling Stones continued to receive the accolade of being considered hip. One of the early rural communes in California was called Strawberry Fields. Yablonsky describes a visit to another, on the misty slopes of the Big Sur:

> It was either a scene from Man In The Beginning or a small troupe of human stragglers who had survived the desolation of the earth by atomic destruction...

At first, Yablonsky could make out about eighty people, then came to realize that within a radius of several hundred yards there were 200 or more:

> a twenty-year-old boy with an Indian headband holding his long hair sat in the center of a hole in the middle of a blanket staring straight into space. The crowd blended with the surrealistic scene. Several children dressed in ragged clothes pranced about, evidently part of the family. The clothes were bizarre but not casually bizarre. There were many leather garments, buckskins, and Indian head-dresses. Several young girls wore long colonial-style dresses.

There was grumbling, and mention of a stabbing incident the previous night. Yablonsky had with him a hippie leader, Gridley Wright, who responded by telling the others that the problems of this commune were not as great as those at Strawberry Fields.

The group began its random dialogue. At first it became a gripe session. 'People are steal-
ing around here, man'. 'We are split up, there is no unity'. 'No-one helps anyone else do
anything'. 'I'm cutting out tomorrow'. Gridley intervened at various points and it became
increasingly apparent that he was truly the leader of the movement. To Pan he said,
'Don't quit, man. Make your light shine. Here is where it's happening. It's happening all
over. We felt like this many times at Strawberry, but we stayed with it. You can hang on
here, too. Let's not quit now. There's nothing better over the ridge. Do it here where you
are, Brothers'.

One hippie suggested they all join in a chant; Gridley suggested prayer.... Everybody
said, 'Too much. Let's pray'.

Yablonsky had already noticed an attractive blonde with a four-year-old son. She was clearly
impressed that the famous Gridley had joined the group. A deplorable feature of hippie
communes, indeed, was the excessive influence wielded by certain charismatic figures—most
notoriously the murderous exprisoner Charles Manson.

Some of the communes were known as 'tribes'. Yablonsky visited the Rising Sun Tribe, in the
East Village in New York. He interviewed a boy from a wealthy Georgia family, who had been
a rioter but was now a complete drop-out. Yablonsky asked him if there was more sex in the
Tribe than there had been back at high school in Georgia, getting this response:

I think there's more at my school. It isn't hidden that much here. Back at school, sex is a
taboo thing. I mean the teachers don't talk about it, the students ain't supposed to talk
about it, the moms and pops don't talk about it. Nobody talks about it. If you do anything
you do it behind everybody's back. Up here it is open, it's a thing, it's a real part of life,
and I think it's beautiful. I enjoy it very much myself. Here, what happens is that the girls
don't play so many games. They play a few, but they don't play so many You just ask a
girl and she'll say yes or no.[72]

A loyal statement on behalf of the Tribe, inflected with the customary male chauvinism; is it also
admitting that sexual permissiveness among the young (whatever the attitudes of the old) was as
prevalent in bourgeois Georgia as it was in a New York hippie commune? My point, anyway, is
that sexual liberation was a general phenomenon, not one limited to hippies. Drugs, of course,
were basic; often taken in nearby Tomkins Square Park—to the intense resentment, no doubt, of
long-established locals, just as the goings-on in Haight-Ashbury and the Panhandle infuriated
long-established citizens of that part of San Francisco.

Sociologist Gilbert Zicklin carried out a survey of rural communes between June and October
1968, and then another one, specifically focused on child-rearing, in 1970. He reported on hippie
ideals, but could not avoid revealing the enormous stresses hippie life placed on ordinary products of prosperous American society (70 per cent of hippies, Yablonsky reckoned, came from

middle- or upper-middle-class families).[73] An integral part of the hippie faith in nature was the eating of healthy, natural food. But Zicklin found that at birthdays and other times of celebration hippies tended to go off for a binge on junk food. There should be no concealment of the natural-ness of the body and bodily functions:

> From the communal bathrooms and toilets to the communal bath house or sauna, from the occasional open farters and belchers to the ever-present naked children, from work-a-day hot-weather gardening in the nude to the idyllic frolic of nude swimming, from long hugs and friendship kisses to mutual massages, one finds acceptance, sometimes halting, sometimes aggressive, of bodily exhibition, bodily functions and bodily plea-sures, and all this in the name of greater naturalness.

Of two communes, he reported that, 'on occasions the entire group might engage in sexual activ-ity, especially after a particular solidarity-filled group meeting or group encounter'.[74] But Yablonsky made it clear that hippie communes did not offer easy sex just for any comer.

> I closely observed in many situations and under many conditions that the hip sex scene is not 'free love'. Many 'untuned-in' sailors, students, and 'dirty old men' who gravitated to the hip community for sex become angry when they are rejected by the love children. Sex is not free—one must be resonant to the feelings of the potential sex mate. For people fully tuned-in, sex is 'free', plentiful, and, from all reports, 'a groove' (great) in the hippie world.

The establishment, and the abandonment, of hippie communities continued into and through-out the seventies. Many were set up by thoughtful, successful professionals. I conclude this discussion of the full-time hippies with a married woman's mildly ironic memoirs of the summer of 1970 in a two-family commune in rural British Columbia, Canada:

> From Vancouver, San Francisco, Los Angeles, Montreal, young seekers came to the Slocan Valley in VW vans, old trucks, converted school buses. They pitched tents, tepees, lean-to's. With brand-fresh chain saws they inexpertly felled trees to build log cabins and feed firewood to old-fashioned cook stores.
>
> Rules were many. One should not eat produce grown outside a 25-mile radius. Marriages should be open. Children should be allowed to run free. Long hair, longjohns, long skirts were the only proper attire. And bare feet; or, for the wet springs we soon learned were common to the Valley, mud-boots.
>
> Communes sprang up—because families should group together, share work and pleasure. Share mates. Join in song, play the harmonica; knead their own bread, brew their own beer, drink it.

Impatience with old constraints brought, I have suggested, a desirable frankness throughout all society. Frankness and naturalness was certainly a hippie ideal; inconsistencies were perhaps too harshly exposed:

> The morning grows hot… Madeleine has stripped naked. On her face she still wears the oatmeal-honey beauty mash she mixed up after breakfast—taking the recipe from a paperback entitled Natural Beauty… She is thinning the beets, and stands bent over at the waist, straddling the row. Her breasts hang down, swinging, her naked buttocks lifted to the sun with the naturalness of a grazing deer…
>
> The dog Rufus barks a warning, but we don't hear the engine until just before the truck rounds the last bend in the driveway. Madeleine shrieks. She will never make it to the cottage in time. And although a nude body is no longer considered a cause for embarrassment, a beauty mask—even an organic one—represents a direct link to white middle-class culture.[75]

In the next chapter I shall be looking at the student activist, New Left end of counter-cultural behaviour. Sticking with the freak-out end for the time being, here is an almost pitying account by a British academic who went to California in 1969 as a visiting professor of sociology:

> The counter culture was luxuriant and highly visible on the university campus. The Beatles had been deified, and in Monday morning lectures one witnessed a languid process of re-surfacing after the weekend freak-out. One also noted all the pet dogs, often secreted in lecture theatres, wandering out into the aisles at the lecture's climacteric; and one wondered at the probable loneliness and desolation behind the apparent togetherness.[76]

Richard Mills conducted interviews with eighty or so 'heads' or 'freaks' in London in 1970, some of them French or American. Basic to almost all was that they had made, or were about to make, the pilgrimage to the Orient, or at least to Morocco, this, in part, being symbolic of their rejection of industrial society; the other basic was the use of drugs. One French girl had had a very strict upbringing, saying that she had had no teenage, and that while her friends went out in the evenings she did not:

> And then I became a Beatles fan, and I started to have fun, and it made things worse at home, because when I would go back home my parents couldn't understand why I was enjoying myself.[77]

In the Bayswater area of west London, Mills found a household, or commune, consisting of Maggie and her baby Sarah, Lucie and her baby Jo, and Barbara and her boyfriend Keith:

> MAGGIE. I feed Sarah and get her clean, and go out into the kitchen and clean up in there. Try to get everything straight before everyone starts coming in. Because we get a lot of

people here. And then we go to the park. At three o'clock I go and look after the kids over the road, who go to school, and so have quite a straight, organised day. I clean up their house and give them their dinner. Until their parents come back, and I have a smoke with them, then come back here and play music or go out. I try to get some writing done, or try to get some mending done.

Maggie remarks that Barbara tends to go to her own room, putting a notice on the door asking people to knock.

BARBARA. Oh, that's just because we're fucking and people come in. I don't mind people coming in, but they ask me a bunch of draggy questions about where the raisin bread is, and I'm trying to get it on. I mean, I don't mind if people come in and go out, but that's why I put knock first, because I don't want to have to be conscious about raisin bread when I'm trying to make love to somebody.[78]

Mills also interviewed hippies centred on Piccadilly Circus. Jimmy had had 70–75 jobs, and had come to the West End two or three years previously.

When I need bread I can go out and sell shit for someone and that gives me bread. I used to get £130 a week in the West End, but then the fuzz moved in and they cut me off. Now I only get a few pounds, get stoned and go to sleep.

I suppose I am a dealer. I don't like heroin though. I don't sell it too much. I have never used it. I take a lot of acid. Well, I used to take a lot of acid. But after a while it just fucks you up.

I smoke shit every day of the week. And I drink every day of the week. I have got a bottle out there. I drink cider and whisky.

Jimmy provided interesting clues as to the distinction between the real hard core of hippies and others, of whom he was very contemptuous, who perhaps hardly even merit the description 'fellow-travellers'.

The people I hate are the King's Road type. Chelsea. The Ravers. Weekend hippies. They wear what they call groovy clothes. They have long hair. But they're about as plastic as the cover of that tape recorder case. Maybe they have a pair of jeans like me— but when they first get outside you can still smell the moth-balls because they've had them hanging around all the year. They're hanging on the peg for 50 weeks of the year and they just take them out and wear them up town one night, smoke one joint and really think they've tuned in, they've done it all.[79]

France in the High Sixties was a country of student activism, of Situationist protest, of happenings and of radical theatre; full-time hippieism was seen as an invention of foreigners,

442

Americans first, then the British, the Scandinavians, the Dutch and the Germans (the hippies of the Leopoldstrasse in Munich being known as 'gammlers'), and those who wanted to practise it tended to go abroad—though there were hippies to be found in the traditional student and bohemian quarters of Paris, as well as on the Cote d'Azur at Cannes and at Nice, while in November 1967 there was a psychedelic night at the Palais des Sports in Paris. Some went straight to the Orient, Turkey, Lebanon, India, Nepal, but there was a quite well-travelled route which took French hippies first to London, then out to the East.[80] Or one could head straight for the United States. Bernard Plossu dropped out when he failed his Bac, Luc Vidal was a well-paid electronics engineer, Brigitte Axel was another successful professional succumbing to the lure of the Orient and the hippie life. Vidal first travelled on the European continent, then went to Turkey and the Lebanon. After that he went to London, where he took a menial job in a hospital and lived in a hippie commune. The commune was joined by another Frenchman who saw London as a first step on the road to India and Nepal. Vidal himself returned to France, where he trained as a nurse before setting out for the Third World.[81] Axel travelled on her own across the entire Orient.[82] Plossu went first to Mexico, then to the United States, where he lived in communes on the Big Sur, in San Francisco, and in Berkeley. In the interview he gave on his experiences he placed a total emphasis on the influence of America and leading American figures. But then he was asked about the Beatles; his reply recalls the points I was making at the beginning of the chapter:

> Absolutely: they are the best. What is astonishing is that through being the idols of young people, they have taken up their proper role. Nowadays they wear beards and long hair, and have become perfect hippies, although to begin with they were merely very gifted stars.[83]

As hippies, or at least honorary hippies, Plossu also mentioned the Rolling Stones; and, while all but one of the photographs in the book were of American scenes or persons, the one rock/pop group photographed was the Who.[84]

Now to the non-travelling 'fellow-travellers', and, what I see as a major gain from the challenges and developments of the time: the greater frankness, openness, and honesty in ordinary personal interchange. For its Eastern audience, *Harper's Magazine* in January 1967 reported on the 'Turned-On and Super-Sincere in California'.

> To a surprising degree, California intellectuals, particularly young ones, have forsaken traditional ironic speech, with its insistence on a certain distance between the speaker and his inner self. As a result, self-deprecation, wit, insouciance—all the cherished intellectual habits—are out of fashion here. If anything, they are taken as a badge of hated phoniness...
>
> You are on the top floor of a San Francisco apartment house on the edge of the Haight-Ashbury district—the West Coast, if not the world-wide center for psychedelic experiences. Cigarette smoke, only lightly laced with pot, thickens the air... Across the

table from you is an authentic Haight-Ashbury denizen, a bearded Dane, swathed in corduroy, his head a torrent of hair. His wife is next to him, a Roger Vadim girl, with pouting insolent lips. When the Dane speaks, his English is immaculate, so perfect that his accent seems an affectation. But the Dane does not speak often. Indeed, he has sat, silent, sullen, but intense, for most of the evening. Suddenly, despite the late hour and the general grogginess, he whirls upon you. You have made an error, filling in a silence with empty remarks about the hour, the distance home, the necessity of a departure. The Dane exclaims, 'Stop playing games. We do not know each other.... Tell me your opinion of me, and I will be candid with you, and perhaps we can get to know one another, but no more of this game.'

The author of the article wonders whether there is a 'hopeful development' here. Others, he says, have thought so, and he quotes from an article in rival magazine *Look,* which had discovered 'surprising openness in personal relations, a new intensity of personal commitment, a radical shift in the morally admissible, an expanding definition of education', leading to a situation in which 'Relations between people will gain a new depth and subtlety'.

Let us give the hippies, and their fellow-travellers, credit for genuinely striving for a new honesty. The striving was carried to unpleasant extremes, there were inconsistencies, the reliance on LSD made it very insecure. As I have said before, the rapid interactions and accelerations of sixties society meant that there could be no positive advances without extremes. But the important point is not that the hippies contributed to a new honesty, but that that new honesty was being created anyway by a convergence of other forces: hippie extremes were a part of it, not the creator of it.

We have had the 'hep', the 'hip', the 'hippies', and the 'flower children': what of 'the underground' and the 'yippies'? At least 'underground' is a more specific term than 'counter-culture', particularly if limited to adjectival use: inherent in the word is some sense of communication, as in newspapers, films, or even rock concerts. It seems that the word itself first came into use in New York in 1964;[85] already what can claim to be the world's first under-ground newspaper, the *Village Voice,* had been in existence for a decade—it was, naturally, fairly openly on sale. The new cohort of underground papers began to come into existence in 1966; imaginative in design though not always easy to read, they strove for a generally psychedelic effect, and often made use of a kind of art nouveau style. Titles could be expressive and to the point, as with *Screw,* and *Fuck You: A Magazine of the Arts.* Other American titles were: *The Oracle of Southern California, Los Angeles Free Press, Other Scenes, San Francisco Oracle, Open City, Berkeley Barb* (associated both with student radicals on the campus and with the hippie communes which grew up around it), and, in New York, *East Village Other.* The Fugs were a burlesque rock-folk group led by Ed Sanders, who was also responsible for *Fuck You* and *The Fug Songbook.* Ted Berrigan was responsible for publishing *C.* Here is a sample of the wisdom dispensed by the *Oracle of Southern California:*

Man's need to surrender is helped by psychedelic sacraments. Psychedelics are more aphrodisiac than scientific studies of fucking can ever show. The sexual energy aroused on acid is general, god-like, cosmic. Hence most people are not interested in merely genital fucking on an acid trip; they are fucking the universe.[86]

Among underground films produced around 1964 were Jack Smith's *Flaming Creatures*, about a Tangiers drag club, *Scorpio Rising*, by Kenneth Anger, and *Towers Open Fire*, by Tony Balch and William Burroughs.

In Britain of the High Sixties, the two major underground papers were *IT*, founded in October 1966 as *International Times*, the change coming when 'top people's paper' *The Times* threatened legal action, and *Oz*, founded in February 1967 by Richard Neville, who had previously run a similar paper in Australia. *IT* was the more stolid publication, discussing the great international political issues (Vietnam, China, Latin America, student protest on the European continent), editorializing (somewhat vaguely) about the alternative society, and, particularly through Jim Haynes, in touch with what cash-paying customers of the Traverse or the Arts Lab would tolerate—*IT* was deliberately less shocking and disgusting than the most advanced American organs. 'London 1967', it declared, 'is not ready for a completely flipped out newspaper.'[87] *IT* had a huge launch party at the Roundhouse: Paul McCartney came, dressed as an Arab; Antonioni and his leading actress Monica Vitti also came.[88] Oz was more daring, more witty, really embodying, to use Richard Neville's phrases, the 'fun revolution' and 'playpower'. Printers were not always happy, and were sometimes downright unwilling, to print the scandalous and scatological pages. If one firm refused, another had to be found: 'the printers often went to jelly at the sight of our camera-ready pages. At such times, we would fan out across the country, searching for another willing web-offset.'[89] Artist and poet Jeff Nuttall, a CND campaigner, drew cartoons for the early issues of *IT;* his book of 1968, *Bomb Culture*, grossly exaggerated the way people's actions were motivated by fear of nuclear holocaust—in fact, in 1967 and 1968 both *IT* and *Oz* were highly optimistic about the caring alternative society (as represented, in particular, by the San Francisco Diggers) they felt they could see emerging. Nuttall's book is divided into five parts, the fifth, 'The Underground', taking up nearly half of the book. Nuttall attributes the beginnings of his 'underground' thinking to his days doing National Service in the fifties.

I can remember realising these ideas for myself in my corner of the threatened world, as Ginsberg, Sanders, Kupferberg, Burroughs, Leary must have done in theirs... I remember waking in my National Service wanking pit, with Nasser and Eden flipping their idiot wigs on the radio networks and the strontium 90 thickening in the atmosphere and seeing that we were fleeing from that human condition that we had already refused by our piddling fastidiousness, that, having made unmentionable those alimentary and sexual functions by *grace*, yes by *grace*, of which we are on earth... we further sought to destroy it, to escape by nuclear suicide... I remember seeing clearly that if the doors could be torn off the lavatories, off the birth chambers, if those lost and desperate railway station embraces I'd seen so often during the war could be carried through to a healthy public consummation, if we

445

could again dance around the phallus and grow golden corn from our dung, then that would be a start.[90]

In this strident harping on facing the facts of life, Nuttall and his excremental allies were ignoring the facts of life: excrement is not nice, and if not disposed of decently is the source of appalling disease; the freeing of sex acts from taboos and shame does not require them to be performed in public, when in fact it is in the clear interest of undrugged sensibilities that they be performed in private.

The strident male chauvinism of the underground, a great motivator for the nascent women's liberation movement, is strikingly illustrated in *IT* 89, for 8–22 October 1970. A photograph of a nude woman has this caption:

Hi there! We wish to welcome into our folds Miss Brenda ('You got the money, I got the space') Anderson, 37–24–36, our new advertising manageress. Says 21-year-old Brenda, 'I'd love to handle your insert. Call me at…'

Charlie Gillett has spoken of an 'underworld', where the 'underground' groups played,

a new underworld of basement cellars which sprang up during 1966 and 1967 as an alternative to the beer-and-cigarettes world of pubs and clubs that spawned the British blues groups. At the Middle Earth and UFO in London's West End, the audience took acid or smoked dope in the gloom, while a grandly-titled 'light show' projectionist lit up the wall at the back of the stage with oil-slides that stirred under the heat of his lamp. The erratic rhythms of the musicians threw the audience into spasm-dance movements, while the guitarists carried themselves off into space. This was the spirit of San Francisco, 6,000 miles East.[91]

This was the world, most notably, in which the group Pink Floyd began, before emerging into commercial success.

Richard Neville speaks of going to the 'smart Hampstead dinner party' of journalists Claire and Nicholas Tomalin.[92] For a much wider sector of the population, who didn't go to smart dinner parties or associate with the official leaders of the underground, alternative ways of enjoying themselves were developing vigorously in some of the traditional pubs—in Hampstead it was the Flask. It was largely in these pubs that young, and youngish, people picked up the addresses of parties, which were then cheerfully gatecrashed, save that the very phrase was hardly used since it did not sit well with this cheerfully loose way of life: parties might or might not involve drugs; they were considered a wasted effort if they did not lead to sex. Fred Vermorel, in his fascinating memoir of the sixties, during which he studied at the Harrow Art School, did various jobs, and visited France, provides a neat account of the party-going business in the London suburbs:

Party hunting around the Ruislip-Harrow-Pinner circuit in the sixties began with the reconnoitring of certain pubs with a reputation for party intelligence. You would visit these and have a drink, mill about, eye the girls. Then someone would arrive with an address. We would travel in Gordon's car, crammed also with freeloaders, and possibly a couple of girls, and arrive at some poor fucker's leafy residence, unannounced and uninvited, and without a bottle to our name.

Vermorel also makes a perceptive comment on the tendency to suggest that everyone lived their life through rock/pop music:

> But we lived our lives the other way round. Music was a backdrop to our noisy and fragile aspirations. We hardly noticed—and who cared?—which Beatles single was in the chart, or what band Eric Clapton had just joined, whether Bob Dylan was in Europe or New York, or dead or alive. Pop and rock only happened on certain occasions in our lives, and then not a lot of it; it was limited in time, space, space and technology, and by our taking it for granted.[93]

In the true heart of underground and hippie society, raids and arrests by the police ('busts') had to be expected. The great were not exempt; indeed were specially targeted. In March 1967 *IT* was raided, and one of its key figures, 'Hoppy' Hopkins, jailed for possession of cannabis. In May two of the Rolling Stones, Mick Jagger and Keith Richard, were arrested, and in June at the Sussex quarter sessions sentenced to prison—Jagger for three months for possession of four amphetamine tablets bought in Italy. To the editor of *The Times*, William Rees-Mogg, this was a judgement which went well beyond the measured, and in a famous leading article, headed 'Who Breaks a Butterfly on a Wheel?', he spoke out against what he saw as a violation of 'tolerance and equity'. Measured judgement prevailed: the two rock stars were released, first on bail and then by the Appeal Court, which, while upholding the convictions against Jagger (that against Richard was quashed), substituted one year's conditional discharge (on the whole, the higher you went up the system, the more balanced counsels prevailed).[94]

To meet the yippies we have to return to the United States. If we accept the distinction between 'counter-cultural' and New Left, then the yippies straddled it. They were radical and militant. They were—as hippies were not—a political party of a sort, the Youth International Party, founded by the radical socialist Jerry Rubin. But they also, adding much to human gaiety, adopted the Dadaist techniques of the Provos and Situationists. We shall meet them again in Chicago, 1968, where their finest stroke was to put up a pig for the presidency of the United States.

As in France, counter-cultural youth movements in Italy tended to have a political, or at least satirical, edge to them. However, the wine and sun of Italy had a strong attraction for north European hippies (generally known in Italy, from the length of their hair, as *capelloni*). The summer of 1965 was the first in which the appearance of foreign *capelloni* was noted in Rome. In his diary in August the journalist Sandro Mayer wrote:

447

They are young people from England, France, and Germany, who, having bombed around all over Europe, have ended up spending a few days in the Italian capital. Their meeting-point is the flight of steps at the piazza di Spagna: it is here that they converse, eat, play the guitar, sleep. In a style tried and tested at home they wear tight-fitting blue jeans, bright coloured T-shirts, high-heeled boots and fantasy jackets. Their motto is: 'Don't make war, make love.'[95]

Open hostility on the part of the authorities and the police towards these foreigners began to manifest itself towards the end of the year. The incident which attracted national attention was highly symbolic: it involved a uniformed Italian conscript, a hippie, who was apparently asking for money, and the soldier's girlfriend, and ended in the hippie and the soldier coming to blows. In a famous article in the Milan *Corriere della Sera* on 5 November 1965 Paolo Bugialli (the name is important, since, as we shall see, the same journalist reversed his stance in an article of a few years later) wrote:

They say they don't do any harm to anyone and that they gather at the steps at the piazza di Spagna because it's a beautiful spot which they like. This is not a good reason. These people are ugly and pleasing to no one...

There followed the standard reference to the Beatles and to the *'capelloni*, as they are called here in Rome' being 'those types apparently of masculine sex who wear their hair long like women'; Bugialli concluded by saying that they should be thrown out of the country. Showing that there was no absolute split between the generations, some letters in support of the Beats or hippies or *capelloni* were published, most notably an ironic one in *La Stampa* of Turin by the celebrated novelist Elsa Morante, who wrote that if they were to be thrown out of the country she herself would have to consider going into exile, as both Dante and Einstein had been exiled: Einstein, she added, remained a *'capellone* till his death'.[96] From the beginning of 1966 a naturalization process set in, initially confined to Rome:

The phenomenon which in the beginning was confined to a small group of foreigners has become more and more 'Italian'. Thousands of our young people between 16 and 22 years old have grown their hair long and dressed in the uniform of the *capelloni*. Many have armed themselves with electric guitars, joined up in groups of four or five, composed songs, cut discs; the first music groups of the *capelloni* have been born: L'Equipe 84, I Rebelli, I Satelliti.

A female journalist in *Corriere della Sera* could still boast:

If by *capelloni* you mean the very young who dress in rags, who have no fixed occupation, seldom see their families, but instead spend a whole day with a gang of youngsters exactly like themselves; who, in short, wear a Beatles haircut as a sign of their status, one has to say that there are no *capelloni* in Milan...[97]

By the autumn *capelloni* were very much in evidence in Milan, many simply part of the general youth scene, preoccupied with dress, sex, perhaps drugs, and a general contempt for conventional society, rather than with politics. Even for the most apolitical and most individualistic there was some form of organization or network with respect to places for eating and drinking and shared dwellings. The political aspect manifested itself first and most clearly in the appearance of 'newspapers', particularly *Mondo Beat* from 15 October 1966 in Milan (now definitely replacing Rome as a serious centre of *capelloni* activity) and the emergence of activist groups, particularly Onda Verde ('Green Wave'), again in Milan. Onda Verde, it is important to note, consisted mostly of students. It issued a first manifesto in verse form:

To remain united we shall not obey the bosses

Karl Marx, Aristotle, the Ministry of War, Saint Thomas are good for being used like American chewing-gum or shoe polish

When the government makes you feel bad, L'Equipe 84 makes you feel good

The war in Vietnam is not bad because it's a war of reds or whites, but because it's a war

First and last principle of sexual morality: the accuser is always in the wrong

Our method is non-violence. Violence is the method of the impotent

Censorship exists whenever anyone says to the others: 'I will do your thinking for you, so relax'

Between the museum and the fun-fair, the artist must choose the fun-fair: for the museum, time is up

The first big demonstration by the new groups—specifically an anti-military demonstration—took place in Milan on 4 November 1966; Vittoria Di Russo, who was shortly to become the moving spirit behind the first issue of *Mondo Beat*, publicly destroyed his passport, declaring himself a 'citizen of the world'. On 10 November copies of the Onda Verde manifesto were distributed at the entrances of Milan's schools. A poll was organized of 500 Milan secondary school pupils: the result—32 per cent voting in favour of school administration entirely by the pupils themselves—may well be quite an accurate reflection of the balance of opinion, revealing the radicals as a substantial minority. On 15 November there appeared the first number of the cyclostyled *Mondo Beat* produced by Di Russo and Paolo Gerbino. At the end of November the three Milanese groups of Provos, Onda Verde, and *Mondo Beat* joined together in another anti-militarist demonstration. On Christmas eve the three groups took part in a pro-peace demonstration. At the very end of the year a second issue of *Mondo Beat* appeared, produced with the participation of Onda Verde. In Rome attention focused on police action to clear the *capelloni* from the piazza di Spagna. That the non-political aspects were still strong was apparent in the demonstrations beginning on 24 December against the closing of the famous Rome rock club Piper.

With the taking over in April of a campsite at the end of via Ripamonti on the outskirts of Milan, a different kind of *capelloni* culture manifested itself. Barbonia (vagabond) City, with probably fewer than 100 inhabitants, was really a rather minor matter, but it served to scandalize the citizens of Milan, particularly those in that part of the city, and also respectable people further afield. After three months the police moved in force, and by 5 a.m. on 11 June the camp was destroyed.[98] In central Milan, the main place for hippies (or 'beatniks' as they were often also called) was the large subterranean hall under the piazza Cordusio, which formed the vestibule to the metro station.

Two contrasting diaries kept respectively by two Italian *capelloni*, one male, one female, demonstrate two different sides to sexual permissiveness. The first is of a 19-year-old young man who decided to leave his (apparently reasonably well-off) parents in Bologna and hitchhike to Milan, where he joined about fifty 'beatniks' at piazza Cordusio:

Friday 11 Nov.: I met Carmen, a blonde, lovely, good figure, the type I fancy. She's exquisite. We were snogging all day at Cordusio and together got totally turned on. So in the evening we went out into the fields to make love. It was a fortnight since I'd made love, so I was completely charged up: I came four times and Carmen told me I was a real man. I felt more relaxed and that evening at home I fell asleep at once.

Sunday 13 Nov.: [He begs money for the juke-box at Cordusio. Says he would like to work but can't get employment because of his long hair.] I have seen Carmen again, but she was with someone else. I didn't feel jealous, even though I love her.

The 18-year-old young woman had apparently had less of a choice, taking to the roads as a beatnik when both of her parents were killed in a car crash. She got chatting in a bar with a well-dressed man of about 30, and she went home with him. 'Aren't you for free love?' he expostulated as she (unsuccessfully) tried to resist him.[99]

As more and more people adopted the hippie lifestyle, plastic society would be sapped, or converted: that was the story. Through the underground press the ideas of a better, more natural society would be transmitted, thus also contributing to the triumph of the alternative society. There was not really the faintest likelihood of any of this coming to pass. What we have been looking at in these first two sections is the continuation, proliferation, diversification of the youth subcultures we examined in Chapter 3, interacting with the other movements and developments I have been discussing. The hippies, the yippies, the underground, the subject-matter for this section, were important as the souped-up motor, often spluttering, and sometimes malfunctioning, of a wider movement critical of the plastic and the artificial, supportive of the simple and the natural and above all asserting the virtues of frankness and honesty in personal relations. Some did merge into the student movements of 1967–9, and their ideas certainly continued to influence schoolchildren until well into the seventies. At a more mundane level, for good or ill, hippie, counter-cultural, underground practices had a lasting effect on the lifestyles and leisure activities of important sections of the population. First, drugs. The late sixties was the first era in which almost everyone in certain age groups, and in certain professions (mainly to do with the arts, entertainment, and education) had at least some contact with drugs, even if that amounted to no more than the offer, and refusal, of a joint or a few amphetamines. The LSD phase passed, and few in later decades believed the rubbish which had been talked about the beneficial, mind-expanding qualities of drugs. None the less all societies today have serious drug problems, and if I am to praise sixties society for some of its legacies, I must surely condemn it for being the society in which drug abuse began to run out of control. It can, however, be seriously questioned whether the recreational use of drugs, and certainly cannabis, is any more reprehensible than the recreational use of alcohol. That was a case the hippies were making, and it is still before us today. Actually, after the busts of the sixties, and the measured reactions to them of leader-writers and superior court judges, the attitudes of judiciary and police have become steadily more relaxed and less punitive.

The emergence of the early youth subculture had been accompanied by boutiques, sources of the latest fashions in clothing. New sorts of boutiques appeared in the period I have just been discussing: known as 'head shops', they stocked the beads, the headbands, the leather apparel, the old army uniforms, the oriental dress, the incense, all the other vital ingredients and miscellaneous junk relating to the underground, hippie, and fellow-travelling existence. Other things which survived were: 'acid rock', a kind of rock music, pioneered in San Francisco, which tried to re-create for listeners and dancers the sensory experiences produced by LSD; the use of strobe lights at rock concerts and dances, to give a psychedelic effect; and 'light shows', rock concerts where strobe and other lighting, and slides, were used to try to reproduce the effects of LSD.

Rock music (and the idolatry it inspired), nature, love, drugs, and mass togetherness—where they all joined hands was in the open-air music festivals, the greatest of all the types of spectacle invented in the sixties. The culminating event of the Summer of Love, 1967, was the pop festival at Monterey, the prototype for the others. From all directions hippies, fellow-travellers, camp-followers, and all descriptions of people filled with a lust for life, converged on the small town on the Californian coast, south of San Francisco. Subsequently, in London, there were several free concerts in Hyde Park, the great British spectacle being the Isle of Wight festival of 1970—an event French and Italian hippies made a point of attending. But the biggest and best-remembered—great care and preparation went into the filming of it—was the Woodstock Music and Arts Fair, held at Bethel in up-state New York, in August 1969. *Time* was perhaps at least half-right when it saluted 'history's largest happening... one of the significant political and social events of the age'. Actually none of the most 'significant' performers were there—no Beatles, Rolling Stones, Bob Dylan, Simon and Garfunkel, Doors, Led Zeppelin, Aretha Franklin, Stevie Wonder, Marvin Gaye, or Temptations. But then the point was more the people who participated, all 250,000 of them, rather than the stars who performed (ones who did well from the publicity were Janis Joplin, Joe Cocker, Jimi Hendrix, and the Who).[100] Assisted by the warm nights of August, Woodstock presented an incomplete, though not wholly inaccurate, image of the joyous new world of rock music.

To bring this section to a close I want to quote a young female student in America, writing in *Harper's* in October 1967. She perhaps overstates the rigidity and universality of the generation gap, but she brings out well how the waves of change radiated out from the activists, affecting almost the whole of a generation of young people, and she touches on that important issue of openness.

> The wisdom that may or may not be on the other side of the generation gap simply isn't relevant to my life, and to the conditions in which I live. An older generation's claim to insight as a result of greater experience is spurious because my experiences are qualitatively different from anything that has gone before.
>
> I deeply feel the inadequacy of the values I learned while growing up. Categories of social worth; drive for possession of things and people; the academic definitions of what is worth knowing and doing; the myth of America's good intentions around the world— all of these break down in the search for what is really important, and for a style of life that has dignity.
>
> The Negro revolution has significantly touched far more young people than just the activists who made the revolution. The reality changes; Negroes became visible on campuses, and even could be seen holding hands with whites. One could not continue to be shocked by everyday occurrences...
>
> Most recently, the easy accessibility and acceptability of drugs has opened a whole new area of possible experiences, of moving inward as well as outward in order to gain self-awareness... The ethics of the hippie culture—indiscriminate love and openness, the dignity of the individual and the value of human relationships, the destructiveness of rigid external authority—have influenced students who are demanding flexibility and personal relevance of the college curriculum...
>
> Finally, Vietnam has given the lie to the values we learned at home and in school.[101]

Some of those in the older generation, and in positions of authority, were concerned about existing systems of education, and also, in particular, about the treatment of crime and offenders—as we shall see in the next section.


### British and American 'Progressives' and 'Do-Gooders'

Myths of the hippie paradise, and of the proximity of the alternative society, were constructed at the time and have inspired believers ever since. So too with myths about how progressives ruined the educational systems of Britain and America, and how softness towards criminals opened the floodgates for the torrent of crime which engulfs us today. Let me start off with a straight statement of the facts. Sixties societies did, as we saw clearly in Chapter 7, generate extreme, absurd ideas—and not just about repressive tolerance or the death of the author, but also about education as a tool of bourgeois indoctrination, and crime as exclusively the creation of an evil society. But the ideas actually put forward by reformers with any practical influence were generally moderate, and almost always related to direct knowledge and experience, rather than to abstract theory. It is true that the events of 1968 were a great stimulus to educational reform, but these reforms were essentially responses to weaknesses now vividly exposed. Those who objected to the changes of 1968 and after, mainly with respect to American university education, were extreme conservatives who had directly experienced student activism and had been outraged by student challenges to their own authority. One can agree that, while it was undoubtedly right to bring new courses in black studies and women's studies into the curriculum, many of these courses were unbalanced and propagandist, and lacking in critical and intellectual depth; but these unfortunate developments came about in the middle and later seventies, not in the sixties at all. In their positive aspects their origins without doubt lay in the sixties: militant activism at the end of the sixties led to a right-wing reaction in the early seventies, which in turn produced an extreme radical response: in between, measured judgement was greatly weakened. The same chronology holds true in Britain, where the alleged decline was in primary and secondary schooling. Some of the changes to which critics objected did begin in the sixties; however, the great (and overdone) swing to pupil-centred learning, and the introduction of nonsense about speaking and writing correctly and grammatically being an unwarranted accommodation to bourgeois values, together with the catastrophic slide in standards, was very much a phenomenon of the later seventies. In the realm of crime and punishment, changes were not very great in any case. What changes there were did come in the early and mid-sixties, expanding at the end of our period—the 'long sixties'—and affecting France and Italy as well as Britain and America. These were changes congruent with the best aspects of sixties challenges and innovations, making penal regimes more civilized and humane. If there is cause for condemnation, it is of the vengeful, know-nothing regimes introduced in the eighties and nineties by the very British and American politicians who fostered the myth of the 'soft sixties'.

If we turn to secondary and primary schools we find an interesting contrast between the two countries. The alleged pernicious advance of progressive methods was already being attacked in Britain at the end of the sixties, while at that very time nearly all the polemical literature in America was critical of existing methods, denounced as conservative and authoritarian—Britain being eulogized as the pioneer of enlightened education. One of Britain's most famous educational progressives was A. S. Neill, the founder much earlier in the century of the experimental school Summerhill, where children had practically complete freedom. A popular edition of one of his books, *Summerhill*, was published in America in 1960. But the key document in the controversy over progressive approaches in Britain was the report of the official committee on the primary schools, set up by the Conservative secretary of state for education and science, Sir Edward Boyle, in August 1963. Chaired by Lady Plowden, and reporting in 1967, it is always known as the 'Plowden Report'. The Plowden Committee was a committee of 'the great and the good', the voices of measured judgement. In their very fibre, such people were moderate progressives, believing above all in dispassionate sifting of the evidence, and in listening to the professional experts. That, if there was a problem, was the problem; and indeed some critics of sixties developments have directed their fire at 'experts' rather than progressives and do-gooders. It may be that professional opinion (in this case that developed in the civil service, by psychologists, and in the university departments of education) suffered from being essentially that of an élite, educated in privileged institutions, protagonists of enlightened and civilized attitudes and eager to empathize with the problems of the poor and untutored, without, however, being exposed to the blasts of scepticism and cynicism generated in ordinary families struggling to make their way. I make this criticism only very tentatively. Above all, what the Plowden Committee represented was the coming to a kind of climax of views about, and even changing practices in, British education which had been forming since at least the Second World War.

The report took the view that what it called 'the modern regime', what was soon to be thought of as the 'child-centred' approach, already existed in quite a number of English primary schools, and essentially set out to evaluate that regime, as against the more traditional one prevalent in the other schools. The tone is measured, civilized, enlightened; the report considers arguments on both sides, but there is no doubt that its heart lay with the 'modern regime'. In discussing the 'Aims of Primary Education', it suggested that a list of what could be called 'danger signs' could be drawn up, these, rather obviously, being indicators of a too-traditional approach:

> fragmented knowledge, no changes in the past decade, creative work very limited, much time spent on teaching, few questions for children, too many exercises, too many rules, frequent punishments, and concentration on tests.

What immediately follows almost says it all about the simultaneously open and closed attitudes of the committee.

> Such a list, of course, involves value judgements at the outset, but it is an invitation to thought and argument and not simply to compliance. Then it could be asked what aims are implicit in, for example, the new mathematics, learning by heart, grammar and so on. To subject all educational practices to this kind of questioning might be healthy. Habit is an immensely strong influence in schools and it is one that should be weakened though it is never likely to be removed. These words are particularly addressed to practising teachers and especially to head teachers, rather than to educational theorists, who seldom fear innovation, but whose ideas may flounder because of their ignorance of what schools (and sometimes teachers) are really like.
> 
> If these methods were applied to all primary schools it would be appropriate that the trend of their practices and outlook corresponds to a recognisable philosophy of education, and to a view of society, which may be summarised as follows.

And what follows that is the most quoted passage from the report, one which has some elements in common with 'doing your own thing', 'playpower', and even to neo-Marxist and structuralist ideas about society and the transmission of values, and, above all, argues that happy self-fulfilment for the child is more important than learning the things which will be useful in adult society:

> A school is not merely a teaching shop, it must transmit values and attitudes. It is a community in which children learn to live first and foremost as children and not as future adults... The school sets out deliberately to devise the right environment for children, to allow them to be themselves and to develop in the way and at the pace appropriate to

454

them... It insists that knowledge does not fall into neatly separate compartments and that work and play are not opposite but complementary.

The report denied that the 'older virtues' of 'accuracy', 'care', 'perseverance', and 'sheer knowledge' were in decline,[102] but this is exactly what critics claimed, referring to the aggressive, recalcitrant students of the end of the decade. Critics did not necessarily rejoice either over the Plowden recommendations that corporal punishment in primary schools should be abolished, or over their criticisms of statutory religious education. It was in direct response to the recommendation about corporal punishment, which Plowden also said should be extended to secondary schools, that Gene Adams, Nick Peacey, and others founded STOPP (Society of Teachers Opposed to Physical Punishment), with Lady Plowden herself as patron, aiming at bringing Britain in this matter up to the level of civilization which had always existed in Italy; it took another twenty years. It was clear where the Plowden Committee stood: it identified 'one of the main educational tasks of primary school' as being 'to build on and strengthen children's intrinsic interest in learning and lead them to learn for themselves rather than from a fear of disapproval or desire for praise'; and it concluded that 'finding out has proved to be better for children than being told', while boldly announcing that 'the gloomy forebodings of the decline of knowledge which would follow progressive methods have been discredited'.

The most perceptive criticism of the Plowden Report was presented by a group of teachers who broadly accepted much of what Plowden was trying to achieve, and strongly agreed that there should be no reversion to 'archaic methods', but did accuse the report of a 'one-sided and misleading set of beliefs'. Rather than teachers swallowing whole, or applying by rote, the progressive philosophy of Plowden, they should be 'critical, empirical', responsive to the precise needs of their own pupils, and be able 'to think on their feet'.[103] A thundering denunciation came in a collection of essays edited by two unfashionably right-wing academics, *Fight for Education: A Black Paper Edited by C. B. Cox and A. E. Dyson*, published in March 1969. The editors stated their belief 'that disastrous mistakes are being made in modern education, and that an urgent reappraisal is required of the assumptions on which "progressive" ideas, now in the ascendant are based'.

In its general denunciation of 'progressive ideas', of the Labour government's policy of abolishing grammar schools and converting them into comprehensive schools, and also of the then prevalent student demonstrations, the paper quoted lurid examples of ignorance and illiteracy among pupils and students.[104] A fatter *Black Paper Two* was published later the same year; more *Black Papers* followed in the early seventies. Their editors and contributors represented a different kind of sixties nonconformity from that featured throughout most of this book: that of the belligerent, radical right, determined to expose smooth progressive platitudes. Far further out on the right were the fundamentalist religious cults,[105] and the anti-Darwinian Creationists in the United States, in their own ways as rebellious and as weird as the hippies. It is the spread of new, as distinct from traditional, forms of personal commitment and belief among ordinary people which is distinctive of the sixties.

Expert professional opinion in Britain in the sixties was turning strongly against the selective educational system, whereby at the age of '11+' some pupils, usually those from the more prosperous backgrounds, were selected for grammar schools, leading to professional careers, while others, usually from poorer backgrounds, were selected for secondary modern schools, which generally led nowhere. The Labour government was responsible for DES Circular 10/65 of 1965 which declared that selection for secondary schools was to be abolished, and grammar schools (to be replaced by comprehensive schools) along with it. When the Conservatives returned to power in 1970, their education secretary, Margaret Thatcher, still a few years from emerging as the leader of the radical right (though she did, at this time, abolish free milk for schoolchildren), accelerated the process of converting grammar schools into comprehensive schools, the official progressive orthodoxy. The Labour government also gave encouragement to the ideas of team teaching and individual learning. On the whole, the policy of extending comprehensive education, in the abstract clearly the policy best calculated to provide equal opportunities for all, had popular support; the main problem was that standards and facilities varied greatly between comprehensives in prospering areas and comprehensives in run-down areas. Apart from the *Black Papers*, there was a critical study published in 1973, *Why Tommy Isn't Learning*.[106] More objective studies were provided by the Central Advisory Council for Education, and by the Inspectors of Schools. The latter study defined the two approaches, coinciding with 'traditional' and 'modern or progressive', as 'broadly didactic' and 'broadly exploratory'. The report brought out that fears of a takeover by progressive approaches were quite unfounded, while at the same time it was itself slightly critical of such approaches. The statistics it gave were that the 'broadly didactic' approach was being followed by 75 per cent of teachers, the 'broadly exploratory' by only 5 per cent; 25 per cent were following an 'appropriate combination'. Its general comment was:

> Limiting teaching to a form that relies on posing questions, or allowing children to pose questions, and then encouraging them to ferret out the answers seems to be less effective than a more controlled form of teaching with explanations provided step by step. But a combination of the two approaches was consistently associated with better scores on the NSER tests and with the best match between tasks to be done and the children's ability to undertake them.[107]

Even by the later seventies, then, claims that progressive methods were ruining English education were still pretty groundless.

During 1964, a couple of important books were published in the United States criticizing the authoritarian and unimaginative nature of American education, *Compulsory Mis-Education*, by Paul Goodman, and *How Children Fail*, by John Holt. That grand piece of Great Society legislation, the Elementary and Secondary Education Act of 1965, did include a provision which permitted funding for innovative teaching programmes in the elementary schools. However, in parallel with the counter-cultural critiques we have studied, there followed a clutch of texts intensifying the criticism of American education, including *Our Children Are Dying*, by Nat Hentoff, and *36 Children*, by Herbert Kohl, which described the author's own experiments in progressive education.[108] Educational journalist Joseph Featherstone had gone to England in 1966, specifically to study schools in Leicestershire. In the immediate aftermath of the publication of the Plowden Report he published three articles in *New Republic*. Featherstone spoke of 'a profound and sweeping revolution in English primary education, involving new ways of thinking about how young children learn, classroom organisation, the curriculum, and the role of the teacher'. This was surely slightly exaggerated, but, perhaps in part because of the good work already put in on behalf of Britain by the Beatles, it had a great impact.[109] By 1969 study teams from twenty American cities had gone to England to learn about what was beginning to be called 'open education'. Already Lillian Weber, a professor at City College, New York, had spent eighteen months observing British primary schools in 1965–6. In the autumn of 1967 she began what she called an 'open corridor programme' in a Harlem public school. This led in 1969 to her getting funding both from the federal government and from the Ford Foundation for the establishment of an advisory service on open education. Charles Silberman had also visited England before publishing his *Crisis in the Classroom* (New York, 1970), which advocated the extension of the open-education principle to secondary schools. President Nixon produced funding for an experimental schools programme, and the New York State commissioner for education, Ewald B. Nyquist, publicly endorsed open education, publishing a book in collaboration with Gene R. Hawes on *Open Education*.[110] In 1974 there appeared *The Teachers' Guide to Open Education:*

> Open education is characterised by a classroom environment in which there is a minimum of teaching to the class as a whole, in which provision is made for children to pursue individual interests and to be actively involved with materials, and in which children are trusted to direct many aspects of their own learning.[111]

The most fundamentalist, the most extremist book, and the one with the greatest international impact, was Ivan Illich, *Deschooling Society*. According to Illich, existing schools were pillars of bourgeois society and must be replaced. In Britain such ideas were advocated by Marxist 'free schoolers',[112] and as British politics became more polarized in the late seventies and early eighties, with Conservatives dominated by the radical right and Labour, particularly on the local authorities which ran education, moving to the 'loony left', 'open' or 'progressive' ideas really did begin to have a destructive effect on English education.

Crime was a steadily growing problem in both countries, to the extent of being essentially out of control in the United States. Despite the mythology, nothing was done by reformers or do-gooders which increased the danger to the public. In Britain we can again detect the influence of the great and the good and of a reform-minded Labour government. Baroness Wootton, at the end of the 1950s, had cast doubt on the whole notion that the extent of the personal responsibility of a criminal could be assessed, and had expressed the view that punishment was inherently bad, and only 'becomes necessary when the nuisance to the community becomes intolerable'. Frank Pakenham, Lord Longford, presented the Christian case against the punitive approach, and in 1964 a publication of his on behalf of the Labour party pinpointed the punitive element in the current judicial system, something which had already been done by the official Kilbrandon

Report on the workings of crime and punishment in Scotland.[113] In the statement of government policy (the 'Queen's Speech') after the Labour government came into office in 1964, the Queen said (interestingly, given the new fixation on the family of the late nineties and the allegations about 'anti-family' policies in the sixties): 'My Government will be actively concerned to make more effective the means of sustaining the family and of preventing and treating delinquency.' In August 1965 the Home Office published a discussion paper, *The Child, the Family and the Young Offender*. This proposed that offenders under 16 should be taken 'as far as possible outside the ambit of the criminal law and of the courts', and that the emphasis should be on treatment and, with the agreement of parents or guardians, on making arrangements for their welfare. With offenders in the 16–21 age group, the aim should be to remove them as far as possible 'from the penal system as it applies to adults... In both cases the determining factor in deciding what is to be done must be the welfare of the particular child or young person.' The close connections between government initiatives and private and voluntary ones in the sphere of reform are, contrary to accounts which privilege collectivist action, very important. In this paper the government clearly expressed its wish for voluntary work to be maintained and strengthened.[114]

In December 1965 there followed a further Home Office discussion paper, *The Adult Offender*. This paper made the bold and enlightened statement: 'It does none of us any good to enjoy a sense of revenge.' Long-term imprisonment was to be imposed only 'with the greatest reluctance, when the protection of the public rendered it clearly essential'. Long sentences inevitably led to progressive deterioration in the condition of the prisoners; thus 'their conditions in confinement must be humane and tolerable'. The government's aim was that 'prisoners whose character and record make them suitable' should be released on licence much earlier than current practices allowed for. The old notion of 'corrective training' should be abolished, all prisoners being provided with useful training. Every prisoner should be provided 'with the best type of work of which he is capable and the best industrial training for which he is fitted'. Family visits to prisoners should be made easier. If prisons were to be greatly humanized, it would have to be recognized that prison staff need 'special qualities of insight and tolerance'. The question of after-care of released prisoners was an important one, and the best way forward was 'to integrate the prison welfare service with the probation and after-care service'. Again great use should be made of voluntary agencies. The final words of the report were that the government wished to support Rule 1 of the Prison Rules of 1964: 'The purpose of the training and treatment of convicted prisoners shall be to encourage and assist them to lead a good and useful life.'[115] Most of these reforms were put into practice by the 1967 Criminal Justice Act: in particular, prisoners could be released on licence after serving one-third, or one year, of their sentence, whichever was the longer. The sponsoring of prison reform, as well as the abolition of capital punishment, was really quite bold in a decade in which had taken place the horrific serial murders of young children, the 'Moors Murders', followed by the evil exploits of the Kray brothers.

In 1969 another horrific series of six child murders was carried out by a telephone engineer who subsequently committed suicide. The father of an 8-year-old girl who had been raped and strangled wrote an almost heart-breakingly brave and enlightened article, published in the *Sunday Times* on 29 March 1970, on the question of capital punishment:

458

For my part I believe that we know almost nothing about the state of mind of men who commit these crimes. The abolition of capital punishment would be right, for one reason alone, if the state, through the agency of the most knowledgeable men and women in the appropriate fields, would attempt to enlist the assistance of the men who are convicted of these murders to give us some kind of insight into their motives.

Perhaps they were maddened by the influences of commercial pornography or by the conditions of life in our industrial society, perhaps they could never find normal sex. Who knows? But we should try to find out, because only through knowledge can there be some hope of preventing these disasters in the future.[116]

Almost certainly not a majority view, but representative of the kind of unquenchable spirit which had, away from hippie communes and underground conclaves, developed among thoughtful ordinary people.

Already by the middle sixties crime was so out of control in the United States that it was reckoned that only one-tenth of all crimes were actually reported. Hence the establishment of the President's Commission on Law Enforcement and the Administration of Justice, which resulted in the publication in 1967 of *The Challenge of Crime in a Free Society*. The report put in at least half a good word on behalf of the police, recognizing them as being 'subject to an incredible amount of uncertainty, anxiety, reproach, misunderstanding, misgivings, and temptations'. The report was slightly confused and short of clear proposals, though full of the expression of moderately progressive attitudes: reflecting the profound impact of the civil rights movement, it described prison as 'segregation'; it aspired to better ways of dealing with offenders, 'so that the system of criminal justice can win the respect and co-operation of all citizens'; it roundly declared that 'individual citizens, social-service agencies, universities, religious institutions, civic and business groups, and all kinds of governmental agencies at all levels must become involved in planning and executing changes in the criminal justice system'.[117] The leading proponent of progressive reform in the system was the psychiatrist, and expert on penal policy in the state of Kansas, Karl Menninger, who in 1968 published the expressively titled *The Crime of Punishment*. 'The secret of success', Menninger said, 'is the replacement of the punitive attitude with a therapeutic attitude.' Menninger wrote that the public has a fascination for violence, clinging tenaciously to its desire for vengeance, and completely unaware of 'the expense, futility, and dangerousness of the result-ing penal system'. His hope was that

The public will grow increasingly ashamed of its cry for retaliation, its persistent demand to punish. This is its crime, *our* crime against criminals—and incidentally our crime against ourselves. For before we can diminish our sufferings from the ill-controlled aggressive assaults of fellow citizens, we must renounce the philosophy of punishment, the obsolete, vengeful penal attitudes.[118]

There were perhaps some slight grounds for hope that that might really happen in the High Sixties; it is not easy to be quite so hopeful today.

459

Complaints about softness and do-goodery in the America and Britain of the sixties really do not stand up to investigation. Similar complaints about their own countries are not usually made by the French and the Italians. In France and Italy at the beginning of the seventies there were, related directly to the great protest movements of 1968 and 1969, movements on behalf of prisoners' rights. There were similar movements in Britain. PROP, Preservation of the Rights of Prisoners, was launched on 12 May 1972 by a small group of ex-prisoners, during protests at Brixton prison in London. The founders of PROP make a colourful group, perhaps the sort of people only to take this kind of committed action when stimulated by the participatory spirit of the time: a former safe-blower, Dick Pooley, who had served a total of twenty years, a certain Ted Ward, who had served two years for breaking *into* Dartmoor prison in Devon to help a successful escape attempt, and a conman who had served a couple of sentences for petty theft, Douglas Curtis, now a mature student at Cambridge University.[119] One begins to feel still more that one is in the middle of a traditional, gentle, British comic film when one reads the press release issued by the Wakefield branch of PROP, on 4 June 1972, with reference to a prisoners' sit-in in Wakefield prison:

> On the night of 29th/30th May a 15 hour sit-in was held in the exercise yard of Wakefield prison by 161 members and supporters of PROP, the prisoners' union. The purpose of this all-night demonstration was to highlight the demands of prisoners in all British prisons for basic civil rights.

These were the right to organize, the right of elected representatives to communicate with other prisons and with Parliament and other bodies, the right to vote, and the right to access to the mass media. The press release continued:

> The Wakefield demonstration was carried out in an orderly, disciplined and good-humoured manner. At no time was there any animosity between prisoners and staff. During the night the prisoners built shelters and lit small fires on which tea was brewed. During the demonstration one delegate was elected from each of the four prison wings to represent the prisoners of that wing. Early on the morning of the 30th the area of the demonstration was cleaned up and at 6 a.m. all prisoners returned to the prison. The 161 prisoners were kept in solitary confinement for the following three days while the authorities carried out an investigation. On the evening of Thursday, 1st June all privileges were restored. To date no further action has been taken by the authorities.
>
> It is not expected that the demands will be met at this stage.[120]

No hints of gentle comedy in France and Italy. In Clervaux prison, France, in 1970, two inmates, Buffet and Bontaud, took a guard and a nurse hostage, demanding that in return for their release they should be allowed safe passage out of the prison. When the minister of justice did not accede to their demands, they killed both hostages. During 1972–3 the prisons at Toul and Nancy were destroyed by the inmates. In 1972 the revolutionary GIP (Groupe d'Information des Prisons) was founded. This was followed in January 1973 by the more moderate, reformist CAP (Comité d'Action des Prisonniers). In a highly practical manifesto issued on 15 January 1973 CAP made demands which, being no more than what was already standard practice in Britain, reveal how repressive the French system was: the manifesto called for the abolition of the death penalty and of transportation overseas, the right to unrestricted visits and correspondence, and the reorganization of prison work and training.[121]

Conditions were about as bad in Italy, though there was no death penalty or transportation, for, as in some other areas, despite a guarantee of prison reform in the constitution, little had changed since the days of the Fascists. In the general turmoil obtaining in Italy between the end of the sixties and the beginning of the seventies there were utterly unprecedented prison revolts, concentrated into waves of action in 1968–70, 1971–2, and 1973. The Italian government at this time was more reform-minded than was the French. Minister of Justice Zagari went to talk to prisoners in Rome, and at the San Vittore prison in Milan meetings were held between prisoners and the press. A reform bill was brought before parliament, and did finally pass into law at the end of 1974.[122]

### Windows on the Nations

In reading novels and looking at films, I have been searching for evidence which might support some of my generalizations about the sixties, and also for evidence which might suggest other generalizations which I had previously missed; I am also looking for characteristics peculiar to the countries in which the novels or films were produced. The novels I propose to discuss, all currently available in cheap reprints are: *Les Choses: une histoire des années soixante* (Things, 1965) by Georges Perec, *Il padrone* (The Boss, 1965) by Goffredo Parise, *A ciascuno il suo* (To Each His Own, 1966) by Leonardo Sciascia, *Myra Breckinridge* (1968) by Gore Vidal, *The Bluest Eye* (1970) by Toni Morrison, *Vogliamo tutto* (We Want the Lot, 1971) by Nanni Balestrini, *La Clé sur la porte* (The Key in the Door, 1972) by Marie Cardinale.[123] Having already exhaustively assessed the validity of the term 'les années anglaises', in this section I concentrate solely on the cultural products of France, Italy and America.

Georges Perec was born in Paris in 1936, the son of Jewish immigrants from Poland: his father died in 1940 fighting in the French army, his mother in 1943, after being deported. There was enough family money for him to complete his secondary education at a boarding-school thirty miles south of Paris, and for him to go on to the Sorbonne, where he spent two years studying sociology; after a short period as a market researcher he married; he and his wife spent the academic year 1960–1 as teachers in Sfax, Tunisia. On his return Perec took a job as an archivist in a medical research laboratory in Paris, a job he retained until the enormous success in 1978 of *La Vie: mode d'emploi* freed him from all financial cares (he died two years later). Perec's first novel was begun in 1962 under the provisional title of *La Grande Aventure*, reaching its final form and title in 1964, and being accepted for the *Lettres Nouvelles* series, edited for Julliard by a leading figure in the literary establishment, Maurice Nadeau; such collections offered opportunities to new writers, though certainly did not guarantee them success. Within a year or two *Les Choses* sold

100,000 copies, a success not initiated but considerably accelerated by the winning of the Prix Renaudot within two months of publication. It has for many years been a set text in French secondary schools. However, despite an American translation for Grove Press, no translation was available in Britain till the 1980s.[124]

*Les Choses* opens with this sentence: 'L'œil, d'abord, glisserait sur la moquette grise d'un long couloir, haut et étroit.' The first substantive, 'The eye', establishes the note of distance, of impersonality, maintained throughout the novel; the third word, 'would slip', very significantly, is in the conditional tense. The first sentence of the second chapter administers a mild shock: 'They would have liked to have been rich.' The opening eight pages have described in meticulous and caressing detail a luxury apartment, together with all the accoutrements that the truly prosperous in this dawning age of consumerism in France could expect to possess. We now move into an equally meticulous description of the physical environment and lifestyle of young people doing well in the new consumer society, but not nearly as rich as they would like to be. 'They' are a particular couple, identified when we get to the third chapter as Jérôme and Sylvie, and a host of other couples very similar to themselves, people who have not persevered with higher education because it only leads to low-paid teaching jobs, and have instead entered enthusiastically into the new world of marketing and market research. Jérôme is the son of a white-collar worker and a hairdresser, though the anonymous narrator, whose position 'neither above the characters, nor inside them' (as Bellos puts it),[125] together with the voluptuous use of marketing language, gives the novel much of its special quality, does not tell us this until page 97. Sometimes the couple, and the couples, feel exultation in their freedom and purchasing power; much of the time they feel cast down that there is so much still beyond their reach. Part I, which takes up ten chapters (part II consists of only three chapters, together with an epilogue), covers the years from around 1958 to around 1964, but without following a strict chronological sequence. We learn of the common interests and attitudes of Jérôme, Sylvie, and their group. We are constantly reminded of the general discontent that richer prizes are always beyond reach. We learn that Sylvie and Jérôme *are* slightly different in that they want to prolong the freedom of temporary jobs, while their contemporaries begin to try to build secure careers for themselves. We learn that throughout the Algerian war Sylvie and Jérôme had shown a sort of commitment to the 'antifascist' cause, but that with the ending of that war (historically, July 1962) all trace of political consciousness vanished and they became preoccupied with somehow winning large sums of money. We learn of their sense of time having passed without their achieving what they wanted; of how the group begins to fall apart. We learn of the research trip the couple make through all parts of booming France, of the joys of this, and, more, of the profound feelings of depression. In part II, learning by chance of teaching opportunities in Tunisia, they decide to flee there. But they find that, instead of living in Tunis, they will have to live in the desolate outpost of Sfax. From a world too full of things, they are transferred into a world too empty. After existing through the academic year, they return to Paris. Their varied experience enables them to get reasonably decent and secure jobs, in Bordeaux.

With a slight adjustment of dates, and the exception of the final move, the outlines of the story follow closely that of Perec (though not his social origins) and his wife. Perec's experiences in the world of market research bear closely on the content of the novel. It is clear that much of the success of the novel at the time depended upon its perceived sociological accuracy, a large swathe of upwardly mobile, middle-class young adults identifying with the characters and their milieu. But, of course, *Les Choses* was a novel, not a sociological analysis; as literary artefact (historian beware!) it is a kind of friendly parody of Flaubert's *L'éducation sentimentale*.[126] Another governing influence was Barthes's *Mythologies*, published in 1958; Perec was to declare that the main idea of the book was to explore the way 'the language of advertising is reflected in us'.[127]

Parise was born in December 1929, son of Ida Wanda Bertoli and an unknown father. Bertoli was herself the adopted daughter of a bicycle manufacturer whose business was wiped out in the crash of 1929, so that Parise was brought up in severe poverty. In 1937 his mother married a journalist, Oswaldo Parise, and from this point on Parise (he took the name in 1943) received a good education in state schools. At university he tried first medicine, then maths, but gave up altogether in 1950, at which point he had already embarked, in Venice, on a career in journalism. In the early 1950s he published two non-naturalistic parables, *Il ragazzo morto e le comete* (1951) and *La grande vacanza* (1953), neither commercially successful. However, the three naturalistic works which followed, *Il prete bello* (1954), *Il fidanzamento* (1956), and *Amore e fervore* (1960), together with the play *La moglie a cavallo*, presented in Milan in 1959, brought him great acclaim. In 1960 he moved to Rome, where to his already considerable circle of literary friends were added the film-makers Rossellini and Fellini: he wrote one episode for *Boccaccio '70*, and collaborated on 8½.[128] Despite the non-naturalistic mode, *Il padrone* is packed with detail. When we move on to evaluating that detail, it will be important to remember Parise's involvement in one of the distinctive cultural activities of the sixties, film-making, and that his eye was that of a journalist. *Il padrone* is a parable, akin to the Italian novels I discussed in Chapter 4. Nevertheless, it won the Viareggio prize, and enjoyed great commercial success.

In chapter 1, the longest in the book, the young narrator (who remains anonymous throughout) arrives from a small town to take up a post in a commercial enterprise (whose activities are never specified) in a large city (never named). His origins are clearly somewhere within the lower ranges of the middle classes, since he has obtained the post through family connections. Although the firm is actually owned by Doctor Satturno, power, apparently, is in the hands of his son, always known as 'il dottor Max'. At first the new recruit is the responsibility of a senior fellow employee, Diabete, who invites him to his own flat, and finds him lodgings. Il dottor Max, however, makes something of a favourite of the young narrator, addressing him on the difficulties of being both a boss and a human being: indeed, vast sections of the book are in the form of long dialogues of a quasi-philosophical character, putting one in mind of the theatrical tradition of Pirandello and Dario Fo. In fact, il dottor Max requires complete subservience and conformity, and becomes more and more irritated with his favourite's quizzical and sceptical responses in their many dialogues. Matters take a sinister turn when the narrator is required to undergo regular injections by Lotar, il dottor Max's bodyguard, though the injections themselves are of harmless, or perhaps beneficial, vitamins. The narrator meets, and visits the houses of, two characteristic employees, Pippo and Pluto, and their wives, who are themselves always unwell; Pippo is an alcoholic, who subsequently commits suicide. The narrator learns that Max's mother, 'la dottoressa Uraza', is keen that he should marry her ward, Zilietta, a girl beautiful in feature and figure, but with deformed hands and feet, and incapable of any conversation beyond the correct naming of objects; the girl is in fact a sufferer from Down's syndrome. The narrator, who, apparently, has had quite a number of sexual adventures since coming to the city, and who has abandoned his fiancée in his own town, is naturally not taken by the idea. He decides that he must find another job, but since his bosses also own all other suitable enterprises, his prospects are not great.

In the final chapter he has married the girl, and now, as a fully integrated employee, has a fine apartment and all the trappings. His life with Zilietta, contrary to all expectations, is a normal one:

> the only thing lacking is speech. Having given each object its name, nothing remains to her but silence. But what purpose is served by speech? It is said that speech enables men to communicate among themselves and to become poets. Perhaps that was once its purpose. But to my mind it is solely an instrument of defence and offence in the struggle. Between me and Zilietta there was neither speech, nor struggle, and, in contrast with other couples, who speak to each other and struggle with each other, we are very happy.[129]

Zilietta is pregnant. Although the doctors are certain that she has only from two to five years to live, she has time to become a mother. 'My son will be, like her, mentally handicapped, something I hope for with all my heart, and over which I shall fret until the last moment.' His hope is that his son will not be like himself, a man with some glimmerings of reason, but happy like his mother in the pure attitude of existing. As he will never employ speech he will never know what is moral and what is immoral. 'I will wish him'—this is the last sentence of the novel—'a life similar to that of the jar which at this very moment his mother is holding in her hand, for only in this way will it be impossible for anyone to do him harm.'

A gloomy and perhaps rather distasteful tale? (William Weaver's American translation of 1966 directly transliterates the Italian '*mongoloîde*', where I, perhaps over-sensitively, have used 'Down's syndrome'.) A long expression of revulsion against modern society in general, rather than a story offering insights specifically into the sixties? Parise himself, in an interview at the time of his acceptance of the Viareggio prize for *Il padrone*, declared that there was a direct link between that novel and his first one, *Il ragazzo morto e le comete*, published in 1951, both in content and in style: 'In that also the mode was non-naturalistic and there was a total absence of the individual psychology (though not the feelings) of the characters.'[130] The key historical point, I think, is the utterly different reception accorded the later novel, published in an age when the readers of difficult novels were being told that 'structure' or 'system' was everything, individual psychology nothing.

As novelist, Perec probably achieved the greatest fame of the French and Italians discussed here; Leonardo Sciascia achieved a certain political eminence—after serving on the Palermo city council from 1975 to 1977 as an independent on the Italian Communist party list, he joined the Radical party, becoming both an Italian and a Euro MP. However, at the time of *A ciascuno il suo* he was known only as a writer and as a primary schoolteacher and educational administrator in his native Sicily (he was born at Racalmuto in the province of Agrigenti, in January 1921).[131] In 1956 Sciascia published a classic of neo-realism, a collection of nine documentary essays on his home town, *Le parrochie di Regalpetra* (his fictional name for Racalmuto). Between 1961 and 1974 he published the four gialli (literally 'yellows', the popular term for the detective story) for which he is most famous, and of which A *ciascuno il suo* was the second (the others are *Il giorno della civetta*, 1961, *Il contesto*, 1971, and *Todo modo*, 1974). Sciascia has made it clear that he used this form in order to grab the attention of the reader;[132] however, there is more self-consciousness than that, the opening of chapter 7 of A *ciascuno il suo* actually being a disquisition on the unreality of the conventional detective story. All the 'detective stories' concern the corruption of Sicilian life and the central role of the Mafia in business and politics; in none of them is a murderer ever brought to justice. The period in which, and about which, Sciascia was writing, quite specifically the sixties, was the period of the Fafundi Commission (1963–8), investigating the Mafia in Sicily, and the period of the centre-left *rapprochement* in national politics, as well as the period of population migration to the Sicilian towns, particularly Palermo (and to the major cities of the north).[133]

The novel (set very precisely in 1964) opens with a village pharmacist receiving an anonymous letter threatening him with death for some sin committed in the past. Shortly thereafter the pharmacist and his friend, Dr Roscio, are gunned down on the first day of the hunting season. It is remembered that an attractive young woman had been coming to the pharmacy with unusual frequency: her reputation, as well as that of the pharmacist himself, is blackened and her engagement broken off. It mattered nothing that actually she had travelled to the pharmacy to obtain medicines for a sick family member. The police lose interest (the one physical clue is a cigar butt left at the scene of the crime), but the local secondary school teacher, Laurana, finds his curiosity aroused when he recognizes that the anonymous letter is made up of the distinctive typeface of *L'Osservatore Romano*, the Catholic weekly. Laurana is a dull pedant, a timid bachelor, and 'victim', as one literary critic put it in colourful Italian, 'of *mammismo*' (dominance by his mother).[134] It is *by chance* (a central point in Sciascia's disquisition on how detection actually progresses in the real world) that he learns that Dr Roscio had been consulting a prominent Communist MP in Rome about an eminent local figure, whose corrupt activities he had discovered. Roscio, it begins to appear, was the real target, the anonymous letter simply a blind. From a parish priest (one of only three characters in the novel represented as disinterested and clear-headed, the others being Roscio's father, a famous oculist, now himself blind, and the allegedly mad aristocrat, Don Benito), Laurana learns of the interlocking industrial, commercial, and political concerns of the advocate, Rosello, who, according to the priest, is by a long way the most eminent and powerful local figure.

Laurana decides to learn to drive. Visiting the palace of justice in Palermo to obtain a provisional driving licence, he happens to encounter Rosello, with another influential advocate and a cigar-smoking third man. From Don Benito, Laurana learns that this man is Ragania, a hired killer; Laurana himself is able to match Ragania's cigars to the butt found near the dead bodies. Roscio's widow, niece of Archbishop Rosello and cousin of the advocate Rosello, is an exceptionally beautiful woman. As Laurana pursues his inquiries, it begins to appear that the cousins have been having an affair. Laurana is repelled and fascinated by the beautiful widow. She persuades him of her grief over her husband's death, of her interest in him and of her determination to help him bring his investigation to a successful conclusion. A rendezvous is arranged in the café Romeris in Palermo. The widow Roscio does not show up. Returning to the station, Laurana accepts a lift. The last words of chapter 16 are: 'The car shot off at a furious pace.' In the next brief chapter there are perfunctory police inquiries into Laurana's disappearance. It is presumed he has gone off with a woman. But, that chapter ended, 'the teacher's body was lying under a pile of stones in an abandoned sulphur mine, half way between his home and the capital' (140). In the final pages we learn of the marriage of Rosello and the widow Roscio. It becomes clear that, rather than acting as a disinterested exposer of corruption, Roscio had simply been the jealous husband, blackmailing both the advocate and the archbishop in the hope of retaining his beautiful wife. It becomes clear, too, that the entire community had known the full story from the beginning. One character also volunteers to another, in secret, that he knows something about the fate of 'poor Laurana'. The book concludes on the words of his confidant: 'He was a fool'

Born in 1925 into the American upper class, Gore Vidal is a true aristocrat, a man of prodigious energy and talent, a patrician critic of American society, active in politics but too far to the left to secure any elected post. He knew Hollywood intimately, and in the fifties wrote both films and television plays. In the sixties he began to concentrate on writing novels, both a famous historical series, running from *Burr* and *Lincoln* to *Washington* D.C., and modernist satirical fables, beginning with *Myra Breckinridge*. Vidal is not one of my favourite novelists (nor is Parise—but, then, what has liking to do with art or, more to the point, with writing history?), and *Myra Breckinridge* is not one of my favourite novels, yet, if I were asked to pick *the* novel around which to structure an illuminating discussion of significant characteristics of the High Sixties, this would be it. In one of the punishingly cynical remarks which punctuate his novels, we learn, on the very last page of the book, that Myra Breckinridge, 'like so many would-be intellectuals back East... never actually read books, only books about books': *Myra Breckinridge* is full of references to Robbe-Grillet and the New French Novel, to Lévi-Strauss and to Marshall McLuhan, clues to the reader, rather than pretentiously dropped names, but the whole novel is an expression (with tongue at least partly in cheek) of some of the more extreme ideas discussed in my Chapter 7. At the same time, in its more naturalistic phases, it comments sharply and comprehensively on the rapidly changing culture of sixties America. That the book is in full modernist mode is made clear first by the brief opening chapters, a parody of Robbe-Grillet. There, in disavowal of the omniscient author, we are informed explicitly how the novel has come into existence: Myra's analyst friend and dentist, Dr Randolph Spenser Montag, has proposed that she write 'this notebook' as therapy. From time to time this 'notebook' is interrupted by transcripts of recordings made on to disc by Buck Loner, Myra's uncle, and head of the Hollywood Film Academy where she was given a job as a lecturer; at one point an unedited telephone conversation by the Golden State Detective Agency is inserted.

The opening chapter consists of fewer than ten lines, and the next four, making it clear to the reader that this is a modernist fable, are not much longer. The opening chapter tells us:

I am Myra Breckinridge whom no man will ever possess. Clad only in garter belt and one dress shield, I held off the entire elite of the Trobriand Islanders, a race who possess no words for 'why' or 'because'. Wielding a stone axe, I broke the arms, the limbs, the balls of their finest warriors, my beauty blinding them, as it does all men, unmanning them in the way that King Kong was reduced to a mere simian whimper by beauteous Fay Wray whom I resemble left three-quarter profile if the key light is no more than five feet high during the close shot.

Hollywood movies of the golden age of the thirties and the forties are to be a rich resource pool throughout the book: the French *nouvelle vague* directors, Umberto Eco, and the new sociologists were all making Hollywood movies, and popular culture generally, a fully respectable subject for study. Myra refers to her late husband, Myron, who was drowned in New York Harbour and who was writing a book in support of his thesis that Hollywood movies between 1935 and 1945 formed the high point of Western culture. But we begin to get hints—and this forms the narrative drive of the novel—that perhaps Myron and Myra are really the same person: by page 84 Loner is recording on his disc that his lawyers have discovered that Myra Breckinridge was never married to his nephew Myron. In fact, the master theme of the novel is that of sexual ambiguity, anticipating the fashionable post-structuralist theories, soon to be taken up by certain feminists, of sex or gender essentially being socially constructed. Myra writes:

I alone have the intuition as well as the profound grasp of philosophy and psychology to trace for man not only what he is but what he must become, once he has ceased to be confined to a single sexual role, to a single person... once he has become free to blend with others, to exchange personalities with both men and women, to play out the most elaborate of dreams in a world where there will soon be no limits to the human spirit's play.[135]

Eventually we learn that Myra had existed previously as Myron, before willing the sex change. Myron had homosexual tendencies. So had Myra, as the beginning of the passage in which she is with the beautiful student Mary-Ann makes clear:

I squeezed her bare shoulders; our breasts touched, teasingly. Mine are even larger than hers, filled with silicone, the result of a new process discovered in France and not always successful in its application (recently a French stripper died when the silicone was injected by mistake into an artery). I was fortunate, however, and no one, not even a trained physician, can tell that my beautiful firm breasts are not the real thing.

Shyly, Mary-Ann once said, 'they are just super, Myra! I bet the boys were really after you in high school.' An amusing thought, since, in those days, it was I who was after the boys. At fourteen Myron vowed that he would, in one way or another, extract the essence of every good-looking boy in school and he succeeded in one hundred and one cases over a three-year period...[136]

Myra is contemptuous of her students, noting the drugs, the British influence, and the division between the reactionary majority and the counter-cultural minority. Following a student party she is very ill, as a result of mixing gin (which she is used to) and marijuana (which she is not). The party was a 'far-out' one, with a different sort of student:

> They wear buttons which, among other things, accuse the Governor of California of being a Lesbian, the President of being God, and Frodo (a character in a fairytale by Tolkien) of actually existing. This is all a bit fey for my taste. But one must be open to every experience and the young, in a sense, lead us since there are now more of them.[137]

Later Myra notes:

> One must not underestimate the influence of these young people on our society. It is true that the swingers, as they are called, make up only a small minority of our society; yet they hold a great attraction for the young and bored who are the majority...[138]

There is an immediate progression to the master theme: this majority 'must appear to accept without question our culture's myth that the male must be dominant, aggressive, woman-oriented'. Earlier Myra has declared: 'The roof has fallen in on the male and we now live at the dawn of the age of Woman Triumphant, of Myra Breckinridge!' In the ideas it expresses and the scenes it describes, this book is by some way more liberated in sexual matters than the ones by Updike and McCarthy I quoted earlier. It is Myra's set purpose to crush and humiliate the handsome and sexually successful student, Rusty. In a protracted and thoroughly explicit sequence, on the pretext of giving him a medical examination, she brutally handles his genitals, jeers at their size, and then thrusts an enormous dildo up his anus. I shall, in Chapter 13, be discussing some of the wilder extremes of fundamentalist, man-hating feminism. Earlier we have learned that: 'Myron and I met Dr Montag some years ago at a lecture Myron gave on "The Uterine Vision in the Films of the Forties" '; this is intended to be highly satirical—the real irony is that such a title would have been quite routine in women's studies courses from the mid-seventies onwards. Myra's views are consistently radical: she reckons the Chinese would run Los Angeles better than the current authorities; she notes that in that city 'only professional criminals are safe from harassment by the local police'; she comments that while 'there are nine Negro teachers in the academy, there are only seven Negro students'.

Reading *Myra Breckinridge* one is reminded of the story of the old lady who said she didn't much like Shakespeare's *Hamlet* because it was 'so full of quotations'. It was Vidal who put into circulation criticisms of aspects of American society—specifically the practice of circumcision by American doctors, and the risks of going on foot rather than by car, 'since it is a part of California folklore that only the queer or criminal walk'.

At the beginning of chapter 39 'Myra is hit by an automobile and remains unconscious for ten days. As she comes to, she feels she is growing a beard.' Chapter 41 consists of one short line: 'Where are my breasts? *Where are my breasts?* The next, and final, chapter is set some years later.

Myron tells the reader about how he came across the notebooks and other documents in an attic. He is now married to Mary-Ann. In his Introduction, Vidal proudly refers to the 'outrage' caused by Myra Breckinridge—'has literary decency fallen so low?' *Time* lamented—but, this being 1968, it was a circumscribed outrage, and no obstacles were placed to the novel going on 'to be a world best-seller'.

Toni Morrison, a black American, was born Chloe Anthony Wofford, the second of four children, in Lorain, Ohio, in 1931. Both her parents were from southern families; her maternal grandparents were from Greenville and Birmingham, Alabama, and had moved first to Kentucky, where her grandfather had worked as a coalminer, before coming on to Lorain. Her father had come to Ohio, taking a job as a shipyard worker in Lorain, to escape the racial violence of Georgia. In the thirties Lorain was basically a steel mill town, population 30,000, with a small port on Lake Erie. Apart from a heavy enough job in the shipyards, her father, for seventeen years, took on a couple of other part-time jobs, so that he was able to send his daughter to the prestigious though highly traditional all-black Howard University in Washington. Because people there had difficulty with her name, she changed it to Toni. Discrimination was obvious enough in Lorain, but there was no full-scale segregation and no ghetto: it was while out on the road with the university theatrical touring group the Howard University Players that Morrison came into direct contact with the vicious reality of segregation in the South. A brilliant student, she was able to profit from the absence of overt prejudice in the North in the fifties, and take an MA in English literature at prestigious Cornell University in New York State. She went back to teach at Howard, and while there experimented with colleagues in the production of a short story. Her basic idea came from memories of a little girl she had known back in Lorain who had claimed she knew God didn't exist because she had prayed for two years for blue eyes without any effect. Thus, the book which eventually became *The Bluest Eye* got its vague beginnings around 1961 or 1962. She married a young black architect from Jamaica, and in the summer of 1964 went to Europe with her husband and two sons. But she returned without the husband, and so had to go back to her parents in Lorain. 'I am from the Midwest,' Toni Morrison has said, 'so I have a special affection for it'.[139]

She got a job with an educational publisher in Syracuse, not far, as it happened, from Cornell. Here, without ever having thought of that as a possible career, she turned, because of loneliness and the absence of anyone to converse with, to trying to turn her short story idea into a novel.[140] Very conscious of, but not directly active in, the civil rights movement, she believed that as an editor of school textbooks she could use her position to change the ways in which blacks were presented in them. In one delightful indication of changing times, she had a white 'maid' to look after her sons. She has described the impetus for getting *The Bluest Eye* written as the desire 'to write a book about a kind of person that was never in literature anywhere, never taken seriously by anybody, all those peripheral little girls. So I wanted to write a book that—if that child ever picked it up—would look representational.' It was to be a book about 'the whole business of what is physical beauty'—a topic, as we saw in the previous chapter, which was very much at the centre of a whole new way of thinking and behaving in the sixties. Such was the drive to follow the ideas once they had formed themselves (though the process was an extended one, involving many revisions) that, Toni Morrison has said, even if 'all the publishers had disappeared one night' she would have continued until she had produced the book she was satisfied with, and then would have xeroxed it and passed it around among her friends. The fact that she was already working for one publisher when another accepted it was a slight embarrassment, and this was the reason for her final change of name to Toni Morrison.[141]

*The Bluest Eye* is set in Lorain, and she has commented: 'I was clearly pulling out of what autobiographical information I had', at the same time expressing what was obviously a strong emotion: 'I never felt like an American or an Ohioan or even a Lorainite. I never felt like a citizen.' The little girl that Morrison wanted to write about emerged as Pecola Breedlove, with her two little childhood friends, Claudia (who is the main narrator of the novel) and Frieda MacTeer, with Pecola's parents, Cholly and Pauline. It eventually becomes apparent that Claudia is telling her parts of the story retrospectively from the standpoint of adulthood. The novel is modernistic in presenting different narrative standpoints. But, much more than this, it is counterpointed throughout by a simple children's reading book which tells the story of a happy white family. This was the kind of book, with its imagery of a little golden-haired girl with blue eyes, which was also presented to black children. After first being printed clearly and correctly, the extracts from the reading book, printed at the head of chapters, become typographically confused and scrambled, to echo the confusion of black children as they find this image of external white civilization does not coincide with their own reality.

After the first paragraph from the reading book about the mother and father and Dick and Jane, we get the narrative and commentary by Claudia:

> Adults, older girls, shops, magazines, newspapers, window signs—all the world had agreed that a blue-eyed, yellow-haired, pink-skinned doll was what every girl child treasures.

Claudia makes it clear that she didn't and that indeed, 'I destroyed white baby dolls'.

Early in the book little Pecola climbs up the four wooden steps to Yacobowski's Fresh Veg Meat and Sundries Store, with three cent pieces in her shoe.

> He does not see her, because for him there is nothing to see. How can a fifty-two-year-old white immigrant storekeeper with the taste of potatoes and beer in his mouth, his mind honed on the doe-eyed Virgin Mary, his sensibilities blunted by a permanent awareness of loss, *see* a little black girl? Nothing in his life even suggested that the feat was possible, not to say desirable or necessary.

Pecola opts for her favourite sweet, three packets each of three Mary Janes (very much a Midwest confection, caramel round a peanut butter centre). She holds out her three cents to the storekeeper:

> He hesitates, not wanting to touch her hand. She does not know how to move the

finger of her right hand from the display counter or how to get the coins out of her left hand... Outside, Pecola feels the inexplicable shame ebb...

Each yellow wrapper has a picture on it. A picture of little Mary Jane, for whom the candy is named. Smiling white face. Blonde hair in gentle disarray, blue eyes looking out at her out of a world of clean comfort. The eyes are petulant, mischievous. To Pecola they are simply pretty. She eats the candy, and its sweetness is good. To eat the candy is somehow to eat the eyes, eat Mary Jane. Love Mary Jane. Be Mary Jane.[142]

We learn of the courtship between Cholly and Pauline. Though the book is restrained in its lack of set-piece, explicit sexual passages, we have a sensitive description of Pauline's experience of orgasm. There are the black prostitutes who are good friends to the children. There is the crummy environment, and the harsh physical punishment administered to the girls. One afternoon Pecola is washing dishes in the dark kitchen. Her father enters: 'What could a burned-out black man say to the hunched back of his eleven-year-old daughter?' He approaches her on hands and knees, and he rapes her. Pecola becomes pregnant, and has her own father's child. There are no overt moral judgements, though the language is powerful and resonant. Pecola goes insane, but not, apparently, so much because of her traumatic experience but because of her persistent wish to have the bluest eyes. Nothing is overtly stated, but from the form as well as from the narrative it is clear that white society and what it has done to blacks is the source of the tragedy. 'I think that everybody knows, deep down, that black men were emasculated by white men, period.'[143] Another black female writer later said that *The Bluest Eye* 'encouraged many of us to speak for the first time about the enormous damage to the psyche which results from trying to adopt an alien standard of beauty'.[144] In the James Baldwin novel we looked at earlier there were fully realized white characters as well as black ones. *The Bluest Eye* has no fully realized white characters, and its only complete black characters are female. In its relation to race issues it is implicitly on the side of black separatism, not integration into white society; and in that it sees black males as emasculated, and deals with a problem specific to black females, it is a feminist book.

*The Bluest Eye* sold 2,000 copies, respectable though far from spectacular. The breakthrough to success came with *Song of Solomon* of 1977, which won two prestigious awards and sold very well. Thereafter Toni Morrison has had an extremely distinguished academic and literary career. The unique talent cannot be in dispute. She was the creator of black women's consciousness, more than its creature; but her success cannot be entirely divorced from the changing status of blacks, particularly educated blacks; there is significance for us, too, in that, though Morrison's books and consciousness are black, she was openly cognizant of the influence upon *The Bluest Eye* of the ideas of Barthes and Althusser, particularly with respect to the invincibility of white bourgeois power because it is carried in language.[145]

As student and working-class activism intensified into 1968 and 1969 (discussed in my next two chapters), Nanni Balestrini (introduced in Chapter 4) participated directly. The highly theoretical Gruppo 63, to which he had belonged, was disbanded. Instead the extremist left-wing organization Potere Operaio (Workers' Power) was formed, with Balestrini as a founding member. It is with the working-class struggles of 1968–9, focused on the Fiat plant in Turin, that Balestrini's next, very different novel, *Vogliamo tutto*, is concerned. In physical appearance, this novel is not very different from *Tristano*. It is built up of short paragraphs, about five to every two pages, each isolated from the other by double-spacing and, though contributing to a continuing story, generally containing complete mini-episodes. There are two parts, each of five chapters. The narrator is a young labourer from the south. The language is foul, gloriously so—one does not need a laser scanner and computer to calculate that the most used substantive is *cazzo*, manfully serving as 'prick', 'arsehole', 'balls', and every other demeaning and insulting sense one could think of. There is much use of 'etc' (a common Italian conversational gambit), much repetition, and, as often in genuine oral testimony, strict chronology is not followed: historical facts are mingled with personal reminiscences. Sentences are short. Although there is a good deal of direct speech, quotation marks are not used at all, not even in the relatively sparse manner common to continental writers. On the verso of both covers is a plan of the Fiat Mirafiori plant in Turin, taken from issue no. 1 of the new organization's newspaper, also called *Potere Operaio*, of 1969; later chapters, in the modernist way, incorporate pamphlets and reports from the Fiat strikes of that year. The overall effect is of the freshness and disorganization of an oral and documentary history, mediated by a strange formalism.

Entitled 'The South', the first chapter opens with details of recent economic change which would, the politicians had claimed, bring a new human dignity for all. Instead what came was emigration to the north: Turin became 'a southern city', while there was little change for the proletariat of Salerno. The narrator has taken 'a sackload' of government-funded technical courses, all valueless. Only through an uncle had he been able to get a government-subsidized apprenticeship at Ideal Standard, making lavatory bowls, and that had meant moving to Brescia in the north. He was involved in a strike there, and then another back in Salerno. Prior to all this (the reader only becomes aware of the jump in time in the next chapter) he had lived at home, financing cigarettes, trendy clothes and going dancing with his girlfriend every Saturday night by drawing benefits for signing on at a nonexistent training school, and doing a month's intensive work, twelve hours a day, seven days a week, in a tomato-canning factory. He makes his third visit to Milan, gets a job in a suburban furniture factory, but is sacked for repeatedly turning up late. Back in the south he takes on coffin-making, and then summer beach jobs. Then, topped up with cash, he returns to Milan, but this time to live in the swinging city centre, spending his evenings in the Gran Bar where there are *fiche meravigliose*, and all the colourful figures of the alternative culture. He works on a building site, gets drunk, misses an afternoon, is fired. For a while, he makes pasta for one of the Alemagna cafés, and when fired manages to talk himself into getting a month's pay. Totally out of money, he decides to try the Fiat factories in Turin. Chapter 4 is titled 'Fiat': though still as uncommitted and hedonistic as an Italian Arthur Seaton *(Saturday Night and Sunday Morning)*, he becomes aware of the demonstrations and strikes. He joins in shouting the names 'Mao Tzetong, Ho Ci Min', and also such enjoyable irrelevancies as 'Viva Gigi Riva' (a star footballer from the southern club, Il Cagliari) and 'Viva la fica'. He joins workers and students in a local bar and meets two of the leading militants. They are to assemble at the university. Part I ends: 'and that was the beginning of the grand struggle at Fiat. Which took place on 29th May, Thursday'

Chapter 6, the first chapter in part II, is titled 'Wages'. The opening is reminiscent of the opening of chapter one, a kind of historical survey of the industrial scene (the narrator explains that these are facts he learned later). The system of production at the Mirafiori plant is described, followed by an explanation of the distinction between the basic hourly wage, and the 'variable' component of a worker's earnings. Piece-work, variable rates, and bonuses are 'a capitalist invention'. The 'prostitute's part' is played by the unions. A carefully dated account of the escalation of industrial action then follows: by Thursday 29 May, production of all cars had been brought to a stop. The title of chapter 7 is 'Comrades'. What he has learned is that workers of all types and students, on the one side, are all the same, as bosses, professors, and professional people, on the other side, are all the same. The only purpose of the system is to make people work, and to produce commodities: 'work is the one enemy, the one sickness'—this was the idea which united workers and students, who were now talking the same language. In face of all the industrial action the bosses propose new contracts, supported by the unions but opposed by the autonomous workers because they preserve differentials. Other Fiat factories are now being affected, the technicians are joining in. Fiat bring in goon squads. There is to be a big assembly at the university, and chapter 9 is titled 'The Assembly'. The style and format are not notably different from previous chapters, but it quickly becomes apparent that most of this chapter consists of directly quoted speeches at the assembly. 'We must fight against a state founded upon work. We say: Yes to working-class violence.' The final chapter is entitled 'The Insurrection', and the graphic and colourful description of this runs to the end of the book. In face of police tear-gas attacks, women distribute wet handkerchiefs (apart from one casual mention earlier, this is the first recognition of any involvement of women). Although the demonstration is concentrated on the corso Triano, at the Fiat factory, the struggle spreads all over the proletarian quarters of Turin. Barricades of cars are then set on fire. Molotov cocktails are in use. What affected the crowd, 'more than rage, was joy': the joy of at last being strong. The book ends when, exhausted, the narrator takes himself off home.

Communist party politicians and critics strongly attacked *Vogliamo tutto*. But Balestrini had resources a British novelist could only dream of: he used Potere Operaio to organize conferences at which he defended the revolutionary integrity of his novel, his arguments being published as *Prendiamoci tutto*. One feels bound to comment that Balestrini, the ideologue defending his revolutionary purity, seems very different from Balestrini the gifted novelist. The narrator, he maintains, is completely typical of the 'new worker', unskilled, able to turn his hand to anything, hedonistic, politically totally ignorant, destined to destroy the system.[146] (How often ideologues, disappointed in the existing working class, are forced to invent a new one—Balestrini's being utterly different from Serge Mallet's technocrats.[147]) The picaresque part I, says Balestrini, is essential for drawing out the character of his historic figure.[148] (A historian may doubt the typicality, but can only welcome the richness of the accounts of the narrator's teenage activities, and then of his later association with the Milan *capelloni*.) In part II the 'new worker', still dedicated to consumption, still hostile to all work, learns where his true interests lie. From that moment capitalism is finally doomed, says Balestrini, cheerfully predicting the outbreak of an era of extreme violence.[149]

Questioned about the directly autobiographical character of her novels, Marie Cardinale somewhat disingenuously responded that 'all novels are autobiographical'.[150] *Les Mots pour le dire* (1976), the story of the seven years during which she underwent psychoanalysis, is explicitly termed 'an autobiographical novel'. *La Clé sur la porte* is not so described, but the narrator clearly is Cardinale herself, a 40-year-old mother living with her three children in an apartment in Paris, taking them to visit her husband in Canada each summer. The novel is about her relationship with her children, and her attempt to give them as open an upbringing as possible. To that end she allows their friends and acquaintances to drift in and out of the flat, and even to reside there for considerable periods at a time. Very explicitly the novel becomes a novel about youth—a subject in which, anyway, Cardinale, as joint author with her sister of *Guide Junior à Paris* (1966), had something of a professional interest. And while there are autobiographical (in the normal sense of the term) reminiscences of an Algerian childhood, the main part of the novel was actually being written at the same time as the various experiences were taking place, that is between 1969 and 1972. In fact, one could say that Cardinale deliberately set up a certain situation in order to be able to write about it. The novel is in the form of a series of loose episodes, most focused on one or more of the children's friends or on a particular incident: there are no chapters, and the episodes are separated by a little extra space between paragraphs. The effect is of a kind of journalism, almost of the sort of articles which might appear in *Elle* or even *L'Express*. Occasionally some deliberate factual information on youth is introduced. Considered as a source for the attitudes and behaviour of young people in Paris at the beginning of the seventies, *La Clé sur la porte* is the counterpart of Perec's observations on the aspiring young couples at the beginning of the previous decade. In the Cardinale there is a clear author's (journalist's?) voice, drawing conclusions, expressing criticisms; this contrasts with the disembodied, floating narrator of the Perec.

Marie Cardinale was born in 1929 to upper-class French colonial parents just at the time that her mother and father were getting divorced. Although she married someone from the same class, both she and her husband reacted against the traditional, very Catholic, very correct society in which they had both been raised. After first moving to France, they adopted a mode of life by which he lived in Canada while she lived with their three children in Paris. She had earlier made the traumatic discovery that her mother had tried to abort her. The novel opens with the express wish of the author/narrator:

> to throw myself into these pages, to open the sluice-gates, so that all of my complex thoughts can flow out like lava, covering the sides of the volcano and finally entering into the sea to solidify; far away from me, far away from my heart which, for the moment is so full as to be about to break.[151]

There is a brief memory of how her own mother neglected her, followed quickly by another of how, during the night, she had taken great care to comfort her own daughter, Dorothée, then four or five. She has three children now, living *à quart* in the Paris flat where the key is always in the door. Grégoire, who wears his blond hair afro-style, 'was 18 last week'. Charlotte, who has the gorgeous blue eyes of her father, Jean-Pierre, and loves to fantasize and meditate, 'will soon be 16'. Of her three children, Charlotte is the only one who is truly attracted by the youth culture which the author/narrator has just discovered this year, the culture which has caused her to write these pages: 'Not to bear testimony but to try to see things clearly, to establish my bearings day after day'. The word for this culture, this universe, is *débile* (debilitated), which, we learn as the novel progresses, is used, as such esoteric key words often are, both in admiration of the attitudes and lifestyles of the young people themselves and in criticism of the manners and morals of their elders. Finally, there is Dorothée, 'who will be 14 in a few days', with chestnut eyes like her mother, a critic of everything, including the lifestyles of her brother and sister.

It is Charlotte who introduces the first group on which the text focuses, the Clamart gang of very beautiful boys—'you don't find that kind of beauty running around in the streets'. The author/narrator's mind goes back a couple of years to Charlotte's first love affair, to which she had responded by ensuring that her daughter went on the pill, unnecessarily, as it happened, since Charlotte subsequently reported that she did not feel herself to be mature enough to enter into a sexual relationship. The Clamarts are fairly quickly dismissed as rich kids lacking in any real purpose. We move to Françoise, for whom the author/narrator has arranged an abortion in London. Françoise is full of enthusiasm for London, still apparently the city of unconventionality, the city where the police are still benign. We make a couple of visits to Canada.

The narrator reflects on the post-1968 educational reforms. Attending a parent-teacher meeting, she finds to her disgust that the parents want to go back to the old disciplines, the old orthodoxies. But she herself is deeply concerned about the spread of drugs. First Cécile and then the Algerian Lakbar tell her about their experiences with drugs. This leads to the story of Sophie, with whom Grégoire falls desperately in love. The narrator is happy to have Sophie stay at the flat, but it transpires that, following a drug offence, she lives in a hostel in Belgium, under the supervision of the police, and so on...

We meet the Daltons, supreme exponents of *la débilité* and 'tricky' fashion (their name, conferred by the author, not themselves, is that of a trio of cartoon villains—reminding us that the tale has been shaped and ornamented, and is not straight reportage). We visit Canada (it is the summer of 1970), where Jean-Pierre's flat is destroyed by fire. Back home, a small boy from the dilapidated houses nearby is crushed to death in the lift. The flat is taken over by Americans, the worst visitors yet. The only narrative element centres on the question of whether the open-house policy should be abandoned. Some valuable antique silver is stolen. The cleaning lady (never previously mentioned) leaves to help her husband in his shop. The household tasks are to be shared according to individual choice. Grégoire does not do his share, but he gets a job as a film editor. The lanky, volatile Moussia confides in the narrator that her mother had wanted her aborted. Next day the gold objects in the narrator's private drawer are stolen, along with Grégoire's camera and the rest of the silverware. The Daltons are suspected, but it could be anybody. 'Still the key is left in the door, but I am no longer sure that I will continue to keep it there.' Moussia is obviously an invention, designed to establish a bond with the author's own experience and to bring the novel to a close. Moussia delivers a prose poem she has written, 'a sort of ballad of an unwanted foetus. I shall transcribe it.' This poem—rather sophisticated for a teenager—takes up the final two pages of the novel.

What windows are opened into the different societies and into the general transformations of the time? The two American novels make no mention of industrial conflict, trade unions, or conventional political parties. On the other hand, specific Italian characteristics on these matters burst forth from *A ciascuno* and *Vogliamo*. For quick insights into the sociopolitical fabric, and the shifts taking place in the middle sixties, the former is unrivalled. The murdered Rosello had been 'Socialist in national elections, in tribute to family tradition and memory of youth; Christian Democrat in local elections, through love of his native heath, from whose Christian Democrat administration he could always squeeze some concessions and ensure that his tax bill was kept low'.

The kind of industrial action we first encounter at Fiat, strikes of only a few hours' duration, would be found in France, but certainly never in Britain or America. Both novels are deeply impregnated with a profound sense of the separation of north and south, a structural fact which not even the transformations of the sixties would overcome. Neither (and this is true also of *Il padrone*) is set in Rome: much of what continued to be distinctive about Italy in the sixties was due to the absence of a recognized metropolis; both the French novels are set in Paris. The murder in *A ciascuno* takes place on a most important day in Italian culture of the time: the opening of the hunting season. All characters in *Il padrone* have comic-strip names; prominent in the Milan alternative culture of *Vogliamo tutto* are comic-strip artists: *fumetti*, indeed, have an important role in 'ordinary' Italian popular culture (today at popular open-air opera performances, audiences are offered a comic-strip version of the libretto!).

The greatest extremes of sexual permissiveness are, appropriately enough, expressed in the American novel *Myra*. *La Cle* is full of serious talk about sex. *Vogliamo tutto* offers insights into the permissive sexual culture of the late sixties Italy; the relevant passages, I believe, could not have been freely published any earlier. *Il padrone* is less transparent. Early on the narrator is subjected to the temptations of the sexy office-girl, Selene; at one point she asks if he is familiar with the trendy drink 'il Sexi Gin'. Towards the end the efficiency expert Rebo questions him about his sex life, to discover that from the chastity of his early upbringing the narrator has moved to a very active sex life (with whom is not specified). It is hard to be certain, but *Il padrone* does seem to be making period-specific observations. Although marital infidelity is fundamental to the plot of *A ciascuno*, it does not really deal with sex in a manner that would have been out of place in the previous hundred years.

The reflections on swinging Milan in *Vogliamo tutto* are of great value, since they confirm what, from other sources, I have already said about hippies in Italy:

I loved that life-style which had nothing to do with factories, with fields, with religion. A world totally cut off from the one I have known, which delighted me. And I was primed for every adventure, even if all I did in the end was to go to the pictures. Or I might end up playing the swinger, trying to pick up foreign girls on the streets, or chatting up birds in the dance-halls and bars... There was lots of spare in Milan, girls from the provinces who'd left home and come to Milan because they wanted to be with the *capelloni*.[152]

Dealing wittingly with youth and youth culture, Cardinale inevitably has much to say about rock/pop music. Several times she drives home the point already alluded to in this chapter that this is *the* language, the central activity—with links to so many others—of the age. Camping in Canada, the family appeared in danger from some new arrivals on motorbikes—then the playing of current rock songs takes substance as a pipe of peace. What gives special force to this contention is the way in which, unwittingly, the significance of pop music surfaces in other novels, most especially in *A ciascuno il suo*. When Laurana is interviewing the almost blind but very clear-headed oculist, father of the murdered doctor, the old man pauses to grumble about the ghastly voice of the actor performing on his records of the *Divine Comedy* (his 12-year-old nephew would do better, he mutters), the noises from the street, and the maid who 'for seven months has been singing about a tear on her face'—a reference to the 1964 hit song of Italy's schoolboy Elvis Presley, Bobby Solo (his real name was Roberto Satti, the song was 'Una lacrima sul viso'). In Salerno, the narrator of *Vogliamo tutto* notes the purchase, along with blue jeans and knitwear, of records: 'Rock and roll, rhythm and blues, all that stuff'. *La Clé* inevitably brings in the Beatles: some of the young *débilés* are critical of the Beatles for 'selling out'; others challenge this. Towards the end of the book, the author/narrator runs together these thoughts:

> As long as my mother is dead and [childhood memories] can no longer touch me. As long as I am forty. As long as I love the Beatles. As long as my children are still full of life![153]

Let us move from novels to films, lingering a little in Hollywood, then to other things in which the different countries excelled. In *Italian National Cinema 1896–1996*, Pierre Sorlin refers to the decade 1960–69 as 'the heyday' of Italian cinematic production: 2,405 films were produced, of which 312 were exhibited in the United Kingdom, and 280 in the United States; but a disproportionate number belonged to the period before 1964:[154] by the High Sixties Italian and French cinema had both made their revolutionary statements—then, of course, continuing to develop them. A rather different mode was commanding international attention at the end of the decade—stylish, relaxing, verbal: I think in particular of two of the later films in Eric Rohmer's series of 'Six Moral Tales', produced between 1963 and 1972: *Ma Nuit chez Maud* (My Night with Maud, 1969) and *Le Genou de Claire* (Claire's Knee, 1970). In an era of rumbustious tumbling and coupling, Jean-Louis (Jean-Louis Trintignant) does not actually have sex with Maud (Françoise Fabin) during his night with her. The film is sophisticated, satisfying to watch, full of good conversation about philosophy, religion, literature, personal relationships: it is about that great double subject, physical beauty and sexual attraction. In *Le Genou de Claire* we see a lot of the beautiful legs and sweetly enticing face of Laurence de Monaghan (Claire); her admirer achieves sexual satisfaction by rubbing her knee. Counter-counter-cultural perhaps, but these films could not have been made at any time other than the High Sixties; they could not have been made in any country other than France.

Few Hollywood films of the middle sixties are of outstanding quality on an international scale; most are instantly recognizable for a particular, slightly mannered stylishness, usually apparent at once in the opening credits (not utterly unrelated to developments in alternative or underground graphics—well seen in the divided-screen technique used at the beginning of *The Thomas Crown Affair* directed by Norman Jewison) and for a quality of sheer *enjoyability*. There were no biblical epics, and not too many musicals (though *The Sound of Music*, Robert Wise, 1965, was the most commercially successful film of the decade—one woman in Wales was reputed to have gone to see it every day for a year). Villains were often given great allure, and sometimes came out on top (Steve McQueen as Thomas Crown); there were heist films issuing in villains coming off best, or in colossal cock-ups; there were comedy Westerns (with, incidentally, black characters becoming increasingly prominent); much humour, much down-to-earth cynicism. Throughout, without any risk of overstatement and in a very relaxed way, movies bore evidence of the society changing around them. Both love and violence became more realistic. Blacks began to appear in key roles; other ethnic minorities were treated with a new sensitivity; women got more assertive parts; films aimed at independent, self-aware youth began to appear, sometimes with explicit references to counter-cultural developments.

First, the question of censorship. In Britain from the late fifties, John Trevelyan administered the British film censorship in a manner thoroughly sensitive to the changing standards of society outside. In America, somewhat later in the day, the equivalent figure was Jack Valenti, a former special assistant to President Johnson, who in 1966 became head of the Motion Picture Association of America, the organization responsible for the censorship system. As a result of his efforts the code was replaced in 1968 by a rating system, analogous to that operating in Britain and other European countries. The 1968 ratings (since altered many times) were: G for general audience; M for mature audiences of adults and mature young people (an unsatisfactory classification, soon changed to PG, for parental guidance); R for restricted, persons under sixteen years only being admitted with an adult; and X for no one under 16 being admitted. The new system run by the Code and Rating Administration was no doubt arbitrary, as all forms of censorship tend to be, but there can be no doubt about the general liberalizing tendency.[155]

For the period immediately before the censorship relaxation, a good film to consider is *Sunday in New York* (Peter Tewkesbury, 1966). This had its origins in a play by Norman Krasna which Thomas Kiernan not unfairly describes as 'a minor trite Broadway sex comedy', continuing:

> It was transformed for the screen by director Peter Tewkesbury into a stylish but still trite Hollywood sex gambol—a bit more daring than similar comedies of previous years, but cut from the same cloth.[156]

But it was very funny, and immensely believable, even though the characters go to enormous lengths to avoid pronouncing the word 'virgin'. The virgin is Jane Fonda, a Mary Quant dollybird, warm and adventurous. Rod Taylor has picked her up; she takes him back to her brother's flat; he has to pretend to be her brother; her brother (played by Cliff Robertson), an airline pilot, is also cheerfully predatory. It is Fonda's serious, prudish fiancé who comes off worst. Most of the residual delicacy had gone by the time *Carnal Knowledge* was released in 1970, one of the first general release films to get the new X certificate: it 'flirted deliberately with areas that until the last few years were unmentionable except among men in private'; and it had the 'first onscreen unsheathing of a condom in a major American movie'.[157]

The transformation in the portrayal of blacks in American films came in 1967, with two films, each of which had just one central black character, portrayed (with Sidney Poitier in the role both times) as a highly successful, highly intelligent, middle-class member of American society. In Norman Jewison's *In the Heat of the Night*, Poitier plays a detective from the North who is assisting the local police chief (played by Rod Steiger) of a southern town in a murder investigation. The film centres on how, within an ambience fevered with segregationist sentiment, the two men accommodate to each other. This was no minority film; it won the 1967 Academy Award for best picture. The other film, *Guess Who's Coming to Dinner?*, directed by Stanley Kramer, was in box office terms the second most successful film of the year. A progressive Californian couple (played by Katharine Hepburn and Spencer Tracy) have to confront the fact that their daughter has got herself engaged to a distinguished black scientist who works with the United Nations. We also encounter the Sidney Poitier character's parents: from a lower social class, they are shown to share some of the same basic values and, in reverse, the same prejudices as the white couple. This is a sensitive (though we do have the black father telling his son that it is highly appropriate that a husband should be considerably older than his wife—a notion which would have seemed strongly male chauvinist within a few years), polished, intelligent, enjoyable, and relaxed film—very much of the sixties.

The films usually selected as having a high quotient of youth-appeal are *The Graduate* (1967), directed by Mike Nichols, about an affair between a student (Dustin Hoffman) and an older woman, the first Hollywood film openly to discuss contraception and the second greatest box office success of the decade; *Bonnie and Clyde* (1967), directed by Arthur Penn, the story of two thirties gangsters, sympathetically portrayed (by Warren Beatty and Faye Dunaway) as two youthful rebels against conventional society; and *Easy Rider* (1969), about two young drug-dealers (Dennis Hopper and Peter Fonda) riding across America on their motorbikes, encountering a drunken civil-rights lawyer and a hippie community—Hopper (b. 1936) directed, while Fonda (b. 1940) was producer. *Midnight Cowboy* suggests a number of themes of this chapter. It was a Hollywood film directed by a star of the British film supremacy, John Schlesinger. Its fundamental theme is sexual in that it features a young Texan (played by Jon Voight) who, sure of himself as a 'stud', comes to New York expecting to make a good living from rich women; in fact he ends up performing a homosexual act for a crippled New York derelict, Ratso (Dustin Hoffman), with whom he then establishes a kind of relationship. Ratso belongs to the underground of the outcast and miserable, but we also encounter the more glamorous underground in the form of a party at the Factory and a couple of Warhol's film actors. Both this film and *Easy Rider* make great use in their music scores of rock songs. Cult status, among the young in particular, was achieved by Stanley Kubrick's *2001: A Space Odyssey* (1968)—science fiction backed by spectacular special effects, and including a psychedelic trip sequence.

Only one film at this time dealt overtly with the Vietnam war, John Wayne's *The Green Berets* (1968), crude jingoism, in which the Vietcong are portrayed in the same racist way that traditional Westerns had portrayed the Indians. *M\*A\*S\*H* (1970), début film of Robert Altman, a central figure in the renaissance of American films which developed and intensified in the seventies, is important for that reason, and several others. It is the first Hollywood movie to employ the 'art film' styles of European cinema in a big way—in the use of alienation techniques, non-realistic sequences, innovative deployment of sound, including overlapping of sounds, and bleeding of sound from one image to another.[158] Vulgar, irreverent, sexually explicit, and very funny, M\*A\*S\*H is about a mobile army surgical hospital, ostensibly during the Korean war, though nobody could be in any doubt that the classical, senseless war being portrayed was the current one in Vitenam. *Little Big Man* (1970), directed by Arthur Penn, was one of the most important of the Westerns to treat Indians sympathetically, and to indict their brutal treatment by American whites. Penn's Indians were made up to look very like Vietnamese. Nobody missed the point. The legendary film critic Pauline Kael, while not altogether approving of the film, made the central point in her *New Yorker* review in December 1970:

> This film is about genocide—about the Indians and about Vietnam... The massacres of the helpless Indians on the screen are, of course, like the massacres of Vietnamese villagers, and make a powerful emotional connection.[159]

Britain's hour was really over, and American film-making primacy was being re-established. Nor were France or Italy ever again to command quite the concentrated gaze they had attracted at the end of the fifties and the beginning of the sixties. However, each made at least one distinctive, perhaps even unique, contribution to civilization. In France, in the later sixties, there emerged *la nouvelle cuisine*, characterized by: small portions arranged on a large plate so as to resemble a carefully composed work of art; the use of very high-quality cuts of meat or fish, usually only lightly cooked; the incorporation of ultra-fresh vegetables, firm to the tooth; the eschewal of, on the one hand, the rich heavy sauces of traditional *haute cuisine*, and, on the other, the hearty casseroles and cheap cuts of traditional peasant cooking. The name associated with *nouvelle cuisine* is that of Paul Bocuse, but in reality there were several inventors. We do not need to strain too hard to see possible connections between this new way of cooking and eating, excoriated by elderly traditionalists, and some of the trends I have been discussing throughout this book: the emphasis on the natural; the desire to be youthful—and preserve a youthful figure; the rejection of the pomposity and rituals of former established society (though *nouvelle cuisine* quickly became almost as ritualistic in its own way); the sense (spurious in part) of a classlessness in which easeful enjoyment was available to the majority. *Nouvelle cuisine* could not have been invented in Italy, where a meal had to be constructed of two basic courses, a first course of pasta (possibly preceded by a prior course) and a second course of meat or fish (perhaps succeeded by some sweet, fruit, or cheese course or courses); the popular Italian conception of French food is that it is *troppo elaborato*, 'too elaborate'. But pick up any book on design and it becomes immediately clear that one of the most important ways in which the Italians expressed their newly burgeoning élan and energy of the late fifties and early sixties was in the world of design.

In this chapter I am concerned both to reiterate my emphasis on the great velocity with which new ideas and new modes of expression circulated from one country to another and to bring out the special characteristics of individual countries. Design was, to the very highest degree, an international phenomenon, drawing its inspiration from innovations in an enormous variety of different countries: the invention of the new material Lycra by Du Pont in America in 1958; British pop styles; the space-age clothes collections of Pierre Cardin and André Courrèges and the plastic and metal clothes of Paco Rabanne; Japanese styles, displayed at the First World Conference on Design in Japan in 1960, and the Tokyo Olympics of 1964; and organic lettering and psychedelic graphics from San Francisco and from the Netherlands. Yet, just as primacy in rock/pop music tended to be conceded to Britain, so, in design, recognition tended to be given to Italy, Italian dominance in design continuing to grow throughout the seventies. In 1972 the Museum of Modern Art in New York held the exhibition 'Italy: The New Domestic Landscape'.[160] A number of points may be made. The relationship between manufacture and design was particularly close in Italy, as seen in the production of the Vespa and Lambretta at the end of the forties, and the continuous elegance of the productions of Fiat and Pininfarina. In *Stile Industria* (Industrial Style), which he founded in 1953, Alberto Rosselli contrasted industrial design in the United States, which he saw simply as 'one of the fruits of a free competition system in which peculiar economic and production conditions have led to a continuous market expansion', with that in Italy, where 'the true nature of design... results from a harmonic relationship between production and culture'.[161] Leading designer Ettore Sottsass put it still more strongly: 'Industry should not buy culture, industry should be culture.'[162] These were not simply pious aspirations: there was in Italy a very close integration between the massive economic powers, like the car manufacturers and Montecatini Edison, the individual designers, such as Professor Mario Zanuso of the faculty of architecture at the Milan polytechnic, the design studios, such as Archizoom founded in 1966, and the small artisan workshops, a particularly important feature of the Italian economy. Good design was not just for those who could pay big sums for it, but was diffused throughout middle Italy. The designer Andrea Branzi put it this way:

> Even the smallest joiner's shop soon learned how to make bar counters that looked like Gio Ponti's own designs, the smallest electric workshop soon learned to make lamps that looked like Vigano's, and upholstery played on armchair models that might be reminiscent of Zanuso's. This sort of indiscriminate profane looting afforded a formal renovation of the entire middle layer of Italian society. It was a style that finally replaced Fascist tinsel, and the provincial neo-classical...[163]

It is often the conceit of designers that they are envisaging the future. Italian designers, perhaps more than any others, appreciated that the present was exciting enough, and that design should focus directly on that. The 13th Triennial Milan Exhibition of 1964, entitled 'Leisure Time' *(Tempo libero)*, was a key event as the catalogue said:

> the XIII Triennale... is all in the present... This is the first time that the Triennale... has been dedicated to a theme, to leisure time... a theme extremely current for Italy now increasingly industrialised and witnessing the phenomena of social transformations.[164]

The most striking representation of the 'living in the present' concept was the brightly coloured, easily movable furniture of 'the new domestic landscape'—beanbag chairs, inflatable cushions, collapsible tables, and so on, all crafted in small artisan workshops where personal, expressive, risk-taking styles could be undertaken.

And America? The leader, no question, in science and technology. This was driven home sensationally in 1968, and even more so on 21 July 1969. The Russians had put the first man in space on 12 April 1961, and in 1965 accomplished the first 'space walk'. But during 1966–7 the Americans began to realize their full potential, and clearly overtook their superpower rivals. The year of 1968 was famous for a number of things on *terra firma;* it was also the year in which the Americans succeeded in putting a three-man vehicle in orbit around the moon, transmitting to earth pictures of the moon surface. On 20 July 1969 a lunar module landed on the moon; the next day Neil Armstrong, commander of the mission, took the first steps on the moon. 'One giant leap for mankind'? Or one giant waste of money? Certainly a giant demonstration of human ingenuity and courage. Above all, a giant spectacle in this decade of spectacles.

Achievements in technology, in design, in cuisine, in film, in literature, in popular music, and in creating new subcultures and lifestyles are important in themselves: in assessing them we are also assessing the proclivities, the health, the dynamism of the individual societies during this period of intense change—unhappy the country with *nul points* under every heading. They play a part, too, in helping us to understand the nature of that change, both generally and with respect to the distinctive characteristics of the different countries. Films and novels have to be handled with particular care: invoking the occasional fictional character or quoting the odd striking phrase may ornament the historian's discourse, but seldom adds weight to it. I hope that by discussing a select number of individual novels and films at some length I have done justice to novel-writing and filmmaking as major activities in their own right, while (without imposing reductive parallels or relationships) suggesting how they fit into the greater continuum of change. We need to have understood the essentials of this 'greater continuum of change' as we now limit our range and concentrate on activism and protest, and the events they generated.

# 11

# Freedom, Turbulence, and Death

## *Confrontation and Violence*

There had been bitter civil strife, with substantial loss of life, in both the United States and France during the interwar years—about 200 civilian deaths in France. In Italy, the Fascists had come to power on the wave of violence afflicting Italy at the end of the First World War, and they had maintained power in a thoroughly brutal fashion. There was violence in Britain in the immediate aftermath of the First World War—the bringing in of troops resulted in one civilian death, and a violent confrontation between police and unemployed in Hyde Park, London, in 1934, while violent incidents attended Fascist marches in the East End of London; there were a couple of IRA bomb attacks, with one fatality. But the fact that the British police were not armed meant that, in contrast with the other countries, they did not cause any deaths. The Second World War, of course, was immensely destructive of human life, and for most of the population in Europe the war experience was either of occupation by a brutal power or of being in the midst of war actually being waged in towns and villages across the countryside. The period after 1945 appeared relatively peaceful, though appearances were in some ways deceptive. Many American historians, as I have noted, have seen the sixties as a time when the cohesion of American society was irreparably damaged. All commentators, naturally, have referred to the urban riots in America in 1965 and 1967, and to the violent confrontations of 1967, 1968, and 1969 in France and Italy as well as the US in which students were the main protagonists. In Chapter 3 I remarked on the distinct age groups which could be conflated under the term 'youth'. It was now, in America, that the groups were brought together under the all-embracing slogan: 'Don't trust anyone over thirty'.

So far I have been stressing improved material conditions and greatly enhanced personal freedoms. Over the whole period, *c*.1958-*c*.1974, these were, I believe, what mattered most for most people. Violence, when it came, affected only certain areas and for relatively short periods. However, it would be quite wrong to gloss over the violence, which could be terrifying for those caught up in it and which certainly brought about great suffering and tragic loss of life. Some commentators present a picture of the civil rights movement in the United States making steady and peaceful progress in the early sixties, then of everything being lost in the violence of the latter half of the decade. Many Italian commentators see the events of 1967–9 as ending a period of peaceful economic growth and ushering in the years of terrorism, 'the years of the bullet'.[1] On the left in particular there was much lamentation over the violent repression of the protests and demonstrations of 1967–9 and over (as they saw it) the conservative reaction that followed. Given less inflexible authority structures, and less confrontational attitudes on the part of the police (and politicians who were afraid not to back them), there would have been much less destruction of life, limb, and property. For many involved in the protests and disturbances of the time, aims were limited and pragmatic: better living conditions, freedom from indignities and restrictions, the right to self-expression, and, among students, to a share in university government. However, some subscribed to the fundamentalist philosophies discussed in Chapter 7, those who, one way or another, were aiming at the overthrow of existing institutions and who were determined to provoke and to prolong violence. Because of the way in which movements and subcultures expanded and interacted, moderate majorities with vague discontents and limited aims found themselves, often unwittingly, swept up in the militant activities of fundamentalist minorities. The civil rights movement of the early sixties formally subscribed to non-violence, but was frequently responded to with extreme violence. The aim was integration within existing society. But fundamentalists called for separatism, and all-out war on white society. As frustration mounted, their extremism gained in attractiveness. And some blacks, particularly young males, welcomed any opportunity to assert themselves, and to direct their rage against whites and middle-class blacks.

Chronologically the civil rights protests and demonstrations in the American South came first, with black students often being prominent. The first big student demonstrations of the sixties took place in France. Both France and Italy had traditions of student involvement in street politics, absent in America and Britain; students also began to copy the working-class tradition of factory occupations—occupying university buildings to demonstrate that universities 'belonged to students', not just to the authorities. In Italy left-wing students feared the re-emergence of Fascist elements in positions of power; in France there was hostility both to French colonialism and to worsening conditions within the French universities. Architecture students formed the radical vanguard in Italy; in 1963 occupations took place of every architecture faculty in the country. A new kind of activism on the part of white (and largely middle-class and, indeed, upper-class) American students, mainly against their own university authorities, began in 1964, with the Berkeley 'Free Speech' movement. Already (i.e. by the later 1950s) in France, there had been violent incidents associated with the colonial conflict in Algeria, mainly in the form of marches, first in support of Algerian independence, then after 1962, when independence was granted, in protest against the OAS, the organization of French officers dedicated to resisting

Algerian independence. Hostility to imperialism was a cause which united committed left-wingers everywhere, who made heroes of such prominent figures in the South American anti-colonialist struggle as Che Guevara and Franz Fanon. Closely linked to the anti-imperialist stance was the opposition to the production and testing of nuclear weapons. But then, in 1965, the expanding American involvement in Vietnam, and the brutal measures inflicted on civilians there, became the central issue, soon closely bound up with the resistance of many young American men to being conscripted into fighting in Vietnam (as there had been resistance in France to conscription to fight in Algeria). Many commentators have maintained that the Vietnam war brought an end to 'the Great Society', 'the War on Poverty', the peaceful advance of civil rights, that it brought the end of cohesion, provoked the 'unravelling of American society', 'the great schism'.[2]

Without question, American involvement in Vietnam was an unmitigated disaster; having got involved, the politicians should have aimed at extricating American troops as quickly as possible through implementation of the Geneva Agreements, the settlement made following French withdrawal from Indo-China. But it simply cannot be said that without the Vietnam war there would have been no demonstrations, no violence. There were too many other issues. What is true is that Vietnam became the great universal issue, binding together protests within America over race, poverty, consumerism, and alleged repression of student freedoms, and providing a focal point for youth and anti-establishment protests throughout the European countries. At the same time, although blacks made a grossly disproportionate contribution to the armed forces who suffered and died in Vietnam, for many blacks Vietnam was not a major issue; for some, even, conscription into the army meant a welcome escape from the ghettos.[3]

The violence of the late sixties was neither desirable nor particularly effective; yet it did have a distinctive character of its own, springing out of idealistic movements of the young and the racially oppressed. Though often accompanied by absurd ideas of counter-cultural revolution and the creation of an alternative society, it was far from being totally futile. It is pointless to divide the sixties into a peaceful, optimistic first half and a violent, pessimistic second half—as it is pointless to isolate 1968 as some kind of astonishing, self-contained year of near-revolution. The violence of the second half of the decade arose from the movements of the first half, and the events of 1968 had their origins firmly bedded in the changes of an entire decade. Some rioters were vandals, but practically every violent episode could be traced back to some stupid or brutal (often both) action by the police. Many of those caught up in violent situations were intensely peace-loving and would have wished to have been anywhere but at the centre of a storm of aggression; at the same time most of those peace-loving people who found themselves trapped in a situation of violence had set out knowing that extreme and life-threatening violence was always a strong possibility in any kind of march or demonstration; while some felt a certain sense of exultation and even heroism, most suffered from a constant and debilitating sense of fear—yet such was their sense that they must bear testimony against evil that they fought against that fear. The sixties was a time of great gains for ordinary people; it was also a time when many ordinary people showed great bravery.

I shall start with the birth of the free speech movement, continuing with the anti-Vietnam war movement, up to the vicious suppression of the Washington demonstration in October 1967;

then I shall turn to the youth and protest movements in Italy, France, and Britain, finally returning to the civil rights movement and the devastating urban riots of 1965 and 1967. The climactic events of 1968 and 1969 are left to Chapter 12.

## Free Speech and Vietnam

By the end of the decade it was customary in America to talk of 'the Movement'—a loose association of the New Left, whose most important organization in the United States was the Students for a Democratic Society (SDS), the civil rights movement, the student free speech movement, which made its most dramatic opening appearance at the University of California campus at Berkeley in September 1964, and the anti-Vietnam war movement, which came into being towards the end of 1964 as the American government was preparing to escalate its involvement in Vietnam. Prior to, and simultaneously with, the events at Berkeley, there were protest movements in French universities, and also in other parts of the United States but for various reasons it was at Berkeley that the organized free speech movement began, and at Berkeley that the first significant confrontations took place.

To the critics of advanced capitalism America was the extreme example, and within America, California was the extreme case. It was actually the former Republican president, General Eisenhower, who had warned of the dangerous articulation between corporate America and preparations for war in the 'military-industrial complex'. The phrase applied particularly aptly to California, the site for the production of much of America's most advanced military technology; here the interpénétration between business, government, and university had reached the highest levels, and while the prestigious Ivy League universities of the East were private institutions, the University of California, with its many campuses, heavily funded from both business and federal sources, belonged to the state of California. New Left commentators represented the universities—and the University of California seemed to fit the bill particularly well—as complicit in the capitalist system, carrying out its military research, turning out carefully brainwashed graduates to staff its higher echelons. For their part, senior academics and administrators generally shared the liberal attitudes now prevailing in the federal capital, and also the optimism and pride in America as the world leader in prosperity and freedom. The doors of the University of California, after all, were open to competent students from, roughly, the upper working class upwards. Students, above all at beautiful Berkeley, situated on its little hill rising from the east side of San Francisco Bay, could scarcely not be aware that they were privileged compared with any previous generation. Some, showing great idealism and bravery, were already participating in the voter registration in the South; the 'Freedom Summer' of 1964 (with which I begin the final section of this chapter) leads directly to the free speech protests, since, justly or otherwise, returning freedom fighters began to draw comparisons between the oppression which was so manifest in Mississippi and the oppression they felt they detected within the university and in corporate capitalism as a whole; they had also become sensitized to the less obvious discrimination practised in California.

Universities everywhere *were* authoritarian. In the United States there was a special complacency about their role in the running of ever-improving American society: Clark Kerr, president of the massive California 'multiversity' (his word), actually spoke, in all pride and sincerity, of the university's role in 'knowledge production' and the 'knowledge industry'.[4] At the very least, the big state universities, from the point of view of individual students, were remote and excessively bureaucratic. Everywhere, and at all levels, the academic system was highly paternalistic, and even very liberal academics failed sometimes to see how that gave offence to students who genuinely wanted to think things out for themselves. Many of those who were to take themselves so spectacularly out of established culture played no part in political activism; however, to many political fundamentalists it was axiomatic that they must adopt counter-cultural manners and morals if they were to bring about the complete revolution they sought, while others in the Movement adopted some of the badges of counter-culture such as drugs, permissive sex, or uninhibited use of expletives. Liberated lifestyles could attract followers, but could also antagonize older, traditional political sympathizers.

In the unfolding of student activism from 1964 to the spectacular events of 1968, the important actors were: the university authorities; the politicians, always responsive to powerful vested interests and to the conservative, red-hating sentiments of America's by no means completely silent 'silent majority'; the police and, at times, the military; and, on the other side, a range of students from the dedicated activists to the moderately resentful and vaguely ideal-istic. In the middle were strongly liberal academics, usually attracted to what they saw as a new sense of commitment on the part of students, sometimes alienated by their behaviour, but generally unable to comprehend the deep illiberalism of some of the fundamentalists. There continued to be plenty of students of conventional outlook and broadly right-wing allegiance, some of whom, indeed, became involved in violent confrontations with the activists. But, true to the way things tended to work in the sixties, there were other students, who, though unsym-pathetic to the doctrines of the fundamentalists, felt attracted by some of their causes, and some of their attitudes. Actual outcomes in each country, with respect to levels and frequency of violence, depended on four factors: the extent to which a tradition of violent confrontation between the forces of law and order and students or radical groups was already embedded in a particular country's past; the actual organization of the police and military forces (discussed in Chapter 2); the firepower at the disposal of these forces; and the attitudes and responses of the university authorities. On the continent of Europe universities had been centres of revolu-tionary and nationalistic action in the nineteenth century, and it was not uncommon for military barracks, or at least substantial police stations, to be situated near to them. In a way, America had gone a stage further. Every university campus had its campus police force—before the sixties, it should be said, concerned more with protecting the privileged inmates from the endemic lawlessness and violence without than with policing students themselves. Senior university administrators usually thought of themselves as liberal: as American wealth, power, and scientific and scholarly achievement grew, they became, as it were, dizzy with success, while at the same time haunted by a fear of Communist subversion of the wonderful interconnected edifice they had helped to construct. Thus they became increasingly resentful, and then suspicious, of student rebelliousness. More and more they felt the pressure from their political and business paymasters, and from the heavily conservative sentiments of what has come to be known as middle America. Among the citizens of California there was a strong feeling that students who had enjoyed relatively open entry, and were now enjoying subsidized study at the expense of the California taxpayer (in contrast with students paying hefty fees at the private universities), ought to show gratitude and loyalty. It was customary in America, whenever trouble of any kind broke out, for there to be a massive response from armed police. The university authorities had their own campus police ready to hand; to them it was almost second nature to see challenges to their authority, and threats to order, as being matters for the police.

The area immediately outside the main gate to the Berkeley campus on Bancroft Way was where the various student organizations set up their stalls. At the beginning of September, as Freedom Fighters were returning from the South, a newly formed group began to discuss action against the discriminatory employment policies practised by the local newspaper, the *Oakland Tribune*. When, on 4 September, a picket was established outside the *Tribune* offices, the newspaper protested to the university administration. Fearful of what a hostile press campaign might entail, the university management reacted crudely and illiberally, declaring the area outside the gates closed to all student organizations. Prompt and united protest resulted in the policy being diluted: the right to foregather was restored, but organizations were prohibited from proselytizing, raising funds, or recruiting—their very reasons for being there in the first place. The new policy was simply ignored: when the attempt was made to discipline five students, graduate student and SDS member Mario Savio (urged on by his good-looking wife, Suzanne Goldberg, a Communist party member) led a protest of 500 students. Eight students were suspended. The next day the authorities challenged a dropped-out graduate student called Jack Weinberg who (illuminating the continuing significance of the civil rights theme at this stage) was manning the Council on Racial Equality stall, and doubtless proselytizing and attempting to raise funds and recruit. The campus police were called: Weinberg offered non-violent resistance, while many of the students who had meantime gathered sat down round the police car, civil rights style. For thirty-two hours there followed a series of speeches made from the roof of the police car. The protesting students were denounced by the eminent liberal sociologist Professor Seymour Martin Lipset and, the next day, by President Clark Kerr himself. Several hundred police from the city of Oakland, from the county of Oakland, and from the state highway patrol were brought on campus.

Certainly neither Kerr nor senior academics like Lipset wanted violent confrontation, though they were under some pressure from the regents, the governors of the university appointed by the state of California. On 23 November Kerr threatened Savio and another student leader, both of whom had been promised an amnesty, with expulsion. This kind of petty breaking of undertakings was to recur again and again, always provoking massive student resentment. On 2 December 6,000 joined a sit-in at the main administrative offices, Sproul Hall, organized by what was now calling itself the 'free speech movement.' Mario Savio was very much a Movement leader. Standing beside him was the person who perhaps more than anyone else embodied the bridge between movement and counter-cultural elements, the folk singer Joan Baez (Mexican father,

Scottish mother), her feet bare, and her long dark hair flapping naturally round her head. Before starting to strum her guitar and launching into 'We Shall Overcome' she asked the students not to enter the administration building in anger, but with love in their hearts. Eight hundred students were arrested; their fellow students at once went on strike, bringing all teaching to a stop. At a meeting addressed by Kerr on 8 December there was an ugly incident when two policemen grabbed Savio by the throat; but in face of manifest student anger Savio was released and allowed to address the meeting. Most of the academic staff, champions of measured judgement and aghast at the massive police intervention, supported the students, as was shown by their vote on that afternoon by 824 to 115 to accept the basic student demand for freedom of political activity on the campus.[5]

With the support of most of their teachers, the free speech movement had won. Just how these teachers were swinging behind the protesting students is brought out in the slightly guilt-stricken open letter written in December 1964 by certain Berkeley academics:

> As long as the 'Free Speech Movement' involved only a small portion of the Berkeley students, it was possible—all the more in the light of their actions—for many to regard them simply as a vociferous and sometimes disorderly minority.
>
> But when among the 800 who were arrested on December 3 and the thousands who supported them we found a large proportion of our most mature and thoughtful students, we were impelled to take a more penetrating look at the reasons for their commitment. The young people are part of a generation which is quite different from those who, as educators, we have faced in the recent past. Many find themselves alienated from what they regard as a bureaucratised society, and from the increasingly impersonal University through which they have their major contact with that society. They are trying to find meaning for their lives, and finding it often outside the University in a commitment to the active social movements of today. To an unfortunate extent, we, their faculties have lost touch with them...[6]

However, a private letter of 11 January 1965 written to a young colleague in Britain reveals much more of the agonies and frustrations well-disposed academics were suffering:

> It seems to me that for months I have hardly had a chance to glance at dog-eared notes before pretending to lecture to my classes. All the rest of the time has gone into activities resembling my idea of what the French Underground was doing during the German occupation, even to the composing, mimeographing (after night fall), and clandestine distribution of dozens of propaganda leaflets and the like... The community is politicized to an inconceivable degree, with the inevitable consequence that we live bathed in political rhetoric of the most exultant kind, and exultation of this sort, even in the best of causes, threatens constantly to be mere flatulence.
>
> Doubtless something has been gained, although it seems to me, at an exorbitant cost in time and energy.[7]

More misery for those committed to free speech but worried and frustrated by the terrible setbacks to academic work was caused by the appearance of free speech of a different sort. At the beginning of March, the first poster appeared heralding the word 'FUCK', followed by the shouting of the same word into their microphones by some of the free speech activists. It did not help that some wit maintained that the word was really an acronym for 'Freedom Under Clark Kerr'.[8]

Scurrilous activity from the other side was no less offensive. There is a whole file of 'hate letters' in the free speech movement papers in the Bancroft Library. An anonymous holograph letter to Mario Savio reads: 'We are weary of paying taxes for bums and beatniks like you. You deserve a sentence at hard labor.' There were many repetitions of the theme I mentioned earlier, that agitators had no place in a state subsidized university, but should seek education in private colleges. According to a typed missive headed 'Student & Professor Agitator's, 'the reason you left wing so-called Freedom of Speech Civil Rights Agitators are causing so much trouble is that you are SEXUALLY AND HOMOSEXUALLY QUEER FOR NEGRO'S [sic].' It continued: 'Why don't you get out of the tax payers [sic] school and go to a private school that allows you to make fools of yourselves in the name of civil rights. What you sex mad agitators need to learn is that NORMAL WHITE PEOPLE ALSO HAVE RIGHTS.'

Before the Vietnam war and the draft began to dominate the campuses, there were student demonstrations across the United States, mainly in the spring of 1965. In addition to the general issue of the university as an oppressive institution in an oppressive society, particular issues related to regulations governing women's dormitories, alcohol on campuses, and student partici-pation in decision-making. Specifically student, university, and local community issues were to continue to provoke intense bouts of student activism even after the Vietnam war had become the dominant national issue. The crucial escalation in America's involvement in the war, deeply disturbing the consciences of older liberals and bringing to students the threat of actually being involved in the fighting, came in March 1965, when President Johnson made the twin decisions to send actual combat troops (as distinct from 'military advisers') to Vietnam and to authorize the bombing of North Vietnam.

The initiatives which quickly led to the nationwide anti-Vietnam war movement began, not with students, not at Berkeley, but with a group of academics at the University of Michigan at Ann Arbor, including several veterans of old left and pacifist campaigns. According to the recent comprehensive account by Tom Wells, they felt desperate over the failure of their newspaper advertisements warning about developments in Vietnam to affect events, and angry at the way in which, in response to their direct representations, the State Department 'had had the gall to treat them like children: they answered their letters with pamphlets explaining the diabolical nature of communism illustrated by a leering Khrushchev.'[9] Their first idea was to organize a one-day suspension of classes, with the day instead being devoted to (to use the word which was quickly coined) a 'teach-in' on the war. Because of threats of disciplinary action from the Michigan state government and the university authorities, the teach-in was rearranged to take place overnight, thus avoiding any disruption of normal teaching. Over the night of 24–5 March 1965, more than 3,000 people participated in the first ever teach-in on the Vietnam war; advance notice of how middle America was going to react was given when proceedings were interrupted at midnight by a bomb threat (though, to be fair, this may have been engineered by antiwar extremists). The multi-faceted consequences of this portentous event are well brought out in the summary provided by Wells.

Exchanges were both reasoned and passionate. 'Facts were demanded and assumptions were exposed,' one participant wrote. 'On that night, people who really cared talked of things that really mattered.' Hierarchical relations between faculty and students received a stiff jolt; students locked horns with professors whose classes they had hardly spoken in. Opponents of the war gained valuable social support, inciting many to plan future protests. Pro-war participants were asked to explain their positions; some began questioning their allegiances... The campus was now alive with debate on Vietnam. It was impossible to avoid the controversy whether one wanted to or not.[10]

Within the next couple of months over 100 similar events took place in campuses across the United States. The biggest teach-in was organized at Berkeley by members of the free speech movement, including Jerry Rubin: it lasted for thirty-six hours and involved more than 30,000 people. Already, on 18 February, the free speech movement had organized a protest at the nearby Oakland army terminal, with further marches on 9 and 23 March, the last resulting in fifteen arrests and all involving violent confrontations with the police. From out of the free speech movement there emerged the Vietnam Day Committee, which linked up with the activists at Ann Arbor. A committee there had a broad responsibility for coordinating plans for two days of mass protests across America on 15 and 16 October; what actually happened in the different cities very much depended upon the outcomes of power struggles between old-guard left-wing organizations such as the Communist party and the Socialist Workers' party, the new formations like SDS, the Vietnam Day Committee, and the politically moderate bodies such as the Inter-Religious Committee on Vietnam, the Committee for Nonviolent Action, and SANE (Committee for a Sane Nuclear Policy). Quietly effective at spreading the message were Women Strike for Peace (WSP), another product of that new mood among middle-class housewives which I discussed in Chapter 3. The National Coordinating Committee to end the war in Vietnam was never very effective, though, sometimes called the Vietnam Coordinating Committee, it did provide a name which was imitated in other countries as anti-Vietnam war protests were coordinated there.

Young people were not the only or even the prime organizers, but young people formed the bulk of the demonstrators, and young people (partly, no doubt, because they were needed to do the fighting) attracted most of the venomous hostility of the authorities. Former President Eisenhower spoke of the 'moral deterioration' of America's youth; the president of Yale University, another erstwhile liberal figure, Kingman Brewster, referred to the 'tragedy' of 'college rebels' who 'hurt their own cause when they demonstrate first and think about it later'. Acting in the spirit of the worst redneck reactionaries, the director of the Selective Service System, General Lewis Hershey, revoked the deferments of thirty students, boasting that this would place them on 'the belt that runs toward the induction station'. Responsible newspapers and broadcasting organizations denounced this action, and there was much uneasiness over it in the administration; it did nothing to add to support for the war policy, and increased sympathy for the protesters.[11] Young male students, if they failed to get good grades or dropped out, could be on the fast route to a nasty war which made no appeal to their patriotism; the temptation to lie low and not participate in high-profile demonstrations must have been strong. Of all the organizations, the SDS was particularly singled out, especially because of its encouragement of conscientious objection to conscription into the war. In Berkeley the target was once again the Oakland army terminal; elsewhere protesters marched on military bases or draft board offices. Those who marched knew what they might expect from the police; there was also fear of freelance right-wing thugs and, most chilling of all, snipers.[12] Around 100,000 people took part in the two-day protests. Earlier, at Berkeley, the son of a professor there had torn up his draft card; a federal law making this an offence was quickly enacted. It was in defiance of this law that, during the New York demonstration, a Catholic pacifist called David Miller burned his draft card, subsequently being imprisoned for two years for the offence. Individual witness went further. Buddhist monks in Vietnam had burned themselves alive in protest against the war: in November, in the United States, first the Quaker Norman Morrison and then the Catholic Roger LaPorte did the same.

Vietnam was an American war: American loyalties and American sensitivities were intimately bound up with it. Among left-wing groups in Europe, quite a strong anti-Americanism already existed: the Vietnam war served mainly to confirm their belief in the evils of American imperialism. And, since their own governments refused to condemn American involvement, it became yet another issue to add to their own more immediate grievances. To traditionalists and middle Americans, protests against the war were attacks on American honour; thus the polarization between all associated with the Movement and the rest intensified. While some progressives felt that protests about the war distracted attention from the more immediate problems of civil rights and economic deprivation, the more important phenomenon was the way in which the Vietnam issue served to bring together protesters of different ages and different types. Many who had little in common with the fundamentalist militants none the less felt that the cause was a universal one, and sometimes found it difficult to resist the argument that American atrocities in Vietnamese jungles and villages justified the strongest possible responses. Within the non-violent civil rights movement there were divisions: some leaders feared the diversion of effort and alienation of the government. But Martin Luther King made clear his adhesion to the anti-war cause at a rally of the Southern Christian Leadership Conference at Petersburg, Virginia, in July 1965:

> I am not going to sit by and see war escalated without saying anything about it... It is worthless to talk about integrating if there is no world to integrate in... The war in Vietnam must be stopped.[13]

At the annual SCLC convention in Miami in April 1966, he called for the withdrawal of

American forces from Vietnam.[14]

Figures from the Old Left, and liberals whose consciences were now deeply troubled, spoke out against the war, while trying to make it clear that they were not in any way supporters of communism; young militants felt less inhibited. In April 1966 Dr Benjamin Spock, the best-selling author of books on the raising of children, and William Sloane Coffin, the chaplain to Yale University, formed 'Clergy and Laymen Concerned About Vietnam', inviting King to accept a co-chairmanship. Their first massive anti-war rally took place in Washington DC on 16 May 1966. King was not present, but provided the following statement: 'The pursuit of widened war has narrowed welfare programmes, making the poor, the Negro, bear the heaviest burdens at the front and at home.'[15]

At a conference sponsored by the left-leaning journal *The Nation* in February 1967, King delivered his first speech entirely devoted to Vietnam, concluding with a call for the civil rights movement and the peace movement to be combined. King repeated this call at a rally in Chicago in March, and shortly afterwards the SCLC put itself officially behind the anti-war cause. As a member of the congregation in Riverside church, New York City, in April 1967, brought together by 'Clergy and Laymen Concerned About Vietnam', King attacked the United States as 'the greatest purveyor of violence in the world today'.[16] It was the SCLC's James Bevel who organized the 'Spring Mobilization to End the War in Vietnam' of 1967: on 15 April, 125,000 demonstrators marched from Central Park in New York to the United Nations headquarters.

In November 1966 trouble broke out again at Berkeley, not this time in the hallowed open territory outside the college entrance but inside the students' union. Objecting to a recruiting table set up there by the US Navy, the SDS had a female student set up a rival table advertising 'Alternatives to Military Service'. Just how close even universities sat to the precipice of violence was evident in the confrontation between police and SDS pickets which started almost at once. Mario Savio and Jerry Rubin, student activists still, though no longer actually students, were arrested with six others, who were not students either. But a meeting of 8,000 students on 2 December voted for another strike. The academic senate, on 5 December, supporting the students rather less wholeheartedly than in 1964, condemned the use of police on the campus, and called for an amnesty. But the new state governor, Ronald Reagan, who had made student radicalism a main issue in his campaign, was insisting on a strong line, probably aided by the fact that many of the students involved in the protest this time were hippies rather than political radicals. To the singing of the Beatles song 'We All Live in a Yellow Submarine', the strike was called off. Confrontation with Reagan was postponed, to break out again as part of the intense violence of 1968–9.[17]

The biggest show of unity by the many different organizations critical in one way or another of the Vietnam war occurred in October 1967. During 'Stop the Draft Week' demonstrations took place at induction centres throughout the country. More than 100,000 pacifists, students, militants, ordinary Americans were brought together on 21 October in a carefully planned march on, and demonstration at, the Pentagon, known as 'the Mobilization', or just 'the Mobe'. The organizers had prepared carefully, securing the necessary permits; so had the authorities—at hand were 1,500 Washington police, 2,500 national guardsmen, 200 US marshals, and 6,000 soldiers of the 82nd Airborne Division. The leading figures were Dr Spock, Noam Chomsky, moderate anti-war organizer Sidney Lowis, poet Robert Lowell, and journalist Dwight Macdonald. Also present was novelist Norman Mailer, who wrote the classic account of the demonstration, published the following year, *The Armies of the Night*. The book, written in the third person, offers psychological explanations for the actions of the various participants; its greatest value to historians lies in the direct quotations from newspapers, notably the *Washington Free Press,* and other eyewitness testimony.

The most aggressively active groups were students from SDS, and a radical group calling themselves the Revolutionary Contingent, who carried out violent assaults on right-wing counter demonstrators. Various aggressive sorties were made by flying squads of militants, breaking down barriers and attempting to breach the Pentagon building itself. Without doubt, considerable strain was placed on the young soldiers of the 82nd Airborne Division guarding the Pentagon itself. They faced what was, in effect, a mixture of demonstration, teach-in, and hippie love-in. Some female hippies bared their breasts; some placed flowers in the barrels of soldiers' guns: a few patted the soldiers' trouser-fronts and invited them off into the bushes, bushes already occupied by a number of enthusiastic practitioners of the precept 'Make love not war'. There was a good deal of taunting, and worse. It was reported in the *New York Times* that some of the demonstrators 'spat on some of the soldiers in the front line and goaded them with the most vicious personal slander'. However, overall it was a most impressive demonstration, as noteworthy for the steady ranks of solid citizens as for the direct enactment of hippie philosophy. A definite victory, a powerful affirmation of opposition to the war, had been achieved, when the crowds began to seek out their buses and to make their way home. As darkness fell, a few hundred were left immediately in front of the Pentagon, a few thousand on the stairs and mall below. Draft cards were burned; food and blankets were dispensed; fires were started. On the announcement of a 'piss call' a substantial group of males faced the Pentagon and urinated *en masse*.

Up to this point the authorities could not be seriously faulted; if anything, the provocation had all come from the other side. It was just before midnight that the terrifying attack began on the remainder of the crowd, described as follows by a woman reporter for the *Washington Free Press:*

> Slowly the wedge began to move in on people. With bayonets and rifle butts, they moved first on the girls in the front line, kicking them, jabbing at them again and again with the guns, busting their heads and arms to break the chain of locked arms.

A professor from the English department at Hunter College witnessed the brutality of the soldiers towards one female demonstrator:

> One soldier spilled the water from his canteen on the ground in order to add to the discomfort of the female demonstrator at his feet. She cursed him—understandably, I think, and shifted her body. She lost her balance and her shoulder hit the rifle at the soldier's side. He raised the rifle, and with its butt, came down hard on the girl's leg. The

girl tried to move back but was not fast enough to avoid the billy-club of a soldier in the second row of troops. At least four times that soldier hit her with all his force, then as she lay covering her head with her arms, thrust his club swordlike between her hands into her face. Two more troopers came up and began dragging the girl toward the Pentagon... She twisted her body so we could see her face. But there was no face there. All we saw were some raw skin and blood. We couldn't even see if she was crying—her eyes had filled with the blood pouring down her head. She vomited and that too was blood. They then rushed her away.[18]

Injuries were serious, but there were no deaths. That was one force in the triangle of forces I identified in Chapter 2—the force of brutal reaction. But in the aftermath the force of measured judgement prevailed. One thousand demonstrators were arrested; of the 600 actually charged, only two were sent for trial—they were both acquitted.[19]

## Italy, France and Britain

Over the period 1967-9 destruction and death from every kind of internal disorder was greatest in the United States, there being so many different sources of conflict. Within the other three countries the most extended, the most widespread, and the most potentially destabilizing (partly because of the thorough involvement of industrial workers but also because of the emergence of neo-fascist and then left-wing fundamentalist organizations) challenges to authority took place in Italy, though the events in France (or rather Paris) were to command more international attention, both at the time and ever since. There are both geographical and historical reasons for this discrepancy between reality and image. The centres of critical activity were spread quite widely over Italy: pioneering protests in the universities of Trento, Pisa, and Naples, explosive ones in Rome, several institutions affected in Milan, major strikes at the Fiat works in Turin. Italy lacked a single metropolitan focus whereas in Paris, where there was a history of popular risings menacing governments, the student insurrections directly impinged upon government. As in America, activism was provoked by a mixture of frustration, genuine anger over the oppression of, and lack of opportunity for, the weak and the disadvantaged both at home and abroad, legitimate grievances, and daft ideas. Reactions to events on the world scene, imperialist interventions and Third World struggles, resentment over restrictions on personal liberties, and the desire for sexual freedom all mixed with the other issues. While in Italy there was good cause for concern over the deprivation among, and discrimination against, some Italians, as in France there was against Moroccans and Algerians, there was no real analogue of the American race issue. On the other hand the direct frustrations and grievances arising from the educational system and attempted educational reforms were far more salient in Italy and France than in America. Events in Italy and France are also distinguished by the important part played in them by secondary-school pupils. Many accounts have tended to suggest that trouble in the schools was a subsequent byproduct of student activism; but a strict attention to chronology shows that some of the earliest protests occurred in the schools, and indicates that it was when those pupils moved on to university, bringing their radical ideas with them, that major protest began to disturb the universities. Contrasts between pragmatic Anglo-Saxons and overly theoretical continentals may have a platitudinous ring to them, but it is simple fact that modes of abstract thinking, either purely Marxist or stressing a dialectic between Catholic approaches and Marxist ones, were integral to Italian and French education and intellectual culture generally; thus what I refer to very deliberately as 'daft ideas' tended to be even dafter and more unilateral. In Italy there was the heart-warming but curious phenomenon of Catholic Marxism.

In concentrating first on Italy, I shall look in turn at the educational system, its problems, and the proposals for reform, at the secondary schools, where powerful protest movements began to appear in 1966, at Catholic Marxism, which produced some of its most powerful statements in 1967, and then at the violent confrontations beginning to take place in 1967; finally (in Chapter 12) I shall look at the workers' protests of 1968–9, discussing how far, if at all, they were related to the student protests. Over the entire period several hundreds of students, workers, and police, and some bystanders, were seriously wounded; twenty-eight people were killed.

One of the first major stirrings of social change in sixties Italy was the education reform of 1962, principally aimed at increasing the numbers obtaining a secondary education (up to the age of 14). But the expansion in numbers was not fully met by an expansion in resources; if anything, conditions in the elementary schools (not affected by the reform) worsened; and even in the secondary schools the old authoritarian attitudes remained and much of the extra work was done by part-time and temporary teachers. Most relevant of all to our topic, tremendous additional pressure was placed on the upper secondary schools, and the universities; further-more, the old distinction between the *liceo* and the technical institute continued. Untouched by reform, the upper secondary schools of both types had to cope with a doubling in numbers. Standards dropped. Drop-out rose: by 1969 20 per cent of pupils at the technical institutes were leaving at the end of their first year, while the figure at the *liceo classico* (drawing mainly from middle-class families) was 10 per cent. Formerly access to universities had been entirely limited to those educated in a *liceo*. However, in 1961 access to science faculties was opened to students from the technical institutes. An even more sweeping gesture in favour of democratic higher education was made in 1965, when entrance by examination and fixed quotas were abolished. The consequence of these two measures was that the percentage of students coming from work-ing-class backgrounds increased from 14 per cent in 1961 to 21 per cent in 1967–8. That, of course, was still a small figure considering the working-class proportion of the entire popula-tion—in fact, only one in sixteen of the relevant age group was going to university. Over the same period the number of women students doubled, so that in 1968 they made up just under one third of the total intake. Far more students were getting into university than was the case in Britain (though in Britain, there was a higher proportion of working-class students among those who did qualify for entry), but the facilities were much poorer and the obstacles much greater: conditions generally militated against those with the most limited resources and the least in the way of family backup—i.e. working-class students. All students suffered from deteriorating staff-student ratios, lack of books, and lecture theatres too small to accommodate the numbers enrolled.[20]

A substantial proportion of Italian students lived at home, but university life did none the less offer a certain amount of the freedom traditionally associated with it ('neglect' might actually be a more appropriate word). Many students came well prepared to exploit this freedom (or neglect), since certain leading Italian secondary schools were already much less authoritarian than their French counterparts. Two episodes of early 1966 concerning two different prestigious Milan schools wonderfully illuminate the conflicts and cross-currents among pupils, schools, parents, puritanical Catholics, progressive teachers, liberal politicians, the legal system (with its aristo-cratic, liberal, and neo-fascist components), and, of course, the police—and, in the case of the second and more famous incident, the 'Zanzara' case, behaviour of an almost perverted nature. The first episode began on 4 November 1965, when two female pupils at the Liceo Berchet, acting in concert with some older university students, distributed leaflets published by the Milan Anti-Imperialist Centre, which were anti-Nato and supportive of the rights of American consci-entious objectors to refuse to fight in the Vietnam war. Italy had both conscription and highly militarized police forces. The Milanese authorities, generally reckoned to be reactionary (and very ready to censor films, as we have seen), considered the case for some time, then suddenly ordered arrests. In the standard way, the homes of all the young people were raided during the night of 9–10 March and all were then sent into San Vittore prison, to spend the rest of the night there. Whatever the eventual outcome—in fact the cases were dismissed and the prisoners imme-diately released—a particularly nasty form of intimidation had been successfully implemented (one of the girls was just sixteen).[21]

Meantime the February issue of the Liceo Parini school magazine, *La Zanzara* (Mosquito) had appeared. It contained an article, 'School and Society', by the 17-year-old editor, Marco de Poli, and a report on the responses to a questionnaire de Poli, and two fellow-pupils, Marco Sassano and Claudia Beltramo Ceppi (also each 17), had circulated among the female pupils, asking them about their sexual attitudes and behaviour, entitled 'What do the girls of today think?' Topics covered included contraception, sexual intercourse outside marriage, unmarried mothers, and illegitimate children. The responses replicated the strong sense we have found elsewhere, among young people and radical thinkers, of Italy lagging behind other Western countries with respect to sexual liberation. Nine students were recorded as protesting against 'control of their sexuality by the state and society' and demanding that 'everyone should be free to do what they want', with 'absolute sexual liberty and a total change in social attitudes'. One female student declared that she imposed limits on her sexual activities purely because of the risks, adding that if she had free access to contraceptives she would impose no such limits. By law four copies should have been deposited at the police headquarters, the Questura, and the contents should have been approved in advance by the headmaster, Professor Daniele Mattalia, a man of very liberal views. Mattalia had been on holiday when the issue was being prepared, and he had not striven officiously to scrutinize it on his return. No copies had been deposited with the police. But all would almost certainly have been well had not the Catholic organization 'Student Youth', which was active in most schools and universities, decided to bring the matter to the attention of parents, the press, and the legal authorities. Fourteen parents immediately phoned to threaten withdrawal of their children. The major newspapers were not very interested at this stage, but the local paper, *Corriere*

*Lombardo*, published a scare-mongering piece under the seven-column headline, 'Scandal Breaks Out at Parini Survey Published in Student Paper'. Throughout this book I am at pains to argue that any notions of crude intergenerational conflict between children and their parents are misplaced, and that parents in the sixties were often as much party to changing ideas as their offspring. In Italy—and especially among the comfortably off—relations between parents, children, *and* teachers were frequently good. The fourteen alarmed parents were now, by the satisfying factor of exactly ten to one, eclipsed by the 140 parents who sent in telegrams expressing solidarity with the three students and their headmaster. But the (very right-wing) chief procurator, Oscar Lanzi, had already decided to institute formal proceedings, putting the vice-questore (deputy chief constable) on to interviewing Mattalia and his deputy, and then, successively, de Poli, Sassano, and Beltramo Ceppi. On 16 March the three students were brought before the procurator substitute of the republic, Pasquale Carcasio.

Carcasio took Sassano first, and it is at this point that the episode takes a strange turn, both sinister and sensational. The detailed evidence rests on the testimony of Sassano, and, almost unbelievably, de Poli, who from a room across the courtyard could see part of what was happening during Carcasio's examination of Sassano. But not only were Carcasio's actions never denied, they were defended, particularly by Lanzi. What de Poli saw was Sassano with his trousers off. Carcasio had brought in a doctor and insisted that Sassano undergo an intimate medical examination. Apparently his case was that any young man who could be so dissolute as to associate himself with the *Zanzara* survey must also be a frequenter of prostitutes, and thus at risk from venereal disease. Carcasio considered himself covered by circular 2326 of 21 September 1933, which decreed that, under certain circumstances, a young person could be forced to submit to medical examination: no prizes for recalling that in 1933 Italy was under the Fascist regime of Benito Mussolini. De Poli was also forced to submit, but Claudia Beltramo Ceppi, having spoken to her father on the phone, and backed up by the two young men, refused to enter the room. The doctor was male, and it was clearly established later that Carcasio intended to be present throughout the inspection. She was instructed to return the next day, accompanied by her mother.[22]

These three students belonged to the fringes of the upper class. Claudia's father was the director of an advertising agency and, as an anti-fascist hero, had been vice-questore of Milan at the end of the war. Sassano's father was an influential journalist. Immediately after the medical inspection contact was being made with top lawyers—and with top politicians, not excluding President of the Republic Saragat himself. De Poli's lawyer, Professor Alberto Dall'Ora, protested to the procurator of the republic, with a copy to President Saragat, about 'an act which by its gravity merits immediate and firm intervention by your office'. Professor Giacomo Delitala, Beltramo Ceppi's lawyer, had already pointed out publicly that the Fascist circular, basically intended to deal with young prostitutes, was, since it involved personal humiliation, outlawed by article 13 of the 1948 constitution. On 2 March the National Association of Evening Students, workers who studied in the evenings (and the most radical of all students), had indicated their support by declaring a one-hour strike at their places of work to be held on 7 March.

Knowing that he had powerful support within the Milanese judicial system, Lanzi decided to go for broke—reactionaries on the run usually do. The three young people, together with their head-master and the printer of *Zanzara*, a woman called Aurelia Terzaghi, were brought to trial on 31 March. The offences charged dated back to Fascist legislation: 'offending the moral sentiments of children and adolescents and thus inciting them to corruption'; and failing to lodge copies with the police. To the dismay of the defence, Lanzi had secured as presiding judge the traditionalist aristo-crat Luigi Bianchi d'Espinosa. Opening proceedings, the prosecutor declared that the trial had been brought about by public opinion as expressed through the press (certainly, since what became known as *lo spogliarello in Procura*—the striptease in the Procurator's office—press coverage had been enor-mous, and there was much criticism of the 'immoral' nature of the survey, but also a great deal of indignation against Carcasio's actions). The defence fielded many expert witnesses and a team of distinguished advocates led by Professor Delitala, who vigorously maintained that there cannot be one morality for adults and another one for children (a point that goes to the very heart of changing ideas about personal relationships), which led to his being greeted with prolonged applause when he sat down. The trial lasted a second day, till 1 April. Then Presiding Judge Bianchi d'Espinosa, on behalf of his tribunal of fellow-judges, delivered a judgment worthy of the patrician traditions of his family. All the defendants were acquitted, save that Terzaghi was fined the minor sum of 15,000 lire, and costs, for failing to deposit copies of the magazine with the authorities. Bianchi concluded with these words.

At tribunals for minors it is usual to conclude with a homily. I do this anyway when it's a normal court case. The tribunal has instructed me to say that it has recognised that your survey did not contain anything that was notably criminal. The task of the penal law stops at that point. Whether what you were trying to do was appropriate or inappropriate the school authorities will decide. Over this whole process an exaggerated fuss has been made. Don't let your heads be swollen, go back to your school and try to forget this expe-rience without thinking that you are people of greater importance than you really are.[23]

Not repressive tolerance, simply measured judgement. Carcasio was subjected to an investigation which brought up some evidence of peculiar behaviour on his part in the past, but no proceed-ings were taken against him.[24]

While luxuriating in all aspects of the trial, the press also demonstrated that passion for explaining young people to the wider world which was one of the constant elements in assisting dissident subcultures to become part of majority culture. *Epoca* undertook to 'give youth a voice', organizing discussion sessions in Milan, Turin, and Rome. What came through most strongly was an antipathy among school and university students towards an education which claimed to be apolitical, combined with a powerful wish for a greater involvement in current politics. As one female student of the Liceo Visconti in Rome put it: 'In practice it's not really apolitical, because, above all in certain subjects like history and philosophy, it is impossible for the teachers not to influence the way pupils think.' The events at the Liceo Parini in 1966 were certainly not isolated ones. A number of school magazines were noted for their provocative tone, including *Mister Gioue* at the Liceo Carducci, Milan, and *Il Vitellone* at the Liceo Gioberti, Turin. There were a number of strikes and demonstrations, with placards bearing such messages as 'Less Latin, more liberty'.[25]

One point seized on by the press was that de Poli admitted to being an atheist. However, a very strong impetus towards protest came from within Catholicism itself. By 1966 Catholic Marxism was an important force, particularly since, though the state educational system was formally secular, much education at all levels, in elementary schools, and in private secondary schools and universities, was in the hands of priests. The effects were also felt through the two Catholic workers' organizations, ACLI and CISL. One form in which Catholic Marxism manifested itself was in a strong sympathy for those primary school children from disadvantaged backgrounds who, in Italy, were unceremoniously 'failed' by their primary school teachers and slung out of the education system and into the lowest sector of the labour market. Don Lorenzo Milani, who ran a small school (about twenty pupils) in the Tuscan village of Barbiana, where he specialized in taking in pupils who had been failed in elementary school and would not otherwise have had any further education, was very much tuned in to the advanced intellectual ideas of the time (or perhaps it would be better to say that he was an instigator of such ideas): he understood the power of language, and he believed in encouraging the active participation of his pupils in educational activities. He wanted to encourage the poor to develop their own powers of writing and speaking; he understood the discriminatory power of correct Italian:

> We need anyway to understand what is correct language. The poor create languages and then continue to renew them. The rich crystallize them so that they can take advantage of whoever doesn't talk like they do. Or they fail them in exams.[26]

The famous *Lettera a una professoressa* (Letter to a Primary Schoolmistress), published in 1967, which Don Milani concocted in collaboration with his pupils, dealt, on the basis of the personal experiences of his pupils, with the scandal of the unceremonious failing of primary schoolchildren. The ambitiousness of Don Milani's methods is demonstrated by the fact that in September 1966 one of his boys, Gostino, was actually in London. It was in a letter to him that Don Milani explained the origins of the *Letter*:

> We are working on an important 'open letter' to the schoolmistress who failed Il Biondo and Enrico last year. The three failed pupils of this year have re-ignited my anger and I think that a masterpiece is going to emerge from it. It will be a hymn of faith in the school and a manifesto of the parents' union of which you and Michele one day will be the moving spirits.[27]

As originally conceived the letter was to be only two or three pages, but it quickly expanded into a short book, denouncing the snobbish and hardhearted schoolmistress who blighted the lives of so many of her pupils.[28] The book was a mixture of personal reminiscences and factual statements about the educational system, and educational law, and the discrepancies between them, and had an appendix of educational statistics. One of the most interesting aspects is the parallel drawn between underprivileged Italians and American blacks. Here is a sample:

> At the elementary level the state offered me a second-class school. Five classes crammed
> into one room. One fifth of the school to which I had a right.
>
> Exactly the system they have in America to create the differences between whites and
> blacks. The poor have the worst schools from the very earliest years.
>
> My elementary schooling finished, I had the right to three further years of schooling.
> The Constitution says that I had an obligation to undergo them. But at [the village of]
> Vicchio there no longer was a secondary school. To travel to Borgo costs money. Anyone
> who tried to do this spent a heap of money and then was spurned like a dog.
>
> In my case the school-marm told me there was no point wasting my money: 'Get back
> to the fields. You are not made for studying'... And not once in a whole year did we ever
> read a newspaper in class.[29]

*Lettera a una professoressa* was an exposé of the class basis of, and the class prejudices inherent in, the Italian educational system. After the citation of figures demonstrating the grossly unequal nature of university entry and university graduation, there followed a reference to Black Power leader Stokely Carmichael's famous pronouncement that no white person could ever be trusted; the implication obviously was that the Italian poor could never trust even one member of the Italian middle class. The reference to the absence of the study of newspapers in school is a pregnant one. Throughout both Italian and French schools this demand for a schooling more relevant to the contemporary world and its political issues was a constant theme. Among the proposals being made in the book were: an ending to the system of summary failure; special full-time schooling for those who appeared to have educational difficulties; and, for the lazy, the identification of positive goals. *Lettera a una professoressa* is one of the classic products of the sixties: almost immediately it became something of a sacred text among those university students in Italy who were now beginning to mount open protests against the appallingly inadequate accommodation and shockingly low teaching standards in the Italian universities.

The common feature of the many different subcultures of the sixties was that, in some way or another, they were expressing a rejection of convention and authority. Often there were links between different movements and different styles of protest, but the richness, and the enduring qualities, of sixties subcultures are missed if we fail to make distinctions between the different sorts of protest. Beatniks, hippies, and great swathes of 'alternative' and 'underground' culture were essentially specific and non-confrontational, and often hedonistic and self-indulgent: to drop out was to drop out of any political engagement with society. Non-violent protesters undoubtedly expected to provoke confrontation; though they hoped to avoid violence, they knew that violence might well eventuate. Then there were the preachers of open violence: for some, violent talk was more than anything intended to shock; for others, no doubt, the belief was that fighting talk backed by resolution and solidarity would result in opposition melting away; but for others again violence itself was an integral part of the revolutionary process. Official Marxism, whether as represented by the Italian Communist party or by the Soviet Union, was seen as ossified and compromising; if international leadership was needed it was to be found in Mao Tse-tung's 'Cultural Revolution' in China, in Ho Chi Minh's resistance in North Vietnam, and in Third World leaders like Fidel Castro. Indigenous Italian Marxism produced the idea of students themselves as members of the proletariat, and therefore as primary agents, along with the workers, of revolution. From outside Italy came the influences of the Provos and the Situationists and, in a more general way, of beatniks and hippies. A unifying cause was that of anti-militarism and hostility to anyone implicated in support for American actions in Vietnam. Opposition to the educational system intensified with the promulgation of the Gui educational programme, which proposed university 'reform' through limiting student intake and replacing some full degree courses with shorter diplomas. A relatively small number of students boasted a complete revolutionary philosophy. For students of a liberal and generous disposition there were enough major political issues—particularly, of course, Vietnam and militarism—to get upset over. For all students there were plenty of grievances within the university system itself: the Gui reforms acted as a general trigger, while there were specific triggers in the form of unwise actions on the part of individual university authorities. An English expert on Italy remarked that he had 'never met an Italian university student who thought he was getting a good education', adding:

> The system seems all wrong, from the Professors at the top to the students at the bottom, most of whom are not qualified to be at either end of the ladder. The universities are the rigid feudal domain of the older professors. They are the refuge of sons and daughters of the middle-class who usually have no intention of pursuing after graduation the field they are training for.[30]

In April 1965 there were marches everywhere against the Gui proposals. In the following years many students were involved in the *capelloni* and Onda Verde demonstrations. In December 1966 Gruppo-Provo Roma I was formed, with the first number of the cyclostyled *Provo 1* appearing in January 1967. This group was responsible for organizing a demonstration against the visit to Rome of British prime minister Harold Wilson, seen as an accomplice in the Vietnam war. Almost immediately there was an anti-Vietnam demonstration in Milan.[31] At the same time architecture students at the Milan polytechnic began what they claimed was a new type of occupation, different from those of 1963, and the beginning of 'the mass mobilization of student power'.[32] But events in Pisa in February were more dramatic and more violent. A conference of university rectors was disrupted, several buildings were occupied, and there were clashes with the police. The Pisan students formulated the 'Pisan Theses', whose primary contention was that students formed part of the proletariat struggling to overthrow the bourgeoisie.[33] Although 1968 remains the year always associated with student activism, in Italy 1967 was in fact a year of almost continuous student activism, blended with the other radical and hippie elements discussed in Chapter 10. In essence there were two overlapping sets of demonstrations: those on the streets ostensibly focused mainly on political ('Fascist laws', and 'Fascists in power'), and above all, international issues, especially Vietnam: and those within university buildings, concerned basically with conditions there and with the proposed reforms. Both sets carried implications of revolutionary resistance to existing society.

French students of the 1960s had the longest tradition of political activism and, in their class-rooms and dormitories, the worst conditions to endure. If anything, sexual taboos were even stronger than in Italy, so that the sexual liberation theme, and specifically male access to female dormitories, has sometimes been represented as the central one in the new phase of extreme turbulence in student affairs which began in late 1963, ten months before the free speech episode at Berkeley; only 1963 in France did not mark such a sharp break from the past as autumn 1964 did in America. Activist French students had opposed the Algerian war, and then the OAS: in June 1960 the government subvention to the National Union of French Students (UNEF) was suspended, being restored again by the education minister, Christian Fouchet, in April 1963.[34] The sexual freedom question did dominate certain episodes and at certain times, but there were many other aspects to the student troubles. While the influence of the Communist party declined drastically, the new doctrines of Situationism and structuralism offered alluring arguments for anti-university and 'anti-bourgeois' activities. It should be noted, too, that secondary pupils in the lycées were consistently active (more so than in Italy) in protesting against the state-imposed educational system.

While in Britain, with much more restricted university entry, eight new universities—Sussex, York, Kent, Warwick, Lancaster, East Anglia, Essex, and Stirling—were created, there was insufficient building in France to meet the ever-growing numbers of students possessed of the baccalauréat. Of course all city-centre universities in all countries were expanding into neigh-bouring buildings, not all of them perfectly suitable. But there was something especially symbolic about the way the Sorbonne took over the vast wholesale wine market (the Halle aux Vins) as well as the leather market (Halle aux Cuirs), impressive buildings both, but neither exactly fash-ioned to the purpose. New residential campuses were built in the outer suburbs, at Nanterre and Orsay. The first blocks at Nanterre were opened in 1964, with 2,300 students. By 1968 this unap-pealing, austere wasteland campus had nearly 15,000 students, but no library, let alone such amenities as cinemas, cafés, or discothèques. New universities were built at Amiens, Orléans, Reims, and Rouen.

It was against inadequate amenities and poor, irrelevant teaching which avoided live politi-cal topics that the leaders of UNEF wished to mobilize; already in 1963 a new cohort of militants wished to use attacks on the university as the basis for attacks on established society. At the April 1963 conference at Dijon the platform won approval for proposals turning UNEF from a representative council into an activist trade union, prepared to resort to demonstrations and strikes in the pursuit of drastic university reform. The beginning of the new academic year (always the likely time for action) came in November, and was immediately dubbed *catastroph-ique rentrée*, 'catastrophic return to classes', by *L'Express*.[35] Demonstrations at the Sorbonne in support of more staff, more and larger lecture-rooms, and better amenities attracted the atten-tion of 4,000 police. Faced with overwhelming force, violently deployed, the students resorted instead, on 25 November, to a strike. The troubles, together with discussions between student leaders and the authorities, continued throughout December and January. As part of his state visit in February, President Segni of Italy was scheduled to visit the Sorbonne: in the end the visit did go ahead, to the accompaniment of pictures of students being marched off in hand-cuffs. The use of superior force resulted in victory for Fouchet, but it was, *L'Express* warned, 'a poisoned victory'.[36]

By September (just when the free speech movement was starting at Berkeley) a new set of troubles had broken out at Paris's original student residential area, Antony, to the south of the city. Here male students were trying forcefully to assert a right to visit female students in their dormitories. The response of the administrators was to order the building of a new warden's lodge to guard the entrance to the women's residence. Almost 2,000 students took immediate direct action, physically preventing building workers from getting on with the job. Once again there was no hesitation about calling in the police, who were then given the tedious task of stand-ing guard, day and night, over the site; this did not increase their affection for the students. Even after the lodge was completed the protests continued, and even intensified. *L'Express* commented particularly on the way in which the demonstrators (just like ordinary trade unionists) were employing banners and placards and shouting slogans. In fact October 1965 it identified a student 'malaise' which signified 'a profound transformation' and 'something like the end of a world'.

*L'Express* was making a class point. What had gone, now that the over-whelming majority of students were middle-class and lower-middle-class, was the universe of the aristocratic student, the *jeunesse dorée*, with its respect for French institutions and traditions and for the special rituals of student life. All that, in the new student argot of the day was *Folklo* (literally, 'folklore', perhaps best translated as 'old hat'). *Folklo* to the young students of 1965 were 'political parties, historic locations, student unions, French education, heroes of the Resistance, historic battles of any sort, Dreyfus, Zola, Hitler, Blum, novels, the army, poverty and the guards who prevent you from climbing into the girls' rooms', and also, the 'Boul' Mich' (boulevard St Michel, historically the central boulevard of Paris's student quarter), rag day parades *(des 'monômes')*, and ritual initiation ceremonies for freshers *(les 'bizuthages')*. Good luck to the students, one might well think. The snide hostility of this journal of the aspiring middle class is revealing. These students no doubt were privileged, but not that privileged—something *L'Express* held against them. The students themselves were often very conscious of how little freedom, and little money, they had in comparison with those of their age group who were already in paid employment. Here is direct testimony of hardship from a female student:

> I detach myself from the hordes in the lecture theatre or lab in order, on the other side of Paris, to dive into a nursery. Like a large number of my comrades, I have to look after tiny children in order to make ends meet. I am shattered. At the end of my tether. Screaming kids and a seventy-hour week. My studies are very strongly affected. The risks of failure are multiplied by ten. It's depressing. Holding up, physically and morally, that's a problem.[37]

The son of a white-collar worker, living on a state grant, touched on some of the gains of student life:

Money problems I have known since childhood. Here, for me, it's a palace. It's luxury! And even a bit more. Living in the city has, thanks to contact with other people, contact with blacks, orientals, North Africans, of whom there are so many here, allowed me to lose my blinkers. I have changed... [my grant] is nothing... It is nothing and it is a lot... I live in a room in Paris. [I pay half my grant] for an attic without electricity and without running water...

*L'Express* based its important perception of 1965 as the critical year of change on evidence from a range of universities across the country. A science student at Montpellier spoke strongly against the new residential universities built in the suburbs—as he saw it, a moat was being constructed between students and life in the cities. Shopkeepers in the suburbs, he claimed, were not interested in the custom of students: 'There are scarcely any cafés where we can meet and certainly no night-clubs which are accessible to us.' Students were not looking forward to army service following their deferment: according to *L'Express* three out of four expected to escape because of mental problems, a real enough affliction for many students.[38]

The students at Antony won at least a partial victory—one, however, which was not extended elsewhere. Taking office in January 1966, a new rector agreed that male and female students over 21 could visit each other, and those under 21 if they received written parental permission, which in fact nine out of ten did (supporting my earlier arguments about liberalization *within* the family). While this local difficulty was being sorted out, a national one was being matured—a new Fouchet Law which, if it went ahead, would impose restrictions on university entry. Many of those with the Baccalauréat, traditionally the open passport to a university education, would be rejected, and others would be forced to take a two-year rather than a four-year course. News that the Fouchet reforms were about to be implemented was released while students were still on vacation, in October 1967.

Meantime the next major event had taken place at the University of Strasbourg in November 1966, written up by its protagonists as 'Ten Days That Shook the University'.[39] The disenchantment and apathy of the majority, together with a substantial minority who shared in the widespread resentment over the way universities were organized and run and, in some cases, the contempt for society in general, ensured that a group of Situationists and Provos were elected to control of the student union. Immediately the new student leaders directed union resources towards advocacy of student revolution and Situationism. In particular, a substantial cyclostyled pamphlet was produced, both in French and in English (that version was subsequently made available to students at the London School of Economics when the troubles broke out there). The Dadaesque, mocking quality, which was the most endearing feature of Situationism, is strongly marked. After the short title, 'Ten Days That Shook the University', there is a second title: 'Of Student Poverty—Considered in its economic, political, psychological, sexual, and in particular intellectual, aspects, and a modest proposal for its remedy.' The university and the city authorities very quickly combined to eject the new student leadership, closing down the union on 14 December.

However, the event could not but excite students both at Strasbourg, and elsewhere. Situationist philosophy might not be particularly popular, but the idea of students taking more of their destiny into their own hands certainly was. Given that most students were thoroughly disillusioned with official Marxism and the French Communist party, Situationism was important in helping to formulate the phrases and slogans which could invest protests against immediate practical grievances with a sense of grander purpose. Following up their second title, authors of the Strasbourg pamphlet commiserated with students: the student is a 'pauper: 80 per cent of students come from income groups well above the working class, yet 90 per cent have less money than the meanest labourer'. They were also highly contemptuous of students, their attack on the contemporary student being shrewd and cruel:

> He thinks he is avant-garde if he has seen the latest Godard or 'participated' in the latest happening. He discovers 'modernity' as fast as the market can produce its ersatz version of long outmoded (though once important) ideas; for him every rehash is a cultural revolution.

However, significantly with regard to the events of 1967–9, they were now prepared to join with Marcuse in recognizing students as the new revolutionary leaders: 'After years of slumber and permanent counter-revolution, there are signs of a new period of struggle, with youth as the new carriers of revolutionary infection.' The final paragraph expressed the joyousness of Situationism, and was not an altogether inaccurate prevision of the famous events of May 1968: 'For proletarian revolt is a festival or it is nothing; in revolution the road to excess leads once and for all to the palace of wisdom.'[40]

Late 1966 was also the period in which extreme discontent within the secondary schools began to become very apparent. A fundamental problem was the contrast between the liberalizing of family life and the continuance in schools of paternalistic and autocratic traditions. Complaints ranged from embargoes on the wearing of long hair to suppression of the discussion of contemporary political issues. Historically, Indo-China had been an important part of the French empire, and in the 1950s a realm of French defeat and tragedy. It was not surprising that feelings about American activities in Vietnam ran particularly high in France. When the National Vietnam Committee, concerned both with general protest at American actions and with pressuring the French government to take a strong anti-American stand, was established in 1966, secondary school pupils formed almost as important a part of the membership as university students. In 1967 special committees of action for pupils at the lycées were set up *(comités d'actions lycéens)*.[41] If 1967 was a year of action over Vietnam it was also, symbolically representing the two polar concerns of youth, another year of action over segregated dormitories. At Nanterre conditions had been improving slightly: there were, for instance, weekly dances, though obviously nothing which could compare with life in the student quarter around the Sorbonne. Female students over 21 could visit male dormitories, but all male students were excluded from female dormitories. In April a group of male students took direct action in the form of a sit-in in the entrance-hall to one of the women's dormitories. Among them was Daniel Cohn-Bendit, a sociology student, whose parents were German Jews who had fled from the Nazis to France, where

Cohn-Bendit was born in 1945; registered as stateless, he had adopted German citizenship in 1959 to avoid French military service. The German connection, as we shall see in the next chapter, was to become increasingly important. Meantime, once again, student action was brought to an end by police intervention.[42] The cup of bitterness, it could be said, was filling up; students had yet to try to meet the police with anything like the force the police wielded against them.

That kind of talk seems quite out of place when we cross the Channel to Britain, where the rights to, and rules governing, peaceful protest were long established, where students were docile and considered either hard-working or licensed members of the aristocracy, and where, above all, the police did not carry firearms. If directed anywhere, the wrath of certain reactionaries in authority was directed towards nonconformist youth from the classes which did not aspire to a university education. This was made clear in the first notorious 'spectacle' of the High Sixties, a spectacle which was more press and television myth-making than reality, the much written-about clashes between mods and rockers at such seaside resorts as Margate and Brighton over the bank holiday weekend of Whitsun 1964. Over-excited magistrates handed out excessive sentences, accompanied by ludicrous speeches—describing short-haired, neatly dressed mods, for instance, as 'long-haired beatniks'. Calmer accounts in the quality newspapers from the Tuesday onwards made it clear that many of the young people involved had certainly not come looking for trouble, but that much of the trouble had been provoked by the hostile and suspicious attitudes of local landladies and café owners, and above all by the over-large and over-active presence of the police.[43] May 1964 in fact marked the end of a short era in which it had been possible to regard large sections of youth as potential delinquents; with the swing towards regarding young people as in the van of cultural change, those who continued to hold such views felt it better to keep them concealed. For students of a politically activist turn, the main vehicle had been CND. The continuing emotional commitment to this cause was shown by the large number of students and other young people who wore the CND badge, but the marches themselves were coming to seem dated and pervaded by the scruffiness of an older generation of pacifists and left-wingers. CND leaders gave youthful political activism a new lease of life, but hastened the path of their own organization into a condition of suspended animation, when they took a key role in planning the first anti-Vietnam war demonstration in 1965. CND was completely eclipsed by the Vietnam Solidarity Campaign, a widely based movement which had considerable support among students— there were teach-ins on Vietnam at the London School of Economics and Oxford University in the summer of 1965; the Vietnam Ad-Hoc Committee was an élite, militant group, responsible for organizing the mass demonstrations of 1968. The ageing but increasingly radical British aristocratic philosopher, Bertrand Russell, in November 1966 launched his Vietnam War Crimes Tribunal, in cooperation with Jean-Paul Sartre. It finally convened in Stockholm in May 1967, the United States being condemned on all counts.

British secondary schools were notably untroubled by the activism apparent in France and Italy. Probably British young people of school age were less mature, and also less prone to political commitment and direct action; perhaps also they had less to complain about—while the secondary moderns which ditched their pupils at the age of 15 were often pretty appalling, the grammar schools, catering for pupils up to the age of 18, were generally quite well equipped; and British schools, unlike those in France and Italy, still employed the sanction of corporal punishment which almost certainly dissuaded too much adventurous nonconformity. The new university campuses were richer in facilities and far better designed than places like Nanterre. Usually remoteness from city centres was not as sharply felt a problem as it was at Nanterre. It was at the austere and relatively isolated campus of the University of Essex that complaints about lack of amenity had most substance; but then complaints began to be made about the cramped city-centre facilities of the London School of Economics; reasonable cases could also be made at the less privileged urban art colleges and technical colleges. Other students at the big civic universities got hold of the notion that their universities were 'too big', though in fact staff-student ratios were remarkably favourable compared with anything which existed in any of the other three countries and, if anything, improving during the sixties. These considerations were all slow to form, and often had strong overtones of emulating what was happening abroad. What was a genuine indigenous issue to at least a significant minority of students throughout Britain from 1964 onwards was that of 'student power'. Most students, and practically all academics, considered that with respect to curriculum, teaching methods, and the organization and running of the university, there was no place for student opinion or student influence (it should be said that, whereas American universities were largely run by administrators answerable to outside interests, and by former academics who upon becoming deans or presidents often became *plus administratif que les administrateurs,* British universities were much more in the hands of their senior academics). Founded in 1966, the Radical Students' Alliance never amounted to anything in terms of numbers, but did proselytize actively on behalf of student power and student commitment on such issues as Vietnam.[44] But before 1968, student power scarcely got beyond the columns of the student newspapers or speakers in student unions or councils.

The London School of Economics (a component college of the University of London) shared the intellectual standards of the best Oxford and Cambridge colleges, had a highly centralized and concentrated student body—not divided among autonomous colleges—and a very cosmopolitan character. Notions of student power were probably strongest here. Outbreaks of student agitation, as we have seen, nearly always had some precipitating cause. Britain's only major student disturbances before 1968 came at LSE in the autumn of 1966 as a consequence of the announcement that Dr Walter Adams, previously principal of University College, Rhodesia, had been appointed the next director of the college. Rhodesia had recently declared itself independent of Britain, and its regime, in the eyes of leftists and liberals, represented all the evils of white supremacism and racial segregation. Adams was seen as standing for these evils. The president of the students' union, still only 19 years old, was Jewish South African by birth, a former pupil of Manchester Grammar School and a leader in the student power movement, David Adelstein. Adelstein took up the matter with the chairman of the LSE board of governors, Lord Bridges, former secretary to the war cabinet and head of the civil service. Bridges took the matter into the public domain, or at least into the domain of the select public educated at élite institutions, in the time-honoured establishment manner, by writing a letter to *The Times* in support of Adams's character and qualifications. The students' union council drafted a response intended for publication as an official students' union statement. However, the retiring director, Sir Sydney Caine, ruled that neither the name of the college nor of its union could be used in such a letter. In response, the union council decided by 306 votes to 23 that Adelstein should sign the letter as LSE union president and seek publication in *The Times*, where it duly appeared on 29 October. The school's moribund board of discipline was given a hasty kiss of life in order that charges could be brought against Adelstein. Making it clear that he would not accept the unilateral action of any little university committee, Adelstein demanded proper legal process; meantime the union organized a demonstration in the street outside, and a strike against lectures and tutorials. The strong transatlantic influence was apparent in the singing by the demonstrators of civil rights songs, and in the banner which read: 'Berkeley 1964: LSE 1966: We'll bring *this* school to a halt too.' But this was still Great Britain: there were no police attacks on the demonstrators, and measured judgement prevailed amongst the university authorities—no action was taken against Adelstein.[45]

However, the central grievance, for left-wing students at least, remained: a 'stop Adams meeting' was arranged for 31 January 1967, to be held in the main college lecture hall, the Old Theatre. When leaflets threatening 'direct action' were discovered, Caine banned the meeting, reinforcing his decision with a neat piece of British pragmatism: he had all the electrical fuses removed from the lecture theatre. On the evening of the putative meeting there was a confrontation outside the closed doors of the lecture theatre between Caine on the one side and Adelstein and a large crowd of students on the other. As students pushed into the theatre, it did not help that it was in darkness: there were scuffles, in one of which a 64-year-old porter slipped and died of a heart attack.[46] At first the crowd seemed seized by an uncompromising rage, then, as news of the death sunk in, they melted away. Adelstein and five other union leaders were charged with going ahead with the meeting after the director had banned it; there was something resembling a proper trial, with three members of the law department, including the celebrated supporter of civil liberties Professor J. A. G. Griffith, speaking on behalf of the accused. Adelstein and one other student, an American postgraduate, were suspended for the rest of the academic year, the other four being acquitted. At five o'clock on 13 March the student occupation of the college began; it lasted nine days. Meantime, there was an attempted occupation of the administrative building, Connaught House. This time the police were brought in, and using the minimum force necessary they ejected the students. On Friday 17 March the 'Daffodil march' of nearly 40 per cent of LSE students, together with 1,500 students from other London colleges and universities, took place down Fleet Street: accompanied in the usual British way by an escort of police, it was completely peaceful.[47]

There exists a professional survey of student attitudes at LSE at this time, to which 2,239 students out of 2,806 contributed. Levels of activism were affected both by subject of study and political allegiance. Of sociology students, 62 per cent took some part in the occupation or strikes, whereas for those studying history, geography, or industrial subjects, the figure varied from 25 to 34 per cent. The relevant figures for Marxists were 96 per cent, for Labour supporters 77 per cent, 70 per cent for Liberals, and 55 per cent for Conservatives. With regard to the issue which had begun the whole business, only 13 per cent actually felt that students should have a role in appointing the director, and only 9 per cent thought that students should have a say in academic appointments. The issues which concerned the majority were essentially practical, commonsense ones: 69 per cent wanted effective power in the running of the library, 54 per cent in disciplinary matters. Only substantial minorities wanted student influence over teaching arrangements (43 per cent), course content (34 per cent), and examination policy (28 per cent). On the general question of strikes and sit-ins 70 per cent were prepared to approve of such tactics, but only with the proviso that they did not interfere with the work of the school. Any action which did this, and thus interfered with the freedom of choice of other students, was condemned by 53 per cent, partly justified by 18 per cent, and wholly justified by 22 per cent. Overall, 56 per cent of undergraduates and 40 per cent of postgraduates played at least some part in the strikes. Overall 36 per cent took part in the occupation for at least one day; only 7 per cent had stayed overnight for from four to six days. Twenty per cent had acted as pickets.[48] Given actual student sentiments about their rights in regard to the appointment of a director, it was perhaps understandable that when Dr Adams came to take up his appointment in September, there was little in the way of open protest.

## *Civil Rights and Urban Riots in the USA*

The cataclysmic violence and destruction which took place in Watts (officially, South Central Los Angeles) in the summer of 1965 was perceived then, and clearly stands out now, as beginning a new phase in race relations in the United States; even so, the implications are not straightforward. Hopelessness breeds violence; but violence itself breeds further violence. There is a direct line between Watts 1965 and Watts 1992, and a situation in which the hope of peaceful integration of the two races had given way to one of the two races forming opposed armed camps. If most of the power still remained with the whites, blacks were savouring a kind of power they had never previously possessed, the power, for however brief a period, to terrorize whites. However, the forces making for a more bitter and explosive divide between the races were matched by rather different reactions on the part of members of both races: many whites, as well as blacks, could see that the problem lay in the slow pace of civil rights advances, and that much more profound and immediate initiatives were required. If the riots sprang from a sense of frustration and powerlessness, they also showed ordinary blacks, untouched for the most part by civil rights aspirations, taking their destiny into their own hands.

Violence associated with the race issue was nothing new. But prior to the mid-sixties, the violence was almost always started by whites reacting to peaceful action on the part of blacks, with the location usually (though very far from invariably) being in the South. The standard trigger for the new wave of black urban violence was heavy-handed action by white policemen, but without doubt the riots were initiated and carried through by blacks. Watts was followed in 1966 by a large number of separate episodes, followed in 1967 by the worst summer yet, with particularly destructive riots in Newark, New Jersey, and Detroit. Such riots undoubtedly expressed an elemental resentment over the appallingly deprived conditions in which many blacks, who had moved to the North in search of better things, actually lived. A deep structural cause, indeed, was the overcrowding resulting from population movements from the South, leading in turn to a situation in which the white authorities simply failed to provide basic amenities, and, also, such basic citizenship entitlements as the right to vote. The riots also expressed the frustration felt by blacks as the major Acts on Civil Rights and Economic Opportunity failed to deliver what they seemed to promise. Finally, the riots showed that blacks were no longer prepared to play the pacific, subservient role. As ideas of Black Power spread, blacks manifested the will to take action on their own behalf, even if that could take no more effective form than burning, looting, and attacking all signs, and all representatives, of white authority.

But devastating and attention-focusing as the riots were, they took up only a small part of each year, and they are far from encapsulating all aspects of race relations between 1964 and the end of 1967. Many of the initiatives which were well under way by the former year continued, as of course did more traditional black aspirations after prosperity within white society. Before turning to the summer riots of 1965–7, I want to consider in turn: the Freedom Summer of 1964, and especially the heroic part played by a handful of young whites, and the gradual deterioration of relations between black and white civil rights activists which followed; the stumbling continuation of community initiatives in that prototypical mid-South city of Memphis; and the quiet advances made by certain prosperous blacks.

By the summer of 1964 the activities of the freedom fighters may have lost some of their novelty, but they continued to carry very high personal risks. The registration drive conducted in 1963 by the students from Yale and Stanford recruited by Bob Moses had been successful. As the Democratic party in the South was a pillar of segregation, the plan for 1964 was to organize a Mississippi Summer Project in which voters would be registered to support the new Mississippi Freedom Democratic party, established in April 1964. Hundreds more white students were to be recruited from the best colleges and trained by black veterans; meantime the state legislature of Mississippi prepared its defences by enacting seven new statutes designed to curb demonstrations and protests; during the first half of 1964 the rules for voter registration took up four pages, and embodied twenty questions. In February a new branch of the historic white supremacist body was established, the White Knights of the Ku Klux Klan; as a special federal report on *Law Enforcement in Mississippi*, published on 14 July 1964, put it: 'The long anticipated, long dreaded, summer of 1964 is here, and the confrontation which may achieve epic stature between old Mississippi and young America has begun.'[49]

The student volunteers were just arriving in late June when they heard that two whites and one black already engaged in voter registration, Andrew Goodman, James Chaney, and Michael Schwerner, had been arrested and then had gone missing in Neshoba County, Mississippi. All the powers that the federal authorities could muster were brought in, but to little avail. Eventually the three bodies were discovered in a newly erected earthen dam six miles from the town of Philadelphia, Mississippi. The three men had been viciously beaten and then shot forty-four days earlier, late on the night of 21 June. In December, federal charges (technically of violating the civil rights of the three men by taking their lives) were brought against the sheriff and deputy sheriff of Neshoba County and nineteen others. But since it proved impossible to get direct witnesses, the charges were dropped within a week.[50]

There is much invaluable personal reminiscence, including Sally Belfrage's classic

511

autobiographical account *Freedom Summer* (1965), but historians are particularly lucky to have systematic interviews conducted at the time with voter registration volunteers (principally from Berkeley and Stanford). These reveal splits between students and their parents, the influence of Existentialism, the significance of first encounters with blacks, the bewilderment of most students within the California 'multiversity', and some delightful personal idiosyncrasies. Sally Belfrage quoted a discussion from back at the training school in Ohio:

> *White boy:* for me there is only one race, the human race. It's one nation. Mississippi is our back yard as much as Harlem. I have had it good for a long time. But I've seen too many people hungry for too long.
> *Negro boy:* we have to try to change the South so that the people of the North will want to do better. The South is a battlefield: the North is a stalemate. For us, it's all intolerable. But we have to work where the situation is flexible enough for change. Open hate is preferable to hypocrisy—it can be moved.[51]

Since they were going into a situation in which civil rights workers were brutally beaten up and murdered, in which they were deliberately run over, in which shots were fired into cars, and cars were forced off the road, and where, indeed, one destination was Greenwood, Leflore county, where Medgar Evers had been murdered the year before, the young volunteers were provided with various pieces of chilling advice: 'Never leave a jail at night'; 'Jail is safer than the mob'.[52] Mixed groups travelling by car, as the Neshoba County murder was to show, were specially at risk. There was also advice about how to avoid upsetting the local black population: atheism should be concealed, church could be attended, there should be no arguments over religious beliefs, conservative clothes should be worn, and the volunteers should not get drunk. For the local black population great courage was called for in going through the registration process: often they had to run the considerable risks of registering over and over again in order to try to get a defaulting registrar dismissed by the federal government. Sally Belfrage noted that at their meetings there were more women than men, although the women all had jobs as well as being homemakers. At the Free Democratic party county convention, thirteen of the seventeen delegates were women. A slightly different impression was given by a story told by the black activist Stokely Carmichael, already on the way to abandoning non-violence and collaboration with whites. A woman he was trying to persuade to register replied:

> 'Our people are dirty, they don't go to school, they are lazy, they smell—we are not ready for the vote. We had to be more like white folks to be ready for the vote.' 'That's right!', I said to her. 'We got to bomb their churches, shoot them at night, wear hoods, lynch them, beat on their heads, be just like they are, *then* we'll be ready for the vote!'[53]

After stating that his relations had always been good with his parents, one young white male, whose father worked for the government in Washington, remarked on the gap opening between the generations:

there's been a breakdown in the way of... a division in the way we look at the world... they don't have any idea of the necessity for people to make commitments... uh to things like civil rights or to take another current topic—to the war in Vietnam and they don't understand the motives either that would impel somebody to take a stand... [54]

A white male aged 20 from Natchez recounted:

I got involved for a while with French existentialism and things around that and, you know, intellectual thought had something to do with it—the two ideas, the one that as man is defined by his acts not his words, and two that it's not a question so much of what you accomplish as that you are doing something—the Camus idea from *Sisyphus*... It's the struggle that's important.

He had grown up in the New York suburbs but was now a student at Wesleyan University, Connecticut. His father, a businessman and financier, 'is a Northern quite liberal in the most derogatory sense of the term. He's thinking he's doing well when he hires a Negro who's not qualified for a job and then when the Negro doesn't do well, he says, "See, look what I told you". He thinks my work down south is increasing crime on the New York Subways...'

Most intriguing is the account of a 27-year-old female graduate student at San Francisco State College, her father a high school teacher, her parents 'white liberal, left liberal', she herself involved in civil rights and other protest movements since 1960, who had had experience as a croupier. When she graduated she 'needed money to go to Europe', so she had taken a job dealing blackjack at the California mountain resort of Lake Tahoe—'it's very good money—it's about twenty-five bucks a day plus tips. And then I went to Europe for a year, when I came back from Europe I was broke. So I went there, dealt some more, and then I went back to graduate school.' She had found Lake Tahoe 'terribly segregated'. Only within the last three or four years had 'Negroes' been allowed to work there, but they were brought 'up in the night time in busloads from San Francisco and Oakland', then the owners 'get them out during the day'. If anybody working there was 'caught with a Negro, they're fired'.

The events in Mississippi in the summer of 1964 did indeed achieve a kind of 'epic stature', but that involved more than confrontation 'between old Mississippi and young America'. In a situation of great tension and fear the inevitable differences between blacks and whites broke through to the surface. These differences showed themselves in many different ways—smart white college kids easily became impatient with what they saw as the disorganized approach of the blacks and were also (strange as it seems in the light of subsequent developments) taken aback by the marijuana-smoking habits of the blacks; and were not least in sexual matters, as Godfrey Hodgson, a leading journalist closely in touch with events at the time, explained:

The black boys would say to the white girls, 'Prove you're not prejudiced; come to bed with me.' What could the girls do but prove it? The white boys would be jealous and say nothing. The black girls would be furious and show it. In some places, by the end of the

513

summer, black-white tension had flared into open hostility.[55]

Black activists effectively abandoned the notion of non-violence, and took to the carrying of guns as essential to their own self-protection. White activists began to see their commitment to civil rights as inadequate and in some sense unrewarding: their activism must be broadened into an attack on the whole nature of American society.

Institutionally, the growing break between black activism and white liberalism was represented in the decision of the Mississippi Freedom Democratic party to send its own, all-black delegation to the 1964 Democratic convention in Atlantic City. Their aim was to oust the all-white, pro-segregationist, official delegation. President Johnson and the party leadership endeavoured to work out a compromise whereby two of the Freedom delegation (one of whom, however, was to be white) and three of the official delegation would be seated. The Freedom delegation refused and attracted enormous attention on television, middle-aged Fanny Lou Hamer proving particularly charismatic. Actually she was but one of the hundreds of blacks who from circumstances of the most unbelievable deprivation rose up to lead the civil rights movement. Fanny Lou Hamer herself was born to a sharecropping family in Sunflower County, Mississippi, the youngest of twenty children. Learning of her right to vote at a SNCC meeting, she decided to exercise it: 'The only thing they could do to me was kill me and it seemed like they'd been trying to do that a little bit at a time ever since I could remember.' She was arrested, jailed, and evicted from her land. She joined the staff of SNCC.[56] Among the Democratic party managers there was a great fear of uncontrolled black action: already in the summer of 1964 there were forewarnings of increasing black independence and violence in the urban riots in Harlem and Rochester.

In the autumn of 1964 SNCC, under the leadership of Stokely Carmichael, decided to move its voter registration efforts to the area around Selma, Alabama—an area notorious for violent intimidation. On 2 January 1965 Martin Luther King arrived in Selma, announcing that he was going to head a voter registration drive there. There is no doubt that King could achieve things which SNCC could not. After demonstrations in late January, King (and 770 other demonstrators) were arrested and jailed. On his release five days later King went to Washington, where he secured a promise that the administration would bring in a bill enforcing registration of qualified voters. The first of the infamous Selma marches took place on 7 March: peaceful and dignified (though without King, who was himself back in Atlanta), this march was first halted by state troopers under the orders of Governor George Wallace, then viciously assaulted from the rear by the local police. Two days later King himself started another march, but then gave way to an injunction forbidding it issued by a federal judge. That night a white Unitarian minister was viciously beaten with iron bars, dying two days later. It was this incident which led to President Johnson, on 15 March, in addressing a joint session of Congress, to make his powerful commitment to civil rights: 'It is not just Negroes, but really it is all of us who must overcome the crippling legacy of bigotry and injustice.' The third Selma march contained many white dignitaries—it was the embodiment of the official black-white civil rights coalition: it had the protection of the National Guard and of army helicopters on its five-day triumphal progress to Montgomery, where it arrived on 25 March. King made a celebratory speech.[57]

Many of the black activists continued their movement towards separatism and the repudiation of non-violence. However, the respected journal the *Afro-American* drew optimistic lessons, particularly from the manner in which the voting rights bill was indeed enacted in 1965:

> The democratising effect of the 1965 Voting Rights Act is already being felt, most appropriately in Alabama. Had it not been for the harsh actions of Alabama's Governor George Wallace during the Selma demonstrations, the law would not now be on the books... Mr Wallace, the self-styled white hope of the racists in 1964, has made such an about-face this year he has actually learned how to pronounce the word 'Negro' and has yet to mention the word 'segregation'.

In his comprehensive study, *Free at Last?*, Fred Powledge shares this optimism, ending his account on 25 March 1965: 'the deep pervading fear that had always infested Negro Southerners... had been beaten, abolished, vanquished; segregation had been broken'.[58] Be that as it may, there was still horror and nastiness to come. The night after King's celebratory speech, a white woman from Detroit who had been using her car to transport black protesters was murdered. Local bigots produced their own version of the third Selma march, a picture book entitled *Sex and Civil Rights: The True Selma Story,* which appeared in Birmingham, Alabama, in the summer of 1965. This consisted of rather feeble photographs of casually attired young people, black and white, freely mixing. The text spoke of: 'open promiscuous, degenerate activity engaged in by large numbers of beatnik-types who participated in the demonstrations' and of 'couples who made no particular effort to hide their sexual activities'.[59] This was actually tame stuff compared with the way in which white female office workers in the 1964 voter registration drive had been pestered with repetitious phone calls: 'How many Nigger cocks y'all got to suck 'fore you can go to sleep at night?'[60] On the other hand, civil rights consciousness was now beginning to develop more widely among white students in the southern universities. But, as elsewhere, voter registration in Tennessee continued to meet all the old resistances. The mayor of Brownsville declared menacingly of the white volunteers: 'We don't want them here, they just cause trouble with the colored. "Anything can happen" to those outsiders if they don't go home.'[61]

As late as November 1966, the Memphis Committee on Community Relations was still hearing reports from various stores on their hiring of black workers. A black minister, the Revd Kyle, chairman of the NAACP employment committee, commented:

> In his opinion this was still token employment and attitudes must change. Much more publicity should be given to the retail stores about the availability of job opportunities for Negroes. This is suggested for Negro news media and radio. He further stated that he believes that there has been discrimination against dark skinned Negroes. He would like to see more Negroes in first floor selling positions so that Negroes coming into a store can see firsthand that there are job opportunities in the selling field.[62]

At a meeting in April 1967 Edmund Orgill from the chair identified (again!) the most important areas with respect to continuing discrimination as education, employment, and housing. He was reported as saying 'that it would be hoped that more would have been accomplished in the area of employment and that of course, the housing problem was the most difficult'. A major new item of discussion, never featured in the deliberations of the late fifties and early sixties, was that of police brutality against blacks. The Revd Kyle complained about the continued evasion of this issue by the press, editor Ahlgren making the feeble excuse that it was difficult for newspapermen to get at the truth.[63] A couple of weeks earlier the black dentist Vasco A. Smith had resigned from the committee, claiming that it 'functioned only as a fire department'.

> I have also suffered the indignity of sitting silently while members of our committee pronounce the word Negro in such a fashion that it sounded like 'Nigger'... Finally, I have called your attention time and time again to this matter of police brutality. Negroes are having their skulls cracked right and left, but you won't do anything creative to remedy this situation until the possibility of a riot threatens the previous 'peace and tranquillity' of the business community.[64]

Lucius Burch tried unsuccessfully to secure a withdrawal of the resignation, explaining that white Memphians could not help pronouncing 'Negro' 'Nigra'. Orville and his associates did manage to pressure Mayor Loeb into making a statement, towards the end of 1967, drafted by them:

> I will actively work to improve relations between white and Negro citizens. Negro citizens will be appointed to City boards and commissions. I will make sure that there is no racial discrimination within the City government with regard to job opportunities and advancement. I will do all in my power to prevent violence by whites and Negroes and will not countenance police brutality toward either the white or Negro race.[65]

Some black newspapers expressed satisfaction with the progress of educational integration throughout the South: in 1965 it appeared that the number of black children in desegregated schools was double that of 1964— but this was still only 2.5 per cent of the eligible black students in the eleven states of the South.[66] The continuing realities in the South, 1964–6, were graphically brought out in a research report:

> As Negro children began what some newspapers termed 'massive' integration of southern public schools in September, 1965, the nation was surprised that Southerners accepted the change in a peaceful manner. The truth is that conditions in the South were neither integrated nor peaceful. Between five and six per cent of the region's 3,014,025 Negro school-age children attended classes with whites, and often these children and their parents paid a very high price for the experience. Men and women who were already desperately poor were evicted from sharecroppers cabins or tenant farms. Many without the training for good jobs lost the meagre ones they had held for years. Some were beaten

and shot at. Others saw their children abused and imprisoned. Yet the headlines continued to reassure the nation that 'School Integration continues to Spread Quietly Across the South.'[67]

The *Commercial Appeal* reported sympathetically on a white mother getting 'sick at my stomach' on hearing that her daughter would have a black teacher.[68]

And what of the blacks who had so ungraciously been 'integrated' into Memphis State University? For the first time ever, on 14 January 1966, *Tiger Rag* published an article on the feelings of black students:

> Most first semester freshmen do enjoy MSU. Many said it was the freedom they liked so much. For the incoming freshmen, college means no more reporting for homeroom role call [as at school], no more sneaking to smoke, no more cliques.

'Most all Negro students and some white students are helpful and friendly after you get to know them,' a black first-year female student was reported as saying. But, the report continued, college life was

> drudgery for the average Negro student at Memphis State. 'All I do is come to school, study, eat, go home or to work, hear my parents nag, go to sleep, get up next morning and start the little merry-go-round again,' said one boy as he sat reading a math book. If a Negro student has any social life, it is sponsored through someone of his own race.... College life including sorority and fraternity dances, open houses, beauty contests... cheerleading, and being a majorette excludes the Negro student.

Apparently senior students had fewer complaints about their instructors than junior ones. A senior remarked that instructors had become less prejudiced since the Civil Rights Act of 1965, whereas a junior commented that he couldn't help thinking 'that the man behind the desk hates to see me succeed in life'. Most of the students interviewed had done well at high school, where they had had trust in their teachers, but had lost confidence in themselves after coming to university, where they did not have the same trust in their instructors. The article concluded that since desegregation in 1959 the university had 'made a great transition'. Although many of the black students complained, 'they realised the situation will be better in the future'. What comes through most strongly in the report is the persistence of prejudice and, indeed, discrimination.

Life was very different both for long-established black leadership figures such as George W. Lee, proponent of the Beale Street project, and black judge Thurgood Marshall, nominated by President Johnson to the United States Supreme Court in June 1967, and for the young middle-class blacks celebrated in the pages of *Ebony*—within the framework of a society in which de facto discrimination was still strong, they were quietly achieving material success and, up to a point, recognition scarcely thinkable ten years previously. A. Miceo Walker was the son of a black doctor turned businessman, and had become president and chairman of the two companies

517

founded by his father, Universal Life Insurance Company and Tri-State Bank of Memphis, both of which, he said, were proud to be 'run by Negroes for Negroes'. He had been the first black to hold a substantial position in Memphis city government (on the Memphis Transit Authority) in 1961; the following year he became the first black to serve on the board of the main Memphis charitable organization, the Shelby United Neighbors. Both Walker and his wife had life memberships of the NAACP, and had participated in the sit-ins at segregated restaurants in the early sixties. Now he was coming to the attention of national government, and in 1964 he headed a US trade delegation to Mali. In 1966 he was invited to a White House dinner in honour of the president of Israel. Walker was then reported as being

> optimistic about the future for Negroes. In his life insurance business he now finds himself competing with white companies seeking Negro employees. But when he was graduated in 1935 from the University of Michigan with a Master's Degree the only jobs open to him in the white companies involved 'sweeping floors, pushing brooms'.[69]

Some middle-class blacks, then, were doing pretty well, while things were still changing only slowly for lower-class ones, who were not necessarily highly impressed by the achievers. According to Sally Belfrage, blacks in Mississippi considered the Revd Jesse Jackson and other middle-class blacks 'snobby', while SNCC workers referred to Martin Luther King as 'De Lawd'.[70]

The idea that there should, from the late fifties onwards, have been a steady, peaceful evolution of race relationships, but that instead there was in the mid-sixties a shocking unravelling of this ideal, is to misread the deeper realities. The extreme violence in Watts was no aberration, but the product of circumstances which had been growing increasingly explosive for at least a generation. A sizeable black community had begun to develop at the time of America's entry into the First World War in 1916, in the area then known as Mud Town; with the great influx of black migrants from the South during and after that war, this community spread along Central Avenue. During the era of intensive social investigation between the wars, Watts was logged as an appalling slum, and much written about. However, in the great boom of the Second World War and after, and the consequent expansion of Los Angeles, this slum was rather lost sight of, creating, as a knowledgeable survey of 1965 pointed out, the illusion that Los Angeles had no serious 'race problem' and was still a much better city in this respect than Chicago or New York. In the post-1945 period blacks had been flocking into Los Angeles at the rate of 2,000 a month; now the rate was 1,000 a month.

In its levels of deprivation, Watts rivalled the slums of southern Memphis: none of the thirteen elementary schools had cafeterias, since their pupils simply could not afford to eat; some children were not enrolled in the schools at all, since they had no shoes. We have also noted in Memphis the increasing attention concerned citizens were giving to the problem of police brutality towards blacks. It was police action which initiated the Watts riots. On 11 August 1965 one Marquette Frye (black, of course) was charged for alleged drunken driving. When his mother and brother protested, they were arrested too, and Marquette Frye was beaten up by the police. A

518

crowd of two hundred quickly gathered and started hurling stones. That night a crowd of 1,000 assembled; but there was no serious violence till twenty-five squad cars came screaming in. The traditional leaders of the Los Angeles black community tried to organize a mass meeting in the local open space, Athens Park: this turned into a denunciation of police brutalities and, by a fairly straightforward process, led to the crowds spilling out along 103rd Street, in the heart of Watts, where store windows were smashed and looting took place.[71] Jerry Furber of the Non-Violent Action Committee based within the ghetto itself wrote:

> By this second night the people of Watts were in possession of a good deal of their own community. People were proud. The overall mood was joyful. The looting itself was done with joy but it was no joke. They wanted that food.[72]

It was on this night that the comedian Dick Gregory, a civil rights activist, spoke to the rebels through a police loudspeaker. His appeals to go home were ignored. A stray bullet grazed his thigh.[73]

On Friday 13 August the arson attacks began. In one sector 3,000 local residents were confronted by 9,000 armed police. Groceries, liquor stores, and overturned cars burned unchecked in an eight-block area along Avalon Boulevard. Police admitted that the situation was completely out of control. All fire engines and ambulances were ordered to keep out of the area because they were liable to be immediately attacked by the rampaging mobs. All whites, apart from police and firemen, were warned to keep clear of the ghetto. As fires blazed from 41st Street to 108th Street, and all of south-east Los Angeles was covered in a pall of smoke, the National Guard were called in. Around 9.45 p.m. on 13 August 2,000 national guardsmen arrived. The catch phrase of a local disc jockey, 'Burn, baby, burn!', became the popular slogan of rebellion. The quoted remark of Police-Chief Parker managed to concentrate into one short sentence the essence of the generations of prejudice which had given rise to the crisis in the first place: 'Somebody threw a rock, and then, like monkeys in a zoo, everybody else started throwing rocks.'[74] The following day (14 August) Los Angeles was proclaimed a disaster area, and an 8.00 p.m. curfew was imposed. Generally, white reactions were uncomprehending. To the *Los Angeles Times*, 'There are no words to express the shock, the sick horror, the first grim order of business is to put down what amounts to civil insurrection, using every method available.'[75] Governor Brown declared (his notion of a 'we-them' relationship being most illuminating): 'Here in California we have a wonderful working relation with the Negroes. We got along fine till this happened.'[76]

On the evening of 16 August Brown declared that the riot was over, and on 17 August the curfew was lifted. Altogether 34 people died, 600 buildings were destroyed or severely damaged, and 4,200 arrests were made. The whole of south-east Los Angeles, an area of 50 square miles, was affected, and there were lesser riots in nearby Pasadena, Long Beach, and San Diego—the total estimated damage to white shop owners being $40 million. Even when the riot was supposed to be over, the police, on 17 August, mounted an attack on a Muslim mosque. Martin Luther King came, but his assertions that the devastation at Watts marked a setback for the civil rights movement was not well received: local blacks felt that, in drawing attention to themselves so dramatically, they had won a victory.[77]

A *Los Angeles Times* reporter had already reported two things shouted at him when he entered the area on 13 August. From a teenage girl: 'White man, you started all this the day you brought the first slave to this country' From a man: 'It's too late white man. You had your chances. Now it's our turn.'[78] The moderate left-wing weekly *Nation* summed up thus:

> Now at last Watts has recovered its social identity. Those who say that the riots have set the civil rights movement back—that they have left permanent scars, etc.— simply do not know the history of big-city based riots. The sad fact is that most race riots have brought some relief and improvement in race relations and the Los Angeles riots will not be an exception... Now that the community knows once again that Watts exists, it will begin to pay some attention to its problems.[79]

The citizens of Watts had made their protest, drawn attention to themselves. Federal money was channelled into the area, though, because of the growing demands of the Vietnam war, not nearly as much as Governor Brown requested; the main emphasis was placed on job training and self-help. In July 1968 the *Los Angeles Times* boasted that 'in the 40 square miles of Los Angeles where there were fires in the summer of 1965, there are now more than 300 social agencies', not mentioning that there had been further rioting in the middle of March 1966, when two people were killed.[80] Within the local context material conditions were slightly improved, some of the worst deprivations remedied; but the essential nature of ghetto life, as being different from that of mainstream America, remained, and even, with the large-scale advent of drugs, worsened. Within the national scene Watts played a small part in the overall reworking of race relations which, for all the continuing inequalities, did bring blacks to a very different position from the one they had been in throughout the sixties so far.

Similar comments could be made about the large number of smaller riots which took place in the summer of 1966, and, with greater force, about the major riots of 1967. Above all, the riots made impossible the maintenance of comfortable myths about racial harmony. This was particularly true of the September 1966 riots in Atlanta:

> Here is a city where one third of the population is Negro, where schools were peacefully integrated, where the police department has many Negro officers and where business has gone the extra mile to offer employment opportunities to Negroes. It is a city regarded as a Mecca for Negroes living in the less-advantaged areas of the South and for the past few years they have flocked into Atlanta to live.[81]

But, screamed the headline, 'Racially Calm City Suddenly Finds Hate Outburst'. Some of the blame was placed on SNCC's 'new leader', Stokely Carmichael, 'who commutes between Lowndes County Alabama, and the second floor of 360 Nelson Street, S.W. in the midst of Atlanta's trouble zone', and who 'can assemble large and dangerous crowds of reckless demonstrators'. But the deeper cause, the newspaper recognized, lay in 'the slums' of the south-east and south-west, 'an area left adrift and gaunt by old age and a new expressway system that meanders like spaghetti through the section'. The immediate cause was a very familiar one: 'Atlanta Police Officers on a routine search for law breakers, spotted a Negro wanted for car theft. They gave chase. He ran. They shot. And the trouble was on.'[82]

Before moving to 1967 and the urban riots in Newark and Detroit, I want to examine a series of interrelated events between late 1965 and the autumn of 1966 straddling North and South (specifically Chicago and Mississippi) within which were implicated some crucial issues and matters of controversy, both then and subsequently. Was segregated housing a bastion of racism over which ordinary white families could never yield? Could Martin Luther King's methods of non-violent protest be applied in the northern ghettoes? Was his Chicago Movement a failure, and a brilliant victory for Chicago's Mayor Daley, his ethnic white clients (Poles, Italians, Irish), and his Democratic party machine? Could a Freedom March now take place unmolested in Mississippi? Was segregation and 'black power' now the only recourse for blacks?

The Chicago Movement had its origins in a campaign launched in 1963 by the local Coordinating Council of Community Organizations (CCCO) against what in practice was segregation in Chicago's schools. The Southern Christian Leadership Conference was anxious to institute action in the North, particularly against housing segregation and appalling ghetto conditions, hoping thereby to provoke federal initiatives. As King remarked, 'there are more Negroes in Chicago than in the whole state of Mississippi'[83]— in fact one million out of the city's total population of three and a half million. CCCO and SCLC came together in the Chicago Movement, planned in the autumn of 1965 and kicked into motion when, on 26 January 1966, King took up residence in Chicago's West Side ghetto, announcing on 29 January that he would lead a rent strike if landlords did not undertake immediate improvements. King deliberately sought the support of black teenage gangs and of Black Muslim leader Elijah Muhammad for his nonviolent tactics; but he was unable, amid the nihilism of the endless northern ghettos, to arouse the kind of religious fervour which had been so potent in smaller southern towns. More, he had to face the power and cunning of Daley and his black henchman, Congressman William L. Dawson. Throughout his political career Daley received 77.4 per cent of the black vote. Daley did not provoke confrontation as southern bigots had done, but instead announced his agreement with King's principle, declaring that there was no segregation in Chicago and that housing improvements were constantly being carried out.

The failure of the Chicago Movement to secure the spectacular success King desperately wanted should not blind us to the fact that Daley did force the landlords to carry out some improvements. However, by June the Movement was certainly being openly criticized, even by leading SCLC members. King was actually based in Atlanta when James Meredith, of 'Ole Miss' fame, set out on 5 June on a Freedom March from Memphis to Jackson. On 6 June a white Mississippian emptied a load of shotgun pellets into his back. Meredith was taken to Memphis Municipal Hospital, where he agreed with King, Stokely Carmichael of SNCC, and Floyd McKissick of CORE that the march should be continued. The NAACP, the Urban League, and many white individuals also became involved. By threatening to withdraw, King prevented

Carmichael from turning the march into an all-black one; for their part Roy Wilkins (NAACP) and Whitney Young (Urban League) did withdraw, over a manifesto, drawn up by Carmichael and McKissick, totally critical of American society and of the government. When the march reached Greenwood a new slogan, 'Black Power', was chanted for the first time. Short only of the slogan, the basic, separatist, uncompromisingly revolutionary ideas of Black Power had, prior to his murder in Harlem on 21 February 1965, been elaborated by Malcolm X, first as a Black Muslim, then as founder of the Organization for Afro-American Unity. At the final demonstration in Jackson on 27 June, the 'Black Power' slogan dominated, though King persevered with the language of integration and non-violence. If one can ever identify a 'correct' course, it surely was that of King and his colleagues, a course which required, and was accorded, uncommon forbearance and uncommon bravery. But it is not appropriate, it seems to me, for white historians to criticize the general, and actually rather diffuse, Black Power movement (as distinct from individual excesses) for, allegedly, bringing about 'schism' and 'unravelling'. In existing circumstances Black Power was an understandable response, and Black Power proponents made measurable contributions to the attack on self-evident evils. Their ultimate cause (where they really had one) was unreal (like several other causes of the sixties): they were right to oppose integration when that really meant assimilation; they failed to see that in the end the only way is that of integration in the form of multiculturalism.

King went back to Chicago determined, first, to create a mighty interracial coalition of blacks, the churches, and white liberals, and second, to use that coalition to create almighty disruptions in the ordinary life of the city of Chicago. He suffered two immediate setbacks. The rally on 'Freedom Sunday', 10 July, to inaugurate the new highly militant campaign was a disappointment, with 40,000 participants rather than the 100,000 hoped for. A couple of days later a violent two-day riot broke out in the west side, in which two people were killed. Daley put the blame on King. However, the two did share a press conference at which it was announced that black youths would be allowed to use fire hydrants to cool themselves in the heat of the ghetto, and that swimming pools would be built. Again, gains which are not negligible. But to refocus attention on the major issues, King decided to move his demonstrations into the white communities. The white denizens, some waving confederate flags, were so violent in their responses that they were actually subject themselves to clubbings by Daley's police forces— something which had considerable shock value for television audiences, generally disposed to believe that the police were always justified in whatever actions they took. Daley successfully obtained an injunction against further marches (within his jurisdiction of Cook County). King announced that he would lead a march to neighbouring Cicero, once home of Al Capone, and where in May 1966 a black teenager seeking employment there had been beaten to death by white youths.

Desperate to avert the inevitable bloodshed, Daley convened a 'summit' with King and his associates, the Chicago real estate board, the Chicago housing authority, and the business community: open housing was not only to be implemented, it was to be positively encouraged. King called the march off. Two hundred SNCC and CORE militants persisted (on 4 September) but, though given the protection of 3,000 national guardsmen, were forced by stone-throwing white mobs to retreat. The 'summit' promises did not amount to much, though they were something, and they were built upon through direct black boycotts along the lines of the southern ones we have already noted. King's major aim had been to stimulate federal housing legislation. In fact the 1966 Open Housing bill was talked out—Democrat politicians blaming urban riots and Black Power, southern obstructionism actually being rather more responsible. A much stronger Fair Housing Act became law on 10 April 1968. Taking a balanced view, as James R. Ralph Jr. has done in his recent exhaustive study of the topic, one is surely right to conclude, as he has done, that King's Chicago Movement was very far from the failure it is often represented as being.[84]

In the riots in Newark, New Jersey, which broke out on 13 July 1967 and lasted five days, twenty-three people were killed, 1,200 injured, and 1,300 arrested. Two characteristics stood out. The rioters themselves seemed remarkably disciplined, singling out white-owned businesses for attack, but avoiding burning them, since the upper rooms in the wooden buildings were generally occupied by black families. The second feature was a complete lack of discipline among the national guardsmen, who behaved in a completely trigger-happy fashion. Police Director Dominick Spina, it should be noted, attempted in vain to maintain the counsels of measured judgement. When on 15 July a guardsman fired suddenly at a man near an apartment window, a hundred other guardsmen jumped into readiness, assuming there must be a sniper. Spina exploded: 'Do you know what you just did? You have now created a state of hysteria.' Remaining on hand for three hours, Spina maintained an atmosphere of calm. Thereafter guardsmen and state troopers began firing on apartment buildings, killing a mother of four and a grandmother. Shortly afterwards a young woman, pulling her 2-year-old daughter away from the window, was also shot dead. Out of the total death toll, six were women, two were children, and one was a 73-year-old man. It was only when the guardsmen were withdrawn that the riots came to an end.[85] Black writer, poet, and militant community organizer Le Roi Jones stated:

> We understand that this unrest was a retaliation against the forces of oppression, brutality and legalised evil that exist within the city of Newark and that we citizens have the right to rebel against an oppressive, illiterate governmental structure that does not even represent our will. We will rule Newark or no one will! We will govern ourselves or no one will![86]

Le Roi Jones, naturally enough given his own ideological position, exaggerated the extent to which the riot was an organized rebellion. Although the rioters did show considerable discipline, there was much of the inevitable looting, and of the usual sense of events progressing under their own momentum. Unusually, there was no particular trigger. Race relations were not good in New Jersey, and resentment had accumulated over slum clearance and redevelopment programmes which destroyed black communities and left blacks to fend for themselves in ever more overcrowded slums. There was also a strong copycat element in New Jersey, with smaller riots breaking out in various other cities.[87]

Detroit, like Atlanta, had been thought to be a model city with respect to race relations. It had long been the northern city with the biggest southern-born black population, and there had been a notorious racial riot in 1943 in which twenty-four blacks and ten whites had died. Deliberate attempts at integration had been made thereafter. During the riots elsewhere in the summers of 1964, 1965, and 1966, Detroit remained unscathed; deservedly so, many thought. As a centre for prostitution, 12th Street was the kind of potential trouble spot that existed in most cities. But it was also an area in which many ordinary blacks lived, and they were increasingly blaming the police for not doing more to control the nuisance, particularly in so far as it entailed an influx of white clients. The police department was beginning to intervene when a rumour began to circulate that they had beaten up a prostitute and her pimp (possibly the rumour had been started by pimps). On 1 July 1967 a prostitute was shot, allegedly by two plain-clothes vice-squad officers. In this heated atmosphere of rumour and counter-rumour the actual riot was triggered by a police raid on a property formally registered as the United Community League for Civic Action, but in effect a well-known 'blind pig', that is to say an illegal after-hours drinking den, frequented by blacks. This place had actually been checked out first by a black vice-squad officer. The raid met considerable resistance, but eventually the police took eighty-two prisoners, being pelted with bottles as they drove off. The raid had begun at 3.45 a.m. on Sunday 23 July. Window-smashing, looting, arson began almost immediately; and there was what appeared to be rifle fire. The first victim was Krikor Messerlian, an immigrant shoemaker clubbed to death in the street by looters in full view of many onlookers.[88] It does no good to pretend that black mobs could not at times be viciously brutal.

A state of public emergency was declared, a curfew imposed, and national guardsmen and state troopers brought in. At 12.25 a.m. the following day (Monday 24 July) a 45-year-old white man was shot by a white store owner, allegedly for looting. Then a 23-year-old white woman was shot, by whom it was not then clear. At 4.00 a.m. next morning a 23-year-old white man was shot by a guardsman, allegedly for sniping. In Watts and Newark the rioters had singled out white businesses; in Detroit, perhaps in some perverse tribute to the more integrated nature of that city, there was no pattern, simply total anarchy in which black businesses and black homes were burned down with white ones. Middle-class blacks, careful in other cities to distance themselves from such untoward events, joined in the looting; children joined in the general fun. The national guardsmen fanned the flames in the usual way, but were quite overwhelmed. On 25 July the state governor, George Romney, requested the assistance of federal forces; 4,700 more troops were brought in. The destruction had been appalling: forty-three dead, 7,000 arrested, 1,300 buildings destroyed, and 2,700 businesses looted.[89]

Immediately after the Detroit riot, an account of it was published by Hubert J. Locke, administrative assistant to the Detroit Police Commissioner.


### The Fourth Day, Wednesday

... four years old at the time of her death, Tanya Blanding was huddled in the living room of a second floor apartment... in the heart of the original riot area... Sporadic sniper fire had been reported in the immediate area earlier in the evening and on the previous night. Guardsmen reported one of their units coming under fire... and believed they had

524

pinpointed it as coming from the apartment in which Tanya and her family lived. Precisely what happened next is unclear; apparently as a Guard tank was being moved into position directly in front of the building, one of the occupants of the building apartment lit a cigarette. Guardsmen opened fire with rifles and the tank's .50-calibre machine gun. At 1.20 a.m. Tanya Blanding was dead.[90]

It was subsequently established that there were no civilian snipers; the police were actually being shot at by inexperienced national guardsmen. Again the escalating consequences of the indiscriminate use of rifles and pistols is demonstrated. Though he is trying to defend the police, Locke shows how incredibly casual the police were in the use of firepower. The firepower is unbelievably excessive in the case of the little girl who was killed. [91]

The Louis Harris organization conducted an opinion poll in the aftermath of Newark and Detroit. Both whites and blacks expressed support for public works programmes as a means of ameliorating conditions in the ghettos.

> In addition white people also showed a greater willingness than they did a year ago to lower the bars to Negroes in public eating places, movie theatres, use of public rest rooms, patronising the same clothing stores and in other areas of the exercise of personal rights. 58 per cent of all Negroes and 49 per cent whites believe Negroes are the chief victims of the riots.[92]

The cost had been appalling, but there clearly was a case here that the riots had brought the black cause, and the need for white responses, to the attention of whites. That the riots had harmed the civil rights cause was believed by 89 per cent of whites and 60 per cent of blacks. In identifying the main reason for the riots, 45 per cent of the whites opted for 'outside radical agitators', but 40 per cent referred to the 'way Negroes have been treated in the slums and ghettos'. Both blacks and whites 'agree that Negro hatred for whites was less a cause of the outbreaks than Negro frustrations over lack of progress on jobs, education and housing'. By more than two to one blacks identified police brutality as a major cause, while whites disagreed to the extent of eight to one. At the same time imitation, or perhaps emulation would be a better word, and suggestion, conveyed by word of mouth and local news reports, had undoubtedly been a subsidiary factor in all of the disturbances. Immediately the Newark riots broke out, there were disturbances in other New Jersey cities—Plainfield, Patterson, Jersey City, Inglewood. Immediately after the first outbreak in Detroit there was rioting in Grand Rapids, Flint, Pontiac, Saginaw, and Toledo.

Much of the conventional wisdom was that blacks were simply harming themselves, and that militant leaders were betraying their followers. The condemnation by Martin Luther King, Roy Wilkins, Whitney M. Young Jr., and A. Philip Randolph of 'killing, arson, looting', and the implied criticism of Black Power leaders Stokely Carmichael and H. Rap Brown, was widely quoted. The essence was captured by the government's own national advisory commission on civil disorders, chaired by Governor Otto Kerner of Illinois. In its report the Commission warned that 'our nation is moving toward two societies, one black, one white—separate but unequal'.[93] It referred to the 'squalor and deprivation in ghetto neighborhoods', and condemned the insensitivity, ineptitude, and sheer indifference to human life displayed by officials, and particularly the police:

> What white Americans have never fully understood—but what the Negro American can never forget—is that white society is deeply implicated in the ghetto. White institutions created it, white institutions maintain it, and white society condones it.[94]

The commission concluded that 'programmes on a scale beyond anything hitherto envisaged were vital: there must be a commitment, compassionate, massive, and sustained, backed by the resources of the most powerful and the richest nation on this earth.'

Striking evidence of the positive consequences of the riots in changing minds among whites appeared in an article by successful businessman and mayor of St Louis, Alfonso J. Cervantes:

> A few years ago, when I was an executive of several companies and a member of the board of directors of various others, I devoutly maintained these puritan tenets:
>
> • Poverty is the result of indolence; anyone who really *wants* a job can obtain one.
> • The poor we will always have with us.
> • Businessmen should commit themselves to making money, politicians to saving the cities, do-gooders to saving the disadvantaged, and preachers to saving souls.
>
> But since then, as Mayor of one of the older mid-western cities, a great deal of my time has been spent figuring out ways to find employment for the thousands of St. Louisans who belong to minority groups... Observing the riots of Watts (and now Newark, Detroit, and other Harlems throughout the country) has converted me to an updated social orthodoxy.
>
> Because of new exposures and later-day revelations, I now devoutly hold—even see in a new vision—that it is primarily up to industry, and not to government, to upgrade the disadvantaged, to provide training for the unemployed, to break down the complexities of job components, to employ the willing to make them able, to push for social betterment, to dissolve the ghettos, to break through the vicious circle of welfareism, to integrate the poor into an affluent economy, and to rebuild the cities—all within the framework of private enterprise and meaningful democratic government.[95]

This is individualistic and entrepreneurial—central elements in sixties thinking—but it expresses a clear change in attitude. Its importance as a source is enhanced both through its publication in a highly influential business journal and by the fact that the clipping I have used is to be found among the papers of former Memphis Mayor Edmund Orgill.

The positive shock to white consciences is not to be gainsaid, but the more apparent immediate outcome was a paralysing sense of crisis. The deputy director of the federal community relations service, George W. Culberson, was clearly a knowledgeable and sensitive man. While recognizing that rioting did gain attention for blacks, and perhaps even some temporary gain, he felt that the total effect was devastating in that it increased hostilities and polarized the differences between whites and blacks. He recognized the need to deal with housing, education, and unemployment, but foresaw no quick results. The fact was that no vast sums were forthcoming, and the main tangible outcome was a sense of foreboding and crisis. In the early spring of 1968 a left-wing journal was already recording (with scarcely any exaggeration) a universal expectation that the summer of that year would be devastating:

> The Long Hot Summer of 1968 opened, unseasonably, early in March in Omaha, Nebraska. It was a bush league effort as racial disorders go—one dead, some windows smashed, a few cars stoned. As might have been expected, the sole fatality was a Negro youth, sixteen-year-old Howard Stevenson, felled by a white police officer's shotgun blast. *The New York Times* ran the story on page 30 and some newspapers didn't bother with it at all. Perhaps they decided that bigger, better riots would soon be making demands on their space.[96]

What populist politicians say in their speeches offers one kind of guide to opinion among their constituents; an even better one is to be found in the letters constituents send to their elected representative. I am going to conclude this chapter about growing turbulence in the years prior to 1968 with one quotation from a speech by a southern Democratic congressman mocking northern civil rights supporters now that their cities were being put to the torch, two quotations from the middle American constituents of a Los Angeles congressman, and a fifth—the one inspiring one in this collection—from a 14-year-old girl.[97] But that I must, finally, balance against a verse being chanted by still younger children in working-class Chicago.

Here is a Mississippi Democrat addressing the House of Representatives on 25 July 1967:

> Even now, some of you are accusing us of starving the Negro people to death, all at a time when the colored in your own areas are burning you to the ground. You have more trouble with this issue in one Northern State than you will find in all of the South combined. Some of you who have made Southern civil rights junkets to get your pictures made and be seen on television are sitting on this floor at this moment. And you are as quiet as the grave... In fact I do not seem to be seeing any of these civil rights experts from the Department of Justice or the Congress headed for Detroit, for Newark, for Spanish Harlem, for Cambridge MD, or one of the other scores of cities now burning from riotous racial conduct.

The first of my Los Angeles constituents had enlisted in the navy for four years in the 1920s, and had served throughout the Second World War. His letter is dated 16 August:

> My love for my country is still real and active—I am convinced that the rioting, burning,

looting and sniping over the past few years, and especially of recent weeks, will certainly destroy our nation... I feel the best deterrent to crime is swift and sure punishment... I believe that the constitutional rights of the criminal are being used to destroy our Nation because they are being so regarded that the rights of the good citizen are disregarded and crime is made to pay—for the criminal!

The writer concludes that although he has always considered the (racist) ex-governor of Alabama, George Wallace, 'the most unqualified candidate possible', he is now 'beginning to wonder' if he 'would be the one who could and would help'.

'I think', began the second letter, of 1 August 1967,

it is high time that the Federal Government do something about the riot situations which are taking place in most all of the major cities of this grand country of ours today. It appears to me that the negro race seems to have developed a minority complex and believe the only manner in which they can gain recognition is by breaking laws and, in general, acting as though they had just emerged from the jungle last week. I believe that if something radical in the way of laws are not instituted shortly and enforced with dispatch, you will see the greatest civil war between the whites and blacks this country could ever dream of... My forebears came from a minority group, but gained recognition by hard work, study, and responsibility.

The writer had an Irish name.

The 14-year-old's letter of 8 May 1967 ranks with the interview with the French student I quoted earlier in this chapter, and with the Freedom Fighter interviews in Chapter 5, as testimony to the hope-inspiring learning processes taking place in the sixties and presaging the advent of multiculturalism:

As a citizen of the United States I am very concerned over the Civil Rights down South and even in San Francisco. During the previous years several unpleasant incidents have been brought to my attention... Negroes are murdered and their murderers are released with no charge... The people of San Francisco are separated into two main areas. The Negroes live in a ghetto-type area. At the school that I go to there is not one Negroe *[sic]*. These conditions do not sound very like the United States to me. Isn't there something that can be done to help smoothe *[sic]* matters out?

But, alas, in 1965 little white girls in Chicago had learned new words to chant as they jumped over their skipping ropes:

I'd like to be an Alabama trooper,
That's what I'd truly like to be

528

'Cause if I were an Alabama trooper,
I could kill the niggers legally.[98]

Segregation had been 'broken', but it was still flailing about it with all the venom and viciousness of a creature grievously wounded. Politicians, pundits, and people were right to expect 'a
new round of escalation in the racial war'. But, as it turned out, students were to be in the van of
the events of 1968 and 1969.

# 12

# 1968 (and 1969)

*1968: A Date to Remember?*

1968 is always remembered as the historic year. May 1968 is always remembered as the historic month. Indeed, for that one month events in France, and particularly in Paris, echoed great historic moments of the past, 1789, 1830, 1848, 1870. Carrying reminders too of 1936 (the year when the election of the leftist Popular Front government was reinforced by a wave of worker occupations of the factories), May 1968 seemed to almost all observers to hold the promise of definitive change in government and society: politicians expected the end of the Gaullist regime, students and radicals expected a root-and-branch reformation of society, for it did appear that in universities, in theatres, in factories, in the offices of professional societies, the representatives of the alternative society were taking power. It was all over rather quickly in France; in a hastily organized general election the French people edged slightly to the right, rather than swinging sharply to the left; de Gaulle and his conservative regime were confirmed in power. But for a brief period the existing system had been brought to a halt by the combined action of students and workers.

However, it was not quite like that anywhere else. What characterized 1968 was the wide geographical spread of student activism affecting Japan and the Iron Curtain countries as well as the West, not the imminence at any point of revolution: this study is confined to four countries, but we shall have to glance at events in Germany. In the United States, while there were renewed troubles in Berkeley, some of the most shocking episodes took place at the hitherto relatively unaffected, highly respectable Columbia University in New York. From early in 1968 there were links between Italian workers' strikes and student activism, though this never brought the paralysis which briefly affected France. On the other hand, Italian industrial militancy gathered strength right through 1969, creating what was dubbed 'the hot autumn' *(l'autunno caldo)* and in effect eclipsing student activism. So, on the wide view we have 'events' spreading through from November 1967 to late 1969: what happened within a shorter space in France left more traces than it is now fashionable to recall, though these traces are faint enough compared with the elephant tracks left by all the innovations and new beginnings since around 1958. If Britain suffered what were mainly 'echoes from the storm'—though heads *were* broken, and blood *was* shed (a little)— in part this was because British students already possessed many of the liberties and amenities being demanded elsewhere; and military service had long since ended. France, throughout the sixties, had had the most rigid and authoritarian government: elsewhere in Europe, politics was characterized by 'openings to the left', but in Italy (and Germany) formation of coalitions between 'bourgeois' and 'socialist' parties simply added yet one further source of anger. In Britain similar anger was aroused by the moderate policies of the Wilson Labour government, while in America President Johnson forfeited all the credit he ought to have received for his 'Great Society' reforms because of the Vietnam war: rage against the Democratic party organization climaxed in the riots accompanying the Democratic party convention in Chicago at the end of August 1968.

The notion of 1968 as a pivotal year received its final endorsement from events in Czechoslovakia: the 'Prague spring', Alexander Dubcek's liberalization of the grim Communist regime, followed by the crushing Soviet invasion in August 1968. There were some contacts between the Prague students and protest movements elsewhere, but effectively these movements were independent of developments in East Europe, except insofar as they intensified the hatred Western student protesters already felt for Soviet Communism, equated, Marcusean style, with Western 'democratic totalitarianism'.

West Germany, and West Berlin, marooned in the middle of Communist East Germany, are important. Rudi Dutschke rivals Daniel Cohn-Bendit as student agitator-in-chief. Dutschke came from an East German Lutheran family and had moved to West Berlin just before the building of the Berlin Wall in August 1961. Here he enrolled at the Free University, itself founded in 1948 in a deliberate attempt to break with the traditional autocratic German university system dominated by overbearing professors, and in the sixties very much a centre of radical thought, both among the academics and among the students, particularly those who had come to the Free University to escape military service in West Germany. Dutschke was a charismatic leader, physically notable for his lean, mobile face and lick of black hair (as Cohn-Bendit was appropriately distinguished by his red hair), an energetic apostle of the idea that the apathetic public must be provoked by spectacular action into taking note of radical ideas about the rottenness of existing society. West Germany could with some justice be represented as the ultimate expression of the consumer society attacked by Marcuse: the very division of Germany could be blamed on bourgeois politicians; the older generation could readily be condemned as accessories to Nazism, while right-wing newspaper magnate Axel Springer manifestly personified bloated capitalist power; and the two regimes on the opposite sides of a divided Germany could be cited as prime examples of Marcuse's theories of convergence and the similarities between oppressive modern societies, whether theoretically capitalist or Communist. Marcuse himself came to the Free University in 1967: this was a significant stage in the transmission of his ideas to Europe via Germany.

The most effective student demonstrations were usually those with a single focal point, such as the visit of some foreign dignitary with, in the eyes of radical students, unclean hands. The incident which began the intensified phase of German student activism reminds us that to radical students there were many other instances of imperialism and international capitalism apart from the all-pervasive Vietnam war. At the end of May 1967 the Shah of Persia visited West Berlin. He was seen as a puppet of the West, as a protagonist of westernization and a suppressor of Iranian nationalism; and he had with him his own cohort of thugs to deal with hostile demonstrations. Television film of the demonstrations and marches, in which Dutschke was prominent, indicates that the violence was initiated by these alien mobsters.[1] There is some footage of the police intervening on the side of the demonstrators, but it was in fact a plain-clothes policeman who fired the shot which struck down a non-activist student, taking part in his first demonstration, Benno Ohnesorg. Ohnesorg was the first martyr of the student 'revolution'. His killing, together with the massive funeral march which followed, in the space of days initiated that process, to be found everywhere in 1968, whereby students with only vaguely leftist sentiments, or merely a slight uneasiness over the current events, were swept towards a more deliberate activism.

A year later there was another martyr but—what was much better—a martyr who survived. Dutschke had acquired a special notoriety when he delivered a speech against the Vietnam war at a Christmas Eve service in the Kaiser Wilhelm memorial church in Berlin, following which he was struck on the head by a member of the congregation with such force that he had to be taken to hospital. Few ordinary West Germans shared the perception expressed by thirty Evangelical pastors that Dutschke's action was analogous to that of Christ driving the money changers from the temple,[2] and Dutschke was in fact charged with 'severe disturbances of the peace'. Out riding on his bicycle, while awaiting trial, he was shot at by a disturbed individual called Josef Bachmann, and seriously wounded.

## Italy Hots Up: November 1967–April 1968

The three spheres of militant action were the universities, the factories, and the secondary schools. The student agitations in the different universities followed similar patterns, as did those in the schools. The factories, however, varied between the most traditional and the most high-tech, and the workers involved ranged from the most highly qualified to those exercising traditional skills, to assembly-line workers, to white-collar workers in the company offices. As the universities reassembled for the new academic year in November, trouble broke out immediately. At about the same time, though without any connection whatsoever, workers in the small town of Valdagno, near Venice, were engaging in a series of stoppages against the archaic working conditions imposed in the old-style textile factories owned by the Marzotto family. Nationwide, one of the main trade union federations, the CGIL, was contemplating the calling of a general strike in support of its claim for better pensions; belatedly the government offered negotiations, and this brought a suspension for the time being of the proposed strike.[3]

The fundamental grievance in the state universities was the proposed Gui Law, now back before parliament for final discussions and enactment. This was the issue to which the activists of the sociology faculty at the University of Trento, most notably 23-year-old Marco Boato, gave most prominence in declaring a student strike from the first day of term, 1 November; it was the issue which most students everywhere could most readily understand and identify with.[4] Equally important to the activists was the question of student power to control the organization and curriculum of the university, but they could always command wider support among their more moderate fellows by making specific demands for better amenities, and such innovations as the use of seminars in teaching, and the elimination of tests and 'exams' (in Italy no more than oral tests conducted by professors on a one-to-one basis, not formal written exams in the British sense). The more idealistic continued to harp on the theme of the socially loaded nature of the secondary schools, and of the way in which the road to university was closed off to working-class children.

The large Catholic university in Milan, the 'Cattolica', was independent of the state, and although many students and some staff had been affected by the notions of Catholic Marxism, it had been largely immune to the student agitations which had occurred sporadically throughout the sixties. But now the authorities there were proposing a sharp rise in fees. Here was an issue on which student anger could easily be aroused and one which also merged readily with the general critique of Italian higher education as being class-based and reserved for the privileged. On 18 November a student occupation of the Cattolica began; a leading figure was 23-year-old philosophy student Marco Capanna, a devout Catholic from a relatively humble background, very sensitive to existing social inequalities. Two other distinctive factors were in operation at the Cattolica. First, a considerable number of students were finding a Catholic regime particularly authoritarian and restrictive of personal liberties, and a Catholic curriculum unduly stifling and inattentive to the greater issues of the wider world. Secondly, the Cattolica had a high proportion of 'worker-students', students working during the day and taking classes in the evening. Higher fees would bear particularly heavily on them; at the same time their cause touched the consciences of the middle-class Catholic students who wished to express solidarity with the proletariat.[5]

The dean of the Cattolica at once brought in the police, who, it should be recorded, cleared the building with little violence, then closed the university. In a motion approved on 19 November 1967, the 'general assembly of students occupying the Cattolica' responded by expressing

> their contempt, pain and sense of affront to the human conscience, civil and Christian, at the behaviour of Authority in response to the occupation. In particular it protests over the massive police force brought in by Rector Franceschini, which was inconsistent with his position as a university rector. It also condemns the closing of the university which is in violation of the fundamental right students have of access to a university 'which also belongs to them'.

Now, gathered outside in the largo Gemelli, they further announced that they had decided to

533

remain in position in front of the university. They would continue 'the appropriate agitation right up to the moment when a new academic life is established'.[6]

In their manifesto against 'examinations', the Cattolica protesters made the following points:

1. Students have to eliminate their own point of view and faithfully repeat only the professor's opinions.
2. In exams students have to present themselves one by one, nervous and defenceless in front of the professor.
3. In fact students are often forced to resort to a series of tricks to put the professor in a good enough humour to pass them, making more use of their knowledge of the pet theories of the academic than a proper course of critical preparation.
4. The actual organization of the exams and the summoning of the students are done on a completely irrational basis.

Later, they described lectures as 'mechanical, without the option of student participation'.[7] The worker-students or *seriali* (evening students) were very much in the forefront of the agitation which led to the occupation of the Cattolica. As a document produced by one of the more traditionalist student unions, the *Unione Goliardica Italiana*, put it:

> The evening students felt that they were pushed out onto the margins of life at university. Just to give one example, they were deeply offended that the rector gave a talk 'to all students' every Wednesday at 3.30 when they were still at work.[8]

Third of the universities to suffer a strike or occupation before November was out, was Turin. On 27 November the university's most magnificent building, the Palazzo Campagna, was occupied. The student leaders at Turin, drawn from the faculties of letters, philosophy, education, law, and political science, were among the most consistent in advocating a new kind of university for a new kind of society, though one precipitating issue was actually the decision of the university administration, without consulting students, to relocate the faculty of science in the suburbs.[9] The occupation was described as being 'against the existing structure and against the structure proposed in Law 2314 [the Gui Law]'. The cyclostyled document produced by 'the Turin student movement' in early December, under the title 'What We Are Doing at the Palazzo Campagna', stated:

> The university should not be organized by courses (with each teacher a feudal title-holder), but by problems (for each problem a staff of qualified people who put their qualifications at the service of the students)...
>
> At Palazzo Campagna we have initiated a completely new teaching experience. The faculty assembly is divided into commissions (letters, philosophy, social analysis, education), each of these into subgroups. Each subgroup has chosen a debate relating to how the interests of the students in the subgroup converge (Vietnam, Latin America, the pedagogy of dissent, psychoanalysis, philosophy of science, the connections between

534

philosophy and culture, the relations between school and society, the different directions the law is taking—penal, civil, constitutional, philosophical).

The University remains a barony. With respect to this Law 2314 will not do. It would perpetuate the current structure of power within the university, that is the subjection of the students, the authoritarianism of the teachers, and the inadequacies of our education.

A document of 9 December on 'The Attitude of the Academic Body Towards our Occupation' described it as 'very hostile'. It claimed that over previous years the academics had expressed agreement in principle to requests for university reform, 'but when their own rights are touched even the most open professors become elusive'. The attitude of the professors was not perhaps totally surprising given the tone of another document entitled 'Didactics and Repression': the professors, their names set out in full, were accused of regarding themselves as having a secure stipend permitting them to concentrate entirely on their own private work. There was no link between research and teaching: 'research in our University means writing books and getting them published!', the insult being added that 'those books simply repeated other books'. Beyond the strong words were open threats of 'an action of force'.[10]

Across Italy there was, inevitably, an element of emulation; committed leaders of this rapidly consolidating student movement, too, travelled around; but grievances were real enough. Genoa followed Turin, then Naples in December, then other southern universities, so that by January practically all the Italian universities, including Rome, Florence, and Venice, were undergoing strikes or occupations. On 27 January came the first of the new wave of actions in the secondary schools starting with a pupil occupation of the Liceo Berchet.[11] Much of the action was sporadic, supported enthusiastically only by the minority of the deeply politically committed. There was a difference between strikes and occupations (strike—not turning up—did not become occupation—not going home—in Trento until 31 January). Strikes, while they might put academics and administrators out of countenance, were scarcely devastating in effect; occupations obviously directly challenged the authority of both academics and, above all, administrators; but they were not nearly so easy to sustain. In theory occupations were intended to provide students with the opportunity to debate the great issues of the day among themselves. But only the most dedicated relished staying in night after night—and failure to do this, as often happened, would lead to premises being reoccupied and students excluded. Furthermore, even activists often preferred to do other things, such as going out on demonstrations or holding joint meetings with other institutions. Faced with determined occupiers, the authorities had several possibilities. They could refuse to set examinations, though this was not unproblematic since the students themselves were protesting about the nature of examinations; they could declare all classes suspended and whole faculties or universities closed. The repercussions for male students could be serious in that lack of progress with studies could lead to loss of deferment and call-up into the army. Equally, the authorities could try negotiating with the students, though it must be said that most of the written student demands look more like calls for unconditional surrender than bases for negotiation. Even so, there was room for frank recognition that the students did have very many legitimate grievances. In fact, almost all of the rectors of the major universities, very far from following policies of measured judgement, themselves took up the most extreme positions and were all too ready to call in the police, when calling in the police inevitably meant that students would immediately be subjected to extreme brutality. It is clear from the documents that some student leaders, and some older figures from the extreme left, were, from the earliest stages, prepared themselves to resort to violence. On the other hand, it is the fact that, certainly throughout 1968, no attempts were made by student leaders to obtain firearms. Students began to wear helmets and to arm themselves with stones and staves, and began to organize in semi-military fashion. But this was all part of an evolving scene. It was the actions of the rectors, and then, more directly, of the police, which turned the situation which over December to January was patchy, and for the university authorities no doubt irritating but not particularly violent, into one characterized by clashes between students and police, where police clearly felt free to act with the utmost viciousness while, if student songs and slogans are anything to go by, students were themselves more and more rejoicing in the escalation of violence. I shall return to that.

At Turin the rector, Mario Allara, had no compunction about bringing in the police and calling for the strongest action against the student leaders: 'a small group of revolutionaries', he said, 'want to impose their insane and impractical ideas on me and 25,000 students—the principle of majority rule is flagrantly ignored.'[12] The police did clear the Palazzo Campagna and charges were brought against 487 of the activists. Of these, 95 were not actually students at the university—72 being from secondary schools or other colleges in Milan, 21 were graduates, most of them being junior lecturers, while two came from outside Turin. Of the genuine Turin students, 70 were studying philosophy, 58 literature, 57 architecture, 54 political sciences, 42 natural sciences, 37 education, 31 law, 20 engineering, 13 medicine, 8 economics, 1 agriculture, and 1 veterinary studies. Twelve students were imprisoned and held for several weeks under severe conditions, before, once again, the higher, more measured judicial authorities ordered their release on suspended sentence.[13]

The authorities at Genoa were uncompromising from the start. At 1.30 a.m. on 13 December 1967 police burst into the university to clear out the students in occupation there. Expressing outrage at this first violation of the university community, the students claimed that they were simply holding an electoral assembly, but now called upon the student body to turn this assembly 'into a permanent assembly of occupation'. The students also printed the less than wise comments of, respectively, the dean of the faculty of letters, and the rector himself:

> If you are not satisfied with any of the teaching which is imparted to you, you don't have to join the Faculty. You can be anarchists excluded from the University.
>
> Tomorrow you students will be the whited sepulchre *[lo scheletro]* of the nation.[14]

Apart from the Cattolica, whose students had proved surprisingly militant, Milan had two major state institutions, the university (known as 'the Statale'), housed in the magnificent sixteenth-century Grand Hospital, and the Politecnico, whose most important components were the architecture and engineering faculties—here students protested that they were being given a professional training designed purely to make them props of the capitalist system. In addition, for two years Milan had been a centre of provocative actions on the part of the Situationists and Provos, some of whom were students but many of whom were professional agitators and drop-outs of various sorts. When to all this is added the fact that Milan had the most vibrant secondary schools of the calibre of Berchet and Parini, it is not surprising that this northern centre of high fashion and high-tech industry became the hub of continuous agitation in the form of assemblies, occupations, and street demonstrations. The first occupation at the Statale took place in the faculty of medicine, anything but the bastion of conservatism that would usually be the case in Britain and America: medical education was a special scandal in Italy, with professors spending most of their time in their own luxury clinics rather than with their students, whose training was conducted under primitive conditions with antiquated equipment.[15] However, the radicals, though vociferous, were inevitably in a minority and a powerful group of right-wing medical students, calling themselves, revealingly, the Western Group of Medics, contended that the activists were simply subserving the interests of Russia and the Eastern bloc. Across the Statale faculties student leaders were putting forward the following demands: that academic and administrative councils should sit in public; that all students should have maintenance grants; that courses of study should be agreed between academics and students; that the assessment system should be reformed, including the abolition of certificates of attendance, and the granting of the right to discuss publicly and to contest marks awarded; the introduction of seminar teaching; finally, the withdrawal of all criminal charges against students who had been involved in public protests.[16]

Protests at Florence University culminated in the events of 30 January 1968, when students attempted to deliver their demands to the rector's office on the piazza San Marco, at the edge of the main university area in central Florence. The police were already there in considerable numbers and in what could quite reasonably be described as 'battle dress'. One group of students, in which members of the architecture faculty were strongly represented, wanted to storm the office, and took to flicking coins at the police. A more moderate group tried to restrain them. The police made no distinction between the two groups, or indeed between students and passers-by, when, without the legally prescribed forms of warning, they began their violent attack. As it happens, a photographer called Giovanni Spinoso took a series of photographs at around midday. They are fuzzy, but shocking. As 'the organization representing the University of Florence', who published the photographs put it, there was no need for written comment, though in fact an investigation by students and academic staff collected a series of important eye-witness statements. Strictly speaking, before ordering the attack, the chief of police should have donned the Sash of the Republic and called for warning trumpets to be sounded; as police charges against students became a regular occurrence, this formality was quickly forgotten. However, within the university, civilized standards were perhaps stronger in Florence than in some other places. A concordat between the rector and 'various sections of the university' was struck, though its vagueness in speaking of 'experiments' and 'improvements' was to leave the way open for greater troubles in the future as students claimed that no real reforms had been implemented. The faculty council gave its approval on 1 March. Throughout the agreement was bitterly contested by the architecture students, who saw it (not altogether without reason) as a sham and a sell-out.[17]

In Pisa, centre of action in early 1967, the new phase of demonstrations culminated towards the end of February.

> Pisan students have put at the centre of their general struggle the problem of the right to study... the first and specific objective... is that of income, in the sense of big increases in family supplements for all children up to the age of eighteen, and of grants direct to university students.

Even students from well-off families, the document explained, found it very difficult to make ends meet.[18]

By the end of February 1968 Italian newspapers were presenting the view that student troubles had entered upon a new dimension. The main headline in *Epoca* for 3 March was 'The Revolt of the Students'. Under the heading 'Why they are Rebelling?' *Epoca* explained that 'students are not demanding more reform or particular concessions: they want instead to liquidate totally the old university and affirm themselves as a new ruling class destined for power'. While *Epoca* and the right-wing press spoke of 'chaos', the left-wing press was beginning, in a phrase which was to be repeated over and over again, the talk of 'a student revolution from the Alps to Sicily'. *Epoca* identified the university cities where interventions by the police, and the use of violence, including rudimentary bombs, by students, had been most sustained: Turin, Milan, Pavia, Trento, Venice, Padua, Genoa, Bologna, Modena, Ferrara, Palma, Florence, Pisa, Sienna, Perugia, Rome, Naples, Lecce, and Messina. Italy, it said, 'is at peace, but the students consider themselves at war'.

> And their agitation, effectively, has the appearance of guerrilla warfare in the cities, of a systematic revolt against constituted authority. Why have we not been able to bring this state of affairs to an end? Why is a truce never possible? How many students are participating in the struggle? To reply to these questions we must among other things ask what the students want. And this is where the difficulty begins, given that their demands include everything: the methods of instruction and study, the construction of the new university, relations with the professors, the exam calendar, set books, the mode of conferring degrees, fees, the administration of funds, right up to the examination of global problems like the structure of society, the organization of the State and the exercise of political power.

The writer of the *Epoca* article, obviously not wishing to overstate the extent of the crisis, then turned to a couple of lighter stories, one about three Roman architecture students climbing to the top of the highest university building and joking with journalists. The second concerned the Communist mayor of Bologna, who took his 19-year-old daughter, a literature student, in his car so that she could participate in the occupation of the faculty of political sciences and

538

letters. The daughter was summonsed, and the mayor fined by his own local police for the illegal parking of his car outside the university. The account in *Epoca*, similar to ones given in the other illustrated magazines, is a good source for the way in which the student disturbances were presented to the public, and indeed for majority, liberal attitudes, involving a mix of puzzlement, sympathy, and hostility. On the whole it complements rather than contradicts what one derives from student documents. It brings out something of the self-righteousness and arrogance of certain of the student extremists but also their genuine desire to involve the majority of students—they did not conspire in secret. It is significant, with regard in particular to my general theme of measured judgement, that, after going on to refer to episodes of violence and confrontation, the *Epoca* article works round to stating the best parts of the student case; violence is represented as sporadic, not something to bring great concern to ordinary readers. The article then goes on to say that the responsibility 'does not entirely lie with the students'.

> To attend classes, squeezed in like sardines, students have to secure a place several hours in advance... University professors are accused of imparting an education which is old, out-dated and facile. They are called 'chair-holding barons' *[baroni in cathedra]*, 'snake charmers', or worse. They are declared 'blind and deaf' to the needs of modern society, guilty of wanting to perpetuate a 'closed caste', manipulating 'academic power' and the 'sources of profit', arising from the holding of funds and from the publication of text books... In the protest writings of the students, published on cyclostyled leaflets entitled *J'accuse*, or published in faculty news-sheets, there are burning accusations, perhaps exaggerated, but which it is not possible to laugh away...

Students at the University of Trieste, away out on the far north-eastern corner of Italy in the city whose ownership had been long contested with Yugoslavia, were very anxious to represent themselves as being involved in an Italy-wide student movement. Action came relatively late here, with the first occupation of the faculty of letters and philosophy taking place towards the end of February 1968. Trieste provides a good example of the way things developed on a campus where moderate student opinion was relatively strong. The students in occupation issued their justificatory statement on 26 February. Their main point was the general one, clearly derived from the protests at other universities, that 'the entire edifice of secondary and higher education is based on selection by class'. The Gui plan was then attacked as deliberately devised to reinforce this. Thirdly, the Trieste students said, occupation was the only means of struggle at their disposal, and one which expressed the rights of students to debate political issues. However, the same day a manifesto was issued by students opposed to the occupation. Their objections were very much to do with what they saw as violation of democratic processes, and the deployment of tactics which would not actually produce results. Very significantly, they were 'not in principle against the occupation'; the broad tolerance of moderates towards the principle of student action helps to explain how they too eventually found themselves swept up in more extreme action. The rector himself also issued a statement on that same 26 February, pointing out that the occupation had interrupted a dialogue between the university authorities and the properly qualified representatives from the official student organizations, and that those actually carrying out the occupation numbered no more than thirty—not, he pointed out, much more than 1 per cent of the total student population. The students, he insisted, must be out by nine o'clock the following morning. Showing a more conciliatory and less egocentric attitude than most of his fellow-rectors, he concluded with the remark that the university senate 'believes in the good sense of students'.[19]

The protesting students had no faith in the traditional student representative bodies and any negotiations they might have with university authorities (this is a feature common to all the 1968 movements), but looked for support to the wider world. In fact, the following day expressions of support came in from the trade union federations, CGIL, CISL and UIL, as also from the local executive of the United Socialist party and, most revealingly, from the Youth Movement of the Christian Democrats. The university senate then (28 February) took the very strong action which was actually far more likely to bring about the desired results than any resort to the police, and which in addition had a certain natural appeal to academics: all teaching, but not research, was suspended and, most crucially from the point of view of students with careers to consider, all exams and all awarding of degrees were also suspended. The immediate response of the occupying students was that such actions were 'illegal'; their number, they said, was actually 204, not a 'tiny minority', since they formed 'a majority of those who participate actively in faculty life'—an argument which obviously lay behind much of the militant action everywhere, though one which was not readily stated so publicly, since the leaders of the student movement liked to envisage it as a mass movement. The embattled 204 issued their *Carta*. Their demands were: free student choices with regard to topics studied; grants for *all* students; all academic staff to work full-time at the university; the introduction of seminars and individual and group study; the abolition of all marks and examinations, these being replaced by 'collective assessment'; recognition of departments rather than faculties as the fundamental units (in Britain at that time the new universities were doing the opposite, replacing departmental structures with interdisciplinary ones; the Italian students craved smaller units over which they would share power); university funds to be administered jointly with students; free access to rooms for student assemblies and meetings; courses detached from the particular interests of individual professors and given a critical function, including criticism of the university. In the final, eleventh point, block capitals were used to express the resentment of the radicals at the mocking criticisms which had been made of them: 'NONE OF THIS IS INFANTILE EXTREMISM, OR UTOPIANISM'—many of these points, they added, had already been conceded at Turin, Trento, and Venice. Some professors and teaching assistants issued their own manifesto supporting the student protesters, and denouncing what they termed the divisive action of the senate. At this point also, typical of the way in which protest tended to spread outwards, the local secondary school students issued their own *Carta*, demanding reform of authoritarian teaching methods, the right for all of study up to the age of 18, full-time employment for all teachers, reform of the state examination system, and pupil participation in all governing bodies, especially those relating to matters of discipline. Utopianism, if not exactly infantile extremism, reared its head in the most radical of their demands—the right to choose their own courses, involving discussion and debates over themes chosen by themselves, with *teachers participating as equals* (my emphasis).

On 1 March, the occupying students, who had not surrendered as requested by the rector, responded again to the two strongest points made against them. They rejected calculations as to legitimacy based on numbers: 'the force of the occupation does not lie in numbers, but in the validity of the theses on which the occupation is based.' And they rejected all existing student organizations, in particular the most important one at Trieste, the ORUG. This was the situation when events in Rome moved the student protests, whose more endearing and ambiguous characteristics had been well brought out by the *Epoca* article, into a new, more remorseless phase.

By late February the occupation of the faculty of letters at Rome was suffering severely from the inevitable wear and tear. It seemed to the students that they had gained one of their most important points. Ordinary, liberal-minded academics had accepted—how could they not?—that the so-called examination system was absurd, and had indicated their willingness to adopt open sessions which would meet the main objections of the students. Exams had in fact gone ahead in the faculty of letters in this way, which was one of the reasons for the run-down of the occupation. However, the rector of Rome University, Professor Pietro Agostino D'Avack, the prototype of all that was wrong in Italian universities, was not prepared to see students gaining a victory and establishing new precedents for the conduct of examinations. D'Avack first had a meeting with the more reactionary professors, then contacted the minister of public instruction, none other than Gui of the Plan; it was agreed that the examinations held under these new conditions would be annulled, and that the remaining occupants of the faculty of letters must be cleared out forthwith. At 1.30 p.m. on Thursday 29 February 1968 D'Avack, standing right in the centre of the university, used a loudspeaker to announce that he would not accept the reformed exam system, and that those continuing the occupation must desist immediately or be arrested. Within an hour 1,500 police and carabinieri were on the university site.[20]

For students looking simply for reform of the most obvious abuses within the system, this was a devastating blow. For the extremists it was a gift. Few students questioned that some kind of mass demonstration must be organized for the next day, Friday 1 March. Word went round that the initial meeting-place would be that spot favoured both by tourists and by the hippies and Beats of 1966 and 1967, the piazza di Spagna. By ten o'clock 4,000 had gathered, with many more on the way, secondary school pupils as well as university students. Questioned by journalists, the protesters did not seem to have any clear ideas as to where they were going from there. Basically, they needed a meeting-place to discuss responses to the latest provocative actions of the rector. Ever-active architecture students suggested another occupation of the architecture faculty, the Architettura. This is a modern classical building, pink and white, not quite as impressive as its site, high on a hill at the western edge of the park of the Villa Borghese. Two flights of about twenty steps lead up from the via Gramsci which, itself in parkland at this point, runs across the side of the hill, with quite a steep drop below to the via Belle Arti. Close beside the Architettura stands the elegant white marble British School at Rome, previously with the address via Gramsci 61, Gramsci being Italy's leading Marxist thinker of the twentieth century; but the short stretch of street outside had been more appropriately renamed and the address was now piazza Winston Churchill 5. On the other side, behind high railings across the via Gramsci, stands the fine modernist building of the Japanese Cultural Institute. This entire bosky enclave is known as the Valle Giulia. Many accounts of the momentous events which were to follow confuse the location (and sometimes even the date): there is no via Valle Giulia; the via Valle Giulio is a short distance away in the middle of the Villa Borghese park, while the via Giulia is a busy city street near the River Tiber. The Villa Giulia, also in the Villa Borghese park, is of course what it says, a villa (housing the archaeological museum), and the via Villa Giulia is the narrow lane leading to it from the via Flaminia (having collected much misinformation on these points from Roman waiters and barmen, I sometimes think I am the only person who knows these things). Only if one has the topography firmly in mind can one grasp the nature of what was to be known as the Battle of Valle Giulia. Still today, the painted slogan high up on the Architettura has not been completely obliterated; 'Police Get Out of the University' *(Via La Polizia dal'Università)*, though whether that particular version dates back to March 1968 or is from the encounters which continued into the early seventies I don't know.

Having at last decided where it was going, the procession marched north up the via Flaminia, turned east into the via Belle Arti, then forked left up the fairly steep hill of the via Bruno Duozzi. To get to the steps at the foot of the Architettura it was then necessary to turn right along the via Gramsci. Journalists reported that the march was orderly, flanked by police and press photographers, though hints that activists did have some deeper plans were apparent in the appearance for the first time of student stewards with green sashes on their arms. Small placards had appeared also: 'Student Power' and 'Police Get Out of the University'. Two small Fascist groups, Primula and Caravelle, attempted to attack the march, but were fairly easily repulsed. The via Gramsci was filled as the procession came to a stop at the steps leading up to the Architettura. Above, immediately in front of the entrance to the Architettura, stood several rows of the special force, the Celere, helmeted and with truncheons drawn.

The police stance was undoubtedly provocative; to students, they had no business standing in the entrance-way of a university building, preventing student access to that building. However, there can be no doubt that in this case it was the students who attacked first, marking a real break from what had happened hitherto. Actually, the students began by hurling no more than insults and eggs; since eggs do not grow on trees there was obviously a strong element of premeditation here, even if eggs can scarcely be rated as dangerous weapons. Then the students began to arm themselves with stones, with branches of trees, and with sections of park benches ripped out of their foundations. With immense courage, or incredible foolhardiness, depending on the way one looks at it, the students charged up the two flights of steps. They had the advantage of numbers, but nothing else. The police did not hesitate to throw stones back, and also wielded their truncheons mercilessly. Students collapsed with blood pouring from their heads. Some were carried to the Japanese Cultural Institute, where medical students provided first aid. The press took many dramatic photographs at the time of injured students, and one of a student lying unconscious beside a fountain. But the students did manage to battle through to the doorway of the Architettura and to establish an occupation. Only for ten minutes, however.

Police buses arriving with reinforcements had their windows smashed, and from one police vehicle which was half-destroyed a young policeman was carried out, unconscious and covered in blood. Several police vehicles were set on fire. But reinforcements kept getting through, while water cannon projected jets of foam.[21] 'Soon', *L'Espresso* reported, 'the battlefield was white as if after a snow storm.' From this moment, the same journal reported, police fury seemed to go completely out of control. The students who had managed to break through were now cut off at the top of the staircase, and were beaten and pushed down it, before being bundled into police vans or ambulances. The battle had begun about 11 a.m. and ran for just over two hours. Throughout that time, practically all of Rome could hear the constant sound of police and ambulance sirens. Smoke and flames from burning vehicles could be seen from miles away. A police van very nearly ran down a group of students carrying a wounded colleague; at the same moment a policeman raised his automatic rifle. Actually (and this is an important point to record) in the whole encounter firearms were not used, save for the case of one policeman who fired one shot in the air. But those taken into custody were beaten up, and in some cases had pistols held to their foreheads. According to a couple of journalists who were taken prisoner along with the students, all were forced to sit, 'like', as the police put it, 'Arabs who are better than you'. 'We are going to make you pay, you're worse than criminals,' the students were also told. Apparently the rumour had gone round among the police that first one, and then a second, of their number had been killed. This was not in fact true, but even relatives and friends who came enquiring after those arrested were liable to beatings. 'The University: The Blackest Day,' read the headline in *Epoca;* 'War at the Valle Giulia,' said *L'Espresso.* Injuries among students and passers-by were recorded at only 53, but this was because students wished at all costs to avoid falling into the hands of the police; injuries in fact amounted to several hundred. However—a matter for satisfaction among some students—the police had also, for the first time, suffered quite heavily: 160 were injured.[22]

Those among the students who argued that violence was inevitable, and perhaps even desirable, were now greatly strengthened. 'What dialogue is possible with academics who, faced with the facts of Rome, say only that they feel "profound grief"?' cried students at hitherto peaceful Trieste;[23] because of their early press deadlines the illustrated journals did not report the Rome events for ten days, but at all universities throughout Italy they were known about within twenty-four hours, and in all of them produced the same kind of reactions as at Trieste. The city of most intense and continuous action was Milan. Trouble broke out again in the Liceo Parini: the Milan authorities, still resentful over the outcome of the Zanzara case, suspended Headmaster Mattalia for being too tolerant towards student protests. This immediately brought strikes and demonstrations all across the Milan secondary schools. There were occupations in all the major institutions of higher education, and frequent demonstrations in the main piazzas. Students in Pisa, meantime, began to initiate violence against the police, wearing crash helmets and organizing themselves in 'defence units' *(servizi d'ordine).* Then, on 25 March, came the most violent event yet in Milan. Clearly some students, led by Marco Capanna, were out to attack the police—this is not in any way to defend or excuse the police, but simply to point out the way in which, since Valle Giulia, student activism was moving into a new deliberately violent dimension. Students gathered in the piazza San Ambrogio, which runs alongside Milan's most beautiful medieval basilica and which at one end abuts onto the Cattolica. As they faced up to police who, in the first instance, were guarding the Cattolica, students chanted 'Val-le-Giu-lia, Val-le-Giu-lia'. Thirty-eight police and fifteen ordinary civilians were injured, probably at least twice as many students.[24] This event is sometimes described as 'Milan's Valle Giulia', but its shock effect did not really measure up to that of the real Valle Giulia.

Ultra-conservative, out-of-touch, authoritarian rectors, deans, and professors. Over-large police forces, long used to far too much licence from politicians afraid to curb them, and to employing extreme violence against working-class demonstrators and strikers, and who were now only too happy to employ similar violence against students seen as both privileged and dangerous enemies of established order. But why did the students act as they did, and how far were they responsible for the violence? Students had genuine grievances; few questioned that. The failure to get more than temporizing responses bred frustration. Occupations were resorted to partly because sit-in strikes were a tradition in Italy among factory workers, with whom many students were anxious to identify themselves. What many students wanted to do was to sit and discuss, debate, and pass resolutions; Italian universities were very short of suitable meeting-places open to students, so occupation seemed an easy route to the sort of continuous talking-shops many craved. And carrying through an occupation was one of the easiest ways of taking some definite action, and one guaranteed to make some impact. Many students had a feeling that they must do something; then, once the first steps had been taken, were swept along in the increasingly extreme actions. The police were indisputably the enemy, not just in forcibly terminating occupations but in their more general role of upholding existing society and, in particular, of resisting workers' strikes and demonstrations—students, as I said, were anxious to identify with workers. Behind everything was the absurd Marxist doctrine that, pushed and squeezed enough, existing 'bourgeois society' was bound to collapse, making way for a better one. Thus, however unfocused, wild, or unspecific actions might be, they could all be justified as contributing to the great general cause.

Violence is very apparent in student songs and slogans. To begin with much of this may have been a kind of joking bravado, but steadily participation in violence became a kind of badge of honour, a badge of belonging; militant activists sought to encourage this attitude—violent acts could be represented as positive denials of the codes of bourgeois society upon which there could be no going back. The refrain of the most popular song of the student movement, *Violence*, was: 'Those who weren't there this time, won't be with us tomorrow'. Other slogans brought in revolution and workers' power, as well as Vietnam:

'Revolution yes, revisionism no'.
Workers' Power—arms to the workers.
Power comes out of the barrel of the gun.
Guevara doesn't talk, he shoots.[25]

Among the many rare and fascinating documents in the Feltrinelli archive one of the most illuminating, emanating from the Rome student movement, undated but possibly as early as February 1968, is headed 'Rules for Self-Defence during Processions, Assemblies, etc'. Badly typed, and even more incompetently cyclostyled, it is a set of instructions for student marchers', beginning thus:

1. Workers and students must participate furnished with simple instruments of defence such as protective helmets, red handkerchiefs and motor cycle goggles against gas.
2. The presence of agents of the police must not be tolerated, in uniform or plain clothes, in the body of the procession...

    In case of unexpected attack from the Celere, whether on foot or in motor vehicles, it is necessary:
3. not to flee in a disorganized fashion because this impedes any resistance and encourages police violence against comrades physically weaker and less expert.
4. Immediately form defence cordons obstructing the approach of the police, and their infiltration of the body of the procession. Police thugs in plain clothes will thus be identified and expelled.[26]

The occupying students of the faculty of architecture in Venice issued their communication number one on 1 March 1968, late in the day, obviously, when news had already got through of the events in Valle Giulia, posing the question, with reference to recent events in Venice, 'Why the attack of the police?' The answer, apparently, was that now that the students had emerged as challengers to the capitalist system, this was the moment when 'the social democratic regime organizes systematic repression'. The communication continued:

With every new act of repression there is a corresponding increase in our action. To the systemization of police intervention we counterpoise the construction of an organization no longer limited to the ambit of the university, but firmly united with all the revolutionary forces. For these reasons the violent agents of police repression at Rome will find here, as in the other universities, their response.[27]

While the student agitations were moving towards the violent events of March, several types of trouble, different in origins and in circumstances, were affecting the factories. The unskilled car workers in the Autobianchi car factory at Desio, near Milan, first had a speed-up imposed on them, then were taken over by Fiat. In mid-February the workers put forward demands to be paid at the same level as workers in the other Fiat factories. When this was refused there was a series of lightning strikes in March, with violent threats to managerial staff. At the same time the skilled workers at the Innocenti engineering works at Lambrate, on the outskirts of Milan, went on strike because they feared their privileges were being attacked. There were wildcat strikes at the high-tech Montedison Porto Marghera petroleum plant, near Venice, while at the opposite end of the technology scale trouble continued to escalate in Valdagno. A total strike was followed by a lock-out in April, accompanied by street battles and the pulling down, on 19 April, of the statue of the founder of the Marzotto dynasty, Gaetano Marzotto, from its pedestal in the town square. In these demonstrations and battles, students from two of the nearest universities, Padua and Trento, were prominent. However, the most important development, starting in the Pirelli

545

rubber factory in Milan, was the formation of United Base-Line Committees, which began the potentially devastating (from the employer's point of view) policy of *autoriduzione*, worker-controlled reduction in output. The big public issue, postponed from November, was that of improved pension rights. Since the government had taken no initiatives, the CGIL called for a general strike in March. As with other industrial disputes, students tried to involve themselves in this one; some student demonstrations, particularly in Milan, added the issue of workers' pensions to all the other ones we have already encountered. When, in April, workers went on strike in the Magnetti Marelli light engineering factories at Crescenzago (in the Milan area), students were active in organizing demonstration marches.[28]

By April, the hackneyed metaphor of the cauldron would not be altogether inappropriate for the by-now interlinked agitations by students, factory workers, and secondary school pupils (though older workers and trade union leaders generally tried to keep at a distance from the students), all spiced up by the clattering brutality of the police. Independently, for some years there had been restlessness in the secondary schools. Increasingly, action there became integrated with action in the universities. As already mentioned, the first secondary school occupation took place at the Liceo Berchet in Milan on 26 January. Then a month later there came the Liceo Parini demonstrations, which in turn led to the setting up of coordinating structures, based at the university, for all the Milan secondary schools; this then became a national movement, organized and orchestrated by university militants.[29] Italy, with respect to widespread violence, came near to equalling even Germany.

## *The Events in Paris*

In the early months of 1968 it appeared from the French press that student rebellion was something taking place elsewhere, in Germany in particular, but also in Italy; as late as March 1968 French commentators were congratulating themselves on the relative tranquillity still obtaining in the French universities.[30] The main story in *L'Express* of 22–8 April, 'Europe: Youth Rebels', focused on West Germany and Rome. It spoke of the influence of Marcuse, of 'a sort of international organization of intellectual revolt', and speculated that rebellious students would have little effect on society: 'In writing he [Marcuse] made a sin of affluence,' the article ended; 'the students are isolating themselves from a popular majority which is far from having eschewed the profits and joys of that affluence.' The following week's issue declared 'France's Number 1 Crisis' to be 'Housing'. A minor piece was headed: 'Students: The New Hussars Don't Have Much Luck', and glossed over obvious acts of violence:

> We are perhaps getting a little bored in France. But no longer in the Latin Quarter. Friday 19 April, 3,000 left-wing students demonstrated on the Boul'Mich in support of Rudi Dutschke, and tried to attack a police vehicle. The following Sunday there was a general assembly of UNEF in the Sorbonne annex: four injured... The 'bourgeois politicians' don't seem particularly menaced by these new hussars launched against 'their' society. M. Edouard Frederick-Duport, deputy for the bourgeois bastion of the 2nd

arrondissement of Paris, calmly explained to *L'Express:* 'All of this is positive. It is a new romanticism which pushes the young students to escape from the family ambience. It's not of a nature to affect the course of events.'[31]

A number of reasons explained the sang-froid and patronizing good humour of French journalists and politicians. First, some sort of student disturbances, often accompanied by vigorous police responses, were a fairly commonplace feature, which could be seen as both quite healthy and utterly harmless. Then, without question, anything happening in France *was* eclipsed by events in Germany and Italy. Knowledge that the threat of the implementation of the Fouchet Law would generate protests was largely confined to the limited circle of those familiar with university politics. 'Never', said a history students' statement of November 1967, 'has the beginning of a new academic year been so catastrophic. More than ever the worst conditions of students are deplorable.' It then went on to warn that for three months the press had been campaigning for the introduction of selective university entry, along the lines of the Fouchet proposals.[32]

At Nanterre, Cohn-Bendit had already served his apprenticeship as an agitator. The opening action in November was moderate in motive and moderate in manner. Worried by the announcements that the Fouchet reforms were about to be put into practice, about 10,000 students went on a ten-day strike. Their basic concern was with how the reforms would affect them personally, and they put forward linked claims concerning the size of classes, examination standards, and student representation in university councils. In keeping with the moderate atmosphere at this stage, a committee of staff and students was actually set up to promulgate changes which could then be put to the ministry of education. But little progress was made, and the moderate student leadership lost credibility.[33] A new militant phase opened with the 'swimming-pool incident' of 8 January 1968. Nanterre, unprepossessing, but not without a steady accumulation of amenities, was to have a new swimming-pool, and the well-intentioned minister for youth, François Missoffe, was there to carry out the official opening ceremony. Referring to the fact that Missoffe was the editor of a massive anthology on the problems of French youth, Cohn-Bendit, supported by a group of jeering students, confronted the minister with the complaint that the book said nothing about the sexual problems of the young. Missoffe's response was actually quite funny, though definitely ill-advised: 'With your looks, no wonder you have a problem. But you can always take a dip in the swimming pool to cool off.' Much less witty, though obviously deeply felt, was Cohn-Bendit's rejoinder that Missoffe was behaving like a member of the Hitler Youth.[34]

Nanterre had actually experienced some relaxation in regulations governing women's dormitories. Other universities had not; a spate of protests across the country demonstrated that the sexual issue was always one among the several which eventually brought France to crisis point. In a Paris lycee an activist student was expelled, leading to an unprecedented wave of action and clashes with police. Workers on strike at the Saviem lorry factory in Caen were joined by students—still an unusual action at this time—and in struggles with the police eighteen were injured and thirty arrested.[35] Meanwhile at Nanterre rumours began to spread that Cohn-Bendit was to be forcibly repatriated to Germany, and that the university was compiling a black list of militant students. On 6 January an occupation was staged in the sociology building. Attempts by the dean, Pierre Grappin, and university administrators to persuade the demonstrators to leave were met with uncompromising resistance. Calling in the police had a longer tradition behind it than was even the case in Italy; Grappin was a humane and liberal-minded figure, but faced with what genuinely could be termed a tiny minority of extremists, he took what must have seemed the obvious course. It was not, however, the wisest. There were violent struggles between students and police before the former were finally ejected from the campus.[36] Tiny minorities subjected to police brutality tended to turn into substantial minorities and, indeed, to win majority support.

A further sharp turn of the screw on the Vietnam issue brought the sporadic outbreaks of trouble, so calmly faced by press and politicians, a massive stage nearer to general crisis. In January the Vietnamese Communists launched their 'Tet Offensive' (called after the name of the month in the Buddhist calendar), which achieved stunning gains against the American-backed South Vietnam government. This brought an intense bout of anti-American demonstrations outside various American organizations; some bombs were exploded, and stones shattered the windows of the American Express office in Paris. Not altogether surprisingly, the police were desperate to make arrests, activists in the National Vietnam Committee being obvious targets. Demonstrators were picked up in the streets, and homes were raided. Plain-clothes police invaded the University of Nantes, and the campus at Nanterre; a Nanterre student was arrested. Cohn-Bendit now had a much larger following than he had had on 6 January: on 22 March he led a band of protesters into the university conference chamber at Nanterre.[37] While discussions continued far into the night, the militant core had already decided to baptize this development 'the Movement of 22 March', and managed to rush out a tract blessed with that magic date. This explained that the movement had come into being as a consequence of the police arrests of National Vietnam Committee militants who had organized a demonstration 'for the victory of the Vietnamese people against American imperialism', and of the other police actions I have just described. Typically of the way in which so often different sorts of grievance and protest were melded together, there was also reference to the 'thirty-odd workers and students imprisoned at Caen, of whom some are still in prison'.[38]

The Movement of 22 March, operating at Nanterre but within the ambit of the University of Paris and its historic centre, the Sorbonne, specifically brought together the anti-imperialist cause, the anti-capitalist cause, and the immediate student grievances, focusing in particular on the Fouchet reforms. The actions of its members led directly to the events of May. In direct imitation of the American anti-Vietnam war movement, a teach-in on the evils of imperialism was planned for 29 March. To stop this from taking place, Grappin, again most unwisely, declared the campus closed from 28 March to 1 April.[39] During the short Easter vacation two news items brought a simmering situation to the boil; the first was that at last the long-threatened Fouchet restrictions on university entrance were to be put into immediate practice; the second was that Rudi Dutschke had very nearly been assassinated. Without doubt the Movement of 22 March was perfectly capable on its own of creating total disruption at Nanterre, but in fact it had the help of various extreme right-wing groups, which attacked the offices of student and left-wing organizations and engaged in direct physical combat. On 3 May the dean, for the second time, took the decision to close down the campus.[40]

Meantime, eight members of the Movement of 22 March, who might perhaps have considered themselves lucky not to be in the hands of the police, had been ordered to appear before a university disciplinary committee at the Sorbonne on 6 May. The closing of Nanterre, and the action pending against the eight students, provided the immediate twin causes for demonstrations to be held at the Sorbonne on Friday 3 May. About 500, drawn from all the main student organizations, took part. The right-wing organization Occident also sought to join in. Police forces were massed outside the Sorbonne, poised to take action against the radical students. In fact they served to repel the forces of Occident.[41] However, it does seem clear that the police authorities had decided that if they were going to become involved they were going to be involved in a way which made itself forcefully felt. They were also very aware of the difference between taking action in the dreary suburban campus of Nanterre and invading the hallowed courtyard of the Sorbonne. It was pure coincidence that on 2 May the French prime minister, Pompidou, had left on a long-planned nine-day visit to Iran and Afghanistan; the fact that three lesser politicians, lacking his wily head and restraining hand, were left in charge probably contributed to the way in which events so very quickly ran out of control, though the origins of these events very definitely lie elsewhere. In any case, it was the rector of the University of Paris himself who took the decision to ask the police to enter the Sorbonne and remove the student demonstrators. According to Police Prefect Grimaud, Rector Paul Roche had watched with apprehension the arrival of Cohn-Bendit and his Nanterre squad at the Sorbonne. Grimaud records that he was ready to help the rector, but 'to tell the truth, we were not enthusiastic about it if we could avoid it, knowing too well, from experience, that our interventions created more problems than they solved'.[42] Certainly the police, usually ready to act at the drop of a hat, this time insisted on receiving written instructions. They also then offered the students the option of leaving quietly. This the students themselves, aware of exactly where they were, agreed to.

But the police, having secured their written instructions from the rector, all along had had a different plan in mind; in the act of treachery which, in the last analysis, was what set off 'the events', whose start can be precisely dated to this moment on 3 May 1968, the police bundled the students into police vans. The sight of young faces appearing through the bars of Black Marias was profoundly affecting, even for otherwise uninvolved passers-by, and aroused many apart from students to anger. Militants who escaped the attentions of the police sprang into immediate action; many other students with no previous history of violence joined them. The first weapons to be called into action were the brick-shaped paving-stones generally in use in much of Paris, and particularly in this quarter; the first stones were ready to hand where street repairs were being carried out. Very quickly tools were brought into operation to dig up the top layer of street paving. The police had acted treacherously, but the physical aggression came from the students. The police inevitably responded with truncheons and tear-gas. Disposing of the students took far longer than the police expected, resulting in increasing police frustration, spilling over into attacks on passers-by and local residents. On that opening

549

day of 3 May, eighty policemen and several hundred students and ordinary civilians were injured; 590 people were arrested.[43]

The news from Paris provoked outrage throughout the universities of France. Everywhere there were demonstrations, followed by violent clashes with the police. At Strasbourg 1,500 students gathered on Monday 6 May. By the next day the number had risen to 2,500: 'Each one arrived revolted by the events in the Latin Quarter and discovered that his disquiet, his problems, his confused anguish was shared by all those who surrounded him.' A self-reinforcing process had come into being. Decisive and conciliatory action by the government might possibly have disrupted that process, though it is difficult to see that anything would have altered police behaviour, now on an exponential curve of brutality. Certainly Grimaud, whose views I will explore further shortly, believed that the students were dangerous revolutionaries who had to be suppressed.[44] The rector had not been wise in calling the police in in the first place; nor was he wise to close the Sorbonne. The judiciary played its part in maximizing grievances which could be felt by almost all students. Four of the students arrested on 3 May were sentenced to two months' imprisonment; this in turn was the cause of a demonstration on 6 May, which produced yet more violent responses from the police. Resentment over this violence produced the demonstrations of 7 and 8 May.[45]

Cohn-Bendit and his colleagues had nothing good to say for the French Communist party, and that party reciprocated with bitter attacks on the students as 'false revolutionaries'. But the police repression, apparently fully supported by government, was so palpable that from 8 May both Communist deputies in the Assembly and the Communist press took up the student cause against the government. In response, the government appeared to hold out the promise of both the Sorbonne and Nanterre being reopened, but on 9 May, quite unambiguously placing itself in confrontation with the students, it announced that the Sorbonne would remain closed.[46] Fighting of a viciousness not yet seen began in the small hours of 11 May. It was at this point that *L'Express* recognized that 'the malady which for several months has shaken the Italian and German universities has come to France'.[47] The cover for the issue of 13–19 May carried the simple statement: 'STUDENTS: INSURRECTION'.

> In less than a week, in a spring without precedent, a tempest has raised over Paris the paving stones of the rioters, the guns of the forces of order, and the ideologies of all sides. In days of violent and bitter revolt, the students have put into the streets more trouble makers than the Fifth Republic had ever known, provoking the intervention of General de Gaulle, setting off—for the first time in ten years—an emergency opening of Parliament, seeing the closing of the University of Nanterre and of the very tabernacle of the ancient university, the Sorbonne...

By Friday 10 May moderate students had become sufficiently radicalized, the wider public sufficiently scandalized, and the militants and ideological extremists sufficiently organized for it to be possible for the students to go on to a systematic offensive. The night of 10–11 May is the first night of the barricades. Although most of the initiatives came from quickly formed and relatively informal organizations, such as the Movement of 22 March, the official student organization, the National Union of French Students, did formally support all of the demonstrations. It was anxious to keep up pressure on the government and the university authorities, while, at the same time, it was anxious to disengage from the accelerating violence. The general attitude held by UNEF, and probably shared by a majority of students, was that the university quarter belonged to students, and should be freely available to them as a meeting-place, and as a place, as appropriate, for demonstrations. UNEF had three priority demands: a halt to the judicial and administrative procedures against demonstrators who have been imprisoned and their immediate release; withdrawal from the university quarter by all police forces; the reopening of the university. To students, it said:

> we do not wish to be responsible for any violence, and demonstrators must abstain from any provocation towards the police. They should occupy the Latin Quarter, forming discussion groups while preparing themselves for eventual defence against attack by the considerable strength of the police forces massing around the Sorbonne.[48]

In envisaging 'eventual defence against attack', UNEF was of course also envisaging at least the possibility of eventual violent confrontation. Others had a more proactive policy in mind. All could agree upon the necessity of erecting barricades—these would mark off 'student territory' from which the police should be excluded.

Since the building of barricades involved the commandeering (and upturning) of cars and vans as well as the produce of building-sites and road works in progress, no student could really believe this to be an entirely unprovocative action. No student, either, could be unaware of the tense, warlike atmosphere as dusk approached on Friday 10 May. At the prefecture the police were equipped with telephone lines and TV screens in order to monitor developments around the barricades.[49] For students, building barricades was an exciting activity which assumed its own momentum. Some young workers joined in, perhaps more because it was fun than to express class solidarity—though there is no doubt that the very labour of building created a kind of solidarity, most importantly between activists and ordinary moderate students. Using materials from a building site, young workers built a particularly effective barricade in the rue de l'Abbé-de-l'épée. The most spectacular one was in the rue d'Ulm, three metres high.[50] Militant students formed their own special units, on bikes or mopeds, allocated to telephones in cafés or at street corners, and equipped with transistor radios tuned in to Europe 1 and Radio Luxembourg. As well as the intimate narrow streets of the Latin Quarter, they made use of the roofs. The students had Molotov cocktails made of camping gas and a form of smoke-bomb produced by chemistry students.[51] The main weapon remained the paving stone. At 2.15 a.m. the police went on the offensive. First, using grenade guns they mounted intensive attacks on the barricades; then, throwing grenades by hand and wielding their truncheons, they attacked the students. Most of the grenades contained tear-gas, which could cause blindness for days or weeks as well as spasms and vomiting. And the *grenade offensive* (stun grenade) had an explosive effect which could be very dangerous over a short distance or in a confined space. Thirdly there was the *grenade criquet* (gas grenade) which contained CB gas used in Vietnam; this caused burning and could be fatal.[52]

Local residents offered support to the students, particularly in the form of food and water, but also allowed those fleeing from the police to take refuge in their flats. It was in pursuit that the police were at their most brutal, beating up often already injured students when they caught up with them, deliberately and often violently impeding the work of ambulance services, bursting into flats, and also throwing grenades through the windows. This had people rushing out into the streets whether they were students or not.[53] As an eye-witness reported:

> a young girl thus came rushing out into the street practically naked and was manhandled from one cop to another; then beaten like the other wounded students. For 150 metres, in front of all the inhabitants of the quarter, she was taken from the rue Roger-Collard to the rue Fossees-Saint-Jacques and thrown into a Black Maria, where a journalist, who had already been arrested had to give her his shirt.[54]

One local resident interviewed in June provided this account which both indicated local support for the students and how that support subsequently faded away, perhaps through fear of the police:

> We all passed the night of 10–11 May in the street. All our neighbours were there, with shopkeepers, profs., laundry staff. We were curious, a little tense. Everybody was carrying materials to help the young people build their barricades: we emptied our cellars, we supplied crates, flowerpots, etc. In front of my place, level with the boulevard Saint Michel and the School of Mines, the first barricade was bristling with tricolour flags. Because of that, we said 'it's like 1848'. A plainclothes officer issued a warning but no one heard him because we were all singing, not the Internationale, but the Marseillaise... We saw the appearance for the first time of those grenade-launcher things.... We were forced back onto the courtyard of my flat and the brutality had broken out. I was afraid—and all the residents around me, for once the grenades began to explode, it was the noise of war.... I was very afraid for my son, who was in rue Gay-Lussac. A car engine had exploded and everyone had had the same reaction: 'Some people will have been killed'. I grabbed a policeman by the buttons of his uniform, saying to him: 'It's my kid who is in there, he is more intelligent than all of you men put together.' At that time one said things to the police one would not dare say today. Because, for us, they were still the men who, in the morning had directed the traffic. They were 'guardians of the peace'. When I returned to rue Roger-Collard, the police were shooting water and grenades at the demonstrators. At that, everyone opened their doors so that they could hide. That hasn't been done since.... I learned, in the aftermath, that people became afraid.[55]

In fact the Internationale was sung rather more frequently than the Marseillaise. Much damage was inflicted on the police. Where student columns marched forwards, those at the rear gouged up paving stones; these were passed forward to the front, then hurled at the police. Cohn-Bendit, it was said, was seen popping up everywhere.[56] At one point students made use of a compressor to blast sand at the police. In order to make still more effective barricades, cars were set on fire. (Someone commented later that while students burned cars, the workers with whom they wished to identify wanted to buy them.) Students attempted to throw back grenades, but risked limbs being blown off when those exploded on being lifted up. Some academics got through to ministers begging them to call off the police 'massacre'. But to no avail: the police must 'clean up the streets', said Fouchet. 'That's all.'[57]

Ministers constantly feared the consequences of not giving the police their full support. But practically everyone could see that the force used had been excessive, crossing into the realm of the sadistic. Thirty thousand (including 5,000 secondary school pupils) turned out to demonstrate on 11 and 12 May.[58] The most powerful response came from the French trade union leaders, who, though not at all enthusiastic about becoming involved with the students, at noon on the morning after the night before called for a twenty-four-hour general strike to be held on 13 May.[59] Pompidou arrived back at Orly airport at 7.15 in the evening. He saw his ministers, he saw de Gaulle; at 11.15 he made a statement on television, also broadcast on all radio stations. His appeal was for 'a rapid and total reconciliation'. He announced that the Sorbonne would be reopened and that, after the formality of an appeal court hearing, the imprisoned students would be released.[60] Too late!

Almost before the great strike against police brutality had had time to make itself felt, at 8.30 on the morning of Monday 13 May Rector Roche opened the gates of the Sorbonne. The consequence was not quite what he would have wanted: students poured in, declaring 'the very tabernacle of the ancient university' to be under occupation. On the afternoon of that same day, the four students who had been imprisoned for two months were released.[61] The 13 May strike marked at least a temporary unity between unions and students, with pupils from the lycées also joining in, together with many professional organizations; there was much tacit support from the general public.[62] This day of general strike (supported by 30–40 per cent of the workers)[63] and demonstrations, was followed by almost continuous parades, occupations, and sit-ins, in mines, factories, offices, colleges, schools, and theatres. The demonstrations in Paris were attended by anything between half a million and one million people; and there were demonstrations in cities and towns all over France as well.

Lyon was to have its most violent episodes on the night of 26 May, as evidenced in a leaflet issued by the three main student unions there:

> Friday at 6.30 p.m., a procession of 5,000 to 6,000 students and workers left the place Bellecour.... Despite the careful planning of the demonstration, from 8 p.m. onwards there were many engagements between demonstrators and the CRS. After a police charge, in which one of our comrades was savagely stamped on and batoned, the demonstrators mostly moved towards the place des Cordeliers, where they set up barricades to protect themselves, while the police threw grenades of different types, some containing noxious gases unfamiliar to the civilian medical services.

It was during the confrontation around 11 p.m. on the Lafayette bridge that the accident took place which caused the death of a police commissioner, knocked down by a lorry wheel the demonstrators were using for cover after a counter-attack.[64]

Opinion polls had already indicated that the students had considerable support (a poll in Paris showed that 61 per cent thought student claims justified, and 71 per cent that they were being unjustly attacked).[65] Inside the Sorbonne Cohn-Bendit gave a press conference, while the students elected an occupation committee and settled down to a festival of talk[66] interspersed with the painting of rather punchier slogans, the art form of May 1968. Slogans, in fact, appeared on walls and buildings all over central Paris, particularly the Left Bank. Here is a selection:[67]

It is prohibited to prohibit. Liberty begins with one prohibition: that against harming the liberty of others.

The dream is reality.

The aggressor is not the one who rebels but the one who upholds authority.

To exaggerate is to begin to create.

Be realistic, demand the impossible. I am a Marxist, Groucho tendency.

Long live de Gaulle (signed, a masochistic Frenchman).

The one who shits in the bed is hidden.

This last was a riposte to de Gaulle's inelegant, much quoted, and much resented description of the student protestors as 'ones who shit in the bed' *(chienlit)*.

While older trade union leaders anxiously prevented too close a fraternization with students, the younger workers enthusiastically took up the idea of occupying their factories. Within just over a week about seven million were engaged in this particularly evocative form of strike action, reminiscent of the factory occupations which accompanied the establishment of the Popular Front government in 1936. The fact that not dissimilar action was taken by a large number of middle-class people, who carried out strikes and sit-ins in the name of greater independence and a reorganization of their professions,[68] indicates once more that the movements of the sixties were essentially movements of personal liberation, not movements of class against class, or of alternative society against established society.

Occupation of the Sorbonne was followed by the occupation of the main science building, the Halle aux Vins, by science students and staff who in June decreed it the 'Summer University', open to all in perpetuity.[69] Then came the occupation of the Odéon theatre, described thus in a tract issued by the occupiers:

After the events of these last ten years. After the political occupation of the Latin Quarter and of Nanterre. After the barricades of the night of 10 May. And the savage police repression. After the general strike of 13 May and the occupation of the Sorbonne. A group of artists and theatrical people, students and workers, constituted as a Committee of Revolutionary Action have tonight occupied... the France-Odéon Theatre, a symbol of bourgeois culture which they fundamentally oppose as they oppose capitalist society.... In order to further this movement we call upon all of you to come this evening, Thursday 16 May at 12 midnight to the ex-theatre of France.[70]

The document is signed by 'the Commission of Information at the Odéon'. On the reverse are listed 'safety measures'. The first must have been hard to bear—'comrades' were instructed that they must not smoke. At the first 'Assembly General', held in the theatre on 16 May, it was resolved that the theatre, for an unlimited duration, should cease to operate as a theatre. Instead it had become 'a meeting-place for workers, students and artists', 'a place of permanent creative revolution', 'a continuous political meeting-place'. A third document, suffused with the creative extremism I discussed in Chapter 7, spoke of the virtues of improvisation—'to improvise is to feel something and then express it'. It was in this spirit that there was to be organized at the School of Mime, 270 rue St Jacques, at 9 p.m. on Saturday 1 June, a 'spectacle of collective improvisation of music, poetry and dance'— 'there will be no barrier between the artists and the public, the goal aimed at being communication.'[71]

Just as many academics supported their students, many teachers, and even head teachers, supported their pupils. The difficulty sometimes lay with parents, who either did not wish their progeny to be involved in revolutionary activity or, at the very least, were worried about the dangers they might incur in schools where occupations and demonstrations had become permanent features. In the fabulous collections of documents relating to the events of 1968 at the Centre de Recherches d'Histoire des Mouvements Sociaux et du Syndicalisme in the Marais in Paris is the letter the headmaster of the école Boulle (a technical lycée) wrote to all parents on 17 May. He supports his pupils, plays down their tendencies to radicalism and violence, and reassures parents that their children are still being fed:

> I can assure all parents that the pupils constituting the Strike Committee have demonstrated organization and method and are the best guarantee of the order and smooth running of their school. The midday meal is served as usual. I affirm, furthermore, that their positions are entirely apolitical and that they are not animated by any spirit of violence.
>
> Finally I reply to the very natural question which may be asked by many families: should I send my son back to the School? My response would be 'YES' if it is a question of a sufficiently mature pupil and one conscious of the problems currently being debated. But each family must reach its own conclusions on this point.[72]

The head concludes the letter by saying he hopes soon to invite the parents to a meeting for a discussion of all of these matters. Rather belying their teacher's gentle estimate of them, the Strike Committee then belligerently wrote demanding that all students should return to the school; contempt for the rights and concerns of adults had reached its extreme. Very much in the role of the liberal sympathizer not really understanding just how intransigent the young people were, the head organized his parent-teacher-pupil meeting for 22 May, striving to keep afloat the notions of participation, discussion, and conciliation.

Ordinary life was coming to a standstill, in a manner completely different from what was happening in other countries. Instead of doing their jobs, going about their business, people in all social classes were involved in strikes, occupations, endless discussions, massive street processions; only the police were in overdrive, the general passivity being punctuated at intervals by violent police-engendered confrontations, both in the streets and inside and outside factories and other premises. After a day of demonstrations on 23 May, Paris suffered the most extreme violence on the third of the 'Black Fridays', 24 May (the other two were 3 and 10–11 May). The students had absorbed all the lessons of previous encounters: they had now perfected their building of barricades, their maintenance of communications, and their offensive weaponry. They used mechanical saws to cut down trees for use as weapons and in barricades.[73] (In general, it should be noted, the students were not distinguished by their concern for the environment, or for artistic and architectural treasures—such as those to be found in the various buildings they occupied.) The near-paralysis lasted from early May to well into June. 'The government shrieks, thunders, threatens, orders. Not a single response: it is like the baby that says "I want" when its parents don't want.'[74] French broadcasting was closed down for five weeks; petrol queues began appearing on 21 May, and shortly thereafter coupons were issued to try to secure supplies for priority occupations.[75] It had all begun on 3 May; when, on 16 June, the police cleared the student occupants out of the Sorbonne, without any violence to speak of (restless students were beginning to feel the call of summer), it began to seem as if things were coming to an end. 'Between these two days', Police Prefect Grimaud recorded,

> there unfolded the strangest events that Paris, and indeed France, had ever lived through. There were paroxysms of violence, but without a single death. Talk submerged the streets and the squares, the amphitheatres, the stage at the Odéon and elsewhere. The most brutal encounters were succeeded by periods of almost idyllic peace in which songs and poetry alternated, spontaneous meetings were held, with the most resolute revolutionary phraseology. The government of France appeared a theatre of shadows.[76]

Grimaud's moderate words have to be taken along with the convictions he expressed—which explain the orders from above, if not the brutality on the ground, that 'there existed two powers in Paris, that of the left in their redoubts and others in the rest of the city'; 'in the fire of action, we never doubted, my colleagues and I, the possibility of the insurgents taking power.'[77] It is true that no students were killed, though by 16 June one bystander and a police commissioner in Lyon had died; there were shortly to be more deaths.

A very important and sometimes neglected force on the course, and cooling, of events was that of parents and parents' organizations. Most shared the criticisms of the systems made by their children, but they were determined that the taking of the Baccalauréat would not be disrupted. In an impressive demonstration of parent power, parents of children of the Lycée

Janson-de-Sailly organized an assembly to include teachers, strikers, and revolutionary pupils; 5,000 parents turned up.[78] That was only one of many manifestations which succeeded in putting pressure on pupils, teachers, and, most important, government. These important exams went ahead, but with many of the improvements for which secondary school pupils had been agitating throughout the sixties. To divide solely by generations is to misunderstand the sixties.

France was different largely because of the way in which a kind of generalized Marxism was taken as read by many in all sections of society, even those who saw themselves as formally anti-Marxist; this acceptance was reinforced by France's own history, in which the Revolution of 1789 could (erroneously) be represented as marking the transition from feudalism to capitalism, and in which street demonstrations and further revolutions had threatened, and sometimes even toppled, regimes. There were many resentments against enduring institutions, and against the narrow and authoritarian regime of de Gaulle; once the process had begun on 3 May there were manifold reasons for joining in. The basic Marxist belief was that bourgeois society was in a state of crisis, and that a little continuous pressure would bring about its collapse: the revolution would simply take place without the need for precise actions, such as assassinating de Gaulle, blowing up the chamber of deputies, or taking control of the television stations. (There were many arson attacks, in particular on the Paris stock exchange on 24 May—great spectacle, but not seriously effective.) The violent confrontations had a ritualistic quality, but in that they took place almost continuously in the centre of Paris they did seem more menacing to central political power than the more scattered confrontations in the other countries. In the Odeon, in the Sorbonne, in many other places, institutions of the alternative society seemed to have taken more tangible form than their analogues elsewhere in Europe and North America. But they operated very much as parallel talking-shops, never in fact taking over from the traditional institutions, which were expected just to disappear.

In the end France was not that different, since the whole theory that a revolution *ought* to take place was simply false. Everybody piled in with their own particular fads and philosophies, then just left it to happen. A badly typed statement from the 'Children's Cell of the Revolutionary Communist (Trotskyite) Party' declared that children were part of the struggle. 'The Association for the Support of Pierre Mendes-France' published a leaflet containing a statement by the political leader supporting 'the workers, students and peasants' and declaring that the crisis had 'put a whole way of life under scrutiny'. A 'Handbill of Christians' of 21 May announced: 'The undersigned Christians, Catholic and Protestant laymen, priests and pastors, declare their solidarity with the actions of the students and workers.' Teachers from the various colleges of applied arts and fine arts formed an 'Action Committee of the Art Schools': their basic idea was cooperation between teachers and pupils, the particular problem 'the neglect into which the authorities had allowed artistic matters to sink'. It is not surprising that one persistent call was for voting rights at the age of 18. Still more important with regard to the positive aspects of the crisis were the calls for rights for the straightforwardly misfortunate. One handbill announced a strike at the école Nationale in support of the disabled. Another was issued jointly by bodies representing the blind, the deaf, the old, and the infirm: 'they also fight: the new society will not forget anyone'... 'The healthy young person of today may perhaps be the infirm and very probably will be the old of tomorrow.'[79]

On 21–2 May the National Assembly appeared briefly to take on again the solid flesh of live politics. There were enough deputies who supported the protesters, or saw the opportunity to overthrow the government, for the debate to be closely fought, but not enough to carry a censure motion against the government. There followed the extreme violence in the streets of 23 and 24 May. One precipitating factor was the news that Cohn-Bendit, who had gone to Germany, was not to be allowed back into France. Now came de Gaulle's first major intervention; on 24 May, in a brief TV appearance, he promised a referendum on the constitution.[80] A slogan painted on the Grand Palais, some distance from the university quarter, sought to cut the president neatly down to size: 'He took three weeks to announce in five minutes that he was going to undertake in one month what he had not succeeded in doing in ten years.'[81] Pompidou, however, went into direct and down-to-earth action, and from 25 to 27 May entered into negotiations with both unions and employers. The Grenelle Agreements offered the workers respectable gains: a general wage increase of 10 per cent; a 35 per cent rise in minimum agricultural and industrial wages; an agreement in principle on a shorter working week; a 5 per cent increase in the proportion of medical expenses reimbursed by social security; strike pay at 50 per cent of normal wages; and a promise to produce legislation giving unions greater shop-floor rights.[82] However, the euphoria had not yet faded: the car workers at Boulogne-Billancourt in the Paris suburbs took the lead in rejecting the package. Occupations followed immediately at Sud Aviation in Nantes and at Renault-Cléon near Rouen.[83] As other factories rejected the peace terms, a new phase of coordinated political and industrial action (different from the street fighting and sit-ins) began. Along with two of the main student organizations, the Party of Socialist Unity (in which Pierre Mendès-France was a leading member) organized a rally at the Charlety stadium on the evening of 27 May. Attending the rally, Mendès-France attracted some applause (contemporary estimates as to whether this constituted an ovation differ, demonstrating the bitter jealousies that existed between the politicians who might have given a lead to the anti-government cause), but he refused to speak. The situation was not greatly improved when the next day François Mitterrand, leader of yet another grouping, the Federation of the Democratic and Socialist Left, proposed the formation of a provisional government under Mendès-France, should Pompidou's ministry in fact (as was widely predicted) fall; Mitterrand himself would be a presidential candidate if de Gaulle resigned.[84]

While opposition politicians seemed incapable of concerted action, de Gaulle produced a *coup de théâtre*. He 'disappeared', thus distracting attention from events in Paris; although the story was that he was simply relaxing at his home in Colombey-les-Deux-Eglises, what he was actually doing was visiting General Massu, commander of the French armed forces stationed in Baden-Baden, to ascertain if he had the general support of the military. If de Gaulle had occasional flashes of genius, Pompidou was consistently a very clever politician. He advised de Gaulle to hold an immediate general election. On his return the following day (30 May), de Gaulle announced in a radio broadcast that the referendum (promised on 24 May) was being deferred, that he was not going to resign, or get rid of Pompidou, but that he was dissolving the National

Assembly and holding immediate elections—the first round on 23 June, the second on 30 June. The first consequence was that the opposition politicians and the leaders of the CGT switched their attentions away from mass demonstrations to the coming election, from which, of course, they hoped they would secure power.

The clever political manoeuvres of the government were reinforced by a carefully organized anti-Communist demonstration on the evening of 30 May, with the participation of 3–400,000 people. The students' union UNEF, together with the PSU, organized counter-demonstrations on 1 June, but against the opposition of the CGT. The 'unity' of workers and students had come about because the older workers and union leaders had been outraged by the police violence against students and because the younger workers had grievances of their own, but it was never very profound; it was now falling apart again.[85] The workers were finding it difficult to maintain their strikes, as money ran out and as the authorities made carefully calculated applications of force. On 10 June police charged strikers at the Renault car factory at Flins, and on 11 June at the Peugeot factory at Sochaux. At both places students and *lycéens* were still trying to show solidarity. Fleeing from the CRS at Flins, twelve *lycéens* found themselves surrounded, jumped into the Seine, became entrapped in the mud, and were attacked with truncheons; one, Gilles Tautin, was drowned.[86] At Sochaux two workers were killed.[87] Inevitably these tragedies were the occasion for further protest demonstrations held on 11 June in Paris and elsewhere—Toulouse had a night of barricades and street fires:[88] the fighting between police and students was extremely violent, but in the perception of many it was the students who appeared to be the aggressors, rather than the police. Though the overthrow of existing society was extremely unlikely in any event, two circumstances had changed since May: the government had recovered its confidence and ordinary French people no longer felt sympathetic towards the students.[89] The police acted decisively on 14 June, clearing out the Odéon, the Beaux-Arts, and then the Sorbonne, now rat-infested and showing the depredations of hippie, rather than intellectual, opposition.[90]

The paper war continued to be waged furiously. To radical students, an election was simply a bourgeois fraud. Issues of *Action*, which first appeared on 7 May, the journal of UNEF, SNR, and CAL, assisted by a team of qualified journalists, continued to appear, and the first issue of *Barricades*, the journal of CAL, was published for the first time on 8 June. The second issue expressed the anger felt over the death of 'comrade Gilíes Tautin'. There was a delightful scurrilous undergraduate humour about these journals. Issue no. 3 of *Action* had a cartoon featuring a teacher taking out his penis, and announcing to the class that he has been charged with giving them a course of sex education. Another one had President Johnson with an erect penis labelled 'NASA', and saying 'Shit, all the same it's still me that has the biggest one'.

Altogether, between the beginning of May and the end of July, there were eight deaths directly arising from incidents between protesters and police: no student was killed in any of the big city demonstrations—the only person killed in Paris being a young male bystander at a barricade in the rue des Ecoles on 24 May. On that same day a police commissioner was killed in Lyon by a lorry whose brakes students had released. All the other deaths, including that of the 17-year-old Gilíes Tautin, were associated with factory disputes, and the remaining five dead were all workers.

Four were shot and one was thrown from a parapet by the explosion of a grenade. The total of those seriously enough injured to be hospitalized (and this did include a considerable number of policemen) amounted to 1,798, of which 953 were in the Paris region and 845 in the whole of the rest of France.[91] These figures in themselves justify giving most attention to Paris; and, of course, it was the apparent paralysis in Paris which gave rise to the belief that the entire regime was about to collapse.

It should be noted that before ever the election took place students had already gained acknowledgement of the justness of their complaints about the university system, the workers had received some concessions, and liberalization of French broadcasting had been promised. Gaullist propaganda against the Left was very effective, while ordinary French people were beginning to suffer from the disruptions to everyday life. The Gaullist victory—a 3 per cent swing yielding, on the second ballot, 358 seats out of 485—was crushing. But parliamentary seats won could not compensate for the profound shock to the regime. Although there was no question of society being turned upside-down as the students had hoped, grave weaknesses in the system had certainly been exposed. A new law of November 1968 attempted reform of the discredited higher education system; everywhere there were moves towards autonomy and decentralization; workers were given formal rights of representation on boards of management.[92] Most important was the fact that people had seen the system shake, and that many felt that they had directly participated in that shaking, at least vicariously, through sons and daughters.

A particularly valuable document is the special edition which *Elle* managed to bring out on 17 June, skinny and without advertisements (issues of all the main newspapers and periodicals were lost over May-June). The editor, Helen Gordon-Lazereff, spoke directly to her readers saying that, without taking one side or another in the political debate, she understood how traumatic their experiences had been. In addition to noting how parents had become involved through their children, she remarked on the large part played by girls and young women in the protests, in which they had shown 'an amazing courage'. She hoped this special edition would bring magazine and readers closer together: 'we want to participate much more closely in your preoccupations of today, and your cares of tomorrow, and to get you to participate in ours...' Admitting that this might sound pretentious she continued with a sentence which, at first, perhaps sounds even more pretentious: 'But the new epoch which has now begun and which has shaken the foundations of our lives demands from you and us an intensity of heart and spirit greater than ever in the past.' The article tells of how parents often had difficulty in understanding children who participated in the lycée protests, but of how some came to understand the rightness of their children's actions. Emotional, intangible, yet (I believe) real. But perhaps the neatest summary of the relationship of French people to the events of May was the formulation attributed to Michel de Certeau: 'Last May we took to speaking up, just as in 1789 we took the Bastille.'[93]

De Gaulle revived his proposal for a constitutional referendum in April 1969: the 51 per cent of the vote he secured for his proposals for regional reform and reform of the senate was not enough for the general, at once arrogant as ever and profoundly shocked by the disrespect for authority recently so openly expressed, and he resigned.[94] Outwardly there was no great change, since Pompidou was elected president in June 1969; and for those who insist on looking in the wrong direction, that is, towards mythical revolution and non-existent alternative societies, there *was* no change—but for the mass of the French people the transformations of a decade had climaxed, and could never be reversed. There were noteworthy relaxations in the authoritarian regime: the events of 1968 were the precipitating factor, though they in turn derived from a framework established throughout the sixties, not suddenly assembled in May 1968. Disturbances and sporadic violence inside and outside universities, schools, and factories continued for several years, but there was now something of a routine quality to it all.

### *Italy, 1968–1969: The 'Hot Autumn'*

For a short period France was in extreme crisis; then, bar the ritualistic prolongations of the next few years, it was all over. By May, Italy had had several months of different kinds of protest, all over the country, with bouts of intense violence. Somehow this never quite added up to a concentrated and direct threat either to the centre-left government in office or to the regime as a whole. To the activists and idealogues, proponents of united revolutionary action by workers and students, the French events of May came as a shining example. The French are more theoretically correct, their workers more rigorously class-conscious: that was the sentiment, redolent of that inferiority complex that manifests itself from time to time among certain Italians, which began to be expressed, together with the view that Italian students and workers must at once follow the French example. The press presented the situation in Paris as being far more serious than that in Italy; and several leaders of the Italian student movement went to Paris to see what lessons could be learned. Student radicals in Genoa issued a manifesto on 4 May declaring that their expression of solidarity with the worker and student struggles in France signalled 'the most acute moment in the crisis of the class movement in Genoa and Liguria'.[95] At Piadena, near Cremona, some adult political figures on the left joined with students in organizing a conference on 22 May to study the French experience.[96] But perhaps, in the end, the French events were more important for the *frisson* of excitement they generated, and the dramatic headlines and pictures they provided for the Italian press, than for any practical effects.

The transcript of the conference at Piadena would sink under the weight of the sterile debates about revolutionary tactics were it not for the unconscious humour of the chair's repeated attempts to get those students who had been to Paris to recount their experiences.[97] Giuseppe Morandi, a clerical worker, member of the United Socialist party and representative of the Cultural League of Piadena, opened the conference, explaining that the Cultural League had organized it with the student movement in order to hear at first-hand about the events in Paris. His first speaker resolutely refused to discuss anything other than her experiences at the University of Trento. After several interventions, Morandi insisted that it was now time to hear from students who had been in Paris. The discussion of Trento continued, before moving on to Pisa, then Milan, Bologna, and Rome. After a long discussion, Morandi intervened to say that it now really was time to talk about France, being greeted by several voices from the floor crying, 'It's always time to talk about France.' Again no one did actually speak about France, though there were a number of (mainly critical) references to Marcuse. Once more Morandi tried to bring up the subject of France, but found himself much heckled and interrupted. Finally, at the end of the transcript, there is a note that 'it was decided to postpone the debate on the French situation'.

Events in Italy, being both more diverse and less decisive, generated their own stumbling momentum, which continued throughout 1968 then turned quite markedly more violent from the beginning of 1969. Occupations, demonstrations, clashes between protesters and police, new relationships, *de facto*, between teachers and taught, became almost institutionalized in universities, colleges, and secondary schools; the speeches and manifestos begin to seem repetitive—things kept going (often, apparently, in circles) partly because the protesters had enough in the way of satisfying successes (buildings occupied and reoccupied, policemen knocked unconscious, new courses and teaching methods installed) without ever changing fundamental conditions, partly because there was a sufficiency of experienced student agitators to keep travelling round the country maintaining high levels of tension, and partly because, if animosity ever did seem like cooling, there was always some police atrocity to refuel the flames. Basic student attitudes and basic student grievances did not change; but increasingly important was the increasingly self-evident fact that Italian workers and white-collar employees, practically across the board, were getting a lesser rather than a greater share in Italy's overall growing prosperity.[98] Continuous worker unrest, and willingness to resort to strong action, steadily began to replace student discontent as the basis of disturbance and violence in Italy. Once again it became perfectly plain that whatever reticence the police might have about using firearms against students did not apply where workers were concerned. By middle and late 1968, particularly as unofficial action steadily eclipsed official trade union action, it was less a case of student activists trying to politicize workers than of students trying to fall in behind highly combative workers.

None of the different industrial disputes which I identified in the second section of this chapter was resolved. By the autumn the Pirelli rubber works in Milan was emerging as the classic site for what left-wing commentators referred to as 'the new struggles' *(lotte nuove)*, struggles in which shop-floor workers themselves, without reference to their unions, slowed down and disrupted production.[99] In such direct shop-floor action there was, of course, no place for students, and, ironically, no real place either for the intellectual theorizers of the newly formed Potere Operaio. The Pirelli high-rise office block in Milan became a focal point for constant marches and picketing involving all sections of the Milan working class. The methods of the 'new struggles' spread not only in the more traditional motor factories but also among the factories making the new consumer goods, such as Candy and Ignis. To some extent, the official unions had to try to keep up: with the pensions issue still not satisfactorily resolved, the three union confederations called general strikes on 14 November 1968 and 5 February 1969; in May 1969 the unions launched a general campaign in favour of large wage increases and the abolition of piece-work. Meantime, in December 1968, the Pirelli management had lost patience and declared a lock-out. But within weeks the lock-out was withdrawn, piece-work rates were increased, and bargaining procedures put in place for the resolving of disputes.[100] However, although all this was agreed by the unions, many workers quietly reserved the right to resume their disruptive actions whenever they felt it necessary. That white-coated workers were getting restless was shown by the occupation in October 1968 of SNAM Progetti; the same type of technical workers began to take action at Sit Siemens in Milan. However, such workers could not necessarily count on the support of blue-collar workers, who were often extremely hostile to office workers.[101] The general sense of anarchy and even terror was reinforced by well-authenticated accounts of worker violence against managers, and even against clerical workers, particularly women. The writings of Potere Operaio and other militant organizations, and in the extreme left-wing press, make it clear that extreme violence was regarded as perfectly legitimate by this small minority.[102]

The targets attacked and the causes espoused by students widened further, increasing the occasions for violent clashes with the police; militant action by secondary school pupils became more universal. On 29 May 1968, 5,000 students and workers together demonstrated in the centre of Trento. Enthusiastically, if not necessarily accurately, a leading trade union figure yelled into the microphone: 'In this united struggle with the student movement, in twenty days we have advanced further than in twenty years.'[103] Just as working-class evening students were particularly active in the student movement, pupils from the commercial secondary schools greatly reinforced the activities from the classical ones. A second mass demonstration by secondary school pupils in Milan took place in December 1968, in support of 'political rights'. One of these was that students should have the right to hold assemblies, organized by themselves, to discuss current political matters. This, though with enough of the usual limitations attached to keep up the students' sense of grievance, was conceded by the minister of education.[104] Secondary school and university students combined in December to disrupt archetypal 'bourgeois' enjoyments at the Rinascente department store, and at the La Scala opera house. 'Enjoy yourselves, aristocrats, it's for the last time' was the cry.[105] In Rome, secondary school pupils organized a demonstration in the piazza S. Maria Maggiore, which led to a confrontation with police.[106] A constant source of violence, more dangerous than in France, was the existence of a number of Fascist groups. A further cause for demonstrations came in November 1968 when the right-wing colonels seized power in Greece.[107] Milan students in December took over an old hotel and set it up as a 'house for students and workers'. In April 1969 this was firebombed by a Fascist group.[108] Endeavouring to establish a headquarters for themselves, activist students in Naples took over a section of the university in December. On 20 January 1969 three Fascist groups, FUAN, GUF and Potere Europeo, occupied the faculty of law opposite the recently established offices of the student movement. Four days later Fascist groups from other southern cities, accompanied by members of parliament from the neo-Fascist party the MSI (Italian Social Movement), conducted a fire attack on the offices occupied by the Student Movement. The students were forced out and beaten up, while the Fascists moved in. The students complained, with perhaps less than a perfect case, that the press treated both them and the Fascists as equally dangerous groups of extremists. They also protested, with accuracy, that the police had given support to the Fascists.[109] This was fairly widespread, and we have a marvellous actuality shot by photographer Uliano Lucas of a right-wing counter-demonstrator, with a stone in his hand ready to throw, talking amicably to a helmeted policeman during one of the episodes at Milan University.[110]

However, the violence which began to dominate the headlines, and also to be strongly featured in student flyers, was police violence against working-class protesters. 'Police have inaugurated 1969 firing on students and workers,' claimed one.[111] On 12 December 1968 police fired on an agricultural workers' demonstration at Avola in Calabria in the south, killing two workers, and seriously wounding forty-four others.[112] On the last night of the year a protest had been mounted outside the Bussola night-club in the seaside resort of Viareggio, a protest allegedly against 'bourgeois luxury': a 17-year-old student was paralysed by a plastic bullet to the spine, and thirty students were imprisoned.[113] The worst incident so far happened at Battipaglia, again in the south, where proposals to close a tobacco and sugar factory there provoked a demonstration on 9 April 1969. The demonstrators attacked and set fire to the town hall. A young schoolteacher standing at her window was killed by a police bullet; a young typist was killed by a plastic bullet. The people of Battipaglia turned out in full themselves the next day, to the tune of 35,000.[114] There were protests organized by students in other cities, with the extreme militants known in the press as *cinesi* ('Chinese') taking a prominent part. A group of *cinesi* were photographed beating up a solitary policeman.[115]

In the midst of these violent events came another episode involving students and police in Rome, to rank with Valle Giulia. The focal point for several days of student action was the visit to Rome on 28 February of President Nixon. The first big march from the university area into the centre of Rome took place on 26 February. It was only towards the end of the demonstration that the tail of the procession was violently charged by the police. The political authorities were anxious that Nixon's visit should not be disturbed and on the following day the police were waiting in readiness, and attacked the students in the precincts of the university as they were forming into a column; none the less, several hundred students got through to march once again into central Rome. On the day of the visit, 6,000 police did carry out what could plausibly be described in the student literature as 'the military invasion of the University of Rome', supported by water cannon, armoured cars, lorries, jeeps, special units, and tanks. Fascist groups joined in and one student was killed in a Fascist assault.[116] The students made their own film of these events, *Nixon in Italia*, in which the police violence comes out clearly enough. This, ironically, became a cause for complaint among those who were beginning to glory in the extremes of violence which eventually were to underpin the terrorism of the Red Brigades: a statement in the summer of 1969 by 'Student Power' criticized the film for going on about police violence, which it described as a habitual and not particularly significant occurrence, instead of stressing the way the student movement had reached a new stage, taking the initiative in the streets as the centre of destructive attacks on capitalism.[117]

*Epoca*s main story of 22 June 1969 was headlined, 'Scandals, Confrontations, Strikes': 'Not a day passes without the press giving news of a new scandal, strike or occupation.' Corruption scandals were nothing new in Italy, but the rapid succession of major ones at this time, continuing throughout the autumn, intensified the notion of a country in decay, and certainly encouraged the protesters in their attacks on capitalism. *Epoca* thought the student revolt, relatively recent in comparison with age-old scandals and industrial disputes, was possibly the most lethal of all the dangers facing the state. It printed a picture of the Milan student leader Marco Capanna with some of his fellow-protesters, noting that Capanna had recently been arrested for his part in the kidnapping of a senior professor at the Milan Statale. Following the second pensions strike, the main issue taken up by the official trade unions was that of housing reform: a big official trade union demonstration over housing in Turin in July led to riots and street battles with the police. Throughout the summer, all types of unofficial disruptive action continued, including what were called 'hiccup strikes' and 'chequerboard strikes'. The most intensive action was to be found in the car factories of Turin, what was in effect guerrilla warfare only coming to an end with the August holiday.[118]

With echoes of America's recent experiences of 'long, hot summers', the press began to speak of a forthcoming 'hot autumn'. The moderate and rational Christian Democrat minister of labour, with a pointed reference to current scandals and revelations of tax evasion, remarked: 'By the end of this autumn we shall all be changed people. A system that waves the Italian flag for the workers and the Swiss flag for the industrialists is not a healthy one.'[119] Troubles broke out in the factories immediately after the holiday break, but were once again more than equalled by developments in Milan, where the Pirelli factory was again a centre of conflict, along with the Milan Fiat factories. The slogan linking the two mighty owners of these concerns was 'Agnelli, Pirelli—ladri gemelli' (Agnelli, Pirelli—the thieving twins). On 25 September there was a national demonstration by 5,000 engineering workers, and throughout the autumn on every day there was some strike on somewhere in Italy.[120] Again certain Christian Democratic members of the government were to present themselves as reasonable and level-headed, and it was through them that agreements with the unions were negotiated on 14 November, meeting official union demands for: a forty-hour week within three years; progress towards parity between manual and clerical workers; elimination of differentials for those under 20; and union rights to be guaranteed inside factories.[121]

However, the more profound personal grievances of the workers remained unresolved, concerning such things as unpleasant working conditions and the lack of respect shown to them as skilled and experienced practitioners in their own fields. A popular slogan, showing how radicals connected international issues to local grievances, was 'The factory is our Vietnam'.[122] Almost any type of protest could result in street fighting involving the police and also, often, Fascist assault groups. On 6 November, on the corso Sempione in Milan, a mass protest was organized against the way in which Italian television and radio was reporting the industrial confrontations, with placards reading 'RAI—the bosses' voice'. This deteriorated into a running street battle, with several workers being arrested and imprisoned.[123] The same process, but this time more disastrous, occurred when demonstrations took place in support of the trade union campaign for housing reforms, at the via Larga near the Statale: a young policeman from the south, Antonio Annarumma, was killed. Most of the left-wing literature identified Annarumma as an innocent and downtrodden worker, the victim of a battle initiated by the bourgeoisie and of capitalist exploitation of the south. His funeral was attended by a procession of 30–50,000.[124] The death-toll since April 1968 was still in single figures, but the death of Annarumma suggested that it might be on the point of a sharp increase. The extremist organization Lotta Continua (The Struggle

Continues) openly boasted about the lethal intentions of the demonstrations it was involved in.[125] On 12 December a bomb went off at the Bank of Agriculture in the piazza Fontana in Milan, killing twelve people. A well-known anarchist was arrested; while under questioning he fell from a window and was killed—the hotly contested official account formed the basis of Dario Fo's comedy *The Accidental Death of an Anarchist*. At the funeral procession for those killed, 300,000 turned out: there was a deep sense that student agitation, then workers' agitation, was now giving way to haphazard terrorism.[126]

That was certainly not what the overwhelming majority of university and secondary school students had wanted. Let us take a more intimate look at some of them, helped in particular by the invaluable collection of diaries and letters preserved in the Archivio Diaristico in Pieve Santo Stefano in southern Tuscany. How did the young people see themselves, and each other? How did their mothers see them? Catholic influences, totally absent from the mountains of student movement leaflets and pamphlets preserved in the Istituto Feltrinelli, are very apparent, either strongly positive or strongly negative. 'The Diary of Fourteen Days, 1968–69' of a pupil in a Catholic secondary school in Padua—'I am imprisoned in a commune of Jesuits'—is bitterly hostile to Catholicism. As a student radical he has completely internalized the usual stuff about Marx, exams, monolithic instruction being part of the bourgeois power structure, which makes the testimony of an entry for 30 October 1969 all the more impressive: he not only recognizes the desperation of some parents whose children are cut off from them in schools which are in a state of occupation, but he goes as far as to recognize that their only hope of retrieving the children lies with the *Celere* coming in and using force.[127]

The fascinating fragments of correspondence starting in October 1967 between two seven-teen-year-olds, one female, one male, former childhood friends, now at school in separate cities, she in Rome, he still in Pisa, offer some sharply contrasting views, though both are activists. He writes that at his school they are looking for a suitable text to put on as a play (reminding us incidentally of the protean character of experimental theatre). He is reading the poetry of the Beat generation, and comments that what he likes above all is 'the hatred of Ginsberg against the Moloch of American capitalism'; he is also reading *The Destruction of Reason* by the leading twen-tieth-century Marxist intellectual Luckacs. He is, he says, 'reading all the time'; he is also taking 'stimulants', presumably amphetamines. In a reply of early November 1967 she urges him to read *Thus Spake Zarathustra* (an English translation of Nietzsche's work from the late nineteenth century). Evidently, they both prefer to read works in English rather than in German. Her next extant letter dates from July 1969: she has taken her final school exams. His reply is the classic one of the student protester: 'In taking these exams we prostitute ourselves', reiterating in appro-priate block capitals: 'WE PROSTITUTE OURSELVES CONTINUOUSLY'.

> The most squalid thing is that I myself have not managed to do anything to cause fear to anyone. I have completed my second topic, have completed such a revolutionary topic, that Fascist examiners have given me excellent marks.... To escape from the economic control of my parents (they maintain me and they make sure that I know that they main-tain me) I am sitting the exams so that I can go to the medical school at Pisa.[128]

At the end of his letter he refers to the feebleness of young men like himself, quoting from Osborne's *Look Back in Anger* (the title is given in Italian— the play, which, of course, dates back to 1956, was popular with Italian young people because of its very association with anger): 'Men are destined to suck the blood out of women.' He awaits, he writes, her 'next move'. In fact, she berates him for both his rage and his inactivity. She, as a Christian, believes in working for others: her friends intend to practise medicine in the Third World, while she is meantime helping a retarded child prepare for exams. He doesn't act, he replies, because he 'can't see any clear end'. Her last letter to him, dated 1 December 1970, informs him that she has a boyfriend, quite probably enough to end the correspondence from his end, and what she describes as a friendship which 'has been something splendid, a perfect integration of adolescent love and adult rules'.

The sort of everyday, apolitical irritation which might turn a mature schoolgirl into an active rebel is apparent in this letter from an 18-year-old female secondary school pupil to a friend:

> The case of Margherita Tuccinei, expelled for two days from F. De Sanctis School because she entered the classroom with a little eyeshadow on her eyes, leaves me perplexed... We are in the era of sexual liberty, of miniskirts, of space voyages, of technological progress, and someone is punished for a little eyeliner on her eyes. Crazy...[129]

It would be wrong to make a rigid distinction between those whose primary aim was the destruction of bourgeois society and those, like volunteers in the American Peace Corps, in the Florence and Venice flood rescue operations, in Shelter in Britain, or working with the mentally handicapped or with the sick in the Third World, who sought constructive amelioration of existing conditions, for almost all were touched with genuine idealism; but when some of the behaviour of 1968–9 does begin to seem vicious and mindless, it is good to remember the acts of genuine selflessness.

In an earlier chapter I quoted the married woman who, by January 1958, though living in a cramped house with shabby furnishings, had a car, a refrigerator, a gramophone and television, a vacuum cleaner and an electric iron; she was legally separated from her husband in April 1967. Personal problems dominate her diary till 1968, when they are eclipsed by the occupations at the school to which she sends her sons. She takes a rather detached and almost dismissive view of what she sees as 'interminable discussions to clarify the most simple issues' and an unwelcome interruption to the natural and healthy activities of the school, such as concerts, theatrical performances, and the school magazine, which, she says, in an obvious reference to one of the issues students were now constantly complaining about, was committed to avoiding 'religion, politics, and sex'.[130] A correspondence between a secondary schoolgirl and her teacher reveals a constructive relationship in which criticisms of the existing school system are shared— to the extent that the teacher has given her pupil a copy of the famous *Letter to a Schoolmistress*.[131]

In fact, relationships between activist pupils and liberal-minded teachers were not always very easy. We are lucky to have the published record, roughly in the form of a diary, of the Florentine secondary school teacher Adriano Guerini, well known locally as a socialist and a democrat. With his entry covering March-April 1969 he begins with the new assemblies, run by the students, which now began the day in many schools. He expresses, with slight irony, the admiration of the teachers for the orderliness of the proceedings: 'a lesson in civilization', 'better than the deputies in parliament'. He notes how self-effacing the 'ten or twenty notorious members of the student movement' are, but then expresses revulsion over his discovery that these activists have planned everything out in advance. One of his ablest students had told him that in a period of politicization many things have to be done which are not strictly speaking democratic.[132] He noted how the boys 'with some difficulty forced themselves to speak the technical language of the left-wing cultural reviews'; the girls had less difficulty. In fact, Guerini thought that, as radical leaders, the girls stood out.[133]

Guerini had long experimented with fairer and more systematic systems of testing and with collective marking: he was known to parents as a friend to their children. While the school was undergoing its regime of assemblies and occupations, he maintained his weekly meetings with parents, but confessed to being able to offer little help with respect to the discomfiture they felt over the behaviour of their children. He saw the problem as being located in the changing attitudes of children towards adults, parents as well as teachers. One mother spoke desolately of the 'hot head' of her son:

You speak to him, professor: your name comes up often, and is always spoken with respect. We no longer know what to do, we are no longer able to talk to him. You should hear how arrogant he is to his father.

Guerini's reflection was that such arrogance was part and parcel of what had changed, and that without a restoration of the traditional civilities of life nothing much could be done.[134] For him, 'the autumn is already "hot" enough', and his tone is one of depression and sense of waste. For this teacher, socialist, democrat, and supporter of progressive teaching methods, there were no excitements in the events of 1968 and 1969.[135]

Let us look at another teacher, a widowed mother, who found herself increasingly infuriated by the attitudes of her son, Sergio, a secondary school student. He insisted, early in 1967, that she too should read *Letter to a Schoolmistress*. She thought the book 'shocking' and 'upsetting', and found herself engaged in increasingly bitter discussions about the book with her son.[136] She ponders the fact that her husband had come from a peasant background, while her father had been a poor official in the south who had had to sacrifice much to send her to university. She feels that teachers like herself are hard-working, underpaid, and constantly tired. Her son insists that teachers are authoritarian and that pupils are their victims. One evening in June 1967 Sergio invited some of his fellow students to supper. They talked all evening about Marcuse's *One Dimensional Man*. When she went into the sitting room with a box of caramels, the students were stretched out on the carpet, across the arms of her chair, and a girl was sitting on the knees of a boy. As the various phrases of Marcuse rang in her ears, she went to her bedroom musing on the hard life her mother had led, and the tiny pleasures of her own childhood. The students left without thanking her, leaving a mess of coffee cups and caramel papers. 'That no one had thought of saying good-bye or thanking me, I had more or less expected... Leaving the room in a mess while continuing to submerge me with their prefabricated and pseudo philosophical phrases, will always seem to me a sign of very bad upbringing.' A few days later she is commenting that Sergio is a brilliant boy with a terrific memory, spouting 'this Marcuse stuff about the irrational becoming the seat of what is truly rational'. She tries to read *One Dimensional Man,* but she can't follow it: her thoughts go back to the war when one of her brothers was a prisoner of the Germans in Venice, and another deported to Austria.

The entry of 26 June mentions Sergio's girlfriend, Giulia: she would be very happy with Giulia save that she is also in the student movement, and, 'a new thing', she calls herself a 'feminist'. Sergio's mother starts wondering if 'our way of thinking truly is too retrograde with respect to theirs; we think we can do good, make others happy by imposing our ways of being happy; and thus, through too much love, we take from them their joy of living, remove their illusions, block their spontaneous activities, and spoil their dreams'. The news for next day is that Sergio has got top marks in his exams. For the Ferragosto, the Italian August holiday, mother, son, and girlfriend are together in the mountains. Later in August she notes: 'All talk is of war: Vietnam, Cuba, Che Guevara, and the words of R. Dutschke.' She is Marxisant in the broad European sense of a general philosophy as to how history and society work, without being committed to a belief in the necessity of conflict and violence. She is afraid that the movement to which her son and his friends belong will be infiltrated by terrorists, while she perceives them as pure idealists: young people who rebel against the hypocrisy of modern society, against the power of consumerism which crushes individual liberty, against capitalism and authoritarianism: for a better world which does not deny basic needs, which gives real dignity to government, to work and to study.

In October, Sergio goes to Turin University. He gets lodgings with friends which she has to pay for. She is surprised to find that they are not as humble as she had expected, given all the talk about class equality and contempt for the bourgeoisie. By later November she is increasingly convinced

> that the student movement will not be an occasional episode, because the rebellion comprises an entire generation of young people on an international scale: a kind of chain reaction between contracting states, in which each zone has its own particular ferment.

She is writing down the causes of all this, industrial growth, the famous economic boom, the American student revolt beginning in 1964 at Berkeley, the rebellions of black minorities, the hippies, the Provos of Amsterdam, the revolts of Berlin, Frankfurt, Nanterre, Paris, when she is interrupted by a phone call from the administrator of her son's lodgings, complaining that the students are behaving appallingly. His tone to her is vicious:

> ... I really am in the midst of the most appallingly ill-brought-up people! The family next door are complaining: the noise keeps everyone awake and, in particular, old people and babies; the coming-and-going is continuous, and the friends of your boys jump on the gate, climb in without going through the doorway, and behave rowdily without the

minimum respect for other people. Notices and banners fall from their balcony into the courtyard creating a mess which upsets everyone.

She confesses to weeping for the first time since her husband's death, but then adds that in her heart of hearts 'she felt some slight sympathy for these young ill-brought-up hippies'.

'The student protest gets more and more bitter. Yesterday they occupied the Palazzo Campana' (entry for 28 November). Her son is arrested as one of the student leaders, but released the next day. He continues to come and visit her on Saturdays and Sundays, but there seems to be nothing to say between them, 'still less when we discuss the inhibitions and disinhibitions of sex'. But this warm and profoundly honest document continues, 'I have to recognize that these kids are good; they will do anything for each other; they defend each other, they help each other... if one of them is ill, they will visit him at home or in hospital... if anyone needs anything they will make any sacrifice to get it.' There is no secret about what is happening all over Italy: the entry for 27 December notes occupations at the universities of Cagliari, Sassari, Pavia, and Naples, where students have been attacked by the police. Then there have been risings at Venice, Padua, and Bologna. 'Nearly always', she writes, 'the police intervene.' So the catalogue of events continues, faithfully recorded in the diary. Events in Turin are naturally of special concern, especially when in February there was another occupation of the Palazzo Campana, with police intervention and the arrest of fifty-two students. She notes that Sergio's and Giulia's names do not appear in the newspapers. But the events leading up to, and the horrors of, the battle of the Valle Giulia in Rome are also chronicled. Student protests and police violence continue to dominate the pages, till there is a brief personal entry for 8 July: Sergio and Giulia have called in on her on the way to visit Giulia's 'modern' and 'permissive' parents. On 9 August she records what she calls 'confused thoughts': 'free love and sex have become the important topics of the day, self-fulfilment psychologically and physically, denial of any regulation and religion. They show nudes and couplings in films, and contempt for relationships and affections...'

On 10 October she records apprehensively that the new academic year is about to begin. Her son seems further away than ever. She finds her own pupils in a lower secondary school attentive—'they couldn't write on the door: "my class is a class of shit" ' (this phrase from *Letter to a Schoolmistress* clearly still rankled). The first entry for the new year (7 January 1969) speaks of classes and courses established by students, of working groups and discussions organized with well-disposed professors, but also of academics resistant to any innovation and even of some who had been subjected to such ill treatment from students that they had attempted to commit suicide.

I am completely estranged from the student discussions, but I have listened attentively to the voices and the problems which are now at the basis of their life, and I have tried to understand; I must confess that I have understood that many of their ideas are concerned with good things which others, even if they should have taken a lead, have not tried to put into practice. Much more than political interventions and useless circulars, they need to be helped and encouraged. That our past and present respectability irritates them is now

570

very clear, and responding to their demonstrations with violence is counter-productive and could produce very regrettable reactions.

This line of thought is pushed further by events recorded in the diary next day:

> I was invited by some acquaintances to tea, and I didn't have the courage to refuse. I felt as if my brains were being washed out: they spoke of nothing but the new winter models, of suppers, of servants who no longer stay in their jobs as they used to do and who are hard to find. Of cakes and biscuits, of wines of a particular vintage, etc. I felt a great urge to burst out shouting: 'for you, has nothing changed in the last year? Don't you see how superficial we are, hypocrites, and attached to a society in full decline?'
>
> But it would have been useless: they would have thought me hysterical and badly brought up.

This is a period of very intensive diary-writing, matching the developing sentiments of the diarist. First, however, her feelings take a sudden turn in the opposite direction. Most of the entry for 9 January is taken up with an account of the proposals of Sergio and Giulia. There must be a complete rejection of the conventional school, of existing exams, marks, authoritarian teaching: all the points we have encountered several times. Middle-school teachers like herself, they say, must enter into this new rebellious order. 'The discussion continued, then they asked, in an almost arrogant tone for the key of house (it was 11 pm).' At that, she records, she couldn't control herself, and uttered the words she

> never would have wanted to say or should have said: 'This house, for you, has become a hotel, just go, but I will not give you the key so that you can come back in; that has never been a custom in this house!' They looked at me as if to challenge, but also to commiserate, with me, and left. And they did not return.

The entry for 13 January records that she has received a letter from Sergio which is so painful that she is not able to transcribe it into the diary, though she quotes the gist:

> She is so bourgeois, she is an insurmountable obstacle to their ideas of a new life. They are in different worlds: they want permanent revolution, continuous struggle, total absence of sexual inhibitions, suppression of all useless taboos.

A couple of days later she sets out for Turin to try to find Sergio, no longer living in the accommodation she had financed, but in a very poor area. Towards the end of March Sergio is taken ill and she goes to visit him. In the same entry she states that she is beginning to move towards Sergio's ideas, while she herself is feeling younger. There is a full statement for 31 March: 'I have faith in Sergio and I greatly appreciated Giulia's feminist ideas, because I began work when, in the family, a woman who was not housewifely was thought badly of.' On 10 May she begins reading the *Communist Manifesto,* wanting to understand the reason for the cooperation between students and workers, and their unions, in the protests. On 24 August Sergio and Giulia are married, Giulia wearing a miniskirt. The remaining entries for 1969 are taken up with strikes and escalating violence, culminating in the bomb at piazza Fontana. No single document can carry too much explanatory freight, but this story of a mother's anger at her son, and her reconciliation with, and developing understanding of, both him and his girlfriend does give an insight into the deeper developments taking place beneath the surface of sloganizing and fighting.

One of the enormous attractions for students, and most certainly male ones, was the existence not just of the theory but of the practice of free love. All the student leaders were male, and most were to be seen accompanied by one or more girlfriends. One woman student described it as part of the mythology of the time that young women wished to be in the roles of lovers to the heroic male figures. She insisted that in the groups she was involved in there was never any question of women not having space to themselves, and that she did not feel diminished by the fact that all the leaders were men.[137] To begin with, at any rate, it seems that young women were much more concerned with getting rid of the special restrictions on their freedoms that they suffered in comparison with men than with any sense of being exploited by men (that was only to come slowly). In the generally liberated atmosphere young women, perforce, had to learn about contraception. Whether all (or most) young women enjoyed this concentrated bout of sexual liberation in the way in which, according to the slogans, they ought to have done may be open to question. But, taking into account the evidence I brought forward in Chapter 8, there can be little doubt that, as well as being times of political and intellectual excitement, and of some danger, these were also times, for young people of both sexes, of sexual liberation.

But what happened also (though more slowly than in, in particular, America) was that much thought was stirred up on the nature of this 'liberation', from the point of view of women. Also—a point not much noted by feminist and other commentators—girls coming into the movement from the secondary schools were sometimes less tied to the older conventions than those a few years older than them already at university. Guerini had said that the girls in his school stood out. He went on to pick one out as an undisputed leader. He was very precise in describing her personal appearance. She was blonde, but squat *(tozza)* and rather plain *(bruttina).*[138] When this young woman moved into the university world she would not be any male leader's choice as adoring companion; she would be a leader in her own right. We will, in our next chapter, see how part of the student movement rapidly diverged into a new feminist movement. A letter written by a young woman in January 1971, now in the Archivio Diaristico, credits reflection on the experiences of 1968 with stimulating a new examination of the role of women not only in the revolutionary Left (including the student movement), but also in the traditional parties, such as the Communist party, and society at large.[139] The student movement did have, by early 1969, a women's committee, and the earliest document presenting the new understanding of sexual liberation that I have found appears to date from March 1969. It is headed: 'Women: A Revolution Within the Revolution':

The liberation of women will obviously come from the overthrow of the society of domination and classes which has produced the destruction and subjection of women. But it is also true that a revolution within the revolution is necessary... It would be an error if during the revolution women did not also reconstruct their own lacerated and manipulated identity: the revolution would not be complete, but women would simply have a new form of slavery... Only in this way will it be possible also to give men a concrete hand in their emancipation from the racist structure...

Then comes the point about sexual liberation: 'The erotic explosion which dominates our social life, hailed for removing repression and being emancipatory, is nothing more than the more refined version of ancient sexual slavery.'[140]

The new challenges of feminism were yet to be effectively raised in any of our countries. In France, although troubles in the universities and more especially in the secondary schools were to continue into the seventies, the worst of what we associate with 'the events' of May was over. That, unfortunately, could not be said for Italy. Here, with respect to violence, the worst was only beginning.

### Echoes from the Storm: Great Britain

Although Britain never endured the sustained and horrifying violence of Rome and Milan, the Paris Left Bank, Berkeley and Columbia, the British disturbances of 1968 and 1969 did have distinctive colourings. The British Empire remained an issue in a way the French Empire no longer was in France, and racism, closely bound up with Empire, had a salience it did not possess in either France or Italy. The notion of free speech stirred resonances which were different from those of Berkeley in 1964, and almost non-existent in France and Italy. Student representation and student rights of various sorts *were* the central matters which linked together the rather isolated and sporadic outbreaks; at Oxford and Cambridge the right to distribute political tracts had still to be won, yet many disturbances centred on attempts to *deny* a hearing to guest speakers associated with right-wing, imperialist, and racist causes. Facilities at British universities were vastly superior to those in France and Italy; on the other hand, questions of student representation and of a student say in the courses taught had scarcely even been raised. Facilities were poorest, and concern about the curriculum often greatest, outside the still highly elitist universities, particularly in those centres of audacity and innovation I have mentioned several times, the art colleges. As in all four countries, Vietnam was the topic which generated most anger and energy, brought most protesters together, and gave greatest scope to the violent extremists. The only event which began to compare in scale and violence with any of those in America or on the Continent was the attempt of the demonstrators to attack the American embassy in Grosvenor Square in March 1968. A majority of those involved in Vietnam protests of all types were students and young people. However, an intellectual left-wing subculture brought together the older and the younger, articulating causes which were not directly tied to university issues. This subculture included the older left-wing journals (such as *New Statesman, Tribune,* and *Left Review),* the underground papers, experimental theatre, and the new radical Marxist journal founded by

Tariq Ali, appearing on 15 May 1968, *Black Dwarf* On the other side were the police—the *British* police—unarmed, vicious enough at times in the wielding of batons, but reluctant to use tear-gas, very loath to interfere in university matters, and generally precluded from bringing prosecutions unless a really secure case at law could be made.

Following the earlier troubles at the LSE the first event in the new phase of more widespread disruption, punctuated by the occasional bout of violence in the streets, was the anti-Vietnam war demonstration of 22 October 1967, originally conceived by the traditional Left as a 'peace' demonstration, but which the Vietnam Solidarity Campaign consciously tried to turn into a 'Victory to the NLF!' (the Vietnamese National Liberation Front) campaign. Some VSC militants just about managed to fight their way through the police to reach the steps of the American embassy in Grosvenor Square. 'The Great Peace Punch-up' was the view of the *Daily Express* (23 October 1967): 'Mobs howling for peace in Vietnam warred with police.' In its own words, the Vietnam Solidarity Campaign

> is a movement committee to the victory of the Vietnamese people against the war of aggression and atrocity waged by the United States. We regard the struggle of the people of Vietnam as heroic and just.[141]

Though small, the VSC tapped into that long-standing British Marxism which brought together activists in both university and unions, and into folk song rather than rock. One of our richest sources is the collection of papers (housed in the Modern Records Centre, University of Warwick) of Joe Askins, a Manchester busman and secretary of the affiliated North West Regional Council for Peace in Vietnam. The minutes of the VSC national executive tell us that the folk song concert at the Roundhouse on 22 December 1967 made a profit of £150, which would be used to fund the next London demonstration on 24 March.[142]

Early in 1969 Tariq Ali, wealthy Pakistani, Trotskyite, and former president of the Oxford Union, brought out a little book, *New Revolutionaries: Left Opposition,* which explained the nature and philosophy of this movement of which he was the leading figure; it also had as a frontispiece a diagram showing 'how to make a Molotov Cocktail'. It was international in character, opening with the testimony of French revolutionary anti-imperialist Régis Debray at his court martial in Bolivia, and including pieces by Eldridge Cleaver and Stokely Carmichael, president and prime minister of the Black Panther party respectively, Fidel Castro, Pierre Frank, leader of the French Trotskyites 'in the forefront of the May Revolution in France', Inti Peredo, successor to Che Guevara as leader of the Bolivian guerrillas, and Fritz Tuefel, leading member of the Marxist section of the West German Socialist Students' Association. Referring to the second and third Vietnam demonstrations in March and October 1968, Ali wrote, with no false deprecation of violence:

> The movement was on the increase and in subsequent demonstrations the numbers doubled and trebled as did the violence. The new revolutionaries were quite open about their aims: it was hypocritical to protest against violence at home while justifying it in

Vietnam; we were not pacifists, and if a policeman hit us we would defend ourselves. Our violence was defensive—a response to the repressive violence of the State machine. Moreover we were not going to be told how to demonstrate. We would occupy the streets, march with linked arms and not let our comrades be arrested...[143]

Ali had (and has) a distinctive, slightly nasal, voice, a mixture of Pakistani English and upper-class Oxford English, which somehow always sounded particularly well suited to the dogmatic tosh he pounded out about capitalist crises and near-revolution in France, which always found ready listeners.

It is now abundantly clear that the problems which arise from the functioning of modern or neo-capitalism cannot be solved within the framework of the existing social structures. They can be dealt with in the short term by classic capitalist remedies (deflation, import controls, export subsidies, devaluation, etc.), but in the long run they will continue to plague imperialist societies. These societies will continue to be afflicted by the internal contradictions of the system; contradictions which will finally tear them apart.[144]

The phrases—'within the framework of the existing social structures', 'classic capitalist remedies', 'the internal contradictions of the system'—all had the familiarity and comfort of a battered old armchair; challenging so many other things, the brightest and best of a generation never blinked at this weary old Marxist claptrap, but that only demonstrates how inherently hopeless the 'capitalist' case appeared to be, and how powerful was the faith that the world could and must be changed.

The particularly turbulent beginnings to the new academic year on the Continent were echoed in Britain's December troubles, not in the élite college of London University, LSE, but in two lowly, non-university institutions, both housed in shabby buildings in central London, the Regent Street Polytechnic and the Holborn College of Law and Commerce. In both there were short sit-ins in support of demands for student representation. In almost all universities and colleges, now, discussions were under way over securing some form of student representation on the main governing bodies, usually called senates and councils ('courts' in Scotland). In Aston University in Birmingham, then Leicester University, there were small demonstrations. However, more attention was attracted by the more or less violent attempts to prevent unpopular speakers from gaining a hearing. At the University of Sussex a speaker on Vietnam from the American embassy was covered in red paint. At the University of Essex two Conservative MPs, including Enoch Powell, who was now beginning to take an extreme white racist line, were attacked. The Labour secretary of state for education and science, Patrick Gordon-Walker, was shouted down at Manchester, while Labour defence secretary Denis Healey almost had his car overturned by Cambridge students, and home secretary James Callaghan ran into similar threats at Oxford. Two of the students involved at Manchester were suspended.[145] In the working-class district of Shoreditch, somewhat to the east of LSE, there was a sort of Anti-University, substantially the work of the American Allen Krebs, following the example of the Free School of New York: a mixture of left-wing academics and figures from experimental theatre provided rather fragmented educational experiences which petered out by the summer of 1968. With perhaps more real intellectual talent to draw on, Cambridge did manage to offer a rather more credible 'Free University'.[146]

But all developments were eclipsed by the Vietnam demonstration on 17 March, in which 25,000 participated. This time the Vietnam Solidarity Campaign, bolstered by the profits of the Roundhouse concert, was better prepared, and the scenes broadcast from Grosvenor Square were the most violent yet seen on British television. In fact, no Molotov cocktails were used, the main offensive weapons of the demonstrators being firecrackers aimed at police horses, and the poles of banners, which were hurled at the police. A mounted police charge caused much screaming, and the use of truncheons many injuries, but tear-gas was not used. In fact, only forty-five demonstrators received medical treatment, as against 117 police; charges were brought against 246 people.[147] Most sloganizing inevitably has its mindless quality: 'Ho-Ho-Ho Chi Minh!' had exactly the right exultant and triumphalist sound. Another demonstration was held the following week, this time, though still dominated by young people, kept largely under the control of CND. CND then had its not very spectacular Easter March: from this Tariq Ali sought recruits for demonstrations at the German embassy and at the Springer building in Fleet Street, as a slightly belated response to news of the attempted murder of Dutschke. Ali complained on television that while all other countries had had protests over Dutschke, only Britain had not.[148]

Further instalments of something could be expected after the Easter holidays; in fact they particularly located themselves in the new University of Essex, remote, but with fine amenities, and in some shabby urban art colleges. At Essex, a scientist from the Ministry of Defence's chemical warfare establishment at Porton Down was prevented from giving a lecture. The vice-chancellor, Sir Alfred Sloman, took immediate and drastic action, expelling three students, on the grounds that while there were no designated disciplinary proceedings for dealing with this offence, to deny free speech was to destroy the whole basis on which a university existed. It was an argument which many students, and quite a number of staff, did not find persuasive. A sit-in, supported by members of staff, resulted in the students being reinstated. With its self-contained campus, a large number of innovative practices, and young staff, strong in the social sciences, Essex became Britain's model centre of protest, with a 'Free University' attracting 1,000 staff and students. Plans were made for a completely new government structure, new kinds of degrees, the abolition of exams.[149] At Hornsey Art School, in a working-class district of north-east London, the initial cause of friction was a very specific matter concerning student rights. For some years at the universities, student office-holders in unions or representative bodies had been successfully arguing that they could not both carry out their duties and continue full-time studies. Students were beginning to seek this privilege in less prestigious places as well. In Hornsey the union president was claiming the right to a sabbatical. As an art college, Hornsey did not have the autonomy of a university, but fell under the control of the local authority. The concession was actually granted, but it took rather a long time, and in the meantime, prodded by rumours of the college being taken over by a polytechnic, a student movement for total reform, rather on the model of the Beaux-Arts in Paris, took over the college, with the support of most of the staff.[150] Programmes were put forward for courses which would be socially and politically aware, but there were also demands for courses which would provide jobs. The Hornsey episode has the honour of producing one of the best known of counter-revolutionary, or bourgeois, or silent majority, or common-sense documents of the time, an editorial in the local paper, the *Wood Green, Southgate and Palmers Green Weekly Herald*:

> ... a bunch of crackpots, here in Haringey, or in Grosvenor Square, or Paris, or Berlin, or Mexico, can never overthrow an established system... They may dislike having to conform to a system in which they are required to study, and follow set programmes, and take examinations or their equivalents; and acknowledge that in doing so they are through the indulgence of others, preparing themselves for a lifetime of earning... The system is ours. We are the ordinary people, the nine-to-five, Monday-to-Friday-semi-detached, suburban wage-earners, who are the system. We are not victims of it. We are not slaves to it. We are it, and we like it. Does any bunch of twopenny-halfpenny kids think they can turn us upside down? They'll learn.[151]

Occupations followed at Croydon College of Art in south London and Guildford School of Art to the south-west of London. At Hornsey, the local authority used security guards and dogs to chase out the small number of students still maintaining the occupation, shortly before the summer vacation. Although the principal was keen to make some accommodation with the students, the local authority locked the college at the beginning of the autumn term, dismissing all students and part-time staff who had been involved in the revolt. At Guildford the college was also closed, with students expelled, and nearly fifty staff dismissed.[152] We are lucky in having preserved in the Modern Records Centre at the University of Warwick a clutch of typescript documents, originated by those involved and by the Association of Teachers in Technical Institutions (ATTI), which not only provide enough detail to convey a palpable sense of the atmosphere at Guildford but at the same time illuminate both the archaeology of a sit-in and the nature of the conflict. The main document is the report compiled by ATTI, dated 28 October 1968.[153] This began by identifying the two main areas of dispute: 'the general state of art education in the country', and specific issues at Guildford. Since the arrival of the principal three years previously there had been no staff meetings; at meetings of heads of departments, the heads were 'simply told what they had to do'. Early in 1968 the local authority had taken the decision to amalgamate Guildford with the Farnham Art School: this had the general agreement of the Guildford staff, 'but as is frequently the case in an amalgamation, staff felt on edge because they did not know what their own future was going to be'. During the last week of May some lecturers became aware that the students were planning a meeting to voice their own complaints, and informed the principal in the hope that he would meet with the students; but no action was taken. On 5 June students asked for, and were granted, permission from the principal to hold their meeting (showing a subservience unheard of on the Continent!). The report continues:

> Certain members of staff attended this student meeting at the invitation of students. The

meeting went on all night and continued into the next day. At first the meeting appears to have been loosely organized, with students going out to classes, but within several days it was clear that the meeting had become a 'sit-in'. Nobody in authority other than certain members of staff appear to have gone to this sit-in. At a fairly early point, certain members of staff called a meeting of staff to discuss what was happening. The Principal appears to have forbidden members of staff to attend this meeting. About 30 staff (the estimates vary) attended, but in view of the Principal's opposition the meeting broke up within 10 to 15 minutes.

On 12 June a meeting of full-time staff (like most art colleges, Guildford had a large complement of part-time staff) was called by the principal, who had with him the local authority assistant education officer responsible for further education.

At an early point the Principal indicated what steps he had taken to end the student sit-in. He then asked all those staff who agreed with what he had done and who were loyal to him to leave the meeting.

About fifty or sixty left, but some remained.

Information in the hands of the Association makes it clear that the intention had been to suspend those staff who remained, but in view of the numbers involved it was decided that there should be a further staff meeting in the afternoon including both part-time and full-time staff.

This meeting agreed to the setting up (amazingly, for the first time in this autocracy) of an academic board, which was perceived as the 'first necessary step towards resolving the difficulties and ending the sit-in'. On being informed of this decision, the students gave it their support, 'believing that if this was set up the difficulties could be resolved'. This agreement between staff and students, along with a statement that it was thought to provide the basis for a solution, was conveyed to the chairman of the governors on 13 June. At their meeting next day the governors decided to make no response to this attempt to institute a form of representative government, instead insisting that the school must return to 'normal' conditions, that is to say, autocracy. On 19 June all staff (full-time and part-time) returned to their duties—but the students remained on a one-hour sit-in. On 21 June the governors decided to close the college and to instruct staff and students to leave the premises. Members of staff were informed by letter that failure to observe this instruction would be regarded as a major breach of discipline; there would be no consideration of the proposal for an academic board till the college buildings had been vacated. Security guards were brought in; lighting and heating were cut off. Several members of staff joined with students in seeing these as provocative actions on the part of the local authority, and refused to leave. The local authority issued writs for trespass against the students and twelve staff members. The writs against the twelve were withdrawn when they agreed to leave on the understanding that a full staff meeting would be held. The meeting was not held.

Now that running question of the relationship between students and their parents comes into focus once more. In fact, the Guildford students acted through their parents in contesting the writs; once again the courts acted in a liberal and rational manner and the writs were quashed. The students remained in the school till 29 July, when, in the familiar way, they succumbed to the call of summer and ended the occupation. The local authority resolved to dismiss twelve full-time staff, subsequently changed to seven, with five being subjected to disciplinary interviews. Forty part-time staff would not have their contracts renewed. Action by ATTI secured the reemployment of a mere eight of them. The student leaders were expelled. With a view to eventual amalgamation, fine art courses were transferred to Farnham. A document produced by the sacked staff got to the heart of student discontent:

> It is implicitly assumed from the very beginning of a student's course that he *[sic*— but students at this sort of college were almost exclusively male] is fitted for no more than a comparatively low-level 'operative' or *'executant'* status in industry or commerce. His 'education' is simply that of being introduced to established skills and fashionable commercial practices.[154]

Another unfashionable centre of protest was Enfield College in north London: the authorities were planning to reduce the numbers of overseas admissions, interpreted by students as a racist move: in the face of a sit-in the authorities withdrew their proposals. Relatively minor action of one sort or another took place at Birmingham Art School and at Hull, Keele, Leeds, and Bradford universities. There was a surge of trouble at Essex again in December, when a well-known radical student was expelled for drugs offences: the computer centre was invaded, and damage done to research.[155]

Meantime, at LSE plans for student involvement in college government were due to be announced in October; however, the next Vietnam demonstration, scheduled for that month, was a much greater source of excitement. At the meeting of the student union on 17 October discussion of university government was trumped by a proposal from VSC supporters to take the school into occupation throughout the weekend of the Vietnam demonstration, so that it could provide sanctuary and medical assistance to demonstrators, and also a centre for political discussion open to all comers. In a thin meeting this surprise proposal was carried. The Conservative Society insisted on a fresh meeting; at this the decision was overthrown by sixty votes, but then when a recount was called for the majority had melted away, and so in a nice illumination of the nature of student politics, a decision ended up being taken formally in favour of the occupation. The majority might well feel aggrieved. However, an announcement that the governors would prevent the occupation probably turned quite a substantial number of students in favour of it. Wisely, the college authorities did not in the event interfere with the occupation, which was conducted with great respect for college property and was, indeed, a highly successful part of the massive Vietnam demonstration.[156]

The police took the precaution of searching marchers for weapons, but nothing very sinister was discovered. This time the demonstration split, with only a minority of about 3,000 once again making for Grosvenor Square (the only precise aim articulated in the VSC executive minutes was to immobilize the American embassy for a token period).[157] Even this section was handled with great restraint by the police:[158] there had been one battle of Grosvenor Square in March, but there was scarcely a second one. The imaginative, and relatively recently founded magazine *New Society* took the opportunity, during the main Sunday of the demonstration, to try to establish the profile and attitudes of demonstrators. Out of 300 questionnaires distributed, 270 were completed. Students made up just over half of the sample, with one tenth of these still being at school. While the demonstrators came from conviction, with two-thirds of the sample having demonstrated before, many tourists came simply for the spectacle, to the extent that, the *New Society* article maintained, ultimately in Grosvenor Square there were more spectators than demonstrators. Most demonstrators had come to protest at United States policies in Vietnam—96 per cent (97 per cent of students), United States policies in general—69 per cent (70 per cent of students), British policies on Vietnam—85 per cent (87 per cent of students), the general structure of British society—65 per cent (67 per cent of students), capitalism in general—68 per cent both for all demonstrators and students, all forms of authority—23 per cent (22 per cent of students). Asked if they were hoping for a Vietnamese victory, or simply a compromise, 53 per cent (and 56 per cent of students) said the former, 42 per cent (38 per cent of students) the latter. Altogether 25 per cent of all of the demonstrators were under the age of 25; only 20 per cent were female (18 per cent of students). Paul Barker of *New Society* thought the demonstration characterized by 'non-militancy' and thought the 'chant of "ho-ho-Ho Chi Minh" was more like a US cheerleader's chant than a call to revolution'. Perhaps the clinching remark was that of a man in Grosvenor Square who commented sadly: 'The whole of swinging London seems to be here.'[159] The visual record we have of this demonstration is enhanced by the fact that since the previous one in March colour television had arrived.[160]

LSE, throughout the weekend, presented a festive appearance, particularly with its perky banner: 'Adams Closed It, We Opened It'. But then things began to turn sour. With the Commonwealth prime ministers' conference scheduled to take place in January, it seemed pertinent to organize a teach-in on South Africa and Rhodesia. The new chairman of the governors, Lord Robbins, author of one of the key sixties texts, his expansionist report on higher education, warned academic staff that they could be dismissed if they encouraged or took part in disorderly conduct.[161] Already unfortunate art lecturers had been dismissed out of hand in a manner which would have been almost impossible on the Continent; it had certainly been thought that such threats could never be applied to incumbents of university posts. About a quarter of the academic staff signed a letter drawing attention to their rights to free expression, while the students' union resolved on resistance to the governors' threats through direct action. Meantime, short sit-ins took place at both Birmingham and Bristol universities, albeit without serious incident.

Adams expressed willingness to address the teach-in, but then some very stern challenges were thrown down at him. It was demanded that the school should publish a list of its holdings in Rhodesia and South Africa; that the school's governors should resign from the boards of companies trading with Rhodesia and South Africa; and that such companies should not be able to recruit inside the school. Adams reappeared two days later, but failed to match the demands of his inquisitors. After something of a shouting match he left. With that combination of persistence and boorishness which endeared them to few outside the peer group, the militant students attempted to summon the director back. As one might expect, he refused. Angry and self-righteous students then went in pursuit, but were prevented from getting to his office by a set of closed fire-doors. They had to make do instead with an impromptu teach-in in the senior common room. Attention now became fixated upon the notorious case of 'the Gates', iron gates recently installed by the administration at strategic points. The militants managed to get a hurried union resolution passed by 51 votes out of 513 in favour of taking direct action to remove the gates forthwith. Despite the attempts of left-wing staff to the get the militants to desist, they none the less waded in with pickaxes, crowbars, and a sledgehammer. Now Adams did summon the police: the students after all were destroying property and wielding dangerous implements. But the police were very loath to show up, and by the time they did the students were gone, many to the bar. Students then had to be identified by members of staff and then taken to Bow Street Magistrates' Court; here another demonstration took place, followed by more arrests.

Once more LSE was closed, rigorously this time with the help of the police, and lasting for four weeks until 19 February. A sort of 'LSE in exile' was established within the London University student union. Disciplinary charges were brought against three LSE lecturers for their part in the 'Gates' episode. A parliamentary committee of inquiry which visited both Essex and LSE was met with disruptive behaviour.[162] Still in exile, the LSE union held a meeting in the Friends Meeting House in Euston Road, which called for the removal of the gates, the removal of the police, and the reopening of LSE. In March criminal summonses were taken out against two of the lecturers and eight students. Open again, LSE was again occupied, this time to the accompaniment of a good deal of vandalism. There was personal violence against those members of staff who had given evidence against students or the three members of staff. Altogether, a thoroughly embittered and poisoned atmosphere was created. In the end, two of the staff dismissals were maintained, harsh and untoward action for a British university. After the general good spirits of 17 October it was a pity that a level of conciliation could not have been maintained; but there were too many irresponsible and unpleasant spirits on both sides. With the summer vacation, the main spasm of turbulence in the British universities faded somewhat, though over the next few years there were to be incidents of a sort which a few years previously would have been thought entirely alien to British higher education.[163]

## America's Annus Horribilis

The long hot summer which commentators were already envisaging early in 1968 was one that they expected would be battled out in the ghettos. In fact, April was the month in which the cities burned. This was because of a portentous chain of events which began with a strike of black workers in Memphis in February. But it was not for violence in the ghettos that 1968 became infamous. First, in a kind of unhinged awfulness which had no equivalent in France or Italy, there were two political assassinations, of the two men who offered, respectively, the best prospect of imaginative yet moderate leadership to whites and to blacks, Robert Kennedy and Martin Luther King. Firearms had not been lightly used in Italy, still less in France, but, in America guns were now quite forcefully setting the agenda: for some militants, guns coloured the kind of threats they most readily made; the police were only too ready to react lethally to any suggestion that the other side had firearms. The geography of confrontation was not entirely as would have been predicted. Massive, intense anti-Vietnam war demonstrations continued; Martin Luther King was planning a new March on Washington, a 'Poor People's March', switching from the civil rights of 1963 to economic rights. Students could be expected to participate actively in the various protest movements; but, for all the continuing energy of the Free Speech Movement, there was no special educational crisis as there was in France and Italy, though events in France were certainly to have their reverberations. But, quite early in the year, a major crisis did indeed break out in one of America's most important universities. Columbia, in New York, was a privileged private university—however, a university in which students were expected to be silently appreciative of the trainee position they occupied within the world of business, respectful towards their elders, and tolerant of the bumbling, arrogant, uncaring bureaucracy. There were some other problems as well.

One of these involved issues of race. Columbia (like a number of other big urban universities, Chicago being a notorious example) had been wont to carry out its development plans without regard to the impact on the housing and amenities of both whites and blacks living in the vicinity. A specific point of contention arose over the desire of the university authorities to build a new gymnasium, encroaching upon the precious open space, Morningside Park, which could reasonably be regarded as a necessary amenity for local blacks. There were other university protests and confrontations throughout 1968, though those at Columbia were the most violent. While the race issue was only a component of the problem at Columbia, race did come to assume a completely new, and extremely dangerous, function on certain other campuses, particularly towards the end of the year. Already I have several times quoted some of the demented utterances of white racists, particularly with respect to sexual matters. The whole move to secure places for blacks within prosperous white colleges was understandable and laudable, as indeed were the moves to replace courses entirely presented from a white point of view with various courses within the realm of black studies. Circumstances varied from campus to campus, but obviously black students and newly appointed black academics could be seen as being at a disadvantage compared with long-established white ones. However, some blacks saw, not just the curriculum, but actual physical space and territory as an arena in which to assert black power and impose black separatism, or even supremacy; and a few held notions of black supremacism with something of that demented quality so obvious in white supremacists. In almost all cases white academics and white students, partly from genuine liberal-mindedness, partly from guilt, partly perhaps also from fear, were only too eager to make accommodations to black colleagues and students, and to make space for black studies; for those skilled in the politics of race and, sometimes, the tricks of the ghetto, opportunities were there for exploitation, and even for blackmail. The new 'black power of the campuses' was an important ingredient in certain distinctive types of violence towards the end of the year.

Before many months of 1969 had passed, one familiar trouble-spot in the university world was back in the headlines, Berkeley. The new source of tension, 'the People's Park', need not have caused violence at all; but with Ronald Reagan governor of California, and determined to crush all agitation by students and hippies, Berkeley entered upon the most awful period in its history at the Easter of 1969, when it is scarcely an abuse of words to say that it fell under military occupation. I started this section by mentioning a black workers' strike; then I moved to various kinds of university activism; but the spot on the map which is most notorious, is the one encompassing the surroundings of the Chicago Democratic Convention of August 1968—where there were episodes of the most appalling brutality on the part of the police towards young protesters against the conservative Democratic party leadership. The social welfare improvements which I mentioned in Chapter 6 continued to be implemented in 1968 and 1969; lifestyles were enriched, perceptions broadened, personal freedoms enhanced. These important matters are all to be taken up again in a later chapter: we should never lose sight of the more profound and more enduring developments; but for the moment we must fix our eyes on events which can be described as nothing other than horrible.

On Monday 12 February, 1,375 employees of the Memphis Department of Public Works, overwhelmingly 'sanitation workers' (or, in British English, 'dustmen'), almost exclusively black, went on strike.[164] The trouble, in fact, had begun among a group of twenty-two black sewer workers. After reporting for work on 31 January these workers were sent home when it began to rain. But white workers on the same job were not sent home, and, when the rain stopped after an hour or so, they were put to work and paid for the full day. The black workers complained, and found at the end of the week that all that the city was paying them for that day was two hours' 'call-up pay'. Deeply dissatisfied, the black workers called for a meeting of Memphis Local 1733 of the American Federation of State, County, and Municipal Employees (affiliated to the AFL-CIO). This particular branch consisted entirely of black members. The Memphis city council recognized neither the union nor the right of public employees to go on strike. A recent nine-day garbage workers' strike in New York had had devastating effects, but outside the city itself the Memphis strike attracted little attention. Hardline Mayor Henry Loeb, 'a tall, big-boned, darkly handsome man' (educated, incidentally, at two upper-class northern institutions, Phillips Exeter Academy and Brown University), appeared to relish the conflict and at once began to hire non-union workers and supervisors.[165] A satisfactory service was maintained downtown, and for such vital institutions as hospitals. For the suburbs a rota system was put into operation, with the two Memphis daily papers printing maps showing which neighbourhoods would have their refuse removed on that particular day, together with the location of city dumps so that people could dispose of their own accumulations of rubbish if they wished. Loeb proudly announced that he had other plans in reserve, such as placing garbage trucks in shopping centres to which, again, people could bring their own refuse. On the seventeenth day of the strike, 317 men reported for work, consisting of 108 non-strikers, 62 strikers who had given up, and 147 new non-union recruits: Loeb expressed delight, and spoke of the possibility of scaling down on hiring as soon as the force 'gets high enough to provide once-a-week pick-ups'.[166]

Loeb's complacent aggressiveness was misplaced. The strike became the focal point for the long-felt discontents of the majority of black Memphis workers: it became a strike on behalf of decent wages, union recognition, and the right to have union dues deducted at source from wage packets. The strike also exposed the fraudulence of the façade of racial tolerance put up by many of Memphis's white 'moderates'. There was heavy irony in the fact that Ahlgren, editor of the *Commercial Appeal*, had received a Brotherhood Award from the local National Conference of Christians and Jews, two days before his paper published an editorial bitterly hostile to the strikers, together with one of those particularly unpleasant racist cartoons in which southern newspapers had long specialized: a fat black man is pictured sitting atop a garbage can surrounded by a pile of rubbish and overturned dustbins. The garbage can is labelled 'City Hall Sit-in'. Wavy lines indicate unpleasant odours arising from the garbage heap and the black man himself. Above his head the lines form into the legend 'Threat of anarchy'. The cartoon is titled 'Beyond the Bounds of Tolerance'.[167] The union sent in a couple of officials from New York, local black ministers attempted mediation, and the Memphis NAACP threatened massive demonstrations, the first of which took the form of a picketing of City Hall on Monday 19 February. At a public hearing of the city committee on public works on Thursday 22 February, striking workers forced their way in (this was the 'sit-in' and 'threat of anarchy' referred to by the *Commercial Appeal)*, so that the hearing was recessed. When the hearing reopened the committee itself actually recommended that Union recognition and the direct collection of union dues be conceded.[168] The equable response at this stage of the more broad-minded moderates is represented in a letter to Edmund Orgill, who was out of town at this time, from his own company vice-president. The letter began with the weather: 'We woke up with about an inch of snow and ice on the ground.' Only in the second paragraph did this piece of news emerge:

> Our garbage men went on strike. I think this is either the tenth or eleventh day and Mayor Loeb has had his hands full. There are a couple of union leaders in here from New York and they really have the men stirred up....

The third paragraph says that sales are good, and the fourth expresses the hope that the absent boss is having a 'wonderful time'. The letter concludes: 'No worthwhile news other than the weather and the garbage strike.'[169]

The case for the strikers was most persuasively put in an editorial entitled 'Memphians Should Be Ashamed' in the March edition of the black paper the *Tri-State Press*. The paper included among the causes of shame:

> That city employees had to strike because they had inadequate wages, no grievance procedure, no workmen's compensation, no unemployment compensation, no recognition of their right to organize, and a denial of their right to strike to redress these wrongs.
>
> That many Memphians were so eager to volunteer for temporary duty as strikebreakers in order to help hold down the wages of garbage collectors—whose jobs they wouldn't have at three times the price.

That some Memphians fooled Boy Scouts into thinking they were doing a 'good turn' when they donated their services as strike-breakers in the sanitation workers strike.

The April issue commented that Loeb was spending more to fight the strike than it would take to settle it—'And he's using your tax money in the effort to annihilate the union'. It was only in January that Memphis had moved from the commission form of government to a properly constituted city council: the strike had its immediate occasion in the sewer workers' grievances, and was essentially the product of long-maturing discontent; but a further triggering factor was probably disappointment that the change to formal city government brought no benefit to blacks.

Loeb undoubtedly had considerable white support. When, because of the vast crowds wishing to attend, the city council meeting on 23 March moved to the music auditorium, a resolution supporting Loeb was passed, while the public works committee recommendations with regard to union recognition and check-off rights were rejected. In an address nine years later a leading black middle-class figure, Patricia W. Shaw, invited her listeners to 'think back' to

> When a Mayor called Henry Loeb almost destroyed this city... His administration was so shackled by tradition and so terrified of change that they trembled at the sound of guitar music or even a mention of the United Nations... They shuddered at the sight of long hair and at black people and white people holding hands. There were bumper stickers every-where—remember those?—red, white and blue bumper stickers reading: MEMPHIS LOVE IT OR LEAVE IT. There were flags in every lapel— with the implication that anyone who didn't wear one was less patriotic, less American than he ought to be.[170]

By the mid-seventies it had also been revealed, during police scandals fully reported in the Memphis newspapers, that the police had mounted surveillance operations against the strik-ers and the union they were trying to join, not to mention a whole range of civil rights, labour, and anti-Vietnam war organizations.

'Let our position be crystal clear,' read the March 1968 typescript 'Statement By Memphis AFL-CIO Labor Council on the Sanitation Department Strike':

> The 1300 employees of the Public Works Department of the city of Memphis must have the right to be represented by the organization of their choice for the purpose of collective bargaining...
> These employees must have the right to have any sum of money they voluntarily choose to authorize deducted from their pay-cheques to support their organization.
> These employees must have the right to a wage that will allow them to live decently.
> These employees must have the right to withhold their services in order to raise their standard of living and preserve their dignity.
> The absolute refusal of Mayor Loeb to bargain with the union and to sign an

agreement demonstrates his Anti-Labor views and his utter disregard for the rights of the employees and his callousness toward the dignity of the individual.[171]

From 26 February marches, boycotts (in particular of all Loeb businesses, downtown stores, and both newspapers), protests, and mass meetings were daily occurrences: the march on 4 March was joined by 500 white trade unionists. Police reacted in the traditional way, and began deploying the new weapon Mace, a disabling and potentially dangerous spray.[172] On 5 March, 121 strike leaders were arrested after a sit-in at City Hall. Some blacks retaliated by dumping garbage in the streets and breaking the windows of laundries and restaurants owned by Mayor Loeb's brother. By the end of that week what was happening in Memphis had reached the *Wall Street Journal*, which, under the headline 'Garbage Strike Piles Up Negro Unity', reported that 'a powerful Negro coalition has risen from the garbage of "America's Cleanest City", as Memphis likes to call itself'. The article drew explicit comparisons with the recent New York garbage strike, declaring that Loeb's measures had prevented a major health hazard developing, at least in white areas, though garbage was piling up in black neighbourhoods.

> The New York strike never developed the racial overtones of the Memphis conflict. Regardless of the merits of either side's contentions in the strike the disquiet here has turned into an all-out assault by Negroes on political, social and economic customs of this Deep-South city, threatening to shatter the surface calm in racial matters that has prevailed in recent years.

The article then noted that, on the grounds that strikes against the public interest were illegal in Tennessee, an injunction had been issued against the strike, and that Loeb was using the excuse of the unions' defiance of his injunction to refuse any negotiations till there was a return to work. 'Legal considerations aside, the Memphis strike has galvanized the Negro community into a unified effort, led by Negro clergymen. There are daily marches on city hall, and a boycott of down-town businesses and the city's two daily newspapers.'

The article then referred to the cartoon I have already mentioned, also to the regular cartoon feature 'Hambone's Meditations', 'depicting an obsequious Negro who spouts homilies in pidgin-English'.

> 'Hambone must go,' says Jesse Turner, President of the Memphis NAACP. Mr Ahlgren replies that the Negro unity drive consists of 'a bunch of rabble-rousing preachers' and says the 'Threat of Anarchy' cartoon was an 'accurate portrayal of Negro strikers in open defiance of law and order.'

The article went on to report that prayer meetings at black churches were jammed not only with sanitation workers and civil rights leaders but also with blacks from the neighbourhoods in which the meetings were held. It reported that in less than a week black ministers had raised more than $15,000 for the strikers, and quoted Dr H. Ralph Jackson, a national officer of the African

Methodist Episcopal Church and a long-time Memphis minister, as saying: 'The Negro community is more united than it was during the sit-ins of the early 1960s or any other time I can remember.' 'And garbage is only the beginning,' the Revd Ezekial Bell, a leader of COME (Community in the Move for Equality), a group of more than 125 Negro ministers who had advocated the boycott from their pulpits, declared. 'We are going to get more and better jobs from the city and the down-town merchants. And those businesses that are patronized by blacks alone are going to be owned and managed by blacks.'

> Dr Jackson, considered a moderate among the city's Negro ministers, says that the use of Mace, 'nearly destroyed in two minutes my self-discipline and a belief in the non-violence that I have preached for 30 years.'
>
> Most whites have seemingly supported Mayor Loeb and the police department's use of Mace. They agree with him that a strike by public employees is illegal. Although many believe that his unwillingness to compromise has prolonged the strike, they share his distaste for a dues check-off. And they argue that the use of Mace prevented violence and saved lives.[173]

While the Memphis strike was developing, Martin Luther King was planning his greatest campaign yet, a second, more massive and more confrontational march on Washington. While the 1963 march had been a celebration of the advance of desegregation and the introduction of the civil rights bill into Congress, the new march was an integral part of a Poor People's Campaign aimed directly at economic disadvantage and housing discrimination. King declared himself to be concerned now with 'human rights' rather than just civil rights, and his specific objective was the enactment of his proposed $12 billion bill of rights for the disadvantaged, guaranteeing jobs for all able to work and an income for those unable, together with an end to discrimination in housing. Ghetto reconstruction and job training schemes were also part of the programme.[174] It was intended that an initial force of 3,000 poor blacks, whites, Puerto Ricans, Mexican Americans, and Indians (soon, as a result of sixties consciousness-raising, to be known as 'Native Americans') should march from ten cities and five rural communities across the country, where at the same time there would be demonstrations and boycotts—all this to begin on 22 April. On the banks of the Potomac River a shanty town to be called Resurrection City was to be built, which would accommodate more and more protesters if Congress failed to respond. If necessary, demonstrations and disruptions would be used to bring the nation's capital and the seat of government to a complete halt. Many of King's closest associates strongly opposed these plans. Much of the goodwill that had surrounded the civil rights movement had evaporated. To standard-issue American liberals, King seemed to have turned in a dangerously socialistic direction. His outspoken attacks on the Vietnam war and American foreign policy generally had alienated many supporters, including black ones. With the costs of the war escalating, politicians were in no mood for passing expensive social legislation. In the aftermath of the 1967 riots, hostility among whites was high towards blacks in general, and demonstrations in particular. An election was on the way. At the same time, while President Johnson had become a hate figure for activists, he was not a racist in the bull-headed southern mould: while he and his associates would be unreceptive to demands for reform, they were unlikely to be provoked into the kind of vicious action which might bring a rush of sympathy for the protesters. These were the arguments deployed by James Bevel, Andrew Young, Jesse Jackson, and Hosea Williams, and also by Bayard Rustin and Michael Harrington. Rustin feared both that King would be unable to control the protest and that it would be infiltrated by extremist elements with no commitment to non-violence, and that widespread revulsion against the protesters would be combined with heavily repressive measures by the authorities. King recognized the risks, appreciating that failure would bring discredit on himself and on the non-violent method, but felt he must go ahead with a protest intended to be 'as dramatic, as dislocative, as disruptive, as attention-getting as the riots without destroying life and property'.

Meeting at Miami in January 1968, the SCLC ministers by a majority gave their approval for the Poor People's Campaign; an all-day meeting between King and his staff in Atlanta on 12 February evolved the grand plan, and King set out on an exhausting series of People-to-People Tours, meeting leaders of the various ethnic groups and striving to secure financial support and the recruitment of volunteers. It was sheer chance that King was fully engaged as the Memphis strike reached its first crisis points: Loeb's ultimatum of 21 February threatening the sack for all workers who refused to return to work, and the police use of clubs on 23 February to attack the strikers' march. The leading SCLC figure in Memphis, James Lawson, was a member of COME, the directing force behind the strike. During the week following these two crisis points he telephoned King and invited him to come to Memphis to address a mass meeting, hoping that this would broaden the base of the Memphis action and attract the national attention which so far was proving elusive. King and his associates, for their part, calculated that, if King could achieve a major success for his non-violent methods in Memphis, this would give the Poor People's Campaign the kind of advance publicity it dearly needed. And it would demonstrate that there was no cause to fear that that campaign would become submerged in violence. In fact a march in Memphis led by King would be the perfect prelude to the massive march and campaign scheduled for 22 April. 'We're going to Washington, by way of Memphis,' Ralph Abernathy, King's closest aide, explained to the leader's wife. King's first address in Memphis took place before 15,000 people at the Masonic Temple on Monday 18 March. The enthusiasm of the audience boded well, and King promised to come back to lead a non-violent demonstration the following Friday. This time he had the support of many of those who were dubious about the march on Washington itself. Continuing his quest for support, King crossed the state line into Mississippi; on the day of his intended return a blizzard dumped a foot of snow on the Memphis streets, meaning that the demonstration had to be postponed to the following Thursday. Further criticisms from within the main campaign forced King to travel to New York to deal with them, from whence he returned on Thursday 28 March, tired but eager to demonstrate what a non-violent march of 6,000 protesters could achieve.[175]

It was intended that the march should pass the corner of Beale Street and continue through downtown Memphis to the city hall. King had not apprised himself of the strength in Memphis

of Black Power sentiment, nor of the alienation felt by young blacks from their moderate leadership. The local group known as the Invaders was prominent in the rioting which took place on
Beale Street, the remaining hard-pressed, white-owned shops being subject to attack. Thus, in
place of a non-violent march, there ensued what seemed very like a reprise of the sort of behaviour associated with the previous summer. One hundred and fifty-five shops were damaged, sixty
people were injured, and one person was killed—a black youth. Only after the national guard
arrived was order restored.[176] The Dalstrom Papers in the Mississippi Valley collection contain a
folder very consciously labelled 'The Memphis "Riot" ', containing eyewitness accounts of
'events in Memphis, March 28-April 1, 1968', provided by a group of high school black students
who had been waiting at their school to be bussed downtown to join the march.[177] At 8.30 a.m.
the only hint of trouble was that most of the students were talking very loudly. Then, as a bus
arrived, some of the students surrounded it and forced their way on to it. According to the
account, this could have been prevented if the NAACP workers had sent a representative to take
charge of the students. With no movement taking place, the students became impatient, blocking
the streets, throwing bricks at garbage trucks, police cars, and a laundry truck. A white woman,
trying to pass down the blocked street, kept her finger on the horn, then found her car being
kicked and dented.

> Police cars began to arrive and a helicopter appeared circling the school overhead. The
> students quietened down a bit then another bus came down Wilson and four more police
> cars arrived. The officers in these cars jumped out suddenly with night sticks and shot-
> guns in their hands and charging toward the students who were fleeing toward the
> buildings. One girl was hurt...
> Around 9.30 the students settled down and proceeded to march down-town to join
> the march.

Although there was not a great deal of disorder, ten to fifteen police patrol cars were already
making their presence felt.

> Dr King arrived at approximately 10.45. It was at this point that there was a good indica-
> tion that events would not proceed as well as planned. The people who had been milling
> around swarmed around Dr King's car and it was a good ten minutes before Dr King was
> able to get out of the car. When he finally did get out of the car he never was able to get
> ahead of those two or three hundred marchers who refused to fall into the ranks of the
> crowd.
> As the march turned on Beale I ran to get in front of Dr King in order to take some
> pictures of the leaders of the march. About a block and a half up Beale Street I heard the
> first window break.

Looking back, this writer became struck by the absence of police at the start of the march on
Beale Street. Shortly afterwards the march came to a complete stop.

589

However if the march was over much of the confusion was just beginning. I looked down Main and saw a line of policemen stretched across Main Street. Some of the policemen were wearing gas masks. As the policemen came forward mass confusion broke loose. People started running, women and children were crying and those on the sidelines were continuing to break windows and loot the stores. It was at this point that what is in my opinion, the most significant event of the whole afternoon occurred.

... as the policemen sought to push the march backwards, they turned not on the looters in particular but on the marchers and Negroes in general. They did this with such enthusiasm and with such utter disregard of justice that many people began to encourage the few who started the window breaking and began to take part in the looting themselves.

The police began using tear-gas, spraying Mace; one white protester was clubbed. According to another eyewitness account things began to get out of hand when a white supermarket owner shot and injured a black youth. This same account attributed the disturbances at Hamilton High School to pupils threatening and beating blackleg garbage workers. Anger against the blacklegs was increased through the presence of police cars as escorts. Other accounts seem to divide responsibility between black youths and the police. One witness saw 'fellows on the street drinking liquor that was stolen from the package store', and commented that 'back at Clayborne Temple fellows were trying to sell some of the things they had stolen'. Then on his way home he saw two teenagers on Vance Avenue stop and beat up a white taxi-driver. Another account probably got it just about right: 'The young looters started it; the police turned it into a disaster.' According to this account, the first shop looted was a menswear specialist, quickly followed by pawnshops yielding a haul of guitars, radios, and so on. But the next account placed the primary guilt firmly with the police:

After the police had beaten so many of the people with their Billy Sticks, some of the boys decided to fight back... I saw a policeman get his head busted by a flying brick. I saw a fellow stab a policeman in the back with a knife. The policemen did things I never thought they would do. Some of them look [sic] as if they got great joy out of beating Negroes... I wish all of this hadn't happen [sic] but, I feel that it is the fault of Mayor Loeb.

Another candidate for blame was the poor organization that led to waiting around for the march to start between 10.00 a.m. and 11.20 a.m.: 'There were quite a few incidents of drinking on the sidelines, many signs were brought past us advocating black power, and the helicopter— the one that, as of now patrols the city—kept flying over head.' There was systematic breaking of windows, but not those of black shops. Particular outrage was expressed that the police had even used Mace inside a black church. But, worst of all, a black pupil at Mitchell Road High School, Larry Paine, had been shot in the stomach at point-blank range. With the march abandoned, and the national guard moving in, there were arson attacks throughout the night. 'It seemed that the rioters tried to burn down the city,' said one student; 'Burn Baby Burn', another (female) reported, was once more the chant.

Other details emerging from eyewitness accounts are that, while Jewish and Italian stores were torched, a Chinese one was left untouched, the owner having shut up shop with a notice 'gone to march', and that, rather than the 'Black Invaders', the principal troublemakers were a local group of drunken thugs, known as the T and P Gang.

The collapse of the intended march into complete anarchy was a desperate blow for King, and for the prospects of the Poor People's Campaign. He must, he felt, make another attempt at a peaceful march in Memphis and carry it through successfully. To the press he admitted that the SCLC had been ignorant of the true situation in Memphis, but claimed also, somewhat disingenuously, that they had been placed at the head of a demonstration they had not actually planned. He went out of his way to meet the leaders of the Invaders, convincing them to give non-violence a chance, while at the same time he had to fight off the claims of his own associates that risking another failure in Memphis was risking the entire Poor People's Campaign. A new march was scheduled for Friday 5 April.[178] On Wednesday 3 April King and his staff arrived at the Lorraine Motel in the black quarter of Memphis to the south of Beale Street. However, it was decided to defer the march to Monday 8 April to encourage the participation of labour and civil rights groups from across the country, and in order to make more thorough preparations against any outbreaks of violence. By 3 April Mayor Loeb had secured a temporary injunction from the Federal District Court against 'non-residents' taking part in any march. King was supposed to be addressing a mass meeting at the Masonic Temple that evening, but was then advised by his staff not to go, since they feared that the heavy rain that day would result in a damagingly low turnout. Actually the turnout was high and enthusiastic, so King was summoned at the last moment. It was in his address here that he used what later seemed portentous words:

> Like anybody, I would like to live a long life. Longevity has its place. But I'm not concerned about that now. I just want to do God's will. And he's allowed me to go to the mountain. And I have looked over. And I have seen the promised land. I may not get there with you.[179]

The gains of the early and mid-sixties did not go for nothing. Not all the odds were stacked against King. On the afternoon of 4 April the injunction against the march was overturned, on condition that demonstrators marched only six abreast and were accompanied by march organizers trained in nonviolence.[180]

The Memphis sanitation workers strike deserves close attention, not just for the way a local (and at first totally neglected) cause came together with a national leader in a tragic dénouement, but because of what it further revealed about the complexities of the changing Memphis microcosm itself. Luckily there exists a magnificent book-length account of the strike written by a former journalist and, at the time of the strike, academic researcher at Memphis State University who herself participated in the demonstrations associated with the strike. In writing *At the River I Stand*, originally published privately in 1985, Joan Turner Beifuss also used interviews and the considerable wealth of documentation available in the two major Memphis archives, resources which, obviously, I have also used. Henry Loeb continued to be a central figure in the strike and the bitter conflict which attended it. Tall and handsome, with many of the attractive personal qualities of the self-conscious southern white male, Loeb had a considerable body of supporters, and it would not be correct to blame him alone for the manner in which the strike crisis developed. Like almost all of his kind (that is, civic leaders with realistic aspirations to office) Loeb had shifted from outspoken support of segregation in the late 1950s to a public accommodation with the notion of equal civil rights. But many of the traditional Memphis white moderates, together with all moderate black leaders, came to see Loeb as the hateful proponent of an unremitting intransigence, which brought shame to the city of whose (alleged) moderate and consensual ways they had always been proud. Loeb, without doubt, set out quite deliberately to break the strike, rather than arrive at any compromise. In some of his written communications something of the Hollywood stereotype of expressing respect for the other person's point of view while holding rigorously to one's own comes through. At one point a white trade union leader was keeping lonely vigil in the freezing cold outside the mayor's office; Loeb, in the warmest form of that stereotype, invited him in for coffee.[181] The striking of the sanitation workers themselves was a rising of the downtrodden, a turning of the most disregarded of worms. It was most important for what it did for the pride and consciousness of these poor, unconsidered men themselves; but the formal involvement of the white-led union was also an important stage in the partial merging of race issues into class ones.

Beifuss is critical of the white Memphis middle-class housewives who were very seriously inconvenienced by the interruptions to the removal of their household rubbish.[182] My impression is slightly different. No doubt the first stimulus was inconvenience, but my conclusion is that some middle-class women, at least, did come to appreciate for the first time the disgraceful conditions, and the indignities, suffered by black unskilled workers;[183] I believe that pressure from these women did play some part (though, of course, the assassination of Martin Luther King was the crucial event) in bringing the strike to a resolution; and I believe that these women were a permanent component in that change in national consciousness which, for all the continuing brutality and deprivation, is a major consequence of the events of the sixties. Inevitably the troubles in Memphis, like the troubles in the ghettos the previous summer, offered opportunities for Black Power advocates. Actually, in so far as certain local Black Power leaders acceded to the request from King to avoid violence, the strike did bring out the possibilities for continued adherence to non-violence. At the same time it became clear, as in the other cities the previous summer, that large numbers of blacks, particularly young ones, felt free of all restraints and were ready to seize any opportunity to loot, destroy, and create every kind of mayhem. At the level of basic human experience, events in Memphis brought out how a well-intentioned, peaceful demonstration (quite different from the rioting in Detroit and elsewhere) could suddenly turn into a terrifying riot, in which ordinary decent people suddenly found themselves caught between violent black elements and a police force which, from a stance of apparent restraint and tolerance, suddenly (once one or two officers had set a violent example) swung into an almost uncontrolled instrument of violence. One other major point emerges during the unfolding of the strike and the crisis associated with it: the difficult relationships that often existed between those involved locally in an issue relating to black rights and Martin Luther King, as a national figure anxious to involve himself in such issues and turn them to the advantage of the national struggle.[184]

On the evening of 4 April, then, it was known that the march postponed to the following Monday could go ahead legally. There was to be a mass meeting that very evening. First, King and his closest associates would have dinner at the Lorraine Motel. It was after dressing for dinner that King went out on to the balcony for a breath of air: it was there that he was hit fatally by an assassin's bullet. A nonentity called James Earl Ray later confessed to the murder. Once again events in Memphis seemed to separate themselves from those in the rest of the United States. The march planned for Monday 8 April took the form of a dignified memorial march, led by Coretta King and Ralph Abernathy, which passed off with remarkably little incident. The tragedy itself had a decisive effect on the Memphis situation. Many moderates now felt irrevocably alienated from Loeb; the initiatives which were already in train towards settling the strike were immeasurably strengthened.[185] Television played a crucial part in bringing home to the entire nation the portentous nature of the long, slow funeral held in Atlanta.

In the ghettos, the assassination was the signal that the long hot summer had arrived. Anger, grief, the sense of some terrible white conspiracy, all were felt. But for the typical young male black the name Martin Luther King may not have meant very much. There were causes aplenty already: here was a good enough excuse for looting and destruction. The rioting, arson, and looting lasted for a week: it began in the South, but quickly spread to all the main northern cities. One hundred and ten cities were affected in all, including Baltimore, Harlem, and Brooklyn in New York, Newark, Boston, Detroit, Chicago, and, most striking of all, Washington. Troops were deployed round the White House as fires burned and looting took place in the city centre. Altogether, across the country 75,000 national guardsmen had to be called in; 3,500 people were injured, 46 killed.[186]

Memphis enjoyed a relative calm. Ahlgren's editorial in the *Commercial Appeal* the day after the memorial march was headed: 'Quiet March, Loud Talk':

> With thousands of quiet marchers stretching down the Main Street of Memphis, yesterday's demonstration in tribute to Dr Martin Luther King went by peacefully. Mrs King spoke movingly about her slain husband as the crowd gathered before City Hall. The peaceful prelude was in vivid contrast to the fiery oratory which followed, not so much as homage to Dr King and his belief in non violence, but on the repeated theme of 'we'll take what we want.'

The editorial continued in this hostile vein, speaking of strife being inevitable when 'one group' is 'working to exert its will over the will of the American majority', then relapsed into complacent satisfaction:

> In marked contrast to many other major cities, Memphis citizens and their law enforcement representatives had maintained relative calm while havoc reigned elsewhere. The Memphis spirit was personified by the turnout of Negroes and whites who filled one stand

at Crump Stadium on Sunday afternoon to show that 'Memphis Cares'. The gathering exemplified brotherhood, a recognition of failures but also desire to move ahead toward common goals and needs.[187]

It was at this meeting in Crump Stadium that a pledge was taken by all present 'to the building of a city where people can trust one another, respect one another and respond to the needs of one another'. This was a characteristically Memphis occasion, deeply uneasy beneath the pomp, full of the letter of 'brotherhood' with little of its spirit. The whites who went manifestly did want reconciliation, but they wanted reconciliation on their own terms: they wanted, in the conservative spirit of the editorial just quoted, admission that rioting was wrong, without any exploration at all of possible causes underlying the rioting. Certain black speakers took the opportunity of referring to the strike, saying that it must now be settled—at which point some whites ostentatiously left. When certain white speakers made it clear that this was not the kind of reconciliation they had in mind, some blacks left.[188] The importance of the occasion lies in the fact that the question of now bringing the strike to a speedy end had been openly broached, and that whites, even if they were not yet prepared to make that connection, recognized that the assassination of King was not an event which could simply be shrugged off.

The principals in the negotiations were the two union leaders, a group of ministers of religion, and the mayor. On the morning after the assassination the ministers, including Rabbi Wax, who had previously held off from such action, felt impelled to make their way in a two-by-two procession to face the mayor with the resolution they had agreed to calling for an acceptance of the strikers' main terms. This was a small but dramatic incident. Wax was provoked out of his normal compromising stance, and spoke hotly to Loeb, who, it became clear, was still not going to budge. A black minister, and a Catholic academic and nun decided to mount a hunger strike there and then in Loeb's office. Loeb showed a certain consideration for the would-be hunger strikers, who eventually settled into a week-long routine outside the office, making use of a room in a nearby hotel. He also wrote a conciliatory letter to Wax—which did not prevent Wax setting down his own bitter thoughts about Loeb: 'The record shows clearly that had the Mayor had a different attitude the strike would have been quickly settled at terms more advantageous to the City of Memphis.'[189]

President Johnson sent Under-Secretary of Labor James Reynolds to Memphis with instructions to do everything possible to achieve a quick settlement. Loeb persisted with his stubborn resistance and day and night meetings continued till 16 April. Union recognition was conceded first; problems remained with the dues checkoff and with the question of a wage rise. The first problem was solved through the direct help of the Labor Department in Washington, the second by a device which strikes one as peculiarly American—a local philanthropist put up the $60,000 needed to enable a rise of ten cents an hour to be paid till the end of the current financial year; from 1 July the city would be responsible for that sum, and for an additional five cents from 1 September.[190] Meantime, the matter that had really been at the top of King's agenda until his diversion to Memphis and his death, the Poor People's March on Washington, went ahead. Resurrection City was set up on 13 May, and dismantled by the police in late June—with 1,600

594

regular troops on standby. Protesting on the steps of the Capitol, the Revd Ralph Abernathy and 343 of his followers were arrested. Some of the refugees from Resurrection City merged into the ghetto and another bout of rioting began.[191]

Now we must return to the major actors of 1968–9: students. All the sources speak of a sharp change in student attitudes at what was, after all, one of the Ivy League universities, Columbia, between the early and the mid- to late sixties. That reminds us once again to think in terms of an entire decade of transformation, rather than putting too much emphasis on 1968 as one single year of change. From 1965–6 onwards, half-a-dozen broad, and rather different, issues were clearly causing concern to a majority of students. The first of these touched on race, community relations, and the environment, matters which would have scarcely ruffled Columbia's white students half a dozen years earlier. Now there was great sensitivity to the way in which Columbia was ruthlessly expanding into the local community, frequently taking over what had formerly been low-cost housing. A neat encapsulation of the whole debate emerged in the form of the new gymnasium which the university authorities wished to build, gobbling up a piece of Morningside Park. Various compromises were put forward whereby local blacks would get some use out of the gymnasium, but all came out in a most offensive and patronizing format, suggesting an offer to the locals of a very limited amount of inferior and racially segregated accommodation. The building of the gymnasium was a local issue with national reverberations. The Institute of Defense Analysis (IDA) was a national body which had particularly strong reverberations at Columbia. Founded in 1955, it was a consortium of twelve universities which organized university research projects financed by government contracts, projects, of course, closely integrated with the military-industrial complex. Columbia's president, Grayson Kirk, was a professor of political science and businessman, sitting on the boards of Socony, Mobil Oil, Con Edison, IBM, and various financial institutions. He was on the board of IDA and openly boastful of the amount of government defence money which came to Columbia.[192] This was perhaps more of a specialist issue than the one involving community relations, but the whole university was undergoing a revulsion against all things militaristic. One special source of resentment arose from the facilities made available by the university authorities to enable recruitment to take place on campus. Columbia had a traditionally close association with the Naval ROTC (Officers' Training Corps): as far back as May 1965 there had been such a strongly and directly expressed demonstration against this that police had in fact been called in. There were also demonstrations against CIA recruiting. This issue continued to be bitter, and merged with one even more fraught, that of handing over students' class results to the draft boards: male students falling below a certain level could find themselves losing their deferment and, in short order, on the way to Vietnam.[193]

Both separate from these issues and running through all of them was the general question of student freedoms and student rights. President Kirk dealt with this matter in exactly the way calculated to turn it into an immediate crisis. A committee actually was set up in November 1965 to look at that great range of mighty issues, running from the rules governing women's dormitories to student representation on decision-making bodies. The committee had five student members, nominated by the student council, the body traditionally taken as representative of all students; with the other places taken up by four senior deans, five senior faculty members, and the chaplain, this President's Advisory Committee on Student Life reported to the president in August 1967. The president did not like what he read, particularly the unanimous recommendation that students should be guaranteed the right to peaceful demonstrations within university buildings. Four of the five student members, in addition, recommended significant student representation on decision-making bodies; however, any such sweeping changes were opposed by the majority. Demonstrations were what particularly bothered Kirk, and even after receiving the committee's unanimous recommendations he unilaterally instituted a ban on all indoor demonstrations, even those conducted peacefully—thus blowing out of the water one of the few genuine compromises that had been patiently put together between students and administrators. The actual occasion for the outbreak of violent troubles at Columbia was this one of free speech, intensified by a very strong sense that Kirk was simply not a man that it was possible to come to any reasonable accommodation with.

However, one other, almost bread-and-butter issue sharply intensified the hostility towards Kirk and the administration felt by students who might not necessarily have been so disturbed by political matters. At the beginning of the academic year in 1966 students suddenly found that the loan scheme on which they had long relied to help even out their finances had been withdrawn. Not only did this put students in extreme financial difficulties, but both Kirk and his officials took the offensive line that students using the scheme had for too long been exploiting the university, and refused to consider any of the real issues of hardship. Still worse, the university treated the matter as one between the university and parents, rather than between the university and students, thus, in a manner which students found insulting, stressing their dependence on their families and their lack of independent adult status.[194]

Over the same period of time that the student body as a whole was finding itself in opposition to the administration over more and more issues, the increasingly bitter national struggles over Vietnam had produced a cohort of SDS zealots, much tougher and more uncompromising than those who had appeared earlier in the sixties. Columbia, which does after all sit in the heart of New York City, by 1968 had a particularly unyielding and unaccommodating (and in some ways unappetizing) chapter of the SDS, led by gangly, cold, foul-mouthed Mark Rudd and Dotson Rader, of the priapic, predatory tendency (he has left an entertaining account of an unexpected encumbrance arising from the joint occupation of the Barnard College women's dormitory—a permanent erection).[195] The Cox Commission, which later carried out a very measured investigation into the Columbia troubles, referred to the deliberate use by the SDS of 'tactics offensive to the manners and spirit of much of the University'.[196] The most uncompromising actions were carried out by SDS activists; often, as votes and opinion surveys[197] from time to time showed, they did not have the support of the majority of students; but throughout there were substantial bodies of students prepared in one way or another to line up against Kirk and the administration; and, of course, in the usual way, there was always enough police sadism to keep converting the waverers.

The Report on Student Life was not released until April 1968. This, anyway, would have returned the free speech issue to the forefront of everyone's consciousness, but Kirk further decided to take action against six students who had already been found guilty of violating his own personal proscription of demonstrations of any sort: this particular protest, by six SDS militants, had been against Columbia's involvement with the IDA— these students, 'the IDA six', were put on probation. Of course, if you punish students for demonstrating, what you do is produce further demonstrations. The intense phase of strikes and demonstrations began on Monday 22 April 1968. Columbia SDS members had already committed a prime example of what came over to many as extreme tastelessness when they had disrupted the memorial service at Columbia on 4 April for Martin Luther King. No doubt there was some truth in their claim that it was hypocrisy for a racist institution to pay tribute to a black leader, but many, of course, were perfectly sincere in expressing their remorse and loss. The complete and violent rejection of all bourgeois standards of taste was signalled in the open letter Mark Rudd wrote to Kirk over the matter of the probations:

> There is only one thing left to say. It may sound nihilistic to you, since it is the opening shot in a war of liberation. I'll use the words of LeRoi Jones, whom I am sure you don't like a whole lot: 'Up against the wall, mother fucker, this is a stick-up.' Yours for freedom, Mark.[198]

Tuesday 23 April was a long day. At around noon, supporters of the IDA six gathered at the traditional (and legal) assembly point in the main campus, the sundial. The crowd then moved out to the construction site for the gymnasium. The evidence suggests that this was not a deliberately planned move by the SDS mainly preoccupied at this time with the issues of IDA and Free Speech; it seems that there was just sufficient disgruntlement of various types to create a crowd desirous of moving somewhere and staging a protest, that the gym was an immediately felt local issue for whites, and one which made a convenient focal point for blacks who were beginning to see the opportunity for making special claims of their own. The consensus is that the SDS were not in control at this stage, and that the rather carefree, undisciplined atmosphere had an appeal for students not completely clear about which particular issue they wished to make a stand on. Some academics attempted to persuade the students to move away from the gym site, and soon the police did in fact disperse them. A rather larger crowd reassembled at the sundial. With night beginning to fall, it was not unnatural that the students should then think of moving indoors, making a particular target of the office of Acting Dean Henry Coleman in Hamilton Hall. The continuing light side of the episode was evidenced by the arrival of a rock band, while the more threatening side appeared in the taking hostage of Dean Coleman, together with the occupation of Hamilton Hall, and still more in the way in which SDS on the one hand sent out for professional organizers while some of the black students on the other brought in SNCC organizers.[199]

All of the white protesters felt particularly sympathetic towards the grievances of blacks, but the blacks both had special grievances of their own (they were forced, for instance, to show identity cards within college buildings in a way that whites were not) and were beginning to feel that they could gain more for themselves by operating independently. In the small hours of the morning of 24 April the black students independently reached the decision which set the Columbia occupation off on another distinctive stage. The white students were requested to leave Hamilton Hall, leaving that exclusively in black occupation. What happened, especially during the first part of the morning as students returned to the campus to find that the action was still continuing, was that a number of separate occupations of different buildings were embarked on, each one broadly reflective of greater or lesser degrees of radicalism or moderation. Together they showed that some even quite moderate students were getting the sense that now was the time when some kind of statement must be made, and that the one effective means to hand was that of occupying a building. Altogether, five buildings were occupied. Having been expelled from Hamilton Hall, the SDS group were on their mettle. They, unlike the other groups, used physical force to overcome the university guards and break their way into the building misleadingly known as the Low Library, in fact the real heart of the administration and the area housing President Kirk's office. Leading SDS members (not Columbia students) and visiting left-wing dignitaries held court in Kirk's office.[200]

Most of the occupations continued the good-natured, festive atmosphere which had attended the open-air demonstrations the previous day. Some wit in the crowd outside Hamilton Hall was quoted as yelling out: 'You've got to get those kids out of Hamilton. They've been in there so long they're going to get tenure.'[201] As in the European universities, occupation basically meant talking shop, or talking-shops. Common policy for all of the occupied buildings, save for Hamilton Hall, was to be evolved democratically by a strike coordinating committee. On the second full day of the occupation, 25 April, an important group of academics, generally supportive of student demands and anxious to avoid violent confrontation, formed the Faculty Ad Hoc Negotiating Committee (subsequently usually known as the Ad Hoc Faculty Group, AHFG). The main agreed strategic objectives were: suspension of the building of the gym; termination of relations between the university and the IDA; new student representative institutions; full restoration of free speech on campus; and suspension of all sanctions against students. All occupying students wanted a guarantee of an amnesty for themselves, with the black students in Hamilton being particularly concerned about their own situation.[202] The evidence is that what most students were interested in was reform of the university; the more extreme SDS statements that the occupations marked the beginning of a wider revolution were generally laughed at. However, the SDS group did command attention with the documents from Kirk's office which it published, showing university involvement in defence contracts.

For seven days the normal work of the university was at a complete standstill. The AHFG tried to develop proposals which would win the support of the majority of students, difficulties mainly being over whether students could really expect to escape totally from any sanctions against their infractions of discipline. But the administration announced that there could be no alteration in the disciplinary powers possessed by the president, and that there could only be a temporary suspension in the building of the gymnasium; on the other side, Mark Rudd and the SDS group declared that there could be no compromise. Even while the generally festive atmosphere persisted, there were always fears that at any point the police might be called in. Members of the AHFG, perhaps too sympathetic towards SDS, donned white armbands and took on a kind of policing, or monitoring, role, in the hope of preventing any final clash, or at least of keeping some observation over the police should they be brought in. The administration maintained that the police would not be brought in; the problem here was that there were differences of opinion between different officers, the trustees, and the president. One eyewitness account spoke of 'the Revolution' beginning 'in earnest' on Thursday 25 April as a band of students occupied Fayerweather Hall, the building housing graduate social sciences. Later in the day another group seized Mathematics Hall, while white students from the school of general studies occupied their classroom building, Lewisohn Hall, in order to 'neutralize' it and prevent its occupation by either SDS or any other faction. According to this account: 'The faculty was meeting around the clock in Philosophy Hall. The Administration was invisible, powerless.' Fayerweather is described as 'a commune of up to 400:

> Girls—about 40 per cent—were not expected to do the kitchen work alone, for this was a 'liberated' area, and boys had to help. Couples slept together in public view, nobody cared, we were 'liberated': here was a single commune in which the adult hypocrisy did not apply any longer, where people shared and shared alike, where democracy decided everything, where people were free of adult values and codes.'[203]

The police were briefly on the campus on 26 April, when, as a number of pieces of testimony showed, they attacked several academics.

> As members of the Ad Hoc Faculty Group, we knew that our representatives were inside demanding the withdrawal of the police force from the campus, so ours was a delaying action. We asked for identification and received no answer. Instead the plain clothes men formed themselves into a rough wedge and hurled themselves upon me. We had linked arms at the last minute, but my grasp was broken by a vicious karate blow on the upper arm. I was then punched, pushed aside, trodden upon by several of them, and I saw Mr R Greenman struck over the head by a billy club, Professor Taylor bleeding from the nose.... The extreme violence, amounting to brutality, was totally unwarranted, unprovoked and unpardonable. Moreover, it should have given the administration a foretaste of what was to come when the police were again invited to intervene.[204]

Whether the occupation of Fayerweather and the other buildings were genuinely as idyllic as described, or not, all that came to an end about 2 a.m. on the morning of Tuesday 30 April, as a student, not actually a participant in any of the occupations, recounted:

> The bust was definitely on, everyone knew it. People were running around in a frenzy, everyone was rushing. The faculty meeting hastily adjourned, and the faculty placed themselves at the entrances to the occupied buildings, in front of crowds of sympathisers who also sat down on the steps, determined to passively resist the police assault.... A hush settled over the crowd. They heard what the police could and would do, and they were afraid, sorely afraid. Then, softly at first, but with ever increasing volume, came the song. 'We shall overcome.'

Being on the sidelines, I was forced away from the scene by the plain clothes men, of whom there were hundreds, and did not see the actual charge. I did hear the shrieks of the wounded and the cries which pierced the warm night air. And still the haunting refrain, 'We shall overcome some day...'

Weeping over the ruins of Columbia University, weeping over the injured that were and that were yet to come, weeping over the death of an illusion as to the nature of the University I loved, I joined the students on the South steps of Fayerweather Hall.

... The police suddenly charged the next entrance, and as the roar of battle, bloody battle, reached us, we began a new song, a new chant. Students and their teachers together: We ARE Columbia...

All was confusion. Flying bodies, bloody heads and arms, blue coats swinging hand-cuffs like clubs rained down on us. I was pulled and beaten, kicked and battered, lifted from the steps.

He was arrested and charged along with a professor from the department of government.

Buses had dropped more than 1,000 policemen at the campus at about 2 a.m. on that terrible morning. At 2.20 a.m. a large force marched to Hamilton Hall under the command of an assistant chief inspector and accompanied by university representatives. Another police group entered the building through underground tunnels which led direct from Broadway into certain buildings. The black occupants of Hamilton were arrested and peacefully removed to police vans outside. Between 2.30 and 2.45 a.m. a force of approximately seventy-five police-men charged into a group of faculty and students in front of the south-east entrance to the Low Library, inflicting injuries. At 2.45 a.m. police entered Avery, violently removing occupants and causing injuries. At approximately 3 a.m. 100 police forced their way through a large number of academics and students on the steps of Fayerweather, the building itself not being fully cleared until 4.30 a.m. Also at 3 a.m. the police entered the Low Library through tunnels, violently removing students. At 3.15 a.m. the police unit which had charged Low moved against a second large group of academics and students at the south steps, and against a crowd of spectators in the quadrangle of Fayerweather. Between 3 and 3.15 a large contingent cleared the lawns in front of the mathematics building; during the succeeding half-hour the building itself was cleared, again with many injuries. Now, spectators standing near the math-ematics building were charged by the police so that they had to flee out into the main road outside, Broadway. Also at this time spectators near 116th Street and Broadway were charged by police. Police vans pulled away loaded up with prisoners. At 4 a.m. a mass charge on a large crowd of spectators on the college wall drove them across the South Lawn. Several hundred students and a handful of academics had received quite severe injuries. One policeman was permanently paralysed as a result of a student jumping on him from a window-ledge. Seven hundred and five arrests were made.

The following day Columbia University, together with interested parties across the nation, was in a condition of deep shock. Students immediately began to mass in another demonstration which, in the evening, ended with more police violence; a condition of general strike was declared. The AHFG, which had enjoyed a sadly ineffective existence for five days, was disbanded; instead a Faculty Executive Committee was established whose most important achievement, in fact, was to set up the Commission of Investigation (the Cox Commission) which provides us with so much detailed evidence about these appalling events. Differences within the student body produced a sharp split between the continuing strike coordinating committee and those now calling themselves Students for a Restructured University. In return for broken heads, the students did find some of their claims being met; the torrent of condemnation of the university for having been responsible for such dreadful violence against its own students forced the university authorities into making concessions, including the consideration of 'changes in the basic structure of the university'. Where the authorities were not prepared to give way was over sanctions against the SDS leaders—opinion polls did indeed show that a majority of students were not in favour of an amnesty for the ringleaders. Four SDS students summoned to appear before the deans failed to do so, and thus were subject to instant suspension.[205] It was basically over the issue of disciplinary action that the SDS students instituted a new occupation of Hamilton Hall on 13 May. The overwhelming evidence is that these students did not have the sympathies of the vast majority. However, there could be no question that that majority totally opposed any resumed use of the police against fellow students, however wide the gap in political attitudes might be. In what it obviously hoped was a balanced policy of concession and firmness, the administration called in the police on the late evening of 21 May, with the object of removing the SDS students from Hamilton (when embarked on around 2.30 a.m. this operation, involving only the arrest of about 100 students, was carried out without undue brutality). But the very presence of the police was enough to attract large numbers of angry students ready themselves to take aggressive action against the enemy. One academic witness brought out how things had changed since the first mass police operation on 30 April.

> The expectations and emotions of the students on campus were significantly different. Many had been through the first police action and were horrified and embittered by what they had seen and experienced. Support for the demonstrating students was stronger in the student body as a whole than on April 30; the first police action had been a major factor in drawing most of the students behind the general strike that followed April 30. The issues involved in that particular situation in Hamilton also appeared much clearer to those outside the building.

According to this report, police began arriving about 10 p.m. The crowds outside Hamilton joined in chants of 'Cops Off Campus', 'No Cops', 'Cops Must Go', and 'Strike, Strike'.

> Students began taking the police saw-horses or barricades which were blocking the main gates and built their own barricades at each end of College Walk to keep police from using these entrances. Since all the other campus gates had been locked by the Administration since April 30, the campus was now virtually sealed.... Around 2.30 a.m. police entered Hamilton through tunnels... As the news that the police were inside

Hamilton spread, hundreds of students crowded against the front of the building booing and jeering the police. The police attempt to open the front door was thwarted by the crush of people outside and their shouting 'Cops Must Go'.... The sit-ins were finally removed quietly... The police, however, remained inside Hamilton, appearing on every floor, and their continued presence served to excite the crowd.[206]

As Hamilton Hall was being cleared, about 200 students began a march on Schernerhorne Hall. Then, starting at around 3 a.m., students began to throw bricks and stones through the windows of the Low Library building, Schernerhorne, and other buildings. Fires were started in both Hamilton and Fayerweather Halls; fire-engines had to be brought to the campus. The situation was not quite as clearcut as on 30 April, when the police were manifestly the sole aggressors. At 4.05 a.m. Dr Kirk made a statement over the radio:

> The police have also been requested to clear the campus of all persons under penalty of arrest. Dormitory residents are to remain in their rooms. All other persons, including dormitory residents not in their rooms, must leave the campus immediately via the nearest campus gate.

The announcement was also made directly to students by a dean at the sundial.[207] It seems clear that both the university administration and the police authorities were hoping for an orderly operation. But with students acting on the basis that the police were the enemy, with no right to be on the campus in the first place ('It's our university too' was the cry across the nation), and the police losing control and showing all their most sadistic impulses, immediately the major sweeping-up operation began, disaster was again at hand. Here is one student's eyewitness account of the beginning of the confrontation:

> About 1–1 ½ hours after the removal of the students from inside Hamilton Hall, between 500 and 1,000 helmeted policemen, armed with billy clubs broke through the barricades at the corner of 116th Street and Amsterdam Avenue, and massed in formation rapidly. They began to move forward to students opposite them inside the campus. These students, or at least a number of them, began to move towards the police with arms linked. As they approached each other, some police broke rank, and began to beat students in their paths. Then the police broke into a full gallop, sweeping down College Walk, beating severely any students who were too slow to escape, or who tripped. Most of us were forced to the steps of Low Library and into Furnald Hall or Ferris Booth Hall, where we stayed until they began to retreat back onto South Field and College Walk. This pattern was repeated twice more, as the Tactical Police Force swept us back into the two buildings. Then for reasons for which I am not aware, approximately 50 patrol men charged those who were standing outside Ferris Booth Hall, throwing one girl and one man through the plate glass doors, injuring them both. It was at this particular time that I saw some demonstrators begin to throw bricks and other objects at the police standing

outside Ferris Booth Hall, who then retreated. I should state that by this time there were already many visible head injuries to demonstrators, many arrests, and much blood outside Furnald and on College Walk. At this point a girl and a man who were injured outside were carried on litters from Ferris Booth Hall, where an emergency medical team was treating some of the injured students.

At the same time, a group of about 200 plain-clothes men, who were not displaying badges began advancing from the lawn in front of the Butler Library, moving at a slow pace along the hedge toward Ferris Booth Hall and Furnald Hall. As the man on the litter passed by them, I saw, as did about 30 others, a plain clothes man pull out a blackjack and begin to beat the student on the stretcher. The medical team carrying him can also verify this information. At this point, a number of students on the lawn in front of Furnald Hall began to hurl bricks and stones at the still advancing plain clothes men, who under this volley, began to run at us wielding clubs and blackjacks...[208]

Others testified that inside Furnald Hall some policemen did draw their guns. Dean Platt testified that he had drawn the attention of two police officers to the 'brutal charge of the plainclothesmen in front of Furnald Hall' and that 'the officers replied that they could see no policemen.[209]

At 5.30 a.m. the police began to withdraw. Fifty-one students and seventeen police needed hospital treatment. Most of the student statements denied student responsibility for any of the fires and some described students actually putting fires out. However, certain students were undoubtedly guilty of the most appalling vandalism, in particular the attack on the office of Professor Orest Ranum and the destruction of both his notes and original sixteenth- and seventeenth-century French manuscripts—manifestations, no doubt, of bourgeois culture. Still, the students did gain concessions on all of their main issues, and one huge symbolic victory, the resignation of President Kirk. But the police invasions left a poisoned atmosphere. Life at the university remained disturbed and unpleasant for another year, with all the old tensions breaking out again in another short occupation in the spring of 1969.[210]

The Chicago riots of August 1968 were a microcosm of the bitter and violent national division between those who supported, and those who opposed the Vietnam war. Lyndon Johnson, so bitterly taunted as the slayer of innocent Vietnamese children, had announced that he was not going to stand again for the presidency; the students, the protesters, the radicals, wanted there to be a Democratic candidate who shared their aspirations and, above all, their opposition to the Vietnam war. Robert Kennedy could have been such a candidate, but Kennedy had been assassinated. As a possible replacement the opponents of the war were left with the unsatisfactorily stiff and proud academic, Eugene McCarthy. The students, and radicals, and yippies, who descended on the Chicago Democratic convention had the surface purpose of winning the nomination for McCarthy, and the adoption by the convention of a peace platform. But those deeply imbued with the ideology of the radical Left believed they had to do far more than secure a candidate and a platform: just as SDS students at Columbia believed they were revealing the brutal violence underpinning that university, so protesters at Chicago aimed to reveal the total system of violence they believed underpinned the Democratic establishment and its support for the Vietnam war.[211]

It was a perfectly chosen battleground, if such a battleground could ever really be perfectly chosen. Chicago was dominated by the Democratic political machine of Mayor Richard Daley, itself supported by a ruthless and brutal police force. The Democratic establishment, almost as ruthlessly, was determined that Johnson's vice-president, Hubert Humphrey, a supporter of his Vietnam policies, should secure the nomination. Humphrey did get the nomination, but then, partly because of the bitter divisions in the Democratic party, lost to Richard Nixon.

America is the country of incredible technological sophistication; it is also the country of crude Old Testament literalism, of coarse nationalism, of company towns, brutal fiefdoms, and the ethics of the frontier. The new movements and subcultures of the late fifties onwards challenged these primitive circumstances. We have watched Memphis change: in 1968 it was in a mess, but it was no longer complacently in the hands of moderate white racists. Chicago had changed less (though Martin Luther King had mounted some partially successful attacks on the entrenched racism of Poles, Italians, and Irish), perhaps because Mayor Daley's Democratic machine ostensibly governed on behalf of the working-class and lower-middle-class majority, with many in that majority recognizing that he did indeed look after them very well. A man in Mayor Daley's position exercised power, he did not share it: federal authorities, state authorities, those with fancy principles of minority rights and abstract morality could mind their own business—running Chicago was his job. Situations came nearest to this in Italy, where we have noted troubles in the northern company town of Valdagno and in some southern towns, and in parts of the south there was an interpénétration between politics and the Mafia. But there was no figure in Italy quite like Mayor Daley. The Italian police had their own forms of uncontrolled violence which the politicians preferred not to try to check: but Italian police actions against students were a matter of concern to the central government, ineffectual though it usually was. Even more so in France: individual officers and groups of officers were responsible for some of the worst brutalities; it was also true that during the time of government paralysis the police were left to fill the gap; yet, all said, the extent of, and the limitations on, police repression in France during the events were very much set by the central government. This was where America was different: as it happened, Daley was acting utterly in the interests of his crony, President Johnson, but even if the federal government had been totally opposed to the actions taken by Mayor Daley and his police forces at the Democratic convention in Chicago in August 1968, there is nothing they could have done about it.

A Democratic convention is supposed to be an integral part of the peaceful democratic process whereby citizens not only elect a president but are enabled to make a prior choice of presidential candidates. It might be thought that the American public and, more critically, the journalists and broadcasters who mediated the news were by August 1968 becoming inured to violence. What was so shocking to journalists was that the violence surrounded and intruded upon the convention. It was all very public, outside and even inside the Hilton hotel, where convention delegates were staying; it was not tucked away in some university, it was invading their world, to the extent that some journalists and cameramen suffered quite severe injuries.[212] The journalists should not have been surprised, but then they belonged to that persuasion which saw the sixties as the time of 'the unravelling of America', underestimating the violence and repression endemic in that society, and then overreacting when they came up against passionate protest, missing what was positive. Mayor Daley had made it absolutely clear what radicals attending the convention could expect: in fact, it could be said that his first line of defence of the interests of the Democratic establishment was open intimidation. SDS leader Tom Hayden certainly said that in going to Chicago he was 'expecting death, expecting the worst'.[213] Daley and his cops were fully convinced of the righteousness of their cause. However, there is always a certain amount of dissimulation in such police actions (found at Columbia, found in Italy and France as well): individual officers were very ready to take the precaution of concealing any means of identification— beating up the enemy was perfectly justified, but none the less it was best not to have allegations of excessive brutality linked to named officers. In these American fiefdoms the rules did not matter. And while Daley boasted of the reception that would greet anti-war protesters, he preferred to keep the police actions as far away as possible from the Hilton and the news cameras: this proved impossible and thus, of course, the police quickly developed an interest in 'taking out' cameramen and reporters.

Twelve thousand police were at the ready, supported by 6,000 national guardsmen. The convention centre, the International Amphitheatre, was protected by barbed wire. In the event there was no mass invasion of Chicago by anti-war protesters. Tom Wells reckons that Daley's intimidatory tactics worked to the extent that the total was limited to about 5,000, an assortment of anti-war protesters from pacifists to revolutionaries, together with icons from the original Beat movement like Allen Ginsberg and the more recently evolved Yippies, the American version of the Situationists.[214] At the beginning of the week (Friday 23 August) the humourists and the pacifists seemed to be in the ascendant. But the committed political activists and revolutionaries had it as their overriding purpose to carry out a march on the Amphitheatre. Events began in the peripheral parks, then came to their vicious climax on the evening of Wednesday 28 August on Wisconsin Avenue and outside the Hilton hotel, when there took place, as a subsequent investigation made clear, what could only be described as 'a police riot'.[215] On the Thursday, while the street riots continued, there was also violence inside the Amphitheatre perpetrated on delegates opposed to Humphrey.

On the evening of Friday 23 August the Yippies, at the Chicago Civic Center, made their own distinctive protest, nominating as their presidential candidate, with all due ceremony, a pig, singing 'God Bless America', and demanding that 'Pigasus' be flown to Johnson's Texas White House for foreign policy briefings like other presidential candidates. The police intervened, but without untoward violence.[216] Next day, representing almost an opposite pole of anti-war testimony, the utterly rational women of WSP (Women Strike for Peace) picketed convention delegates at the Hilton Hotel. The police did not intervene. There was only a relatively slight upping of the temperature that evening when Allen Ginsberg sat at the centre of a peaceable group of hippies round a bonfire in Lincoln Park. At 11 p.m. closing time some had to be forcibly ejected by the police, but that was about it. Lincoln Park was the venue the following evening for a rock concert and Festival of Life. The Yippies put on another of their fetchingly absurd shows. This was a less docile crowd, especially as the evening wore on. At eleven o'clock the police used tear-gas to clear the park; the demonstrators hurled stones, and in turn were attacked with police truncheons. Out on the streets groups of protesters up-ended dustbins and hammered on cars. In this, the first night in which the police tested out their strength, many people had to receive medical attention for the effects of gas and for open wounds. On the Monday evening, 25 August, there were happenings again in Lincoln Park, and also an anti-birthday party (in execration of the president) in the Chicago Coliseum. The protesters at Lincoln Park this time attacked the police with bottles and stones before the police could begin clearing the park: inevitably this meant that the clearance, when it came, was just a little more vicious. On the Tuesday evening almost the entire range of anti-war protesters—SDS, Yippies, the National Mobilization Committee, and local clergy—joined together to try to keep the protest going beyond the usual curfew. In face of a straight refusal to obey orders, the police action was the most brutal yet. That was the last of the sideshows.

The mass centrepiece demonstration was to be held in Grant Park, almost within the shadow of the massive hulk of the Hilton hotel, on the Wednesday afternoon. Daley had prepared his ground well: permits had been granted for the rally in the park, but marches towards the Amphitheatre were strictly prohibited. While the speeches began before a crowd of 10,000, the police appeared to be waiting for any kind of act of a provocative or insulting character which could be used as an excuse for going into the attack. One such attack occurred when a hippie climbed up a flagpole to turn the union flag upside down. Then a red flag was hoisted—possibly by *agents provocateurs* (Daley's men had managed to infiltrate most of the anti-war organizations). Substantial numbers of demonstrators, it has to be said, had come not unprepared, and while the police picked on certain individuals, bricks, stones, and balloons filled with urine were thrown at them (the last needed quite careful preparation!). Dave Dillinger of Mobilization was ostensibly in charge, and he appealed for a cessation of attacks on the police; then, with the rally reduced to pointless chaos, he called for a march—a non-violent march—to the Amphitheatre. Hayden and Neumann of the SDS called for the war to be taken out into the streets and waged actively against the police, telling people that SDS colleague Rennie Davis was already lying uncon- scious, blood covering his face and being soaked up by his shirt. Even following Dillinger's instructions was far from easy. The police were battering anyone attempting to leave the park, while the national guardsmen had particularly effective devices, jeeps with barbed wire across the front, ferocious mobile barricades.

What the demonstrators decided to do was to make their way in small numbers towards the Hilton hotel. Most got there eventually, though it was a perilous journey, in which gas was released against them in almost blanket quantities—so much so that it wafted into the Hilton, bringing home to the elegant residents there the realities of police and army action in particularly nauseous fashion. The demonstrators had won a kind of double victory: they had got to the Hilton, within the purview of their enemies, the Democratic party establishment, and in doing this they got themselves onto evening television, revealing to all America, or so they believed, the naked evil of a police state. But they had also set themselves up as sacrificial lambs: the police, roused to a state of fury, though lining up in systematic military style, were now to exact a terrible revenge, which was aimed at protesters and journalists but which did not spare bystanders. Busloads of extra helmeted police arrived. They lined up, began jogging on the spot, raising their arms and chanting, 'Kill, kill, kill'. Then they swung round and charged into the demonstrators in front of the Hilton. Heads were smashed, limbs were wrenched from sockets, people were trampled underfoot: as a result of the tremendous pressure the huge plate-glass window of the Hilton Haymarket Lounge shattered inwards; demonstrators and ordinary passers-by crashed through, many suffering horrific wounds from the shards of glass. The police poured in behind, clubbing indiscriminately. The Paris police violence was only three months away; but this was worse. It was within a confined space, though those fleeing were pursued back into the park and thoroughly beaten in relative obscurity. It was quite plainly and simply an exercise in revenge and punishment; the protesters had been provocative, and some of them dangerous, but this continued after any possible threat had been extinguished.

On the Thursday protesters were back out on the streets, and now they were joined by some of the sober political workers for McCarthy, who were coming to see that this enemy outside the hall was the same as the enemy inside the hall. Open violence broke out within the convention, with the chair of the New Hampshire delegation and the Democratic candidate for New York senator both being roughly manhandled, while a CBS reporter was punched on the jaw. Thursday was more mopping-up operation against brave show of defiance than the all-out war of Wednesday, but it was still ugly enough. At 5 a.m. on the Friday morning the police actually broke into the McCarthy headquarters on the fifteenth floor of the Hilton, beating up McCarthy's young workers.

Some delegates on the convention floor joined with press and television in condemning the police actions, but the American public, though presented with graphic evidence on their television screens, were not affected as many had earlier been affected by scenes of police brutality in the South: even among those who supported McCarthy a majority rejected the view that the police had used too much force. Provocative, violent, obscene, manifestly unpatriotic, anti-war demonstrators were deeply unpopular. The belief that force, even in dangerous quantities, was an essential adjunct to the police force went deep. The revolutionary zealots were pushed towards still more violence; those who had been prepared to demonstrate tirelessly lost much of their appetite; it seemed that peaceful protest was becoming impossible in America. Immediate reflections have to be gloomy. Public opinion confirmed Daley in power as well as in office; but then a general election had confirmed de Gaulle in power. We will return to more rounded judgements shortly; meantime we have two further sets of episodes to work through.

In addition to being a centre of student activism, the San Francisco Bay area had become a powerpoint for the Black Panthers. In a manner which I have already explained, racial issues became embedded in the politics of many colleges in the area. The SDS was being supplanted as the most militant body by the Black Student Union (BSU), and that was being joined by a body representing Orientals and Latin Americans, the Third World Liberation Front (TWLF). Throughout 1967 San Francisco State College had been disrupted by issues relating to Vietnam; by 1968 these were being eclipsed by issues relating to the rights of black students and black teachers. Two problem figures were Dr Nathan Hare, Director of the recently established black studies programme, and George Murray, a graduate student and part-time instructor. Hare made no secret of his support for Black Power and his aim of physically taking over 'racist' learning. Murray had been accused by the student newspaper of planning to bring Black Power into the college, and had retaliated by severely beating up members of the paper's editorial staff. President Smith was ordered by the college trustees to suspend Murray. The BSU began a strike on 6 November, demanding the reinstatement of Murray and the promotion of Hare to full professorial status. The TWLF joined in: both organizations sent squads round the classrooms, intimidating staff and students and destroying equipment. The bringing in of police was not altogether unjustified, but inevitably led to open warfare, particularly serious on 13 November. To protect life and limb Smith closed the campus and then, when ordered to reopen it, resigned. He was replaced by a hard-line right-wing figure of some academic distinction, S. I. Hayakawa. Murray was imprisoned, and Hayakawa governed unashamedly through the power of the police. In January, Hare and his colleagues disrupted a speech by Hayakawa and were arrested. Hare boasted that he proposed to recruit revolutionary nationalists for his department. Before the end of the month (23 January 1969) a massive BSU/TWLF rally was organized in the college. When the police order to disperse was ignored, 453 protesters were arrested. Hayakawa had the support of the public and of the State of California under Governor Ronald Reagan. As those arrested now ran a severe risk of jail sentences, many were prepared to plead for suspended sentences and probation. The draconian policy had drawn the sting of both separatist movements, both of which, it has to be said, were tinged with deep irrationality. Murray was back in jail; Hare was dismissed as chair of the black studies programme.[217]

The original Berkeley Free Speech Movement of 1964 had focused on a piece of territory, the territory outside the campus gates over which students claimed the right to set up their stalls and seek recruits. The last Berkeley episode of the sixties, in the spring and summer of 1969, a horrible and in some ways pathetic one, was over another piece of territory not far away, 'The People's Park'. Berkeley was now more than a major university campus with a small town attached; it was a centre of hippiedom, the local variety being 'the street people'. Some were drop-outs, some were students, more or less, some had never been students. They were in the music business, they were in selling, they were in the underground press, they were in drugs, they were beggars. Black Power groups operated both with the street people and independently. As elsewhere, they were an important force in Berkeley by 1969. One link between young people inside the college and young people outside had been established in the autumn of 1967:

The Free University of Berkeley is people like yourself, students, workers, and citizens, sensitive to a hostile environment and committed to examine and act against all forms of establishment suppression... The Free University of Berkeley was founded out of anger to preserve that anger and make it meaningful. We are working to involve the suppressed and dissenting members of our community by encouraging them to act together in a common learning experiment which gives a direction to dissent with the goal of eliminating suppression.... Through our action oriented learning we can move with strength and meaning to counter the institution of power and the men who exploit and manage our society.[218]

It was in June 1967 that the university regents announced that $1.3 million was being allocated for the purchase of a piece of land on Telegraph Avenue, 'the scene of hippie concentration and rising crime', for playing-fields, faculty offices, and parking spaces. During the early months of 1968 Berkeley was disrupted by the actions of the Third World Liberation Front, but news of the French police repression against French students in May provided the occasion for a combined protest in support of the French students and against the proposed development of this piece of land. On Friday 28 June it was almost as if the Berkeley students, with the enthusiastic cooperation of the police, were using the piece of wasteland as a kind of film set on which to re-enact the Paris events: barricades were built and set on fire, the police used tear-gas, running battles took place.[219] It was not until April 1969 that the idea emerged of converting the rubble-strewn piece of wasteland into a 'People's Park'. The announcement inviting people to come and help in the building of the park was published in the Berkeley underground newspaper, the *Berkeley Barb*. The supporters of the People's Park produced some curious arguments. The land, they said, had been stolen from the American Indians: it was now being restored to the people.[220] There was the obvious symbolism of environmentalism, and flower power resistance to an authoritarian university was represented as a good in itself. A pamphlet, *Our Park and Our Struggle,* presented the struggle as being against 'an unresponsive and inequitable arrangement of power', against 'illegitimate authority', and associated with the struggle against conscription; it is described as being ' "creative" Marxist-Leninist'. Widespread support for the People's Park was claimed because the park demonstrated to people 'that they did not have to accept an urban experience that was both sterile and unjust, both disagreeable and oppressive'.[221] One of the earliest actions of the newly established Women's Liberation Front was a march in support of the park. No doubt those who laboured to build the People's Park felt a profound sense of personal commitment to it, but to the rational mind the arguments in its support scarcely seemed to make it the life-and-death matter that it proved to be. Equally, it seems incredible that the authorities adopted the extreme methods they did simply in order to repossess this piece of land. Still, Reagan was now governor, tough tactics had paid off at San Francisco State College, and it could be argued that there was public support for a policy of crushing hippies and student radicals once and for all. The builders of People's Park, certainly, had made it clear that they intended to occupy it and defend it. On the other hand, there was a petition against the park, protesting against the noise, the beggars, and the drug-pushers: but it got no more than forty-eight signatures. To begin with the university authorities were conciliatory: they made much of the point that it was intended to build a soccer field, obviously thought to be a good selling line in this age of British pubs and reaction against the more violent, regimented American sports.

Actually, there were only three street people in the park when, at three o'clock on the morning of 15 May, 200 police moved in, preparing the way for workmen to fence it off. That afternoon a massive attempt was made to reoccupy the park: this was the most concentrated afternoon of violence, with the police firing warning shots from their pistols. By their own statements, some of the students were aiming at permanent revolution. A typed sheet on the 'People's Park' by the Bay Area Revolutionary Union declared:

We will fight and fight from this generation to the next. The south campus community has no park. It is a community of street people who have dropped out of the rat race that capitalism offers as a way of life and who have come to associate labor with oppression; it is a community of students who only work with their hands; it is a community of thousands in all types of jobs terribly conscious that their labor is alienated labor.... Just hang in and keep your powder dry... We'll merge the spirit of the people with our own technology and we'll oppose anyone who puts technology ahead of people. That's what we'll do.... That's why the ruling classes tremble and get uptight. We are everywhere. Communism is everywhere.[222]

It seems unlikely that Reagan believed this nonsense (though one has to say it was absolutely playing into his hands for students to spread it around). Experience showed that after a student occupation had ended, it was always liable to start again; Reagan wanted to bring a continuing nuisance to an end. What he did was to put Berkeley under permanent occupation. A letter from Professor Smith once again tells us what it was really like:

Berkeley has been plunged for ten days into by far the worst of our many periods of turmoil. The city is literally an occupied zone; there are more than 2,000 National Guardsmen with fixed bayonets who patrol the streets and are encamped in parks; and they are merely assisting some four or five-hundred policemen of various sorts mobilized from several communities. On most days three helicopters circle overhead with a maddening beep of rotor blades: they are spotting-planes, observing the formation of dangerous or supposedly dangerous assemblies in the streets or signalling to troops on the ground where they should go in order to disperse guerrilla bands. On one occasion a monster of an army helicopter flew over Sproul Plaza spraying a highly concentrated cloud of tear gas on some thousands of people gathered below. One man has been killed by buckshot fired by police, and some thirty or forty others injured by birdshot and buckshot; one of these other wounded may be permanently blinded.[223]

Nine secretaries wrote a letter of protest to the university authorities:

The special background of our protest and request is the injury of Miss Mary Lange, the receptionist in our department, yesterday afternoon when she was trying to leave the campus to go home, and ended up being herded into the Sproul Plaza, gassed, clubbed and sent to the Highland Hospital... we ask that you immediately seek the removal of the National Guard and police forces occupying Berkeley. Until the troops are gone, we feel that the only responsible action you can take is closing the campus.[224]

Reagan was bitterly attacked by Bishop C. Kilmer Myers: declaring himself 'an old-fashioned conservative', the bishop described Reagan as 'the one who has unleashed the dogs of war on Berkeley... a full-scale military operation replete with strong-armed and brutal methods which as a student I observed in Germany in 1939'. In a press interview, Reagan 'conceded that use of a helicopter spraying tear gas to clear crowds from the Berkeley Central Campus... may have been a "tactical mistake" '; but, he added, apparently rejoicing in the phrase which the bishop also had used, 'once the dogs of war are unleashed, you must expect things will happen, and people being human will make mistakes on both sides.'[225]

Events, December 1968-June 1969, at posh Cornell University in upstate New York deserve a glance. Guns on campus were shocking; but right-wing commentators have grossly overstated the threat of an armed black takeover. By Saturday 19 April when, at 6.00 a.m., 80–100 black students occupied the student union, blacks feared for their lives from white extremists (a cross had been burned outside a black female residence). Gun purchases by white fraternities being reported, the black students sent out for rifles. At 4.00 p.m. on Saturday 20 April, after talks, they voluntarily came out, not 'brandishing' their rifles, but holding them empty and disabled as required by law. President John A. Perkins, who had been deliberately recruiting blacks since 1965 was himself a model of measured judgement, but was pushed out by the usual uncomprehending bigots in authority. The overwhelming majority of students took a centrist stance, moderately sympathetic to black grievances, and welcoming the opportunity to put the whole running of the University under scrutiny. Their letters home show a strong desire to *share* their moral dilemmas with their parents.[226]

Students in all countries, often activated by the best of motives, spouted nonsense; but they were embarked on a learning process which would eventually apply its own antidotes to that nonsense. I have referred several times to the great Marxisant fallacy, but there was no great Vietnam fallacy. Outrage over the evil of American involvement was completely justified. Commentators disillusioned with, or opposed to, radical protest in the sixties, most notably Adam Garfinkle in *Telltale Hearts*, have argued that the anti-war movement actually helped to prolong the war, on the grounds that 'the image of irresponsibility and wilful antipatriotism'... 'had the general effect of muting the expression of disaffection' among liberals and ordinary decent people.[227] This strikes me as wilfully nonsensical (and entirely in keeping with the right-wing view of the sixties, which is just as totalizing as that of the metaphysical Left). The protesters were wrong in their idealization of Ho Chi Minh and the Vietcong, but they were not wrong in making the war the issue nobody could ignore.

In 1969, both Reagan and Daley were swaggering high; there was more tragic violence to come, but eventually the kinds of action they had sponsored would become impossible. The violence in Rome, in Paris, in Battipaglia, in these various parts of the United States was appalling, but in no case, let us just remember, would it be appropriate to apply the term 'massacre'. Shortly things were to get worse in two of our countries, and one other one, with three kinds of terrorists: the Baader-Meinhoff gang in Germany, the Red Brigades in Italy, and the Weathermen in America. The bitter clashes and the violent confrontations were the product of ideas and movements which had been accumulating and converging since the end of the fifties; but they affected only minorities within the entire population we are concerned with, and they are of minor significance compared with the transformations which that same process of accumulation and convergence brought to these entire populations.

We have already noted rapid changes in the role and status of women. But with respect to rights and freedoms there was still much catching-up to accomplish. As we move to the final period of the 'long sixties', the phase of (in the urban centres of change) 'everything goes' and (in the backward regions) 'catching up', we must start by bringing into pole position the women activists and the major outstanding issues still affecting women.

Why chronicle all these events—the battles of the Quartier Latin, the Valle Giulia, Grosvenor Square, Columbia, Chicago, Berkeley? First, because events are important (and sorting them out is quite a difficult task—it is much easier to pontificate about 'hidden structures', since nobody can possibly tell whether you are right or wrong). Second, because study of these events brings out two vital aspects of the sixties: on the one hand, the dedication, the idealism, the bravery of those who participated in them; on the other, the folly of their obedience to the great Marxisant fallacy, the absurd faith that there was a promised land ready—given sufficient protest, sufficient violence, sufficient unconventionality, sufficient vulgarity—for the taking. I do not mock the protesters; I salute them, recognizing that they never had a hope of success in their revolutionary aspirations. I do mock commentators since, who, looking for the revolution decreed in the Marxist scriptures, have gone on and on picking over their failure, missing the real cultural revolution.

# Part IV

# Everything Goes, and Catching Up, 1969–1974

# 13

# Women's Turn

*From Civil Rights and Student Protest to Women's Liberation and Fundamentalist Feminism*

Amid the tension, the exultation, the heightened sensitivities engendered in the turmoil of 1968–9, women participating in the great causes of the time became sharply conscious of their own subordinate position, of their own rights, and of the blatant withholding of them. Some women, in isolation, had harboured rebellious thoughts; now they were brought together in stimulating interaction, in a period when all authority systems, all power relationships, open or concealed, real or imagined, were subject to the most intensive scrutiny—aided by the new neo-Marxist theories, much more subtle and appealing than the vulgar Marxism which had had to serve the radical young right through from the interwar years till the end of the fifties. Women came together in radical feminist groups, different from all previous feminist organizations in that they could not avoid taking on the defining characteristics of the other protest movements of the sixties, anarchic anti-authoritarianism and ruthless fundamentalism. But, just as the civil rights movement had a wider if largely tacit support, and protesting students, at certain points in time, had majority sympathy, so the radical feminists were not operating entirely in isolation. Earlier in the sixties a gentler, more traditional feminism, propagated in Europe by the successors to Simone de Beauvoir and inspired in America by Betty Friedan's perception that the American dream was in many ways a nightmare for American women, had begun to affect wider sections of society. Allied to this element were movements in favour of causes which all feminists would necessarily support, represented specifically in the President's Commission on Women's Rights, and the important legislation enacted in Great Britain: equal pay, equal job opportunities, free dissemination of contraceptives and contraceptive advice, easier divorce, legally available abortions: these were all issues on which many more people, men as well as women, could give their support. The National Organization for Women (NOW) was established by 300 men and women meeting in Washington in October 1966 in the belief that 'the time has come for a new movement toward free equality for all women in America, and toward a truly equal partnership of the sexes, as part of the world-wide revolution of human rights now taking place within and beyond our national borders'.[1] In Italy a new, moderate 'review of research and documentation', *Donna e Società* (Woman and Society), was first published in March 1967.

It is widely agreed that it was during the exhilarating and lacerating period of student activism that the new women's liberation groups were formed and new fundamentalist policies formulated, though much of the preliminary thinking and sharpening of consciousness had taken place in the civil rights movement (in America) and in the anti-Vietnam war movements in America and Europe. The evidence from Italy as from America, from Britain as from France, all confirms the importance of the activism of 1968 and 1969; indeed, one simply has to list the dates on which first meetings were held, first groups announced themselves, first manifestos were promulgated, to perceive the concentration in these two key years. One can see clearly how intensive activity on behalf of manifold student causes brought to the surface questions about secondary and inferior roles being performed by women. But how far is it true that during the time of the student protests young women actually had new oppressions imposed upon them, and that this was the real detonator of women's liberation? Greater permissiveness, the abandonment of many of the taboos and restrictions affecting women were crucial parts of the changes we have followed throughout the decade; the free granting of sexual favours by young women was very much part of the general male expectation during civil rights actions and organized protests, as well, of course, as in the hippie communes; free access to women's dormitories and a general abolition of the special codes imposed on women were absolutely central to the student movement, as was everything implied in the portentous slogan: 'Make love not war.' The orthodoxy was one of sexual liberation, and sexual liberation was taken, without much questioning to begin with, to mean males and females freely engaging in sexual activity without any of the conventional female reticence, and without any of what were now held to be the old possessive and selfish monogamous shibboleths.

But was this sexual liberation for women, or simply enhanced liberation for men, a grand occasion for the even more ruthless sexual exploitation of women? It would be hard to deny that the general loosening of prohibitions and inhibitions and the equalizing of rules and codes as between males and females was of enormous benefit to women, and increased opportunities for fulfilment and happiness. But that could be true in general, while at the same time the intense pressures, the almost compulsory promiscuity, could be bearing down excessively on women, depriving them of genuinely free choices and forcing them into activities which they did not enjoy, and perhaps even found unpleasant; or at any rate left them feeling oppressed, used, exploited, treated as objects without individuality, without humanity except as expressed through the sexual interest of a male lover. Certainly the leaders in the student movement were almost all male, and such leaders expected, and indeed generally attracted, the sexual ministrations of young women in the movement. Was it not also true that the young women were expected to do the chores: making the coffee, ironing the jeans, doing the typing and providing the other secretarial services?

We have to separate two distinct questions. What were the sexual experiences of women involved in the new activism and new heightened participation? And how far did a sufficient number of the women feel such a sense of aggravated oppression and exploitation as to provoke directly the creation of the new fundamentalist groups? It is a cliché that often you do not know you are being exploited until you have it pointed out to you. The whole (male-led) attack on capitalist, consumer society aimed at exposing the falsity, the deliberate generation of unnecessary wants, and the lulling of people into accepting an empty existence: the putative women's liberationists were operating within this ideological framework as they reflected on Simone de Beauvoir's earlier revelations about the cultural construction of female behaviour and Betty Friedan's exposure of the feminine mystique. Those women most thoroughly sensitized to the many manifestations and nuances of oppression did begin to articulate their perception that the alleged new sexual freedom was actually intensified sexual slavery. Against that one does have to recognize that in matters of intimate personal relationships nobody can possibly enjoy happiness and fulfilment all the time, and still more, that there were real gains. There are reminiscences enough to establish that large numbers of young women felt their lives to be driven by new-found freedoms and new-found joys, and unclouded by *arrières-pensées* about possible abuse and dehumanization. On freedom rides, protest marches, university sit-ins, they had available to them a much wider choice of men than ever home or campus provided, with a complete disruption of the conventions about the upper limits of the age range within which it was becoming for them to date—we saw a préfiguration of this in the work of Edna O'Brien.[2] To answer my first question: it would be unhistorical to read back the austere and accusatory fundamentalist feminist orthodoxy of the early seventies into the late sixties. For most women life was better and in that betterment men usually played an indispensable part, though for some women freedom and fulfilment were undoubtedly to be found in openly acknowledged lesbian lifestyles (treated warmly, it may be remembered, by Helen Gurley Brown) and a part also of the disruption of conventional living patterns and the complexity of life during the events of 1968–9. In brief, there was more sex, in more variations, and, crucially, there was less guilt, less fear, and less furtiveness.

The answer to the second question is: yes, direct personal experience of closer, and often more frequent, intimate personal contact with men created in some women a very strong reaction against unrestricted male licentiousness in its predatory, arrogant, and inconsiderate aspects, and was a force behind the new aggressive demand for women's liberation. At the same time as there was a more naked (in several senses) experience of the male, there was anyway a new frankness and openness with regard to bodily functions and bodily parts which, not long before, women had been supposed not to think about and certainly not put names to. Certain women, angry about male attitudes and behaviour, began to scrutinize the precise male role, or lack of it, in their own sexual fulfilment. Just as this scrutiny was taking place, the general rejection of old rules and old canons of behaviour was making it possible for lesbian preferences to be openly acknowledged. Female lovers, it seemed, paid far more attention to the clitoris than did most males, hell-bent on their own satisfaction. Questions were raised about the real value with respect to female pleasure of the vagina, and thence of the value of the male organ. All the great feminists of the past had been concerned about female pleasure within the context of sexual congress with men; now the new, uninhibited exploration of the female body and its relationships with the male was leading to the adumbration of a scenario in which women could find sexual fulfilment while dispensing entirely with men—an exact echo of the separatist doctrines of the Black Power movement. Feminists, reacting to all the exhortations to be uninhibited, to be liberated, to 'make love not war' were beginning to talk of 'the personal being the political', of their own bodies being a site of power politics, of the sex act being an imposition on them of male political power. An exaggerated version claimed that a 'terrorism of coitus' had replaced that of chastity.[3] It was noted later by Italian feminists that while German female students had been to the fore in taking up leadership roles, Italian ones, on the contrary, were happy to 'play the girlfriend' *(fanno le ragazze)* or be the women of the comrades *(donne dei compagni)*, which may partly account for the subsequent extreme anti-male reaction in some branches of Italian feminism.[4] Before the big books came out, the key text, circulated 'underground' as it were, was the typed and cyclostyled document 'The Myth of the Vaginal Orgasm', prepared in November 1968 for the first American National Women's Liberation Conference; it achieved slightly wider circulation in *Notes for the Second Year* produced by the New York Radical Feminists in 1970.[5] Anne Koedt, the author, was Danish-born, but had worked in both the civil rights organization, CORE, and the socialist SDS.

It is a measure of the complexities with which we have to deal, and a clear indication that Catholic, and in so many ways ultra-traditionalist, Italy was the country in which women suffered the most unfavourable conditions, that the first ever radical feminist organization had appeared in Milan on 1 December 1966, DEMAU (the Group for the Démystification of Authoritarianism, to which the adjective 'Patriarchal' was quickly added). Although this body was minuscule, its first manifesto, signed by Daniela Pellegrini, Elena Rasi, and Lia Cigarini, deserves to be quoted because of its historical primacy. Its first point was opposition to the integration of women into a society where there is forced division of tasks and compulsory domesticity for women. Second is the 'démystification of authoritarianism, with regard to rights, sexual relations, conflict of roles in family and society, education, work and intellectual and scientific production'. The third point called for a research programme into the establishment of the autonomy of women, 'towards a conscious valuation of her own essential values and historical position'. Only thus, it was concluded, 'can women participate in elaborating the values of a new society'. All of this, according to the fourth point, would lead to the emancipation of men, currently 'deprived because of the devaluation of values considered feminine'. It was characteristic of the notably intellectual cast of the Italian movement to insist on the need for programmes of research and study, the Italians being less certain than Americans that the nature and causes of women's oppression were self-evident. The twofold programme of action of DEMAU called for studies in biology, anthropology, mythology, psychoanalysis, sociology, pedagogy, and psychology, as well as the preparation of propaganda, organization of debates, and cooperation with other feminist groups.[6] Certain Italian feminists were to be among the most uninhibited in promoting the claims of the clitoris.

But without question the first home of active, effective, radical feminism was America, just as the new phase of liberal feminism had earlier received its stimulus from Betty Friedan's *The Feminine Mystique*. Only in 1970 did there appear a British counterpart of Friedan's book, *The Female Eunuch*, by Australian-born Germaine Greer. However, this was a counterpart for an utterly different generation, rumbustious and confrontational, where Friedan's work had been gentle and conciliatory. *The Female Eunuch* was rapidly reissued in paperback in Britain and America, and in translation in both France and Italy. As the British feminist movement took shape in 1970 and 1971 it presented a more united front than was to be found in America or Italy; it also carried with it much of the colour and vivacity of 'swinging Britain'. Thanks to the 'civilized society' legislation of 1967, Britain already had legal abortion and freely available contraception; legislation on divorce and equal pay (enacted in 1969 and 1970 respectively) were on the way. The country with an established tradition of intellectual feminism, thoroughly integrated into intellectual and political life, and the world of journalism, was France. Evelyne Sullerot and Françoise Giroud continued the tradition of the (still very active) Simone de Beauvoir, together with such novelists as Claire Etcherelli, Christiane Rochefort, and Marie Cardinale. Organized campaigns on contraception and abortion were already in existence, but these remained, as in Italy, very fraught issues. As with all social development in the sixties, international exchange was of great importance. On the continent of Europe the 'Anglo-Saxons' were frequently invoked, the British for their legislation, the Americans for their radical ideas and actions.

The fundamentalist feminist movement in America had its roots in civil rights agitation and SDS. In both, young women developed a professional sense of self-worth and of their own potential for altering the lives of others and of themselves. In both they found themselves belittled and taken for granted. Attempts to bring women's issues onto the agendas at the 1965 and 1966 SDS conferences were greeted with jeers. It was at the SDS national convention in the summer of 1967 that some radical women began to realize that they could no longer work through the existing organizations of the Left, that even having their own caucus within SDS was insufficient, and that they must start organizing independently. The inevitability of a split seemed confirmed at the National Conference for a New Politics held in Chicago in the first week of September.[7] At the end of 1967 Shulamith Firestone and others formed New York Radical Women. Feminist meetings began to be arranged, and feminist tracts issued from the autumn of 1967, accelerating after the turn of the year. *Women: A Journal of Liberation* first appeared in the autumn of 1967; nationwide contacts were being established by January 1968. A first national meeting of the various radical women's groups was held at Sandy Springs, Maryland, in August.

Two more groups were set up in New York, Firestone being a member of both of them: Redstockings and New York Radical Feminists. Inevitably there was Women's Liberation of Berkeley, while Boston had Cell 16 and then, in 1969, Bread and Roses. WITCH had branches in several cities, with a particularly active group in Cleveland. The Chicago Women's Liberation Union was founded in 1969. In November 1969 over 500 women from an assortment of different groups in the East met in New York as the Congress to Unite Women. Another New York group, founded in 1969, was simply called the Feminists.[8] In January 1968 there appeared the leaflet 'The Ostentatious Orgasm' by Jill Scharf:

> The orgasm may seem ostentatious because, for the first time in history, it can be discussed openly. The ability and right for women as well as men to enjoy sexual expression and satisfaction is as important and relevant a subject today as any other physical ability or civil right. However, mention the word orgasm in some circles and eyebrows still go up two inches, women giggle or look guilty, and men look vaguely hostile or protective. By the defence of silence that ensues you get the feeling with married couples particularly, that the subject is simply not discussed, at least not with each other. It's about time the defences came down... what we have here,... is a failure to communicate.[9]

A mimeographed document of June 1968, emanating from a southern students' organization, drove home the argument that sex was an issue in exactly the same way that race was, and that separate action was as necessary for women as it was for blacks. The document conceded that female students were really treated fairly equally and did not understand the real oppression of women which lay in the bearing of children and in marriage.

> Marriage as we know it is for women, as integration is for blacks. It is the atomisation of a sex so as to render it politically powerless... While sexual and emotional alliances with men may continue to be of some benefit, the peculiar domestic constitution is not... We are brainwashed by the media with sexy commercials and talk in the movement about screwing as often as possible; many of us have already been on the pill for longer than we can medically afford. And a good many of us, I would suspect, are desperately screwing some guy because we think we should and wonder what our friends would think if we didn't at all for a while. Celibacy has always been a tool for those who wish, for a time, to 'stop the world and get off'... We must stop being pawns in the media's sexuality game and reconsider the whole scene... The territory ahead is new, frightening, and appears lonely... In the life of each woman, the most immediate oppressor, however unwilling he may be in theory to play that role, is 'the man'.

Even if the larger enemy is still bourgeois society, the immediate one is being identified as husband or boyfriend, who, in an analogy which is starkly effective, if on the slightest reflection highly overdrawn, is likened to an upholder of black slavery: even if women prefer to view him as 'merely a pawn in the game, he is still the foreman on the big plantation'.[10]

Such views were circulating across the country among small committed groups, including the ones I have mentioned; they commanded none of the attention of the violent student protests. Then came the event which put women's liberation on television, and brought it to the attention of a national public. The event used the methods of the yippies and of street theatre to make a profound feminist statement against another event, seen as embodying society's reduction of women to mere objects in the sexual game, the Miss America contest at Atlantic City on Saturday 7 September 1968. The organizers, New York Women, distributed a leaflet inviting women to bring to the event 'old bras, girdles, high-heeled shoes, women's magazines, curlers, and other instruments of torture to women'. A 'freedom trash-can' was set up so that women could chuck into it the relics of traditional femininity which they had brought with them. The throwing away of bras was transmuted by the press into 'the burning of bras', an image which stuck, though in fact no bras were burnt. A live sheep was crowned Miss America, while the protesters chained themselves to a replica of Miss America in a red, white, and blue bathing-suit, and displayed placards declaring 'Miss America Sells It' and 'Miss America Is a Big Falsie'.[11] It should be said that, great publicity success though this demonstration was, it did meet with criticism from other feminists, for seeming to be directing their attack on beautiful women in particular and non-feminist women in general.[12] The bra-burning legend was perpetuated in a bantering article a year later (1 September 1969) in *Newsweek* with the punning title 'The Big Letdown':

> It all began last fall when some 150 uprighteous members of the Women's Liberation Movement gathered in front of Convention Hall in Atlantic City and burned their brassieres... With that, a solid grass roots rebellion was underway to threaten the foundations (possibly moral, certainly garment) of this country.

Articles in *Life*, 'An "Oppressed Majority" Demands Its Rights' (12 December 1969) and *Time*, 'The New Feminists: Revolt Against "Sexism"' (21 November 1969) were not entirely serious either.[13]

For publication in 1969, the New York Radical Feminists prepared *Politics of the Ego: a Manifesto for the New York Radical Feminists* which spoke of 'the supremacist male ego'. This manifesto also made clear where these Radical Feminists parted company with such movements as NOW, which envisaged men and women working together, declaring: 'while we realise that the liberation of women will ultimately mean the liberation of men from their destructive role as oppressor, we have no illusion that men will welcome this liberation without a struggle.'[14] In September 1969 a young French scholar went to Smith College, Northampton, Massachusetts, to carry out research on the American novel. After several weeks she began to hear about 'women's liberation', and was invited to attend the inaugural meetings of the local group. She recorded her 'great joy at those women saying out loud what she had never dared think save only very deep down'. 'These Americans', she continued, 'were passionate; I had the feeling of rediscovering a living philosophy: I had lost that sense in France.' In the spring of 1970, Kate Millett, one of the leading pioneers of radical feminism, visited Smith College: 'her verve was regenerating.' This young French scholar decided to abandon her academic researches in favour of writing a book on American feminism, which she believed was completely misunderstood in France. But while she was quite clear that the American radicals deserved the credit for initiating a new phase in feminism, she was also aware of their obsessiveness, fissility, and personal egotism. She described herself as 'sympathizing but not engaged', and more interested in the national movement than what she called 'local avatars'; she also recorded that the local militants took her for an agent of the FBI.

> One must remember the notorious antifeminism of the American tradition, as it appears in novels, for instance; that if the American woman seems to her European counterparts infinitely privileged because her standard of life is so superior, she is perhaps more harassed than her European counterpart. More than European women, American ones are obliged to devote many hours to their child because of the educational system; paid maternity leave is practically non-existent; women occupy the lowest jobs; the percentage of female doctorates is minute; the female student must have higher marks than the male to be admitted to the same university.[15]

Although the 'bra-burning' at Atlantic City provided publicity, it served also to pigeonhole women's liberation as a fringe activity. Three developments made 1970 the year in which feminism was recognized as a movement to be taken just as seriously as the black civil rights movement had been taken from 1964 onwards. These three developments were: the *Newsweek* special report of 23 March called 'Women's Lib.: The War on Sexism', which among other things explained how the term 'sexist' applied to activities and attitudes which could be regarded as just as obnoxious as those of a 'racist'; the publication of two key texts, in the form of substantial books by the radical leaders I have already mentioned, Kate Millett and Shulamith Firestone (the feminist texts I have quoted so far were all unpublished or published by minority presses—only now was there a market for books); and the Women's Strike Day demonstrations of 26 August, commemorating the fiftieth anniversary of the winning of the vote by American women, and the immense media coverage of them. The background report on the demonstrations prepared for CBS television subsequently emerged in 1971 as a book, *Rebirth of Feminism*, by Judith Hole and Ellen Levine. A paperback edition came out in 1973, and the preface to this edition well encapsulated the expansion from 1970 and 1971 on into 1972, reporting that in August 1971 when *Rebirth of Feminism* was completed:

> hundreds of thousands of women had directly participated in movement activities as well as felt the impact of feminist ideas. Nonetheless, women's issues were not yet viewed as serious by most traditional political analysts, right, left, or center.
>
> In the intervening year, although the critics remain, the movement has expanded so dramatically that even the most established institutions have been forced to recognise women's issues... almost daily the press reported the election, appointment, or hiring of women to jobs previously held only by men; conscious-raising groups proliferated and became almost as accepted in their communities as the PTA; and dozens of books and periodicals on feminism were published and widely read.[16]

The key texts presenting the fundamental radical feminist thesis that patriarchy is as much a dominant force in society as is (allegedly) capitalism, that all aspects of life at large are pervaded by assumptions of male superiority, and that all aspects of personal relationships, and most particularly, of course, sexual relationships, are political in that they always involve women's oppression by men, are *Sexual Politics* by Kate Millett and *The Dialectic of Sex: The Case for Feminist Revolution* by Shulamith Firestone (somehow the very names of the two authors are profoundly evocative: harsh, uncompromising, scholarly Kate Millett—much of *Sexual Politics* is in fact an analysis of representations of sex in literature—and exotic, inflammatory Shulamith Firestone). Behind this feminist thesis lay the modifications to Marxism carried out by the intellectuals of the sixties, stressing cultural determinism and the social construction of reality. Here is Millett on the sex act itself as essentially a political act:

> Coitus can scarcely be said to take place in a vacuum; although of itself it appears a biological and physical activity, it is set so deeply within the larger context of human affairs that it serves as a charged microcosm of the variety of attitudes and values to which culture subscribes. Among other things, it may serve as a model of sexual politics on an individual or personal plane.

And on patriarchy:

> ... What goes largely unexamined, often even unacknowledged (yet is institutionalized nonetheless) in our social order, is the birthright priority whereby males rule females. Through this system a most ingenious form of 'interior colonization' has been achieved. It is one which tends moreover to be sturdier than any form of segregation, and more rigorous than class stratification, more uniform, certainly more enduring.

The book concludes with an assessment of the place of feminism in the mass movements of the day, and an invocation of its potential as the most revolutionary movement yet.

> As the largest alienated element in our society, and because of their numbers, passion, and length of oppression its largest revolutionary base, women might come to play a leadership part in social revolution, quite unknown before in history...[17]

In making such large claims Millett was only showing herself a prisoner of the other movements she mentions and their absurd faith in the imminent collapse of bourgeois society: still, the changes taking place in the lives of ordinary women were already considerable, and over the next few years were to be enormous.

Firestone repeated the point that sexual attraction to a man, or even sexual satisfaction through a man, is a dangerous drug best avoided. 'Love', said Firestone, 'perhaps more than childbearing is the pivot of women's oppression today.' 'Nature', she wrote, 'produced the fundamental inequality—half the human race must bear and rear the children of all of them—which was later consolidated, institutionalized, in the interests of men.' The upshot, she continued, was great cultural sacrifice: 'men and women developed only half of themselves, at the expense of the other half.' The first demand of feminist revolution, therefore, must be 'The freeing of women from the tyranny of their reproductive biology by every means available, and the diffusion of the childbearing and child rearing role to the society as a whole, men as well as women.' In setting out the means by which women were to free themselves from this 'tyranny' Firestone, as so many of the innovators of the time did, pushed the paradigm beyond its utmost limits, toppling over into the realm of cultural extremism: women would no longer be expected to become pregnant; instead there would be extra-uterine gestation in test-tubes.[18]

As with the new British popular culture of the sixties, women's liberation in Britain had its own unique history, while also owing something to American influences—distant in that there was a vague general knowledge of the early feminist initiatives in the United States, and contingent in that certain American women in the Vietnam Solidarity Campaign in London founded one of the first British women's liberation groups in 1968. Much of the impetus, as in America, came from left-wing and radical groups, such as the International Socialists, the International Marxist Group, the Vietnam Solidarity Campaign, and CND. Specifically British were the contributions of a more traditionalist group of pacifists and moderate feminists who, in February 1968, organized celebrations for the fiftieth anniversary of a most important event in British history, the granting of the vote to women, and of a handful of highly practical women trade unionists. In Hull, in the spring of 1968, Lil Bilocca led a campaign of fishermen's wives for improved safety at sea. In June, Rose Boland led the sewing machinists at the Ford Dagenham plant in east London in a three-week strike for the right to undertake higher-grade work on equal terms with men.[19] At around the same time a group of London bus conductresses demanded the right to become bus drivers.[20] We are here at the very heart of what was truly significant in the changes in consciousness brought about by sixties developments: action not just by gilded youth, but by ordinary, under-privileged working-class women. The upshot was the establishment at top trade union level of the National Joint Action Campaign for Women's Equal Rights (NJACWER), which was both successful in pressuring for the 1970 Equal Pay Act and a stimulus to the budding women's liberation movement.[21]

Sheila Rowbotham, who in 1969 produced a crucial statement about the need for socialists to understand and internalize the concrete realities of the cultural oppression of women, *Women's Liberation and the New Politics,* has given a sharp insight into how many women felt *before* the convergence of circumstances in 1968–9 got things moving:

> In the diary I kept during 1967 there are persistent references to incidents I'd seen and books I'd read from a women's liberation point of view. I can remember odd conversations with women who were friends of mine, and particular very intense moments when I was hurt and made angry by the attitudes of men on the left. But it was still at an intellectual level. We didn't think of meeting consciously as a group, far less of forming a movement. We were floundering around. The organizational initiative came from elsewhere.[22]

In this book I have not concealed my atheism with regard to Marxisant visions of society and

624

'historical process'. However there can be no doubt that many 'floundering' feminists of the time did turn to Marxism for inspiration. The 'underground' journal *Black Dwarf* obliged in January 1969 with an entire issue offering Marxist interpretations of the oppression of women.[23] To the group formed in Tufnell Park, north London, by the American expatriates were added groups at Essex University and in Peckham, south London. In May 1969 a first newsletter was issued. That British women's libbers had a sense of humour was made clear in the title chosen for the second issue, 'Harpies Bizarre'; thereafter the publication settled down as *Shrew*. By the end of 1969 there were about seventy groups spread across Great Britain.[24]

One important intellectual development of the sixties was the sponsorship of 'democratic' history, best seen in the 'history workshops' (discussing the history of ordinary working people) held at Ruskin, the 'workers' college', at Oxford. It was at a history workshop there in September 1969 that the idea was matured of having a women's liberation conference at the same venue in February 1970.[25] This was attended by 600 delegates, and out of it came the Women's National Co-ordinating Committee, putting forward the following four highly reasonable demands: equal pay; equal educational and work opportunities; free contraception and abortion on request; free twenty-four-hour child care for working mothers.[26]

This was the moderate, practical tone of *The Female Eunuch*, a book which, at the same time, presented a very individualistic (some were later to say idiosyncratic) version of feminism. Germaine Greer was a graduate in English from Australia who had come to Cambridge to do a Ph.D., and who subsequently obtained an academic appointment at the University of Warwick. Tall, good-looking, and intellectually brilliant, she was the embodiment of the emancipated female enjoying the permissive society to the full, associating with the underground, and turning her talents to earning fame and fortune. Contemptuous of the sexual prowess of British males, she wrote a series for *Oz* on 'In Bed with the English'; she had her own 'alternative' comedy show, *Nice Time,* on Granada TV.[27] Perhaps the contrast between Greer's book and the canonical American texts does demonstrate that women in sixties Britain simply had more fun than did women in America. However, the more usual kind of feminism, that deriving from the New Left and Marxism, was represented in Britain by the psychoanalyst Juliet Mitchell. In 'Women: The Longest Revolution', published in *New Left Review* in November 1966, Mitchell had identified the family as a key institution of capitalism, through which women reproduce and maintain the workforce, while they are fooled into believing that these are their natural tasks in which they find fulfilment. Where Greer was rumbustious and in touch with life as it was lived at the end of the sixties, Mitchell was erudite and theoretical: she developed her views in the weighty book *Woman's Estate* (1971).

The new feminists all broke with the romantic idealism which had pervaded the *Feminine Mystique;* but while it was becoming commonplace to speak of men as oppressing and exploiting women, Greer sought to shake her readers out of their illusions by warning them that they did not realize, as she put it, 'how much men hate women'. Much of the essence of her arguments and style come through in this statement: 'A woman should not continue to apologise and disguise herself, while accepting her male's potbelly, wattles, bad breath, farting, stubble, baldness and other ugliness without complaint.'[28] Towards the end of the book Greer dwells on the

625

question of women's preoccupation with trying to beautify themselves, and also with other accepted activities such as cooking and housekeeping. *The Female Eunuch* acknowledges that women, or at least younger ones, are already changing, and breaking with convention. With regard to fashionable hairstyles, she suggests:

> women could find the way their hair grows best and keep it that way, working the possible changes according to their own style and mood instead of coiffing themselves in a shape ordained by fashion but not by their heads.

She then goes on to recognize that such trends

> are already apparent. Most young girls do not inhabit the hairdressers anything like as much as their mothers do. They have vanquished the couturier single-handed with whatever they pleased, from the boldest and most romantic to the most crass adaptations of men's sporting gear.

Critical of 'women's liberation' in the political, banner-waving sense, Greer proposes liberation within the home:

> The chief means of liberating women is replacing of compulsiveness and compulsion by the pleasure principle. Cooking, clothes, beauty, and housekeeping are all compulsive activities in which the anxiety quotient has long since replaced the pleasure or achievement quotient. It is possible to use even cooking, clothes, cosmetics and housekeeping for *fun*. The essence of pleasure is spontaneity. In these cases spontaneity means rejecting the norm, the standard that one must live up to, and establishing a self-regulating principle... it could be possible to cook a meal that you want to cook, that everybody wants to eat, and to serve it in any way you please, instead of following a timetable, serving Tuesday's meal or the tastefully varied menu of all new and difficult dishes you have set yourself as a new cross, and if you simply cannot feel any interest in it, not to do it.

As many feminists were openly and honestly doing, Greer recognized the very deep fear that existed among women over doing anything as drastic as abandoning compulsive activities. Women must accept the existence of risk when they 'refuse to accept the polarity of masculine-feminine.'[29]

Rather more than two years after their American counterparts, British radical feminists took direct action against a beauty contest, this time against the Miss World competition taking place at the Royal Albert Hall on 20 November 1970. A fluoride bomb was exploded outside the hall; but the demonstrators also managed to get inside and, witnessed by millions of television viewers, created a great din with whistles and rattles, while throwing flour, smoke-bombs and stink-bombs at the ageing American comedian presenting the show, Bob Hope, and displaying placards referring to the event as a 'cattle market degrading to women'. They also distributed leaflets declaring

'We're not beautiful, we're not ugly, we're angry', and attacking the way beauty contests treated women as objects, and represented 'the traditional female road to success'. Two women were arrested as the show continued with Bob Hope cracking a few feebly defensive jokes.[30] This certainly gained for British feminism the same kind of notoriety as the Atlantic City event had gained for American. Meantime, in the summer of 1970, the Women's Street Theatre Group was formed. On the following 11 March, Women's Day marches were held; as an offshoot of the massive London one, the Women's Street Theatre Group produced in Trafalgar Square one of the most spectacular shows ever, *Sugar and Spice*, featuring huge models of a deodorant, a sanitary towel, and a gigantic red, white, and blue penis.[31] Tight police security meant that the group's attempt at a second Miss World demonstration (also attended by the newly formed Gay Street Theatre Group) was confined to a parade outside the Albert Hall. The contest was parodied in The Flashing Nipple Show, in which the actresses had flashing lights at breasts and crotch.[32] These were minority but highly dramatic activities. Of more enduring significance was the founding in 1972 of the monthly journal *Spare Rib*.

Organized radical feminism in France appeared in the universities with the beginning of the new academic year in November 1969, but for the time being was eclipsed by the rapidly developing moderate women's movement.[33] When Greer's book appeared in France in 1971, with noun and adjective transposed, as *La Femme eunuque* (The Eunuch Woman), the blurb presented it as a work of moderation hostile to men in only a limited way, and not really 'feminist' in the American sense, which, to the French, connoted extreme fundamentalism. Greer's own special introduction, dated 14 February 1971, declared that the success of the book in Britain had only come about because the women's movement was then already in existence; it was now, she added, in full flood. The quintessence of the moderate, male-supported movement in France, to which of course the publishers were deliberately making an appeal, can be found in two developments of 1970. In October the French government, with much fanfare, announced a major new initiative, 'France for French Women'. *L'Express* (always well-informed with regard to this part of the political spectrum) offered four reasons for this remarkable development. First of all, crude electoral calculation— women tended to vote Gaullist anyway, so this was a move to consolidate the government's natural constituency. Secondly, *L'Express* referred to the strikes then taking place in the big department stores which had once more drawn attention to the dismal conditions suffered by female shop workers (a fairly constant issue in French social history, though this particular action was part of the continuing post-1968 effervescence). Then, very significantly with respect to my general theme of international exchange and my particular one of the primacy of American feminism, the paper stressed the impact on France of the feminist demonstrations currently taking place in New York. In putting forward its fourth factor, *L'Express* was perhaps being less than rigorously analytical: still, it is historically significant, and an apt summary of important trends throughout the sixties, that *L'Express* should single out what it called 'the new importance of everything concerning women'. Under this very general heading it made two rather different points: first, the immense importance of women in the workforce, one worker out of three now being female; second, the disgraceful inequalities in the payment of men and women, women's salaries and wages being stuck at 36 per cent below men's. The government's proposals, described by *L'Express* as 'modest', though 'traditional (but far from negligible)' might have been a more appropriate description, were: more professional training for women; the creation, within government itself, of part-time employment for women; state benefits for female heads of families even if they were in employment; a requirement upon employers to pay women 90 per cent of their normal salary during maternity leave, instead of the current 50 per cent; more crèches. In tune with the basic feminist perception that what most needed changing were attitudes, especially those of men, *L'Express* summed up sardonically: 'The prime minister has taken a timid step in the right direction. What now remains is to change the outlook of men. A vast programme!'[34]

A little more adventurous, though still very much related to established politics as well as to the profit-making women's magazine industry, was the 'Estates General' organized by the fashion and beauty editors of *Elle* magazine, held in Versailles on 20-22 November. An inquiry presented to *Elle* readers in October 1969 had determined the themes for the 14,000 question-naires distributed and collected between 5 March and 15 October 1970: love, the couple, and marriage; cultural life; education; political life; work; leisure; health; women's rights in law; the content and presentation of news; teaching; fashion and beauty; the urban environment; daily life. Three hundred and ninety delegates and several politicians of all political parties attended the conference.[35] On fashion and beauty (anathema to the fundamentalists), resolutions including the following were adopted by a majority of 175 to 23, with six abstentions:

1. That women should find in the woman's press the means and elements to enable them to attain the full blossoming of their personality.
2. That ready-made styles should be available for a price appropriate to the quality.
3. That this should also apply to beauty products.
4. From childhood, introduction to beauty should be given as a part of art subjects, physical education, hygiene and diet, all within a coherent scholarly education.
5. Social security payments should be extended to cover dermatological treatments and certain plastic surgery.[36]

At the end of the conference twelve general motions were adopted, which directly addressed discriminatory language, attitudes, and actions, some going beyond women to embrace in partic-ular the disabled, a highly visible concern of 1968 and after. According to the first two:

1. There must be an end to contrasts between the 'strong sex' and the 'weak sex' and to use of terms implying male superiority.
2. Women should be given not just equal rights, but equal opportunities, and rights of choice in relation to differences said to be imposed by biology, though too often in fact confused with those imposed by society.

Others demanded: an end to all 'Laws and arrangements regulating civil, professional, and family life' which uphold the last traces of a society founded on the superiority of the male, and to all segregation in work or in education; equal rights for the elderly, foreign workers, single women, those with mental and physical handicaps, orphans. The ninth resolution echoed the first in demanding that journalists and politicians, especially, should take care in their language not to treat women as children, as immature, or as of lesser worth than men.[37] The final resolution expressed the conviction of the conference that it was 'responding to the deepest wishes of all women' in 'solemnly' demanding that 'men and women of goodwill should unite to secure the victory by all methods of the spread of *tolerance* which is the superior dimension of liberty of expression and *generosity* which is the superior dimension of intelligence'[38]—a call to measured judgement indeed. Among the fourteen resolutions on sex, the most striking are those which reveal the need to combat the persistence in France of heavily traditional morality: one insisted that there should be no moral condemnation or material punishment of those who chose to live together; another that the penal code against adultery should be abrogated. There was a declaration in favour of premarital sex, coupled with the insistence that 'women should have the maximum opportunity for physical pleasure'.[39] There is no mention anywhere of lesbianism. The final general resolution at the congress demanded 'equality of opportunities, of rights, and of duties'. This very practical topic became the focus of the thirteen associated public debates organized across the country at Marseille, Toulouse, Bordeaux, Clermont-Ferrand, Grenoble, Dijon, Metz, Loudeac, Rouen, Lille, Tours, and Sarcelles. In Paris itself, there were twenty-six additional discussion sessions *(tables rondes)*.[40]

The central argument of this book is that the liberation of the sixties affected, and was participated in by, majorities: it was not the prerogative of ultimately frustrated revolutionary minorities. *Elle* was a successful magazine which clearly appealed to large numbers of women (unless we are to adopt the patronizing position that the women who purchased *Elle* and followed its hints on 'beauty', housekeeping, and so on were dupes suffering from 'false consciousness'). The issues discussed at *Elle's* 'Estates General' were those raised by readers themselves; the resolutions adopted quite clearly identified and condemned existing male dominance, and directly challenged much existing law and custom in French society. Some commentators found the contrast a 'strange phenomenon', an apparent reversal of Elle's devotion since its foundation to 'feminizing' women, 'representing them as beautiful, dynamic, modern, good housekeepers, good mothers, and good wives';[41] that 'devotion' could well have been characteristic of an earlier *Elle,* but, like so many other institutions of established society, it could not stay immune to the infection of High Sixties change. Nevertheless the Estates General was ridiculed by radical feminists, who had undergone their own two defining events in May and August. In May a 'General Assembly' (the echoes of 1789 are striking) was held in Vincennes, men being firmly excluded: an invasion by men shouting obscene sexual slogans served to confirm the movement in the radical separatist direction.[42] In July a special number of *Partisans,* 'Liberation des Femmes—Année Zéro', was issued, with two crucial articles, a Marxist analysis of housework and a French version of 'The Myth of the Vaginal Orgasm'; then on 28 August a dozen women staged a protest in front of the Tomb of the Unknown Soldier in homage to 'the Unknown Soldier's Wife' with the slogans, 'There is someone even more unknown than the soldier; his wife' and 'One man out of two is a woman'. The intervention of the police ensured attention in the press who, fully mindful of the American precedents, dubbed the group the Women's Liberation Movement.[43] This was the baptism of the French radical feminist MLF. These fundamentalists took their hostility to *Elle's* Estates General direct to Versailles, invading and disrupting the opening cocktail party, and distributing a brilliant but bitter mock questionnaire, parodying the one so carefully drawn up by *Elle*, with questions such as:

> When you are pregnant and you do not want to keep the child, do you prefer: Knitting needles? The branch of a vine? A wire of steel, of copper, of barbed wire? Going on the streets to procure 2,000 francs?

or

> When a man speaks to a woman should he address himself: To her breasts and her legs? To her bottom and her breasts? To her bottom only?[44]

Three hundred and forty-three well-known women, including famous film stars, achieved the greatest publicity yet for women's liberation and one of its major causes when, in April 1971, they published a manifesto declaring that they themselves had all had abortions.[45] Other events demonstrated that a form of feminism, or certainly women's activism, was affecting all social classes: the strikes of the department store workers were followed by sit-in strikes by women in a number of workshops and factories, culminating in spectacular strikes of women workers at Troyes in 1971 and Thionville in 1972. For the municipal elections of March 1971, lists of exclusively women candidates were drawn up; International Women's Day, 20 November 1971, brought out impressive demonstrations.[46]

Effective cooperation across ideology and across sex in France (of which there is further evidence in the next section) was not replicated in Italy, largely because of the geographical sectionalism, and the absence of one single metropolitan centre, but also because of the Italian proclivity for indulging in highly theoretical, and therefore highly divisive, debate, as a result of which Italian radical feminism splintered into many different tiny groups. As DEMAU began to fade, there came into existence over 1969–70 the Rome University Women's Collective, the Women's Liberation Movement (MLD), the Revolt of Women (Rivolta Femminile), the Italian Front for the Liberation of Women, and the Feminist Group of Trento. In a cyclostyled document circulated in 1969, the Rome University Women's Collective specified its three tasks as:

1. A specific attack on the capitalist mode of production, in particular the division of labour through which is operated a separation and differentiation of the work of women, thus rupturing class unity in this sphere as well.
2. Pressing this attack on capital right to its institutional origin, the family, the instrument of capital as a source for private production through domestic labour and ideological basis of the maintenance of the entire system.

3. To develop an anti-capitalist front with a cultural revolution at its very heart for the clarification of the role of women in the revolutionary process and the préfiguration of the phase of transition to socialism.[47]

This group seemed very stuck in the conventional wisdom of 1968: it was very strongly against the family (represented primarily as a capitalist institution) but not very strongly against men as such.

In contrast to this collective of Roman students, the MLD was an offshoot of the Radical party, reformed in 1967, combining a presence in parliamentary politics with a belief (adapted from British and American protest movements) in non-violent action, and genuinely living up to its title in its attitudes towards drugs, abortion, and the workings of the Italian constitution. A leading figure was the academic Massimo Teodori, who returned to Italy in 1970 after spells in Britain and in America: it was from his experiences in America that in January 1970 he began a series of seminars on the role and status of women. The MLD had its first national conference in February 1971. Briefly, there seemed a possibility of a united radical feminist movement, but crucial issues arose immediately, the lesser one concerning the role of Marxism, and the all-important one relating to whether men could participate in the movement or whether it should be exclusively confined to women. Rivolta Femminile, which had been founded in the summer of 1970, was totally opposed to the inclusion of men; the Italian Front for Women's Liberation continued to take a Marxist line.[48]

The MLD spoke of: 'our present repressive and oppressive society with its oppression and exploitation which are special and peculiar to women whether considered individually or as a social group'.[49] The special oppressions of women took five forms: first, 'the biological functions of procreation', despite the evolution of science and the transformation of economic, demographic, and social reality, had continued to be used 'to restrict and limit' the subjective development of women and the fulfilment of their social functions. Secondly, 'the principles of patriarchal society' had 'subjected women to the authority of men' and led to them being 'considered inferior beings under the economic, legal and moral tutelage of men'. Thirdly, 'the economic exploitation of women' had confined their working role 'above all to that of serving within the institution of the family. Since the industrial revolution women have been considered as reserve manual labour to be manipulated according to the needs of the trade cycle.' Fourth was 'psychological conditioning', which had led to women themselves accepting their inferior role. Fifth was 'the repression of female sexuality', resulting in women remaining the sexual property of men.

The MLD's objectives included: information on contraceptives to be available in schools (and elsewhere) and contraceptives to be freely distributed; the legalization of abortion; the end of separate education in schools; fighting the myths of the separate roles of men and women; publicly funded day nurseries; action against all manifestations of male authoritarianism—particularly the forcing of women to take their husband's name.[50]

As in France, there was a broad general movement sympathetic to women's claims and involving figures from the government and the learned professions. A convention endeavouring to bring together establishment figures and the various feminist groups was held in Rome on 24–5 June 1970. Three government ministers as well as magistrates, university professors, and

631

journalists attended; one third of the speakers were men.[51] There was a moment of excitement when a woman rose to say: 'My name is not important. I am from the movement Rivolta Femminile', at which another voice responded: 'you just want to be duplicates of men'. The woman continued:

> For us women there is an alternative, a cultural revolution. Because for us culture is masculine... We want to create a society which is opposed to existing models which are masculine and authoritarian.[52]

Rivolta Femminile issued its manifesto in Rome in July 1970.[53] It is in the characteristic staccato format of manifestos as they emerged from 1967 onwards (particularly noticeable in hippie and Situationist pronouncements); it is prefaced by a quotation of 1791 from Olympe de Gouges, author of the Declaration of the Rights of Women: 'Must women always be divided one from the other? Can they never form one united body?' The manifesto is long, repetitive, uncompromising, quaint, full of intellectual resonance, frequently obscure, a nagging poem which belongs absolutely to its era; divorce, the great liberal issue of the time and one which profoundly engaged the mass of the Italian people, is treated very dismissively; consorting sexually with men appears to be acceptable, communicating with them not; there is no patience with Shulamith Firestone's line that differences between men and women are largely culturally constructed; it is interesting that the events of 1968/9 are termed 'the popular revolution'. This 'poem' expresses the essence of one brand of Italian feminism; it begins:

> Women are not to be defined by their relationship to men. On that consciousness is founded our struggle and our liberty.
>
> Men do not provide the model for the process of women's self-discovery. Women are different from men. Men are different from women. Equality is an ideological initiative designed to raise women to a higher level.
>
> Identifying women with men entails blocking the ultimate road to liberation. Liberation for women does not mean accepting the same life as men because it is unliveable, but expressing their own sense of existence.
>
> Women as subjects do not refute men as subjects, but refute them in their exercise of absolutist rule. In social life women refute men in their authoritarian role.

and ends: 'We will communicate solely with women.'[54]

Most of the pioneers of the new radical feminism were of student age, or were young university teachers. A most important phenomenon by the early seventies was the way in which certain women of an older generation were enthusiastically taking up the cause. The art critic Carla Lonzi, whose publications dated back to the late fifties, in effect took on the role of leading publicist for Rivolta Femminile. Disturbed, as she put it, that the totality of Italian feminists gave more weight to the class struggle than to their own oppression, she took up the notion that it was male philosophers who had brainwashed women into accepting their own oppression, cannibalizing a verse from the poem/manifesto I have just quoted in producing the tract *Sputiamo su Hegel* (We Spit on Hegel): 'The Hegelian account of the master-servant relationship', she wrote, 'belongs entirely to the masculine world.'[55] Lonzi was the chief contributor to two further tracts published by Rivolta Femminile, *The Withdrawal of Women from the Celebration of Male Creativity* (March 1971) and *Female Sexuality and Abortion* (July 1971), almost immediately followed by Lonzi's own publication, *Clitoral Woman and Vaginal Woman*.

*Female Sexuality and Abortion* is not really part of the abortion campaign at all, which is identified as an essentially male demand which simply continues 'the myth of the genital act concluded by a man having an orgasm inside the vagina'. All women needed to do was to stop allowing themselves to be used by 'phallocratic sexual culture', in other words (though such unambiguous language is never used), to refuse to submit to penetrative sex. The conclusion then is:

> It would no longer be a case of preparing for a sexual encounter between a ruler and his instrument, but between two human beings, the woman and the man, and their sex organs (in every possible permutation and combination). From being a place of violence and male pleasure, the vagina will become, as a matter of choice, one of the places for sexual gains. When that level of civilization has been reached it will become clear that contraceptives are only needed by those engaging in sexual activity of the old procreative type, and that abortion is no concern of liberated women, but is only needed by women colonized by the patriarchal system.[56]

From this it was only a few short steps to Lonzi's polemic with the nakedly explicit title, a continuation of the discourse established by Milana Mileni's novel *A Girl Named Jules,* entailing direct and shocking confrontation with Catholic prudery, now transformed, partly under American radical feminist influence, into rude confrontation with patriarchy. One of the central arguments is very much in keeping with general sixties liberationist thinking, that sex is a biological necessity but is entirely separable from procreation: it can be experienced between two people, or it can be experienced by one person alone. But (and this is the break from the more male chauvinist aspects of sixties liberation) if a man and a woman do do it together, they should do it freely, and each, as it were, should do their own thing. The precise analogue of the penis is the clitoris, not the vagina. And so to the rather more contentious assertions. The erect penis is a symbol of power (some—a thought too literal for Lonzi to contemplate—might think that it was a symbol of sexual arousal). Thus women can be divided into 'the free, clitoral women, and the unfree, vaginal women'. The strictures with respect to the latter have all the narrow censoriousness of any other sect: couples practising penal-vaginal sex are condemned as being 'patriarchal couples'. Vaginal pleasure is not for the woman the most profound and complete pleasure, but is the official pleasure of patriarchal sexual culture. If she achieves this she is limiting herself to one model: 'that which gratifies the expectations of the man'. The vaginal woman is the woman 'who upholds the myth of the mighty penis and who maintains the ideology of patriarchal virility'.[57]

The University of Trento had been in the vanguard of all sixties movements; it is surprising that the Feminist Group of Trento was founded there only in 1971, unsurprising that it represents the most extreme reaction against the stereotype of *le donne dei compagni* of 1968. It became the most vociferous of the men-hating, separatist groups, taking up the analogy between masculine supremacism and racism and declaring: 'Our movement must be solely a movement of women.'[58] The major organization of the opposite persuasion was the Italian Front for the Liberation of Women, formed in 1970 and publishing the first edition of its journal *Quarto Mondo* (Fourth World) in March 1971. The Front expressed itself as being concerned with all the major problems of humanity, including imperialism, and the environmental threat of uncontrolled industrial development. Thus it was prepared to involve men in struggles against the problems which 'menace all humanity'. Men, it explained, needed to be released from their 'frustrating and limiting sexual role'.[59] Given the Front's uncompromising rhetoric on the one side and attitudes of the Trento feminists and of Rivolta Femminile on the other, it is not surprising that the Italian feminist movement was bitterly split between those who could work with men and those who could not. The seventies, 'the years of the bullet', were in any case years of extreme violence in the politics of protest; in feminism, as elsewhere, ideas of compromise had little attraction. Even the MLD, the body most adapted to achieving practical gains, split in 1975.[60] However, developments of real consequence to the majority of women were continuing elsewhere. We have already seen something of the genuine reality of sexual liberation. The astonishing triumph of the masses in the battle over divorce will feature in the last section of this chapter.

### The Battles Over Contraception and Abortion

When talking of abortion, contraception, and divorce as elements in the liberalization projects of the sixties, it is important to be precise about exactly what we mean in each case. The more traditional the society, the more total the opposition to the practice of any of these three; to the Catholic hierarchy, and to many humble Catholics, all were sins. At the opposite extreme, in the completely libertarian state, there would be abortion 'on demand', and paid for by the state; contraceptive information and advice would be disseminated by the state, and contraceptive devices themselves would be free. Divorce was more difficult, since obviously two parties were involved: what if one wanted a divorce and the other did not? In the adversarial legal systems of the Protestant countries, divorces could be obtained upon such grounds as 'cruelty', 'desertion', or 'adultery'. In Catholic countries one aim of reformers was simply to make such provisions available in their own countries. The full libertarian position tended to be based on ideas such as divorce 'by mutual consent', or upon 'the irretrievable breakdown' of the marriage. However, matters were far from uncomplicated with the other two issues as well. Most reformers shrank from the notion of abortion entirely on demand: debates focused on extending the range of reasons for which an abortion might be legal, from the physical well-being of the woman to her mental wellbeing, and then to the social and economic circumstances into which the child would be born. The other debate concerned how late in a pregnancy an abortion might be performed (there were both medical and moral arguments here). But behind all this argumentation lay a much more desperate fact: whatever the law said, women were having abortions in the most appalling and dangerous conditions. Reformers did not ignore the point that there is something tragic about a woman being in the position of wanting an abortion, but this aspect did tend to get lost among those who felt they must put the pro-abortion case as strongly as possible, often abetted by those who too mindlessly adapted to the carefree, permissive spirit of the time.

The main debate over contraception concerned whether advice and availability should be confined to married women, and if not, at what age and under what circumstances it should be available to girls. Within even the radical feminist movement there was a division between those who enthusiastically took up the liberationist cause on all fronts and those fundamentalists who saw all three causes as arising from a female submission to male dominance which should be ended as quickly as possible. An American radical feminist tract denounced the pill:

> How is birth control practised in our society? It's a familiar story to women. We go to a doctor and lowering our eyes, embarrassed at our dependency, with a mixture of fear and anger, we stumble through that horrible sentence, 'What do I do not to get pregnant?' Remember, we are asking this of a male doctor, behind whom stands the whole power-penis-potency complex (PPP). What do you think he's going to tell us? Right! 'Get high on our latest special, the PPP's Pill!' 'Great new wonder drug! It launches formal attack on the pituitary gland (fondly known as the master gland of the body—which means that our entire hormonal system is assaulted) and 'saves us from pregnancy' in exchange for a two-page long list of side effects— nausea, edema, vomiting, bleeding, cramp, mental depression, bloating, changes in menstrual period, etc., with risk of thrombophlebitis, pulmonary embolism, cerebral thrombosis, etc., etc.—which our male pharmacist or male doctor threw in the waste basket, and which we will never see. What we do see are little booklets from the drug companies, deco-rated with roses, tulips, and peach blossoms full of reassuring babbling.[61]

If, for some extreme radicals, abortion, and even contraception were not genuine feminist issues but simply components of patriarchally imposed 'Vaginal sex', unwanted pregnancies and back-street abortions were in fact among the severest burdens still being borne by large numbers of ordinary women across France, Italy, and the United States (the British 1967 Abortion Act could not work miracles, but was the envy of campaigners in the other countries).

Across the United States, with very few exceptions, it had since the nineteenth century been legal to carry out an abortion when the mother's life, and, in many states, her health, was in danger; but in the sixties, more than a million illegal abortions a year were still being carried out, about a third of which resulted in serious complications, with 500–1,000 deaths.[62] By the High Sixties there was open discussion of the issue of substantially relaxing these laws: in 1967 California and Colorado did just that. 'Abortion', a campaigning group in California reported, 'is no longer a hot potato, but it's not a cold potato either... The subject used to be taboo in polite society. The enactment of the (California) law changed that. The climate of opinion is changing. England has gone far beyond any state in this nation to permit abortion... That's going to speed up the shift of opinion in this country.'[63] Laws enacted in Georgia, Maryland, North Carolina, Delaware, and Oregon over 1968 and 1969 also were much more restrictive than the British one.

Partly stimulated by the stirrings of radical feminism, the National Association for the Repeal of Abortion Laws was founded in 1969. On the one hand, partly because of ambiguities in the new laws and because of the gross discrepancies remaining between the different states, progressive lawyers and clergy were drawn in; on the other, radical women's liberation organizations took up the cause. The Protestant and Jewish ministers in the 'Clergy Counseling Service for Problem Pregnancies' did sometimes help women to secure legal abortions, while usually being very ready with advice on such alternatives as keeping the child or making it available for adoption. Anti-abortion groups such as the Right to Life League were very active. Some extreme feminist groups worked with the (mainly male) reform groups, others refused to do so. A flyer issued by the Los Angeles Women's Abortion Action Committee advertising a march in San Francisco on 20 November 1971 included this concession: 'Men', it said, were 'welcome to march'. However, a meeting in July on the topic 'Women Speak Out for Abortion Law Repeal' was 'open to women only'.[64] The trend in the early seventies was towards recognition of a woman's right to choose abortion, but there was much confusion, and many bitter counter-offensives. A Supreme Court ruling in *Roe* v. *Wade*, announced on 22 January 1973, did establish that abortions could be carried out legally.[65]

In France the Neuwirth law of 28 December 1967, legalizing the spreading of information on, and the sale of, contraceptives, had left the way clear for campaigners to focus their attention on abortion reform. A further stage in the general, issues-related, liberal movement (as distinct from any radical feminist one) was marked by the formation in 1969 of the National Association for the Study of Abortion.[66] Books about abortion, mainly technical in content and generally directed against the evils of clandestine abortions, continued to be published. At the *Elle* Estates General in November 1970, two-thirds of the participants favoured the legalization of abortion on social grounds. Opinion polls of the French people as a whole revealed that, while there was overwhelming support for abortions on medical grounds, still only a minority favoured abortions on social grounds. A SOFRES poll taken in November 1970 yielded typical results. People were asked whether they were for or against abortion in certain specific circumstances (see Table 13.1).

The MLF group invading the *Elle* Estates General in the month of this poll engaged actively in the discussion on abortion there, and in fact the MLF took up abortion as a major issue.[67] The movement in informed middle-class opinion is signalled by *L'Express* of 11–17 January 1971: blazoned on the cover was 'Abortion: Yes or No'; the extensive coverage inside contained a horrifying first-hand description of a clandestine operation carried out by a drunken doctor, and a very fair assessment of the number of abortions actually carried out in France and of the state

**Table 13.1** *Opinions (%) for or against abortion according to circumstance*

|  | For | Against |
|---|---|---|
| If the mother is in danger | 86 | 10 |
| If the baby is likely to be abnormal | 84 | 9 |
| If the mother is a young girl without resources | 40 | 48 |
| If the family already has too many children | 37 | 52 |
| If the family is without resources | 28 | 63 |

of public opinion. The figures for abortions carried out were given as 400,000–500,000 a year; it was said that public opinion in favour of abortion in special cases had recently jumped to as high as 80 or 90 per cent, but remained at 30 per cent in social cases.[68] Then at the beginning of April 1971 came the *Nouvel Observateur* manifesto of the 343 French women prominent in public life or the world of entertainment, demanding free abortion on demand and, with respect to some of the very well-known ones, admitting that they themselves had had abortions. In the aftermath of the manifesto there emerged the Movement for Free Abortions (MLA), which arranged a series of debates and demonstrations throughout 1972. Meantime the medical and legal case was being quietly developed by the newly formed organization Association Choisir (Choice).[69]

What the various types of campaigning, restrained and factual, flamboyant and extrovert, were combining to do was to show that the existing law making abortion a crime had fallen into complete disrepect. Those who ruled the Church and those who ruled the medical profession remained resolutely opposed to abortion on any grounds; but politicians, publicists, and members of the ordinary public were shifting uncomfortably: it was the function of the activists to make them face up to issues they would have preferred to ignore. The actual situation was that while more and more people were becoming aware of the appalling number of abortions which did take place in France, the authorities and the police were making no very strenuous efforts to enforce the law. Then came one of the most affecting dramas of contemporary social history, the drama of a working-class girl, her mother, and a couple of fellow-workers on the Paris Métro, a drama which is integral to my general argument about the period we are studying being one of a people's revolution, not simply one of protesting (and in their ultimate aims, futile) minorities, and a revolution, in the end, largely by consent—at the core of this drama were a courageous 16-year-old girl and her equally courageous mother, but among the vital supporting players were top medical professors prepared to defy the geriatric chiefs of their profession.

Marie-Claire Chevalier was a 16-year-old student at a technical college, the eldest of three daughters. Her mother, Michèle Chevalier, unmarried, had lived for four or five years with a working man, who had then deserted her. This single-parent family lived in one of those housing estates on the outskirts of Paris well described in *Les Petis Enfants du siècle*, Bobigny. A fellow-student, Daniel, aged 18, took Marie-Claire for a ride in a car he had acquired, then took her to his house, which was empty since his mother was on holiday. Daniel was an unpleasant character, leader of a local gang (which may, of course, have added to his attractiveness); whether he was actually guilty of rape must be a very open question (Marie-Claire was clearly a mature, intelligent, and independent young woman, who neither complained nor severed all contact with Daniel), but certainly she became pregnant by him.[70] When this became apparent she immediately confided in her mother, with whom she had a very close relationship. Michèle Chevalier's response was that they could rear the child together, but Marie-Claire had made her own independent decision that she did not wish to go ahead with the birth. Mother and daughter went first to a respectable gynaecologist. In keeping with the social realities of the day he had no qualms about providing an abortion; also in keeping with the social realities of the day he demanded a fee of Fr. 4,500—three months' salary for Michèle Chevalier. She turned to her fellow Métro worker, Mme Duboucheix, a practising Catholic, married with one child.

Catholic dogma could not, of course, govern the exigencies of the ordinary lives of working-class women. Mme Duboucheix contacted her friend, Mme Sausset. Abandoned by her parents, Mme Sausset had been brought up by the public assistance, where she had become friendly with another unfortunate, now Mme Bambuk. Mme Bambuk had been twice married, had three children, and had herself had an abortion by the usual primitive method. She was now working as a secretary; her husband had recently committed suicide; she had considerable financial problems. She was prepared to carry out the primitive operation for a fee of Fr. 1,200. The barbaric business was carried out at the Chevaliers' flat, where the first two attempts failed and a third provoked a haemorrhage, at two in the morning. Rain was pouring down, there was no telephone in the flat, and Mme Chevalier did not dare have recourse to any of her neighbours; she ran for a public telephone box, managed to make an emergency call, and was given the address of a clinic. On the brink of collapse, Marie-Claire was rushed to the clinic in a taxi. There she was refused admission until a deposit of Fr. 1,200 was made; all Michèle Chevalier could do was to offer Fr. 200 in cash and sign a cheque for Fr. 1,000.

Conditions in the clinic were to the highest standards, and three days later Marie-Claire was discharged, the danger over, and the abortion successfully completed. Michèle Chevalier now had enormous bills to meet; Marie-Claire, back at college, told Daniel of the abortion. Some weeks later, Daniel was arrested in connection with some car thefts: to ingratiate himself with the police, he told them about Marie-Claire's abortion (even if no longer actively pursued, still a very serious offence when thrust in front of the eyes of the police). With all their customary finesse, the police raided the flat while Marie-Claire was in bed, and by threatening that both she and her mother would be immediately thrown into prison, terrorized her into making a full confession implicating her mother and the three other women.

Because Marie-Claire (now 17) was a minor, the ensuing procedures were split into two. Marie-Claire, on her own, but supported by leading Association Choisir figure Gisèle Halimi, the barrister acting for Marie-Claire and her mother, was summoned to a hearing behind closed doors, before the children's tribunal in the palace of justice, Bobigny; there was subsequently to be a trial of the four women, in the same building at Bobigny, but this time in the adult criminal court. Marie-Claire's hearing was scheduled for 11 October 1972, before a president and two assessors, both specialists in children's problems. Association Choisir drew up a leaflet, 'Tract pour Marie-Claire', and called for demonstrations both in the place de l'Opéra in the centre of Paris and then, on the day of the hearing, outside the children's tribunal. The 'Tract pour Marie-Claire' was direct and potent:

A YOUNG GIRL OF 17 IS ABOUT TO BE TRIED FOR HAVING AN ABORTION... BECAUSE SHE did not have 3,000 Francs to go and have a comfortable abortion in a clinic in Geneva, London or even Paris.

BECAUSE SHE is the illegitimate daughter of an unmarried mother, a worker on the Métro, who has brought up three daughters on her own.

BECAUSE THERE IS NO SEXUAL EDUCATION at school and because there is a total muddle over contraception.[71]

Both men and women participated in the demonstration at the Opéra on 9 October, with the police once again doing their bit for the cause. They wielded their batons with such ferocity that the press reported it, and in so doing gave publicity to the case. On the day of the hearing there was an impressive gathering of all ages and both sexes outside the windows of the children's tribunal. The basic slogan was 'Free Marie-Claire', but there were two other richly evocative chants: 'We have all had abortions' and 'England for the rich, prison for the poor'.[72] Gisèle Halimi expressed the view that this was quite a new kind of demonstration. Certainly, it was not exclusively confined to political activists, to students, to radical feminists: the range of people there, in support of a working-class teenager and the right to choose abortion, was symbolic of the interacting transformations which had been developing through the sixties.

The tribunal which Marie-Claire had to face was in fact totally sympathetic to her predicament. It could not, of course, openly flout the law, and it could not impinge upon the trial still to come of the four adults. It ignored the fact that the decision to have an abortion had actually been Marie-Claire's own; and it could not, of course, have vindicated such a decision. In the strict letter of its judgement, the tribunal, in a sense, was dishonest, and perhaps also patronizing towards Marie-Claire. But in principle the judgement was a masterpiece of wisdom and compassion, and in reporting it the press was in no doubt as to its real implications. The tribunal gave Marie-Claire unconditional acquittal, ruling that she was not complicit in the abortion since she had endured 'constraints of a moral, social, and familial character which were irresistible'. The next day the press was full of the verdict. The headline in *Figaro* was representative: 'The Law on Abortion Appears Out-dated even in the Eyes of Justice.' The article concluded:

> Once again a judicial process has publicly opened to question our legislation on abortion. Will the law of 1920 now be considered in law, as it is in actuality, as having fallen into disuse? Such a divorce between law and fact has for more than fifty years encouraged the clandestine practice of abortion with all that means in injustice and inequality. Will yesterday's decision institute a precedent? That is the principal question emerging from the proceedings. Above all, in the longer term, will the heavy penalties prescribed by law, continue to be meted out to the infinitesimal number of those carrying out abortions actually brought before the courts?[73]

*France-Soir* had gone for the personal angle, and on the whole got it right. On the eve of the proceedings it quoted Michèle Chevalier as saying of her daughter's abortion, with reference presumably to the birth and rearing of her own children: 'It was essential that she should not relive my calvary.' In reporting the verdict, it carried interviews with first the daughter and then the mother:

> 'I was moved to tears', the young girl said. 'All through the hearing I heard the shouts, the songs, the slogans; I said to myself: this is what it is all for. I'll stick it out.'
>
> At the end of the hearing, Marie-Claire's mother said to us: 'I hope that my case, the unhappiness of my daughter, will help other mothers, other children.'

But the release of an under-age girl was one thing, the trial of four adults something else. The strategy to be followed at the trial was discussed at a plenary session of Association Choisir. The fullest account we have is that given by defence barrister Gisèle Halimi. Halimi found herself opposed by the more fundamentalist feminists of the MLF, and it may be that her account is a little unfair to them. I have thought it best to quote her own words directly. I believe she fairly records the matters at issue, though, in allegedly giving verbatim reports of what people said, she is probably guilty of oversimplification, a certain sentimental romanticism, and sarcasm at the expense of the MLF. With regard to the differences between herself and the radical feminists, it is important to point out that, being Tunisian, she belonged to an ethnic minority, and that she had a magnificent record of acting as defence counsel for Algerian nationalists, several of whom had been on trial for their lives. Prior to the discussion she had contacted Professor Jacques Monod, Nobel prizewinner in physiology and medicine, and, though she did not know him personally, had put him in touch with Michèle Chevalier. According to Halimi the two got on well, and the Métro worker derived enormous confidence from the encounter, saying: 'Do you understand: someone like that, on our side...' Monod advised Halimi to visit Professors Paul Milliez, dean of the Paris medical faculties, and Raoul Palmer, professor of gynaecology.[74]

I arranged to meet them. On entering, Paul Milliez said to me: 'I am against abortion...' I closed my briefcase and got ready to leave.

'In these circumstances, I can hardly ask you to come as a witness...'

The eminent doctor had risen to his feet. His tormented face revealed an interior struggle.

'I could write a letter to the court...' he was speaking solely, as if to himself. This case was so unfair, so unbearable... he himself, when he was still an intern, hadn't he carried out abortions for the poor women who came to the hospital... in such a state... and since then, he's seen so much of that...

'No... to write, that would be to shirk the issue... It would be cowardice... I will go to Bobigny'.

I wanted to be sure there would be no misunderstandings: 'I ask you publicly: "If Marie-Claire had come to consult you, what would you have done?"' He looked me straight in the face: 'I would have carried out the abortion...'

Halimi's commitment to these distinguished gentlemen is clear enough; she saw them as key players in her defence strategy. This, she tells us, was strongly opposed by the MLF representatives at the Association Choisir conference: they did not want 'grand witnesses', they wanted no men, no Nobel prizewinners. Bobigny must be exclusively a matter for women—and for women who were not big stars. They could just about accept a Simone de Beauvoir, a Delphine Seyrig, a Françoise Fabian, 'but they also wanted to have anonymous women'.

They wanted Michèle and the other two to go before the court and say: 'You stand for bourgeois justice and phallocratic justice.' We do not recognize your authority... condemn us if you will... We don't care!'

It was useless, Halimi claimed, to point out that the three women themselves opposed such tactics. According to Halimi, Michèle Chevalier 'shouted out' her opposition:

I don't want to have you at my trial, you don't have any relationship with my life story; the proof of that is that you are free and have never been prosecuted, while I am the one that has to appear before the court.

For her part Mme Duboucheix, according to Halimi, declared:

I don't understand your attitudes. You are intellectuals, and you speak a language I can't understand. You say, 'There is nothing to explain', but for myself, a woman of the people, I do feel a bit guilty, and I need to have in the witness box Professors Monod, Jacob, Rostand saying to me, to me who doesn't understand anything, that I am not guilty. What's more, I need to feel them at my side defending me, saying 'We demand the acquittal of this woman'...[75]

Halimi continues her account, saying that 'the daughters of the MLF jeered at her'. It is hard to believe that the radicals, however militant, actually jeered, though no doubt they found difficulty in controlling their feelings. If the account is over-drawn, Halimi was describing a genuine difference of view. If there was to be no comprehensive attack on bourgeois patriarchal society, it was agreed that the case would be used to put the anti-abortion law of 1920 on trial.

Summing up his case at the trial itself, the prosecutor warned that any publication of the proceedings would be a serious offence against the law (in fact Association Choisir printed the entire transcript of the trial, and it is upon that that my own account here is based).[76] He questioned whether Marie-Claire really had been subjected to violence and rape, suggested that a proper course would have been for Marie-Claire to marry Daniel, and made a great issue of the fact that the possibility of marriage had never been pursued by Marie-Claire and her mother. Then he turned to the law itself:

And so, is the law today really so bad as people say? I think that the proposition upon which it is founded lives on since it is based on respect for life, on the respect for oneself and the respect for other people. We must remember that all of us, wherever we are, rich or poor, educated or not, we have all emerged from the state of being a foetus [laughter], we must quietly affirm, whether our birth was desired or not, that in general we are happy to have life. If our parents had been free to commission abortions, it is probable that a certain number among us, even among the most distinguished, would not now be in this world.[77]

After this somewhat factitious excursion (properly rewarded with ironic laughter) the prosecutor

641

went out of his way to express sympathy for Mme Bambuk (known formally in the court indictment as Micheline Deiss) who, separately defended, had distanced herself from the other three by admitting her guilt and expressing contrition.

> She is the only one who seems to feel guilt, and he spent a moment or two on the very hard life she had had, losing her husbands. However, he was not going to neglect his duty: I must of course demand a sentence which amounts to more than simply a token penalty. I would ask for a suspended prison sentence, together with a fine amounting to the fee she was paid for the abortion.[78]

It was becoming clear that the prosecution was gunning for Marie-Claire's mother:

> As far as Mme Michèle Chevalier is concerned, she bears a heavy responsibility in this matter. She is the one who made the arrangements, who was actually present at the abortion, and she is the one who deliberately and in full awareness gambled with the life of the one she calls her little daughter. She also has had her difficulties; I bear these in mind and recognize that apart from this case she is an honourable woman. There are of course extenuating circumstances, but in her case I must demand a serious sentence.

Perhaps, indeed, the prosecutor's own heart was not altogether in the prosecution. He dealt very cursorily with the other two:

> As far as Mme Duboucheix and Mme Sausset are concerned, the matters which they are accused of stand somewhat apart from the actual crime, since they simply served as intermediaries, putting the abortionist in contact with Mme Chevalier. For them I request a token sentence.[79]

Mme Bambuk was defended by a male barrister, not part of the Association Choisir team: according to his statement, Mme Bambuk expressed her sorrow that she had broken the law, said she did not feel she had acted wrongly, but that she would never do it again. The barrister selected for Mme Duboucheix was also a man. He called upon the judges not to apply the law. She was being accused by a cold, distant law, not by society. She had acted out of pity. 'The prosecutor, in demanding that you apply that law—and it would quite possibly be the last application of that law—gave me the impression of trying to provoke the final spasms of a moribund text.'[80]

Earlier, in her own testimony Lucette Duboucheix had declared that she would rather 'die than carry out an abortion':

> Only, I could not work things out... when Mme Chevalier came to see me, my duty was to help her, for she had decided to get an abortion for her daughter or Marie-Claire had decided to have an abortion... In the name of what, or in whom, should I impose my

convictions on other women? I am for every woman having a free choice and so, even if in my case it is clear that I would never have had an abortion, I find it perfectly normal that someone who has made a contrary choice should go ahead, without having to go through this drama which I have gone through and shared with Mme Chevalier, my fellow-worker from the Métro.[81]

Testimony was given by the other accused women and also by Marie-Claire herself. There then followed the expert testimonies in favour of the defendants. Repeating what he had said in private to Halimi, Professor Paul Milliez declared that he himself would have been prepared to give Marie-Claire an abortion, and that he himself, at the age of 19, had performed an abortion. There followed Professor Raoul Palmer, the gynaecologist, Mme Simone Iff, national vice-president of Planning Familial, Mme Jacqueline Mancou, midwife, Gérard Mendel, neuro-psychiatrist, Louis Vallim, parliamentary deputy for Paris, and Jacques Monod: he admitted complicity in that he had contributed Fr. 3,000 to ease Michèle Chevalier's financial problems caused by the bungled abortion and its aftermath, and insisted that many good doctors gave abortions free as a matter of conscience. 'This law', he said, 'is inapplicable.' A foetus, he added, is not a human being. Two actresses who had been signatories to the famous Manifesto, Françoise Fabian and Delphine Seyrig, repeated that they had had abortions. Then the testimony of two 18-year-old working-class, single mothers, as to their serious plight since they had been unable to have abortions, was read out. Finally, in confirming the point that the case for the defence was not based on the views of any fundamentalist minority, the journalist Mme Claude Servan-Schreiber gave testimony based on the *Elle* article of 17 April 1972, denouncing the evil of clandestine abortions.[82]

Mme Renée Sausset was born on 31 July 1930, in Paris, at the Hôpital de la Pitié. Three weeks later her unmarried mother abandoned her to the public assistance. At the age of eight months she was handed over to a couple, very poor people, who were also products of the public assistance. She went to school until the age of 14, then found a job as a maid of all work. In the words of her barrister (also Halimi), 'She earned a miserable living, and she ate the leftovers of her employers.' At 19 the public assistance enrolled her in courses in French and shorthand and typing. At the age of 21 she set out to find her mother. Finally after three months she found her, but her mother rejected her for a second time.[83] In her own testimony Mme Sausset said:

When Mme Chevalier asked me to help her, I had a choice: to be the accomplice to an abortion or the accomplice in abandoning a baby. For it was quite clear—and Marie-Claire had said it over and over again—that if she were obliged to have the baby, she would abandon it to the public assistance. And so, Mr President, I did not hesitate. Between being the accomplice to an abortion and the accomplice to abandoning a baby, I chose to be the accomplice to an abortion, and that is why I am here, accused...[84]

Halimi made much of the problems of working-class families driven out of Paris by the rich into the remote housing estates. She concluded to loud applause: 'What game are we playing in making judgements by virtue of a law which is quite irrelevant and therefore, inapplicable, a law in which no one in France any longer believes?'[85]

Then came Halimi's defence of Michèle Chevalier. She launched straight in on the point that it was always women of the working class who got punished; upper-class women who had abortions were never prosecuted. But this 'class justice' was in fact ineffective in preventing abortions, as she demonstrated by giving the dismal annual figures of back-street abortions actually carried out. Continuing to make important political points, she then pointed out that Marie-Claire had had no sex education, had no knowledge of how to avoid pregnancy through contraception (this point, one may note, rather conflicts with Halimi's own allegation that Marie-Claire had been raped). Having earlier made the fullest possible use of the expert testimony of prestigious male witnesses, Halimi now went in hard with the pure feminist line:

> If there are still serfs in the world, they are women; she is a serf, since she is brought before you, gentlemen, when she has disobeyed your law, when she aborts. She is brought before you. Is that not the most certain sign of our oppression? Excuse me, gentlemen, but I have decided to say everything tonight. Look at yourselves and look at us... these four women in front of these four men!...
>
> Would you be willing, Gentlemen, to be brought before a tribunal of women because of what you do with your own bodies?... That would seem crazy![86]

There was loud applause. Halimi concluded: 'Gentlemen, it is your duty today to say that a new era begins in which the old world is abandoned.' Again there was loud applause. The president announced that judgement and sentences would be pronounced in a fortnight's time. The judgement, when it came, was brief. Duboucheix and Sausset were simply acquitted. Chevalier was sentenced to a fine of Fr. 500, immediately suspended. Deiss (Bambuk) was sentenced to one year in prison, with immediate suspension. Chevalier and Deiss were further sentenced to pay the costs of the action, limited, however, to the (unrealistically small) sum of Fr. 319.80, together with the cost (also in practice small) of promulgating the verdicts. A final technical phrase made it clear that the two women would not be held in prison while the final settlements were being made.

Milliez was censured by the national council of the medical profession, but if anything that simply added to the salience of the whole affair. His photograph appeared in *France-Soir* over the caption, 'I would have agreed to abort Marie-Claire'; millions of French women and French men, as Halimi put it, 'discovered that back street abortion could be discussed in public and took note that great Parisian professors were placing themselves openly against the law and on the side of those who had had abortions'. The press had no doubt about the significance of the verdicts. Noting that two of the accused were sentenced to merely token penalties and the other two acquitted, *Figaro* declared: 'The obsolescence of the law becomes more and more obvious.' *L'Humanité* commented, 'The law against abortion has become nul and void.' The defendants themselves were delighted: Michèle Chevalier confided to *L'Aurore*. 'It's fantastic, we are practically acquitted.'[87] Association Choisir did actually mount an appeal (on the grounds that two of the defendants had technically been found guilty), but with infinite wisdom the French judicial authorities simply suspended the case *sine die.*

The Association (together, in fact, with the press) won a more important second victory. Despite the prosecutor's warning, publication of the entire proceedings of the trial went ahead, and there was never any question of prosecution for this. Similarly, the very full press reporting of the trial (also illegal) provoked no response. It was not until 1975 that the law of 1920 was replaced by another one specifying the grounds upon which and the limits within which an abortion could be legal. But between 1972 and the passing of the new law there were no further prosecutions. The pain and suffering of ordinary people, evoking the support of some of the greatest liberal figures, female and male, in the land, had had truly historic consequences. Of course, the matter was not finally satisfactorily settled. How can such a question be 'satisfactorily settled'? Fundamentalist feminists continued to resist the notion of abortion as something to be conceded under particular conditions (as distinct from an absolute right), and to argue that often the need for abortions only arose as a consequence of the infliction upon women of male sexual demands. Such were the arguments printed in the fundamentalist organ *Le Torchon Brule* (The Torch Burns). Total right to abortion was 'the most elementary liberty, one which men exercise to the full'; it was certainly not just a question of the law having become obsolete.[88]

While some militants demanded total access to abortion, others argued that what women wanted was not the general availability of abortion but the total disappearance of any necessity for it:

We are told to be 'active' to increase the pleasure of men, we are told to be efficiently equipped with contraceptives so to be always available to the desire of men. Mystification! for the wave of sexual pseudo-liberation always entails the same roles between men and women.[89]

The course of events, for France, demonstrates again the power, in this era, of people, as against politicians and their formal alignments, and the force of contingency and convergence. The courage and energy of feminists (of both sexes) allied to the skill of Maître Halimi and the measured judgement of the tribunals in both Bobigny trials made abortion reform a pressing issue for some time in the ensuing decade. Such, indeed, was the impact of the Bobigny trial that the government immediately brought in a bill which would have made legal abortion possible provided a special commission (not the woman herself) pronounced in favour. This bill was strongly opposed by most of the women's groups, and, in fact, with the death of President Pompidou it lapsed. Meanwhile, in April 1973, a group of doctors, feminists, and the film-makers Mariella Issartel and Charles Belmont produced the film *Histoires d'A,* which not only advocated, but demonstrated, abortion by the relatively straightforward Karman method; the film was immediately banned, with the police rejoicing in the opportunity, offered by the few occasions on which it was shown, to wade in with extreme violence. In keeping with his role as the Gallic Kennedy, the new president, Giscard d'Estaing (whose minister of culture raised the ban on *Histoire d'A),* was determined to bring in a new law, and for that purpose he chose as his minister of health the heroic judge and women's champion Simone Veil: this led to a bill being introduced in the National Assembly in November 1974. But of the president's own party (UDF) and his Gaullist allies (RPR) only 99 out of 314 deputies supported the bill. The brave 99 were listening to the majority outside parliament, and with practically the total support of the Socialists and Communists carried the decision for abortion law reform by 284 to 189. Abortion had to be carried out within ten weeks (it was twenty-eight in Britain), and there had to be physical or mental risk to the mother—but the final decision on this was left to the woman herself; the law was only valid for five years; doctors could refuse to participate, with the result that a third of public hospitals effectively opted out of the new dispensation. Over a third of the 150,000 abortions a year carried out under the act were in private clinics. Only under the Socialist presidency of François Mitterrand in 1983—legalization having been confirmed in November 1979—was IVG (voluntary interruption of pregnancy) made a charge reimbursable from social security. The Giscard presidency had long since done this for contraception. The law of 1974 can be seen as yet another victory for young people: not only would social security repay the cost of contraceptives, but under-age girls could legally obtain them without having to get their parents' consent.[90]

In Italy there were several little dramas but none on the scale of Bobigny. Italy differed significantly from France in that the influence of the Catholic Church was much more comprehensive, and levels of general sophistication and knowledge about sexual matters were considerably lower. Specifically, there were far more clandestine abortions than in France, probably as many as 3–3.5 million in a year: this was probably mainly due to lack of diffusion of contraceptive knowledge and techniques, but also owed something to the horrific combination of general ignorance among the unmarried, and acceptance among the married that abortion was the normative method of family limitation.[91] Secondly, the case for legalized abortion was less well developed among liberal and expert pressure groups. This in turn, finally, meant that much of the discussion of the question of abortion was left in the hands of the radical feminists. Their arguments tended to follow two courses. First, certainly, they did take the empirical line of publicizing the dreadful nature of back-street abortions conducted in appalling conditions without anaesthetics. But, secondly, they presented abortion as an inevitable byproduct of male sexual dominance—even at times seeming to suggest that contraception as well as abortion would be unnecessary in the kind of perfect society they envisaged. The classic expression of the combination of these two courses, the practical and the fundamentalist, is the 1972 tract published by the New Left, *In Support of the Right of Abortion, with an appendix on contraceptive techniques,* by Lara Foletti and Clelia Boesi. In fact, apart from the brief preface, this was actually two separate, sometimes overlapping tracts, by the two individual authors. The bringing together of the two approaches is very apparent in the preface:

> Already the experience of one of us of working and living among country folk and among workers in the cities has made very clear the vastness of the tragedy of the phenomenon of 'abortion'...
>
> Now, having worked our way through this book, we are more than ever convinced of the significance of the rejection of pregnancies imposed by violence, which relegate

women to the totally restrictive role of reproducing the species. At the same time, we are more than ever aware of the way in which the system will try to preserve itself by conceding abortion as a limited reform. The struggle for this must be carried out personally by us women, deriving from our experience and our history, in order to make it an enrichment of our collective consciousness on the universality of our sexual, social and political oppression.[92]

Lara Foletti opens her contribution by looking at the way in which the Italian penal code put 'the crime of abortion' in a mass of 'crimes against the integrity and health of the nation', saying very shrewdly that the use of the word 'nation' is 'more poetic than juridical'. Both the woman having the abortion and the abortionist are liable to two to five years' imprisonment. She then discussed arguments over the growth and status of the foetus, coming to the conclusion that the primary right lies with 'the entity which is definitely a human being', that is to say the mother. The recent questioning by Minister of Health Marcotti of the continuing reality of the legal prohibition upon pro-contraceptive propaganda and diffusion of contraceptives gains few plaudits from her. Marcotti had argued that this was necessary because of the continuing growth in population.

> Once again the interests of the state are more important than the needs of women and maternity is being discussed solely as a demographic fact. Naturally, in giving a clear road for the marketing of 'the pill', the interests of the big pharmaceutical companies have had a considerable role, even if these were originally on sale as 'for ovarian disorders'.

The important issue is not contraception but 'the sexual slavery outside and inside marriage' which forces sexual relations on a woman 'even when she doesn't desire them'. Because a woman has no independent economic means of her own she is forced into 'the prostitution of marriage'. In order to survive she has to become 'a sexual object', without any choice in finding satisfactory sexual relations. Inevitably there follows a discussion of vaginal and clitoral orgasms. Foletti is very even-handed. Both exist: the value of the controversy is in 'challenging traditional coitus as the only type of sexual relations'. She mentions, without supporting or rejecting it, Freud's view of the clitoris as the 'principal residue of the adolescent masculinity of women'.[93] This is a prelude to an entirely technical discussion of the different methods of contraception, where her basic refrain is that no method is absolutely safe. She suggests that the possible development of a morning-after pill will further blur the abortion issue and make impossible traditional moral arguments.

The remainder of the tract is essentially a survey of the existing situation with regard to clandestine abortions, making use of interview material which makes clear, first, the frequent complicity of the police in this widely tolerated form of 'birth control' and, secondly, the unspeakable nastiness created by a system in which abortion was formally illegal, and in which it was considered proper to make the experience as painful as possible, indeed to administer a kind of punishment, which often seems to have been the intention of the woman (known as the *'mammand)*

647

wielding the crude implement *(la sonda)*. Foletti's first horror story was that of a student in Bologna from a working-class family:

> When I saw that house and the evil-looking woman, they had told me the *mammana* was a former nurse, but this woman looked like something totally different. Later I became aware that she had run a house of prostitution... What struck me was her manner between hostility and complicity, especially when she spoke of the money I'd have to pay her. I had 70,000 lire and had to support myself in the city for several days. She wanted the lot. For my part, I no longer had the courage to turn back, but I didn't feel like going through with the abortion with that woman in that filthy house... In the room there was an untidy divan with lots of cushions... I saw that she had taken the *sonda* from the cupboard, then she told me to stretch out on the back and prepare myself; I was terrified, and I wanted to tell her to wash her hands, feeling that a minimum of hygiene was necessary. I didn't have the courage and when she drew back the covers of the bed for me to stretch out, I experienced such nausea that I felt ill. She told me I was a 'faint-heart'. I also felt some fear, but what I felt most was something different: disgust.... the ultimate extremity of being a woman. I stretched out on the bed and let her get on with it. I didn't feel very bad just then, but the whole thing was repugnant, and I will never forget it.[94]

The second interviewee was an unemployed working girl and former evening student, whose boyfriend had fixed her up with someone who was supposed to be a professor of gynaecology:

> The evening of the termination arrived, but I was hoping that the moment when they would start using the *sonda* would never arrive... Instead I was stretched out on the table of the dining room with a sheet underneath me. The assistant took a firm grip of me and told me not to scream. I felt awful, I felt as if they were tearing out all my insides, I was vomiting and they had to stop the intervention for a moment... The woman who was doing the abortion kept saying that I was too narrow, and also too advanced, that I was three months and I hadn't told them. I didn't have the strength to reply that I had been honest, that I thought it was only two. I begged her only to stop and not do any more.[95]

Boesi recorded an interview with a married woman of 31, who apparently had a reasonably sympathetic *mammana:*

> I have had eight abortions, all with a *mammana* with a *sonda*. This woman knows me and knows that I have no money, and what's more have four little children, and this woman gives me a discount, so that I pay only 10 or 15 thousand lire for each abortion. Now I am separated from my husband, each time we separate then get together again for the sake of the children. I also have another man and I get on a little better with him than with my husband. As a result of all those abortions I have had I finished up in hospital...

Boesi asked: 'Have you ever tried to avoid becoming pregnant?'

What could I do? I've heard many basic things about the pill, with the fear of getting still fatter... now however a doctor has given me some boxes of the pill and I use them, I am perhaps thinner, which makes me feel quite well. I hope not to have any more abortions, in any case the hospital won't take me in again.[96]

There can be no doubt as to the effectiveness with which the case against the prevailing system is built up. But there is some inconsistency. At one point, Foletti equates abortion with male violence on women, practised, she says in a striking metaphor, like a vet on an animal. But the worst abortionist cited in her evidence is a woman. And then, further, she goes on to say, somewhat insensitively, that abortion is no problem for the privileged, who can afford to have an anaesthetic and a completely hygienic environment. Boesi's contribution covers much of the same ground. An introductory sentence again contains the sense of two not necessarily consistent basic ideas: 'It is important to demand the immediate liberalization of abortion because the inequities imposed on women are so serious, but in making the demand the fundamental thing is the consciousness of the global oppression of women.'[97]

In essence, the Italian radical feminists wanted to change the entire biological circumstances of women; although they did not propose Firestone's remedies, they really wanted the condition of pregnancy to disappear; above all, they did not want easy abortions that would simply make life easier for men. The most utopian sentiments were expressed in the often youthfully cheerful document, *Maternity and Abortion,* circulated by the Women's Struggle Movement of Padua in June 1971:

The problem is not abortion. *The problem is to have the opportunity to become mothers every time we want to become mothers. Only the times that we want to but all the times we want to...,*[98]

In all the circumstances it is not surprising that no great progress was made with abortion law reform. After the middle of the decade the idea of separatism and the exclusion of men began to be abandoned by feminists. A coalition similar to the one behind divorce reform was built up, and in 1978 an act was passed which did make legal abortions possible, though under very restricted conditions. Still, that was progress. And in all countries matters which had been ignored, or treated too lightly, were being brought under rigorous scrutiny: rape, violence against women, pornography.

### Divorce and Equal Rights

At the beginning of the sixties France, because of its long anti-clerical tradition—a strong counterpoise to Catholicism—together with the powerful institution of civil marriage, originating in the Revolution, had on paper the most liberal divorce provisions of any of our four countries, though in practice Americans enjoyed 'strict laws and easy evasion', while there were growing complaints about the way divorce procedures actually operated in France. Overall, divorce was not such a pressing issue in France as was abortion, and the relaxations and improvements in divorce law actually did not come until July 1975, some months after the historic legalization of abortion. At the opposite extreme was Italy. Here, the battle for divorce had all the drama and intensity of the battle for abortion, as concentrated in the Bobigny trial, in France. I shall end this chapter with divorce reform in Italy because it brings me back again to my fundamental point that the changes of the sixties were changes involving majorities, not simply radical activists. Before that, I shall look at developments with regard to divorce in America and France, and then at some of the other issues affecting women's rights and their ability to live a full and free life.

By the end of the sixties in America there had been some modification of the principles of 'strict laws and easy evasion'. In all the discussion of individual rights, doing your own thing, sexual fulfilment, the changing roles of women, there had emerged a consensus in many states that the letter of the old divorce laws needed to be amended. Matters of concern were: the way in which existing laws insisted on identifying a 'guilty' party; the question of divorced husbands paying alimony to their former wives; and the fact that divorce proceedings were expensive, and therefore unavailable to large sections of the population. There were no spectacular campaigns. That there was a perceived need for reform was a product of the social and sexual changes which had interacted and climaxed throughout the sixties. That there was a willingness to enact reform without fuss was a product of the liberalization of thought which had also developed steadily throughout the sixties. In March 1971 the Supreme Court ruled that all states must open their divorce courts to people unable to pay court costs. A cluster of states enacted laws allowing 'irretrievable breakdown' or some similar phrase as a basis for divorce: Vermont (1969), California (1970), Iowa (1970), Alabama (1971), Florida (1971), New Hampshire (1971), Oregon (1971), Colorado (1972), Hawaii (1972), Nebraska (1972).[99] In a lawyer-ridden country, it was inevitable that much attention was given to questions of how exactly property should be divided up after a divorce by consent. At the same time certain lawyers did form associations to try to help the larger numbers of poorer people now coming forward to the divorce courts. In early 1971 the Memphis and Shelby Bar Association mounted 'Operation Divorce', with each member working free to help mop up the flood. Tennessee proceeded cautiously: the new law of June 1971 maintained the old grounds of marital offence, but decreed that the specific details did not have to be brought out in court. In December Dr Margaret DiCanio, professor at Memphis State University and head of the Memphis chapter of NOW, spoke out strongly against alimony as an integral part of divorce settlements: 'Both the man and the woman should be tied to tight rules which consider men to be at least equal with women.' In the summer of 1973 hearings began to be held on a proposed new Tennessee family law: under its provisions irretrievable breakdown would be the only ground for divorce; alimony would be abolished, though temporary maintenance might be paid, depending on their respective economic circumstances, to either the man or the woman. Support in the local press was strong, with Britain once again being presented as the model and Italy as the miracle: 'Divorce laws are changing around the world. Even Italy has relaxed its ban. In England, the only ground for divorce is that the marriage "has irretrievably broken down".' In fact Tennessee had to wait until April 1977 for its law; and even then a further law of July 1977

650

insisted that before a divorce could be confirmed there must be a written property settlement.[100]

Events in France offer a classic demonstration of change brought about by the forces and circumstances discussed throughout this book, modified by the traditions of French law and French religious and secular life. By the early sixties one in ten French marriages ended in divorce, no longer a cause for scandal; a learned treatise of 1964 presented it as an essential component of individual liberty.[101] Yet, just as much as in English, Scottish, and American legislation, grounds for divorce involved the concept of one or other marriage partner being at fault, though sometimes the 'fault' could be stretched to simply little more than unintentional conduct making for incompatibility. But where British and American proceedings had been adversarial, French ones were intrusive and inquisitorial: judges had to establish the full 'facts' of the case, determine whether reconciliation was possible, and rule on the settlement, first interviewing each spouse separately.[102] At law women were seriously disadvantaged until, still a decade ahead of Italy, the Matrimonial Act of 1965 granted women full civil rights, so that (among other things) they could now obtain a passport, start a business, or open a bank account without first being obliged to secure the husband's permission. Completion of divorce proceedings could take two years, yet the amount of time available for discussing the possibilities of reconciliation, or the nature of settlements, was often ludicrously short: in the late sixties the civil courts in Paris were handling ninety divorces a day. More profound objections to the system were to the over-large presence of the state in what was increasingly seen as a purely personal matter, and to the persistence of the notion of fault. As in other spheres, the shake-up of 1968 had its positive effects, though in this case purely on the procedural side. A new family court was created, relieving the pressure on the civil courts and making a more specialized service available.

The most critical development was the changing consciousness among Catholics, with Catholic women preferring divorce to separation, and many clerics in effect arguing that a marriage which was in personal terms not completely fulfilling for both partners was not worth preserving. On the whole the outburst of feminist activities I have just described also contributed to growing pressure for moving totally towards divorce on the basis of the marriage having broken down, with the British 1969 act frequently being cited. In 1972 a senate commission proposed that legal grounds for divorce should be extended to include divorce by consent. As with many other matters, final enactment did not come till 1975. The Lecanuet Law of 11 July was not, in the end, as sweeping as the British and American laws. Instead of one fundamental basis for divorce, it legislated for three, splitting up the concept of breakdown into two—'mutual consent' and 'breakdown', established, very restrictively, by the couple having lived apart for six years; the third basis retained the traditional notion of 'fault', though adultery was at last removed from the list.

Traditional marriage had been based on the notion that the husband had a job and supported his wife and family, while the wife brought up the children and did the household chores. Some of the resistance to making divorce more readily available was based on the perceived problem that a divorced wife might have no means of support. An integral part of the heightened preoccupation with the status and rights of women was a concern to ensure that women could be independent earners, and could have earnings equal to those of men. In the event of divorce, alimony, continuing payments from the ex-husband as determined by the courts, was intended to give the ex-wife some security. However, as we have seen with respect to Dr DiCanio, feminists were beginning to argue that if women were to be truly independent they should not be relying on payments from their ex-husbands. At the same time, there was in the same quarters a feeling that all that a woman might have contributed to the matrimonial home throughout the years of marriage was not properly recognized. Once again, Britain set an example to the rest of the world: the Matrimonial Property Act of 1970 established that a wife's work, whether as a housewife within the home or as a money-earner outside it, should be considered as an equal contribution towards creating the family home if, as a result of the divorce, that had to be divided. In the same year was passed the Equal Pay Act. There were exceptions and loop-holes, and the act was voluntary for the first five years, not coming fully into law until 1975. In France an equalization of wages act became law in 1971; if anything this was less rigorously applied than the British law, but at least in both cases a vital principle had been laid down.

In all countries the proportion of women in the most responsible and the highest-paid jobs remained low. In France, for instance, in 1974 only 1 per cent of executives were women, 3 per cent of engineers, and 6 per cent of foremen (and forewomen); on the other hand, 60 per cent of white-collar workers were women. However, while radical feminists were undoubtedly in the van in perceiving aspects of inequality to which men were blind, there was everywhere support for improving the condition of women, even if within the limits of what males thought appropriate. It was in France, very much on the initiative of the new president from 1974, Giscard d'Estaing, that the idea was seriously put forward of there being a minister for women in the government. A poll of 15 June 1974 showed that 74 per cent of the public at large favoured the creation of such a post. The post was indeed created, in the person of Françoise Giroud, the leading journalist and a founder of *Elle*.[103]

An issue on which it was particularly difficult to make progress was that of child care, a plank in practically all of the radical feminist programmes. The moderate, both-sex NOW put forward the demand that 'childcare facilities be established by law on the same basis as parks, libraries, and public schools, adequate to the needs of children from the preschool years through adolescence, as a community resource to be used by citizens from all income levels'. An act in this sense was promulgated in Congress, but it was vetoed by President Nixon on the grounds that it would be destructive of the family. Again we see America as the country of radical pioneers, constructive liberals, and the most pig-headed reactionaries. Radical feminists themselves were active in setting up their own private child care centres, sometimes in conjunction with universities.

Another concern, further back down the line as it were, was that of childbirth itself. Without the radical feminists, probably the cry would never have been heard that women in childbirth are subject to a regime imposed by male doctors to suit their own convenience and their own theories, not the comfort or welfare of the women involved. The Boston Women's Health Collective was prominent in discussing questions of women's health care, and of childbirth: a classic work is the Collective's publication *Our Bodies, Ourselves* (1973). In the same year (June) feminists organized the First International Childbirth Conference, in Stamford, Connecticut. In a fashion which was less available to women in the European countries, American feminists established their own maternity clinics in which the old male regulations could be abandoned in favour of practices of natural childbirth. Tending to come from a left-wing intellectual background, tinged by the ideas of Marcuse and other philosophers of the 'social construction of reality', radical feminists were from the start arguing that women's nature and functions were not determined by biology but by the roles constructed for them by male-dominated society. This in fact had been a major contention of Simone de Beauvoir in her publication of the forties, *The Second Sex,* but it was now put forward with renewed intensity and conviction. It would be appropriate to say that it was in this area, despite the often ludicrous exaggeration, that radical feminists performed a singular service, drawing attention to a whole arena of the subordination of women which most males, and many females, were blissfully unaware of. The more extreme, and absurd, developments were to come later, but already in 1970 a 'liberation nursery' was being described in which boys and girls played with the same toys, without sexual stereotyping. Boys and girls played with both lorries and dolls, 'and we invested $22 in a petit frère boy doll with genitals because we didn't want to give the impression that all dolls were female.'[104]

It may be remembered that in that very liberated but strongly male-oriented book, *Sex and the Single Girl,* Helen Gurley Brown had been quite relaxed about the idea of women who preferred girlfriends to boyfriends, and had supported their right to go about their affairs without interference or criticism. The last of the civil rights to find vigorous spokespersons in the closing months of the decade were those of gays and lesbians. The exhaustive anatomical exploration of the virtues of the clitoris, and of the alleged mythical nature of the vaginal orgasm, together with the general condemnation of men and the heavy warnings about the dangers of falling in love with, or even just having an intimate relationship with, a man inevitably added force to lesbian discourse. The main practical concern in the early stages of the radical feminist movement was over the rights of lesbian women to the custody of children born in former heterosexual relationships; questions of lesbian marriages and of the rights of lesbians to raise children entirely in isolation from any male were some way ahead. Still, from the start, many radical lesbians were claiming that they were the only true and perfect feminists in that they had severed all contact with men, and all need for them. This, inevitably, was a powerful source of tension within the radical feminist movement, most particularly in the United States, though to a lesser degree also in Italy.[105] Other inherent sources of tension concerned, in all countries, class and, most specifically in the United States, race. American radical feminists were well aware that black American women suffered a double oppression; yet all of the early radical feminist movements were extremely white and extremely middle-class. When a meeting was held in Memphis in April 1970 to establish the first branch of the moderate NOW, the organizers made a deliberate attempt 'to get some of the working-class blacks to attend'.[106] For their part, black radical women were already following black men in the direction of Black Power and separatism. As early as 1969 a black woman, Frances Deale, produced an article 'Double Jeopardy: To Be Black and Female'. Separatist black feminist organizations began to appear in 1973/4: the Sisterhood of Black Single Mothers in Brooklyn, the National Black Feminist Organization in New York City, and the Combahee River Collective in Boston. Because of greater trade union activism, and because of the closer links, however spurious in many ways, between workers' activism and student radicalism, working-class women were involved in forms of feminist protest in France, Italy, and Britain. None the less a strong sense of distinction between working-class women and intellectual and middle-class feminists remained, despite the genuine efforts of radical feminists to campaign on behalf of their worse-off compatriots. The distinction existed in America as well. Here is a furious complaint from a working-class woman, published in August 1970:

> Everyone keeps talking about a mass women's movement. But the women's movement clearly doesn't want anything to do with the masses, or even a few women like us; we're too needy for them. It's an elite movement exuding slimy contempt as it slips along in cahoots with various ruling class men... Seems things are falling along old class lines. Seems some of us aren't nice enough, aren't polite enough, aren't smart enough, aren't slick enough, aren't revolutionary enough, aren't cool enough for the classy women's movement.[107]

Historians of the many different factions and cells which made up the early radical feminist movement have felt bound, therefore, to point to the tensions and the splinterings, the mutual hostility, apparent from practically the very beginning. By the end of 1973 the National Black Feminist Organization had been founded. In a remark which has become canonical, Ti-Grace Atkinson declared as early as 1970: 'Sisterhood is powerful. It kills sisters.' In 1973 the editors of the Boston feminist journal *Second Wave* wrote:

> Tensions have recently re-emerged in Female Liberation around questions of sexuality: Lesbians and straight women each feeling oppressed by the other; women confused about their own sexuality and shy of labeling it; women concerned about a lack of support for Lesbian issues. Conflicts about sexuality in general have been responsible for cross-intimidation of straight women and Lesbians; women who have not defined their sexuality have been lost in the shuffle.

The other source of tension made itself felt not only in heterosexual circles but in lesbian ones: a contributor to *Lesbian Tide* spoke of being 'discouraged by the polarization and angry dialog, particularly that stemming from the issue of racism in our movement'.[108] In the broad perspective, this internecine warfare does not really require much attention. The true achievements of the radical feminists were in propaganda, in consciousness-raising and encouragement of self-confidence among themselves, and in the stretching of their own talents. Great changes have taken place in the role and status of women: the radical feminist groups played a crucial part, but they would not have been successful without the much wider movement of moderates and liberals, and the sense among the unpolitical majority of women that the time had come for past indignities to be rejected, and for new opportunities to be seized.

With that thought firmly in mind, let us turn finally to the 'miracle' in Italy. There the crucial opening moves stemmed from mainstream culture, not from radical feminism. The fundamental campaigning had been done throughout the sixties by *ABC*, a commercial magazine, increasingly successful because of its sexy articles and photography, by the Italian League for Divorce, a conventional pressure group, and by the socialist deputy Loris Fortuna, with certain parliamentary associates. To intelligent politicians and publicists, opposed to the obscurantism of the Catholic Church, making divorce possible seemed an obvious reform; the fight was essentially that of politicians and lobbyists, though through public meetings and frequent items in the press and on television the issue had an increasing impact on ordinary people. New legislation came first; then, four years later, came the intervention of the Italian people, an intervention so decisive it took everyone by surprise. In November 1969 Fortuna's bill, amended and supported by the Liberal deputy Antonia Bislini, came before the chamber of deputies. The Italian League for Divorce organized demonstrations outside. In this era, when the political mood was against traditional authoritarianism in parliament, only ultra-conservative Christian Democrats and the neo-Fascists opposed the bill, which was passed by 325 votes to 283.[109] Many radical feminists, who lumped marriage and divorce together as interdependent aspects of patriarchy, were not enthusiastic. Nor, it must be noted, were many young people, though others took part enthusiastically in the demonstrations organized by the League for Divorce. One 17-year-old female student replied to a male friend who had written enthusiastically about the massive prodivorce demonstration in Rome in November 1969:

> Divorce is nothing more than one regulation on top of another regulation... Marriage for me is nothing more than the record of a legal-economic agreement, and divorce is simply another legal process... instead of fighting for divorce, we should be fighting to eliminate marriage.[110]

A 20-year-old male student replying to a male friend who had written, also enthusiastically, about the Rome demonstration wrote: 'For me it's all balls *[balle]*... No one understands that love is an act of freedom, without rights or duties, without laws.'[111] Parliamentary opposition was stiffer in the senate, where the majority enforced a number of diluting amendments. But on 1 December 1970 a modest act, making divorce possible, once (after a five-year delay) a marriage could be shown to have broken down, became law.

It was only now that the true public battle began. The Catholic hierarchy began a double campaign, first for a referendum to be held on the divorce law, then to ensure that if a referendum were held, the faithful would vote on the side of the angels. *Epocd's* headline of 18 April 1971 read: 'The Battle over Divorce Begins Again', its report noting that the campaign for a referendum was now well under way. On 8 October 1972 it published a debate between Bislini and Professor Gabrio Lombardi, leader of the campaign for a referendum. It also remarked, sharing a certain sympathy for the pro-divorce side, that the number of divorces had not suddenly risen as the opponents of the law had predicted (in fact, the number of divorces did soon rise sharply— showing how much needed the legislation was). It is a sign of the changes in perceptions and assumptions which had come about as a result of the movements and events of the sixties that the attempted obstruction of the Catholic Church actually encouraged popular support for divorce. On 14 April 1973 *Epoca* announced the results of a poll organized by the University of Bologna:

70 per cent of the sample expressed support for the new divorce law. The poll also recorded changes in the nature of the Italian family: 'The parents of today are much less authoritarian and much more likely to have a relationship of genuine friendship with their children.' This went to the heart of the matter. There had been real changes within the depths of Italian society. The divorce issue had begun among a middle-class minority: now it was a direct reflection of these changes. The power of the Church, and the enormous resources it mobilized, ensured that, of course, a referendum was held, and also that the country was swamped in anti-divorce material. *Donna e Società*, that brave token of moderate change at the end of the sixties, took a strong anti-divorce line: 'Supporters of divorce were wrong in thinking that the sanctity of marriage was a Catholic matter—it's a basic human matter.'

The early months of 1974 were months of demonstrations and counter-demonstrations. The referendum was to be held on 12 May 1974. Politicians and other middle-class supporters of divorce feared the worst—traditionally, ordinary Italian people had been very much in awe of the Church. The Christian Democrats saw political advantage in coming out totally against divorce, and their prime minister, Fanfani, made the sort of speeches which would certainly have once been very effective: but remote politicians were no longer able to reach the substantial numbers of Italian people who had left behind the old restricted lifestyles and authoritarian ways. What was really at stake, the prime minister said, was the preservation of the Italian family, that 'instrument of progress, guarantor of continuity, fertilizer of the earth, procreator; that lamp which keeps alive ideas and affections, that cradle of the most fervent sanctity'. He predicted: 'If divorce is allowed in Italy, it will then be possible to have marriages between homosexuals and perhaps your wife will leave you to run off with some young girl or other.'[112] This address exclusively to men, this over-spiced reactionary rhetoric, placed Fanfani with Nixon, Daley, de Gaulle, and the others who, whatever the future vagaries in the narrow course of politics, were the true losers of the sixties. In fact, the leftward move of many Catholics which began in the middle sixties had not run its course: some priests said divorce was simply a matter of individual choice, others gave it active support; the principles of measured judgement pervaded all ideologies.[113] In the upshot, 59.1 per cent voted to endorse the divorce reform law; 40.9 per cent voted against—as these things go, an overwhelming victory. A key document expressing the essential truth of the matter takes the form of an article by the veteran Socialist leader Pietro Nenni: he confessed that this unequivocal verdict had come as a total surprise to himself and to his fellow-politicians, including those on the Left: this demonstrated, he said, in a comment of immense significance, 'how far the politicians had drifted from the sentiments of the Italian people'.[114] Indeed, the Italian people, like people everywhere in the West, had changed.

# 14

# Full Effrontery

## *Gay Liberation*

Recent surveys, conducted entirely independently of each other, in Britain and in the United States have been remarkably consistent in indicating that gay males in each country amount to no more than about 3 per cent of the total male populations.[1] That there was some surprise in both countries that the gay population was so small is a measure of the success of the gay liberation movement in drawing attention to the gay cause. Gay liberation shares one of the most salient characteristics of all the protest movements of the sixties: an insistence that it was a genuinely revolutionary movement (as distinct from a movement simply on behalf of a special interest); and like the other movements it encountered both violent repression from the police and a certain tolerance from those liberal upholders of humanist values and measured judgement whom I have identified as also being important actors in sixties developments. Gay liberation emerged in the wake of women's liberation. There was some exchange of ideas and sympathies between the two, though there was not necessarily any fundamental reason why feminists should feel any sense of identity with gay liberationists, who in many ways manifested just those same predatory and unprincipled attitudes towards the fulfilment of their own desires as the feminists detested in heterosexual males. In common with radical socialists and radical feminists, gays enthusiastically embraced fashionable theories about the social construction of reality. And, as with much else, it happened first in California, in particular the Bay area.

The earliest signs of gay activism here date from the late summer of 1969. A flyer of 15 October 1969 is headed: 'No Vietnamese Ever Called Me a Queer...' In an echo of the way the feminist movement grew out of unhappy experiences in the student radical movement, the message continues: 'Nor are we going to fight in a revolution that puts us down.'[2] On the whole, however, the early tracts associate the movement with the various other civil rights and liberation movements. Another flyer, headed 'Homosexuals for Peace', announced a march in San Francisco to be held on 15 November 1969: 'We will not help to perpetuate a society that oppresses us and discriminates against us, nor will we fight in its army. We will join the fight to end racism and exploitation of all minorities in every phase of every institution.' Then, more specifically to the immediate cause, it concluded: 'Not only is it QUEER that young men are sent halfway around the world to kill each other while they are imprisoned for loving each other, it is perverted and unnatural.'[3] A 'Fact Sheet' of January 1970 with, incidentally, an interesting early use of the term 'counter culture', explained:

> The Gay Liberation Front is a nation-wide coalition of revolutionary homosexual organisations creating a radical Counter Culture within the homosexual lifestyles. Politically it's part of the radical 'Movement' working to suppress and eliminate discrimination and oppression against homosexuals in industry, the mass media, government, schools, and churches.[4]

Obviously consciousness-raising and building of confidence were urgent priorities at this stage. A Berkeley flyer from the spring of 1970 asked: 'Homosexual? Uptight?', responding, 'Don't be: you're beautiful!' 'Gay Liberation' is the phrase most frequently used, but several times the slogan 'Gay Power' makes its appearance. Many of the more extensive mimeographed documents were issued by a body calling itself the Committee of Concern for Homosexuals (Berkeley). A broad idea of the nature of the movement, the influences on it, the insistence that homosexuality is a deliberate political choice, the confessions and the special pleading, can be derived from 'Refugees from Amerika: A Gay Manifesto', of the autumn of 1970. This, along the way, referred to the gay 'ghetto' now being formed in the Castro district of San Francisco.

> 1. *What homosexuality is:* Nature leaves undefined the object of sexual desire. The gender of that object is imposed socially. Humans originally made homosexuality taboo because they needed every bit of energy to produce and raise children: survival of species was a priority. With over population and technological change, that taboo continues only to exploit us and enslave us. As kids we refused to capitulate to demands that we ignore our feelings toward each other. Somewhere we found the strength to resist being indoctrinated, and we should count that among our assets. We have to realise that our loving each other is a good thing, not an unfortunate thing, and that we have a lot to teach straights about sex, love, strength, and resistance. Homosexuality is not a lot of things. It is not a makeshift in the absence of the opposite sex; it is not genetic, it is not the result of broken homes except in as much as we could see the sham of American marriage. *Homosexuality is the capacity to love someone of the same sex.* Exclusive heterosexuality is fucked up. It is a fear of people of the same sex, it's anti-homosexual, and it is fraught with frustrations... We need to purge male chauvinism, both in behaviour and in thought among us. Chick equals Nigger equals queer...

A note on the exploitation of children: kids can take care of themselves, and are sexual beings way earlier than we'd like to admit.

The sudden switch from the glimmering of self-awareness of the male chauvinism of gays to the special pleading with respect to sexual relationships with children is staggering.

In the gay flyers which refer to Lesbianism there is a particularly strong whiff of Foucault and the cultural construction of reality:

> It should first be understood that lesbianism, like male homosexuality, is a category of behaviour possible only in a sexless society characterized by rigid sex roles and dominated by male supremacy. In a society in which men did not oppress women, and sexual expression is allowed to follow feelings, the categories of homosexuality and heterosexuality would disappear.[5]

A tract dated March 1971 headed 'Smash Phallic Imperialism' is certainly powerful enough, though special pleading begins to shade into something very like hypocrisy (I don't single out gay propaganda for special criticism: all the most powerful statements of sixties protest had elements of the weird and unsustainable):

> Sex is an Institution. In an oppressive society like America, it reflects the same ideology as other major institutions. It is gratification-oriented, profit and productivity oriented. It is a prescribed system, with a series of correct and building activities aimed towards a production of a single goal: climax.[6]

Long before the emergence of gay liberation there had been a well-established gay community in Greenwich Village in New York City with its own pub, the Stonewall. Men using the pub were subject to constant harassment by the police, then on 27 June 1969, in one of the great events in gay liberation history, symptomatic of the changes in consciousness and assertiveness which the agitations of the sixties engendered, gays at the Stonewall went on the attack and engaged the police in heroic battle. That day the American Gay Liberation Front was founded.[7]

In May 1968 there had briefly appeared at the Sorbonne a 'Committee of Action of Revolutionary Pederasts'. Gays had a powerful supporter in (the very actively heterosexual) Jean-Paul Sartre, and he joined with them in the launching in September 1970 of a new journal, *Tout*. This contained the first public statement of the French gay liberation movement, including this exhortation: 'Do not be afraid of seeking out experiences, of showing that, for example in face of family life, there already exists for a mass of young people another way'. Reference was made to 'groups who live, not in the shadow, not in the false security of the little world of crippled desires and frustrated passions, but where the exultation of our desires makes even more clear to us the necessity for our struggle'.[8] For Sartre, no doubt, this was boldest Existentialism, asserting individual choice, denying that homosexuality was part of an essentialist genetic inheritance. The link between homosexuality and revolution was asserted through the proposition that revolution must mean the overthrow of the family, and that homosexuality in itself performed a desirable function in destroying the family. The aspirants after unreal Marxist revolution failed to perceive the real cultural revolution taking place around them: children were decreasingly submitting to parents, wives to husbands.

The second issue of *Tout* invoked the American example:

> 'do it', say the young Americans of the 'Youth Culture'... don't be ashamed of your body, especially of your naked body; rely on yourself to construct your dreams, your sensibility. Don't let them impose on you the romantic ideas of *Nous Deux* and *Elle*.[9]

American influences showed also in the first number of yet another new homosexual paper, *L'Idiot Liberté*, of January 1971, together with a refusal to associate gay liberation with rock/pop music:

> In the United States, it makes sense to talk about pop: young people there have created as many bands as there are universities or communities; what is pop(ular) there is elitist here. In Italy the revolution is shaping up against pop (try talking to a Fiat worker about Jimi Hendrix). In Britain, pop is developing as a counter-revolutionary soporific (fall asleep to the sound of the Beatles).[10]

Much more characteristic is the linkage made by *Tout* in February 1971, when it denounced in equal terms laws against drug-taking and laws against homosexuality. However, despite the early Sartrean overtones, and in contrast to the attitude taken up by many American gay activists, the nascent gay liberation movement in France tended towards presenting homosexuality as biologically determined, rather than as a revolutionary choice. In the early stages, as in Britain, there were close attachments to the apron strings of the women's liberation movement: gays expressed solidarity with lesbians, and some joined the MLF. 'Gays and women have the same enemy,' declared *Tout*: 'phallocratism.' In the April issue gays were given four pages in which to express themselves under the title 'The Free Disposal of Our Own Bodies'. This number was circulated quite widely before being seized by the police, perhaps mainly because it contained a rather bathetic echo of the famous abortion manifesto, in the 'Manifesto of 343 sods who have performed homosexual acts'.[11]

Following the issue of *Partisans* dedicated to the liberation of women, a group of lesbians who wanted to organize themselves into a revolutionary movement had contacted the Mouvement de Libération des Femmes (MLF). In February 1971 a number of male homosexuals joined this group of autonomous women. One of the first actions of the augmented group, which did not yet have a name, was to sabotage an anti-abortion meeting organized by the 'Let Them Live' group at the Mutuality conference hall. In March, the group joined with some members of the MLF in interrupting a radio broadcast whose cast was indicated by its loaded (and slightly risible) title: 'Homosexuality: This Painful Problem'. The speakers were chased from the microphones with calls of 'down with the hetero-cops' and 'transvestites are with us'. It was during this action that the title 'Homosexual Front for Revolutionary Action' (FHAR) was coined. Now organized activity began in earnest, with the distribution of tracts at homosexual clubs, reunions at the Beaux-Arts, and workshops.

There followed the publication of the *Report Against Normality*, a collection of texts by 'comrades from the FHAR', including some previously published in *Tout*. Two important statements of April 1971 are quoted. First, an 'Address to Those Who Think Themselves Normal':

> Along with women we are the moral mat on which you wipe your conscience. We state here that we have had enough of it, that you will no longer keep our mouths shut, because we will defend ourselves, that we will hunt down your racism against us including that in language. We say further: we won't be content with defending ourselves, we will attack.

Second was an 'Address to Those Who Are Like Us', that is to say, lesbians:

> For us homosexuality is not a means of attacking society, in the first instance it is simply our condition and it is society which forces us to attack. We make no distinction between us. We know that male and female homosexuals suffer a different oppression. Male homosexuals share the thoughts of male society. Lesbians are oppressed as women. Male homosexuals benefit as men from advantages that are denied to women. But lesbianism is perhaps less scandalous to men, who view it as a spectacle... We want to know how your alliance with the women's liberation movement can continue without involving submission to heterosexual ideology.[12]

In the May Day parades of 1971 *pédés et gouines* (gays and lesbians—'poofs and dikes' might be a more accurate translation, save that these insulting labels were, at this time, accepted by the gays and lesbians themselves) took part together under the banner of the FHAR, next to, but separate from, the MLF. In a reminder of the relationship between such movements and experimental theatre the event was turned into a spectacle, and filmed by members of the FHAR. In echoes of the Sorbonne in May 1968, discussions lasting more than a week were held in the philosophy department at Vincennes. At Censier discussions continued on sexuality, the family, and so on. FHAR began to expand, with twelve local committees by the middle of 1971. Groups were organized in the provinces, there being a particularly active one in Marseille (historically, as a seaport, notorious as a venue for homosexual activity). The continued close association between gays and women's liberation was marked by the participation of FHAR in the 'mothers' fête' organized by the MLF in June 1971. There was also a close link to another of the major developments of the post-1968 'everything goes' climax of the sixties, the movement towards the abolition of censorship. That same evening a hundred members of FHAR went to Tours to join in the Anti-Censorship Day and Fête (in which the experimental theatre group Great Magic Circus was also involved). Three FHAR members were arrested. On 27 June 1971 small demonstrations were held in the Tuileries in Paris in celebration of the anniversary of the Stonewall battle and the founding of the American Gay Liberation Front: massive police action followed immediately and there were four arrests. There was an involvement with the environmental movement too, when FHAR participated in the last Festival of Les Halles (before demolition and redevelopment).[13] But gay protests did not make news in the way that feminist ones did. The sexual element in feminism was fascinating to most male journalists and readers, while the same element in gay liberation seemed (reprehensibly, no doubt) merely disgusting. And the feminists, after all, were claiming to speak for half the human race; gays spoke only for a tiny percentage, though claiming also to speak for many more with 'repressed secret desires'. Typical of the balance of press coverage was a *Paris-Match* report of 15 May 1971: describing a pro-abortion demonstration, it gave great prominence to 'bare-breasted majorettes', merely adding in parentheses that also present were 'a dozen or so homosexuals'.

In Italy, just as conditions for women were toughest, so also were they for homosexuals. But while Italian radical feminism had a spirited character of its own (and, indeed, in the form of DEMAU had produced the first ever organized movement), Italian gay liberation was highly derivative from movements in the other three countries. In the sixties, homosexuality was at best treated as a medical or psychological condition; amid the events of 1968–9 there are no signs of homosexual protest movements being provoked into life. The one clear sign that the general reassessments taking place in these years could include a consideration of the social disabilities suffered by homosexuals is the way in which a new series of books, established in Bologna in 1970, entitled 'The Outcasts', included as its second volume a book entitled *The Homosexuals*. The general editorial introduction to the series suggested that there were faults in society which made certain groups 'outcasts'.[14] In the same year there was published *Diary of a Homosexual*. This was in fact a composite account made up from various case studies by a neuropathologist and psychiatrist. There is no mention at all of gay rights, but the treatment, as in *The Homosexuals*, is sympathetic. The author of the latter book explained why he had chosen to remain anonymous:

> It is not possible for me to bring everything out into the light if I don't want to be forced to play for the rest of my life a role which others impose upon me, a stereotype, either a colourful character or one of the dregs of society. So there is no use talking of freedom. But silence no longer springs from fear or respect for the views of others; it is intended to preserve the freedom to scratch the sore, because a discovery will have been made when you have begun to understand and when you have begun to support our freedom and to see us through different eyes.[15]

The actual content of the book is not very liberationist, the chapters dealing with: the origins and mechanisms of sexual inversion; psychological considerations; opportunities for meeting; the aggravating factors in society; choosing to be different and the automatic exclusion from society; prevention and therapy. However, the conclusion looks forward to developments soon to take place:

> These pages have certainly been an attempt by 'one of them' to open up an understanding of their anxieties and hopes... Precisely from this agony and from the joy which arises

from it is born the authenticity of those who refuse to think of their lives as predestined, irredeemably consigned to 'difference' and to exclusion.

The writer hopes for 'liberation' from the 'servitude' and 'colonialism' which have been 'at the roots of "difference" '.[16]

In August 1971 the Front for the Liberation of Homosexuals was founded. Three months later there followed the United Front of Italian Revolutionary Homosexuals (FUORI—a neat acronym, since *fuori* normally means 'outside'). The first number of their publication, *FUORI*, in December 1971 stated: 'We are convinced of the need for "Sexual Revolution" parallel with, and integrated into, the political revolution which is taking place in all countries.'[17] Gay liberation had arrived in Italy, and perhaps, after all, there was a specifically Italian colouring. In a first major public demonstration, the two groups joined together in demonstrating at a sexology congress at San Remo, where, of course, homosexuality was being treated as a condition needing therapy. The first major publication appeared in late 1972: *The Homosexual Movements of Liberation: Documents, Testimony and Photographs of the Homosexual Revolution*, which described itself as a survey of 'the first two years of struggle for homosexual liberation'. The prefatory chapter was entitled 'Sexual Racism':

> In our country homosexuality is seen as an attack on the family, on procreation, on religion. Catholicism and fascism have been its most bitter enemies. But even among revolutionaries homosexuality is not accepted. Male and female are considered two eternal and immutable categories.[18]

The Berkeley gay activists are quoted approvingly, and in the long section of documents the 'Refugees from Amerika' manifesto which I have already quoted is given in full in Italian translation. The scale of external influences on the Italian movement is well represented by the order in which documents are quoted: first from America, second from France, and then from what is referred to as 'England'.[19]

There had at least been some form of homosexual law reform in Britain, though it still left under-21s at risk and, most critically, those over 21 consorting with those under. The first meeting of the London Gay Liberation Front was held at LSE on 13 October 1970. The earliest GLF demands (November 1970) included:

> That all discrimination against gay people, male and female, by the law, by employers, and by society at large, should end.
>
> That all people who feel attracted to a member of their own sex be taught that such feelings are perfectly normal.
>
> That sex education in schools stop being exclusively heterosexual.
>
> That psychiatrists stop treating homosexuality as though it were a problem or sickness, thereby giving gay people senseless guilt complexes.
>
> GAY POWER TO GAY PEOPLE AND POWER TO OPPRESSED PEOPLE.[20]

If gays, like feminists, sometimes took their own revolutionary pretentions far too seriously, and were at times guilty of double-think, they could, also like the feminists, mount the funniest and punchiest street theatre. At first gay liberation joined in the feminist demonstrations, then each group went its own way. Gay Liberation Front street theatre was just one of the many agents through which the liveliest innovations of the sixties were carried on into the seventies.

## Uncut Film and Superrealism in Art

It is always tempting to indulge the nostalgia of representing the sixties as a lost golden age, already, perhaps, losing its innocence in the aftermath of 1968, or to fantasize over the alleged 'crisis' of the later sixties, overdramatizing 1968 as marking 'defeat' for the high aspirations of the earlier years of the decade. Thus in his *Sixties Design* the distinguished design historian Philippe Garner writes of

> a major socio-political upheaval which changed the mood of western society in the critical period of 1966–68. The promise of the early sixties faded into anger, frustration and unrest.[21]

Looking back from the eighties, Jim Haynes of the Traverse and the Arts Lab saw the end of the sixties as a time of 'incredible collapse', succeeded by depression and cynicism:

> a collapse of hope, and of the innocence and naivety of the decade when everyone felt that they were changing the world, that we could change the world. Then maybe a few people began to realise that through the music, through long hair and colourful costumes, through our attitudes, hopes and fears, we weren't going to change the world. We could only maybe change ourselves a bit. And I think this resulted in depression for some people and a rush of cynicism.[22]

This book is saying something very different. The changes which arose from the special circumstances and the many interactions in the years from the late fifties onwards were deep, and they were long-lasting. The notion that they were accompanied by naivety—as many, including the two schoolteachers looking back on the Liverpool 'mini-Renaissance' I quoted in Chapter 1, insisted—and innocence has been greatly overstated. To be open-hearted and tolerant, to communicate joy and optimism—that is not necessarily to be naive and innocent. And there was certainly nothing truly innocent about the hedonism, the pretence that the only alternative to unbridled lust was bourgeois repression, the drugtaking, the money-making—from club-licence booze, from head shops, from the latest piece of creative extremism. The world did change, but often in far corners, out of sight of the counter-cultural impresarios, entrepreneurs, and performers, and not by way of dramatically substituting one entire culture for another. Jim Haynes—let us take him as a representative figure—was no naive failure: experimental theatre, with which he had been intimately associated, the 'mighty atom of change', as I called it, grew throughout the seventies. Many, probably most, of the activists and protesters were warm and generous in their fundamental motivation (as their elders often came to recognize). They were scarcely naive; if they were, they shared these characteristics with the greatest thinkers of the time, victims together of the Great Marxisant Fallacy. Some were ruthless to the extent of being totally blind to the legitimate interests of other people, while others were utterly unscrupulous in their self-absorption. But, along with the more alluring and ultimately more influential fun-loving tolerance, experimentation, and colour, ruthlessness was important for providing the searching gaze and ferocious truculence which exposed hidden hypocrisies and oppressions in mainstream society, the sort of things the more rational and tolerant would probably have missed. None the less, change, as it actually came, owed much to those in positions of influence who did practise the traditional humanist virtues of tolerance and rationality. It is not a matter of allocating praise and blame. The people I am talking about lived comfortable lives whose only justification, really, was that they applied their expensive education and their intelligence in an open-minded way to the problems of the day (too many of them did not do this). Brutal things did happen in the sixties, yet there was a remarkable balance between this humanism and the extremes of innovation. For many reasons this balance could not have lasted, above all because the economic buoyancy upon which almost everything depended was punctured by the oil crisis. There was no 'collapse', but the fine balance upon which the unique civilization of the sixties was based began to falter in the early seventies. Most people continued, or began for the first time, to feel the benefits of the main changes of the sixties, and many of these changes developed and accelerated in a most desirable way—experimentation, having fun, optimism over improving lifestyles most assuredly continued, as we shall see in my final chapter. The more fundamentalist and uncompromising movements had already brought conflict and violence, though usually in the form of brief destructive outbursts which then faded into relative quiescence.

The debate continues to rage today over the particular topic for the first part of this section. To many thoughtful people, any kind of censorship of free expression, and specifically censorship of film or television, is in itself an evil: it is an infringement of a basic freedom, it denies people potentially life-enhancing experiences or necessary revelations, it imposes the thinking and prejudices of one person or group upon others. Censorship restrictions as they had existed in all four countries in the fifties were restrictive and absurd. Liberalization of censorship had been one of the most striking products of the combination of radical protest and measured judgement. The events of 1968 had forced on the authorities a thorough appraisal of all their most basic instincts. As there was liberalization in professional institutions, in education, with regard to abortion, divorce, drink laws, so also was it a logical development that there should be a collapse in most of surviving censorship. Yet, it might be claimed that the arguments I have just rehearsed for total abolition of censorship belong in the same fundamentalist realm as radical feminism or radical gay liberation. In looking at how society actually is, and how individuals and groups actually behave and react, it is not axiomatic that total abolition of censorship is integral to the good of society. I suggest that while measured judgement held up till the beginning of the seventies, thereafter what happened in the way of release from censorship, while a logical continuation of certain sixties trends, was very much part of the 'everything goes' ambience in which the unique and, as one can now see, precarious balance between liberation and sensibility was lost. That is a comment, not a condemnation. If a relaxed censorship brought an explosion of porn and exploitation, it was also accompanied by a remarkable continuity in the revival in serious American film-making whose beginnings I noted in Chapter 10, leading to what the doyenne of American film critics, Pauline Kael, has described as Hollywood's 'authentic golden age'.[23] Such films as *The Godfather* (Francis Ford Coppola, 1972), *American Graffiti* (George Lucas, 1973), *The Conversation* (Francis Ford Coppola, 1974), *Chinatown* (Roman Polanski, 1974), *Nashville* (Robert Altman, 1975), and *Taxi Driver* (Martin Scorsese, 1976) present the truly creative aspect of 'everything goes'. Here, to make my point, I concentrate on the tawdry side.

Three Swedish films exhibited in America between 1967 and 1969 were *I, A Woman* (about a nymphomaniac, this showed the heroine's breasts and implied the sex act, but avoided any glimpses of the sex organs),[24] *The Language of Love* (which claimed to be educational and had explicit sexual elements), and *I Am Curious—Yellow* (whose simulated sex scenes were said to be 'franker and more explicitly visualized than anything previously seen in a 35 mm feature for general release').[25] Both the latter two films had trouble, first with the American customs authorities and then with various local courts. But they always ended up being exhibited in various parts of America, usually to packed houses with long queues forming outside.[26]

To concentrate too exclusively on censorship alone is, however, to fall into the traditional error of focusing on the state rather than on society. At least as interesting as what the state permitted is what individuals and groups within society were proposing. I have already suggested that key cultural artefacts for summing up and publicizing some of the most significant trends of their time are *Room at the Top* (the film) for 1958–9 and *Hair* (the stage show) for 1968; for the period I am now discussing one might choose the film *Deep Throat* (1972)—which I come to in a moment. It is important, however, that I do not confuse the chronology with too many generalizations. First, we must distinguish between films intended for general theatrical exhibition and films designed for specialist outlets. Short films, lasting about ten minutes, usually featuring one act of copulation, for exhibition in the shabby clubs to be found in the sleazier parts of town, or for private parties, were known as 'loops'. Longer films, often of Scandinavian origin, for exhibition in cinema clubs, usually had some alleged educational or didactic purpose, as for instance in the *1000 Love Positions* of 1969. A more elaborate kind of loop appeared in 1970, *Mona: The Virgin Nymph*. This lasted for an hour and allegedly presented a discussion of the appropriateness of Victorian prudishness: Mona is willing to have every kind of sex with her fiancé except actual intercourse, which must be reserved for her wedding night. *Dark Dreams* of later the same year concerns the encounter of two virgin newly-weds with devil-worshippers.[27]

Loops were blatantly exploitation films for male audiences, without any pretence at seeing women as anything other than instruments of male pleasure. However, many competing views were being advanced as to what actually constituted sexual liberation for women. *How to Become the Sensuous Woman* by 'J' appeared in the United States in 1969, and Britain in 1971, becoming a worldwide best-seller. The blurb read as follows:

666

Every female has the ability and the right to be fully sensuous. But most women never learn how. *The Sensuous Woman* will show you how to attract a man worth your attention, drive him wild with pleasure and keep him eagerly coming back for more. And *The Sensuous Woman* will show you how to reach peaks of erotic and loving pleasure you never dreamed were available to you.

For my purposes, *The Sensuous Woman* is a perfect specimen in the way it brings together the notions of women's rights, individual fulfilment, the abolition of all inhibitions, and faith in proselytizing on behalf of all of these. The opening itself reads like a hilarious parody, though presumably intended to be taken quite seriously. Inevitably there could be no avoiding frank references to the importance of looks (later works of this general type would often invoke the possibilities of plastic surgery).

For the last five years men have been telling me the most delicious things—that I am sexy, all woman, that perfect combination of a lady in the living room and a marvellous bitch in bed, sensual, beautiful, a modern Aphrodite, maddeningly exciting, the epitome of the Sensuous Woman.

Some of the most interesting men have fallen in love with me. I have received marriage proposals from such diverse personalities as a concert pianist, a best selling author, the producer of three of America's most popular television shows, a bomb expert for the CIA, a trial counsel, an apple grower, a TV and radio star, and a tax expert.

Yet you'd never believe it if we came face to face on the street, for I'm not particularly pretty. I have heavy thighs, lumpy hips, protruding teeth, a ski jump nose, poor posture, flat feet and uneven ears.

I am not brilliant and I don't have a magnetic personality. In fact, I'm shy.

Mothers, wives and girlfriends think of me as the wholesome, apple pie, girl-next-door type (which, translated, means non-sexy).

But while these mothers, wives and girlfriends are burning up over that spectacular blond undulating provocatively in the peekaboo leopard print, I'm the one that's having the wonderful time—and getting and *keeping* men.

... through intelligence and hard work I have become a Sensuous Woman.

After a quick discussion of why sex is 'the nation's number one sport', the book moves rapidly on to masturbation, joining with Italian and other feminists in the song of the clitoris.[28] The feminists, of course, were concerned to show how women could be independent of men, whereas what *The Sensuous Woman* (like *Sex and the Single Girl* before it) was claiming to offer was uttermost success in heterosexual relationships.

The Italian writer Maryat Rollet-Andriane (pseudonym Emmanuelle Arsan), who had participated in the Paris events of May 1968, identified herself with what she perceived as an alternative, or 'parallel', hippie culture. She was involved in the Italian divorce reform campaign; she supported black civil rights and gay liberation. In Paris in 1969, she published an *Epistle to*

*Paul VI* on the pill, recycling the same material in Italian feminist journals and the American magazine *Evergreen Review*. The *Epistle* began: 'I am reading your Encyclical [Humane Vitae, 25 July 1968], naked on the terrace of my house. I am looking at my body in the sun and am forcing myself to understand why you and your people, for nearly 2,000 years, have wished it so much harm.' She belonged, she said, 'to that category of people—a minority it seems—who force themselves to live in accordance with what they think'. 'Erotic culture', she continued, 'is one of several parallel cultures': its basic belief is 'that every conception of liberty is fraudulent, if it excludes the most precious and the most desirable of liberties: that of pleasure.' The revolution she was concerned with was 'the one that would substitute pleasure for money and power'.[29] Thus spoke the author of the best-selling erotic novel *Emmanuelle* (1970), soon turned by Italian film director Bruno Zincone into a full-length film; the film (1972) may also be regarded as a key text in the entry of what would recently have been regarded as pornography into mainstream film-making. Arsan, understandably enough, claimed not to like the film, but did not disassociate herself from it. The relationship between pornography, women's rights, and exploitation are complicated. It should not be forgotten that the original begetter of this famous film was an ultra-active women's liberationist.

On 28 June 1972 there opened at the World Theatre off Times Square in New York City the film *Deep Throat*. This film, originally called *The Doctor Makes a House Call*, was written and directed by a specialist in pornographic loops, Gerard Damiano, who had had a superior budget of $25,000 which had allowed for six days' shooting and three months' editing. It brought together some of the most profound obsessions of the time, to be found equally in the most scatological 'fun-loving' male chauvinist literature and the most earnestly anatomical feminist literature. Under the subheading 'Nibbling, Nipping, Eating, Licking and Sucking', *The Sensuous Woman* had declared:

> Now don't turn up your nose and make that ugly face! oral sex is, for most people who will give it a real try, delicious. It is part of the Sensuous Woman's bag of pleasures and has the added advantage, if you're a snob, of being a status style of love making. (It's the preferred way with many movie stars, artists, titled Europeans and jet-setters.)[30]

Linda Lovelace, the star of the film (born Linda Boreman, daughter of a heavy-drinking Yonkers cop), was already a practised performer in pornographic films and at private parties, with a fall-back career as a prostitute. In the film she is, its makers insisted, playing 'as herself', a woman dedicated to sex but unable to achieve orgasm. So she consults her doctor (hence the doctor featured in the original title), played by another regular in the pornographic shorts of the time, Harry Reems (real name Herbert Streicher). His diagnosis (which could be seen as a tribute to, or a spoof on, *The Myth of the Vaginal Orgasm* and subsequent literature, or, of course, mere pandering to male sexual fantasy) is that her clitoris is in her throat. Thus the erotic content of the film consists of repeated episodes of oral sex between Lovelace and Reems, and also between Lovelace and three of Reems's 'patients'. At the end Lovelace finds 'true love' in the person of a masked man with sadistic fantasies. Damiano said that 'the truly amazing thing' about Lovelace 'is that she looks so sweet and innocent'. When, in accordance with the script, finally achieving orgasm, she genuinely appeared, according to critics, to be achieving those 'peaks of erotic and loving pleasure' never previously dreamed of. Lovelace's realistic performance was intercut with the ancient clichés of fireworks exploding and a Saturn rocket being launched.[31]

*Deep Throat* took $33,000 in its first week. At the beginning of the previous decade, Carol Cheesman in California had been executed for forcing women to have oral sex with him, his case also providing one of the earliest radical causes of the sixties. Now here was something for women to watch as well as men. The word spread. It was natural that the film should be mentioned in the magazine *Screw;* however, editor-publisher Al Goldstein, while rating the film highly for its unambiguous erotic qualities, seemed to suggest that it had other qualities as well. The entirely serious film critics of the *Village Voice* and the *New York Times* gave the film earnest attention. As leading personalities in entertainment and in politics went to see it, the *New York Times* described its appeal as that of 'pornochic'.[32] In a study of 1974, two American critics summed up what had become almost received critical opinion:

> It is not degrading or ugly. It is, rather, expertly made, funny, and almost unique amongst sex films in its celebration of individual response. The plot is more than just a pretext for a series of compulsive sexual encounters, and women are not portrayed as objects of sexual hatred and perversion, a perspective that is scored—or perhaps shaped—by Linda Lovelace's extraordinary erotic talent. She appears to be genuinely turned on by what she is doing, with a result that her performance shows none of the boredom, inadvertent laughter, or undisguised disgust that breaks the sensual reality of many films.[33]

While many women went to the film, and apparently enjoyed it, it had its opponents among women critics. Writing in *New York Review of Books,* Ellen Willis declared it 'as erotic as a tonsillectomy'. Nora Ephron, in *Esquire,* announced that she came out of the cinema 'a quivering fanatic', after what she called 'one of the most unpleasant, disturbing films I have ever seen'. She found it 'not just anti-female but anti-sex as well'. However, it is a tribute to the power the film exerted, and to the favourable reactions it had elicited from other distinguished people, that Ephron interviewed Lovelace and honourably quoted her own declaration that she 'totally enjoyed myself making the movie', and that she ended up by questioning her own reactions, wondering whether, in fact, she was simply 'a puritanical feminist who had lost her sense of humour at a skin flick'.[34]

Whether Linda Lovelace really enjoyed playing the part, or whether in fact she had been brutalized and terrorized into doing this and her earlier performances, subsequently became a matter of controversy. It seems clear that she suffered treatment which no woman in the post-feminist generation would endure. At the same time, she gave every sign of enjoying and playing out to the full the celebrity which the film brought her. Her remark to Ephron seems genuine enough, and is supported by what she said subsequently in her autobiography, *Inside Linda Lovelace* (New York, 1974). Her celebrity had passed, and her sweet and innocent good looks were no longer so much in evidence, when she came to write *Ordeal* (New York, 1981), which she claimed as a more accurate account of the horrors she had endured. Doubtless with hindsight, and the wisdom developed by the women's movement, her experiences at the end of the sixties and the beginning of the seventies seemed a good deal less liberating (though they did continue to be some kind of liberation from her repressive Catholic upbringing). But however inauthentic (and a film, after all, is a film), *Deep Throat* remained, and was at the time seen to be, some kind of statement about female sexual liberation. There is no call to defend it, nor conceal the fact that its essential function was to make money (most of which seems to have gone to the Mafia, with the actual participants all being poorly paid). Make money it certainly did: $5 million by July 1973, and ultimately, with all spin-offs, something like $600 million. Its immediate successors were *Behind the Green Door* and *The Devil in Miss Jones*. Many others followed. The courageous experiments and challenges of the sixties had resulted in a deeply vulgar industry.

However, though much of the sting of censorship had been drawn in the post-1968 retreat from authoritarianism, *Deep Throat* did not go unchallenged by the authorities. In August 1972 a New York judge ordered the film to be seized, and its sponsors tried for obscenity. There were inescapable echoes of trials at the beginning of the previous decade; again expert witnesses provided arguments on 'redeeming social value' for something which, a few years previously, would without doubt have been thought by lawyers and audiences alike totally unsuitable for public exhibition; a distinguished film historian declared that 'there was a kind of sophisticated filming with the sexual content'; directly germane to the main point I have just made, a medical professor, Dr John Money, insisted: 'It indicates that women have a right to a sex life of their own.'[35] Linda Lovelace herself, still playing the character she had played in the film, declared:

> It makes me so mad that sex films are called obscene when movies full of slaughter are called PG. Kids learn that killing is accepted; what they should learn is that sex is good. Then there wouldn't be so many neurotics in the world.[36]

But the judge, by no means a total victim of myopia, could find no redeeming social value: World Theatre was fined $3 million and the film banned. However *Deep Throat* continued to be shown in seventy other cities, and eventually made a return to New York. The manager of the Theatre betrayed a certain justified optimism when he put up the notice: 'Judge Cuts Throat, World Mourns'.[37] In 1974 the film went on trial before a Federal Court in—how inevitable it begins to seem—Memphis: the main effect was to give it a renewed lease of life.[38]

The long-term change, in which 1972 was a fulcrum, was from cheaply produced, rather stilted pornography, either dressed up as educational material or shown to very small audiences, to big-budget films for mass exhibition, containing scenes which once would even have been considered impossible even in small-audience specialist porn. Usually there was a strong horror element associated with the eroticism, as with *The Exorcist*, which, though containing what not long before would have been regarded as sexual obscenities, such as a girl masturbating with a crucifix, was granted an X certificate in 1973. But the two most sensational films of these years, breath-stoppingly explicit yet so deeply serious as to be in no slightest sense exploitation films, were both European: *W.R.: Mysteries of the Organism* (1971), by the Yugoslav director Dusan

Makavejev, and *Last Tango in Paris* (1972), an Italian-French co-production directed by an Italian director already making a considerable name for himself, Bernardo Bertolucci (b. 1940). The release and success in the West of *W.R.* neatly marks the consummation of the sexual transformation which began at the end of the fifties, having Wilhelm Reich—to sixties students the revered apostle of sexual liberation—as its central character, and being loosely structured on his writings. Among the episodes that flash past we have a young lady who collects plaster casts of the erections of pop stars (another neat consummation of an important aspect of sixties life). The film was given an X certificate by John Trevelyan's successor as film censor. Trevelyan's comment reveals more than he realized (and that he failed to appreciate that the days of art cinemas exclusively for toffs were over): 'This must have been the first time an erection was to be seen on the screen of a public cinema with a Board's certificate, though admittedly this was an art film which would have a limited distribution.' Once it had its certificate, of course, there were no necessary limits to *W.R's* distribution. *Last Tango in Paris,* as a classic cross-national production, featured American megastar Marlon Brando as a middle-aged man who forsakes his nagging wife for lashings of sex of all kinds with a young woman—famously a packet of butter is used in an act of sodomy. She is an independent woman: she kills him.

From upmarket movies back down to straight bottom-of-the-market pornography. An article in the *Los Angeles Times* of 3 November 1973 described Los Angeles as 'the capital of mail-order erotica firms'. Bare statistics of numbers of films banned, or cuts imposed, do not necessarily say anything about the strengthening or weakening of censorship. A rise in the number of films banned may simply testify to the increasing daring of film-makers. In 1960, in France, ten films were banned and thirty-one subject to cuts. From then till 1964 only one film was banned a year, with none in 1963. In 1965 the figure goes up to two, then in 1966 to eight. The figures for the succeeding years are shown in Table 14.1, which suggests increasing daringness around 1968, with corresponding reactions from the censorship. It also supports what we know from other sources: in France, 1974 was the key year of liberalization in French film censorship. In July

**Table 14.1** *Film censorship in France*

| Year | Films banned | Films cut |
|------|-------------|-----------|
| 1967 | 10 | 56 |
| 1968 | 12 | 65 |
| 1969 | 17 | 69 |
| 1970 | 13 | 37 |
| 1971 | 15 | 21 |
| 1972 | 9 | 28 |
| 1973 | 11 | 39 |
| 1974 | 3 | 59 |
| 1975 | 3 | 17 |
| 1976 | 4 | 8 |
| 1977 | 5 | 4 |
| 1978 | 4 | 5 |
| 1979 | 6 | 3 |
| 1980 | 3 | 5 |

1974, commenting on the great success in France of the film *Emmanuelle*, *L'Express* noted that fifty-six cinemas in Paris were screening twenty-six erotic films. Since 1968, the year of *I am Curious—Yellow* and *The Love Life of Romeo and Juliet,* there had been, it said, an irresistible rise of more or less 'lascivious films'.[39]

There is nothing like the study of pornography to demonstrate that, whatever else the period 1958–74 was, it was most certainly an era of liberated private enterprise. Tom Peart, a builder, was a working-class participant in the mixed-class Chelsea subculture. He sent out a mailshot of two million letters advertising *Variations on a Sexual Theme* by Terence Hendrickson (himself), published by the Julian Press (also himself), at a price of fifty-seven shillings and sixpence, with postage and packing at two shillings and sixpence (also known as 'half-a-crown' in the wonderfully archaic currency which was still an evocative part of life in sixties Britain):

> This book sets out to explain in concise and lucid terms, with the aid of accompanying photographic illustrations, the physical means whereby enjoyment of the act of sexual intercourse between married couples may be both heightened and prolonged, by the adoption of an infinitely greater variety of critical positions than would previously lie within the knowledge and experience of the average man.[40]

There were 110,000 subscribers, yielding a nice profit of £50,000.[41] That the photographs now seem yawn-makingly tame did not prevent the book falling foul of the Marylebone Magistrates. The tone is actually the benevolent and reassuring one of the great and the good of the time: men are encouraged not to worry about their small penises, and it is explained that the clitoris is situated rather higher up than might be expected.[42]

British television continued its innovative path into the 1970s. A new series of *Till Death Us Do Part* was thought to be still more uninhibited in its thought and explicit in its language than its predecessors. A constituent complained to his MP:

> I would like to raise my voice in protest at the ultimate in blasphemy permitted in the BBC programme 'Till Death do us part' *[sic]*. I would ask you take rigorous action against the perpetrators, J Speight and his crew and attempt to protect the public from this sort of thing. The permissive society is rapidly becoming the corrupt society with the permission of our legislators.

In his reply, the MP regretted that he had not had a chance to see the new series but noted that this letter was the only one of complaint out of the thousands who had seen it: 'If the programme is as you say, I would have expected to have heard from others of my constituents.' Having seen the programme, the MP wrote a further letter saying that he could see nothing to protest about. To this the constituent replied with an expression of thanks and of hostility to other aspects of permissiveness, recording that, though a lifelong Labour supporter, he would not be voting for the MP again, 'due to your views on hanging, abortion, etc. etc.[43]' (The delicious irony of *Till Death Us Do Part,* of course, was that on these issues Alf Garnett shared the views of this bigoted constituent.) Whatever the excesses of the radicals and pioneers, there frequently came points when lines had to be drawn which set reactionaries firmly on one side, leaving the moderates stuck with the radicals on the other.

One example of a noble dream of the sixties going sour in the seventies was that of the Bit community agency in the well-known black area of central London, Notting Hill. *IT*, much later, at the beginning of 1980, provided a disillusioned account:

> Finally it was the dregs of the hippie dream that finally destroyed Bit, with certain individuals insisting that 'Everyone must do their thing—Bit is open to everyone man'. This meant that in the end Bit was only open to rip-offs, free loaders and a few unfortunate wrecks who were prepared to put up with the disgusting state of the offices because they had nowhere else to go—and no-one cared enough to help them.
>
> The many dedicated and hard working people who devoted years in some cases to keeping Bit going, normally did not last long in these latter years; these gave up in frustration and often in total disillusionment; Bit ended up in the hands of a bunch of petty crooks, speed freaks, con-artists and jaded hypocrites mouthing meaningless platitudes about 'The Alternative Society' while they dealt barbs and stole from their friends. Always ready to shout 'Fuck the Pigs' but having as much love and peace in them as any member of the Special Patrol Groups, probably less.[44]

Decline, disillusionment, unrestrained excess: that is not the central story. The central story is of the freedoms won, the movements, the innovations, and the ideas of the sixties continuing through the 1970s. To take an example: there were actually far more experimental theatre groups in the seventies than ever there had been in the sixties, though arguably the period of greatest innovation was now over. Arguably, too, while the new departures in painting and sculpture proceeded unhindered, innovation was giving place to the derivative or commercialized, with a conceptual art that was becoming self-indulgent and self-defeating, and a political art which was often banal.

If we wanted to look at early seventies art as representing sixties innovations overstated and then made banal, an appropriate place to start would be with the English artists Gilbert and George. Gilbert (b. 1943) and George (b. 1942) were still sculpture students at the St Martin's School of Art when they attracted international attention for a peculiar and highly personal twist on the notions of art as 'performance' and as being 'temporal': in what was first called 'Our New Sculpture', then 'Underneath the Arches', and finally 'The Singing Sculpture', they themselves posed as their own 'sculptures'. The next stage was to seek a permanent form for these 'living sculptures': 'they began to use the traditional media of painting and drawing, in a novel and witty way', creating numerous 'drawing pieces', 'charcoal on paper sculptures', and one huge 'painting sculpture', in all of which the posed image of the artists appeared life-size.[45] In 1971 Gilbert and George turned to photography, creating the 'photo-piece' which henceforth was to be the basic form of their art.

The photo-piece consists basically of an arrangement of a number of separately framed photographic images adding up to a unified expressive whole. The photographs them-selves are manipulated in various ways through the printing process to enhance their expressive potential and in the early photo-pieces the framed images were hung in config-urations which were emblematic of the theme of the piece.[46]

Words and phrases often appear on these photo-pieces, seeming to maintain a link with Conceptual art: but Gilbert and George saw themselves as 'New Realists'. From 1973 there was an emphasis on urban settings: many appeared to be about drinking and drunkenness—in his note for the 1986 retrospective exhibition Simon Smith explained this as being 'a particularly apt metaphor to express what was clearly a state of considerable alienation and existential angst which gripped them at that time'.[47] The Nature photo-pieces of the early seventies seemed to have much in common with Earth Art. But Gilbert and George were great self-publicists, and very soon they began to insist that they were not of the narrow world of conceptualism: theirs was an art of the people.

> We want Our Art to speak across the barriers of knowledge directly to People about their Life and not about their knowledge of art. The 20th century has been cursed with an art that cannot be understood.[48]

To many critics their art was merely simplistic and meretricious. The 'Life of People' seemed, particularly in the painting of the middle and later seventies, to be the life of the lavatory wall: titles ran from 'Prostitute Poof', 'Shag Stiff', and 'Wanker' to the less and less printable, the photo-pieces incorporating graffiti, photographs (sometimes of male sex organs), and red paint. The unmediated photographs of Robert Mapplethorpe (1946–89), who had his first exhibition in New York in 1972, aroused not dissimilar reactions, many being of male genitalia (black and white) or of sadomasochistic male homosexual encounters.

The driving forces behind Superrealism, as well as the label itself, were American, but in fact many Europeans were independently going in the same direction, and the label was very easily adapted into the European languages—it is *Iperrealismo* in Italian. In Italy the hyper-inventive Pistoletto, with his life-size photographs pasted onto sheets of steel which reflected the spectator, was already developing his own type of Superrealism. The leading figure in France was Jacques Monory (b. 1934), and in Germany Gerard Richter. In Britain Lucian Freud (b. 1922) had long been producing meticulous warts-and-all nudes which, as has been said, appear naked rather than nude.[49] The arrival of Superrealism as a main trend in European art was signalled by the Documenta V exhibition in Kassel in West Germany in 1972. The leading Superrealists are the Americans Duane Hanson (b. 1925), Ralph Goings (b. 1928), Richard Estes (b. 1936), Chuck Close (b. 1940), and John De Anviea (b. 1941); Malcolm Morley (b. 1931) was English, but had worked from New York since 1964. At its best, Superrealism was exploring the nature of reality; most Superrealist paintings (though not all) were based on photographs, not directly on reality. They present a very intense, cold, distant take on life, totally without sentiment or rhetoric. Sculptor Duane Hanson did go beyond neutrality, seemingly commenting on the emptiness of materialist society: 'I just want to express my feelings of dissatisfaction.' He has commented on such works as *Couple with Shopping Bags* (1976):

> My most successful pieces are naturalistic or illusionistic, which results in an element of shock, surprise or psychological impact for the viewer. The subject matter that I like best deals with the familiar lower- and middle-class American types of today.

He has said that his work reveals 'the emptiness and loneliness of their existence'.[50]

However, 'empty', 'brittle', 'frozen' are adjectives which readily suggest themselves to describe most Superrealist art. To me it marks a climax of the calculating, introverted aspects of sixties movements, and is a sad culmination to the colour and innovativeness of the decade. I like the description of Italian art critic Lea Vergine, 'il rigurgito reazionario'—the reactionary regurgitation![51] However, no more than at any other time in the period we have been studying did this one 'ism' monopolize. If any one figure dominates the world art scene it is Joseph Beuys, who now entered on his period of greatest fame as he presented himself both as research scientist and high priest, creating happenings and installations, and his many works made of felt and fat, old bottles, and practically everything else.[52] Beuys incarnated much of the spirit of the sixties, best and worst, and his eminence is symbolic of the way in which the innovations of the sixties flooded on through the seventies.

## Bullets, Bombs, and a Break-in

For those eager to lead the prosecution in indicting the innovators and the activists of the sixties for the corruption of morals, the subversion of social harmony, and the destruction of public order, the early seventies would seem to provide material for the perfect peroration, the clinching appeal to the jury. Student protests and demonstrations in 1968 and 1969 had set new precedents and established new thresholds: there were none of the same sustained actions in the seventies, but universities and, more particularly in France and Italy, secondary schools had become very uncomfortable places to be.

As in Italy, secondary schools in France remained centres of disturbance: many of the issues of 1968 were kept on the boil, while the government added a couple of new ones of its own. The question of limiting the right of entry of all who achieved the Bac to enter overcrowded and under-resourced universities had been on the agenda for a long time: in 1973 the government brought forward proposals for ending deferment of military service for male pupils who had achieved the right of university entry, and in 1974 it came up with the idea of instituting two Bacs, only one of which would lead to university. In fact, discontent had been almost continuous, but—and this is very important in understanding the crucial point—was seldom straightforwardly dialectical (counter-culture versus established culture, youth versus age). Between June and August 1971 two journalists conducted a series of interviews with 16–18-year-olds. A 17-year-old at the Lycée Grandmont in Tours described how, following a strike in March at another Tours lycée, her school had gone on strike as well, simply out of solidarity.

It was the first time, it was fabulous. It was an explosion... Something very important happened during that strike: the students discovered that they could demonstrate solidarity and thus exercise power. And this right to voice their views which they had seized, they were determined to hold on to it. A 'committee of vigilance' was created, together with a clandestine journal called *Le Trait d'Union* [the standard translation would be *The Hyphen*, though perhaps *The Active Union* might be more resonant here] and then we organized the collection for some striking workers.

Some of the students were expelled; the others then went on hunger strike. The parents of the strikers published a letter supporting their children, commenting on the 'psychological marasmus' and the 'reign of fear' obtaining at the school, and concluding by inviting all parents to join in a demonstration with the pupils. On the day of the demonstration, according to this 17-year-old's account, pupils, parents, teachers, and workers found themselves faced by a police cordon.

On seeing this everybody decided to go to a university restaurant to hold a meeting. It was at that point that the cops charged: people were beaten with batons and chased through the streets. Quite a festival, that! Fifteen pupils were arrested. But the parents saw the kind of repression we were suffering, and the role those in power give to the police. And that proved also that what one hears on the radio every evening is not true, that it is not a problem of generations, parents against young people... [53]

It was never as simple as that, of course. The very next interview is with the 16-year-old daughter of a lorry driver who hated, she said, young people and their protests and demonstrations. On the other side, as it were, several of the pupils admitted to belonging to gangs of a more or less violent nature, and to the prevalence of drug-taking.[54] Trouble in the lycées rumbled on and were the subject of *L'Express's* leading article in the issue of 18–24 March 1974: 'What Do the Lycéens Want?' was the cover headline. Lycéens were not the sole problem: the previous September the same magazine had run an article on youth violence in the suburbs.[55]

On the whole, in 1968 and 1969, most of the violence had been initiated by the police, though among extreme radical elements both language and actions had become increasingly menacing. From 1969 onwards acts of terrorism were being perpetrated by left-wing extremists, briefly in America, on a sustained basis in Italy: civil rights agitation in Northern Ireland became subsumed into a terrorist campaign by the IRA, which moved to the British mainland: a new phase of violent trade union action there provoked a brief fad for posing the question as to whether Britain had become 'ungovernable'.[56] These were not the only unpleasant things happening in the early seventies, though the others—reprehensible behaviour by the president of the United States resulting in his enforced resignation, and a worsening of race relations in Britain and France—could scarcely be blamed on sixties activists.

Terrorism reached its deadliest proportions in West Germany, where the Red Army Faction and its most important component, the Baader-Meinhof gang, were in action from 1968 onwards. Their activities—bombing, robbery, assassination, and kidnap—intensified after 1970, then declined after the arrest of Andreas Baader and some of his leading associates in 1972; after 1974 there was a further intense wave of terrorism culminating in 1977, and including two air hijackings as well as further murders and hostage-taking. The German operations were highly sophisticated, for (often with the help of Soviet finance) the terrorists received training in the Middle East or in Eastern Europe.[57] Red terrorism in Italy, though deadly enough, was never quite so sophisticated or dangerous. Threatening language and violent behaviour had been more widespread in the Italian student movements than in the any of the other three we are concerned with; Italian demonstrations, with their *servizi d'ordine*, paramilitary stewards, were the most militarized. In Italy there was a very real fear of Fascist connections in high places, in both police and politics. Violent Fascist gangs were a palpable presence on the streets. For their part the revolutionary groups, Lotta Continua and Potere Operaio, both constantly at work in student and above all worker demonstrations, openly advocated revolutionary violence. There was a link between the movements of 1968 and 1969 and the main terrorist organization, the Red Brigades *(Brigate Rosse, BR)*, formed in October 1970; but in opting for clandestinity and premeditated terror the Red Brigades, with probably well below 100 members, marked a distinctive break from the student movements, which had operated publicly and carried large numbers of moderate students with them. While the Baader-Meinhof gang had mainly been drawn from the pampered upper class, the Red Brigades drew mainly from the working and lower middle class. Among the leaders, Renato Curcio and Mara Cagol belonged to Maoist groups at Trento University, while Alberto Franceschini had belonged to the Young Communist movement. Many came from Potere Operaio and Lotta Continua, disillusioned that these groups, for all their fiery words, had not brought the revolution any closer.[58]

The first actions of the Red Brigades must have been frightening for the victims, but there was no loss of life. The early attacks concentrated entirely on employers, foremen, or right-wing trade unionists at the major Milan and Turin factories. In September 1971 two incendiary bombs were sent to the personnel director of Sit Siemens, but did no damage. Flyers were distributed at various factories giving the names of those on a Red Brigades proscribed list: in November the car of a Pirelli manager was set on fire. The following March a Sit Siemens manager was kidnapped for about twenty minutes, long enough for his captors to tie on a placard with this statement: 'Macchirini, Idalgo, Fascist manager of Sit Siemens, tried by the BR. The proletarians have taken up arms, for the bosses it is the "beginning of the end".' In November the cars of nine members of the right-wing union at Mirafiori were set on fire in various parts of Milan. In December seven more cars of targeted individuals went up in smoke and flame; messages were left warning 'We have lost patience with Mirafiori and Rivalta [another major factory]. We shall pursue you to your homes.'[59] On 12 February 1973 a commando group of the Red Brigades kidnapped from his house the provincial secretary of the right-wing union CISNAL. After being kept in confinement for several days he was released, but still in chains, and with a placard round his neck indicting him as 'secretary of the Fascist pseudounion'. In June a senior professional engineer for Alfa Romeo was kidnapped. In December the personnel director of the Fiat motor group was taken, and held for eight days before being released. Up until the end of 1973 there were about a dozen incidents of this sort; in May 1972 a bomb exploded at the entrance to Sit Siemens and injured a guard. At the beginning of 1974 the campaign widened, the Red Brigades announcing that from attacking industrial targets they were now going to attack the state itself. Through the kidnapping of the Genoa judge Mario Sossi, in March—a kidnapping which lasted for thirty-five days, Sossi eventually being released unharmed—the Red Brigades achieved national attention, and also the systematic attention of the police. On a number of occasions bullets were exchanged as the police attempted to make arrests; in October 1974 a carabiniere was killed in one of these engagements. The wealthy left-wing publisher, Gian Giacomo Feltrinelli (founder of the archive which has been so useful to me in my researches) had a terrorist organization of his own, the GAP (Group for Partisan Action); in March 1972 he blew himself up in an attempt at dynamiting an electricity pylon near Milan. Another terrorist organization had a brief, inglorious existence: the NAP (Nuclei of the Armed Proletariat) recruited mainly from ex-prisoners and from Lotta Continua.[60]

But there were other continuing sources of violence. Among several disturbances in the south, the longest-lasting and most violent was that which took up most of 1970 and part of 1971 in Reggio Calabria. The cause was not, at first sight, a very noble one. Suffering from chronic underemployment, Reggio Calabria hoped to be named capital of the newly established region of Calabria, thus securing the government jobs which would go with that status. But the gravy train was routed to Catanzara. The protests were led by a Christian Democratic former mayor with the combative name of Pietro Battagli. In the usual way brutal police suppression came first, but subsequently the citizens of Reggio Calabria showed a fine talent for violence, with occupations of the railway station and other main buildings, the establishment of barriers and roadblocks, and a dozen dynamite attacks. Three people were killed.[61] It should always be remembered that this period of instability and terror was inaugurated by right-wing elements with the bombs in Milan and Rome on 12 December 1969. An anti-Fascist demonstration being held in the main square at Brescia on 28 May 1974 was brought to a tragic climax when some of those against whom the demonstration was aimed exploded a bomb, killing eight people. Twelve people were killed on 4 August when right-wingers left a bomb to explode on an international express as it was travelling between Florence and Bologna. There were violent clashes in early 1975 between Fascist gangs and student and left groups. The first to be killed, in Rome, was actually a neo-Fascist sympathizer, a Greek student. Then, in April, a member of the student movement was killed in Milan; during the protest demonstration the next day another left-wing figure was killed by a police vehicle. Matters got worse in Italy before they got better. The 1976 general election was fought against a background of violence, and in 1978 came the kidnap and appallingly cruel murder of the decent, middle-of-the-road but left-inclining politician Aldo Moro. In the actual kidnapping attempt seven policemen were killed.[62]

In America, on the contrary, the left-inspired violence was largely concentrated into 1969 and 1970. But first, the untoward event which seemed to signal the end of the magic of rock, particularly British rock, and of love-in pop concerts. At the Woodstock festival in August 1969 practically everything that could go right had gone right, presenting, as I remarked, an incomplete though not totally inaccurate image of the joyous new world of rock music. At Altamont,

San Francisco, in the final month of the sixties puristically defined, practically everything that could go wrong did go wrong, thus presenting a nightmarish image of the world of rock music and all its denizens, also incomplete, but also far from inaccurate. Like practically all the great triumphs and all the great disasters of the sixties, the Altamont pop festival (in December 1969) was inspired by good intentions. It was not altogether untypical of the age that along with good intentions went some crass decisions. San Francisco enjoys fresh breezes for much of the year; in December its nights are very cold. One can make an immediate contrast between balmy Woodstock and freezing Altamont. There are many good things to say about the Rolling Stones. They went on touring and giving live concerts long after the Beatles, and many other groups, had stopped. In 1969 they had had an outstandingly successful US tour, not least of course, financially. In a gesture of gratitude, they announced a final free concert which, in an expression of recognition of what they owed to the music of the Bay City, would be in the Bay area. Actually, the too-hastily chosen venue was a decrepit disused speedway situated in a run-down district on the other side of the Bay, thirty miles beyond Berkeley. On the advice of the leading San Francisco group, the Grateful Dead, the Stones hired the Hell's Angels to provide 'security' and to equip the Rolling Stones with a suitably demonic personal guard. It was a disastrous choice. Not totally disinterested, as no performers ever were, the Stones were also having a film shot. By the time of their deliberately delayed arrival by helicopter, the Hell's Angels, drunk and high on LSD, were already ruthlessly beating up members of the audience. Soon after Jagger, in his red satin cloak, launched into *Sympathy for the Devil,* he thought he saw a black man in the audience pointing a gun at him. The Hell's Angels pounced on the man and beat and stabbed him to death. There were two other deaths by violence, and a fourth when a drug-bedazed hippie walked into an irrigation ditch and drowned; hundreds were injured.[63]

The first mention of the Weathermen occurred at the SDS convention in Chicago in June 1969, when a manifesto headed by a line from a Bob Dylan song was handed out: 'You don't need a weatherman to know which way the wind blows'.[64] Like the Red Brigades in Italy, the Weathermen were a tiny minority of the utterly disillusioned and pathologically violent: linked to the student movement (the most famous Weatherman was Mark Rudd, the Columbia agitator), they in fact marked a sharp break from the generous emotions which had always informed it. A common note among all of the post-1969 terrorist groups was that of 'anger' or 'rage', of having 'run out of patience'. It sounded nasty in a way in which pre-1968 slogans had not quite managed to do, and it was. The first public performance by the Weathermen came in what they declared as 'Days of Rage', beginning shortly before midnight on Monday 6 October when they blew up a monument to policemen, situated in Chicago's Haymarket Square. Chunks of masonry were blasted into the surroundings, windows shattered. More ominously, a Chicago police official declared, 'We now feel that it is kill or be killed.'[65] Between 8 and 11 October, in the same city, the Weathermen smashed up cars and business property. Thereafter, chief resort was had to high explosives, with another group, Revolutionary Force 9, joining in the series of bombings in New York. The damage to property was enormous, but most of the almost fifty deaths were of Weathermen who blew themselves up in error. The most spectacular example was when a bomb factory in a house in Greenwich Village blew up on 6 March 1970, demolishing the house and killing three bomb-makers. Some students had caught the fever: on 26 February students at the Santa Barbara campus of the University of California burned down a branch of the Bank of America there.[66]

Meantime, the kind of violence perpetrated by the Panthers and other black militants discussed in Chapter 12 intensified, though if ever there was justification for violence, the appalling, utterly inhumane story of 'Soledad Brother' George Jackson provided it. Jackson—black, need I say?—at the age of 18 in 1960 was sentenced to 'one year to life' for driving the getaway car when a friend robbed a petrol station of seventy dollars. The friend was released in 1963, but Jackson was kept in foul conditions, first in Soledad prison, then San Quentin, then, in January 1969, back in Soledad, annual parole boards always turning him down. On 13 January 1970 a new exercise yard was opened on O Wing of Soledad jail. A fight broke out between black and white prisoners. A prison guard opened fire, killing three blacks. Following a verdict of 'justifiable homicide', a white guard was found dying in Jackson's wing, having been beaten up and thrown down one floor. Jackson and two other black prisoners were arrested for murder—together they formed the Soledad Brothers. Technically on a life sentence (for being involved in the theft of seventy dollars), Jackson now faced a mandatory death sentence. On 7 August 1970 Jackson's younger brother, Jonathan, led an attempt to kidnap Judge Harold Haley and four other hostages from the Court House at San Rafael, California, in order to force the release of the Soledad Brothers. The police foiled the attempt in a bloody shoot-out which resulted in the death of Jonathan and two accomplices, and of Judge Haley. Jackson had been moved again to San Quentin: on 21 August 1971 he was shot dead in an alleged escape attempt, there being a well-founded belief that the prison authorities had conspired to murder him.[67] But if centuries of prejudice and punishment did not change much, the world outside really was yielding to measured judgement: in April 1972 the other two Soledad Brothers were acquitted on all charges.[68]

The massive slaughter which, for protesters, fully justified their own minor acts of terrorism, the Vietnam war, took another twist when it became known that American troops had moved into Cambodia. It was in protest against this that students throughout the country staged a new set of demonstrations. At Kent State University, Ohio, and also at Jackson State, a black college in Mississippi, the forces of law and order demonstrated once more that when it came to sheer callous disregard for human life they could easily eclipse the Weathermen, the Red Brigades, and the Baader-Meinhoff gang. The events of 4 May 1970 at Kent State stand out as the most horrific and the most appallingly wasteful of promising young life in all the sixties turmoil in the United States, and as a terrible indictment of the evils of American society against which students and radicals had been continuously protesting. Absolutely without justification, members of the Ohio national guard opened fire on the students, killing four and wounding nine. On 15 May police shot and killed two students at Jackson State and wounded nine others.[69] Throughout this same period, the horrors of the Vietnam war were being brought to the American people in a new way: from 12 November 1969 to 29 March 1971 Lieutenant William Calley was before a court martial on the charge of the massacre of at least twenty civilians at My Lai in South Vietnam. Calley was found guilty, but this scarcely expiated the systematic use over many years of the most horrific methods and weapons against civilians by the American forces.[70] On 13 June 1971 the *New York Times* began publishing documents, leaked by a former Pentagon official, Daniel Elsberg, which confirmed that Presidents Kennedy and Johnson had consistently misled the public over their intentions in Vietnam. These became known as the 'Pentagon Papers'.

Richard Nixon had not instigated the disastrous American involvement in Vietnam, though it is possible that had Hubert Humphrey won in 1968 there might have been a scaling down sooner, and a more forceful search for a means of ending the military operations. Nixon was re-elected president in November 1972 in a landslide victory. Nemesis was shortly to overtake him. Already in June his agents had, still unknown to anyone, carried out a break-in at the Democratic national headquarters in the Watergate building in Washington. During the following year, thanks in part to some brilliant investigative journalism, the essential features of what became known as the Watergate Affair became known, and a senate committee was appointed to investigate it fully. The upshot was the resignation of Nixon in 1974. It cannot be said that Nixon was brought down by radicals and protesters, even in the indirect way it can be said that de Gaulle was brought down by the events of 1968. The strategy of Nixon and his henchmen, indeed, had been to draw exaggerated attention to demonstrations and protests, in order to make, rather successfully, an appeal to middle America.[71] So, if we were to concentrate on politics, and on the more dramatic events, we might well conclude that America, in the immediate aftermath of the sixties, was in a sorry mess. But politics and events are not everything and, in the development of human societies, not the most important things.

That is an issue I shall return to at the end of the chapter. Meantime: perhaps Britain was immune to the rage of shooting and bombing? Britain had its own Angry Brigade, modelled, distantly, on the Weathermen. During 1970, this minuscule organization exploded several bombs, though always with the apparent intention of avoiding any loss of life or limb—most notably two outside the house of the home secretary, Robert Carr, and one at that cathedral of innovatory sixties fashion and consumer enjoyment, Biba.[72] Unrest continued sporadically at universities, and even reached some schools. The most noteworthy episode involving students was in Cambridge, where, at the end of a 'Greek Week' designed to confer respectability on the shabby and cruel dictatorship of the colonels, some 400 students picketed the reception at the Garden House hotel on Friday 13 February. The arrival of the police, combined with the presence of some socialist militants, produced a flurry of flying bricks and an unplanned invasion of the hotel; among those injured were a university proctor and a policeman. Six students were arrested at the time, followed, on information received from university authorities, by a further thirteen members (including one don) of the University Socialist Society. At the end of June twelve were put on trial at Hertford and found guilty of 'unlawful assembly' and 'riot'. Judge Melford Stevenson was no representative of measured judgement: handing down sentences ranging from several months in Borstal to eighteen months in prison, he made it clear that his anger was not directed at the younger generation alone; the sentences, he said, would have been even more severe were he not aware that the defendants had been exposed to 'the evil influence of some senior members of your university'.[73] Reforms of university procedures were taking place piecemeal, but in many places of learning comfortable relations between administration, academics, and students were still not fully established. There were troubles in 1972, then again in 1974, most notably at the University of Essex.[74]

Much more menacing than continuing discomfort in the universities was the new violent phase in industrial relations. During the miners' strike in 1972 'flying pickets' were deployed to prevent coal movements. There was violence at the Saltley coke depot in Birmingham in February 1972; in an unfortunate accident, a picket was killed under the wheels of a lorry. That summer there was further violence in the building workers' strike: the brutal intimidation by pickets at Shrewsbury resulted in arrests and prison sentences. The IRA had already embarked on a terrorist campaign in Northern Ireland; but it was unarmed, peacefully demonstrating civilians, thirteen of them, who were shot dead by the Parachute Regiment on 30 January 1972, 'Bloody Sunday'. The IRA began operations on the British mainland, five civilians being killed in a bomb attack at Aldershot. An intense phase of IRA attacks was initiated in July 1974, when a bomb explosion at the Tower of London killed one woman and badly injured forty-one children. In October and November there were IRA pub bombings near army barracks in Guildford and Woolwich: seven were killed. Then in Birmingham in November, in a horrific pub attack, twenty-one were killed and 162 injured. As the race issue became ever more prominent (see below), the right-wing National Front grew in strength. Yet a further civilian fatality occurred in June, in Red Lion Square, London, when Kevin Gateley was killed as a Trotskyist counter-demonstration met a right-wing National Front demonstration. During the miners' strike of 1973–4 the country was reduced to a three-day working week, with power cuts and periods of darkness: 'Is Britain ungovernable?', 'Who governs Britain?' seemed reasonable questions.[75] But these were surface and temporary issues, while in the depths of society more profound changes continued to work themselves out.

France had its clandestine 'angry' organization as well, Action Directe.[76] But violence in France was mainly associated with an abysmal new phase in race relations. Indeed, the greatest failures of those who had sought progress and change (apart from the energy and resources wasted on the futile pursuit of a revolution which was never in prospect) were in housing and, in Britain and France, in race relations. The Franco-Algerian accord of 10 April 1964 set agreed limits on Algerian immigration and was accompanied by similar accords with Mali, Mauretania, and Senegal. An expanded social action fund after 1966 assumed responsibility for all foreign workers.[77] For the Algerian immigrant and his family, whom we left crammed into the cells of an ancient hospital, conditions improved when he was housed in a building specially built for foreign workers, theoretically in transit:

We had water, an interior WC. We cooked with butane gas, and, in winter, we kept warm with oil. It was fine. There were no showers, but we got by...

He reckoned he was better off than those living in the HLM, public housing at low rent for French workers (such as those inhabited by the characters in Christiane Rochefort's novel or the individuals in the Bobigny saga). Facilities were fewer, but there were no stairs to climb. 'Besides,' he said, 'I have a large washing-machine'—and there were gardens.[78] Not magnificent, but adequate. Then suddenly conditions worsened. With regard to the French events of 1968 it is possible to say that in practically every area of French life there were, indirectly if not directly, in the longer term if not immediately, benefits of some sort. For North African immigrants, on the contrary, the effects were an almost unmitigated disaster. Wherever they could in any way be suspected of involvement in any of the strikes or other actions, they were instantly deported. Mass expulsions was one part of government reaction; the other was a unilateral limitation, on 1 July 1968, of the number of immigrants coming in from Algeria to 1,000 per month. In December, with the Algerians wanting a total of 50,000 a year, a negotiated total of 35,000 was reached. In February plans were adopted whereby Algerian immigrants would have been permitted only temporary stays in France; since no such limitations were proposed on European immigrants, this would have been the beginning of a selective, racist policy—however, it was not put into practice.

   An appalling though all too predictable accident in January 1970 galvanized the government into action. A five-room building in the working-class district of Aubervilliers housed fifty immigrants. Because the landlord had not paid the bills, electricity supplies were cut off. To keep warm the inhabitants were reduced to lighting fires of wood and charcoal: while asleep, five North Africans were asphyxiated from fumes from one of these fires. The prime minister, Jacques Chaban-Delmas, visited the area and promised immediate action. The Viveen Act provided funds with which the government could buy up the *bidonvilles* and raze them to the ground; that, of course, simply made the problems of homeless immigrants even worse. During 1970 and 1971 the proto-terrorist groups forming in France, as elsewhere, staged commando raids on the government offices which dealt with immigrants.[79] In February 1972 the Fontenat Circular continued the policy of trying to clean up immigrant housing, while again bearing down very heavily on the immigrants themselves: it attempted to insist that only those who already had decent housing, as well as work prospects, could enter the country. Clearly there was a recognition within the government that direct action against racism was required: in July 1972 it enacted the first law since the Second World War outlawing discriminatory practices. At the same time, however, the prominence being given to racial issues was oxygen for the neo-fascist New Order, which in June 1973 launched a campaign demanding an end to immigration. By the worst of misfortune, it was just as this campaign was beginning to work its mischief that a mentally disturbed Arab killed a bus driver in Marseille. Immediately there was a massive outbreak of violence against North Africans, resulting in at least eleven deaths during the period 29 August-21 September; the police made no arrests.[80]

   The first chapter of a contemporary biography of Giscard d'Estaing, elected president in 1974, is entitled 'Le Kennedy Gaulois' ('The Gallic Kennedy').[81] Giscard, conservative but non-Gaullist, sought to project an image of youthful energy combating the immobilism of Gaullism as Kennedy had sought to combat the inertia of fifties America. The parallel has many resonances, not all intended by Giscard and his admirers. Kennedy, reluctantly, had made some important interventions on behalf of black civil rights, but scarcely carried through a transformation. Giscard, who created the post of secretary of state for women, certainly altered the official rhetoric of race relations (and also created the post of secretary of state for immigration). In a speech of 28 February 1975, welcomed by reformers as genuine in the intentions it expressed, the president featured the 'immigrant who, being a part of our national productive community, should have in the French society that I am trying to organize, a place which will be at once dignified, humane, and equitable'.[82] But, critically, it was of 'the immigrant', not of 'the new French citizen', that he spoke. Immigration was actually temporarily suspended while a programme of building low-cost housing for immigrants was instituted. Racism continued to be deeply embedded in French society, and right-wing racist organizations continued to prosper. No very powerful signs of multiculturalism, it must be admitted; still, by the mid-1990s the French international rugby team was being captained by an Algerian.

Under Home Secretary Roy Jenkins, sponsor of so much of the 'civilized society' legislation, Britain in 1968 seemed to be on the way towards also formulating civilized policies with regard to race relations. Persuasive propaganda was being disseminated by another couple of important sixties voluntary organizations, the Campaign Against Racial Discrimination and the Institute of Race Relations. In a series of speeches Jenkins tried to weaken the obsession with immigration and turn attention towards questions of discrimination and integration. A phrase from the speech he gave on 23 May 1966 deserves to be treasured in any anthology of 'sayings of the sixties': he offered a vision of integration 'not as a flattening process of assimilation but of equal opportunity, accompanied by cultural diversity, in an atmosphere of mutual tolerance',[83] a vision, in fact, of a true multicultural society. Then a double dose of contingency sabotaged the entire optimistic process. Before the fruits of his labours reached the statute-book as the Race Relations Act of 1968, which extended the previous act by covering discrimination in employment, housing, credit, banking, and insurance facilities, Jenkins was moved to the post of chancellor of the exchequer, being replaced by James Callaghan. The Race Relations Board was strengthened and the Community Relations Commission established to replace the old National Committee for Commonwealth Immigrants, the new title clearly expressing the new emphasis. But Callaghan did not have Jenkins's patrician sensitivities to the appeal of a multiracial society; his attitudes to race were very much those of the conservative British working class. Then an equally virulent form of racism struck, the racism of an independent black African country. The adoption by Kenya in 1968 of an Africanization programme meant that the Asians long resident there, who had passports as citizens of the Commonwealth, immediately sought refuge in Britain. As at the end of the fifties, the government panicked over the prospect of a further flood of immigrants, and in February 1968 a new immigration bill was rushed through Parliament: this simply took away from passport-holders the right of free entry unless they could demonstrate some clear family connection with Britain—relatively easy for whites from Australia or Canada, practically impossible for Asians. The rate of entry for East African Asians was reduced to 1,500 per year.[84]

Simultaneously, the front-bench Conservative politician Enoch Powell, once thought to be on the left of the party, took up the race issue in the most mischievous and unscrupulous manner. He delivered speeches in which he spoke of defenceless old ladies in areas with growing immigrant populations having excrement pushed through their letter-boxes, and on

20 April 1968, while the stronger and more comprehensive Race Relations Bill was actually being discussed in Parliament, he delivered a speech in Birmingham in which he envisaged a staggering growth of the non-white population: 'Like the Romans, I seem to see "the river Tiber flowing with much blood".' This went far beyond the measured views of the Conservative leadership, and Powell was instantly dismissed from his position in the Conservative shadow cabinet.[85] However, a Gallup poll showed that 75 per cent of the population were broadly sympathetic to the sentiments expressed by Powell, and there were a number of working-class demonstrations in his support. The racist National Front assumed a more prominent and more confident stance. During 1969 and 1970 physical attacks on Asians reached a new peak.[86] All of these developments were noted in the conclusion to the report which the Institute of Race Relations had been compiling since 1963, *Colour and Citizenship*. After stressing the need for much greater direct government intervention, the Conclusion referred both to the positive policies embodied in the Race Relations Act and to the negative ones embodied in the Immigration Act:

> We are very much encouraged by the constructive action taken in some fields in the course of the last year, while this Report was being written; we are also encouraged by the existence of new agencies with the capacity to intervene constructively. But in other directions the situation seems profoundly disturbing. We refer here particularly to the open sore of immigration policy. While this wound remains unhealed, the basis for constructive action in other directions is constantly undermined. Like nineteenth-century British governments in their Irish policy, contemporary administrations have followed a policy of 'kicks and kindness'. It is the kicks that those at the receiving end tend to remember...

The report was a clear expression of sanity and compassion in what was admitted to be a difficult subject, almost the last expression of sanity and compassion before the politicians allowed the issue to run out of their control. The report concluded with a touching, if not altogether justified, expression of faith in a continuing moral leadership vested in Great Britain:

> A society which has provided the model for other societies by evolving democratic forms that respect the individual, and which has known how to combine tolerance with dissent, now has the chance to set a further example by proving that men of many races can live together in justice and harmony...[87]

That was a fine aspiration, expressed not by radical protesters but by weighty figures on the liberal wing of the establishment. But Britain was not in fact setting much of an example, although, as an Institute of Race Relations survey brought out once more, the majority of Britons were not actively racist: according to the answers to the institute's 1967 questionnaire, in areas with a relatively high proportion of 'coloured residents' over a third of the white population showed no prejudice, while a further two-fifths made only 'an isolated prejudiced response'; a further sixth could be regarded as prejudiced, though (in the somewhat opaque words of the report) they were prepared to 'make exceptions', leaving a tenth whose antipathy to 'coloured people' seemed to be unconditional.[88] What was manifestly lacking was any kind of active support for the multiculturalism advocated by Roy Jenkins and expressed in *Colour and Citizenship*. And the crude fact was that racist attacks continued unchecked, partly at least because of the racist attitudes entrenched within the police. The Select Committee on Race Relations and Immigration carried out an investigation in 1971. This found that police officers held the belief that blacks were more involved in crime than other sections of the community, despite the objective finding of the committee:

> Of all the police forces from whom we took evidence not one had found that crime committed by black people was proportionately greater than that by the rest of the population. Indeed in many places it was somewhat less.[89]

An investigation published in 1973 found that many policemen considered 'niggers were in the main... pimps and layabouts living off what we pay in taxes'.[90] Asian organizations, however, reported that relations with the police were cordial; Asians, it was clear, avoided situations which might lead to confrontation with the police.[91] At the opposite extreme were young Afro-Caribbeans whose relations with the police were consistently hostile and explosive. A survey among West Indians living in London in 1972, commissioned by the British Caribbean Association, found that almost all West Indians believed that the police discriminated against them, with 20 per cent claiming to have had direct experience of unfair treatment.[92]

At the beginning of the seventies, government preoccupation had swung away from issues of integration and of racial prejudice back to immigration itself: in 1971 the Conservative government, returned to power in 1970, passed a new Immigration Act which was still more overtly racist than its predecessor, and very nearly brought Britain into line with France in imposing immigration controls which openly discriminated against non-whites. The original bill had the infamous 'grandfather clause', which required the prospective immigrant to have had a grandfather resident in this country; this clause was actually taken out of the text of the act, but in 1973 sneaked back in again in the 'rules' by which the act was to be interpreted.[93] Only at the end of the fifties had Britain begun to be aware of the problems involved in having several racial groups living within the one society. Briefly, a version of what the boons might be of a genuinely multicultural society had opened up. But there is no shirking the fact that, at the end of the long sixties, in Britain, as in France, the 'dominant question of our century' was very far from resolution.

We have been mainly looking at the evil and unsavoury aspects of the early seventies, including terrorism of left and right and Fascist and racist outrages, though with the very positive development of growing liberation for gays. But what was important about the beginning of the seventies was that more people than ever before were thinking and acting for themselves. Overall, despite the absurdities and the outrages, this meant a notable gain with respect to the quality of life of most people. That is the topic to which I return in my final chapter.

# 15

# Living Life to the Full

## *Incomes and Aspirations*

In the early seventies there was tension and violence in all four of the countries we are studying; there was much intolerance, and there were areas of extreme poverty and deprivation. But over the countries as a whole, in all classes, races, age groups, the vast majority of people were better fed, had more varied and interesting lives, were less subject to stress than the analogous populations at the end of the fifties. Living standards were still highest in the United States, but the catching-up process within the European countries had accelerated considerably; gaps between south and north, in both the USA and in Italy, had decreased. Modern amenities, with respect both to domestic life and to leisure activities, were more widely diffused than ever before. There are problems with all such generalizations, of course, particularly with the more basically economic ones, those concerned with purchasing power. There had, in the different countries, been fluctuations in the sixties, and in the autumn of 1973 there came the biggest threat to standards of living in the West since the Second World War: the international oil crisis, and the doubling of oil prices. In many ways this event—or perhaps its first significant repercussions in 1974—can be taken as marking the end of an epoch which began in the later fifties. But in fact, in the West—though profits fell, and entrepreneurs, relatively speaking, suffered—ordinary workers, thanks in part to the protection they had secured in the sixties, maintained and improved their real incomes.

It is congruent with the cultural changes taking place both earliest and most harmoniously in Britain that, of the European nations, the British should have expressed the highest sense of optimism and satisfaction, even though the British economy was in many ways the weakest. Both the general trend and interesting comparisons between countries emerged from an EEC

687

survey of 1973.[1] The first table concerns levels of satisfaction in the different countries (the pedantic may cavil at the phrases 'level of satisfaction', 'level of optimism', and 'level of happiness', but historians have to use the evidence that is available, and mine here is taken from scientific surveys which recorded the attitudes of real individuals in language these people themselves accepted) (see Tables 15.1-4).

**Table 15.1** *Levels of satisfaction*

| Level of satisfaction | EEC | France | Germany | Great Britain | Italy |
|---|---|---|---|---|---|
| Very satisfied | 21 | 15 | 16 | 33 | 8 |
| Quite satisfied | 58 | 62 | 66 | 52 | 57 |
| Quite dissatisfied | 16 | 17 | 15 | 11 | 27 |
| Not satisfied | 4 | 4 | 2 | 3 | 7 |
| Don't know | 1 | 2 | 1 | 1 | 1 |

**Table 15.2** *Levels of satisfaction with regard to particular areas* (+100 to −100)

| Area | EEC | France | Germany | Great Britain | Italy |
|---|---|---|---|---|---|
| Relationship with others | 54 | 49 | 44 | 68 | 42 |
| Housing | 47 | 50 | 42 | 56 | 29 |
| Work | 37 | 40 | 28 | 48 | 19 |
| Leisure | 25 | 16 | 26 | 44 | −6 |
| Education of children | 19 | 8 | 20 | 31 | −6 |
| Position in society | 18 | 30 | 21 | 9 | −4 |
| Relations between generations | 10 | 16 | −2 | 16 | 2 |
| Income | 6 | 1 | 10 | 6 | −12 |
| State of society | −4 | −10 | 9 | 1 | −28 |
| State of democracy | −14 | −10 | −8 | −37 | 8 |

**Table 15.3** *Reactions to changes in the previous five years*

| Level of satisfaction | EEC | France | Germany | Great Britain | Italy |
|---|---|---|---|---|---|
| More | 42 | 35 | 40 | 45 | 48 |
| Less | 24 | 26 | 21 | 31 | 25 |
| No change | 32 | 36 | 36 | 22 | 25 |
| Don't know | 2 | 3 | 3 | 2 | 2 |

**Table 15.4** *Levels of optimism about what will happen in the succeeding five years*

| Level of optimism | EEC | France | Germany | Great Britain | Italy |
|---|---|---|---|---|---|
| Very optimistic | 13 | 14 | 8 | 17 | 14 |
| Quite optimistic | 36 | 38 | 31 | 31 | 39 |
| Pessimistic | 34 | 32 | 41 | 34 | 26 |
| Don't know | 17 | 16 | 17 | 18 | 21 |

In Tables 15.1 and 15.2 the Italians emerge as overall the least satisfied, yet Tables 15.3 and 15.4 show them as both most satisfied with the changes of the previous five years and most optimistic about the next five, supporting what I have already suggested about change coming relatively late in Italy, as well as the perception that, however horrific the early 'years of the bullet', life for ordinary Italians was continuing to get fuller and freer. The growth in the percentage of Italian families possessing the main consumer goods is striking (see Table 15.5).

**Table 15.5** *Ownership of consumer goods in Italy*

|  | % of families in | |
|---|---|---|
|  | 1965 | 1975 |
| Owning TV sets | 49 | 92 |
| Owning refrigerators | 55 | 94 |
| Owning washing machines | 23 | 76 |

While Britain emerges in the first two EEC tables as overall the most satisfied of nations, it is the most sharply divided with respect to the previous five years and the coming five years (in both cases both the positive and the negative ratings are relatively high), suggesting that already in Britain there was a perception among a substantial number of people that the best days of the sixties were now over. In the first two EEC tables the British also stand out as being the ones least satisfied both with society as a whole and with their own position in it, suggesting that perceptions of the continuing inequalities of British society were strong (despite the generally high ratings, relatively speaking, for relations with others, housing, work, leisure, education, and relations between the generations).

For France we have some particularly illuminating material from early 1969 commissioned by *L'Express* from the French Institute for Public Opinion, and presenting comparisons with results of a similar survey conducted in 1957 (see Tables 15.6-15.11).[2] The particular population sampled was that of the ten million or so in the age group 15–21. Figures never quite speak for themselves, but apart from the slight overall swing towards representing themselves as 'happy' as against 'not very happy', the truly striking thing is the substantially increased numbers giving the positive and unambiguous response of 'very happy'. The general impression given by responses to this question is fortified by the answers shown in Table 15.7. Apart from the actual figures, the much greater positiveness is particularly noteworthy.

**Table 15.6** *How the interviewees rated their own happiness*

|  | 1969 (%) | 1957 (%) |
|---|---|---|
| Very happy | 35 | 24 |
| Quite happy | 54 | 61 |
| Not very happy | 9 | 14 |

**Table 15.7** *Opinion as to whether it was 'good luck or bad luck to live in this epoch'*

|  | 1969 (%) | 1957 (%) |
|---|---|---|
| More good | 77 | 53 |
| More bad | 13 | 18 |
| No opinion | 10 | 29 |

**Table 15.8** *Answers to the question, 'In material terms, what do you feel deprived of?'*

|  | 1969 (%) | 1957 (%) |
|---|---|---|
| Holidays | 30 | 42 |
| Distractions | 30 | 35 |
| Personal transport | 20 | 39 |
| Housing | 15 | 27 |
| Clothing | 13 | 18 |
| Furniture | 13 | 22 |
| Mod cons | 11 | 33 |
| Food | 0 | 2 |
| Nothing | 35 | 10 |

**Table 15.9** *Answers to the question, 'Do you feel free?'*

|  | Yes (%) | No (%) |
|---|---|---|
| In relations with parents | 85 | 11 |
| In employing leisure | 80 | 18 |
| In love relationships | 78 | 8 |
| In purchases | 71 | 27 |
| In choice of job | 64 | 26 |
| In the exercise of your occupation, educational or professional | 62 | 26 |
| In politics | 58 | 23 |

**Table 15.10** *Answers to the question, 'Can people like you influence the future of France, or are you at the mercy of events?'*

|  | 1969 (%) | 1957 (%) |
|---|---|---|
| Can influence the future of France | 32 | 20 |
| At the mercy of events | 62 | 72 |

*Source: L'Express, 24 Feb.–2 Mar. 1969.*

**Table 15.11** *American opinion of what was harmful to women*

|  | Harmful (%) | Not very harmful (%) |
|---|---|---|
| Nudes in *Playboy*, etc. | 43 | 55 |
| Cracks about blondes | 32 | 67 |
| Men calling females 'girls', not 'women' | 31 | 65 |
| Beauty competitions | 17 | 79 |

*Source:* Opinion poll results published in Claire Masnata-Rubattel, *La Révolte des américaines: analyse du féminisme contemporaine* (Paris, 1972).

The next question concerned material circumstances and possession of consumer goods and services (see Table 15.8). The biggest change is in the realm of 'mod cons'—one of my main arguments throughout this book has been the perhaps rather unexciting one that one of the most significant achievements of society in the sixties was the bringing of the basic amenities of civilized living to the vast majority of the people. The next biggest change is in regard to 'personal transport': for good or for ill a major element in the growth of private freedom in the sixties was the private motor vehicle. It is a condemnation of the austere policies of both the Gaullist government and the private companies that holidays still stood at the top of the list of deprivations. 'Distractions' refers to entertainments and leisure activities of all sorts: can we perhaps blame the French people themselves for being unwilling to direct a greater proportion of their incomes in this direction, or is this a measure of persisting, or maybe even increasing, poverty of life in the provinces? One can only guess at the different (and quite possibly self-cancelling and contradictory) components going to make up the figures here.

Interviewees were then asked the question, 'Do you feel free?' This question had no counterpart in the 1957 survey, so the responses, rather impressive testimony none the less in support of what I have been saying about the sixties as essentially an era of increasing personal freedom, refer only to 1969 (see Table 15.9). The 'no opinions' have been excluded (but can be worked out by simple arithmetic): it is noteworthy that these account for only 4 per cent in the affirmation that relationships within the family were being steadily liberated. The biggest 'no' score, and also the lowest 'no opinion' one, relates to 'purchases': more than a quarter of the French people still lack the freedom—presumably because insufficiently affluent—to purchase all that their hearts desire (echoes of Perec's *Les Choses!*). There are relatively low positive scores for the closely inter-related 'choice of job' and 'exercise of occupation': that, one might say, is life, though the scores are surely high compared with what would have been recorded by previous generations. Politics gets the lowest positive score, though also the highest 'no opinion' score, suggesting (once more) that for most people the decisions of daily life are what are really important. This result can be amplified with the results of a further question (see Table 15.10) specially helpful since in this case again a comparison can be made with 1957. It is not surprising that a majority still felt that they had no influence over events; but the shift since 1957 is sufficiently sizeable to support my claims that, whatever the continuing privacy of the issues of ordinary social life, people were becoming more knowledgeable, more aware of their own potential.

*L'Express* supported the tables with direct quotations from interviewees. As sources these can bear less weight of interpretation than the statistical tables, but since they do not conflict with the quantitative evidence, and are indeed corroborated in other discursive sources, they are worthy of citation here. First, feelings about living in this particular epoch. A barber commented: 'The world is in the midst of change. That is what makes life more exciting.' A printer spoke of 'a prodigiously exciting and interesting era'; youth, he said, 'understands that it is much more free than its elders, and that if it wishes, many opportunities await it'. To a student, this was 'A sensational era, when everything is in question. This generation must, if it is to survive in this enticing world, find new values.' Another student recorded his belief that he had had 'a "sacred chance". My father is a worker, twenty or thirty years ago, I would certainly not have undertaken university level studies.' 'Everything is possible,' said an agricultural expert, 'because of the freedom of spirit which permeates the epoch.' An architect and a professional engineer each put it epigrammatically: 'Epics occur daily,' declared the former; 'It is the springtime of knowledge,' said the latter.

With reference to the questions of happiness and of relations within the family, the responses of three teenagers are of particular interest. First, a girl at a lycée in Marseille: 'I am following quite normally my studies in a lycée which I like. I can discuss things very freely with my parents, who have a very full understanding of the development of young people.' A boy of 15 from Toulon sounded particularly self-satisfied: 'I reckon I am good-looking, quite intelligent, am working quite well, I have good and kind parents, and I know how to accept earthly happiness.' The third is a boy of sixteen-and-a-half from Châlons-sur-Marne: 'I will have the opportunity of going to university and my parents respect my political ideas, leaving me with considerable freedom in my leisure time.'

The whole question of family relationships, set within the context of class, was thoroughly explored in a survey carried out between March and July 1971 on behalf of the Centre for Research and Documentation on Consumer Behaviour. The survey concentrated particularly on the question of women working, and the attitudes towards this of married women and of their husbands. A first finding here was that the most radical marriages, with the wife working full-time, even when she had very young children, were often among those who had risen out of modest origins into quite well-paid employment. The married women most hostile to work outside the home were those enduring the worst conditions: wives of manual workers with many children. They secured the least employment outside the home, and when they did work they got the lowest pay. In general, it was concluded, opposition to women's work increased as one went down the social scale. A large number of women, particularly in the middle classes, were neither strongly for nor strongly against taking a job. Men at all social levels were more opposed to women's employment than were women themselves. This hostility could affect outcomes, the report said, since in the case of conflict the man's view usually prevailed. None the less, women's employment had accelerated greatly during the previous decade, women's employment being the highest in the managerial and executive class. The main exception was agriculture, where women's employment had formerly been high, but was now falling steadily. Among younger women the existence of young children was becoming less and less of a barrier to taking up employment, and 'the most revealing phenomenon was the rapid spread of work among the well-off categories'. In fact, in the higher classes the wife's view was now tending to prevail, while in the working class the husband's views were still prevailing. The survey concluded that while the overall level of female employment had not changed greatly between 1962 and 1968, more and more young women with children were taking up employment, and there had been spectacular growth among the upper middle classes. Women who worked also had more other activities ('distractions'!).[3]

What, during the first sorties of the new feminism, was the state of consciousness of American women across the Union? 'The Virginia Slims American Women's Opinion Poll' (the title a reminder, incidentally, that nobody as yet was seriously challenging the status of tobacco as an adjunct to the good life), conducted by Harris in 1970, reported that a 'majority' of American women were 'satisfied' with their condition, but that 51 per cent (not a staggering statistic, though perhaps a percipient one) thought their opinion did not count for very much, while two out of five (rather depressing if taken at face value—but perhaps to be seen as a token of new aspirations) 'never' did what they wished to in life. In another Harris Poll, this time published in the *Washington Post* on 20 March 1971, women were asked whether or not they supported the current efforts of the women's liberation movement to improve women's conditions: those under 30 were 48 per cent for and 40 per cent against; those between 30 and 39 were 41 per cent for and 45 per cent against; those over 50 were 37 per cent for and 46 per cent against. Overall the figure was finely balanced: 42 per cent for, 43 per cent against. But definitely, as suggested in Chapter 13, things were on the move: an analogous poll reported in the *New York Times* of 24 March 1972 revealed a truly substantial change: 48 per cent to 36 per cent. My larger concern in this book, however, is changing consciousness among both women and men. Americans of both sexes were questioned as to what was harmful to women, yielding the results shown in Table 15.11. Fifteen years before, to the vast majority of Americans of both sexes such matters would have been non-issues. The pointer to the future was that they—and particularly the third question—were now up for serious discussion.

Changing sexual morality among the student generation has already come up frequently. Towards the end of 1974 *Epoca* was moved to ask, 'Does sin exist any more?'

During the last few years there has been a radical upset in the moral rules which regulate our everyday life. Practically none of the Ten Commandments are observed any longer. Sexual taboos have gone. The idea of abortion has grown along with the values of justice, authenticity, and participation... Young people no longer give much recognition to the traditional sins; but in their consciousness the sense of natural justice has become much more profound.[4]

Some interviews conducted by a female journalist with French girls and young women between the ages of 16 and 23 indicate emancipated, rational, attitudes, but no signs of conceding to the 'tyranny of coitus' which some feminists perceived as having replaced the older sexual taboos. A 19-year-old secretary from a working-class background stated that she had no objections to sex before marriage, though she herself was still a virgin: she had many propositions, but did not like being taken for a sex object. A 16-year-old at a lycée, on the other hand, was sleeping with her boyfriend but, as she explained very carefully, she was making sure that her parents, though upper-middle-class professionals, were not aware of this.[5] An opinion poll in 1971 among French 15–20-year-olds posed the question: 'Do you think a man and a woman living together ought to marry?' Opinion was against the proposition, though perhaps less overwhelmingly than might have been expected. Only 17 per cent gave a direct 'yes'; 28 per cent took what might well be regarded as the highly rational line that 'it would be better if they did', while avoiding any sense of compulsion. However, on the other side, 46 per cent were far from taking a strong line, simply saying that marriage should not be forced on the couple, with only 9 per cent giving a positive no, saying that marriage would be 'useless'.[6] A 1973 survey of 13–17-year-olds suggested considerable sophistication among this age group in the finding, not of strong moral stands one way or another about marriage, but that 67 per cent were simply worried about the lack of solidity and durability in that institution.[7]

Two young French factory workers, interviewed by François Cerutti in 1972, expressed hostility to traditional sex roles, but some recognition that they would be difficult to avoid. Josette said that marriage was not worth talking about, her interest was 'in living with someone': 'But being free all the same, doing what one wants to. I have no wish to be under the domination of a man, in most cases it turns out like that.' Agnès continued: 'It doesn't matter how, but if you live with someone you have to take a job, because if you don't work and you stay in the house, automatically you will be obliged to do the house work.'[8]

Against my earlier rather fragmentary evidence of 'happy' young people, contented in their relationships with their parents, one must place the testimony of a survey conducted in 1972–3 by Michèle Aumont among 16–25-year-olds. Aumont found their most characteristic feature a lack of any respect for their parents, their teachers, or the educational system. 'All adults', she reported, 'are on trial.' She noted a libertarian attitude towards sex, and contempt for the traditional romanticism of the highly conventional and sentimental 1971 Hollywood film *Love Story* ('golden age' or not, Hollywood's preoccupation, inevitably, was box-office appeal):

> Among the young people I met, many had no hesitation in dismissing it as a story seen through rose-coloured spectacles, and above all considering it as 'a swindle in which the love story was written by a computer'.[9]

Such sentiments recall the sort of things young people were saying during the formation of youth subculture at the very beginning of the sixties. This book is not exclusively about constant change and continuing acceleration towards extremes; it is also about the reiteration, more and more insistently, of certain themes.

In Italy, Rivolta Femminile sponsored some interviews between October 1970 and October 1971 with two cohorts of schoolgirls, the first of 11–12 and the second of 13–14. The interviews with the younger children struck me as being very contrived, but some interesting points emerge from those with the 13–14-year-olds, identified as 'B', 'D', 'F', and so on:

694

B: But what I want to say is, weren't our mothers girls like us? Didn't they have the same problems as us?... Of course, they had the same problems as us when they were girls, perhaps even worse, since their parents were even more severe with them, so I don't know why today, having had their problems as children, they are so unsympathetic to us. I am going to keep a diary of how things seem to me now, so that I can note down some advice. Then when I'm grown up I will look it up so that I can remember how I used to think so that I can be more sympathetic towards my children.

F: Listen, that's a mistake, my mother also makes, because she always says to me: 'You realize that I had the same problems as you at your age, but now that I am grown up and have some experience' (we are always being told about experience!)... she says: 'I have thought about it and you mustn't do what I did.'

The discussion turned to the attitudes of men, with the girl identified as 'D' taking up the discussion: 'Men have always wanted to show themselves as superior to women, and that fact has always existed, not just today... it is only we today who discuss this problem.'[10] The discussion switched to the question of virginity. Some of the girls expressed some puzzlement over whether virginity was an anatomical phenomenon (a 'Veil inside us') or a condition. Apparently they were continually pestered by boys asking them if they were still virgins. It was agreed that a girl would have to be very self-confident to respond as one was reputed to have done, by asking the same question of the boys.[11]

But were there not millions of families across our four countries where basic standards were so low that it is absurd to speak of living life to the full, of emancipated attitudes, and of happy and optimistic perceptions of the uniqueness of the age? There is no question that as life got richer for the majority, it was by contrast more bitter for the remaining poor and unfortunate. No society at the beginning of the seventies was a just society. In all societies there were minorities of the outrageously rich and absurdly privileged. But all that said, we are decisively into an era when the majority themselves—urban and rural workers, the lower and middle classes, the non-earning young—were privileged, as that majority certainly had not been in any country up till, and after, the Second World War.

The country with the bitterest contrasts, and the largest number of poor, was the United States. I have already said much about the blacks in their ghettos, and the poor whites in their rotting industrial, or formerly industrial, environments. The complex pattern of deprivation, involving Mexicans, Puerto Ricans, Orientals, and native Americans, meant that throughout the sixties the issue of poverty had been inseparable from the cruelties and absurdities of racism (often poor whites did not want to be helped if that made them 'no better than' racial 'inferiors'). Central, as always, was the position of the substantial Afro-American minorities. In looking at poverty and the position of blacks in the United States there are five points to be made.

First, from the late fifties to the early seventies, the total number of human beings in poverty substantially diminished. In 1975, there were three million fewer Americans below the poverty line of $5,500 a year than in 1970. Since 1959 the proportion of the population below the poverty line had declined from 22.4 to 11.4 per cent, still, of course, a disgracefully large number, amounting to 23.9 million (these last two figures apply to 1973; they both rose sharply in the recession of 1975, before falling again in the latter half of the seventies).[12] However, the social welfare programmes, on the whole rendered more efficient by the changes under the Nixon presidency, though still incomplete and ill-organized, did have a marked effect.[13] Governments, of course, tell lies, and one of the classic ways is through the statistics they release. Still, given that the Congressional Budget Office operated independently of the executive, we can take its figures as broadly accurate. The CBO published comprehensive figures indicating that, in 1975, welfare programmes, including in particular 'in-kind services' such as Medicaid, food stamps, housing subsidies, and the like, actually reduced the number in poverty by half. The claim was that, with the services taken into account, the number in poverty dropped to 5.4 million, or 6.9 per cent.[14] To get a measure of the way in which changes initiated in the sixties accelerated into the seventies we need only look back to 1965, the year when the Great Society was into its first full year: the comparable figures then were 9.5 million families, or 15.8 per cent.[15] Thirdly, to keep the racial situation in perspective, it has to be noted that about 70 per cent of families in poverty were white;[16] since whites made up more than 85 per cent of the total population this still meant that the burden of poverty fell disproportionately on blacks, while making it clear that poverty was not purely a race issue.

All of which leads on to my fourth point: poverty was beginning to become as much a class as a race matter. Blacks in low-grade but unionized, working-class jobs could now get the same rates as whites: the classic case was the revolution taking place in the conditions of Memphis sanitation workers. The poor were more and more made up of unfortunates from all races, those in areas where local industries had collapsed, those suffering from chronic illness, single-parent families. Working-class blacks were beginning to share the prosperity of working-class whites: the real problem was falling into the under-class. There were still plenty of badly paid jobs: members of the under-class forced to take them then found that they were not eligible for government assistance. Yet at the same time, the black middle class continued to expand and prosper— making the lot of ghetto blacks all the worse by comparison. And that leads on to my final point: the aspirations of American blacks. These aspirations, some actually realized, are an important legacy of both the struggles and the tenacious strivings of the sixties, whether motivated by the drive for personal advancement, the desire to beat the white man at his own game, or the deter- mination to prove the viability of a separate Afro-American community. In fact, separatism and the doctrines of Black Power waned in the early seventies. Meantime, in public discourse, the word 'Negro' was steadily disappearing, being replaced almost entirely by 'black', if not 'African- American'—'Negro' continued to be used in interviews when irate whites expressed their indignation over what they saw as forced integration. Where prejudice is so deeply ingrained, the change in formal language was quite an achievement, and those who persisted with racial language were really pointing fingers at themselves. (There was a problem that most southern whites tended anyway to pronounce 'Negro' as 'nigra'. Memphis 'moderate' Lucius Birch tried to calm one of his outraged black friends by remarking 'the truth is when it comes to cultivated enunciation, both you and I would sound pretty quaint in a London drawing-room'.[17]) All of this must be expressed extremely cautiously, as racist attacks by white policemen and race rioting in the nineties make one very aware. But, in what was of course still basically a white-run society, there now were opportunities at all levels for blacks which simply had not existed in the fifties.

Appropriate caution was shown by the Memphis *Press-Scimitar* when, on 2 August 1971, it posed the question, 'How Can Blacks Break Poverty Cycle?' in an article which, suggesting a recent growth in racial harmony rather than a continuing 'unravelling' of American society, referred both to new black aspirations and to the immense obstacles still confronting them. Remarking that a few years previously, angry black mobs had 'vented an anger in the streets of America that frightened and shocked the rest of the nation', the writer claimed that 'out of the resultant death and destruction came wide spread efforts to rectify the injustices that have been wrought against blacks for decades'. These efforts were 'important in reorienting the attitude of many black citizens'.

> Where black power had once been virtually synonymous with revolution in the streets, it gradually came to mean a greater self-pride and an effort to acquire leverage by partici-pating in the economic and political system.
>
> Black power today is not necessarily a clenched fist but an appreciation of the cultural heritage of black America—it is a dashiki, and afro hair style, it is the power of a people to appreciate from whence they came and thereby more effectively to determine their destiny...

None the less, 'the injustices of the past' had left most blacks seriously disadvantaged.

> The most distressing aspect of the poverty cycle is the denial of education, which comes about for various reasons which do not relate to lack of motivation or ability. An educa-tion is a critically important asset to those who would participate effectively in today's economic and political structure...
>
> But there are too many blacks who, through no fault of their own, simply cannot eradicate in one generation the effects of enslavement and oppression.

Maternal love, extending beyond one's natural offspring, grit and determination, pride in one's home (however unfavourable the environment), are qualities to be found in all eras. Perhaps the only significant point about this account of the life of a black single parent from the same newspaper is the tone of the report itself, so different from what it would have been ten, or even half-a-dozen years before. Is it fanciful to see here a form of aspiration born of sixties struggles, and perhaps even elements of opportunity, however circumscribed and physically punishing, opened up by sixties changes? It is about Mrs Lucille Johnson, mother of eight chil-dren, one of whom is adopted.

> Mrs Johnson, whose large family lives in two rooms, has an immaculate house. She also works five or six nights a week as a waitress at a nearby drive-in, her pay ranging from $37 to $42 a week. She bundles all of the children and carries them a few blocks to a

baby-sitter and wakes them up again after work at midnight or 1.00 am and walks them home. A hard schedule.[18]

Let a United Press International journalist, writing at the end of 1970, sum up for America: 'The nation is making dramatic progress towards ending poverty defined on the basis of a minimum human diet. But it seems to be moving far less quickly toward closing the gap between the rich and the poor.'[19]

## *Who Cares?*

Those who objected particularly strongly to the economic and social policies of Ronald Reagan and Margaret Thatcher sometimes looked back nostalgically to the sixties as a 'caring society' compared with the 'uncaring' and atomized societies created by the restoration of the values of Scrooge and Gradgrind. A caring society is presumably one where both the state and voluntary organizations endeavour to look after those unfortunates who are unable to look after themselves, a society where there is a strong sense of community as against unrestricted individualism, where there is a fully developed welfare state. As we have seen, many of the activities and attitudes which characterized sixties societies were highly individualistic and entrepreneurial; but, I have suggested, a fair balance was established with, in all countries, new initiatives in social policy (with some waste of money) and the creation of new voluntary organizations concerned with social welfare. Traditional charity, conceived as a Christian duty and dispensed in a manner best calculated to induce humility in the poor, has rightly been seen as inimical to a truly caring polity; but it is wrong to see state action and voluntary action as incompatible (as left-wing ideologues tended to do); in fact, while societies are inevitably replete with contradictions and paradoxes, the quality of caring is something of a seamless web, made up of the attitudes of individual citizens, their willingness to sponsor and support voluntary organizations, their acceptance of certain levels of taxation, and the actual policies put into practice by governments.

Individual wellbeing generally comes from being in decent employment, skilled or professional, whether in the private or public sector. To attain this prerequisite for wellbeing the individual requires education and training. The greatest source of inequity, and also of potential economic decline, was the large number of children in all four countries denied a decent education. The other most obvious social evil was bad housing; and bad housing and bad education were often closely interrelated. Even though in theory there was, in all four countries, an egalitarian, publicly funded education system, publicly funded schools in areas of decaying housing were often themselves in substandard condition, frequently, therefore—whatever valiant efforts might be made by dedicated teachers—purveying substandard education. These interconnected facets of deprivation were in turn related to the structures of politics and power. As we saw in the previous section, even the optimistic, generally prospering citizens tended not to rate highly their ability to influence political decisions. Yet, with regard to the condition of the poor, the political complexion of governments in power was less relevant than the overall state of the economy; this is particularly true with reference to the severe economic downturns of 1974 and 1975. In any case, there was no universal swing to the right in the seventies. Italy had a centre-right government for about a year in 1974, but that proved to be an unsustainable interruption to the general pattern of centre-left governments. France continued to have right-wing governments, but the first one, under the presidency of Giscard d'Estaing after 1974, was anxious to strike a note of youthful reformism. Britain had a moderate Conservative government under Edward Heath after 1970, then a rather weak Labour government. President Nixon made no complete break with 'Great Society' policies; there was a Democratic presidency after 1976. In this section I shall continue to devote some space to the United States, in many ways the hard case in arguing for the enduring and beneficent character of the legacy of the sixties. I shall start with the seamless web of private attitudes and public policies with respect to social welfare, moving on to education, and then to housing. Then comes the moment to continue the story of what had been well started in the sixties in regard to protecting the environment. Finally I will look at the question of the relationships of ordinary people to authority and power, at the police, and at participation in politics.

The American system, it will be remembered, was to try to involve representatives of the poor themselves as much as possible in the administration of welfare systems. In Memphis, the proportion of the poor who were black was much higher than the national average figure I quoted earlier. Because the proportion was 95 per cent black and 5 per cent non-black, so the ethnic composition of the staff actually making the grants for the Community Action Agency (successor to the War on Poverty Committee) was 95 per cent black and 5 per cent non-black, made up of four whites and 'one Spanish-speaking person'. The fevered anxiety to seek out disadvantaged ethnic minorities, showing how far away we are from the world of the late fifties, is revealed in the comment of the agency that 'concerted efforts are being made to recruit American Indians, Orientals, and other national minorities'.[20] Among the poor as well as the rich, there was little active discontent with the inadequacies of existing programmes, and no strong drive towards improvement. In its outcomes, the Memphis poverty programme was one of the weakest in the country: 'Welfare and Social Services in Memphis Receive Poor Marks', was a headline in the *Press-Scimitar* of 24 March 1975; yet a poll published in the same issue showed a remarkable congruence in the attitudes of both rich and poor towards the existing system in Memphis (see Table 15.12). For the purposes of the poll the sample of the 'rich' was taken among those earning more than $20,000 a year, and

**Table 15.12** *Answers to the question, 'How would you rate the welfare system being operated in Memphis?'*

|  | Poor (%) | Rich (%) |
|---|---|---|
| Very good | 4 | 3 |
| Good | 24 | 18 |
| Average | 47 | 57 |
| Poor | 21 | 18 |
| Very poor | 4 | 4 |

that of the 'poor' taken among those earning less than $5,000. Where the prevailing ideology leads to low expectations from public services, the result is low-quality public services.

However, the true answer to poverty is to get people into proper jobs, with education and training the key facilitator. But, of course, where there is racism there is the crude blockage of employment discrimination. Private enterprise, particularly under the auspices of that premier voluntary organization the NAACP, in the realm of direct affirmative action, was rather impressive. Madison Cadillac Inc. in Memphis had an abysmal record in the employment of black staff, who could hope for nothing better than jobs as janitors or 'drive-out boys' (those driving the cars in and out of the showrooms). In March 1972 Mrs Maxine Smith, NAACP executive secretary, announced the beginning of 'an immediate affirmative programme to employ blacks at all levels'. Mrs Smith declared that their Labor and Industrial Committee, chaired by a black minister, the Revd W. R. Johnson, had been 'rudely treated' by the Madison owner-president, A. F. Madison, Jr., when it attempted to investigate the lack of black salesmen working for the firm. Madison commented that he had met the committee, but that he had not been given a chance to explain the company's position. There was, he said, little turnover in personnel within the company, adding: 'But we definitely have plans to add a black salesman to our used-car department, which is the only way anyone here moves into the new car department' (quite untrue, as subsequent events were to show). The affirmative action took three forms: picketing; a total black boycott on all purchases from the company (very effective, and very revealing of black economic power); and a series of formal letters from the NAACP to the president, chairman of the board, and zone manager of the parent company, General Motors, informing them of the 'discriminatory employment practices of the local dealer', and requesting the establishment of a second Cadillac dealer, 'preferably a black'. Within two months, total victory had been won. On 20 May the boycott was called off, with the local NAACP leader announcing that ' "discriminatory employment practices" at the dealership have ended'. Two black salesmen, one in the new department and one in the used-car department, had been hired. 'The company is also seeking a black service representative', the NAACP figure said, 'and has generally promised to hire and upgrade blacks in other positions as they become available.'[21]

The great sixties panacea for the inequality in education which followed formal desegregation was bussing. The free provision of colourful yellow buses to take children to the nearest publicly provided school was an admirable American tradition. It was now adapted so that buses took black children out of the ghettos, away from the badly equipped, low-quality schools there, and out to the high-quality schools in the white suburbs. In some cases, white children were bussed to what had formerly been black schools. Among most white families the policy was hated with the same sort of venom that was directed towards attempts to integrate housing. Already, by the beginning of the seventies, some bussing projects were being abandoned in the face of local opposition, and as a result of President Nixon's dislike of expensive social engineering. A rotten little story was popular with white parents in Memphis in March 1975:

There was a little boy who always did well in spelling in school and his parents were very proud of him. But the city decided it had to bus him to a new school a long way away where he would have black classmates and a black teacher. When the little boy came home with his first report card from his new school his mother noticed his spelling was quite bad and decided to go and see his new black teacher about it.

'My little boy's spelling has always been quite good,' the mother said.

'Well, I'ze gives him the tests just like all the other lil' boys and girls,' the teacher answered.

The irate mother insisted that her boy be given a spelling test then and there and the teacher agreed. As the teacher gave the words the mother jotted them down as well. At the end, the teacher said the little boy had missed 5 of 10 words and the mother insisted he hadn't.

'He spelled "flow" right. It's FLOW,' the mother said.

'No, I didn't say "FLOW",' the teacher snapped back. 'I said FLO-, like the Flo I'm standin' on.'[22]

Alas, there is just the possibility that the story was true, at least symbolically, in its basic premiss that slum schools provided an inadequate education compared with suburban schools. I showed in Chapter 10 that most of the accusations subsequently levelled at sixties educational progressives were without foundation. However, it is true that the pressing question sixties reforms left unanswered is that of how you create educational equality without pushing standards downwards.

A news item in the same month reported that 'bussing was almost exclusively a complaint of whites', although 'a few blacks said they would prefer that their children went to neighborhood schools'. A television repair man who lived in a 'modest home' with his wife and children was quoted as saying: 'The one thing that hurts me is to have to pay taxes to bus them niggers around when I have to pay to send mine to a private school.' If he sent his son to the local public school, he added, 'I know they would kill him'. A man described as living in a 'middle-class frame house' was reported as saying:

> I have three kids and all are in private schools—church schools. I took them out of public schools because we would have had to furnish them transportation to take them down to nigger-town.[23]

The opposite case had been put in a statement of policy on 'Busing and the Schools', published on the second anniversary of the assassination of Martin Luther King, 5 April 1970, and paid for by a mixture of black leaders and white liberals.

> During the decade of the sixties just past, our nation witnessed unprecedented strides towards desegregation. Presently, however, at the beginning the seventies, there appears to be a dramatic reversal from the progress already made—in fact, a retreat to the turn of the century when segregation and separatism became the pattern of race relations, fastened on our nation both by practice and by law...

However, the statement continued, veering towards a vision of multi-culturalism, society was now infinitely more complex than it had been at the beginning the century. Whether they liked it or not, people today 'are citizens of the world'; and 'this world requires a breadth of insight and knowledge, understanding, and skills unparalleled in the history of mankind'.

> The thrust of the civil rights movement in the sixties has been to place the black people of our nation in the mainstream of American life. If such is to be possible, black people must have access to the places where education and training for the mainstream take place. The US Supreme Court has ruled that segregated education is inherently unequal education. Black people have learned that segregated education is also inferior education. Certainly no one can contend, rationally, that segregated education has ever prepared Negroes to compete in our society.

The statement now identified an apparent 'conspiracy' seeking a return to segregated education, consisting of racist whites determined to maintain existing patterns, some liberal whites, weary of the fight for equal justice, soothing their consciences by supporting the status quo until all sections of the nation changed their segregationist practices, and some blacks motivated by fear, resentment, frustration, or pride, who were calling for the continuation of segregated schools. A key slogan in this 'conspiracy' was that of 'neighborhood schools'.

> The Neighborhood Schools concept is being promulgated to create opposition to bussing. These proponents piously argue that they are not attempting to maintain a segregated school system, but simply trying to keep schools within walking distance of the students they serve... The opponents of an integrated society loudly proclaim what they contend are the evils of bussing for racial balance; yet, they proudly support bussing for racial imbalance; i.e. bussing white students past black schools and black students past white schools.

> Negroes have learned through bitter experience that the best schools are likely to serve white majorities.

Good education, the statement continued, demands a community atmosphere; it cannot take place 'in an atmosphere of dope peddling, disruption, rowdiness, and disrespect for the purposes of education and the teaching-learning process itself. 'At this point in history,' it concluded:

> the black community will neither retreat into re-segregation, nor will it be intimidated or given false guidance regardless of how 'high-sounding' the name of it might be called. If there is another betrayal of past hopes and promises, the black community will have no basis for trust in the future. Our one great hope is that out of all the rhetoric relating to the problems facing American schools, the result will be that the American dream of equal educational opportunity for all will be realized...

'Blacks', 'Negroes', 'the American dream'. Still quite a mixed vocabulary; but then, as we have just seen, ordinary citizens, five years later, were openly speaking of 'niggers'. The Southern Regional Council's publication *The South and Her Children* revealed both the gloom of the false dawn and some of the glimmerings of a true one. It challenged the federal government's claim that 1970 marked a watershed in the desegregation of southern schools, 'unmasking' what it called 'the deceptive game of numbers', detailed unsatisfactory and sometimes violent happenings in schools, and criticized the manipulating of allocations so that there was never a minority of whites in any class.

On the other hand, the changes that have taken place in the schools—some of them quite extraordinary—must be acknowledged, and the issues and challenges that lie ahead defined. At one level, the kind of change that the South is witnessing can be measured by the grudging adjustment of whites who now accept desegregation as an inevitable fact of life. In Perry County, Mississippi, for example, a white construction worker was waiting nervously for his daughter at the end of her first day in the newly desegregated school. If anything happens to my girl, he remarked, if she is insulted by a nigger, I'll come over here and knock hell out of Adcox. Mr Adcox, the Principal, was pleased by the news; 'That's great; that's progress,' he observed. 'Last year, the same man said he would shoot me if we desegregated the school.'[24]

In Italy in the mid-sixties, the classic of personal protest against the educational system had been *Lettera ad una professoressa*. In the early seventies another great attempt was made to stir consciousness over the nature of Italian elementary schooling in poorer areas, again by one strong individual, enlisting the cooperation of school children. In this case the individual was the film director Vittorio De Sica, who decided in April 1969 to make a television film *Diario di un maestro* (Diary of a Teacher), documenting the everyday activities and problems of an elementary school in a deprived area in the south-east corner of Rome. The film, shot during 1970 and 1971, focuses on the children, and on one teacher with original methods who falls foul of the system. The first thing De Sica did was read the Don Milani classic.[25] His educational consultant explained the director's aims:

The crisis really arises from the fact that today in our society a teacher who works with and for the boys, and not against them, has the whole system against him, and thus our school is engaged in a constant battle... To whom can the teacher turn? Should his kids be chucked out? How can a teacher deal with a situation which is so complex?

Our teacher, from profound conviction, has made these decisions:

1. School must prepare each child to live his own life and not simply to enter it in a passive and resigned manner.... [This] means trusting the boys, helping them to develop the powers of critically analysing the world. Preparation for life means never being detached.

2. School is an open environment. Children in school cannot be isolated from the world outside.

3. In learning, there is no room for the distinction between the teacher who knows and the child who does not know...

In his pursuit of relevance, this teacher insists on teaching about the Second World War, but not about the Risorgimento (the nineteenth-century movement for national unity, the bedrock of all history teaching in Italy). The teacher loses his job, and so, in a powerful scene, states his views, finally asking the headmaster if he realizes how many of the boys are destined for reformatory or prison.[26]

*Diary of a Teacher* was broadcast over four Sundays in February-March 1972, to an audience of 12.5 million.[27] It was extensively reviewed, and almost universally praised. The critic of the conservative newspaper *Paese Sera* recorded: 'the film is the testimony heard, seen and re-created of a profound disquiet and of despairing contradictions. The extraordinary boys in this film offer a truthfulness that approached poetry'. The critic of the socialist *Avanti* declared that the programme presented 'in the most terse and effective way the sad and squalid reality of the Roman suburbs'.[28] This television film, then—and, more critically, the responses to it—demonstrate a continuing and, indeed, deepening responsiveness to a very severe problem in Italian society. Solving it was not so easy. The minister of education, Franco Maria Malfatti, should be given credit for endeavouring to do something about the still deeply authoritarian nature of the Italian education system during 1973 and 1974, by introducing representative committees at every stage, on which pupils, parents, and teachers could express their views. But, as might be expected, given the continuing turbulence in Italian schools, pupils boycotted the committees, while parents showed little enthusiasm for them.[29]

Greatest attempts to remedy the inequalities in the educational system took place in Great Britain, where the Conservative secretary of state for education, Margaret Thatcher, continued the process of converting (mainly middle-class) grammar schools into comprehensive schools, intended to recruit from all classes. France moved in the same direction when the law of July 1975 introduced the comprehensive principle into secondary education.[30]

We have already noted something of the nature of European housing problems, and especially those of immigrants in France and Britain, and of southern migrants to the north Italian cities. A new Italian law of October 1971 allocated large sums of money for new public housing programmes; but the legislation was too complex and Italian procedures too cumbersome, so that by January 1974, out of the grant of L. 1,062 billion, only L. 42 billion had been spent.[31] In Britain, government recognition of the problem of the homeless was signalled in the shift of responsibility for them from the social services to the housing authorities. For those who did have homes, housing standards rose slightly but steadily between 1971 and 1978.[32]

But, as I said at the outset, it is America which is our hard, if fascinating, case. In the early days of attempted housing integration in the sixties, newspapers had tended to support the alleged property and personal rights of whites who adopted all possible means to avoid integration. In the seventies, discrimination in housing had become a scandal to be exposed. In January 1975 the Memphis *Commercial Appeal* ran an investigation into the renting of apartments, sending out one young female black reporter and one young female white reporter each ostensibly in search of an apartment. In one random check the former was told there were no vacancies, while the latter was offered several. Elsewhere the former was shown inferior apartments or put on a waiting-list, while the latter, after being assured that there were few or no blacks in the neighbourhood, was shown vacant apartments. However, the story has at least a mildly encouraging ending. Asked for his comments, the president of a major property agency did not seek refuge in the stock bluster of the type I quoted in discussing housing in Los Angeles in the mid-sixties. 'The facts are accepted,' he said. 'We are going to strive to see that this does not continue.'[33] The cause of slum housing was energetically taken up by some of those middle-class women whose consciences had been aroused by the Memphis sanitation workers' strike. Enterprisingly, they toured the ghettos with a television crew, and they made a series of stubborn speeches at City Hall.[34] White liberals continued to try to develop an interracial community near to South Western College through the Vollentine-Evergreen Community Action Association, which in the autumn of 1972 affiliated itself to National Neighbors, a nationwide non-profit-making organization of interracial neighbourhoods.[35] Such voluntary initiatives were of the highest importance, while private enterprise in itself was neither good nor evil. However, there were still some pretty evil estate agents around, exploiting the accelerating opportunities to sell houses to upwardly mobile blacks, having frightened white house owners into selling at a loss under the threat that the whole area would soon become black-dominated. That, and other problems of integration, of bigotry, and of intolerance, of enduring sexual fears about blacks 'mixing' with whites, and of being a white minority within a black majority, were exposed in a captivating series of interviews included in the same article in the *Commercial Appeal*. The white fear of being swamped in a black majority deserves some contemplation: all-black ghettos were certainly not a good idea (whether in America or, indeed, in Britain), so one might feel that the right balance in any community ought to reflect the white-black balance nationally, something like 86 per cent to 14 per cent in America; at the same time blacks were not immigrants in America, but had been established there just as long as whites and longer than most. Whatever the rights and wrongs, the fear was a strong one. The interviews are, I am certain, accurate records of what people actually said; of course, decent people tend to say decent and even optimistic things. But I do not think the optimism is overdone, and the final note is a slightly sour one. One other comment: when researching on the fifties, to provide the baseline for my examination of the sixties, I was very struck by the tolerant and sympathetic attitudes of white Memphis nurses towards their black co-workers—as in the fifties, so in the seventies, though even more so. The interviews begin with a reference to the estate agents.

> Here are some of the sales tactics they used, as related by Mrs Martin and others in the neighborhood:
> 'Your schools will be solid Negro in two years. You don't want your children to grow up in an all-Negro neighborhood. Your property will lose value. I have someone who is interested in your home. I have a cash customer.'
> Mrs Martin has a sign in her yard which says: 'I shall not be moved'. Others in

the areas have signs in their porches or in the yard which say: 'Our House is not for Sale'.

'I think the Real-estate people realized "here is a gold mine"—250 houses we can get, and they sell them as fast as they can to make commissions', Mrs Martin said. 'Oh, they tell us they're not "block busting", but that doesn't change the character of their practices.'...

Mrs Martin, a nurse at Baptist Hospital, said, 'I find the Negro families have similar backgrounds'. They are nurses, doctors, school teachers, and mostly professional people, she said.

'If white people would stay in the neighborhood six months after the integration, they would see it's not going to kill them', said Mrs Martin. 'The black families have made good neighbors'.

Dr and Mrs Lawrence Seymour... were among the first Negro families to move into the neighborhood. Along with Dr and Mrs Andrew Dancy, who live next door, the Seymours have built a swimming-pool. They share it jointly with the Dancys, also Negro. Mrs Seymour said she had difficulty in getting acquainted with some of her white neighbors.

'They would turn their heads the other way and I never had a chance to wave', she said. 'Before I could, they had moved.'

There has been no harassment of the Negro families they said. Some Negroes feel hurt when they see their white neighbors move away, knowing the only reason is because they don't want to live next door to black families.

'It doesn't bother me now', said Mrs Seymour. 'We've lived in mixed neighborhoods before in various cities when my husband was in the military service. I don't care whether my neighborhood is all-Negro, or all white, or all-professional people so long as neighbors can live together in peace and harmony.'...

Mrs Lillian Neal..., white, lives with her son and daughter-in-law... who have two children.

'We've moved once before and a great many others in the area have also,' said Mrs Neal. 'We lost $2,000 the first time we moved so we're going to stay here'.

Mrs Neal said, 'I come from the old South. Period. I had a black mammy when growing up. If a few Negro families moved in on the street, it wouldn't bother me, but I would hate to see the neighborhood go all black. I would like to see a few white faces still on the street.'

'I try to live a Christian life and I want to treat the black families right. When we all get to heaven, they are going to be there, too. I hate to see the races mix—like dating and marrying. That's all that bothers me. We are going to stay and do the best we can by them. I think those moving in are a good class of people.'...

White families moving away give various reasons—the need for a bigger den, house notes too high, house too big, but one white housewife said, frankly, 'I am prejudiced and don't want to live in a mixed neighborhood'. Several Negro families said they respected that woman more than the neighbors who pretended to be friends and then moved away as soon as they could sell their house.

That text, I would say, despite the sour notes, is pregnant with change, rather than impregnated with reaction. But the blacks here are middle-class and well-educated. Poverty-stricken ghettos, now filling up with the poor of other racial minorities, remained.

On racial matters both Memphis newspapers were now speaking in enlightened tones, their fundamental cause continuing to be business enterprise and economic expansion. Thus they were still resolute supporters of the building of the expressway through Overton Park. Opinion polls indicated that they carried a majority of Memphis citizens with them. But the race was to the energetic and the dedicated, those with vision, and by now it was clear that the road would never be built. And at the end of September 1972 the *Commercial Appeal*, however reluctantly, had to report that throughout the South environmentalists were having increasing success in stopping urban expressways: in particular, the proposed expressway through the French Quarter in New Orleans had been embargoed.[36]

Beale Street, on the other hand, reached a condition of ultimate degradation. A syndicated *Chicago Sun-Times* article of 28 May 1975 was headed, dispassionately enough, 'Death of Beale Street'. Indeed, Beale Street, at the end of the twentieth century, though it has a few venues for jazz, is still a massive disappointment; the main construction completed is a vast car park. Beale Street had suffered from neglect and a narrow calculation of commercial possibilities. The alternative was not necessarily paradise: 'conservation' could mean formerly lived-in urban quarters being turned into centres for people-watching—another form of sixties spectacle—tricked out as slices of national cultural heritage, filled with the shining entrepreneurial ventures of the time, cafés, boutiques, restaurants, art galleries, agencies of various kinds. In my view, the gains far outweighed the losses.

But there are other views. In the library of the National Museum of Popular Arts and Traditions in Paris, there is a survey conducted by the Association for a Humane City into the reactions of residents, in a small triangle of the 14th arrondissement to the south of the boulevard Montparnasse, to the changes which took place there between 1968 and 1975, involving, in the words of the survey, the displacement of long-time ordinary residents *(classes moyennes* in French, not the same as 'middle classes' in English) by middle-class intellectuals *(petite bourgeoisie intellectuelle)*.[37] Since all the interviews express hostile reactions, with a harsh reference to the British influence, it is worth bearing in mind that, though the survey refers to the years 1968–75, the actual interviews were not carried out till 1978–9. Laurence, a 30-year-old psychiatric nurse, declared:

> The squalor of modernism is in the process of taking over rue Daguerre. Montparnasse is being swamped by fashionable entrepreneurs. I detest these things. It's a tourist trap. I detest this sort of marketing of tourist knick-knacks which comes from England. We don't need it. And, what's more, with exorbitant prices. It *terrifies* me, because it has a completely artificial side which I don't like.

Twenty-six-year-old Christine expressed her 'fear that it will become like rue Mouffetard [on the fringes of the Quartier Latin, and by this time almost exclusively a street of tourist restaurants]. A real ghetto of phoney intellectuals, the whole place totally artificial and totally fucked-up [*complètement foutue*].' Anne, an architecture student aged 22 (perhaps not the most typical of local residents), remembered the past:

> This quarter used to be fantastic. You had some stunningly picturesque people living here. But I'm afraid it's going to become different. People are already talking about that and I'm afraid that in five or ten years you will have more and more young people wanting to live here and that will make it like the Latin Quarter. From the point of view of living here, that will make it superficial.

Béatrice, an unemployed medical graduate of 28, was of the opinion that 'It is becoming completely corrupted. The little cafés which used to be so appealing are now filled with hippies [*babas cools*]. It's full of phoney intellectuals. Ghastly!'[38] There are serious points in this testimony, but clearly the group as a whole was out of sympathy with the cultural initiatives of the sixties.

The citizen activists of Memphis, by their own exertions, had saved Overton Park. The citizens of Paris had done enough to change the contour of the plan for Les Halles, but major decisions continued to be made from on high. De Gaulle's successor, Pompidou, suddenly decided that the museum of contemporary art being planned for La Défense should be incorporated within the Les Halles plan; meantime it was decided that the library should go to the renovated Beaubourg plateau. Because it was going to take longer to clear the Les Halles site and begin reconstruction, and since Pompidou wanted to see the new museum in business before his presidency ended, it was decided to locate that also on the Beaubourg side.[39] What ensured the renewal of Paris as both a beautiful and a continually exciting city was the combination of conservation with the imaginative deployment of the latest architectural ideas. Some ideas were less pleasing than others, however. The notion of a major reconstruction of the area around Montparnasse station went back to the early sixties: it was actually in 1969 that the construction of Paris's first skyscraper, the Tour Montparnasse, was begun, this new feature of the Paris skyline being completed in 1973.[40] It was in 1971 that the architects Piano and Rogers, putting forward one of the earliest examples of what was to become known as postmodernism in architecture, won the competition for the Centre Pompidou, the building which was to combine both the museum of contemporary art and the projected library.[41] Ruthlessness and good taste remained the keynotes of French policies with respect to architecture and the urban environment: in the middle sixties it looked as though the balance was tipping towards the former; participation and protest in the late sixties ensured that it swung again towards the latter, and that, indeed, the element of participation was written into the new urban landscapes.

*L'Express* presented a neatly balanced piece on 'Urbanism: The Mutation of Les Halles', featuring current agonies and coming benefits, past protests and future hopes. The main picture accompanying the article presented, absolutely bare, the site where once the markets had been,

St Eustache rising at the back. The small picture was of a demonstration the previous summer with the banner, 'Enough Scandals: Les Halles for the Parisians'. One section of the article was entitled 'A Fatal Blow'.

> For everyone, the problems of daily life come before all others: they have to survive in a quarter which is in total upheaval, in spite of the works, the noise, the dust. The old inhabitants of les Halles view the future pessimistically: their bistros and their small businesses are slowly becoming deserted; the departure of the wholesale meat market for Rungis will deal a fatal blow.

Then a paragraph putting the opposite case:

> On the contrary, the new-style les Halles will be big box office: fashion and design boutiques flourish under signs saying 'Fruit and Vegetables', the sordid bars are putting on a fresh face to attract the wealthy trendies and the tourists. Publishers and architects are setting up office in the rue Saint-Denis and the rue du Cygne. Three hundred new boutiques have been opened since March 1969. 'Les Halles, today, is somewhere, like St-Germain-des-Prés fifteen years ago,' declares Mme Claude Cadiot, 'Zozo', who sells avant-garde clothes in the rue Pierre Lescot where things are happening. Opposite her, the American restaurant Joe Allen puts the 'Restaurant full' sign up every evening.

For our friends from the triangle of the 14th arrondissement south of the boulevard Montparnasse, this catalogue of changes would not be an occasion for rejoicing, especially with the further information that the construction of the new combined Métro station Châtelet-Les Halles would make the area accessible to ten million people from the Paris region.[42] This time, the only documents are 'the documents on the ground'. Go there, dear 'indentured' reader (the adjective is Hayden White's in his Preface to *The Content of the Form*), and reflect upon what this magnificent piece of urban renewal owes to the activism of the sixties.

The trouble with Italy was that the laws of the 1960s aimed at protecting the urban environment were (in keeping with an old Italian custom) honoured only in the breach. But the Italian liberal establishment was tenacious: thus a new law to protect historic city centres was enacted, described by two Italian experts as having 'an almost charismatic' value attached to it',[43] meaning (I think) that this law was actually obeyed. A special law of April 1973 undertaking the complete protection of Venice was followed in December 1974 by the establishment of a new ministry for cultural heritage and environment.[44]

Urban environments and historic city centres were all very well, but the issue beginning to generate enthusiastic commitment among young and old was that of the menace to the natural world and to the survival of humankind, resulting, as Rachel Carson had pointed out a decade earlier, from the commercial exploitation of technology. Looming large were the new, grossly swollen oil-tankers as well as offshore oil-rigs: the tanker *Torrey Canyon* dumped 117,000 tons of crude oil off Land's End, England, in March 1967; two years later there was a blow-out at a Union

Oil Company platform off Santa Barbara, California. Also nuclear power stations—on 17 October 1969 there was a partial meltdown at the Saint-Laurent I nuclear reactor in the Loire valley in France,[45]—and—caused, to be fair, by the non-use of (contraceptive) technology—over-population. Paul R. Ehrlich, professor of biology at Stanford University, published *The Population Bomb* in 1968. The following year David R. Brower founded Friends of the Earth in New York, 'a non-profit-making organization created to undertake aggressive political and legislative activity aimed at restoring an environment misused by man, and at preserving the Earth's remaining wilderness'.[46] The UK Friends of the Earth was established in 1970. In another of several Domesday texts, *The Closing Circle*, Barry Commoner wrote:

> To survive on earth human beings require the stable, continuing existence of a suitable environment. Yet the evidence is overwhelming that the way in which we now live on earth is driving its thin, life-supporting skin, and ourselves with it, to destruction.[47]

Though the initial impetus came from concerned individuals, the official international agencies did quickly become involved. In 1972 the United Nations organized the Stockholm Conference on the Human Environment, out of which Barbara Ward and René Duboi compiled (for production in nine languages) *Only One Earth*. The Club of Rome (a group of economic experts from the affluent nations) mounted a 'Project on the Predicament of Mankind', culminating in a report, *The Limits to Growth*.[48]

Questions of social and cultural change cannot be totally divorced from those of international politics, still less from those of domestic politics. With regard to the political representation of blacks in America, three different developments were of importance. First was the increase both in the registration of black voters and, still more critically, in their willingness to turn out to vote. As a result of this a whole new cohort of black candidates offered themselves for election, which led in the first years of the 1970s to the arrival of substantial numbers of blacks in positions of power. The third development is more complex. In the first aftermath of the voter registration drives the next imperative was to encourage voter solidarity, so that, as black candidates began to stand, blacks tended to vote for them. To an even greater degree whites voted white, being sure not to support black candidates. But in the early seventies many voters, both white and black, began to vote on the issues rather than along crudely racist lines.[49] Memphis, we have seen, had some distinguished black figures. A new name just emerging into prominence at the beginning of the seventies was that of Willie Otis Higgs, Jnr., born in August 1939 in the Orange Mound section of Memphis. In 1953 he had won a Ford Foundation early admission to college scholarship when only 16, and had gone to Morehouse College, Atlanta. Because of financial difficulties he left Morehouse and took jobs as a waiter, factory worker, and—the traditional black job celebrated in so many Hollywood movies—Pullman porter. Returning to Memphis in 1957, he completed a BA in American history at Lemoyne-Owen College. After employment as a schoolteacher, he enrolled in the Memphis State University Law School. He then, as a beneficiary of the gentle loosening of segregation in Memphis in the early and middle sixties, became the first black to hold the post of deputy criminal court clerk in the Shelby County criminal court.

He went into practice with the already well-established Russell Sugarmon and buried himself in civil rights cases. In July 1970 Higgs became a judge in the Shelby County criminal court, being the youngest criminal court judge, and the only black state trial judge in the state of Tennessee.

The 1974 Congressional elections produced Memphis's biggest black/white confrontation so far: the white Republican incumbent, Dan Kuykendall, closely associated with the disgraced President Nixon, was defeated by 774 votes by the young black Democratic state legislator Harold Ford. This predominantly white congressional district had turned out 91,000 white votes in 1972; now, in 1974, the number was only 70,000. As Ford got only 17 per cent of the white vote, the black turnout had to be (and was) exceptional.[50] In this encouraging situation Higgs, very late in the day, decided to give up his judgeship and enter the Memphis mayoral race. He made, for a Memphis black, pioneering use of television, putting over the message: 'If you can vote for me on my qualifications, then you get my blackness as a bonus.' Here we see the elements of the transition from black politician seeking to benefit from a unified black vote to black politician presenting himself simply as a politician. Publicly, in his challenge to the incumbent, Wyeth Chandler, race was not an issue. Significantly, it was the white, Chandler, who had to make some mention of race, but only to stress his record in appointing blacks to city boards and commissions: 'It's nothing particular to brag about,' he said, 'but it represents a significant change in the city's history' Change would not go further for the time being: Chandler won the run-off comfortably by 58 per cent to 42 per cent for Higgs. Still, in some black precincts, voter turnout was as high as 65 per cent.[51]

Nationally, blacks had done reasonably well in the November 1972 elections. The most striking black victory was in Atlanta, where the Revd Andrew Young, Jr., former aide to Martin Luther King, Jr., defeated Republican state representative Rodney Cook by 68,974 votes to 59,838. Young said his victory, as the first black congressman from Georgia since Reconstruction, was 'due to a coalition of moderate whites and blacks and a city bent on breaking away from its "racist past" '.

> I think if the blacks take the next two to four years to build this kind of coalition, they will be able to pull this off anywhere, North or South. This is a district with a white voting majority in a Deep South city where the voters picked a black man—from the civil rights movement—for Congress. With everything going for Richard Nixon, I think this is a tremendous testimony to Atlanta's willingness to struggle against its racial heritage, or racist past, whichever you prefer.[52]

Altogether, sixteen blacks were elected to the House of Representatives, three of them women, Shirley Chisholm of Brooklyn, Barbara Jordan of Houston, and Yvonne Brathwaite Burke of Los Angeles. A black journalist commented:

> For a hundred years an unholy alliance between Dixiecrats and Tory Republicans in Congress has served to kill or emasculate most efforts to move America forward in a liberal direction. Most of the dirty work has been done behind closed legislative doors, far from

711

the public view. They talk with forked tongues and the biggest bigots are the first to deny their bigotry. The growing numbers of blacks in the Congress is threatening that alliance and no longer can the racists play the old anti-black games and escape notice and retaliation. The number of blacks in Congress and other positions of power is still far too small. Nevertheless, we made some gains in 1972 and our victories should inspire greater political strides in the campaigns to come.[53]

Andrew Young was quickly to become a statesman of international renown. Such figures had simply not existed in the 1950s. The classic black leader then was in the mould of George W. Lee, scarcely known outside the city of Memphis, and confined to a conservative, conformist role within the segregated structure of that city. The classic black leader in the 1960s was in the mould of Martin Luther King, Jr.: a great spokesman for blacks, but not a spokesman for America in the way that Andrew Young was to become.

With respect to changes affecting substantial numbers of voters, Italy came second to America. Two reforms provided for in the 1948 constitution were brought into effect in 1970: the establishment of fifteen regional governments (in addition to the five already in existence round the fringes of the country—Val d'Aosta, Trento-Alto Adige, Friuli-Venezia Giulia, Sicily, and Sardinia); and the right to the holding of a referendum if 500,000 citizens requested it. The referendum, as we saw, was used as a device to sabotage the divorce law, but in the event provided a magnificent opportunity for ordinary Italians to speak their minds. Regional government did bring government on important social matters closer to the people. Better: there was a stirring into life of voluntary organizations and pressure groups, operating in the spirit of 1968 but on much more reasoned and sophisticated formulations. Of immense significance was the movement Magistratura Democratica, consisting of officials low down in the judicial system, who made a point of resisting and exposing the procrastinations and corruption of vested interests.[54] On a larger scale was the relaunching in the early seventies of the tiny and hitherto uninfluential Radical party as the party of civil rights. The Radicals achieved a presence in parliament for the first time after the general election of 1976, when they secured 1.1 per cent of the popular vote; their support rose exponentially throughout the rest of the decade, so that they secured 3.4 per cent of the popular vote in the election of 1979. An important figure was the historian Massimo Teodori, who had been responsible for bringing some of the latest radical feminist ideas to Italy: the Radical party devoted itself both to all the issues related to women's liberation, and also to questions of constitutional reform and participatory democracy. It was socialist in the sense in which the student movements of the 1960s were socialist (humanist, activist, free of bureaucracy). It was a pressure group, a think-tank, and also a party of street demonstrations: it sought to achieve drastic change in Italian society through (above all) organizing referendums. The splendid title of its 1974 manifesto conveys the flavour fully: *Against the Regime: Eight Referendums for the Abrogation of Repressive, Clerical, Fascist, Corporatist, Militarist and Class-based Legislation*. The Radicals were 'For a Republic Which Is Authentically Constitutional' and 'For a Democratic Alternative Based on the Reality of Class'. The first chapter was titled 'A Project of Struggle Against the Regime'; it was explained that, in initiating this project, the Radical party had had the support of the PDUP, Lotta Continua, Il Manifesto, Avanguardia Operaia, PC(ml)I, FGSI, FGR, Sinistra Liberale, Sinistra Repubblicana, Federazione Giovanile Ebraica, Federazione delle Chiese Evangeliche in Italia—a magnificent roll-call of the activist groups born in the late sixties or early seventies; the breadth of the concern for minorities is seen in the inclusion not just of a Protestant church organization but of one representing young Jews. The text opens by making a point which I myself advanced in Chapter 2 as one of the explanations for the outburst of activism in the 1960s: the sense that the reorganization of society (and in this case, in particular, the constitution) promised in the concluding stages of the war had never actually been put into effect.

A quarter of a century after being approved the Constitution still remains in large measure unimplemented and Italian society continues for the most part to be governed by laws which are fascist, clerical, nationalist, militaristic, class-based, authoritarian and inhuman.

Chapter 2 explains the focus on referendums, which, it was recognized, might seem not only ambitious but utterly unrealistic, since to launch a referendum it was necessary to secure 500,000 signatures. There then followed a remarkable anticipation of the campaign of the 1990s (spearheaded by the Radical party and in great part carried through by young magistrates) which was to bring down the Italian political system as it had existed since the Second World War: this statement can be seen as forming the bridge between the agitation of the sixties and the attempt in the nineties to remodel Italian government. There is condemnation of the way in which power throughout Italy was monopolized either by the Church or by the Communist party, of 'majority rule without responsibility', 'the tight intertwining of the political parties', Christian democracy 'with its clerical cement and philosophy of class collaboration', and 'the corporatism of our society'. The eight referendums called for were on the following subjects: the concordat between Church and State of 1929; the prohibition of divorce contained in that concordat; compulsory military service; the legal powers of the military; freedom of information; censorship of the press; the Radical party's own proposal to abrogate the television censorship law of March 1973; and various provisions of the penal code constraining trade union rights, freedom of association, sexual behaviour, and abortion.[55]

Britain and France could boast of being free of the kind of denial of electoral rights which had existed for so long in the United States, and of the inertia, muddle, and corruption which existed in Italy. Without question their executive governments were far more powerful, far less subject to checks and balances, than those in the other two countries. And thereby hang not a few tales of executive abuse. Britain came up with a remedy, borrowing from the Scandinavian countries the institution of the Ombudsman—this term always being preferred to the boring English rendering, 'parliamentary commissioner'. Established in 1968, the Ombudsman existed to deal with the complaints of humble citizens against the sovereign parliament—the government, really—and its agents. It was in the very last months of his presidency, in 1974, that Pompidou established an Ombudsman for France.

With regard to legal majority and voting rights for 18-year-olds, Britain again had led the way with, respectively, the Family Law Reform and Representation of the People Acts of 1968. The United States (with, as it happened, West Germany following closely) came next, the Voting Rights Act being passed in 1970. But since the Supreme Court ruled the act only enforceable in federal elections, the 26th Amendment to the Constitution was proposed and ratified the following year. Given everything that had happened since the early sixties, the accompanying report from the Senate committee makes rich reading:

> the Committee is convinced that the time has come to extend the vote to 18 year-olds in all elections: because they are mature enough in every way to exercise the franchise; they have earned the right to vote by bearing the responsibilities of citizenship; and because our society has much to gain by bringing the force of their idealism and concern and energy into the constructive mechanism of elective government.[56]

In Italy 18-year-olds demonstrated in the streets in 1974—not with the intention of overthrowing bourgeois society, but in support of the right to vote in parliamentary elections. France granted the right in June 1974, and Italy followed suit within the same year. These major electoral reforms could well mark the point at which I should bring this book to a summary conclusion. They certainly demonstrated what nonsense it is to envisage the events of the sixties in terms of some implacable generational conflict. Young people, as I have said, were part of society, part of the larger culture; those who thought they could will their way out of it into an oppositional 'non-bourgeois' society, those who thought that there was a unified 'counterculture' diametrically opposed to 'mainstream' culture, had been fooling themselves. Young people had not brought society crashing down; but they had played a full part in the transformation of society, including that of the attitudes of US senators. Young people were not enemies of a transforming society: they had proved themselves to be 'mature', capable of 'bearing the responsibilities of citizenship', idealistic, concerned, and energetic.

The relationship of young people to other institutions and subcultures had been steadily changing for over a decade. What of young people and the police? Very early on the Pompidou regime attempted to open up dialogue between police and public, and in particular between police and young people, clearly with the intention of modifying the appalling image the police had acquired from their repression of the student demonstrations. Shortly thereafter the Paris prefecture of police produced a pamphlet for internal use, *Le Policier et les jeunes* (The Police and Young People). That lightness of touch was desired all round was signalled by the fact that cartoons appeared on every second page. The first represents a very French-looking policeman flying like an angel above the street which contains three conventional-looking older people, two tots hand in hand, and two young lovers, he with long hair and flares, she in a miniskirt. The section which follows is headed 'How to behave with young people':

> Conscious of the authority which society confers on you, maintain an attitude preserving respect, without slipping into authoritarianism, nor, the opposite, paternalism. You must show yourself to be good-natured, but rule out all excessive familiarity. Be very

714

discriminating in your employment of the familiar 'tu'. Perfectly natural with a child, this form of speech must be avoided with adolescents and above all with girls!... avoid all prejudgements! Do not systematically catalogue young people in accordance with their physical appearance or dress: a black lumber jacket is not necessarily the dress of a hooligan; a hippie is not always a drug addict; long hair is not the external symbol of delinquency.... You will often be the first policeman with whom a young person has any dealings: it will be through you and through your actions that he will judge the police as a whole.[57]

Actions speak louder than words. First, we must remember that the worst brutalities had always been committed by the French Special Forces. It cannot be said that over the years there has been a great improvement here. But it is impossible to conceive of a document of this sort being written at any time before the end of the 1960s.

Drug-taking was a new activity which brought young people everywhere into confrontation with the police. That fact was the objective circumstance which brought into existence in Britain an organization which was a true microcosm of caring and commitment among young people of the time, Release. Release was started in July 1967 at the time when a new Dangerous Drugs Act was passed, giving the police powers to search anyone they suspected of carrying drugs. The two founder-members were Caroline Coon and Rufus Harris. Coon, born in London in 1945, trained at the Royal Ballet School from the age of 10 to 16, then led the full emancipated life of a sixties teenager, for several years earning her living as a waitress, a factory worker, and a model. She went to a secretarial college during the day and took A-level art at evening classes, enabling her, at the age of 19, to go to Northampton College of Art in 1964. She then moved to the Central School of Arts and Crafts in London, leaving before completing her Diploma in Fine Art since she was now caught up in the work of Release. Harris was born in 1946, had separate years at St Martin's School of Art and Kingston College of Art, before dropping out to live in a caravan in north Wales. Release, in its own straightforward words, 'was established to help those who have been arrested for drug offences', providing a twenty-four-hour telephone service.[58] Like Shelter, it was one of the great sixties successes which grew steadily throughout the seventies.

On the whole, the subsequent history of the various police forces continues to support the thesis that the police operated as independent polities of their own, which politicians dared not interfere with, and which remained largely insulated from surrounding society: the Memphis police department, for instance, was subject throughout the seventies to criticism and investigation, with public hearings being held in 1976/7 after the police themselves had carried out a massive bonfire of their own files in September 1976; police misconduct was labelled 'the most critical civil rights problem in Tennessee'.[59] Sometimes, of course, the police did have to tread carefully. In February 1974 a leading black businesswoman and active figure in the public life of the city complained of the disrespectful way she was treated by a white police officer. She was an important enough figure first for the precinct commander to telephone her and then for the director of the police department to write in apologetic fashion:

715

Further response to your letter of 20 February 1974 reporting undue familiarity on the part of [a police officer]... in his addressing you recently. You are absolutely correct in taking the time to bring this incident to our attention.... I hope that you will accept my personal apology for having such an unpleasant encounter with us. Also, please extend my best wishes to your husband who gives so generously of his time to our Community Relations Program.[60]

Very difficult to envisage anything like this happening ten years earlier.

In all countries accelerated efforts were made to recruit women police officers, and some efforts to recruit members of racial minorities. The triangle young people-black officers-white graft and influence produced disconcerting results, as a report from August 1976 indicates:

'What can you do?' asked a black officer. 'A buddy of mine was in a club in Overton Square. Taking names of kids under 18 drinking. The manager came over to him and said, 'You don't have to bother taking all those names. You're not going to be on this beat tomorrow.' Sure enough my buddy was moved to another beat—that same night.

'You didn't have to tell the two cops who took their place not to bother Overton Square. They knew what happened to the other two there.' He spread his hands. 'What can you do?'[61]

I return to this matter in the next section.

One matter of life and death ends this discussion of policing in America. In 1972, through a Supreme Court ruling declaring the death penalty unconstitutional, as a 'cruel and unusual punishment', that country joined Britain and Italy as countries which recognized that the first duty of a judicial system is to the innocent. Giscard, personally, wished to abolish capital punishment in France, but dared not do so since opinion polls told him of the continuing popularity of the guillotine if used on other people.

Plenty of expressions of concern, plenty of grounds for concern. In one area of social concern there were striking advances as cares voiced in the sixties were converted into action, the area of physical disability. The keynote act was the British Chronic Sick and Disabled Persons Act of 1970, the basic act governing so many developments with which we are familiar today: kerbs smoothed, ramps built alongside steps for the easy passage of wheelchairs, special lifts and special lavatories, with their distinctive signs (cause of some upset in the early days when people thought they actually represented someone sitting on a toilet seat, rather than the wheel of a wheelchair). In France Pompidou had, in 1969, commissioned a report on the problems of the disabled: this stressed the urgency of the problem, and the need for a national programme which would integrate the disabled into ordinary life rather than making them the perpetual subject of social welfare. Two laws were passed immediately; then came the major law of June 1975, whose four key points were: replacement of the notion of National Assistance with that of joint liability (involving employers); greater respect for the disabled person as a complete citizen; maximum integration of the disabled in the social and economic life of the country; simplification of

716

legislation.[62] Legislation followed in the various American states and in Italy. Taken together, the legislation and its implementation was one of the finest memorials to the extended vision of civil and personal rights which rose out of the flux and agitations of the sixties.

Other monuments were raised in Italy as that country, in a genuine period of reform, caught up with, and in some ways surpassed, welfare state legislation already existing in France and Britain. With regard to employment protection Britain fell behind Italy until the passing of the Employment Protection Act of 1975, whose provisions covered the right not to be unfairly dismissed, entitlements to a written statement of terms and conditions of employment, guaranteed pay, time off work for trade union duties, and also redundancy pay, minimum periods of notice, and maternity rights. It also covered suspension from work on medical grounds and an employee's rights when the employer became insolvent. The major reforms in Italy were the pensions law of 1969, which consolidated the existing fragmentary legislation and guaranteed all workers a state pension, the law of May 1970 establishing the workers' charter, which guaranteed workers the right to organize trade unions, the right of assembly at the workplace, and the right to appeal to the courts against unfair dismissal, and the law of 1975, which provided for the indexing of wage rates to the cost of living (abolished in the austerity programmes of 1995). Meantime, the workers' own initiative in the strike of 1973 established the 150 hours' education scheme, whereby workers were to get 150 hours a year of paid study leave to attend courses organized by the trade unions.[63] The events of the sixties had changed millions of lives. One changed life was that of the widowed schoolteacher whose diary I have quoted from extensively. Another was the *donna borghese* who from the time of the occupation of her son's school in March 1968 was drawn into discussion groups concerned with the claims being made by young people and workers, and who became involved in teaching in the 150 hours programme. She was amazed at the capacity of her students, whose ages ranged from 16 to 50, to learn. 'Their culture', she wrote,

> is based on comics, photo romances, popular cinema and television variety shows. They don't read newspapers, or listen to the news on the radio because these are difficult and we can't understand a word...

But by the end of the academic year:

> I no longer needed to look for simple words in order to make myself understood, for by this time we were speaking the same language, and they were asking me for the titles of books to buy for they were anxious to read and learn more.

During 1975 she became involved in conferences involving professional engineers, architects, poets, and in particular the two famous writers Pasolini and Moravia. In April 1976 she was writing in her diary: 'In one year I have learned more than in the previous fifty'; she had now become fully conscious of 'the unwritten laws against women'.[64] Exceptional, perhaps. But let us also recall the diary of Anna Avallone, the school teacher who had been upset by *Lettera ad una professoressa*, and hostile to the early manifestations of the student movement, and had come to accept the outlook of her son and his girlfriend. These experiences are at least symbolic of the sense of expanding horizons felt by so many people of the time.

Returning to the solid ground of legislation, we can conclude with the Italian family law of 1975. This was another of those laws which brought into being what had been expressed as intention in the constitution of 1948. Coming together here we have three major themes: the outburst of reform, 1958–74, being in part caused by the fifteen-year frustration of the aspirations aroused by the war and liberation; the changing position of children within the family; the changing position of women. Wives and husbands were henceforth to be absolutely equal partners, sharing in all decisions; the idea of the man as head of the household with a duty of oversight over his wife's activities was abandoned. Dowries were abolished; wives were formally allowed to keep their maiden names (many were already doing this). In the spirit of the new, relaxed, non-hierarchical family, parents were not only to 'maintain, instruct and educate' their children, but were also to respect their 'capacity, natural inclinations and aspirations'. Almost all legal discriminations against children born out of wedlock were abolished.[65] By this law, Italy, in legal terms, recognized the transformations in ordinary life of the sixties, and caught up with our other three countries. Discussion of the Italian family law of 1975 marks a good point at which to bring to an end this section demonstrating that, on balance, caring ideas initiated in the sixties expanded and developed in the early seventies.

## *Going Out*

The real importance of the changes and developments of the sixties is that they transformed the lives of ordinary people, in material conditions, in family and personal relationships, and in leisure activities. Certainly a ruling component in the spending of leisure everywhere was now television. In the ownership of sets, the French and the Italians caught up with the Americans and the British in the early seventies. In Britain by the middle seventies average hours of television viewed per person per week were sixteen in the summer and twenty in the winter.[66] But the dominating presence of television did not prevent people from also going out to enjoy themselves. It was characteristic of France that there should be a serious concern in government circles for the cultural health of the people: hence the vast study whose results were published in two volumes in December 1974 as *The Cultural Practices of the French* (Table 15.13). Television viewing had certainly increased since 1967, but so also had going out in the evening.

There is comfort in the halving of that sad figure of 52 per cent in 1967 never going out in the evening; perhaps too in the figure that suggests that by 1973 certain people had taken a positive decision not to watch any television. It should be hastily added that the figures for 'going out' do not include going out for a meal, not considered an exceptional occurrence in France or in Italy. An important development in both Britain and America is the increase in the practice of going out for a meal, seconded by the growing number of restaurants, and particularly the growing number of restaurants able to provide wine. A not dissimilar development in all countries was the mass development, particularly for young people, male as well as female, of shopping

718

**Table 15.13** *Relative popularity of watching television and going out in the evening*

| Activity | 1967 (%) | 1973 (%) |
|---|---|---|
| *Watching television* | | |
| Every day | 51.1 | 65.1 |
| Approximately every second day | 5.4 | 9.3 |
| Once or twice a week | 11.9 | 13.0 |
| Once or twice a month | 7.6 | 5.9 |
| More rarely or never | 4.0 | 6.7 |
| *Going out in the evening* | | |
| Several times a week | 6.2 | 14.7 |
| Around once a week | 10.8 | 16.5 |
| Once or twice a month | 13.2 | 15.9 |
| Less | 17.8 | 16.0 |
| Never | 52.0 | 26.6 |

*Source*: Ministère de la Culture et de la Communication, *Pratiques culturelles des français* (Paris, 1974), i. 8.

as a recreational rather than just a utilitarian activity.

In the realm of rock/pop music one or two native stars held their popularity in France and Italy—most notably Johnny Hallyday in France, and Ornella Vanoni and Mina, 'the two eternal prima donnas of Italian song', in Italy—but the native popular music industries in both countries were perceived as being in deep crisis,[67] with British and American recording stars dominating, even though the peak of 'the British years' had now passed.

An official household survey carried out in Britain in 1973 gives us some idea of the most important leisure activities apart from watching television. Questions were asked about activities participated in over a four-week period.[68] The hallowed custom of centuries of 'going out for a drink' got a total of 38.4 per cent; however, the relatively new activity of 'going out for a meal' got the respectable total of 29.1 per cent. A distinction (interestingly enough) was not made at that time between watching television, and listening to records or tapes: in the 1977 household survey the figures were 64 per cent of men and 60 per cent of women. Reading books, again in 1977, scored 57 per cent of women and 52 per cent of men; the French study I quoted noted a revival in book-reading in France in 1973; figures for Britain and France were higher than those for Italy or the United States. After that, for men, came house repairs and do-it-yourself (51 per cent, 22 per cent of women) and gardening (49 per cent, 35 per cent of women) and for women needlework and knitting (51 per cent, as against a not altogether surprising 2 per cent for men). Against 10.4 per cent for watching sports and games (1973 figures), one can place 17.7 per cent for actually playing outdoor sports and games and 9.8 per cent for indoor sports and games, 15 per cent for dancing, 2.4 per cent for open-air outings, 8.8 per cent for visits to buildings, museums etc., 11.8 per cent for going to clubs, 7.4 per cent for social and voluntary work, and 1.9 per cent for leisure classes. The total for 'cultural outings', films, theatres, concerts, and opera, was 17.7 per cent; that for films alone 10.9 per cent. The 1977 survey gave a separate heading for 'countryside activities', mainly walking and climbing, which involved 31 per cent of men and 27 per cent of women; and also amateur music and drama, involving 4 per cent of men and 3 per cent of women.

Big cities—London, New York, San Francisco, Paris—could relax on the tides of change which had swept through half a dozen years before. Other places—in Italy, in the American South—were still catching up; Berkeley, still in 1971 centre of the Reagan-led 'occupation', acquired its first gourmet restaurant that same year, when Alice Waters set up Chez Panisse, which was to become as much a monument to the sixties as the 'People's Park'. In reflecting on the spread of hedonistic living, does one feel outrage over a black policeman being moved to another beat for doing his duty in enforcing the Tennessee state law prohibiting the consumption of alcohol by anyone under the age of 21? Or does one feel pleased that the young people of Memphis should be left in peace to enjoy a drink in the newly created restaurant precinct of Overton Square? The development of a hitherto somewhat anonymous area of warehouses into a trendy centre for dining out, specially christened Overton Square (the famous Overton Park was a mile or so away), is directly linked to the changes in the liquor laws discussed in Chapter 9. The day after mixed drinks were legalized in Tennessee was, by a marvellous serendipity, actually Thanksgiving Day, and it was on that auspicious day that the thirteen stockholders of Overton Square Inc. announced their plan to develop a number of restaurants exploiting the new freedom to dispense and consume alcohol in a civilized way. The members of the board of Overton Square Inc. were not, on the whole, products of cultural change and social mobility, though it was in part due to recent cultural change that men so young were so readily able to assume considerable responsibility and raise money for such a project; in fact, they were young members of the mid-South upper class. Chairman of the board was Frank Doggrell III, aged 24, educated at the University of Tennessee. The general manager was George Jones, educated at 'Ole Miss', son of Dr Paul Tudor Jones, minister at one of Memphis's most important churches, Idlewild Presbyterian. The vice-presidents were Ben Woodson, educated at the University of Tennessee, and Charles Hull, 'son of the late Horace Hull, a major personality in Memphis finance' and a graduate of Yale. Without too much difficulty this group of privileged young men raised the sum of $750,000 for their Overton Square project. They studied the famous sixties projects in other cities: Ghirardelli Square in San Francisco, Underground Atlanta, Westfort Square in Kansas City, Market Square in Houston, Old Town in Chicago, the Quadrangle in Dallas. All, as Woodson told a reporter, 'had one central authority, which could maintain a proper balance of tenants, keep out the undesirable element'. The single most successful restaurant which the group hoped to emulate was, of course, Friday's in New York. At this stage Friday's was not a franchising organization. The original Friday's had merely expanded into the TGIF group, which was now operating further singles bar-restaurants in New York called Tuesday's, Wednesday's, Thursday's, Friday's, and Kitty Hawk. There were no operations outside New York City.[69]

Doggrell went to New York to discuss the Memphis possibilities with Al Stillman, now aged 38, head of the TGIF group. He was happy to take up the idea of the Memphis restaurant being the first in a franchise operation. The group offered expertise and, in particular, quality and inventory control of the food and bar business; once a deal was struck, their representatives came to Memphis for several weeks; and their cooks trained the Memphis cooks in the difficult art of cooking hamburgers, steaks, and fantail shrimps. The decor of the first franchised Friday's essentially echoed that of the First Avenue Friday's, faint elements of the British pub thoroughly submerged in Tiffany glass and a sixties vision of the early 1900s. Waiters were to be college students wearing white and red striped polo shirts. Ten years previously, young adults in their 30s in Memphis were expected to be married and raising a family: this new Friday's was openly targeted at successful singles in that age group, though it was to attract many younger and some older customers. The Overton Square Friday's opened on 21 May 1972. The hours were 11.00 a.m. to 2.00 a.m. weekdays and Saturdays, with a Sunday opening time which did not clash with church (as if…), but allowed for the serving of a champagne brunch, with Eggs Benedict, at 1.00 p.m. The new venture was a colossal success, with queues forming outside every evening. Woodson, who became the manager of the new restaurant, put matters with rare succinctness: 'Memphis was hungry for something like Friday's.'[70]

The trouble with the early seventies is that many of the vaunted innovations seem merely to be reruns of the genuine innovations of the sixties. However, it would appear that even large Italian cities still had some catching up to do. Much attention, in 1974 and 1975, was given to the entrepreneur Elio Fiorucci. The rule of high fashion has never, of course, been completely overthrown; but in looking at Fiorucci, I can drive home the point that the developments of the sixties associated with Mary Quant, John Stephen, Pierre Cardin, Twiggy, and so on had brought to an end, for those who cared to escape, the old tyranny of fashion. Rather quaintly, *Epoca* attempted to capture Fiorucci's democratic intentions in the headline 'Marx at the Boutique' (20 July 1974). The article predicted a difficult autumn for the clothing trade, reporting that many of the grand fashion houses had closed. However, Elio Fiorucci, 'the man who revolutionized the sector', was not worrying about the trend.

> 'The fashion of the billionaires is finished,' he says, 'the society to which it belonged is dead. Equality today has one name: jeans, faded and torn. And even rich ladies from the international set queue up to buy them…

There is a picture of Fiorucci, a Milanese of Abruzzese origins aged 39 known as 'king of the rags', outside 'his picturesque shop' in Milan. And also of two models taking a walk in that city, one wearing a complete pair of jeans, the other with jeans cut down to the size of sixties hot pants. *Epoca* credits Fiorucci with having brought great changes: 'faded jeans, printed T-shorts, bowling-alley vests, vest gowns in eighteenth-century style, half Aunt Carlotta, half gypsy, sandals and clogs', and, above all, 'a supreme contempt for conventional dress'. Asked to name the best fashion, he replied, 'That which doesn't exist', continuing:

> The word 'fashion' should be abolished from our vocabulary… Blue is beautiful this year, the next year it must be green. But who says so? Where is it written down? Why couldn't people dress as they wanted to? Our fashion is founded on liberty. One basic element, a

skirt or trousers made of denim, and then whatever else you want. I have built my shop like a souk, or a bazaar. People come in to look for what they want, without restriction or pressure. Comfortable, practical, free, personalized in the choice of accessories: that's how I think people should dress.

Fiorucci fully shared in the spirit of the great reform movements of the time; with millions of others, he feared that the referendum would remove the right to divorce, and was overjoyed at the convincing vote which preserved it. The specific task he set himself was to bring the informality of his apparel to eating out. He wanted, he said, to get away from what he called the 'hypocrisy' of waiters in white jackets and black bow ties. Again *Epoca* sought to sum up the essence of Elio Fiorucci in a headline: 'Jeans and Spaghetti'. What he was envisaging was a combination of boutique and eating-place, 'a place where, after buying all kinds of objects, one can consume a light meal or treat friends to a cocktail', 'a meeting-place which breaks all conventions', with 'the atmosphere of just turning up in a Parisian drugstore, with a very youthful feel, and a great range of goods for sale, from scarves to soap, from a skirt to a well-cooked steak'. As much as Overton Square Inc., or the Open Space, or Andy Warhol's Factory, Fiorucci's project needed commercial investment. Standa, itself a new venture in the early sixties, was now a very successful department store chain: it was with Standa that Fiorucci entered into a commercial deal.[71]

It was a characteristic of the sixties that more people had more time and more money to spend on more and more leisure activities. The dangers of homogenization, of passivity, and of blandness were real, yet many key developments in the sixties threw into reverse the relentless march towards a faceless mass society. Against the family viewing of television one can place the individual use of transistor radios and earphones. Against blockbuster films one can place experimental theatre, which went on in the seventies to its greatest successes. Local initiatives and do-it-yourself activities multiplied. In Britain pirate radio had been suppressed in the sixties; properly established local radio, commercial and public, arrived at the beginning of the seventies. The great battle against the big brewery combines with their mass-produced, gassy, tasteless beer also began at the same time in Britain. The Campaign for Real Ale, founded in 1971, was eventually to have a counterpart in the United States. Professional football certainly became a thoroughly commercialized industry, but played by highly paid, highly entertaining stars. The attempt to get professional football started in America faded away. Nevertheless 'soccer' blossomed as a game for amateurs, for women, and above all for children of both sexes. A later generation was to refer to the kind of youngish-to-middle-aged activist women whose emergence has been chronicled in the earlier chapters of this book as 'soccer mums'.

I have made the case for seeing the 'long sixties' as a distinctive period in cultural and social history, but of course it was not a 'closed' era. The new movements, subcultures, and developments, weird and wonderful, positive and destructive, but transforming the lives of the majority of people much for the better, did not come to a sudden end in 1969, nor even in 1974; whatever the political complexion of governments, these developments have continued to work away in society, among ordinary individuals and families, right up to the present.

# Part V

# Conclusion

# 16

# The Consummation of a Cultural Revolution

Uring the long period in which I was writing this book, I took part in a radio discussion on the sixties. The academic (not a historian!) chairing the discussion put to me the suggestion that 'the sixties was a dry run for the nineties'. Behind such a notion lies the metaphysical assumption that there is some immanent presence or process which divides the flux of human affairs and the developments and changes in human societies into periods, each with some purposive identity. A 'dry run' is the dried-up bed of a river. In the remark just quoted, it is being used as a metaphor—a very dead metaphor, in fact a cliché—to make the suggestion that in some way the sixties was a 'try-out', or 'rehearsal', for the nineties. As I started, so I finish: resort to the sloppy clichés of everyday conversation does not make for clear, rigorous history, nor does the belief that periods have some intrinsic existence, as distinct from being merely the products of the analytical methodology of historians. Were my interests in economic history, diplomatic history, the history of political institutions, or, indeed, the history of the Third World, I would not feel that anything particularly important or unique happened between 1958 and 1974. It is because I am interested in what happens to majorities, rather than minorities, because I am a social and cultural historian, and because I am a historian of the West, that I do feel that the years 1958 to 1974 form a period, as self-contained as a period can ever be; that is to say, I believe that 1958 to 1959 was a point of change, that in the years which followed the manifold activities and developments which took place are integrated together by certain distinctive and, in some cases, unique characteristics, and that another point of change is apparent by 1974. As these things go, it is reasonable, I would argue, to apply the term 'cultural revolution' to this period, though only if we evacuate from both adjective and noun any Marxist implications of violent confrontation or of one discrete and integrated culture totally replacing another. If we prefer the route of semantic caution, then 'social and cultural transformation' will do very well. The period 'integrated by distinctive, and even unique, characteristics' does not exactly coincide with the decade 1960–69, but there is no problem about referring to it as 'the sixties', especially if we keep in mind the fruitful concept of 'the long sixties'.

The flabby phrase about the sixties being a 'dry run' for the nineties would seem to be suggesting, not so much that in the nineties there was a return to the practices and values of the sixties, but that in the nineties these practices and values reappeared in a perfected form. At once, one must comment that any notion that the practices and values of the sixties disappeared during some intervening period, in consequence (the implication usually is) of the reactionary policies and new moral piety associated with the administrations of President Ronald Reagan and Prime Minister Margaret Thatcher, is quite mistaken. The sixties was a time of entrepreneuralism and private enterprise, a time of the creation and satisfaction of new consumer needs, a time of expansion in the service and entertainment industries. Such developments anticipated aspects of 'Thatcherism' (an international phenomenon), rather than being antithetical to them. More critically, those elements of sixties lifestyles which Reagan and Thatcher detested continued to be present during the seventies and were very evident throughout the eighties. All the statistical evidence suggests that permissive attitudes and permissive behaviour continued to spread at accelerating rates, with only the utterly unforeseen occurrence of AIDS to bring any kind of caution; single-parent families proliferated, the term 'husband' and 'wife' became almost quaint, giving place to 'lover' and 'partner'. It took a long time in coming, but by the mid-nineties topless sunbathing was evident even on some Italian beaches. The appearance, also, of moralistic crusades simply testifies to the strength of the by now well-established behaviour patterns which the crusades, vainly, hoped to eliminate. The cultural revolution, in short, had continuous, uninterrupted, and lasting consequences.

The essence of the cultural revolution was its involvement of vast numbers of ordinary people: from peasant families in rural Italy getting the basics of civilized living to black children in the ghettos of the American South being admitted for the first time to properly equipped schools; from paraplegics whose needs as integrated members of the community were for the first time being recognized, to women everywhere freed from the confinements of the feminine mystique; from Italian, French, British, and American workers with freshly negotiated wages and conditions of employment to young people in once-dreary provincial cities, now provided with boutiques and discos. All sections of society (workers, blacks, women, provincials) hitherto ignored became visible. At the beginning of the decade, in America, what hit the headlines with respect to segregated housing was the right of whites to safeguard the value of their properties; by the end of the decade what was discussed in the newspapers was the intrinsic unfairness of racial discrimination in housing. Everywhere, as we saw, there was a growth both in state action and voluntary action aimed at the ordinary problems of social welfare. At the same time people gained power to make decisions for themselves. Life became more varied and enjoyable. With less rigid conceptions of marriage and new opportunities for divorce, with changing attitudes to fashion and to education, with the abandonment of comfortable fictions about the nature of beauty and the arrival of informal, body-hugging clothing, there was a healthier openness to ordinary living, less need for lies, fewer cover-ups—literally in the case of female sunbathers no longer constrained to go through incredible contortions in endeavouring to combine maximum exposure to the sun with minimum outrage to public pudicity. The testimony that the new universal language of rock was genuinely liberating, and not just for the young, is overwhelming.

It is important not to exaggerate the extent of change, or its novelty. Not everything in the sixties that I have picked out to discuss was entirely new; what was new was that so many things happened at once. Much of what was done in the sixties was downright stupid: I referred at the start to the Great Marxisant Fallacy, and we have seen that there was much pointless violence in pursuit of a revolution that was never there to be grasped. Faith in drugs as the key to a better society was mindless, self-deluding, and destructive; many other counter-cultural activities owed far more to self-indulgence than to serious protest against established ways of doing things. The desire to silence pompous, hidebound males and to give voices to females and oppressed minorities was entirely laudable; unfortunately, even before the decade was out there were intimations of what small minds were later to turn into the sour prescriptiveness which the right, with less than the usual exaggeration, denounced as 'political correctness'. But if we are looking at what was not done, or what was done badly, then we have to turn to those in authority, those who had the power to make a difference. That is why it is absurd to accuse, as latter-day right-wing revisionists and turncoat radicals have done, anti-war extremists of prolonging the Vietnam war; the protesters gave witness as conscience dictated, and in the end they won. Governments often did badly on domestic issues as well. In all countries housing policies were misguided, and sometimes downright inadequate. Environmental protection began late, and too many disasters were allowed to happen. But this *was* an area in which ordinary people had taken action, and *did* make a difference. So, above all, in civil rights. The greatest advances in race relations as between the beginning and the end of my long sixties were made in the United States. As we have seen, great tranches of white prejudice remained, while militant black separatism did nothing to further peaceful and just accommodation.

Of course, the issue of the proper relations between two different races had existed since the foundation of the United States. It only began to become truly significant in Britain and France in the sixties, when, also, the question of the treatment in north and central Italy of southern immigrants became pressing; only at the very end of our period did blacks begin to arrive from the territories in the Horn of Africa that Italy under Mussolini had once tried to conquer. Only then, too, did the rights of American Indians begin to be recognized, particularly after the generally peaceful occupation of the deserted former penitentiary on Alcatraz Island, San Francisco Bay, by about thirty American Indians, mainly local students, with some children, from 20 November 1969 to 11 June 1971. Addressing Congress on 9 July 1970, President Nixon spoke some measured, indeed progressive words, referring to 'aggression, broken agreements, intermittent remorse and prolonged failure', and proposing a wide-ranging programme to give American Indians dignity and control over their own lives.[1] Putting things another way: it was in the sixties that an important stage was passed in the passage to our contemporary world made up of multicultural societies—a process caused not by deliberate human agency but by the great demographic movements of our time. The question which has to be asked about individuals, groups, and governments in the sixties is: what did they do to foster or to frustrate the advance of multiculturalism? The counter-cultural and movement groups, with their genuine celebration of the colour, the variety, and the mutual stimulus to be found in a multicultural society, score well. So do some of the liberal Democrats in America, politicians like Roy Jenkins in Britain, and some Hollywood film-makers. Those who advocated segregation, discrimination, or separatism (including Enoch Powell and Toni Morrison) were the unseeing and distinctive members of their time.

Of the sixteen characteristics of the sixties I outlined in Chapter 1, this one is probably the most contentious. But some readers, perhaps, are still unpersuaded by my concept of 'measured judgement'. Let me quote from the autobiography of the leader of the radical socialist group SDS, Tom Hayden. Hayden and many others suffered grievously at the hands of the most reactionary elements in the 'justice' system, George Jackson most atrociously of all. In the following couple of sentences Hayden is wittingly making the case that he and his fellow-protesters were basically right (I do not demur); unwittingly he brings out that deep within the American system as it developed during the sixties, there was measured judgement:

> It was remarkable that during these several years of political trials on conspiracy charges, the federal government failed to win against *any* of the sixty-five conspiracy defendants. Such defendants as the Harrisburg Seven, the Camden Seventeen, and the Gainesville Eight always managed to win, either before juries or appeals courts, a dramatic difference from the McCarthy era, only fifteen years before.[2]

Testimony on sexual liberation in the sixties is less supportive than we have sometimes been led to believe of the position that liberation was purely for males to exploit females. The new freedom for girls and women was real, though so also was a strong determination among males to exploit new opportunities to the full. Even so, male chauvinism had its positive consequences in providing a stimulus to the nascent women's liberation movement. Feminist ideas, never monolithic in any case, have since gone through a number of phases, including some very extreme ones. Self-evidently, discrimination against women has not yet ended, but it would be a sour commentator indeed who would not concede that a movement initiated in the sixties has resulted at the end of the second millennium in more humane and balanced relationships between the sexes than ever existed previously.

There was no economic revolution, no political revolution, no advent of the proletariat to power, no classless society, no destruction of mainstream culture, no obliteration of language. The gospel according to Marcuse was that, since the mass of the ordinary workers were so content with the boons of consumer society that they had no interest in revolution, the revolutionary forces would have to come from the outcast and deprived, including in particular racial minorities—not, in other words, from the working class but from the under-class—and the revolutionary leadership would have to come from the student activists. But why have a revolution? If the majority are already contented, would it not be better to concentrate in a systematic and pragmatic way on raising the living standards of the minority, and thus abolishing the under-class? What possible reason, anyway, was there for believing that even if a revolution could be carried out it would bring anything but further misery to the lowest class of people? Governments with their welfare policies actually achieved far more for the under-class than did the Movement or the New Left. But not nearly enough. And with market economics rampant in later decades, the under-class greatly expanded. Revolution was never the answer. Nor were badly conceived and badly applied welfare schemes. Not so much unfinished business as business for which neither the radicals nor the apostles of measured judgement had found effective answers.

Democratic institutions survived, if somewhat fitfully, in Italy, where special problems (identified in Chapter 2) were never resolved. But the Italian people became more self-aware during the sixties, more responsible for their own destinies. The seventies was a time of violence and terrorism, but there was enough confidence, enough resilience among the people for democratic Italy to survive. Austerity measures in the mid-nineties, designed to equip Italy for European Monetary Union, have stripped the workers of many of the gains they made at the end of the sixties. For all that, Italy remains a freer, more affluent, more joyful society than it was in the fifties. That stands across the four countries. Today, in all four countries, the proportion of the disadvantaged is growing all the time, and too much power is still held by too few people. But it is senseless to dismiss the developments of the sixties because they did not have revolutionary consequences. It is perfectly true that many of the most spectacular features—the music of the Beatles, the fashion of Mary Quant, the art of Andy Warhol—were thoroughly implicated with the profit-making commercialism of the time, but suggestions that they averted revolution by lulling people into a false contentment are absurd; what they did do was to contribute their mite to the people's liberation.

After the end of the sixties, despite the economic crisis of 1973–4, living conditions for most people continued to improve. However, I would not want to claim that the sixties have been followed by an irreversible upward trend in material circumstances. The world economy has been much more unstable than seemed likely in the sixties; 'globalization' has meant that developments anywhere in the world can threaten the job security of people in the West. Without question, global economic stability was indispensable to the happy circumstances of the sixties; but no recipes for permanent economic success were produced then. As I have said, there is certainly no case to be made that people in the sixties were somehow more moral, more unselfish, or more far-sighted than people in any other age: circumstances were different, though, given the favourable circumstances, people did show extraordinary energy, imagination, and critical awareness directed at their own society. A vital factor was the existence, and expansion, of the liberal and progressive element within the structures of authority, who practised measured judgement. That was what gave the societies of the sixties much of their unique quality: gone was the stuffy conservatism of previous decades, while the radical, divisive, philistine conservatism of Reagan and Thatcher was yet to come. Yet, whatever the political changes, the consequences of what happened in the sixties were long-lasting: the sixties cultural revolution in effect established the enduring cultural values and social behaviour for the rest of the century. This had been no transient time of ecstasy and excess, fit only for nostalgia or contempt. I began this short concluding chapter carping at someone else's cliché. But now, in making my closing pronouncements on the sixties, I cannot improve upon these two clichés: there has been nothing quite like it; nothing would ever be quite the same again.

# Notes

## Part I. Introduction

### Chapter 1. Was There a Cultural Revolution, c.1958–c.1974?

1. There are many picture books on the sixties, generally of a remarkably high quality, and also accounts by both journalists and leading cultural figures of the time—all containing valuable insights. Most recently a thoughtful new autobiography by the sixties supermodel Twiggy has appeared: Twiggy Lawson, with Penelope Denning, *Twiggy in Black and White* (1997). There have been many television accounts of the sixties, and it is worth consulting the book associated with a Channel 4 series, Frances Wheen, *The Sixties: A Fresh Look at the Decade of Change* (1982). With respect to serious scholarly studies of sixties society and aspects of it, America is far ahead of the field, and already there is an invaluable guide to the literature, Rebecca Jackson, *The 1960s: An Annotated Bibliography of Social and Political Movements in the United States* (Westport, Conn., 1992). Adam Garfinkle, *Telltale Heart: The Origins and Impact of the Vietnam Anti-War Movement* (Basingstoke, 1995) has a notably extensive bibliography. There are no other comparative studies of quite the type I am attempting here, though David Caute's splendid *1968: The Year of the Barricades* (1988) covers an impressive range of countries.
2. *Daily Mail*, 30 Mar. 1982; cited in Brian Masters, *The Swinging Sixties* (1985), 14.
3. Allan Bloom, *The Closing of the American Mind: How Higher Education Has Failed Democracy and Impoverished the Souls of Today's Students* (New York, 1987), 322, 313–14; Paul Bearman, *A Tale of Two Utopias: The Political Journey of the Generation of 1968* (New York, 1997); Stephen Macedo (ed.), *Reassessing the Sixties: Debating the Political and Cultural Legacy* (New York, 1997).
4. 'Afterword' to the 1989 edition of his *Revolt into Style*, originally published in 1970, 257. Jim Haynes and his autobiography are discussed in Ch. 14. See also the semi-autobiographical *High Sixties: The Summer of Riot and Love* (1992), by Roger Hutchinson. Marta Bonesea has recently defined the alleged cultural changes in sixties Italy as a 'great illusion': *La grande illusione* (Milan, 1997).

5. Maureen Nolan and Roma Singleton, 'Mini-Renaissance', in Sara Maitland (ed.), *Very Heaven: Looking Back at the 1960s* (1988), 25.

6. Jacob Burckhardt, *The Civilization of the Renaissance in Italy* (1955 edn), 341, 1.

7. Jean Fourastié, *Les Trente Glorieuses ou la révolution invisible de 1946 à 1975* (Paris, 1976); E. J. Lacombe (ed.), *Les changements de la société française* (Paris, 1971).

8. Alberto Ronchey, *Accade in Italia, millenove sessantotto a millanove sessantasette* (Milan, 1977); Luigi Mistrorigo, *L'utopia dell'innocenza dal '68 ad oggi: la scomposizione della storia* (Rome, 1979)—'the decomposition of history', the same notion for this later period as Matusow, O'Neill, Blum, and Burner hold for America in the sixties; Martin Clark, *Modern Italy* (2nd edn, 1996), ch. 18.

9. Allen J. Matusow, *The Unraveling of America: A History of Liberalism in the 1960s* (New York, 1984); W. L. O'Neill, *Coming Apart: An Informal History of America in the 1960s* (Chicago, 1971); John M. Blum, *Years of Discord: American Politics and Society 1961–1974* (New York, 1991); David Burner, *Making Peace With the 60s* (Princeton, NJ, 1996); Peter Collier and David Horowitz, *Destructive Generation: Second Thoughts about the Sixties* (New York, 1989). Positive views of sixties changes in America are presented in the magnificent book by Terry H. Anderson, *The Movement and the Sixties: Protest in America from Greensboro to Wounded Knee* (New York, 1995), and in two excellent textbooks, David Chalmers, *And The Crooked Places Made Straight: The Struggles for Social Change in the 1960s* (Baltimore, 1991), and David Farber, *The Age of Great Dreams: America in the 1960s* (New York, 1994). In *Berkeley at War: The 1960s* (New York, 1989), W. J. Rorabaugh has produced his own telling riposte to the 'unravelling' thesis: 'it was only centralized authority which was in decline. At the local level, those on the bottom saw less a disintegration of society than a rebirth of community spirit and individual liberty' (p. x).

10. One can always learn from those one disagrees with. An outstanding example is the collection edited by Bart Moore-Gilbert and John Seed, *Cultural Revolution? The Challenge of the Arts in the 1960s* (1992). Classic Marxist accounts are: Stuart Hall and Tony Jefferson (eds.), *Resistance Through Rituals: Youth Subcultures in Postwar Britain* (1976); Dick Hebdige, *Subculture: The Meaning of Style* (1979); Geoff Mungham and Geoff Pearson (eds.), *Working Class Youth Culture* (1976). Sohnia Sayres, Anders Stephanson, Stanley Aronowitz, and Frederick Jameson (eds.), *The Sixties Without Apology* (Minneapolis, 1984) is an American collection of readings of broadly Marxist outlook.

11. Theodore Roszak, *The Making of a Counter Culture: Reflections on the Technocratic Society and Its Youthful Opposition* (New York, 1970), pp. xi-xiii.

12. Charles Reich, *The Greening of America* (New York, 1970), esp. the final chapter.

13. The distinction is neatly explained in Lauri Umansky, *Motherhood Reconceived: Feminism and the Legacies of the Sixties* (New York, 1996), 14–15. See also Judith C. Albert and Stewart E. Albert (eds.), *The Sixties Papers: Documents of a Rebellious Decade* (New York, 1984); Wini Breines, *The Great Refusal: Community and Organization in the New Left, 1962–1968* (New Brunswick, NJ, 1989), esp. pp. 8–9; Cyril Levitt, *Children of Privilege: Student Revolt in the Sixties, a Study of Student Movements in Canada, the United States, and West Germany* (Toronto, 1984); and Anderson, *The Movement and the Sixties*.

732

14. I should note here that Ian MacDonald, working on a very different style of project, independently came to a similar conclusion in his indispensable *Revolution in the Head: The Beatles' Records and the Sixties* (1994), 28–30.

15. Herbert Marcuse, 'Repressive Tolerance', in Robert Paul Wolff, Barrington Moore, Jr, and Herbert Marcuse, *A Critique of Pure Tolerance* (New York, 1965).

16. Serge Mallet, *La Nouvelle Classe ouvrière* (Paris, 1962).

17. Nino Balestrini, *Prendiamo tutto: conferenza per un romanzo: letterature e lotta di classe* (Milan, 1972). This argument with his fellow Marxists explains the philosophy underlying Balestrini's novel, *Vogliamo tutto (We Want the Lot*, Milan, 1970), discussed by me in Ch. 10.

18. This is how the term is used by Godfrey Hodgson, *In Our Time: America from World War II to Nixon* (New York, 1976), when he speaks of 'Triumph and failure of a Cultural Revolution' (pp. 326–64); and by Bernice Martin in the final chapter, 'A Cultural Revolution?' of her excellent book, *A Sociology of Contemporary Cultural Change* (Oxford, 1981). I first used the term in the wider sense, associating it with transformation in the lives of ordinary people, in *Class: Image and Reality in Britain, France and the USA since 1930* (1980), ch. 14; and *British Society Since 1945* (1982), ch. 8. Marxist disputations are well summarized in ch. 1 of Elizabeth Nelson, *The British Counter-Culture 1966–73* (1989).

19. This view was put to me very forcefully by Dr Owen Dudley Edwards of Edinburgh University when I had presented a summary of my own views on the sixties to history students and staff at that university in Dec. 1996.

20. In Felix Gross, *Il Paese: Values and Social Change in an Italian Village* (New York, 1974), 137.

21. The advent of multiculturalism in America is noted by Anderson, *The Movement and the Sixties*, 414.

22. For a full frontal exposure of these 'committed theories', see the work of two wholehearted enthusiasts, Rosalind Coward and John Ellis, *Language and Materialism: Developments in Semiology and the Theory of the Subject* (1977), which begins: 'Perhaps the most significant feature of twentieth-century intellectual development has been the way in which the study of language has opened the route to an understanding of mankind, social history and the laws of how society functions' (p. 1). It may be noted that in introducing his defence of metaphysical history, or 'large-scale theories about the historical process as a whole', Alex Callinicos declares that 'showing that such theories are philosophically respectable... is *politically important*' (my emphasis)—*Theories and Narratives: Reflections on the Philosophy of History* (Cambridge, 1995), p. ix. In my view historians should not be concerned to get it *politically* right, just right.

23. This comes out very strongly in Hayden White's 'Response' (*Journal of Contemporary History*, Apr. 1995) to my article 'Two Approaches to Historical Study: The Metaphysical (including Postmodernism) and the Historical' (*Journal of Contemporary History*, Jan. 1995). The original debate took place at the Open University in Oct. 1993. My own views are also developed in *The Nature of History* (3rd edn, 1980); and ' "A Fetishism of Documents"?: The Salience of Source-Based History', in Henry Kozicki (ed.), *The Development of Modern Historiography*, ii (1993), 107–38. The arguments against postmodernist criticisms of the history of historians are well summarized in Richard J. Evans, *In Defence of History* (1997).

*Chapter 2. If So, Why?*

1. The very influential (at the time) book, *The Status Seekers* (New York, 1960) by Vance Packard, presented fifties America as conformist, dominated by vast corporate entities, and devoid of individuality and spontaneity.

2. Richard O. Collin, 'The Blunt Instruments: Italy and the Police', in John Roach and Jurgen Thomaneck (eds.), *The Police and Public Order in Europe* (1985), ch. 7, esp. p. 185; John Roach, 'The French Police', ibid., ch. 5; Ian K. McKenzie and G. Patrick Gallagher, *Behind the Uniform: Policing in Britain and America* (Hemel Hempstead, 1989), esp. 3; Romano Canosa, *La polizia in Italia del 1945 ad oggi* (Bologna, 1976).

3. Roach, 'The French Police', 119 ff.; Philip John Stead, *The Police of France* (New York, 1983), 6.

4. Roach, 'The French Police', 113.

5. Collin, 'Blunt Instruments', 186.

6. Ibid. 204; Alexander Stille, *Excellent Cadavers: The Mafia and the Death of the First Italian Republic* (New York, 1995), 17–28.

7. Collin, 'Blunt Instruments', 204–5; Stille, *Excellent Cadavers*, 17–28.

8. Quoted in John L. Cooper, *You Can Hear Them Knocking: A Study in the Policing of America* (Port Washington, NY, 1981), 214–15.

9. McKenzie and Gallagher, *Behind the Uniform*, 161; Cooper, *You Can Hear Them Knocking*, 25; Godfrey Hodgson, *In Our Time: America from World War II to Nixon* (New York, 1976), 282.

10. McKenzie and Gallagher, *Behind the Uniform*, 38.

11. Stead, *Police of France*, 4.

12. STOPP (Society of Teachers Opposed to Physical Punishment), 'The European Example: The Abolition of Corporal Punishment in European Schools' (TS, 1986).

13. Copy of letter of 12 Sept. 1950, Nowland Van Powell MSS, Box 23, Folder 2, Mississippi Valley Collection, Memphis State University; theatre programmes in Julie Bensdorf Isenberg Papers, Box 1, Folder 15, Mississippi Valley Collection.

14. Sadie Plant, *Most Radical Gesture: The Situationist International in a Postmodern Age* (1992), 61. The quotations, from *International Situationist*, 1 (1958), can be found in Charles Gray (ed.), *The Incomplete Work of the Situationist International* (Brussels, 1974).

15. Simone de Beauvoir, *The Second Sex* (1949; 1968 edn translated by H. M. Parshley), 734–5.

16. Verbatim report of the trial, J. W. Ehrlich (ed.), *Howl of the Censor* (San Carlos, Calif., 1960), 126.

17. Ann Charters, 'Foreword' to Ann Charters (ed.), *The Beats: Literary Bohemians in Postwar America* (Detroit, 1983), p. x.

18. Ibid.

19. Ibid. p. xi.

20. John L. McKenzie, *The Roman Catholic Church* (1969).

21. *Commercial Appeal*, 27 Apr. 1968.

22. Ibid.

23. Hinds MSS, Box II, Mississippi Valley Collection.

24. Paul Yonnet, *Jeux, modes et masses: la société française et le moderne* (Paris, 1986), 192.

25. Ken Jameson, 'The Castle or the Tipi: Rationalization or Irrationality in the American Economy', in Ronald Weber (ed.), *America in Change: Reflection on the 60's and 70's* (Notre Dame, Ind., 1972), 18.

26. Paul Vaughan, *The Pill on Trial* (1970), 49, 56.

27. See Arthur Marwick, *War and Social Change in the Twentieth Century: A Comparative Study of Britain, France, Germany, Russia and the United States* (1974), chs. 5 and 6.

## Part II. The First Stirrings of a Cultural Revolution, 1958–1963

### Chapter 3. New Actors, New Activities

1. For Macmillan the best brief account is John Turner, *Harold Macmillan* (1994). For the sexist joke, see my *British Society since 1945* (3rd edn, 1996), 110–11.

2. Mark Abrams, *The Teenage Consumer* (1959); Colin MacInnes, *Absolute Beginners* (1959); Ministry of Education, *The Youth Service in England and Wales* (the Albemarle Report), Cmnd. 929 (1960).

3. Among the most useful studies are: John Davis, *Youth and the Condition of Britain: Images of Adolescent Conflict* (1990); James S. Coleman, *The Adolescent Society: The Social Life of Teenagers and Its Impact on Education* (New York, 1961); Thomas Doherty, *Teenagers and Teenpics: The Juvenilization of American Movies in the 1950s* (Boston, 1988): James Gilbert, A *Cycle of Outrage: America's Reactions to the Juvenile Delinquent in the 1950s* (New York, 1986); Elgar Z. Friedenberg, *The Vanishing Adolescents* (New York, 1959).

4. Albemarle Report, 15.

5. James Monroe Hughes, *Education in America* (3rd edn, New York, 1970), 5–17, 278.

6. *American Mercury*, Sept. 1958.

7. Doherty, *Teenagers and Teenpics*, 42–83.

8. Van Dyke Papers, Box 7, Folder 192, Mississippi Valley Collection, Memphis State University.

9. Paul Goodman, *Growing Up Absurd* (New York, 1960), 27–62.

10. Ibid. 240.

11. Kenneth Keniston, 'Social Change and Youth in America', in Erik H. Erikson (ed.), *Youth: Change and Challenge* (New York, 1963).

12. *Tiger Rag*, 9 Dec. 1960, University Archives, Mississippi Valley Collection.

13. Ibid. 9 Dec. 1960.

14. Ibid. 14, 21 Apr., 6 Oct. 1961.

15. Keniston, 'Social Change and Youth in America', 170, 171, 173, 175. See David Riesman, *The Lonely Crowd* (New York, 1962).

16. Keniston, 'Social Change and Youth in America', 175–7.

17. Goodman, *Growing Up Absurd*, 24.

18. Ibid. 13.

19. Robert Coles, 'Serpents and Doves: Non-violent Youth in the South', in Erikson, *Youth*, 138.

20. Quoted by Joseph F. Kauffman, 'Youth and the Peace Corps', in Erikson, *Youth*, 152.

21. Quoted ibid. 158.

22. The Port Huron Statement is printed in Massimo Teodori, *The New Left: A Documentary History* (1970), 163–72. See also Tom Hayden, *Reunion: A Memoir* (New York, 1988), 84–102; John P. Diggins, *The Rise and Fall of the American Left* (New York, 1992), 222 ff.; and Godfrey Hodgson (a journalist who conducted many interviews at the time), *In Our Time: America from World War II to Nixon* (New York 1976), 278–83.

23. Interview in Jonathon Green, *Days in the Life: Voices from the English Underground 1961–1971* (1988), 11.

24. Mary Quant, *Quant by Quant* (1966), 35.

25. Interview in Green, *Days in the Life*, 32. For an exploration of the significance of British art colleges, see Simon Frith and Howard House, *Art into Pop* (1987).

26. Interview in Green, *Days in the Life*, 46–7.

27. Albemarle Report, 1, 13, 53.

28. Abrams, *The Teenage Consumer*, 18.

29. Mark Abrams, *Teenage Consumer Spending in 1959* (1961), 5.

30. Albemarle Report, 24.

31. Ibid. 15.

32. Home Office, *Report of Committee on Children and Young Persons*, Cmnd. 1191 (1960), 7–8.

33. Albemarle Report, 32.

34. Ibid. 33.

35. In Green, *Days in the Life*, 10.

36. Albemarle Report, 19–20.

37. As in such works as Stuart Hall and Tony Jefferson (eds.), *Resistance Through Rituals: Youth Subcultures in Postwar Britain* (1976), and Geoff Mungham and Geoff Pearson (eds.), *Working Class Youth Culture* (1976).

38. Interview in Peter Laurie, *The Teenage Revolution* (1968), 110.

39. Ferdynand Zweig, *The Student in an Age of Anxiety: A Survey of Oxford and Manchester Students* (1963), 198; Michael Young, *The Observer*, 22 Sept. 1963, quoted by Frank Musgrove, *Youth and the Social Order* (1964), 21; ibid. 22; George Paloczi-Horvath, *Youth Up in Arms: A Political and Social World Survey 1955–1970* (1971), 155.

40. Zweig, *Age of Anxiety*, 200.

41. Ibid. 208.

42. Ibid. 201.

43. Paul Byrne, *The Campaign for Nuclear Disarmament* (1988); John Minnion and Philip Bolsover, *The CND Story: The First 25 Years of CND in the Words of the People Interviewed* (1983); Richard Taylor and Colin Pritchard, *The Protest Makers: The British Nuclear Disarmament Movement of 1958–1965, Twenty Years On* (1980).

44. Quoted in Barbara Bernard, *Fashion in the Sixties* (1978), 16.

45. Ibid. 27.

46. Quoted in *Quant by Quant*, 105.

47. Ibid. 111.

48. David Laing, *The Sound of Our Time* (1969), 106. For a full list of books on rock music, see ch. 10, n. 11.

49. Quoted in Peter Wicke, *Rock Music: Culture, Aesthetics and Sociology* (Cambridge, 1987), 64.

50. Laing, *The Sound of Our Time*, 97.

51. Anthony Bicât, 'Fifties Children: Sixties People', in Vernon Bogdanor and Robert Skidelsky, *The Age of Affluence 1951–1964* (1970), 325.

52. Ibid. 323–4.

53. Michael Cable, *The Pop Industry Inside Out* (1977), 8.

54. Quoted in Wicke, *Rock Music*, 64.

55. Charlie Gillett, *The Sound of the City* (1983), 263. See also Richard Middleton, *Pop Music and the Blues* (1972), 167–74, 182–4, 235–5; Ian MacDonald, *Revolution in the Head: The Beatles' Records and the Sixties* (1994), 40–83; Laing, *Sound of Our Time*, 115–16.

56. Philip Norman, *Shout! The True Story of the Beatles* (1981), 141–73.

57. H. N. Smith Papers, Box 6F8, Bancroft Library, University of California at Berkeley.

58. Frances Rust, *Dance in Society* (1969), 113.

59. Ibid. 111–12.

60. Quoted ibid. 115.

61. Abrams, *The Teenage Consumer*, 15.

62. *Mirabelle*, Sept. 1959-July 1960.

63. Charles Hamblett and Jane Deverson, *Generation X* (London, 1965), 26–7.

64. Ibid. 19–24.

65. Michael Schofield, *The Sexual Behaviour of Young People* (1965), 263–4.

66. Registrar-General, *Statistical Review for England and Wales for 1960*, ii: *population* (1961).

67. G. M. Carstairs, *This Island Now: The BBC Reith Lectures 1962* (1963), 50–1.

68. Marianne Faithfull, *Faithfull* (1964), 13.

69. Steve Humphries and John Taylor, *The Making of Modern London, 1945–1985* (1986), 36.

70. Ibid. 36–7.

71. Green, *Days in the Life*, 47.

72. Humphries and Taylor, *Making of Modern London*, 48.

73. Ibid.

74. Ibid. 40.

75. Green, *Days in the Life*, 49.

76. Vidal Sassoon, *Sorry I Kept You Waiting, Madam* (1967), 121.

77. Ibid. 105.

78. Ibid. 105, 120–8.

79. M. P. Carter, *Education, Employment and Leisure* (1963), 155.

80. Simon Frith, *Sound Effects: Youth, Leisure and the Politics of Rock* (1983), 239.

81. Paul Ginsborg, *A History of Contemporary Italy: Society and Politics 1945–1988* (1990), 214.

82. David W. Jones, Jr., 'California's Freeway Era in Historical Perspective', Institute of Transportation Studies, University of California at Berkeley, for California Department of

Transportation, June 1989; TS in Documents Department, San Francisco Public Library, 256–90; *San Francisco Chronicle,* 29 Jan. 1991.

83. See the proposals of the engineering and planning firm Wilsey, Hain & Blair, *Earth Fill Study for the San Mateo County Board of Supervisors* (Milbrae, Calif., 1962), cited in Mel Scott, 'The Future of San Francisco Bay', Institute of Government Study at the University of California at Berkeley, Sept. 1963, in Documents Dept, San Francisco Public Library.

84. Jones, 'California's Freeway Era', 268.

85. Ibid. 290.

86. Ibid. 293.

87. Ibid. 299.

88. Ibid. 300.

89. *San Francisco Chronicle,* 29 Jan. 1991.

90. Jane Jacobs, *The Death and Life of Great American Cities: The Failure of Town Planning* (New York, 1961), 40. My page references are to the British paperback edition of 1964.

91. Ibid. 14, 39, 622.

92. 'Save San Francisco Bay Association', Social Protest Collection, Carton 7, F.20, Bancroft Library.

93. Scott, 'The Future of San Francisco Bay', p. i.

94. Ibid. 68.

95. Documents in Handy-Ruffin Papers, Boxes 4 and 5, Mississippi Valley Collection.

96. Ibid. Box 5.

97. Ibid.

98. Mrs Horace Wright to President J. F. Kennedy, 27 Mar. 1961; copy in Handy-Ruffin Papers, Box 4.

99. Rachel Carson, *Silent Spring* (1962, Penguin edn. 1965), 256–7.

100. Betty Friedan, *The Feminine Mystique* (New York, 1983), 18, 43.

101. Ibid. 22.

102. Ibid. 378

103. Helen Gurley Brown, *Sex and the Single Girl* (New York, 1962), 227.

104. *Paris-Match,* 8 Sept. 1962; André Gauron, *Histoire économique et sociale de la cinquième république, i: Le Temps des modernistes* (Paris, 1983), 95.

105. Ibid. 22.

106. Henri Mendras, *Sociologie de la campagne française* (Paris, 1959), 107–9.

107. Ibid. 105–6.

108. *L'Express,* 18–24 Feb. 1960.

109. Paolo Ammassari, *Worker Satisfaction and Occupational Life: A Study of the Automobile Worker in Italy* (Rome, 1970), 61–3, 67–8, 80, 90, 128, 135, 137.

110. *Epoca,* 23, 30 Oct. 1960; 5, 12 Feb. 1961.

111. Lieta Harrison, *Le svergognate* (Rome, 1963), 4–150.

112. Full account in Eustace Chesser, *Is Chastity Outmoded?* (1960), 7–14.

113. Carstairs, *This Island Now,* 70–2.

114. Laurence Wylie, 'Youth in France and the United States', in Erikson, *Youth*, 243–60.

115. Alfred Sauvy, *La Montée des jeunes* (Paris, 1959), 115.

116. La Documentation Française, *The Young Face of France* (Paris, 1959), 6.

117. Reprinted in *La Génération du twist et la presse française* (Paris, 1962).

118. Antonin Bondat, *Jeunesse et famille à l'heure de l'atome* (Paris, 1962), 101.

119. Pierre Lavonde in 'L'Histoire au jour le jour', *La Génération du twist et la presse française*, 6.

120. Documentation Française, *Young Face of France*, 3.

121. Jacques Duquesne, *Les 16–24 ans: ce qu'ils sont, ce qu'ils pensent. D'après une enquête de l'Institut français d'Opinion Publique* (Paris, 1963), 5.

122. Ibid. 232–7.

123. Edgar Morin, *Commune en France: la métamorphose de Plodémet* (Paris, 1967), 149.

124. *La Génération du twist*, 5; *Paris-Match*, 4 Apr. 1964; Les Cahiers de cepec, *La Jeunesse d'aujourd'hui*, ed. Michel de Saint-Pierre (Paris, 1964), 3–12.

125. Ibid. 12–49.

126. A. Belden Fields, *Student Politics in France: A Study of the Union Nationale des étudiants de France* (New York, 1970), 33–73.

127. Cepec, *La Jeunesse*, 31–2.

128. Quoted in *La Generation du twist*, 48.

129. The memoirs of Moustache, ed. Guillaume Hanoteau, *Tambour battant* (Paris, 1975), 183.

130. Copies in the newspaper section of the Bibliothèque Nationale.

131. *Salut les Copains*, July/Aug. 1962.

132. Ibid.

133. *Le Monde*, 6–8 July 1963.

134. Yvonne Delandres, *Le Costume image de l'homme* (Paris, 1976), esp. 168; Bruno du Roselli, *La Crise de la mode: la revolution des jeunes et la mode* (Paris, 1973), esp. 75–106.

135. I am grateful to Professor Pierre Sorlin for putting me right on this matter.

136. 'Le Trecce del Vento', diary of Margherita Nicotra, entries for 11 Jan. and 13 Apr. 1960, Archivio Diaristico, Pieve Santa Stefano.

137. Giancarlo Riccio, *Percorsi del rock italiano* (Milan, 1980), 132. See also Alessandro Carrera, *Musica e pubblico giovanile* (Milan, 1980).

138. Ginsborg, *Contemporary Italy*, 256–7.

139. Ugoberto Alfassio-Grimaldi and I. Bertoni, *I giovani degli anni sessanta* (Bari, 1964), 47, 379–80.

140. Ibid. 380.

*Chapter 4. Art, Morality, and Social Relations*

1. 'The most unfailing herald, companion, and follower of the awakening of a great people to want a beneficial change in opinions or institutions is poetry... It is impossible to read the compositions of the most celebrated writers of the present day without being startled with the electric life which burns within their words. They measure the circumference and

sound the depths of human nature with a comprehensive and all-penetrating spirit, and they are themselves perhaps the most sincerely astonished at its manifestations: for it is less their spirit than the spirit of the age... Poets are the unacknowledged legislators of the world.' Percy Bysshe Shelley, *Defence of Poetry* (1821).

2. Transport and General Workers' Union Archives 1/4/12, Modern Records Centre, University of Warwick.

3. Josephine Klein, *Samples from English Cultures* (1955), 184.

4. Alison Davis, *Psychology of the Child in the Middle Class* (1960), 4–5.

5. Stephan Thernstrom, *The Other Bostonians* (1973), 104.

6. Ibid.

7. Caesar L. Donnaruma to Laurence F. O'Brien, Special Assistant to the President, 9 Feb. 1961; O'Brien to Donnaruma, 16 Feb. 1961. Donnaruma Collection, Immigration History Research Center, University of Minnesota Libraries, St Paul.

8. John Bodnar (ed.), *The Ethnic Experience in Pennsylvania* (1973), 185.

9. Anthony Aldgate, *Censorship and the Permissive Society: British Cinema and Theatre 1955–1965* (Oxford, 1995).

10. At an Open University 'Sixties Research Group' seminar, 1993.

11. Eyre and Spottiswoode to Penguin Books, 16 Apr., 13 May 1957; Penguin Books to Eyre and Spottiswoode, 7 May 1957. By courtesy of Peter Carson, Penguin Books.

12. Aldgate, *Censorship*, 5–6, 33–5, 38–47.

13. Ibid. 43–4.

14. Ibid. 44.

15. Ibid. 45.

16. Censorship file, *Room at the Top:* Note from examiners, 4 Feb. 1959. Dr Aldgate generously made this file, kindly loaned to him by James Ferman, available to me when I was preparing 'Room at the Top, Saturday Night and Sunday Morning, and the "Cultural Revolution in Britain" ', *Journal of Contemporary History*, 19(1) (1984); and 'Room at the Top: The Novel and the Film', in Arthur Marwick (ed.), *The Arts, Literature and Society* (1990), 249–79.

17. John Braine, *Room at the Top* (Penguin edn, 1959), 90–1.

18. Alan Sillitoe, Introduction to 'Heritage of Literature' repr. of *Saturday Night and Sunday Morning* (1968), p. xii.

19. Alan Sillitoe, *Saturday Night and Sunday Morning* (Star edn, 1975), 29–30.

20. Ibid. 74–5.

21. Ibid. 136.

22. Quoted in Aldgate, *Censorship*, 94.

23. Publicity material in British Film Institute file on *Saturday Night and Sunday Morning*.

24. Ibid.

25. Aldgate, *Censorship*, 97–8.

26. Ibid. 99.

27. Stan Barstow, *A Kind of Loving* (Penguin edn, 1962), 171.

28. Ibid. 272.

29. Aldgate, *Censorship*, 147–8.

30. All quoted ibid. 121.

31. Ibid. 128.

32. Ibid. 104.

33. Ibid. 108.

34. Ibid. 110 (my italics).

35. Ibid. 163.

36. John Sutherland, *Offensive Literature: Decensorship in Britain 1960–1982* (1982), 10.

37. For the trial, see J. Ehrlich (ed.), *Howl of the Censor* (San Carlos, Calif., 1959).

38. Sutherland, *Offensive Literature*, 14.

39. Record in Civil Rights Movement Papers, Box 3, University of California at Los Angeles Library Special Collections.

40. Sutherland, *Offensive Literature*, 14.

41. Ibid. 16.

42. Reported in C. H. Rolf, *The Trial of Lady Chatterley* (1961).

43. Documents in Civil Rights Movement Papers, Boxes 3 and 4.

44. *Los Angeles Daily Journal*, 30 Jan. 1962.

45. *Daily Bruin*, 4 Apr. 1962: Civil Rights Movement Papers, University of California at Los Angeles, Box 3; *Los Angeles Times*, 3 July 1963.

46. Statement by Aldous Huxley, 30 Jan. 1962; Civil Rights Movement Papers, Box 4.

47. Jerome Klinkowitz, 'John Updike', in Jeffrey Helterman and Richard Layman (eds.), *American Novelists Since World War II*, Gale Research Company, *Dictionary of Literary Biography*, ii (Detroit, 1978), 484–6.

48. John Updike, *Rabbit, Run* (Penguin edn, 1964), 8.

49. Ibid. 26–7.

50. Ibid. 76–7.

51. Ibid. 97.

52. Ibid. 118.

53. Ibid. 160.

54. Ibid. 13, 23.

55. Quoted by Fred L. Standley, 'James Baldwin', ibid. 15.

56. James Baldwin, *Another Country* (Penguin edn, 1990), 229, 398.

57. James Baldwin, *The Fire Next Time* (New York, 1963).

58. Eugenia Collier, quoted in Standley, 'James Baldwin', 18.

59. Robert Bone, quoted ibid. 18.

60. Baldwin, *Another Country*, 30–1.

61. Ibid. 271–2.

62. Ibid. 379.

63. Ibid. 409.

64. Mary McCarthy, *The Group* (Penguin edn, 1964), 33–7.

65. Ibid. 313.

66. Camilla Van Dyke to her parents, 11 Oct. 1963, Van Dyke Papers, Memphis State University, Box 8, Folder 211.

67. Richard Brautigan Papers, Box 2, Bancroft Library, University of California at Berkeley.

68. Stephen L. Tanner, 'Ken Kesey', in Helterman and Layman, *American Novelists*, 261.

69. Inge Kutt, 'Joseph Heller', ibid. 233.

70. Arthur D. Casciato, 'John Barth', ibid. 26.

71. Harold Robbins, *The Carpetbaggers* (1961), 45–6.

72. Ibid. 459.

73. Edna O'Brien, *The Girl with Green Eyes* (Penguin edn, 1964), 191.

74. Ibid. 22, 213.

75. I use the edition published in Britain in 1985 by Thomas Nelson, Walton-on-Thames, with an introduction and notes by P. M. W. Thody; the British translation by Edward Hyams of 1963 is called *Josyane and the Welfare*, a title which focuses on the name of the child-narrator and gives a somewhat reductionist impression of the content.

76. Christopher Robinson, *French Literature in the Twentieth Century* (Newton Abbot, 1980), 108.

77. Details from the invaluable introduction by P. M. W. Thody to his edition of Christiane Rochefort, *Les Petits Enfants du siècle* (Walton-on-Thames, 1985), and Jacques Bersani, M. Autrand et al. (eds.), *La Littérature en France depuis 1945* (Paris, 1970), 308–11.

78. Again I have depended heavily on Thody.

79. *John Lennon en flagrant délire, tentative désespérée de traduction par Christiane Rochefort et Rachel Mizraki* (Paris, 1965), 12–13.

80. Thody, introd. to *Les Petits Enfants du siècle*, p. vii.

81. Anna Koedt's essay 'The Myth of the Vaginal Orgasm' was written and distributed to close feminist associates in Oct. 1968, then published in mimeographed form in 'Notes for the First Year' (1969, published by New York Radical Women). See Ch. 13.

82. The letter is printed in the introduction by Giovanni Tesio to the combined volumes. This book also has informative appendices by Italo Calvino and Gian Carlo Ferretti. I have also used the collection of papers given at Vigerano, 6–7 June 1981, and published as M. Antonietta Grignani (ed.), *Per Mastronardi* (Vigerano, 1983).

83. I have used the Einaudi Tascabile (pocket-book) No. 226, published in Turin in 1994, which contains the complete *Vigerano* trilogy, of which the third, first published in 1964, was *Il meridionale di Vigerano* (The Southerner of Vigerano)—the focus here being on a major social phenomenon of the time, an immigrant from southern Italy in a northern town.

84. Tesio, introduction.

85. I know of no cheap Italian edition, and myself own the expensive reprint of 1993, which has a useful preface by Sergio Pautasso; my references are all to the original 1962 edition. For certain connoisseurs of Italian life, it may be of interest that the book was dedicated 'to my noble friend Carlo Ripa de Meana'— disgraced politician of much more recent times, and in 1962 undoubtedly a vigorous and predatory pursuer of the good life just beginning to be created in the early sixties.

86. Luciano Bianciardi, *La vita agra* (Milan, 1962), 29.

87. Ibid. 74.

88. Ibid. 176.

89. Ibid. 197.

90. Pierre Sorlin, *European Cinemas, European Societies 1939–1990* (1991), 158.

91. Philippe J. Maarek, *La Censure cinématographique* (Paris, 1982), 17–18.

92. *L'Espresso*, 21 June 1960.

93. *Osservatore Romano*, quoted in Federico Fellini, *La dolce vita* (Bologna, 1959), 187. The cast list is also included in the Fellini volume.

94. Quoted ibid. 171.

95. *La Civiltà Cattolica*, 5 Mar. 1960, quoted in Fellini, *La dolce vita*, 188.

96. Interview with Fellini in *Il Giorno*, 7 Feb. 1960, quoted in Fellini, *La dolce vita*, 164; Mino Argentieri, *La censura nel cinema italiana* (Rome, 1974), 152–5.

97. Ibid. 157–8.

98. Quoted in Ian Cameron and Robin Wood, *Antonioni* (1968), 25.

99. Michelangelo Antonioni, *L'avventura* (1960), 122.

100. *Il Contemporaneo*, 32 (1960), quoted in Sergio Pastore, *Proibitissimo: la censura nel tempo* (Naples, 1980), 91.

101. Edward Lucie-Smith, *Movements in Art Since 1945* (rev. edn, 1984).

102. Ibid. 225. Apart from permanent collections, temporary exhibitions, and their catalogues, I have also made great use of Lea Vergine, *L'arte in trincea: lessico delle tendenze artistiche 1960– 1990* (Milan, 1996).

103. Mel Scott, for Institute of Government Studies, *Partnerships in the Arts: Public and Private Support of Cultural Activities in the San Francisco Bay Area* (San Francisco, Calif., 1963), 7.

104. Lucie-Smith, *Movements*, 80.

105. Tate Gallery, *Richard Hamilton, 17 June-6 September 1992*.

106. Royal Academy of Art, *The Pop Art Show* (1996).

107. Ibid.

108. The critical notes provided in the relevant rooms of the Beaubourg Gallery in Paris are particularly helpful.

109. Vergine, *L'arte in trincea*, 87, 205; Lucie-Smith, *Movements*, 131.

110. Frances Spalding, *British Art Since 1900* (1986), 189.

111. Lucie-Smith, *Movements*, 139.

112. Peter Fuller, 'The Visual Arts', in Boris Ford (ed.), *The Cambridge Guide to the Arts in Britain Since the Second World War* (Cambridge, 1988), 138.

113. Quoted in John Rothenstein, *Modern English Painters: Wood to Hockney* (1974), 215.

114. RCA, *The Pop Art Show*.


*Chapter 5. Race*

1. Dalstrom Papers, Box 5, MS 189, Mississippi Valley Collection, Memphis State University. Important books relating to the first two sections of this chapter are: Earle and Merle Black,

*Politics and Society in the South* (Cambridge, Mass., 1987); Rhoda Lois Blumberg, *Civil Rights: The 1960s Freedom Struggles* (Boston, 1991); Taylor Branch, *Parting the Waters: Martin Luther King and the Civil Rights Movement, 1954–63* (1988); Clayborne Carson, *In Struggle: SNCC and the Black Awakening of the 1960s* (Cambridge, Mass., 1981); James A. Colaiaco, *Martin Luther King, Jr.: Apostle of Militant Nonviolence* (New York, 1988); John Dittmer, *Local People: The Struggle for Civil Rights in Mississippi* (Urbana, Ill., 1994); Charles Eagles (ed.), *The Civil Rights Movement in America: Essays* (Oxford, Miss., 1986); David J. Garrow (ed.), *We Shall Overcome: The Civil Rights Movement in the United States in the 1950s and 1960s* (3 vols., New York, 1989); David J. Garrow, *Bearing the Cross: Martin Luther King, Jr. and the Southern Christian Leadership Conference* (New York, 1986); Hugh D. Graham, *The Civil Rights Era: Origins and Development of National Policy, 1960–1972* (New York, 1990); Nicolaus Mills, *Like a Holy Crusade: Mississippi 1964—The Turning of the Civil Rights Movement in America* (Chicago, 1992); Charles M. Payne, I've *Got the Light of Freedom: The Organizing Tradition and the Mississippi Freedom Struggle* (Berkeley, Calif., 1995); Fred Powledge, *Free at Last? The Civil Rights Movement and the People Who Made It* (Boston, 1991); Harvard Sitkoff, *The Struggle for Black Equality, 1954–1992* (1993); Robert Weisbrot, *Freedom Bound: A History of America's Civil Rights Movement* (New York, 1990); Juan Williams, *Eyes on the Prize: America's Civil Rights Years, 1954–1965* (New York, 1987).

There are useful oral accounts in: Howell Raines (ed.), *My Soul Is Rested: Movement Days in the Deep South Remembered* (New York, 1977). Published autobiographies include: Roy Wilkins, *Standing Fast: the Autobiography of Roy Wilkins* (New York, 1982); James Farmer, *Lay Bare the Heart: An Autobiography of the Civil Rights Movement* (New York, 1986); Anne Moody, *Coming of Age in Mississippi* (US, 1968; London, 1974); David J. Garrow (ed.), *The Montgomery Bus Boycott and the Woman Who Started It: The Memoir of Jo Ann Gibson Robinson* (Knoxville, Tenn., 1987). Other important books are cited in the notes to Ch. 11.

2. Edmund Orgill Papers, Box 24, Folder 2, MS 87, Mississippi Valley Collection.

3. Ibid. David L. Chappell, *Inside Agitators: White Southerners in the Civil Rights Movement* (Baltimore, 1991) is an excellent account of the growing 'flexibility' (his word) of white moderates up to 1965.

4. Rabbi J. A. Wax Collection, Box VI, Folder 7, Memphis and Shelby County Library Special Collections.

5. Edmund Orgill Papers, Box 16, Folder 9.

6. Ibid.

7. Ibid.

8. Ibid.

9. Ibid.

10. Wax Collection, Box VI, Folder 8.

11. Ibid.

12. *Wall Street Journal*, 16 Jan. 1962.

13. Ibid.

14. *Tiger Rag*, 25 Sept. 1959, Memphis State University Papers, Mississippi Valley Collection.

15. William H. Chafe, *Civilities and Civil Rights: Greensboro, North Carolina, and the Black Struggle for Freedom* (New York, 1980), 114–37; August Meier and Elliott Rudwick, *CORE: A Study of the Civil Rights Movement 1942–1968* (New York, 1973), 101–31.

16. Carson, *In Struggle*, 33–5.

17. Meeman Papers, Box 19, Folder 1, Mississippi Valley Collection.

18. Oral History Project, UCLA Library Special Collections—on which the rest of this paragraph is also based.

19. Dr Lucy Turnbull Collection, Folder 7, University of Mississippi, Oxford, Miss.

20. *New York Times*, 13 Jan. 1963.

21. Milbourn Hinds Papers, Box 19, Folder 666, Mississippi Valley Collection.

22. Ibid., Box 15, Folder 473.

23. Ibid., Box 13, Folder 432.

24. Ibid.

25. Memphis Typographical Union Papers, Box 20, Mississippi Valley Collection.

26. *Albany Herald*, 8 Mar. 1963.

27. *Los Angeles Times*, 17 Mar. 1963.

28. John F. Kennedy, *Public Papers of the Presidents, 1963* (Washington, DC, 1964), 221–30.

29. Printed in Martin Luther King, *Why We Can't Wait* (New York, 1964), 76–95.

30. Ibid. 194–5.

31. Ibid.

32. *Commercial Appeal*, 12 June 1963.

33. Letter of 31 Mar. 1963, Van Dyke Papers, Mississippi Valley Collection, Box 8, Folder 209.

34. Los Angeles County Commission on Human Relations, *Notes on the History and Activities of the Human Relations Commission*, July 1963, Civil Rights Movement Papers, Box IIIB, UCLA Special Collections.

35. Social Protest Collection, 86/157C, Carton 7, Folder 42, Mississippi Valley Collection.

36. Colaiaco, *Martin Luther King*, 70.

37. Civil Rights Movement Papers, University of California at Los Angeles, Box 1.

38. 'Committee to Fight Police Brutality' (mimeographed report), Civil Rights Movement Papers, Box IIIB.

39. Documents in Japanese-American Research Project, Box 521, Folder 3, and Box 523, Folder 4, UCLA Special Collections.

40. In Edward M. Ainsworth Papers, Box 70, UCLA Special Collections.

41. Quoted in Colaiaco, *Martin Luther King*, 71.

42. Ibid. 72.

43. James Melvin Washington (ed.), *I Have a Dream: Writings and Speeches That Changed the World, Martin Luther King Jr.* (San Francisco, Calif., 1992), 102–6.

44. University Civil Rights Committee, 'Articles of Organization', 18 Nov. 1963, Civil Rights Movement Papers, Box IIIB.

45. *Epoca, Oggi, Panorama, L'Espresso*, 14 Oct. 1962.

46. Dilip Hero, *Black British White British: A History of Race Relations in Britain* (1991), 331.

47. Gary P. Freeman, *Immigrant Labor and Racial Conflict in Industrial Societies: The French and British Experience 1945–1975* (Princeton, NJ, 1978), 23.

48. Ibid. 78; Paulette and Pierre Calmane, *Les Travailleurs étrangers en France* (Paris, 1972).

49. Hero, *Black British White British*, 40.

50. Ibid. 39.

51. Ibid. 39–40. James Wickenden, *Colour in Britain* (Institute of Race Relations, 1 Oct. 1958), 38–40.

52. Hero, *Black British White British*, 41.

53. Wickenden, *Colour in Britain*, 44.

54. Ibid.

55. Maurice Edelman Papers, 'Coventry Immigration File', MS 125, Modern Records Centre, University of Warwick.

56. Sheila Patterson, *Dark Strangers: A Sociological Study of the Absorption of a Recent West Indian Migrant Group in Brixton, South London* (1963), 365.

57. Wickenden, *Colour in Britain*, 26, 30.

58. Patterson, *Dark Strangers*, 237.

59. Ibid. 199.

60. Hero, *Black British White British*, 39; Wickenden, *Colour in Britain*, 15.

61. Hero, *Black British White British*, 42–3.

62. Ibid. 44.

63. Quoted in Paul Foot, *Immigration and Race in British Politics* (Harmondsworth, 1965), 212.

64. Sheila Patterson, *Immigration and Race Relations in Britain, 1960–1967* (Institute of Race Relations, 1968), 168–9.

65. Paul H. Maucorps, Albert Memmi, and Jean-Francis Held, *Les Français et le racisme* (Paris, 1965), 79–105.

66. Ibid. 105.

67. Freeman, *Immigrant Labor and Racial Conflict*, 81.

68. Juliette Mince, *Les Travailleurs étrangers en France* (Paris, 1973), 102.

69. Printed in Goffredo Foffi, *L'immigrazione meridionale a Torino* (Milan, 1966), 160–8.

70. Ibid. 179.

71. Ibid. 181.

## Part III. The High Sixties, 1964–1969

### Chapter 6. Acts of God and Acts of Government

1. Cited by Godfrey Hodgson, *In Our Time: America from World War II to Nixon* (New York, 1976), 6.

2. Maurice Larkin, *France since the Popular Front: Government and People 1936–1986* (1988), 184.

3. Paul Vaughan, *The Pill on Trial* (1970), 49.

4. Kevin Allen and Andrew Stevenson, *An Introduction to the Italian Economy* (1974), 49.

5. Augusto Graziani (ed.), *L'economia italiana dal 1945 a oggi* (Bologna, 1972), 78–9.

6. Elbert W. Stewart, *The Troubled Land: Social Problems in Modern America* (New York, 1972), 195.

7. Allen J. Matusow, *The Unraveling of America: A History of Liberalism in the 1960s* (New York, 1984), 212.

8. Graziani, *L'economia italiana*, 69.

9. Gisèle Podbielski, *Twenty-five Years of Special Action for the Development of Southern Italy* (Milan, 1978), 144.

10. Ibid. 127.

11. Andrée Gauron, *Histoire économique et sociale de la cinquième république*, i: *Le Temps des modernistes* (Paris, 1983), 20–1.

12. Ibid.

13. Ibid.

14. Ralph Nader, *Unsafe at Any Speed: The Designed-in Dangers of the American Automobile* (New York, 1965); Sidney Margoles, *The Innocent Consumer Versus the Exploiters* (New York, 1968).

15. Central Statistical Office, *Social Trends*, i (1971); *Social Trends*, iii (1973); Jean-Marcel Jeanneney and Elisabeth Barbier-Jeanneney, *Les économies occidentales du XIX$^e$ siècle à nos jours*, i (Paris, 1985), 132–3.

16. Calculated from National Census statistics, 1955–75.

17. Michael Harrington, *The Other America: Poverty in the United States* (New York, 1962), 158–9.

18. Walter I. Trattner, *From Poor Law to Welfare State: A History of Social Welfare in America* (2nd edn, New York, 1979), 255. For recent books on the Kennedy years, see Note on Sources.

19. Hodgson, *In Our Time*, 173.

20. Trattner, *Poor Law to Welfare State*, 256.

21. Maurizio Ferrera, *Il Welfare State in Italia: sviluppo e crisi in prospettiva comparata* (Bologna, 1984), 27.

22. Jean-Pierre Dumont, *La Sécurité sociale toujours en chantier: historique, bilan, perspectives* (Paris, 1981), 40.

23. Ferrera, *Il Welfare State in Italia*, 27.

24. Ugo Ascoli (ed.), *Welfare State all'italiana* (Bari, 1984).

25. Patrizia David, 'Il sistema assistenziale in Italia', ibid. 92.

26. James T. Patterson, *The Welfare State in America 1930–1980* (1981), 25.

27. Ibid. 26; Trattner, *Poor Law to Welfare State*, 256.

28. Ibid. 258.

29. Patterson, *Welfare State in America*, 29.

30. Centro Studi Investimenti Sociali (CENSIS), ed. Franco Angeli, *Gli anni di cambiamento* (Milan, 1982), 72.

31. Or so I have argued at length in *Class: Image and Reality in Britain, France and the USA since 1930* (1980; 2nd edn 1990).

32. See my forthcoming chapter on Alison Lurie's *Love and Friendship* (1962) in Anthony Aldgate, James Chapman, and Arthur Marwick (eds.), *Windows on the Sixties: Significant Texts* (London, forthcoming, 1999).

33. Richard P. Coleman and Bernice L. Neugarten, *Social Status in the City* (1971), 18.

34. Herbert J. Gans, *The Levittowners: Ways of Life and Politics in a New Suburban Community* (1967), 373–8.

35. *Chicago Tribune*, 4 Nov. 1976.

36. *New York Times*, 7 Aug. 1977.

37. John C. Leggett, *Class, Race and Labor: Working Class Consciousness in Detroit* (1968).

38. Serge Mallet, *La Nouvelle Classe ouvrière* (Paris, 1963).

39. Alan Touraine, *La Conscience ouvrière* (Paris, 1966), 60–8, 116–19.

40. Ibid. 119.

41. Janich Arbois and Joshka Schidlow, *La Vraie Vie des français* (Paris, 1978), 150.

42. Ibid. 166, 169, 172.

43. Michael Kahan, David Butler, and Donald Stokes, 'On the Analytical Division of Social Class', *British Journal of Sociology*, 17 (2) (June 1966).

44. Colin Bell, *Middle Class Families* (1968), 28–32.

45. Brian Jackson and Denis Marsden, *Working-Class Community: Some General Notions Raised by a Series of Studies in Northern England* (1962).

46. Ibid.

47. J. Goldthorpe, D. Lockwood, J. Beckhofer, and J. Platt, *The Affluent Worker in the Class Structure* (1969), 140–56.

48. Suzanne Keller, *Beyond the Ruling Class: Strategic Elites in Modern Society* (New York, 1963), 205.

49. *New York Times*, 5 Aug. 1977.

50. *Life*, 21 Mar. 1960.

51. *Time*, 27 Nov. 1978.

52. Ronald Blythe, *Akenfield: A Study of Rural Life* (1969), 101–8.

53. Richard Crossman, *The Diaries of a Cabinet Minister*, ii (1976), 190.

54. Steven B. Levine, 'The Rise of American Boarding Schools and the Development of a National Upper Class', *Social Problems* (Oct. 1980), 63–94.

55. *Esquire*, Sept. 1977.

56. George Katona, Burkhard Strempel, and Ernest Zahn, *Aspirations and Affluence: Comparative Studies in the United States and Western Europe* (New York, 1976), 225.

57. Anna Laura Zanatta, *Il sistema scolastico italiano* (Bologna, 1971), 201.

58. Larkin, *France since the Popular Front*, 211.

*Chapter 7. Pushing Paradigms to Their Utmost Limits*

1. Michael Crozier, 'France's Cultural Anxieties under Gaullism: The Cultural Revolution Revisited', in Stanley Hoffman and Paschalis Kitromilides (eds.), *Culture and Society in Contemporary Europe: A Casebook* (Cambridge, Mass., 1981), 107–8.

2. Angela Davis, *Angela Davis: An Autobiography* (1975), 133–4. Biographical information on Marcuse in Barry Katz, *Herbert Marcuse and the Art of Liberation: An Intellectual Biography* (1982).

3. Herbert Marcuse, 'Repressive Tolerance', in Robert Paul Wolff, Barrington Moore, Jr., and Herbert Marcuse (eds.), *A Critique of Pure Tolerance* (1965).

4. Ibid. 130; *Daily Californian* (Berkeley), 26 Mar. 1966; *L'Express,* 23–9 Sept. 1968; Daniel Cohn-Bendit, *The French Student Revolt* (1969), 58.

5. Didier Eribon, *Michel Foucault,* trans. Betsy Wing (1992).

6. Ferdinand de Saussure, *Cours de Linguistique Générale,* published by Charles Bally and Albert Sachehaye, with Albert Rudlinger (Lausanne, 1916), esp. 33–4, 101–2.

7. Noam Chomsky, *Language and the Problems of Knowledge* (Cambridge, Mass., 1988); John Lyons, *Language and Linguistics* (Cambridge, 1981), esp. 38, 221, 261–2, 304–8; Guilio Lepschy, *A Survey of Structural Linguistics* (London, 1982); Steven Pinker, *The Language Instinct: The New Science of Language and Mind* (1994).

8. Edmund Leach, *Lévi-Strauss* (1950), 8.

9. The essay 'Historical Discourse', in translation, is conveniently available in Michael Lane (ed.), *Structuralism: A Reader* (1970), 145–55. Biographical information and critical comment on Barthes are from: Louis-Jean Calvet, *Roland Barthes 1915–1980* (Paris, 1990); Michael Moriarty, *Roland Barthes* (Cambridge, 1991); Steven Ungar, *Roland Barthes: The Professor of Desire* (Lincoln, Neb., 1983); Philip Thody, *Roland Barthes: A Conservative Estimate* (1977). The first two quotations are in Moriarty, *Barthes,* 31, 34.

10. Roland Barthes, *Mythologies* (Paris, 1957), 223.

11. Roland Barthes, 'The Death of the Author', in *Image-Music-Text: Essays Selected and Translated by Stephen Heath* (1971), 142–8. Background information is from Sean Burke, *The Death and Return of the Author: Criticism and Subjectivity in Barthes, Foucault, and Derrida* (Edinburgh, 1992), 9–12, 20, 178.

12. Moriarty, *Barthes,* 1.

13. Thody, *Barthes,* 136.

14. Celia Britton, *The Nouveau Roman: Fiction, Theory and Politics* (New York, 1992), 101–2.

15. John Fletcher and John Calder (eds.), *The Nouveau Roman Reader* (1986), 20–2, 32, 36; Britton, *Nouveau Roman,* 58–9, 87–8. In much of what follows I have drawn heavily on these two books.

16. Philippe Forest, *Philippe Sollers* (Paris, 1992), 11–14.

17. Alain Robbe-Grillet, *Pour un nouveau roman* (Paris, 1963), 36–7. Background information is from Ben Stoltzfus, *Alain Robbe-Grillet: Life, Work and Criticism* (Frederickton, NB, Canada, 1987).

18. Alain Robbe-Grillet, *La Maison des rendez-vous* (Paris, 1965): translated by A. M. Sheridan Smith as *The House of Assignation* (London, 1970).

19. J. A. E. Louberè, *The Novels of Claude Simon* (Ithaca, NY, 1975), 92–4.

20. Forest, *Sollers,* 14.

21. Ibid. 18.

22. Ted Benton, *The Rise and Fall of Structural Marxism: Althusser and His Influence* (1988), 13.

23. François Furet, 'French Intellectuals: From Marxism to Structuralism' (1967); repr. in Furet, *In the Workshop of History* (Chicago, 1984), 35.

24. Madan Sarup, *Jacques Lacan* (Hemel Hempstead, 1992), 80.

25. Althusser's articles were collected in *Pour Marx* (Paris, 1965).

26. Benton, *Rise and Fall;* Edith Kurzweil, *The Age of Structuralism: Lévi-Strauss to Foucault* (New York, 1980), 8.

27. Michel Foucault, *Folie et déraison: histoire de folie à l'âge classique* (always appearing in English as *History of Madness in the Classical Age*, dropping the main title of 'Madness and Unreason').

28. All of the fascinating details come from Eribon, *Foucault*. Also helpful are: David Macey, *The Lives of Michel Foucault* (1993); Barry Smart, *Michel Foucault* (1985); Alan Sheridan, *Michel Foucault: The Will to Truth* (1980); Mark Poster, *Foucault, Marxism and History* (Cambridge, 1984); Michel Foucault, *Power/Knowledge: Selected Interviews and Other Writings, 1972–1977*, ed. Colin Gordon (1980).

29. Foucault, *Power/Knowledge*, 53; Jeffrey Weeks, 'Foucault for Historians', *History Workshop*, 14 (1982), 108. Foucault's Marxism also comes through clearly in the debate he had with Chomsky, printed (under a curious title) as Fons Elders (ed.), *Reflexive Water: Basic Concerns of Mankind* (1974).

30. Quoted in Eribon, *Foucault*, 155.

31. Quoted ibid. 346–7.

32. Ibid. 193.

33. Ibid. 187.

34. Ibid. 202–3.

35. Ibid. 210.

36. Ibid. 211.

37. Sean Burke, *Death and Return of the Author: Criticism and Subjectivity in Barthes, Foucault and Derrida* (Edinburgh, 1992), 9; Christopher Norris, *Derrida* (1987).

38. For Balestrini, see biographical details in Marco Spinelli's introd. to Nanni Balestrini, *Vogliamo tutto* (Milan, 1988). See also Christopher Wagstaff, 'The New-Avantgarde', in Michael Caeser and Peter Hainsworth (eds.), *Writers and Society in Contemporary Italy: A Collection of Essays* (Leamington Spa, 1984), 36–49; François Livi, *Les écrivains italiens d'aujourd'hui* (Paris, 1982), 81; *Magazine Littéraire*, 165 (Paris, Oct. 1980)—issue devoted to Italian literature of the 1960s; Marinella Colummi Caemarino, *I contemporanei* (Rome, 1979); Giorgio Pullini, *Volti e risvolti del romanzo italiano contemporaneo* (Milan, 1971). For Eco on James Bond, see Oreste del Buono and Umberto Eco, *The Bond Affair* (trans. R. A. Dowie, 1966).

39. Claude T. Bissell, 'Herbert Marshall McLuhan', in George Sanderson and Frank Macdonald (eds.), *Marshall McLuhan: The Man and His Message* (Golden, Colo., 1989), 8.

40. Quoted ibid.

41. Gunther M. Weil, Ralph Metzner, and Timothy Leary, *The Psychedelic Reader: Selected from the Psychedelic Review* (New Hyde Park, NY, 1965), 191.

42. Ibid. p. vii.

43. Ibid. 198–209.

44. Timothy Leary, with Richard Alpert, 'The Fifth Freedom: The Right to Get High', *Harvard Review*, 1 (4) (Summer 1963).

45. Timothy Leary, *The Politics of Ecstasy* (1968), 102. The full *Playboy* interview is printed on 99–120.

46. Leary interviewed in *Playboy* (Sept. 1966), 111, 117.

47. Norman O. Brown, *Life Against Death: The Psychoanalytical Meaning of History* (1959).

48. John Clay, *R. D. Laing: A Divided Self* (1996), 147–8.

49. Ibid. 84.

50. Ibid. 268. The Manifesto of the Dialectics of Liberation Conference is printed in Peter Stansill and David Zain Mairowits (eds.), *BAMN (By Any Means Necessary): Outlaw Manifestos and Ephemera 1965–70* (1971), 89.

51. David Bourdon, *Warhol* (New York, 1989), 14–16.

52. Ibid. 248–9.

53. Quoted ibid. 299.

54. Ibid. 301.

55. Quoted in John Rothenstein, *Modern English Painters: Wood to Hockney* (1974), 230.

56. Peter Webb, *Portrait of David Hockney* (1988), 244.

57. Quoted in Rothenstein, *Modern English Painters*, 228.

58. See John Ashberry, Joe Shannon, Jane Livingstone, and Timothy Hyman, *Kitaj, Paintings, Drawings, Pastels* (1983); *R. B. Kitaj: A Retrospective* (Tate Gallery, 16 June-4 September 1994).

59. Germano Celant, *Art Povera: Conceptual, Actual or Impossible Art?* (1969), 6.

60. Peter Fuller, 'The Visual Arts', in Boris Ford (ed.), *The Cambridge Guide to the Arts in Britain since the Second World War* (1988), 139.

61. Quoted in Mary Ellen Solt (ed.), *Concrete Poetry: A World View* (Bloomington, Ind., 1980), 7.

62. Ibid. 16, 32–49; Lawrence R. Smith, *The New Italian Poetry: 1945 to the Present. A Bilingual Anthology* (Berkeley, Calif., 1981), esp. 4, 29, 33.

63. Pierre Garnier, 'Manifesto', *Les Lettres: Poésie Nouvelle*, 29 (Jan. 1963), quoted in David W. Seaman, *Concrete Poetry in France* (Ann Arbor, Mich., 1981), 237.

64. *Les Lettres*, 30 (May 1963).

65. Solt, *Concrete Poetry*, 35.

66. Graham Dunstan Martin, *Anthology of Contemporary French Poetry* (Edinburgh, 1972), 2, 6.

67. Michael Horowitz, *Children of Albion: Poetry of the 'Underground'* (1969), 337.

68. Edwin Morgan, 'Scottish Poetry in the 1960s', in Michael Schmidt and Grevel Lindop (eds.), *British Poetry Since 1960* (1972).

69. Ibid.

70. Quoted in Glyn Jones, 'Second Flowering: Poetry in Wales', ibid. 130.

71. I have relied heavily on Michael Kurz's 1988 biography, translated into English by Richard Toop as *Stockhausen: A Biography* (1992), and in general on Robert P. Morgan, *Twentieth-Century Music: A History of Musical Style in Modern Europe and America* (New York, 1991).

72. Karlheinz Stockhausen, 'Manifesto for the Young', repr. in Tim Nevill (ed.), *Towards a Cosmic Music* (1989), 44–7.

73. Kurz, *Stockhausen*, 171. For *Hymnen* and *Stimmung*, see Robin Maconie, *The Works of Karlheinz Stockhausen* (1976), 217–26, 239–43.

74. Luigi Nono, *Intolleranza* (Mainz, 1962), 22—my translation.

75. Leonard Bernstein, *The Infinite Variety of Music* (1961), 10.

76. Steve Reich, *Writings about Music* (New York, 1974), 50.

77. Apart from Steve Reich, *Writings about Music* (New York, 1974), I have used *Steve Reich and Musicians* (1989), and Wim Mertens, *American Minimal Music*, trans. J. Hantenkiet (1983).

78. Reich, *Writings about Music*, 56.

79. Yasuhiro Fujioka, with Lewis Porter and Yoh-Ichi Hamada, *John Coltrane: A Discography and Musical Biography* (Metuchen, NJ, 1995), 180. See also Brian Priestley, *John Coltrane* (1987).

80. Bourdon, *Warhol*, 179.

81. Lewis Mumford, *The Highway and the City* (1964), 156, quoted in Charles Jencks, *Modern Movements in Architecture* (1973), 96.

82. Ibid. 95.

83. Vincent Scully, *American Architecture and Urbanism* (1969), 230.

84. William J. R. Curtis, *Modern Architecture since 1900* (Oxford, 1982), 350.

85. Vincent Scully, *American Architecture and Design* (1969), 20; Curtis, *Modern Architecture*, 349.

86. Ibid. 294.

87. Ibid. 345–6.

88. Ibid. 291–2.

89. William Wilson Papers, Box A2, Modern Records Centre, Warwick University Library.

90. Jencks, *Modern Movements in Architecture*, 269.

91. Stefan Brecht, *Peter Schumann's Bread and Puppet Theatre* (New York, 1988), 609; Andrew Davies, *Other Theatres: The Development of Alternative and Experimental Theatre in Britain* (1987), 170. See also Françoise Kouvilsky, *Le Bread and Puppet Theatre* (Lausanne, 1971).

92. Ferlinghetti Papers, Bancroft Library, University of California at Berkeley.

93. James Roose-Evans, *Experimental Theatre from Stanislavsky to Today* (1973), 215.

94. Ibid. 151–2.

95. Richard Neville, *Hippie Hippie Shake: The Dreams, the Trips, the Love-ins, the Screw Ups... the Sixties* (1996), 155–7.

96. Stuart W. Lilte, *Off-Broadway: The Prophetic Theater* (New York, 1972), 197.

97. *Village Voice* (18 Oct. 1968); *Drama Review* (spring 1969), both quoted by Donald L. Loeffler, *An Analysis of the Treatment of the Homosexual Character in Drama Produced in New York Theatre from 1950 to 1968* (New York, 1975), 185.

98. Stefan Brecht, *Peter Schumann's Bread and Puppet Theatre* (New York, 1988), 607.

99. Ibid. 343.

100. Ibid. 608.

101. Quoted ibid. 501.

102. Quoted ibid. 646.

103. Barbara Lee Horn, *Joseph Papp: A Biography* (Westport, Conn., 1992), 16.

104. David Jeffrey, 'Towards Collective Creation', in Ralph Yarrow (ed.), *European Theatre 1960–1990: Cross-Cultural Perspectives* (1992), 20.

105. Jennie Lee to Ritchie Calder, Ritchie Calder Papers, Folder 10, National Library of Scotland.

106. There is an excellent history, Joyce McMillan's *The Traverse Theatre Story 1963–1988* (1988); this I have amplified from my own researches in the Traverse Theatre archives, housed in the National Library of Scotland.

107. Letter of 2 Dec. 1962, Ginsberg Papers, Box 1, Columbia University Special Collections.

108. McMillan, *Traverse Theatre*, 12.

109. 'Constitution', Traverse Theatre Papers, Box 1, National Library of Scotland.

110. Ibid. Box 2.

111. Minutes of AGM, 27 Apr. 1966, Folder for 1966–7, Traverse Theatre Papers.

112. Traverse Theatre Papers, Box 1.

113. Folder for 1968–9, Traverse Papers.

114. Ibid.

115. McMillan, *Traverse Theatre*, 28.

116. Jim Haynes, *Thanks for Coming! An Autobiography* (1984), 123–54.

117. Peter Brook et al., *The Book of US* (1968), 9.

118. Suzanne Cowan, 'Theatre, Politics and Social Change in Italy since the Second World War', *Theatre Quarterly*, 7 (27) (autumn 1977), 30.

119. Printed in Franco Quadri, *L'avanguardia teatrale in Italia: materiali 1960–1976* (Turin, 1977), 1. 137.

120. Cowan, 'Theatre, Politics', 35.

121. Printed in Quadri, *L'avanguardia*, 348.

122. Elizabeth J. Natalle, *Feminist Theatre: A Study in Persuasion* (New York, 1985).

123. Loeffler, *Analysis*, 40.

124. Quoted ibid. 41.

125. Edward Bond, *Early Morning* (published in 1968 by John Calder's firm of Calder and Boyars), 71.

126. Charles Marowitz, *Plays and Players* (Nov. 1969).

### Chapter 8. Affluence, Poverty, Permissiveness

1. Feliks Gross, *Il Paese: Values and Social Change in an Italian Village* (New York, 1974). Quotations on the pages which follow are from pp. 45, 123, 124, 125, 150–1, 126, 137, 131–2, and 134.

2. I am deeply indebted to the generous and helpful staff at L'Istituto Regionale Ferruccio Parri in Bologna, where I was able to study these videos.

3. Lawrence Wylie, *Village in Vaucluse* (3rd edn, New York, 1974), 371.

4. Edgar Morin, *Commune en France: le métamorphose de Plodémet* (Paris, 1967), 28.

5. Ibid. 71 ff.

6. Ibid. 73.

7. Ibid. 90.

8. Ibid. 170.

9. *L'Express*, 12 and 18 Oct. 1970.

10. André Gauron, *Histoire économique et sociale de la Cinquième République, i: Le Temps des modernistes* (Paris, 1983), 32.

11. Jean-Daniel Reynaud (ed.), *Tendances et volontés de la société française* (Paris, 1966), 155.

12. Thérèse Jolly, *Les Bergers* (Paris, 1974), 110, 128.

13. N. M. Hansen, *Public Policy and Regional Economic Development: The Experience of Nine Western Countries* (Cambridge, Mass., 1974), 26.

14. John B. Williamson, *Strategies against Poverty in America* (Cambridge, Mass., 1975), 10–18.

15. Survey Research Center, Institute for Social Research, University of Michigan, *Five Thousand American Families: Patterns of Economic Progress* (Ann Arbor, 1974), vol. i, p. ix.

16. Memphis *Commercial Appeal*, 20–3 Nov. 1967.

17. The Civil Rights Movement Papers, Box III, B8, UCLA Library Special Collections.

18. News Enterprise Association Special, New York, 27 Mar. 1964.

19. *Press-Scimitar*, 25 Apr. 1964.

20. *Commercial Appeal*, 9 Apr. 1964.

21. *Your Money's Worth*, 5 Nov. 1964.

22. *Press-Scimitar*, 11 Aug. 1967.

23. *Commercial Appeal*, 27 Apr. 1968.

24. Wylie, *Village in Vaucluse*, 583.

25. 'Témoignages 1985: Lulu', Maison de la Villette, Paris.

26. Hannah Gavron, *The Captive Wife: Conflicts of Housebound Mothers* (1964, paperback 1968), 34.

27. Jacqueline Chabaud, Évelyne Sullerot, and Claude Ulin, *Un Métier pour quoi faire?* (Paris, 1969), 9–13.

28. Vahé Katcha, *Dix filles qui se lèvent à midi* (Paris, 1968). My quotations are from pp. 15 and 33–6.

29. Lieta Harrison, *L'iniziazione: come le adolescenti italiani diventano donne* (Milan, 1966), 1, 39–132.

30. *Detroit Free Press*, 16 Aug. 1967.

31. Ibid. 30 Sept., 6 Dec. 1966, 14 Feb. 1967.

32. Ibid. 15 Mar. 1968.

33. Ibid. 25 Feb. 1969.

34. See e.g. David Caute, *Sixty-eight: The Year of the Barricades* (1988); Charles Kaiser, *1968 in America: Music, Politics, Chaos, Counterculture and the Shaping of a Generation* (1988); and W. J. Rorabaugh, *Berkeley at War: The 1960s* (New York, 1989).

35. Milena Milani, *Italia Sexy* (Milan, 1967), 118.

36. *L'Express*, 8–15 Nov. 1966.

37. *Marie-Claire*, 6 Aug. 1966.

38. *L'Express*, 21–8 May 1966.

39. Ibid. 8–14 Aug. 1966.

40. *Epoca*, May 1967; Lara Foletti and Clelia Boesi, *Per il diretto del aborto* (Rome, 1972), 14.

41. Morin, *Plodémet*, 179.

42. William Masters and Virginia Johnson, *Human Sexual Response* (Boston, 1966).

43. *L'Express*, 28 Aug-5 Sept., 24–31 Dec. 1966.

44. There is a splendid general account in David J. Garrow, *Liberty and Sexuality: The Right to Privacy and the Making of* Roe v. Wade (New York, 1994), esp. 354–88.

45. Alan F. Guttmacher, *The Case for Legalised Abortion Now* (Berkeley, Calif., 1967), preface.

46. Anne Edwards and Drusilla Beyfus, *Lady Behave* (1956), 9.

47. Ibid., 1969 edn., p. ix.

48. Ibid. 187.

49. Interview in *TV Times*, 1 and 8 Nov. 1966.

50. Drusilla Beyfus, *The English Marriage: What It Is Like to Be Married Today* (1968), 80.

51. Ibid. 73–101.

52. Gavron, *Captive Wife*, 83–8, 146.

53. Lieta Harrison, *La donna sposata: mille mogli accusano* (Milan, 1972), 17–79, 207–32.

54. Ibid. 229.

55. Evelyne Sullerot, *La Femme dans le monde moderne* (Paris, 1974), 87.

56. Diary of Loredana Valmori, Archivio Diaristico, Pieve Santo Stefano, Tuscany.

*Chapter 9. Beauty, Booze, and the Built Environment*

1. The arguments in my opening paragraphs are fully developed in my *Beauty in History: Society, Politics and Personal Appearance, c.1500 to the Present* (1988), where full references are given for the various quotations.

2. Ibid. 34; see also 195, 228, 253, 254.

3. Quoted ibid. 70, 80, 81.

4. Ibid. 345–6.

5. *Paris-Match*, 20 May 1967.

6. David Bailey, *David Bailey's Box of Pin-Ups* (1965).

7. Michael Gross, *Model: The Ugly Business of Beautiful Women* (1995, repr. 1996), 223.

8. Ibid. 255–62.

9. Anne Edwards and Drusilla Beyfus, *Lady Behave: A Guide to Modern Manners for the 1970s* (1969).

10. Marilyn Bender, *The Beautiful People* (New York, 1967), 23; *Life*, 26 Dec. 1969.

11. *Ebony*, July 1956, Nov. 1965.

12. Ibid. Nov. 1958.

13. Ibid. June 1964, June 1965.

14. Ibid. Mar. 1964; these and the following paragraphs are based on Marwick, *Beauty*, 368–9.

15. Jean Shrimpton, *The Truth about Modelling* (1964), 12–153.

16. Marwick, *Beauty*, esp. 33, 55–8.

17. Shrimpton, *The Truth about Modelling*, 20.

18. Ibid. 66.

19. Ibid. 68.

20. Twiggy, *An Autobiography* (1975), 6–8.

21. Ibid. 24; see also Justin de Villeneuve, *An Affectionate Punch* (1986), 39 ff.

22. Ibid. 25.

23. Ibid. 29.

24. Ibid. 36.

25. Ibid. 53–68.

26. Michael Parkinson, *George Best: An Intimate Biography* (1975), 69.

27. *Ladies' Home Journal*, Aug. 1979.

28. *Life*, 18 Mar. 1966.

29. Ibid. 9 Jan. 1970.

30. *Le Figaro*, 1 Dec. 1965.

31. Erving Goffman, 'On Calling the Mark Out: Some Aspects of Adaptation to Failure', *Psychiatry*, 15 (1952), 456.

32. Marwick, *Beauty*, 385–7.

33. E. Walster, V. Aronson, D. Abrahams, and I. Rottman, 'Importance of Physical Attractiveness in Dating Behaviour', *Journal of Personality and Social Psychology*, 5 (1966), 508–16.

34. W. Stroebe, C. A. Insho, V. D. Thompson, and B. D. Layton, 'Effects of Physical Attractiveness, Attitude Similarity, and Sex on Various Aspects of Interpersonal Attraction', *Journal of Personality and Social Psychology*, 18 (1971), 79–89; E. Berscheid, K. K. Dion, E. Walster, and G. W. Walster, 'Physical Attractiveness and Dating Choice', *Journal of Experimental Social Psychology*, 7 (1971), 173–89.

35. T. L. Huston, 'Ambiguity of Acceptance, Social Desirability, and Dating Choice', *Journal of Experimental Psychology*, 9 (1973), 32–42.

36. Stroebe et al., 'Effects of Physical Attractiveness'.

37. Ibid. 89.

38. K. K. Dion, E. Berscheid, and E. Walster, 'What Is Beautiful Is Good', *Journal of Personality and Social Psychology*, 24 (1972), 205–90.

39. D. Krebs and A. A. Adinolfi, 'Physical Attractiveness, Social Relations and Personality Style', *Journal of Personality and Social Psychology*, 31 (1975), 245–53.

40. M. Dermer and D. J. Thiel, 'When Beauty May Fail', *Journal of Personality and Social Psychology*, 31 (1975), 1168–76.

41. e.g. Brigitte Baer, *Grande Forme: être bien dans sa peau* (Paris, 1970), 16; *L'Encyclopédie beauté bien-être* (Paris, 1964), 5; Josette Lyon, *La Femme et la beauté* (Paris, 1965), 9, 12; Helen Whitcombe and Rosalind Lancy, *Charm: The Career Girl's Guide to Business and Personal Success* (New York, 1964). Italian guides still tended to peddle the old myths—e.g. Mila Cantani, *Cure di bellezza* (Milan, 1967).

42. Gilda Lund, *Beauty* (1983), 7.

43. e.g. Helen M. McLachlan, *Poise, Personality and Charm* (New York, 1965); Elizabeth Kendall, *Good Looks, Good Grooming* (New York, 1963).

44. e.g. 'Famille 2000', *Beauté et hygiene* (Paris, 1971); Pierre Desjardin, *Le Guide de la santé et de la beauté* (Paris, 1971), 9–11.

45. Ibid. *passim*, Robert Schwartz, *Médecine et beauté* (Paris, 1969), esp. 157 ff.

46. e.g. Franke Guez, *Masculin quotidien: guide pratique à l'usage des hommes* (Paris, 1969), 7–8; 'Marabout Flash', *Le Guide Flash de l'homme* (Verviers, Belgium, 1970), 8–9.

47. Guez, *Masculin quotidien*, 8; *Guide Flash*, 11.

48. *Life*, 12 Mar. 1965.

49. Pierette Sartin, *La Réussite professionelle* (Paris, 1971), 37–8.

50. Marwick, *Beauty*, 393 and references given there.

51. e.g. *Life*, 24 Aug. 1959.

52. W. L. O'Neill, *Coming Apart: An Informal History of America in the 1960s* (Chicago, 1971), 387 fn.

53. *Life*, 26 May 1961.

54. Ibid. 28 May 1965.

55. Ibid. 21 Jan. 1966.

56. Edmund G. Brown, *Reagan and Reality: The Two Californias* (New York, 1970), 40–1.

57. *Tiger Rag*, 15 Nov. 1968.

58. Edmund Orgill Papers, Box 27, Mississippi Valley Collection.

59. *Press-Scimitar*, 22 Oct. 1960.

60. Ibid. 23, 30 Nov., 8 Dec. 1964.

61. Ibid.

62. *Commercial Appeal*, 7 Apr. 1965.

63. Ibid. 7 May 1965.

64. Associated Press item of 9 July 1971.

65. *Press-Scimitar*, 3 Mar. 1969.

66. Ibid. 17 Mar. 1967.

67. Ibid. 18 Aug. 1967, 26 Nov., 16 Dec. 1969; *Commercial Appeal*, 20 June 1968.

68. Ibid. 22 Sept. 1968.

69. Evan Broadman, *Broadman's Social Guide to New York Bars* (New York, 1973), 40–90. On the 'body shop', see Donald E. Lundberg, *The Restaurant: From Concept to Operation* (New York, 1985), 10.

70. Myra Waldo, *Myra Waldo's Restaurant Guide to New York City and Vicinity* (New York, 1971), 142, 249–50.

71. David Bourdon, *Warhol* (New York, 1989), 250.

72. Feliks Gross, *Il Paese: Values and Social Change in an Italian Village* (New York, 1974), 174.

73. Ernesto Galli della Loggia, 'Ideologica, classi e costume', in Valerio Castronova (ed.), *L'Italia contemporanea 1945–1975* (Turin, 1976), 416–19, 423.

74. Harold Gillian, *Between the Devil and the Deep Blue Bay: The Struggle to Save San Francisco Bay* (San Francisco, Calif., 1969), 10 and *passim;* US Dept. of Transportation, *The Freeway in the City: Principles of Planning and Design* (Washington, DC, May 1968); *The Quality of Urban Life: Hearings Before the Ad Hoc Subcommittee on Urban Growth of the Committee on Banking and Currency: House of Representatives, 91st Congress*, pt. 2 (Washington, DC, 1970), 43–9.

75. Anonymous letter, 25 June 1964, Handy-Ruffin Papers, Box 4, Mississippi Valley Collection.

76. Mrs Stoner to Tennessee State Highway Dept., 20 July 1964; Mrs Handy to Commissioner Pack, 11 Aug. 1964; State Programming Engineer to Mrs Handy, 20 Aug. 1964; Memorandum from State Programming Engineer to Commissioner Pack, 28 Aug. 1964; Memphis Citizens Committee Memo, Oct. 1964; all ibid. Box 5.

77. Tennessee Commissioner for Public Service to Mrs Handy, 25 May 1965, ibid.

78. Taken from the accounts by Mrs Sara N. Hines in *Commercial Appeal*, 22 Feb. 1976.

79. *Press-Scimitar*, 5 Jan. 1972.

80. *The Quality of Urban Life*, 2.

81. Roger Kain, 'Conservation Planning in France'; Norma Evenson, 'The City as Artefact: Building Control in Modern Paris'; in Roger Kain (ed.), *Planning for Conservation* (1985), 199, 191–3.

82. Speech by Amédée Brousset, 21 May 1964, Théâtre des Ambassadeurs, Paris, printed as *Transfert des Halles et rénovation de Paris* (Paris, 1964), esp. 10–12.

83. Ibid., esp. 12–15.

84. Robert Franc, *Le Scandale de Paris* (Paris, 1971), 149. See also Préfecture de Paris, 'Les Grandes Problèmes de l'urbanisme à Paris' (mimeographed report, 9 Feb. 1971); Louis Chevalier, *l'Assassinat de Paris* (Paris, 1977).

85. Franc, *Scandale*, 149–50.

86. Ibid. 152–60.

87. OECD, *Streets for People* (Paris, 1974), 108–10.

88. Ibid. 110.

89. Associazione Nazionale Centri Storico-Artistici, *Riequilibrio territoriale e centri storici* (Venice, 1974); Roberto Pane, *Attualità dell'ambiente antico* (Florence, 1967).

90. Graeme Buicks, 'Integrated Conservation', in Brian Bassett (ed.), *Conservation and Development* (Cape Town, SA, 1978), 9.

91. A. Wood, *The Pedestrianisation of Traditional Central Areas* (Norwich, 1968); OECD, *Streets for People*, 98–103; Bassett, *Conservation and Development*, 3.

92. Letter of 19 Oct. 1965, G. W. Lee papers, Box III, Folder 16, Memphis Shelby County Library, Special Collections.

93. *Press-Scimitar*, 22 July 1965, 25 Mar. 1966.

94. Ibid. 3 Feb. 1967.

95. Ibid. 17 Feb. 1967.

96. Ibid. 10 Mar. 1967.

97. *Commercial Appeal*, 3 Feb. 1967.

98. *Press-Scimitar*, 17 Feb. 1967.

99. Ibid. 4 Mar. 1967.

100. Ibid. 13 Jan., 2 Mar. 1967.

101. Ibid. 22 July 1965.

102. Ibid. 13 Mar. 1967.

103. Ibid. 17 July, 1 Aug. 1973.

104. Celestine Sibleif, *Peachtree Street, USA: An Affectionate Portrait of Atlanta* (New York, 1963), 30.

105. Rivers Siddons, *Go Straight on Peachtree* (New York, 1978), 88.

106. Ibid. 14–15.

107. Quoted in Pane, *Attualità*, 86.

*Chapter 10. National and Other Identities*

1. J. B. Priestley, *English Journey* (1934), 401–7. From sixties France there is the best-seller of the decade, *Le Défi américain* (The American Challenge, Paris, 1967) in which Jean-Jacques

Servan-Schreiber argued that the French should imitate the Americans. Authoritative recent studies are: David W. Ellwood, *Rebuilding Europe: Western Europe, America and Postwar Reconstruction* (1988); Richard F. Kuisel, *Seducing the French: The Dilemma of Americanization* (Berkeley, Calif., 1993); Simon Frith, 'Anglo-America and Its Discontents', *Cultural Studies,* 5 (3) (1991), 263–9; and the excellent collection of essays, Rob Kroes, Robert W. Rydell, and Doeko F. J. Bosscher (eds.), *Cultural Transmission and Reception: American Mass Culture in Europe* (Amsterdam, 1993).

2. Michel Winock, *Chronique des années soixante* (Paris, 1987), 103.

3. *L'Express,* 2–8 May 1966; *Time,* special number, Apr. 1966; *Epoca,* 14 Nov. 1965.

4. Ibid. 17 July 1966.

5. Ray Coleman, *Brian Epstein: The Man Who Made the Beatles* (1989), 222–33.

6. Ian MacDonald, *Revolution in the Head: The Beatles' Records and the Sixties* (1994), 321.

7. Letter of 23 Sept. 1964, Allen Ginsberg Papers, Box 13, Columbia University Library Special Collections.

8. Quoted in Hunter Davies, *The Beatles* (1985), 290.

9. MacDonald, *Revolution in the Head,* 113.

10. Charlie Gillett, *The Sound of the City* (1983), 266; Paul Griffiths, 'Music', in Boris Ford (ed.), *The Cambridge Guide to the Arts in Britain,* ix: *Since the Second World War* (1988), 79.

11. I have of course drawn on all the distinguished Beatles and rock/pop experts, far more knowledgeable than myself, among them: Carl Belz, *The Story of Rock* (New York, 1969); Dick Bradley, *Understanding Rock'n'Roll: Popular Music in Britain 1955–1964* (Buckingham, 1992); Peter Brown and Pat Broeske, *Down at the End of Lonely Street: The Life and Death of Elvis Presley* (1977); Michael Cable, *The Pop Industry Inside Out* (1977); Steve Chapple and Reebee Garofalo, *Rock'n'Roll Is Here to Pay: The History and Politics of the Music Industry* (Chicago, 1977); Sara Cohen, *Rock Culture in Liverpool: Popular Music in the Making* (Oxford, 1991); Hunter Davies, *The Beatles: The Only Authorised Biography* (1992); Robin Denselow, *When the Music's Over* (1990); Jonathan Eisen (ed.), *The Age of Rock* (New York, 1969); Simon Frith, *Sound Effects: Youth, Leisure and the Politics of Rock* (1983); Simon Frith, *Music for Pleasure* (Cambridge, 1988); Simon Frith, *Sociology of Rock* (1978); Simon Frith (ed.), *Facing the Music* (1990); Gillett, *Sound of the City*; Albert Goldman, *Elvis* (New York, 1981); Marcus Greil, *Mystery Train: Images of America in Rock'n'Roll Music* (4th rev. edn, New York, 1997); Peter Guralnick, *Last Train to Memphis: The Rise of Elvis Presley* (Boston, 1994); C. Hamm, B. Nettl, and R. Byrnside (eds.), *Contemporary Music and Music Cultures* (Englewood Cliffs, NJ, 1975); Dave Harker, *One for the Money: Politics and Popular Song* (1980); Chris Hutchins and Peter Thompson, *Elvis Meets the Beatles* (1994); Michael Bryan Kelly, *The Beatle Myth: The British Invasion of American Popular Music, 1956–1969* (Jefferson, NC, 1991); Dave Laing, *The Sound of Our Time* (1969); Peter Laurie, *The Teenage Revolution* (1965); Richard Mabey, *The Pop Process* (1969); Wilfrid Mellers, *Twilight of the Gods: The Beatles in Retrospect* (1973); Richard Middleton, *Pop Music and the Blues* (1972); Barry Miles, *Paul McCartney: Many Years From Now* (1997); Philip Norman, *Shout! The True Story of the Beatles* (1981); Philip Norman, *The Stones* (1993); Tony Palmer, *All You Need Is Love* (1977); Anthony Picat, 'Fifties Children: Sixties People', in Vernon Bogdanor and Robert Skidelsky (eds.), *The Age of Affluence 1951–1964*

(1970), 321–40; David Pichaske, *A Generation in Motion: Popular Music and Culture in the Sixties* (1979); Patricia Jobe Pierce, *The Ultimate Elvis: Elvis Presley Day by Day* (New York, 1994); Anthony Scaduto, *Bob Dylan* (1972); Arnold Shaw, *Black Popular Music in America* (New York, 1986); John Street, 'Youth Culture and the Emergence of Popular Music', in Terry Gourvish and Alan O'Day (eds.), *Britain since 1945* (1992); Peter Wicke, *Rock Music: Culture, Aesthetics and Sociology*, trans. Rachael Fogg (Cambridge, 1990). For the particular thoughts expressed here I would like to record a special debt to Ian MacDonald's *Revolution in the Head*.

12. Ibid 135, 143, 156–7, 172, 179, 184–5, 199.

13. Griffiths, 'Music', 80.

14. MacDonald, *Revolution in the Head*, 223–9, 230–4.

15. Gillett, *Sound of the City*, 269–70.

16. Ibid. 270.

17. Ibid. 270–9.

18. John Swenson, *Stevie Wonder* (1986), 14, 49, 53, 57, 131.

19. 'Interview d'un rocker: Jean-Louis R.', 1985, Maison de la Villette, Paris.

20. *J2 Jeunes*, 11 Feb. 1965.

21. *L'Express*, 21–7 June 1965.

22. F. Seloron, *Les Beatles* (Paris, 1972), 1.

23. Suzanne Frère, *La Jeunesse bagnolaise* (Bagnoles-sur-Clèze, 1968), 83.

24. Kelly, *The Beatle Myth*, 9.

25. Letter of 13 Sept. 1964, Van Dyke Papers, Box 8, F216, Memphis State University Libraries.

26. *Evening Standard*, 4 Mar. 1966. I gladly acknowledge the Middlesex Polytechnic BA thesis of May 1988, 'The Film *A Hard Day's Night*', by Rowana Agajanian, for the full text of this much misquoted passage, and for a number of stimulating ideas.

27. MacDonald, *Revolution in the Head*, 170.

28. *Tiger Rag*, 15 Mar. 1968.

29. Carl Pelz, *The Story of Rock* (New York, 1969), 118.

30. Eric Lefbowitz, *The Monkees Tale* (New York, 1985).

31. *Paris-Match*, 30 Nov. 1963.

32. *L'Express*, 22–8 Mar. 1965, 21–7 Nov., 19–25 Dec. 1966; *Salut les Copains*, Mar. 1966.

33. Yvonne Deslandres, *Le Costume image de l'homme* (1976), 168.

34. Vidal Sassoon, *Sorry I Kept You Waiting, Madam* (1968), 131.

35. Letter of 12 Sept. 1967, Van Dyke Papers, Box 8, F226.

36. *Press-Scimitar*, 22 Sept. 1969.

37. Ibid.

38. Ibid. 3 Apr. 1970, 26 Jan. 1971.

39. *Ciao Amici*, 5 Apr. 1967.

40. Ibid.; *Epoca*, 19 Mar. 1967.

41. *Life*, 14 Apr. 1967.

42. *Press-Scimitar,* 17 Apr. 1967.

43. *Epoca,* 30 Jan. 1966.

44. Alexander Walker, *Hollywood England: The British Film Industry in the Sixties* (1974), 16.

45. In general, reference may be made to J. Philip di Franco, *The Beatles in Richard Lester's 'A Hard Day's Night': A Complete Pictorial Record of the Movie* (New York, 1977). I have been greatly helped by Agajanian, '*A Hard Day's Night*'.

46. Oreste de Buono and Umberto Eco, *The Bond Affair,* trans. R. A. Downie (1966).

47. Andrew J. Edelstein, *The Swinging Sixties* (New York, 1986), 140–1.

48. Anthony Aldgate, 'Alfie', *History Today,* Oct. 1996.

49. See the excellent chapter on this film by Jeffrey Richards in Jeffrey Richards and Anthony Aldgate, *Best of British: Cinema and Society 1930–1970* (1983).

50. *L'Express,* 30 May–5 June 1966.

51. *Salut les Copains,* Apr. 1966.

52. Nicholas Wapshott, *Peter O'Toole* (New York, 1983), 130.

53. Alexander Walker, *Peter Sellers: The Authorized Biography* (1981), 139–40.

54. *L'Express,* 30 May–5 June 1966.

55. *Ciao Amici,* 10 Jan. 1966; *Nuova Generazione,* 5 Nov. 1967.

56. In the Henry Nash Smith Papers, Bancroft Library, University of California at Berkeley.

57. For British television, see Hilary Kingsley and Geoff Tibballs, *Box of Delights: The Golden Years of Television* (1989).

58. See Tony Lambrianou, with Carol Clark, *Inside the Firm: The Untold Story of the Krays' Reign of Terror* (1992); and Colin Fry, with Charlie Kray, *Doing the Business: Inside the Krays' Secret Network of Glamour and Violence* (1994).

59. Terence Stamp, *Double Feature* (1989), 151.

60. Lewis Yablonsky, *The Hippie Trip* (New York, 1968), 36–7.

61. Lois Rather, *Bohemians to Hippies: Wars of Rebellion* (Oakland, Calif., 1977), 109.

62. Suzanne Labin, *Hippies, drogues et sexe* (Paris, 1970), 136.

63. *Esquire,* Oct. 1965.

64. George Paloczi-Horvath, *Youth Up in Arms: A Political and Social World Survey 1955–1970* (1971), 242–5.

65. Ibid.

66. *Esquire,* Oct. 1965.

67. Yablonsky, *Hippie Trip,* 22.

68. Quoted ibid. 24.

69. Gillett, *Sound of the City,* 350–9.

70. Yablonsky, *Hippie Trip,* 29.

71. Rather, *Bohemians to Hippies,* 110–13.

72. Yablonsky, *Hippie Trip,* 121.

73. Ibid. 26.

74. Gilbert Zicklin, *Countercultural Communes: A Sociological Perspective* (Westport, Conn., 1983), 34–42.

75. Diana Hartog, *No Hippies Allowed* (Silverton, BC, Canada, 1994), 5.

76. Frank Musgrove, *Ecstasy and Holiness: Counter Culture and the Open Society* (1974), 19.

77. Richard Mills, *Young Outsiders: A Study of Alternative Communities* (1973), 35.

78. Ibid. 46–7.

79. Ibid. 59–82.

80. Labin, *Hippies, drogues et sexe*, 10–46.

81. Luc Vidal, *La Route: mon journal de hippy* (Paris, 1976), 9, 11.

82. Brigitte Axel, *H* (Paris, 1970).

83. Bernard Plossu, *Pourquoi n'êtes vous pas hippie?* (Paris, 1970), 56.

84. Ibid. 67, 114–15.

85. Jeff Nuttall, *Bomb Culture* (1968), 175.

86. Roger Lewis, *Outlaws of America: The Underground Press and Its Context* (New York, 1972). See also Laurence Leamer, *The Paper Revolutionaries: The Rise of the Underground Press* (New York, 1972); Robert J. Glessing, *The Underground Press in America* (Bloomington, Ind., 1970).

87. Elizabeth Nelson, *The British Counter-Culture, 1966–73: A Study of the Underground Press* (1989), 55.

88. Ibid. 45. In general see the excellent Nigel Fountain, *Underground: The London Alternative Press, 1966–1974* (1988).

89. Richard Neville, *Hippie Hippie Shake: The Dreams, the Trips, the Trials, the Love-ins, the Screw Ups... The Sixties* (1995), 145.

90. Nuttall, *Bomb Culture*, 249.

91. Gillett, *Sound of the City*, 397.

92. Neville, *Hippie Hippie Shake*, 169.

93. Fred Vermorel, *Fashion and Perversity: A Life of Vivienne Westwood and the Sixties Laid Bare* (1996), 115.

94. Philip Norman, *The Stones* (1993), 189–211; Anthony Scaduto, *Mick Jagger* (1975), 184–7.

95. Sandro Mayer (ed.), *Lettere capelloni* (Milan, 1968), 11.

96. Ibid. 12–14.

97. Ibid. 17.

98. Giorgio Galli, 'La stampa giovanile in Europa come elemento di cultura politica', *IKON*, 71 (1969), 79–84; Mayer, *Lettere*, 18–43; Gianni-Emilio Simonetti,... *Ma l'amor mio non muove: origini documenti strategichi della 'cultura alternativa' e dell' 'underground' in Italia* (Rome, 1971), 15–181.

99. Mayer, *Lettere*, 153–4.

100. Gillett, *Sound of the City*, 403–4; David Caute, *Sixty-Eight: The Year of the Barricades* (1988), 394.

101. *Harper's Magazine*, Oct. 1967.

102. Department of Education and Science, *Children and Their Primary Schools: A Report of the Central Advisory Council for Education (England) Cmnd.* (1967), i., 187–8.

103. Richard Peters (ed.), *Perspectives on Plowden* (1969), 1, 20.

104. C. B. Cox and A. E. Dyson (eds.), *Fight for Education: A Black Paper (Critical Quarterly* Society, Mar. 1967), 6 and *passim*.

105. See Robert S. Ellwood, *The Sixties Spiritual Awakening: American Religion Moving from Modern to Postmodern* (Brunswick, NJ, 1994).

106. S. Froome, *Why Tommy Isn't Learning* (1973).

107. Dept of Education and Science, *Primary Education in England: A Survey by HM Inspectors of Schools* (Sept. 1978), 26–7, 123; Neville Bennett, *Teaching Styles and Pupil Progress* (1976).

108. Maurice R. Berube, *American School Reform: Progressive, Equality and Excellent Movements, 1883–1993* (Westport, Conn., 1994), 64; Diane Ravitch, *The Troubled Crusade; American Education, 1945–1980* (New York, 1983), 236 ff.

109. Ibid. 239.

110. Ibid. 241–8.

111. L. S. Stephens, *The Teacher's Guide to Open Education* (New York, 1974), 27.

112. Ivan Illich, *Deschooling Society* (New York, 1971; Penguin, 1973). Kathleen M. Evans, *Development and Structure of the English Educational System* (1975), 14.

113. Baroness Wootton, *Social Science and Social Pathology* (1959), 68–9; Frank Pakenham, Lord Longford, *The Idea of Punishment* (1961).

114. Home Office, *The Child, the Family and the Young Offender* (Aug. 1965), 3, 5, 10–11,12.

115. Home Office, *The Adult Offender* (Dec. 1965), 3–4, 7, 9, 10–11.

116. Quoted in Giles Playfair, *The Punitive Obsession: An Unvarnished History of the English Prison System* (1971), 247.

117. Cited in Karl Menninger, *The Crime of Punishment* (New York, 1968), 269, 248.

118. Ibid. 262, 280.

119. Mike Fitzgerald, in Herman Bianchi, Mario Simondi, and Ian Taylor (eds.), *Deviance and Control in Europe: Papers for the European Group for the Study of Deviance and Social Control* (1975), 98–9.

120. Ibid. 106–7.

121. Jacques Donzelot, ibid. 111–13.

122. Raffaele Rauty, ibid. 116, 118, 120–1, 125.

123. My references are to the following editions: Perec, *Les Choses:* a 1991 reprint of the original 1965 paperback, published by Julliard (Paris); Parise, *Il padrone:* the 1992 Mondadori edition (Milan), with an introduction by Silvia Perella; Sciascia, *A ciascuno il suo:* the 1988 Einaudi edition (Turin), with introduction and notes by Jole Magri and pedagogic commentary by Carlo Minois and Gabriella Salvini, in a series intended for secondary schools Vidal, *Myra Breckinridge:* the 1993 Abacus combined edition with the 1974 sequel, *Myron,* and a short introduction by Vidal himself; Morrison, *The Bluest Eye:* the Chatto 8c Windus edition of 1979; Balestrini, *Vogliamo tutto:* the 1988 Mondadori edition (Milan), with an introduction by Mario Spinello; Cardinale, *La Clé sur la porte* (Paris, 1972).

124. Georges Perec, *Things: A Story of the Sixties* and *A Man Asleep,* ed. David Bellos (1982). In addition, biographical details are drawn from Paul Schwarz, *Georges Perec, Traces of His Passage* (Birmingham, Ala., 1988), 1–76; Catherine Savage Brosman, *Dictionary of Literary Biography,* lxxxiii: *French Novelists since 1960* (Detroit, 1989), 166–8; Jacques Bersani, M. Autrand, et al. (eds.), *La littérature en France depuis 1945* (Paris, 1970); *L'Arc,* 76 (Aix-en-Provence, 1979), issue devoted to Perec.

125. Perec, *Things*, 10.

126. Schwarz, *Perec*, 5; Perec, *Things*, 9; Bersani and Autrand, *Littérature en France*, 621.

127. Perec, *Things*, 9.

128. Details from Perella's introd. to Parise, *Il padrone*. In general, see Michael Caesar and Peter Hainsworth (eds.), *Writers and Society in Contemporary Italy: A Collection of Essays* (Leamington Spa, Warwickshire, 1984).

129. Parise, *Il padrone*, 261.

130. Quoted in Paolo Petroni, *Invito alla lettura di Parise* (Milan, 1975), 79. Apart from Petroni and Perella, I have been helped by Giorgio Pullini, *Volti e risvolti del romanzo italiano contemporane* (Milan, 1971), 241–4; Paolo Volpone, *La macchina mondiale* (Milan, 1972), 242; and Carlo Ferrucci, *Letteratura dell' utopia: sociologia del romanzo contemporaneo* (Rome, 1980), 206–27.

131. Biographical details from Magri's introd. to Sciascia, *a ciascuno il suo;* and Matteo Collura, *Il maestro di Regalpetra: vita di Leonardo Sciascia* (Milan, 1996). See also Claude Ambroise, *Invito alla lettura di Leonardo Sciascia* (Milan, 1974); Giovanni Ghetti Abruzze, *Leonardo Sciascia e la Sicilia* (Rome, 1974).

132. *Il Castro*, 48 (Dec. 1970), issue devoted to Sciascia. Interview with Walter Mauro, *Il Castro*, 48 (Dec. 1970), 2; Leonardo Sciascia, *Le parrochie di Regalpetra* (new edn, Bari, 1967), new preface by Sciascia, 6.

133. Ambroise, *Invito*, 128.

134. Ibid. 59.

135. Vidal, *Myra Breckinridge*, 186–7.

136. Ibid. 200–1.

137. Ibid. 52.

138. Ibid. 94.

139. Linden Peach, *Toni Morrison* (1995), 3–7; Claudia Tate, *Black Women Writers at Work* (New York, 1983), 119; Danielle Taylor-Guthrie (ed.) *Conversation with Toni Morrison* (Jackson, Miss., 1994), 49.

140. Peach, *Toni Morrison*, 7–8; Taylor-Guthrie, *Conversation*, 30, 44, 50, 88–90.

141. Ibid. 10.

142. Morrison, *The Bluest Eye*, 36–7.

143. Taylor-Guthrie, *Conversation*, 17.

144. Judith Wilson, ibid. 129.

145. Peach, *Toni Morrison*, 13.

146. Nanni Balestrini, *Prendiamoci tutto: conferenza per un romanzo: letterature e lotte di classe* (Milan, 1972), 7–9. For orthodox Communist party criticism of *Vogliamo tutto*, see Giampaolo Borghello, *Linea rossa: intellettuali, letteratura e lotta di classe 1965–1975* (Venice, 1982), 135–44.

147. Serge Mallet, *La Nouvelle Classe ouvrière* (Paris, 1963).

148. Balestrini, *Prendiamoci tutto*, 8–12.

149. Ibid. 13–15, 32–3.

150. Marie Cardinale, *Autrement dit* (Paris, 1977), 86. For comments on *La Clé*, see pp. 201–2. I have been enormously helped by the introduction of Colin Roberts to Lesbron, *Chiens perdus sans collier* and Cardinale, *La Clé sur la porte* (Glasgow, 1988).

151. Marie Cardinale, *La Clé sur la porte* (Paris, 1972), 7.

152. Balestrini, *Vogliamo tutto*, 65.

153. Cardinale, *La Clé sur la porte*, 179.

154. Pierre Sorlin, *Italian National Cinema 1896–1996* (1996), 7.

155. Robert Sklar, *Film: An International History of the Medium* (New York, 1993), 422–3.

156. Thomas Kiernan, *Jane Fonda* (1982), 146.

157. Richard McGuinness, 'Carnal Knowledge', in Thomas R. Atkins (ed.), *Sexuality in the Movies* (Bloomington, Ind., 1975), 209.

158. Sklar, *Film*, 429, 433.

159. Repr. in Pauline Kael, *Deeper into the Movies* (New York, 1973), 217. I am indebted to Rowana Agajanian, Royal College of Art MA thesis, 'Hearts of Darkness: Vietnam at the Movies' (May 1993), 34, for this reference.

160. Peter Dormer, *Design since 1945* (1993), 104, 160–1, 170, 205; Stephen Bayley, Philippe Garner, and Deyan Sudjic, *Twentieth-Century Style and Design* (1986), 256, 260; Philippe Garner, *Sixties Design* (Cologne, 1996), 8; Andrea Branzi, *The Hot House: Italian New Wave Design* (1984), 51–60.

161. Stephen Bayley (ed.), *The Conran Directory of Design* (1985), 51–2.

162. Ibid. 52.

163. Ibid. 53.

164. Philadelphia Museum of Art, *Design since 1945* (1983), p. xx.

*Chapter 11. Freedom, Turbulence, and Death*

1. A. Ronchey, *Accade in Italia, 1968–1977* (Milan, 1977); Luigi Mistrorigo, *L'utopia dell'innocenza dal '68 ad oggi: la scomposizione della storia* (Rome, 1979).

2. e.g. Allen J. Matusow, *The Unraveling of America: A History of Liberalism in the 1960s* (New York, 1984); W. L. O'Neill, *Coming Apart: An Informal History of America in the 1960s* (Chicago, 1971); Godfrey Hodgson, *In Our Time: America from World War II to Nixon* (New York, 1976), ch. 18.

3. James A. Colaiaco, *Martin Luther King, Jr.: Apostle of Militant Nonviolence* (New York, 1988; 1993 edn), 181–2.

4. Clark Kerr, *The Uses of the University* (Cambridge, Mass., 1963), 88, 87.

5. See Joan Baez, *And a Voice to Sing With: A Memoir* (New York, 1987), 118–19. W. J. Rorabaugh, *Berkeley at War: The 1960s* (New York, 1989) is invaluable. S. M. Lipset, *The Berkeley Student Protest: Facts and Interpretations* (New York, 1965) offers a contemporary conservative account. I am indebted to Professor Dan Leab for the personal information about Mario Savio.

6. Civil Rights Movement Papers, Box III, UCLA Library Special Collections.

7. Henry Nash Smith Collection, Box 6, F8, Bancroft Library, University of California at Berkeley.

8. Hodgson, *In Our Time*, 296.

9. Tom Wells, *The War Within: America's Battle over Vietnam* (Berkeley, Calif., 1994), 23.

10. Ibid. 24.

11. Ibid. 57.

12. Ibid.

13. Colaiaco, *Martin Luther King*, 136.

14. Ibid. 158.

15. Ibid.

16. Ibid. 179.

17. Hodgson, *In Our Time*, 301.

18. Norman Mailer, *The Armies of the Night: History as a Novel, the Novel as History* (New York, 1968), 272–6. See Wells, *The War Within*, 195–203.

19. Mailer, *Armies of the Night*, 284–5.

20. Fiorella Padoa-Schioppa, *Scuola e classi sociali in Italia* (Milan, 1974), 18.

21. *L'Espresso*, 20 Mar. 1966; Guido Nozzoli and Pier Maria Paoletti, *La Zanzara: cronache e documenti di uno scandalo* (Milan, 1966), 11–12.

22. Ibid. 15 This is an excellent contemporary account, with an appendix of key documents. There are also invaluable accounts in *L'Espresso*, 27 Mar. 1966.

23. L'Espresso Documenti, 'Il processo contro "La Zanzara". Testo stenografico del dibatimento. Tribunale de Milano 30 marzo-i aprile', Archivio MSI (Movimento Studentesco Italiano) 11.1.3, Istituto Feltrinelli, Milan. I am deeply indebted to Professor Gianfranco Petrillo and the Institute for providing me with a photocopy of this document to take home with me.

24. Nozzoli and Paoletti, *La Zanzara*, 152.

25. *Epoca*, 3 Apr. 1966.

26. Don Lorenzo Milani, *Lettera ad una professoressa* (Florence, 1967), 4.

27. Nazareno Fattretti, *Don Mazzolari, Don Milani: i 'disubbidienti'* (Milan, 1972), 187.

28. Niera Fallaci, *Dalla porta dell'ultimo: vita del prete Lorenzo Milani* (Milan, 1974), 481.

29. Milani, *Lettera*, 10–11.

30. George Armstrong, 'Italy's Student Strikes', *New Statesman*, 5 Apr. 1968.

31. Giorgio Galli, 'La stampa giovanile in Europa come elemento di cultura politica', *IKON*, 71 (1969), 83, 906; Gianni-Emilio Simonetti, *Ma l'amor mio non muove: origini documenti strategichi della 'cultura alternativa' e del 'underground' in Italia* (documents and commentary, Rome 1971), 178–81.

32. 'Librobianco sulla facoltà di architettura di Milano: occupazione 1967', pt. 1, p. viii, Archivio MSI, 10.1.16

33. Documents in Archivio MSI, 10.4.

34. A. Beldon Fields, *Student Politics in France: A Study of the Union Nationale des étudiants de France* (New York, 1970), 30–2.

35. *L'Express*, 27 Feb. 1964 (a retrospective article covering the student world in 1963).

36. Ibid.

37. This and the next quotation are from interviews by Gérard Marin for his *Les Nouveaux Français* (Paris, 1967), 136–8.

38. *L'Express*, 18–24 Oct. 1965 (*L'Express* adopted this dating system when, with the issue of 21–7 Sept. 1964, it became a colour magazine).

39. The original French version of Nov. 1966 is printed in René Viénet, *Enragés et situationistes dans le mouvement des occupations* (Paris, 1968), 219–43. See also *L'Express*, 5–11 Dec. 1966.

40. In Viénet, *Enragés*, 8, 26.

41. Alain Schnapp and Pierre Vidal-Naquet, *Journal de la commune étudiante: textes et documents Novembre 67-Juin 68* (Paris, 1969), 472–3, 745–6.

42. 'Alain Touraine parle', in Philippe Labo, *Mai/Juin 68: ce n'est qu'un début* (Paris, 1968), 38–44; Schnapp and Vidal-Naquet, *Journal*, 101–3; Bernard E. Brown, *Protest in Paris: Anatomy of a Revolt* (New Brunswick, NJ, 1974), 6.

43. George Palaczi-Horvath, *Youth Up in Arms: A Political and Social World Survey* (1971), 175–80.

44. Colin Crouch. *The Student Revolt* (1970), 99, 116; David Widgery, 'The Failure of Student Institutions', in Alexander Cockburn and Robin Blackburn (eds.), *Student Power: Problems, Diagnosis, Action* (Harmondsworth, 1969), 126–33; Harry Kidd, *The Trouble at L.S.E. 1966–1967* (1969), 41–3.

45. Crouch, *Student Revolt*, 36–46; Kidd, *Trouble*, 17–40.

46. Crouch, *Student Revolt*, 46–9.

47. Ibid. 51–71; Kidd, *Trouble*, 61–119.

48. Tessa Blackstone, Kathleen Gales, Roger Hadley, and Wyn Lewis, *Students in Conflict: L.S.E. in 1967* (1970).

49. On Freedom Summer, see Mary Aicken Rothschild, *A Case of Black and White: Northern Volunteers and the Southern Freedom Summers, 1964–1965* (Westport, Conn., 1982), and John Dittmer, *Local People: The Struggle for Civil Rights in Mississippi* (Urbana, Ill., 1994), 242–71. On the Mississippi Freedom Democratic party, see ibid. 272–302.

50. Hodgson, *In Our Time*, 209.

51. Sally Belfrage, *Freedom Summer* (New York, 1965), 7.

52. Ibid. 42–3.

53. Ibid. 203, 41–2, 135.

54. Project South Collection, Stanford University Library Special Collections.

55. Hodgson, *In Our Time*, 210.

56. Robert Weisbrot, *Freedom Bound: A History of America's Civil Rights Movement* (New York, 1990), 117–20. William H. Chafe, *'Mississippi Burning'*, in Mark C. Carnes (ed.), *Past Imperfect: History According to the Movies* (1996), 275.

57. Clayborne Carson, *In Struggle: SNCC and the Black Awakening of the 1960s* (Cambridge, Mass, 1981).

58. Fred Powledge, *Free at Last?: The Civil Rights Movement and the People Who Made It* (Boston, 1991), 627.

59. Colaiaco, *Martin Luther King*, 134; Albert C. Buck Persons, *Sex and Civil Rights: The True Selma Story* (Birmingham, Ala., 1965). (In Orgill Papers, Box 24, Mississippi Valley Collection.)

60. Belfrage, *Freedom Summer*, 64.

61. West Tennessee voters' project 'Immediate Press Release', 5 Aug. 1965, Sugarmon Papers, Box 2, Mississippi Valley Collection.

62. *Commercial Appeal*, 20 Nov. 1966.

63. Minutes of Memphis Committee on Community Relations, YWCA, 4 p.m., 1 Nov. 1966, Orgill Papers, Box 24, Folder 1.

64. Ibid.

65. Letter from Loeb's attorney, 26 Oct., 1967, ibid.

66. Southern Regional Council, *Segregation and Education* (Atlanta, 1967), 8.

67. Ibid. 15.

68. *Commercial Appeal,* 20 Nov. 1966.

69. *Press-Scimitar,* 17 Aug. 1966.

70. Belfrage, *Freedom Summer,* 166–8.

71. Los Angeles Socialist Workers' Party, *Why Watts Exploded: How the Ghetto Fought Back* (Los Angeles, 1965), 5–6.

72. Ibid. 6.

73. Ibid. 9.

74. Ibid. 12.

75. *Los Angeles Times,* 15 Aug. 1965.

76. LA Socialist Workers' Party, *Why Watts Exploded,* 10.

77. Ibid. 13.

78. Ibid. 14.

79. *The Nation,* 3 Aug. 1965.

80. *Los Angeles Times,* July 1968.

81. Ibid. 30 Sept. 1966.

82. Ibid.

83. Colaiaco, *Martin Luther King,* 152–3. James R. Ralph, Jr., *Northern Protest: Martin Luther King Jr., Chicago, and the Civil Rights Movement* (Cambridge, Mass., 1993), is a splendid detailed account of the Chicago episode; Colaiaco, *Martin Luther King,* 149–73, offers an excellent summary of both the Chicago and the Mississippi aspects.

84. Ralph, *Northern Protest,* 220–1.

85. *Report of the National Advisory Commission on Civil Disorders* (New York, 1968), esp. 67–9; Weisbrot, *Freedom Bound,* 262–3.

86. Interview in the black newspaper the *Washington Free Press,* 4 Aug. 1967, quoted in Thomas Powers, *The War at Home: Vietnam and the American People, 1964–1967* (New York, 1973), 218.

87. *Report on Civil Disorders* (New York, 1968), 56–82.

88. Herbert G. Locke, *The Detroit Riot of 1967* (Detroit, 1969), 26–7, 32, 35; John Swenson, *Stevie Wonder* (1986), 59.

89. Locke, *Detroit Riot,* 51.

90. Ibid. 43–5.

91. Powers, *The War at Home,* 219.

92. *Detroit Free Press,* 16 Aug. 1967.

93. *Report on Civil Disorders,* 1; see also 398–400, 404–7.

94. Ibid. 2; see also 397–9.

95. Alfonso J. Cervantes, *Harvard Business Review,* Sept./Oct. 1967.

96. *The Progressive,* Apr. 1968.

97. All five letters are in J. Arthur Younger Additional Papers, M216, Box 1 Folder 58, Stanford University Library Special Collections.

98. *The Nation,* 30 Aug. 1965.


Chapter 12. 1968 (and 1969)

1. This film can be seen in the Open University television programme, made for Course A309, *Images of Conflict.* In general see Dennis L. Bark and David R. Guess, *A History of West Germany,* ii; *Democracy and Its Discontents 1963–1988* (Oxford, 1989), 122–4.

2. David Caute, *Sixty-eight: The Year of the Barricades* (1988), 78.

3. Robert Lumley, *States of Emergency: Cultures of Revolt in Italy from 1968 to 1978* (1990), 167–9; Rossana Rossanda, *L'anno degli studenti* (Bari, 1968), 13.

4. Archivio MSI, 10.6.1, Istituto Feltrinelli, Milan; Mario Boato, *Il 68 è morto: viva il 68* (Verona, 1979), 316–33.

5. Alba Tiberto Beluffi, *Il rospo: testimonianze sulla contestazione del 'Sessantotto' a Milano* (Milan, 1983), 14–16.

6. Archivio MSI, 10.1.20.

7. Ibid. 10.1.7–9; 10.1.16; 10.1.20.

8. Copy ibid. 10.1.20.

9. Referred to in several documents ibid. 10.8.1.

10. These documents are all ibid. 10.8.1.

11. Ibid. 11.1.3; Lumley, *States of Emergency,* 95.

12. Quoted in Archivio MSI, 10.1.7.

13. Figures in Romolo Gobbi, *Il '68 alla rovescia* (1968 Inside Out, Milan, 1984)— mainly interviews and eyewitness accounts, 14–15. Other details in Archivio MSI, 10.1.7, and *L'Espresso,* 14 May 1968.

14. Documents in Archivio MSI, 10.15.

15. Ibid. 10.1.1, 10.1.12; *Epoca,* 3 Mar. 1968 (articles on 'The Revolt of the Students' and 'Why They Are Rebelling').

16. Archivio MSI, 10.1.1; Beluffi, *Il rospo,* 23–4.

17. The collection of photographs and eyewitness accounts are in Archivio MSI, 10.5.1. The other documents are in 10.5.2–5.

18. 'Documenti sul salario...', ibid. 10.4.1.

19. The documents on which this and the next two paragraphs are based are neatly bound into the volume 'Documenti studentesco: occupazione... febbraiomarzo 1968', ibid. 10.13.

20. My account is based on articles in *Epoca* and *L'Espresso,* 10 Mar. 1968.

21. Ibid.

22. Ibid.; and *Epoca,* 10 Mar. 1968.

23. Archivio MSI, 10.13.

24. Ibid. 10.1.7, 10.1.3, 10.1.17; *Gente,* 20 Mar. 1968; Egidio Sterpa, *I figli sulle barricate* (Milan, 1968), Beluffi, *Il Rospo,* 8–9; Lumley, *States of Emergency,* 66–7, 87, 95–6.

25. *L'Espresso*, 15 Dec. 1968; Emilio Tiberi, *La contestazione murale* (Milan, 1972); Lumley, *States of Emergency*, 68–9.

26. Archivio MSI, 10.11.1.

27. Ibid. 10.9.4.

28. Lumley, *States of Emergency*, 170–6, 185 ff., 167; Alessandro Pizzorno (ed.), *Lotte operaie e sindicato in Italia: 1968–1972* (Rome, 1974–8), esp. i, iii, iv; Boato, *Il 68*, 25, 332; Archivio MSI, 10.1.4, C, 'Verso le fabbriche'.

29. Ibid. 10.8.1, 11.1.3–5; Beluffi, *Il rospo*, 8–9.

30. *L'Express*, 18–24 Mar. 1968. In the student magazine *Droit-Sciences-Eau* for Mar.–Apr. 1968 there are no hints of the storms to come: Documents concernant les mouvements universitaires 1968–1970, 14AS250, Archives Nationales, Paris.

31. Ibid. 29 Apr.–5 May 1968.

32. Archives 1968, Fonds 1, Carton 5, Centre de recherches histoire des mouvements sociaux et du syndicalisme (CRHMSS), Paris.

33. Alain Schnapp and Pierre Vidal-Naquet, *Journal de la commune étudiante: textes et documents novembre 1967–juin 1968* (Paris, 1969), 101–3. This is a magnificent collection of primary sources with helpful commentary. Philippe Labro et al., *Mai/juin 1968: ce n'est qu'un début* (Paris, 1968), 38–44. (A collection of documents and eyewitness accounts, with editorial commentary.) A well-documented recent work is Geneviève Dreyfus-Armand and Laurent Gervereau, *Mai 68: les mouvements étudiants en France et dans le monde* (Paris, 1988).

34. Bernard E. Brown, *Protest in Paris: Anatomy of a Revolt* (New Brunswick, NJ), 6.

35. Ibid. 7.

36. Schnapp and Vidal-Naquet, *Journal*, 101–3; Labro et al., *Mai/juin 1968*, 38–44; René Viénet, *Enragés et Situationnistes dans le mouvement des occupations* (Paris, 1968), 27.

37. Labro et al., *Mai/juin 1968*, 51.

38. Printed in Adrien Dansette, *Mai 1968* (Paris, 1971), 411.

39. Lucien Rioux and René Backmann, *L'Explosion de mai* (Paris, 1968), 54–62 (a contemporary account by two journalists, completed in July 1968).

40. Schnapp and Vidal-Naquet, *Journal*.

41. Ibid. 181.

42. Maurice Grimaud, *En mai, fais ce qu'il te plait: le préfet de police de mai 68 parle* (Paris, 1970), 13.

43. *L'Express*, 13–19 May 1968.

44. Grimaud, *En mai*, 11.

45. Schnapp and Vidal-Naquet, *Journal*, 192–3.

46. Labro et al., *Mai/juin*, 17.

47. *L'Express*, 6–12 May 1968.

48. UNEF statement, 'La vérité sur les événements de la nuit de 10 au 11 mai', 11 May 1968, in Schnapp and Vidal-Naquet, *Journal*, 224–5.

49. Rioux and Backmann, *Explosion de mai*, 190.

50. Ibid. 192–3.

51. Labro et al., *Mai/juin*, 102–3.

52. Ibid. 107–8; Rioux and Backmann, *L'Explosion de mai*, 195, 203–8; Alain Delale and Gilles Ragache, *La France de 68* (Paris, 1978), 75.

53. Rioux and Backmann, *Explosion de mai*, 194 ff. There are unpublished accounts of police brutality in Archives 1968, Carton 6, CRHMSS.

54. Quoted in Rioux and Backmann, *L'Explosion de mai*, 197.

55. Printed in Labro et al., *Mai/juin*, 93–4.

56. Rioux and Backmann, *L'Explosion de mai*, 194.

57. Ibid. 196–7.

58. Schnapp and Vidal-Naquet, *Journal*, 227.

59. Rioux and Backmann, *L'Explosion de mai*, 234.

60. Ibid.

61. Ibid. 239.

62. Ibid. 240, 256.

63. Rioux and Backmann, *L'Explosion de mai*, 256.

64. Schnapp and Vidal-Naquet, *Journal*, 289–90.

65. IFOP poll in *L'Express*, 13–19 May 1968.

66. Rioux and Backmann, *L'Explosion de mai*, 269.

67. From Julien Besançon, *Les Murs ont la parole: journal mural mai 1968* (Paris, 1968), 14–173.

68. Rioux and Backmann, *L'Explosion de mai*, 279, 298; Delale and Ragache, *La France de 68*, 195; Brown, *Protest in Paris*, 15.

69. Archives 1968, Carton G, CRHMSS; Labro et al., *Mai/juin*, 334 ff.

70. 14 AS 238, Archives Nationales.

71. Ibid.

72. Ibid.

73. Labro et al., *Mai/juin*, 357–65.

74. Rioux and Backmann, *Explosion de mai*, 298.

75. Delale and Ragache, *La France de 68*, 195; Labro et al., *Mai/juin*, 326–7.

76. Grimaud, *En mai*, 19–20.

77. Ibid. 9.

78. Documents in 14AS: 238, Archives Nationales.

79. Ibid.

80. Text in Dansette, *Mai 1968*, 461–2.

81. Brown, *Protest in Paris*, 19.

82. Rioux and Backmann, *L'Explosion de mai*, 402; Maurice Larkin, *France Since the Popular Front* (1988), 324–5.

83. Rioux and Backmann, *L'Explosion de mai*, 256 ff.; Brown, *Protest in Paris*, 13–15.

84. Larkin, *France*, 325.

85. Ibid. 325–7.

86. Delale and Ragache, *La France de 68*, 150.

87. Ibid. 230.

88. Dreyfus-Armand and Gervereau, *Mai 68*, 203.

89. Labro et al., *Mai/juin*, 323.

90. Ibid. 232.

91. Delale and Ragache, *La France de 68*, 230.

92. Larkin, *France*, 327–9.

93. Quoted in Rioux and Backmann, *L'Explosion de mai*, 298. There is a copy of the *Elle* special issue for 17 June in Brochures mai '68, 14 AS.238, Archives Nationales, Paris.

94. Larkin, *France*, 330–1.

95. Archivio MSI, 10.15.

96. 'Movimentio studentesco 1968: verbale della riunione organizzata a Piadena della Biblioteca Popolare e della Liga di Cultura la sera del 22, 6, 1968', Archivio MSI, 10.16.1.

97. Ibid.

98. Paul Ginsborg, *History of Contemporary Italy: Society and Politics 1945–1988* (1990), 238–9, 309–18.

99. Pizzorno, *Lotte operaie* i, pt. 1, 81.

100. Lumley, *States of Emergency*, 186–7.

101. Ibid. 203.

102. Patrizia Violi, *Giornale dell'estrema sinistra* (Rome, 1977), 174.

103. Boato, *Il 1968*, 25.

104. Archivio MSI, 11.1.

105. Lumley, *States of Emergency*, 201.

106. Archivio MSI, 11.1.1.

107. Ibid.

108. Ibid. 10.1.3.

109. Ibid. 10.10.1.

110. Uliano Lucas, *Cinque anni a Milano* (Milan, 1973), 92.

111. Archivio MSI, 10.8.5.

112. Ibid. 10.4.6, 10.8.5.

113. Ibid. 10.8.3.

114. 'Battipaglia: una svolta nella lotta politica del sud', ibid. 10.8.4. See also *Epoca*, 20 Apr. 1969.

115. Ibid.

116. Archivio MSI, 10.11.1–2.

117. Ibid. 10.11.1.

118. Lumley, *States of Emergency*, 210, 227–8.

119. Ibid. 209.

120. Ibid. 210.

121. Ibid. 217 ff.

122. Ibid. 227.

123. Ibid. 234.

124. Archivio MSI, 10.4.4, 10.17; Lumley, *States of Emergency*, 234–5.

125. Violi, *Giornale*, 173–4.

126. Lumley, *States of Emergency*, 23.

127. 'Diario di quattordici giorni, 1968–1969', Archivio Diaristico, Pieve Sant. Stefano.

128. 'Due ragazzi intorno al '68', Archivio Diaristico.

129. Sandro Mayer (ed.), *Lettere capelloni* (Milan, 1968), 108.

130. Diario Loredana Valmori, Archivio Diaristico.

131. Diario Patrizia Papili, Archivio Diaristico.

132. Adriano Guerrini, *La rivoluzione al liceo* (Florence, 1971), 4–6.

133. Ibid. 7.

134. Ibid. 21.

135. Ibid. 39–41.

136. Anna Avallone, 'Il mio sessantotto: ricordi di una "madre" e "insegnante"', Archivio Diaristico.

137. Gobbi, *Il 68*, interview no. 7. The same sense is conveyed in the 3 other interviews Gobbi prints, nos. 25, 26, and 75 (14, 55).

138. Guerrini, *Rivoluzione al liceo*, 7.

139. Anna Morizi, 'Lettere 1967–1977', Archivio Diaristico.

140. Archivio MSI, 11.11.

141. Vietnam Solidarity Campaign, Bulletin no. 5, June 1967, Jack Askins Papers, MSS 189 V, Box 1, Modern Records Centre (MRC), University of Warwick.

142. VSC National Executive Minutes, 4 Jan. 1968, ibid.

143. Tariq Ali, 'The Extra-Parliament Opposition', in Tariq Ali (ed.), *The New Revolutionaries: A Handbook of the International Radical Left* (Toronto, Canada), 72.

144. Ibid. 67.

145. Crouch, *The Student Revolt* (1970), 98–107, 115–19.

146. Caute, *Sixty-eight*.

147. Television film has been preserved in the Open University programme *Images of Conflict*.

148. See ibid.

149. My best source has been the specially written inside account, 'Developments at Essex', by Luke Hodgkin, part of the section on 'Student Revolt' in the David Spencer Papers, MSS 164, Box 2, MRC. An excellent contemporary published source which ranges widely is Bernard Crick and William A. Robson (eds.), *Protest and Discontent* (Harmondsworth, 1970).

150. Students and staff of Hornsey College, *The Hornsey Affair* (1969).

151. Quoted ibid. 207.

152. ATTI, Guildford College of Design (formerly Guildford School of Art), 28.10.68, Collard MSS 155, Box 2, Folder 2, MRC.

153. Ibid.

154. Summary of Reasons for Supporting the Students by Victimized Staff', ibid.

155. Crouch, *Student Revolt*, 102; Caute, *Sixty-eight*, 303–5.

156. Crouch, *Student Revolt*, 72–9.

157. VSC Executive Minutes, Askins Papers, V, Box 1.

158. Caute, *Sixty-eight*, 314.

159. *New Society*, 31 Oct. 1968.

160. *Images of Conflict*.

161. Crouch, *Student Revolt*, 78–83.

162. Ibid. 80–94, 124.

163. Ibid. 87–96.

164. My main source for the opening month of the strike is 'Southern Regional Council Special Report: In Memphis: More than a Garbage Strike', by J. Edwin Stanfield, 22 Mar. 1968, Edmund Orgill Papers, MSS 87, Box 16, Folder 9, Mississippi Valley Collection; Joan Turner Beifuss, *At the River I Stand* (Memphis, 1985), is a magnificent local account, using interviews, personal recollection, and a vast array of documentation.

165. 'More than a Garbage Strike', 2.

166. Ibid. 3.

167. *Commercial Appeal*, 23 Feb. 1968.

168. 'More than a Garbage Strike', 4.

169. Letter of 21 Feb. 1968, Orgill Papers, MSS 87, Box 16, Folder 9.

170. Address by Patricia W. Shaw, 3 Mar. 1977, Patricia W. Shaw Papers, MSS. 109, Folder 2, Mississippi Valley Collection.

171. Copy in Rabbi James A. Wax Collection, Folder 6, Memphis/Shelby County Archives.

172. 'More than a Garbage Strike', 7.

173. *Wall Street Journal*, 8 Mar. 1968.

174. James A. Colaiaco, *Martin Luther King, Jr.* (New York, 1993), 189–91, on which the rest of this paragraph is based.

175. Ibid. 192–4; Southern Regional Council, 'In Memphis: Tragedy Unaverted, by J. Edwin Stanfield, Supplement of Special Report of March 22, 1968', 3 Apr. 1968, in Orgill Papers, MSS 87, Box 16, Folder 9.

176. Ibid.

177. MSS 154, Box 5, Mississippi Valley Collection.

178. Colaiaco, *Martin Luther King*, 193–4.

179. Ibid. 196–7.

180. Ibid. 197.

181. Beifuss, *At the River I Stand*, 271.

182. Ibid. 237.

183. Based on my reading of the reports on their activities in the Memphis newspapers.

184. 'Tragedy Unaverted'; Colaiaco, *Martin Luther King*, 194.

185. Letter of 29 May 1968, and memo 'not to be quoted till after my death' in Wax Collection, Box 5, Folder 6.

186. Godfrey Hodgson, *In Our Time: America from World War II to Nixon* (New York, 1976), 361–2; Colaiaco, *Martin Luther King*, 197.

187. *Commercial Appeal*, 9 Apr. 1968.

188. Beifuss, *At the River I Stand*, 438–40.

189. Wax Collection, Box 5, Folder 6.

190. Beifuss, *At the River I Stand*, 451–8.

191. Caute, *Sixty-eight*, 126.

192. Cox Commission Hearings, Box 7, Columbia Administration Records, Columbia University Rare Book and Manuscript Library. My account is based partly on the published Report of the Cox Commission, but more on the 'raw' hearings and testimony on which the Report was based. *Crisis at Columbia: Report of the Fact Finding Commission Appointed to Investigate the Disturbances at Columbia University in April and May 1968* (New York, 1968).

193. Cox Commission Hearings, Box 1, vol. ii.

194. Ibid.

195. Dotson Rader, *I Ain't Marching Anymore!* (New York, 1969), 115.

196. *Cox Commission Report*, 74.

197. Cox Commission Hearings, *passim*.

198. Ibid. Box 1, vol. iv.

199. *Cox Commission Report*, 99–106.

200. Cox Commission Hearings, esp. Box 2, vols. ix-xi.

201. Ibid. xi, 1732 ff.

202. *Cox Commission Report*, 122–51.

203. Cox Commission Hearings, Box 5.

204. Ibid. 'Police on Campus Collection', Box 1.

205. *Cox Commission Report*, 153.

206. Cox Commission Hearings, Box 2, i., 90.

207. Ibid. vol. ix.

208. Ibid. Box 6.

209. Ibid. Box 2, vol. xi.

210. Caute, *Sixty-eight*, 156.

211. Tom Wells, *The War Within* (Berkeley, Calif., 1994), 270–6.

212. Hodgson, *In Our Time*, 373.

213. Ibid. 277.

214. Ibid. 276–7.

215. *Official Report of National Commission on Violence*, 1 Dec. 1963, quoted in Caute, *Sixty-eight*, 285.

216. Wells, *The War Within*, 277. My account in the following paragraphs is based on ibid. 277–80.

217. Caute, *Sixty-eight*, 368–78.

218. Free Speech Collection, Box 6, Bancroft Library, University of California at Berkeley. Once again W. J. Rorabaugh, *Berkeley at War: The 1960s* (New York, 1980) is invaluable.

219. Free Speech Collection, Box 6.

220. Ibid.

221. 'Our Park and Our Struggle' (n.d., May 1969), in Eric C. Bellquist Collection, Box 59, Hoover Institution Library, Stanford, Calif.

222. Free Speech Collection, Box 6.

223. Letter of 29 May 1969, Henry Nash Smith Papers, Bancroft Library.

224. Letter of 20 May 1969, Bellquist Collection, Box 142.

225. Letter of 29 May 1969, Henry Nash Smith Papers.

226. My conclusions are based on documents in the rich 'Challenge to Governance Project', Division of Rare and Manuscript Collections, 47/5/1309, Cornell University Library, Ithaca, NY.

227. Adam Garfinkle, *Telltale Hearts: The Origins and Impact of the Vietnam Antiwar Movement* (Basingstoke, 1995), 2.


*Chapter 13. Women's Turn*

1. National Organization of Women Circular, Oct. 1966. Copy in Free Speech Movement Collection, Box 10, F23, Bancroft Library, University of California at Berkeley.

2. These issues are complicated. I would refer to the primary sources I have already quoted in Chs. 8 and 12, and particularly to the testimony (for Britain) in Sara Maitland, *Very Heaven: Women's Voices from the 1960s* (1988) and (for Italy) in the interviews with women students in Romolo Gobbi, *Il 68 alla rovescia* (1968 Inside Out, Milan, 1984). More of the evidence, on both sides of the main debates, can be studied in: Judith Clavir Albert and Stewart Albert (eds.), *The Sixties Papers: Documents of a Rebellious Decade* (New York, 1984); Sally Belfrage, *Freedom Summer* (New York, 1965); Sara Evans, *Personal Politics: The Roots of Women's Liberation in the Civil Rights Movement and the New Left* (New York, 1979); Judith Hole and Ellen Levine, *The Rebirth of Feminism* (New York, 1971); Mary King, *Freedom Song: A Personal Story of the 1960s Civil Rights Movement* (New York, 1967); Keith Melville, *Communes in the Counterculture: Organs, Theories, Styles of Life* (New York, 1972); Robin Morgan (ed.), *Sisterhood Is Powerful: An Anthology of Writings from the Women's Liberation Movement* (New York, 1970); Geoffrey O'Brien, *Dream Time: Chapters from the Sixties* (New York, 1988); Leslie B. Tanner (ed.), *Voices from Women's Liberation* (Boston, 1970); and in other books cited in this chapter.

3. Jean Rabout, *Histoire des féminismes français* (Paris, 1978), 334.

4. Paolo Gaiotti de Biase, 'La posizione della donna nel movimento studentesco europeo', *Donna e Società*, 11 (Sept. 1969); Camilla Pozione, *Breve storia del movimento femminile in Italia* (Rome, 1978), 250–1, 283; Ferdinando Antoniotti et al. (eds.), *Donna oggi in Italia* (Rome, 1975), 30, 31.

5. There is a copy of the original in Social Protest Collection, Box 25, F9, Bancroft Library. It was reprinted in *Notes from the Second Year: Women's Liberation* (New York, 1970).

6. Gruppo Demistificazione Autoritarismo (DEMAU), Manifesto, 1 Dec. 1966, repr. in the excellent collection of documents edited by Rosalba Spagnoletti, *I movimenti femministi in Italia* (Rome, 1971), 25–8.

7. Hole and Levine, *Rebirth of Feminism*, 112; Evans, *Personal Politics*.

8. Hole and Levine, 220 ff.; Lauri Umansky, *Motherhood Reconceived: Feminism and the Legacies of the Sixties* (New York, 1996), 35–45.

9. Social Protest Collection, Box 25, Folder 32, Bancroft Library.

10. Women's Liberation Collection, Box 177, Folder 1, UCLA Library Special Collections.

11. Hole and Levine, *Rebirth of Feminism*, 123–5; Umansky, *Motherhood Reconceived*, 37–8.

12. Ibid. 38–9.

13. Ibid. 177, n. 66.

14. Hole and Levine, *Rebirth of Feminism* (1973 edn.), 441.

15. Roland Bellorain, *Le Nouveau Féminisme américain* (Paris, 1972), 11–13.

16. Hole and Levine, *Rebirth of Feminism* (1973 edn.), p. xv.

17. Kate Millett, *Sexual Politics* (New York, 1970). My quotations are from the Virago paperback of 1977, pp. 12, 25, 29, 362, 363.

18. Shulamith Firestone, *The Dialectic of Sex: The Case for Feminist Revolutions* (New York, 1970), 142, 232–3.

19. Sheila Rowbotham, 'The Beginnings of Women's Liberation in Britain', in Micheline Wandor, *The Body Politic: Women's Liberation in Britain* (1972), 91–3.

20. David Bouchier, *The Feminist Challenge: The Movement for Women's Liberation in Britain and the USA* (1983), 57.

21. Rowbotham, 'Beginnings', 92; Anna Coote and Beatrix Campbell, *Sweet Freedom: The Struggle for Women's Liberation* (1982), 18.

22. Rowbotham, 'Beginnings', 91.

23. Bouchier, *Feminist Challenge*, 58; Rowbotham, 'Beginnings', 94.

24. Ibid. 93–6; Bouchier, *Feminist Challenge*, 59.

25. Rowbotham, 'Beginnings', 96–7.

26. Bouchier, *Feminist Challenge*, 93–4.

27. Richard Neville, *Hippie Hippie Shake: The Dreams, the Trips, the Trials, the Love-ins, the Screw Ups, the Sixties,* (1995), 71, 145.

28. Germaine Greer, *The Female Eunuch* (1970), 325.

29. Ibid. 249, 261.

30. Micheline Wandor, *Carry On, Understudies: Theatre and Sexual Politics* (1986), 326–7.

31. Ibid. 37

32. Ibid. 328.

33. Nicole Benoit, Edgar Morin, and Bernard Paillard, *La Femme majeure: nouvelle fémininité, nouveau féminisme* (Paris, 1973), 107.

34. *L'Express*, 21–7 Oct. 1970.

35. The Estates General is reported in full in Jean Mauduit, *La Révolte des femmes: après les états Généraux de 'Elle'* (Paris, 1971).

36. Ibid. 245–6.

37. Ibid. 247–9.

38. Ibid. 250.

39. Ibid. 259.

40. Benoit et al., *La Femme majeure*, 58.

41. Ibid. 9.

42. Ibid. 113.

43. Anne Tristan and Annie de Pisan, *Histoires de MLF* (Paris, 1977), 48–59. Issues 54 and 55 (July and Oct.) of *Partisans* were reissued together as *Partisans libération des femmes année zéro* (Paris, 1972).

44. Tristan and Pisan, *Histoires*, 61–2.

45. Benoit et al., *La Femme majeure*, 9.

46. Ibid.

47. Spagnoletti *Movimenti femministi*, 54–5.

48. Antoniotti, *Donna oggi*, 30 ff.

49. Spagnoletti, *Movimenti femministi*, 62.

50. Ibid. 68.

51. Carla Ravaioli, 'Le donne', in Antonio Gambino et al., *Dal '68 a oggi: come siamo e come eravamo* (Bari, 1979), 319 ff.

52. Ibid. 319.

53. Printed in Carla Lonzi, *'Sputiamo su Hegel', 'La donna clitoridea e la donna vaginale', e altri scritti* (Milan, 1974), 11–18.

54. Since I produced my own translation of the Rivolta Femminile manifesto, another English version has appeared in the admirable collection by Paolo Bono and Sandra Kent, *Italian Feminist Thought: A Reader* (Oxford, 1991).

55. Ibid. 23.

56. 'Premessa', in Lonzi, *Sputiamo su Hegel*, 9; 'Sessualità femminile e aborto', ibid. 67–75.

57. Lonzi, *La donna clitoridea*, 77–140.

58. Antoniotti, *Donna oggi*, 29.

59. *Quarto Mondo*, 1 (Mar. 1971), repr. in Spagnoletti, *Movimenti femministi*, 126–55. My direct quotation is from p. 134.

60. Antoniotti, *Donna oggi*, 31.

61. Quoted in Paul Vaughan, *The Pill* (1970), 45.

62. Flora Davis, *Moving the Mountain: The Women's Movement in America since 1960* (New York, 1991), 157.

63. Social Protest Collection, Box 25, F25, 'Abortion Counselling Service', Bancroft Library. For abortion reform across America, see Davis, *Moving the Mountain*, 157–83; David J. Garrow, *Liberty and Sexuality: The Right to Privacy and the Making of Roe v. Wade* (New York, 1994), 354–88.

64. Documents in David S. Hall Papers, Boxes 1–3, UCLA Library Special Collections.

65. Garrow, *Liberty and Sexuality*, 586–99.

66. François and Michel Guy, *L'Avortement: documents pour une information et une réflexion sur un problème d'actualité* (Paris, 1971), 21.

67. Mauduit, *Révolte des femmes*, 248.

68. Guy, *Avortement*, 23–4.

69. Tristan and Pisan, *Histoires*, 65.

70. My account is based on ch. 3, 'Le Procès de Bobigny', in *La Cause des femmes* (Paris, 1976) by Gisèle Halimi, the main defence counsel and a leading figure in Association Choisir, amplified by newspaper reports. Halimi speaks confidently of 'rape' (69).

71. Quoted ibid. 73.

72. Ibid.

73. These press reports are all printed in J. Gouazé, M. Mouilland, E. Severin, and J. F. Têtu, *Stratégies de la presse et du droit* (Lyon, 1979), 142–205.

74. Halimi, *La Cause*, 63–8.

75. Ibid. 65–8.

76. Association Choisir, *Avortement: une loi en procès: l'affaire de Bobigny*, 'Sténotypie intégrale des débats an tribunal de Bobigny (8 Novembre 1972)' (Paris, 1973).

77. Ibid. 141–2, 146.

78. Ibid. 147.

79. Ibid.

80. Ibid. 151–63.

81. Ibid. 50.

82. Ibid. 61–123.

83. Ibid. 165.

84. Ibid. 55.

85. Halimi, *La Cause*, 85.

86. Ibid. 209, 220.

87. Press reports quoted in Gouazé et al., *Stratégies de la presse*.

88. *Le Torchon Brûle,* 1, quoted in François A. Isambert and Paul Labrière, 'Contraception et avortement: dix ans de débat dans la presse' (1965–74), éditions du Centre Matériel de la Recherche Scientifique (TS, Paris, 1979), 105.

89. 'Maternité/Sexualité/Libération/Politique', supplement 2 of *Pétroleuses* (Nov. 1974), ibid. 117.

90. Nelly Mauchamp, *La France d'aujourdhui: civilisation* (Paris, 1991), 11.

91. Lara Foletti e Clelia Boesi, *Per il diritto di aborto con un appendice sulle tecniche contracettive* (Rome, 1972), 8–14; E. Banotti, *La sfida femminile: maternità e aborto* (Bari, 1971); Cristina Papa, *Dibattito sull'aborto: documenti e confronti* (Rimini, 1975), 37 ff.

92. Foletti and Boesi, *Per il diritto,* 7.

93. Ibid. 14 ff.

94. Ibid. 28–30.

95. Ibid. 30.

96. Ibid. 66–7.

97. Ibid. 68–72.

98. Lotta di Donna, *Maternità ed aborto* (Padua, 1971), 5.

99. Article on 'Divorce' in *Commercial Appeal,* 11 Nov. 1973.

100. *Press-Scimitar,* 30 July 1977.

101. Jean-Charles Laurent, *Le Divorce: essai de sociologie juridique* (Paris, 1964), 44, cited by Antony Copley, *Sexual Moralities in France 1730–1980: New Ideas on the Family, Divorce and Homosexuality* (1989), 207.

102. My account is based on ibid. 204–15; also *Press-Scimitar*, 4 Mar. 1971.

103. Ibid. 22 Jan., 27 Aug. 1973, 4 May 1977.

104. Umansky, *Motherhood Reconceived*, 46–76.

105. Ibid. 106–97; Antoniotti, *Donna oggi*, 30 ff.

106. *Commercial Appeal*, 30 Apr. 1970.

107. Umansky, *Motherhood Reconceived*, 106.

108. Ibid. 104–8.

109. Paul Ginsborg, *History of Contemporary Italy: Society and Politics 1945–1988* (1990), 328; *Epoca*, 18 Oct. 1970.

110. Sandro Mayer (ed.), *Lettere capelloni* (Milan, 1968), 109.

111. Ibid. 111.

112. *Epoca*, 14, 18 Apr. 1973; *Donna e Società*, Jan-Mar. 1974; Ginsborg, *History*, 350.

113. Ibid., 35.

114. *Epoca*, 25 May 1974.

*Chapter 14. Full Effrontery*

1. The research for Britain and America, and some other countries, is summarized in Kaye Wellings, Julia Field, Anne M. Johnson, and Jane Wadsworth, *Sexual Behaviour in Britain: The National Survey of Sexual Attitudes and Lifestyles* (1994), 185–90.

2. Social Protest Collection, Box 8, F21, Bancroft Library, University of California at Berkeley.

3. Ibid.

4. Ibid. F38; repr. in Aubrey Walter (ed.), *Come Together: The Years of Gay Liberation 1970–73* (1980), 7.

5. Social Protest Collection, Box 8, F30.

6. Ibid.

7. 'Fact Sheet', Jan. 1970, ibid. F38.

8. Printed in Guy Hocquemghem, *L'Après-mai des faunes* (Paris, 1974), 76–81.

9. Ibid. 61, 84.

10. Ibid. 118–19.

11. Le Front Homosexuel d'Action Révolutionnaire, *Rapport contre la normalità* (Paris, 1971), 7; Hocquemghem, *Après-mai*, 188.

12. Front Homosexuel, *Rapport*, 7–18.

13. Ibid. 18.

14. Giacomo Dacquino, *Diario di un omosessuale* (Milan, 1970), 9; *Gli omosessuali* (Bologna, 1970), editorial introduction.

15. Ibid. frontispiece.

16. Ibid. 166.

17. Printed in Mariasilvia Spolato (ed.), *I movimenti omosessuali di liberazione: documenti testimonianze e foto della rivoluzione omosessuale* (Rome, 1972), 133.

18. Ibid. 7.

19. Ibid. 16 ff., 90.

20. Printed in Walter, *Come Together*, 11.

21. Philippe Garner, *Sixties Design* (Cologne, 1996), 148.

22. Jim Haynes, *Thanks for Coming! An Autobiography* (1984), 174.

23. Quote in Robert Sklar, *Film: An International History of the Medium* (1990), 461.

24. Arthur Lennig, 'A History of Censorship in the American Film', in Thomas L. Atkins (ed.), *Sexuality in the Movies* (Bloomington, Ind., 1975), 70.

25. David S. Lenfest, 'I Am Curious—Yellow: A Practical Education', in Atkins, *Sexuality*, 193.

26. Lennig, 'History', 71.

27. Linda Williams, *Hard Core: Power, Pleasure and the 'Frenzy of the Visible'* (1990), 96–8; Al Di Lauro and Gerald Rabkin, Dirty *Movies: An Illustrated History of Stag Film* (New York, 1976); Kenneth Turan and Stephen Zito, *Sinema: American Pornographic Films and the People Who Make Them* (New York, 1974); Walter Kendrick, *The Secret Museum: Pornography in Modern Culture* (new edn., New York, 1996).

28. 'J', *The Sensuous Woman* (New York, 1969; London, 1971), 7, 9, 27 ff.

29. Emmanuelle Arsan, *Mon 'Emmanuelle', leur pape et mon éros* (Paris, 1974).

30. 'J', *Sensuous Woman*, 78.

31. Ellen Willis, *'Deep Throat:* Hard to Swallow', in Atkins, *Sexuality*, 216 ff.; Simon Garfield, *'Deep Throat* Revisited', *Independent on Sunday*, 28 June 1992.

32. Richard Smith, *Getting into Deep Throat* (New York, 1973); Williams, *Hard Core*, 99–103, 110–15; Gloria Steinem, 'The Real Linda Lovelace', in *Outrageous Acts and Everyday Rebellions* (1984), 243–51; Alan Dershowitz, *The Best Defense* (New York, 1982), 155–92.

33. Turan and Zito, *Sinema*, 202.

34. Williams, *Hard Core*, 111; Garfield, *'Deep Throat* Revisited'.

35. Linda Lovelace, *Inside Linda Lovelance* (New York, 1974), 73–104; Garfield, *'Deep Throat* Revisited'.

36. Ibid.

37. Ibid.

38. John Trevelyan, *What the Censor Saw* (1973), 104.

39. *L'Express*, 15–21 July 1974.

40. Terence Hendrickson, *Variations on a Sexual Theme* (1969); covering letter still preserved with British Library copy.

41. Information from the author.

42. Hendrickson, *Variations*, 13–14.

43. Letters of Sept.–Oct. 1972 in William Wilson, MP Papers, Modern Records Centre, University of Warwick.

44. *IT,* Jan.-Feb., 1980.

45. *Gilbert and George: Pictures 1982–86* (Hayward Gallery, 1986).

46. Ibid.

47. Ibid. In general, see *Gilbert and George: The Complete Pictures 1971–1985* (1986).

48. Ibid. p. vii.

49. David Piper (ed.), *The Mitchell Beazley History of Painting and Sculpture*, iii: *New Horizons* (1981), 252.

50. Lea Vergine, *L'arte in trincea: lessico delle tendenze artistiche 1960–1990* (Milan, 1996); Piper, *History*, 252–3, Edward Lucie-Smith, *Movements in Art since 1945* (1984), ch. 9.

51. Vergine, *L'arte*, 187

52. Götz Adriani, Winfried Konnertz, and Karen Thomas, *Joseph Beuys: Life and Works* (Woodbury, NY, 1979).

53. Gilles Bresson and Noèl Monier, *Avoir 16 ans* (Paris, 1972), 39.

54. Ibid. 45–6, 70 ff.

55. *L'Express*, 12–18 Sept. 1973.

56. See the brief account in Arthur Marwick, *British Society since 1945* (3rd edn, 1996), 184–5, 254–69.

57. Dennis L. Bark and David R. Guess, *History of West Germany*, ii: *Democracy and Its Discontents 1913–1988* (Oxford, 1989), 348.

58. Paul Ginsborg, *History of Contemporary Italy: Society and Politics 1943–1988* (1990), 361 ff.

59. There are chronologies of these incidents in Massimo Cavallini, *Il terrorismo in fabbrica: interviste di Massimo Cavallini con gli operai della FIAT, Sit-Siemens, Magnetti Marelli, Alfa Romeo* (Rome, 1978).

60. Ibid.; Ginsborg, *History*, 362–3.

61. Ibid. 338–40.

62. Ibid. 371, 384–5.

63. David Caute, *Sixty-eight: The Year of the Barricades* (1988), 394–6.

64. Ibid. 387; Tom Wells, *The War Within: America's Battle over Vietnam* (Berkeley, Calif., 1994), 304.

65. Ibid. 366.

66. Ibid. 452–3.

67. Roxy Harris, *Being Black: Selections from 'Soledad Brother' and 'Soul on Ice'* (1981), 7. See David Burner, *Making Peace with the 60s* (Princeton, NJ), 59.

68. See new edn. of George Jackson, *Soledad Brother: The Prison Letters of George Jackson* (Chicago, 1994), p. x.

69. George C. Herring, *America's Longest War: The United States and Vietnam, 1950–1975* (3rd edn., New York, 1996), 262; John M. Blum, *Years of Discord: American Politics and Society 1961–1974* (New York, 1991), 386–7.

70. Herring, *America's Longest War*, 266; Blum, *Years of Discord*, 368.

71. Stephen E. Ambrose, *Nixon*, ii. *The Triumph of a Politician 1962–1972* (New York, 1989), esp. 373–7, 392–4, 579–86, 599–600, 623–4, 636–7.

72. Nigel Fountain, *Underground: The London Alternative Press 1966–1974* (1980), 141, 157, 159–60.

73. Mark Weatherall, *From Our Cambridge Correspondent: Cambridge Student Life 1945–95 as seen in the pages of 'Varsity'* (Cambridge, 1995), 35–7.

74. Norman Shrapnel, *The Seventies: Britain's Inward March* (1980), 158–60.

75. Marwick, *British Society*, 184–5, 254–69.

76. Gary P. Freeman, *Immigrant Labor and Racial Conflict in Industrial Societies: The French and British Experience 1945–1975* (Princeton, NJ, 1979), 92.

77. Ibid. 83.

78. Juliette Minces, *Les Travailleurs étrangers en France: enquête* (Paris, 1973), 102–3.

79. Freeman, *Immigrant Labor*, 91.

80. Ibid. 93.

81. Xavier de la Fournière, *Giscard d'Estaing et nous* (Paris, 1977).

82. Freeman, *Immigrant Labor*, 98.

83. Ibid. 57.

84. Ibid. 59.

85. Ibid. 59–60.

86. Zig Layton-Henry, *The Politics of Immigration* (1992), 126.

87. Institute of Race Relations, *Colour and Citizenship: A Report on British Race Relations* (1969), 756.

88. Ibid. 319.

89. House of Commons Select Committee on Race Relations and Immigration, *Police-Immigrant Relations* (1972), quoted in Layton-Henry, *Politics of Immigration*, 126.

90. M. Cain, *Society and the Policeman's Role* (1973), 117.

91. Ibid. 127.

92. Layton-Henry, *Politics of Immigration*, 127.

93. Freeman, *Immigrant Labor*, 60.

*Chapter 15. Living Life to the Full*

1. Results printed in Frederick Villiers, *Vivre en France: étude sur les revenus et le pouvoir d'achat* (Paris, 1974), 21.

2. *L'Express*, 17–23 Feb. 1969.

3. Nicole Tabard, *Besoins et aspirations des familles et des jeunes* (Paris, 1975), 85, 119, 137, 182–90, 390.

4. *Epoca*, 23 Nov. 1974.

5. Monique Hébrard, *Les Parents, les jeunes et l'amour* (Paris, 1975), 20–30.

6. SOFRES survey, cited ibid. 31.

7. IFOP survey, cited ibid. 32.

8. François Cerutti, *Les Jeunes au boulot* (Paris, 1974), 103.

9. Michèle Aumont, *Jeunes dans un monde* (Paris, 1973), 52–6, 84–5.

10. Caria Accardi, *Superiore e inferiore: conversazioni fra le ragazzine delle scuole medie* (Scritti di Rivolta Femminile 4, Rome, Feb. 1972), 95, 96, 99.

11. Ibid. 106, 107, 111–12.

12. US Census Bureau figures reported by UPI, 12 Oct. 1976 and 5 Dec. 1977.

13. See Ch. 6, p. 261.

14. Congressional Budget Office figures, UPI, 5 Dec. 1977.

15. Ibid.

16. Ibid.

17. Letter of 10 Apr. 1967, Box 24, Folder 1, Orgill Papers, Mississippi Valley Collection, Memphis.

18. Ibid. 5 Jan. 1969.

19. UPI press release, 4 Dec. 1970.

20. '1972 Affirmative Action Plan for the Community Action Agency of Memphis and Shelby County', in Orgill Papers, Box 35, II.

21. *Press-Scimitar,* 20 May 1972.

22. *Commercial Appeal,* 17 Mar. 1975.

23. *Press-Scimitar,* 5 Apr. 1970.

24. Southern Regional Council, *The South and Her Children: School Segregation 1970–1977* (Atlanta, Ga., 1978).

25. Vittorio De Sica, *Diario di un maestro in TV* (Turin, Apr. 1973), 29.

26. Ibid.

27. Ibid. 40.

28. Newspapers quoted ibid. 20–1.

29. Paul Ginsborg, *A History of Contemporary Italy: Society and Politics 1943–1986* (1990), 371.

30. Maurice Larkin, *France Since the Popular Front* (Oxford, 1988), 348.

31. Paul Ginsborg, *History of Contemporary Italy: Society and Politics 1945–1988* (1990), 329.

32. Central Statistical Office, *Social Trends 10* (1980), 200

33. *Commercial Appeal,* 1 Jan. 1975.

34. Featured in Memphis press throughout June 1969. See esp. *Press-Scimitar,* 18 June, and *Commercial Appeal,* 19 and 23 June.

35. Ibid. 14 Sept. 1972.

36. Ibid. 28 Sept. 1972.

37. Association Ville Humaine: Sabine Chalvon-Demersay, 'Le Triangle du XIV$^{ième}$: mythologie urbaine et socialité dans le XIV$^{ième}$ arrondissement de Paris' (n.d.), Musée Nationale des Arts et Traditions Populaires 23.

38. Ibid.

39. Robert Franc, *Le Scandale de Paris* (Paris, 1971), 157.

40. Confédération Française pour l'Habitation et l'Urbanisme, *35 ans d'urbanisme* (Paris, n.d., 1981), 169.

41. Ibid. 187.

42. *VExpress,* 21–7 Aug. 1972.

43. Guiseppe Morbidelli and Guiseppe Stancanelli, La tutela dell'ambiente con particolare riferimento ai centri storici', in ISGEA, *La tutela dell'ambiente con particolare riferimento ai centri storici* (Varese, 1977), 92.

784

44. Ibid. 63.

45. John McCormick, *The Global Environmental Movement: Reclaiming Paradise* (1992), 57–8; Georges Lamiral, *Chronique de trente années d'équipement nucléaire á électricité de France* (Paris, 1988), ii. 109–12,

46. Friends of the Earth, *Environmental Handbook (New York 1970)*.

47. Barry Commoner, *The Closing Circle: Confronting the Environmental Crisis* (New York, 1971), 14.

48. Barbara Ward and René Duboi, *Only One Earth: The Care and Maintenance of a Small Planet* (New York, 1972), Donella H Meadows et al., *The Limits to Growth* (New York and London, 1972).

49. *Pittsburgh Courier*, 18 Nov. 1972.

50. *Commercial Appeal*, 17 Nov. 1975.

51. Documents in Russell Sugarmon Papers, Box 1, Folder 3, Mississippi Valley Collection.

52. Ibid.; *Press-Scimitar*, 12 Feb. 1976; *Commercial Appeal*, 24 Oct. 1976.

53. *Pittsburgh Courier*, 18 Nov. 1972.

54. Partito Radicale, *Contro il regime: otto referendum per abrogare legge repressive, clericale, fasciste, corporative, militariste e classiste* (Rome, 1974), 7.

55. Ibid. 23–42.

56. Harold W. Chase, 'Twenty-sixth Amendment', in *Dictionary of American History* (rev. edn., New York, 1976), vii. 133.

57. Imprimerie des Services Techniques de la Préfecture de Police, *Le Policier et les jeunes: guide à l'usage des fonctionnaires de police* (Paris?, n.d., 1976?).

58. See Caroline Coon and Rufus Harris, *The Release Report on Drug Offenders and the Law* (1969).

59. *Press-Scimitar*, 11 Sept. 1976.

60. Patricia W. Shaw Papers, Folder 4, Mississippi Valley Collection.

61. *Press-Scimitar*, 6 Aug. 1976.

62. Rassemblement pour la République, *Le RPR propose égalité pour les handicapés* (Paris, Dec. 1977).

63. Ginsborg, *Contemporary Italy*, 322.

64. Silvana Sabatini, 'Pagine e giorni-diario di una donna borghese', entries for 18 Mar., 21 Apr., 25 July 1968, 25 Aug. 1972, 20 June 1974, 31 Aug. 1975, 29 Apr. 1976.

65. Ginsborg, *History*, 370.

66. Arthur Marwick, *British Society since 1945* (3rd edn., 1996), 246.

67. Paul Yonnet, *Jeunes, modes et masses: La société française et le moderne* (Paris, 1986), 194–203; Giancarlo Riccio, *Percorsi del rock italiano* (Milan, 1980), 136.

68. *Press-Scimitar*, 15 June 1970.

69. Ibid.

70. Ibid. 19 Jan. 1973.

71. *Epoca*, 20 July 1974.

*Part V. Conclusion*

*Chapter 16. The Consummation of a Cultural Revolution*

1. Troy Johnson, Joane Nagel, and Duane Champagne (eds.), *American Indian Activism: Alcatraz to the Longest Walk* (Urbana, Ill., 1997). For the Nixon speech, see the chapter by John Garvey and Troy Johnson, 'The Government and the Indians: the American Indian Occupation of Alcatraz Island, 1969–71', 167.

2. Tom Hayden, *Reunion: A Memoir* (New York, 1988), 452.

# Note on Sources

*Archive Sources*

(The collections listed are confined to those which provided substantial information used in this book)

*Britain*

Modern Records Centre, University of Warwick Library
    J. Askins Papers (Anti-Vietnam War), MSS189
    Cyril Collard Papers, MSS155
    Derek Coombs, MP Papers, MSS132
    Maurice Edelman, MP Papers, MSS125
    David Spencer Papers, MSS164
    William Wilson, MP Papers, MSS76

National Library of Scotland
    Ritchie Calder Papers, AC10318
    John P. Mackintosh, MP Papers, Dep.323
    W. J. Taylor Papers, Acc.9575
    Traverse Theatre Archive, Acc.4850 and Acc.10365

*France*

Archives Nationales: Institut Français d'Histoire Sociale, Paris
    Dossier sur l'affaire Lipp, 14 AS 317
    Mai 1968 (brochures et tracts), 14 AS 238 and 250
    Renault régie (tracts 1962–5), 14 AS 238

Centre de Recherches, Histoire des Mouvements Sociaux et du Syndicalisme, Paris
    Archive 1968

Musée Nationale des Arts et Traditions Populaires, Paris
    Various documents on popular art and the environment

Maison de la Villette, Paris
    Various *témoignages* (oral histories and interviews)


*Italy*

Archivio Diaristico, Pieve Santo Stefano, Tuscany
    Anna Avallone, 'Il mio sessantotto: ricordi di una "madre" e "insegnante"'
    Ivana Cavaletti, 'Diario di una teenager, 1958–1960'
    Loredana Valmori, 'Diario Firenze-Sesto Fiorentino 1963–1981'
    Vincenzo Fazio, 'Lettere alla fidanzata, 1961–1962'
    Franca Morigi, 'Lettere 1967–1977'; e autori vari, Lettere a Franca Morigi'
    Giordano Moretti, 'Diario di 14 giorni del 1968/69'
    Margherita Nicotra, 'Le trecce del vento'
    Patrizia Papili, 'Al di là del mare'
    Silvana Sabatini, 'Pagine e giorni: diario di una donna borghese'
    Nunzia Stano, 'Diario'
    Roberto Stocchi, 'Diario'
    Giuseppe Corlito, 'Due ragazzi informo al '68'

Istituto Ferruccio Parri, Bologna
    important for its collection of video material relating to the 1960s

Fondazione Giangiacomo Feltrinelli, Milan
    Archivio Movimento Studentesco Italiano


*United States*

Mississippi Valley Collection/Special Collections Department, Memphis State University
Libraries, Memphis, Tennessee
    Oscar Clark Carr Papers, MSS134
    Dalstrom Papers, MSS189
    Myra Dreifus Papers, MSS12
    Handy-Ruffin (Overton Park Expressway) Papers, MSS61
    Joan Hassell Papers, MSS205
    Berta Hill Harris Collection on Women, MSS204
    Julie Bensdorf Isenberg Papers, MSS276
    Meeman Papers, MSS85
    Memphis Poverty Program Papers, MSS54
    Memphis Typographical Union Papers, MSS68
    Milbourn Hinds Papers, MSS70
    Edmund Orgill Papers, MSS87

Race Relations Collection, MSS200
Patricia W. Shaw Papers, MSS109
Russell Sugarmon Papers, MSS108
Tennessee Nurses' Association Records, MSS323
Van Dyke (Annie Pope) Papers, MSS257
Nowland Van Powell Papers, MSS258

Memphis and Shelby County Library Special Collections
Beale Street Collection
George W. Lee Collection
Rabbi James A. Wax Collection

University of Mississippi Library Special Collections, Oxford
Dr Lucy Turnbull Collection

University of California at Los Angeles Library Special Collections
Edward M. Ainsworth Papers, MSS405
Paul Bullock Papers, MSS1303
Civil Rights Movement Papers, MSS1111
Extremist Literature, Collection 50
Mrs Bernardine Fritz Papers, Collection 1298
David S. Hall Papers, MSS1193
Japanese-American Research Project Papers, MSS2010
Carey McWilliams Papers, MSS1319
Norris Poulson Papers, Collection 787
Paul J. Smith Papers, Collection 267
UCLA Oral History Programme Papers, MSS300
Women's Liberation Papers, Collection 50

San Francisco Public Library, Reference Section and Documents Department
Documents on the Bay Area environment

Stanford University Library Special Collections
Delmer Daves Papers, M192
Bruce Ormitz Bliven Papers, M294
Project South Collection, SC 066
Lorna D. Smith Papers, M194
J. Arthur Younger Papers, M216

Hoover Institution on War, Revolution and Peace, Stanford University
Eric C. Bellquist Papers
French Subject Collection
Sidney Hook Papers
Frank L. Price Papers
Ronald Reagan Papers (most of the collection was closed, but the press releases, clippings,

and other printed material were useful)
Venena Collection

Bancroft Library, University of California at Berkeley
Richard Brautigan Papers, 87/173C
Philip Burton Papers, 87/233C
Free Speech Movement Collection, CU309
Jack Micheline Papers, 87/174
Henry Nash Smith Papers, 87/136C
Social Protest Collection, 68/157C

Columbia University Rare Book and Manuscript Library
Gregory Corso Papers
Cox Commission Hearings
Allen Ginsberg Collection
Jack Kerouac Papers
Louis Kirk Grayson Papers
Barry Miles Collection
Peter Stafford Collection

Cornell University Division of Rare and Manuscript Collections, Ithaca, New York
Challenge to Governance Project, 47/5/1309

Schlesinger Library, Radcliffe College, Cambridge, Massachusetts
Susan Bolotin Papers
Betty Friedan Papers
MS Magazine Letters
Barbara Seaman Papers

Grayson History Research Center, University of Minnesota Libraries, St Paul
Donnaruma Collection

*Printed Primary Sources*

These, which I take to include studies of aspects of the sixties published at the time or shortly after, are too extensive to be listed here, but can be traced through my chapter notes. I should make it clear that while I have worked systematically through such magazines as Time, *Ebony, Paris-Match, L'Express, Epoca, ABC, L'Espresso,* the various youth magazines, and *Tiger Rag* (from the summer of 1972 called *The Helmsman,* to be found, along with the 'counter-cultural' student magazine *Rodent,* in the Mississippi Valley Archives), my use of newspapers is almost exclusively through the cuttings to be found in the many archive collections I have consulted; the delightfully named 'Morgue Files' of the two main Memphis newspapers, again to be found in the Mississippi Valley Collection, were particularly useful. It will be clear that I have made considerable use of films, novels, works of art and music of many sorts: again these must be tracked through my chapter notes.

## Secondary Sources

The literature is immense. I hope my chapter notes do justice to the many authors from whose work I have benefited. I confine myself here to a select list of books published or reprinted after 1986. Since autobiographical works are classified as primary sources, I do not list again here such illuminating works as Richard Neville, *Hippie Hippie Shake: The Dreams, the Trips, the Trials, the Love-ins, the Screw Ups... the Sixties* (London, Bloomsbury, 1995), Danille Taylor-Guthrie (ed.), *Conversations with Toni Morrison* (University Press of Mississippi, 1994), Mary King, *Freedom Song: A Personal Story of the 1960s Civil Rights Movement* (New York, Morrow, 1987), or Tom Hayden, *Reunion: A Memoir* (New York, Random House, 1988); slightly inconsistently, I do include some collections of readings from primary sources.

ALDGATE, ANTHONY, *Censorship and the Permissive Society: British Cinema and Theatre, 1955–1965* (Oxford, Clarendon Press, 1995).

ANDERSON, TERRY H., *The Movement and the Sixties: Protest in America from Greensboro to Wounded Knee* (New York, Oxford University Press, 1995).

APPLEYARD, BRYAN, *The Pleasures of Peace: Art and Imagination in Post-War Britain* (London, Faber & Faber, 1989).

BARK, DENNIS L., and GRESS, DAVID R., *A History of West Germany, ii: Democracy and Its Discontents 1963–1988* (Oxford, Blackwell, 1989).

BARNARD, STEPHEN, *On the Radio: Music Radio in Britain* (Milton Keynes, Open University Press, 1989).

—*The Rolling Stones: Street Fighting Years.* Foreword by Bill Wyman (London, Studio Editions, 1993).

BASSNETT, SUSAN, *Magdalena: International Women and Experimental Theatre* (Oxford, Berg, 1989).

BAYLEY, STEPHEN, GARNER, PHILIPPE, and SUDJIC, DAYAN, *Twentieth-Century Style and Design* (London, Thames & Hudson, 1986).

BEARMAN, PAUL, *A Tale of Two Utopias: The Political Journey of the Generation of 1968* (New York, Norton, 1997).

—(ed.), *Debating PC: The Controversy over Political Correctness on College Campuses* (New York, Norton, 1992).

BEIFUSS, JOAN TURNER, *At the River I Stand* (Memphis, St Luke's Press, 1990).

BENTON, TED, *The Rise and Fall of Structural Marxism: Althusser and His Influence* (London, Macmillan, 1988).

BIANCHINO, GLORIA, and QUINTAVALLE, CARLO, *Moda dalla fiaba al design: Italia 1951–1989* (Novara, Europia, 1989).

BLACK, EARLE, and BLACK, MERLE, *Politics and Society in the South* (Cambridge, Mass., Harvard University Press, 1987).

BLUM, JOHN M., *Years of Discord: American Politics and Society 1961–1974* (New York, Norton, 1991).

BLUMBERG, RHODA LOIS, *Civil Rights: The 1960s Freedom Struggles* (Boston, Twayne, 1984; repr. 1991).

BONESEA, MARTA, *La grande illusione* (Milan, Mondadori, 1997).

BONO, PAOLO, and KENT, SANDRA, *Italian Feminist Thought: A Reader* (Oxford, 1991).

BOURDON, DAVID, *Warhol* (New York, Abrams, 1989).

BRADLEY, DICK, *Understanding Rock'n'Roll: Popular Music in Britain 1955–1964* (Buckingham, Open University Press, 1992).

BRANCH, TAYLOR, *Parting the Waters: America in the King Years, 1954–63* (New York, Simon & Schuster, 1988).

BRAUN, EMILY (ed.), *Italian Art in the 20th Century: Painting and Sculpture* (Munich, Prestel Verlag Museum, and London, Royal Academy, 1969).

BRECHT, STEFAN, *Peter Schumann's Bread and Puppet Theatre* (London, Methuen, 1988).

BREINES, WINI, *Young, White and Miserable: Growing Up Female in the Fifties* (Boston, Beacon Press, 1992).

—*The Great Refusal: Community and Organization in the New Left, 1962–1968* (New Brunswick, NJ, New Edition, 1989).

BRITTON, CELIA, *The Nouveau Roman: Fiction, Theory and Politics* (Basingstoke, Macmillan, 1992).

BROSMAN, CATHARINE SAVAGE (ed.), *French Novelists since 1960* (Chicago, Gale Research, 1989).

BROWN, MICHAEL K. (ed.), *Remaking the Welfare State: Retrenchment and Social Policy in America and Europe* (Philadelphia, Temple University Press, 1988).

BROWN, PETER, and BROESKE, PAT, *Down at the End of Lonely Street: The Life and Death of Elvis Presley* (London, Heinemann, 1997).

BURKE, SEAN, *The Death and Return of the Author: Criticism and Subjectivity in Barthes, Foucault and Derrida* (Edinburgh University Press, 1992).

BURNER, DAVID, *Making Peace With the 60s* (Princeton, NJ, Princeton University Press, 1996).

BYRNE, PAUL, *The Campaign for Nuclear Disarmament* (London, Croom Helm, 1988).

CALVET, LOUIS-JEAN, *Roland Barthes 1915–1980* (Paris, Flammarion, 1990).

CASTRO, GINETTE, *American Feminism: A Contemporary History.* Translated from the French by Elizabeth Loverde-Bagwell (New York University Press, 1990).

CAUTE, DAVID, *Sixty-eight: The Year of the Barricades* (London, Paladin, 1988).

CHAFE, WILLIAM H., *The Unfinished Journey: America since World War II,* 2nd edn. (New York, Oxford University Press, 1991).

CHALMERS, DAVID, *And the Crooked Places Made Straight: The Struggle for Social Change in the 1960s* (London, Johns Hopkins University Press, 1991).

CHAPPELL, DAVID L., *Inside Agitators: White Southerners in the Civil Rights Movement* (Baltimore, Johns Hopkins University Press, 1994).

CHOMSKY, NOAM, *Language and the Problem of Knowledge: The Managua Lectures* (Cambridge, Mass., MIT Press, 1988).

CHURCHILL, WARD, and VANDER WALL, JIM, *The COINTELPRO Papers: Documents from the FBI's Secret Wars Against Domestic Dissent* (Boston, Southend Press, 1990).

CLARK, MARTIN, *Modern Italy 1871–1995* (London, Longman, 1996).

CLAY, JOHN, *R. D. Laing: A Divided Self* (London, Hodder & Stoughton, 1996).

COHEN, SARA, *Rock Culture in Liverpool: Popular Music in the Making* (Oxford, Clarendon Press, 1991).

COLAIACO, JAMES A., *Martin Luther King, Jr.: Apostle of Militant Nonviolence* (New York, St. Martin's Press, 1988).

COLLIER, PETER, and HOROWITZ, DAVID, *Destructive Generation: Second Thoughts About the Sixties* (New York, Summit Books, 1989).

——*Second Thoughts: Former Radicals Look Back at the Sixties* (New York, Madison Books, 1989).

COLLURA, MATTEO, *Il maestro di Regalpetra: vita di Leonardo Sciascia* (Milan, Longanesi, 1996).

COMPTON, SUSAN (ed.), *British Art in the 20th Century: The Modern Movement* (Munich, Prestel, 1987).

COPLEY, ANTONY, *Sexual Moralities in France, 1780–1980: New Ideas on the Family, Divorce, and Homosexuality* (London, Routledge, 1989).

CRESPI, FRANCO, and MUCCHI FAINA, ANGELICA (eds.), *Le strategie delle minoranze attive: una ricerca empirica sul movimento delle donne* (Naples, Liguori, 1988).

CRUIKSHANK, MARGARET, *The Gay and Lesbian Liberation Movement* (London, Routledge, 1992).

DAVIES, ANDREW, *Other Theatres: The Development of Alternative and Experimental Theatre in Britain* (London, Macmillan, 1987).

DAVIES, HUNTER, *The Beatles: The Only Authorised Biography*, rev. edn. (London, Cape, 1992).

DAVIS, FLORA, *Moving the Mountain: The Women's Movement in America Since 1960* (New York, Simon & Schuster, 1991).

DAVIS, JOHN, *Youth and the Condition of Britain: Images of Adolescent Conflict* (London, Athlone, 1990).

DEBENEDETTI, CHARLES, *An American Ordeal: The Anti-War Movement of the Vietnam Era* (Syracuse, NY, Syracuse University Press, 1990).

DENSELOW, ROBIN, *When the Music's Over: The Story of Political Pop* (London, Faber & Faber, 1989).

DICKSTEIN, MORRIS, *Gates of Eden: American Culture in the Sixties*, 2nd edn. with new introd. (Cambridge, Mass., Harvard University Press, 1997).

DIGGINS, JOHN P., *The Proud Decades: America in War and Peace, 1941–1960* (New York, Norton, 1988).

——*The Rise and Fall of the American Left* (New York, Norton, 1992).

DITTMER, JOHN, *Local People: The Struggle for Civil Rights in Mississippi* (Urbana, University of Illinois Press, 1994).

DOHERTY, THOMAS, *Teenagers and Teenpics: The Juvenilization of American Movies in the 1950s* (Boston, Mass., Unwin Hyman, 1988).

DONAVAN, ROBERT J., and SCHERER, RAY, *Unsilent Revolution: Television News and American Public Life* (Cambridge University Press, 1992).

DORMER, PETER, *Design since 1945* (London, Thames & Hudson, 1993).

DRAPER, ROBERT, *The Rolling Stone Story: The Magazine That Moved a Generation* (Edinburgh, Mainstream, 1990).

793

DREYFUS-ARMAND, GENEVIEVE, and GERVEREAU, LAURENT, *Mai 68: les mouvements étudiants en France et dans le monde* (Paris, Bibliothèque de Documentation Internationale Contemporaine, Nanterre, 1988).

EAGLES, CHARLES (ed.), *The Civil Rights Movement in America: Essays* (University of Mississippi Press, 1986).

ECHOLS, ALICE, *Daring to Be Bad: Radical Feminism in America 1967–1975* (Minneapolis, University of Minnesota Press, Minneapolis, 1989).

ELLWOOD, ROBERT S., *The Sixties Spiritual Awakening: American Religion Moving from Modern to Postmodern* (New Brunswick, NJ, Rutgers University Press, 1994).

ERIBON, DIDIER, *Michel Foucault,* trans. Betsy Wing (London, Faber & Faber, 1992).

FARBER, DAVID (ed.), *The 1960s: From Memory to History* (Chapel Hill, University of North Carolina Press, 1994).

—*The Age of Great Dreams: America in the 1960s* (New York, Hill & Wang, 1994).

—*Chicago '68* (University of Chicago Press, 1988).

FLETCHER, JOHN, and CALDER, JOHN, *The Nouveau Roman Reader* (London, Calder, 1986).

FOLENA, GIANFRANCO (ed.), *Tre narratori: Calvino, Primo Levi, Parise* (Padua, Liviana, 1989).

FOREST, PHILIPPE, *Philippe Sollers* (Paris, Seuil, 1992).

FORGACS, DAVID, *Italian Culture in the Industrial Era 1880–1980: Cultural Industries, Politics and the Public* (Manchester University Press, 1990).

FOSTER, EDWARD HALSEY, *Understanding the Beats* (Columbia, University of South Carolina Press, 1992).

FOUNTAIN, NIGEL, *Underground: The London Alternative Press, 1966–1974* (London, Routledge, 1988).

FOWLER, DAVID, *The First Teenagers: The Lifestyle of Young Wage-Earners in Inter-War Britain* (London, Woburn Press, 1995).

FRASER, RONALD, et al., *1968: A Student Generation in Revolt* (London, Chatto & Windus, 1988).

FRITH, SIMON (ed.), *Facing the Music: Essays on Pop, Rock and Culture* (London, Mandarin, 1990).

—*Music for Pleasure* (Cambridge, Polity Press, 1988).

GALE RESEARCH COMPANY, *Dictionary of Literary Biography* (Detroit, 1978- ).

GANN, LEWIS H., and DUIGNAN, PETER, *The New Left and the Cultural Revolution of the 1960s: A Re-evaluation* (Stanford, Hoover Institution, 1995).

GANS, HERBERT J., *The War Against the Poor: The Underclass and Antipoverty Policy* (New York, Basic Books, 1995).

GARFINKLE, ADAM, *Telltale Hearts: The Origins and Impact of the Vietnam Anti-War Movement* (Basingstoke, Macmillan, 1995).

GARNER, PHILIPPE, *Sixties Design* (Cologne, Taschen, 1996).

GARROW, DAVID J. (ed.), *We Shall Overcome: The Civil Rights Movement in the United States in the 1950s and 1960s* (3 vols., Brooklyn, NY, Careson, 1989).

—*Bearing the Cross: Martin Luther King, Jr. and the Southern Christian Leadership Conference* (New York, Morrow, 1986).

—*Liberty and Sexuality: The Right to Privacy and the Making of Roe v. Wade* (New York, Macmillan, 1994).

GENTRY, CURT, *J. Edgar Hoover: The Man and the Secrets* (New York, Norton, 1991).

GILBERT, JAMES, *A Cycle of Outrage: America's Reaction to the Juvenile Delinquent in the 1950s* (New York, Oxford University Press, 1986).

GINSBORG, PAUL, *A History of Contemporary Italy: Society and Politics 1943–1988* (Harmondsworth, Penguin, 1990).

GITLIN, TODD, *The Sixties: Years of Hope, Days of Rage* (New York, Pantheon, 1987; new edn. with new Preface, New York, Bantam, 1993).

GOBBI, ROMOLO, *Il '68 alla rovescia* (Milan, Mondadori, 1988).

GOODMAN, LIZBETH, *Contemporary Feminist Theatres: To Each Her Own* (London, Routledge, 1993).

GOTTLIEB, ANNIE, *Do You Believe in Magic? The Second Coming of the Sixties Generation* (New York, Times Books, 1987).

GRAHAM, HUGH D., *The Civil Rights Era: Origins and Development of National Policy, 1960–1972* (New York, Oxford University Press, 1990).

GRAY, CHRISTOPHER (ed.), *The Incomplete Work of the Situationist International*, translated from the French (London, Free Fall, 1974).

GREEN, JONATHON, *Days in the Life: Voices from the English Underground 1961–1971* (London, Heinemann, 1988; new edn., 1998).

GROSS, MICHAEL, *Model: The Ugly Business of Beautiful Women* (London, Bantam, 1996).

GROSSINI, GIANCARLO, *Firme in passerella: Italian Style, modo e spettacolo* (Bari, Dedalo, 1986).

GURALNICK, PETER, *Last Train to Memphis: The Rise of Elvis Presley* (Boston, Little, Brown, 1994).

HALIMI, GISèLE, *La Cause des femmes*, new rev. edn. (Paris, Gallimard, 1992).

HALLIN, DANIEL C., *The 'Uncensored War': The Media and Vietnam* (New York, Oxford University Press, 1986).

HAMPTON, HENRY, and FAYER, STEVE, with FLYNN, SARAH, *Voices of Freedom: An Oral History of the Civil Rights Movement from the 1950's through the 1980's* (New York, Bantam, 1990).

HARMAN, CHRIS, *The Fire Last Time: 1968 and After* (London, Bookmarks, 1988).

HASKINS, JAMES, and BENSON, KATHLEEN, *The 60s Reader* (New York, Viking, 1988).

HEATLEY, MICHAEL, and FORD, DANIEL, *Football Grounds, Then and Now* (Shepperton, Dial Press, 1994).

HERO, DILIP, *Black British White British: A History of Race Relations in Britain* (London, Grafton, 1991).

HERRING, GEORGE C., *America's Longest War: The United States and Vietnam 1950–1975*, 3rd edn. (New York, McGraw-Hill, 1996).

HEWISON, ROBERT, *Too Much: Art and Society in the Sixties 1960–75* (London, Methuen, 1986).

HILL, JOHN, *Sex, Class and Realism: British Cinema 1956–1963* (London, British Film Institute, 1986).

HOBSBAWM, ERIC, *The Age of Extremes: The Short Twentieth Century 1914–1991* (London, Michael Joseph, 1994).

HONEY, MICHAEL K., *Southern Labor and Black Civil Rights: Organizing Memphis Workers* (Urbana, University of Illinois Press, 1993).

HOTCHNER, A. E., *Blown Away: The Rolling Stones and the Death of the Sixties* (New York, Simon & Schuster, 1990).

HUMPHRIES, STEVE, and TAYLOR, JOHN, *The Making of Modern London 1945–1985* (London, Sidgwick & Jackson, 1986).

HUTCHINS, CHRIS, and THOMPSON, PETER, *Elvis Meets the Beatles* (London, Smith Gryphon, 1994).

INGLIS, SIMON, *Football Grounds of Europe* (London, Collins, 1990).

JACKSON, REBECCA, *The 1960s: An Annotated Bibliography of Social and Political Movements in the United States* (Westport, Conn., Greenwood, 1992).

JOHNSON, TROY, NAGEL, JOANE, and CHAMPAGNE, DUANE (eds.), *American Indian Activism: Alcatraz to the Longest Walk* (Urbana, Ill., University of Illinois Press, 1997).

KAIN, ROGER (ed.), *Planning and the Environment in the Modern World, iii: Planning for Conservation* (London, Mansell, 1981).

KAISER, CHARLES, *1968 in America: Music, Politics, Chaos, Counterculture, and the Shaping of a Generation* (London, Weidenfeld & Nicolson, 1988).

KELLY, MICHAEL BRYAN, *The Beatle Myth: The British Invasion of American Popular Music, 1956–1969* (Folkestone, McFarland, 1991).

KING, TERRY, *The Politics of Corporal Punishment* (Sheffield City Polytechnic, 1987).

KINGSLEY, HILARY, and TIBBALS, GEOFF, *Box of Delights: The Golden Years of Television* (London, Macmillan, 1989).

KNIGHT, DOUGLAS, *Streets of Dreams: The Nature and Legacy of the 1960s* (Durham, NC, Duke University Press, 1989).

KROES, ROB, RYDELL, ROBERT W., and BOSSCHER, DOEKO F. J. (eds.), *Cultural Transmission and Perception: American Mass Culture in Europe* (Amsterdam, VU Press, 1993).

KUISEL, RICHARD F., *Seducing the French: The Dilemma of Americanization* (Berkeley, University of California Press, 1993).

KURZ, MICHAEL, *Stockhausen: A Biography*, trans. Richard Toop (London, Faber & Faber, 1992).

LARKIN, MAURICE, *France Since the Popular Front: Government and People 1936–1986* (Oxford, Clarendon Press, 1988).

LAYTON-HENRY, ZIG, *The Politics of Immigration: Immigration, 'Race' and 'Race' Relations in Postwar Britain* (Oxford, Blackwell, 1992).

LECHTE, JOHN, *Julia Kristeva* (London, Routledge, 1990).

—*Fifty Key Contemporary Thinkers: From Structuralism to Postmodernity* (London, Routledge, 1994).

LEWIS, JANE (ed.), *Women and Social Policies in Europe: Work, Family and the State* (Aldershot, Elgar, 1993).

LOUVRE, ALF, and WALSH, JEFFREY (eds.), *Tell Me Lies About Vietnam: Cultural Battles for the Meaning of the War* (Milton Keynes, Open University Press, 1988).

LOVELL, TERRY (ed.), *British Feminist Thought: A Reader* (Oxford, Blackwell, 1990).

LOWE, RODNEY, *The Welfare State in Britain since 1945* (London, Macmillan, 1993).

LUMLEY, ROBERT, *States of Emergency: Cultures of Revolt in Italy from 1968–1978* (London, Verso, 1990).

LYONS, JOHN, et al. (eds.), *New Horizons in Linguistics, iii* (Harmondsworth, Penguin, 1987).

MCCORMICK, JOHN, *The Global Environmental Movement: Reclaiming Paradise* (London, Belhaven Press, 1992).

MCCULLOUGH, KATHLEEN, *Concrete Poetry: An Annotated International Bibliography with an Index of Poets and Poems* (Troy, NY, Whitston, 1989).

MACDONALD, IAN, *Revolution in the Head: The Beatles' Records and the Sixties* (London, Fourth Estate, 1994).

MACEDO, STEPHEN (ed.), *Reassessing the Sixties: Debating the Political and Cultural Legacy* (New York, Norton, 1997).

MACEY, DAVID, *The Lives of Michel Foucault* (London, Hutchinson, 1993).

McMILLAN, JOYCE, *The Traverse Theatre Story 1963–1988* (London, Methuen, 1988).

McROBBIE, ANGELA, *Feminism and Youth Culture: From 'Jackie' to 'Just Seventeen'* (Basingstoke, Macmillan, 1991).

MARCUS, GREIL, *Mystery Train: Images of America in Rock'n'Roll Music,* 4th edn. (New York, Plume, 1997).

MELLOR, DAVID ALAN, *The Sixties Art Scene in London* (Oxford, Phaidon, 1993).

—and GERVEREAU, LAURENT, *The Sixties, Britain and France, 1962–1973: The Utopian Years* (London, Philip Wilson, 1997).

MENDRAS, HENRI, and COLE, ALISTAIR, *Social Change in Modern France: Towards a Cultural Anthropology of the Fifth Republic* (Cambridge University Press, 1991).

MILES, BARRY, *Paul McCartney: Many Years from Now* (London, Seeker & Warburg, 1997).

MILLER, JAMES, *'Democracy is in the streets': From Port Huron to the Siege of Chicago* (New York, Touchstone, 1987).

MILLER, TIMOTHY, *The Hippies and American Values* (Knoxville, University of Tennessee Press, 1991).

MILLS, NICOLAUS, *Like a Holy Crusade; Mississippi 1964—The Turning of the Civil Rights Movement in America* (Chicago, I. R. Dee, 1992).

MOI, TORIL (ed.), *French Feminist Thought: A Reader* (Oxford, Blackwell, 1987).

MOORE-GILBERT, BART, and SEED, JOHN (eds.), *Cultural Revolution? The Challenge of the Arts in the 1960s* (London, Routledge, 1992).

MORGAN, EDWARD P., *The 60s Experience: Hard Lessons about Modern America* (Philadelphia, Temple University Press, 1991).

MORGAN, ROBERT P., *Twentieth-Century Music: A History of Musical Style in Modern Europe and America* (New York, Norton, 1991).

MORIARTY, MICHAEL, *Roland Barthes* (Cambridge, Polity Press, 1991).

MORRISON, JOAN, and MORRISON, ROBERT K. (eds.), *From Camelot to Kent State: The Sixties Experience in the Words of Those Who Lived It* (New York, Times Books, 1987).

MURRAY, CHARLES S., *Crosstown Traffic: Jimi Hendrix and Post-War Pop* (London, Faber & Faber, 1989).

797

NATALLE, ELIZABETH J., *Feminist Theatre: A Study in Persuasion* (London, Scarecrow, 1985).

NELSON, ELIZABETH, *The British Counter Culture, 1966–73: A Study of the Underground Press* (Basingstoke, Macmillan, 1989).

NEVE, BRIAN, *Film and Politics in America: A Social Tradition* (London, Routledge, 1992).

NEVERS, GUY, *Les français vus par les français* (Paris, Barrault, 1985).

NORMAN, PHILIP, *Shout! The True Story of the Beatles*, new edn. (Harmondsworth, Penguin, 1993).

—*The Stones*, new edn. (Harmondsworth, Penguin, 1993).

NORRIS, CHRISTOPHER, *Derrida* (London, Fontana, 1987).

O'NEILL, WILLIAM L., *American High: The Years of Confidence, 1945–1960* (New York, Free Press, 1986).

OSGERBY, BILL, *Youth in Britain Since 1945* (Oxford, Blackwell, 1997).

PALMER, JERRY, *Logic of the Absurd in Film and Television Comedy* (London, British Film Institute, 1987).

PATTERSON, JAMES, *Grand Expectations: The United States, 1945–74* (New York, Oxford University Press, 1996).

PAYNE, CHARLES M., *I've Got the Light of Freedom: The Organizing Tradition and the Mississippi Freedom Struggle* (Berkeley, University of California Press, 1995).

PEACH, LINDEN, *Toni Morrison* (London, Macmillan, 1995).

PIERCE, PATRICIA JOBE, *The Ultimate Elvis: Elvis Presley Day by Day* (New York, Simon & Schuster, 1994).

PINKER, STEVEN, *The Language Instinct: The New Science of Language and Mind* (London, Allen Lane, 1994).

PLANT, SADIE, *Most Radical Gesture: Situationist International in a Postmodern Age* (London, Routledge, 1992).

POWLEDGE, FRED, *Free at Last? The Civil Rights Movement and the People Who Made It* (Boston, Little, Brown, 1991).

RALPH, JAMES R., JR., *Northern Protest: Martin Luther King, Jr., Chicago, and the Civil Rights Movement* (Cambridge, Mass., Harvard University Press, 1993).

ROBERTS, COLIN, *Chiens perdus sans collier, Gilbert Cestron; La Clé sur la porte, Marie Cardinal* (Glasgow Introductory Guides to French Literature 5, University of Glasgow, 1988).

RORABAUGH, W. J., *Berkeley at War: The 1960s* (New York, Oxford University Press, 1989).

ROUDINESCO, ELIZABETH, *Jacques Lacan* (Cambridge, Polity, 1997).

ROWE, JOHN CARLOS, and BERG, RICK (eds.), *The Vietnam War and American Culture* (New York, Columbia University Press, 1991).

SARUP, MADAN, *Jacques Lacan* (London, Harvester Wheatsheaf, 1992).

SCHULZINGER, ROBERT D., *A Time for War: The United States and Vietnam, 1941–1975* (Oxford University Press, 1997).

SCHWARTZ, PAUL, *Georges Perec: Traces of His Passage* (Birmingham, Ala., Summa Publications, 1988).

SHAW, ARNOLD, *Black Popular Music in America* (New York, Macmillan, 1986).

SILVER, KENNETH, *David Hockney* (New York, Rizzoli, 1994).

SITKOFF, HARVARD, *The Struggle for Black Equality, 1954–1992* (New York, Hill & Wang, 1993).

SKLAR, ROBERT, *Film: An International History of the Medium* (London, Thames & Hudson, 1993).

SMALL, MELVIN, *Johnson, Nixon and the Doves* (New Brunswick, NJ, Rutgers University Press, 1988).

SORLIN, PIERRE, *The Film in History: Restaging the Past* (Oxford, Blackwell, 1980).

—*European Cinemas, European Societies, 1939–1990* (London, Routledge, 1991).

—*Italian National Cinema 1896–1996* (London, Routledge, 1996).

STEAD, PETER, *Film and the Working Class: The Feature Film in British and American Society* (London, Routledge, 1989).

STEIGERWALD, DAVID, *The Sixties and the End of Modern America* (New York, St. Martin's Press, 1995).

STEVENS, JAY, *Storming Heaven: LSD and the American Dream* (New York, Atlantic Monthly Press, 1987; London, Paladin, 1989).

STILLE, ALEXANDER, *Excellent Cadavers: The Mafia and the Death of the First Italian Republic* (London, Jonathan Cape, 1995).

STOLZFUS, BEN, *Alain Robbe-Grillet: Life, Work and Criticism* (Fredericton, NB, Canada, 1987).

STRAMACCIONI, ALBERTO, *Il sessantotto e la sinistra* (Perugia, Protagon, 1988).

—*Il movimento studentesco e la sinistra in Umbria: documenti e testimonianze 1966–1972* (Perugia, Protagon, 1988).

STREET, JOHN, 'Youth Culture and the Emergence of Popular Music', in Terry Gourvish and Alan O'Day (eds.), *Britain since 1945* (Basingstoke, Macmillan, 1991), 305–23.

SWERDLOW, AMY, *Women Strike For Peace: Traditional Motherhood and Radical Politics in the 1960s* (University of Chicago Press, 1993).

TANITCH, ROBERT, *Sean Connery* (London, Chapmans, 1992).

THOMPSON, BILL, *Soft Core: The Battle over Pornography in Britain and America* (London, Cassell, 1994).

TIMMINS, NICHOLAS, *The Five Giants: A Biography of the Welfare State* (London, HarperCollins, 1995).

TODD, EMMANUEL, *La Nouvelle France* (Paris, Seuil, 1988).

UMANSKY, LAURI, *Motherhood Reconceived: Feminism and the Legacies of the Sixties* (New York University Press, 1996).

VAN DEBURG, WILLIAM L., *New Day in Babylon: The Black Power Movement and American Culture, 1965–1975* (University of Chicago Press, 1992).

VERGINE, LEA, *L'arte in trincea: lessico delle tendenze artistiche 1960–1990* (Milan, Skira, 1996).

VERMOREL, FRED, *Fashion and Perversity: A Life of Vivienne Westwood and the Sixties Laid Bare* (London, Bloomsbury, 1996).

WALTER, AUBURY (ed.), *Come Together: The Years of Gay Liberation 1970–73* (London, Gay Men's Press, 1980).

WANDOR, MICHELINE, *Carry On Understudies: Theatre and Sexual Politics* (London, Routledge & Kegan Paul, 1986).

WARD, KEN, *Mass Communication and the Modern World* (Basingstoke, Macmillan, 1989).

WASHINGTON, JAMES MELVIN, 'I *have a dream': Writings and Speeches That Changed the World, Martin Luther King Jr.* (New York, HarperCollins, San Francisco, 1992).

WATSON, STEVEN, *The Birth of the Beat Generation: 1944–1960* (New York, Pantheon, 1995).

WEATHERALL, MARK, *From Our Cambridge Correspondent: Cambridge Student Life 1945–95 as Seen in the Pages of Varsity* (Cambridge, Varsity Publication, 1995).

WEBER, HENRI, *Vingt ans après, que reste-t-il de 68?* (Paris, Seuil, 1988).

WEISBROT, ROBERT, *Freedom Bound: A History of America's Civil Rights Movement* (New York, Norton, 1990).

WELLS, TOM, *The War Within: America's Battle over Vietnam* (Berkeley, University of California Press, 1994).

WHITMER, PETER O., *Aquarius Revisited: Seven Who Created the Sixties Counterculture that Changed America* (New York, Macmillan, 1987).

WICKE, PETER, *Rock Music: Culture, Aesthetics and Sociology*, trans. Rachel Fogg (Cambridge University Press, 1990).

WIEVIORKA, MICHEL (ed.), *Racisme et xénophobie en Europe: une comparaison internationale* (Paris, éditions La Découverte, 1994).

WILLIAMS, JUAN, *Eyes on the Prize: America's Civil Rights Years, 1954–1965* (New York, Viking, 1987).

WILLIAMS, LINDA, *Hard Core: Power, Pleasure and the 'Frenzy of the Visible'* (London, Pandora Press, 1990).

WINOCK, MICHEL, *Chronique des années soixante* (Paris, Seuil, 1987).

YARROW, RALPH (ed.), *European Theatre 1960–1990: Cross-Cultural Perspectives* (London, Routledge, 1992).

YONNET, PAUL, *Jeux, modes et masses: la société française et le moderne 1945–1985* (Paris, Gallimard, 1986).

YOUNG, LOLA, *Fear of the Dark: 'Race', Gender and Sexuality in the Cinema* (London, Routledge, 1996).

# A NOTE ON THE AUTHOR

Arthur John Brereton Marwick was born in Edinburgh in 1936, and was a graduate of Edinburgh University and Balliol College, Oxford. Marwick was appointed the first Professor of History at the Open University in 1969, after lecturing at Edinburgh for ten years. He held visiting professorships at the State University of New York at Buffalo, Stanford University, Rhodes College and the École des Hautes Études en Sciences Sociales in Paris.

Marwick was a left-wing social and cultural historian but was critical of Marxism and other approaches to history that he believed stressed the importance of metanarrative over archival research. He was also a critic of postmodernism, seeing it as a "menace to serious historical study". It was also the methodology of the postmodernists to which he was opposed, "the techniques to deconstruction or discourse analysis have little value compared with the sophisticated methods historians have been developing over years".

Marwick died in 2006.